AA

guide to GOLF courses

Shirehampton one

AA Lifestyle Guides

Produced by AA Publishing
Maps prepared by the Cartographic Department of
Automobile Association Developments Ltd
Maps © The Automobile Association 2001
Directory generated by the AA Establishment
Database, Information Research, AA Hotel Services
Design by Nautilus Design UK Ltd, Basingstoke,
Hampshire

The Automobile Association would like to
thank the following photographers and
libraries for their assistance in preparation
of this book:

Cover Photographs: Action Images/
S Franklin
All main images come from the Automobile
Association's own library (AA PHOTO
LIBRARY) and were taken by the following
photographers

AA Photo Library 4tl, 9b, 13; Adrian Baker 8;
Jamie Blandford 9t, 430; Caroline Jones 4t, 5c; Rob
Moore 3 (main); Rich Newton 401; Ken Paterson 2t,
10, 11; Clive Sawyer 7; Peter Sharpe 323; Rick Strange
2c, 3 (inset), 5tr; Peter Zollier 1

Abbreviations for terms appearing above: (t) top: (b)
bottom; (l) left; (r) right; (c) centre

Advertisement Sales
Telephone Karen Weeks 01256 491545

Typeset/Repro by Avonset, 11 Kelso Place, Bath

Printed in Italy by Rotolito Lombarda SpA

The contents of this book are believed correct at the
time of printing. Nevertheless, the Publisher cannot be
held responsible for any errors or omissions or for
changes in the details given in this guide or for the
consequences of any reliance on the information
provided in the same. We have tried to ensure accuracy
in this guide but things do change and we would be
grateful if readers would advise us of any inaccuracies
they may encounter.

© The Automobile Association 2001

Mapping produced by the Cartographic Department of
The Automobile Association.

A CIP catalogue record for this book is available from
the British Library

Published by AA Publishing, which is a trading name
of Automobile Association Developments Limited
whose registered office is Norfolk House, Priestley
Road, Basingstoke,
Hampshire RG24 9NY,

Registered number 1878835.

ISBN 0 7495 3032 4

Contents

How to Use the Guide 4
Accommodation 5
AA Star Classification 6
AA Rosette Awards 7
Feature: Golfing Getaways 8–11
Directory of Golf Courses 13–492

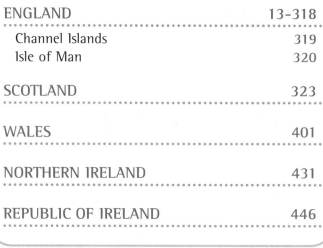

ENGLAND	13–318
Channel Islands	319
Isle of Man	320
SCOTLAND	323
WALES	401
NORTHERN IRELAND	431
REPUBLIC OF IRELAND	446

REFERENCE LISTS

Maps of Britain & Ireland 493–509

Hotels with special arrangements for golf 510–522

Driving Ranges 523–528

Index of Golf Courses 529–544

How to Use the Guide

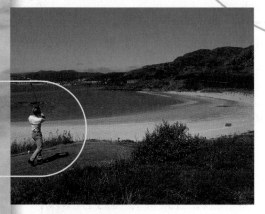

General Information

The AA Guide to Golf Courses aims to provide useful information about a large number of courses across Britain and Ireland. Entries include the contact details for each course, a brief description of the type of course and details of green fees, leisure, club or catering facilities. AA recommended accommodation follows the golf course entry.

Arranging to visit a golf course

The guide includes information on special requirements such as advance notice, handicap certificates or letters of introduction. It is always a good idea to check this with courses in advance as details in the directory, particularly green fees, may change during the currency of the guide.

Key to Symbols and Abbreviations

A number of symbols and abbreviations may appear under the **Facilities** heading for each entry as follows:

Finding a golf course in the directory

The directory is arranged in countries: England, Scotland, Wales, Northern Ireland and the Republic of Ireland. Golf courses appear alphabetically by town within each county. The index at the back of the book lists golf course names.

AA Hotels with special arrangements for golf are listed at the back of the guide. Arrangements may include reduced green fees, preferential tee times or golfing packages.

Map References and Directions

The 16 page atlas at the back of the book has a black dot and town name marking the location of towns with golf courses listed in the guide. Map references are shown alongside the town headings throughout the guide. These include the map page number and National Grid reference. The grid references for the Republic of Ireland are unique to this atlas. Brief directions for each course appear under the heading **Location** in each entry. It is advisable to contact the course for full directions if you are unsure of the exact location.

Highlighted Courses

Green boxes in the guide highlight selected courses considered to be of particular merit or interest. These may include historic clubs, particularly testing or enjoyable courses or those in holiday areas popular with visiting golfers. The selection cannot be either exhaustive or totally objective and these courses do not represent any formal category on quality or other grounds. Major Championship Courses are shown with a full page entry which includes a selection of AA recommended restaurants as well as hotels.

Entries in Bold Italics

We make every effort to obtain current information from golf clubs however in some cases we have been unable to verify details with the club. In this case the course name is shown in bold italics and you are strongly advised to check any details with the club in advance of your visit.

☎	Telephone number	🖻	Well-stocked shop
IEP	Irish Punts (Republic only, the exchange rate between Punts and pounds sterling is liable to fluctuate)	⚐	Clubs for hire
		↝	Motorised cart/trolley for hire
		⚒	Buggies for hire
⊗	Lunch	⚑	Trolley for hire
ⅷ	Dinner	⁴	Driving range
⅃	Bar snacks	★	AA star classification for hotels
☟	Tea/coffee	◉	AA Rosette Award (applicable to championship course entries)
♀	Bar open midday and evenings		
⋈	accommodation at club	◆	AA Guest house classification
⌂	Changing rooms	TH	Town House hotel

KEY

Accommodation

Telephone for details

Where we have been unable to obtain recent information on a course we recommend that you telephone for current details. The contact details including the address and telephone number are provided in the entry.

Restricted membership

A small number of courses included in this guide are not open to visitors however we have included limited details where possible.

Green fees not confirmed

Where green fees are not confirmed we recommend that you telephone for details.

Telephone Codes

The area telephone codes shown for the Republic of Ireland apply only within the Republic. The area telephone codes shown for Great Britain and Northern Ireland do not apply when dialling from the Republic of Ireland. Check your telephone directory for details.

Hotels

Golf course entries in the guide are followed by details of a nearby AA recognised hotel. In some cases the hotel will be in the grounds of the golf course. Most of the recommended hotels fall within the two, three and four star classifications. Where there is no nearby AA recognised hotel AA Guest Accommodation is recommended with a diamond classification from 1 to five diamonds.

AA Classification and Inspection

The AA inspects and classifies hotels and guest accommodation under quality standards agreed between the AA, English Tourism Council and RAC. Hotels receive a star classification from one to five stars and Guest Accommodation establishments receive between one and five diamonds. AA recognised establishments pay an annual fee, this varies according to the classification level and the number of bedrooms. The establishment receives an unannounced inspection visit from a qualified AA inspector who recommends the appropriate classification. Return visits are made to check that standards are maintained and the classification is not transferable if an establishment changes hands. The Hotel Guide and Bed & Breakfast Guide, published annually by the AA, give further details of AA recognised establishments and the classification schemes. A summary of the star classification for hotels is shown on page 6.

Quality Percentage Score and Red Star Hotels

The quality percentage score is an additional assessment made by AA hotel inspectors. This assessment of quality covers everything the hotel has to offer, including hospitality. The quality percentage score appears in red after the star classification in the guide and allows a comparison between hotels with the same number of stars. A three star hotel with a score of 79% therefore compares favourably with a three star hotel with a score of 65%. To gain AA recognition a hotel must score a minimum of 50%, while hotels scoring over 80% generally qualify for AA Red Star Awards. Red Star Awards are the highest accolade awarded by the AA to hotels and the stars are shown in red in the guide. No percentage score is shown for red star hotels.

Club Accommodation at golf courses

Where courses offer club accommodation the bed symbol appears under club facilities in the entry. This is listed as an option for readers wishing to stay at the course, however, unless the club accommodation has an AA star classification, the only AA recommended accommodation is the hotel or guest house which follows each entry.

AA Star Classification

Quality standards you can expect from an AA recognised hotel

All hotels recognised by the AA should have the highest standards of cleanliness, proper records of booking, give prompt and professional service to guests, assist with luggage on request, accept and deliver messages, provide a designated area for breakfast and dinner with drinks available in a bar or lounge, provide an early morning call on request, good quality furniture and fittings, adequate heating and lighting and proper maintenance. A guide to some of the general expectations for each star classification is as follows:

What you can expect from a one star hotel ★

Polite, courteous staff providing a relatively informal yet competent style of service, available during the day and evening to receive guests. At least one designated eating area open to residents for breakfast and dinner. Last orders for dinner no earlier than 6.30pm, a reasonable choice of hot and cold dishes and a short range of wines available. Television in lounge or bedroom. Majority of rooms en suite, bath or shower room available at all times.

What you can expect from a two star hotel ★★

Smartly and professionally presented management and staff providing competent, often informal service, available throughout the day and evening to greet guests. At least one restaurant or dining room open to residents for breakfast and dinner. Last orders for dinner no earlier than 7pm, a choice of substantial hot and cold dishes and a short range of wines available. Television in bedrooms. En suite or private bath or shower and WC.

What you can expect from a three star hotel ★★★

Management and staff smartly and professionally presented and usually uniformed. Technical and social skills of a good standard in responding to requests. A dedicated receptionist on duty, clear direction to rooms and some explanation of hotel facilities. At least one restaurant or dining room open to residents and non-residents for breakfast and dinner whenever the hotel is open. A wide selection of drinks served in a bar or lounge, available to residents and their guests throughout the day and evening. Last orders for dinner no earlier than 8pm, full dinner service provided. Remote-control television, direct-dial telephone. En suite bath or shower and WC.

What you can expect from a four star hotel ★★★★

A formal, professional staffing structure with smartly presented, uniformed staff, anticipating and responding to your needs or requests. Usually spacious, well-appointed public areas. Bedrooms offering superior quality and comfort than at three star. A strong emphasis on food and beverages and a serious approach to cuisine. Reception staffed 24 hours per day by well-trained staff. Express checkout facilities where appropriate. Porterage available on request and readily provided by uniformed staff. Night porter available. Newspapers can be ordered and delivered to your room, additional services and concierge as appropriate to the style and location of the hotel. At least one restaurant open to residents and non-residents for all meals seven days per week. Drinks available to residents and their guests throughout the day and evening, table service available. Last orders for dinner no earlier than 9pm, an extensive choice of hot and cold dishes and comprehensive list of wines. Remote-control television, direct-dial telephone, a range of high-quality toiletries. En suite bath with fixed overhead shower, WC.

What you can expect from a five star hotel ★★★★★

Flawless guest services, professional, attentive staff, technical and social skills of the highest order. Spacious and luxurious accommodation and public areas with a range of extra facilities. As a minimum, first-time guests shown to their bedroom. Multilingual service consistent with the needs of the hotel's normal clientele. Guest accounts well explained and presented. Porterage offered and provided by uniformed staff. Luggage handling on arrival and departure. Doorman or means of greeting guests at the hotel entrance, full concierge service. At least one restaurant open to residents and non-residents for all meals seven days per week. Staff showing knowledge of food and wine. A wide selection of drinks, including cocktails, available in a bar or lounge, table service provided. Last orders for dinner no earlier than 10pm. High-quality menu and wine list properly reflecting and complementing the style of cooking and providing exceptional quality. Evening turn-down service. Remote-control television, direct-dial telephone at bedside and desk, a range of luxury toiletries, bath sheets and robes. En suite bath with fixed overhead shower, WC.

AA Rosette Awards

How the AA assesses restaurants for Rosette Awards

The AA's rosette award scheme was the first nationwide scheme for assessing the quality of food served by restaurants and hotels. The rosette scheme is an award scheme, not a classification scheme and although there is necessarily an element of subjectivity when it comes to assessing taste, we aim for a consistent approach to our awards throughout the UK. It is important, however, to remember that many places serve enjoyable food but do not qualify for an AA award.

Our awards are made solely on the basis of a meal visit or visits by one or more of our hotel and restaurant inspectors who have an unrivalled breadth and depth of experience in assessing quality. They award rosettes annually on a rising scale of one to five.

So what makes a restaurant worthy of a Rosette Award?

For our inspectors the top and bottom line is the food. The taste of the food is what counts for them, and whether the dish successfully delivers to the diner what the menu promises. A restaurant is only as good as its worst meal. Although presentation and competent service should be appropriate to the style of the restaurant and the quality of the food, they cannot affect the rosette assessment as such, either up or down.

The following summaries attempt to explain what our inspectors look for, but are intended only as guidelines. The AA is constantly reviewing its award criteria and competition usually results in an all-round improvement in standards, so it becomes increasingly difficult for restaurants to reach award level.

One rosette

At the simplest level, one rosette, the chef should display a mastery of basic techniques and be able to produce dishes of sound quality and clarity of flavours, using good, fresh ingredients.

Two rosettes

To gain two rosettes, the chef must show greater technical skill, more consistency and judgement in combining and balancing ingredients and a clear ambition to achieve high standards. Inspectors will look for evidence of innovation to test the dedication of the kitchen brigade, and the use of seasonal ingredients sourced from quality suppliers.

Three rosettes

This award takes a restaurant into the big league, and, in a typical year, fewer than 10 per cent of restaurants in our scheme achieve this distinction. Expectations of the kitchen are high, and inspectors find little room for inconsistencies. Exact technique, flair and imagination will come through in every dish, and balance and depth of flavour are all-important.

Four rosettes

This is an exciting award because, at this level, not only should all technical skills be exemplary, but there should also be daring ideas, and they must work. There is no room for disappointment. Flavours should be accurate and vibrant.

Five rosettes

This award is the ultimate awarded only when the cooking is at the pinnacle of achievement. Technique should be of such perfection that flavours, combinations and textures show a faultless sense of balance, giving each dish an extra dimension. The sort of cooking that never falters and always strives to give diners a truly memorable taste experience.

Further details of all restaurants with AA rosette awards can be found in The Restaurant Guide published annually by the AA and available from bookshops.

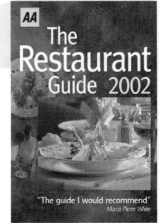

AA

The Restaurant Guide 2002

"The guide I would recommend"
Marco Pierre White

Golfing Getaways

There are many ways to plan a golfing break using this guide. Why not treat yourself and choose a course in the guide that you have always wanted to play at, then stay at one of the AA rated and inspected hotels or Be&Bs nearby? There are recommendations after each golf course in the guide to help you make arrangements direct, or choose a hotel or Be&B from the AA's internet site www.theAA.com, you can book online and find out about the latest special offers on accommodation.

A large number of AA rated hotels have special arrangements for golfers, these hotels are listed for you at the back of the guide, with contact telephone numbers. The hotels may have their own course or may have special arrangements with local courses.

Give them a call, and please tell them you found them in the AA Guide to Golf Courses.

Whether you are arranging a corporate golf day, a golf society trip or a weekend escape with some golf tuition, there is a great choice of destinations in this guide. Many AA hotels offer special packages and we have listed just a small selection here.

AA Hotels offering breaks:

Channel Islands

GUERNSEY

ST PETER PORT
St Pierre Park Hotel
tel 01481 728282
e-mail stppark@itl.net

Weekend breaks for minimum two nights, includes bed and breakfast and free hire car, from £155 per couple per night. 18 holes for £15 or two half hour golf lessons for £40.

England

BERKSHIRE

NEWBURY
Donnington Valley Hotel & Golf Course
tel 01635 551199
e-mail
general@donningtonvalley.co.uk

Weekend breaks from £75 per person for two nights bed & breakfast, the Golf Clubhouse can also be hired for social occasions or corporate golf events.

CAMBRIDGESHIRE

ST NEOTS
Abbotsley Golf Hotel & Country Club
tel 01480 474000
e-mail
abbotsley@americangolf.uk.com

Golf breaks for 1-5 nights with dinner, bed and breakfast and golf.

CORNWALL & ISLES OF SCILLY

ST MELLION
St Mellion International
tel 01579 351351
e-mail
stmellion@americangolf.uk.com

Golfing breaks including dinner, bed and breakfast. Other leisure and family breaks available, health club and spa, skincare centre, sauna and steam room.

EAST RIDING OF YORKSHIRE

POCKLINGTON
Yorkway Motel Ltd
tel 01759 303071

e-mail info@yorkway-motel.co.uk
Golf breaks and weekend special breaks, play at a variety of courses including Allerthorpe Park and Kilnwick Percy Golf.

ESSEX

TOLLESHUNT KNIGHTS
Five Lakes Hotel, Golf, Country Club & Spa
tel 01621 868888
e-mail enquiries@fivelakes.co.uk

Two nights dinner bed and breakfast and two rounds of golf from £205 per person, or for golfing societies prices start at £65 per person per night including dinner, bed and breakfast and a round of golf.

HAMPSHIRE

BROOK
Bell Inn
tel 23 8081 2214
e-mail bell@bramshaw.co.uk

Golf inclusive breaks including dinner, bed and breakfast. Golf on the 3 18-hole golf courses.

LIPHOOK
Old Thorns Hotel, Golf & Country Club
tel 01428 724555
e-mail kflockhart@oldthorns.com
Golf breakaway with 18 holes or half hour beauty treatment, two nights dinner, bed and breakfast.

KENT
SEVENOAKS
Donnington Manor
tel 01732 462681
Golf breaks with dinner, bed and breakfast.

LANCASHIRE
CHORLEY
Shaw Hill Hotel Golf & Country Club
tel 01257 269221
e-mail info@shaw-hill.co.uk
Golfing weekends or mini-breaks with one complimentary round and others at a reduced cost. Society and corporate golf days with a variety of options to choose from.

LINCOLNSHIRE
SCUNTHORPE
Forest Pines Hotel
tel 01652 650770
e-mail enquiries@forestpines.co.uk
Golfing breaks, telephone 01652 650756 for details. Beauty, spa and health treatments also available.

MERSEYSIDE
SOUTHPORT
Stutelea Hotel & Leisure Club
tel 01704 544220
e-mail info@stutelea.co.uk
Minimum two nights golfing break, with dinner, bed and breakfast. Stutelea Challenge Cup Trophy for parties of ten. Winter offer from £41.50 per person per night.

NORTH YORKSHIRE
HUNMANBY
Wrangham House Hotel
tel 01723 891333
e-mail mervynpoulter@lineone.net
Breaks include two nights accommodation with dinner, English breakfast and a complimentary bottle of wine. From £77.75 per person per day including 18 holes.

THORNTON WATLASS
Buck Inn
tel 01677 422461
e-mail buckwatlass@btconnect.com
From £44 per person per night for two nights or more, golf and fishing breaks, packages for groups.

STAFFORDSHIRE
PATTINGHAM
Patshull Park Hotel Golf & Country Club
tel 01902 700100
e-mail sales@patshull-park.co.uk
Dinner, bed and breakfast and a round of golf, or fishing.

SUFFOLK
WOODBRIDGE
Ufford Park Hotel Golf & Leisure
tel 01394 383555
e-mail uffordparkltd@btinternet.com
Golf and leisure breaks and golf tuition available.

SURREY
OCKLEY
Gatton Manor Hotel Golf & Country Club
tel 01306 627555
e-mail gattonmanor@enterprise.net
Golfing breaks including dinner, bed and breakfast.

WARWICKSHIRE
STRATFORD-UPON-AVON
Welcombe Hotel and Golf Course
tel 01789 295252
e-mail sales@welcombe.co.uk
Dinner, bed and breakfast with either golf, theatre or health and beauty treatments. Two night breaks from £244.00 per person.

WARWICK
Ardencote Manor Hotel & Country Club
tel 01926 843111
e-mail hotel@ardencote.com
Play at Ardencote's own 9-hole course, or enjoy preferential rates for hotel guests at The Warwickshire, Leek Wooton, £20 per person for 18 holes Monday to Friday and weekends after 12.

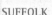

Scotland

ANGUS

CARNOUSTIE
Carnoustie Links Hotel
tel 01241 853273
e-mail enquiries@carnoustielinks.com

Golf packages available, telephone for details.

ARGYLL & BUTE

ERISKA
Isle of Eriska
tel 01631 720371
e-mail office@eriska-hotel.co.uk

Unique island setting, April to October three day breaks with dinner, bed and breakfast from £445, golf tuition also available.

DUMFRIES & GALLOWAY

NEWTON STEWART
Creebridge House Hotel
tel 01671 402121
e-mail creebridge.hotel@daelnet.co.uk

Midweek or weekend breaks with golf at a choice of courses, from around £195 for a 3 night midweek break including dinner, bed and breakfast and 3 rounds of 18 holes.

FIFE

CRAIL
Balcomie Links Hotel
tel 01333 450237
e-mail
mikekadir@balcomie.fsnet.co.uk

Bed and breakfast with three rounds

of golf in winter time, also special rates for shooting parties.

MARKINCH
Balbirnie House
tel 01592 610066
e-mail balbirnie@breathemail.net

Golfing Enthusiasts break, 4-course dinner, accommodation, full Scottish breakfast and a round of golf on Balbirnie park, from £117.50 per person.

ST ANDREWS
The Old Course Hotel, Golf Resort & Spa
tel 01334 474371
e-mail info@oldcoursehotel.co.uk

Various seasonal golf packages for accommodation and golf.

HIGHLAND

BRORA
The Links Hotel
tel 01408 621225
e-mail
highlandescape@btinternet.com

Dinner, bed and breakfast with free use of the leisure club, golf, fishing and walking breaks available.

NAIRN
Golf View Hotel & Leisure Club
tel 01667 452301
e-mail golfview@morton-hotels.com

Golf breaks including dinner, bed and breakfast. Spa, health and leisure facilities, bridge breaks are also offered.

TAIN
Mansfield House Hotel
tel 01862 892052
e-mail mansfield@cali.co.uk

Play on any of the eight courses within a 25 mile radius including the Royal Dornoch, the most northerly and oldest championship course in the world. Discounts and passes available from the hotel.

NORTH AYRSHIRE

BRODICK
Auchrannie Country House Hotel
tel 01770 302234
e-mail info@auchrannie.co.uk

Seasonal breaks include car and passenger ferry travel and a 40 minute aromatherapy massage or 2 rounds of golf per person at Brodick Golf Course, from around £66 per person per night based on two sharing.

PERTH & KINROSS

AUCHTERARDER
The Gleneagles Hotel
tel 01764 662231
e-mail resort.sales@gleneagles.com

Special interest breaks include one night's accommodation for two people, full Scottish breakfast, lunch and dinner and the activity of your choice. Prices from around £475.

CRIEFF
Crieff Hotel
tel 01764 652632
Tailor-made golf packages, for example three nights bed and breakfast for the price of two.

PERTH

Murrayshall Country House Hotel & Golf Course
tel 01738 551171
Accommodation, breakfast and a round of golf from £67.50 per person based on two sharing.

ST FILLANS
The Four Seasons Hotel
tel 01764 685333
e-mail
info@thefourseasonshotel.co.uk

Over twenty-five courses within an hour's drive. Choose from parkland, steep hilly courses or even one of only two island courses in the world. Prices from around £41 per night for bed and breakfast.

Wales

DENBIGHSHIRE

LLANGOLLEN
The Wild Pheasant Hotel &
Restaurant
tel 01978 860629
e-mail
reception@wildpheasanthotel.co.uk

One night breaks with a round of
golf, dinner, bed and breakfast from
£70 per person, other options
available and alternative activities
including white water rafting and
canoeing.

NEWPORT
The Celtic Manor Resort
tel 01633 413000
e-mail postbox@celtic-manor.com

Weekend overnight golf breaks from
£125 per person per night sharing,
includes a round of golf, dinner, bed
and breakfast and use of the health
clubs. Choose from the three Trent
Jones championship courses.

N. Ireland

DOWN

BANGOR
Marine Court Hotel
tel 0289145 1100
e-mail marine.court@dial.pipex.com

Golf packages including dinner, bed
and breakfast, leisure facilities.

Ireland

CO CAVAN

BALLYCONNELL
Slieve Russell Hotel Golf & Country
Club
tel 049 9526444
Golf breaks with two nights dinner,
bed and breakfast.

England

ENGLAND

BEDFORDSHIRE

ASPLEY GUISE   Map 04 SP93

Aspley Guise & Woburn Sands West Hill MK17 8DX
☎ 01908 583596 Fax 01908 583596 (Secretary)
A fine undulating course in expansive heathland
interspersed with many attractive clumps of gorse,
broom and bracken. Some well-established silver birch
are a feature. The 7th, 8th and 9th are really tough holes
to complete the first half.
18 holes, 6079yds, Par 71, SSS 70, Course record 67.
Club membership 560.
Visitors	with member only at weekends.
Societies	Wed & Fri normally booked 6 mths ahead.
Green Fees	£35 per day; £26 per round weekdays only.
Prof	Joe Awuku
Designer	Sandy Herd
Facilities	⊗ by prior arrangement ⫚ by prior arrangement ⬱ ♥ ♀ ⬥ ⛳ ♦ ⚐
Location	2m W of M1 junc 13

Hotel	★★★ 68% Moore Place Hotel, The Square, ASPLEY GUISE ☎ 01908 282000 39 ⇆ ♣ Annexe15 ⇆ ♣

BEDFORD   Map 04 TL04

Bedford Great Denham Golf Village, Carnoustie Dr,
Biddenham MK40 4FF
☎ 01234 320022 Fax 01234 320023
e-mail: thebedford1@ukonline.co.uk
American styled course with 89 bunkers, 8 large water
features and large contoured greens. Built on sand and gravel
the course is open all year round.
18 holes, 6471yds, Par 72, SSS 72, Course record 67.
Club membership 600.
Visitors	contact in advance, limited weekends.
Societies	telephone for details.
Green Fees	£25 per round (£35 weekends and bank holidays).
Cards	🖩 ▬ ▬ 🄿 ▬ ▬ ◨
Prof	Zac Thompson
Designer	David Pottage
Facilities	⊗ ⫚ ⬱ ♥ ♀ ⬥ ⛳ ♦ ⚐ ♦ ⚐ ℓ
Location	2.5m W of Bedford off A428

Hotel	★★★ Woodlands Manor Hotel, Green Ln, Clapham, BEDFORD ☎ 01234 363281 30 ⇆ ♣ Annexe3 ⇆ ♣

Bedford & County Green Ln, Clapham MK41 6ET
☎ 01234 352617 Fax 01234 357195
A mature parkland course established in 1912 with views
over Bedford and surrounding countryside. Beware of the
brook that discreetly meanders through the 7th, 10th, 11th
and 15th holes. The testing par 4 15th is one of the most
challenging holes in the area.
18 holes, 6347yds, Par 70, SSS 70.
Club membership 600.

Visitors	handicap certificate required, weekends with member only.
Societies	welcome Mon,Tue,Thu & Fri, telephone in advance.
Green Fees	£24 per round; £30 per 2 rounds.
Prof	R Tattersall
Facilities	⊗ ⫚ by prior arrangement ⬱ ♥ ♀ ⬥ ⛳ ♦
Location	2m N off A6

Hotel	★★★ Woodlands Manor Hotel, Green Ln, Clapham, BEDFORD ☎ 01234 363281 30 ⇆ ♣ Annexe3 ⇆ ♣

Bedfordshire Bromham Rd, Biddenham MK40 4AF
☎ 01234 261669 Fax 01234 261669
An attractive and easy walking parkland course with plenty
of trees providing a problem for 'off-line' golfers.
18 holes, 6305yds, Par 70, SSS 70, Course record 63.
Club membership 700.
Visitors	may not play at weekends except with member.
Societies	must telephone in advance/confirm in writing.
Green Fees	not confirmed.
Prof	Peter Saunders
Facilities	⬥ ⛳ ♦ ⚐ ℓ
Location	1m W on A428

Hotel	★★★ Woodlands Manor Hotel, Green Ln, Clapham, BEDFORD ☎ 01234 363281 30 ⇆ ♣ Annexe3 ⇆ ♣

Mowsbury Cleat Hill, Kimbolton Rd, Ravensden
MK41 8DQ
☎ 01234 771041 & 216374 (pro) Fax 01234 771041
e-mail: mgc@freenet.co.uk
Parkland municipal course in rural surroundings. Long and
testing 14-bay driving range and squash facilities.
18 holes, 6451yds, Par 72, SSS 71, Course record 66.
Club membership 550.
Visitors	no restrictions.
Societies	apply in writing.
Green Fees	£10 per round (£13.50 weekends).
Prof	Malcolm Summers
Designer	Hawtree
Facilities	⊗ ⫚ by prior arrangement ⬱ ♥ ♀ ⬥ ⛳ ♦ ⚐ ♦ ℓ
& Leisure	squash.
Location	2m N of town centre on B660

Hotel	★★★ Woodlands Manor Hotel, Green Ln, Clapham, BEDFORD ☎ 01234 363281 30 ⇆ ♣ Annexe3 ⇆ ♣

CHALGRAVE   Map 04 TL02

Chalgrave Manor Dunstable Rd LU5 6JN
☎ 01525 876556 Fax 01525 876556
Undulating course constructed in 1994 offering a good test of
golf for all standards of golfer. Feature holes include the
short 10th (150 yards) that requires an accurate shot across
water to a splendid sloping green, and the Par 4 11th which
incorporates an elevated tee, a ditch, several bunkers, a pond
and perilously close out of bounds.
18 holes, 6382yds, Par 72, SSS 70, Course record 69.
Club membership 450.
Visitors	welcome, dress code smart casual, after 11am at weekends.
Societies	apply in writing or telephone, in advance.
Green Fees	£15 (£20 weekends & bank holidays).

▶

Cards	🖩 💳 💳 💳 💷
Prof	Terry Bunyan
Designer	M Palmer
Facilities	⊗ 🛏 🍴 ♀ ⛳ 🏪 🚃 ✐
Location	From M1 junct 12 take A5120 through Toddington, entrance about 1m out, well signposted
Hotel	★★★ 67% Hanover International Hotel, Church St, DUNSTABLE ☎ 01582 662201 68 ⇄ ⏽

COLMWORTH   Map 04 TL15

Colmworth & North Bedfordshire New Rd MK44 2NU
☎ 01234 378181 Fax 01234 376235
An easy walking course with well-bunkered greens, opened in 1991. The course is often windy and plays longer than the yardage suggests. Water comes into play on 3 holes.
18 holes, 6435yds, Par 72, SSS 71, Course record 71.
Club membership 200.

Visitors	advisable to contact in advance, may only play at weekends after 9.30am.
Societies	telephone in advance.
Green Fees	£12 per 18 holes; £9 per 12 holes; £7 per 9 holes (£18/£13/£10 weekends).
Prof	M Fields/S Bonham/S Richardson
Designer	John Glasgow
Facilities	⊗ 🛏 🍴 ♀ ⛳ 🏪 🍴 🚗 🚃 ✐ ⛳
& Leisure	fishing, par 3 course.
Location	7m NE of Bedford, off B660
Hotel	★★★ 70% The Barns Hotel, Cardington Rd, BEDFORD ☎ 01234 270044 48 ⇄ ⏽

DUNSTABLE   Map 04 TL02

Dunstable Downs Whipsnade Rd LU6 2NB
☎ 01582 604472 Fax 01582 478700
e-mail: dunstabledownsgc@aol.com
A fine downland course set on two levels with far-reaching views and frequent sightings of graceful gliders. The 9th hole is one of the best short holes in the country. There is a modernised clubhouse.
18 holes, 6251yds, Par 70, SSS 70, Course record 64.
Club membership 600.

Visitors	welcome Mon, Tue, Thur and Fri, weekends with member only. Handicap certificate required.
Societies	apply in advance.

Green Fees	£40 per day; £25 per round.
Prof	Michael Weldon
Designer	James Braid
Facilities	⊗ 🍴 by prior arrangement 🛏 🍴 ♀ ⛳ 🏪 🚃 ✐
Location	2m S off B4541
Hotel	★★★ 67% Hanover International Hotel, Church St, DUNSTABLE ☎ 01582 662201 68 ⇄ ⏽

Griffin Chaul End Rd, Caddington LU1 4AX
☎ 01582 415573 Fax 01582 415314
A challenging 18-hole course with ponds and lakes.
18 holes, 6240yds, Par 71, SSS 70.
Club membership 510.

Visitors	welcome Mon-Fri & after 2pm weekends no need to book.
Societies	welcome midweek and Sat/Sun pm summer. Book by telephone.
Green Fees	£13 per round Mon-Thu (£15 Fri, £18 weekends).
Facilities	⊗ 🍴 🛏 🍴 ♀ ⛳ 🏪
Location	Off A505 Luton/Dunstable
Hotel	★★★ 67% Hanover International Hotel, Church St, DUNSTABLE ☎ 01582 662201 68 ⇄ ⏽

LEIGHTON BUZZARD   Map 04 SP92

Leighton Buzzard Plantation Rd LU7 7JF ☎ 01525 244800 (Office) & 244805 (Club) Fax 01525 244801
Parkland course with easy walking. The 17th and 18th holes are challenging tree-lined finishing holes with tight fairways. 11th par 3 is signature hole.
18 holes, 6101yds, Par 71, SSS 70, Course record 66.
Club membership 700.

Visitors	may play yellow tees, may not play Tue (Ladies Day). May only play with member weekends and bank holidays. Handicap certificate required unless playing with member.
Societies	prior booking required.
Green Fees	not confirmed.
Prof	Lee Scarbrow
Facilities	⊗ 🍴 🛏 🍴 ♀ ⛳ 🏪 🍴 🏌 🚃 ✐
Location	1.5m N of town centre off A4146
Hotel	★★★ 67% Hanover International Hotel, Church St, DUNSTABLE ☎ 01582 662201 68 ⇄ ⏽

LOWER STONDON   Map 04 TL13

Mount Pleasant Station Rd SG16 6JL ☎ 01462 850999
e-mail: davidsimsmpgolf@aol.com
A 9-hole course which, when played over 18 totals some 6003 yards. The course is undulating meadowland with mature hedges and trees and also 10,000 new trees. Two small ponds are crossed and there is a significant ditch in play on several holes. The 5th, 11th and 14th holes are all 400yds and play long into the prevailing West wind. Visitors consider the greens some of the best conditioned in the area and with good drainage the course rarely has to close.

▶

9 holes, 6003yds, Par 70, SSS 69, Course record 71.
Club membership 300.

Visitors   no restrictions, can book 2 days in advance,
                booking advisable weekends & evenings May-
                Sep.
Societies   telephone or apply in writing.
Green Fees   18 holes £12, 9 holes £7 (£16/£9 weekends &
                bank holidays).
Cards   ▨▨ ▨▨ ▨▨ ▨▨ ▨▨ ▨
Prof   Mike Roberts
Designer   Derek Young
Facilities   ⊗ ⧛ ᵇ ♥ ♀ ♨ 🖿 ⌁ ♨ ✧
Location   0.75m W of A600, 4m N of Hitchin

Hotel   ★★★ 81% Menzies Flitwick Manor, Church
                Rd, FLITWICK ☎ 0870 6003013 17 ⇌ ♠

LUTON   Map 04 TL02

South Beds Warden Hill LU2 7AE
☎ 01582 591500 Fax 01582 495381
18 and 9 hole downland courses, slightly undulating.
Galley Hill Course: 18 holes, 6397yds, Par 71, SSS 71,
Course record 64.
Warden Hill Course: 9 holes, 2424yds, Par 32, SSS 32.
Club membership 1000.

Visitors   must contact in advance and have a handicap
                certificate.
Societies   telephone for details.
Green Fees   telephone for fees.
Prof   Eddie Cogle
Facilities   ⊗ ⧛ ᵇ ♥ ♀ ♨ 🖿 ⌁ ✧
Location   2m N of Luton on A6

Hotel   ★★★ 57% The Chiltern, Waller Av, LUTON
                ☎ 01582 575911 91 ⇌ ♠

Stockwood Park London Rd LU1 4LX
☎ 01582 413704 (pro shop)
Well laid out municipal parkland course with established
trees and several challenging holes.
18 holes, 6049yds, Par 69, SSS 69, Course record 67.
Club membership 800.

Visitors   no restrictions.
Societies   Mon, Tue & Thu only, telephone for
                application.
Green Fees   £9 per round (£12 weekends).
Prof   Glyn McCarthy
Facilities   ⊗ ⧛ ᵇ ♥ ♀ ♨ 🖿 ⌁ ❧ ♨ ✧ ୧
Location   1m S

Hotel   ★★★ 57% The Chiltern, Waller Av, LUTON
                ☎ 01582 575911 91 ⇌ ♠

MILLBROOK   Map 04 TL03

Lyshott Heath Millbrook Village MK45 2JB
☎ 01525 840252 Fax 01525 406249
e-mail: enquiries@lyshott-heath.com
Long parkland course, on rolling countryside high above the
Bedfordshire plains. Laid out on well-drained sandy soil with
many fairways lined with silver birch, pine and larch.
18 holes, 7100yds, Par 74, SSS 73, Course record 69.
Club membership 366.

Visitors   must contact in advance, may not play after
                11am on Thu or after 11.30am at weekends.
Societies   telephone for details.

Green Fees £20 per 18 holes (£35 weekends).
Prof   Geraint Dixon
Designer   William Sutherland
Facilities   ⊗ ⧛ ᵇ ♥ ♀ ♨ 🖿 ⌁ ♨ ✧
Location   M1 junct 12 & 13, then take A507 Woburn to
                Ampthill road

Hotel   ★★★ 81% Menzies Flitwick Manor, Church
                Rd, FLITWICK ☎ 0870 6003013 17 ⇌ ♠

PAVENHAM   Map 04 SP95

Pavenham Park MK43 7PE
☎ 01234 822202 Fax 01234 826602
e-mail: kolvengolf@ukonline.co.uk
Mature, undulating parkland course with fast contoured
greens.
18 holes, 6400yds, Par 72, SSS 71, Course record 63.
Club membership 790.

Visitors   welcome weekdays, weekends as members
                guests only.
Societies   telephone in advance.
Green Fees £20 per 18 holes.
Cards   ▨▨ ▨▨ ▨
Prof   Zac Thompson
Designer   Zac Thompson
Facilities   ⊗ ⧛ ᵇ ♥ ♀ ♨ 🖿 ⌁ ❧ ♨ ✧
Location   1.5m from A6, N of Bedford

Hotel   ★★★ Woodlands Manor Hotel, Green Ln,
                Clapham, BEDFORD ☎ 01234 363281
                30 ⇌ ♠ Annexe3 ⇌ ♠

SANDY   Map 04 TL14

John O'Gaunt Sutton Park SG19 2LY
☎ 01767 260360 Fax 01767 262834
Two magnificent parkland courses - John O'Gaunt and
Carthagena - covering a gently undulating and tree-lined
terrain. The John O'Gaunt course makes the most of
numerous natural features, notably a river which crosses the
fairways of four holes. The Carthagena course has larger
greens, longer tees and from the back tees is a challenging
course. Fine clubhouse.
John O'Gaunt Course: 18 holes, 6513yds, Par 71, SSS 71,
Course record 64.
Carthagena Course: 18 holes, 5869yds, Par 69, SSS 69.
Club membership 1500.

Visitors   must contact in advance.
Societies   must pre-book.
Green Fees not confirmed.
Prof   Peter Round
Designer   John O'Gaunt/Others
Facilities   ⊗ ⧛ ᵇ ♥ ♀ ♨ 🖿 ❧ ♨ ✧
Location   3m NE of Biggleswade on B1040

Hotel   ★★ 69% Abbotsley Golf Hotel & Country
                Club, Potton Rd, Eynesbury Hardwicke, ST
                NEOTS ☎ 01480 474000 Annexe42 ⇌ ♠

┌───┐
│   AA Hotels that have special   │
│ arrangements with golf courses are listed at │
│   the back of the guide   │
└───┘

SHEFFORD
Map 04 TL13

Beadlow Manor Hotel & Golf & Country Club SG17 5PH
☎ 01525 860800 Fax 01525 861345
e-mail: beadlow@kbnet.co.uk
A 36-hole golf and leisure complex. The Baroness Manhattan and the Baron Manhattan golf courses are undulating with water hazards on numerous holes. These are good challenging courses for both the beginner and low handicap player.
Baroness Course: 18 holes, 6072yds, Par 71, SSS 69, Course record 67.
Baron Course: 18 holes, 6619yds, Par 73, SSS 72, Course record 67.
Club membership 300.
Visitors book in advance & must adhere to dress code.
Societies apply in writing or telephone in advance.
Green Fees not confirmed.
Cards 🏧 💳 💳 💳 💳 💳 💳
Prof Geraint Dixon
Facilities ⊗ ⊞ 🏌 🏌 ♀ 👥 🏠 🍴 🏌 🐦 🏌 ♂ ⛳
& Leisure sauna, solarium, gymnasium.
Location On A507

Hotel ★★ 67% Stratton House Hotel, London Rd, BIGGLESWADE ☎ 01767 312442 31 🛏 🐦

TILSWORTH
Map 04 SP92

Tilsworth Dunstable Rd LU7 9PU
☎ 01525 210721/2 Fax 01525 210465
e-mail: www.tilsworthgolf.co.uk
An undulating 18 hole parkland course with a 30-bay floodlit driving range.
18 holes, 5306yds, Par 69, SSS 66, Course record 66.
Club membership 400.
Visitors may book up to 7 days in advance. May not play before 10am Sundays.
Societies welcome weekdays, apply in advance to W Payne
Green Fees £12 per 18 holes;(£14 weekends & bank holidays).
Cards 🏧 💳 💳 💳 💳
Prof Nick Webb
Facilities ⊗ ⊞ 🏌 🏌 ♀ 👥 🏠 🍴 🐦 🏌 ♂ ⛳
Location 0.5m NE off A5, N of Dunstable

Hotel ★★★ 67% Hanover International Hotel, Church St, DUNSTABLE ☎ 01582 662201 68 🛏 🐦

WHIPSNADE
Map 04 TL01

Whipsnade Park Studham Ln, Dagnall HP4 1RH
☎ 01442 842330 Fax 01442 842090
e-mail: whipsnadeparkgc@talk21.com
Parkland course situated on downs overlooking the Chilterns adjoining Whipsnade Zoo. Easy walking, good views.
18 holes, 6800yds, Par 73, SSS 72, Course record 66.
Club membership 600.
Visitors welcome weekdays, with member only at weekends. Must contact in advance.
Societies by prior arrangement.
Green Fees £36 per day; £26 per round.
Cards 🏧 💳 💳
Prof Roland Perry

Facilities ⊗ ⊞ 🏌 🏌 ♀ 👥 🏠 🍴 🐦 🏌 ♂ ⛳
Location 1m E off B4506 between villages of Dagnall & Studham

Hotel ★★★ 67% Hanover International Hotel, Church St, DUNSTABLE ☎ 01582 662201 68 🛏 🐦

WYBOSTON
Map 04 TL15

Wyboston Lakes MK44 3AL ☎ 01480 223004
Fax 01480 407330 e-mail: venue@wybostonlakes.co.uk
Parkland course, with narrow fairways, small greens, set around four lakes and a river which provide the biggest challenge on this very scenic course.
18 holes, 5955yds, Par 70, SSS 69, Course record 65.
Club membership 300.

Visitors a booking system is in operation at weekends, book no more than 8 days in advance.
Societies telephone in advance.
Green Fees £12.50 per 18 holes (£16.50 weekends & bank holidays).
Cards 🏧 💳
Prof Paul Ashwell
Designer N Oakden
Facilities ⊗ ⊞ 🏌 🏌 ♀ 👥 🏠 🍴 🐦 🏌 ♂ ⛳
& Leisure heated indoor swimming pool, fishing, sauna, solarium, gymnasium, watersports.
Location 1m S of St Neots off A1/A428

Hotel ★★★ Woodlands Manor Hotel, Green Ln, Clapham, BEDFORD ☎ 01234 363281 30 🛏 🐦 Annexe3 🛏 🐦

ASCOT
Map 04 SU96

Berkshire Swinley Rd SL5 8AY ☎ 01344 621495
Two heathland courses with splendid tree-lined fairways. The Red Course, on slightly higher ground is a little longer than the Blue. It has an unusual assortment of holes, 6 par threes, 6 par fours and 6 par five, the short holes, particularly the 10th and 16th, being the most intimidating. The Blue Course starts with a par 3 and shares with the 16th the reputation of being the finest holes of the 18. ▶

Red Course: 18 holes, 6379yds, Par 72, SSS 71.
Blue Course: 18 holes, 6260yds, Par 71, SSS 71.

Visitors	by prior arrangement
Societies	applications in writing only and must be registered.
Green Fees	£80 per day; £60 per round.
Cards	🔲 🔲 💳
Prof	P Anderson
Designer	H Fowler
Facilities	⊗ ⊪ 🍺 ♍ ♀ ♨ 🏠 ⌁ ➘ ⚒ ⌂ ⟨
Location	2.5m NW of M3 jct 3 on A332
Hotel	★★★★ 64% The Berystede, Bagshot Rd, Sunninghill, ASCOT ☎ 0870 400 8111 90 ⇌ ⌂

Lavender Park Swinley Rd SL5 8BD ☎ 01344 893344
Public parkland course, ideal for the short game featuring challenging narrow fairways. Driving range with 9-hole par 3 course, floodlit until 22.00 hrs.
9 holes, 1102yds, Par 27, SSS 28.

Visitors	no restrictions.
Societies	welcome, notice preferred.
Green Fees	£3.50 per 9 holes;£5 per 18 holes (£5/£8 weekends).
Cards	🔲 🔲 🔲 💳 🔲 🔲 💳
Prof	David Johnson/Andy Piper
Facilities	🍺 ♀ 🏠 ⌁ ⟨
& Leisure	snooker.
Location	3.5m SW of Ascot, on A332
Hotel	★★★★ 64% The Berystede, Bagshot Rd, Sunninghill, ASCOT ☎ 0870 400 8111 90 ⇌ ⌂

Mill Ride Mill Ride SL5 8LT
☎ 01344 886777 Fax 01344 886820
e-mail: archie@millride.com
Opened for play in 1991, this 18-hole course combines links and parkland styles. The holes require as much thinking as playing.
18 holes, 6807yds, Par 72, SSS 72, Course record 64.
Club membership 400.

Visitors	must contact in advance, limited access at weekends.
Societies	apply in advance.
Green Fees	not confirmed.
Cards	🔲 🔲 🔲 💳 🔲 🔲 💳
Prof	Terry Wild
Designer	Donald Steel

Facilities	⊗ ⧉ ⊪ 🍺 ♀ 🏠 ⌁ 🏠 ⟨
& Leisure	sauna.
Location	2m W of Ascot
Hotel	★★★★ 64% The Berystede, Bagshot Rd, Sunninghill, ASCOT ☎ 0870 400 8111 90 ⇌ ⌂

Royal Ascot Winkfield Rd SL5 7LJ
☎ 01344 625175 Fax 01344 872330
Heathland course inside Ascot racecourse and exposed to weather.
18 holes, 5716yds, Par 68, SSS 68, Course record 65.
Club membership 620.

Visitors	must be guest of member or contact secretary in advance. Not weekends.
Societies	telephone for provisional booking.
Green Fees	not confirmed.
Prof	Alistair White
Designer	J H Taylor
Facilities	♨ 🏠 ⟨
Location	0.5m N on A330
Hotel	★★★★ 64% The Berystede, Bagshot Rd, Sunninghill, ASCOT ☎ 0870 400 8111 90 ⇌ ⌂

Swinley Forest Coronation Rd SL5 9LE
☎ 01344 874979 (Secretary) Fax 01344 874733
e-mail: swinleyfgc@aol.com
An attractive and immaculate course of heather and pine situated in the heart of Swinley Forest. The 17th is as good a short hole as will be found, with a bunkered plateau green and the 12th hole is one of the most challenging par 4's.
18 holes, 6100yds, Par 69, SSS 70, Course record 62.
Club membership 350.

Visitors	on introduction of a member or by invitation only.
Societies	must contact in writing.
Green Fees	£70 per round.
Cards	🔲 🔲 💳
Prof	R C Parker
Designer	Harry Colt
Facilities	⊗ ⊪ 🍺 ♀ ♨ 🏠 ⌁ ➘ ⚒ ⟨
Location	1.5m S, off A330
Hotel	★★★★ 64% The Berystede, Bagshot Rd, Sunninghill, ASCOT ☎ 0870 400 8111 90 ⇌ ⌂

BINFIELD   Map 04 SU87

Blue Mountain Golf Centre Wood Ln RG42 4EX
☎ 01344 300200 Fax 01344 360960
An 18-hole Pay and Play course with many testing holes with water hazards. Greens are large, undulating and strategically placed bunkers provide a fair challenge.
18 holes, 6097yds, Par 70, SSS 69, Course record 63.
Club membership 1250.

Visitors	tee times bookable in advance by phoning 01344 300220,
Societies	must contact in advance.
Green Fees	not confirmed.
Cards	🔲 🔲 🔲 💳 🔲 🔲 💳
Prof	Iain Looms

▶

Blue Mountain Golf Centre

Facilities	⊗ ⅏ ⅊ ⬥ ♀ ⚲ 🏠 ⚑ ⚓ ✂ ⚗
Location	2m from junct 10 of the M4

Hotel ★★★★ 76% Coppid Beech, John Nike Way, BRACKNELL ☎ 01344 303333 205 ⇆ ⋔

CHADDLEWORTH — Map 04 SU47

West Berkshire RG20 7DU
☎ 01488 638574 & 638851 Fax 01488 638781
Challenging and interesting downland course with views of the Berkshire Downs. The course is bordered by ancient woodland and golfers will find manicured fairways with well constructed greens and strategically placed hazards. The testing 627yds 5th hole is one of the longest par 5's in southern England. Bunkers are well placed from tees and around the greens to catch any wayward shots.
18 holes, 7001yds, Par 73, SSS 74.
Club membership 650.

Visitors	must contact in advance, may play weekends pm only.
Societies	telephone in advance.
Green Fees	£35 per day; £25 per round (£35 weekends pm only).
Cards	⬜ ⬛ 💳 🔲
Prof	Paul Simpson
Designer	Robin Stagg
Facilities	⊗ ⅊ ⬥ ♀ ⚲ 🏠 ⚓ ✂ ⚗
Location	1m S of village off A338

Hotel ★★★ 65% The Chequers, Oxford St, NEWBURY ☎ 01635 38000 45 ⇆ ⋔ Annexe11 ⇆ ⋔

COOKHAM — Map 04 SU88

Winter Hill Grange Ln SL6 9RP
☎ 01628 527613 (Secretary) Fax 01628 527479
Parkland course set in a curve of the Thames with wonderful views across the river to Cliveden.
18 holes, 6408yds, Par 72, SSS 71, Course record 63.
Club membership 850.

Visitors	phone in advance, not permitted weekends.
Societies	welcome Wed & Fri, telephone initially.
Green Fees	£28 per day; £20 after 2pm.
Prof	Roger Frost
Designer	Charles Lawrie
Facilities	⊗ ⅊ ⬥ ♀ ⚲ 🏠 ✂ ⚗
Location	1m NW off B4447

Hotel ★★★★ 71% The Compleat Angler, Marlow Bridge, MARLOW ☎ 0870 400 8100 65 ⇆ ⋔

CROWTHORNE — Map 04 SU86

East Berkshire Ravenswood Ave RG45 6BD
☎ 01344 772041 Fax 01344 777378
An attractive heathland course with an abundance of heather and pine trees. Walking is easy and the greens are exceptionally good. Some fairways become tight where the heather encroaches on the line of play. The course is testing and demands great accuracy.
18 holes, 6344yds, Par 69, SSS 70.
Club membership 766.

Visitors	must contact in advance and have a handicap certificate; must play with member at weekends & bank holidays.
Societies	telephone for availability.
Green Fees	not confirmed.
Prof	Arthur Roe
Designer	P Paxton
Facilities	⚲ 🏠 ⚑ ✂ ⚗
Location	W side of town centre off B3348

Hotel ★★★★★ 72% Pennyhill Park Hotel & Country Club, London Rd, BAGSHOT ☎ 01276 471774 26 ⇆ ⋔ Annexe97 ⇆ ⋔

DATCHET — Map 04 SU97

Datchet Buccleuch Rd SL3 9BP
☎ 01753 543887 & 541872 Fax 01753 541872
Meadowland course, easy walking.
9 holes, 5978yds, Par 70, SSS 69, Course record 63.
Club membership 430.

Visitors	may play weekdays before 3pm.
Societies	Tue only. (Other times by prior arrangement)
Green Fees	not confirmed.
Facilities	⊗ ⅏ ⅊ ⬥ ♀ ⚲ 🏠 ⚗
Location	NW side of Datchet off B470

Hotel ★★★ 67% The Castle Hotel, 18 High St, WINDSOR ☎ 0870 400 8300 41 ⇆ ⋔ Annexe70 ⇆ ⋔

MAIDENHEAD — Map 04 SU88

Bird Hills Drift Rd, Hawthorn Hill SL6 3ST
☎ 01628 771030 Fax 01628 631023

A gently undulating course with easy walking and many water hazards. Some challenging holes are the Par 5 6th dogleg, Par 3 9th surrounded by water and bunkers, and the 16th which is a long uphill Par 4 and a two-tier green. ▶

19

18 holes, 6176yds, Par 72, SSS 69, Course record 65.
Club membership 400.

Visitors	to book ring 7 days in advance.
Societies	write or telephone in advance.
Green Fees	not confirmed.
Cards	〰 〰 〰 〰 〰
Prof	Nick Slimming
Facilities	⊗ ⏍ ⅃ ⅃ ⅃ ⅃ ⅃ ⅃ ⅃
Location	4m SW of Bray on A330

Hotel	★★★ 72% Stirrups Country House, Maidens Green, BRACKNELL ☎ 01344 882284 29 ⇋ ↑

Maidenhead Shoppenhangers Rd SL6 2PZ
☎ 01628 624693 Fax 01628 624693
A pleasant parkland course on level ground with easy walking to good greens. Perhaps a little short but there are many natural features and some first-rate short holes.
18 holes, 6364yds, Par 70, SSS 70.
Club membership 650.

Visitors	may not play after noon on Fri or at weekends. Must contact in advance and have a handicap certificate.
Societies	must contact in writing.
Green Fees	£35 per day; £27 per round.
Cards	〰
Prof	Steve Geary
Designer	Alex Simpson
Facilities	⊗ ⏍ ⅃ ⅃ ⅃ ⅃ ⅃ ⅃
Location	S side of town centre off A308

Hotel	★★★★ Fredrick's Hotel, Shoppenhangers Rd, MAIDENHEAD ☎ 01628 581000 37 ⇋ ↑

Temple Henley Rd, Hurley SL6 5LH ☎ 01628 824795
Fax 01628 828119
An open parkland course offering extensive views over the Thames Valley. Firm, relatively fast greens, natural slopes and subtle contours provide a challenging test to golfers of all abilities. Excellent drainage assures play during inclement weather.
18 holes, 6232yds, Par 70, SSS 70, Course record 63.
Club membership 480.

Visitors	must contact in advance, limited weekend access.
Societies	contact Secretary for details.
Green Fees	£50 per day; £33 per round (£55/£38 weekends & bank holidays).
Cards	〰 〰 〰 〰
Prof	James Whiteley
Designer	Willie Park (Jnr)
Facilities	⊗ ⅃ ⅃ ⅃ ⅃ ⅃ ⅃ ⅃
Location	Exit M4 jct 8/9 take A404M then A4130, or M40 exit jct 4 take A404 then A4130,signposted Henley

Hotel	★★★★ 71% The Compleat Angler, Marlow Bridge, MARLOW ☎ 0870 400 8100 65 ⇋ ↑

Looking for a driving range?
See the index at the back of the guide

MORTIMER

Map 04 SU66

Wokefield Park Wokefield Park RG7 3AE
☎ 0118 9334018 Fax 0118 9334162
Set in a prime location amid the peaceful and picturesque Berkshire countryside. The course architect has retained the numerous mature trees, and these, together with the winding streams, nine lakes and large bunkers, contribute to the beauty and challenge of this championship course.
18 holes, 6577yds, Par 72, SSS 72.
Club membership 252.

Visitors	no restrictions.
Societies	apply in writing/telephone in advance
Green Fees	not confirmed.
Cards	〰 〰 〰 〰 〰 〰
Prof	Gary Smith
Designer	Jonathan Gaunt
Facilities & Leisure	⊗ ⏍ ⅃ ⅃ ⅃ ⅃ ⅃ ⅃ ⅃ ⅃ ⅃ ⅃ ⅃ hard tennis courts, heated indoor swimming pool, fishing, sauna, gymnasium, jacuzzi.
Location	M4 junct11, on Grazeley/Mortimer road

Hotel	★★★ 74% Romans Country House Hotel, Little London Rd, SILCHESTER ☎ 0118 970 0421 11 ⇋ ↑ Annexe14 ⇋ ↑

NEWBURY

Map 04 SU46

Donnington Valley Snelsmore House, Snelsmore Common RG14 3BG ☎ 01635 568140 Fax 01635 568141
e-mail: golf@donningtonvalley.co.uk
Undulating, testing course with mature trees and elevated greens, some protected by water.
18 holes, 6353yds, Par 71, SSS 71.
Club membership 520.

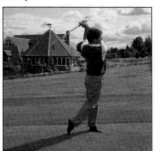

Visitors	booking system up to 7 days in advance, members have priority weekends.
Societies	write or telephone in advance.
Green Fees	£18 per 18 holes(£25 weekends).
Cards	〰 〰 〰
Prof	Edward Lainchbury
Designer	Mike Smith
Facilities	⊗ ⏍ ⅃ ⅃ ⅃ ⅃ ⅃ ⅃ ⅃ ⅃ ⅃
Location	2m N of Newbury

Hotel	★★★★ 79% Donnington Valley Hotel & Golf Course, Old Oxford Rd, Donnington, NEWBURY ☎ 01635 551199 58 ⇋ ↑ *See advertisement on page 512*

Newbury & Crookham Bury's Bank Rd, Greenham
RG19 8BZ ☎ 01635 40035 Fax 01635 40045
e-mail: june.hearsey@newburygolf.co.uk
A well-laid out, attractive course running mostly through
woodland, and giving more of a challenge than its length
suggests.
18 holes, 5940yds, Par 69, SSS 68.
Club membership 800.

Visitors	must play with member on weekends & bank holidays. Handicap certificate required.
Societies	must contact in advance.
Green Fees	£30 per day; £25 per round.
Cards	🔲 🔲 🔲
Prof	David Harris
Facilities	⊗ ﹐ 🝙 🝙 ♀ 🝙 🝙 ✆
Location	2m SE off A34
Hotel	★★★ 65% The Chequers, Oxford St, NEWBURY ☎ 01635 38000 45 ⇆ ᒃ Annexe11 ⇆ ᒃ

READING   Map 04 SU77

Calcot Park Bath Rd, Calcot RG31 7RN
☎ 0118 942 7124 Fax 0118 945 3373
A delightfully sporting, slightly undulating parkland
course just outside the town. Hazards include streams, a
lake and many trees. The 6th is the longest, 507 yard par
5, with the tee-shot hit downhill over cross-bunkers to a
well-guarded green, the 7th (162 yards) is played over
the lake to an elevated green and the 13th (194 yards)
requires a big carry over a gully to a plateau green.
18 holes, 6283yds, Par 70, SSS 70, Course record 63.
Club membership 750.

Visitors	must have handicap certificate or letter of introduction from club. May play weekdays only, excluding bank holidays.
Societies	must apply in writing.
Green Fees	£36 per day/round.
Prof	Ian Campbell
Designer	H S Colt
Facilities	⊗ ﹐ 🝙 🝙 ♀ 🝙 🝙 🝙 ✆
& Leisure	fishing.
Location	1.5m from M4 junct 12 on A4 towards Reading
Hotel	★★★ 75% The Copper Inn Hotel & Restaurant, PANGBOURNE ☎ 0118 984 2244 14 ⇆ ᒃ Annexe8 ⇆ ᒃ

Hennerton Crazies Hill Rd, Wargrave RG10 8LT
☎ 0118 940 1000 Fax 0118 940 1042
Overlooking the Thames Valley, this Par 68 course has many
existing natural features and a good number of hazards such
as bunkers, mature trees and two small lakes. The most
memorable hole is probably the 7th which is a par 3, 183
yards crossing a sharp valley to the green from which there
are spectacular views of the course.
9 holes, 5460yds, Par 68, SSS 67, Course record 66.
Club membership 450.

Visitors	book 48 hours in advance, play weekends after 10am.
Societies	telephone or write for information.
Green Fees	£15(£18 weekends).
Cards	🔲 🔲 🔲
Prof	William Farrow

Designer	Col D Beard
Facilities	⊗ 🝙 🝙 ♀ 🝙 🝙 🝙 ✆
Location	Follow signs from A321 Wargrave High Street
Hotel	★★★ 71% Red Lion Hotel, Hart St, HENLEY-ON-THAMES ☎ 01491 572161 26 ⇆ ᒃ

Mapledurham Chazey Heath, Mapledurham RG4 7UD
☎ 0118 946 3353 Fax 0118 946 3363
18-hole course designed by Bob Sandow. Flanked by
hedgerows and mature woods, it is testing for players of all
levels.
*Mapledurham Golf Club: 18 holes, 5635yds, Par 69, SSS 67,
Course record 66.*
Club membership 1800.

Visitors	advanced booking required. No play before 2pm at weekends.
Societies	must contact in advance.
Green Fees	not confirmed.
Cards	🔲 🔲 🔲 🔲 🔲 🔲
Prof	Symon O'Keefe
Designer	Robert Sandow
Facilities	⊗ ﹐ 🝙 🝙 ♀ 🝙 ✆
& Leisure	sauna, gymnasium.
Location	On A4074 to Oxford
Hotel	★★★★ 58% Holiday Inn, Caversham Bridge, Richfield Av, READING ☎ 0118 925 9988 112 ⇆ ᒃ

Reading 17 Kidmore End Rd, Emmer Green RG4 8SG
☎ 0118 947 2909 (Secretary) Fax 0118 946 4468
e-mail: secretary@readinggolfclub.golfagent.co.uk
Pleasant tree-lined parkland course, part hilly and part flat
with interesting views and several challenging par 3's.
18 holes, 6212yds, Par 70, SSS 70, Course record 65.
Club membership 585.

Visitors	contact the professional. Welcome weekdays, with member only Fridays & weekends.
Societies	apply by telephone,tues,wed,thur only.
Green Fees	£33 per day.
Cards	🔲 🔲 🔲 🔲 🔲 🔲
Prof	Scott Fotheringham
Designer	James Braid
Facilities	⊗ ﹐ 🝙 🝙 ♀ 🝙 🝙 ✆
& Leisure	indoor nets.
Location	2m N off B481
Hotel	★★★ 64% Royal County Hotel, 4-8 Duke St, READING ☎ 0118 958 3455 52 ⇆ ᒃ

SINDLESHAM   Map 04 SU76

Bearwood Mole Rd RG41 5DB ☎ 0118 976 0060
Flat parkland course with one water hazard, the 40 acre lake
which features on the challenging 6th and 7th holes. Also
driving range.
9 holes, 5610yds, Par 70, SSS 68, Course record 66.
Club membership 500.

Visitors	welcome weekdays and weekend afternoons (contact in advance for pm weekend bookings)
Societies	apply in writing.
Green Fees	£18 per 18 holes; £12 per 9 holes(£22/£16 weekends).
Cards	🔲 🔲 🔲 🔲 🔲
Prof	Bayley Tustin
Designer	Barry Tustin

▶

Facilities ⊗ ⅃ ♨ ♀ ♨ 📷 🏌 ♂ 𝄞

Location 1m SW on B3030

Hotel ★★★ 64% Edward Court Hotel, Wellington Rd, WOKINGHAM ☎ 0118 977 5886 27 ⇆ ♠

SONNING   Map 04 SU77

Sonning Duffield Rd RG4 6GJ
☎ 0118 969 3332 Fax 0118 944 8409
e-mail: at@sonning-golf-club.co.uk
A quality parkland course and the scene of many county championships. Wide fairways, not overbunkered, and very good greens. Holes of changing character through wooded belts.
18 holes, 6366yds, Par 70, SSS 70, Course record 65.
Club membership 750.

Visitors weekdays only. Handicap certificate or proof of membership of another club required.
Societies must apply in writing. Wed only. Min 16
Green Fees £40 per day (£30 after 10.30am).
Prof R McDougall
Designer Hawtree
Facilities ⊗ ⅃ by prior arrangement ⅃ ♨ ♀ ♨ 📷 ♂

Location 1m S off A4

Hotel ★★★ 77% The French Horn, SONNING ON THAMES ☎ 0118 969 2204 12 ⇆ ♠ Annexe8 ⇆ ♠

STREATLEY   Map 04 SU58

Goring & Streatley RG8 9QA
☎ 01491 873229 Fax 01491 875224
e-mail: goringgc@aol.com
A parkland/moorland course that requires 'negotiating'. Four well-known first holes lead up to the heights of the 5th tee, to which there is a 300ft climb. Wide fairways, not overbunkered, with nice rewards on the way home down the last few holes. A delightful course that commands magnificent views of the Ridgeway and the River Thames.
18 holes, 6320yds, Par 71, SSS 70, Course record 65.
Club membership 740.

Visitors must contact in advance, with member only at weekends. Handicap certificate required.
Societies telephone in advance.
Green Fees not confirmed.
Cards 💳
Prof Jason Hadland
Designer Tom Morris
Facilities ⊗ ⅃ ⅃ ♨ ♀ ♨ 📷 ♂
Location N of village off A417

Hotel ★★★★ 68% The Swan Diplomat Hotel, High St, STREATLEY ☎ 01491 878800 46 ⇆ ♠

SUNNINGDALE   See page 23

SUNNINGDALE   Map 04 SU96

Sunningdale Ladies Cross Rd SL5 9RX ☎ 01344 620507
A short 18-hole course with a typical Surrey heathland layout. A very tight course, making for a challenging game.
18 holes, 3616yds, Par 60, SSS 60, Course record 51.
Club membership 350.

Visitors telephone in advance.
Societies Ladies societies only.
Green Fees not confirmed.
Facilities ⊗ ⅃ ♨ ♀ ♨ ♂
& Leisure Practice net.
Location 1m S off A30

Hotel ★★★★ 64% The Berystede, Bagshot Rd, Sunninghill, ASCOT ☎ 0870 400 8111 90 ⇆ ♠

WOKINGHAM   Map 04 SU86

Downshire Wayne Owers RG40 3DH
☎ 01344 302030 Fax 01344 301020
18 holes, 6416yds, Par 73, SSS 71.
Location 3m SW of Bracknell
Telephone for further details

Hotel ★★★★ 76% Coppid Beech, John Nike Way, BRACKNELL ☎ 01344 303333 205 ⇆ ♠

Sand Martins Finchampstead Rd RG40 3RQ
☎ 0118 9792711 Fax 0118 977 0282
e-mail: lizroginski@sandmartins.com
Two different 9-hole loops: the front nine is mostly tree-lined with ponds and the back nine is similar to a links course.
18 holes, 6212yds, Par 70, SSS 70, Course record 65.
Club membership 800.

Visitors must telephone in advance. Restricted Thu, with member only at weekends.
Societies prior arrangement by telephone.
Green Fees £17.50 per 9 holes;£30.50 per 18 holes;£50.50 per day weekdays only.
Cards 💳💳💳💳💳
Prof Andrew Hall
Designer Edward Fox
Facilities ⊗ ⅃ ⅃ ♨ ♀ ♨ 📷 🏌 🏌 ♂ 𝄞
Location 1m S of Wokingham

Hotel ★★★ 64% Edward Court Hotel, Wellington Rd, WOKINGHAM ☎ 0118 977 5886 27 ⇆ ♠

Sunningdale

Sunningdale, *Berkshire*   ☎ 01344 621681   Fax 01344 624154   Map 04 SU96

The Old Course, founded in 1900, was designed by Willie Park. It is a classic course at just 6308 yards long, with gorse and pine trees, silver birch, heather and immaculate turf. The new course is no less a challenge, created by HS Holt in 1922 it is 6443 yards. There is a long wait for anyone wishing to become a member of this prestigious club, its location within easy reach of London is an attraction in itself. Visitors playing two rounds will be asked to alternate onto the other course in the afternoon. Short rounds may be played by finishing at the 10th or 13th green on the Old Course, and the 10th or 11th green on the New Course. On Monday one course is designated the two ball course until 3.00pm, check when booking a tee time.

Visitors may not play Fri, Sat, Sun or public holidays. Must contact in advance, and have a handicap certificate and letter of introduction

Societies Tue, Wed, Thu by arrangement

Green Fees Old Course £120 per round; New Course £85 (Day ticket for both courses £145) ▭ ▬ ▬ ▣

Facilities ⊗ ▙ ▆ ♀ ⅄ 🏠 ⛳🏌 Professional (Keith Maxwell)

Location Ridgemount Rd, Sunningdale, Ascot SL5 9RR (1m S of Sunningdale, off A30)

Holes/Par/Course record 36 holes. Old Course: 18 holes, 6308 yds, Par 70, SSS 70
New Course: 18 holes, 6443 yds, Par 71, SSS 72

Championship Course

WHERE TO STAY AND EAT NEARBY

Hotels
ASCOT

★★★★⊛ 68% The Royal Berkshire, London Rd, Sunninghill.
☎ 01344 623322. 63 ⇆ 🏠

★★★★ 64% The Berystede, Bagshot Rd, Sunninghill. ☎ 0870 400 8111.
90 (89 ⇆ 🏠 1 🏠)

★★ 74% Highclere, 19 Kings Rd, Sunninghill. ☎ 01344 625220. 11 🏠

★★ 66% Brockenhurst, Brockenhurst Rd. ☎ 01344 621912.
11 (10 ⇆ 1 🏠) Annexe 5 (2 ⇆ 3 🏠)

BAGSHOT

★★★★★⊛⊛⊛ 72% Pennyhill Park, London Rd. ☎ 01276 471774.
26 ⇆ 🏠 Annexe 97 ⇆ 🏠

Restaurant
BRAY

⊛⊛⊛⊛ Waterside Inn, Ferry Rd. ☎ 01628 620691.

BRISTOL

BRISTOL   Map 03 ST57

Bristol and Clifton Beggar Bush Ln, Failand BS8 3TH
☎ 01275 393474 Fax 01275 394611
e-mail: mansec@bristolgolf.co.uk
A downland course with splendid turf and fine tree-lined
fairways. The 222-yard (par 3) 13th with the green well
below, and the par 4 16th, with its second shot across an
old quarry, are outstanding. There are splendid views
over the Bristol Channel towards Wales.
18 holes, 6316yds, Par 70, SSS 70, Course record 65.
Club membership 650.

Visitors	must have a handicap certificate. Weekends restricted.
Societies	telephone to enquire.
Green Fees	£32 per day (£35 weekends).
Cards	▦ ▦ ▦ ▧
Prof	Peter Mawson
Facilities	⊗ �𝄞 🐾 🍺 🖤 ♀ ⚲ 🏠 🍴 ⚑ ✎ ⚲ (
& Leisure	chipping green, practical bunkers.
Location	M5 junct19, follow A369 for 4m, then take B3129. Club 1m on right
Hotel	★★★ 66% Redwood Lodge Hotel, Beggar Bush Ln, Failand, BRISTOL ☎ 01275 393901 112 ⇌ ♠

Filton Golf Course Ln, Filton BS34 7QS ☎ 0117 969 4169
Fax 0117 931 4359
Challenging parkland course situated on high ground in a
pleasant suburb to the north of the city. Extensive views can
be enjoyed from the course, especially from the second tee
and the clubhouse, where on a clear day the Cotswold Hills
and the Brecon Beacons can be seen. Good par 4 testing hole
'dog-leg' 383 yds.
18 holes, 6318yds, Par 70, SSS 70, Course record 63.
Club membership 750.

Visitors	advisable to contact in advance for availability, may not play at weekends unless with member. Must have a handicap certificate.
Societies	apply in writing/phone for details.
Green Fees	£27 per day; £22 per round.
Prof	D Robinson
Facilities	⊗ �𝄞 🐾 🍺 ♀ ⚲ 🏠 🍴 ⚲
Location	5m NW off A38
Hotel	★★★ 69% Posthouse Bristol, Filton Rd, Hambrook, BRISTOL ☎ 0870 400 9014 198 ⇌ ♠

Henbury Henbury Hill, Westbury-on-Trym BS10 7QB
☎ 0117 950 0044 & 950 2121 (Prof)
Fax 0117 959 1928
e-mail: thesecretary@henburygolfclub.co.uk
A parkland course tree-lined and on two levels. The
River Trym comes into play on the 7th drop-hole with its
green set just over the stream. The last nine holes have
the beautiful Blaise Castle woods for company.
18 holes, 6007yds, Par 69, SSS 70, Course record 65.
Club membership 825.

Visitors	handicap certificate required, with member only at weekends. Advisable to contact in advance for availability.
Societies	apply in writing or telephone well in advance. Tue & Fri only.
Green Fees	£25 per round /day.
Cards	▦ ▦ ▧
Prof	Nick Riley
Facilities	⊗ ⟩⟩⟩ by prior arrangement 🐾 🍺 ♀ ⚲ 🏠 🍴 ⚲ ✎
Location	3m NW of city centre on B4055 off A4018
Hotel	★★★ 65% Henbury Lodge Hotel, Station Rd, Henbury, BRISTOL ☎ 0117 950 2615 12 ⇌ ♠ Annexe9 ⇌ ♠

Knowle West Town Ln, Brislington BS4 5DF
☎ 0117 977 0660 Fax 0117 972 0615
A parkland course with nice turf. The first five holes
climb up and down hill but the remainder are on a more
even plane.
18 holes, 6016yds, Par 69, SSS 69, Course record 61.
Club membership 700.

Visitors	must have handicap certificate, must telephone professional 0117 977 9193 for weekends.
Societies	Thu only, apply in writing.
Green Fees	£22 per round weekdays(£27 weekends & bank holidays).
Prof	Gordon Brand Snr
Designer	Hawtree/J H Taylor
Facilities	⊗ ⟩⟩⟩ 🐾 🍺 ♀ ⚲ 🏠 🍴 ⚲ ✎
Location	3m SE of city centre off A37
Hotel	★★★ 77% Hunstrete House Hotel, HUNSTRETE ☎ 01761 490490 22 ⇌ ♠

Mangotsfield Carsons Rd, Mangotsfield BS17 3LW
☎ 0117 956 5501
18 holes, 5337yds, Par 68, SSS 66, Course record 61.
Location 6m NE of city centre off B4465
Telephone for further details

Hotel	★★★ 69% Posthouse Bristol, Filton Rd, Hambrook, BRISTOL ☎ 0870 400 9014 198 ⇌ ♠

Shirehampton Park Park Hill, Shirehampton BS11 0UL
☎ 0117 982 2082 & 982 3059 Fax 0117 982 5280 e-
mail: info@shirehamptonparkgolfclub.co.uk
A lovely parkland course with views across the Avon Gorge.
18 holes, 5430yds, Par 67, SSS 66, Course record 63.
Club membership 600.

Visitors	with member only at weekends. Must have a handicap certificate.
Societies	weekdays (book through Secretary)
Green Fees	£30 per 36 holes; £25 per 27 holes, £20 per round.
Cards	▦ ▦ ▦ ▦ ▦ ▧
Prof	Brent Ellis
Facilities	⊗ ⟩⟩⟩ 🐾 🍺 ♀ ⚲ 🏠 🍴 ⚲
Location	2m E of junct 18 M5 on B4054
Hotel	★★★ 66% Redwood Lodge Hotel, Beggar Bush Ln, Failand, BRISTOL ☎ 01275 393901 112 ⇌ ♠

Woodlands Trench Ln, Almondsbury BS32 4JZ
☎ 01454 619319 Fax 01454 619397
e-mail: woodlands@tracypark.com
Situated on the edge of the Severn Valley, bordered by
Hortham Brook and Shepherds Wood, this interesting
parkland course features five testing par 3's set around the
course's five lakes, notably the 206 yd 5th hole which
extends over water.
Woodlands Golf Course: 18 holes, 6068yds, Par 70, SSS 69.
Club membership 45.
Visitors   no restrictions.
Societies   Phone or write in advance.
Green Fees   £12 per round (£14 weekends & bank holidays).
Cards   ⬜⬜⬜⬜
Prof   Nigel Warburton & Andy Lowen
Facilities   ⊗ ℳ ᴸ ▐ �sᴸ ⌂ ⛳ ⛳
& Leisure   fishing.
Location   N of Bristol off A38

Hotel   ★★★ 69% Posthouse Bristol, Filton Rd,
                  Hambrook, BRISTOL ☎ 0870 400 9014
                  198 ⇄ ℟

BUCKINGHAMSHIRE

AYLESBURY   Map 04 SP81

Aylesbury Golf Centre Hulcott Ln, Bierton HP22 5GA
☎ 01296 393644
A parkland course with magnificent views to the Chiltern
Hills. A good test of golf with out of bounds coming into
play on 9 of the holes, also a number of water hazards and
bunkers.
18 holes, 5965yds, Par 71, SSS 69.
Club membership 200.
Visitors   no restrictions, but booking advisable.
Societies   telephone for details.
Green Fees   £10 per round (£14 weekends).
Cards   ⬜⬜
Prof   Alex Saary
Designer   T S Benwell
Facilities   ⊗ ℳ ᴸ ▐ ⵙ ⌂ ⛳ ⛳
Location   1m N of Aylesbury on A418

Hotel   ★★★ 69% Posthouse Aylesbury, Aston
                  Clinton Rd, AYLESBURY
                  ☎ 0870 400 9002 140 ⇄ ℟

Aylesbury Park Off Coldharbour Way, Oxford Rd
HP17 8QQ ☎ 01296 399196 Fax 01296 336830
Parkland course with mature trees, located just south-west of
Aylesbury.
18 holes, 6148yds, Par 70, SSS 69, Course record 69.
Club membership 340.
Visitors   may book up to 1 week in advance.
Societies   telephone for Society Pack
Green Fees   not confirmed.
Designer   M Hawtree
Facilities   ⊗ ᴸ ▐ ⵙ ⌂ ⛳ ⛳ ⛳
Location   0.5m SW of Aylesbury, on the A418

Hotel   ★★★ 69% Posthouse Aylesbury, Aston
                  Clinton Rd, AYLESBURY
                  ☎ 0870 400 9002 140 ⇄ ℟

Chiltern Forest Aston Hill, Halton HP22 5NQ
☎ 01296 631267 Fax 01296 632709
e-mail: secretary@chilternforest.co.uk
This very hilly wooded parkland course is on two levels. It is
a true test of skill to the low handicap golfer, as well as being
a fair challenge to higher handicap golfers. The surrounding
woodland makes the course very scenic.
18 holes, 5765yds, Par 70, SSS 70, Course record 69.
Club membership 650.
Visitors   welcome weekdays, must play with member at
                  weekends.
Societies   contact in advance for booking form.
Green Fees   £30 per day; £25 per round.
Cards   ⬜⬜⬜⬜
Prof   A Lavers
Facilities   ⊗ ℳ ᴸ ▐ ⵙ ⌂ ⛳ ⛳
Location   1m NE off A4011

Hotel   ★★★ 69% Posthouse Aylesbury, Aston
                  Clinton Rd, AYLESBURY
                  ☎ 0870 400 9002 140 ⇄ ℟

Ellesborough Butlers Cross HP17 0TZ
☎ 01296 622114 Fax 01296 622114
Once part of the property of Chequers, and under the
shadow of the famous monument at the Wendover end of
the Chilterns. A downland course, it is rather hilly with
most holes enhanced by far-ranging views over the
Aylesbury countryside.
18 holes, 6360yds, Par 71, SSS 71, Course record 64.
Club membership 700.
Visitors   welcome on weekdays, handicap certificate
                  required.
Societies   Wed & Thu only, by prior arrangement with
                  General Manager.
Green Fees   not confirmed.
Prof   Mark Squire
Designer   James Braid
Facilities   ⊗ ᴸ ▐ ⵙ ⌂ ⛳
Location   1m E of Ellesborough on B4010

Hotel   ★★★ 69% Posthouse Aylesbury, Aston
                  Clinton Rd, AYLESBURY
                  ☎ 0870 400 9002 140 ⇄ ℟

BEACONSFIELD   Map 04 SU99

Beaconsfield Seer Green HP9 2UR
☎ 01494 676545 Fax 01494 681148
e-mail: secretary@beaconsfieldgolfclub.golfagent.co.uk
An interesting and, at times, testing tree-lined and
parkland course which frequently plays longer than
appears on the card! Each hole differs to a considerable
degree and here lies the charm. Walking is easy, except
perhaps to the 6th and 8th. Well bunkered.
18 holes, 6493yds, Par 72, SSS 71, Course record 63.
Club membership 850.
Visitors   must contact in advance and have a
                  handicap certificate. May not play
                  weekends.
Societies   phone for details
Green Fees   £48 per day; £35 per round.
Prof   Michael Brothers
Designer   H S Colt
Facilities   ⊗ ᴸ ▐ ⵙ ⌂ ⛳ ⛳ ⛳
Location   Adjacent to Seer Green railway station   ▶

Hotel	★★★★ 69% The Bellhouse, Oxford Rd, BEACONSFIELD ☎ 01753 887211 136 ⇔ 🐾

BLETCHLEY   Map 04 SP83

Windmill Hill Tattenhoe Ln MK3 7RB
☎ 01908 631113 & 366457 (Sec) Fax 01908 630034
Long, open-parkland course, the first championship course designed by Henry Cotton, opened in 1972. Proprietary Pay & Play. No winter greens.
18 holes, 6720yds, Par 73, SSS 72, Course record 68.
Club membership 400.

Visitors	booking system in operation up to 7 days in advance.
Societies	packages available, contact for details.
Green Fees	not confirmed.
Prof	Colin Clingan
Designer	Henry Cotton
Facilities	⊗ �𝄞 ⅃ ⚑ ♉ ⚷ ⌂ ☙ ❟ ➘ 🏌 ✿ (
& Leisure	pool t.
Location	W side of town centre on A421

Hotel	★★★ 63% Posthouse Milton Keynes, 500 Saxon Gate West, MILTON KEYNES ☎ 0870 400 9057 150 ⇔ 🐾

BOW BRICKHILL   Map 04 SP93

WOBURN See page 27

BUCKINGHAM   Map 04 SP63

Buckingham Tingewick Rd MK18 4AE
☎ 01280 815566 Fax 01280 821812
Undulating parkland course with a stream and river affecting 8 holes.
18 holes, 6082yds, Par 70, SSS 69, Course record 67.
Club membership 690.

Visitors	welcome Mon-Fri, with member only at weekends.
Societies	by prior arrangement.
Green Fees	£28 per day.
Prof	Tom Gates
Facilities	⊗ �𝄞 ⅃ ⚑ ♉ ⌂ ✿
& Leisure	snooker roomo.
Location	1.5m W on A421

Hotel	★★★ 65% Buckingham Four Pillars Hotel, Buckingham Ring Rd South, BUCKINGHAM ☎ 01280 822622 70 ⇔ 🐾

BURNHAM   Map 04 SU98

Burnham Beeches Green Ln SL1 8EG
☎ 01628 661448 Fax 01628 668968
A wooded parkland course on the edge of the historic Burnham Beeches Forests with a good variety of holes.
18 holes, 6449yds, Par 70, SSS 71.
Club membership 670.

Visitors	must contact in advance. May play on weekdays only. Handicap certificate required.
	welcome Apr-Oct, write or telephone for information.
Green Fees	not confirmed.
Prof	Ronnie Bolton
Facilities	⚷ ⌂ ♉ ❟ ➘ 🏌 ✿
Location	0.5m NE of Burnham

Hotel	★★★ 67% Burnham Beeches, Grove Rd, BURNHAM ☎ 01628 429955 82 ⇔ 🐾

Lambourne Dropmore Rd SL1 8NF
☎ 01628 666755 Fax 01628 663301
A championship standard 18-hole parkland course. Undulating terrain with many trees and several lakes, notably on the tricky 7th hole which has a tightly guarded green reached via a shot over a lake. Seven par 4's over 400yds with six picturesque lakes, excellent drainage and full irrigation.
18 holes, 6771yds, Par 72, SSS 73, Course record 67.
Club membership 740.

Visitors	must contact in advance & have a handicap certificate. May not play at weekends.
Green Fees	£40 per round,£50 per day,£50(per round weekends).
Cards	🔲 🔲 🔲 🔲 🔲
Prof	David Hart
Designer	Donald Steel
Facilities	⊗ �𝄞 ⅃ ⚑ ♉ ⌂ ☙ ❟ ➘ 🏌 ✿ (
& Leisure	sauna.
Location	Access via M4 junct 7 towards Burnham or M40 junct 2 towards Slough/Burnham

Hotel	★★★ 67% Burnham Beeches, Grove Rd, BURNHAM ☎ 01628 429955 82 ⇔ 🐾

CHALFONT ST GILES   Map 04 SU99

Harewood Downs Cokes Ln HP8 4TA
☎ 01494 762184 Fax 01494 766869
A testing undulating parkland course with sloping greens and plenty of trees.
18 holes, 5958yds, Par 69, SSS 69, Course record 64.

Visitors	must contact in advance.
Societies	apply in writing or telephone.
Green Fees	£40 per day; £30 per round (£45/£35 weekends & bank holidays).
Cards	🔲 🔲 🔲 🔲 🔲 🔲
Prof	G C Morris
Facilities	⊗ ⟋ ⅃ ⚑ ♉ ⌂ ☙ ❟ ➘ ✿
Location	2m E of Amersham on A413

▶

Woburn

Bow Brickhill, *Buckinghamshire* ☎ 01908 370756 | Fax 01908 378436 | Map 04 SP93

Conveniently accessed from the M1, Woburn is famed not only for its golf courses, but also for the magnificent stately home and wildlife park. If you are unable to play the courses yourself these are well worth a visit. Charles Lawrie of Cotton Pennink designed two great golf courses here amongst the trees and beautiful countryside. From the back tees, they are rather long for the weekend amateur golfer. The Duke's is a tough challenge for golfers at all levels, while the Duchess Course although relatively easier, still demands a high level of skill to negotiate the fairways guarded by towering pines.

The Dukes course has become the home of the increasingly popular Weetabix Women's British Open, held here since 1990.

The town of Woburn and the Abbey are both within Bedfordshire, while the golf and country club are over the border in Buckinghamshire. Just 45 miles from London, visitors will enjoy the wonderful countryside, excellent local pubs and friendly people.

Visitors must play with a member at weekends. Midweek by arrangement.

Societies must contact in advance.

Green Fees Credit card and charge cards accepted, current fees not available.

Facilities ⊗ ⬛ ♀ ♨ 🏠 🐎 🐕

Location Bow Brickhill, Milton Keynes MK17 9LJ (SE of Bow Brickhill) 4m W of J13 M1, off A5130.

Holes/Par/Course record 36 holes: Dukes Course: 18 holes 6973 yds, Par 72, SSS 74. Duchess Course: 18 holes, 6651 yds, Par 72, SSS 72

Championship Course

WHERE TO STAY AND EAT NEARBY

Hotels and Restaurants
★★★ 80% ◎◎ Menzies Flitwick Manor, Church Road MK45 JAE ☎ 0870 6003013/7 Fax 01773 880321 e-mail info@menzies-hotels.co.uk. 17 ⇔ 🐾

NEWPORT PAGNELL
◆◆◆◆◆ The Limes, North Square MK16 8EP ☎ 01908 617041 Fax 01908 217292. 4 (bath & shower symbols)

WOBURN
◎◎ Paris House Restaurant, Woburn Park MK17 9QP ☎ 01525 290692 Fax 01525 290471

GREAT BRICKHILL
The Old Red Lion, Ivy Lane MK17 9AH ☎ 01525 261715 Fax 01525 261716
★★ 72% ◎ Penhelig Arms Hotel & Restaurant, Aberdyfi LL35 OLT ☎ 01654 767215 Fax 01654 767690 e-mail penheligarms@saqnet.co.uk. 10 ⇔ 🐾

Hotel   ★★★★ 69% The Bellhouse, Oxford Rd,
BEACONSFIELD ☎ 01753 887211
136 ⇄ ⁅

Oakland Park Threehouseholds HP8 4LW
☎ 01494 876293 Fax 01494 874692
Parkland with mature trees, hedgerows and water features,
designed to respect the natural features of the land and lakes
whilst providing a good challenge for players at all levels.
18 holes, 5246yds, Par 67, SSS 66.
Club membership 750.
Visitors   weekdays only.
Societies   Mon, Wed & Fri. Must apply in writing.
Green Fees not confirmed.
Cards   ⬜ ⬛ ⬛ ⬛ ⬜
Prof   Allistair Thatcher
Designer   Johnathan Gaunt
Facilities   ⊗ ⫴ by prior arrangement ⬛ ⬛ ⬟ ⬟ ⬟ ⫟
                 ⬟ ⬟ ⬟
Location   3m N of M40 junct 3

Hotel   ★★★★ 69% The Bellhouse, Oxford Rd,
BEACONSFIELD ☎ 01753 887211
136 ⇄ ⁅

CHARTRIDGE   Map 04 SP90

Chartridge Park HP5 2TF ☎ 01494 791772
A family run, easy walking parkland course set high in the
beautiful Chiltern Hills, affording breathtaking views.
18 holes, 5516yds, Par 69, SSS 67, Course record 65.
Club membership 700.
Visitors   may not play before 10.30am weekends.
Societies   must telephone in advance.
Green Fees £30 weekends.
Prof   Peter Gibbins
Designer   John Jacobs
Facilities   ⊗ ⫴ ⬛ ⬛ ⬟ ⬟ ⬟ ⬟ ⬟ ⬟
Location   3m NW of Chesham

Hotel   ★★★ 68% The Crown, High St,
AMERSHAM ☎ 0870 400 8103
19 ⇄ ⁅ Annexe18 ⇄ ⁅

CHESHAM   Map 04 SP90

Chesham & Ley Hill Ley Hill Common HP5 1UZ
☎ 01494 784541 Fax 01494 785506
Wooded parkland course on hilltop with easy walking.
9 holes, 5296yds, Par 66, SSS 65, Course record 62.
Club membership 400.
Visitors   may play Mon & Thu all day, Wed after noon,
                  Fri up to 4pm.
Societies   subject to approval, Thu only.
Green Fees not confirmed.
Facilities   ⊗ ⫴ ⬛ ⬛ ⬟ ⬟ ⬟
& Leisure   practice net.
Location   2m E of Chesham

Hotel   ★★★ 68% The Crown, High St,
AMERSHAM ☎ 0870 400 8103
19 ⇄ ⁅ Annexe18 ⇄ ⁅

DENHAM   Map 04 TQ08

Buckinghamshire Denham Court Dr UB9 5BG
☎ 01895 835777 Fax 01895 835210
e-mail: bucks@dircon.co.uk
A John Jacobs designed championship-standard course.
Visitors only welcome as guests of members to this beautiful
course in 269 acres of lovely grounds including mature trees,
five lakes and two rivers. The testing 7th hole requires a 185
yd carry over a stream, followed by a second shot over a
river to a green guarded by a lake.
18 holes, 6880yds, Par 72, SSS 73, Course record 70.
Club membership 600.
Visitors   contact 48 hours in advance, subject to
                 availability.
Societies   must contact in advance.
Green Fees £70 per 18 holes (£80 weekends & bank
                 holidays).
Cards   ⬜ ⬛ ⬛ ⬛ ⬜
Prof   John O'Leary
Designer   John Jacobs
Facilities   ⊗ ⫴ ⬛ ⬛ ⬟ ⬟ ⬟ ⬟ ⬟ ⬟
Location   Just beyond junct 1 on M40

Hotel   ★★★★ 69% The Bellhouse, Oxford Rd,
BEACONSFIELD ☎ 01753 887211 136 ⇄ ⁅

Denham Tilehouse Ln UB9 5DE
☎ 01895 832022 Fax 01895 835340
A beautifully maintained parkland/heathland course,
home of many county champions. Slightly hilly and
calling for good judgement of distance in the wooded
areas.
18 holes, 6462yds, Par 70, SSS 71, Course record 66.
Club membership 790.
Visitors   must contact in advance & have handicap
                 certificate. Must play with member Fri-Sun.
Societies   Tue-Thu. Must book in advance.
Green Fees £62 per day; £44 per round.
Prof   Stuart Campbell
Designer   H S Colt
Facilities   ⊗ ⫴ by prior arrangement ⬛ ⬛ ⬟ ⬟ ⬟
                 ⬟ ⬟ ⬟
Location   0.5m N of North Orbital Road, 2m from
                 Uxbridge

Hotel   ★★★★ 69% The Bellhouse, Oxford Rd,
BEACONSFIELD ☎ 01753 887211
136 ⇄ ⁅

FLACKWELL HEATH   Map 04 SU89

Flackwell Heath Treadaway Rd, High Wycombe HP10 9PE
☎ 01628 520929 Fax 01628 530040
Open sloping heath and tree-lined course on hills
overlooking Loudwater and the M40. Some good challenging
par 3's and several testing small greens.
18 holes, 6211yds, Par 71, SSS 70, Course record 63.
Club membership 800.
Visitors   with member only at weekends. Must contact in
                 advance and hold a handicap certificate.
Societies   Wed & Thu only, by prior booking.
Green Fees £36 per day; £24 per round.
Prof   Paul Watson
Facilities   ⊗ ⫴ ⬛ ⬛ ⬟ ⬟ ⬟ ⬟ ⬟
Location   NE side of town centre

▶

Hotel   ★★★★ 69% The Bellhouse, Oxford Rd,
BEACONSFIELD ☎ 01753 887211 136 ⇄ ↟

GERRARDS CROSS   Map 04 TQ08

Gerrards Cross Chalfont Park SL9 0QA
☎ 01753 278500 Fax 01753 883593
A wooded parkland course which has been modernised
in recent years and is now a very pleasant circuit with
infinite variety. The best part lies on the plateau above
the clubhouse where there are some testing holes.
18 holes, 6295yds, Par 69, SSS 70, Course record 64.
Club membership 773.

Visitors	must contact professional in advance, a handicap certificate is required, may not play Tuesday, weekends or public holidays.
Societies	booking well in advance necessary, handicap certicates required, packages to suit.
Green Fees	£48 per day; £35 per round.
Cards	▭▭ ▬▬ ▨▨ 🔲
Prof	Matthew Barr
Designer	Bill Pedlar
Facilities	⊗ ⫇ 🅻 ➿ ♀ ♨ 🛎 🗇 ⚲
Location	NE side of town centre off A413

Hotel   ★★★★ 69% The Bellhouse, Oxford Rd,
BEACONSFIELD ☎ 01753 887211
136 ⇄ ↟

HIGH WYCOMBE   Map 04 SU89

Hazlemere Penn Rd, Hazlemere HP15 7LR
☎ 01494 719300 Fax 01494 713914
e-mail: hazelgolf@aol.com
Undulating parkland course in beautiful countryside with
water hazards in play on some holes. Two long par 5s and a
fine par 4 closing hole.
18 holes, 5873yds, Par 70, SSS 68, Course record 62.
Club membership 700.

Visitors	weekdays all day. Weekends by prior arrangement through Pro. shop telephone 01494 719306
Societies	by prior telephone arrangement.
Green Fees	not confirmed.
Cards	▭▭ ▬▬ ▨▨ 🔲
Prof	Gavin Cousins/Paul Harrison
Designer	Terry Murray
Facilities	⊗ ⫇ 🅻 ➿ ♀ ♨ 🛎 🗇 ⚲ ⚲ 🦽 ⚲
Location	2m NE, A404 towards Amersham

Hotel   ★★★ 68% The Crown, High St,
AMERSHAM ☎ 0870 400 8103
19 ⇄ ↟ Annexe18 ⇄ ↟

IVER   Map 04 TQ08

Iver Hollow Hill Ln, Langley Park Rd SL0 0JJ
☎ 01753 655615 Fax 01753 654225
Fairly flat, pay and play parkland course with challenging par
5s, plenty of hazards - water and ditches - and strong
crosswinds to contend with.
9 holes, 6288yds, Par 72, SSS 72, Course record 66.
Club membership 275.

Visitors	competitions at weekends, telephone to pre book tee times.
Societies	telephone in advance.
Green Fees	£12 per 18 holes; £6.50 per 9 holes (£15.50/£8 weekends and bank holidays).
Cards	▭▭ ▬▬ ▨▨ 🔲
Prof	Karl Teschner
Facilities & Leisure	⊗ 🅻 ➿ ♀ ♨ 🛎 🗇 ⚲ ⚲ bunker & chipping area.
Location	1.5m SW off B470

Hotel   ★★★★ 68% Slough/Windsor Marriott Hotel,
Ditton Rd, Langley, SLOUGH
☎ 01753 544244 380 ⇄ ↟

Richings Park Golf & Country Club North Park SL0 9DL
☎ 01753 655370 & 655352(pro shop) Fax 01753 655409
Set amongst mature trees and attractive lakes, this testing par
70 parkland course provides a suitable challenge to golfers of
all abilities. Well irrigated greens and abundant wildlife.
There is an academy course with 5 short holes and teaching
facilities on the driving range.
18 holes, 6144yds, Par 70, SSS 69.
Club membership 560.

Visitors	welcome but may not play until after 12 noon at weekends.
Societies	apply in writing or telephone.
Green Fees	£22 per 18 holes;£14 per 9 holes(£30/£16 weekends).
Cards	▭▭ ▬▬ 🔲 ▨▨ 🔲
Prof	Sean Kelly
Designer	Alan Higgins
Facilities	⊗ ⫇ 🅻 ➿ ♀ ♨ 🛎 🗇 ⚲ 🦽 🦽 ⚲ ⚲
Location	Junct 5 on M4, A4 towards Heathrow, left at lights, Sutton Lane, right at next lights North Park

Hotel   ★★★ 68% Courtyard by Marriott
Slough/Windsor, Church St, SLOUGH
☎ 01753 551551 150 ⇄ ↟

Thorney Park Thorney Mill Rd SL0 9AL
☎ 01895 422095 Fax 01895 431307
Thorney Park is a 9 hole parkland course, which will test
both the beginner and established golfer. Fairway irrigation
ensures lush green fairways and smooth putting surfaces.
Many interesting holes including the testing par 4 ninth
which needs a long drive to the waters edge and a well hit
iron onto the bunker guarded green.
9 holes, 2834yds, Par 34, SSS 33, Course record 65.
Club membership 180.

Visitors	must telephone in advance.
Societies	must telephone in advance.
Green Fees	£13 per 18 holes; £8 per 9 holes (£16/£9.50 weekends).
Cards	▭▭ ▬▬ 🔲 ▨▨ 🔲
Prof	Andrew Killing
Facilities	⊗ ⫇ 🅻 ➿ ♀ ♨ 🛎 🗇 ⚲
Location	From M4 junct 5 left onto A4. Left into Sutton Lane and right for Thorney Mill Road

Hotel   ★★★★ 68% Slough/Windsor Marriott Hotel,
Ditton Rd, Langley, SLOUGH
☎ 01753 544244 380 ⇄ ↟

LITTLE CHALFONT   Map 04 SU99

Little Chalfont Lodge Ln HP8 4AJ
☎ 01494 764877 Fax 01494 762860
Gently undulating parkland course surrounded by mature trees.
9 holes, 5852yds, Par 68, SSS 68, Course record 66.
Club membership 300.
Visitors   no restrictions, please phone to ensure there are no competitions in progress. Must contact for weekend play.
Societies   please telephone in advance.
Green Fees not confirmed.
Cards   ▭ ▭ ▭ ▭ ▭
Prof   M Dunne
Facilities   ⊗ ⫶ by prior arrangement ▯ ▯ ▯ ▯ ▯ ▯ ▯
& Leisure   one motorised cart for hire by arrangement.
Location   Between Little Chalfont & Chorleywood

Hotel   ★★★ 68% The Crown, High St,
                 AMERSHAM ☎ 0870 400 8103
                 19 ⇄ ▮ Annexe18 ⇄ ▮

LOUDWATER   Map 04 SU89

Wycombe Heights Golf Centre Rayners Ave HP10 9SW
☎ 01494 816686 Fax 01494 816728
e-mail: trilwm@aol.com
Opened in 1991 and designed by the John Jacobs Partnership. The golf centre includes a 24-bay driving range.
18 holes, 6253yds, Par 70, SSS 72, Course record 64.
Club membership 750.
Visitors   booking advisable 6 days in advance.
Societies   telephone in advance & confirm in writing.
Green Fees not confirmed.
Cards   ▭ ▭ ▭ ▭ ▭
Prof   Adam Bishop
Designer   John Jacobs
Facilities   ⊗ ⫶ ▯ ▯ ▯ ▯ ▯ ▯ ▯ ▯ ▯

Hotel   ★★★ 66% Posthouse High Wycombe, Handy
                 Cross, HIGH WYCOMBE
                 ☎ 0870 400 9042 109 ⇄ ▮

MARLOW   Map 04 SU88

Harleyford Harleyford Estate, Henley Rd SL7 2SP
☎ 01628 402300 Fax 01628 478434
e-mail: harleyfordgolf@msn.com
Set in 160 acres, this Donald Steel designed course, founded in 1996, makes the most of the natural rolling contours of the beautiful parkland of the historic Harleyford Estate. A challenging course to golfers of all handicaps. Stunning views across the Thames Valley.
18 holes, 6653yds, Par 72, SSS 72, Course record 72.
Club membership 800.
Visitors   soft spikes only. Must contact in advance and have a handicap certificate.Can play after 10am weekdays and !pm weekends.
Societies   handicap cert required, Tel 01628 402344 Groups co-ordinator.
Green Fees £40 per round (£60 weekends & bank holidays).
Cards   ▭ ▭ ▭ ▭
Prof   Christian Donald
Designer   Donald Steel
Facilities   ⊗ ⫶ ▯ ▯ ▯ ▯ ▯ ▯ ▯ ▯ ▯

Location   S side A4156 Marlow/Henley road, close to A404 Marlow bypass linking junct 4 M40/junct 8/9 M4

Hotel   ★★★★ 75% Danesfield House, Henley Rd, MARLOW-ON-THAMES
                 ☎ 01628 891010 87 ⇄ ▮

MENTMORE   Map 04 SP91

Mentmore Golf & Country Club LU7 0UA
☎ 01296 662020 Fax 01296 662592
Two 18-hole courses - Rosebery and Rothschild - set within the wooded estate grounds of Mentmore Towers. Gently rolling parkland course with mature trees and lakes and two interesting feature holes; the long par 5 (606 yds) 9th on the Rosebery course with fine views of the Chilterns and the par 4 (340yd) 14th on the Rothschild course, in front of the Towers.
Rosebery Course: 18 holes, 6777yds, Par 72, SSS 72, Course record 68.
Rothschild Course: 18 holes, 6700yds, Par 72, SSS 72.
Club membership 1100.
Visitors   must contact in advance, may not play weekends before 11am.
Societies   by prior arrangement.
Green Fees not confirmed.
Cards   ▭ ▭ ▭ ▭ ▭
Prof   Pip Elson
Designer   Bob Sandow
Facilities   ⊗ ⫶ ▯ ▯ ▯ ▯ ▯ ▯ ▯ ▯ ▯ ▯ ▯
& Leisure   hard tennis courts, heated indoor swimming pool, fishing, sauna, gymnasium.
Location   4m S of Leighton Buzzard

Hotel   ★★★ 69% Posthouse Aylesbury, Aston Clinton Rd, AYLESBURY
                 ☎ 0870 400 9002 140 ⇄ ▮

MILTON KEYNES   Map 04 SP83

Abbey Hill Monks Way, Two Mile Ash MK8 8AA
☎ 01908 562408
Undulating municipal course within the new town. Tight fairways and well-placed bunkers. Stream comes into play on five holes. Also Par 3 course.
18 holes, 6122yds, Par 71, SSS 69, Course record 71.
Club membership 500.
Visitors   no restrictions.
Societies   must telephone (01908) 562408 in advance.
Green Fees not confirmed.
Cards   ▭ ▭ ▭ ▭ ▭
Prof   Keith Bond
Facilities   ⊗ ⫶ ▯ ▯ ▯ ▯ ▯ ▯ ▯ ▯ ▯
Location   2m W of new town centre off A5

Hotel   ★★★ 63% Quality Hotel & Suites Milton Keynes, Monks Way, Two Mile Ash, MILTON KEYNES ☎ 01908 561666 88 ⇄ ▮

Three Locks Great Brickhill MK17 9BH
☎ 01525 270470 & 270050 Fax 01525 270470
Parkland course offering a challenge to beginners and experienced golfers, with water coming into play on ten holes. Magnificent views.
18 holes, 6036yds, Par 71, SSS 68, Course record 69.
Club membership 300.   ▶

Visitors	telephone 01525 270050 to book tee times.
Societies	write or telephone for details.
Green Fees	£15 (£18 weekends& bank holidays).
Cards	〰 🖅 🖅 🖅 🈸
Prof	G Harding
Designer	MRM Sandown
Facilities	⊗ 🖫 ♥ ♀ 🏌 📠 ℿ 🏠 🖘 ⚓ ✐
& Leisure	fishing.
Location	A4146 between Leighton Buzzard/Bletchley

Hotel	★★★ 63% Posthouse Milton Keynes, 500 Saxon Gate West, MILTON KEYNES ☎ 0870 400 9057 150 ⇆ 🐾

PRINCES RISBOROUGH   Map 04 SP80

Whiteleaf Upper Icknield Way, Whiteleaf HP27 0LY
☎ 01844 274058 Fax 01844 275551
e-mail: whiteleafgc@genie.co.uk
Short, hilly and tricky 9-hole parkland course, requiring great accuracy, set high in the Chilterns with beautiful views.
9 holes, 5391yds, Par 66, SSS 66, Course record 64.
Club membership 300.

Visitors	advisable to contact in advance, with member only at weekends.
Societies	on Thu only, must contact the secretary in advance.
Green Fees	£25 per day; £18 per round.
Prof	Ken Ward
Facilities	⊗ ℿ 🖫 ♥ ♀ 🏌 📠 ✐
Location	1m NE off A4010

Hotel	★★ 64% Rose & Crown Hotel, Wycombe Rd, SAUNDERTON ☎ 01844 345299 15 ⇆ 🐾

STOKE POGES   Map 04 SU98

Farnham Park Park Rd SL2 4PJ
☎ 01753 643332 & 647065 Fax 01753 643332 & 647065
Fine, public parkland course in pleasing setting.
18 holes, 6172yds, Par 71, SSS 70, Course record 68.
Club membership 500.

Visitors	telephone in advance for tee times.
Societies	apply in writing.
Green Fees	£10.50 per round(£14.50 weekends).
Cards	〰 🖅 🖅 🖅 🈸
Prof	Paul Warner
Designer	Hawtree
Facilities	⊗ 🖫 ♥ ♀ 🏌 📠 ℿ ✐
Location	W side of village off B416

Hotel	★★★★ 68% Slough/Windsor Marriott Hotel, Ditton Rd, Langley, SLOUGH ☎ 01753 544244 380 ⇆ 🐾

Stoke Poges Stoke Park, Park Rd SL2 4PG
☎ 01753 717171 Fax 01753 717181
e-mail: info@stokepark.co.uk
Judgement of the distance from the tee is all important on this first-class parkland course. Fairways are wide and the challenge seemingly innocuous. The 7th hole being the model for the well known 12th hole at Augusta. Stoke Poges is a 27 hole course and is considered the best traditional course in the British Isles.
Course 1: 18 holes, 6721yds, Par 72, SSS 72.
Course 2: 18 holes, 6551yds, Par 72, SSS 73.
Course 3: 18 holes, 6318yds, Par 71, SSS 70.
Club membership 750.

Visitors	must contact in advance.
Societies	telephone in advance.
Green Fees	not confirmed.
Cards	〰 🖅 🖅 🖅 🈸
Prof	David Woodward
Designer	Harry Shapland Colt
Facilities	⊗ ℿ 🖫 ♥ ♀ 🏌 📠 ℿ 🏠 🖘 ⚓ ✐ ℓ
& Leisure	hard and grass tennis courts, fishing.
Location	Turn off A4 at Slough into Stoke Poges Lane B416, club is 1.5m on left

Hotel	★★★★ 68% Slough/Windsor Marriott Hotel, Ditton Rd, Langley, SLOUGH ☎ 01753 544244 380 ⇆ 🐾

WAVENDON   Map 04 SP93

Wavendon Golf Centre Lower End Rd MK17 8DA
☎ 01908 281811 Fax 01908 281257
e-mail: wavendon@jack-barker.co.uk
Pleasant parkland course set within mature oak and lime trees and incorporating several small lakes as water hazards. Easy walking.
18 holes, 5540yds, Par 68, SSS 68.
Club membership 300.

Visitors	booking advised.
Societies	must contact in advance by telephone.
Green Fees	£12 (£17.50 weekends).
Cards	〰 🖅 🖅 🖅 🈸
Prof	Greg Iron
Designer	J Drake/N Elmer
Facilities	⊗ ℿ 🖫 ♥ ♀ 🏌 📠 ℿ 🖘 ⚓ ✐ ℓ
Location	Just off A421

Hotel	★★★ 68% Moore Place Hotel, The Square, ASPLEY GUISE ☎ 01908 282000 39 ⇆ 🐾 Annexe15 ⇆ 🐾

WESTON TURVILLE   Map 04 SP81

Weston Turville Golf & Squash Club New Rd HP22 5QT
☎ 01296 424084 Fax 01296 395376
Parkland course situated at the foot of the Chiltern Hills and providing an excellent challenge for the accomplished golfer, yet not too daunting for the higher handicap player. Flat easy walking with water hazards and many interesting holes, notably the testing dog-leg 5th (418yds).
18 holes, 6008yds, Par 69, SSS 69, Course record 68.
Club membership 600.

Visitors	no restrictions.
Societies	must contact in advance.
Green Fees	not confirmed.
Cards	🖅 🖅 🈸
Prof	Gary George
Facilities	⊗ 🖫 ♥ ♀ 🏌 📠 ℿ 🖘 ⚓ ✐
& Leisure	squash.
Location	2m SE of Aylesbury, off A41

Hotel	★★★ 69% Posthouse Aylesbury, Aston Clinton Rd, AYLESBURY ☎ 0870 400 9002 140 ⇆ 🐾

Where to stay, where to eat?
Visit the AA internet site
www.theAA.com

WEXHAM STREET   Map 04 SU98

Wexham Park SL3 6ND
☎ 01753 663271 Fax 01753 663318
Gently undulating parkland course. Three courses. One 18
hole, one challenging 9 hole and another 9 hole suitable for
beginners.
Blue: 18 holes, 5346yds, Par 68, SSS 66.
Red: 9 holes, 2822yds, Par 34.
Green: 9 holes, 2233yds, Par 32.
Club membership 850.

Visitors	no restrictions
Societies	must contact in advance.
Green Fees	£7 per 9 holes;£12.50 per 18 holes(£9/£16 weekends).
Cards	🃏 🃏 🃏 🃏
Prof	John Kennedy
Designer	E Lawrence/D Morgan
Facilities	⊗ ᴸ 🍴 🎮 🛋 🍽 🏌 🚗 ⚑
Location	0.5m S

Hotel   ★★★★ 68% Slough/Windsor Marriott Hotel,
            Ditton Rd, Langley, SLOUGH
            ☎ 01753 544244 380 🛏 🏌

WING   Map 04 SP82

Aylesbury Vale Stewkley Rd LU7 0UJ
☎ 01525 240196 Fax 01525 240848
The course set in quiet countryside is gently undulating.
There are five ponds to add interest, notably on the par 4 420
yd 13th - unlucky for some - where the second shot is all
downhill with an inviting pond spanning the approach to the
green. In addition there is a 10-bay driving range and practice
putting green.
18 holes, 6612yds, Par 72, SSS 72, Course record 67.
Club membership 545.

Visitors	must adhere to dress regulations. Must contact in advance.
Societies	telephone to book in advance.
Green Fees	£13 per 18 holes;call for weekend rates.
Cards	🃏 🃏 🃏 🃏
Prof	Guy Goble
Designer	D Wright
Facilities	⊗ 🏋 ᴸ 🍴 🎮 🛋 🍽 🏌 🚗 ⚑
Location	2m NW of Leighton Buzzard on unclassified Stewkley road, between Wing/Stewkley

Hotel   ★★★ 69% Posthouse Aylesbury, Aston
            Clinton Rd, AYLESBURY
            ☎ 0870 400 9002 140 🛏 🏌

CAMBRIDGESHIRE

BAR HILL   Map 05 TL36

Cambridgeshire Moat House Moat House Hotel,
Bar Hill CB3 8EU
☎ 01954 780098 & 249971 Fax 01954 780010
Mature undulating parkland course with tree-lined
fairways, easy walking.

18 holes, 6734yds, Par 72, SSS 73, Course record 68.
Club membership 600.

Visitors	must book in advance. Weekdays subject to availability, weekends after noon.
Societies	must telephone in advance.
Green Fees	£21 per round (£30 weekends & bank holidays).
Cards	🃏 🃏 🃏 🃏 🃏
Prof	Paul Simpson
Facilities & Leisure	⊗ 🏋 ᴸ 🍴 🎮 🛋 🍽 🏌 🚗 ⚑ hard tennis courts, heated indoor swimming pool, sauna, solarium, gymnasium.
Location	5m NW of Cambridge

Hotel   ★★★ 69% Posthouse Cambridge,
            Lakeview, Bridge Rd, Impington,
            CAMBRIDGE ☎ 0870 400 9015
            165 🛏 🏌

BRAMPTON   Map 04 TL27

Brampton Park Buckden Rd PE28 4NF
☎ 01480 434700 Fax 01480 411145
Set in truly attractive countryside, bounded by the River
Great Ouse and bisected by the River Lane. Great variety
with mature trees, lakes and water hazards. One of the most
difficult holes is the 4th, a Par 3 island green, 175 yards in
length.
18 holes, 6300yds, Par 71, SSS 72, Course record 64.
Club membership 650.

Visitors	must contact in advance.
Societies	apply in advance.
Green Fees	not confirmed.
Cards	🃏 🃏 🃏 🃏
Prof	Alisdair Currie
Designer	Simon Gidman
Facilities	⊗ 🏋 ᴸ 🍴 🎮 🛋 🍽 ⚑
Location	Follow signs from A1 or A14 to RAF Brampton

Hotel   ★★★ 76% The Old Bridge Hotel, 1 High St,
            HUNTINGDON ☎ 01480 424300 24 🛏 🏌

CAMBRIDGE   Map 05 TL45

Gog Magog Shelford Bottom CB2 4AB
☎ 01223 247626 Fax 01223 414990
e-mail: secretary@gogmagog.co.uk
Situated just outside the centre of the university town,
Gog Magog, established in 1901, is known as the nursery
of Cambridge undergraduate golf. The courses are on
high ground, and it is said that if you stand on the highest
point and could see far enough to the east the next
highest ground would be the Ural Mountains! The
courses are open but there are enough trees and other
hazards to provide plenty of problems. Views from the
high parts are superb. The nature of the ground ensures
good winter golf. The area has been designated a Site of
Special Scientific Interest (SSSI).
*Old Course: 18 holes, 6400yds, Par 70, SSS 70, Course
record 60.*
Wandlebury: 18 holes, 6700yds, Par 72, SSS 72.
Club membership 1280.

Visitors	Must contact in advance. Mon-Fri only.
Societies	Tue & Thu by reservation.
Green Fees	£42 per day; £35 per round.

▶

Prof	Ian Bamborough
Designer	Hawtree Ltd
Facilities	⊗ 🕮 🖪 🍺 ♀ 🛆 🏠 ⛳ ↘ ✎ (
Location	3m SE on A1307

Hotel	★★★ 71% Gonville Hotel, Gonville Place, CAMBRIDGE ☎ 01223 366611 & 221111 Fax 01223 315470 64 ⇌ ☞

ELY
Map 05 TL58

Ely City 107 Cambridge Rd CB7 4HX
☎ 01353 662751 (Office) Fax 01353 668636 e-mail: elygolf@lineone.net
Parkland course slightly undulating with water hazards formed by lakes and natural dykes. Demanding par 4 5th hole (467yds), often into a headwind, and a testing par 3 2nd hole (160yds) played over 2 ponds. Magnificent views of Cathedral.
18 holes, 6627yds, Par 72, SSS 72, Course record 65.
Club membership 825.

Visitors	advisable to contact the club in advance,handicap certificate required.
Societies	Tue to Fri, advisable to contact club well in advance.
Green Fees	£30 per day (£36 weekends & bank holidays).
Prof	Andrew George
Designer	Sir Henry Cotton
Facilities	⊗ 🕮 🖪 🍺 ♀ 🛆 🏠 ⛳ ✎
& Leisure	snooker.
Location	S of city on A10

Hotel	★★ 62% The Nyton Hotel, 7 Barton Rd, ELY ☎ 01353 662459 10 ⇌ ☞

GIRTON
Map 05 TL46

Girton Dodford Ln CB3 0QE
☎ 01223 276169 Fax 01223 277150
e-mail: secretary@girtongolfclub.sagehost.co.uk
Flat, open parkland course with many trees and ditches. Easy walking.
18 holes, 6012yds, Par 69, SSS 69, Course record 66.
Club membership 800.

Visitors	with member only at weekends. Contact professional in advance (01223 276991).
Societies	apply writing.
Green Fees	£30 per day; £20 per round.
Prof	Scott Thomson
Designer	Allan Gow
Facilities	⊗ 🕮 🖪 🍺 ♀ 🛆 🏠 ⛳ ✎
Location	NW side of village

Hotel	★★★ 69% Posthouse Cambridge, Lakeview, Bridge Rd, Impington, CAMBRIDGE ☎ 0870 400 9015 165 ⇌ ☞

HEMINGFORD ABBOTS
Map 04 TL27

Hemingford Abbots Cambridge Rd PE28 9HQ
☎ 01480 495000 & 493900 Fax 01480 4960000
Interesting 9-hole course featuring a par 5 dog-leg 4th with a testing tapering fairway, two ponds at the entrance to the 8th green and an island green on the 9th.
9 holes, 5468yds, Par 68, SSS 68, Course record 69.
Club membership 170.

Visitors	advisable to phone in advance, particularly for weekends.
Societies	advise in writing or telephone.
Green Fees	£12 per 18 holes; £8 per 9 holes (£15/£10 weekends).
Prof	Jamie Donaldson
Designer	Ray Paton
Facilities	⊗ 🖪 🍺 ♀ 🛆 🏠 ⛳ ✎ (
Location	A14 Hemingford Abbots turning

Hotel	★★★ 76% The Old Bridge Hotel, 1 High St, HUNTINGDON ☎ 01480 424300 24 ⇌ ☞

LONGSTANTON
Map 05 TL36

Cambridge Station Rd CB4 5DR ☎ 01954 789388
An undulating parkland course with bunkers and ponds.
18 holes, 6736yds, Par 72, SSS 73.
Club membership 300.

Visitors	must contact in advance.
Societies	must telephone in advance.
Green Fees	£7/10 (£13 weekends).
Cards	🗋 🗋 🗋 🗋
Prof	Geoff Huggett/A Engelman
Facilities	⊗ 🕮 🖪 🍺 ♀ 🛆 ⛳ ↘ 🛥 ✎ (
& Leisure	fishing, hot air ballons.

Hotel	★★★ 69% Posthouse Cambridge, Lakeview, Bridge Rd, Impington, CAMBRIDGE ☎ 0870 400 9015 165 ⇌ ☞

MARCH
Map 05 TL49

March Frogs Abbey, Grange Rd PE15 0YH
☎ 01354 652364 Fax 01354 652364
Nine-hole parkland course with a particularly challenging par 3 9th hole, with out of bounds on the right and high hedges to the right.
9 holes, 6204yds, Par 70, SSS 70, Course record 65.
Club membership 400.

Visitors	contact in advance, with member only at weekends.
Societies	must contact in advance.
Green Fees	£16.50 per day.
Cards	🗋 🗋 🗋
Prof	Stewart Brown
Facilities	🍺 ♀ 🛆 🏠 ✎
Location	0.5m off A141, March bypass

Hotel	★★ 64% Olde Griffin Hotel, High St, MARCH ☎ 01354 652517 20rm(19 ⇌ ☞)

AA Hotels that have special arrangements with golf courses are listed at the back of the guide

---

Entries with a green background identify courses considered to be particularly interesting

PETERBOROUGH   Map 04 TL19

Elton Furze Bullock Rd, Haddon PE7 3TT
☎ 01832 280189 & 280614 (Pro shop) Fax 01832 280299
e-mail: secretary@eltonfurzegolfclub.co.uk
Wooded parkland 18-hole course in lovely surroundings.
18 holes, 6289yds, Par 70, SSS 70, Course record 67.
Club membership 620.
Visitors welcome, preferably Mon-Fri, weekends only
with prior permission (phone in advance).
Societies by prior arrangement telephone for details.
Green Fees £22 per round (£32 weekends & bank holidays).
Cards 🔲🔲
Prof Frank Kiddie
Designer Roger Fitton
Facilities ⊗ 🗏 🖺 💄 💟 ⚑ 🕋 🏌 ⚐ ℓ
Location 4m SW of Peterborough, off A605/A1

Hotel ★★★★ 65% Swallow Hotel, Peterborough
Business Park, Lynchwood,
PETERBOROUGH ☎ 01733 371111
157 ⇔ 🏌

Orton Meadows Ham Ln, Orton Waterville PE2 5UU
☎ 01733 237478 Fax 01733 332774
Pretty public parkland course set within the Nene Valley
Country Park with large lakes and water hazards.
Challenging 3rd hole (480yards from white tee)
incorporating lots of water and 'out of bounds' areas.
Also 12-hole pitch and putt course.
18 holes, 5269yds, Par 67, SSS 68, Course record 69.
Club membership 650.
Visitors phone for reservations 7 days in advance.
Societies apply in advance.
Green Fees not confirmed.
Cards 🔲 🔲 🔲 🔲 🗏
Prof Jason Mitchell
Designer D & R Fitton
Facilities ⊗ 🗏 🖺 💄 💟 ⚑ 🕋 🏌 ⚐ ℓ
& Leisure 12 hole pitch & putt.
Location 3m W of town on A605

Hotel ★★★ 69% Orton Hall Hotel, Orton
Longueville, PETERBOROUGH
☎ 01733 391111 65 ⇔ 🏌

Peterborough Milton Milton Ferry PE6 7AG
☎ 01733 380489 Fax 01733 380489
e-mail: miltongolfclub@aol.com
Designed by James Braid, this well-bunkered parkland
course is set in the grounds of the Milton Estate, many of the
holes being played in full view of Milton Hall. Challenging
holes are the difficult dog-leg 10th and 15th. Easy walking.
18 holes, 6479yds, Par 71, SSS 72, Course record 62.
Club membership 800.
Visitors must contact in advance. Handicap certificate
required.
Societies bookings by telephone to secretary.
Green Fees £35 per day; £25 per round.
Cards 🔲 🔲 🔲 🗏
Prof Mike Gallagher
Designer James Braid
Facilities ⊗ 🗏 🖺 💄 💟 ⚑ 🕋 ⚐ ℓ
Location 2m W of Peterborough on A47,near the villages
of Castor & Ailsworth

Hotel ★★★ Butterfly Hotel, Thorpe Meadows,
Longthorpe Parkway, PETERBOROUGH
☎ 01733 564240 70 ⇔ 🏌

Thorpe Wood Thorpe Wood, Nene Parkway PE3 6SE
☎ 01733 267701 Fax 01733 332774
e-mail: enquiries@thorpewoodgolfcourse.co.uk
Gently undulating parkland course, designed by Peter Alliss
and Dave Thomas. Challenging holes include the 5th, the
longest hole usually played with prevailing wind and the
14th, entailing a difficult approach shot over water to a two-
tier green.
18 holes, 7086yds, Par 73, SSS 74, Course record 68.
Club membership 750.
Visitors phone for reservations 7 days in advance.
Societies must telephone in advance, society bookings
taken up to year ahead.
Green Fees £10.70 per round (£13.75 weekends & bank
holidays).
Cards 🔲 🔲 🔲 🔲 🗏
Prof Roger Fitton
Designer Peter Allis/Dave Thomas
Facilities ⊗ 🗏 🖺 💄 💟 ⚑ 🕋 🏌 ⚐ ℓ
Location 3m W of city centre on A47

Hotel ★★★ Butterfly Hotel, Thorpe Meadows,
Longthorpe Parkway, PETERBOROUGH
☎ 01733 564240 70 ⇔ 🏌

PIDLEY   Map 05 TL37

Lakeside Lodge Fen Rd PE28 3DF
☎ 01487 740540 Fax 01487 740852
e-mail: info@golf-lakeside-lodge.co.uk
A well designed, spacious course incorporating eight lakes,
12,000 trees and a modern clubhouse. The 9th and 18th holes
both finish dramatically alongside a lake in front of the
clubhouse. Also 9-hole Par 3 and 25-bay driving range. The
Manor provides an interesting contrast with its undulating
fairways and angular greens.
*Lodge Course: 18 holes, 6821yds, Par 72, SSS 73, Course
record 72.*
The Manor: 9 holes, 3202yds, Par 68.
The Church: 12 holes, 3290yds, Par 44.
Club membership 850.
Visitors no restrictions.
Societies must telephone in advance.
Green Fees £11 (£17 weekends).
Cards 🔲 🔲 🔲 🗏
Prof Scott Waterman
Designer A W Headley
Facilities ⊗ 🗏 🖺 💄 💟 ⚑ 🕋 🏌 ⚐ 🏌 🏌 ⚐ ℓ
& Leisure fishing, ten pin bowling, smart golf simulator.

Hotel ★★★ 69% Slepe Hall Hotel, Ramsey Rd,
ST IVES ☎ 01480 463122 16 ⇔ 🏌

RAMSEY   Map 04 TL28

Old Nene Golf & Country Club Muchwood Ln, Bodsey
PE26 2XQ ☎ 01487 813519 & 815622
A flat well-drained course with water hazards. There are
excellent greens and there are many challenging holes across
water in either a head wind or cross wind.
9 holes, 5605yds, Par 68, SSS 68, Course record 64.
Club membership 170.

▶

Visitors	book in advance especially evenings & weekends. Dress code must be adhered to.
Societies	arrange in advance with Secretary.
Green Fees	£7 per 9 holes;£11 per 18 holes(£9/£16 weekends).
Prof	Ian Galloway
Designer	R Edrich
Facilities	⊗ ⅢⅢ ⅃ ▬ ♀ ᇫ ᗆ ⏀ ⅍ ⅏ ∅ ⅃
& Leisure	fishing, practice area.
Location	0.75m N of Ramsey towards Ramsey Mereside

Hotel	★★★ 76% The Old Bridge Hotel, 1 High St, HUNTINGDON ☎ 01480 424300 24 ⇆ ♈

Ramsey 4 Abbey Ter PE17 1DD
☎ 01487 812600 Fax 01487 815746
Flat, parkland course with water hazards and well irrigated greens, mature tees and fairways, assuring a good surface whatever the conditions. It gives the impression of wide open spaces, but the wayward shot is soon punished.
18 holes, 5830yds, Par 71, SSS 68, Course record 65.
Club membership 750.

Visitors	contact professional in advance 01487 813022, may only play with member at weekends & bank holidays.
Societies	apply in writing.
Green Fees	not confirmed.
Prof	Stuart Scott
Designer	J Hamilton Stutt
Facilities	⊗ by prior arrangement ⅢⅢ by prior arrangement ⅃ ♀ ᇫ ᗆ ⏀ ∅
& Leisure	snooker tables, bowls rinks.
Location	12m SE of Peterborough on B1040

Hotel	★★★ 76% The Old Bridge Hotel, 1 High St, HUNTINGDON ☎ 01480 424300 24 ⇆ ♈

St Ives   Map 05 TL37

St Ives (Cambs) Westwood Rd PE27 6DH
☎ 01480 468392 Fax 01480 468392
e-mail: stivesgolfclub@talk21.com
Picturesque parkland course.
9 holes, 6100yds, Par 70, SSS 70, Course record 68.
Club membership 500.

Visitors	may not play weekends.
Societies	welcome Wed & Fri.
Green Fees	not confirmed.
Prof	Darren Glasby
Facilities	⊗ ⅢⅢ ⅃ ▬ ♀ ᇫ ᗆ ⏀ ∅
Location	W side of town centre off A1123

Hotel	★★★ 69% Slepe Hall Hotel, Ramsey Rd, ST IVES ☎ 01480 463122 16 ⇆ ♈

St Neots   Map 04 TL16

Abbotsley Golf & Squash Club Eynesbury Hardwicke
PE19 6XN ☎ 01480 474000 & 215153 Fax 01480 403280
Two courses - main Abbotsley course featuring mature parkland with tree-lined fairways, plenty of water hazards and a particularly testing par 3 2nd hole - the 'Mousehole'. Cromwell course is less demanding with tricky driving holes and sloping greens. Courses surround moated country house and hotel. Residential golf schools 30 weeks of the year plus floodlit, covered driving range, par 3 course and grass practice area.

Abbotsley Course: 18 holes, 6311yds, Par 73, SSS 52, Course record 69.
Cromwell Course: 18 holes, 6087yds, Par 70, SSS 69, Course record 66.
Club membership 550.

Visitors	welcome all times. Necessary to book weekends.
Societies	prior booking essential.
Green Fees	Abbotsley:£19 per 18 holes;£13 per 9 holes(£30/£19 weekends & bank holidays).Cromwell:££10 per 18 holes;£6 per 9 holes(£17/£9 weekends & bank holidays).
Cards	▬ ▬ ▬ ▬ ▬ ▬ ▬
Prof	Denise Hastings
Designer	D Young/V Saunders
Facilities	⊗ ⅢⅢ ⅃ ▬ ♀ ᇫ ᗆ ⏀ ⅍ ⅏ ∅ ⅃
& Leisure	squash, gymnasium, Holistic Health & Beauty salon.
Location	10 mins from A1 & A428

Hotel	★★ 69% Abbotsley Golf Hotel & Country Club, Potton Rd, Eynesbury Hardwicke, ST NEOTS ☎ 01480 474000 Annexe42 ⇆ ♈

St Neots Crosshall Rd PE19 4AE ☎ 01480 472363
e-mail: office@stneots-golfclub.co.uk
Undulating and very picturesque parkland course with lake and water hazards and exceptional greens, close to the Kym and Great Ouse rivers. Easy, level walking.
18 holes, 6074yds, Par 69, SSS 69, Course record 64.
Club membership 630.

Visitors	must book in advance. with member only at weekends.
Societies	must contact in advance.
Green Fees	not confirmed.
Prof	Graham Bithrey
Designer	H Vardon
Facilities	⊗ ⅢⅢ ⅃ ▬ ♀ ᇫ ᗆ ⏀ ⅍ ⅏ ∅
Location	Just off the A1 with the jct B1048 heading into St Neots

Hotel	★★ 69% Abbotsley Golf Hotel & Country Club, Potton Rd, Eynesbury Hardwicke, ST NEOTS ☎ 01480 474000 Annexe42 ⇆ ♈

Thorney   Map 04 TF20

Thorney English Drove, Thorney PE6 0TJ
☎ 01733 270570 Fax 01733 270842
The 18-hole Fen course is ideal for the beginner, while the Lakes course has a challenging links-style layout with eight holes around water.
Fen Course: 18 holes, 6104yds, Par 70, SSS 69, Course record 66.
Lakes Course: 18 holes, 6402yds, Par 71, SSS 70, Course record 65.
Club membership 400.

Visitors	book in advance for Fen course, limited weekend play Lakes course.
Societies	contact in advance.
Green Fees	not confirmed.
Cards	▬ ▬ ▬ ▬ ▬
Prof	Mark Templeman
Designer	A Dow
Facilities	⊗ ⅢⅢ ⅃ ▬ ♀ ᇫ ᗆ ⏀ ⅍ ⅏ ∅ ⅃
& Leisure	gymnasium.
Location	Off A47, 7m NE of Peterborough ▶

Hotel ★★★ Butterfly Hotel, Thorpe Meadows, Longthorpe Parkway, PETERBOROUGH ☎ 01733 564240 70 ⇄ ⊮

TOFT   Map 05 TL35

Cambridge Meridian Comberton Rd CB3 7RY ☎ 01223 264700 Fax 01223 264701
Set in 207 acres to a Peter Allis/Clive Clark design with sweeping fairways, lakes and well bunkered greens. The 4th hole has bunker complexes, a sharp dog-leg and a river with the green heavily guarded by bunkers. The 9th and 10th holes challenge the golfer with river crossings.
18 holes, 6651yds, Par 73, SSS 72, Course record 72.
Club membership 600.
Visitors must contact in advance.
Societies telephone for provisional booking
Green Fees not confirmed.
Cards ⊞ ▩
Prof Michael Clemons
Designer Peter Alliss/Clive Clark
Facilities ⊗ �𝍖 ⮞ 🍺 ♀ ♨ 🏌 ⛳ 🐾 🛒 ⚷
Location 3m W of Cambridge, on B1046

Hotel ★★ 69% Abbotsley Golf Hotel & Country Club, Potton Rd, Eynesbury Hardwicke, ST NEOTS ☎ 01480 474000 Annexe42 ⇄ ⊮

CHESHIRE

ALDERLEY EDGE   Map 07 SJ87

Alderley Edge Brook Ln SK9 7RU ☎ 01625 585583
Well-wooded, undulating pastureland course. A stream crosses 7 of the 9 holes.
9 holes, 5823yds, Par 68, SSS 68, Course record 62.
Club membership 400.
Visitors by arrangement on Thu.
Societies Thu only, apply in writing or telephone.
Green Fees not confirmed.
Prof Peter Bowring
Facilities ⊗ 𝍖 ⮞ 🍺 ♀ ♨ ⛳ ⚷
Location 1m NW on B5085

Hotel ★★★ 73% Alderley Edge Hotel, Macclesfield Rd, ALDERLEY EDGE ☎ 01625 583033 46 ⇄ ⊮

ALSAGER   Map 07 SJ75

Alsager Golf & Country Club Audley Rd ST7 2UR ☎ 01270 875700 Fax 01270 882207
An 18-hole parkland course situated in rolling Cheshire countryside and offering a challenge to all golfers whatever their standard. Clubhouse is well appointed with good facilities and a friendly atmosphere.
18 holes, 6225yds, Par 70, SSS 70, Course record 68.
Club membership 640.

Visitors must contact in advance, may not play Fri afternoon, can only play with member at weekends.
Societies must contact in advance.
Green Fees £25 per day.
Prof Richard Brown
Facilities ⮞ 🍺 ♀ ♨ ⛳ ⚷
Location 2m NE of M6 junct 16

Hotel ★★★ 71% Manor House Hotel, Audley Rd, ALSAGER ☎ 01270 884000 57 ⇄ ⊮

CHESTER   Map 07 SJ46

Carden Park Hotel Carden Park CH3 9DQ ☎ 01829 731000 Fax 01829 731032
e-mail: reservations@cardenpark.co.uk
A superb golf resort set in 750 acres of beautiful Cheshire countryside. Facilities include the mature parkland Cheshire Course, the Nicklaus Course, the 9 hole par 3 Azalea Course, Europe's first Jack Nicklaus Residential Golf School and a luxurious clubhouse.
Cheshire: 18 holes, 6891yds, Par 72, SSS 71, Course record 69.
Nicklaus: 18 holes, 6302yds, Par 72, SSS 72.
Club membership 250.

Visitors must contact in advance, handicap certificate required for the Nicklaus Course. To help maintain the highest quality metal spikes cannot be worn.
Societies contact for details, tel: 01829 731594.
Green Fees not confirmed.
Cards ⊞ ▩ ▦ 💳 🎱
Prof Simon Edwards
Facilities ⊗ 𝍖 ⮞ 🍺 ♀ ♨ ⛳ 🏌 📧 🐾 🛒 ⚷ ⚏
& Leisure hard tennis courts, heated indoor swimming pool, sauna, solarium, gymnasium, residential golf school, snooker room, dance studio.
Location Off A534

Hotel ★★★★ 70% De Vere Carden Park Hotel, Carden Park, BROXTON ☎ 01829 731000 115 ⇄ ⊮ Annexe77 ⇄ ⊮

Chester Curzon Park CH4 8AR ☎ 01244 677760 Fax 01244 676667
Meadowland course on two levels contained within a loop of the River Dee. The car park overlooks the racecourse across the river.
18 holes, 6508yds, Par 72, SSS 71, Course record 66.
Club membership 820.

▶

Visitors	must contact in advance.
Societies	must telephone or write in advance.
Green Fees	£25 (£30 weekends).
Prof	George Parton
Facilities	⊗ ⦀ ⮞ ⮚ ▼ ♀ ⥁ 🖿 🛒 ⛳
Location	1m W of city centre

Hotel	★★★ 66% Grosvenor Pulford Hotel, Wrexham Rd, Pulford, CHESTER ☎ 01244 570560 76 ⇆ 🏌

Eaton Guy Ln, Waverton CH3 7PH
☎ 01244 335885 & 335826 Fax 01244 335782
A parkland course with a liberal covering of both mature trees and new planting enhanced by natural water hazards.
18 holes, 6562yds, Par 72, SSS 71, Course record 69.
Club membership 550.

Visitors	must contact in advance particularly for weekends.
Societies	must contact in advance. May not play weekends or Wednesdays.
Green Fees	not confirmed.
Cards	🖃
Prof	Neil Dunroe
Designer	Donald Steel
Facilities	⊗ ⦀ ⮞ ⮚ ▼ ♀ ⥁ 🖿 🛒 ⛳
Location	3m SE of Chester off A41

Hotel	★★★★★ 78% The Chester Grosvenor, Eastgate, CHESTER ☎ 01244 324024 85 ⇆ 🏌

Upton-by-Chester Upton Ln, Upton-by-Chester CH2 1EE
☎ 01244 381183 Fax 01244 376955
Pleasant, tree-lined, parkland course. Not easy for low-handicap players to score well. Testing holes are 2nd (par 4), 14th (par 4) and 15th (par 3).
18 holes, 5808yds, Par 69, SSS 68, Course record 63.
Club membership 750.

Visitors	must contact in advance.
Societies	apply in writing.
Green Fees	£30 per day; £20 per round.
Cards	🖃 🖃 🖃
Prof	P A Gardner
Facilities	⊗ ⦀ ⮞ ⮚ ▼ ♀ ⥁ 🖿 🛒 ⛳
Location	N side off A5116

Hotel	★★★★ 68% Mollington Banastre Hotel, Parkgate Rd, CHESTER ☎ 01244 851471 63 ⇆

Vicars Cross Tarvin Rd, Great Barrow CH3 7HN
☎ 01244 335595 Fax 01244 335686
Tree-lined parkland course, with undulating terrain.
18 holes, 6428yds, Par 72, SSS 71, Course record 64.
Club membership 750.

Visitors	advisable to contact in advance, visitors may not play competition days or Wed.
Societies	Tue & Thu only. Must book in advance.
Green Fees	£27 per day (£32 weekends & bank holidays).
Prof	J A Forsythe
Designer	J Richardson
Facilities	⊗ ⦀ by prior arrangement ⮞ ⮚ ▼ ♀ ⥁ 🖿 ⛳ ⥁
Location	4m E on A51

Hotel	★★★ 68% Rowton Hall Country House Hotel, Whitchurch Rd, Rowton, CHESTER ☎ 01244 335262 38 ⇆ 🏌

CONGLETON   Map 07 SJ86

Astbury Peel Ln, Astbury CW12 4RE
☎ 01260 279139 Fax 01260 291300
e-mail: admin@astburygolfclub.com
Parkland course in open countryside, bisected by a canal. The testing 12th hole involves a long carry over a tree-filled ravine. Large practice area.
18 holes, 6296yds, Par 71, SSS 70, Course record 61.
Club membership 720.

Visitors	must be a member of a recognised golf club and possess official handicap. May only play weekdays Apr-Nov.
Societies	contact for details.
Green Fees	not confirmed.
Prof	Ashley Salt
Facilities	⊗ ▼ ♀ ⥁ 🖿 ⛳
Location	1.5m S between A34 and A527

Congleton Biddulph Rd CW12 3LZ ☎ 01260 273540
Superbly-manicured parkland course with views over three counties from the balcony of the clubhouse.
9 holes, 5103yds, Par 68, SSS 65.
Club membership 400.

Visitors	may not play during competitions. Must contact in advance.
Societies	must apply in writing to Secretary.
Green Fees	not confirmed.
Prof	John Colclough
Facilities	⮞ ▼ by prior arrangement ♀ ⥁ 🖿
Location	1.5m SE on A527

CREWE   Map 07 SJ75

Crewe Fields Rd, Haslington CW1 5TB
☎ 01270 584099 Fax 01270 584099
e-mail: secretary@crewsgolfclub.co.uk
Undulating parkland course.
18 holes, 6424yds, Par 71, SSS 71, Course record 66.
Club membership 674.

Visitors	may not play at weekends, contact professional for details.
Societies	Tue only, prior arrangement with the secretary.
Green Fees	not confirmed.
Prof	Mike Booker
Facilities	⊗ ⦀ by prior arrangement ⮞ ▼ ♀ ⥁ 🖿 ⛳
Location	2.25m NE off A534

Hotel	★★★ 66% Hunters Lodge Hotel, Sydney Rd, Sydney, CREWE ☎ 01270 583440 47 ⇆ 🏌

Queen's Park Queen's Park Dr CW2 7SB
☎ 01270 666724 Fax 01270 569902
A short but testing municipal course, the 9 holes are highlighted by the tight dog-leg 4th hole and 450yard Par 4 7th hole. There is a testing Par 4 on finishing hole with a bomb crater on left and outerbounds on the right.
9 holes, 4920yds, Par 68, SSS 64, Course record 67.
Club membership 400.

Visitors	booking for weekends, cannot play Wed or Sun before 10.30am.
Societies	must book at least 2 weeks in advance.
Green Fees	not confirmed.
Cards	🖃 🖃 🖃 🖃 🖃 🖃
Prof	David Evanson
Facilities	⊗ ⮞ ▼ ♀ ⥁ 🖿 ⛳ ⥁
& Leisure	hard tennis courts, bowling green.
Location	Located behind Queen's Park. Well signposted ▶

Hotel   ★★★ 66% Hunters Lodge Hotel, Sydney Rd, Sydney, CREWE ☎ 01270 583440 47 ⇄ ☞

DELAMERE   Map 07 SJ56

Delamere Forest Station Rd CW8 2JE
☎ 01606 883264 (Office) 883307 (Pro)
Fax 01606 883800 (Sec)
Played mostly on undulating open heath there is great charm in the way this course drops down into the occasional pine sheltered valley. Six of the first testing nine hole are between 420 and 455 yards in length.
18 holes, 6328yds, Par 72, SSS 70, Course record 63.
Club membership 500.

Visitors   must contact in advance.
Societies   apply in writing or by telephone.
Green Fees not confirmed.
Prof   Ellis B Jones
Designer   H Fowler
Facilities   ⊗ �🏊 by prior arrangement 🏌 💷 ♀ ⛳ 🏠 🐎 ♨ ⚲
Location   1.5m NE, off B5152

Hotel   ★★★ Nunsmere Hall Country House Hotel, Tarporley Rd, SANDIWAY ☎ 01606 889100 36 ⇄ ☞

DISLEY   Map 07 SJ98

Disley Stanley Hall Ln SK12 2JX
☎ 01663 762071 & 764001 (Sec) Fax 01663 762678
Straddling a hilltop site above Lyme Park, this undulating parkland/moorland course affords good views and requires accuracy of approach to almost all the greens which lie on either a ledge or plateau. Testing holes are the 3rd and 4th.
18 holes, 6015yds, Par 71, SSS 69, Course record 63.
Club membership 658.
Visitors   contact in advance, may not normally play at weekends.
Societies   by prior arrangement.
Green Fees £25 per day(£30 weekends).
Prof   Andrew Esplin
Facilities   ⊗ ⼘ 🏌 💷 ♀ ⛳ 🏠 ♨ ⚲
Location   NW side of village off A6

Hotel   ★★★ 65% County Hotel Bramhall, Bramhall Ln South, BRAMHALL ☎ 0161 455 9988 65 ⇄ ☞

ELLESMERE PORT   Map 07 SJ47

Ellesmere Port Chester Rd, Childer Thornton CH66 1QF
☎ 0151 339 7689 Fax 0151 339 7689
Municipal parkland course that is easy walking, with natural hazards of woods, brook and ponds.
18 holes, 6432yds, Par 71, SSS 70.
Club membership 300.
Visitors   must book with professional & send a deposit.
Societies   by arrangement with professional.
Green Fees not confirmed.
Cards   💳 💳 💳 💳 💳 💳
Prof   Tony Roberts
Designer   Cotton, Pennick & Lawrie
Facilities   ⊗ ⼘ 🏌 💷 ♀ ⛳ 🏠 ♨ ⚲
& Leisure squash.
Location   NW side of town centre on A41

Hotel   ★★★ Quality Hotel Chester, Welsh Road/Berwick Rd, Little Sutton, ☎ 0151 339 5121 53 ⇄ ☞

FRODSHAM   Map 07 SJ57

Frodsham Simons Ln WA6 6HE
☎ 01928 732159 Fax 01928 734070
e-mail: office@frodshamgc.golfagent.co.uk
Undulating parkland course with pleasant views from all parts. Emphasis on accuracy over the whole course, the long and difficult par 5 18th necessitating a drive across water to the green. Crossed by two footpaths so extreme care needed.
18 holes, 6298yds, Par 70, SSS 70, Course record 63.
Club membership 600.
Visitors   must contact in advance. May not play at weekends.
Societies   telephone for bookings.
Green Fees not confirmed.
Cards   💳 💳 💳 💳 💳
Prof   Graham Tonge
Designer   John Day
Facilities   ⊗ ⼘ 🏌 💷 ♀ ⛳ 🏠 ♨ ⚲
& Leisure snooker.
Location   1.5m SW,M56 junct 12,follow signs for Forest Hills Hotel,Golf Club 1st left on Simons Lane

Hotel   ★★★ Forest Hills Hotel & Leisure Complex, Overton Hill, FRODSHAM ☎ 01928 735255 58 ⇄ ☞

HELSBY   Map 07 SJ47

Helsby Towers Ln WA6 0JB
☎ 01928 722021 Fax 01928 725384
Parkland course with several tree plantations and natural pits as water hazards. Total of 41 bunkers.
18 holes, 6221yds, Par 70, SSS 70, Course record 69.
Club membership 590.
Visitors   must contact in advance. Weekends and bank holidays with member only.
Societies   Tue & Thu. Booking through Hon Secretary.
Green Fees not confirmed.
Prof   Matthew Jones
Designer   James Braid (part)
Facilities   ⊗ ⼘ 🏌 💷 ♀ ⛳ 🏠 ♨ ⚲
Location   1m S off A56   ▶

Hotel   ★★★★★ 78% The Chester Grosvenor,
               Eastgate, CHESTER ☎ 01244 324024
               85 ⇦ ♞

KNUTSFORD   Map 07 SJ77

Heyrose Budworth Rd, Tabley WA16 0HZ
☎ 01565 733664 Fax 01565 734267
e-mail: heyrose.freeuk.com
An 18-hole course in wooded and gently undulating terrain.
The par 3 16th (237yds), bounded by a small river in a
wooded valley, is an interesting and testing hole - one of the
toughest par 3s in Cheshire. Several water hazards. Both the
course and the comfortable clubhouse have attractive views.
18 holes, 6515yds, Par 73, SSS 71, Course record 66.
Club membership 600.
Visitors   not before 3.30pm Sat, ladies priority Wed and
                seniors priority Thu am.
Societies   must contact in advance.
Green Fees not confirmed.
Cards   〰 💳
Prof   Colin Iddon
Designer   C N Bridge
Facilities ⊗ ⅷ by prior arrangement ⅃ ♥ ♀ ⅄ 🛄 ♂
Location   1.5m from junc 19 on M6

Hotel   ★★★★ 67% Cottons Hotel, Manchester Rd,
                KNUTSFORD ☎ 01565 650333   99 ⇦ ♞

Knutsford Mereheath Ln WA16 6HS ☎ 01565 633355
Parkland course set in a beautiful old deer park. It demands
some precise iron play.
9 holes, 6288yds, Par 70, SSS 70.
Club membership 230.
Visitors   restricted Wed and weekends. Must contact in
                advance.
Societies   Thursday only by prior arrangement.
Green Fees £25 per round.
Prof   G Ogdon
Facilities ⊗ ⅃ ♥ ♀ ⅄ ♂
Location   N side of town centre off A50

Hotel   ★★★★ 67% Cottons Hotel, Manchester Rd,
                KNUTSFORD ☎ 01565 650333   99 ⇦ ♞

Mere Golf & Country Club Chester Rd, Mere
CW12 3DE ☎ 01565 830155 Fax 01565 830713
e-mail: enquiries@meregolf.co.uk

A gracious parkland championship course designed by
James Braid in the Cheshire sand belt, with several holes
close to a lake. The round has a tight finish with four
testing holes.

18 holes, 6817yds, Par 71, SSS 73, Course record 64.
Club membership 550.
Visitors   by prior arrangement only, not able to play
                Wed, Fri, Sat & Sun.
Societies   apply by telephone to Karen Gallagher.
Green Fees £70 per day April-Oct (£45 Nov-April).
Cards   〰 💳 ▦ 📇 🔲 💳 ⅃
Prof   Peter Eyre
Designer   James Braid/George Duncan
Facilities ⊗ ⅷ ⅃ ♥ ♀ ⅄ 🛄 ♛ ♝ 🏊 ♂ ₰
& Leisure   hard tennis courts, heated indoor swimming
                pool, squash, sauna, solarium, gymnasium.
Location   1m E of junc 19 of M6

Hotel   ★★★★ 67% Cottons Hotel, Manchester
                Rd, KNUTSFORD ☎ 01565 650333
                99 ⇦ ♞

Peover Plumley Moor Rd, Lower Peover WA16 9SE
☎ 01565 723337 Fax 01565 723311
e-mail: mail@peovergolfclub.co.uk
Tees and greens have been positioned to maximise the
benefits of the natural contours of the land. An excellent mix
of holes varying in design and character with many doglegs
and water hazards including a river which three of the
fairways cross, including the first.
18 holes, 6702yds, Par 72, SSS 72, Course record 69.
Club membership 400.
Visitors   full golfing attire required. Please book for tee
                times.
Societies   apply in writing/telephone in advance
Green Fees £20 weekdays (£25 weekends).
Cards   〰 ▦ 📇 🔲 💳 ⅃
Prof   Bobby Young
Designer   P A Naylor
Facilities ⊗ ⅷ ⅃ ♥ ♀ ⅄ 🛄 ♛ 🏊 ♂
Location   M6 junct19/A556 onto Plumley Moor Rd

Hotel   ★★ 74% The Longview Hotel & Restaurant,
                55 Manchester Rd, KNUTSFORD
                ☎ 01565 632119   13 ⇦ ♞ Annexe13 ⇦ ♞

LYMM   Map 07 SJ68

Lymm Whitbarrow Rd WA13 9AN
☎ 01925 755020 Fax 01925 755020
e-mail: mail@lymmgolfclub.fsnet.co.uk
First ten holes are gently undulating with the Manchester
Ship Canal running alongside the 6th hole. The remaining
holes are comparatively flat.
18 holes, 6304yds, Par 71, SSS 70.
Club membership 800.
Visitors   may not play at weekends except with member.
Societies   Wed only, must contact in advance.
Green Fees £22.
Prof   Steve McCarthy
Facilities ⊗ ⅷ ⅃ ♥ ♀ ⅄ 🛄 ♂
Location   0.5m N off A6144

Hotel   ★★ 75% Rockfield Hotel, Alexandra Rd,
                Grappenhall, WARRINGTON
                ☎ 01925 262898 6 ⇦ ♞ Annexe6 ⇦ ♞

Looking for a driving range?
See the index at the back of the guide

MACCLESFIELD   Map 07 SJ97

Macclesfield The Hollins SK11 7EA
☎ 01625 616952(Professional) Fax 01625 260061
e-mail: secretary@maccgolfclub.co.uk
Hillside heathland course situated on the edge of the Pennines
with excellent views across the Cheshire Plain. A pleasant
course providing a good test for players of all abilities.
18 holes, 5769yds, Par 70, SSS 68, Course record 66.
Club membership 620.
Visitors   apply in advance and have a handicap
                   certificate.
Societies   telephone initially.
Green Fees   £20(£25 weekends & bank holidays).
Prof   Tony Taylor
Designer   Hawtree & Son
Facilities   ⊗ ⋔ 🏌 🍺 🍴 ⚲ 🛖 🎯 ✓
Location   SE side of town centre off A523

Hotel   ★★★ 68% Belgrade Hotel & Restaurant,
                   Jackson Ln, Kerridge, Bollington,
                   MACCLESFIELD ☎ 01625 573246   54 ⇆ ➤

Shrigley Hall Hotel Shrigley Park, Pott Shrigley SK10 5SB
☎ 01625 575757 Fax 01625 575437
Parkland course set in 262-acre estate with breathtaking views
over the Peak District and Cheshire Plain. Designed by Donald
Steel, this championship standard course provides a real sporting challenge while the magnificent hotel provides a wealth of
sporting facilities as well as accommodation and food.
18 holes, 6281yds, Par 71, SSS 71, Course record 68.
Club membership 500.

Visitors   must contact in advance by telephone.
Societies   contact in advance.
Green Fees   not confirmed.
Cards   💳 💳 💳
Prof   Tony Stevens
Designer   Donald Steel
Facilities   ⊗ ⋔ 🏌 🍺 🍴 ⚲ 🛖 🎯 🍴 🛖 ✓
& Leisure   hard tennis courts, heated indoor swimming
                   pool, fishing, sauna, solarium, gymnasium.

Hotel   ★★★★ 64% Shrigley Hall Hotel Golf &
                   Country Club, Shrigley Park, Pott Shrigley,
                   MACCLESFIELD ☎ 01625 575757 150 ⇆ ➤

Tytherington Dorchester Way, Tytherington SK10 5EU
☎ 01625 506000 Fax 01625 506040
e-mail: tytherington.pulse@clubhaus.com
Modern championship course in beautiful, mature
parkland setting with numerous water features and over
100 bunkers. Testing holes, notably the signature 12th

---

hole (par 5), played from an elevated tee with adjacent
snaking ditch and a lake guarding the green.
18 hole3s, 6765yds, Par 72, SSS 74.
Visitors   subject to availability and may not play
                   weekends am.
Societies   telephone and apply in writing.
Green Fees not confirmed.
Cards   💳 💳 💳 💳 💳
Designer   Dave Thomas/Patrick Dawson
Facilities   ⊗ ⋔ 🏌 🍺 🍴 ⚲ 🛖 🎯 🛖 ✓
& Leisure   hard tennis courts, heated indoor swimming
                   pool, squash, sauna, solarium, gymnasium.
Location   1m N of Macclesfield off A523

Hotel   ★★★★ 64% Shrigley Hall Hotel Golf &
                   Country Club, Shrigley Park, Pott Shrigley,
                   MACCLESFIELD
                   ☎ 01625 575757 150 ⇆ ➤

NANTWICH   Map 07 SJ65

Reaseheath Reaseheath College CW5 6DF
☎ 01270 625131
The course at Reaseheath is attached to Reaseheath College,
which is one of the major centres of greenkeeper training in
the UK. It is a short 9-hole which can only be played with a
member.
9 holes, 1882yds, Par 62, SSS 58.
Club membership 550.
Visitors   with member only.
Societies   by prior arrangement, apply in writing.
Green Fees £7 per 18 holes with a member.
Designer   D Mortram
Facilities   ⚲
Location   1.5m NE of Nantwich, off A51

OSCROFT   Map 07 SJ56

Pryors Hayes Willington Rd CH3 8NL
☎ 01829 741250 & 740140 Fax 01829 749077
e-mail: info@pryors-hayes.co.uk
Picturesque 18-hole parkland course set in the heart of
Cheshire. Gently undulating fairways demand accurate
drives, and numerous trees and water hazards make the
course a challenging test of golf.
18 holes, 6054yds, Par 69, SSS 69.
Club membership 530.
Visitors   no restrictions.
Societies   apply for application form.
Green Fees £20 (£25 weekends).
Cards   💳 💳 💳 💳 💳
Prof   Martin Redrup
Designer   John Day
Facilities   ⊗ ⋔ 🏌 🍺 🍴 ⚲ 🛖 🎯 🛖 ✓
Location   Between A54 & A51 roads, approx 6m E of
                   Chester, village of Oscroft near Tarvin

Hotel   ★★★ 66% Blossoms Hotel, St John St,
                   CHESTER ☎ 0870 400 8108 64 ⇆ ➤

POYNTON   Map 07 SJ98

Davenport Worth Hall, Middlewood Rd SK12 1TS
☎ 01625 876951 Fax 01625 877489
Undulating parkland course. Extensive view over Cheshire
Plain from elevated 5th tee. Testing 17th hole, par 4.
18 holes, 6027yds, Par 69, SSS 69, Course record 64.
Club membership 700.   ▶

Visitors contact professional in advance, 01625 858387. May not play Wed or Sat.
Societies Tue and Thu only. Must apply in advance.
Green Fees £27per day(£32 weekends & bank holidays).
Cards ▭ ▬ ▬ ▭
Prof Gary Norcott
Facilities ⊗ ⅧℕⓄ▭♀⚐☎♂
& Leisure snooker.
Location 1m E off A523

Hotel ★★★ 65% County Hotel Bramhall, Bramhall Ln South, BRAMHALL ☎ 0161 455 9988 65 ⇆ ⋔

PRESTBURY Map 07 SJ97

Prestbury Macclesfield Rd SK10 4BJ
☎ 01625 828241 Fax 01625 828241
e-mail: wrightneil@talk21.com
Undulating parkland course, with many plateau greens. The 9th hole has a challenging uphill 3-tier green and the 17th is over a valley. Host to county and inter-county championships.
18 holes, 6359yds, Par 71, SSS 71, Course record 64.
Club membership 702.

Visitors must contact in advance and have an introduction from own club, with member only at weekends.
Societies apply in writing, Thu only.
Green Fees £42.50 per day.
Cards ▭ ▬ ▬
Prof Nick Summerfield
Designer Harry S Colt
Facilities ⊗ ⅧℕⓄ▭♀⚐☎♂♂♀
Location S side of village off A538

Hotel ★★★★ 68% Mottram Hall Hotel, Wilmslow Rd, Mottram St Andrew, Prestbury, ☎ 01625 828135 132 ⇆ ⋔

RUNCORN Map 07 SJ58

Runcorn Clifton Rd WA7 4SU
☎ 01928 574214 Fax 01928 574214
Parkland course with tree-lined fairways and easy walking. Fine views over Mersey and Weaver valleys. Testing holes: 7th par 5; 14th par 5; 17th par 4.
18 holes, 6048yds, Par 69, SSS 69, Course record 63.
Club membership 570.
Visitors weekends restricted to playing with member only, Tuesday Ladies Day.
Societies telephone in advance.

Green Fees not confirmed.
Prof A Franklin
Facilities ⊗ Ⅷ by prior arrangement ℕⓄ▭♀⚐☎♂
Location 1.25m S of Runcorn Station

Hotel ★★★ 66% Posthouse Warrington/Runcorn, Wood Ln, Beechwood, RUNCORN ☎ 0870 400 9070 150 ⇆ ⋔

SANDBACH Map 07 SJ76

Malkins Bank Betchton Rd, Malkins Bank CW11 4XN
☎ 01270 765931 Fax 01270 764730
Parkland course. Tight 13th hole with stream running through.
18 holes, 6071yds, Par 70, SSS 69, Course record 65.
Club membership 500.
Visitors no restrictions. Advisable to book in advance.
Societies apply for booking form to course professional
Green Fees £9.30 (£10 weekends).
Prof David Wheeler
Designer Hawtree
Facilities ⊗ ⅧℕⓄ▭♀⚐☎♂♂
Location 1.5m SE off A533

Hotel ★★★ 65% Chimney House Hotel, Congleton Rd, SANDBACH ☎ 01270 764141 49 ⇆ ⋔

SANDIWAY Map 07 SJ67

Sandiway Chester Rd CW8 2DJ
☎ 01606 883247 (Secretary) Fax 01606 888548
Delightful undulating wood and heathland course with long hills up to the 8th, 16th and 17th holes. Many dog-legged and tree-lined holes give opportunities for the deliberate fade or draw.
18 holes, 6404yds, Par 70, SSS 71, Course record 65.
Club membership 750.
Visitors book through secretary, members have reserved tees 8.30-9.30 and 12.30-1.30 (11.30-12.30 winter). Handicap certificate required
Societies book in advance through Secretary/Manager.
Green Fees not confirmed.
Prof William Laird
Designer Ted Ray
Facilities ⊗ ⅧℕⓄ▭♀⚐☎♂♂
Location 2m W of Northwich on A556

Hotel ★★ 66% Wincham Hall, Hall Ln, Wincham, NORTHWICH ☎ 01606 43453 10rm(9 ⇆ ⋔)

TARPORLEY Map 07 SJ56

Portal Golf & Country Club Cobbler's Cross Ln CW6 0DJ
☎ 01829 733933 Fax 01829 733928
e-mail: portalgolf@aol.com
Opened in 1991, there are two 18-hole courses here - Championship and Premier - one 9-hole course - Arderne - and the largest indoor golf academy in Britain. They are set in mature, wooded parkland. There are fine views over the Cheshire Plain and numerous water hazards. The Championship 14th is just a short iron through trees, but its green is virtually an island surrounded by water. ▶

Championship Course: 18 holes, 7037yds, Par 73, SSS 74, Course record 64.
Premier Course: 18 holes, 6508yds, Par 71, SSS 72, Course record 64.
Arderne Course: 9 holes, 1724yds, Par 30.
Club membership 300.

Portal Golf & Country Club

Visitors   must contact in advance.
Societies must pre-book.
Green Fees not confirmed.
Cards
Prof   Mike Slater/Adrian Hill
Designer Donald Steel
Facilities
& Leisure hard tennis courts, indoor golf academy.
Location Off A49

Hotel   ★★★ The Wild Boar, Whitchurch Rd, Beeston, TARPORLEY ☎ 01829 260309 37

WARRINGTON   Map 07 SJ68

Birchwood Kelvin Close, Science Park North, Birchwood WA3 7PB
☎ 01925 818819 (Club) & 816574 (Pro) Fax 01925 822403
Very testing parkland course with many natural water hazards and the prevailing wind creating a problem on each hole. The 11th hole is particularly challenging.
Pilgrims: 18 holes, 6727yds, Par 71, SSS 73, Course record 66.
Progress: 18 holes, 6359yds, Par 71, SSS 72.
Mayflower (ladies course): 18 holes, 5849yds, Par 74, SSS 74.
Club membership 745.
Visitors   advisable to check with the professional to determine if course is fully booked.
Societies Mon, Wed & Thu. Apply in writing, or telephone.
Green Fees not confirmed.
Cards
Prof   Paul McEwan
Designer T J A Macauley
Facilities
& Leisure sauna.
Location Junct 11 on M62, follow signs for Science Park North, 2m from the junct

Hotel   ★★★ 66% Posthouse Haydock, Lodge Ln, HAYDOCK ☎ 0870 400 9039 138

Leigh Kenyon Hall, Broseley Ln, Culcheth WA3 4BG
☎ 01925 762943 (Secretary) Fax 01925 765097
A pleasant, well-wooded parkland course. Any discrepancy in length is compensated by the wide variety of golf offered here. The course is well maintained and there is a comfortable clubhouse.
18 holes, 5853yds, Par 69, SSS 68, Course record 64.
Club membership 550.
Visitors   contact professional for details.
Societies Mon (ex bank holidays) & Tue, apply by telephone.
Green Fees not confirmed.
Prof   Andrew Baguley
Designer James Braid
Facilities
Location 5m NE off A579

Hotel   ★★★ 72% Fir Grove Hotel, Knutsford Old Rd, WARRINGTON ☎ 01925 267471 40

Poulton Park Dig Ln, Cinnamon Brow, Padgate WA2 0SH
☎ 01925 822802 Fax 01925 822802
Tight, flat parkland course with good greens and many trees. A straight drive off each tee is important. The 4/13th has a fairway curving to the left with water and out-of-bounds on left and trees on right.
9 holes, 4978mtrs, Par 68, SSS 66, Course record 66.
Club membership 350.
Visitors   midweek only. Contact professional for details 01925 825220.
Societies apply in advance.
Green Fees £15per round(£17 weekends).
Prof   Andrew Matthews
Facilities
Location 3m from Warrington on A574

Hotel   ★★★ 72% Fir Grove Hotel, Knutsford Old Rd, WARRINGTON ☎ 01925 267471 40

Walton Hall Warrington Rd, Higher Walton WA4 5LU
☎ 01925 263061 (bookings)
A quiet, wooded, municipal parkland course on Walton Hall estate.
18 holes, 6647yds, Par 72, SSS 73, Course record 70.
Club membership 250.
Visitors   must book 6 days in advance.
Societies must contact in writing.
Green Fees £11.50(£13.50 weekends).
Prof   John Jackson
Facilities
Location 2m from junct 11 of M56

Hotel   ★★★ 72% Fir Grove Hotel, Knutsford Old Rd, WARRINGTON ☎ 01925 267471 40

Warrington Hill Warren, London Rd, Appleton WA4 5HR
☎ 01925 261775 (Secretary) Fax 01925 265933
Meadowland, with varied terrain and natural hazards. Major work has recently been carried out on both the clubhouse and the course to ensure high standards. The course is a constant challenge with with ponds, trees and bunkers threatening the errant shot!
18 holes, 6305yds, Par 72, SSS 70, Course record 61.
Club membership 840.

▶

Visitors	contact in advance.
Societies	by prior arrangement with Secretary.
Green Fees	£27 per day (£32 weekends & bank holidays).
Prof	Reay Mackay
Designer	James Braid
Facilities	⊗ ⫘ ⅃ 🛈 🏌 ♀ 🍴 🛆 ➔ ⚑ ✓
Location	1.5m N of junct 10 of M56 on A49

Hotel	★★ 75% Rockfield Hotel, Alexandra Rd, Grappenhall, WARRINGTON ☎ 01925 262898 6 ⇆ 🐾 Annexe6 ⇆ 🐾

WIDNES   Map 07 SJ58

St Michael Jubilee Dundalk Rd WA8 8BS
☎ 0151 424 6230 Fax 0151 495 2124
18 holes, 5925yds, Par 69, SSS 67.
Location   W side of town centre off A562
Telephone for further details

Hotel	★★★ 64% Everglades Park Hotel, Derby Rd, WIDNES ☎ 0151 495 2040 65 ⇆ 🐾

Widnes Highfield Rd WA8 7DT
☎ 0151 424 2440 & 424 2995 Fax 0151 495 2849
Parkland course, easy walking.
18 holes, 5719yds, Par 69, SSS 68, Course record 64.
Club membership 700.

Visitors	may play after 9am & after 4pm on competition days. Must contact in advance.
Societies	must contact the secretary in writing.
Green Fees	£15 per round(plus £1 insurance);£25 weekends.
Prof	J O'Brien
Facilities	⊗ ⫘ ⅃ 🛈 🏌 ♀ 🛆 🍴
Hotel	★★★ 64% Everglades Park Hotel, Derby Rd, WIDNES ☎ 0151 495 2040 65 ⇆ 🐾

WILMSLOW   Map 07 SJ88

Mottram Hall Wilmslow Rd, Mottram St Andrew SK10
4QT ☎ 01625 828135 Fax 01625 828950
e-mail: dmh.sales@devere-hotels.com
Championship standard course with flat meadowland on the
front nine and undulating woodland on the back with well
guarded greens. The course is unusual as each half opens and
closes with Par 5's. The hotel offers many leisure facilities.
18 holes, 7006yds, Par 72, SSS 74, Course record 65.
Club membership 500.

Visitors	must contact in advance. Cannot play before 11am Sat/Sun. Handicap certificate required.
Societies	must contact in advance.
Green Fees	£39 per round(£44 weekends).

Cards	🖃 🖃 🖃 🖃 🖃 🖃 🖃
Prof	Tim Rastall
Designer	Dave Thomas
Facilities	⊗ ⫘ ⅃ 🛈 🏌 ♀ 🛆 🍴 🏊 ➔ ⚑ ✓ 🐾
& Leisure	hard tennis courts, heated indoor swimming pool, squash, sauna, solarium, gymnasium.
Location	On A538 between Wilmslow and Presbury

Hotel	★★★★ 68% Mottram Hall Hotel, Wilmslow Rd, Mottram St Andrew, Prestbury, ☎ 01625 828135 132 ⇆ 🐾

Styal Station Rd, Styal SK9 4JN
☎ 01625 531359 Fax 01625 530063
Well designed flat parkland course with testing bunkers and
water hazards. Boasts the longest hole in Cheshire!
18 holes, 6301yds, Par 71, SSS 70, Course record 66.
Club membership 800.

Visitors	contact to reserve tee time.
Societies	telephone in advance.
Green Fees	£16 per round;£24 per day(£20/£30 weekends).
Cards	🖃 🖃 🖃 🖃 🖃 🖃
Prof	Simon Forrest
Designer	Tony Holmes
Facilities	⊗ ⫘ ⅃ 🛈 🏌 ♀ 🛆 🍴 ➔ ⚑ ✓ 🐾
Location	M56 junct 5, 5min drive from Wilmslow

Hotel	★★★★ 65% Belfry House Hotel, Stanley Rd, HANDFORTH ☎ 0161 437 0511 80 ⇆ 🐾

Wilmslow Great Warford, Mobberley WA16 7AY
☎ 01565 872148 Fax 01565 872172
e-mail: wilmslowgolfclub@ukf.net
A fine parkland championship course, of middle length,
fair to all classes of player and almost in perfect
condition.
18 holes, 6607yds, Par 72, SSS 72, Course record 62.
Club membership 800.

Visitors	must contact in advance.
Societies	Tue & Thu only application in writing.
Green Fees	£50 per day; £40 per round (£60/£50 weekends & bank holidays).
Prof	John Nowicki
Facilities	⊗ ⫘ ⅃ 🛈 🏌 ♀ 🛆 🍴 ⚑ ✓
Location	2m SW off B5058

Hotel	★★★ 73% Alderley Edge Hotel, Macclesfield Rd, ALDERLEY EDGE ☎ 01625 583033 46 ⇆ 🐾

WINSFORD   Map 07 SJ66

Knights Grange Grange Ln CW7 2PT ☎ 01606 552780
Attractive, well maintained municipal parkland course with
water hazards. Within a large recreation complex including a
public house and childrens' play area.
18 holes, 6010yds, Par 71, SSS 70.

Visitors	24 hr booking system for weekly play, after 10am Wed for weekend bookings.
Societies	apply in writing.
Green Fees	apply to reception.
Prof	Graham Moore
Facilities	🍴 🛆 ⚑ ✓
& Leisure	hard and grass tennis courts.
Location	N side of town off A54

▶

Hotel ★★ 66% Wincham Hall, Hall Ln, Wincham, NORTHWICH ☎ 01606 43453 10rm(9 ⇄ ♠)

WINWICK   Map 07 SJ69

Alder Root Alder Root Ln WA2 8R2
☎ 01925 291919 Fax 01925 291919
A woodland course, flat in nature but with many undulations. Several holes have water hazards. One of the most testing nine hole courses in the north west.
9 holes, 5837yds, Par 69, SSS 68, Course record 67.
Club membership 400.

Visitors	telephone for details of dress code.
Societies	must telephone in advance.
Green Fees	not confirmed.
Prof	C McKevitt
Designer	Mr Lander/Mr Millington
Facilities	⊗ ⓑ ♥ ♀ ♣ ♠ ♣ ♠ ♂
Location	From M62 junct 9 take A49 N for 800mtrs then left at lights and 1st right into Alder Root Lane

Hotel ★★ 64% Paddington House Hotel, 514 Old Manchester Rd, WARRINGTON ☎ 01925 816767 37 ⇄ ♠

CORNWALL & ISLES OF SCILLY

BODMIN   Map 02 SX06

Lanhydrock Lostwithiel Rd, Lanhydrock PL30 5AQ
☎ 01208 73600 Fax 01208 77325 e-mail: lanhydrock-golf-club@eclipse.co.uk
An acclaimed parkland/moorland course adjacent to the National Trust property Lanhydrock House. Nestling in a picturesque wooded valley of oak and birch, this undulating course provides an exciting and enjoyable challenge to all abilities with discreet use of water and bunkers.
18 holes, 6100yds, Par 70, SSS 70, Course record 66.
Club membership 400.

Visitors	no restrictions.
Societies	please telephone in advance.
Green Fees	not confirmed.
Cards	▭ ▬ ▭ ▭ ▩ ▨
Prof	Jason Broadway
Designer	Hamilton Stutt
Facilities	⊗ Ⅲⓑ♥♀♣♠♂♣♠♣♠♂ᵗ
Location	1m S of Bodmin from B3268

Hotel ★★★ 64% Restormel Lodge Hotel, Hillside Gardens, LOSTWITHIEL ☎ 01208 872223 21 ⇄ ♠ Annexe12 ⇄

BUDE   Map 02 SS20

Bude & North Cornwall Burn View EX23 8DA
☎ 01288 352006 Fax 01288 356855
Seaside links course with natural sand bunkers, superb greens and breathtaking views. Club established in 1893.
18 holes, 6205yds, Par 71, SSS 70.
Club membership 1000.

Visitors	book by telephone 6 days in advance for starting time - or before 6 days with a deposit. Limited tee times at weekends.
Societies	apply in writing or by telephone/fax.
Green Fees	£25 per day (£30 weekends & bank holidays).
Cards	▭ ▬ ▭ ▩
Prof	John Yeo
Facilities	⊗ Ⅲ ⓑ ♥ ♀ ♣ ♠ ♂ ᵗ ♂
& Leisure	snooker room.
Location	N side of town

Hotel ★★ 68% Camelot Hotel, Downs View, BUDE ☎ 01288 352361 24 ⇄ ♠

BUDOCK VEAN   Map 02 SW73

Budock Vean Golf & Country House Hotel Mawnan Smith TR11 5LG
☎ 01326 250288 (hotel) & 252102 (shop)
Fax 01326 250892 e-mail: relax@budockvean.co.uk
Set in 65 acres of mature grounds with a private foreshore to the Helford River, this 18 tee undulating parkland course has a tough par 4 5th hole (456yds) which dog-legs at halfway around an oak tree. The 16th hole measures 572 yds, par 5.
9 holes, 5227yds, Par 68, SSS 65, Course record 61.
Club membership 140.

Visitors	must contact in advance.
Societies	apply in writing or telephone in advance.
Green Fees	£18 per day.
Cards	▭ ▬ ▩ ▨ ▩
Prof	Tony Ramsden
Designer	James Braid
Facilities	⊗ Ⅲ ⓑ ♥ ♀ ♣ ♠ ♂ ᵗ ♠ ♣ ♠ ♂
& Leisure	hard tennis courts, heated indoor swimming pool, boating facilitiesu.
Location	1.5m SW

Hotel ★★★★ 72% Budock Vean-The Hotel on the River, MAWNAN SMITH ☎ 01326 252100 & Freephone 0800 833927 Fax 01326 250892 58 ⇄ ♠

CAMBORNE — Map 02 SW64

Tehidy Park TR14 0HH
☎ 01209 842208 Fax 01209 843680
A well-maintained parkland course providing good
holiday golf.
18 holes, 6241yds, Par 71, SSS 71, Course record 62.
Club membership 850.
Visitors	must contact in advance and have a handicap certificate.
Societies	telephone followed by letter.
Green Fees	£25 per day (£30 weekends and bank holidays).
Prof	James Dumbreck
Facilities	⊗ ⅷ ᥢ ᴗ ⌾ ♁ ☖ ☎ ⚐ ♂
Location	On Portreath/Pool road, 2m S of Camborne

Hotel ★★★ 65% Penventon Hotel, REDRUTH
☎ 01209 203000 50 ⇆ ℝ

CAMELFORD — Map 02 SX18

Bowood Park Lanteglos PL32 9RF
☎ 01840 213017 Fax 01840 212622
A testing parkland course situated in Bowood Park, formerly
the largest deer park in Cornwall. The first nine holes are designed around rolling hills; the back nine being played through
the River Allen Valley. Plenty of wildlife, water and trees.
18 holes, 6692yds, Par 72, SSS 72.
Club membership 300.
Visitors	booking system in operation
Societies	contact for details.
Green Fees	not confirmed.
Cards	⊟ ⌷⌷ 🞕 ᥨ
Prof	Richard Jenkins
Designer	Sandow
Facilities	⊗ ⅷ ᥢ ᴗ ⌾ ♁ ☖ ☎ ⚐ ↺ ♚ ♂ ♭
Location	Through Camelford, 0.5m turn right Tintagel/Boscastle B3266, 1st left at garage

Hotel ★★♨♨ 78% Trebrea Lodge, Trenale,
TINTAGEL ☎ 01840 770410
6 ⇆ ℝ Annexe1 ⇆ ℝ

CARLYON BAY — Map 02 SX05

Carlyon Bay Hotel Sea Rd PL25 3RD
☎ 01726 814250 Fax 01726 814250
Championship-length, cliff-top course moving into
parkland. Magnificent views surpassed only by the
quality of the course. The 230-yard (par 3) 18th with
railway and road out-of-bounds, holds the player's
interest to the end.
18 holes, 6597yds, Par 72, SSS 71, Course record 66.
Club membership 500.
Visitors	must contact in advance.
Societies	must contact in advance.
Green Fees	£25-£35 per round depending on season.
Cards	⊟ ⌷⌷ 🞕 ᥨ
Prof	Mark Rowe
Facilities	ᥢ ᴗ ⌾ ♁ ☖ ☎ ⚐ ↺ ♚ ♂
& Leisure	hard tennis courts, outdoor and indoor heated swimming pools, sauna, solarium.
Hotel	★★★★ 74% Carlyon Bay Hotel, Sea Rd, Carlyon Bay, ST AUSTELL ☎ 01726 812304 73 ⇆ ℝ

See advertisement on page 50.

CONSTANTINE BAY — Map 02 SW87

Trevose PL28 8JB ☎ 01841 520208 Fax 01841 521057
e-mail: info@trevose-gc.co.uk
Well known links course with early holes close to the sea on
excellent springy turf. A championship course affording
varying degrees of difficulty appealing to both the professional and higher handicap player. It is a good test with
well-positioned bunkers, and a meandering stream, and the
wind playing a decisive role in preventing low scoring.
Self-catering accommodation is available at the club.
Championship Course: 18 holes, 6461yds, Par 71, SSS
71, Course record 66.
New Course: 9 holes, 3031yds, Par 35.
Short Course: 9 holes, 1360yds, Par 29.
Club membership 1500.
Visitors	subject to reservations, handicap certificate required for championship course. Advisable to contact in advance.
Societies	telephone or write to the secretary.
Green Fees	£25-£38 per day dependent on time of day (championship course).
Cards	⊟ ⌷⌷ 🞕 ᥨ
Prof	Gary Alliss
Designer	H S Colt
Facilities	⊗ ⅷ ᥢ ᴗ ⌾ ♁ ☖ ☎ ⚐ ↺ ♚ ♂
& Leisure	hard tennis courts, heated outdoor swimming pool, snooker & games room.
Location	N of Constantine Bay, off B3276

Hotel ★★★ 77% Treglos Hotel, CONSTANTINE
BAY ☎ 01841 520727 44 ⇆ ℝ

FALMOUTH — Map 02 SW83

Falmouth Swanpool Rd TR11 5BQ
☎ 01326 311262 & 314296 Fax 01326 317783
e-mail: falmouthgolfclub@freezone.co.uk
Seaside/parkland course with outstanding coastal views.
Sufficiently bunkered to punish any inaccurate shots. Five
acres of practice grounds.
18 holes, 5937yds, Par 71, SSS 70.
Club membership 500.

Visitors	please book for tee time.
Societies	must contact in advance.
Green Fees	£35 per day; £25 per round.
Cards	⊟ ⌷⌷ 🞕 ᥨ
Prof	Bryan Patterson
Facilities	⊗ ⅷ ᥢ ᴗ ⌾ ♁ ☖ ☎ ⚐ ♚ ♂ ♭
Location	SW side of town centre

Hotel ★★★★ 70% Royal Duchy Hotel, Cliff Rd,
FALMOUTH ☎ 01326 313042 43 ⇆ ℝ

HOLYWELL BAY   Map 02 SW75

Holywell Bay TR8 5PW
☎ 01637 830095 Fax 01637 831000
e-mail: golf@trevornick.co.uk
Holywell Golf Club is situated beside a family fun park with many amenities. The course is an 18 hole Par 3 with excellent sea views. Fresh Atlantic winds make the course hard to play and there are several tricky holes, particularly the 18th over the trout pond. The site also has an excellent 18 hole Pitch & Putt course for the whole family.
18 holes, 2784yds, Par 61, Course record 58.
Club membership 100.

Visitors   no restrictions.
Societies   telephone in advance.
Green Fees   not confirmed.
Designer   Hartley
Facilities   ⊗ ⅶ ⓛ ⴹ ♀ 🖻 ⵜ ⸜
& Leisure   heated outdoor swimming pool, fishing.
Location   Off A3075 Newquay/Perranporth road

Hotel   ★★★ 70% Barrowfield Hotel, Hilgrove Rd, NEWQUAY ☎ 01637 878878
                   81 ⇆ ⵕ Annexe2 ⇆ ⵕ

LAUNCESTON   Map 02 SX38

Launceston St Stephens PL15 8HF
☎ 01566 773442 Fax 01566 777506
Undulating parkland course with views over Tamar Valley to Dartmoor and Bodmin Moor. Dominated by the 'The Hill' up which the 8th and 11th fairways rise, and on which the 8th, 9th, 11th and 12th greens sit.
18 holes, 6407yds, Par 70, SSS 71, Course record 65.
Club membership 800.
Visitors   must contact in advance, may not play weekends Apr-Oct.
Societies   telephone in first instance.
Green Fees   £20 per day.
Prof   John Tozer
Facilities   ⊗ ⅶ ⓛ ⴹ ♀ ⴷ 🖻 ⵜ ⸜
Location   NW side of town centre on B3254

Hotel   ★★ 64% Eagle House, Castle St, LAUNCESTON ☎ 01566 772036 14 ⇆ ⵕ

Trethorne Kennards House PL15 8QE
☎ 01566 86324 Fax 01566 86903
Rolling parkland course with well maintained fairways and computer irrigated greens. Plenty of trees and natural water hazards make this well respected course a good challenge.
18 holes, 6432yds, Par 71, SSS 71.
Club membership 630.

Visitors   must contact in advance.
Societies   write or telephone Colin Willis.
Green Fees   £24 per round-April-Oct(£15 Nov-March).
Cards   ▱ 🖿 ⊞ 🄭 ⊡
Prof   Mark Boundy
Designer   Frank Frayne
Facilities   ⊗ ⅶ ⓛ ⴹ ♀ ⴷ 🖻 ⵜ ⸜ ⵘ ⵝ ⸜ ⸜
Location   Just off the A30, 3m W of Launceston, on junct with the A395 (Camelford)

Hotel   ★★ 75% Penhallow Manor Hotel, ALTARNUN ☎ 01566 86206 6 ⇆ ⵕ

LELANT   Map 02 SW53

West Cornwall TR26 3DZ
☎ 01736 753401 & 753177 Fax 01736 753401
e-mail: malcolm@westcornwallgolfclub.fsnet.uk.co
A seaside links with sandhills and lovely turf adjacent to the Hayle estuary and St Ives Bay. A real test of the player's skill, especially 'Calamity Corner' starting at the 5th on the lower land by the River Hayle. A small (3 hole) course is available for practice.
18 holes, 5884yds, Par 69, SSS 69, Course record 63.
Club membership 748.

Visitors   must prove handicap certificate, be a member of a club affiliated to the EGU, advisable to contact in advance.
Societies   must apply in writing.
Green Fees   £25 per day (£30 weekends & bank holidays) plus 50p insurance charge.
Prof   Paul Atherton
Designer   Reverend Tyack
Facilities   ⊗ ⅶ ⓛ ⴹ ♀ ⴷ 🖻 ⵜ ⸜
& Leisure   snooker.
Location   N side of village off A3074

Hotel   ★★ 73% Pedn-Olva Hotel, West Porthminster Beach, ST IVES ☎ 01736 796222 26 ⇆ ⵕ Annexe4 ⇆ ⵕ

LOOE   Map 02 SX25

Looe Widegates PL13 1PX
☎ 01503 240239 Fax 01503 240864
Designed by Harry Vardon in 1935, this downland/parkland course commands panoramic views over south-east Cornwall and the coast. Easy walking.
18 holes, 5940yds, Par 70, SSS 69, Course record 64.
Club membership 600.

▶

Visitors	handicap certificate preferred, booking in advance recommended, no limitations subject to availability.
Societies	telephone in advance, booking to be confirmed in writing.
Green Fees	£25 per 18 holes.
Cards	
Prof	Alistair Macdonald
Designer	Harry Vardon
Facilities	
Location	3.5m NE off B3253

Hotel ★★★ 64% Hannafore Point Hotel, Marine Dr, West Looe, LOOE ☎ 01503 263273 37 ⇆ ⋔

LOSTWITHIEL
Map 02 SX15

Lostwithiel Hotel, Golf & Country Club Lower Polscoe
PL22 0HQ ☎ 01208 873550 Fax 01208 87479
e-mail: reception@golf-hotel.co.uk

An undulating, parkland course with water hazards. Overlooked by Restormel Castle, and the River Fowey flows alongside the course. Driving range.
18 holes, 5984yds, Par 72, SSS 71, Course record 67. Club membership 500.

Visitors	must contact in advance.
Societies	contact in advance.
Green Fees	£26 (£29 weekends).
Cards	
Prof	Tony Nash
Designer	S Wood
Facilities	
& Leisure	hard tennis courts, heated indoor swimming pool, fishing, gymnasium.
Location	1m outside Lostwithiel off A390

Hotel ★★ 66% Lostwithiel Hotel Golf & Country Club, Lower Polscoe, LOSTWITHIEL ☎ 01208 873550 19 ⇆ ⋔

MAWGAN PORTH
Map 02 SW86

Merlin TR8 4DN ☎ 01841 540222 Fax 01841 541031
A heathland course. The most challenging hole is the Par 5 12th with out of bounds along the lefthand side. The course is being lengthened to a par 72.
18 holes, 5227yds, Par 67, SSS 67. Club membership 350.

Visitors	no restrictions, except during club competitions.
Societies	telephone in advance.
Green Fees	£13 per day/round; £9.50 per 9 holes.
Cards	
Designer	Ross Oliver
Facilities	

▶

Location   On the coast rd Newquay/Padstow. After
              Mawgan Porth follow signs for St Eval,
              golf course on right

Hotel   ★★ 68% Tredragon Hotel, MAWGAN
            PORTH ☎ 01637 860213   26 ⇔ ♙

MAWNAN SMITH

See **Budock Vean**

MULLION   Map 02 SW61

Mullion Cury TR12 7BP
☎ 01326 240685 & 241176(pro) Fax 01326 240685
Founded in 1895, a clifftop and links course with
panoramic views over Mounts Bay. A steep downhill
slope on 6th and the 10th descends to the beach with a
deep ravine alongside the green. Most southerly course
in the British Isles.
18 holes, 6037yds, Par 70, SSS 70.
Club membership 654.
Visitors   preferable to contact in advance, restricted
               during club competitions.
Societies   must contact in advance.
Green Fees £23 per day/round (£28 weekends& bank
               holidays).
Cards   ▭
Prof   Phil Blundell
Designer   W Sich
Facilities ⊗ ⟩∭ ᴛ ❧ ♟ ♙ ⌂ ℾ ♣ ⚸
& Leisure   golf academy.
Location   1.5m NW of Mullion, off A3083

Hotel   ★★★ 71% Polurrian Hotel, MULLION
            ☎ 01326 240421   39 ⇔ ♙

NEWQUAY   Map 02 SW86

Newquay Tower Rd TR7 1LT
☎ 01637 874354 Fax 01637 874066
e-mail: newquaygolfclub@smartone.co.uk
Gently undulating seaside course running parallel to the
beach and open to wind. Breathtaking views.
18 holes, 6150yds, Par 69, SSS 69, Course record 63.
Visitors   please telephone in advance.
Societies   apply in writing or telephone.
Green Fees £25 per day/round.
Cards   ▭ ▭ ▭
Prof   Mark Bevan
Designer   H Colt
Facilities ⊗ ⟩∭ ᴛ ❧ ♟ ♙ ⌂ ℾ
& Leisure   hard tennis courts.
Location   W side of town

Hotel   ★★★ 69% Hotel Bristol, Narrowcliff,
            NEWQUAY ☎ 01637 875181   74 ⇔ ♙

Treloy TR8 4JN ☎ 01637 878554 Fax 01637 871710
e-mail: paull@treloy.freeserve.co.uk
An executive course constructed in 1991 to American
specifications with large contoured and mounded greens.
Offers an interesting round for all categories of player.
9 holes, 2143yds, Par 32, SSS 31, Course record 63.

Visitors   no restrictions.
Societies   telephone in advance.
Green Fees not confirmed.
Cards   ▭ ▭ ▭
Designer   M R M Sandow
Facilities ᴛ ❧ ♟ ♙ ⌂ ℾ ♣ ⚸
Location   On A3059 Newquay to St Columb Major Road

Hotel   ★★ 71% Whipsiderry Hotel, Trevelgue Rd,
            Porth, NEWQUAY ☎ 01637 874777
            24rm(5 ⇔ 14 ♙)

PADSTOW

See **Constantine Bay**

PERRANPORTH   Map 02 SW75

Perranporth Budnic Hill TR6 0AB
☎ 01872 573701 Fax 01872 573701
e-mail: perranporth@golfclub92.fsnet.co.uk
There are three testing par 5 holes on the links course (2nd,
5th, 11th) and a fine view over Perranporth Beach from all
holes.
18 holes, 6288yds, Par 72, SSS 72, Course record 62.
Club membership 832.
Visitors   no reserved tee times.
Societies   by prior arrangement.
Green Fees £25 per day (£30 weekends).
Cards   ▭ ▭ ▭
Prof   D Michell
Designer   James Braid
Facilities ⊗ ⟩∭ ᴛ ❧ ♟ ♙ ⌂ ℾ ⇢ ⚸
Location   0.75m NE on B3285

Hotel   ★★ 63% Beach Dunes Hotel, Ramoth Way,
            Reen Sands, PERRANPORTH
            ☎ 01872 572263 6rm(5 ⇔ ♙) Annexe3 ⇔ ♙

PRAA SANDS   Map 02 SW52

Praa Sands Germoe Cross Roads TR20 9TQ
☎ 01736 763445 Fax 01736 763399
A beautiful parkland course, overlooking Mount's Bay with
outstanding sea views from every tee and green.
9 holes, 4122yds, Par 62, SSS 60, Course record 59.
Club membership 220.

Visitors   restricted Sun 8-12.30pm, no need to phone.
Societies   telephone in advance for details.
Green Fees £20 per day; £15 per 18 holes; £10 per 9 holes.

▶

Designer	R Hamilton
Facilities	⊗ ℣ ⓛ 🌿 💺 ♀ 🏖 🏠 ⛳ ⚷
& Leisure	pool, darts.
Location	A394 midway between Penzance/Helston

Hotel	★★ 79% Nansloe Manor Hotel, Meneage Rd, HELSTON ☎ 01326 574691 7rm(6 ⇔ 🐾)

ROCK
Map 02 SW97

St Enodoc PL27 6LD
☎ 01208 863216 Fax 01208 862976
Classic links course with huge sand hills and rolling fairways. James Braid laid out the original 18 holes in 1907 and changes were made in 1922 and 1935. On the Church, the 10th is the toughest par 4 on the course and on the 6th is a truly enormous sand hill known as the Himalayas. The Holywell is not as exacting as the Church, it is less demanding on stamina but still a real test of skill for golfers of any handicap.
Church Course: 18 holes, 6243yds, Par 69, SSS 70, Course record 64.
Holywell Course: 18 holes, 4142yds, Par 63, SSS 61.
Club membership 1500.

Visitors	may not play on bank holidays. Must have a handicap certificate of 24 or below for Church Course. Must contact in advance.
Societies	must contact in writing/telephone.
Green Fees	Church: £50 per day; £35 per round (£40 weekends). Holywell: £25 per day; £15 per round.
Cards	⊟ ▦ 💳 💳 ▦ 🔄
Prof	Nick Williams
Designer	James Braid
Facilities	⊗ ℣ ⓛ 🌿 💺 ♀ 🏖 🏠 ⛳ 🏑 🏌 ⚷ ⚷
Location	W side of village

Hotel	★★ 65% The Molesworth Arms Hotel, Molesworth St, WADEBRIDGE ☎ 01208 812055 16rm(14 ⇔ 🐾)

ST AUSTELL
Map 02 SX05

Porthpean Porthpean PL26 6AY ☎ 01726 71643
A picturesque 18 hole course, the outward holes are in a pleasant parkland setting whilst the return holes command spectacular views over St Austell Bay.
18 holes, 5210yds, Par 67, SSS 66.
Club membership 300.

Visitors	no restrictions
Societies	telephone in advance.
Green Fees	£14 per day; £9 per 9 holes.
Cards	⊟ ▦ 💳 🔄 🔄
Facilities	⊗ ⓛ 🌿 💺 ♀ 🏖 🏠 ⛳ ⚷ ⚷
Location	1.5m from St Austell by-pass

Hotel	★★ 70% The Pier House, Harbour Front, Charlestown, ST AUSTELL ☎ 01726 67955 26 ⇔ 🐾

St Austell Tregongeeves Ln PL26 7DS
☎ 01726 74756 Fax 01726 71978
Very interesting inland parkland course designed by James Braid and offering glorious views of the surrounding countryside. Undulating, well-covered with tree plantations and well-bunkered. Notable holes are 8th (par 4) and 16th (par 3).

18 holes, 6089yds, Par 69, SSS 69, Course record 64.
Club membership 700.

Visitors	advisable to contact in advance, weekend play is limited. Must be a member of a recognised golf club and hold a handicap certificate.
Societies	must apply in writing.
Green Fees	£20 per day.
Prof	Tony Pitts
Facilities	⊗ ⓛ 🌿 💺 ♀ 🏖 🏠 ⚷ ⚷ ℓ
Location	1m W of St Austell on A390

Hotel	★★★ 64% Porth Avallen Hotel, Sea Rd, Carlyon Bay, ST AUSTELL ☎ 01726 812802 24 ⇔ 🐾

ST IVES
Map 02 SW54

Tregenna Castle Hotel, Golf & Country Club TR26 2DE
☎ 01736 797381 Fax 01736 796066
Parkland course surrounding a castellated hotel and overlooking St Ives Bay and harbour.
18 holes, 3260yds, Par 60, SSS 58.
Club membership 140.

Visitors	no booking needed. Dress code in operation.
Societies	telephone for details.
Green Fees	£15 per round; 320 per day.
Cards	⊟ ▦ 💳 💳 ▦ 🔄
Designer	Abercrombie
Facilities	⊗ ℣ ⓛ 🌿 💺 ♀ 🏠 ⛳ 🏑 🏌 ⚷
& Leisure	hard tennis courts, outdoor and indoor heated swimming pools, squash, sauna, solarium, gymnasium.
Location	From A30 Penzance road turn off just past Hayle onto A3074

Hotel	★★★ 67% Tregenna Castle Hotel, ST IVES ☎ 01736 795254 84 ⇔ 🐾

ST JUST (NEAR LAND'S END)
Map 02 SW33

Cape Cornwall Golf & Country Club Cape Cornwall
TR19 7NL ☎ 01736 788611 Fax 01736 788611
Coastal parkland, walled course. The walls are an integral part of its design. Country club facilities.
18 holes, 5650yds, Par 70, SSS 68, Course record 69.
Club membership 630.

Visitors	may not play before 11.30am at weekends.
Societies	must contact in advance.
Green Fees	£20 per round; £25 per day.
Cards	⊟ ▦ 💳 💳 ▦ 🔄
Prof	Paul Atherton
Designer	Bob Hamilton
Facilities	⊗ ℣ ⓛ 🌿 💺 ♀ 🏖 🏠 ⛳ 🏑 🏌 🏑 ⚷
& Leisure	heated indoor swimming pool, sauna, solarium, gymnasium.
Location	1m W of St Just

Hotel	★★★ 62% Higher Faugan Hotel, Newlyn, PENZANCE ☎ 01736 362076 11 ⇔ 🐾

ST MELLION
Map 02 SX36

ST MELLION See page 51

St Mellion Hotel

St Mellion, *Cornwall*   ☎ **01579 351351**   **Fax 01579 350537 Map 02 SX36**

e-mail: stay@st-mellion.co.uk

S et amongst 450 acres of glorious undulating Cornish countryside, St Mellion International is heralded as the premier Golf and Country Club in the SouthWest.

St Mellion boasts two outstanding golf courses, the first being the interesting yet demanding Old Course, which is perfect for golfers of all abilities. Complete with ideally sited bunkers, stategically tiered greens and difficult water features, the Old Course is definitely one not to be overlooked.

However, if you really want to test your game, look no further than the renowned Nicklaus Course, designed by the great man himself. On it's opening in 1998 Jack quoted "St Mellion is potentially the finest golf course in Europe". An inspiration to all golfers, the Nicklaus Course offers spectacularly sculptured fairways and carpet-like greens to all who take up its challenge.

Visitors telephone in advance 01579 352002
Societies apply in writing or telephone in advance
Green Fees Nicklaus Course: £70 per day,
£50 per round. Old Course: £35 per round
Facilities ⊗ ⨛ 🍴 ☕ 💺 ♀ ⛹ 🏠 ⛳ 🏌
🛺 ♐ ♟ Professional (David Moon)
Leisure tennis, swimming, sauna, solarium,
gymnasium
Location Saltash PL12 6SD (0.5m NW off A388)
Holes/Par/Course record 36 holes.
Nicklaus Course: 18 holes, 6651 yds,
Par 72, SSS 72, Course record 63
The Old Course: 18 holes, 5782 yds,
Par 68, SSS 68, Course record 60.

Championship Course

WHERE TO STAY NEARBY

Hotels
ST MELLION
★★★⑥ 72% St Mellion International
☎ 01579 351351. Annexe 39 ⇄ 📶

LISKEARD
★★⑥⑥⑥ ♣♣ Well House, St Keyne
☎ 01579 342001. 9 ⇄ 📶
★★ 63% Lord Eliot, Castle St. ☎ 01579
342717. 15 (2 ⇄ 📶 2 ⇄ 10 📶)

ST MINVER
Map 02 SW97

Roserrow Golf & Country Club Roserrow PL27 6QT
☎ 01208 863000 Fax 01208 863002 e-mail: roserrow.co.uk
Challenging par 72 course in an undulating wooded valley.
Stunning views over the Cornish countryside and out to
Hayle Bay. Accommodation and numerous facilities on site.
18 holes, 6551yds, Par 72, SSS 72.
Club membership 400.

Visitors	by arrangement weekdays or weekends, must pre book tee times.
Societies	apply in writing or telephone in advance.
Green Fees	£33 per day, £26 per round.
Cards	💳 💳 💳 💳
Prof	Andrew Cullen
Facilities	⊗ 🎿 🍴 💪 ♀ ♨ 🏠 🍴 🏠 🐎 🛒 ⛳ 🏌
& Leisure	hard tennis courts, heated indoor swimming pool, sauna, solarium, gymnasium.
Location	Between Wadebridge and Polzeath off the B3314

Hotel	★★ 65% The Molesworth Arms Hotel, Molesworth St, WADEBRIDGE ☎ 01208 812055 16rm(14 ⇄ ℝ)

SALTASH
Map 02 SX45

China Fleet Country Club PL12 6LJ
☎ 01752 848668 Fax 01752 848456
e-mail: sales@china-fleet.co.uk
A parkland course with river views. The 14th tee shot has to
carry a lake of approximately 150yards.
18 holes, 6551yds, Par 72, SSS 72, Course record 69.
Club membership 550.

Visitors	may play anytime and can book up to 7 days in advance.
Societies	telephone 01752 854657 for provisional booking.
Green Fees	on application.
Cards	💳 💳 💳 💳
Prof	Robert Moore
Designer	Hawtree
Facilities	🏠 🏠 🍴 🏠 🐎 🛒 ⛳ 🏌
& Leisure	hard tennis courts, heated indoor swimming pool, squash, sauna, solarium, gymnasium.
Location	1m from the Tamar Bridge

> AA Hotels that have special
> arrangements with golf courses are listed at
> the back of the guide

TORPOINT
Map 02 SX45

Whitsand Bay Hotel Golf & Country Club Portwrinkle
PL11 3BU ☎ 01503 230276 Fax 01503 230329
e-mail: earlehotels@btconnect.com
Testing seaside course laid out on cliffs overlooking
Whitsand Bay. Easy walking after 1st hole. The par 3 (3rd)
hole is acknowledged as one of the most attractive holes in
Cornwall.
18 holes, 5998yds, Par 69, SSS 68, Course record 62.
Club membership 400.

Visitors	visitors welcome.
Societies	must contact in advance.
Green Fees	£25 per round.
Cards	💳 💳 💳 💳 💳
Prof	Stephen Poole
Designer	Fernie
Facilities	⊗ 🎿 🍴 💪 ♀ ♨ 🏠 🍴 🏠 🐎 🛒 ⛳
& Leisure	heated indoor swimming pool, sauna, solarium, gymnasium.
Location	5m W off B3247

Hotel	★★ 70% Whitsand Bay Hotel, Golf & Country Club, Portwrinkle, TORPOINT ☎ 01503 230276 39rm(37 ⇄ ℝ)

TRURO
Map 02 SW84

Killiow Park Kea TR3 6AG
☎ 01872 270246 & 240915 Fax 01872 240915
e-mail: killiowoffice@fsnet.co.uk
Picturesque parkland course with mature oaks and woodland
and five holes played across or around water hazards.
Floodlit, all-weather driving range and practice facilities.
18 holes, 3829yds, Par 61.
Club membership 500.

Visitors	must telephone in advance to check on course availability.
Societies	apply in writing/telephone, limited catering facilities at present.
Green Fees	not confirmed.
Designer	Ross Oliver
Facilities	💪 ♀ ♨ 🏠 🛒 ⛳ 🏌
Location	3m SW of Truro, off A39

Hotel	★★★ 69% Alverton Manor, Tregolls Rd, TRURO ☎ 01872 276633 34 ⇄ ℝ

Truro Treliske TR1 3LG
☎ 01872 278684 (manager) & 272640 (club)
Fax 01872 278684
Picturesque and gently undulating parkland course with small
greens requiring accurate play. Lovely views over the
cathedral city of Truro and the surrounding countryside.
18 holes, 5306yds, Par 66, SSS 66, Course record 59.
Club membership 900.

Visitors	must have handicap certificate, advisable to ring for availability although casual fees welcome.
Societies	telephone for details.
Green Fees	£20 per day (£25 weekends & bank holidays).
Prof	Nigel Bicknell
Designer	Colt, Alison & Morrison
Facilities	⊗ 🎿 🍴 💪 ♀ ♨ 🏠 🛒 ⛳
Location	1.5m W on A390 towards Redruth, adjacent to Treliske Hospital

▶

Hotel   ★★★ 69% Alverton Manor, Tregolls Rd, TRURO ☎ 01872 276633   34 ⇆ ⟊

WADEBRIDGE   Map 02 SW97

St Kew St Kew Highway PL30 3EF
☎ 01208 841500 Fax 01208 841500
e-mail: st-kew-golf-club@ic24.net
An interesting, well-laid out 9-hole parkland course with 6 holes with water and 15 bunkers. In a picturesque setting there are 10 par 4s and 8 par 3s. No handicap certificate required but some experience of the game is essential. 9 extra tees have now been provided allowing a different teeing area for the back nine.
18 holes, 4543yds, Par 64, SSS 62, Course record 63.
Club membership 270.
Visitors   no restrictions. Start time system in operation allowing prebooking.
Societies   apply in writing, telephone or fax
Green Fees £9 per 9 holes;£14 per 18 holes.
Cards   ▭ ▭ 🖃
Prof   Nick Rogers
Designer   David Derry
Facilities   ⊗ ⟊ ⯚ 🛢 ♀ ⛳ 🖻 ⛟ ⚲ 🛒 ⌀ ℓ
& Leisure fishing.
Location   2m N,of Wadebridge main A39

Hotel   ★★ 65% The Molesworth Arms Hotel, Molesworth St, WADEBRIDGE
☎ 01208 812055 16rm(14 ⇆ ⟊)

ALSTON   Map 12 NY74

Alston Moor The Hermitage, Middleton in Teesdale Rd
CA9 3DB ☎ 01434 381675 Fax 01434 381675
Parkland and Fell, in process of upgrading to full 18 holes, stunning views of the North Pennines.
10 holes, 5518yds, Par 68, SSS 66, Course record 67.
Club membership 170.
Visitors   usually turn up and play but for weekends telephone secretary for information and availability.
Societies   telephone or write in advance.
Green Fees £9 per day (£11 weekends & bank holidays).
Facilities   🛢 ♀ ⛳
Location   1 S of Alston on B6277

Hotel   ★★ 68% Lowbyer Manor Country House Hotel, ALSTON ☎ 01434 381230
8 ⇆ ⟊ Annexe4 ⇆

APPLEBY-IN-WESTMORLAND   Map 12 NY62

Appleby Brackenber Moor CA16 6LP
☎ 017683 51432 Fax 017683 52773
This remotely situated heather and moorland course offers interesting golf with the rewarding bonus of several long par-4 holes that will be remembered. There are superb views of the Pennines and the Lakeland hills.
18 holes, 5901yds, Par 68, SSS 68, Course record 63.
Club membership 800.

Appleby Manor Country House Hotel
Visitors   phone for details. May not play before 3pm weekends/competition days.
Societies   must contact in advance by letter.
Green Fees £20 per day;£18 per round (£25/£22 weekends and bank holidays).
Prof   Gary Key
Designer   Willie Fernie
Facilities   ⊗ ⟊ ⯚ 🛢 ♀ ⛳ 🖻 ⛟ ⚲ ⌀
Location   2m E of Appleby 0.5m off A66

Hotel   ★★★ 77% Appleby Manor Country House Hotel, Roman Rd, APPLEBY-IN-WESTMORLAND ☎ 017683 51571
23 ⇆ ⟊ Annexe7 ⇆ ⟊

ASKAM-IN-FURNESS   Map 07 SD27

Dunnerholme Duddon Rd LA16 7AW ☎ 01229 462675 & 465095 Fax 01229 462675 e-mail: meg@dunnerholme.co.uk
Unique 10-hole (18 tee) links course with view of the Cumbrian mountains and Morecambe Bay. Two streams run through and around the course, providing water hazards on the 1st, 2nd, 3rd and 9th holes. The par 3, 6th is the feature hole on the course playing to an elevated green on Dunnerholme Rock, an imposing limestone outcrop jutting out into the estuary.
10 holes, 6154yds, Par 72, SSS 70.
Club membership 400.
Visitors   restricted times on Sun.
Societies   apply in writing to the secretary.
Green Fees £10 (£12 weekends).
Facilities   ☕♀⚐
Location   1m N on A595

Hotel   ★★ 60% Lisdoonie Hotel, 307/309 Abbey Rd,
                 BARROW-IN-FURNESS
                 ☎ 01229 827312 12 ⇆ ♙

BARROW-IN-FURNESS   Map 07 SD26

Barrow Rakesmoor Ln, Hawcoat LA14 4QB
☎ 01229 825444 & 832121 (Pro) Fax 01229 832121
Pleasant course laid out on two levels on meadowland with extensive views of the nearby Lakeland fells. Upper level is affected by easterly winds.
18 holes, 6184yds, Par 71, SSS 70, Course record 66.
Club membership 700.
Visitors   must be a member of a recognised golf club or
                 hold a handicap certificate, advisable to contact
                 the professional regarding tee time.
small groups ring professional for details, groups over 12
                 apply to the secretary in advance.
Green Fees £20.
Prof   Andy Whitehall
Facilities   ⊗ �𝕀 ᴸ ▪ ♥ ♀ ⚐ 🏠 ♙ ⚑
Location   2m from Barrow off A590

Hotel   ★★ 60% Lisdoonie Hotel, 307/309 Abbey Rd,
                 BARROW-IN-FURNESS
                 ☎ 01229 827312 12 ⇆ ♙

Furness Central Dr LA14 3LN ☎ 01229 471232
Links golf with a fairly flat first half but a much sterner second nine played across subtle sloping ground. There are good views of the Lakes, North Wales and the Isle of Man.
18 holes, 6363yds, Par 71, SSS 71, Course record 65.
Club membership 630.
Visitors   must contact the secretary in advance.
Societies   apply in writing, must be member of recognised
                 club with handicap certificate.
Green Fees not confirmed.
Facilities   ⊗ �𝕀 ᴸ ▪ ♥ ♀ 🏠 ⚐
Location   1.75 W of town centre off A590 to Walney
                 Island

Hotel   ★★ 60% Lisdoonie Hotel, 307/309 Abbey Rd,
                 BARROW-IN-FURNESS
                 ☎ 01229 827312 12 ⇆ ♙

BOWNESS-ON-WINDERMERE   Map 07 SD49

Windermere Clearbarrow LA23 3NB
☎ 015394 43123 Fax 015394 43123
Enjoyable holiday golf on a short, slightly hilly but sporting course in this delightful area of the Lake District National Park, with superb views of the mountains as the backcloth to the lake and the course.
18 holes, 5122yds, Par 67, SSS 65, Course record 58.
Club membership 1043.
Visitors   contact pro shop 7 days before day of play,
                 10-12 & 2-4.30 or before 9am by
                 arrangement.
Societies   by arrangement contact the secretary.
Green Fees £24 per day (£28 weekends & bank
                 holidays).
Cards   💳 💳 💳 💳 💳 💳
Prof   W S M Rooke
Designer   G Lowe
Facilities   ⊗ �𝕀 ᴸ ▪ ♥ ♀ ⚐ 🏠 ♙ ⚑ ⚐
& Leisure   snooker.
Location   B5284 1.5m from Bowness

Hotel   ★★★ 67% Wild Boar Hotel, Crook,
                 WINDERMERE ☎ 015394 45225 36 ⇆ ♙
                 See advertisement on page 58

BRAMPTON   Map 12 NY56

Brampton Talkin Tarn CA8 1HN
☎ 016977 2255 & 2000 Fax 016877 41487
Challenging golf across glorious rolling fell country demanding solid driving and many long second shots. A number of particularly fine holes, the pick of which may arguably be, the 3rd and 11th. The course offers unrivalled panoramic views from its hilly position.
18 holes, 6407yds, Par 72, SSS 71, Course record 64.
Club membership 800.
Visitors   visitors intending to play at weekends are
                 recommended to telephone in advance.
Societies   apply in writing to M Ogilvie (Hon
                 Commercial Sec), 3 Warwick St, Carlisle,
                 Cumbria CA3 8QW or telephone 01228
                 401996.
Green Fees not confirmed.
Prof   Stewart Wilkinson
Designer   James Braid
Facilities   ⊗ ⟰ ᴸ ▪ ♥ ♀ 🏠 ⚐ ⚑ ⚐
& Leisure   games room.
Location   1.5m SE of Brampton on B6413

Hotel   ★★ 65% The Tarn End House Hotel,
                 Talkin Tarn, BRAMPTON
                 ☎ 01697 72340 7 ⇆ ♙

CARLISLE   Map 11 NY35

Carlisle Aglionby CA4 8AG
☎ 01228 513029 (secretary) & 510164 (bookings)
Fax 01228 513303
Majestic looking parkland course with great appeal. A complete but not too severe test of golf, with fine turf, natural hazards, a stream and many beautiful trees. A qualifying course for the Open Championship.

▶

18 holes, 6278yds, Par 71, SSS 70, Course record 63.
Club membership 800.

Visitors may not play before 9am and between 12-
1.30 and when tee is reserved. Very limited
play Sunday and with member only
Saturday and Tuesday.

Societies Mon, Wed & Fri, contact in advance for
details.

Green Fees £40 per day; £25 per round (Sun £40 per
round).

Prof Martin Heggie
Designer Mackenzie Ross
Facilities ⊗ �III 🔓 ☕ ♀ ♿ 🏠 🛒 ♂
Location On A69 0.5m E of M6 junc 43

Hotel ★★★ 71% Crown Hotel, Wetheral,
CARLISLE ☎ 01228 561888
49 ⇆ 🏠 Annexe2 ⇆ 🏠

Stony Holme Municipal St Aidans Rd CA1 1LS
☎ 01228 625511
18 holes, 5783yds, Par 69, SSS 68, Course record 68.
Location 2m W of M6 (junct 43) and A69
Telephone for further details

Hotel ★★★ 67% Posthouse Carlisle, Parkhouse Rd,
CARLISLE ☎ 0870 400 9018 127 ⇆ 🏠

COCKERMOUTH Map 11 NY13

Cockermouth Embleton CA13 9SG
☎ 017687 76223 & 76941 Fax 017687 76941
Fell-land course, fenced, with exceptional views and a hard
climb on the 3rd and 11th holes. Testing holes: 10th and 16th
(rearranged by James Braid).
18 holes, 5496yds, Par 69, SSS 67, Course record 62.
Club membership 600.

Cockermouth Golf Club

Visitors restricted Wed, Sat & Sun.
Societies apply in writing to the secretary.
Green Fees £15 per day/round (£20 weekends & bank
holidays).
Designer J Braid
Facilities 🔓 ☕ ♀ ♿ ♂
Location 3m E off A66

Hotel ★★★ 71% The Trout Hotel, Crown St,
COCKERMOUTH ☎ 01900 823591
30 ⇆ 🏠

CROSBY-ON-EDEN Map 12 NY45

Eden CA6 4RA
☎ 01228 573003 & 573013 Fax 01228 818435 e-
mail: alistair.wannop@virgin.net
Open, championship-length parkland course following the
River Eden. A large number of water hazards, including the
river on certain holes, demands acuracy, as do the well
designed raised greens. Flood-lit driving range and excellent
clubhouse facilities.
18 holes, 6410yds, Par 72, SSS 72, Course record 64.
Club membership 500. ▶

Eden Golf Course

Visitors must contact in advance.
Societies telephone to check availability.
Green Fees £25 (£30 weekends & bank holidays).
Cards 〰️ 〰️ 🔲
Prof Steve Harrison
Facilities ⊗ �𝄆 ⓛ ▐ ▼ ⓨ ⚖ 🏠 🍴 ♂ ⎰
& Leisure hard tennis courts.
Location 5m from M6 junc 44,on A689 towards
Brampton & Newcastle-Upon-Tyne

Hotel ★★★🏵️ 78% Crosby Lodge Country House
Hotel, High Crosby, Crosby-on-Eden,
CARLISLE ☎ 01228 573618
9 ⇄ 🐾 Annexe2 ⇄ 🐾

GRANGE-OVER-SANDS   Map 07 SD47

Grange Fell Fell Rd LA11 6HB
☎ 015395 32536 Fax 015395 35357
Hillside course with magnificent views over Morecambe
Bay and the surrounding Lakeland mountains.
9 holes, 5278yds, Par 70, SSS 66, Course record 65.
Club membership 400.
Visitors may normally play Mon-Sat.
Green Fees £15 per day (£20 weekends & bank
holidays).
Facilities ▼ ⓨ ⚖
Location 1m W on Grange-Over-Sands/Cartmel

Hotel ★★★ 69% Netherwood Hotel, Lindale Rd,
GRANGE-OVER-SANDS
☎ 015395 32552 28 ⇄ 🐾

Grange-over-Sands Meathop Rd LA11 6QX
☎ 015395 33180 or 33754 Fax 015395 33754
Interesting parkland course with well sited tree plantations,
ditches and water features. The four par 3s are considered to
be some of the best in the area.
18 holes, 5958yds, Par 70, SSS 69, Course record 68.
Club membership 650.
Visitors must be a member of Golf Club or recognised
Golf Society, advisable to contact in advance for
play at weekends.
Societies apply in writing.
Green Fees £25 per day; £20 per round (£30/£25 weekends
& bank holidays).
Cards 〰️ 〰️ 🔲 🔲 🔲
Prof Steve Sumner-Roberts
Designer Mackenzie (part)
Facilities ⊗ �𝄆 ⓛ ▐ ▼ ⓨ ⚖ 🏠 🍴 ⎰
Location NE of town centre off B5277

Hotel ★★★ 64% Graythwaite Manor Hotel, Fernhill
Rd, GRANGE-OVER-SANDS
☎ 015395 32001 & 33755 Fax 015395 35549
21 ⇄ 🐾

KENDAL   Map 07 SD59

Carus Green Burneside Rd LA9 6EB
☎ 01539 721097 Fax 01539 721097
Bounded by the Kent and Sprint rivers (brought into play on
5 holes), this flat course enjoys open views to the Lakeland
Fells.
18 holes, 5691yds, Par 70, SSS 68.
Club membership 500.
Visitors no restrictions except during club competitions
at weekend, check by phone.
Societies telephone for details.
Green Fees £12 per round (£14 weekends & bank holidays).
Designer W Adamson
Facilities ⓛ ▼ ⓨ ⚖ 🏠 🍴 ⎰

Hotel ★★ 64% Garden House Hotel, Fowl-ing Ln,
KENDAL ☎ 01539 731131 11 ⇄ 🐾

Kendal The Heights LA9 4PQ ☎ 01539 723499
Elevated parkland/fell course affording breathtaking views of
Lakeland fells and surrounding district.
18 holes, 5765yds, Par 70, SSS 67, Course record 65.
Club membership 737.
Visitors must have a handicap certificate, weekends
subject to availability. Telephone to reserve tee-
off time.
Societies must contact in advance.
Green Fees £20 per day/round(£25 weekends).
Cards 〰️ 〰️ 🔲 🔲 🔲
Prof Peter Scott
Facilities ⊗ �𝄆 ⓛ ▐ ▼ ⓨ ⚖ 🏠 🍴 ⎰
Location 1m W of town centre

Hotel ★★ 64% Garden House Hotel, Fowl-ing Ln,
KENDAL ☎ 01539 731131 11 ⇄ 🐾

KESWICK   Map 11 NY22

Keswick Threlkeld Hall, Threlkeld CA12 4SX
☎ 017687 79324 Fax 017687 79861 e-
mail: keswickgolfclub@netscapeonline.co.uk
Varied fell and tree-lined course with commanding views of
Lakeland scenery.
18 holes, 6225yds, Par 71, SSS 72, Course record 67.
Club membership 866.
Visitors booking up to 7 days in advance 017687 79010.
Restricted on competition days.
Societies apply in writing to secretary.
Green Fees £20 per day (£25 weekends & bank holidays).
Prof Paul Rawlinson
Designer Eric Brown
Facilities ⊗ �𝄆 ⓛ ▐ ▼ ⓨ ⚖ 🏠 🍴 ⎰
& Leisure fishing.
Location 4m E of Keswick, off A66

Hotel ★★★ 65% Keswick Country House Hotel,
Station Rd, KESWICK ☎ 017687 72020
74 ⇄ 🐾

KIRKBY LONSDALE   Map 07 SD67

Kirkby Lonsdale Scaleber Ln, Barbon LA6 2LJ
☎ 015242 76365 Fax 015242 76503
e-mail: KLGolf@Dial.Pipex.com/
Parkland course on the east bank of the River Lune and
crossed by Barbon Beck. Mainly following the lie of the
land, the gently undulating course uses the beck to provide
water hazards.
18 holes, 6472yds, Par 72, SSS 71, Course record 68.
Club membership 600.

Visitors	restricted on Sunday, must telephone in advance or call in at pro shop.
Societies	apply in writing for society package.
Green Fees	£24 per day (£28 weekends & bank holidays).
Prof	Chris Barrett
Designer	Bill Squires
Facilities	⊗ ⅏ ⓑ ▆ ♀ ♨ ⚑ ⛳ ✦
Location	3m NE of Kirkby Lonsdale on A683

Hotel   ★★ 69% Pheasant Inn, CASTERTON
☎ 015242 71230 11 ⇄ ⏃

MARYPORT   Map 11 NY03

Maryport Bankend CA15 6PA
☎ 01900 812605 Fax 815626
A tight seaside links course exposed to Solway breezes. Fine
views across Solway Firth. Course comprises 9 holes links
and 9 holes parkland and small streams can be hazardous on
several holes. The first three holes have the seashore on their
left and an errant tee shot can land in the water. Holes 6-14
are parkland in quality, gently undulating and quite open.
Holes 15-18 revert to links.
18 holes, 6088yds, Par 70, SSS 69, Course record 65.
Club membership 450.

Visitors	booking advisable for weekends.
Societies	must apply in writing.
Green Fees	£17 per day (£22 weekends & bank holidays).
Facilities	⊗ ⅏ ⓑ ▆ ♀ ♨
Location	1m N on B5300

Hotel   ★★ 67% Broughton Craggs Hotel, Great
Broughton, COCKERMOUTH
☎ 01900 824400 14 ⇄ ⏃

PENRITH   Map 12 NY53

Penrith Salkeld Rd CA11 8SG
☎ 01768 891919 Fax 01768 891919
A beautiful and well-balanced course, always changing
direction, and demanding good length from the tee. It is
set on rolling moorland with occasional pine trees and
some fine views.
18 holes, 6047yds, Par 69, SSS 69, Course record 63.
Club membership 850.

Visitors	contact in advance. Handicap certificate required.
Societies	telephone in advance.
Green Fees	£25 per day; £20 per round (£30/£25 weekends).
Prof	Garry Key
Facilities	⊗ ⅏ ⓑ ▆ ♀ ♨ ⚑ ⛳ ✦ ⏃
Location	0.75m N off A6

Hotel   ★★ 67% Brantwood Country Hotel,
Stainton, PENRITH ☎ 01768 862748
6 ⏃ Annexe5 ⇄ ⏃

ST BEES   Map 11 NX91

St Bees CA27 0EJ ☎ 01946 824300
Links course, down hill and dale, with sea views.
9 holes, 5082yds, Par 64, SSS 65.
Club membership 275.

Visitors	no restrictions.
Green Fees	not confirmed.
Location	0.5m W of village off B5345

Hotel   ★★★ 76% Ennerdale Country House Hotel,
CLEATOR ☎ 01946 813907 30 ⇄ ⏃

SEASCALE   Map 06 NY00

Seascale The Banks CA20 1QL
☎ 019467 28202 Fax 019467 28202
e-mail: secretary@seascalegolfclub.org
A tough links requiring length and control. The natural
terrain is used to give a variety of holes and considerable
character. Undulating greens add to the challenge. Fine
views over the Western Fells, the Irish Sea and Isle of
Man.
18 holes, 6416yds, Par 71, SSS 71, Course record 64.
Club membership 650.

Visitors	no restrictions, but advisable to contact for tee reservation times.
Societies	telephone to make provisional booking.
Green Fees	£29 per day; £24 per round (£32/£29 weekends & bank holidays).
Prof	Sean Rudd
Designer	Willie Campbell
Facilities	⊗ ⅏ ⓑ ▆ ♀ ♨ ⚑ ⛳ ✦ ⏃
Location	NW side of village off B5344

Hotel   ★★ 71% Westlakes Hotel, GOSFORTH
☎ 019467 25221 9 ⇄ ⏃

SEDBERGH   Map 07 SD69

Sedbergh Dent Rd LA10 5SS
☎ 015396 21551 (Club) & 20993 (Sec)
A tree-lined grassland course with superb scenery in the
Yorkshire Dales National Park. Feature hole is the par 3 2nd
(110yds) where the River Dee separates the tee from the
green.
9 holes, 5624yds, Par 70, SSS 68, Course record 66.
Club membership 250.

Visitors	must book to play on weekends & bank holidays.
Societies	must contact in advance.
Green Fees	£18 per day; £14 per round (£21/£16 weekends).
Designer	W G Squires
Facilities	⊗ ⅏ ⓑ ▆ ♀ ♨ ⚑ ⛳ ✦
Location	1m S off A683, 5m junct 37 M6

Hotel   ★★ 64% Garden House Hotel, Fowl-ing Ln,
KENDAL ☎ 01539 731131 11 ⇄ ⏃

SILECROFT

Map 06 SD18

Silecroft 30 Lowther Rd LA18 4PG ☎ 01229 774342
Seaside links course parallel to the coast of the Irish Sea.
Often windy. Easy walking. Spectacular views inland of
Lakeland hills.
9 holes, 5877yds, Par 68, SSS 68, Course record 66.
Club membership 300.
Visitors may be restricted competition days & bank
holidayscontact secretary in advance to check.
Societies must contact in writing.
Green Fees £15 per day.
Facilities ♥ ♀ ♨
Location 3m W of Millom

SILLOTH

Map 11 NY15

Silloth on Solway The Clubhouse CA7 4BL
☎ 016973 31304 & 32404 Fax 016973 31782
e-mail: sillothgc@btinternet
Billowing dunes, narrow fairways, heather and gorse and
the constant subtle problems of tactics and judgement
make these superb links on the Solway an exhilarating
and searching test. The 13th is a good long hole. Superb
views.
18 holes, 6614yds, Par 72, SSS 73, Course record 65.
Club membership 700.
Visitors must contact in advance.
Societies telephone for times available.
Green Fees not confirmed.
Prof J Graham
Designer David Grant/Willie Park Jnr
Facilities ⊗ 川 ┗ ♥ ♀ ♨ 🛍 ♂
Location S side of village off B5300

Hotel ★★ 64% Golf Hotel, Criffel St, SILLOTH
☎ 016973 31438 22 ⇆ 🐾

ULVERSTON

Map 07 SD27

Ulverston Bardsea Park LA12 9QJ
☎ 01229 582824 Fax 01229 588910
Inland golf with many medium length holes on
undulating parkland. The 17th is a testing par 4.
Overlooking Morecambe Bay the course offers extensive
views to the Lakeland Fells.
18 holes, 6201yds, Par 71, SSS 70, Course record 64.
Club membership 750.
Visitors must contact in advance, be a member of an
accredited golf club with a handicap
certificate. May not play on Sat,
competition days & restricted on Tue-
Ladies day.
Societies by arrangement in writing.
Green Fees £25 per round;£27 per 27 holes;£30 per
day(£35 per day weekends)reductions in
winter.
Prof M R Smith
Designer A Herd/H S Colt (1923)
Facilities ⊗ 川 ┗ ♥ ♀ ♨ 🛍 ⚷ ♂
Location 2m S off A5087

Hotel ★★★ Whitewater Hotel, The Lakeland
Village, NEWBY BRIDGE
☎ 015395 31133 35 ⇆ 🐾

WINDERMERE

See **Bowness-on-Windermere**

WORKINGTON

Map 11 NY02

Workington Branthwaite Rd CA14 4SS
☎ 01900 67828 Fax 01900 607123
e-mail: golf@workingtongolfclub.freeserve.co.uk
Meadowland course, undulating, with natural hazards created
by stream and trees. Good views of Solway Firth and
Lakeland Hills. 10th, 13th and 15th holes are particularly
testing.
18 holes, 6217yds, Par 72, SSS 70, Course record 65.
Club membership 735.
Visitors advisable to contact pro for weekday, weekends
are generally very busy & Tue is Ladies Day.
No vistors befire 9.30am.
Societies booking required for over 8 people.
Green Fees not confirmed.
Prof Aidrian Drabble
Designer James Braid
Facilities ⊗ 川 ┗ ♥ ♀ ♨ 🛍 🪣 ♂
& Leisure snooker table.
Location 1.75m E off A596

Hotel ★★★ 79% Washington Central Hotel,
Washington St, WORKINGTON
☎ 01900 65772 46 ⇆ 🐾

DERBYSHIRE

ALFRETON   Map 08 SK45

Alfreton Wingfield Rd, Oakerthorpe DE55 7LH
☎ 01773 832070
A small parkland course with tight fairways and many
natural hazards.
11 holes, 5393yds, Par 67, SSS 66, Course record 67.
Club membership 300.
Visitors   must contact in advance.
Societies   apply in writing or telephone in advance.
Green Fees not confirmed.
Prof   Julian Mellor
Facilities   🏌 🍴 ♀ ⛳ 🏪
Location   1m W on A615

Hotel   ★★★★ 68% Swallow Hotel, Carter Ln East,
SOUTH NORMANTON ☎ 01773 812000
158 ⇌ ⁂

ASHBOURNE   Map 07 SK14

Ashbourne Wyaston Rd DE6 1NB
☎ 01335 342078 & 347960(pro shop) Fax 01335 347937
With fine views over surrounding countryside, the course
uses natural contours and water features.
18 holes, 6402yds, Par 72, SSS 72.
Club membership 650.
Visitors   must contact professional in advance, may not
play on competition days.
Societies   telephone in advance.
Green Fees £20 per 18 holes (£30 weekends & bank
holidays).
Prof   Andrew Smith
Designer   D Hemstock
Facilities   ⊗ 🏌 🍴 ♀ ⛳ 🏪 🏓 ✦
& Leisure   snooker table.
Location   Off Wyaston Road

Hotel   ★★★♨ 73% Callow Hall, Mappleton Rd,
ASHBOURNE ☎ 01335 300900   16 ⇌ ⁂

BAKEWELL   Map 08 SK26

Bakewell Station Rd DE45 1GB ☎ 01629 812307
Parkland course, hilly, with plenty of natural hazards to test
the golfer. Magnificent views across the Wye Valley.
9 holes, 5240yds, Par 68, SSS 66.
Club membership 325.
Visitors   limited at weekends due to competitions.
Societies   apply in writing.
Green Fees £15 (£20 weekends & bank holidays).
Facilities   ⊗ 🏌 🍴 ♀ ⛳
Location   E side of town off A6

Hotel   ★★ 73% Croft Country House Hotel, Great
Longstone, BAKEWELL
☎ 01629 640278 9 ⇌ ⁂

Entries with a green background
identify courses considered to be
particularly interesting

BAMFORD   Map 08 SK28

Sickleholme Saltergate Ln S33 0BN
☎ 01433 651306 Fax 01433 659498
Undulating downland course in the lovely Peak District, with
rivers and ravines and spectacular scenery.
18 holes, 6064yds, Par 69, SSS 69, Course record 62.
Club membership 700.
Visitors   must contact in advance, restricted weekends.
Societies   telephone in advance.
Green Fees £28 per round/day (£32 weekends).
Prof   P H Taylor
Facilities   ⊗ 🏌 🍴 ♀ ⛳ 🏪 ✦
Location   0.75m S on A6013

Hotel   ★★ 70% Yorkshire Bridge Inn, Ashopton Rd,
Hope Valley, BAMFORD
☎ 01433 651361   14 ⇌ ⁂

BREADSALL   Map 08 SK33

Marriot Breadsall Priory Hotel & Country Club Moor Rd,
Morley DE7 6DL ☎ 01332 832235 Fax 01332 833509
Set in 200 acres of mature parkland, the Priory Course is
built on the site of a 13th-century priory. Full use has been
made of natural features and fine old trees. In contrast the
Moorland Course, designed by Donald Steel and built by
Brian Piersen, features Derbyshire stone walls and open
moors heavily affected by winds. Open when most other
clubs are closed in winter.
*Priory Course: 18 holes, 6100yds, Par 72, SSS 69, Course
record 63.*
Moorland Course: 18 holes, 6028yds, Par 70, SSS 69.
Club membership 900.

Visitors   must contact in advance, 10 day booking
service.
Societies   telephone in advance.
Green Fees Priory Course from £26 per round; Moorland
Course from £28. Prices according to season.
Cards   💳 💳 💳 💳 💳 💳
Prof   Darren Steels
Designer   D Steel
Facilities   ⊗ 🏌 🍴 ♀ ⛳ 🏪 🏓 🛒 🏓 ✦ ❙
& Leisure   hard tennis courts, heated indoor swimming
pool, sauna, solarium, gymnasium.
Location   0.75m W

Hotel   ★★★★ 64% Marriott Breadsall Priory Hotel &
Country Club, Moor Rd, MORLEY
☎ 01332 832235   12 ⇌ ⁂ Annexe100 ⇌ ⁂

BUXTON   Map 07 SK07

Buxton & High Peak Waterswallows Rd SK17 7EN
☎ 01298 26263 & 23453 Fax 26333
e-mail: sec@bhpgc.fsnet.co.uk
Bracing, well-drained meadowland course; the highest in
Derbyshire. Challenging course where wind direction is a
major factor on some holes; others require blind shots to
sloping greens.
18 holes, 5966yds, Par 69, SSS 69.
Club membership 650.

Visitors	By prior arrangment only.
Societies	Prior arrangement only. Phone or write to Jane Dobson.
Green Fees	£29 per day, £23 per round (£34/£29 weekends & bank holidays).
Cards	〰️ 💳 💳 📇
Prof	Gary Brown
Designer	J Morris
Facilities	⊗ ﹢ 💺 ♀ ⚲ 🏠 ⛵ 🏌 🚜 ⚘
Location	1m NE off A6
Hotel	★★★★ 64% Palace Hotel, Palace Rd, BUXTON ☎ 01298 22001 122 🛏 🐾

Cavendish Gadley Ln SK17 6XD ☎ 01298 79708
Fax 01298 79708
This parkland/moorland course with its comfortable
clubhouse nestles below the rising hills. Generally open
to the prevailing west wind, it is noted for its excellent
surfaced greens which contain many deceptive subtleties.
Designed by Dr Alastair McKenzie, good holes include
the 8th, 9th and 18th.
18 holes, 5721yds, Par 68, SSS 68, Course record 61.
Club membership 650.

Visitors	must contact in advance, weekends are restricted by competitions. Ladies day Thursday
Societies	telephone professional on 01298 25052.
Green Fees	not confirmed.
Prof	Paul Hunstone
Designer	Dr Mackenzie
Facilities	⊗ ﹢ 💺 ♀ ⚲ 🏠 ⛵ ⚘ ♺
Location	0.75m W of town centre off A53
Hotel	★★★ 76% Best Western Lee Wood Hotel, The Park, BUXTON ☎ 01298 23002 35 🛏 🐾 Annexe5 🛏 🐾

CHAPEL-EN-LE-FRITH   Map 07 SK08

Chapel-en-le-Frith The Cockyard, Manchester Rd
SK23 9UH
☎ 01298 812118 & 813943 (sec) Fax 01298 814990
e-mail: info@chapelgolf.co.uk
Scenic parkland course, with testing holes at the 14th (par 4)
and 18th (517 yds), par 5. Good views.
18 holes, 6054yds, Par 70, SSS 69, Course record 67.
Club membership 676.

Visitors	must contact professional or secretary in advance.
Societies	apply in advance to Secretary.
Green Fees	£30 per day; £22 per round (£30 per round weekends & bank holidays).
Cards	〰️ 💳 💳
Prof	David J Cullen

Designer	David Williams
Facilities	⊗ 🍽 ﹢ 💺 ♀ ⚲ 🏠 ⛵ ⚘
Location	On B5470
Hotel	★★★ 76% Best Western Lee Wood Hotel, The Park, BUXTON ☎ 01298 23002 35 🛏 🐾 Annexe5 🛏 🐾

CHESTERFIELD   Map 08 SK37

Chesterfield Walton S42 7LA ☎ 01246 279256
Fax 01246 276622
A varied and interesting, undulating parkland course with
trees picturesquely adding to the holes and the outlook alike.
Stream hazard on back nine. Views over four counties.
18 holes, 6326yds, Par 71, SSS 70, Course record 65.
Club membership 600.

Visitors	must contact in advance and must play with member at weekends and bank holidays. A handicap certificate is generally required.
Societies	apply in writing.
Green Fees	£35 per day; £26 per round.
Prof	Mike McLean
Facilities	⊗ 🍽 ﹢ 💺 ♀ ⚲ 🏠 ⚘
Location	2m SW off A632
Hotel	★★ 69% Abbeydale Hotel, Cross St, CHESTERFIELD ☎ 01246 277849 11 🛏 🐾

Grassmoor Golf Centre North Wingfield Rd, Grassmoor
S42 5EA ☎ 01246 856044 Fax 01246 853486
e-mail: grassmoorgolf@btconnect.com
An 18-hole heathland course with interesting and challenging
water features. 26-bay floodlit driving range, practice
bunkers and putting area.
18 holes, 5723yds, Par 69, SSS 69, Course record 67.
Club membership 420.

Visitors	contact Manager in advance. Smart dress code.
Societies	telephone Manager in advance.
Green Fees	£15 per round; £10 per day (£12 per round weekends).
Cards	〰️ 💳 📇
Prof	Gary Hagues
Designer	Hawtree
Facilities	⊗ 🍽 ﹢ 💺 ♀ ⚲ 🏠 ⛵ 🚜 ⚘ ♺
Location	Between Chesterfield & Grassmoor, off B6038
Hotel	★★ 69% Abbeydale Hotel, Cross St, CHESTERFIELD ☎ 01246 277849 11 🛏 🐾

Stanedge Walton Hay Farm, Stonedge, Ashover S45 0LW
☎ 01246 566156
Moorland course in hilly situation open to strong winds.
Some tricky short holes with narrow fairways, so accuracy is
paramount. Magnificent views over four counties. Extended
course now open.
9 holes, 5786yds, Par 69, SSS 68, Course record 68.
Club membership 310.

Visitors	with member only Sat & Sun, and may not play after 2pm weekdays.
Societies	apply in writing.
Green Fees	£15 per 18 holes.
Facilities	⊗ by prior arrangement 🍽 by prior arrangement ﹢ 💺 ♀ ⚲
Location	5m SW off B5057 nr Red Lion public house
Hotel	★★ 69% Abbeydale Hotel, Cross St, CHESTERFIELD ☎ 01246 277849 11 🛏 🐾

Tapton Park Municipal Tapton Park, Tapton S41 0EQ
☎ 01246 239500 & 273887 Fax 01246 558024
Municipal parkland course with some fairly hard walking.
The 620 yd (par 5) 5th is a testing hole.
Tapton Main: 18 holes, 6013yds, Par 71, SSS 69.
Dobbin Clough: 9 holes, 2613yds, Par 34, SSS 34.
Club membership 750.
Visitors   must contact in advance. No caddies allowed.
Societies   apply in writing.
Green Fees Tapton; £6.50 per round (£8 weekends).
Prof   Andrew Carnall
Facilities   ⊗ ⅷ ⅃ ⅃ ⅃ ⅃ ⅃ ⅃ ⅃ ⅃
Location   0.5m E of Chesterfield Station

Hotel   ★★ 69% Abbeydale Hotel, Cross St,
CHESTERFIELD ☎ 01246 277849   11 ⇄ ⋔

CODNOR   Map 08 SK44

Ormonde Fields Golf & Country Club Nottingham Rd
DE5 9RG ☎ 01773 570043 (Secretary) & 742987 (Pro)
Fax 01773 742987
Parkland course with undulating fairways and natural
hazards. There is a practice area.
18 holes, 6502yds, Par 71, SSS 72, Course record 68.
Club membership 500.
Visitors   must contact in advance.
Societies   telephone in advance.
Green Fees £20 per day; £17.50 per round (£20 per round
weekends after 3pm).
Cards   ▭
Prof   Peter Buttifant
Designer   John Fearn
Facilities   ⊗ ⅷ ⅃ ⅃ ⅃ ⅃ ⅃ ⅃ ⅃
Location   1m SE on A610

Hotel   ★★★ 73% Makeney Hall Country House
Hotel, Makeney, Milford, BELPER
☎ 01332 842999   27 ⇄ ⋔ Annexe18 ⇄ ⋔

DERBY   Map 08 SK33

Allestree Park Allestree Hall, Duffield Rd, Allestree
DE22 2EU ☎ 01332 550616 Fax 01332 541195
Public course, picturesque and undulating set in 300 acre
park with views across Derbyshire.
18 holes, 5806yds, Par 68, SSS 68.
Visitors   start times may be booked in advance by
telephone, visitors welcome any day.
Societies   apply in writing or by telephone in advance.
Green Fees not confirmed.
Prof   John Siddons
Facilities   ⅃ ⅃ ⅃ ⅃
& Leisure fishing.
Location   N of Derby, from A38 take A6 towards north,
course in 1.5m on left

Hotel   ★★★★ 64% Marriott Breadsall Priory Hotel&
Country Club, Moor Rd, MORLEY
☎ 01332 832235   12 ⇄ ⋔ Annexe100 ⇄ ⋔

Mickleover Uttoxeter Rd, Mickleover DE3 5AD
☎ 01332 518662 Fax 01332 512092
Undulating parkland course of 2 loops of 9 holes, in a
pleasant setting and affording splendid country views. There
is a premium in hitting tee shots in the right place for
approaches to greens, some of which are on elevated
plateaux. Some attractive par 3s which are considered to be
very exacting.
18 holes, 5702yds, Par 68, SSS 68, Course record 64.
Club membership 800.
Visitors   must contact Professional in advance.
Societies   apply in writing/telephone.
Green Fees £22 per day/round (£25 weekends & bank
holidays).
Cards   ▭
Prof   Tim Coxon
Designer   J Pennink
Facilities   ⊗ ⅷ ⅃ ⅃ ⅃ ⅃ ⅃ ⅃ ⅃
Location   3m W of Derby on A516/B5020

Hotel   ★★★★ 75% Menzies Mickleover Court,
Etwall Rd, Mickleover, DERBY
☎ 0870 6003013   99 ⇄ ⋔

Sinfin Wilmore Rd, Sinfin DE24 9HD
☎ 01332 766462 Fax 01332 769004
Municipal parkland course with tree lined fairways an
excellent test of golf. Generally a flat course it is suitable for
golfers of all ages.
18 holes, 6163yds, Par 70, SSS 69.
Visitors   starting time must be booked in advance by
telephone, visitors welcome any day.
Societies   apply in writing or by telephone in advance.
Green Fees £11.20 per 18 holes.
Cards   ▭ ▭ ▭ ▭ ▭
Prof   Steven Lamb
Facilities   ⅃ ⅃ ⅃ ⅃
Location   3.5m S of city centre

Hotel   ★★★ 63% International Hotel, 288 Burton Rd,
DERBY ☎ 01332 369321
41 ⇄ ⋔ Annexe21 ⇄ ⋔

DRONFIELD   Map 08 SK37

Hallowes Hallowes Ln S18 1UR
☎ 01246 411196 Fax 01246 411196
Attractive moorland/parkland course set in the Derbyshire
hills. Several testing par 4's and splendid views.
18 holes, 6342yds, Par 71, SSS 71, Course record 64.
Club membership 630.
Visitors   may only play with member at weekends. Must
contact in advance.
Societies   contact in advance, various packages.
Green Fees £35 per day; £30 per round.
Prof   Philip Dunn
Facilities   ⊗ ⅷ ⅃ ⅃ ⅃ ⅃ ⅃ ⅃
& Leisure snooker.
Location   S side of town

Hotel   ★★ 67% Chantry Hotel, Church St,
DRONFIELD ☎ 01246 413014 7 ⇄ ⋔

AA Hotels that have special
arrangements with golf courses are listed at
the back of the guide

Where to stay, where to eat?
Visit the AA internet site
www.theAA.com

DUFFIELD
Map 08 SK34

Chevin Golf Ln DE56 4EE
☎ 01332 841864 Fax 01332 841864
A mixture of parkland and moorland, this course is rather hilly which makes for some hard walking, but with most rewarding views of the surrounding countryside. The 8th hole, aptly named "Tribulation", requires an accurate tee shot, and is one of the most difficult holes in the country.
18 holes, 6057yds, Par 69, SSS 69, Course record 64.
Club membership 750.

Visitors	not before 9.30am or off first tee between 12.30 and 2pm. Proof of handicap required.
Societies	contact in advance.
Green Fees	£27 per day; £14 per round.
Prof	Willie Bird
Designer	J Braid
Facilities	⊗ ⊞ 🏌 🏆 ⚑ 🏌 ☕ ✆ ⚐
Location	N side of town off A6

Hotel ★★★ 73% Makeney Hall Country House Hotel, Makeney, Milford, BELPER ☎ 01332 842999 27 ⇄ 🏠 Annexe18 ⇄ 🏠

GLOSSOP
Map 07 SK09

Glossop and District Hurst Ln, off Sheffield Rd SK13 7PU
☎ 01457 865247(club house) & 853117(pro shop)
Moorland course in good position, excellent natural hazards. Difficult closing hole (9th & 18th).
11 holes, 5800yds, Par 68, SSS 68, Course record 64.
Club membership 350.

Visitors	no restrictions.
Societies	must apply in writing to professional.
Green Fees	£20 per day (£25 weekends).
Prof	Daniel Marsh
Facilities	⊗ ⊞ 🏌 🏆 ⚑ 🏌 ☕ ⚐
Location	1m E off A57

Hotel ★★ 71% York House Hotel, York Place, Richmond St, ASHTON-UNDER-LYNE ☎ 0161 330 9000 24 ⇄ 🏠 Annexe10 ⇄ 🏠

HORSLEY
Map 08 SK34

Horsley Lodge Smalley Mill Rd DE21 5BL
☎ 01332 780838 Fax 01332 781118
e-mail: @horsleylodge.co.uk.
This lush meadowland course set in 100 acres of Derbyshire countryside, has some challenging holes. Also Par 3 course and floodlit driving range. USGA world class greens designed by former World Champion Peter McEvoy.
18 holes, 6400yds, Par 72, SSS 71, Course record 72.
Club membership 650.

Visitors	must contact professional in advance and have handicap. May not play weekends before noon.
Societies	must telephone in advance.
Green Fees	not confirmed.
Cards	🔲 🔲 🔲 🔲 🔲 🔲
Prof	G Lyall
Designer	Bill White
Facilities	⚑ ☕ 🏌 ⇄ 🏌 ✆ ⚐
& Leisure	fishing, sauna, solarium.
Location	4m NE of Derby, off A38 at Belper then follow tourist signs

Hotel ★★★★ 64% Marriott Breadsall Priory Hotel& Country Club, Moor Rd, MORLEY ☎ 01332 832235 12 ⇄ 🏠 Annexe100 ⇄ 🏠

KEDLESTON
Map 08 SK34

Kedleston Park DE22 5JD
☎ 01332 840035 Fax 01332 840035
The course is laid out in flat mature parkland with fine trees and background views of historic Kedleston Hall (National Trust). Many testing holes are included in each nine and there is an excellent modern clubhouse.
18 holes, 6675yds, Par 72, SSS 72, Course record 66.
Club membership 847.

Visitors	must contact in advance.
Societies	weekdays only, apply in writing.
Green Fees	£35 per round £45 per day (£25 per round winter).
Prof	David J Russell
Designer	James Braid
Facilities	⊗ ⊞ 🏌 🏆 ⚑ 🏌 ☕ 🏌 🛒 ✆ ⚐
& Leisure	sauna.
Location	Signposted Kedleston Hall from A38

Hotel ★★★ 63% International Hotel, 288 Burton Rd, DERBY ☎ 01332 369321 41 ⇄ 🏠 Annexe21 ⇄ 🏠

MATLOCK
Map 08 SK36

Matlock Chesterfield Rd, Matlock Moor DE4 5LZ
☎ 01629 582191
Moorland course with fine views of the beautiful Peak District.
18 holes, 5996yds, Par 70, SSS 69, Course record 63.
Club membership 700.

Visitors	with member only weekends & bank holidays. Members only weekdays 12.30-1.30pm.
Societies	prior arrangement with Secretary.
Green Fees	£30 per day; £25 per round.
Prof	M A Whithorn
Designer	Tom Williamson
Facilities	⊗ ⊞ 🏌 🏆 ⚑ 🏌 ☕ ⚐
Location	1.5m NE of Matlock on A632

Hotel ★★★ 71% New Bath Hotel, New Bath Rd, MATLOCK BATH ☎ 0870 400 8119 55 ⇄ 🏠

MICKLEOVER
Map 08 SK33

Pastures Social Centre, Hospital Ln DE3 5DQ
☎ 01332 521074
Challenging course laid-out on undulating meadowland with good views across the Trent valley. Numerous testing Par 3s.
9 holes, 5095yds, Par 64, SSS 65, Course record 67.
Club membership 320.

Visitors	must be accompanied by a member, may not play on Sun & between noon-4pm Sat. Handicap certificate required.
Societies	Mon & Tue, must contact in advance.
Green Fees	not confirmed.
Designer	J F Pennik
Facilities	🏌 🏆 ⚑ evenings ⇄ 🏠
Location	1m SW off A516

▶

Hotel	★★★ 63% International Hotel, 288 Burton Rd, DERBY ☎ 01332 369321 41 ⇌ ↑ Annexe21 ⇌ ↑

MORLEY
Map 08 SK34

Morley Hayes Main Rd DE7 6DG
☎ 01332 780480 Fax 01332 781094
e-mail: golf@morleyhayes.com
Peaceful pay and play course set in a splendid valley and incorporating charming water features and woodland. Floodlit driving range. Challenging 9 hole short course (Tower Course).
Manor Course: 18 holes, 6726yds, Par 72, SSS 72.
Tower Course: 9 holes, 1614yds, Par 30.

Visitors	welcome.
Societies	booking essential telephone for details.
Green Fees	Manor course: £30 per day; 16.50 per 18 holes per day (£37.50/£22.50 weekends & bank holidays). Tower course £8 per 9 holes(£10 weekends & bank holidays).
Cards	▨ ▨ ▨ ▨ ▨ ▨ ▨
Prof	Mark Whithorn
Facilities	⊗ ⅷ ㄴ ♥ ♀ ♨ 🏠 ↑ ⚑ ✄ ⟨
Location	A608

Hotel	★★★★ 64% Marriott Breadsall Priory Hotel& Country Club, Moor Rd, MORLEY ☎ 01332 832235 12 ⇌ ↑ Annexe100 ⇌ ↑

NEW MILLS
Map 07 SK08

New Mills Shaw Marsh SK22 4QE ☎ 01663 743485
Moorland course with panoramic views and first-class greens.
9 holes, 5633yds, Par 68, SSS 67.
Club membership 389.

Visitors	contact secretary/professional in advance, cannot play during competitions.
Societies	must contact secretary or professional in advance.
Green Fees	£15 per 18 holes (£20 weekends) (£20 weekends).
Prof	Carl Cross
Designer	Williams
Facilities	⊗ ⅷ ㄴ ♥ ♀ ♨ 🏠 ↑ ⚑ ✄ ⟨
Location	0.5m N off B6101

Inn	♦♦♦♦ Matteo's Bar & Country Hotel, Rock Tavern, Glossop Rd, Marple Bridge, MARPLE ☎ 01457 852418 5 ⇌ ↑

RENISHAW
Map 08 SK47

Renishaw Park Club House, Mill Ln S21 3UZ
☎ 01246 432044 & 435484 Fax 01246 432116
Part parkland and part meadowland with easy walking.
18 holes, 6262yds, Par 71, SSS 70, Course record 65.
Club membership 750.

Visitors	Visitors not allowed on competition days.Contact professional on 01246 435484 for other days.
Societies	Telephone Secretarys office to arrange.
Green Fees	£34 per day; £24.50 per round (£38.50 per day/round weekends).
Prof	John Oates

Designer	Sir George Sitwell
Facilities	⊗ ⅷ ㄴ ♥ ♀ ♨ 🏠 ⟨
Location	1.5m W of junct 30 M1

Hotel	★★★ 64% Sitwell Arms Hotel, Station Rd, RENISHAW ☎ 01246 435226 30 ⇌ ↑

RISLEY
Map 08 SK43

Maywood Rushy Ln DE72 3ST ☎ 0115 939 2306
18 holes, 6424yds, Par 72, SSS 72, Course record 70.

Location	Near junct 25 on M1
Telephone for further details	

Hotel	★★★ 72% Risley Hall Hotel, Derby Rd, RISLEY ☎ 0115 939 9000 16 ⇌ ↑

SHIRLAND
Map 08 SK45

Shirland Lower Delves DE55 6AU ☎ 01773 834935
Rolling parkland and tree-lined course with extensive views of Derbyshire countryside.
18 holes, 6072yds, Par 71, SSS 70, Course record 67.
Club membership 450.

Visitors	contact professional in advance.
Societies	contact Professional.
Green Fees	£17 per round;£25 per day(£25 weekends).
Prof	Neville Hallam
Facilities	⊗ ⅷ ㄴ ♥ ♀ ♨ 🏠 ↑ ⚑ ✄ ⟨
Location	S side of village off A61

Hotel	★★★★ 68% Swallow Hotel, Carter Ln East, SOUTH NORMANTON ☎ 01773 812000 158 ⇌ ↑

STANTON-BY-DALE
Map 08 SK43

Erewash Valley DE7 4QR
☎ 0115 932 3258 Fax 0115 932 2984
Parkland/meadowland course overlooking valley and M1. Unique 4th and 5th in Victorian quarry bottom: 5th - testing par 3.
18 holes, 6557yds, Par 72, SSS 71, Course record 67.
Club membership 750.

Visitors	no restrictions except when club events in progress.
Societies	contact in advance.
Green Fees	not confirmed.
Prof	M J Ronan
Designer	Hawtree
Facilities	⊗ ㄴ ♥ ♀ ♨ 🏠 ↑ ⚑ ✄ ⟨
Location	1m W, 2m from junct 25 on M1

Hotel	★★★ 72% Risley Hall Hotel, Derby Rd, RISLEY ☎ 0115 939 9000 16 ⇌ ↑

UNSTONE
Map 08 SK37

Birch Hall Sheffield Rd S18 4DB
☎ 01246 291979 Fax 01246 412912
18 holes, 6379yds, Par 73, SSS 71, Course record 72.

Location	Turn off A61 between Sheffield and Chesterfield, outskirts of Unstone village
Telephone for further details	

Hotel	★★ 67% Chantry Hotel, Church St, DRONFIELD ☎ 01246 413014 7 ⇌ ↑

DEVON

AXMOUTH
Map 03 SY29

Axe Cliff Squires Ln EX12 4AB ☎ 01297 21754 & 24371
Undulating links course with coastal views.
18 holes, 6000yds, Par 70, SSS 70, Course record 64.
Club membership 400.

Visitors	must contact in advance.
Societies	must contact in advance.
Green Fees	£20 per day (£24 weekends & bank holidays).
Prof	Mark Dack
Facilities	⊗ ⊪ 🏌 ♟ ♐ ☆ 🏠 ☕ ⌕
Location	0.75m S on B3172

Hotel ★★ 77% Swallows Eaves, COLYFORD
☎ 01297 553184 8 ⇆ ♞

BIGBURY-ON-SEA
Map 03 SX64

Bigbury TQ7 4BB
☎ 01548 810557 (Secretary) 810412 (Pro Shop)
Fax 01548 810207
Clifftop, heathland course with easy walking. Exposed to winds, but with fine views over the sea and River Avon. 7th hole particularly tricky.
18 holes, 6048yds, Par 70, SSS 69, Course record 65.
Club membership 850.

Visitors	must have handicap certificate. Must contact in advance.
Societies	must apply in writing.
Green Fees	£27 per day (£30 weekends).
Prof	Simon Lloyd
Designer	J H Taylor
Facilities	⊗ ⊪ 🏌 ♟ ♐ ☆ 🏠 ☕ ⌕
Location	1m S on B3392 between Bigbury and Bigbury-on-Sea

Hotel ★★★★ 72% Thurlestone Hotel,
THURLESTONE ☎ 01548 560382 64 ⇆ ♞

BLACKAWTON
Map 03 SX85

Dartmouth Golf & Country Club TQ9 7DE
☎ 01803 712686 & 712650 Fax 01803 712628
e-mail: info@dgcc.co.uk
The 9-hole Club course and the 18-hole Championship course are both worth a visit and not just for the beautiful views. The Championship is one of the most challenging courses in the West Country with 12 water hazards on the course and a daunting par 5 4th hole that visitors will always remember. The spectacular final hole looking downhill and over a water hazard to the green, can be difficult to judge and has been described as one of the most picturesque finishing holes in the country.
Championship Course: 18 holes, 6663yds, Par 72, SSS 72, Course record 68.
Dartmouth Course: 9 holes, 4791yds, Par 66, SSS 64.
Club membership 700.

Visitors	must contact in advance, visitors welcome subject to availability. Normal dress standards apply on both courses.Tee times must be pre booked for both courses.
Societies	telephone in advance.

Green Fees	Championship Course: £27 per round (£35 weekends & bank holidays). Dartmouth Course: £15 per 18 holes; £13 per 18 holes (£14/£16 weekends & bank holidays).
Cards	💳 💳 💳 💳 💳 💳 💳
Prof	Steve Dougan
Designer	Jeremy Pern
Facilities	⊗ ⊪ 🏌 ♟ ♐ ☆ 🏠 ☕ ⌕
& Leisure	heated indoor swimming pool, sauna, solarium, gymnasium.
Location	On A3122 Totnes/Dartmouth road

Hotel ★★★ 68% Stoke Lodge Hotel, Stoke Fleming,
DARTMOUTH ☎ 01803 770523 25 ⇆ ♞

BUDLEIGH SALTERTON
Map 03 SY08

East Devon North View Rd EX9 6DQ
☎ 01395 443370 Fax 01395 445547
An interesting course with downland turf, much heather and gorse, and superb views over the bay. The early holes climb to the cliff edge. The downhill 17th has a heather section in the fairway, leaving a good second to the green.
18 holes, 6239yds, Par 70, SSS 70, Course record 64.
Club membership 850.

Visitors	advisable to contact in advance, no visitors before 9am. Visitors must be member of a recognised club and must produce proof of handicap.
Societies	Thu only, must contact in advance.
Green Fees	£36 per day; £28 per round (£42/£36 weekends & bank holidays).
Cards	💳 💳 💳 💳 💳
Prof	Trevor Underwood
Facilities	⊗ ⊪ 🏌 ♟ ♐ ☆ 🏠 ☕ ⌕
Location	W side of town centre

Hotel ★★ 68% Barn Hotel, Foxholes Hill,
Marine Dr, EXMOUTH
☎ 01395 224411 11 ⇆ ♞

CHITTLEHAMHOLT
Map 03 SS62

Highbullen Hotel EX37 9HD ☎ 01769 540561
Fax 01769 540492 e-mail: info@highbutton.co.uk
Mature parkland course with water hazards and outstanding scenic views to Exmoor and Dartmoor. Excellent facilities offered by the hotel.
18 holes, 5755yds, Par 68, SSS 67.
Club membership 100.

Visitors	to book tee time telephone 01769 540530 daytime, 01769 540561 evenings.
Societies	must contact in advance.
Green Fees	not confirmed.
Prof	Paul Weston
Designer	M Neil/ J Hamilton
Facilities	♐ 🏠 ☕ 🏌 ⌕
& Leisure	hard tennis courts, outdoor and indoor heated swimming pools, squash, fishing, sauna, solarium, gymnasium.
Location	0.5m S of village

Hotel ★★★♨ 69% Highbullen Hotel,
CHITTLEHAMHOLT ☎ 01769 540561
12 ⇆ Annexe25 ⇆ ♞

CHRISTOW
Map 03 SX88

Teign Valley EX6 7PA
☎ 01647 253026 Fax 01647 253026
18 holes, 5913yds, Par 70, SSS 68.

Location Take Teignvalley exit off A38, Exeter/Plymouth Expressway and follow GC signs up valley on B3193
Telephone for further details

Hotel ★★★★ 67% Manor House Hotel, MORETONHAMPSTEAD
☎ 01647 440355 90 ⇄ ʀ

CHULMLEIGH
Map 03 SS61

Chulmleigh Leigh Rd EX18 7BL
☎ 01769 580519 Fax 01769 580519
e-mail: howard@chulmleighgolf.freeserve.co.uk
Situated in a scenic area with views to distant Dartmoor, this undulating meadowland course offers a good test for the most experienced golfer and is enjoyable for newcomers to the game. Short 18 hole summer course with a tricky 1st hole; in winter the course is changed to 9 holes and made longer for players to extend their game.
Summer Short Course: 18 holes, 1450yds, Par 54, SSS 54, Course record 49.
Winter Course: 9 holes, 2310yds, Par 54, SSS 54, Course record 57.
Club membership 85.
Visitors welcome anytime.
Societies telephone in advance.
Green Fees £10 per day; £8.50 per 36 holes; £6.50 per 18 holes.
Prof John Phillips
Designer John Goodban
Facilities ⓑ ▼ ♀ ⌂ 🏠 ⛷ ⊟ ♂
Location SW side of village just off A377

Hotel ★★★ 80% Northcote Manor, BURRINGTON
☎ 01769 560501 11 ⇄ ʀ

CHURSTON FERRERS
Map 03 SX95

Churston Dartmouth Rd TQ5 0LA
☎ 01803 842751 & 842218 Fax 01803 845738
A cliff-top downland course with splendid views over Brixham harbour and Tor Bay. There is some gorse with a wooded area inland. A variety of shot is called for, with particularly testing holes at the 3rd, 9th and 15th, all

par 4. Conference facilities and a well equipped shop are also available.
18 holes, 6219yds, Par 70, SSS 70, Course record 64.
Club membership 700.
Visitors must telephone in advance and be a member of recognised golf club with a handicap certificate.
Societies apply in writing or telephone.
Green Fees not confirmed.
Cards 💳
Prof Neil Holman
Facilities ⊗ ⦀ ⓑ ▼ ♀ ⌂ 🏠 ⛷ ♂
Location NW side of village on A379

Hotel ★★ 65% Dainton Hotel, 95 Dartmouth Rd, Three Beaches, Goodrington, PAIGNTON
☎ 01803 550067 & 525901
Fax 01803 666339 11 ⇄ ʀ

CREDITON
Map 03 SS80

Downes Crediton Hookway EX17 3PT
☎ 01363 773025 & 774464 Fax 01363 775060
Parkland course with water features. Flat front nine. Hilly and wooded back nine.
18 holes, 5951yds, Par 70, SSS 69.
Club membership 700.
Visitors handicap certificate required, must contact in advance, restricted at weekends.
Societies must contact in advance.
Green Fees £22 (£25 weekends).
Prof Howard Finch
Facilities ⊗ ⦀ ⓑ ▼ ♀ ⌂ 🏠 ⛷ ♂
Location 1.5m SE off A377

Hotel ★★★ 73% Barton Cross Hotel & Restaurant, Huxham, Stoke Canon, EXETER
☎ 01392 841245 9 ⇄ ʀ

CULLOMPTON
Map 03 ST00

Padbrook Park EX15 1RU
☎ 01884 38286 Fax 01884 34359
A 9-hole, 18 tee parkland course with many water and woodland hazards and spectacular views. The dog-leg 2nd and pulpit 7th are of particular challenge to golfers of all standards.
9 holes, 6108yds, Par 70, SSS 70, Course record 67.
Club membership 250.
Visitors welcome at all times but preferable to book in advance.
Societies apply in writing or telephone.
Green Fees £12 per 18 holes, £9 per 9 holes (£16/£11 weekends& bank holidays).
Cards 💳 💳 💳
Prof Stewart Adwick
Designer Bob Sandow
Facilities ⊗ ⓑ ▼ ♀ ⌂ 🏠 ⛷ 🎣 ♂ ♂
& Leisure fishing, gymnasium, indoor bowling centre, health suite.
Location Southern edge of Cullompton on B3181

Hotel ★★★ 67% The Tiverton Hotel, Blundells Rd, TIVERTON ☎ 01884 256120 74 ⇄ ʀ

DAWLISH WARREN Map 03 SX97

Warren EX7 0NF
☎ 01626 862255 & 864002 Fax 01626 888005
Typical flat, genuine links course lying on spit between sea
and Exe estuary. Picturesque scenery, a few trees but much
gorse. Testing in windy conditions. The 7th hole provides the
opportunity to go for the green across a bay on the estuary.
18 holes, 5965yds, Par 69, SSS 69, Course record 65.
Club membership 600.

Visitors	must contact in advance & have handicap certificate.
Societies	prior arrangement essential.
Green Fees	£21.50 per day (£24.50 weekends & bank holidays).
Prof	Darren Prowse
Facilities	⊗ ⋔ ⓛ ♥ ♀ ⚘ 🏠 ✐
Location	E side of village

Hotel ★★★ 68% Langstone Cliff Hotel, Dawlish
Warren, DAWLISH ☎ 01626 868000
64 ⇌ ↟ Annexe4 ⇌ ↟

DOWN ST MARY Map 03 SS70

Waterbridge EX17 5LG ☎ 01363 85111
A testing course of 9-holes set in a gently sloping valley. The
Par of 32 will not be easily gained with 1 par 5, 3 par 4's and
5 par 3's, although the course record holder has Par 29! The
3rd hole which is a raised green is surrounded by water and
the 4th (439 yards) is demanding for beginners.
9 holes, 3910yds, Par 64, SSS 64.

Visitors	no restrictions.
Societies	no restrictions.
Green Fees	£10 per 18 holes; £6 per 9 holes (£12/£7 weekends & bank holidays).
Prof	David Ridyard
Designer	D Taylor
Facilities	♥ ⌕ ✐
Location	From Exeter on A377 towards Barnstaple

Hotel ★★★ 80% Northcote Manor, BURRINGTON
☎ 01769 560501 11 ⇌ ↟

EXETER Map 03 SX99

Exeter Golf & Country Club Topsham Rd, Countess Wear
EX2 7AE ☎ 01392 874139 Fax 01392 874914
e-mail: info@exetergcc.fsnet.co.uk
A sheltered parkland course with some very old trees and
known as the flattest course in Devon. 15th & 17th are
testing par 4 holes. Small, well guarded greens.
18 holes, 6008yds, Par 69, SSS 69, Course record 62.
Club membership 800.

Visitors	welcome but may not play during match or competitions, very busy pre booking needed up to 1 week in advance. Must have handicap certificate. Ring starter in advance on 01392 876303
Societies	welcome Thu only, booking available by telephone to manager tel 01392 874139.
Green Fees	£28 per round(£33 weekends).
Cards	⊟ ▬ ▧ ▣
Prof	Mike Rowett
Designer	J Braid

Facilities ⊗ ⋔ ⓛ ♥ ♀ ⚘ 🏠 ✐
& Leisure hard tennis courts, heated indoor plus outdoor
swimming pool, squash, sauna, solarium,
gymnasium.
Location SE side of city centre off A379

Hotel ★★★ 67% The Buckerell Lodge Hotel,
Topsham Rd, EXETER ☎ 01392 221111
53 ⇌ ↟

Woodbury Park Woodbury Castle, Woodbury EX5 1JJ
☎ 01395 233500 Fax 01395 233384
e-mail: woodburypark@eclipse.co.uk
Two courses set in the lovely wooded parkland of Woodbury
Castle.
Oaks: 18 holes, 6870yds, Par 72, SSS 72, Course record 66.
Acorn: 9 holes, 2297yds, Par 32, SSS 32.
Club membership 750.

Visitors	welcome, please reserve tee times in advance.
Societies	contact in advance.
Green Fees	not confirmed.
Cards	⊟ ▬ ▬ ▣ ▧ ▨
Prof	Alan Richards
Designer	J Hamilton-Stutt

Facilities ⊗ ⋔ ⓛ ♥ ♀ ⚘ 🏠 ↟ 🏌 ✈ ⚓ ✐ ⚑
& Leisure hard tennis courts, heated indoor swimming
pool, squash, fishing, sauna, gymnasium.
Hotel ★★ 65% Ebford House Hotel, Exmouth Rd,
EBFORD ☎ 01392 877658 16 ⇌ ↟

HIGH BICKINGTON Map 02 SS52

Libbaton EX37 9BS
☎ 01769 560269 & 560167 Fax 01769 560342
Parkland course on undulating land with no steep slopes.
Floodlit driving range.
18 holes, 6494yds, Par 73, SSS 72, Course record 72.
Club membership 500.

Visitors	book in advance. No jeans, trainers or collarless shirts.
Societies	telephone to book in advance.
Green Fees	£18 (£21 weekends).
Cards	⊟ ▬
Designer	H Col Badham
Facilities	⊗ ⋔ ⓛ ♥ ♀ ⚘ 🏠 ↟ 🏌 ✈ ⚓ ✐ ⚑
Location	B3217,1m of High Bickington, off A377

Hotel ★★★♨ 69% Highbullen Hotel,
CHITTLEHAMHOLT ☎ 01769 540561
12 ⇌ Annexe25 ⇌ ↟

HOLSWORTHY Map 02 SS30

Holsworthy Killatree EX22 6LP
☎ 01409 253177 Fax 01409 253177
e-mail: gngolfsales@aol.com
Pleasant parkland course with gentle slopes and numerous
trees.
18 holes, 6100yds, Par 70, SSS 69, Course record 64.
Club membership 600.

Societies	by arrangement with secretary or professional.
Green Fees	£20 per round/day.
Cards	⊟ ▬ ▬ ▧ ▣
Prof	Graham Webb
Facilities	⊗ ⋔ ⓛ ♥ ♀ ⚘ 🏠 ↟ ✈ ✐
Location	1.5m W on A3072

▶

Hotel   ★★★ 71% Falcon Hotel, Breakwater Rd,
BUDE ☎ 01288 352005 27 ⇌ 🐾

HONITON   Map 03 ST10

Honiton Middlehills EX14 9TR
☎ 01404 44422 & 42943 Fax 01404 46383
Level parkland course on a plateau 850ft above sea level.
Easy walking and good views. The 4th hole is a testing par 3.
The club was founded in 1896.
18 holes, 5902yds, Par 69, SSS 68.
Club membership 800.
Visitors   must contact in advance.
Societies   society bookings on Thursdays.
Green Fees £23 per day (£28 weekends & bank holidays).
Prof   Adrian Cave
Facilities ⊗ ⽊ ⽧ ⬛ ⽤ ⚘ 🏠 🍴 ♂
Location   1.25m SE of Honiton,turn towards Farway at
                Tower Cross on A35

Hotel   ★★ 69% Home Farm Hotel & Restaurant,
            Wilmington, HONITON ☎ 01404 831278
            8 ⇌ Annexe5 ⇌ 🐾

ILFRACOMBE   Map 02 SS54

Ilfracombe Hele Bay EX34 9RT
☎ 01271 862176 & 863328 Fax 01271 867731
e-mail: ilfracombe.golfclub@virgin.net
A sporting, clifftop, heathland course with views over the
Bristol Channel and moors from every tee and green.
18 holes, 5893yds, Par 69, SSS 69, Course record 66.
Club membership 520.

Ilfracombe Golf Club

Visitors   recommended to make tee reservation prior to
                visit, member only before 10am on weekends.
Societies   telephone in advance.
Green Fees £20 per day (£24 weekends).
Prof   Mark Davies
Designer   T K Weir
Facilities ⊗ ⽧ ⬛ ⽤ ⚘ 🏠 🍴 ♂
Location   1.5m E off A399

Hotel   ★★ 71% Elmfield Hotel, Torrs Park,
            ILFRACOMBE ☎ 01271 863377
            11 ⇌ 🐾 Annexe2 ⇌ 🐾

IPPLEPEN   Map 03 SX86

Dainton Park Totnes Rd, Ipplepen TQ12 5TN
☎ 01803 815000 Fax 01803 815009
e-mail: dpgolf@globalnet.co.uk
A challenging parkland type course in typical Devon
countryside, with gentle contours, tree-lined fairways   ▶

and raised tees. Water hazards make the two opening holes particularly testing. The 8th, a dramatic 180yard drop hole totally surrounded by sand, is one of four tough Par 3's on the course. It is advisable to book start times.
18 holes, 6207yds, Par 71, SSS 70, Course record 70.
Club membership 650.

Visitors	prior booking by phone advisable to guarantee start time.
Societies	must contact in advance.
Green Fees	£18 per round (£20 weekends).
Cards	🖾 🖾 🄡
Prof	Martin Tyson
Designer	Adrian Stiff
Facilities	⊗ ⅏ ⅃ ⌁ ⚏ ♀ ♨ 🖾 ☂ ➴ ✎ ⌣
& Leisure	solarium, gymnasium.
Location	2m S of Newton Abbot on A381

IVYBRIDGE   Map 02 SX65

Dinnaton Sporting & Country Club Blachford Rd PL21 9HU ☎ 01752 690020 892512 Fax 01752 698334
9 holes, 4089yds, Par 64, SSS 60.

Location	Leave A38 at Ivybridge junct and continue towards town centre. At first rdbt follow signs for club

Telephone for further details

Hotel	★★ 74% Glazebrook House Hotel & Restaurant, SOUTH BRENT ☎ 01364 73322 11 ⇆ 🛏

MORETONHAMPSTEAD   Map 03 SX78

Manor House Hotel TQ13 8RE ☎ 01647 440998 Fax 01647 440961 e-mail: manortee@aol.com
This enjoyable parkland course has enough hazards to make any golfer think. Most hazards are natural such as the Rivers Bowden and Bovey which meander through the first eight holes.
18 holes, 6016yds, Par 69, SSS 69, Course record 63.
Club membership 120.

Visitors	must contact in advance and pre-arrange starting times.
Societies	must telephone for reservation in advance.
Green Fees	£30 per day; £25 per round (£37/£32 weekends).
Cards	🖾 🖾 🖾 🖾 🄡
Prof	Richard Lewis
Designer	J Abercrombie
Facilities	⊗ ⅏ ⅃ ⌁ ⚏ ♀ ♨ 🖾 ☂ ⇤ ➴ ⚒ ⌣
& Leisure	hard tennis courts, fishing.
Location	3m W of Moretonhampstead, off B3212

Hotel	★★★★ 67% Manor House Hotel, MORETONHAMPSTEAD ☎ 01647 440355 90 ⇆ 🛏

MORTEHOE   Map 02 SS44

Mortehoe & Woolacombe EX34 7EH
☎ 01271 870225 & 870745 (Sec)
Attached to a camping and caravan site, this 9-hole course has 2 par 3s and 7 par 4s. The gently sloping clifftop course has spectacular views across Morte Bay.
9 holes, 4690yds, Par 66, SSS 63, Course record 66.
Club membership 245.

Visitors	no restrictions.
Societies	must telephone or write in advance.
Green Fees	not confirmed.
Designer	D Hoare
Facilities	⊗ ⅏ ⅃ ⌁ ⚏ ♀ ♨ 🖾 ☂ ⌣
& Leisure	heated indoor swimming pool, indoor bowls, skittles, table tennis, pool table.
Location	0.25m before Mortehoe on station road

Hotel	★★★ 75% Watersmeet Hotel, Mortehoe, WOOLACOMBE ☎ 01271 870333 22 ⇆ 🛏

NEWTON ABBOT   Map 03 SX87

Newton Abbot (Stover) Bovey Rd TQ12 6QQ
☎ 01626 352460 (Secretary) Fax 01626 330210
Wooded parkland course with a stream coming into play on eight holes. Fairly flat.
18 holes, 5764yds, Par 69, SSS 68, Course record 63.
Club membership 800.

Visitors	must have proof of membership of recognised club or current handicap certificate. Advised to contact in advance.
Societies	by arrangement on Thu only.
Green Fees	£30 per day; £25 per round (£32/£28 weekends).
Cards	🖾 🖾
Prof	Malcolm Craig
Designer	James Braid
Facilities	⊗ ⅏ ⅃ ⌁ ⚏ ♀ ♨ 🖾 ☂ ⌣
Location	3m N on A382

Hotel	★★ 66% Queens Hotel, Queen St, NEWTON ABBOT ☎ 01626 363133 20 ⇆ 🛏

OKEHAMPTON   Map 02 SX59

Ashbury Higher Maddaford EX20 4NL
☎ 01837 55453 Fax 01837 55468
A parkland style courses with natural undulations and hazards. Set in 235 acres of Devon countryside with 137 bunkers and 18 lakes, the courses comprise a loop of 27 holes, the 18 hole Oakwood course and an 18 hole par 3 course. Each hole has a purpose built alternative green so that greens can be changed in adverse weather.
Ashbury Beeches, Pines Willows: 27 holes, 8100yds.
Ashbury Oakwood: 18 holes, 5343yds, Par 68, SSS 66.
Ashbury Acorns: 18 holes, 2018yds, Par 54.
Club membership 170.

Visitors	must contact in advance.
Green Fees	£15 per day/round (£20 weekends & bank holidays).
Cards	🖾 🖾 🖾 🖾 🄡
Prof	Reg Cade
Designer	David Fensom
Facilities	⊗ ⅃ ⌁ ⚏ ♀ ♨ 🖾 ☂ ⇤ ⚒ ✎ ⌣
& Leisure	hard tennis courts, heated indoor swimming pool, fishing, sauna, solarium, Indoor bowls, Snooker.
Location	Off A3079 Okehampton-Holsworthy

Hotel	★★ 65% Ashbury Hotel, Higher Maddaford, Southcott, OKEHAMPTON ☎ 01837 55453 26 ⇆ 🛏 Annexe29 ⇆ 🛏

Looking for a driving range?
See the index at the back of the guide

Okehampton Tors Rd EX20 1EF
☎ 01837 52113 Fax 01837 52734
A good combination of moorland, woodland and river make
this one of the prettiest, yet testing courses in Devon.
18 holes, 5243yds, Par 68, SSS 67, Course record 66.
Club membership 600.
Visitors	advance booking recommended, limited times available at weekends. Saturdays by prior arrangement only
Societies	by prior arrangement.
Green Fees	not confirmed.
Prof	Simon Jefferies
Designer	J F Taylor
Facilities	⊗ ⅢL⅃ 墨 ⅀ ⅄ 🏛 ⅍ ♂
Location	1m S off A30

Hotel	★★ 67% Oxenham Arms, SOUTH ZEAL ☎ 01837 840244 & 840577 Fax 01837 840791 8rm(7 ⇌ ⋔)

PLYMOUTH   Map 02 SX45

Elfordleigh Colebrook, Plympton PL7 5EB
☎ 01752 336428 (hotel) & 348425 (golf shop)
Fax 01752 344581
Charming, saucer-shaped parkland course with alternate tees
for 18 holes. Tree-lined fairways and three lakes. Fairly hard
walking.
9 holes, 5664yds, Par 68, SSS 67, Course record 66.
Club membership 600.
Visitors	must contact in advance and hold a handicap certificate.
Societies	by arrangement.
Green Fees	not confirmed.
Cards	〰 ▬ ⬛ 📶 🔲
Prof	Ross Troake
Designer	J H Taylor
Facilities	⊗ ⅢL⅃ 墨 ⅀ ⅄ 🏛 ⅍ ⊟ ♂ ℓ
& Leisure	hard tennis courts, heated outdoor swimming pool, squash, gymnasium, golf tuition breaks.
Location	2m NE off A374

Staddon Heights Plymstock PL9 9SP
☎ 01752 402475 Fax 01752 401998
Seaside course affording spectacular views across Plymouth
Sound, Dartmoor and Bodmin Moor. Testing holes include
the par 3 17th with its green cut into a hillside and the par 4
14th across a road. Easy walking.
18 holes, 5869yds, Par 68, SSS 68, Course record 66.
Club membership 750.
Visitors	must have handicap certificate and contact the pro or secretary in advance.
Societies	apply by telephone in advance.
Green Fees	£18 per day(£22 weekends).
Prof	Ian Marshall
Designer	Hamilton Stutt
Facilities	⊗ ⅢL⅃ 墨 ⅀ ⅄ 🏛 ⅍ ⊟ ♂
Location	5m SW of city centre

Hotel	★★★ 66% Posthouse Plymouth, Cliff Rd, The Hoe, PLYMOUTH ☎ 0870 400 9064 113 ⇌ ⋔

Where to stay, where to eat?
Visit the AA internet site
www.theAA.com

SAUNTON   Map 02 SS43

Saunton EX33 1LG
☎ 01271 812436 Fax 01271 814241
e-mail: admin@sauntongolf.co.uk
Two traditional championship links courses. Windy,
with natural hazards.
*East Course: 18 holes, 6373yds, Par 71, SSS 71, Course
record 65.*
*West Course: 18 holes, 6138yds, Par 71, SSS 70, Course
record 67.*
Club membership 1350.

Visitors	prior booking recommended and must have handicap certificate.
Societies	must apply in advance, handicap certificates required.
Green Fees	£45 per 18 holes;£65 per 36 holes,both prices inclusive of a complimentary meal ticket.
Cards	〰 ▬ ⬛ 🔲
Prof	A T MacKenzie
Designer	F Pennick
Facilities	⊗ ⅢL⅃ 墨 ⅀ ⅄ 🏛 ⅍ ♂ ℓ
Location	S side of village off B3231

Hotel	★★★★ 70% Saunton Sands Hotel, SAUNTON ☎ 01271 890212 92 ⇌ ⋔
Additional hotel	★★ 69% Kittiwell House Hotel & Restaurant, St Mary's Rd, CROYDE ☎ 01271 890247 Fax 01271 890469 12 ⇌ ⋔

SIDMOUTH   Map 03 SY18

Sidmouth Cotmaton Rd, Peak Hill EX10 8SX
☎ 01395 513451 & 516407 Fax 01395 514661
Situated on the side of Peak Hill, offering beautiful coastal
views. Club founded in 1889.
18 holes, 5100yds, Par 66, SSS 65, Course record 59.
Club membership 700.
Visitors	by prior arrangement.
Societies	by prior arrangement with the secretary.
Green Fees	£20 per round;£24 per day.
Prof	Gaele Tapper
Designer	J H Taylor
Facilities	⅄ 🏛 ⅍ ♂
Location	W side of town centre

Hotel	★★★★ 72% Victoria Hotel, The Esplanade, SIDMOUTH ☎ 01395 512651 61 ⇌ ⋔

SOUTH BRENT
Map 03 SX66

Wrangaton (S Devon) Golf Links Rd, Wrangaton
TQ10 9HJ ☎ 01364 73229 Fax 01364 73229
Unique 18 hole course with 9 holes on moorland and 9 holes
on parkland. The course lies within Dartmoor National Park.
Spectacular views towards sea and rugged terrain. Natural
fairways and hazards include bracken, sheep and ponies.
18 holes, 6083yds, Par 70, SSS 69, Course record 66.
Club membership 660.

Visitors	contact in advance.
Societies	write or telephone.
Green Fees	£18per 18 holes.
Cards	💳 💳
Prof	Adrian Whitehead
Designer	D M A Steel
Facilities	⊗ ℿ ⅂ ⅃ ♀ ⚐ 🏌 ⏺ ⚑ ⚘
Location	2.25 m SW off A38

Hotel ★★ 74% Glazebrook House Hotel &
Restaurant, SOUTH BRENT
☎ 01364 73322 11 ⇥ ⎈

SPARKWELL
Map 02 SX55

Welbeck Manor & Sparkwell Golf Course Blacklands
PL7 5DF ☎ 01752 837219 Fax 01752 837219
A mature parkland course with several challenging holes, it
features fairway and greenside bunkers, mature trees and
streams. The house on the site, now the hotel, was built by
Isambard Kingdom Brunel. Several holes commemorate his
famous works - the 6th being The Great Western. This very
challenging Par 5 tee is out of bounds all the way up the left.
9 holes, 2886yds, Par 68, SSS 68, Course record 68.
Club membership 200.

Visitors	no restrictions
Societies	telephone in advance.
Green Fees	not confirmed.
Designer	John Gabb
Facilities	⅃ ⚐ 🏌 ⚘
Location	1m N of A38 Plymouth/Ivybridge road

Hotel ★★★ 64% Boringdon Hall, Colebrook,
Plympton, PLYMOUTH ☎ 01752 344455
41 ⇥ ⎈

TAVISTOCK
Map 02 SX47

Hurdwick Tavistock Hamlets PL19 8PZ ☎ 01822 612746
An executive parkland course with many bunkers and fine
views. Executive golf originated in America and the concept
is that a round should take no longer than 3 hours whilst
offering solid challenge.
18 holes, 5200yds, Par 68, SSS 67.
Club membership 180.

Visitors	no restrictions.
Societies	must contact in advance.
Green Fees	not confirmed.
Designer	Hawtree
Facilities	⊗ ⅂ ⅃ ♀ ⚐ 🏌 ⚑ ⚘
Location	1m N of Tavistock

Hotel ★★★ 68% Bedford Hotel, 1 Plymouth Rd,
TAVISTOCK ☎ 01822 613221 30 ⇥ ⎈

Tavistock Down Rd PL19 9AQ
☎ 01822 612344 Fax 01822 612344
e-mail: tavygolf@freeserve.net
Set on Whitchurch Down in south-west Dartmoor with
easy walking and magnificent views over rolling
countryside into Cornwall. Downland turf with some
heather, and interesting holes on undulating ground.
18 holes, 6250yds, Par 70, SSS 70, Course record 64.
Club membership 700.

Visitors	advisable to contact in advance.
Societies	by arrangement with secretary.
Green Fees	not confirmed.
Prof	D Rehaag
Designer	H Fowler
Facilities	⊗ ℿ ⅂ ⅃ ♀ ⚐ 🏌 ⚘
Location	1m SE of town centre, on Whitchurch Down

Hotel ★★★ 68% Bedford Hotel, 1 Plymouth Rd,
TAVISTOCK ☎ 01822 613221 30 ⇥ ⎈

TEDBURN ST MARY
Map 03 SX89

Fingle Glen EX6 6AF ☎ 01647 61817
Fax 01647 61135
9-hole course containing six par 4's and three par 3's set in
52 acres of rolling countryside. Testing 4th, 5th and 9th
holes. 12-bay floodlit driving range.
9 holes, 4818yds, Par 66, SSS 63, Course record 63.
Club membership 500.

Visitors	must contact in advance.
Societies	write or telephone in advance.
Green Fees	£10 per 9 holes;£15 per 18 holes.
Cards	💳 💳 💳 💳
Prof	Stephen Gould
Designer	Bill Pile
Facilities	⊗ ℿ ⅂ ⅃ ♀ ⚐ 🏌 ⚑ ⚘ ⎈
Location	5m W of Exeter, off A30

Hotel ★★★ 68% Lord Haldon Hotel, Dunchideock,
EXETER ☎ 01392 832483 19 ⇥ ⎈

TEIGNMOUTH
Map 03 SX97

Teignmouth Haldon Moor TQ14 9NY
☎ 01626 777070 Fax 01626 777070
e-mail: teignmouth.g.c@btclick.com
This fairly flat heathland course is high up with a fine
panoramic views of sea, moors and river valley. Good
springy turf with some heather and an interesting layout
makes for very enjoyable holiday golf. Designed by Dr
Alister MacKenzie, the world famous architect who also
designed Augusta GC USA.
18 holes, 6200yds, Par 71, SSS 70, Course record 65.
Club membership 900.

Visitors	handicap certificate required, groups must contact in advance, restricted tee off times at weekends.
Societies	Tue & Thu only, telephone in advance and confirm in writing.
Green Fees	£25 per round; £30 per 36 holes (£27.50 per round weekends).
Prof	Peter Ward
Designer	Dr Alister Mackenzie
Facilities	⊗ ℿ ⅂ ⅃ ♀ ⚐ 🏌 ⚘
Location	2m NW off B3192

▶

Hotel	★★ 70% Ness House Hotel, Marine Dr, Shaldon, TEIGNMOUTH ☎ 01626 873480 7 ⇄ ℟ Annexe5 ⇄ ℟

THURLESTONE — Map 03 SX64

Thurlestone TQ7 3NZ
☎ 01548 560405 Fax 01548 562149
Situated on the edge of the cliffs with typical downland turf and good greens. The course, after an interesting opening hole, rises to higher land with fine seaviews, and finishes with an excellent 502-yard downhill hole to the clubhouse.
18 holes, 6340yds, Par 71, SSS 70, Course record 65.
Club membership 770.

Visitors	must contact in advance & have handicap certificate from a recognised club.
Green Fees	£28 per round.
Cards	🖃 🖃 🖃 🖃
Prof	Peter Laugher
Designer	Harry S Colt
Facilities	⊗ 🏌 by prior arrangement 🏌 🍺 🍸 🏌 🏌 🏌
& Leisure	hard and grass tennis courts.
Location	S side of village

Hotel	★★★★ 72% Thurlestone Hotel, THURLESTONE ☎ 01548 560382 64 ⇄ ℟

TIVERTON — Map 03 SS91

Tiverton Post Hill EX16 4NE ☎ 01884 252187
A parkland course where the many different species of tree are a feature and where the lush pastures ensure some of the finest fairways in the south-west. There are a number of interesting holes which visitors will find a real challenge.
18 holes, 6236yds, Par 71, SSS 71, Course record 65.
Club membership 725.

Visitors	must have a current handicap certificate.
Societies	apply in writing or telephone.
Green Fees	not confirmed.
Prof	David Sheppard
Designer	Braid
Facilities	⊗ 🏌 by prior arrangement 🏌 🍺 🍸 🏌 🏌 🏌
Hotel	★★★ 74% Midland Hotel, Midland Rd, DERBY ☎ 01332 345894 100 ⇄ ℟

TORQUAY — Map 03 SX96

Torquay 30 Petitor Rd, St Marychurch TQ1 4QF
☎ 01803 314591 Fax 01803 316116
e-mail: torquaygolfclub@skynow.net
Unusual combination of cliff and parkland golf, with wonderful views over the sea and Dartmoor.
18 holes, 6175yds, Par 69, SSS 70, Course record 63.
Club membership 700.

Visitors	must contact in advance.
Societies	must apply in writing.
Green Fees	£25(£30 weekends).
Prof	Martin Ruth
Facilities	⊗ 🏌 🏌 🍺 🍸 🏌 🏌 🏌 🏌 🏌
Location	1.25m N

Hotel	★★ 62% Norcliffe Hotel, 7 Babbacombe Downs Rd, Babbacombe, TORQUAY ☎ 01803 328456 27 ⇄ ℟

TORRINGTON (GREAT) — Map 02 SS41

Torrington Weare Trees, Great Torrington EX38 7EZ
☎ 01805 622229 & 623878 Fax 01805 623878
Attractive and challenging 9 hole course. Free draining to allow play all year round. Excellent greens and outstanding views.
Torrington Golf Club: 9 holes, 4423yds, Par 64, SSS 62, Course record 58.
Club membership 420.

Visitors	must contact in advance. May not play Tues, Wed, Sat, Sun or bank holidays before noon.
Societies	by arrangement.
Green Fees	£12 per day.
Facilities	⊗ 🏌 🏌 🍺 🍸 🏌 🏌 🏌
Location	1m W of Torringdon

Hotel	★★★ 67% Royal Hotel, Barnstaple St, BIDEFORD ☎ 01237 472005 31 ⇄ ℟

UPOTTERY — Map 03 ST20

Otter Valley Golf Centre
☎ 01404 861266, Fax 01404 861266 (5m NW of Honiton off A30, on Upottery Rd)
This Golf School set in beautiful Devon countryside was established in 1989. There are practice facilities with driving range, approach green, chipping green with bunkers and 8 practice holes. Weekend and 5 day courses are available and there is self catering accommodation, telephone for details. All coaching is given personally by Andrew Thompson P.G.A.

WESTWARD HO! — Map 02 SS42

Royal North Devon Golf Links Rd EX39 1HD
☎ 01237 473817 Fax 01237 423456
e-mail: info@royalnorthdevongolfclub.co.uk
Oldest links course in England with traditional links features and a museum in the clubhouse.
18 holes, 6716yds, Par 72, SSS 72, Course record 68.
Club membership 1150.

Visitors	advisable to telephone and book tee time, handicap certificate preferred or letter of introduction from club.
Societies	apply in writing or telephone.
Green Fees	£36 per day; £30 per round (£40/£36 weekends & bank holidays).
Cards	🖃 🖃 🖃
Prof	Richard Herring
Designer	Old Tom Morris
Facilities	⊗ 🏌 🍺 🍸 🏌 🏌 🏌
& Leisure	museum of Golf Memorabilia, snooker.
Location	N side of village off B3236

Guest house	◆◆◆◆ Culloden House Hotel, Fosketh Hill, WESTWARD HO! ☎ 01237 479421 9rm(2 ⇄5 ♠)

WOOLSERY   Map 02 SS32

Hartland Forest Woolsery EX39 5RA
☎ 01237 431442 Fax 01237 431734
Exceptionally varied course with many water hazards.
18 holes, 6015yds, Par 71, SSS 69.
Club membership 240.
Visitors   no restrictions.
Societies   telephone in advance or apply in writing.
Green Fees   not confirmed.
Cards   ▨▨▨▨▨
Designer   A Cartwright
Facilities   ⊗ by prior arrangement ⅲ ⓛ ☷ ☷ 占 ☂ ☙
& Leisure   ⚓ ☙
                 hard tennis courts, heated indoor swimming
                 pool, fishing, sauna, solarium.
Location   1.7m E of A39

Hotel   ★★★ 73% Penhaven Country House, Rectory
                 Ln, PARKHAM ☎ 01237 451388 & 451711
                 Fax 01237 45187812 ⇄ ♠

YELVERTON   Map 02 SX56

Yelverton Golf Links Rd PL20 6BN
☎ 01822 852824 Fax 01822 855309
e-mail: secretary@yelvertongc.freeserve.co.uk

An excellent course on Dartmoor with plenty of gorse
and heather. Tight lies in the fairways, fast greens and
challenging hazards. Boasts 3 of the best holes in Devon
(12th, 13th & 16th). Outstanding views.
18 holes, 6363yds, Par 71, SSS 72, Course record 67.
Club membership 650.

Visitors   must have handicap certificate and subject
                 to availability, contact in advance.
Societies   must be booked in advance, by telephone
                 initially.
Green Fees   £30 per day (£40 saturdays).
Prof   Tim McSherry
Designer   Herbert Fowler

Facilities   ⊗ ⅲ ⓛ ☷ ☷ ♀ 占 ☎ ☂ ☙
Location   1m S of Yelverton, off A386

Hotel   ★★★ 71% Moorland Links Hotel,
                 YELVERTON ☎ 01822 852245 45 ⇄ ♠

DORSET

BEAMINSTER   Map 03 ST40

Chedington Court South Perrott DT8 3HU
☎ 01935 891413 Fax 01935 891217
This beautiful 18 hole parkland course is set on the Dorset-
Somerset borders with mature trees and interesting water
hazards.
18 holes, 5924yds, Par 70, SSS 70, Course record 71.
Club membership 400.
Visitors   must book tee time in advance at weekends.
Societies   apply in writing or telephone.
Green Fees   not confirmed.
Designer   David Hemstock
Facilities   ⊗ ⅲ ⓛ ☷ ☷ ♀ 占 ☎ ☂ ☙
Location   5m NE of Beaminster on A356 Dorchester-
                 Crewkerne

Hotel   ★★★ 71% Bridge House Hotel, 3 Prout
                 Bridge, BEAMINSTER
                 ☎ 01308 862200 9 ⇄ ♠ Annexe5 ⇄ ♠

BELCHALWELL   Map 03 ST70

Dorset Heights DT11 0EG
☎ 01258 861386 Fax 01258 860900
18 holes, 6138yds, Par 70, SSS 70, Course record 74.
Telephone for further details

Hotel   ★★★ 67% Crown Hotel, West St,
                 BLANDFORD FORUM
                 ☎ 01258 456626 32 ⇄ ♠

BERE REGIS   Map 03 SY89

East Dorset BH20 7NT
☎ 01929 472244 Fax 01929 471294
e-mail: edgc@golf.co.uk
Lakeland is a long 18-hole parkland course with natural
water features. The Woodland is a second 9-hole, 18-tee
course set amongst trees and rhododendrons. Floodlit 22-
bay driving range, golf shop.
Lakeland Course: 18 holes, 6580yds, Par 72, SSS 73,
Course record 69.
Woodland Course: 9 holes, 5032yards, Par 66, SSS 64.
Club membership 550.
Visitors   must book in advance and handicap
                 certificate required for Lakeland course.
Societies   apply in advance.
Green Fees   Lakeland: £35 per day; £30 per round
                 (£40/£35 weekends). Woodland: £23 per
                 day; £21 per round (£25/£23 weekends). ▶

Prof	Derwynne Honan
Designer	Martin Hawtree
Facilities	⊗ 〗 ᴸ ᴸ ♥ ♀ ♨ ᴸ ✆ ↱ ♨ ♣ ♣ ✆ ↿
Location	5m from Bere Regis on Wool Road
Hotel	★★ 70% Kemps Country House Hotel,
	East Stoke, WAREHAM
	☎ 01929 462563
	5rm(4 ⇄ ↾) Annexe10 ⇄ ↾

BLANDFORD FORUM   Map 03 ST80

Ashley Wood Wimborne Rd DT11 9HN
☎ 01258 452253 Fax 01258 450590
Undulating and well drained downland course with superb
views over the Tarrant and Stour Valleys.
18 holes, 6276yds, Par 70, SSS 70, Course record 65.
Club membership 700.

Visitors	phone in advance. Handicap certificate required
	weekends unless with member.
Societies	apply to Secretary.
Green Fees	not confrmed.
Prof	Spencer Taylor
Designer	P Tallack
Facilities	⊗ 〗 ᴸ ᴸ ♥ ♀ ♨ ♣ ♣ ♣ ✆
Location	2m E on B3082
Hotel	★★★ 67% Crown Hotel, West St,
	BLANDFORD FORUM ☎ 01258 456626
	32 ⇄ ↾

BOURNEMOUTH   Map 04 SZ09

The Club at Meyrick Park Central Dr, Meyrick Park
BH2 6LH ☎ 01202 786000 Fax 01202 786020
Picturesque muncipal parkland course founded in 1890.
The Club At Meyrick Park: 18 holes, 5600yds, Par 69, SSS
69.

Visitors	book 7 days in advance.
Societies	telephone in advance.
Green Fees	not confirmed.
Cards	💳 💳 💳 🌐 🖩
Prof	David Miles
Facilities	⊗ 〗 ᴸ ᴸ ♥ ♀ ♨ ✆ ↱ ♨ ✆
& Leisure	heated indoor swimming pool, sauna,
	gymnasium, spa and steam room.
Hotel	★★★ 64% Burley Court Hotel, Bath Rd,
	BOURNEMOUTH
	☎ 01202 552824 & 556704
	Fax 01202 298514 38 ⇄ ↾

Knighton Heath Francis Av, West Howe BH11 8NX
☎ 01202 572633 Fax 01202 590774
e-mail: khgc@btclick.com
Undulating heathland course on high ground inland from
Poole.
18 holes, 6084yds, Par 70, SSS 69.
Club membership 700.

Visitors	may not play weekend. Phone for availability.
Societies	must book in advance.
Green Fees	£25 per round £30 per day.
Facilities	⊗ ᴸ ♥ ♀ ♨ ✆ ✆
Location	N side of Poole, junct of A348/A3409
	signposted at rdbt
Hotel	★★ 75% Beechleas Hotel & Restaurant,
	17 Poole Rd, WIMBORNE MINSTER
	☎ 01202 841684 5 ⇄ ↾ Annexe4 ⇄ ↾

Queen's Park Queens Park Dr West BH8 9BY
☎ 01202 302611 Fax 01202 302611
e-mail: dgibb@qpbgc.fsnet.co.uk
Undulating parkland course of pine and heather, with narrow,
tree-lined fairways. Public course played over by 'Boscombe
Golf Club' and 'Bournemouth Artisans Golf Club'.
18 holes, 6305yds, Par 72, SSS 70, Course record 69.
Club membership 370.

Visitors	Not open for play Sun pm.
Societies	Must book in advance.
Green Fees	not confirmed.
Cards	💳 💳 💳 🌐 🖩
Prof	Richard Hill
Facilities	⊗ 〗 ᴸ ᴸ ♥ ♀ ♨ ✆ ✆
Location	2m NE of Bournemouth town centre off A338
Hotel	★★★ 70% Queens Hotel, Meyrick Rd,
	East Cliff, BOURNEMOUTH
	☎ 01202 554415 109 ⇄ ↾

BRIDPORT   Map 03 SY49

Bridport & West Dorset East Cliff, West Bay DT6 4EP
☎ 01308 421491 & 421095 Fax 01308 421095
Seaside links course on the top of the east cliff, with fine
views over Lyme Bay and surrounding countryside. A
popular feature is the pretty and deceptive 14th hole, its
sunken green lying 90 feet below the tee and guarded by
natural hazards and bunkers.
18 holes, 6488yds, Par 73, SSS 71.
Club membership 600.

Visitors	must contact in advance.
Societies	must contact in writing in advance.
Green Fees	£22 per day; £16 after noon, £10 after 5pm.
Prof	David Parsons
Designer	Hawtree
Facilities	⊗ ᴸ ♥ ♀ ♨ ✆ ✆
& Leisure	pitch & putt (holiday season).
Location	2m S of Bridport
Hotel	★★★ 62% Haddon House Hotel, West Bay,
	BRIDPORT ☎ 01308 423626 & 425323
	Fax 01308 427348 12 ⇄ ↾

> AA Hotels that have special
> arrangements with golf courses are listed at
> the back of the guide

BROADSTONE   Map 04 SZ09

Broadstone (Dorset) Wentworth Dr BH18 8DQ
☎ 01202 692595 Fax 01202 692595
Undulating and demanding heathland course with the
2nd, 7th, 13th and 16th being particularly challenging
holes.
18 holes, 6315yds, Par 70, SSS 70, Course record 66.
Club membership 700.

Visitors	restricted at weekends & bank holidays. Must contact in advance. Handicap certificate required.
Societies	contact in advance.
Green Fees	£45 per day; £32per round (£45 per round weekends).
Prof	Nigel Tokely
Designer	Colt/Dunn
Facilities	⊗ ⅷ ᒻ ᒻ 🖤 ♀ ♙ 🏠 🍴 🏌 ♂
Location	N side of village off B3074

Hotel   ★★ 75% Beechleas Hotel & Restaurant,
17 Poole Rd, WIMBORNE MINSTER
☎ 01202 841684 5 ⇆ ↱ Annexe4 ⇆ ↱

CHRISTCHURCH   Map 04 SZ19

Dudmoor Farm Dudmoor Farm Rd, Off Fairmile Rd
BH23 6AQ ☎ 01202 473826 Fax 01202 480207
A testing par 3 & 4 woodland course in an area of
outstanding natural beauty.
9 holes, 1428mtrs, Par 31.

Visitors	no restrictions.
Societies	telephone in advance.
Green Fees	not confirmed.
Facilities	🖤 ♙ 🍴 🛒 ♂
& Leisure	squash, fishing.
Location	Located on a private road off B3073 Christchurch to Hurn road

Hotel   ★★★ 74% Waterford Lodge Hotel, 87 Bure
Ln, Friars Cliff, Mudeford, CHRISTCHURCH
☎ 01425 272948 & 278801
Fax 01425 279130   18 ⇆

Iford Bridge Barrack Rd BH23 2BA ☎ 01202 473817
9 holes, 2165yds, Par 34, SSS 32.
Location   W side of town centre on A35
Telephone for further details

Hotel   ★★★ 74% Waterford Lodge Hotel, 87 Bure
Ln, Friars Cliff, Mudeford, CHRISTCHURCH
☎ 01425 272948 & 278801
Fax 01425 279130   18 ⇆

DORCHESTER   Map 03 SY69

Came Down Came Down DT2 8NR
☎ 01305 813494 (manager) & 812670 (pro)
Fax 01305 813494
Scene of the West of England Championships on several
occasions, this fine course lies on a high plateau
commanding glorious views over Portland. Three par 5
holes add interest to a round. The turf is of the springy,
downland type.
18 holes, 6244yds, Par 70, SSS 71.
Club membership 750.

Visitors	advisable to phone in advance, must have handicap certificate. May play after 9am weekdays & after noon Sun.
Societies	by arrangement on Wed only.
Green Fees	not confirmed.
Prof	David Holmes
Designer	J H Taylor
Facilities	⊗ ⅷ ᒻ 🖤 ♀ ♙ 🏠 🍴 🛒 ♂
Location	2m S off A354

Guest   ◆◆◆◆ Yalbury Cottage Hotel &
house   Restaurant, Lower Bockhampton,
DORCHESTER ☎ 01305 262382 8 ⇆ ↱

FERNDOWN   Map 04 SU00

Dudsbury 64 Christchurch Rd BH22 8ST
☎ 01202 593499 Fax 01202 594555
e-mail: glegg@dudsbury.demon.co.uk
Set in 160 acres of beautiful Dorset countryside rolling down
to the River Stour. Wide variety of interesting and
challenging hazards, notably water which comes into play on
14 holes. The well-drained greens are protected by large
bunkers and water hazards. A feature hole is the 16th where
the green is over two lakes; the more aggressive the drive the
greater the reward.
Championship Course: 18 holes, 6904yds, Par 71, SSS 73.
Club membership 700.

Visitors	welcome by arrangement with secretary or golf professional.
Societies	telephone in advance.
Green Fees	£42 per 36 holes; £32 per 18 holes (£47/£37 weekend and bank holidays).
Cards	💳 💳
Prof	Mark Thomas
Designer	Donald Steel
Facilities	⊗ ⅷ ᒻ 🖤 ♀ ♙ 🏠 🍴 ♂ 🛒 ♂ ⎮
& Leisure	fishing, 6 Hole Par 3 Academy Course.
Location	3m N of Bournemouth on B3073, between Parley and Longham

Hotel   ★★★★ 70% The Dormy, New Rd,
FERNDOWN ☎ 01202 872121 115 ⇆ ↱

Ferndown 119 Golf Links Rd BH22 8BU
☎ 01202 874602 Fax 01202 873926
e-mail: ferndowngc@lineone.net
Fairways are gently undulating amongst heather, gorse
and pine trees giving the course a most attractive
appearance. There are a number of dog-leg holes, and, on
a clear day, there are views across to the Isle of Wight.
Championship Course: 18 holes, 6452yds, Par 71, SSS
71, Course record 65.
Presidents Course: 18 holes, 5604yds, Par 70, SSS 68.
Club membership 600.

Visitors	must contact in advance & have handicap certificate, no visitors on Thursdays except on Presidents course, numbers restricted at weekends.
Societies	welcome Tue & Fri only, telephone in advance.
Green Fees	Championship; £55 per day; £45 per round (£60/£50 weekends). President ; £20 (£25 weekends).
Prof	Iain Parker
Designer	Harold Hilton

Facilities	⊗ ⍦ 🏌 🍴 ☕ ♀ 🏊 🍽 🏌 🏌
Location	S side of town centre off A347
Hotel	★★★★ 70% The Dormy, New Rd,
	FERNDOWN ☎ 01202 872121 115 ⇆ 🐾

Ferndown Forest Forest Links Rd BH22 9QE
☎ 01202 876096 Fax 01202 894095
Flat parkland course dotted with mature oak trees, several interesting water features, and some tight fairways.
18 holes, 5068yds, Par 67, SSS 65, Course record 60.
Club membership 400.

Visitors	advisable to contact in advance.
Societies	apply in writing.
Green Fees	£15 per day; £11 weekdays (£18/£13 weekends) per day.
Cards	🟦🟦 🟦🟦 🟦🟦 🟦
Prof	Mike Dodd
Designer	Guy Hunt/Richard Graham
Facilities	⊗ ⍦ 🏌 🍴 ☕ ♀ 🏊 ☕ 🏌 🏌 🏌
Location	From London M3 then A31, end of dual carriageway Dolmans Crossing rdbt right exit Forest Links Rd
Hotel	★★★★ 70% The Dormy, New Rd,
	FERNDOWN ☎ 01202 872121 115 ⇆ 🐾

HALSTOCK Map 03 ST50

Halstock Common Ln BA22 9SF
☎ 01935 891689 Fax 01935 891839 e-mail: halstock.golf@feeuk.com
Halstock is a short tight course, but presents an interesting challenge to players of all abilities. The terrain is gently undulating in places and there are plenty of trees and water hazards.
18 holes, 4481yds, Par 66, SSS 63, Course record 63.
Club membership 200.

Visitors	must telephone in advance. Restricted until 10.30am on Sundays.
Societies	telephone in advance.
Green Fees	£16 per day; £11 per 18 holes (£18/£13 weekends).
Cards	🟦🟦 🟦🟦 🟦🟦 🟦
Facilities	☕ ♀ 🏊 ☕ 🏌 🏌 🏌
Location	6m S of Yeovil
Hotel	★★★🏖 Summer Lodge, EVERSHOT
	☎ 01935 83424 11 ⇆ 🐾 Annexe7 ⇆ 🐾

HIGHCLIFFE Map 04 SZ29

Highcliffe Castle 107 Lymington Rd BH23 4LA
☎ 01425 272210 Fax 01425 272210
Picturesque parkland course with easy walking.
18 holes, 4776yds, Par 64, SSS 63, Course record 58.
Club membership 500.

Visitors	must have handicap certificate and be a member of recognised club. Telephone in advance.
Societies	write or telephone in advance.
Green Fees	contact Secretary for charges.
Facilities	⊗ 🏌 🍴 ☕ ♀ 🏊
Location	SW side of town on A337
Hotel	★★★ 74% Waterford Lodge Hotel, 87 Bure Ln, Friars Cliff, Mudeford, CHRISTCHURCH ☎ 01425 272948 & 278801 Fax 01425 279130 18 ⇆

HURN Map 04 SZ19

Parley Parley Green Ln BH23 6BB
☎ 01202 591600 & 593131
Flat parkland course with few hazards and only one par 5. Friendly atmosphere.
9 holes, 4584yds, Par 66, SSS 64, Course record 69.
Club membership 238.

Visitors	good standard of dress expected.
Societies	write or telephone.
Green Fees	not confirmed.
Prof	Ken Gilhespy/Chris Brook
Designer	P Goodfellow
Facilities	⊗ ⍦ 🏌 🍴 ☕ ♀ 🏊 ☕ 🏌 🏌
Location	Opposite Bournemouth airport
Hotel	★★★★ 70% The Dormy, New Rd,
	FERNDOWN ☎ 01202 872121 115 ⇆ 🐾

LYME REGIS Map 03 SY39

Lyme Regis Timber Hill DT7 3HQ ☎ 01297 442963
Undulating cliff-top course with magnificent views of Golden Cap and Lyme Bay.
18 holes, 6283yds, Par 71, SSS 70, Course record 67.
Club membership 575.

Visitors	must contact in advance & have handicap certificate or be a member of recognised golf club. No play on Thu & Sun mornings.
Societies	Tue, Wed & Fri; must contact in writing.
Green Fees	not confirmed.
Prof	Andrew Black
Designer	Donald Steel
Facilities	🏊 ☕ 🏌
Location	1.5m on A3052
Hotel	★★★ 70% Alexandra Hotel, Pound St, LYME REGIS ☎ 01297 442010 26 ⇆ 🐾 Annexe1 ⇆ 🐾

POOLE Map 04 SZ09

Parkstone Links Rd, Parkstone BH14 9QS
☎ 01202 707138 Fax 01202 796027
Very scenic heathland course with views of Poole Bay.
Club founded in 1910.
18 holes, 6250yds, Par 72, SSS 70, Course record 63.
Club membership 700. ▶

Visitors	must contact in advance and have handicap certificate.
Societies	apply in writing/telephone in advance.
Green Fees	£50 per day; £35 per round (£60/£45 weekends & bank holidays).
Prof	Martyn Thompson
Designer	Willie Park Jnr

Facilities	⊗ ⅷ ⅃ ⅃ ♥ ♀ ⅄ 🛆 📣 🏌 ➘ ⌕ 〱
Location	E side of town centre off A35

Hotel	★★★ 80% Salterns Hotel, 38 Salterns Way, Lilliput, POOLE ☎ 01202 707321 20 ⊨ 〱

SHERBORNE   Map 03 ST61

Sherborne Higher Clatcombe DT9 4RN
☎ 01935 814431 Fax 01935 814218 e-mail: enquires@sherbornegolfclub.fsnet.co.uk
A sporting course of first-class fairways with far-reaching views over the lovely Blackmore Vale and the Vale of Sparkford. Parkland in character, the course has many well-placed bunkers. The dog-leg 2nd calls for an accurately placed tee shot, and another testing hole is the 7th, a 194-yard, par 3. There is a practice area.
18 holes, 5882yds, Par 70, SSS 68, Course record 63.
Club membership 600.

Visitors	must contact in advance & have handicap certificate.
Societies	prior booking only (Tue & Wed only).
Green Fees	£28 per day; £22 per round (£36/£30 weekends).
Prof	Stewart Wright

Designer	James Braid (part)
Facilities	⊗ ⅷ ⅃ ⅃ ♥ ♀ ⅄ 🛆 📣 ⌕
Location	2m N off B3145

Hotel	★★★ 69% Eastbury Hotel, Long St, SHERBORNE ☎ 01935 813131 15 ⊨ 〱

SLEPE   Map 03 SY99

Bulbury Woods Bulbury Ln BH16 6EP
☎ 01929 459574 Fax 01929 459000
Parkland course amidst ancient woodland, with a mixture of American and traditional style greens and extensive views over the Purbecks and Poole Harbour.
18 holes, 6350yds, Par 72, SSS 70.
Club membership 600.

Visitors	visitors may book 7 days in advance and subject to availability.
Societies	must contact in advance.
Green Fees	£20 (£24 weekends).
Cards	▭▭ ▭▭ ▭▭ ▭▭ ▯
Facilities	⊗ ⅷ ⅃ ⅃ ♥ ♀ ⅄ 🛆 📣 ➘ 🚜 ⌕
Location	A35 Poole to Dorchester, 3m from Poole centre

Hotel	★★★▲▲ Priory Hotel, Church Green, WAREHAM ☎ 01929 551666 15 ⊨ 〱 Annexe4 ⊨ 〱

STURMINSTER MARSHALL   Map 03 ST90

Sturminster Marshall Moor Ln BH21 4AH
☎ 01258 858444 Fax 01258 858262
Privately owned club with pay & play facilities set in beautiful Dorset countryside. Played off 18 different tees the course is ideal for golfers of all standards.
9 holes, 4882yds, Par 68, SSS 64.
Club membership 350.

Visitors	no restrictions.
Societies	must contact in advance.
Green Fees	not confirmed.
Cards	▭▭ ▭▭
Prof	Graham Howell
Designer	John Sharkey/David Holdsworth
Facilities	⊗ ⅷ ⅃ ⅃ ♥ ♀ ⅄ 🛆 📣 ➘ 🚜 ⌕
Location	On A350. Signposted from village

Hotel	★★★ 67% Crown Hotel, West St, BLANDFORD FORUM ☎ 01258 456626 32 ⊨ 〱

SWANAGE   Map 04 SZ07

Isle of Purbeck BH19 3AB
☎ 01929 450361 & 450354
Fax 01929 450501
A heathland course sited on the Purbeck Hills with grand views across Swanage, the Channel and Poole Harbour. Holes of note include the 5th, 8th, 14th, 15th, and 16th where trees, gorse and heather assert themselves. The very attractive clubhouse is built of the local stone.
Purbeck Course: 18 holes, 6295yds, Par 70, SSS 71, Course record 66.
Dene Course: 9 holes, 4014yds, Par 60.
Club membership 500.

Visitors	advisable to telephone.
Societies	must contact in advance.

▶

Green Fees not confirmed.
Cards
Prof   Ian Brake
Designer   H Colt
Facilities ⊗ ⫘ by prior arrangement �🌭 ☕ ⚲ ⛾ 🏠 ⛳ 🏌 🎣 ⛱ 🏌

Location   2.5m N on B3351

Hotel   ★★★ 66% The Pines Hotel, Burlington Rd, SWANAGE ☎ 01929 425211 49 ⇄ ⛾

VERWOOD   Map 04 SU00

Crane Valley The Club House BH31 7LE
☎ 01202 814088 Fax 01202 813407
Two secluded parkland courses set amid rolling Dorset countryside and mature woodland - a 9-hole Pay and Play and an 18-hole Valley course for golfers holding a handicap certificate.The 6th nestles in the bend of the River Crane and there are 4 long Par 5's ranging from 499 to 545 yards.
Valley: 18 holes, 6445yds, Par 72, SSS 71, Course record 66.
Woodland: 9 holes, 2060yds, Par 33, SSS 30.
Club membership 700.
Visitors   must have handicap certificate for Valley course. Woodland course is pay and play.
Societies telephone in advance.
Green Fees Valley: £25 per round;£35 per day(£32.50/£45 weekends) Woodland:£5.50 per 9 hole;£10.50 per 18 hole(£6.50/£12 weekends).
Cards
Designer   Donald Steel
Facilities ⊗ ⫘ 🌭 ☕ ⚲ ⛾ 🏠 🏌 🎣 ⛱ ⛳ ⛳
Location   6m W of Ringwood on B3081

Hotel   ★★★★ 70% The Dormy, New Rd, FERNDOWN ☎ 01202 872121 115 ⇄ ⛾

WAREHAM   Map 03 SY98

Wareham Sandford Rd BH20 4DH
☎ 01929 554147 Fax 01929 554147
e-mail: admin@warehamgolfclub.com
At the entrance to the Purbecks with splendid views over Poole Harbour and Wareham Forest. A mixture of undulating parkland and heathland fairways. A challenge for golfers of all abilities.
18 holes, 5753yds, Par 69, SSS 68, Course record 66.
Club membership 500.
Visitors   Handicap preferred.Course acailable after 09.30 weekdays and after 13.00 weekends
Societies weekdays only. Weekends after 1pm.
Green Fees £28 per day; £22 per round(£25 per round weekends).

Prof   Gary Prince
Facilities ⊗ ⫘ 🌭 ☕ ⚲ ⛾ 🏠 🏌 🎣 ⛳
Location   Adjacent to A351, nr Wareham railway station

Hotel   ★★★ 68% Springfield Country Hotel & Leisure Club, Grange Rd, WAREHAM ☎ 01929 552177 48 ⇄ ⛾

WEYMOUTH   Map 03 SY67

Weymouth Links Rd DT4 0PF
☎ 01305 773981 (Secretary) & 773997 (Prof)
Fax 01305 788029 e-mail: weymouth-gc@lineone.net
Seaside parkland course. The 5th is played off an elevated tee over copse.
18 holes, 5981yds, Par 70, SSS 69, Course record 63.
Club membership 750.
Visitors   advisable to contact in advance.
Societies apply in writing/telephone/e-mail/fax
Green Fees please enquire.
Prof   Des Lochrie
Designer   James Braid
Facilities ⊗ ⫘ 🌭 ☕ ⚲ ⛾ 🏠 🏌 ⛳
Location   N side of town centre off B3157

Hotel   ★★★ 61% Hotel Rex, 29 The Esplanade, WEYMOUTH ☎ 01305 760400 31 ⇄ ⛾

WIMBORNE   Map 03 SZ09

Canford Magna Knighton Ln BH21 2AS
☎ 01202 592552 Fax 01202 592550
Lying in 350 acres of Dorset countryside, the Canford Magna Golf Club provides 45 holes of challenging golf for the discerning player. The 18 hole Parkland and Riverside courses are quite different and, for the short game, the new 9 hole Knighton course demands the same level of playing skill. For those wishing to improve their handicap, the Golf Academy offers a covered driving range, pitching greens, a chipping green and bunkers, together with a 6 hole par 3 academy course.
Parkland: 18 holes, 6495yds, Par 71, SSS 71, Course record 66.
Riverside: 18 holes, 6214yds, Par 70, SSS 70, Course record 68.
Knighton: 9 holes, 1377yds, Par 27, Course record 26.
Club membership 1000.
Visitors   are advised to contact in advance.
Societies must telephone in advance.
Green Fees not confirmed.
Prof   Martyn Thompson
Designer   Howard Swan
Facilities ⊗ ⫘ 🌭 ☕ ⚲ ⛾ 🏠 🏌 ⛱ ⛳ ⛳
& Leisure Golf lessons.

Location   On A341

Hotel   ★★ 75% Beechleas Hotel & Restaurant, 17
Poole Rd, WIMBORNE MINSTER
☎ 01202 841684 5 ⇄ ſ Annexe4 ⇄ ſ

CO DURHAM

BARNARD CASTLE   Map 12 NZ01

Barnard Castle Harmire Rd DL12 8QN
☎ 01833 638355 & 631980 Fax 01833 638355 e-
mail: christine.sec@talk21.com
Perched high on the steep bank of the River Tees, the
extensive remains of Barnard Castle with its splendid
round tower dates back to the 12th and 13th centuries.
The parkland course is flat and lies in open coutryside.
18 holes, 6406yds, Par 73, SSS 71, Course record 66.
Club membership 650.
Visitors   must contact in advance, restricted at
weekends. Handicap certificate required.
Societies   apply in writing.
Green Fees   from £20 per 18 holes weekdays up to £32
for 27 holes at weekends.
Prof   Darren Pearce
Designer   A Watson
Facilities   ⊗ ⅢⅡ ᴸᴬ ■ ♀ ♨ 🏠 ♈ ♂
Location   1m N of town centre on B6278

Hotel   ★★ 79% Rose & Crown Hotel,
ROMALDKIRK ☎ 01833 650213
7 ⇄ ſ Annexe5 ⇄ ſ

BEAMISH   Map 12 NZ25

Beamish Park DH9 0RH
☎ 0191 370 1382 Fax 0191 370 2937
Parkland course. Designed by Henry Cotton and W
Woodend.
18 holes, 6204yds, Par 71, SSS 70, Course record 64.
Club membership 630.
Visitors   must contact in advance and may only play
weekdays.
Societies   telephone in advance.
Green Fees   not confirmed.
Prof   Chris Cole
Designer   H Cotton
Facilities   ⊗ ⅢⅡ ᴸᴬ ■ ♀ ♨ 🏠 ♂
Location   1m NW off A693

Hotel   ★★★ 69% Beamish Park Hotel, Beamish Burn
Rd, MARLEY HILL ☎ 01207 230666
47 ⇄ ſ

BILLINGHAM   Map 08 NZ42

Billingham Sandy Ln TS22 5NA
☎ 01642 533816 & 554494 Fax 01642 533816
e-mail: eddiedouglas@billgolfclub.fsnet.co.uk
Parkland course on edge of urban-rural district, with hard
walking and water hazards.
18 holes, 6404yds, Par 73, SSS 71, Course record 61.
Club membership 1050.

Visitors   contact professional in advance on 01642
557060 a handicap certificate may be requested.
Societies   apply in writing to Secretary/Manager.
Green Fees £25 per day (£40 weekends).
Prof   Michael Ure
Designer   F Pennick
Facilities   ⊗ ⅢⅡ ᴸᴬ ■ ♀ ♨ 🏠 ♈ ♂
Location   1m W of town centre E of A19

Hotel   ★★★ 71% Parkmore Hotel, 636 Yarm Rd,
Eaglescliffe, STOCKTON-ON-TEES
☎ 01642 786815 55 ⇄ ſ

BISHOP AUCKLAND   Map 08 NZ22

Bishop Auckland High Plains, Durham Rd DL14 8DL
☎ 01388 663648 & 661618 (pro) Fax 01388 607005
e-mail: enquiries@bagc.co.uk
A rather hilly parkland course with many well-
established trees offering a challenging round. A small
ravine adds interest to several holes including the short
7th, from a raised tee to a green surrounded by a stream,
gorse and bushes. Pleasant views down the Wear Valley
and over the residence of the Bishop of Durham.
18 holes, 6420yds, Par 72, SSS 71, Course record 64.
Club membership 950.
Visitors   parties must contact in advance. Handicap
certificate advisable. Dress rules apply.
Societies   weekdays only; must contact in advance.
Green Fees £26 per day; £22 per round.
Prof   David Skiffington
Designer   James Kay
Facilities   ⊗ ⅢⅡ ᴸᴬ ■ ♀ ♨ 🏠 ♂
& Leisure   snooker.
Location   1m NE on A689

Hotel   ★★★ 68% Swallow Eden Arms Hotel,
RUSHYFORD ☎ 01388 720541 45 ⇄ ſ

BURNOPFIELD   Map 12 NZ15

Hobson Municipal Hobson NE16 6BZ
☎ 01207 271605 Fax 01207 271069
e-mail: s_fox@derwentside.org.uk
Meadowland course with very easy walking.
18 holes, 6403yds, Par 69, SSS 68, Course record 65.
Club membership 700.
Visitors   must book in advance at weekends.
Societies   must contact in advance.
Green Fees £15 per round (£18 weekend).
Cards   💳 💳 💳 🔳 🔲
Prof   Jack Ord
Facilities   ⊗ ⅢⅡ ᴸᴬ ■ ♀ ♨ 🏠 ♈ ♂
Location   0.75m S on A692

Hotel   ★★★ 67% Swallow Hotel, High West St,
GATESHEAD ☎ 0191 477 1105 103 ⇄ ſ

CHESTER-LE-STREET   Map 12 NZ25

Chester-le-Street Lumley Park DH3 4NS
☎ 0191 388 3218 (Secretary) Fax 0191 388 1220
Parkland course in castle grounds, good views, easy walking.
18 holes, 6437yds, Par 71, SSS 71, Course record 71.
Club membership 650.

▶

Visitors	must contact in advance and have an introduction from own club or handicap certificate.
Societies	must apply in writing.
Green Fees	not confirmed.
Prof	David Fletcher
Designer	J H Taylor
Facilities	⊗ ⍟ 🕭 ▌ ♀ ♨ 🏠 ✈ ✧
Location	0.5m E off B1284

Hotel	★★★ 70% Ramside Hall Hotel, Carrville, DURHAM ☎ 0191 386 5282 80 ⇄ 🐾

Roseberry Grange Grange Villa DH2 3NF
☎ 0191 370 0670 Fax 0191 370 0660
Testing holes on this parkland course include the uphill par 3 12th (147yds) and the par 4 8th (438yds) with a ditch crossing the fairway.
18 holes, 5628yds, Par 70, SSS 69.
Club membership 550.

Visitors	after 11.30am Sun & 10.30am Sat in summer, pay and play Mon-Fri.
Societies	booking form available on request.
Green Fees	not confirmed.
Cards	🔲 ▨ ▨ ▨ ▨ ▨
Prof	Alan Hartley
Designer	Durham County Council
Facilities	⊗ ⍟ 🕭 ▌ ♀ ♨ 🏠 ✈ ✧ ✟
Hotel	★★★ 65% George Washington Golf & Country Club, Stone Cellar Rd, District 12, High Usworth, WASHINGTON ☎ 0191 402 9988 103 ⇄ 🐾

CONSETT   Map 12 NZ15

Consett & District Elmfield Rd DH8 5NN
☎ 01207 502186 Fax 01207 505060
e-mail: secretary@consettgolfclub.safe.co.uk
Undulating parkland/moorland course with views across the Derwent Valley to the Cheviot Hills.
18 holes, 6023yds, Par 71, SSS 69, Course record 63.
Club membership 900.

Visitors	advised to contact Professional in advance on 01207 580210.
Societies	apply in writing.
Green Fees	£18 per day (£26 weekends).
Prof	Craig Dilley
Designer	Harry Vardon
Facilities	⊗ ⍟ 🕭 ▌ ♀ ♨ 🏠
& Leisure	snooker room.
Location	N side of town on A691

Hotel	★★ 69% Lord Crewe Arms Hotel, BLANCHLAND ☎ 01434 675251 9 ⇄ 🐾 Annexe10 ⇄ 🐾

CROOK   Map 12 NZ13

Crook Low Jobs Hill DL15 9AA
☎ 01388 762429 & 767926
Meadowland/parkland course in elevated position with natural hazards, varied holes and terrain. Panoramic views over Durham and Cleveland Hills.
18 holes, 6102yds, Par 70, SSS 69, Course record 64.
Club membership 550.

Visitors	weekends by arrangement.
Societies	apply in writing to Secretary.

Green Fees	ring for details.
Facilities	△
Location	0.5m E off A690

Hotel	★★ 66% Kensington Hall Hotel, Kensington Ter, WILLINGTON ☎ 01388 745071 10 ⇄ 🐾

DARLINGTON   Map 08 NZ21

Blackwell Grange Briar Close, Blackwell DL3 8QX
☎ 01325 464458 Fax 01325 464458
e-mail: Secretary@blackwell-grange.demon.co.uk
Pleasant parkland course with good views, easy walking.
18 holes, 5621yds, Par 68, SSS 67, Course record 63.
Club membership 1020.

Visitors	restricted Wed & weekends.
Societies	welcome weekdays except Wed (Ladies Day).
Green Fees	£25 per day; £20 per round (£30 per round weekends and bank holidays).
Prof	Ralph Givens
Designer	F Pennink
Facilities	⊗ ⍟ 🕭 ▌ ♀ ♨ 🏠 ✈ ✧
Location	1m SW off A66, turn into Blackwell, signposted

Hotel	★★★ 67% Blackwell Grange, Blackwell Grange, DARLINGTON ☎ 01325 509955 99 ⇄ 🐾 Annexe11 ⇄ 🐾

Darlington Haughton Grange DL1 3JD
☎ 01325 355324 Fax 01325 488126
e-mail: darlingtongolf.club1@virgin.net
Fairly flat parkland course with tree-lined fairways, and large first-class greens.
18 holes, 6271yds, Par 71, SSS 70, Course record 65.
Club membership 850.

Visitors	may not play weekends unless accompanied by member.
Societies	by prior arrangement with the Secretary but not at weekends.
Green Fees	£27 per 36 holes; £22 per 18 holes.
Prof	Mark Rogers
Designer	Dr Alistair McKenzie
Facilities	⊗ ⍟ 🕭 ▌ ♀ ♨ 🏠 ✈ ✧
Location	N side of town centre off A1150

Hotel	★★★🎖 70% Headlam Hall Hotel, Headlam, Gainford, DARLINGTON ☎ 01325 730238 19 ⇄ 🐾 Annexe17 ⇄ 🐾

Hall Garth Golf & Country Club Hotel Coatham Mundeville DL1 3LU ☎ 01325 320246
Fax 01325 310083
A 6621 yard course with mature trees and Victorian deer folly. The challenging 165 yard Par 3 3rd requires teeing over water, whilst the 500 yard Par 5 6th hole features the picturesque River Swale running alongside the fairway and the green.
9 holes, 6621yds, Par 72, SSS 72.

Visitors	tee times bookable 7 days in advance.
Societies	prior booking by telephone.
Green Fees	£10 per 18 holes (£12.50 weekends).
Cards	🔲 ▨ ▨ ▨ ▨ ▨
Designer	Brian Moore
Facilities	⊗ ⍟ 🕭 ▌ ♀ ♨ 🏠 ✈ 🛏 ✧
& Leisure	heated indoor swimming pool, sauna, solarium, gymnasium.
Location	0.5m from A1(M), junct 59 off A167 ▶

Hotel   ★★★ 73% Hall Garth Golf and Country Club
                 Hotel, Coatham Mundeville, DARLINGTON
                 ☎ 01325 300400   30 ⇋ ♦ Annexe11 ⇋ ♦

Stressholme Snipe Ln DL2 2SA
☎ 01325 461002 Fax 01325 351826
Picturesque municipal parkland course, long but wide, with
98 bunkers and a par 3 hole played over a river.
18 holes, 6229yds, Par 70, SSS 69, Course record 68.
Club membership 650.
Visitors   must book 8 days in advance.
Societies   apply to the steward or professional.
Green Fees   £10 per round (£12.10 weekends & bank
                 holidays).
Cards   ⬜ ⬜ ⬜ ⬜
Facilities   ⊗ ↳ ♥ ♀ ♣ ☏ ⛳ ♂ ℓ
Location   SW side of town centre on A67

Hotel   ★★★ 67% Blackwell Grange, Blackwell
                 Grange, DARLINGTON
                 ☎ 01325 509955   99 ⇋ ♦ Annexe11 ⇋ ♦

Durham   Map 12 NZ24

Brancepeth Castle Brancepeth Village DH7 8EA
☎ 0191 378 0075 Fax 0191 3783835
Parkland course overlooked at the 9th hole by beautiful
Brancepeth Castle.
18 holes, 6234yds, Par 70, SSS 70, Course record 64.
Club membership 780.
Visitors   must contact in advance, restricted weekends.
Societies   must contact in advance.
Green Fees   not confirmed.
Cards   ⬜ ⬜ ⬜
Prof   David Howdon
Designer   H S Holt
Facilities   ⊗ ⫴ ↳ ♥ ♀ ♣ ☏ ⛳ ℓ
Location   4m from Durham A690 towards Crook, left at
                 xrds in Brancepath, left turn at Castle Gates,
                 400yds

Hotel   ★★★★ 74% Durham Marriott Hotel, Royal
                 County, Old Elvet, DURHAM
                 ☎ 0191 386 6821 139 ⇋ ♦

Durham City Littleburn, Langley Moor DH8 8HL
☎ 0191 378 0806 & 378 0029 Fax 0191 378 4265
Undulating parkland course bordered on several holes by the
River Browney.
18 holes, 6326yds, Par 71, SSS 70, Course record 67.
Club membership 750.
Visitors   restricted on competition days.
Societies   apply in writing or telephone the club
                 professional on 0191 378 0029
Green Fees   not confirmed.
Prof   Steve Corbally
Designer   C Stanton
Facilities   ⊗ ⫴ ↳ ♥ ♀ ♣ ☏ ⛳ ℓ
Location   2m W of Durham City, turn left off A690 into
                 Littleburn Ind Est

Hotel   ★★★ 69% Swallow Three Tuns Hotel, New
                 Elvet, DURHAM ☎ 0191 386 4326 50 ⇋ ♦

Mount Oswald South Rd DH1 3TQ ☎ 0191 386 7527
Fax 0191 386 0975 e-mail: information@mountoswald.co.uk
Flat, wooded parkland course with a Georgian clubhouse and
good views of Durham Cathedral on the back nine.
18 holes, 6101yds, Par 71, SSS 69.
Club membership 125.
Visitors   must contact in advance for weekends but may
                 not play before 10am on Sun.
Societies   must telephone in advance.
Green Fees   £12 per round Mon-Thu (£14 Fri-Sun & bank
                 holidays).
Cards   ⬜ ⬜ ⬜ ⬜ ⬜
Facilities   ⊗ ⫴ ↳ ♥ ♀ ♣ ⛳ ℓ
Location   On A177, 1m SW of city centre

Hotel   ★★★ 70% Ramside Hall Hotel, Carrville,
                 DURHAM ☎ 0191 386 5282 80 ⇋ ♦

Ramside Hall Carrville DH1 1TD
☎ 0191 386 9514 Fax 0191 386 9519
Three recently constructed 9-hole parkland courses - Princes,
Bishops, Cathedral - with 14 lakes and panoramic views
surrounding an impressive hotel. Excellent golf academy and
driving range.
Princes: 9 holes, 3235yds, Par 36, SSS 36.
Bishops: 9 holes, 3285yds, Par 36.
Cathedral: 9 holes, 2874yds, Par 34.
Club membership 400.
Visitors   open at all times subject to tee availability.
Societies   telephone in advance.
Green Fees   not confirmed.
Cards   ⬜ ⬜ ⬜ ⬜ ⬜ ⬜
Prof   Robert Lister
Designer   Johnathan Gaunt
Facilities   ⊗ ⫴ ↳ ♥ ♀ ♣ ⛳ ⛳ ⛳ ⛳ ♂ ℓ
Location   500m from A1/A690 interchange

Hotel   ★★★ 70% Ramside Hall Hotel, Carrville,
                 DURHAM ☎ 0191 386 5282 80 ⇋ ♦

Eaglescliffe   Map 08 NZ41

Eaglescliffe and District Yarm Rd TS16 0DQ
☎ 01642 780098 Fax 01642 780238
This hilly course offers both pleasant and interesting golf
to all classes of player. It lies in a delightful setting on a
rolling plateau, shelving to the River Tees. There are fine
views to the Cleveland Hills.
18 holes, 6275yds, Par 72, SSS 70, Course record 63.
Club membership 700.
Visitors   restricted Tue, Thu, Fri & weekends.
Societies   must contact in advance, apply to secretary
                 on 01642 780238
Green Fees   £35 per day; £25 per round (£50/£35
                 weekends).
Prof   Paul Bradley
Designer   J Braid/H Cotton
Facilities   ⊗ ⫴ ↳ ♥ ♀ ♣ ☏ ⛳ ℓ
Location   E side of village off A135

Hotel   ★★★★ 63% Swallow Hotel, John Walker
                 Square, STOCKTON-ON-TEES
                 ☎ 01642 679721 0800 7317549
                 Fax 01642 601714 125 ⇋ ♦

HARTLEPOOL Map 08 NZ53

Castle Eden & Peterlee Castle Eden TS27 4SS
☎ 01429 836510 e-mail: derek.livingston@btinternet.com
Beautiful parkland course alongside a nature reserve. Hard
walking but trees provide wind shelter.
18 holes, 6262yds, Par 70, SSS 70, Course record 65.
Club membership 750.
Visitors   with member only at certain times, must contact
in advance.
Societies   must contact in advance tel: 01429 836510.
Green Fees £24.
Prof   Graham J Laidlaw
Designer   Henry Cotton
Facilities   ⊗ �ₘ ⅃ 🛢 ♀ ♨ 🛒 🏌 ➷ ➿ ✐
& Leisure   snooker.
Location   2m S of Peterlee on B1281 off A19

Hotel   ★★ 69% Hardwicke Hall Manor Hotel,
Hesleden, PETERLEE
☎ 01429 836326 15 ⇆ ♝

Hartlepool Hart Warren TS24 9QF
☎ 01429 274398 Fax 01429 274129
A seaside course, half links, overlooking the North Sea. A
good test and equally enjoyable to all handicap players.
The 10th, par 4, demands a precise second shot over a ridge
and between sand dunes to a green down near the edge of
the beach, alongside which several holes are played.
18 holes, 5981yds, Par 70, SSS 70, Course record 62.
Club membership 700.
Visitors   with member only on Sun.
Societies   must apply in writing in advance.
Green Fees £25 per day (£36 weekends).
Prof   Malcolm E Cole
Designer   Partly Braid
Facilities   ⊗ ⚏ ⅃ 🛢 ♀ ♨ 🛒 🏌 ✐
Location   N of Hartlepool, off A1086

Hotel   ★★★ 65% The Grand Hotel, Swainson St,
HARTLEPOOL
☎ 01429 266345 47 ⇆ ♝

MIDDLETON ST GEORGE Map 08 NZ31

Dinsdale Spa Neasham Rd DL2 1DW
☎ 01325 332297 Fax 01325 332297
A mainly flat, parkland course on high land above the
River Tees with views of the Cleveland Hills. Water
hazards in front 10th tee and green, the prevailing west
wind affects the later holes. There is a practice area by
the clubhouse.
18 holes, 6099yds, Par 71, SSS 69, Course record 65.
Club membership 870.
Visitors   welcome Mon & Wed-Fri, contact for
further details.
Societies   bookings through office, no weekends or
Tue. Apply in writing or telephone.
Green Fees £25 per day.
Prof   Neil Metcalfe
Facilities   ⊗ ⚏ ⅃ 🛢 ♀ ♨ 🛒 ✐
Location   1.5m SW

Hotel   ★★★ 64% The St George, Middleton St
George, Darlington, TEES-SIDE
AIRPORT ☎ 01325 332631 59 ⇆ ♝

NEWTON AYCLIFFE Map 08 NZ22

Oakleaf School Aycliffe Ln DL5 4EF ☎ 01325 310820
18 holes, 5732yds, Par 69, SSS 70.
Location   6m N of Darlington, off A6072
Telephone for further details

Hotel   ★★★★ 71% Redworth Hall Hotel,
REDWORTH ☎ 01388 770600 100 ⇆ ♝

Woodham Golf & Country Club Burnhill Way DL5 4PN
☎ 01325 320574 (Office) 315257 (Pro Shop)
Fax 01325 315254
Beautiful parkland course offering golfers a full and varied
challenge with plenty of trees, numerous lakes and
meandering streams.
18 holes, 6771yds, Par 73, SSS 72, Course record 68.
Club membership 694.
Visitors   must book 1 week in advance for weekends.
Societies   telephone or write in advance.
Green Fees £22 per day; £16.50 per round (£33/£26
weekends and bank holidays).
Cards   🖃 📇 💳 🖸 🖂
Prof   Ernie Wilson
Designer   James Hamilton Stutt
Facilities   ⊗ ⚏ ⅃ 🛢 ♀ ♨ 🛒 🏌 ➷ ➿ ✐
Location   Off A167

Hotel   ★★★ 68% Swallow Eden Arms Hotel,
RUSHYFORD ☎ 01388 720541 45 ⇆ ♝

SEAHAM Map 12 NZ44

Seaham Dawdon SR7 7RD
☎ 0191 581 2354 & 581 1268 (Sec)
Heathland links course with several holes affected by strong
prevailing winds.
18 holes, 6017yds, Par 70, SSS 69, Course record 64.
Club membership 600.
Visitors   contact professional at all times, with member
only weekends until 3.30pm.
Societies   must apply in advance.
Green Fees £18 per day; (£23 round weekends).
Prof   Glyn Jones
Facilities   ⊗ ⚏ by prior arrangement ⅃ 🛢 ♀ ♨ 🛒 🏌 ✐
Location   3m E of A19, exit for Seaham

Hotel   ★★★★ 67% Swallow Hotel, Queen's Pde,
Seaburn, SUNDERLAND
☎ 0191 529 2041 98 ⇆ ♝

SEATON CAREW Map 08 NZ52

Seaton Carew Tees Rd TS25 1DE
☎ 01429 261040 & 266249
A championship links course taking full advantage of its
dunes, bents, whins and gorse. Renowned for its par 4
(17th); just enough fairway for an accurate drive
followed by another precise shot to a pear-shaped,
sloping green that is severely trapped.
The Old Course: 18 holes, 6604yds, Par 72, SSS 72.
Brabazon Course: 18 holes, 6900yds, Par 73, SSS 73.
Club membership 650.
Visitors   restricted until after 10am at weekends &
bank holidays,and after 09.30am midweek.
Societies   must apply in writing.   ▶

Green Fees	£32 per day (£42 weekends & bank holidays).
Prof	W Hector
Designer	McKenzie
Facilities	⊗ ⵈ ╟ ┗ ♥ ♀ ♨ 🏠 ⚘ ⚓ ✓
Location	SE side of village off A178

Hotel	★★★ 65% The Grand Hotel, Swainson St, HARTLEPOOL ☎ 01429 266345 47 ⇔ ⌂

SEDGEFIELD   Map 08 NZ32

Knotty Hill Golf Centre TS21 2BB
☎ 01740 620320 Fax 01740 622227
The 18-hole Princes course is set in rolling parkland with
many holes routed through shallow valleys. Several holes are
set wholly or partially within woodland and water hazards
abound. Bishops Course is a developing 18-hole course with
varied water features on attractive terrain. Several holes are
routed through mature woodland.
Princes Course (A+B): 18 holes, 6577yds, Par 72, SSS 71.
Bishops Course (C+D): 18 holes, 5859yds, Par 70.

Visitors	must telephone in advance for tee reservations.
Societies	package available on request.
Green Fees	Mon-Fri:£26 per 36 holes, £21 per 27 holes, £13 per 18 holes, £8 per 9 holes.
Designer	C Stanton
Facilities	⊗ ⵈ ╟ ┗ ♥ ♨ 🏠 ⚘ ♥ ⚓ ✓ ⚑
Location	1m N of Sedgefield on A177, 2m from junct 60 on A1(M)

Hotel	★★★ 65% Hardwick Hall Hotel, SEDGEFIELD ☎ 01740 620253 51 ⇔ ⌂

STANLEY   Map 12 NZ15

South Moor The Middles, Craghead DH9 6AG
☎ 01207 232848 & 283525(pro) Fax 01207 284616
Moorland course with natural hazards designed by Dr
Alistair McKenzie in 1926 and remains one the most
challenging of its type in north east England. Out of bounds
features on 11 holes from the tee and the testing par 5 12th
hole is uphill and usually against a strong headwind.
18 holes, 6271yds, Par 72, SSS 70, Course record 66.
Club membership 650.

Visitors	welcome except sundays, must contact in advance. Handicap certificate required.
Societies	apply in writing to Secretary.
Green Fees	£22 per day; £15 per round (£26 per day/round weekends & bank holidays).
Prof	Shaun Cowell
Designer	Dr Alistair Mackenzie
Facilities	⊗ ⵈ ╟ ┗ ♥ ♨ 🏠 ⚘ ♥ ⚓ ✓
Location	1.5m SE on B6313

Hotel	★★★ 69% Beamish Park Hotel, Beamish Burn Rd, MARLEY HILL ☎ 01207 230666 47 ⇔ ⌂

> Where to stay, where to eat?
> Visit the AA internet site
> www.theAA.com

STOCKTON-ON-TEES   Map 08 NZ41

Norton Norton TS20 1SU
☎ 01642 676385 Fax 01642 608467
An interesting parkland course with long drives from the 7th
and 17th tees. Several water hazards.
18 holes, 5855yds, Par 70.

Visitors	no visiting party tee times booked on weekends.
Societies	apply in advance.
Green Fees	£10 (£12 weekends).
Cards	▭▭ ▭▭ ▭▭ 🎟
Designer	T Harper
Facilities	⊗ ⵈ ╟ ┗ ♥ ♀ ✓
& Leisure	bowling green.
Location	At Norton 2m N off A19

Hotel	★★★ 71% Parkmore Hotel, 636 Yarm Rd, Eaglescliffe, STOCKTON-ON-TEES ☎ 01642 786815 55 ⇔ ⌂

Teesside Acklam Rd, Thornaby TS17 7JS
☎ 01642 616516 & 673822 (pro) Fax 01642 676252 e-mail:
teeside@golfclub76.freeserve.co.uk
Flat parkland course, easy walking.
18 holes, 6535yds, Par 72, SSS 71, Course record 64.
Club membership 700.

Visitors	with member only weekdays after 4.30pm, weekends after 11am.
Societies	must contact in writing.
Green Fees	£26 per day.
Prof	Ken Hall
Designer	Makepiece & Dr Somerville
Facilities	⊗ ⵈ ╟ ┗ ♥ ♀ ♨ 🏠 ✓
Location	1.5m SE on A1130, off A19 at Mandale interchange

Hotel	★★★ 69% Posthouse Middlesbrough/Teesside, low Ln, Stainton Village, Thornaby, STOCKTON-ON-TEES ☎ 0870 400 9081 136 ⇔ ⌂

ESSEX

ABRIDGE   Map 05 TQ49

Abridge Golf and Country Club Epping Ln, Stapleford
Tawney RM4 1ST
☎ 01708 688396 Fax 01708 688550
e-mail: lynn@abridgegolf.freeserve.co.uk
A parkland course with easy walking. The quick drying
course is by no means easy to play. This has been the
venue of several professional tournaments. Abridge is a
Golf and Country Club and has all the attendant
facilities.
18 holes, 6692yds, Par 72, SSS 72, Course record 67.
Club membership 650.

Visitors	must have current handicap certificate, contact in advance. May play weekends after 2pm.
Societies	telephone in advance.
Green Fees	£33 per 18 holes (£35 weekends).
Cards	▭▭ ▭▭ ▭▭ 🎟 ▶

Prof	Stuart Layton
Designer	Henry Cotton
Facilities	⊗ ⅂ ♥ ♀ ♨ 🏠 🏌 ↘ ♘ ✦ ♔
& Leisure	heated outdoor swimming pool, sauna.
Location	1.75m NE

Hotel	★★★ 62% Posthouse Epping, High Rd, Bell Common, EPPING ☎ 0870 400 9027 Annexe79 ⊒ ♙

BASILDON   Map 05 TQ78

Basildon Clay Hill Ln, Kingswood SS16 5JP
☎ 01268 533297 Fax 01268 533849
Undulating municipal parkland course. Testing 13th hole
(par 4).
18 holes, 6236yds, Par 72, SSS 70.
Club membership 350.

Visitors	contact professional in advance 01268 533532.
Societies	may contact for details.
Green Fees	£9.50 (£16 weekends).
Cards	💳 💳
Prof	M Oliver
Designer	A Cotton
Facilities	⊗ 🗏 ⅂ ♥ ♀ ♨ 🏠 🏌 ♘ ✦
Location	1m S off A176

Hotel	★★★ 65% Posthouse Basildon, Cranes Farm Rd, BASILDON ☎ 0870 400 9003 149 ⊒ ♙

BENFLEET   Map 05 TQ78

Boyce Hill Vicarage Hill, South Benfleet SS7 1PD
☎ 01268 793625 & 752565 Fax 01268 750497
e-mail: boycehill@hotmail.com
Hilly parkland course with good views.
18 holes, 5983yds, Par 68, SSS 68, Course record 61.
Club membership 700.

Visitors	must have a handicap certificate, must contact 24hrs in advance, may not play at weekends.
Societies	Thu only, book well in advance by telephone.
Green Fees	£25 up to 36 holes.
Prof	Graham Burroughs
Designer	James Braid
Facilities	⊗ 🗏 ⅂ ♥ ♀ ♨ 🏠 ↘ ✦
Location	0.75m NE of Benfleet Station

Hotel	★★★ 65% Posthouse Basildon, Cranes Farm Rd, BASILDON ☎ 0870 400 9003 149 ⊒ ♙

BILLERICAY   Map 05 TQ69

The Burstead Tye Common Rd, Little Burstead CM12 9SS
☎ 01277 631171 Fax 01277 632766
The Burstead is an attractive parkland course set amidst some
of the most attractive countryside in south Essex. It is an
excellent test of golf to players of all standards with the
greens showing maturity beyond their years. Challenging
holes include the Par 4 16th hole which at 348yds requires an
accurate tee shot to leave a second shot played over a lake
protecting an attractive contoured green. The 18th is the
longest hole on the course.
18 holes, 6275yds, Par 71, SSS 70, Course record 69.
Club membership 850.

Visitors	Must book in advance and may not play weekends am.
Societies	Apply in writing or telephone for reservation.
Green Fees	£25 per day; £19 per 18 holes; £10 per 9 holes (£14 per 9 holes; £25 per 18 holes).
Cards	💳 💳 💳 💳 💳
Prof	Keith Bridges
Designer	Patrick Tallack
Facilities	⊗ 🗏 ⅂ ♥ ♀ ♨ 🏠 ↘ ♘ ✦
Location	M25 onto A127, located off A176.

Hotel	★★★ 69% Chichester Hotel, Old London Rd, Wickford, BASILDON ☎ 01268 560555 2 ⊒ ♙ Annexe32 ⊒ ♙

Stock Brook Golf & Country Club Queens Park Av,
Stock CM12 0SP
☎ 01277 653616 & 650400 Fax 01277 633063
e-mail: events@stockbrook.com

Set in 250 acres of picturesque countryside the 27 holes
comprise three undulating 9's, offering the challenge of
water on a large number of holes. Any combination can be
played, but the Stock and Brook courses make the 18-hole,
6750 yard championship course. There are extensive
clubhouse facilities.
Stock & Brook Courses: 18 holes, 6728yds, Par 72, SSS 72,
Course record 66.
Manor Course: 9 holes, 2997yds, Par 35.

Visitors	handicap certificate required, must contact 24hrs in advance.
Societies	apply in writing or telephone.
Green Fees	not confirmed.
Prof	Kevin Merry
Designer	Martin Gillet
Facilities	⊗ 🗏 ⅂ ♥ ♀ ♨ 🏠 ↘ ♘ ✦ ♔
& Leisure	hard tennis courts, heated outdoor swimming pool, sauna, gymnasium, bowls.

Hotel	★★★ 66% The Heybridge Hotel, Roman Rd, INGATESTONE ☎ 01277 355355 22 ⊒ ♙

BRAINTREE   Map 05 TL72

Braintree Kings Ln, Stisted CM7 8DA
☎ 01376 346079 Fax 01376 348677
e-mail: manager@braintreegolfclub.freeserve.co.uk
Parkland course with many unique mature trees. Good par 3s
with the 14th - 'Devils Lair'-regarded as one of the best in
the county.
18 holes, 6174yds, Par 70, SSS 69, Course record 65.
Club membership 750.

▶

Visitors	contact the pro shop in advance 01376 343465.
Societies	society days Wed & Thu early booking advised.
Green Fees	£32 per day; £25 per round (£42 per day/round weekends ex Sun am).
Prof	Tony Parcell
Designer	Hawtree
Facilities	⊗ �𝍢 ⅃ 🏌 💺 ♀ ⚘ 🏠 ⚲ 🚃 ♂
Location	1m E, off A120

Hotel	★★★61% White Hart Hotel, Bocking End, BRAINTREE ☎ 01376 321401 31 ⇆ ⏘

Towerlands Panfield Rd CM7 5BJ
☎ 01376 326802 Fax 01376 552487
Undulating, grassland course. Driving range and sports hall.
9 holes, 2749yds, Par 34, SSS 66.
Club membership 300.

Visitors	must not play before 12.30pm weekends or before 5pm Wed. Correct dress at all times. Must contact in advance.
Societies	must contact in advance by telephone.
Green Fees	not confirmed.
Cards	▭ ▭ ▭ ▭ ▭
Designer	G Shiels
Facilities	⊗ �𝍢 ⅃ 🏌 💺 ♀ ⚘ 🏠 ♂ ♂
& Leisure	squash, gymnasium.
Location	On B1053

Hotel	★★★61% White Hart Hotel, Bocking End, BRAINTREE ☎ 01376 321401 31 ⇆ ⏘

BRENTWOOD   Map 05 TQ59

Bentley Ongar Rd CM15 9SS
☎ 01277 373179 Fax 01277 375097
Parkland course with water hazards.
18 holes, 6709yds, Par 72, SSS 72.
Club membership 600.

Visitors	should contact in advance, may not play at weekends.
Societies	must write or telephone in advance.
Green Fees	£22 per round; £30 per day.
Cards	▭ ▭ ▭ ▭ ▭
Prof	Nick Garrett
Designer	Alec Swann
Facilities	⅃ 🏌 💺 ♀ ⚘ 🏠 🚃 ♂
Location	3m NW on A128

Hotel	★★★69% Posthouse Brentwood, Brook St, BRENTWOOD ☎ 0870 400 9012 145 ⇆ ⏘

Hartswood King George's Playing Fields, Ingrave Rd
CM14 5AE ☎ 01277 218850 Fax 01277 218850
Municipal parkland course, easy walking.
18 holes, 6192yds, Par 70, SSS 69, Course record 64.
Club membership 500.

Visitors	pre-book by telephone up to five days ahead on 01277 214830
Societies	weekdays only, must contact in advance.
Green Fees	£9.50 (£14 weekends & bank holidays).
Cards	▭ ▭ ▭ ▭ ▭
Prof	Stephen Cole
Facilities	⊗ ⅃ 🏌 💺 ♀ ⚘ 🏠 ♂ ♂
Location	0.75m SE on A128

Hotel	★★★69% Posthouse Brentwood, Brook St, BRENTWOOD ☎ 0870 400 9012 145 ⇆ ⏘

Warley Park Magpie Ln, Little Warley CM13 3DX
☎ 01277 224891 Fax 01277 200679
e-mail: enquiries@warleyparkgc.com
Parkland course with reasonable walking. Numerous water hazards. There is also a golf-practice ground.
1st & 2nd: 18 holes, 5967yds, Par 69, SSS 67,
Course record 66.
1st & 3rd: 18 holes, 5925yds, Par 71, SSS 69,
Course record 65.
2nd & 3rd: 18 holes, 5917yds, Par 70, SSS 69,
Course record 70.
Club membership 800.

Visitors	must have handicap certificate and contact in advance. May not play at weekends.
Societies	telephone in advance for provisional booking.
Green Fees	£30 per round.
Prof	Jason Groat
Designer	Reg Plumbridge
Facilities	⊗ �𝍢 by prior arrangement ⅃ 🏌 💺 ♀ ⚘ 🏠 ⚲ 🚃 ♂ 🏌
Location	0.5m N off junct 29 of M25/A127

Hotel	★★★69% Posthouse Brentwood, Brook St, BRENTWOOD ☎ 0870 400 9012 145 ⇆ ⏘

Weald Park Coxtie Green Rd, South Weald CM14 5RJ
☎ 01277 375101 Fax 01277 374888
e-mail: wealdpark@americangolf.uk.com
Tranquil parkland course with many mature oak trees, lakes, ponds and plentiful wildlife. The undulating terrain and the numerous hedges and ponds make this par 71 course a fair test of golf for all abilities.
18 holes, 6285yds, Par 71, SSS 70, Course record 65.
Club membership 570.

Visitors	telephone booking preferable, no weekday restrictions, weekend afternoons only.
Societies	apply in writing or telephone for package.
Green Fees	£18 per 18 holes (£24 weekends).
Cards	▭ ▭ ▭ ▭ ▭
Prof	Ian Parker
Designer	Reg Plumbridge
Facilities	⊗ ⅃ 🏌 💺 ♀ ⚘ 🏠 🚃 ♂
Location	3m from M25

Hotel	★★★★72% Marygreen Manor Hotel, London Rd, BRENTWOOD ☎ 01277 225252 3 ⇆ ⏘ Annexe40 ⇆ ⏘

BULPHAN   Map 05 TQ68

Langdon Hills Golf Centre Lower Dunton Rd RM14 3TY
☎ 01268 548444 Fax 01268 490084
Well situated with the Langdon Hills on one side and dramatic views across London on the other, the Centre offers an interchangeable 27 hole course, a floodlit 22-bay driving range and three academy holes.
Langdon & Bulphan Course: 18 holes, 6500yds, Par 72,
SSS 71, Course record 67.
Bulphan & Horndon Course: 18 holes, 6422yds, Par 73,
SSS 71.
Horndon & Langdon Course: 18 holes, 6186yds, Par 71,
SSS 70.
Club membership 800.

Visitors	preference given to members on weekend mornings and visitors may not play Langdon course before 10.30am. Cannot book more than 5 days in advance. ▶

Societies   apply in writing or telephone.
Green Fees £14.85 per 18 holes; £10.85 per 9 holes
        (£19.75/£7.95 weekends and bank holidays).
Prof   Terry Moncur
Designer   Howard Swan
Facilities   ⊗ ⅲ ⅃ ♭ ♥ ♀ ⚲ 🖻 ⛳ 🏴 ➘ ⚒ ♂ ⁅
Location   Between A13 & A127 N of A128 S of Basildon

Hotel   ★★★★ 72% Marygreen Manor Hotel, London
        Rd, BRENTWOOD ☎ 01277 225252
        3 ⇆ ♣ Annexe40 ⇆ ♣

BURNHAM-ON-CROUCH   Map 05 TQ99

Burnham-on-Crouch Ferry Rd, Creeksea CM0 8PQ
☎ 01621 782282 Fax 01621 784489
Undulating meadowland riverside course, easy walking.
18 holes, 6056yds, Par 70, SSS 69, Course record 66.
Club membership 586.
Visitors   welcome weekdays. Must play with member at
        weekends.
Societies apply in writing or telephone.
Green Fees £24 per day/round.
Prof   Steven Cardy
Designer Swan
Facilities ⊗ ⅲ ⅃ ♭ ♥ ♀ ⚲ 🖻 ➘ ⚒ ♂
Location 1.25m W off B1010

CANEWDON   Map 05 TQ99

Ballards Gore Gore Rd SS4 2DA
☎ 01702 258917 Fax 01702 258571
A parkland course with several lakes.
18 holes, 6874yds, Par 73, SSS 73, Course record 69.
Club membership 500.
Visitors   must contact in advance. May play weekdays
        and Sun after 2pm.
Societies apply in advance.
Green Fees £25 per day; £20 per round.
Cards   ▬ ▬ ▬ 💳
Prof   Richard Emery
Designer D J J Caton
Facilities ⊗ ⅃ ♭ ♥ ♀ ⚲ 🖻 ➘ ⚒ ♂
Location 2m NE of Rochford

Hotel   ★★★ 69% Hotel Renouf, Bradley Way,
        ROCHFORD ☎ 01702 541334 24 ⇆ ♣

CANVEY ISLAND   Map 05 TQ78

Castle Point Somnes Av SS8 9FG
☎ 01268 696298 (Secretary) & 510830 (Pro)
e-mail: sec@castlepointgolfclub.freeserve.co.uk
A flat seaside links and part parkland course with water
hazards on 13 holes and views of the estuary and Hadleigh
Castle. Always a test for any golfer when the wind starts to
blow.
18 holes, 6176yds, Par 71, SSS 69, Course record 69.
Club membership 275.
Visitors   must book for weekends.
Societies phone or write for details.
Green Fees not confirmed.
Prof   Michael Utteridge
Facilities ⊗ ⅃ ♭ ♥ ♀ ⚲ 🖻 ⛳ ♂ ⁅
Location SE of Basildon, A130 to Canvey Island

Hotel   ★★★ 69% Chichester Hotel, Old London Rd,
        Wickford, BASILDON
        ☎ 01268 560555 2 ⇆ ♣ Annexe32 ⇆ ♣

CHELMSFORD   Map 05 TL70

Channels Belstead Farm Ln, Little Waltham CM3 3PT
☎ 01245 440005 Fax 01245 442032
The Channels course is built on land from reclaimed gravel
pits, 18 very exciting holes with plenty of lakes providing an
excellent test of golf. Belsteads a nine hole course is mainly
flat but has 3 holes where water has to be negotiated.
Channels Course: 18 holes, 6402yds, Par 71, SSS 71,
Course record 67.
Belsteads: 9 holes, 2467yds, Par 34, SSS 32.
Club membership 650.
Visitors   Channels Course; must contact in advance and
        may only play with member at weekends.
        Belsteads Course; available anytime.
Societies telephone starter on 01245 443311.
Green Fees Channels: £36 per day; £36 per round. Belsteads
        ;£12 per 9 holes, £18 per 18 holes (£14/£20
        weekends).
Prof   Ian Sinclair
Designer Cotton & Swan
Facilities ⊗ ⅲ ⅃ ♭ ♥ ♀ ⚲ 🖻 ➘ ⚒ ♂ ⁅
& Leisure fishing.
Location 2m NE on A130

Hotel   ★★★ 70% County Hotel, Rainsford Rd,
        CHELMSFORD ☎ 01245 455700
        54 ⇆ ♣ Annexe8 ⇆ ♣

Chelmsford Widford Rd CM2 9AP
☎ 01245 256483 Fax 01245 256483
e-mail: office@chelmsfordgc.sagehost.co.uk
An undulating parkland course, hilly in parts, with 3
holes in woods and four difficult par 4's. From the
reconstructed clubhouse are fine views over the
course and the wooded hills beyond.
18 holes, 5981yds, Par 68, SSS 69, Course record 63.
Club membership 650.
Visitors   must contact in advance. Society days
        Wed/Thu, Ladies Day Tue. With member
        only at weekends.
Societies must contact in advance.
Green Fees not confirmed.
Prof   Mark Welch
Designer Tom Dunn
Facilities ⊗ ⅃ ♭ ♥ ♀ ⚲ 🖻 ➘ ⚒ ♂
Location 1.5m S of town centre off A12

Hotel   ★★★ 71% Pontlands Park County Hotel,
        West Hanningfield Rd, Great Baddow,
        CHELMSFORD
        ☎ 01245 476444 17 ⇆ ♣

CHIGWELL   Map 05 TQ49

Chigwell High Rd IG7 5BH ☎ 020 8500 2059
Fax 020 8501 3410 e-mail: info@chigwellgolfclub.co.uk
A course of high quality, mixing meadowland with
parkland. For those who believe 'all Essex is flat' the
undulating nature of Chigwell will be a refreshing
surprise. The greens are excellent and the fairways tight
with mature trees.

18 holes, 6279yds, Par 71, SSS 70, Course record 66.
Club membership 670.

Visitors	must contact in advance & have handicap certificate, but must be accompanied by member at weekends.
Societies	recognised societies welcome by prior arrangement.
Green Fees	£35 per 18 holes(Mon/Wed/Thur);£25 after 2.30pm;£45 per day.
Prof	Ray Beard
Designer	Hawtree/Taylor
Facilities	⊗ ⓑ ♥ ♀ ♨ 🖻 ⚑ ✧
Location	0.5m S on A113
Hotel	★★★ 63% Roebuck Hotel, North End, BUCKHURST HILL ☎ 020 8505 4636 28 ⇌ ⓕ

CHIGWELL ROW   Map 05 TQ49

Hainault Forest Romford Rd, Chigwell Row IG7 4QW
☎ 020 8500 2131 Fax 020 8501 5196
Club playing over Borough of Redbridge public courses; hilly parkland subject to wind. Two courses, driving range.
No 1 Course: 18 holes, 5687yds, Par 70, SSS 67, Course record 65.
No 2 Course: 18 holes, 6238yds, Par 71, SSS 71.
Club membership 600.

Visitors	no restrictions.
Societies	must contact in writing.
Green Fees	not confirmed.
Prof	Chris Hope
Designer	Taylor & Hawtree
Facilities	⊗ ⓑ ♥ ♀ ♨ 🖻 ⚑ 🛒 ✧
Location	0.5m S on A1112
Hotel	★★★ 66% County Hotel Epping Forest, 30 Oak Hill, WOODFORD GREEN ☎ 020 8787 9988 99 ⇌ ⓕ

CLACTON-ON-SEA   Map 05 TM11

Clacton West Rd CO15 1AJ
☎ 01255 421919 Fax 01255 424602
Windy, seaside course.
18 holes, 6494yds, Par 71, SSS 69.
Club membership 650.

Visitors	must contact in advance.
Societies	apply in writing/ telephone.
Green Fees	not confirmed.
Prof	S J Levermore
Facilities	⊗ ⫿ ⓑ ♥ ♀ ♨ 🖻 🛒 ✧
Location	1.25m SW of town centre
Hotel	★★ 72% Maplin Hotel, Esplanade, FRINTON-ON-SEA ☎ 01255 673832 11rm(10 ⇌ ⓕ)

> AA Hotels that have special
> arrangements with golf courses are listed at
> the back of the guide

COLCHESTER   Map 05 TL92

Birch Grove Layer Rd, Kingsford CO2 0HS
☎ 01206 734276 Fax 01206 734276
A pretty, undulating course surrounded by woodland - small but challenging with excellent greens. Challenging 6th hole cut through woodland with water hazards and out of bounds.
9 holes, 4532yds, Par 66, SSS 63.
Club membership 280.

Visitors	restricted Sun mornings.
Societies	apply in writing or telephone.
Green Fees	£12 per 18 holes; £9 per 9 holes.
Facilities	⊗ ⫿ ⓑ ♥ ♀ ♨ 🖻 ✧
Location	2.5m S on B1026
Hotel	★★★ 73% George Hotel, 116 High St, COLCHESTER ☎ 01206 578494 47 ⇌ ⓕ

Colchester Braiswick CO4 5AU
☎ 01206 853396 Fax 01206 852698
e-mail: colchester.golf@btinternet.com
A fairly flat, yet scenic, parkland course with tree-lined fairways and small copses. Mainly level walking.
18 holes, 6307yds, Par 70, SSS 70, Course record 64.
Club membership 700.

Visitors	by prior arrangement.
Societies	apply in writing or by telephone, Mon, Thu & Fri only.
Green Fees	fees available on request.
Prof	Mark Angel
Designer	James Braid
Facilities	♨ 🖻 ✧ ⓕ
Location	1.5m NW of town centre on B1508
Hotel	★★★ 73% George Hotel, 116 High St, COLCHESTER ☎ 01206 578494 47 ⇌ ⓕ

Colchester & Lexden Golf Centre Bakers Ln CO3 4AU
☎ 01206 843333 Fax 01206 854775
New 18-hole course within easy reach of the town centre. Also a 9-hole pitch and putt course, and a floodlit driving range.
18 holes, 5500yds, Par 67.
Club membership 500.

Visitors	welcome.
Societies	telephone for details.
Green Fees	not confirmed.
Cards	💳 💳 💳 💳 💳
Prof	Phil Grice
Designer	J Johnson
Facilities	⊗ ⫿ ⓑ ♥ ♀ ♨ 🖻 ⚑ ✧ ⓕ
& Leisure	9 hole par 3.
Location	Adjacent to A12. Take Colchester Central from A12 and then follow tourist signs
Hotel	★★★ 70% Marks Tey Hotel, London Rd, Marks Tey, COLCHESTER ☎ 01206 210001 110 ⇌ ⓕ

Stoke-by-Nayland Keepers Ln, Leavenheath CO6 4PZ
☎ 01206 262836 Fax 01206 263356
e-mail: info@golfclub.co.uk
Two undulating courses (Gainsborough and Constable) situated in Dedham Vale. Some water hazards and hedges. On Gainsborough the 10th (par 4) takes 2 shots over a lake; very testing par 3 at 11th.

▶

Gainsborough Course: 18 holes, 6581yds, Par 72, SSS 71, Course record 68.
Constable Course: 18 holes, 6544yds, Par 72, SSS 71, Course record 67.
Club membership 1360.

Visitors	write or telephone for details.
Societies	write or telephone for brochures and booking forms.
Green Fees	not confirmed.
Cards	🃏 💳 💳 📇 🗒
Prof	Kevin Lovelock
Designer	R Swan
Facilities	ⅢⅢ ⅼ 🍺 🍴 ⑨ △ 🖼 🏄 ↘ 🛒 ¢
& Leisure	heated indoor swimming pool, squash, fishing, sauna, solarium, gymnasium.
Location	1.5m NW of Stoke-by-Nayland on B1068

Hotel	★★★♨♨ Maison Talbooth, Stratford Rd, DEDHAM ☎ 01206 322367 10 ⇄ 📞

EARLS COLNE   Map 05 TL82

Colne Valley Station Rd CO6 2LT
☎ 01787 224233 Fax 01787 224126
An 18-hole course along the valley of the River Colne.
18 holes, 6301yds, Par 70, SSS 70, Course record 68.
Club membership 450.

Visitors	only after 11.00am at weekends, must dress correctly, no sharing of clubs. Must contact in advance.
Societies	apply in writing, minimum of 12 persons.
Green Fees	£18 per round (£23 weekends).
Cards	🃏 💳 💳 📇 🗒
Prof	James Taylor
Designer	Howard Swan
Facilities	⊗ ⅼ 🍺 ⑨ △ 🖼 🏄 ¢
& Leisure	sauna.
Location	Off A604

Hotel	★★★ 70% Marks Tey Hotel, London Rd, Marks Tey, COLCHESTER ☎ 01206 210001 110 ⇄ 📞

Essex Golf & Country Club CO6 2NS
☎ 01787 224466 Fax 01787 224410
Created on the site of a World War II airfield, this challenging course contains 10 lakes and strategically placed bunkering. Also a 9 hole course and a variety of leisure facilities.
County Course: 18 holes, 6907yds, Par 73, SSS 73, Course record 67.
Garden Course: 9 holes, 2190yds, Par 34, SSS 34.
Club membership 600.

Visitors	contact golf reception for bookings up to 1 week in advance.
Societies	apply in writing to the Functions Manager.
Green Fees	Country Course £25 per round (£35 weekends & bank holidays); Garden Course £17 per 18 holes, £12 per 9 holes.
Cards	🃏 💳 💳 📇 🗒
Prof	Lee Cocker
Designer	Reg Plumbridge
Facilities	⊗ ⅢⅢ ⅼ 🍺 ⑨ △ 🖼 ⑨ 🏄 ↘ 🛒 ¢ ¢
& Leisure	hard tennis courts, heated indoor swimming pool, fishing, sauna, solarium, video golf tuition studio.
Location	Off the A120 onto the B1024

Hotel	★★★ 70% Marks Tey Hotel, London Rd, Marks Tey, COLCHESTER ☎ 01206 210001 110 ⇄ 📞

EPPING   Map 05 TL40

Epping Fluxs Ln CM16 7PE
☎ 01992 572282 Fax 01992 575512
e-mail: neilsjoberg@hotmail.com
Rolling tree-lined parkland course with ponds and panoramic country views. Designed to use every club in the bag, the picturesque 4th is driveable but rarely birdied. The spectacular 18th "Happy Valley" is rarely parred.
18 holes, 5104, Par 68, SSS 65, Course record 67.
Club membership 350.

Visitors	welcome.
Societies	telephone in advance.
Green Fees	£8 (£10 weekends).
Designer	Sjoberg
Facilities	⊗ ⅼ 🍺 🍴 ↘ 🏄 ¢ ¢
Location	0.5m downhill from Epping tube station

Hotel	★★★ 62% Posthouse Epping, High Rd, Bell Common, EPPING ☎ 0870 400 9027 Annexe79 ⇄ 📞

Nazeing Middle St, Nazeing EN9 2LW
☎ 01992 893798 Fax 01992 893882
Parkland course built with American sand based greens and tees and five strategically placed lakes. One of the most notable holes is the difficult par 3 13th with out of bounds and a large lake coming into play.
18 holes, 6598yds, Par 72, SSS 71, Course record 68.
Club membership 400.

Visitors	contact for weekend and bank holidays, may only play pm.
Societies	prior arrangement required in writing.
Green Fees	£35 per day; Mon £16 per round (£20 Tue-Fri; £28 weekends).
Cards	🃏 💳 🗒 🗒
Prof	Robert Green
Designer	M Gillete
Facilities	⊗ ⅢⅢ ⅼ 🍺 ⑨ △ 🖼 ↘ 🏄 ¢ ¢
Location	Just outside Waltham Abbey

Hotel	★★★★ 64% Swallow Hotel, Old Shire Ln, WALTHAM ABBEY ☎ 01992 717170 162 ⇄ 📞

FRINTON-ON-SEA   Map 05 TM22

Frinton 1 The Esplanade CO13 9EP
☎ 01255 674618 Fax 01255 674618
e-mail: frintongolf@lineone.net
Deceptive, flat seaside links course providing fast, firm and undulating greens that will test the best putters and tidal ditches that cross many of the fairways, requiring careful placement of shots. Its open character means that every shot has to be evaluated with both wind strength and direction in mind. Easy walking.
Long Course: 18 holes, 6265yds, Par 71, SSS 70, Course record 64.
Short Course: 9 holes, 2734yds, Par 58.
Club membership 850.

Visitors must contact in advance.
Societies by arrangement, apply in writing to the secretary, Wed, Thu and some Fri.
Green Fees not confirmed.
Cards ⊟ ▬ ▬ ▧ ▧
Prof Peter Taggart
Designer Willy Park Jnr
Facilities ⊗ ⅷ by prior arrangement ⅊ ⚑ ♀ ♨ 🏪 ⚐ ♦ 🚜 ✎
Location SW side of town centre,17m East of Colchester

Hotel ★★ 72% Maplin Hotel, Esplanade, FRINTON-ON-SEA
☎ 01255 673832 11rm(10 ⇥ ☞)

GOSFIELD   Map 05 TL72

Gosfield Lake The Manor House, Hall Dr CO9 1RZ
☎ 01787 474747 Fax 01787 476044
e-mail: gosfieldlakegc@btconnect.com
Parkland course with bunkers, lakes and water hazards.
Designed by Sir Henry Cotton/Mr Howard Swan. Also 9-hole course; ideal for beginners and improvers.
Lakes Course: 18 holes, 6615yds, Par 72, SSS 72, Course record 68.
Meadows Course: 9 holes, 4180yds, Par 64, SSS 61.
Club membership 650.
Visitors Lakes Course: must contact in advance. Sat & Sun from 3.30 only. Meadows Course: Booking advisable.
Societies By prior arrangement.
Green Fees available on request.
Prof Richard Wheeler
Designer Henry Cotton/Howard Swan
Facilities ⊗ ⅷ ⅊ ⚑ ♀ ♨ 🏪 ♦ 🚜 ✎
& Leisure sauna.
Location 1m W of Gosfield off B1017

Hotel ★★★ 61% White Hart Hotel, Bocking End, BRAINTREE ☎ 01376 321401 31 ⇥ ☞

HARLOW   Map 05 TL40

Canons Brook Elizabeth Way CM19 5BE
☎ 01279 421482 Fax 01279 626393
Challenging parkland course designed by Henry Cotton. Accuracy is the key requiring straight driving from the tees, especially on the par 5 11th to fly a gap with out of bounds left and right before setting up the shot to the green.
18 holes, 6800yds, Par 73, SSS 72, Course record 65.
Club membership 850.
Visitors may not play at weekends.
Societies welcome Mon, Wed and Fri, must book in advance by telephone.
Green Fees £24 per 18 holes.
Cards ⊟ ▬ ▬ ▧ ▧
Prof Alan McGinn
Designer Henry Cotton
Facilities ♨ 🏪 ⚐ 🚜 ✎
Location 3m NW of junct 7 on M11

Hotel ★★★ 73% Swallow Churchgate Hotel, Churchgate St Village, Old Harlow, HARLOW
☎ 01279 420246 85 ⇥ ☞

North Weald Rayley Ln, North Weald CM16 6AR
☎ 01992 522118 Fax 01992 522881
Although only opened in November 1995, the blend of lakes and meadowland give this testing course an air of maturity.
18 holes, 6311yds, Par 71, SSS 70, Course record 66.
Club membership 500.
Visitors must contact in advance weekday,limited at weekends after 11am.
Societies contact in advance.
Green Fees £20 per round (£27.50 weekends).
Cards ⊟ ▬
Prof David Rawlings
Designer David Williams
Facilities ⊗ ⅷ ⅊ ⚑ ♀ ♨ 🏪 ♦ 🚜 ✎ ☜
& Leisure gymnasium.
Location M11 exit 7,off A414 towards Chipping Ongar & Chelmsford

Hotel ★★★ 62% Posthouse Epping, High Rd, Bell Common, EPPING
☎ 0870 400 9027 Annexe79 ⇥ ☞

HARWICH   Map 05 TM23

Harwich & Dovercourt Station Rd, Parkeston CO12 4NZ
☎ 01255 503616 Fax 01255 503323
Flat parkland course with easy walking.
9 holes, 5900yds, Par 70, SSS 69, Course record 58.
Club membership 420.
Visitors visitors with handicap certificate may play by prior arrangement, with member only at weekends.
Societies prior arrangement essential.
Green Fees £18 per 18 holes; £9 per 9 holes.
Facilities ⊗ ⅷ ⅊ ⚑ ♀ ♨ 🏪 ✎
Location Off A120 near Ferry Terminal

Hotel ★★★ 70% The Pier at Harwich, The Quay, HARWICH ☎ 01255 241212
7 ⇥ ☞ Annexe7 ⇥ ☞

INGRAVE   Map 05 TQ69

Thorndon Park CM13 3RH
☎ 01277 811666 & 01277 810345 Fax 01277 810645
Among the best of the Essex courses with a fine purpose-built clubhouse and a lake. The springy turf is easy on the feet. Many young trees now replace the famous old oaks that were such a feature of this course.
18 holes, 6492yds, Par 71, SSS 71.
Club membership 620.
Visitors must contact in advance, at weekends with member only.
Societies welcome Tue and Fri but must apply in writing.
Green Fees £55 per day; £40 per round.
Prof Brian White
Designer Colt/Alison
Facilities ⊗ ⅷ by prior arrangement ⅊ ⚑ ♀ ♨ 🏪 ⚐ ✎
Location W side of village off A128

Hotel ★★★ 69% Posthouse Brentwood, Brook St, BRENTWOOD
☎ 0870 400 9012 145 ⇥ ☞

LOUGHTON   Map 05 TQ49

High Beech Wellington Hill IG10 4AH ☎ 020 8508 7323
Short 9-hole course set in Epping Forest.
9 holes, 1477, Par 27, Course record 25.
Visitors welcome.
Green Fees not confirmed.
Prof Clark Baker
Facilities ♥ 🏠 ↑ ♂
Location Close to M25 Waltham Abbey junct

Loughton Clays Ln, Debden Green IG10 2RZ
☎ 020 8502 2923
9-hole parkland course on the edge of Epping Forest. A good test of golf.
9 holes, 4652yds, Par 66, SSS 63, Course record 65.
Club membership 180.
Visitors must contact in advance.
Societies telephone in advance.
Green Fees £10 per 18 holes; £7 per 9 holes (£11.50/£8 weekends).
Prof Richard Layton
Facilities ᒪ ♥ ⛳ 🏌 🏠 ↑ ♂
Location 1.5m SE of Theydon Bois

Hotel ★★★ 62% Posthouse Epping, High Rd, Bell Common, EPPING
☎ 0870 400 9027 Annexe79 ⇔ ♜

MALDON   Map 05 TL80

Forrester Park Beckingham Rd, Great Totham CM9 8EA
☎ 01621 891406 Fax 01621 891406
Tight, undulating parkland course with tree-lined fairways and good views over the Blackwater estuary. Easy walking. Attractive 16th-century clubhouse.
18 holes, 6073yds, Par 71, SSS 69, Course record 69.
Club membership 1000.
Visitors must contact in advance but may not play before noon weekends & bank holidays.
Societies must apply in advance.
Green Fees From £8_£18(mon-fri);£9-£20(sat & sun).
Cards 🖅 🖅 🖅 🖅
Prof Gary Pike
Designer T R Forrester-Muir
Facilities ⊗ ᒪ ♥ ⛳ 🏌 🏠 🚗 ♂ ↑
& Leisure hard tennis courts.
Location 3m NE of Maldon off B1022

Hotel ★★★ 71% Pontlands Park Country Hotel, West Hanningfield Rd, Great Baddow, CHELMSFORD ☎ 01245 476444 17 ⇔ ♜

Maldon Beeleigh, Langford CM9 6LL
☎ 01621 853212 Fax 01621 855232
Flat, parkland course in a triangle of land bounded by the River Chelmer, the Blackwater Canal and an old railway embankment. Alternate tees on 2nd nine holes. Testing par 3 14th (166yds) demanding particular accuracy to narrow green guarded by bunkers and large trees.
9 holes, 6253yds, Par 71, SSS 70, Course record 66.
Club membership 380.
Visitors telephone to check availability, may only play with member at weekends. Handicap certificate required.
Societies initially telephone then confirm in writing.
Green Fees not confirmed.

Designer Thompson of Felixstowe
Facilities ⊗ ∭ ᒪ ♥ ⛳ 🏠
Location 1m NW off B1019

Hotel ★★★ 71% Pontlands Park Country Hotel, West Hanningfield Rd, Great Baddow, CHELMSFORD ☎ 01245 476444 17 ⇔ ♜

ORSETT   Map 05 TQ68

Orsett Brentwood Rd RM16 3DS
☎ 01375 891352 Fax 01375 892471
A very good test of golf - this heathland course with its sandy soil is quick drying and provides easy walking. Close to the Thames estuary it is seldom calm and the main hazards are the prevailing wind and thick gorse. Any slight deviation can be exaggerated by the wind and a lost ball in the gorse results. The clubhouse has been modernised to very high standards.
18 holes, 6614yds, Par 72, SSS 72, Course record 68.
Club membership 750.
Visitors weekdays only. Must contact in advance and have a handicap certificate.
Societies must contact in advance.
Green Fees £40 per day; £25 per round.
Prof Paul Joiner
Designer James Braid
Facilities ⊗ ∭ ᒪ ♥ ⛳ 🏠 🏌 🚗 ♂
& Leisure coaching.
Location At junct of A13 off A128

Hotel ★★★ 65% Posthouse Basildon, Cranes Farm Rd, BASILDON
☎ 0870 400 9003 149 ⇔ ♜

PURLEIGH   Map 05 TL80

Three Rivers Stow Rd, Cold Norton CM3 6RR
☎ 01621 828631 Fax 01621 828060
e-mail: devers@clubhaus.com
Set in landscaped wooded parkland, Kings Course is fully matured with 18-holes, affording good valley views over the Crouch, Blackwater and Roach rivers that give the club its name. With ponds and dog-legs among the challenges it is ideal for beginners and seasoned golfers who have the opportunity to improve their short game. The Jubilee Course offers an alternative in both style and challenge.
Kings Course: 18 holes, 6449yds, Par 72, SSS 71.
Jubilee Course: 18 holes, 4501yds, Par 64, SSS 62.
Club membership 900.
Visitors telephone before visit,must book in advance for Kings Course.
Societies apply in writing or telephone.
Green Fees not confirmed.
Cards 🖅 🖅 🖅 🖅 🖅
Prof Scott Clark
Designer Hawtree
Facilities ⊗ ∭ ᒪ ♥ ⛳ 🏠 ↑ 🏌 🚗 ♂
& Leisure hard tennis courts, video swing analysis centre.
Location 2.5m from South Woodham Ferrers

Hotel ★★★ 71% Pontlands Park Country Hotel, West Hanningfield Rd, Great Baddow, CHELMSFORD ☎ 01245 476444 17 ⇔ ♜

ROCHFORD   Map 05 TQ89

Rochford Hundred Hall Rd SS4 1NW
☎ 01702 544302 Fax 01702 541343
Parkland course with ponds and ditches as natural hazards.
18 holes, 6292yds, Par 72, SSS 70, Course record 64.
Club membership 800.
Visitors	must have handicap certificate. Visitors may not play Tue morning (Ladies) or Sun without a member.
Societies	must contact in writing.
Green Fees	£30 per day/round(£40 sat & bank holidays).
Prof	Graham Hill
Designer	James Braid
Facilities	⛳🏠🛒 ⌀
Location	W on B1013

Hotel ★★★ 69% Hotel Renouf, Bradley Way, ROCHFORD ☎ 01702 541334 24 ⇌ ↑

SAFFRON WALDEN   Map 05 TL53

Saffron Walden Windmill Hill CB10 1BX
☎ 01799 522786 Fax 01799 522786
e-mail: office@swgc.com
Undulating parkland course, beautiful views.
18 holes, 6606yds, Par 72, SSS 72, Course record 63.
Club membership 950.
Visitors	must contact in advance and have a handicap certificate. With member only at weekends.
Societies	must contact in advance.
Green Fees	£35 per day/round.
Prof	Philip Davis
Facilities	⊗ ⅢL ♟️♀⛳🏠 ➤🛒 ⌀ ⌐
Location	N side of town centre off B184

Hotel ★★ 68% The Crown House, GREAT CHESTERFORD ☎ 01799 530515 8 ⇌ ↑ Annexe10 ⇌ ↑

SOUTHEND-ON-SEA   Map 05 TQ88

Belfairs Eastwood Rd North, Leigh on Sea SS9 4LR
☎ 01702 525345 & 520202
Municipal parkland course run by the Borough Council.
Tight second half through thick woods, easy walking.
Belfairs Golf Club: 18 holes, 5840yds, Par 70, SSS 68, Course record 68.
Club membership 350.
Visitors	contact for booking, correct dress code must be adhered to.
Societies	contact 01702 520202
Green Fees	£10.40 (£15.80 weekends).
Prof	Martin Foreman
Designer	H S Colt
Facilities	⊗ ⅢL ♟️♀🏠⛳ ⌀
& Leisure	hard tennis courts.
Location	Off A127

Hotel ★★ 70% Balmoral Hotel, 34 Valkyrie Rd, Westcliffe-on-Sea, SOUTHEND-ON-SEA ☎ 01702 342947 29 ⇌ ↑

Thorpe Hall Thorpe Hall Av, Thorpe Bay SS1 3AT
☎ 01702 582205 Fax 01702 584498
e-mail: thgc@hotmail.com
Parkland course with narrow fairways where placement rather than length is essential.
18 holes, 6319yds, Par 71, SSS 71, Course record 68.
Club membership 995.
Visitors	must contact in advance, with member only weekends & bank holidays.
Societies	apply in writing, only a certain number a year.
Green Fees	£32 per day/round.
Prof	Bill McColl
Designer	Various
Facilities	⊗ ⅢL ♟️♀⛳🏠 ⌐🛒 ⌀
& Leisure	squash, sauna, snooker room.
Location	2m E off A13

Hotel ★★ 70% Balmoral Hotel, 34 Valkyrie Rd, Westcliffe-on-Sea, SOUTHEND-ON-SEA ☎ 01702 342947 29 ⇌ ↑

SOUTH OCKENDON   Map 05 TQ58

Belhus Park Belhus Park RM15 4QR
☎ 01708 854260 Fax 01708 851952
A well established 18 hole course set in beautiful parkland.
18 holes, 5589yds, Par 69, SSS 68, Course record 67.
Club membership 200.
Visitors	no restrictions. Must have proper golf shoes and shirts to be worn at all times. Booking advisable at weekends.
Societies	contact in writing or telephone
Green Fees	not confirmed.
Prof	Gary Lunn
Designer	Capability Brown
Facilities	⛳🏠 ⌐ ⌀ ⌐
& Leisure	heated indoor swimming pool, solarium, gymnasium.
Location	Off the B1335, follow brown tourist signs to course

Hotel Hotel Ibis, Weston Av, THURROCK ☎ 01708 686000 102 ↑

Top Meadow Fen Ln, North Ockendon RM14 3PR
☎ 01708 852239
Set in the Essex countryside with a panoramic view of the area. Some holes are very difficult with the variable wind directions, especially 1st, 6th, 7th and 13th.
18 holes, 6348yds, Par 72, SSS 71, Course record 68.
Club membership 600.
Visitors	welcome Mon-Fri.
Societies	telephone in advance.
Green Fees	£12 per round inc breakfast.
Cards	▭ ▬
Prof	Paul King/Kevin Smith
Designer	Burns/Stock
Facilities	⛳🏠 ⌐ ⌖ ➤🛒 ⌀ ⌐
& Leisure	fishing.
Location	Junct 29 off M25, A127 towards Southend, B186 towards Ockendon, Fen Lane

STANFORD-LE-HOPE — Map 05 TQ68

St Clere's Hall London Rd SS17 0LX
☎ 01375 361565 Fax 01375 361565
All year round golf with views of the Thames, with several challenging par 3's, notably the 223 yard 13th.
18 holes, 6474yds, Par 72, SSS 71, Course record 71.
Club membership 460.

Visitors welcome after 9.30am Mon-Fri, and 10am Sat & Sun. Telephone for times.
Societies welcome Mon, Tue and Thu, telephone for details.
Green Fees not confirmed.
Cards ⊞ ▦ ▦ ▦ ▦ ▦ ▦
Prof David Wood
Designer A Stiff
Facilities ⊗ ⅶ ┗ ♥ ♀ ♨ 🏠 ⛳ 🍴 🏌 🛒 ♿ ♪
Location 5m from M25 E of London on A13, take Stanford turn off in direction Linford, St Clere on the left

Hotel ★★★ 65% Posthouse Basildon, Cranes Farm Rd, BASILDON ☎ 0870 400 9003 149 ⇆ ♨

STAPLEFORD ABBOTTS — Map 05 TQ59

Stapleford Abbotts Horsemanside, Tysea Hill RM4 1JU
☎ 01708 381108 Fax 01708 380345
Abbotts course provides a challenging test for players of all abilities as mature trees, large greenside bunkers and many lakes are all brought into play. The Priors course with its links-type layout gives a fresh challenge on each hole.
Abbotts Course: 18 holes, 6501yds, Par 72, SSS 71.
Priors Course: 18 holes, 5735yds, Par 70, SSS 69.
Friars Course: 9 holes, 1140yds, Par 27, SSS 27.
Club membership 800.

Visitors Abbotts Course midweek only. Priors and Friars, 7 days per week. Advisable to telephone starter on 01277 373344 for Priors and 01277 381108 for Abbotts and Friars.
Societies must be pre booked.
Green Fees not confirmed.
Cards ⊞ ▦ ▦ ▦ ▦
Prof Dominic Eagle
Designer Henry Cotton/Howard Swan
Facilities ⊗ ⅶ ┗ ♥ ♀ ♨ 🏠 ⛳ 🛒 ♪
& Leisure sauna.
Location 1m E of Stapleford Abbotts, off B175

Hotel ★★★★ 72% Marygreen Manor Hotel, London Rd, BRENTWOOD ☎ 01277 225252 3 ⇆ ♨ Annexe40 ⇆ ♨

STOCK — Map 05 TQ69

Crondon Park Stock Rd CM4 9DP
☎ 01277 841115 Fax 01277 841356
Undulating parkland course with many water hazards.
18 holes, 6585yards, Par 72, SSS 71, Course record 66.
Club membership 700.

Visitors may play at weekends after mid-day.
Societies telephone in advance.
Green Fees not confirmed.
Cards ⊞ ▦ ▦
Prof Paul Barham/Freddie Sunderland
Designer Mr M Gillet

Facilities ⊗ ⅶ ┗ ♥ ♀ ♨ 🏠 ⛳ 🍴 ♪
Location On B1007, off A12

Hotel ★★★ 66% The Heybridge Hotel, Roman Rd, INGATESTONE ☎ 01277 355355 22 ⇆ ♨

THEYDON BOIS — Map 05 TQ49

Theydon Bois Theydon Rd CM16 4EH
☎ 01992 812460 & 813054 Fax 01992 813054
e-mail: theydongolf@hotmail.com
The course was originally nine holes built into Epping Forest. It was later extended to 18 holes which were well-planned and well-bunkered but in keeping with the 'forest' tradition. The old nine in the Forest are short and have two bunkers between them, but even so a wayward shot can be among the trees. The autumn colours here are truly magnificent.
18 holes, 5480yds, Par 68, SSS 68, Course record 64.
Club membership 600.

Visitors may not play Wed, Thu, Sat & Sun mornings, ring 01992 812460 in advance to be sure tee is available.
Societies book through the secretary.
Green Fees not confirmed.
Prof R Hall
Designer James Braid
Facilities ⊗ ⅶ ┗ ♥ ♀ ♨ 🏠 ⛳ ♪
Location 2m from junct 26 on M25

Hotel ★★★ 62% Posthouse Epping, High Rd, Bell Common, EPPING ☎ 0870 400 9027 Annexe79 ⇆ ♨

TOLLESHUNT KNIGHTS — Map 05 TL91

Five Lakes Hotel Golf & Country Club Colchester Rd CM9 8HX ☎ 01621 868888 Fax 869696
e-mail: enquiries@fivelakes.co.uk
Two 18-hole courses. The Links is a seaside course with a number of greenside ponds and strategically placed bunkers, while the Lakes is a championship course with large water features and mounding between fairways.
Links Course: 18 holes, 6250yds, Par 71.
Lakes Course: 18 holes, 6767yds, Par 72.
Club membership 534.

Visitors must contact in advance.
Societies must contact in advance.
Green Fees not confirmed.
Cards ⊞ ▦ ▦ ▦ ▦
Prof Gary Carter
Designer Neil Cole
Facilities ⊗ ⅶ ┗ ♥ ♀ ♨ 🏠 ⛳ 🍴 🏌 🛒 ♿ ♪
& Leisure hard tennis courts, heated indoor swimming pool, squash, sauna, solarium, gymnasium, putting green.
Location 1.75m NE on B1026

Hotel ★★★★ 72% Five Lakes Hotel, Golf, Country Club & Spa, Colchester Rd, TOLLESHUNT KNIGHTS ☎ 01621 868888 114 ⇆ ♨
See advertisement on page 92

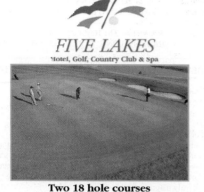

FIVE LAKES
Hotel, Golf, Country Club & Spa

Two 18 hole courses
* The Lakes – championship course
* The Links – par 71
* Covered floodlit driving range
* Putting & chipping greens
* Exclusive Club House
* Hotel with 114 bedrooms
* Fully equipped Country Club & Spa

Colchester Road, Tolleshunt Knights, Maldon,
Essex. CM9 8HX
Tel: 01621 862326
Fax: 01621 869696
E-mail enquiries@fivelakes.co.uk
Web http://www.fivelakes.co.uk

Cards	
Prof	John Hudson/Peter McBride
Designer	Alan Walker/Charles Cox
Facilities	
Location	Witham turn off on A12, signposted

Hotel	★★★ 61% White Hart Hotel, Bocking End, BRAINTREE ☎ 01376 321401 31

Braxted Park Braxted Park Estate CM8 3EN
☎ 01376 572372 Fax 01621 892840
e-mail: estate-office@braxted-park.demon.co.uk
A Pay and Play course in ancient parkland, surrounded by lakes and extremely pretty countryside. Suitable for beginners and experienced players.
9 holes, 2940yds, Par 35, SSS 34.
Club membership 83.

Visitors	welcome weekdays from 7.30am onwards.
Societies	telephone to arrange.
Green Fees	not confirmed.
Prof	Tony Parcell
Designer	Sir Allen Clark
Facilities	
& Leisure	fishing.
Location	2m from A12 near Kelvedon/Witham, at Gt Braxted

Hotel	★★★ 61% White Hart Hotel, Bocking End, BRAINTREE ☎ 01376 321401 31

WOODHAM WALTER   Map 05 TL80

Bunsay Downs Little Baddow Rd CM9 6RU
☎ 01245 222648 Fax 01245 223989
Attractive 9-hole public course, challenging for all abilities. Also Par 3 course.
9 holes, 2932yds, Par 70, SSS 68.
Badgers: 9 holes, 1319yds, Par 54.
Club membership 400.

Visitors	no restrictions.
Societies	Mon-Fri only. Must contact in advance.
Green Fees	not confirmed.
Cards	
Prof	Mickey Walker/Henry Roblin
Designer	John Durham
Facilities	
Location	2m signposted from Danbury on A414

Hotel	★★★ 70% County Hotel, Rainsford Rd, CHELMSFORD ☎ 01245 455700 54 Annexe8

Warren CM9 6RW ☎ 01245 223258 Fax 01245 223989
Attractive parkland course with natural hazards and good views.
18 holes, 6229yds, Par 70, SSS 70, Course record 65.
Club membership 765.

Visitors	contact in advance, weekend pm only, Wed pm only.
Societies	arrange by telephone, confirm in writing, weekdays ex Wed.
Green Fees	not confirmed.
Prof	Mickey Walker
Facilities	
Location	0.5m SW

TOOT HILL   Map 05 TL50

Toot Hill School Rd CM5 9PU
☎ 01277 365523 Fax 01277 364509
Pleasant course with several water hazards and sand greens.
18 holes, 6053yds, Par 70, SSS 69, Course record 65.
Club membership 400.

Visitors	welcome by prior arrangement, handicap certificate may be required.
Societies	Tue & Thu contact in advance.
Green Fees	not confirmed.
Prof	Mark Bishop
Designer	Martin Gillett
Facilities	
Location	7m SE of Harlow, off A414

Hotel	★★★ 62% Posthouse Epping, High Rd, Bell Common, EPPING ☎ 0870 400 9027 Annexe79

WITHAM   Map 05 TL81

Benton Hall Wickham Hill CM8 3LH
☎ 01376 502454 Fax 01376 521050
Set in rolling countryside surrounded by dense woodland, this challenging course provides a severe test even to the best golfers. The River Blackwater dominates the front nine and natural lakes come into play on five other holes.
18 holes, 6574yds, Par 72, SSS 72, Course record 64.
Club membership 470.

Visitors	visitors can book 6 days in advance
Societies	telephone in advance.
Green Fees	not confirmed.

Hotel	★★★ 70% County Hotel, Rainsford Rd, CHELMSFORD ☎ 01245 455700 54 ⇄ ⋔ Annexe8 ⇄ ⋔

GLOUCESTERSHIRE

ALMONDSBURY   Map 03 ST68

Bristol St Swithins Park, Blackhorse Hill BS10 7TQ
☎ 01454 620000 Fax 01454 202700
An undulating parkland course with USGA specified constructed greens, mature trees and numerous water features. Magnificent views over the Severn estuary and surrounding countryside.
18 holes, 6086yds, Par 71, SSS 69.
Club membership 600.

Visitors	must book in advance.
Societies	must contact in advance by telephone/writing
Green Fees	£30 per day; £20 per round (£45/£30 weekends).
Cards	🖃 💳 🖃 📱
Prof	Richard Berry
Facilities	⊗ ⦀ ⓛ ➦ ♟ ⚑ 🛅 ♣ ✧
& Leisure	par 3 academy course.
Location	100yds off M5 junct17

Hotel	★★★ 65% Henbury Lodge Hotel, Station Rd, Henbury, BRISTOL ☎ 0117 950 2615 12 ⇄ ⋔ Annexe9 ⇄ ⋔

CHELTENHAM   Map 03 SO92

Cotswold Hills Ullenwood GL53 9QT
☎ 01242 515264 Fax 01242 515317
A gently undulating course with open aspects and views of the Cotswolds.
18 holes, 6565yds, Par 72, SSS 71, Course record 67.
Club membership 750.

Visitors	telephone in advance, handicap certificate preferred. May play at weekend if no competitions.
Societies	must apply in writing or telephone.
Green Fees	£32 per day; £26 per round (£38/£32 weekends).
Cards	🖃 💳 🖃 📱
Prof	Norman Allen
Designer	M D Little
Facilities	⊗ ⦀ ⓛ ➦ ♟ ⚑ 🛅 ✧
Location	3m SE on A435 and A436

Hotel	★★★ 68% Posthouse Gloucester, Crest Way, Barnwood, GLOUCESTER ☎ 0870 400 9034 122 ⇄ ⋔

Lilley Brook Cirencester Rd, Charlton Kings GL53 8EG
☎ 01242 526785 Fax 01242 256880
e-mail: secretary@lilleybrookgc.fsnet.co.uk
Undulating parkland course. Magnificent views over Cheltenham and surrounding coutryside.
18 holes, 6212yds, Par 69, SSS 70, Course record 61.
Club membership 300.

Visitors	advisable to enquire of availability. Handicap certificate required.May not play Sat or Sun morning

Societies	apply in writing.
Green Fees	£30 per day; £25 round (£35/£30 weekends).
Cards	🖃 🖃
Prof	Forbes Hadden
Designer	Mackenzie
Facilities	⊗ ⦀ ⓛ ➦ ♟ ⚑ 🛅 ♣ ✧
Location	2m S of Cheltenham on A435

Hotel	★★★★ 67% Cheltenham Park Hotel, Cirencester Rd, Charlton Kings, CHELTENHAM ☎ 01242 222021 144 ⇄ ⋔

Shipton Shipton Oliffe, Andoverford GL54 4HT
☎ 01242 890237 Fax 01242 820336
Deceptive, easy walking course situated in the heart of the Cotswolds giving a fair challenge and panoramic views.
9 holes, 2516yds, Par 34, Course record 33.

Visitors	pay & play course no bookings taken.
Societies	welcome.
Green Fees	not confirmed.
Facilities	➦ ♟ ⚑ 🛅 ✧
Location	On A436, south of junct with A40

Hotel	★★★ 68% Charlton Kings Hotel, London Rd, Charlton Kings, CHELTENHAM ☎ 01242 231061 14 ⇄ ⋔

CHIPPING SODBURY   Map 03 ST78

Chipping Sodbury BS37 6PU
☎ 01454 319042 Fax 01454 320052
Parkland courses of championship proportions on the edge of the Cotswolds. The old course may be seen from the large opening tee by the clubhouse at the top of the hill. Two huge drainage dykes cut through the course and form a distinctive hazard on eleven holes. The 527 yard par 5 18th provides a fitting finale.
New Course: 18 holes, 6912yds, Par 73, SSS 73, Course record 65.
Old Course: 9 holes, 6184yds, Par 70, SSS 69.
Club membership 800.

Visitors	no restriction on Old Course, must have a handicap certificate and may only play until after noon at weekends on New Course.
Societies	must contact in writing.
Green Fees	£22 per 27 holes (£27 weekends).
Prof	Mike Watts
Designer	Hawtree
Facilities	⊗ ⦀ ⓛ ➦ ♟ ⚑ 🛅 ♣ ✧
Location	0.5m N

Hotel	★★ 70% Compass Inn, TORMARTON ☎ 01454 218242 & 218577 Fax 01454 218741 26 ⇄ ⋔

CIRENCESTER   Map 04 SP00

Cirencester Cheltenham Rd, Bagendon GL7 7BH
☎ 01285 653939 & 652465 Fax 01285 650665
e-mail: cirencestergolf@compuserve.com
Undulating open Cotswold course with excellent views.
18 holes, 6055yds, Par 70, SSS 69, Course record 65.
Club membership 800.

Visitors	restricted availability at weekends, contact professional shop in advance on 01285 656124.
Societies	telephone Secretary/Manager.

▶

Green Fees £25 per round/day (£30 per weekends & bank holidays).
Cards ▨ ▦ ▨ ▨ ▨
Prof Peter Garratt
Designer J Braid
Facilities ⊗ ℳ ⅃ ■ ♀ ㊀ ⋔ ♦ ♨ ✑ ᵗ
Location 2m N of Cirencester on A435

Hotel ★★★ 68% Stratton House Hotel, Gloucester Rd, CIRENCESTER ☎ 01285 651761 41 ⇆ ↖

CLEEVE HILL
Map 03 SO92

Cleeve Hill GL52 3PW ⟨ *672592* ⟩
☎ 01242 672025 Fax 01242 67444
Undulating and open heathland course affected by crosswinds.
18 holes, 6411yds, Par 72, SSS 71, Course record 69.
Club membership 600.
Visitors bookings taken 7 days in advance. Limited play weekends.
Societies telephone pro shop in advance (01242 672592)
Green Fees £12 per round (£15 weekends).
Cards ▨ ▨ ▨ ▨ ▨
Prof Dave Finch
Facilities ⊗ ℳ ⅃ ■ ♀ ㊀ ⋔ ✑
Location 1m NE on B4632

Hotel ★★★ 64% The Prestbury House Hotel & Restaurant, The Burgage, Prestbury, CHELTENHAM ☎ 01242 529533 8 ⇆ ↖ Annexe9 ⇆ ↖

COLEFORD
Map 03 SO51

Forest Hills Mile End Rd GL16 7BY ☎ 01594 810620 Fax 01594 810623
A parkland course on a plateau with panoramic views of Coleford and Forest of Dean. Some testing holes with the par-5 13th hole sitting tight on a water hazard, and the challenging 18th with 2nd shot over large pond to a green protected by another pond and bunker - all in front of the clubhouse.
18 holes, 6740yds, Par 68, SSS 68, Course record 64.
Club membership 350.
Visitors no restrictions.
Societies contact in advance.
Green Fees not confirmed.
Cards ▨ ▨ ▨
Prof Richard Ballard
Designer A Stiff
Facilities ⊗ ℳ ⅃ ■ ♀ ㊀ ⋔ ♦ ♨ ✑ ᵗ

Hotel ★★★ 67% The Speech House, COLEFORD ☎ 01594 822607 15 ⇆ ↖ Annexe17rm(10 ↖)

Forest of Dean Golf Club & Bells Hotel Lords Hill GL16 8BE ☎ 01594 832583 Fax 01594 832584
Established in 1973 and now matured into an extremely pleasant parkland course. Well bunkered with light rough, a few blind tee shots and water in play on several holes.
18 holes, 6033yds, Par 70, SSS 69.
Club membership 450.
Visitors are required to book tee-off times.
Societies must telephone in advance.
Green Fees not confirmed.
Cards ▨ ▨ ▨ ▨ ▨

Prof John Hansel
Designer John Day
Facilities ⊗ ℳ ⅃ ■ ♀ ㊀ ⋔ ⋔ ♦ ♨ ✑
& Leisure hard tennis courts, bowling green.
Location 0.25m from Coleford town centre on B4431 Coleford to Parkend road

Hotel ★★★ 67% The Speech House, COLEFORD ☎ 01594 822607 15 ⇆ ↖ Annexe17rm(10 ↖)

DURSLEY
Map 03 ST79

Stinchcombe Hill Stinchcombe Hill GL11 6AQ ☎ 01453 542015 Fax 01453 549545
High on the hill with splendid views of the Cotswolds, the River Severn and the Welsh hills. A downland course with good turf, some trees and an interesting variety of greens. Protected greens make this a challenging course in windy conditions.
18 holes, 5734yds, Par 68, SSS 68, Course record 63.
Club membership 550.

Visitors restricted at weekends. Must contact professional in advance 01453 543878.
Societies must apply in advance.
Green Fees £20 per 18 holes in summer (£25 weekends); £13 per 18 holes in winter (£20 weekends).
Cards ▨ ▨ ▨ ▨ ▨ ▨
Prof Paul Bushell
Designer Arthur Hoare
Facilities ⊗ ℳ ⅃ ■ ♀ ㊀ ㊀ ✑
Location 1m W off A4135

Hotel ★★★ 66% Prince Of Wales Hotel, Berkeley Rd, BERKELEY ☎ 01453 810474 43 ⇆ ↖

GLOUCESTER
Map 03 SO81

Brickhampton Court Cheltenham Rd, Churchdown GL2 9QF ☎ 01452 859444 Fax 01452 859333
e-mail: info@brickhampton.co.uk
27 holes, including the county's first intermediate course (9-hole par 31) for the new and developing golfer, set in undulating parkland. The Spa course offers a good golfing challenge, featuring lakes, streams and well placed bunkers.
Spa: 18 holes, 6449yds, Par 71, SSS 71, Course record 66.
Glevum: 9 holes, 1859yds, Par 31.
Club membership 700.
Visitors advance booking recommended, recognised golfing attire to be worn and evidence of golfing ability preferred. ▶

Societies contact for information and booking form.
Green Fees Spa: £30 per day; £19 per round (£35/£25 weekends & bank holidays) Glevum:£6.50 per 9 holes(£8 weekends & bank holidays).
Cards ▨ ▦ ▨ ◪ ▨
Prof Bruce Wilson
Designer Simon Gidman
Facilities ⊗ ⫿ ▱ ♥ ♀ ⚘ ▥ ↘ ⚒ ♦ ⟒
Location Junct 11 M5, A40 towards Gloucester, at Elmbridge Court rdbt B4063 signed Churchdown, approx 2m

Hotel ★★★ 65% Hatherley Manor Hotel, Down Hatherley Ln, GLOUCESTER ☎ 01452 730217 56 ⇄ ☏

Jarvis Gloucester Hotel & Country Club Matson Ln, Robinswood Hill GL4 6EA
☎ 01452 411331 Fax 01452 307212
Undulating, wooded course, built around a hill with superb views over Gloucester and the Cotswolds. The 12th is a drive straight up a hill, nicknamed 'Coronary Hill'.
18 holes, 6170yds, Par 70, SSS 69, Course record 65.
Club membership 600.
Visitors can book up to 7 days in advance.
Societies telephone in advance.
Green Fees £19.50 per 18 holes(£25.50 weekends).
Cards ▨ ▦ ◪ ▨
Prof Chris Gillick/John Whiddon
Facilities ⊗ ⫿ ▱ ♥ ♀ ⚘ ▥ ⌂ ⍾ ↘ ⚒ ♦ ⟒
& Leisure hard tennis courts, heated indoor swimming pool, squash, sauna, solarium, gymnasium.
Location 2.5m SE of Gloucester, off B4073

Hotel ★★★ 72% Hatton Court, Upton Hill, Upton St Leonards, GLOUCESTER ☎ 01452 617412
17 ⇄ ☏ Annexe28 ⇄ ☏

Rodway Hill Newent Rd, Highnam GL2 8DN
☎ 01452 384222
A challenging 18-hole course with superb panoramic views. Testing front 5 holes and the par 3 13th and par 5 16th being affected by strong crosswinds off the River Severn.
18 holes, 6070yds, Par 70, SSS 69, Course record 71.
Club membership 400.
Visitors no restrictions.
Societies telephone in advance.
Green Fees not confirmed.
Prof Tony Grubb
Designer John Gabb
Facilities ⚘ ⌂ ⍾ ⟒
Location 2m outside Gloucester on B4215

Hotel ★★★ 65% Hatherley Manor Hotel, Down Hatherley Ln, GLOUCESTER ☎ 01452 730217 56 ⇄ ☏

Entries with a green background identify courses considered to be particularly interesting

---

LYDNEY   Map 03 SO60

Lydney Lakeside Av GL15 5QA
☎ 01594 843940 (secretary) & 842614
Flat parkland/meadowland course with prevailing wind along fairways.
9 holes, 5298yds, Par 66, SSS 66, Course record 63.
Club membership 350.
Visitors with member only at weekends & bank holidays.
Societies apply in writing to the Secretary.
Green Fees £10.
Facilities ▱ by prior arrangement ♀ ⚘
Location SE side of town centre

Hotel ★★★ 67% The Speech House, COLEFORD ☎ 01594 822607
15 ⇄ ☏ Annexe17rm(10 ☏)

MINCHINHAMPTON   Map 03 SO80

Minchinhampton (New Course) New Course GL6 9BE
☎ 01453 833866 Fax 01453 837360
e-mail: mgc.new@cableclick.net
The Cherington course is set in undulating upland. Large contoured greens, pot bunkers, and, at times, a stiff breeze present a very fair test of skill. The Avening course has a variety of holes including water on the 10th and 13th.
Avening: 18 holes, 6279yds, Par 70, SSS 70, Course record 65.
Cherington: 18 holes, 6387yds, Par 71, SSS 70.
Club membership 1200.
Visitors must contact in advance.
Societies must contact by telephone.
Green Fees £28 per day; (£32 weekends & bank holidays).
Cards ◪ ▨
Prof Chris Steele
Designer Hawtree & Son
Facilities ⊗ ⫿ ▱ ♥ ♀ ⚘ ⌂ ⍾ ⟒ ♦
Location 2m SEof Minchinhampton

Hotel ★★★ 69% Burleigh Court, Minchinhampton, STROUD ☎ 01453 883804
11 ⇄ ☏ Annexe7 ⇄ ☏

Minchinhampton (Old Course) Old Course GL6 9AQ
☎ 01453 832642 & 836382 e-mail: mgc18old@aol.com
An open grassland course 600 feet above sea level. The numerous humps and hollows around the greens tests the golfer's ability to play a variety of shots - often in difficult windy conditions. Panoramic Cotswold views. Two of the par 3's, the 8th and the 16th often require an accurate long iron or wood depending on the strength and direction of the wind.
18 holes, 6019yds, Par 71, SSS 69.
Club membership 700.
Visitors must contact in advance.
Societies must contact in advance.
Green Fees £12 per day/round(£15 weekend).
Cards ▨ ▦ ▨
Facilities ⊗ ▱ ♥ ♀ ⚘ ⌂ ⍾ ⟒
Location 1m NW

Hotel ★★★ 69% Burleigh Court, Minchinhampton, STROUD ☎ 01453 883804
11 ⇄ ☏ Annexe7 ⇄ ☏

NAUNTON   Map 04 SP12

Naunton Downs GL54 3AE
☎ 01451 850090 Fax 01451 850091
Naunton Downs course plays over beautiful Cotswold
countryside. A valley running through the course is one of
the main features, creating 1 par 3 hole that crosses over it.
The prevailing wind adds extra challenge to the par 5's
(which play into the wind), combined with small undulating
greens.
18 holes, 6078yds, Par 71, SSS 70, Course record 67.
Club membership 750.
Visitors   must contact in advance.
Societies   telephone for details.
Green Fees   £19 (£27.50 weekends).
Prof   Nick Ellis
Designer   J Pott
Facilities   ⊗ ⫴ ᒪ ᖯ ■ ♀ ᐃ ☎ ↑ ↘ ♣ ⌀
& Leisure   hard tennis courts.
Location   B4068 Stow/Cheltenham

Hotel   ★★★ Lords of the Manor, UPPER
                  SLAUGHTER ☎ 01451 820243 27 ⇋ ↳

PAINSWICK   Map 03 SO80

Painswick GL6 6TL ☎ 01452 812180
Downland course set on Cotswold Hills at Painswick
Beacon, with fine views. Short course more than
compensated by natural hazards and tight fairways.
18 holes, 4895yds, Par 67, SSS 63, Course record 61.
Club membership 480.
Visitors   member only on Sat pm & Sun.
Societies   must apply in advance.
Green Fees   £20 per day; £15 per round(£20 per round
                  weekends).
Cards   ⊟ ▨ ⑨
Facilities   ⊗ ⫴ ᒪ ᖯ ■ ♀ ᐃ ☎ ↑ ⌀
Location   1m N on A46

Hotel   ★★★ 78% Painswick Hotel, Kemps Ln,
                  PAINSWICK ☎ 01452 812160 19 ⇋ ↳

TEWKESBURY   Map 03 SO83

Hilton Puckrup Hall Puckrup GL20 6EL
☎ 01684 296200 & 271591 (golf shop) Fax 01684 850788
e-mail: puckruphall@hotmail.com

Set in 140 acres of undulating parkland with lakes, existing
trees and marvellous views of the Malvern hills. There are
water hazards at the 5th and a cluster of bunkers on the long

14th before the challenging tee shot across the water to the
par 3 18th.
*Puckrup Hall Hotel & Golf Club: 18 holes, 6189yds, Par 70,
SSS 70, Course record 63.*
Club membership 500.
Visitors   must be a regular golfer familiar with rules and
                  etiquette, must book a tee time, may book up to
                  5 days in advance.
Societies   telephone in advance.
Green Fees   £25 per round (£30 weekends).
Cards   ⊟ ▤ ▦ ▨ ⬛ ⬜ ⑨
Prof   Kevin Pickett
Designer   Simon Gidman
Facilities   ⊗ ⫴ ᒪ ᖯ ■ ♀ ᐃ ☎ ↑ ↘ ♣ ⌀
& Leisure   heated indoor swimming pool, sauna, solarium,
                  gymnasium.
Location   4m N, of Tewkesbury on A38 or junct 1 M50

Tewkesbury Park Hotel Golf & Country Club
Lincoln Green Ln GL20 7DN ☎ 01684 295405
Fax 01684 292386 e-mail: tewkesburypark@corus.com
A parkland course overlooking the Abbey and rivers
Avon and Severn. The par 3, 5th is an exciting hole
calling for accurate distance judgment. The hotel and
country club offer many sports and club facilities
including a well equipped gym with cardio theatre.
18 holes, 6533yds, Par 73, SSS 72, Course record 66.
Club membership 550.
Visitors   must book in advance via pro shop/hotel
                  reservations.
Societies   telephone initially.
Green Fees   not confirmed.
Cards   ⊟ ▤ ▦ ▨ ⬛ ⬜ ⑨
Prof   Charlie Boast
Designer   Frank Pennick
Facilities   ⊗ ⫴ ᒪ ᖯ ■ ♀ ᐃ ☎ ↑ ↘ ♣ ⌀ ↳
& Leisure   hard tennis courts, heated indoor swimming
                  pool, squash, sauna, solarium, gymnasium.
Location   1m SW off A38

Hotel   ★★★ 71% Tewkesbury Park Hotel Golf &
                  Country Club, Lincoln Green Ln,
                  TEWKESBURY ☎ 01684 295405
                  78 ⇋ ↳

THORNBURY   Map 03 ST69

Thornbury Golf Centre Bristol Rd BS35 3XL
☎ 01454 281144 Fax 01454 281177

Two 18 hole Pay & Play courses designed by Hawtree and
set in undulating terrain with exstensive views towards the
Severn estuary. The Low 18 is a Par 3 with holes ranging

▶

from 80 to 207 yards and is ideal for beginners. The High course puts to test the more experienced golfer. Excellent 25 bay floodlit driving range.
High Course: 18 holes, 6154yds, Par 71, SSS 69, Course record 70.
Low Course: 18 holes, 2195yds, Par 54.
Club membership 540.
Visitors welcome at all times, telephone to reserve.
Societies apply in writing.
Green Fees £23 per day; £15 per round(£27/£18 weekends & bank holidays).
Cards ⊟ ⚏ 🗠 ⬡
Prof Simon Hubbard
Designer Hawtree
Facilities ⊗ ⊪ ⬚ ⬤ ♉ ⬠ 🏌 ⬧ 🛺 🏌 ♟ ♦
Location Off A38

Hotel ★★ 67% Thornbury Golf Lodge, Bristol Rd, THORNBURY ☎ 01454 281144 11 ⇆ ⬕

Westonbirt Golf Course

Hotel ★★★ 68% Hare & Hounds Hotel, Westonbirt, TETBURY ☎ 01666 880233
24 ⇆ ⬕ Annexe7 ⇆ ⬕

WESTONBIRT   Map 03 ST88

Westonbirt Westonbirt School GL8 8QG ☎ 01666 880242 Fax 01666 880385
A parkland course with good views.
9 holes, 4504yds, Par 64, SSS 64.
Club membership 150.
Visitors no restrictions.
Societies no reserved tees.
Green Fees £8.50 per day (£8.50 per round;£17 per day weekends).
Facilities ⬤ ⬚
Location E side of village off A433

WICK   Map 03 ST77

Tracy Park Tracy Park, Bath Rd BS30 5RN
☎ 0117 937 2251 Fax 0117 937 4288
e-mail: golf@tracypark.com
Two 18 hole championship courses on the south-western escarpment of the Cotswolds, affording fine views. Both courses present a challenge to all levels of player, with water playing a part on a number of occasions. The clubhouse dates back to 1600 and is a building of great beauty and elegance, set in the 221 acre estate of this golf and country club. ▶

Crown Course: 18 holes, 6443yds, Par 70, SSS 70.
Cromwell Course: 18 holes, 6011yds, Par 70, SSS 69.
Club membership 900.

Visitors	no restrictions, must book tee time(0117 3039123)
Societies	must telephone/write to Robert Ford or Tim Thompson Green
Green Fees	£30 per round (£36 weekends).
Cards	〰️ 🟥 〰️ 🟥 💳
Prof	Tim Thompson Green
Facilities	⊗)Ⅲ ᨒ 💺 ♀ ᗱ 🏠 ⛳ 🏌 ⅋ 🛒 ♂ ✦
& Leisure	hard tennis courts, squash.
Location	S side of village off A420

Hotel	★★★ The Queensberry Hotel, Russel St, BATH ☎ 01225 447928 29 ⇆ ♠

WOTTON-UNDER-EDGE Map 03 ST79

Cotswold Edge Upper Rushmire GL12 7PT
☎ 01453 844167 Fax 01453 845120
Meadowland course situated in a quiet Cotswold valley with magnificent views. First half flat and open, second half more varied.
18 holes, 6170yds, Par 71, SSS 71.
Club membership 800.

Visitors	preferable to contact in advance, at weekends may only play with member.
Societies	must contact in writing or telephone in advance.
Green Fees	not confirmed.
Prof	David Gosling
Facilities	⊗ ᨒ 💺 ♀ ᗱ 🏠 ⅋ 🏌 🛒 ♂
Location	N of town on B4058 Wotton-Tetbury road

Hotel	★★ 70% Egypt Mill Hotel, NAILSWORTH ☎ 01453 833449 8 ⇆ ♠ Annexe10 ⇆ ♠

GREATER LONDON

Those courses which fall within the confines of the London Postal District area (ie have London postcodes - W1, SW1 etc) are listed under the county heading of **London** in the gazetteer (see page 180).

GREATER LONDON

ADDINGTON Map 05 TQ36

The Addington 205 Shirley Church Rd CR0 5AB
☎ 020 8777 1055 Fax 0207 7771701
e-mail: theaddgc@dialstart.net
Designed by Abercromby, the famous golf course architect, and not altered since. Thought and skill are required at every hole.
18 holes, 6242yds, Par 68, SSS 71, Course record 66.

Visitors	handicap certificate required.
Societies	weekdays only, telephone for prior arrangement.
Green Fees	£35.
Designer	Abercromby

Facilities	⊗)Ⅲ 💺 ♀ ᗱ 🏠 ⅋
Hotel	★★★★ 70% Selsdon Park Hotel, Addington Rd, Sanderstead, SOUTH CROYDON ☎ 020 8657 8811 204 ⇆ ♠

Addington Court Featherbed Ln CR0 9AA
☎ 020 8657 0281 (booking) & 8651 5270 (admin)
Fax 020 8651 0282
Challenging, well-drained courses designed by F. Hawtree. Two 18-hole courses, 9-hole course and an 18 hole Par 3 course designed to suit all standards.
Championship Course: 18 holes, 5577yds, Par 68, SSS 67, Course record 60.
Falconwood: 18 holes, 5472yds, Par 68, SSS 67.
9 Hole: 9 holes, 1804yds, Par 31.
Club membership 350.

Visitors	no restrictions. Advisable to phone in advance to play on Championship Course.
Societies	must telephone in advance.
Green Fees	not confirmed.
Cards	〰️ 🟥 〰️ 💳
Prof	Tony Healy
Designer	Hawtree Snr
Facilities	⊗)Ⅲ ᨒ 💺 ♀ ᗱ 🏠 ⅋ 🏌 🛒 ♂ ✦
Location	1m S off A2022

Hotel	★★★★ 70% Selsdon Park Hotel, Addington Rd, Sanderstead, SOUTH CROYDON ☎ 020 8657 8811 204 ⇆ ♠ *See advertisement on page 102*

Addington Palace Addington Park, Gravel Hill CR0 5BB
☎ 020 8654 3061 Fax 020 8655 3632
Hard-walking parkland course, with two (par 4) testing holes (2nd and 10th).
18 holes, 6286yds, Par 71, SSS 71, Course record 63.
Club membership 700.

Visitors	telephone in advance.may play wekdays only.
Societies	weekdays only, telephone in advance.
Green Fees	£30 per day/round.
Prof	Roger Williams
Designer	J H Taylor
Facilities	⊗)Ⅲ ᨒ 💺 ♀ ᗱ 🏠 ⅋
Location	2miles SE of Croydon station on A212

Hotel	★★★★ 70% Selsdon Park Hotel, Addington Rd, Sanderstead, SOUTH CROYDON ☎ 020 8657 8811 204 ⇆ ♠

BARNEHURST   Map 05 TQ57

Barnehurst Mayplace Rd East DA7 6JU
☎ 01322 552952 Fax 01322 552952
Public parkland course with well matured greens. Easy
walking.
9 holes, 4796yds, Par 70, SSS 67.
Visitors   Reasonable standard of dress required. No jeans.
Societies   telephone in advance.
Green Fees £8.45(£11.55 weekends).
Cards   �
Designer   James Braid
Facilities   ⊗ ⅷ ᴸ ♥ ♀ ⚲ 🏠 ⚐ ⚔ ⚙
Location   0.75m NW of Crayford off A2000

Hotel   ★★★ 64% Posthouse Bexley, Black Prince
                  Interchange, Southwold Rd, BEXLEY
                  ☎ 0870 400 9006 105 ⇌ ⋈

BARNET   Map 04 TQ29

Arkley Rowley Green Rd EN5 3HL
☎ 020 8449 0394 Fax 020 8440 5214
Wooded parkland course situated on highest spot in
Hertfordshire with fine views.
9 holes, 6117yds, Par 69, SSS 69.
Club membership 450.
Visitors   may play weekdays only.
Societies   must contact in advance.
Green Fees £22 per day.
Prof   Martin Porter
Designer   Braid
Facilities   ⊗ ⅷ ᴸ ♥ ♀ ⚲ 🏠 ⚙
Location   Off A1 at Arkley sign

Hotel   ★★★ 75% Edgwarebury Hotel, Barnet Ln,
                  ELSTREE ☎ 020 8953 8227 47 ⇌ ⋈

Dyrham Park Country Club Galley Ln EN5 4RA
☎ 020 8440 3361 Fax 020 8441 9836
18 holes, 6369yds, Par 70, SSS 70, Course record 65.
Location   3m NW off A1081
Telephone for further details

Hotel   ★★★ 66% Posthouse South Mimms, SOUTH
                  MIMMS ☎ 0870 400 9072 143 ⇌ ⋈

Old Fold Manor Old Fold Ln, Hadley Green EN5 4QN
☎ 020 8440 9185 Fax 020 8441 4863
e-mail: manager@oldfoldmanor.co.uk
Heathland course, good test of golf.
18 holes, 6447yds, Par 71, SSS 71, Course record 66.
Club membership 520.

Visitors   with member only weekends & bank holidays.
Societies   must apply in writing.
Green Fees £25 per round;£35 per day -midweek(£13/£20
                  Mon-Wed),£30 per round weekends & bank
                  holidays-p.m only.
Cards   ▬ ▬ ▬ ▬ ▬
Prof   Peter McEvoy
Facilities   ⊗ ⅷ ᴸ ♥ ♀ ⚲ 🏠 ⚐ ⚔ ⚙
Location   Off A1000 between Barnet/Potters Bar

Hotel   ★★★★ 71% West Lodge Park Hotel,
                  Cockfosters Rd, HADLEY WOOD
                  ☎ 020 8216 3900 46 ⇌ ⋈ Annexe9 ⇌ ⋈

BECKENHAM   Map 05 TQ36

Beckenham Place Park The Mansion, Beckenham Place
Park BR3 2BP ☎ 020 8650 2292 Fax 020 8663 1201
Picturesque course in the grounds of a public park. The course
varies from open to tight surroundings with the back nine
providing a challenge for both the novice and low handi-
capper. A water-filled ditch comes into play on several holes.
18 holes, 5722yds, Par 68, SSS 68.
Visitors   booked tee times operate contact for details.
Societies   apply in writing or telephone for Society pack.
Green Fees not confirmed.
Cards   ▬ ▬ ▬ ▬ ▬
Prof   Huw Davis-Thomas
Facilities   ⊗ ᴸ ♥ ♀ ⚲ 🏠 ⚐ ⚙
& Leisure   hard tennis courts.
Location   Main Catford/Beckenham road, just off A21

Hotel   ★★★ 71% Bromley Court Hotel, Bromley
                  Hill, BROMLEY ☎ 020 8461 8600 115 ⇌ ⋈

Langley Park Barnfield Wood Rd BR3 6SZ
☎ 020 8658 6849 Fax 020 8658 6310
This is a pleasant, but difficult, well-wooded, parkland
course with natural hazards including a lake at the 18th
hole.
18 holes, 6488yds, Par 69, SSS 71, Course record 65.
Club membership 700.
Visitors   must contact in advance and may not play
                  weekends.
Societies   Wed & Thu only, telephone to book.
Green Fees not confirmed.
Prof   Colin Staff
Designer   J H Taylor
Facilities   ⊗ ⅷ ᴸ ♥ ♀ ⚲ 🏠 ⚐ ⚙
Location   0.5 N on B2015

Hotel   ★★★ 71% Bromley Court Hotel, Bromley
                  Hill, BROMLEY ☎ 020 8461 8600
                  115 ⇌ ⋈

BEXLEYHEATH   Map 05 TQ47

Bexleyheath Mount Rd DA6 8JS ☎ 020 8303 6951
Undulating course.
9 holes, 5162yds, Par 66, SSS 66, Course record 65.
Club membership 330.
Visitors   must contact Secretary in advance, may not play
                   weekends.
Societies   telephone in advance.
Green Fees   not confirmed.
Facilities   ⊗ ⫴ ⤸ ⬤ ♀ ⚒
Location   1m SW

Hotel   ★★★ 64% Posthouse Bexley, Black Prince
                   Interchange, Southwold Rd, BEXLEY
                   ☎ 0870 400 9006 105 ⇥ ⫳

BIGGIN HILL   Map 05 TQ45

Cherry Lodge Jail Ln TN16 3AX
☎ 01959 572250 & 572989 Fax 01959 540672
Undulating parkland course set 600 feet above sea level with
panoramic views of the surrounding Kent countryside. An
enjoyable test of golf for all standards. The 14th is 434 yards
across a valley and uphill, requiring two good shots to reach
the green.
18 holes, 6652yds, Par 72, SSS 73, Course record 66.
Club membership 700.
Visitors   must contact in advance but may not play at
                   weekends.
Societies   must telephone in advance.
Green Fees   not confirmed.
Prof   Nigel Child
Designer   John Day
Facilities   ⊗ ⤸ ⬤ ♀ ⚒ ⌂ ▸ ⛏ ⚒
Location   1m E

Hotel   ★★★ 68% Donnington Manor, London Rd,
                   Dunton Green, SEVENOAKS
                   ☎ 01732 462681 60 ⇥ ⫳

BROMLEY   Map 05 TQ46

Bromley Magpie Hall Ln BR2 8JF
☎ 020 8462 7014 Fax 020 8462 6916 e-
mail: bromley.gov.uk
Flat course, ideal for beginners.
9 holes, 2745yds, Par 70, SSS 67.
Club membership 100.
Visitors   no restrictions.
Societies   apply in writing.
Green Fees   £5.30(£6.95 weekends).
Cards   ▭ ▭ ▭ ▭ ⊙
Prof   Alan Hodgson
Facilities   ⤸ ⬤ ⌂ ▸ ⚒
Location   2m SE off A21

Hotel   ★★★ 71% Bromley Court Hotel, Bromley
                   Hill, BROMLEY ☎ 020 8461 8600 115 ⇥ ⫳

Shortlands Meadow Rd, Shortlands BR2 0DX
☎ 020 8460 8828 Fax 020 8460 8828
Easy walking parkland course with a brook as a natural
hazard.
9 holes, 5261yds, Par 65, SSS 66, Course record 59.
Club membership 500.

Visitors   must be guest of member.
Societies   must contact in advance.
Green Fees   £5 & £10 respectively.
Prof   Mick Taylor
Facilities   ⊗ ⫴ ⤸ ⬤ ♀ ⚒ ⌂ ⚒
Location   0.75m W off A222

Hotel   ★★★ 71% Bromley Court Hotel, Bromley
                   Hill, BROMLEY ☎ 020 8461 8600 115 ⇥ ⫳

Sundridge Park Garden Rd BR1 3NE
☎ 020 8460 0278 Fax 020 8289 3050
The East course is longer than the West but many think
the shorter of the two courses is the more difficult. The
East is surrounded by trees while the West is more hilly,
with good views. Both are certainly a good test of golf.
East Course: 18 holes, 6516yds, Par 71, SSS 71, Course
record 63.
West Course: 18 holes, 6019yds, Par 69, SSS 69, Course
record 65.
Club membership 1200.
Visitors   may only play on weekdays. Must contact
                   in advance and must have a handicap
                   certificate. No advance booking necessary.
Societies   must contact well in advance.
Green Fees   not confirmed.
Prof   Bob Cameron
Designer   Willie Park
Facilities   ⊗ ⫴ ⤸ ⬤ ♀ ⚒ ⌂ ⚒
Location   N side of town centre off A2212

Hotel   ★★★ 71% Bromley Court Hotel, Bromley
                   Hill, BROMLEY ☎ 020 8461 8600
                   115 ⇥ ⫳

CARSHALTON   Map 04 TQ26

Oaks Sports Centre Woodmansterne Rd SM5 4AN
☎ 020 8643 8363 Fax 020 8770 7303
e-mail: golf@oaks.sagehost.co.uk
Public parkland course with floodlit, covered driving range.
18 Holes: 18 holes, 6025yds, Par 70, SSS 69, Course record
65.
The Oaks: 9 holes, 1443yds, Par 28, SSS 28.
Club membership 864.
Visitors   no restrictions weekdays. May not play
                   mornings at weekends.
Societies   must apply in writing.
Green Fees   18 Hole: £14.75 (£18 weekends). The Oaks: £7
                   (£8.50 weekends).
Prof   Horley/Russell/Pilkington
Facilities   ⊗ ⫴ ⤸ ⬤ ♀ ⚒ ⌂ ▸ ⛏ ⚒ ⫳
& Leisure   squash.
Location   0.5m S on B278

Hotel   ★★★ 65% Posthouse Croydon, Purley Way,
                   CROYDON ☎ 0870 400 9022 83 ⇥ ⫳

CHESSINGTON   Map 04 TQ16

Chessington Garrison Ln KT9 2LW ☎ 020 8391 0948
Fax 020 8397 2068
Tree-lined parkland course designed by Patrick Tallack.
9 holes, 1761yds, Par 30, SSS 29.
Club membership 75.   ▸

Visitors	Can't play before 9.00am on Sun.
Societies	Telephone in advance.
Green Fees	£7 per round (£9 weekends).
Cards	⬜ 💳 ⬛ 📳 💋
Prof	Mark Janes
Designer	Patrick Tallack
Facilities	⊗ 🌿 ♣ ♈ 🏠 ⚑ 🏌 🏌 🏏 ∫
Location	M25,junct 9,3miles N on A243

Hotel   ★★ 63% Haven Hotel, Portsmouth Rd,
ESHER ☎ 020 8398 0023
16 ⇄ 🏠 Annexe4 ⇄ 🏠

COULSDON MANOR
HOTEL & GOLF CENTRE
AA ★★★★
GOLF SOCIETIES WELCOME

★ 18 hole course in 140 acre parkland setting
★ Practice Range ★ Golf Tuition ★ Club
Repairs ★ Manor House Hotel ★ Conference
Suites ★ Leisure Facilities including gym,
squash, aerobics, racketball, sauna, sunbed,
tennis ★ Award Winning Restaurant ★ Bars
★ Private Functions

Coulsdon Court Road, Coulsdon,
Nr. Croydon, Surrey CR5 2LL
Tel: 020 8668 0414/Fax: 020 8668 3118
www.marstonhotels.com

CHISLEHURST   Map 05 TQ47

Chislehurst Camden Park Rd BR7 5HJ
☎ 020 8467 2782 Fax 020 8295 0974
Pleasantly wooded undulating parkland/heathland course.
Magnificent clubhouse with historical associations.
18 holes, 5106yds, Par 66, SSS 65, Course record 61.
Club membership 800.

Visitors	with member only weekends.
Societies	weekdays only.
Green Fees	£25 per round/day.
Prof	Mark Lawrence
Designer	Park
Facilities	⊗ 🍴 by prior arrangement 🌿 ♣ ♈ 🏔 🏠 ⚑ ∫

Hotel   ★★★ 71% Bromley Court Hotel, Bromley
Hill, BROMLEY ☎ 020 8461 8600 115 ⇄ 🏠

COULSDON   Map 04 TQ25

Coulsdon Manor Hotel Coulsdon Court Rd CR5 2LL
☎ 020 8668 0414 Fax 020 8668 3118
e-mail: coulsdonmanor@marstonhotels.com
Set in its own 140 acres of landscaped parkland.
18 holes, 6037yds, Par 70, SSS 68.

Visitors	must telephone up to 5 days in advance.
Societies	by arrangement.
Green Fees	£15.25 per round(£18.50 weekends & bank holidays).
Cards	⬜ ⬛ 💳 💷
Prof	David Copsey
Designer	Harry Colt
Facilities	⊗ 🍴 🌿 ♣ ♈ 🏔 🏠 ⚑ 🏌 🏌 ∫
& Leisure	hard tennis courts, squash, sauna, solarium, gymnasium.
Location	0.75m E off A23 on B2030

Hotel   ★★★★ 77% Coulsdon Manor, Coulsdon Court
Rd, Coulsdon, CROYDON
☎ 020 8668 0414 35 ⇄ 🏠

Woodcote Park Meadow Hill, Bridle Way CR5 2QQ
☎ 020 8668 2788 Fax 020 8668 2788
Slightly undulating parkland course.
18 holes, 6669yds, Par 71, SSS 72, Course record 66.
Club membership 650.

Visitors	handicap certificate required, contact professional for details. Visitors may not play weekends.
Societies	must contact Secretary in advance.
Green Fees	not confirmed.
Prof	I Golding
Facilities	🏔 🏠 ∫
Location	1m N of town centre off A237

Hotel   ★★★ 65% Posthouse Croydon, Purley Way,
CROYDON ☎ 0870 400 9022 83 ⇄ 🏠

CROYDON   Map 04 TQ36

Croham Hurst Croham Rd CR2 7HJ
☎ 020 8657 5581 Fax 020 8657 3229
Parkland course with tree-lined fairways and bounded by
wooded hills. Easy walking.
18 holes, 6290yds, Par 70, SSS 70.
Club membership 800.

Visitors	must contact in advance & have handicap certificate. With member only weekends & bank holidays.
Societies	Apply in writing/telephone in advance
Green Fees	£37 per day.
Prof	Eric Stillwell
Designer	Hawtree
Facilities	⊗ 🍴 🌿 ♣ ♈ 🏔 🏠 ⚑ ∫
Location	1.5m SE,of Croydon between South Croydon & Selsdon on B269

Hotel   ★★★★ 70% Selsdon Park Hotel, Addington
Rd, Sanderstead, SOUTH CROYDON
☎ 020 8657 8811 204 ⇄ 🏠

Selsdon Park Addington Rd, Sanderstead CR2 8YA
☎ 020 8657 8811 Fax 020 8651 6171
e-mail: sales.selsdonpark@principalhotels.co.uk
Parkland course. Full use of hotel's sporting facilities by
residents.
18 holes, 6473yds, Par 73, SSS 71, Course record 63.

▶

SELSDON PARK ★★★★
HOTEL & GOLF COURSE   Deluxe
CROYDON, LONDON
Addington Road, Sanderstead, South Croydon, Surrey, CR2 8YA
Telephone: (44) 0208 657 8811 Fax: (44) 0208 651 6171
• 18 hole championship golf course • Visitors welcome 7 days a week • 9 hole putting green • Driving range • Practice area • Relaxed atmosphere everyone welcome • Superb dining facilities • Exceptional weekend breaks • Fully stocked pro-shop • Three PGA golf professionals on site • Set high in the rolling hills of Surrey with panoramic views • Fourball rate – weekday £25.00, weekend £32.50

Visitors welcome, booking advisable, booking 1 week in advance for weekends.
Societies telephone in advance.
Green Fees not confirmed.
Cards ⬤ ■ ■ ▩ ▦ ▩ ▨
Prof Malcolm Churchill
Designer J H Taylor
Facilities & Leisure ⊗ 🕮 ⅃ ♟ ♀ ⚲ 🏠 ⛳ 🍴 ↘ 🚲 ✂ ♦
hard and grass tennis courts, outdoor and indoor heated swimming pools, squash, sauna, solarium, gymnasium.
Location 3m S on A2022

Hotel ★★★★ 70% Selsdon Park Hotel, Addington Rd, Sanderstead, SOUTH CROYDON ☎ 020 8657 8811 204 ⇔ 🐾

Shirley Park 194 Addiscombe Rd CR0 7LB
☎ 020 8654 1143 Fax 020 8654 6733
e-mail: shirleyparkgolfclub.co.uk
This parkland course lies amid fine woodland with good views of Shirley Hills. The more testing holes come in the middle section of the course. The remarkable 7th hole calls for a 187-yard iron or wood shot diagonally across a narrow valley to a shelved green set right-handed into a ridge. The 13th hole, 160yds, is considered to be one of the finest short holes in the county.
18 holes, 6210yds, Par 71, SSS 70, Course record 66.
Club membership 600.

Visitors should contact in advance. With member only at weekends.
Societies by arrangement.
Green Fees £30.
Cards ⬤ ■ ■ ▩ ▩ ▨
Prof Wraith Grant
Facilities ⊗ 🕮 ⅃ ♟ ♀ ⚲ 🏠 ⛳ ♦
Location E side of town centre on A232

Hotel ★★★★ 70% Selsdon Park Hotel, Addington Rd, Sanderstead, SOUTH CROYDON ☎ 020 8657 8811 204 ⇔ 🐾

DOWNE   Map 05 TQ46

High Elms High Elms Rd BR6 7JL
☎ 01689 853232 & 858175 bookings Fax 01689 856326
e-mail: bromley.gov.uk
Municipal parkland course. Very tight 13th, 221 yds (par 3).
18 holes, 6210yds, Par 71, SSS 70, Course record 68.
Club membership 450.
Visitors should phone to book/enquire about availability
Societies telephone to book. Tel 01689 861813.
Green Fees not confirmed.
Prof Peter Remy
Designer Hawthorn
Facilities ⊗ 🕮 ⅃ ♟ ♀ ⚲ 🏠 ⛳ 🍴 ↘ 🚲 ♦
Location 2m E of A21

Hotel ★★★ 71% Bromley Court Hotel, Bromley Hill, BROMLEY ☎ 020 8461 8600 115 ⇔ 🐾

West Kent West Hill BR6 7JJ ☎ 01689 851323
Fax 01689 858693
Partly hilly downland course.
18 holes, 6399yds, Par 70, SSS 70.
Club membership 700.
Visitors with member only at weekends. Must contact in advance.
Societies must apply in writing.
Green Fees £40 per day; £30 per round.
Prof Roger Fidler
Designer W Fowler & J Abercrombie
Facilities ⊗ ⅃ ♟ ♀ ⚲ 🏠 🚲 ♦
Location 0.75m SW

Hotel ★★★ 71% Bromley Court Hotel, Bromley Hill, BROMLEY ☎ 020 8461 8600 115 ⇔ 🐾

ENFIELD   Map 04 TQ39

Crews Hill Cattlegate Rd, Crews Hill EN2 8AZ
☎ 020 8363 6674 Fax 020 8364 5641
Parkland course in country surroundings.
18 holes, 6250yds, Par 70, SSS 70, Course record 65.
Club membership 600.
Visitors all day Mon, 7-9.30am Tue-Fri and after 2pm Wed & Fri,are public timings.Handicap certificate required.Not permitted to use club house facilities.
Societies Wed-Fri; must apply in writing. ▶

Green Fees £13 per 18 holes.
Prof Neil Wichelow
Designer Harry Colt
Facilities ⊗ ⅭⅢ ⅬⅬ ⚑ ⅬⅬ ⚑ ⚑ ⚑ ⚑ ⚑
Location 3m NW off A1005

Hotel ★★ 71% Oak Lodge Hotel, 80 Village Rd,
Bush Hill Park, ENFIELD
☎ 020 8360 7082 7 ⇆ ⌕

Enfield Old Park Rd South EN2 7DA
☎ 020 8363 3970 Fax 020 8342 0381
e-mail: enfieldgolfclub@dial.pipex.com
Parkland course. Salmons Brook crosses 7 holes.
18 holes, 6154yds, Par 72, SSS 70, Course record 61.
Club membership 700.
Visitors must contact the Professional in
advance,weekends and bank holidays by
arrangement only.
Societies must contact the secretary in advance.
Green Fees £27 per round;£36 per day(£36 per round
weekends & bank holidays).
Prof Lee Fickling
Designer James Braid
Facilities ⊗ ⅭⅢ ⅬⅬ ⚑ ⅬⅬ ⚑ ⚑ ⚑
Location M25 jnct 24, A1005 to Enfield to rdbt with church
on left, right down Slades Hill, 1st left to end

Hotel ★★ 71% Oak Lodge Hotel, 80 Village Rd,
Bush Hill Park, ENFIELD
☎ 020 8360 7082 7 ⇆ ⌕

Whitewebbs Park Whitewebbs Ln EN2 9JN
☎ 020 8363 4454
Gently undulating wooded parkland course with an attractive
brook running through four holes.
*Whitewebbs Park Golf Club: 18 holes, 5782yds, Par 68,
SSS 68, Course record 67.*
Club membership 190.
Visitors can play all times, can book in advance
Societies must apply in writing or by phone to Course
Manager.
Green Fees £12.50 (£15.50 weekends).
Cards ▭ ▭ ▭ ▭ ▭
Facilities ⊗ ⅭⅢ ⅬⅬ ⚑ ⅬⅬ ⚑ ⚑ ⚑
Location N side of town centre

Hotel ★★ 71% Oak Lodge Hotel, 80 Village Rd,
Bush Hill Park, ENFIELD
☎ 020 8360 7082 7 ⇆ ⌕

GREENFORD   Map 04 TQ18

C & L Golf & Country Club Westend Rd, Northolt
UB5 6RD ☎ 020 8845 5662
18 holes, 4438yds, Par 64, SSS 63.
Location Junct Westend Road/A40
Telephone for further details

Hotel ★★★ 69% The Bridge Hotel, Western Av,
GREENFORD ☎ 020 8566 6246 68 ⇆ ⌕

Ealing Perivale Ln UB6 8SS
☎ 020 8997 0937 Fax 020 8998 0756
Flat, parkland course relying on natural hazards; trees, tight
fairways, and the River Brent which affects 9 holes.
18 holes, 6216yds, Par 70, SSS 70, Course record 64.
Club membership 600.

Visitors Mon-Fri only on application to pro shop.
Societies Mon, Wed & Thu only by arrangement.
Green Fees £15(7-8am) £30 other times.
Prof Ian Parsons
Designer H S Colt
Facilities ⊗ ⅭⅢ by prior arrangement ⅬⅬ ⚑ ⅬⅬ ⚑ ⚑
⚑ ⚑
Location Off A40 travelling W from London

Hotel ★★★ 69% The Bridge Hotel, Western Av,
GREENFORD
☎ 020 8566 6246 68 ⇆ ⌕

Horsenden Hill Whitton Av, Woodland Rise UB6 0RD
☎ 020 8902 4555
A well-kept, tree-lined short course.
9 holes, 1632yds, Par 28, SSS 28.
Club membership 135.
Visitors no restrictions.
Societies telephone for details.
Green Fees not confirmed.
Prof Simon Hoffman
Facilities ⊗ ⅭⅢ ⅬⅬ ⚑ ⅬⅬ ⚑ ⚑ ⚑
Location 3m NE on A4090

Hotel ★★★ 69% The Bridge Hotel, Western Av,
GREENFORD
☎ 020 8566 6246 68 ⇆ ⌕

Lime Trees Park Ruislip Rd, Northolt UB5 6QZ
☎ 020 8842 0442 Fax 0208 8420542
Parkland course.
9 holes, 5836yds, Par 71, SSS 69.
Club membership 300.
Visitors no restrictions, but advisable to book for
weekends.
Societies contact for details.
Green Fees not confirmed.
Prof Ian Godleman
Facilities ⊗ ⅬⅬ ⚑ ⅬⅬ ⚑ ⚑ ⚑ ⚑ ⚑
Location 300yds off A40 at Polish War Memorial/A4180
towards Hayes

Hotel ★★★ 69% The Bridge Hotel, Western Av,
GREENFORD ☎ 020 8566 6246 68 ⇆ ⌕

Perivale Park Stockdove Way UB6 8TJ
☎ 020 8575 7116
Parkland course.
9 holes, 2667yds, Par 68, SSS 67.
Club membership 250.
Visitors no restrictions.
Societies one weeks notice required.
Green Fees not confirmed.
Cards ▭ ▭ ▭ ▭ ▭
Prof Peter Bryant
Facilities ⚑ ⚑ ⚑ ⚑
Location E side of town centre, off A40

Hotel ★★★ Cumberland Hotel, 1 St Johns Rd,
HARROW ☎ 020 8863 4111
31 ⇆ ⌕ Annexe53 ⇆ ⌕

┌─────────────────────────────────────┐
│   AA Hotels that have special   │
│ arrangements with golf courses are listed at │
│   the back of the guide   │
└─────────────────────────────────────┘

HADLEY WOOD — Map 04 TQ29

Hadley Wood Beech Hill EN4 0JJ
☎ 020 8449 4328 & 4486 Fax 020 8364 8633
e-mail: gen.mgr@hadleywoodgc.com
A parkland course on the northwest edge of London. The gently undulating fairways have a friendly width inviting the player to open his shoulders, though the thick rough can be very punishing to the unwary. The course is pleasantly wooded and there are some admirable views.
18 holes, 6506yds, Par 72, SSS 71, Course record 67.
Club membership 600.

Visitors	handicap certificate required, may not play Tue mornings & weekends.Must contact in advance.
Societies	must contact in advance.
Green Fees	£40 per round:£55 per day.
Prof	Peter Jones
Designer	Alistair Mackenzie
Facilities	⊗ ⅶ ⅐ ♥ ♀ ⅄ 🏠 ⛿ 🦯 ⌇ ⌇
Location	E side of village

Hotel ★★★★♨ 71% West Lodge Park Hotel, Cockfosters Rd, HADLEY WOOD ☎ 020 8216 3900 46 ⇋ ☏ Annexe9 ⇋ ☏

HAMPTON — Map 04 TQ17

Fulwell Wellington Rd, Hampton Hill TW12 1JY
☎ 020 8977 3844 & 020 8977 2733 Fax 020 8977 7732
Championship-length parkland course with easy walking. The 575-yd, 17th, is notable.
18 holes, 6544yds, Par 71, SSS 71.
Club membership 750.

Visitors	may not play Tue & weekends. Must contact in advance and have a handicap certificate.
Societies	must apply in writing.
Green Fees	not confirmed.
Prof	Nigel Turner
Facilities	⅄ 🏠 ⛿ 🦯 ⌇
Location	1.5m N on A311

Hotel ★★★ 69% The Richmond Hill Hotel, Richmond Hill, RICHMOND UPON THAMES ☎ 020 8940 2247 138 ⇋ ☏

HAMPTON WICK — Map 04 TQ16

Home Park KT1 4AD
☎ 020 8977 2423 Fax 020 8977 4414
Flat, parkland course with easy walking.
18 holes, 6584yds, Par 71, SSS 71.
Club membership 550.

Visitors	welcome all week subject to club competitions.
Societies	apply in writing.
Green Fees	not confirmed.
Prof	Len Roberts
Facilities	⊗ ⅐ ♥ ♀ ⅄ 🏠 🦯
Location	Off A308 on W side of Kingston Bridge

Hotel ★★★ 69% The Richmond Hill Hotel, Richmond Hill, RICHMOND UPON THAMES ☎ 020 8940 2247 138 ⇋ ☏

HILLINGDON — Map 04 TQ08

Hillingdon 18 Dorset Way UB10 0JR
☎ 01895 233956 & 239810 Fax 01895 233956
Parkland course west of London, with gentle undulations.
9 holes, 5490yds, Par 68, SSS 67.
Club membership 370.

Visitors	must contact in advance. May not play Thu, weekends, or bank holidays. Handicap certificate required.
Societies	must apply in writing.
Green Fees	not confirmed.
Prof	Phil Smith
Facilities	⊗ ⅶ ⅐ ♥ ♀ ⅄ 🏠 🦯
Location	W side of town off A4020

Hotel ★★★ 70% Novotel Heathrow, Junction 4 M4, Cherry Ln, WEST DRAYTON ☎ 01895 431431 178 ⇋ ☏

HOUNSLOW — Map 04 TQ17

Airlinks Southall Ln TW5 9PE
☎ 020 8561 1418 Fax 88136284
Meadowland/parkland course designed by P. Allis and D. Thomas.
18 holes, 6000yds, Par 71, SSS 69, Course record 65.
Club membership 350.

Visitors	welcome all times. Must contact in advance
Societies	telephone in advance.
Green Fees	£8 per 9 holes;£11 per 18(£14/£17 weekends).
Cards	🪙 ■ 🚊 💳 🗠 🆔
Prof	Tony Martin
Designer	P Alliss/D Thomas
Facilities	⊗ ⅶ ⅐ ♥ ♀ ⅄ 🏠 ⛿ ➘ ⚒ 🦯 ⌇
& Leisure	hard tennis courts, outdoor and indoor heated swimming pools, squash, sauna, solarium, gymnasium.
Location	W of Hounslow off M4 junc 3

Hotel ★★★ 64% Master Robert Hotel, 366 Great West Rd, HOUNSLOW ☎ 020 8570 6261 Annexe94 ⇋ ☏

Hounslow Heath Municipal Staines Rd TW4 5DS
☎ 020 8570 5271
Heathland course in a conservation area, planted with an attractive variety of trees. The 15th hole lies between the fork of two rivers.
18 holes, 5901yds, Par 69, SSS 68, Course record 62.
Club membership 300.

Visitors	pay & play, bookings taken for weekends & bank holidays seven days in advance.
Societies	must telephone and confirm at least 14 days in advance.
Green Fees	not confirmed.
Prof	Joe Smith
Designer	Fraser M Middleton
Facilities	⊗ ⴹ ⅃ ♥ ⚐ ⚑ ⚏ ⚒ ⚘
Location	On A315 towards Bedfont

Hotel   ★★★★ 67% Posthouse Premier Heathrow, Sipson Rd, WEST DRAYTON
☎ 020 8759 2323 610 ⇆ ⁍

ILFORD   Map 05 TQ48

Ilford Wanstead Park Rd IG1 3TR
☎ 020 8554 2930 Fax 020 8554 0822
Fairly flat parkland course with the River Roding running through it. The river borders four holes, and is crossed by three holes. Whilst not a particularly long course, the small greens, and many holes requiring brains rather than brawn, provide a challenging test to all ranges of golfer.
18 holes, 5299yds, Par 67, SSS 66, Course record 61.
Club membership 500.

Visitors	must contact in advance, book with pro on 020 8554 0094.
Societies	telephone for provisional date and booking form.
Green Fees	£20 per day; £16 per round (£19 per round weekends& bank holidays).
Cards	⬜ ⬛ ⬜ ⬛ ⬜
Prof	S Dowsett
Designer	Whitehead
Facilities	⊗ ⅃ ♥ ⴹ ⚐ ⚒
Location	NW side of town centre off A12

Hotel   ★★★ 66% County Hotel Epping Forest, 30 Oak Hill, WOODFORD GREEN
☎ 020 8787 9988 99 ⇆ ⁍

ISLEWORTH   Map 04 TQ17

Wyke Green Syon Ln TW7 5PT
☎ 020 8847 0685 (Prof) & 8560 8777 (Sec)
Fax 020 8569 8392
e-mail: office@wykegreen.golfagent.co.uk
Fairly flat parkland course.
18 holes, 6211yds, Par 69, SSS 70, Course record 64.
Club membership 650.

Visitors	may not play before 3pm weekends and bank holidays
Societies	must apply in writing or telephone in advance.
Green Fees	£35 per day; £25 per round(£28 per round weekends & bank holidays).
Prof	Neil Smith
Designer	Hawtree
Facilities	⊗ ⅃ ⴹ ♥ ⴹ ⚐ ⚒ ⚘ ⚏ ⚒

Location   0.5m N on B454 off A4 at Gillette Corner

Hotel   ★★★ 64% Master Robert Hotel, 366 Great West Rd, HOUNSLOW
☎ 020 8570 6261 Annexe94 ⇆ ⁍

KINGSTON UPON THAMES   Map 04 TQ16

Coombe Hill Golf Club Dr, Coombe Ln West KT2 7DF
☎ 020 8336 7600 Fax 020 8336 7601
A splendid course in wooded terrain. The undulations and trees make it an especially interesting course of great charm. And there is a lovely display of rhododendrons in May and June.
18 holes, 6293yds, Par 71, SSS 71, Course record 67.
Club membership 550.

Visitors	must contact in advance. With member only at weekends.
Societies	must book in advance.
Green Fees	£80 per 36 holes; £60 per 18 holes,reductions in winter.
Cards	⬜ ⬛
Prof	Craig Defoy
Designer	J F Abercromby
Facilities	⊗ ⴹ ♥ ⴹ ⚐ ⚒ ⚏ ⚘ ⚒
& Leisure	sauna.
Location	1.75m E on A238

Hotel   ★★★ 70% Kingston Lodge Hotel, Kingston Hill, KINGSTON UPON THAMES ☎ 0870 400 8115 63 ⇆ ⁍

Coombe Wood George Rd, Kingston Hill KT2 7NS
☎ 020 8942 0388 Fax 020 8942 5665
Mature parkland course with seven varied and challenging par 3's.
18 holes, 5299yds, Par 66, SSS 66, Course record 61.
Club membership 660.

Visitors	must play with member at weekends.
Societies	Wed, Thu & Fri; must contact in advance.
Green Fees	not confirmed.
Cards	⬜ ⬛
Prof	David Butler
Designer	Tom Williamson
Facilities	⊗ ⅃ by prior arrangement ⴹ ♥ ⴹ ⚐ ⚒
Location	1.25m NE on A308

Hotel   ★★★ 70% Kingston Lodge Hotel, Kingston Hill, KINGSTON UPON THAMES
☎ 0870 400 8115 63 ⇆ ⁍

MITCHAM   Map 04 TQ26

Mitcham Carshalton Rd CR4 4HN
☎ 020 8648 4280 Fax 020 8647 4197
A wooded heathland course on a gravel base.
18 holes, 5935yds, Par 69, SSS 68, Course record 65.
Club membership 500.

Visitors	must telephone & book in advance, restricted play at weekends.
Societies	must phone in advance.
Green Fees	£16.
Cards	⬜ ⬛ ⬜ ⬛ ⬜ ⬛ ⬜
Prof	Jeff Godfrey
Designer	T Scott/T Morris
Facilities	ⴹ ⚐ ⚒
Location	1m S

Hotel   ★★★ 65% Posthouse Croydon, Purley Way, CROYDON ☎ 0870 400 9022 83 ⇄ 🐾

NEW MALDEN   Map 04 TQ26

Malden Traps Ln KT3 4RS
☎ 020 8942 0654 Fax 020 8336 2219
18 holes, 6295yds, Par 71, SSS 70.
Location   N side of town centre off B283
Telephone for further details

Hotel   ★★★ 70% Kingston Lodge Hotel, Kingston Hill, KINGSTON UPON THAMES
☎ 0870 400 8115 63 ⇄ 🐾

NORTHWOOD   Map 04 TQ09

Haste Hill The Drive HA6 1HN
☎ 01923 822877 & 829808 Fax 01923 824683
Parkland course with stream running through. Excellent views.
18 holes, 5787yds, Par 68, SSS 68, Course record 67.
Club membership 250.

Visitors   advised to book in advance 01923 825224
Societies   must apply in advance.
Green Fees not confirmed.
Cards   🖴 ▬ ▬ 🖴 ▬ 🖴
Prof   Cameron Smilie
Facilities   ⊗ ⫚ by prior arrangement ⅃ 🍺 🍴 🛒 🏌 ⚐ 🖈 ♣ ♂
Location   0.5m S off A404

Hotel   ★★★ 67% Quality Harrow Hotel, 12-22 Pinner Rd, HARROW ☎ 020 8427 3435
79 ⇄ 🐾 Annexe23 ⇄ 🐾

Northwood Rickmansworth Rd HA6 2QW
☎ 01923 821384 Fax 01923 840150
e-mail: secretary@northwoodgc.com.uk
A very old club to which, it is said, golfers used to drive from London by horse and carriage. They would find their golf interesting as present-day players do. The course is relatively flat although there are some undulations, and trees and whins add not only to the beauty of the course but also to the test of golf.
18 holes, 6535yds, Par 71, SSS 71, Course record 67.
Club membership 650.
Visitors   must contact in advance. May not play weekends.
Societies   must apply in writing.
Green Fees £28 per 18 holes;£36 per day.
Prof   C J Holdsworth
Designer   James Braid

Facilities   ⊗ ⫚ ⅃ 🍺 🍴 🏌 🛒 ⚐ ♂
Location   On main A404

Hotel   ★★★ 67% Quality Harrow Hotel, 12-22 Pinner Rd, HARROW ☎ 020 8427 3435
79 ⇄ 🐾 Annexe23 ⇄ 🐾

Sandy Lodge Sandy Lodge Ln HA6 2JD
☎ 01923 825429 Fax 01923 824319
18 holes, 6347yds, Par 71, SSS 71, Course record 64.
Location   N side of town centre off A4125
Telephone for further details

Hotel   ★★★ The White House, Upton Rd, WATFORD ☎ 01923 237316   60 ⇄ 🐾

ORPINGTON   Map 05 TQ46

Chelsfield Lakes Golf Centre Court Rd BR6 9BX
☎ 01689 896266 Fax 01689 824577
A downland course but some holes are played through the orchards which used to occupy the site. The 9th and 18th holes are separated by a hazardous lake.
18 holes, 6077yds, Par 71, SSS 69, Course record 64.
Warren: 9 holes, 1188yds, Par 27.
Club membership 438.
Visitors   must book in advance.
Societies   telephone in advance.
Green Fees not confirmed.
Cards   🖴 ▬ ▬ ▬ 🖴
Prof   N Lee/B Hodkin
Designer   M Sandow
Facilities   ⊗ ⫚ ⅃ 🍺 🍴 🏌 🛒 ⚐ ♂ ♣
Location   Exit M25 junct 4, on A224 Court Rd

Hotel   ★★★ 71% Bromley Court Hotel, Bromley Hill, BROMLEY ☎ 020 8461 8600 115 ⇄ 🐾

Cray Valley Sandy Ln, St Paul's Cray BR5 3HY
☎ 01689 837909 & 871490 Fax 01689 891428
An easy walking open parkland course comprising an 18 hole par 70 and a 9 hole par 32. Challenging for all standards of golfers.
18 hole: 18 holes, 5669yds, Par 70, SSS 67.
9 holes: 9 holes, 2140yds, Par 32.
Club membership 700.
Visitors   no restrictions, may book up to 7 days in advance.
Societies   by arrangement.
Green Fees £16 (£21 weekends).
Cards   🖴 ▬ ▬ ▬ 🖴
Prof   Gary Stewart
Facilities   ⊗ ⅃ 🍺 🍴 🏌 🛒 ⚐ ♣ ♂ ♣
Location   1m off A20, Critley's Corner junction

Hotel   ★★★ 71% Bromley Court Hotel, Bromley Hill, BROMLEY ☎ 020 8461 8600 115 ⇄ 🐾

Lullingstone Park Parkgate Rd, Chelsfield BR6 7PX
☎ 01959 533793 & 533794 Fax 01959 533795
Popular 27-hole public course set in 690 acres of undulating parkland. Championship length 18 holes, plus 9-hole course and a further 9-hole pitch and putt.
Main Course: 18 holes, 6778yds, Par 72, SSS 72, Course record 71.
9 hole course: 9 holes, 2432yds, Par 33, SSS 31.
Club membership 400. ▶

Visitors	telephone for details.
Societies	must telephone in advance.
Green Fees	not confirmed.
Cards	🖮 🖳 🖳 🖳 🖳
Prof	Mark Watt
Facilities	⊗ ⅏ 🝙 💺 ♀ ⚓ 🏠 🍴 🏌 🚚 ✍ (
Location	Leave M25 junct 4 and take Well Hill turn

Hotel ★★★ 71% Bromley Court Hotel, Bromley Hill, BROMLEY ☎ 020 8461 8600 115 ➯ ♜

Ruxley Park Golf Centre Sandy Ln, St Paul's Cray BR5 3HY ☎ 01689 871490 Fax 01689 891428
Undulating parkland course with public, floodlit driving range. Difficult 6th hole, par 4. Easy walking and good views.
18 holes, 5703yds, Par 70, SSS 68, Course record 63.
Club membership 1000.

Visitors	may book 7 days in advance and regular dress code expected.
Societies	telephone for details 01689 839677.
Green Fees	£16(£21 weekends).
Cards	🖮 🖳 🖳 🖳 🖳 🖳
Prof	Andy Langdon
Facilities	⊗ 🝙 💺 ♀ ⚓ 🏠 🍴 🏌 🚚 ✍ (
Location	2m NE on A223

Hotel ★★★ 71% Bromley Court Hotel, Bromley Hill, BROMLEY ☎ 020 8461 8600 115 ➯ ♜

PINNER   Map 04 TQ18

Grims Dyke Oxhey Ln, Hatch End HA5 4AL
☎ 020 8428 4539 Fax 020 8421 5494
Pleasant, undulating parkland course.
18 holes, 5596yds, Par 69, SSS 67, Course record 61.
Club membership 500.

Visitors	May not play weekends except as guest of a member.
Societies	Apply in writing or by phone.Deposit required.
Green Fees	£25 per round, £30 per day.
Cards	🖮 🖳 🖳 🖳 🖳 🖳
Prof	Nathan Stephens
Designer	James Briad
Facilities	⊗ 🝙 💺 ♀ ⚓ 🏠 ✍
Location	3m N of Harrow on A4008

Hotel ★★★ Cumberland Hotel, 1 St Johns Rd, HARROW ☎ 020 8863 4111 31 ➯ ♜ Annexe53 ➯ ♜

Pinner Hill Southview Rd, Pinner Hill HA5 3YA
☎ 020 8866 0963 Fax 020 8868 4817
A hilly, wooded parkland course.
18 holes, 6330yds, Par 71, SSS 69.
Club membership 710.

Visitors	are required to have handicap certificate on Mon, Tue & Fri. Public days Wed & Thu. Contact in advance.
Societies	Mon, Tue & Fri only, by arrangement.
Green Fees	£30 per day,Mon,Tue & Fri:£15 per round Wed & Thur(£35 per day weekends & bank holidays).
Prof	Mark Grieve
Designer	J H Taylor
Facilities	⊗ ⅏ 🝙 💺 ♀ ⚓ 🏠 🍴 🏌 🚚 ✍
Location	2m NW off A404

Hotel ★★★ 67% Quality Harrow Hotel, 12-22 Pinner Rd, HARROW ☎ 020 8427 3435 79 ➯ ♜ Annexe23 ➯ ♜

PURLEY   Map 05 TQ36

Purley Downs 106 Purley Downs Rd CR2 0RB
☎ 020 8657 8347 Fax 020 8651 5044
e-mail: info@purleydowns.co.uk
Hilly downland course which is a good test for golfers.
18 holes, 6262yds, Par 70, SSS 70, Course record 64.
Club membership 650.

Visitors	must contact in advance & play on weekends only with member.
Societies	must contact in advance.
Green Fees	£35 per day; £25 per round.
Prof	Graham Wilson
Designer	J Taylor/H S Colt
Facilities	⊗ 🝙 💺 ♀ ⚓ 🏠 🚚 ✍
Location	E side of town centre off A235

Hotel ★★★ 65% Posthouse Croydon, Purley Way, CROYDON ☎ 0870 400 9022 83 ➯ ♜

RICHMOND UPON THAMES   Map 04 TQ17

Richmond Sudbrook Park, Petersham TW10 7AS
☎ 020 8940 4351 (office) & 8940 7792 (shop)
Fax 8940 8332/7914
A beautiful and historic wooded, parkland course on the edge of Richmond Park, with six par-3 holes. The 4th is often described as the best short hole in the south of England. Low scores are uncommon because cunningly sited trees call for great accuracy. The clubhouse is one of the most distinguished small Georgian mansions in England.
18 holes, 6007yds, Par 70, SSS 69.
Club membership 700.

Visitors	may not play weekends before 3.30pm.
Societies	must apply in writing.
Green Fees	£50 per day; £32 per 18 holes (£35 per round weekends after 3.30pm).
Prof	Nick Job
Facilities	⊗ ⅏ by prior arrangement 🝙 💺 ♀ ⚓ 🏠 🍴 ✍ (
Location	1.5m S off A307

Hotel ★★★ 69% The Richmond Hill Hotel, Richmond Hill, RICHMOND UPON THAMES ☎ 020 8940 2247 138 ➯ ♜

Royal Mid-Surrey Old Deer Park TW9 2SB
☎ 020 8940 1894 Fax 020 8332 2957
A long playing parkland course. The flat fairways are cleverly bunkered. The 18th provides an exceptionally good par 4 finish with a huge bunker before the green to catch the not quite perfect long second.
Outer Course: 18 holes, 6343yds, Par 69, SSS 70, Course record 62.
Inner Course: 18 holes, 5544yds, Par 68, SSS 67.
Club membership 1400.

Visitors	may not play at weekends. Must contact in advance and bring a handicap certificate.
Societies	must apply in writing.

▶

Green Fees £45 per day winter; £68 per day summer.
Cards ▭▭ ▭▭ ▭▭ ▭
Prof Philip Talbot
Designer J H Taylor
Facilities ⊗ ⓑ ⓟ ♟ ⚲ ⌂ ⌖ ⚐ ⛙ ⚑

Location 0.5m N of Richmond upon Thames off A316

Hotel ★★★ 69% The Richmond Hill Hotel, Richmond Hill, RICHMOND UPON THAMES ☎ 020 8940 2247 138 ⇥ ☏

ROMFORD   Map 05 TQ58

Maylands Golf Club & Country Park Colchester Rd, Harold Park RM3 0AZ
☎ 01708 346466 Fax 01708 373080
Picturesque undulating parkland course.
18 holes, 6361yds, Par 71, SSS 70, Course record 65.
Club membership 700.
Visitors handicap certificate required.
Societies Mon, Wed & Fri only, by arrangement.
Green Fees £20 per 18 holes(£30 weekends).
Cards ▭▭ ▭▭
Prof J Hopkin/D Parker
Designer H S Colt
Facilities ⊗ ⍉ ⓑ ⓟ ♟ ⚲ ⌂ ⌖ ⚐ ⛙ ⚑
Location Junct 28 off M25, 0.5m down A12 towards London, club on right hand side

Hotel ★★★ 69% Posthouse Brentwood, Brook St, BRENTWOOD ☎ 0870 400 9012 145 ⇥ ☏

Risebridge Golf Centre Risebridge Chase, Lower Bedfords Rd RM1 4DG ☎ 01708 741429 Fax 01708 741429
A well matured parkland golf course, with many challenging holes especially the long 12th, the Par 4 13th and Par 5 14th with water and a two tiered green.
18 holes, 6000yds, Par 71, SSS 70, Course record 66.
Club membership 300.
Visitors no restrictions.
Societies must telephone in advance.
Green Fees not confirmed.
Prof Paul Jennings
Designer Hawtree
Facilities ⊗ ⍉ ⓑ ⓟ ♟ ⚲ ⌂ ⌖ ⚐ ⚑
Location Between Colier Row and Harold Hill

Hotel ★★★ 69% Posthouse Brentwood, Brook St, BRENTWOOD ☎ 0870 400 9012 145 ⇥ ☏

Romford Heath Dr, Gidea Park RM2 5QB
☎ 01708 740986 Fax 01708 752157
A many-bunkered parkland course with easy walking. It is said there are as many bunkers as there are days in the year. The ground is quick drying making a good course for winter play when other courses might be too wet.
18 holes, 6410yds, Par 72, SSS 70, Course record 64.
Club membership 693.
Visitors with member only weekends & bank holidays. Must contact proffessional in advance & have handicap certificate.

Societies must telephone in advance.
Green Fees £27.50 per 18 holes;£37.50 per 36 holes.
Prof Chris Goddard
Designer H Colt
Facilities ⊗ ⍉ ⓑ ⓟ ♟ ⚲ ⌂ ⚑
Location 1m NE on A118

Hotel ★★★ 69% Posthouse Brentwood, Brook St, BRENTWOOD ☎ 0870 400 9012 145 ⇥ ☏

RUISLIP   Map 04 TQ08

Ruislip Ickenham Rd HA4 7DQ
☎ 01895 638081 & 638835 Fax 01895 635780
Municipal parkland course. Many trees.
18 holes, 5700yds, Par 69, SSS 68, Course record 65.
Club membership 300.

Visitors telephone in advance.
Societies must contact in advance.
Green Fees £12.50 per round(£18.50 weekends).
Cards ▭▭ ▬▬ ▭▭ ▭▭ ▭
Prof Paul Glozier
Designer Sand Herd
Facilities ⊗ ⍉ ⓑ ⓟ ♟ ⚲ ⌂ ⌖ ⚐ ⛙ ⚑ ⚑
Location 0.5m SW on B466

Hotel ★★★ 67% Quality Harrow Hotel, 12-22 Pinner Rd, HARROW ☎ 020 8427 3435 79 ⇥ ☏ Annexe23 ⇥ ☏

SIDCUP   Map 05 TQ47

Sidcup 7 Hurst Rd DA15 9AE
☎ 020 8300 2150 Fax 0208 3002150
Easy walking parkland course with natural water hazards.
9 holes, 5722yds, Par 68, SSS 68.
Club membership 370.
Visitors contact in advance and may not play weekends or bank holidays.
Societies must contact in advance.
Green Fees £18 per round.
Prof Nigel Willis
Designer James Braid
Facilities ⊗ ⍉ ⓑ ⓟ ♟ ⚲ ⌂
Location N side of town centre off A222

Hotel ★★★★ 71% Bexleyheath Marriott Hotel, 1 Broadway, BEXLEYHEATH ☎ 020 8298 1000 138 ⇥ ☏

SOUTHALL   Map 04 TQ17

West Middlesex Greenford Rd UB1 3EE
☎ 020 8574 3450 Fax 020 8574 2383
e-mail: westmid.gc@virgin.net
Gently undulating parkland course.
18 holes, 6242yds, Par 69, SSS 69, Course record 64.
Club membership 700.
Visitors must contact in advance and may only play at weekends after 3pm
Societies must apply in advance.
Green Fees Tue,Thu,Fri(£20 per round;£35 per day)£10/£12/£25 Mon/Wed/Weekends per round.
Prof I P Harris
Designer James Braid
Facilities ⊗ ⽊ ⅃ ♥ ♀ ♣ 🏠 𝄢
& Leisure squash.
Location W side of town centre on A4127 off A4020

Hotel ★★★ 64% Master Robert Hotel, 366 Great West Rd, HOUNSLOW ☎ 020 8570 6261 Annexe94 ⇄ ♠

STANMORE   Map 04 TQ19

Stanmore 29 Gordon Av HA7 2RL
☎ 020 8954 2599 Fax 0208 9546418
North London parkland course.
18 holes, 5860yds, Par 68, SSS 68, Course record 61.
Club membership 560.
Visitors may not play weekends. Contact professional 0208 954 2646.
Societies phone in advance for booking sheet.
Green Fees £15 per round;£22.50 per day(mon & Fri); £28.50/£36.50(Tues,Wed/Thur).
Prof V Law
Facilities ⊗ ⽊ by prior arrangement ⅃ ♥ ♀ ♣ 🏠 𝄢
Location S side of town centre, between Stanmore & Belmont

Hotel ★★★ 67% Quality Harrow Hotel, 12-22 Pinner Rd, HARROW ☎ 020 8427 3435 79 ⇄ ♠ Annexe23 ⇄ ♠

SURBITON   Map 04 TQ16

Surbiton Woodstock Ln KT9 1UG
☎ 020 8398 3101 (Secretary & 8398 6619 (Pro)
Fax 020 8339 0992 e-mail: surbitongolfclub@hotmail.com
Parkland course with easy walking.
18 holes, 6055yds, Par 70, SSS 69, Course record 63.
Club membership 700.
Visitors must call in advance, handicap certificate required. With member only at weekends & bank holidays. No visitors Tue am (Ladies Day).
Societies Mon & Fri only. Apply year in advance.
Green Fees not confirmed.
Prof Paul Milton
Designer Tom Dunn
Facilities ⊗ ⅃ ♥ ♀ ♣ 🏠 𝄢 𝄢
Location 2m S off A3, take A309 from Hook junct of A3,turn left into Woodstock Lane

Hotel ★★ 63% Haven Hotel, Portsmouth Rd, ESHER ☎ 020 8398 0023 16 ⇄ ♠ Annexe4 ⇄ ♠

TWICKENHAM   Map 04 TQ17

Strawberry Hill Wellesley Rd, Strawberry Hill TW2 5SD
☎ 020 8894 0165
e-mail: secretary@strawberry-hill.fsnet.co.uk
Parkland course with easy walking.
9 holes, 4762yds, Par 64, SSS 63, Course record 59.
Club membership 300.
Visitors must contact in advance, with member only at weekends.
Societies must apply in writing.
Green Fees £20 per 18 holes.
Cards ▦
Prof Peter Buchan
Designer J H Taylor
Facilities ⊗ ⽊ ⅃ ♥ ♀ ♣ 🏠 𝄢
Location S side of town centre off A316

Hotel ★★★ 69% The Richmond Hill Hotel, Richmond Hill, RICHMOND UPON THAMES ☎ 020 8940 2247 138 ⇄ ♠

Twickenham Staines Rd TW2 5JD
☎ 020 8783 1748 & 1698 Fax 020 8941 9134
Interesting tree lined parkland course with water feature.
9 holes, 3180yds, Par 36, SSS 69.
Visitors must book in advance for weekends & bank holidays.
Societies apply in advance
Green Fees £6.50 per 9 holes(£7.50 weekends).
Cards ▦ ▦ ▦ ▦ ▦
Prof Suzy Watt
Facilities ⅃ ♥ ♀ 🏠 𝄢 𝄢 𝄢
Location 2m W on A305

Hotel ★★★ 69% The Richmond Hill Hotel, Richmond Hill, RICHMOND UPON THAMES ☎ 020 8940 2247 138 ⇄ ♠

UPMINSTER   Map 05 TQ58

Upminster 114 Hall Ln RM14 1AU
☎ 01708 222788 (Secretary) 220000 (Pro)
Fax 01708 222788
The meandering River Ingrebourne features on several holes of this partly undulating parkland course situated on one side of the river valley. It provides a challenge for golfers of all abilities. The clubhouse is a beautiful Grade II listed building.
18 holes, 6076yds, Par 69, SSS 69, Course record 66.
Club membership 1000.
Visitors contact in advance, may not play at weekends.
Societies telephone initially.
Green Fees not confirmed.
Prof Steve Cipa
Designer W G Key
Facilities ⊗ ⽊ ⅃ ♥ ♀ ♣ 🏠 𝄢 𝄢
Location 2m W from A127 junct with M25

Hotel ★★★ 69% Posthouse Brentwood, Brook St, BRENTWOOD ☎ 0870 400 9012 145 ⇄ ♠

UXBRIDGE   Map 04 TQ08

Stockley Park Stockley Park UB11 1AQ
☎ 020 8813 5700 8561 6339 tee times Fax 020 8813 5655
Hilly and challenging parkland championship course
designed by Trent Jones in 1993 and situated within two
miles of Heathrow Airport.
18 holes, 6548yds, Par 72, SSS 71.
Visitors	6 day in advance reservation facility.
Societies	please telephone for details.
Green Fees	not confirmed.
Cards	🖾 ■ 🖾 🖾 🖾 🖾
Prof	Alex Knox
Designer	Robert Trent Jones Snr
Facilities	⊗ ⅄ ♊ ♀ ⚲ 🏠 ⚑ ⚘
Location	2m N of junct4 M4

Hotel   ★★★★ 75% Crowne Plaza London -
Heathrow, Stockley Rd, WEST DRAYTON
☎ 01895 445555 458 ⇥ 🐾

Uxbridge The Drive, Harefield Place UB10 8AQ
☎ 01895 237287 Fax 01895 813539
e-mail: higolf@btinternet.com
Municipal parkland course, undulating and tricky.
18 holes, 5750yds, Par 68, SSS 68, Course record 66.
Club membership 270.

Visitors	no restrictions.
Societies	by arrangment.
Green Fees	not confirmed.
Cards	🖾 🖾 🖾 🖾 🖾
Prof	Robert Mullane
Facilities	⊗ ⅄ ♊ ♀ ⚲ 🏠 ⚑ ⚘ 🐾 ⚘ ⚘
Location	2m N off B467

Hotel   ★★★★ 75% Crowne Plaza London -
Heathrow, Stockley Rd, WEST DRAYTON
☎ 01895 445555 458 ⇥ 🐾

WEMBLEY   Map 04 TQ18

Sudbury Bridgewater Rd HA0 1AL
☎ 020 8902 3713 Fax 020 8903 2966
Undulating parkland course very near centre of London.
18 holes, 6282yds, Par 69, SSS 70.
Club membership 650.
Visitors	must have handicap certificate. With member only at weekends.
Societies	must apply in writing.
Green Fees	not confirmed.
Prof	Neil Jordan
Designer	Colt

Facilities	⊗ ⅄ ♊ ♀ ⚲ 🏠 ⚘ ⚘ ⚘
Location	SW side of town centre on A4090

Hotel   ★★★ 69% The Bridge Hotel, Western Av,
GREENFORD ☎ 020 8566 6246 68 ⇥ 🐾

WEST DRAYTON   Map 04 TQ07

Heathpark Stockley Rd UB7 9NA
☎ 01895 444232 Fax 01895 444232
Fairly large, testing, hilly par 4 course suitable both for
beginners and scratch players.
9 holes, 2032yds, Par 64, SSS 60, Course record 64.
Club membership 80.
Visitors	may not play before 11.15am weekends. Restricted play on club compitition days. Telephone for details.
Societies	by arrangement.
Green Fees	£7 per 18 holes(£8 weekends).
Cards	🖾 🖾 🖾 🖾
Designer	Niel Coles
Facilities	⊗ ⅄ ♊ ♀ ⚲ 🏠 ⚑ 🐾 ⚘
& Leisure	heated indoor swimming pool, sauna, solarium, gymnasium.
Location	1m SE off A408 via junct 4 on M4

Hotel   ★★★★ 75% Crowne Plaza London -
Heathrow, Stockley Rd, WEST DRAYTON
☎ 01895 445555 458 ⇥ 🐾

WOODFORD GREEN   Map 05 TQ49

Woodford Sunset Av IG8 0ST
☎ 020 8504 3330 & 8504 0553 Fax 020 8559 0504
Forest land course on the edge of Epping Forest. Views over
the Lea Valley to the London skyline.
9 holes, 5806yds, Par 70, SSS 68, Course record 66.
Club membership 420.
Visitors	advisable to contact in advance. May not play Sat or Sun morning.
Societies	telephone for details.
Green Fees	£14 per round;£16 per day.
Prof	Richard Layton
Designer	Tom Dunn
Facilities	⊗ ♀ ♀ ⚲ 🏠
Location	NW side of town centre off A104

Hotel   ★★★ 66% County Hotel Epping Forest, 30
Oak Hill, WOODFORD GREEN
☎ 020 8787 9988 99 ⇥ 🐾

GREATER MANCHESTER

ALTRINCHAM   Map 07 SJ78

Altrincham Stockport Rd WA15 7LP ☎ 0161 928 0761
Municipal parkland course with easy walking, water on many
holes, rolling contours and many trees. Driving range in
grounds.
18 holes, 6162yds, Par 71, SSS 69.
Club membership 350.

▶

Visitors	must book in advance via course office.
Societies	by prior arrangement.
Green Fees	not confirmed.
Cards	💳
Prof	Scott Partington
Facilities	⛳🏠🏌🔧
Location	0.75 E of Altrincham on A560

Hotel	★★★ 67% Cresta Court Hotel, Church St, ALTRINCHAM ☎ 0161 927 7272 137 ➡ 🐾

Dunham Forest Oldfield Ln WA14 4TY
☎ 0161 928 2605 Fax 0161 929 8975
Attractive parkland course cut through magnificent beech woods.
18 holes, 6636yds, Par 72, SSS 72.
Club membership 680.

Visitors	by prior arrangement. May not play weekends & bank holidays.
Societies	apply in writing or telephone in advance.
Green Fees	£40 per round; £45 per 27 holes (£45 per round weekends).
Prof	Ian Wrigley
Designer	Dave Thomas
Facilities	⊗ ⅢΠ by prior arrangement 🏌 🍺 ♀ ⛳ 🏠 🔧 🛠
& Leisure	hard tennis courts.
Location	1.5m W off A56

Hotel	★★★ 67% Quality Hotel Altrincham, Langham Rd, Bowdon, ALTRINCHAM ☎ 0161 928 7121 89 ➡ 🐾

Ringway Hale Mount, Hale Barns WA15 8SW
☎ 0161 980 8432 (pro) & 0161 980 2630
Fax 0160 980 4414
e-mail: enquiries@ringwaygolfclub.co.uk
Parkland course, with interesting natural hazards. Easy walking, good views.
18 holes, 6494yds, Par 71, SSS 71, Course record 67.
Club membership 700.

Visitors	must have handicap certificate, may not play before 9.30am or between 1-2pm, play restricted Tue, Fri & Sat.
Societies	Thu only May-Sep.
Green Fees	£35 per day Mon-Thu (£45 weekends and bank holidays).
Cards	💳 💳 💳
Prof	Nick Ryan
Designer	Colt
Facilities	⊗ ⅢΠ 🏌 🍺 ♀ ⛳ 🏠 🔧
Location	M56 junct 6, take A538 signposted Hale & Altrincham

Hotel	★★★ 67% Cresta Court Hotel, Church St, ALTRINCHAM ☎ 0161 927 7272 137 ➡ 🐾

ASHTON-IN-MAKERFIELD   Map 07 SJ59

Ashton-in-Makerfield Garswood Park, Liverpool Rd WN4 0YT ☎ 01942 727267 & 719330
Well-wooded parkland course. Easy walking.
18 holes, 6250yds, Par 70, SSS 70, Course record 63.
Club membership 800.

Visitors	with member only weekends & bank holidays. No visitors Wed.
Societies	apply in writing.
Green Fees	£28 per round.

Prof	Peter Allan
Facilities	⊗ ⅢΠ 🏌 🍺 ♀ ⛳ 🏠 🔧
Location	0.5m W of M6 (junc 24) on A58

Hotel	★★★ 66% Posthouse Haydock, Lodge Ln, HAYDOCK ☎ 0870 400 9039 138 ➡ 🐾

ASHTON-UNDER-LYNE   Map 07 SJ99

Ashton-under-Lyne Gorsey Way, Higher Hurst OL6 9HT
☎ 0161 330 1537 Fax 0161 330 1537
A testing, varied moorland course, with large greens. Easy walking.
18 holes, 6209yds, Par 70, SSS 70, Course record 67.
Club membership 700.

Visitors	must contact in advance.
Societies	apply in advance.
Green Fees	£25 per day.
Cards	💳 💳 💳
Prof	Colin Boyle
Facilities	⊗ ⅢΠ 🏌 🍺 ♀ ⛳ 🏠 🛠 🔧
Location	N off B6194

Hotel	★★ 71% York House Hotel, York Place, Richmond St, ASHTON-UNDER-LYNE ☎ 0161 330 9000 24 ➡ 🐾 Annexe10 ➡ 🐾

Dukinfield Lyne Edge, Yew Tree Ln SK16 5DF
☎ 0161 338 2340
18 holes, 5303yds, Par 67, SSS 66.

Location	S off B6175
Telephone for further details	

Hotel	★★ 71% York House Hotel, York Place, Richmond St, ASHTON-UNDER-LYNE ☎ 0161 330 9000 24 ➡ 🐾 Annexe10 ➡ 🐾

BOLTON   Map 07 SD70

Bolton Lostock Park, Chorley New Rd BL6 4AJ
☎ 01204 843067 & 843278 Fax 01204 843067 e-mail: hms@boltongolf.golfagent.co.uk
This well maintained heathland course is always a pleasure to visit. The 12th hole should be treated with respect and so too should the final four holes which have ruined many a card.
18 holes, 6237yds, Par 70, SSS 70, Course record 64.
Club membership 612.

Visitors	not able to play Tue before 2.30pm or on competition days or before 10am and between 12-2pm.
Societies	write or telephone in advance, not accepted Tue, Sat or Sun.
Green Fees	£36 per day; £30 per round (£40/£33 weekends & bank holidays).
Prof	R Longworth
Facilities	⊗ ⅢΠ 🏌 🍺 ♀ ⛳ 🏠 🔧
Location	3m W of Bolton, on A673

Hotel	★★★ 60% Posthouse Bolton, Beaumont Rd, BOLTON ☎ 0870 400 9011 101 ➡ 🐾

Where to stay, where to eat?
Visit the AA internet site
www.theAA.com

Breightmet Red Bridge, Ainsworth BL2 5PA
☎ 01204 527381
Long parkland course.
9 holes, 6416yds, Par 72, SSS 71, Course record 68.
Club membership 350.
Visitors may not play Wed or weekends.
Societies welcome Mon, Tue, Thu & Fri only, apply in advance in writing.
Green Fees £15 (£18 weekends & bank holidays).
Facilities ⊗ ⫵ ⅃ ♥ ♀ ♨
Location E side of town centre off A58

Hotel ★★★ 60% Posthouse Bolton, Beaumont Rd, BOLTON ☎ 0870 400 9011 101 ⇆ ♜

Deane Broadford Rd, Deane BL3 4NS
☎ 01204 61944 (professional) 651808(secretary)
Undulating parkland course with small ravines on approaches to some holes.
18 holes, 5652yds, Par 68, SSS 67, Course record 64.
Club membership 470.
Visitors must be a member of a golf club or member's guest. Restricted weekends. Must contact in advance.
Societies must telephone in advance and confirm in writing.
Green Fees £20 per round (£25 weekends).
Prof David Martindale
Facilities ⊗ ⫵ ⅃ ♥ ♀ ♨ ♜ ♧ ♂
Location 1m from exit 5 on M61 towards Bolton

Hotel ★★★ 60% Posthouse Bolton, Beaumont Rd, BOLTON ☎ 0870 400 9011 101 ⇆ ♜

Dunscar Longworth Ln, Bromley Cross BL7 9QY
☎ 01204 303321
A scenic moorland course with panoramic views. A warm friendly club.
18 holes, 6085yds, Par 71, SSS 69, Course record 65.
Club membership 600.
Visitors must telephone 01204 592992 in advance and have a handicap certificate.
Societies must apply in writing.
Green Fees £20 per round (£30 weekends & bank holidays).
Prof Gary Treadgold
Facilities ⊗ ⫵ ⅃ ♥ ♀ ♨ ♜ ♂
Location 2m N off A666

Hotel ★★★ 60% Posthouse Bolton, Beaumont Rd, BOLTON ☎ 0870 400 9011 101 ⇆ ♜

Great Lever & Farnworth Plodder Ln, Farnworth
BL4 0LQ ☎ 01204 656137 Fax 01204 656137
Downland course with easy walking.
18 holes, 6064yds, Par 70, SSS 69, Course record 67.
Club membership 600.
Visitors must contact in advance, weekend by prior arrangement. handicap certificate required.
Societies must contact in advance.
Green Fees £20 (£27 weekends & bank holidays).
Prof Tony Howarth
Facilities ⊗ ⫵ ⅃ ♥ ♀ ♨ ♂
Location 1m junct 4 M61

Hotel ★★★ 60% Posthouse Bolton, Beaumont Rd, BOLTON ☎ 0870 400 9011 101 ⇆ ♜

Harwood Springfield, Roading Brook Rd, Harwood BL2
4JD ☎ 01204 522878 & 524233 (Sec) Fax 01204 524233
Mainly flat parkland course.
18 holes, 5778yds, Par 70, SSS 69.
Club membership 584.
Visitors must be members of a golf club and hold a current handicap certificate. May not play at weekends.
Societies contact the Secretary by telephone or in writing.
Green Fees not confirmed.
Prof A Rogers
Designer G Shuttleworth
Facilities ⊗ ⫵ ⅃ ♥ ♀ ♨ ♜
Location 2.5m NE off B6196

Hotel ★★★ 60% Posthouse Bolton, Beaumont Rd, BOLTON ☎ 0870 400 9011 101 ⇆ ♜

Old Links Chorley Old Rd, Montserrat BL1 5SU
☎ 01204 842307 Fax 01204 842307 ext 25
Championship moorland course.
18 holes, 6406yds, Par 72, SSS 72.
Club membership 600.
Visitors must contact in advance and may only play weekends with member.
Societies apply by letter or telephone.
Green Fees £30 per day (£40 weekends & bank holidays).
Prof Paul Horridge
Designer Dr Alistair MacKenzie
Facilities ⊗ ⫵ ⅃ ♥ ♀ ♨ ♜ ♂
Location NW of town centre on B6226

Hotel ★★★ 60% Posthouse Bolton, Beaumont Rd, BOLTON ☎ 0870 400 9011 101 ⇆ ♜

Regent Park Links Rd, Chorley New Rd BL2 9XX
☎ 01204 844170
Parkland course.
18 holes, 6130yds, Par 70, SSS 69, Course record 67.
Club membership 200.
Visitors must book 6 days in advance.
Societies must telephone 01204 495421 in advance.
Green Fees not confirmed.
Cards ▣
Prof P A Wells
Facilities ⊗ ⫵ ⅃ ♥ ♀ ♨ ♜ ⚑ ♂
Location 3.5m W off A673

Hotel ★★★ 60% Posthouse Bolton, Beaumont Rd, BOLTON ☎ 0870 400 9011 101 ⇆ ♜

BRAMHALL   Map 07 SJ88

Bramall Park 20 Manor Rd SK7 3LY
☎ 0161 485 3119 & 7101 (secretary) Fax 0161 485 7101
Well-wooded parkland course with splendid views of the Pennines.
18 holes, 6043yds, Par 70, SSS 69.
Club membership 829.
Visitors must contact resident professional or club secretary.
Societies apply in writing.
Green Fees £30 per day/round (£40 weekends & bank holidays).
Prof M Proffitt
Facilities ⊗ ⫵ ⅃ ♥ ♀ ♨ ♜ ♧ ♂
Location NW side of town centre off B5149

▶

Hotel ★★★ 65% County Hotel Bramhall, Bramhall Ln South, BRAMHALL
☎ 0161 455 9988 65 ⇆ ⋔

Bramhall Ladythorn Rd SK7 2EY
☎ 0161 439 6092 Fax 0161 439 0264
Undulating parkland course, easy walking.
18 holes, 6340yds, Par 70, SSS 70.
Club membership 700.
Visitors must contact in advance.
Societies apply in writing.
Green Fees not confirmed.
Prof Richard Green
Facilities ⊗ ⓑ ♥ ♀ ⅄ 🏠 ⋔
Location E side of town centre off A5102

Hotel ★★★ 65% County Hotel Bramhall, Bramhall Ln South, BRAMHALL
☎ 0161 455 9988 65 ⇆ ⋔

BROMLEY CROSS   Map 07 SD71

Turton Wood End Farm, Chapeltown Rd BL7 9QH
☎ 01204 852235
Moorland course with panoramic views. A wide variety of holes which challenge any golfer's technique.
18 holes, 6159yds, Par 70, SSS 70, Course record 70.
Club membership 450.
Visitors avoid 10.30-12.30;2.00-3.00pm. Wed Ladies day. Sat tee available after last competition.Restricted Sun.
Societies must contact in writing.
Green Fees £20 per day (£25 per round weekends & bank holidays).
Designer Alex Herd
Facilities ⊗ ⓑ ♥ ♀ ⅄
Location 3m N on A666

Hotel ★★★ 60% Posthouse Bolton, Beaumont Rd, BOLTON ☎ 0870 400 9011 101 ⇆ ⋔

BURY   Map 07 SD81

Bury Unsworth Hall, Blackford Bridge, Manchester Rd BL9 9TJ ☎ 0161 766 4897 Fax 0161 796 3480
Moorland course, difficult in part. Tight and good test of golf.
18 holes, 5961yds, Par 69, SSS 69, Course record 64.
Club membership 650.
Visitors may not normally play at weekends. Must contact in advance.
Societies telephone 0161 766 4897.
Green Fees not confirmed.
Designer Mackenzie
Facilities ⅄ 🏠 ⋔
Location 2m S on A56

Hotel ★★★ 66% Bolholt Country Park Hotel, Walshaw Rd, BURY
☎ 0161 762 4000 66 ⇆ ⋔

Lowes Park Hilltop, Lowes Rd BL9 6SU
☎ 0161 764 1231 Fax 0161 763 9503
Moorland course, with easy walking. Exposed outlook with good views.
9 holes, 6009yds, Par 70, SSS 69, Course record 65.
Club membership 400.

Visitors may not play Wed & Sat, by appointment Sun. Must contact in advance.
Societies apply in writing.
Green Fees not confirmed.
Facilities ⊗ ⅏ ⓑ ♥ ♀ ⅄
Location N side of town centre off A56

Hotel ★★★ 66% Bolholt Country Park Hotel, Walshaw Rd, BURY
☎ 0161 762 4000 66 ⇆ ⋔

Walmersley Garretts Close, Walmersley BL9 6TE
☎ 0161 764 1429 & 0161 764 7770 Fax 01706 827618
Moorland hillside course, with wide fairways, large greens and extensive views. Testing holes: 2nd (484 yds) par 5; 5th par 4 with severe dogleg and various hazards.
18 holes, 5341yds, Par 69, SSS 67.
Club membership 475.
Visitors welcome by arrangement with Secretary. May only play with member at weekend,
Societies must apply in writing.
Green Fees £20 per day.
Prof P Thorpe
Designer S Marnoch
Facilities ⊗ ⅏ ⓑ ♥ ♀ ⅄ 🏠 ⋔
Location 2m N off A56

Hotel ★★★ 66% Bolholt Country Park Hotel, Walshaw Rd, BURY
☎ 0161 762 4000 66 ⇆ ⋔

CHEADLE   Map 07 SJ88

Cheadle Cheadle Rd SK8 1HW ☎ 0161 491 4452
Parkland course with hazards on every hole, from sand bunkers and copses to a stream across six of the fairways.
9 holes, 5006yds, Par 64, SSS 65.
Club membership 425.
Visitors may not play Tue & Sat, & restricted Sun. Must contact in advance and have a handicap certificate and be member of a bona-fide golf club.
Societies apply in writing to secretary
Green Fees not confirmed.
Prof S Booth
Designer T Renouf
Facilities ⊗ ⅏ ⓑ ♥ ♀ ⅄ 🏠 ⋔
Location S side of village off A5149

Hotel ★★ 67% The Wycliffe Hotel, 74 Edgeley Rd, Edgeley, STOCKPORT
☎ 0161 477 5395 20 ⇆ ⋔

DENTON   Map 07 SJ99

Denton Manchester Rd M34 2GG ☎ 0161 336 3218
Easy, flat parkland course with brook running through. Notable hole is one called 'Death and Glory'.
18 holes, 6541yds, Par 72, SSS 71, Course record 66.
Club membership 585.
Visitors must contact in advance & may not play summer weekends.
Societies apply in advance.
Green Fees not confirmed.
Prof M Hollingworth
Designer R McCauley
Facilities ⊗ ⓑ ♥ ♀ ⅄ 🏠 ⋔
Location 1.5m W on A57

▶

Hotel   ★★ 71% York House Hotel, York Place, Richmond St, ASHTON-UNDER-LYNE ☎ 0161 330 9000 24 ⇔ ╟ Annexe10 ⇔ ╟

FAILSWORTH   Map 07 SD80

Brookdale Medlock Rd M35 9WQ
☎ 0161 681 4534 Fax 0161 688 6872
e-mail: info@brookdalegolfclub.co.uk
Undulating parkland course, with river crossed 5 times in play. Hard walking.
18 holes, 5841yds, Par 68, SSS 68, Course record 64.
Club membership 700.
Visitors   advisable to contact in advance. May only play as guest of member at weekends.
Societies   must contact in advance.
Green Fees not confirmed.
Prof   Tony Cuppello
Facilities ⊗ ╗ ╚ ╘ ♀ ╩ ╣ ➤ ⚒ ♂
Location   N side of Manchester

Hotel   ★★ 71% York House Hotel, York Place, Richmond St, ASHTON-UNDER-LYNE ☎ 0161 330 9000 24 ⇔ ╟ Annexe10 ⇔ ╟

FLIXTON   Map 07 SJ79

William Wroe Municipal Pennybridge Ln, Flixton Rd M41 5DX ☎ 0161 928 9542
18 holes, 4395yds, Par 68, SSS 65.
Location   E side of village off B5158
Telephone for further details

Hotel   ★★ 63% Trafford Hall Hotel, 23 Talbot Rd, Old Trafford, MANCHESTER ☎ 0161 848 7791 31 ⇔ ╟ Annexe3 ⇔ ╟

GATLEY   Map 07 SJ88

Gatley Waterfall Farm, Styal Rd, Heald Green SK8 3TW ☎ 0161 437 2091
Parkland course. Moderately testing.
9 holes, 5934yds, Par 68, SSS 68.
Club membership 400.
Visitors   may not play Tue & Sat. With member only weekends. Handicap certificate required.
Societies   apply in writing.
Green Fees £21.
Prof   James Hopley
Facilities ⊗ ╗ ╚ ╘ ♀ ╩ ╣
Location   S side of village off B5166

Hotel   ★★★★ 65% Belfry House Hotel, Stanley Rd, HANDFORTH ☎ 0161 437 0511 80 ⇔ ╟

HALE   Map 07 SJ78

Hale Rappax Rd WA15 0NU ☎ 0161 980 4225
9 holes, 5780yds, Par 70, SSS 68, Course record 65.
Location   Off Bankhall Lane close to Altrincham Priory Hospital
Telephone for further details

Hotel   ★★★ 67% Quality Hotel Altrincham, Langham Rd, Bowdon, ALTRINCHAM ☎ 0161 928 7121 89 ⇔ ╟

HAZEL GROVE   Map 07 SJ98

Hazel Grove Buxton Rd SK7 6LU ☎ 0161 483 3978
Testing parkland course with tricky greens and water hazards coming into play on several holes.
18 holes, 6310yds, Par 71, SSS 71, Course record 62.
Club membership 600.
Visitors   must contact in advance tel: 0161 483 7272.
Societies   must apply in writing, Thu & Fri only.
Green Fees £30 per day (£35 weekends & bank holidays).
Prof   M E Hill
Facilities ⊗ ╗ ╚ ╘ ♀ ╩ ╣ ➤ ♂
Location   1m E off A6

Hotel   ★★★ 65% County Hotel Bramhall, Bramhall Ln South, BRAMHALL ☎ 0161 455 9988 65 ⇔ ╟

HINDLEY   Map 07 SD60

Hindley Hall Hall Ln WN2 2SQ
☎ 01942 255131 Fax 01942 253871
Parkland course with mostly easy walking.
18 holes, 5913yds, Par 69, SSS 68, Course record 64.
Club membership 430.
Visitors   must contact in advance, may not play on weekend competition days.
Societies   apply in advance to Secretary
Green Fees £20 per day (£27 weekends).
Prof   Neil Brazell
Facilities ⊗ ╗ ╚ ╘ ♀ ╩ ╣ ♂
Location   1m N off A58

Hotel   ★★★ 65% Quality Hotel Wigan, Riverway, WIGAN ☎ 01942 826888 88 ⇔ ╟

HYDE   Map 07 SJ99

Werneth Low Werneth Low Rd, Gee Cross SK14 3AF
☎ 0161 368 2503 336 9496(secretary) Fax 0161 320 0053
e-mail: mel.gregg@btinternet.com
Hard walking but good views from this moorland course. Exposed to wind.
11 holes, 6113yds, Par 70, SSS 70, Course record 66.
Club membership 375.
Visitors   may not play Tue mornings, Thu afternoons or Sun and by prior arrangement on Sat.
Societies   must contact in at least 14 days in advance.
Green Fees £18 (£24 weekends).
Cards   ▭ ▭ ▭ ▭ ▭
Prof   Tony Bacchus
Facilities ⊗ ╗ ╚ ╘ ♀ ╩ ╣ ♂
Location   2m S of town centre

Hotel   ★★ 77% Wind in the Willows Hotel, Derbyshire Level, Sheffield Rd, GLOSSOP ☎ 01457 868001 12 ⇔ ╟

> Entries with a green background identify courses considered to be particularly interesting

KEARSLEY   Map 07 SD70

Manor Moss Ln BL4 8SF
☎ 01204 701027 Fax 01204 796914
Parkland course with water features. Treelined fairways
including evergreen and deciduous trees. Suitable for players
of all levels.
18 holes, 5010yds, Par 66, SSS 64, Course record 65.
Club membership 500.
Visitors   book in advance. Must observe dress code.
Societies   contact in advance for details.
Green Fees not confirmed.
Cards   🔲 ■ 🔳 🔳
Designer   Jeff Yates
Facilities   ⊗ ﹉ ﾋ 🍺 ♀ ⚒ 🏠 ⛳ ✓
& Leisure   fishing.
Location   Off A666, Manchester Rd

Hotel   ★★★ 66% Novotel Manchester West,
Worsley Brow, WORSLEY
☎ 0161 799 3535 119 ⇄ 🐾

LITTLEBOROUGH   Map 07 SD91

Whittaker Whittaker Ln OL15 0LH ☎ 01706 378310
Moorland 9-hole course with outstanding views of
Hollingworth Lake Countryside Park and the Pennine Hills.
9 holes, 5632yds, Par 68, SSS 67, Course record 61.
Club membership 210.
Visitors   welcome except for Tue pm and Sun.
Societies   apply to Secretary.
Green Fees not confirmed.
Facilities   ♀ ⚒
Location   1.5m out of Littleborough off A58

Hotel   ★★★★ 64% Norton Grange Hotel,
Manchester Rd, Castleton, ROCHDALE
☎ 01706 630788   51 ⇄ 🐾

MANCHESTER   Map 07 SJ89

Blackley Victoria Ave East, Blackley M9 7HW
☎ 0161 643 2980 & 654 7770 Fax 0161 653 8300
Parkland course. Course crossed by footpath.
18 holes, 6237yds, Par 70, SSS 70.
Club membership 800.
Visitors   with member only Thu, weekends and bank
holidays.
Societies   apply in advance.
Green Fees £24 per day.
Prof   Craig Gould
Facilities   ⊗ ﹉ ﾋ 🍺 ♀ ⚒ 🏠 ⛳ ✓ ✓
Location   4m N of city centre, on Rochdale Rd

Hotel   ★★★ 72% Malmaison, Piccadilly,
MANCHESTER ☎ 0161 278 1000 112 ⇄ 🐾

Chorlton-cum-Hardy Barlow Hall, Barlow Hall Rd,
Chorlton-cum-Hardy M21 7JJ
☎ 0161 881 5830 Fax 0161 881 4532
Meadowland course with trees, stream and several ditches.
18 holes, 5980yds, Par 70, SSS 69, Course record 64.
Club membership 802.
Visitors   handicap certificate required.
Societies   on Thu & Fri only by prior booking.
Green Fees £26 per day (£30 weekends).
Prof   David Valentine

Facilities   ⊗ ﹉ ﾋ 🍺 ♀ ⚒ 🏠 ⛳ ✓
Location   4m S of Manchester A5103/A5145

Hotel   ★★★ 67% Willow Bank Hotel, 340-342
Wilmslow Rd, Fallowfield, MANCHESTER
☎ 0161 224 0461 117 ⇄ 🐾

Davyhulme Park Gleneagles Rd, Davyhulme M41 8SA
☎ 0161 748 2260 Fax 0161 747 4067
Parkland course.
18 holes, 6237yds, Par 72, SSS 70, Course record 67.
Club membership 680.
Visitors   may play Mon, Tue & Thu.
Societies   telephone in advance.
Green Fees not confirmed.
Prof   Dean Butler
Facilities   ⊗ ﾋ 🍺 ♀ ⚒ 🏠 ✓
& Leisure   snooker.
Location   8m S adj to Trafford General Hospital

Hotel   ★★ 63% Trafford Hall Hotel, 23 Talbot Rd,
Old Trafford, MANCHESTER
☎ 0161 848 7791 31 ⇄ 🐾 Annexe3 ⇄ 🐾

Didsbury Ford Ln, Northenden M22 4NQ
☎ 0161 998 9278 Fax 0161 998 9278
Parkland course.
18 holes, 6273yds, Par 70, SSS 70, Course record 63.
Club membership 750.
Visitors   advised to check dates/times with manager or
professional.
Societies   Thu & Fri, must contact in advance.
Green Fees £28 per day (£32 weekends).
Prof   Peter Barber
Facilities   ⊗ ﹉ ﾋ 🍺 ♀ ⚒ 🏠 ❧ ⚒ ✓
Location   6m S of city centre off A5145

Hotel   ★★★ 64% Posthouse Manchester, Palatine Rd,
Northenden, MANCHESTER
☎ 0870 400 9056 190 ⇄ 🐾

Fairfield "Boothdale", Booth Rd, Audenshaw M34 5GA
☎ 0161 370 1641 & 370 2292
Parkland course set around a reservoir. Course demands
particularly accurate placing of shots.
18 holes, 4956yds, Par 68, SSS 66, Course record 65.
Club membership 450.
Visitors   may not play mornings at weekends & may be
restricted on Wed & Thu.
Societies   prior booking through Secretary.
Green Fees not confirmed.
Prof   Stephen Pownell
Facilities   ⊗ ﹉ ﾋ 🍺 ♀ ⚒ 🏠 ✓
Location   5m E of Manchester, off A635

Hotel   ★★ 71% York House Hotel, York Place,
Richmond St, ASHTON-UNDER-LYNE
☎ 0161 330 9000 24 ⇄ 🐾 Annexe10 ⇄ 🐾

Marriott Worsley Park Hotel & Country Club
Worsley Park, Worsley M28 2QT
☎ 0161 975 2043 Fax 0161 975 2058
Set in 200 acres of parkland with a range of tee positions,
8 lakes and 70 strategically placed bunkers and providing an
exciting challenge to golfers of all abilities, very often
requiring brains rather than brawn to make a successful score.
Marriott Worsley Park Hotel & Country Club: 18 holes,
6611yds, Par 71, SSS 72.
Club membership 400.

▶

Marriott-Worsley Park

Visitors must have a handicap certificate. Must contact in advance.
Societies weekdays only. Telephone in advance.
Green Fees £50 per round (£60 weekends).
Cards ⬜⬛⬛⬜⬜⬛⬜
Prof David Screeton
Designer Ross McMurray
Facilities ⊗ ⅲ ⅊ ⅃ ⅋ ⅌ ⅎ 🏠 ⅏ ⅐ ⅑ ⅒ ⅓
& Leisure heated indoor swimming pool, sauna, solarium, gymnasium.

Hotel ★★★★ 71% Marriott Worsley Park Hotel & Country Club, Worsley Park, Worsley, MANCHESTER ☎ 0161 975 2000 158 ⇋ ⅋

Northenden Palatine Rd, Northenden M22 4FR
☎ 0161 998 4738 Fax 0161 998 5592
Parkland course surrounded by the River Mersey.
18 holes, 6503yds, Par 72, SSS 71, Course record 64.
Club membership 800.
Visitors must contact professional in advance on 0161 945 3386.
Societies Tue & Fri only, apply in advance to Secretary.
Green Fees £28 per day (£32 weekends & bank holidays).
Prof J Curtis
Designer Renouf
Facilities ⊗ ⅲ ⅊ ⅃ ⅋ ⅌ 🏠 ⅎ
Location 6.5m S of city centre on B1567 off A5103

Hotel ★★★ 64% Posthouse Manchester, Palatine Rd, Northenden, MANCHESTER ☎ 0870 400 9056 190 ⇋ ⅋

Withington 243 Palatine Rd, West Didsbury M20 2UE
☎ 0161 445 9544 Fax 0161 445 5210
Flat parkland course bordering the river Mersey. Easy walking with an extremely tough finish.
18 holes, 6410yds, Par 71, SSS 71.
Club membership 600.
Visitors welcome except Thu, must contact in advance, restricted at weekends.
Societies telephone in advance, welcome except Thu, Sat & Sun.
Green Fees not confirmed.
Prof R J Ling
Facilities ⊗ ⅲ ⅊ ⅃ ⅋ ⅌ 🏠 ⅎ
Location 4m SW of city centre off B5167

Hotel ★★★ 64% Posthouse Manchester, Palatine Rd, Northenden, MANCHESTER ☎ 0870 400 9056 190 ⇋ ⅋

Worsley Stableford Av, Worsley M30 8AP
☎ 0161 789 4202 Fax 0161 789 3200
Well-wooded parkland course.
18 holes, 6252yds, Par 71, SSS 70, Course record 65.
Club membership 600.
Visitors must contact professional in advance restricted during club competitions.
Societies apply in advance.
Green Fees not confirmed.
Prof Ceri Cousins
Designer James Braid
Facilities ⊗ ⅲ ⅊ ⅃ ⅋ ⅌ 🏠 ⅎ ⅏
Location 6.5m NW of city centre off A572

Hotel ★★★ 66% Novotel Manchester West, Worsley Brow, WORSLEY
☎ 0161 799 3535 119 ⇋ ⅋

MELLOR Map 07 SJ98

Mellor & Townscliffe Gibb Ln, Tarden SK6 5NA
☎ 0161 427 2208 (secretary) & 427 5759 (pro)
Fax 0161 4270103
Scenic parkland and moorland course, undulating with some hard walking. Good views. Testing 200 yd, 9th hole, par 3.
18 holes, 5925yds, Par 70, SSS 69.
Club membership 650.
Visitors with member only weekends & bank holidays.
Societies apply by letter.
Green Fees £22 per day(£31 weekends).
Prof Gary R Broadley
Facilities ⊗ ⅲ ⅊ ⅃ ⅋ ⅌ 🏠 ⅎ
Location 7m SE of Stockport off A626

Inn ♦♦♦♦ Matteo's Bar & Country Hotel, Rock Tavern, Glossop Rd, Marple Bridge, MARPLE
☎ 01457 852418 5 ⇋ ⅋

MIDDLETON Map 07 SD80

Manchester Hopwood Cottage, Rochdale Rd M24 2QP
☎ 0161 643 3202 Fax 0161 643 9174
e-mail: mec@zen.co.uk
Moorland golf of unique character over a spaciously laid out course with generous fairways sweeping along to large greens. A wide variety of holes will challenge the golfer's technique, particularly the testing last three holes.
18 holes, 6519yds, Par 72, SSS 71, Course record 65.
Club membership 650.
Visitors must contact in advance, limited play weekends and Wed.
Societies telephone in advance.
Green Fees £40 per day; £30 per round.
Cards ⬜⬛⬜
Prof Brian Connor
Designer Shapland Colt
Facilities ⊗ ⅲ ⅊ ⅃ ⅋ ⅌ 🏠 ⅎ ⅏ ⅐ ⅑
& Leisure snooker.
Location 2.5m N off A664. M62 junct 20

Hotel ★★★★ 64% Norton Grange Hotel, Manchester Rd, Castleton, ROCHDALE
☎ 01706 630788 51 ⇋ ⅋

New North Manchester Rhodes House, Manchester Old Rd M24 4PE ☎ 0161 643 9033 Fax 0161 643 7775
e-mail: secretary@nmgc.co.uk
A long, tight heathland course with natural water hazards. Excellent views of the Yorkshire Wolds.
North Manchester Golf Club: 18 holes, 6527yds, Par 72, SSS 72, Course record 66.
Club membership 700.
Visitors	contact Pro Shop on 0161 643 7094 for availability.
Societies	telephone in advance.
Green Fees	not confirmed.
Prof	Jason Peel
Designer	J Braid
Facilities	⊗ ∭ ⅃ ☕ 🏌 ⚐ 🛊 🏌 ✓
Location	W side of town centre off A576

Hotel	★★★★ 64% Menzies Avant Hotel, Windsor Rd, Manchester St, OLDHAM ☎ 0870 6003013 103 ⇄ 🐾

MILNROW   Map 07 SD91

Tunshill Kiln Ln OL16 3TS ☎ 01706 342095
Testing moorland course, particularly 7th and 15th (par 5's).
9 holes, 5743yds, Par 70, SSS 68, Course record 64.
Club membership 275.
Visitors	must contact in advance, restricted weekends & evenings.
Societies	apply in writing.
Green Fees	£16.
Facilities	⊗ ∭ ⅃ ☕ 🏌 ⚐
Location	1m NE M62 exit junc 21 off B6225

Hotel	★★★★ 64% Norton Grange Hotel, Manchester Rd, Castleton, ROCHDALE ☎ 01706 630788 51 ⇄ 🐾

OLDHAM   Map 07 SD90

Crompton & Royton Highbarn OL2 6RW
☎ 0161 624 0986 Fax 0161 652 4711
Undulating moorland course.
18 holes, 6214yds, Par 70, SSS 70, Course record 63.
Club membership 700.
Visitors	must contact in advance and may not play Tue or Sat, limited play Sun pm and Wed.
Societies	apply in advance
Green Fees	not confirmed.
Prof	David Melling
Facilities	⊗ ∭ ⅃ ☕ 🏌 ⚐ 🛊 ✓
Location	0.5m NE of Royton

Hotel	★★★★ 64% Menzies Avant Hotel, Windsor Rd, Manchester St, OLDHAM ☎ 0870 6003013 103 ⇄ 🐾

Oldham Lees New Rd OL4 5PN ☎ 0161 624 4986
Moorland course, with hard walking.
18 holes, 5122yds, Par 66, SSS 65, Course record 62.
Club membership 370.
Visitors	no restrictions.
Societies	must contact in advance.
Green Fees	not confirmed.
Prof	C Atkinson
Facilities	⊗ ∭ ⅃ ☕ 🏌 ⚐ 🛊 ✓
Location	2.5m E off A669

Hotel	★★ 71% York House Hotel, York Place, Richmond St, ASHTON-UNDER-LYNE ☎ 0161 330 9000 24 ⇄ 🐾 Annexe10 ⇄ 🐾

Werneth Green Ln, Garden Suburb OL8 3AZ
☎ 0161 624 1190
Semi-moorland course, with a deep gulley and stream crossing eight fairways. Testing hole: 3rd (par 3).
18 holes, 5363yds, Par 68, SSS 66, Course record 63.
Club membership 460.
Visitors	may not play on Tue or Thu and weekends. Must contact in advance.
Societies	must contact in advance.
Green Fees	£18.50 per 18 holes.
Prof	Roy Penney
Designer	Sandy Herd
Facilities	⊗ ∭ ⅃ ☕ 🏌 ⚐ 🛊 ✓
Location	S side of town centre off A627

Hotel	★★ 71% York House Hotel, York Place, Richmond St, ASHTON-UNDER-LYNE ☎ 0161 330 9000 24 ⇄ 🐾 Annexe10 ⇄ 🐾

PRESTWICH   Map 07 SD80

Heaton Park Municipal Heaton Park, Middleton Rd M25 2SW ☎ 0161 654 9899 Fax 0161 653 2003
18 holes, 5815yds, Par 70, SSS 70.
Location	N of Manchester near junct 18 of M62
Telephone for further details	

Hotel	Premier Lodge (Manchester West), East Lancs Rd, SWINTON ☎ 0870 700 1472 27 ⇄ 🐾

Prestwich Hilton Ln M25 9XB ☎ 0161 773 1404 Fax 0161 772 0700
Parkland course, near to Manchester city centre. A testing course with small greens.
18 holes, 4806yds, Par 64, SSS 63, Course record 60.
Club membership 565.
Visitors	handicap certificate, weekdays by arrangement. Restricted at weekends, ladies day Tue.
Societies	apply in writing or telephone.
Green Fees	not confirmed.
Prof	Simon Wakefield
Facilities	⊗ ∭ ⅃ ☕ 🏌 ⚐ 🛊 ⛳ ✓
Location	N side of town centre on A6044

Hotel	★★★ 66% Novotel Manchester West, Worsley Brow, WORSLEY ☎ 0161 799 3535 119 ⇄ 🐾

ROCHDALE   Map 07 SD81

Castle Hawk Chadwick Ln, Castleton OL11 3BY
☎ 01706 640841 Fax 01706 860587
e-mail: teeoff@castlehawk.co.uk
Two parkland courses, with challenging par 3s, and a driving range.
New Course: 9 holes, 2699yds, Par 34, SSS 34, Course record 30.
Old Course: 18 holes, 3189yds, Par 55, SSS 55.
Club membership 290.

▶

Visitors 9 Holes members only from 9am-6.30 pm in summer.
Societies must contact in advance.
Green Fees £8 (£10 weekends& bank holidays),reductions in winter.
Cards 🟢 ■ 📇 🔳 📇 🗔
Prof Frank Accleton/cRAIG bOWRING
Designer T Wilson
Facilities ⊗ ⫼ ⓑ 🖤 ♀ ⚤ 🖻 ⚐ ♂ ♗
Location S of Rochdale, nr junc 20 (M62)

Hotel ★★★★ 64% Norton Grange Hotel, Manchester Rd, Castleton, ROCHDALE ☎ 01706 630788 51 ⇆ ⚑

Rochdale Edenfield Rd OL11 5YR
☎ 01706 643818 Fax 01706 861113
Parkland course with enjoyable golf and easy walking.
18 holes, 6050yds, Par 71, SSS 69, Course record 65.
Club membership 750.
Visitors must telephone in advance.
Societies apply in writing or telephone
Green Fees £30(£35 weekends)reductions in winter.
Prof Andrew Laverty
Designer George Lowe
Facilities ⊗ ⫼ ⓑ 🖤 ♀ ⚤ 🖻 ⚐ ♗
Location 1.75m W on A680

Hotel ★★★★ 64% Norton Grange Hotel, Manchester Rd, Castleton, ROCHDALE ☎ 01706 630788 51 ⇆ ⚑

Springfield Park Springfield Park, Bolton Rd OL11 4RE
☎ 01706 56401 (weekend only)
18 holes, 5237yds, Par 67, SSS 66, Course record 64.
Location 1.5m SW off A58
Telephone for further details

Hotel ★★★★ 64% Norton Grange Hotel, Manchester Rd, Castleton, ROCHDALE ☎ 01706 630788 51 ⇆ ⚑

ROMILEY   Map 07 SJ99

Romiley Goose House Green SK6 4LJ
☎ 0161 430 2392 Fax 0161 430 7258
Semi-parkland course on the edge of the Derbyshire Hills, providing a good test of golf with a number of outstanding holes, notably the 6th, 9th, 14th and 16th. The latter enjoys magnificent views from the tee.
18 holes, 6454yds, Par 70, SSS 71, Course record 66.
Club membership 700.
Visitors are advised to contact in advance, may not play Thu or Sat before 4pm.
Societies Tue & Wed, must book in advance.
Green Fees £40 per day; £30 per round (£50/£40 weekends).
Prof Robert N Giles
Facilities ⊗ ⫼ ⓑ 🖤 ♀ ⚤ 🖻 ♗
Location E side of town centre off B6104

Hotel ★★ 67% The Wycliffe Hotel, 74 Edgeley Rd, Edgeley, STOCKPORT ☎ 0161 477 5395 20 ⇆ ⚑

> Looking for a driving range?
> See the index at the back of the guide

SALE   Map 07 SJ79

Ashton on Mersey Church Ln M33 5QQ
☎ 0161 976 4390 & 962 3727 Fax 0161 976 4390
Parkland course with easy walking alongside the River Mersey.
9 holes, 6146yds, Par 71, SSS 69, Course record 66.
Club membership 485.
Visitors with member only Sun & bank holidays, not Sat or Tue.
Societies Thu only. Apply in writing.
Green Fees £20.50 incl 3rd party liability insurance.
Prof Mike Williams
Facilities ⊗ ⫼ ⓑ 🖤 ♀ ⚤ 🖻 ♗
& Leisure sauna.
Location 1m W of M60,junc 7, off Glebelands Road

Hotel ★★★ 67% Cresta Court Hotel, Church St, ALTRINCHAM ☎ 0161 927 7272 137 ⇆ ⚑

Sale Golf Rd M33 2XU
☎ 0161 973 1638 (Gen Man) Fax 0161 962 4217
e-mail: billi@sandiway87.fsnet.co.uk
Tree-lined parkland course. Feature holes are the 13th - Watery Gap - and the par 3 (117yd) 17th.
18 holes, 6352yds, Par 71, SSS 70.
Club membership 700.
Visitors contact professional in advance.
Societies apply by letter.
Green Fees £28 per round(£33 weekends 7 bank holidays).
Prof Mike Stewart
Facilities ⊗ ⫼ ⓑ 🖤 ♀ ⚤ 🖻 ♗
Location 0.5m from M60 J6, NW side of town centre off A6144

Hotel ★★★ 67% Cresta Court Hotel, Church St, ALTRINCHAM ☎ 0161 927 7272 137 ⇆ ⚑

SHEVINGTON   Map 07 SD50

Gathurst 62 Miles Ln WN6 8EW
☎ 01257 255235 (Secretary) & 254909 (Pro)
Testing parkland course, slightly hilly.
18 holes, 6016yds, Par 70, SSS 69, Course record 64.
Club membership 575.
Visitors may play anytime except competition days.
Societies welcome Mon, Tue, Thu & Fri. Apply in writing to Secretary.
Green Fees not confirmed.
Prof Rob Eastwood
Designer N Pearson
Facilities ⊗ ⫼ ⓑ 🖤 ♀ ⚤ 🖻 ♗
Location W side of village B5375 off junc 27 of M6

Hotel ★★★★ Kilhey Court Hotel, Chorley Rd, Standish, WIGAN ☎ 01257 472100 62 ⇆ ⚑

STALYBRIDGE   Map 07 SJ99

Stamford Oakfield House, Huddersfield Rd SK15 3PY
☎ 01457 832126 & 834829
e-mail: stamford.golfclub@bigfoot.com
Undulating moorland course.
18 holes, 5701yds, Par 70, SSS 68, Course record 62.
Club membership 600.

▶

Visitors limited play at weekends.
Societies apply in writing or telephone 0161 633 5721
Green Fees not confirmed.
Facilities ⊗ ⫙ ⮱ ☖ ⚲ ⚘ 🛄 ⚘
Location 2m NE off A635

Hotel ★★ 71% York House Hotel, York Place, Richmond St, ASHTON-UNDER-LYNE ☎ 0161 330 9000 24 ⇆ ⋔ Annexe10 ⇆ ⋔

STANDISH   Map 07 SD51

Standish Court Rectory Ln WN6 0XD
☎ 01257 425777 Fax 01257 425888
e-mail: info@standishgolf.co.uk
Undulating 18 hole parkland course, not overly long but provides a good test for all level of players. Front nine more open with room for errors, back nine very scenic through woodland, a number of tight driving holes. Greens in excellent condition.
18 holes, 5625yds, Par 68, SSS 66.
Club membership 375.
Visitors can play anytime, phone in advance for tee time, standard golfing dress required.
Societies telephone in advance.
Green Fees £10 (£15 weekends).
Cards 💳 💳 💳 🖹 🖭
Prof J Kershaw
Designer P Dawson
Facilities ⊗ ⫙ ⮱ ☖ ⚲ ⚘ ⛳ ⚘ ⎿
Location Off M61,junct 6, follow signs to Aspoll/Haigh

Hotel ★★★★ Kilhey Court Hotel, Chorley Rd, Standish, WIGAN ☎ 01257 472100 62 ⇆ ⋔

STOCKPORT   Map 07 SJ89

Heaton Moor Heaton Mersey SK4 3NX
☎ 0161 432 0846
Parkland course, easy walking.
18 holes, 5968, Par 70, SSS 69, Course record 66.
Club membership 400.
Visitors restricted Tue, bank holidays & Sat (summer).
Societies apply in writing.
Green Fees £23 per day (£31 weekends & bank holidays).
Prof Simon Marsh
Facilities ⊗ ⫙ ⮱ ☖ ⚲ ⚘ 🛄 ⚘
Location N of town centre off B5169

Hotel ★★ 68% Saxon Holme Hotel, 230 Wellington Rd, STOCKPORT ☎ 0161 432 2335 33 ⇆ ⋔

Houldsworth Houldsworth Park, Reddish SK5 6BN
☎ 0161 442 1712 Fax 0161 442 1712
Flat parkland course, tree-lined and with water hazards.
Testing holes 9th (par 5) and 13th (par 5).
18 holes, 6209yds, Par 71, SSS 70, Course record 65.
Club membership 680.
Visitors may not play weekends & bank holidays unless by prior arrangement with professional.
Societies by prior arrangement, telephone Secretary.wellcome on Mon,Thur & Fri
Green Fees £24 (£30 weekends).
Prof David Naylor
Designer Dave Thomas
Facilities ⊗ ⫙ ⮱ ☖ ⚲ ⚘ 🛄 ⚘
Location 4m SE of city centre off A6

Hotel ★★★ 67% Willow Bank Hotel, 340-342 Wilmslow Rd, Fallowfield, MANCHESTER ☎ 0161 224 0461 117 ⇆ ⋔

Marple Barnsfold Rd, Hawk Green, Marple SK6 7EL
☎ 0161 427 2311 Fax 0161 427 1125
e-mail: marple.golf.club@ukgateway-net
Parkland course.
18 holes, 5552yds, Par 68, SSS 67, Course record 66.
Club membership 640.
Visitors restricted Thu afternoon & weekend competition days.
Societies apply in writing to professional.
Green Fees £20 per day (£30 weekends & bank holidays).
Prof David Myers
Facilities ⊗ ⫙ ⮱ ☖ ⚲ ⚘ 🛄 ⚘
Location S side of town centre

Hotel ★★★ 67% Bredbury Hall Hotel & Country Club, Goyt Valley, BREDBURY ☎ 0161 430 7421 120 ⇆ ⋔

Reddish Vale Southcliffe Rd, Reddish SK5 7EE
☎ 0161 480 2359 Fax 0161 477 8242
e-mail: admin@reddishvalegolfclub.co.uk
Undulating heathland course designed by Dr A Mackenzie and situated in the River Tame valley.
18 holes, 6100yds, Par 69, SSS 69, Course record 64.
Club membership 550.
Visitors must play with member at weekends. No societies at weekends.
Societies must contact in writing.
Green Fees £25.
Prof Bob Freeman
Designer Dr A Mackenzie
Facilities ⊗ ⫙ ⮱ ☖ ⚲ ⚘ 🛄 ⛳ ⚘
Location Off Reddish Road

Hotel ★★ 67% The Wycliffe Hotel, 74 Edgeley Rd, Edgeley, STOCKPORT ☎ 0161 477 5395 20 ⇆ ⋔

Stockport Offerton Rd, Offerton SK2 5HL
☎ 0161 427 8369 (Secretary) & 427 2421 (Pro)
Fax 0161 449 8293 e-mail: stockportgolf@genie.co.uk
A beautifully situated course in wide open countryside with views of the Cheshire and Derbyshire hills. It is not too long but requires that the player plays all the shots, to excellent greens. Demanding holes include the dog-leg 3rd, 12th, and 18th and the 460 yard opening hole is among the toughest in Cheshire.
18 holes, 6326yds, Par 71, SSS 71, Course record 66.
Club membership 500.
Visitors must contact professional in advance, limited play weekends.
Societies Wed & Thu only, apply in writing to Secretary.
Green Fees £35 (£45 weekends).
Prof Mike Peel
Designer P Barrie/A Herd
Facilities ⊗ ⫙ ⮱ ☖ ⚲ ⚘ 🛄 ⛳ ⚘
Location 4m SE on A627

Hotel ★★★ 67% Bredbury Hall Hotel & Country Club, Goyt Valley, BREDBURY ☎ 0161 430 7421 120 ⇆ ⋔

SWINTON   Map 07 SD70

Swinton Park East Lancashire Rd M27 5LX
☎ 0161 794 0861 Fax 0161 281 0698
One of Lancashire's longest inland courses.
18 holes, 6726yds, Par 73, SSS 72, Course record 66.
Club membership 600.
Visitors   may not play weekends or Thu. Must
               contact in advance and have handicap
               certificate.
Societies   apply by letter.
Green Fees   not confirmed.
Prof   James Wilson
Designer   James Braid
Facilities   ⊗ ⍾ ᒪ ♥ ♀ ♨ 🏠 ⚹
Location   1m W off A580

Hotel   ★★★ 66% Novotel Manchester West,
               Worsley Brow, WORSLEY
               ☎ 0161 799 3535 119 ⇥ ⚑

UPPERMILL   Map 07 SD90

Saddleworth Mountain Ash OL3 6LT
☎ 01457 873653 Fax 01457 820647
Moorland course, with superb views of Pennines.
18 holes, 5976yds, Par 71, SSS 69, Course record 61.
Club membership 800.
Visitors   must contact in advance, restricted at weekends.
Societies   contact in advance.
Green Fees   £23 per round(£30 weekends).
Prof   Robert Johnson
Designer   George Lowe/Dr McKenzie
Facilities   ⊗ ⍾ ᒪ ♥ ♀ ♨ 🏠 ⛳ ⟍ ⚒ ⚹
Location   E side of town centre off A670

Hotel   ★★★ 71% Hotel Smokies Park,
               Ashton Rd, Bardsley, OLDHAM
               ☎ 0161 785 5000 73 ⇥ ⚑

URMSTON   Map 07 SJ79

Flixton Church Rd, Flixton M41 6EP
☎ 0161 748 2116 Fax 0161 748 2116
Meadowland course bounded by River Mersey.
9 holes, 6410yds, Par 71, SSS 71.
Club membership 430.
Visitors   contact professional in advance, with member
               only weekends & bank holidays.
Societies   apply in writing.
Green Fees   £16.
Cards   ⚏ ⚏ ⚏ 🔲
Prof   David Wade
Facilities   ⊗ ⍾ ᒪ ♥ ♀ ♨ 🏠 ⚹
Location   S side of town centre on B5213

Hotel   ★★★★ 66% Copthorne Hotel Manchester,
               Clippers Quay, Salford Quays,
               MANCHESTER ☎ 0161 873 7321 166 ⇥ ⚑

AA Hotels that have special
arrangements with golf courses are listed at
the back of the guide

WALKDEN   Map 07 SD70

Brackley Municipal M38 9TR ☎ 0161 790 6076
Mostly flat course.
9 holes, 3003yds, Par 35, SSS 69.
Visitors   no restrictions.
Green Fees   not confirmed.
Facilities   🏠
Location   2m NW on A6

Hotel   ★★★ 66% Novotel Manchester West, Worsley
               Brow, WORSLEY
               ☎ 0161 799 3535 119 ⇥ ⚑

WESTHOUGHTON   Map 07 SD60

Westhoughton Long Island, School St BL5 2BR
☎ 01942 811085 & 608958 Fax 01942 608958
Compact downland course.
9 holes, 2886yds, Par 70, SSS 68, Course record 64.
Club membership 280.
Visitors   with member only at weekends.
Societies   telephone in advance or apply in writing.
Green Fees   not confirmed.
Prof   Jason Seed
Facilities   ⊗ ⍾ ᒪ ♥ ♀ ♨ 🏠
Location   0.5m NW off A58

Hotel   ★★★ 60% Posthouse Bolton, Beaumont Rd,
               BOLTON ☎ 0870 400 9011 101 ⇥ ⚑

WHITEFIELD   Map 07 SD80

Stand The Dales, Ashbourne Grove M45 7NL
☎ 0161 766 3197 Fax 0161 796 3234
A semi-parkland course with five moorland holes. A fine test
of golf with a very demanding finish.
18 holes, 6411yds, Par 72, SSS 71, Course record 66.
Club membership 500.
Visitors   must contact professional in advance.
Societies   Wed & Fri, apply by telephone.
Green Fees   £25.50 per day(£30.50 weekends).
Cards   ⚏ 🔲
Prof   Mark Dance
Designer   G Lowe/A Herd
Facilities   ⊗ ⍾ ᒪ ♥ ♀ ♨ 🏠 ⛳ ⚹
Location   1m W off A667

Hotel   ★★★ 66% Bolholt Country Park Hotel,
               Walshaw Rd, BURY
               ☎ 0161 762 4000 66 ⇥ ⚑

Whitefield Higher Ln M45 7EZ
☎ 0161 351 2700 Fax 0161 351 2712
e-mail: golfclub@whitefield.u-net.com
Fine sporting parkland course with well-watered greens.
18 holes, 6045yds, Par 69, SSS 69, Course record 64.
Club membership 540.
Visitors   play restricted Tue & Sun. Booking essential
               weekends and bank holidays, contact the
               proffesional shop on 0161 7663096.
Societies   must contact in advance.
Green Fees   £25 per 18 holes;£30 per 27/36 holes(£35 per 18
               holes saturday).
Cards   ⚏ ■ ⚏ ⚏ 🔲
Prof   Paul Reeves

▶

Facilities ⊗ ⍢ ⌕ ⚏ ⚑ ⛳ ⊶ ✦
& Leisure hard tennis courts, snooker room.
Location N side of town centre on A665

Hotel ★★★ 72% Malmaison, Piccadilly,
MANCHESTER ☎ 0161 278 1000 112 ⇄ ♝

WIGAN   Map 07 SD50

Haigh Hall Haigh Country Park, Aspull WN2 1PE
☎ 01942 831107
18 holes, 6423yds, Par 70, SSS 71, Course record 65.
Location 2m NE off B5238
Telephone for further details

Hotel ★★ 65% Bel-Air Hotel, 236 Wigan Ln,
WIGAN ☎ 01942 241410 11 ⇄ ♝

Wigan Arley Hall, Haigh WN1 2UH ☎ 01257 421360
Among the best of Lancashire's 9-hole courses. The fine old
clubhouse is the original Arley Hall, and is surrounded by a
12th century moat.
18 holes, 6009yds, Par 70, SSS 69.
Club membership 200.
Visitors must contact in advance. May not play Tue or
Sat.
Societies apply by telephone.
Green Fees £25 per 18 holes.
Designer Gaunt & Marnoch
Facilities ⊗ ⍢ ⮂ ⌕ ⚏ ⚑ ⛳
Location 3m NE off B5238

Hotel ★★★ 65% Quality Hotel Wigan, Riverway,
WIGAN ☎ 01942 826888 88 ⇄ ♝

WOODFORD   Map 07 SJ88

Avro Old Hall Ln SK7 1QR ☎ 0161 439 2709
9 holes, 5735yds, Par 69, SSS 68.
Location W side of village on A5102
Telephone for further details

Hotel ★★★ 65% County Hotel Bramhall, Bramhall
Ln South, BRAMHALL
☎ 0161 455 9988 65 ⇄ ♝

WORSLEY   Map 07 SD70

Ellesmere Old Clough Ln M28 7HZ
☎ 0161 799 0554 (office) & 790 8591 (pro)
e-mail: honses@ellesmeregolf.fsnet.co.uk
Parkland course with natural hazards. Testing holes: 3rd (par
5), 9th (par 3), 15th (par 5). Hard walking.
18 holes, 6248yds, Par 70, SSS 70, Course record 67.
Club membership 700.
Visitors welcome except club competition days & bank
holidays.
Societies apply in advance.
Green Fees £25 per day; £19 per round (£26 per round/day
weekends).
Prof Terry Morley
Facilities ⊗ ⍢ ⮂ ⌕ ⚏ ⚑ ⛳ ✦
Location N side of village off A580

Hotel ★★★ 66% Novotel Manchester West,
Worsley Brow, WORSLEY
☎ 0161 799 3535 119 ⇄ ♝

ALDERSHOT   Map 04 SU85

Army Laffans Rd GU11 2HF
☎ 01252 337272 Fax 01252 337562 e-mail: agc@ic24.net
The second oldest course in Hampshire. Picturesque
heathland course with three par 3's, over 200 yds.
18 holes, 6550yds, Par 71, SSS 71, Course record 67.
Club membership 825.
Visitors may not play weekends.
Societies apply in writing.
Green Fees £26 per 18 holes; £36 per 36 holes(weekdays
only).
Cards ▭▭ ▭▭ ▭▭ ⚏
Prof Graham Cowley
Facilities ⊗ ⍢ ⮂ ⌕ ⚏ ⚑ ⛳ ✦
Location 1.5m N of town centre off A323/A325

Hotel ★★★ 69% Potters International Hotel,
1 Fleet Rd, ALDERSHOT
☎ 01252 344000 97 ⇄ ♝

ALRESFORD   Map 04 SU53

Alresford Cheriton Rd, Tichborne Down SO24 0PN
☎ 01962 733746 Fax 01962 736040
e-mail: secretary@alresford-golf.demon.co.uk
A testing downland course on well drained chalk. Expanded
to 18 holes, incorporating the original 12, but changing
direction of play to give two starting points and two closing
greens near clubhouse.
18 holes, 5905yds, Par 69, SSS 68, Course record 63.
Club membership 750.
Visitors must contact in advance.
Societies must telephone in advance.
Green Fees £23 per round, £35 per day (£40 per round
weekends).
Prof Malcolm Scott
Designer Scott Webb Young
Facilities ⊗ ⍢ ⮂ ⌕ ⚏ ⚑ ⛳ ⊶ ✦
Location 1m S on B3046

Hotel ★★ 63% Swan Hotel, 11 West St,
ALRESFORD ☎ 01962 732302 & 734427
Fax 01962 735274
11rm(3 ⇄7 ♝) Annexe12 ⇄ ♝

ALTON   Map 04 SU73

Alton Old Odiham Rd GU34 4BU
☎ 01420 82042 & 86518
Undulating meadowland course.
9 holes, 5744yds, Par 68, SSS 68, Course record 62.
Club membership 350.
Visitors must contact in advance and must have a
handicap certificate to play at weekends. Correct
golf attire must be worn.
Societies must contact in advance.
Green Fees not confirmed.
Prof Paul Brown
Designer James Braid
Facilities ⮂ ⌕ ⚏ ⚑ ⛳ ✦
Location 2m N of Alton off B3349 at Golden Pot

▶

Hotel ★★★ 65% Alton House Hotel, Normandy St, ALTON ☎ 01420 80033 39 ⇆ ☍

Worldham Park Cakers Ln, East Worldham GU34 3BF
☎ 01420 543151 Fax 01420 84124
The course is in a picturesque woodland setting with an abundance of challenging holes (doglegs, water and sand).
18 holes, 6209yds, Par 71, SSS 70.
Club membership 500.
Visitors are advised to book in advance at weekends.
Societies must contact in advance.
Green Fees £11 per round (£14 weekends and bank holidays).
Cards ⬓ ⬛ ▨ ▨
Prof Jon Le Roux
Designer F J Whidborne
Facilities ⛏ 🏠 ⛳ ⚑ ⚒ ⛳ ⚐
Location B3004, 2mins from Alton

Hotel ★★★ 66% Alton Grange Hotel, London Rd, ALTON ☎ 01420 86565
26 ⇆ ☍ Annexe4 ⇆ ☍

AMPFIELD   Map 04 SU42

Ampfield Par Three Winchester Rd SO51 9BQ
☎ 01794 368480
Pretty parkland course designed by Henry Cotton in 1963.
Well-bunkered greens.
18 holes, 2478yds, Par 54, SSS 53, Course record 49.
Club membership 470.
Visitors must contact in advance & have a handicap certificate to play at weekends & bank holidays, recognised golfshoes must be worn.
Societies must contact in advance.
Green Fees not confirmed.
Prof Richard Benfield
Designer Henry Cotton
Facilities ⊗ ⫼ ﹆ ⬛ ⚑ ⛏ 🏠 ⛳ ⚐
Location 4m NE of Romsey on A31

Hotel ★★★ 66% Potters Heron Hotel, Winchester Rd, Ampfield, ROMSEY ☎ 023 8026 6611 54 ⇆ ☍

ANDOVER   Map 04 SU34

Andover 51 Winchester Rd SP10 2EF
☎ 01264 358040 Fax 01264 358040
Undulating downland course combining a good test of golf for all abilities with breathtaking views across Hampshire countryside. Well guarded greens and a notable par 3, 9th (225yds) with the tee perched on top of a hill, 100ft above the green.
9 holes, 6096yds, Par 70, SSS 69, Course record 66.
Club membership 450.
Visitors must contact professional in advance tel: 01264 324151.
Societies Mon-Wed only. Must contact in advance.
Green Fees £15 per 9/18 holes; £20 per day (£20 weekends).
Prof D Lawrence
Designer J H Taylor
Facilities ⊗ ⫼ ﹆ ⬛ ⚑ ⛏ 🏠 ⚐
Location 0.5m S on A3057

Hotel ★★★ 63% Quality Hotel Andover, Micheldever Rd, ANDOVER
☎ 01264 369111 13 ⇆ ☍ Annexe36 ⇆ ☍

Hampshire Winchester Rd SP11 7TB
☎ 01264 357555 (pro shop) & 356462
A pleasant undulating parkland course, based on chalk which provides very good drainage, with a superb finishing hole
18 holes, 6359yds, Par 72, SSS 70, Course record 67.
Club membership 600.
Visitors must book 3 days in advance.
Societies apply by phone to Jan Miles (01264 356462)
Green Fees £25 per day; £15 per round (£25 per round weekends).
Cards ⬓ ⬛ ▨
Prof Stewart Cronin
Facilities ⊗ ⫼ ﹆ ⬛ ⚑ ⛏ 🏠 ⛳ ⚑ ⚒ ⛳ ⚐
& Leisure 9 hole par 3 course.
Location located 1.5m S of Andover on A3057 Winchester road

Hotel ★★★ 67% White Hart, Bridge St, ANDOVER
☎ 01264 352266 27 ⇆ ☍

ASHLEY HEATH   Map 04 SU10

Moors Valley Moors Valley Country Park, Horton Rd BH24 2ET ☎ 01425 479776 Fax 01425 472057
This municipal course is set in the beautiful surroundings of a country park. It offers a test for all standards. It is gently undulating, with water hazards on six holes.
18 holes, 6200yds, Par 72, SSS 70.
Club membership 250.
Visitors must contact in advance.
Societies telephone for availability.
Green Fees not confirmed.
Prof Michael Torrens
Designer Hawtree & Son
Facilities ⛏ 🏠 ⛳ ⚐
Location Signposted from A31 Ashley Heath roundabout

Hotel ★★ Moortown Lodge Hotel, 244 Christchurch Rd, RINGWOOD
☎ 01425 471404 6rm(2 ⇆ 3 ☍)

BARTON-ON-SEA   Map 04 SZ29

Barton-on-Sea Milford Rd BH25 5PP
☎ 01425 615308 Fax 01425 621457
Though not strictly a links course, it is situated on a coastal cliff with views over the Solent to the Isle of Wight. With 27 holes (three loops of nine), sea breezes often add to the test.
Becton-Needles: 18 holes, 6521yds, Par 72, SSS 71, Course record 65.
Stroller: 9 holes, Par 35.
Club membership 940.
Visitors must contact in advance and have a handicap certificate.
Societies must telephone in advance.
Green Fees £30 per day (£35 weekends & bank holidays).
Prof Peter Rodgers
Designer Hamilton Stutt
Facilities ⊗ ⫼ by prior arrangement
﹆ ⬛ ⚑ ⛏ 🏠 ⛳ ⚑ ⚒ ⛳ ⚐ ▶

& Leisure snooker tables.
Location B3058 SE side of town

Hotel ★★★★★ ♨ Chewton Glen Hotel, Christchurch Rd, NEW MILTON
☎ 01425 275341   62 ⇆ ⋒

BASINGSTOKE   Map 04 SU65

Basingstoke Kempshott Park RG23 7LL
☎ 01256 465990 Fax 01256 331793
A well-maintained parkland course with wide and inviting fairways. You are inclined to expect longer drives than are actually achieved - partly on account of the trees. There are many two-hundred-year-old beech trees, since the course was built on an old deer park.
18 holes, 6350yds, Par 70, SSS 70, Course record 66.
Club membership 700.
Visitors must contact in advance and play Mon-Fri only (ex bank holidays).
Societies must contact in advance.
Green Fees £38 per day; £28per round.
Cards ⬚ ⬛ ⬚
Prof Guy Shoesmith
Designer James Braid
Facilities ⊗ ⅏ ⮂ ♥ ♀ ⚐ 🖝 ⌂ ⛟ 🦵 ⚷
Location 3.5m SW on A30 M3 exit 7

Hotel ★★★ 65% Posthouse Basingstoke, Grove Rd, BASINGSTOKE
☎ 0870 400 9004   84 ⇆ ⋒

Dummer Dummer RG25 2AR
☎ 01256 397888 Fax 01256 397889
e-mail: golf@dummergc.co.uk
Designed by Peter Alliss/Clive Clark, this course is set in 180 acres of countryside with panoramic views. It provides a challenge for all playing categories and is open all year round. All facilities, including the clubhouse have recently been enhanced.
18 holes, 6385yds, Par 72, SSS 70, Course record 64.
Club membership 720.

Visitors must contact in advance, adhere to dress code, handicap required, limited at weekends.
Societies contact in advance.
Green Fees £28 (£35 weekends).
Cards ⬚ ⬛ ⬚ ⬚ ⬚
Prof Andrew Fannon & Anthony Wain
Designer Peter Alliss
Facilities ⊗ ⅏ ⮂ ♥ ♀ ⚐ 🖝 🦵 ⚷ ⅃
& Leisure sauna.

Location Off junc 7 of M3 towards Dummer village

Hotel ★★★ 70% Hanover International Hotel & Club, Scures Hill, Nately Scures, Hook, BASINGSTOKE ☎ 01256 764161 100 ⇆ ⋒

Weybrook Park Rooksdown Ln RG24 9NT
☎ 01256 320347 Fax 01256 812973
e-mail: secretary@weybrookpark.fsnet.co.uk
A course designed to be enjoyable for all standards of player. Easy walking with fablous views.
18 holes, 6468yds, Par 71, SSS 71.
Club membership 600.
Visitors telephone for availability.
Societies telephone in advance for availability and confirm in writing.
Green Fees not confirmed.
Cards ⬚ ⬛ ⬚
Prof Anthony Dillon
Facilities ⊗ ⅏ ⮂ ♥ ♀ ⚐ 🖝 🦵 ⚷
Location 2m W of town centre, entrance via A339

Hotel ★★★ 65% Ringway Hotel, Popley Way, Aldermaston Roundabout, Ringway North (A339), BASINGSTOKE
☎ 01256 796700 128 ⇆ ⋒

BORDON   Map 04 SU73

Blackmoor Firgrove Rd, Whitehill GU35 9EH
☎ 01420 472775 Fax 01420 487666
e-mail: ctupper@blackmoorgolf.co.uk
A first-class moorland course with a great variety of holes. Fine greens and wide pine tree-lined fairways are a distinguishing feature. The ground is mainly flat and walking easy.
18 holes, 6164yds, Par 69, SSS 69, Course record 64.
Club membership 750.
Visitors must contact in advance, must have handicap certificate and may not play at weekends.
Societies must telephone in advance.
Green Fees not confirmed.
Prof Stephen Clay
Designer H S Colt
Facilities ⊗ by prior arrangement ⅏ by prior arrangement ⮂ ♥ ♀ ⚐ 🖝
Location Travelling S on A325, 6m beyond Farnham, pass through Whitehill and turn right at crossroads

Hotel ★★★ 65% Alton House Hotel, Normandy St, ALTON ☎ 01420 80033 39 ⇆ ⋒

BOTLEY   Map 04 SU51

Botley Park Hotel, Golf & Country Club Winchester Rd, Boorley Green SO32 2UA
☎ 01489 780888 Fax 01489 789242
e-mail: info@botleypark.macdonald.hotels.co.uk
Pleasantly undulating course with water hazards. Driving range and country club facilities.
18 holes, 6341yds, Par 70, SSS 70, Course record 67.
Club membership 1500.
Visitors must play with member at weekends. Must contact in advance & have handicap certificate.
Societies contact in advance. ▶

Green Fees not confirmed.
Cards [symbols]
Prof Tim Barter
Designer Ewan Murray
Facilities [symbols]
& Leisure hard tennis courts, heated indoor swimming pool, squash, sauna, solarium, gymnasium, health and beauty spa.
Location 1m NW of Botley on B3354

Hotel ★★★★ 69% Botley Park Hotel Golf & Country Club, Winchester Rd, Boorley Green, BOTLEY ☎ 01489 780888 100 ⇔ ↾

BROCKENHURST   Map 04 SU20

Brokenhurst Manor Sway Rd SO42 7SG
☎ 01590 623332 (Secretary) Fax 01590 624140
e-mail: pclifford@bmgcltd.freeserve.co.uk
An attractive woodland/heathland course set at the edge of the New Forest, with the unusual feature of three loops of six holes each to complete the round. Fascinating holes include the short 5th and 12th, and the 4th and 17th, both dog-legged. A stream also features on seven of the holes.
18 holes, 6222yds, Par 70, SSS 70, Course record 63.
Club membership 700.
Visitors must contact in advance, numbers limited. Must have a handicap certificate.
Societies Thu only, apply in writing.
Green Fees not confirmed.
Prof Bruce Parker
Designer H S Colt

★★
The Watersplash Hotel
Brockenhurst in the New Forest

The Watersplash Hotel is recommended for its excellent food, friendly service and accommodation. Brockenhurst Manor Golf Club, situated just half a mile away, is one of ten courses within easy reach of the hotel. Personally supervised by resident proprietor Robin Foster who specialise in catering for the individual and small golf parties. Well-stocked bar and extensive wine list. All 23 bedrooms have private bathroom, colour TV, tea and coffee making facilities, direct dial telephone and radio. Four-poster Room with double Jacuzzi Bath. Heated outdoor pool in season. For further details ask for our colour brochure.

The Watersplash Hotel, The Rise, Brockenhurst, Hampshire SO42 7ZP.
Tel: (01590) 622344 Fax: (01590) 624047

Facilities [symbols]
Location 1m S on B3055

Hotel ★★★ 72% Balmer Lawn Hotel, Lyndhurst Rd, BROCKENHURST ☎ 01590 623116 55 ⇔ ↾
Additional ★★ 67% Watersplash Hotel, The Rise,
hotel BROCKENHURST ☎ 01590 622344 Fax 01590 624047 23 ⇔ ↾

BURLEY   Map 04 SU20

Burley Cott Ln BH24 4BB
☎ 01425 402431 & 403737 Fax 01425 402431
Undulating heather and gorseland. The 7th requires an accurately placed tee shot to obtain par 4. Played off different tees on second nine.
9 holes, 6149yds, Par 71, SSS 69, Course record 68.
Club membership 520.
Visitors must contact in advance & preferably have a handicap certificate or be a member of a recognised golf club. May not play before 4pm Sat or 8am Sun.
Societies telephone in advance, parties up to 14 only.
Green Fees £20 per day; £16 per round (£25/£20 weekends & bank holidays).
Facilities [symbols]
Location E side of village

Hotel ★★★ 63% Moorhill House, BURLEY ☎ 01425 403285 24 ⇔ ↾

CORHAMPTON   Map 04 SU62

Corhampton Sheep's Pond Ln SO32 3LP
☎ 01489 877279 Fax 01489 877680
Free draining downland course situated in the heart of the picturesque Meon Valley.
18 holes, 6444yds, Par 71, SSS 71.
Club membership 800.
Visitors weekdays only and must contact in advance.
Societies Mon & Thu only, contact in writing or telephone.
Green Fees £24 per round.
Prof Ian Roper
Facilities [symbols] by prior arrangement [symbols]
Location 1m W of Corhampton, off B3035

Hotel ★★ 67% Old House Hotel, The Square, WICKHAM ☎ 01329 833049 9 ⇔ ↾

CRONDALL   Map 04 SU74

Oak Park Heath Ln GU10 5PB
☎ 01252 850850 Fax 01252 850851
Village: Gently undulating parkland course overlooking pretty village. 16-bay floodlit driving range, practice green and practice bunker. Woodland: Undulating on holes 10 to 13. Panoramic views, mature trees, very challenging.
Woodland: 18 holes, 6352yds, Par 70, SSS 70.
Village: 9 holes, 3279yds, Par 36.
Club membership 500.
Visitors restricted to members until 10.20am Sat. All tee times bookable in advance.

▶

Societies	must telephone and book in advance, min 12 persons.
Green Fees	Woodland: £20 (£30 weekends). Village: £10 (£12 weekends).
Prof	Gary Murton
Designer	Patrick Dawson
Facilities	⊗)Ⅲ by prior arrangement ⓑ ⓦ ♀ ⚲ 🏠 ⚑ 🏌 🟤 ⚙ ⓕ
& Leisure	gymnasium.
Location	0.5m E of village off A287 Farnham-Odiham
Hotel	★★★♨ 59% Farnham House Hotel, Alton Rd, FARNHAM ☎ 01252 716908 25 ⇥ ⓕ

DENMEAD   Map 04 SU61

Furzeley Furzeley Rd PO7 6TX
☎ 023 92231180 Fax 023 92230921
A well laid parkland course with many features including several strategically placed lakes which provide a good test set in beautiful scenery. Straight hitting and club selection on the short holes is the key to manufacturing a low score.
18 holes, 4363yds, Par 62, SSS 61, Course record 56.
Club membership 250.

Visitors	may book 2 days in advance.
Societies	must telephone in advance and confirm in writing.
Green Fees	not confirmed.
Prof	Derek Brown
Designer	Mark Sale/Robert Brown
Facilities	⊗)Ⅲ by prior arrangement ⓑ ⓦ ♀ ⚲ 🏠 ⚑ 🏌 ⚙
Location	From Waterlooville take Hambledon Road NW and follow golf course signs
Hotel	★★★★ 65% Portsmouth Marriott Hotel, North Harbour, PORTSMOUTH ☎ 023 9238 3151 170 ⇥ ⓕ

DIBDEN   Map 04 SU40

Dibden Main Rd SO45 5TB ☎ 023 80207508
Municipal parkland course with views over Southampton Water. A pond guards the green at the par 5, 3rd hole. Twenty-bay driving range.
Course 1: 18 holes, 5931yds, Par 70, SSS 69, Course record 64.
Course 2: 9 holes, 1520yds, Par 29.
Club membership 600.

Visitors	must book in advance for 18 hole course. 9 hole is pay & play.
Societies	must contact in advance.
Green Fees	not confirmed.
Prof	Paul Smith & John Slade
Designer	Hamilton Stutt
Facilities	⊗)Ⅲ ⓑ ⓦ ♀ ⚲ 🏠 ⚑ ⚙ ⓕ
Location	2m NW of Dibden Purlieu, off A326 to Hythe
Hotel	★★★ 66% Forest Lodge Hotel, Pikes Hill, Romsey Rd, LYNDHURST ☎ 023 8028 3677 28 ⇥ ⓕ

Where to stay, where to eat?
Visit the AA internet site
www.theAA.com

EASTLEIGH   Map 04 SU41

Fleming Park Passfield Av SO50 9NL
☎ 023 80612797 Fax 023 80651686
Parkland course with stream - 'Monks Brook' - running through.
18 holes, 4436yds, Par 65, SSS 62, Course record 62.
Club membership 300.

Visitors	must contact in advance, no restrictions.
Societies	must contact in advance.
Green Fees	£8 per 18 holes; £5 per 9 holes (£11.80/£7.85 weekends).
Cards	🟦 🟥 🟩 🟪 🟨
Prof	Chris Strickett
Designer	David Miller
Facilities	⊗)Ⅲ ⓑ ⓦ ♀ ⚲ 🏠 ⚑ 🏌 🟤 ⚙
& Leisure	hard and grass tennis courts, heated indoor swimming pool, squash, sauna, solarium, gymnasium.
Location	E side of town centre
Hotel	★★★ 68% Posthouse Eastleigh/Southampton, Leigh Rd, EASTLEIGH ☎ 0870 400 9075 116 ⇥ ⓕ

EAST WELLOW   Map 04 SU32

Wellow Ryedown Ln SO51 6BD
☎ 01794 323833 & 322872 Fax 01794 323832
Three 9-hole courses set in 217 acres of parkland surrounding Embley Park, former home of Florence Nightingale.
Ryedown & Embley: 18 holes, 5966yds, Par 70, SSS 69, Course record 65.
Embley & Blackwater: 18 holes, 6295yds, Par 72, SSS 70.
Blackwater & Ryedown: 18 holes, 5819yds, Par 70, SSS 68.
Club membership 600.

Visitors	advisable to contact in advance weekdays only.
Societies	telephone in advance, Mon-Fri not bank holidays.
Green Fees	£20 per day; £16 per 18 holes(£23/£19 weekends).
Prof	Neil Bratley
Designer	W Wiltshire
Facilities	⊗)Ⅲ ⓑ ⓦ ♀ ⚲ 🏠 🏌 🟤 ⚙
& Leisure	gymnasium.
Location	Exit2 of M27, then A36 to Salisbury then 1m right
Hotel	★★★ 58% The White Horse, Market Place, ROMSEY ☎ 0870 400 8123 33 ⇥ ⓕ

FAREHAM   Map 04 SU50

Cams Hall Cams Hall Estate PO16 8UP
☎ 01329 827222 Fax 01329 827111
Two Peter Alliss/Clive Clark designed golf courses. The Creek Course is coastal and has salt and fresh water lakes and the fairways are lined with undulating hills. The Park Course is designed in the grounds of Cams Hall.
Creek Course: 18 holes, 6244yds, Par 71, SSS 70, Course record 69.
Park Course: 9 holes, 3247yds, Par 36, SSS 36.
Club membership 950.

Visitors	must contact in advance, tee times available any time. ▸

Societies telephone for details and society golf day pack.
Green Fees not confirmed.
Prof Jason Neve
Designer Peter Alliss
Facilities ⊗ ⑇ ⓛⓁ 🏌 ♀ ♣ 🏠 ⚑ ⛳
& Leisure sauna.
Location M27 exit 11 to A27

Hotel ★★★ 64% Lysses House Hotel, 51 High St,
FAREHAM ☎ 01329 822622 21 ⇆ ⋔

FARNBOROUGH Map 04 SU85

Southwood Ively Rd, Cove GU14 0LJ
☎ 01252 548700 Fax 01252 515855
Municipal parkland course with stream running through.
18 holes, 5738yds, Par 69, SSS 68, Course record 61.
Club membership 650.
Visitors must book in advance.
Societies must contact in advance.
Green Fees not confirmed.
Cards 💳 💳 💳 💳 💳
Prof Bob Hammond
Designer Hawtree & Son
Facilities ♣ 🏠 ⚑ 🏌 ⛳ ⛳
Location 0.5m W

Hotel ★★★ 68% Posthouse Farnborough,
Lynchford Rd, FARNBOROUGH
☎ 0870 400 9029 143 ⇆ ⋔

FLEET Map 04 SU85

North Hants Minley Rd GU13 8RE
☎ 01252 616443 Fax 01252 811627
e-mail: secretary@north-hants-fleetgc.co.uk

Picturesque tree-lined course with much heather and
gorse close to the fairways. A comparatively easy par-4
first hole may lull the golfer into a false sense of
security, only to be rudely awakened at the testing holes
which follow. The ground is rather undulating and,
though not tiring, does offer some excellent 'blind'
shots, and more than a few surprises in judging distance.
18 holes, 6519yds, Par 71, SSS 72.
Club membership 600.
Visitors must contact at least 48 hours in advance.
Must play with member at weekends.
Societies Tue & Wed only. Subject to pre-booking.
Green Fees £32 per 1 round; £44 per 2 rounds (£40/£50
weekends). Twilight 5.30-6.00pm £20 (£25
weekends).
Prof Steve Porter

Designer James Braid
Facilities ⊗ ⑇ ⓛⓁ 🏌 ♀ ♣ 🏠 ⛳
Location 0.25m N of Fleet station on B3013

Hotel ★★★ 63% Lismoyne Hotel, Church Rd,
FLEET ☎ 01252 628555 44 ⇆ ⋔

GOSPORT Map 04 SZ69

Gosport & Stokes Bay Off Fort Rd, Haslar PO12 2AT
☎ 023 92527941 Fax 023 92527941
A testing links course overlooking the Solent, with plenty of
gorse and short rough. Changing winds.
9 holes, 5999yds, Par 70, SSS 69, Course record 65.
Club membership 499.
Visitors may not play Sun and Thu.
Societies must contact in writing.
Green Fees £15 Mon-Fri (Sun £20).
Facilities ⑇ ⓛⓁ 🏌 ♀ ♣ 🏠 ⚑ ⛳
Location A32 S from Fareham, E on Fort rd to Haslar

Hotel ★★★ 60% Belle Vue Hotel, 39 Marine Pde
East, Lee-on-the-Solent, GOSPORT
☎ 023 9255 0258 24 ⇆ ⋔ Annexe3 ⇆ ⋔

HARTLEY WINTNEY Map 04 SU75

Hartley Wintney London Rd RG27 8PT
☎ 01252 844211 (Sec) & 843779 (Prof) Fax 01252 844211
Easy walking, parkland course in pleasant countryside.
Played off different tees on back nine, with testing par 4s at
4th and 13th.
18 holes, 6240yds, Par 71, SSS 71, Course record 63.
Club membership 750.
Visitors must contact in advance, restricted at weekends.
Societies Tue & Thu only by prior arrangement.
Green Fees £35 per day; £25 per round.
Prof Martin Smith
Facilities ⊗ ⓛⓁ 🏌 ♀ ♣ 🏠 ⛳
Location NE side of village on A30

Hotel ★★★ 63% Lismoyne Hotel, Church Rd,
FLEET ☎ 01252 628555 44 ⇆ ⋔

HAYLING ISLAND Map 04 SU70

Hayling Links Ln PO11 0BX
☎ 023 92464446 Fax 023 92464446
e-mail: hgcltd@aol.com
A delightful links course among the dunes offering fine
sea-scapes and views across to the Isle of Wight.
Varying sea breezes and sometimes strong winds ensure
that the course seldom plays the same two days running.
Testing holes at the 12th and 13th, both par 4. Club
selection is important.
18 holes, 6531yds, Par 71, SSS 71, Course record 65.
Club membership 900.
Visitors must contact in advance and have a
handicap certificate, no jeans, denims or
collarless shirts allowed.
Societies welcome Tue & Wed, or half days Mon &
Thu, apply in writing or telephone.
Green Fees £40 per day; £32 per round (£55/£44
weekends).
Cards 💳 💳 💳 💳
Prof Raymond Gadd

▶

Designer Taylor 1905, Simpson 1933
Facilities ⊗ ⑭ 🏌 ♥ ♨ 🏠 ⛳ ✐
Location SW side of island at West Town

Hotel ★★★ 63% Langstone Hotel, Northney Rd,
HAYLING ISLAND
☎ 023 9246 5011 92 ⇄ 🐾

Prof Tony Ashton
Facilities ♥ ♨ ✐
Location 1m SW off A3057

Hotel ★★★ 70% Fifehead Manor, MIDDLE
WALLOP ☎ 01264 781565
10 ⇄ 🐾 Annexe6 ⇄ 🐾

KINGSCLERE   Map 04 SU55

Sandford Springs Wolverton RG26 5RT
☎ 01635 296800 & 296808 (Pro Shop)
Fax 01635 296801
The course has unique variety in beautiful surroundings
and offers three distinctive loops of 9 holes. There are
water hazards, woodlands and gradients to negotiate,
providing a challenge for all playing categories.
The Park: 9 holes, 2963yds, Par 34.
The Lakes: 9 holes, 3042yds, Par 35.
The Wood: 9 holes, 3180yds, Par 36.
Club membership 650.
Visitors must contact in advance. Restricted at
weekends.
Societies must contact in advance.
Green Fees not confirmed.
Cards 🖃 🖃 🖃 🖃
Prof Gary Edmunds/Kim Brake
Designer Hawtree & Son
Facilities ⊗ ⑭ 🏌 ♥ ♨ ♨ 🏠 ⛳ 🏑 ✐
Location On A339 between Basingstoke and
Newbury

Hotel ★★★ 65% The Chequers, Oxford St,
NEWBURY ☎ 01635 38000
45 ⇄ 🐾 Annexe11 ⇄ 🐾

KINGSLEY   Map 04 SU73

Dean Farm GU35 9NG
☎ 01420 489478 & 472313
Undulating downland course.
9 holes, 1500yds, Par 29.
Visitors no restrictions. Course closed Mon until 1pm.
Societies must contact in writing.
Green Fees not confirmed.
Facilities 🏠 ⛳
& Leisure hard tennis courts.
Location W side of village off B3004

Hotel ★★★ 66% Alton Grange Hotel, London Rd,
ALTON ☎ 01420 86565
26 ⇄ 🐾 Annexe4 ⇄ 🐾

LECKFORD   Map 04 SU33

Leckford SO20 6JG ☎ 01264 810320 Fax 01264 811122
e-mail: golf@leckfordestate.co.uk
A testing downland course with good views.
Old Course: 9 holes, 6444yds, Par 70, SSS 71.
New Course: 9 holes, 4562yds, Par 66, SSS 62.
Club membership 200.
Visitors Phone Secretary/Manager.
Societies phone Secretary/Manager
Green Fees £10 per day(£14 weekends & bank holidays).

LEE-ON-THE-SOLENT   Map 04 SU50

Lee-on-Solent Brune Ln PO13 9PB
☎ 023 92551170 Fax 023 92554233
e-mail: leegolfclub@yahoo.com
A modest parkland/heathland course, yet a testing one. The
five short holes always demand a high standard of play and
the 13th is rated one of the best in the country. The last 6
holes are amongst the most difficult in Hampshire.
18 holes, 5933yds, Par 69, SSS 69, Course record 64.
Club membership 750.
Visitors may not play before 9am or after 2.30pm on
weekends. Handicap certificate required.
Societies must contact in advance.
Green Fees £30 per round.
Cards 🖃 🖃 🖃 🖃 🖃
Prof John Richardson
Facilities ⊗ ⑭ 🏌 ♥ ♨ ♨ 🏠 ✐ ₹
Location 1m N off B3385

Hotel ★★★ 60% Belle Vue Hotel, 39 Marine Pde
East, Lee-on-the-Solent, GOSPORT
☎ 023 9255 0258 24 ⇄ 🐾 Annexe3 ⇄ 🐾

LIPHOOK   Map 04 SU83

Liphook Wheatsheaf Enclosure GU30 7EH
☎ 01428 723271 & 723785 Fax 01428 724853
e-mail: liphookgolfclub@btinternet.com
Heathland course with easy walking and fine views.
18 holes, 6167yds, Par 70, SSS 69, Course record 67.
Club membership 800.
Visitors must contact in advance; may not play Tue,
competition days etc.
Societies Wed-Fri only. Must contact in advance.
Green Fees on application.
Prof Geoffrey Lee
Designer A C Croome
Facilities ⊗ 🏌 ♥ ♨ ♨ 🏠 ⛳ ✐
Location 1m S on B2030 (old A3)

Hotel ★★★★ 65% Lythe Hill Hotel,
Petworth Rd, HASLEMERE
☎ 01428 651251 41 ⇄ 🐾

Old Thorns Hotel, Golf & Country Club Griggs Green
GU30 7PE ☎ 01428 724555 Fax 01428 725036
e-mail: generalmanager@oldthorns.freeserve.co.uk
A challenging 18-hole championship-standard course
designed around magnificent oaks, beeches, Scots pine
and lakes.
18 holes, 6581yds, Par 72, SSS 71, Course record 69.
Club membership 250.
Visitors subject to availability.
Societies must telephone in advance.
Green Fees £40 per day; £35 per round (£55/£45
weekends).
Cards 🖃 🖃 🖃 🖃 🖃   ▶

Prof	Kieron Stevenson
Designer	Peter Alliss/Dave Thomas
Facilities	⊗ �𝍄 ㏒ 🍷 ♀ ⌖ 🏠 ⛳ 🚶 🏌 ✂ 🏐
& Leisure	hard tennis courts, heated indoor swimming pool, sauna, solarium, gymnasium.
Location	Leave A3 at Griggs Green, S of Liphook, signposted 'Old Thorns'
Hotel	★★★ 71% Old Thorns Hotel, Golf & Country Club, Longmoor Rd, Griggs Green, LIPHOOK ☎ 01428 724555 29 ⇄ ↿ Annexe4 ↿

LYNDHURST Map 04 SU20

Bramshaw Brook SO43 7HE
☎ 023 80813433 Fax 023 80813460 e-mail: golf@bramshaw.co.uk
Two 18-hole courses. The Manor Course is landscaped parkland with excellent greens, and features mature trees and streams. The Forest course is set amidst beautiful open forest. Easy walking. The Bell Inn Hotel, attached to the club, provides fine accommodation just a wedge shot from the first tee, and reserved tee times for its guests.
Manor Course: 18 holes, 6517yds, Par 71, SSS 71, Course record 65.
Forest Course: 18 holes, 5774yds, Par 69, SSS 68, Course record 65.
Club membership 950.

Visitors	limited availability weekends and bank holidays unless accompanied by member or resident of Bell Inn.Phone in advance.
Societies	apply in writing or telephone in advance.
Green Fees	Manor: £30 per day. Forest £25 per day. Both courses all day £44. Reduced winter rates.
Prof	Clive Bonner
Facilities	⊗ �𝍄 ㏒ 🍷 ♀ ⌖ 🏠 ⛳ 🚶 🏌 ✂ 🏐
Location	On B3079 1m W of M27 junc 1
Hotel	★★★ 67% Bell Inn, BROOK ☎ 023 8081 2214 25 ⇄ ↿

New Forest Southampton Rd SO43 7BU
☎ 023 8028 2752 Fax 023 8028 2484 e-mail: barbara@nfgc.sagehost.co.uk
This picturesque heathland course is laid out in a typical stretch of the New Forest on high ground a little above the village of Lyndhurst. Natural hazards include the inevitable forest ponies. The first two holes are somewhat teasing, as is the 485-yard (par 5) 9th. Walking is easy.
18 holes, 5742yds, Par 69, SSS 68.
Club membership 700.

Visitors	must contact in advance,dress code applies.
Societies	must contact in advance.
Green Fees	£16 per day; £12 per round (£20/£14 weekends).
Prof	Danny Harris ▸

Facilities	⊗)Ⅲ by prior arrangement 🍴 ♨ ♀ ⚲ 🏠 ✓
Location	0.5m NE off A35)
Hotel	★★★ 68% Crown Hotel, High St, LYNDHURST ☎ 023 8028 2922 39 ⇄ 📞

NEW MILTON   Map 04 SZ29

Chewton Glen Hotel Christchurch Rd BH25 6QS
☎ 01425 275341 Fax 01425 272310
e-mail: reservations@chewtonglen.com
A 9-hole, Par 3 course with the hotel grounds plus a practice area. ONLY open to residents of the hotel or as a guest of a member of the club.
9 holes, 854yds, Par 27.
Club membership 150.
Visitors non residents must play with member.
Societies must contact in advance.
Green Fees not confirmed.
Cards 💳 ■■ ⚏ ⚏ ⚏ ⚏
Facilities ⊗ by prior arrangement)Ⅲ by prior arrangement ♨ ♀ ⚲ 🏠 📞 ✓
& Leisure hard tennis courts, outdoor and indoor heated swimming pools, sauna, gymnasium, Health Club, Croquet Lawn, Indoor Tennis Centre.
Hotel ★★★★★🔱 Chewton Glen Hotel, Christchurch Rd, NEW MILTON ☎ 01425 275341 62 ⇄ 📞

OVERTON   Map 04 SU54

Test Valley Micheldever Rd RG25 3DS
☎ 01256 771737 Fax 01256 770916
A downland course with excellent drainage, fine year-round greens and prominent water and bunker features. On undulating terrain with lovely views over the Hampshire countryside. Has hosted the Hampshire Open and the PGA Lombard Trophy.
18 holes, 6165yds, Par 72, SSS 69.
Club membership 500.
Visitors must phone in advance. Must play after 11am weekends & bank holidays.
Societies apply in writing or telephone in advance.
Green Fees £17 per round (£23 weekends).
Cards ⚏ ⚏ ⚏ ⚏
Prof Alastair Briggs
Designer Don Wright
Facilities ⊗)Ⅲ 🍴 ♨ ♀ ⚲ 🏠 📞 ✎ 🏌 ⚲ ✓
Location 1.5m N of A303 on road to Overton
Hotel ★★★ 71% The Hampshire Centrecourt Hotel, Centre Dr, Chineham, BASINGSTOKE ☎ 01256 816664 50 ⇄ 📞

OWER   Map 04 SU31

Paultons Golf Centre Old Salisbury Rd SO51 6AN
☎ 023 80813992 e-mail: paultons@americangolf.uk.com
A Pay and Play 18-hole course built within the original Paultons parkland which was laid out by 'Capability' Brown. There is also a 9-hole academy course, ideal for beginners or players wishing to improve their short games as well as a 20-bay floodlit driving range.
18 holes, 6238yds, Par 71, SSS 70, Course record 67.
Club membership 500.

Visitors	book 7 days in advance.
Societies	telephone for details.
Green Fees	not confirmed.
Cards	💳 ■■ ⚏ ⚏ ⚏ ⚏
Prof	Mark Williamson/Mark Patience
Designer	J R Smith
Facilities	⊗)Ⅲ 🍴 ♨ ♀ ⚲ 🏠 📞 🏌 ⚲ ✓
& Leisure	9 hole academy course.
Hotel	★★★ 71% Bartley Lodge, Lyndhurst Rd, CADNAM ☎ 023 8081 2248 31 ⇄ 📞

PETERSFIELD   Map 04 SU72

Petersfield (New Course) Tankerdale Ln, Liss GU33 7QY
☎ 01730 895165 (office) & 895216 (pro)
Fax 01730 894713 e-mail: richard@petersfieldgolfclub.co.uk
Gently undulating course with mature trees and hedgerows. All the advantages of a course recently built to USGA specifications.
18 holes, 6387yds, Par 72, SSS 71, Course record 70.
Club membership 725.
Visitors start times required at weekends, may play only after 12pm weekends
Societies booking forms and deposit required.
Green Fees £25 per round £35 per day (£30 per round weekends & bank holidays).
Prof Greg Hughes
Designer M Hawtree
Facilities ⊗)Ⅲ 🍴 ⚲ 🏠 📞 🏌 ⚲ ✓
Location Off the A3 (M), between the Liss/Petersfield exits southbound
Hotel ★★★ 74% Spread Eagle Hotel and Health Spa, South St, MIDHURST ☎ 01730 816911 35 ⇄ 📞 Annexe4 📞

Petersfield (Old Course) Sussex Rd GU31 4EJ
☎ 01730 267732 Fax 01730 894713
9 hole parkland course on level ground in an area of outstanding natural beauty. Numerous trees and water features. Part of Petersfield Golf Club although 1.5m away from the 18 hole New Course.
9 holes, 3005yds, Par 72, SSS 69.
Visitors starting times required, pay & play at all times.
Societies booking form must be completed & deposit paid.
Green Fees £10 per 18 holes; £6 per 9 holes (£12/£7 weekends & bank holidays).
Prof Greg Hughes
Facilities ♨ ⚲ 📞 ✓
Location Off Sussex Road, B214
Hotel ★★★ 74% Spread Eagle Hotel and Health Spa, South St, MIDHURST ☎ 01730 816911 35 ⇄ 📞 Annexe4 📞

PORTSMOUTH   Map 04 SU60

Great Salterns Public Course Burrfields Rd PO3 5HH
☎ 023 92664549 Fax 023 92650525
Easy walking, seaside course with open fairways and testing shots onto well-guarded, small greens. Testing 13th hole, par 4, requiring 130yd shot across a lake.
Great Salterns Golf Course: 18 holes, 5575yds, Par 70, SSS 67, Course record 64.
Club membership 700.

▶

129

Visitors book up to 1 week in advance.
Societies must contact in advance.
Green Fees £11(£13 weekends).
Cards [icons]
Prof Terry Healy
Facilities ⊗ �X ⓑ ♀ ⚑ ⛳ ㅑ ✆ (
Location NE of town centre on A2030

Hotel ★★★ 65% Innlodge Hotel, Burrfields Rd,
PORTSMOUTH ☎ 023 9265 0510 74 ⇔ ⚑

Southsea The Clubhouse, Burrfields Rd PO3 5JJ
☎ 023 92664549 Fax 023 92668667
Municipal, meadowland course.
*Great Salterns: 18 holes, 5800yds, Par 71, SSS 68, Course
record 64.*
Club membership 400.
Visitors no restrictions. Booking advisable via pro shop.
Societies must contact in advance.
Green Fees £13.50 per 18 holes.
Cards [icons]
Prof Terry Healy
Facilities ⚑ ㅑ ⚭ (
Location 0.5m off M27

Hotel ★★★ 65% Innlodge Hotel, Burrfields Rd,
PORTSMOUTH ☎ 023 9265 0510 74 ⇔ ⚑

ROMSEY   Map 04 SU32

Dunwood Manor Danes Rd, Awbridge SO51 0GF
☎ 01794 340549 Fax 01794 341215
e-mail: admin@dunwood-golf.co.uk
Undulating parkland course with fine views. Fine holes
running through mature woodland.
18 holes, 5767yds, Par 69, SSS 68, Course record 65.
Club membership 620.
Visitors always welcome advisable to contact in
advance; essential for weekends after 11am.
Societies must contact in advance.
Green Fees £35 per day; £24 per round,summer(£30 per
round weekends)£18 per 18 holes winter.
Prof Heath Teschner
Facilities ⊗ �X ⓑ ♀ ⚭ ⚑ ㅑ ✆ ↘ ⚙ ⚗
Location 4m W off A27

Hotel ★★★ 67% Bell Inn, BROOK
☎ 023 8081 2214 25 ⇔ ⚑

Romsey Romsey Rd, Nursling SO16 0XW
☎ 023 80734637 Fax 023 80741036
e-mail: romseygc@interalpha.net
Parkland/woodland course with narrow tree-lined fairways.
Six holes are undulating, rest are sloping. There are superb
views over the Test valley.
18 holes, 5851yds, Par 69, SSS 68.
Club membership 900.
Visitors welcome Mon-Fri, must play with member
weekends and bank holidays.
Societies Mon, Tue & Thu, must contact in advance.
Green Fees not confirmed.
Prof Mark Desmond
Facilities ⊗ �X ⓑ ♀ ⚭ ⚗ ⚙
Location 3m S on A3057

Hotel ★★★ 58% The White Horse, Market Place,
ROMSEY ☎ 0870 400 8123 33 ⇔ ⚑

ROTHERWICK   Map 04 SU75

Tylney Park RG27 9AY
☎ 01256 762079 Fax 01256 763079
Parkland course. Practice area.
18 holes, 6109yds, Par 70, SSS 69, Course record 67.
Club membership 730.
Visitors must be with member at weekends or have a
handicap certificate.
Societies must apply by phone in advance.
Green Fees not confirmed.
Cards [icons]
Prof Chris de Bruin
Designer W Wiltshire
Facilities ⊗ �X ⓑ by prior arrangement ⓑ ♀ ⚭ ⚑ ㅑ
⚙ ⚗
Location 0.5m SW of Rotherwick, 2m NW of Hook, 2.5m
from M3 junct 5 via Newnham

Hotel ★★★★❦ Tylney Hall Hotel, ROTHERWICK
☎ 01256 764881 35 ⇔ ⚑ Annexe75 ⇔ ⚑

ROWLANDS CASTLE   Map 04 SU71

Rowlands Castle 31 Links Ln PO9 6AE
☎ 023 92412784 Fax 023 92413649
Reasonably dry in winter, the flat parkland course is a
testing one with a number of tricky dog-legs and bunkers
much in evidence. The Par 4 13th is a signature hole
necessitating a drive to a narrow fairway and a second
shot to a two-tiered green. The 7th, at 522yds, is the
longest hole on the course and leads to a well-guarded
armchair green.
18 holes, 6612yds, Par 72, SSS 72, Course record 69.
Club membership 800.
Visitors may not play Sat; must contact in advance
and hold a handicap certificate.
Societies Tue & Thu only; must contact in writing.
Green Fees £30 per day (£35 weekends).
Cards [icon]
Prof Peter Klepacz
Designer Colt
Facilities ⊗ �X ⓑ ♀ ⚭ ⚗ ⚑ ↘ ⚙ ⚗
Location W side of village off B2149

Hotel ★★★ 68% Brookfield Hotel, Havant Rd,
EMSWORTH ☎ 01243 373363 & 376383
Fax 01243 376342 40 ⇔ ⚑

SHEDFIELD   Map 04 SU51

Marriott Meon Valley Hotel & Country Club Sandy
Ln SO32 2HQ ☎ 01329 833455 Fax 01329 834411
It has been said that a golf course architect is as good as
the ground on which he has to work. Here Hamilton Stutt
had magnificent terrain at his disposal and a very good
and lovely parkland course is the result. There are three
holes over water. The hotel provides many sports
facilities.
*Meon Course: 18 holes, 6520yds, Par 71, SSS 71,
Course record 66.*
Valley Course: 9 holes, 2721yds, Par 35, SSS 33.
Club membership 700.
Visitors may book up to seven days in advance.
Societies telephone in advance, written confirmation.

Marriott-Meon Valley

Green Fees Meon:£34(£45 weekends); Valley: £15 per
18 holes(£18 weekends).
Prof Rod Cameron
Designer Hamilton Stutt
Facilities ⊗ 训 ⮜ ⬤ ♀ ⚲ 🏠 ⛳ 🥢 🐾 🏌 ⚑ ⚓
& Leisure hard tennis courts, heated indoor swimming
pool, sauna, solarium, gymnasium, health &
beauty salon, spa bath, aerobics studio.
Location Off A334 between Botley and Wickham.
Access via junct 7 M27

Hotel ★★★★ 65% Marriott Meon Valley Hotel
& Country Club, Sandy Ln, SHEDFIELD
☎ 01329 833455 113 ⇄ 🐾

SOUTHAMPTON   Map 04 SU41

Chilworth Main Rd, Chilworth SO16 7JP
☎ 023 80740544
A course with two loops of nine holes, with a booking
system to allow undisturbed play. The front nine are fairly
long and undulating and include water hazards. The back
nine are tighter and quite a challenge.
*Manor Golf Course: 18 holes, 5740yds, Par 69, SSS 69,
Course record 68.*
Club membership 600.
Visitors no restrictions.
Societies telephone in advance and complete booking
form, various packages available.
Green Fees £12 per round (£15 weekends).
Cards ▦ ▦ 🄿 ▦ ▦ 🄾
Designer J Garner
Facilities ⊗ 训 ⮜ ⬤ ♀ ⚲ 🏠 ⛳ 🏌
Location A27 between Chilworth and Romsey

Hotel ★★★ 64% Highfield House, Highfield Ln,
Portswood, SOUTHAMPTON
☎ 023 8035 9955 66 ⇄ 🐾

Southampton Golf Course Rd, Bassett SO16 7AY
☎ 023 80760478 & 80760546 (booking) Fax 023 80760472
This beautiful municipal parkland course always ensures a
good game, fast in summer, slow in winter. Three par 4's
over 450 yds.
18 holes, 6103yds, Par 69, SSS 70.
9 holes, 2395yds, Par 33.
Visitors 18 hole course: min 2 players (3 weekends and
bank holidays) booking advisable but not always
necessary. 9 hole course: 1-4 players per tee
Societies welcome, book up to 1yr in advance.

Green Fees £39.60 per 18 holes;£4.40 per 9
holes(£13.50/£6.20 weekends & bank holidays).
Prof John Waring
Designer Hockley/A P Taylor
Facilities ⊗ 训 ⮜ ⬤ ♀ ⚲ 🏠 ⛳ ⚓
Location 4m N of city centre off A33

Hotel ★★ 65% The Star Hotel & Restaurant,
26 High St, SOUTHAMPTON
☎ 023 8033 9939 43rm(37 ⇄ 🐾)

Stoneham Monks Wood Close, Bassett SO16 3TT
☎ 023 80769272 Fax 023 80766320
e-mail: stonehamgc@stoneham09.freeserve.co.uk
A hilly, heather course with sand or peat sub-soil; the
fairways are separated by belts of woodland and heather
to present a varied terrain. The interesting 4th is a
difficult par 4 and the fine 11th has cross-bunkers about
150 yards from the tee.
18 holes, 6310yds, Par 72, SSS 70, Course record 63.
Club membership 800.
Visitors advisable to contact in advance, handicap
certificate required.
Societies Mon, Thu & Fri only. Must telephone in
advance or apply in writing.
Green Fees call for details.
Cards ▦ ▦ 🄿 ▦ ▦ 🄾
Prof Ian Young
Designer Willie Park
Facilities ⊗ 训 ⮜ ⬤ ♀ ⚲ 🏠 ⛳ ⚓
Location 4m N of city centre off A27

Hotel ★★★ 64% Highfield House, Highfield Ln,
Portswood, SOUTHAMPTON
☎ 023 8035 9955 66 ⇄ 🐾

SOUTHWICK   Map 04 SU60

Southwick Park Naval Recreation Centre Pinsley Dr
PO17 6EL ☎ 023 92380131 Fax 023 92210289
Set in 100 acres of parkland.
18 holes, 5992yds, Par 69, SSS 69, Course record 64.
Club membership 700.
Visitors contact in advance, welcome weekends after
2pm
Societies Tue only, telephone in advance.
Prof John Green
Designer C Lawrie
Facilities ⊗ 训 ⮜ ⬤ ♀ ⚲ 🏠 ⛳ ⚓
Location 0.5m SE off B2177

Hotel ★★ 67% Old House Hotel, The Square,
WICKHAM ☎ 01329 833049 9 ⇄ 🐾

TADLEY   Map 04 SU66

Bishopswood Bishopswood Ln RG26 4AT
☎ 0118 9812200 Fax 0118 9408606 e-
mail: bishopswood@hampshiregolf.u-net.com
Wooded course, fairly tight, with stream and natural water
hazards.
9 holes, 6474yds, Par 72, SSS 71, Course record 66.
Club membership 485.
Visitors must contact in advance. No play weekends or
bank holidays.
Societies must contact by telephone.
Green Fees £10 per 9 holes; £15 per 18 holes.   ▶

Cards 📧 📧 📧 📧 🗐
Prof Steve Ward
Designer M W Phillips/G Blake
Facilities ⊗ ⊤⊩ 🕮 ⬛ ♀ ♨ 🎂 ✪ ⅋
Location 6m N of Basingstoke off the A340

Hotel ★★★ 74% Romans Country House Hotel,
Little London Rd, SILCHESTER
☎ 0118 970 0421 11 ⇄ ♠ Annexe14 ⇄ ♠

WATERLOOVILLE Map 04 SU60

Portsmouth Crookhorn Ln, Purbrook PO7 5QL
☎ 023 92372210 Fax 023 92200766
Hilly, challenging course with good views of Portsmouth
Harbour. Rarely free from the wind and the picturesque 6th,
17th and 18th holes can test the best.
18 holes, 6139yds, Par 69, SSS 70, Course record 64.
Club membership 600.
Visitors must book in advance.
Societies must book in advance, in writing or by
telephone.
Green Fees £10.50 per 18 holes (£13.50 weekends).
Cards 📧 📧 📧 📧 🗐
Prof Jason Banting
Designer Hawtree
Facilities ⊗ ⊤⊩ 🕮 ⬛ ♀ ♨ 🎂 🖢
Location 2m S, off A3

Hotel ★★★★ 65% Portsmouth Marriott Hotel, North
Harbour, PORTSMOUTH
☎ 023 9238 3151 170 ⇄ ♠

Waterlooville Cherry Tree Av, Cowplain PO8 8AP
☎ 023 92263388 Fax 023 92347513
e-mail: secretary@waterloovillegolfclub.co.uk
Parkland course, easy walking. Challenging course with 5
par 5's over 500 yards and featuring 4 ponds and a stream
running through.
18 holes, 6602yds, Par 72, SSS 72, Course record 64.
Club membership 800.
Visitors must contact in advance & may only play on
weekdays. Handicap certificate required.
Societies Thu only; apply by letter or telephone.
Green Fees not confirmed.
Prof John Hay
Designer Henry Cotton
Facilities ⊗ ⊤⊩ 🕮 ⬛ ♀ ♨ 🎂 ⅋
Location NE side of town centre off A3

Hotel ★★★ 63% Langstone Hotel, Northney Rd,
HAYLING ISLAND
☎ 023 9246 5011 92 ⇄ ♠

WINCHESTER Map 04 SU42

Hockley Twyford SO21 1PL
☎ 01962 713165 Fax 01962 713612
e-mail: hockleygolfclub@aol.com
High downland course with good views.
18 holes, 6336yds, Par 71, SSS 70, Course record 64.
Club membership 750.
Visitors are advised to phone in advance. Restricted
times at weekends. Handicap certificate
required.
Societies must telephone in advance and confirm in
writing with deposit.
Green Fees not confirmed.

Prof Terry Lane
Designer James Braid
Facilities ⊗ ⊤⊩ 🕮 ⬛ ♀ ♨ 🎂 🚜 ⅋
Location Jct 11 M3, follow sign to Twyford

Hotel ★★★★ 65% The Wessex, Paternoster Row,
WINCHESTER ☎ 0870 400 8126 94 ⇄ ♠

Royal Winchester Sarum Rd SO22 5QE
☎ 01962 852462 Fax 01962 865048
e-mail: royalwinchestergolfclub.com
The Royal Winchester course is a sporting downland
course centred on a rolling valley, so the course is hilly
in places. Royal Winchester must be included in any list
of notable clubs, because of its age (it dates from 1888)
and also because the club was involved in one of the
very first professional matches.
18 holes, 6204yds, Par 71, SSS 70, Course record 65.
Club membership 800.
Visitors must play with member at weekends. Must
contact in advance and have a handicap
certificate.
Societies must contact in writing or by telephone.
Green Fees £33 per 18 holes;£40 per 36 holes.
Prof Steven Hunter
Designer J H Taylor
Facilities ♨ 🎂 ⅋
Location 1.5m W off A3090

Hotel ★★★★🟊 73% Lainston House Hotel,
Sparsholt, WINCHESTER
☎ 01962 863588 41 ⇄ ♠

South Winchester Romsey Rd SO22 5QW
☎ 01962 877800 Fax 01962 877900
This Dave Thomas designed course incorporates downland,
meadows and seven lakes. Home of the Hampshire PGA and
the venue for European Ladies Tour Pro-Ams.
18 holes, 7086yds, Par 72, SSS 74, Course record 68.
Club membership 750.

Visitors guests only by arrangement.
Societies must contact in advance.
Green Fees not confirmed.
Cards 📧 📧 📧 📧 🗐
Prof Richard Adams
Designer Dave Thomas
Facilities ⊗ ⊤⊩ 🕮 ⬛ ♀ ♨ 🎂 🖢 🏐 🚜 ⅋ ₹
Location On A3090 Romsey road

Hotel ★★★ 73% The Winchester Royal, Saint Peter
St, WINCHESTER ☎ 01962 840840
75 ⇄ ♠

HEREFORDSHIRE

HEREFORD   Map 03 SO53

Belmont Lodge Belmont HR2 9SA
☎ 01432 352666 Fax 01432 358090
e-mail: info@belmontlodge.co.uk
Parkland course designed in two loops of nine. The first nine
take the higher ground, offering magnificent views over
Herefordshire. The second nine run alongside the River Wye
with five holes in play against the river.
18 holes, 6511yds, Par 72, SSS 71, Course record 66.
Club membership 450.

Visitors	advised to contact in advance at weekends. Tel: 01432 352666 or 352717.
Societies	must telephone in advance.
Green Fees	£19 per round (£26 weekends). Winter reductions.
Cards	[card symbols]
Prof	Mike Welsh
Designer	Bob Sandow
Facilities	⊗ ⫽ ⻏ ♛ ♀ ⚘ ⛪ ⚲ ➤ ⚒ ⛳ ✧
& Leisure	hard tennis courts, fishing.
Location	2m S off A465

Hotel	★★★ 62% Belmont Lodge & Golf Course, Belmont, HEREFORD ☎ 01432 352666 30 ⇌ ↾

Burghill Valley Tillington Rd, Burghill HR4 7RW
☎ 01432 760456 Fax 01432 761654 e-
mail: golf@bvgc.co.uk
The course is situated in typically beautiful Herefordshire
countryside. The walking is easy on gently rolling fairways
with a background of hills and woods and in the distance, the
Welsh mountains. Some holes are played through mature
cider orchards and there are two lakes to negotiate. A fair but
interesting test for players of all abilities.
18 holes, 6239yds, Par 71, SSS 70, Course record 69.
Club membership 700.

Visitors	contact in advance.
Societies	apply in writing or telephone in advance.
Green Fees	£20 per round (£27 weekends & bank holidays).
Cards	[card symbols]
Prof	Nigel Clarke
Designer	M Barnett
Facilities	⊗ ⫽ ⻏ ♛ ♀ ⚘ ⛪ ➤ ⚒ ✧
Location	4m NW of Hereford

Hotel	★★★ 64% The Green Dragon, Broad St, HEREFORD ☎ 0870 400 8113 83 ⇌ ↾

Hereford Municipal Hereford Leisure Centre, Holmer Rd
HR4 9UD ☎ 01432 344376 Fax 01432 266281
This municipal parkland course is more challenging than first
appearance. The well-drained greens are open all year round
with good drainage for excellent winter golf.
9 holes, 3060yds, Par 35, SSS 69.
Club membership 195.

Visitors	restrictions on race days.
Societies	telephone in advance.
Green Fees	£6.75 18 holes, £4.50 9 holes (£8.25/£5.50 weekends).
Cards	[card symbols]
Prof	Gary Morgan
Designer	J Leek
Facilities	⊗ ⫽ ⻏ ♛ ♀ ⚘ ⛪ ⚲ ✧
& Leisure	squash, gymnasium, Leisure centre.
Location	Located with race course on Holmer Rd, on A49 Hereford to Leominster

Hotel	★★★ 64% The Green Dragon, Broad St, HEREFORD ☎ 0870 400 8113 83 ⇌ ↾

KINGTON   Map 03 SO25

Kington Bradnor Hill HR5 3RE
☎ 01544 230340 (club) & 231320 (pro shop)
Fax 01544 230340 /231320 (pro)
The highest 18-hole course in England, with magnificent
views over seven counties. A natural heathland course
with easy walking on mountain turf cropped by sheep.
There is bracken to catch any really bad shots but no
sand traps. The greens play true and fast.
18 holes, 5980yds, Par 70, SSS 68, Course record 63.
Club membership 510.

Visitors	contact the professional, particularly at weekends by phoning 01544 231320.
Societies	must book in advance through the Professional.
Green Fees	£20 per day; £15 per round (£24/£20 weekends).
Prof	Dean Oliver
Designer	Major Hutchison
Facilities	⊗ ⑂ ┗ ⬛ ♀ ♙ 🛆 🏠 ✦ ♂ ♟
Location	0.5m N of Kington, off B4355

Hotel	★★★ 65% Talbot Hotel, West St, LEOMINSTER ☎ 01568 616347 20 ⇄ ♞ *See advertisement on Page 133*

LEOMINSTER   Map 03 SO45

Leominster Ford Bridge HR6 0LE ☎ 01568 611402 (Prof) & 610055 (Sec/Mngr) Fax 01568 610055
e-mail: leominstergolf@freeuk.com
On undulating parkland with the lower holes running alongside the River Lugg and others on the higher part of the course affording fine panoramic views over the surrounding countryside.
18 holes, 6026yds, Par 70, SSS 69.
Club membership 570.

Visitors	must contact in advance.
Societies	must telephone in advance.
Green Fees	Mon & Fri £8, Tue-Thu £12 per round (£16 weekends & bank holidays).
Prof	Andrew Ferriday
Designer	Bob Sandow
Facilities	⊗ ⑂ ┗ ⬛ ♀ 🛆 🏠 ♂
& Leisure	fishing.
Location	3m S of Leominster on A49. Clearly signposted from Leominster by-pass

Talbot Hotel

Hotel	★★★ 65% Talbot Hotel, West St, LEOMINSTER ☎ 01568 616347 20 ⇄ ♞

ROSS-ON-WYE   Map 03 SO62

Ross-on-Wye Two Park, Gorsley HR9 7UT
☎ 01989 720267 Fax 01989 720212
e-mail: secretary@therossonwyegolfclub.co.uk
The undulating, parkland course has been cut out of a silver birch forest; the fairways being well-screened from each other. The fairways are tight, the greens good and the bunkers have been re-structured.

18 holes, 6451yds, Par 72, SSS 71, Course record 68.
Club membership 760.

Visitors	must contact Secretary/Professional in advance 01989 720267/720439
Societies	apply in writing/telephone in advance.
Green Fees	£34 per 18 holes;£40 per 27 holes;£44 per 36 holes.
Cards	💳 💳
Prof	Nick Catchpole
Facilities	⊗ ⑂ ┗ ⬛ ♀ 🛆 🏠 ♂ ♟
Location	On B4221 N side of M50 junc 3

Pengethley Manor

Hotel	★★★ Pengethley Manor, Pengethley Park, ROSS-ON-WYE ☎ 01989 730211 11 ⇄ ♞ Annexe14 ⇄ ♞

South Herefordshire Twin Lakes HR9 7UA
☎ 01989 780535 Fax 01989 740611
e-mail: shgc.golf@clara.co.uk
A parkland course of over 180 acres with fine views. The landscape has enabled the architect to design 18 individual and varied holes and golfers have a chance to use every club in the bag. Free draining soil provides year round play.
Twin Lakes: 18 holes, 6672yds, Par 71, SSS 72, Course record 71.
Club membership 300.

Visitors	must contact in advance.
Societies	phone in advance.
Green Fees	£15 weekdays (£20 weekends) per 18 holes.
Cards	💳 💳 💳 💳
Prof	Edward Litchfield
Designer	John Day
Facilities	⊗ ⑂ ┗ ⬛ ♀ 🛆 🏠 ✦ ♙ ♂ ♟
Location	J4 M50 to Upton Bishop,right to B4224,1m left

Hotel	★★★♨ 68% Pencraig Court Hotel, Pencraig, ROSS-ON-WYE ☎ 01989 770306 11 ⇄

UPPER SAPEY   Map 03 SO66

Sapey WR6 6XT
☎ 01886 853288 & 853567 Fax 01886 853485
e-mail: anybody@sapeygolf.co.uk
Parkland course with views of the Malvern Hills. Trees, lakes and water hazards. Not too strenuous a walk.
The Rowan: 18 holes, 5935yds, Par 69, SSS 68, Course record 63.
Club membership 520.

Visitors	must contact in advance.
Societies	must contact in advance.

▶

Green Fees The Rowan: £18 per round;£25 per day(£23/£30 weekends),The Oaks: £4 per round(£5 weekends).
Cards 🌐 💳 📇
Prof Chris Knowles
Designer R McMurray
Facilities ⊗ ⅲ by prior arrangement 🍴 🏌 ♀ 👤 🏠 ⛳ 🚶
       🛒 ♂
Location B4203 Bromyard/Stourport Rd

Hotel ★★★ 65% Talbot Hotel, West St,
       LEOMINSTER ☎ 01568 616347   20 ⇆ 🏴

WORMSLEY   Map 03 SO44

Herefordshire Ravens Causeway HR4 8LY
☎ 01432 830219 & 830465 (pro) Fax 01432 830095
e-mail: herefordshire@golf.sagehost.co.uk
Undulating parkland course with expansive views.
18 holes, 6078yds, Par 70, SSS 69, Course record 61.
Club membership 750.
Visitors must contact in advance, possibility of weekend play if no competitions are taking place.
Societies must apply in advance.
Green Fees £25 per day; £20 per round (£32/£25 weekends & bank holidays).
Cards 🌐 💳 📇 📇
Prof David Hemming
Designer James Braid
Facilities ⊗ ⅲ 🍴 🏌 ♀ 👤 🏠 ⛳ 🚶 🛒 ♂
Location 7m nw of Hereford on A 'B'road to Weobley

Hotel ★★★ 64% The Green Dragon, Broad St,
       HEREFORD ☎ 0870 400 8113 83 ⇆ 🏴

HERTFORDSHIRE

ALDBURY   Map 04 SP91

Stocks Hotel Golf & Country Club Stocks Rd HP23 5RX
☎ 01442 851341 Fax 01442 851253
An 18-hole parkland course is one of the many facilities at this country club.
Stocks Golf & Country Club: 18 holes, 6804yds, Par 72, SSS 73, Course record 65.
Club membership 450.
Visitors must contact in advance and have a handicap certificate. May not play before 12pm at weekends.
Societies must contact well in advance.
Green Fees £30 per round (£40 weekends & bank holidays,after 12pm only).
Cards 🌐 💳 📇 📇 📇
Prof Peter Lane
Designer Mike Billcliffe
Facilities ⊗ ⅲ 🍴 🏌 ♀ 👤 🏠 ⛳ 🚶 🛒 ♂
& Leisure hard tennis courts, sauna, solarium, chipping green, practice bunker.
Location 2m from A41 at Tring

Hotel ★★★★ 65% Pendley Manor, Cow Ln, TRING
       ☎ 01442 891891   74 ⇆ 🏴

ALDENHAM   Map 04 TQ19

Aldenham Golf and Country Club Church Ln WD25 8NN
☎ 01923 853929 Fax 01923 858472
e-mail: aldenhamgolf@ukonline.co.uk
Undulating parkland course with many specimen trees. Beautiful views across countryside.
Old Course: 18 holes, 6480yds, Par 70, SSS 71.
White Course: 9 holes, 2350yds, Par 33, SSS 32.
Club membership 550.
Visitors Old Course restricted weekends before noon. White Course no restrictions.
Societies must contact in advance.
Green Fees Old Course: £25 per round; £35 per day(£32 weekends). White Course £10 per round (£12 weekends).
Cards 🌐 💳 📇 📇 📇
Prof Tim Dunstan
Facilities ⊗ ⅲ 🍴 🏌 ♀ 👤 🏠 ⛳ 🛒 ♂
Location W side of village

BERKHAMSTED   Map 04 SP90

Berkhamsted The Common HP4 2QB
☎ 01442 865832 Fax 01442 863730
e-mail: golf agent.com/clubsites/Berkhamsted
There are no sand bunkers on this Championship heathland course but this does not make it any easier to play. The natural hazards will test the skill of the most able players, with a particularly testing hole at the 11th, 568 yards, par 5. Fine Greens, long carries and heather and gorse. The clubhouse is very comfortable.
18 holes, 6605yds, Par 71, SSS 72, Course record 65.
Club membership 700.
Visitors must contact in advance and be ccompetent golfer.
Societies must contact in advance.
Green Fees £40 per day; £30 per round (£40 weekends after 11.30am).
Cards 🌐 💳 📇
Prof Basil Proudfoot
Designer Colt/Braid
Facilities ⊗ ⅲ 🍴 🏌 ♀ 👤 🏠 ♂
Location 1.5m E

Hotel ★★★★ 65% Pendley Manor, Cow Ln,
       TRING ☎ 01442 891891   74 ⇆ 🏴

BISHOP'S STORTFORD   Map 05 TL42

Bishop's Stortford Dunmow Rd CM23 5HP
☎ 01279 654715 Fax 01279 655215
e-mail: bishopstortfordgc@hotmail.com
Well established parkland course, fairly flat, but undulating, with easy walking.
18 holes, 6404yds, Par 71, SSS 71, Course record 66.
Club membership 900.
Visitors must have a valid handicap certificate, must play with member at weekends. Ladies day Tue.
Societies must contact in writing.
Green Fees £35 per day; £31 per 27 holes; £27 per 18 holes.
Prof Stephen M Bryan
Designer James Braid
Facilities ⊗ ⅲ 🍴 🏌 ♀ 👤 🏠 ⛳ 🚶 🛒 ♂
& Leisure snooker tables.
Location 0.5m W of M11 junc 8 on A1250   ▶

Bishop's Stortford Golf Club

Hotel   ★★★★ 69% Down Hall Country House Hotel,
               Hatfield Heath, BISHOP'S STORTFORD
               ☎ 01279 731441   99 ⇌ ♠

Great Hadham Golf & Country Club Great Hadham Rd,
Much Hadham SG10 6JE
☎ 01279 843558 Fax 01279 842122
An undulating open meadowland/links course offering
excellent country views and a challenge with its ever present
breeze.
18 holes, 6854yds, Par 72, SSS 73, Course record 67.
Club membership 700.
Visitors   welcome all times except am Mon, Wed, Sat &
                  Sun.
Societies   by advance booking in writing.
Green Fees   not confirmed.
Cards   💳 💳 💳
Prof   Kevin Lunt
Designer   Iain Roberts
Facilities   ⊗ ⅲ Ꮮ 💺 ♀ ⚲ 🏠 ❦ ♂ ⚓
& Leisure   sauna, solarium, gymnasium, health club.
Location   On the B1004, 3m SW of Bishop's Stortford

Hotel   ★★★★ 69% Down Hall Country House Hotel,
               Hatfield Heath, BISHOP'S STORTFORD
               ☎ 01279 731441   99 ⇌ ♠

BRICKENDON   Map 05 TL30

Brickendon Grange Pembridge Ln SG13 8PD
☎ 01992 511258 Fax 01992 511411
e-mail: genman@brickendongrangegc.co.uk
Undulating parkland course with some fine par 4's. 17th hole
reputed to be best in the county.
18 holes, 6395yds, Par 71, SSS 70, Course record 66.
Club membership 680.
Visitors   must have handicap certificate. With member
                  only at weekends & bank holidays.
Societies   by arrangement.
Green Fees   £38 per day; £28 per round.
Prof   Graham Tippett
Designer   C K Cotton
Facilities   ⊗ ⅲ Ꮮ 💺 ♀ ⚲ 🏠 ❦ ♂ ⚓
Location   W side of village

Hotel   ★★★ 65% The White Horse, Hertingfordbury,
               HERTFORD ☎ 0870 400 8114 42 ⇌ ♠

BROOKMANS PARK   Map 04 TL20

Brookmans Park Golf Club Rd AL9 7AT
☎ 01707 652487 Fax 01707 661851
Brookman's Park is an undulating parkland course, with
several cleverly constructed holes. But it is a fair course,
although it can play long. The 11th, par 3, is a testing
hole which plays across a lake.
18 holes, 6460yds, Par 71, SSS 71, Course record 66.
Club membership 750.
Visitors   must contact professional in advance 01707
                  652468 and have a handicap certificate;
                  must play with member at weekends &
                  bank holidays.
Societies   must telephone or write in advance.
Green Fees   not confirmed.
Prof   Ian Jelley
Designer   Hawtree/Taylor
Facilities   ⊗ ⅲ Ꮮ 💺 ♀ ⚲ 🏠 ❦ ♂ ⚓
Location   N side of village off A1000

Hotel   ★★★ 66% Posthouse South Mimms,
               SOUTH MIMMS ☎ 0870 400 9072
               143 ⇌ ♠

BROXBOURNE   Map 05 TL30

Hertfordshire Broxbournebury Mansion, White Stubbs Ln
☎ 01992 466666 & 441268 (pro shop) Fax 01992 470326
e-mail: hertfordshire@americangolf.uk.com
An 18 hole course of a 'Nicklaus' design set around a Grade
II listed clubhouse to full USGA specifications. Considered
to be one of the best 'pay and play' courses to appear in
recent years.
18 holes, 6314yds, Par 70, SSS 70, Course record 62.
Club membership 600.
Visitors   book 7 days in advance, soft spikes only
Societies   telephone in advance, deposit required.
Green Fees   £30 (£35 weekend).
Cards   💳 💳 💳 💳 💳 💳 💳
Prof   Adrian Shearn
Facilities   ⊗ ⅲ Ꮮ 💺 ♀ ⚲ 🏠 ❦ ♂ ⚓
& Leisure   hard tennis courts, heated indoor swimming
                  pool, fishing, sauna, solarium, gymnasium,
                  jacuzzis.
Location   on A10 take Broxbourne exit and follow signs
                  for Paradise Wildlife Park. Turn left at Bell
                  Lane and follow road over A10, course on right.

Hotel   ★★★★ 65% Cheshunt Marriott Hotel,
               Halfhide Ln, Turnford, BROXBOURNE
               ☎ 01992 451245 143 ⇌ ♠

BUNTINGFORD   Map 05 TL32

East Herts Hamels Park SG9 9NA ☎ 01920 821922(Pro)
An attractive undulating parkland course with magnificent
specimen trees.
18 holes, 6456yds, Par 71, SSS 71.
Club membership 750.
Visitors   must contact in advance & have handicap
                  certificate, but may not play on Wed &
                  weekends.
Societies   apply in writing.
Green Fees   £35 per day/round.
Prof   G Culmer

Facilities ⊗ 🅱 ♟ ♀ ♨ ⌂ ⚑ 🖐 ♿ ✐
Location 1m N of Puckeridge off A10

Hotel ★★★ 66% Novotel Stevenage, Knebworth Park, STEVENAGE ☎ 01438 346100 100 ⇄ ☏

BUSHEY   Map 04 TQ19

Bushey Golf & Country Club High St WD23 1TT
☎ 020 8950 2215(pro shop) Fax 020 8386 1181
Undulating parkland with challenging 2nd and 9th holes. The latter has a sweeping dolgleg left, playing to a green in front of the club house. For the rather too enthusiatic golfer, Bushey offers its own physiotherapist!
9 holes, 6120yds, Par 70, SSS 69, Course record 67.
Club membership 411.
Visitors must contact in advance and subject to club competition times.
Societies apply in writing or by telephone.
Green Fees £16 per 18 holes; £10 per 9 holes(£19/£12 weekends).
Cards 🖃
Prof Grahame Atkinson
Facilities ⊗ 🍴 🅱 ♟ ♀ ♨ ⌂ ⚑ 🖐 ♿ ✐ ⚐
& Leisure sauna, solarium, gymnasium, health & fitness club.

Hotel ★★★ 75% Edgwarebury Hotel, Barnet Ln, ELSTREE ☎ 020 8953 8227 47 ⇄ ☏

Bushey Hall Bushey Hall Dr WD23 2EP
☎ 01923 222253 Fax 01923 229759 e-mail: busheyhallgolf@aol.com
Tree lined parkland course.
18 holes, 6099yds, Par 70, SSS 69.
Club membership 500.

Bushey Hall Golf Club

Visitors may book 14 days in advance and may only play after 10.30am weekends.
Societies must contact in writing.
Green Fees £20 per round (£28 weekends & bank holidays).
Cards 🖃 🖃 🖃 🖃 🖃
Prof Ken Wickham
Designer Clouston
Facilities ⊗ 🅱 ♟ ♀ ♨ ⌂ ⚑ 🖐 ♿ ✐
Location 1.5m NW on A4008

Hotel ★★★ 75% Edgwarebury Hotel, Barnet Ln, ELSTREE ☎ 020 8953 8227 47 ⇄ ☏

Hartsbourne Golf & Country Club Hartsbourne Ave WD2 1JW ☎ 020 8950 1133
18 holes, 6305yds, Par 71, SSS 70, Course record 62.
Location 5m SE of Watford
Telephone for further details

Hotel ★★★ 75% Edgwarebury Hotel, Barnet Ln, ELSTREE ☎ 020 8953 8227 47 ⇄ ☏

CHESHUNT   Map 05 TL30

Cheshunt Cheshunt Park, Park Ln EN7 6QD
☎ 01992 624009
Municipal parkland course, well-bunkered with ponds, easy walking.
18 holes, 6613yds, Par 71, SSS 71.
Club membership 350.
Visitors must book Tee-times through Reception. Must contact in advance.
Societies must apply in writing.
Green Fees not confirmed.
Cards 🖃 🖃 🖃 🖃 🖃
Prof Andy Traynor
Designer P Wawtry
Facilities ⊗ 🍴 🅱 ♟ ♀ ♨ ⌂ ⚑ 🖐 ♿ ✐
Location 1.5m NW off B156

Hotel ★★★★ 65% Cheshunt Marriott Hotel, Halfhide Ln, Turnford, BROXBOURNE ☎ 01992 451245 143 ⇄ ☏

CHORLEYWOOD   Map 04 TQ09

Chorleywood Common Rd WD3 5LN
☎ 01923 282009 Fax 01923 286739 e-mail: chorleywood.gc@btclick.com
Very attractive mix of woodland and heathland with natural hazards and good views.
9 holes, 5712yds, Par 68, SSS 67.
Club membership 300.
Visitors must contact in advance, restricted weekends & Tues.
Societies initial contact by telephone.
Green Fees £16 per day (£20 weekends & bank holidays).
Facilities ⊗ 🍴 by prior arrangement 🅱 ♟ ♀ ♨
Location E side of village off A404

Hotel ★★★ 69% The Bedford Arms Chenies, CHENIES ☎ 01923 283301 10 ⇄ ☏

ELSTREE   Map 04 TQ19

Elstree Watling St WD6 3AA
☎ 020 8953 6115 Fax 020 8207 6390
Parkland course.
18 holes, 6556yds, Par 73, SSS 72.
Club membership 650.
Visitors advisable to contact in advance, no restrictions weekdays, may not play until after 2pm weekends unless tee time available day prior.
Societies telephone in advance.
Green Fees not confirmed.
Cards 🖃 🖃
Prof Marc Warwick
Designer Donald Steel
Facilities ⊗ 🅱 ♟ ♀ ♨ ⌂ ⚑ 🖐 ♿ ✐ ⚐
Location A5183 between Radlett and Elstree ▶

Hotel   ★★★ 75% Edgwarebury Hotel, Barnet Ln,
              ELSTREE ☎ 020 8953 8227 47 ⇆ ↿

ESSENDON   Map 04 TL20

Hatfield London Country Club Bedwell Park AL9 6JA
☎ 01707 642624(old course) & 663131(new course)
Fax 01707 646187 & 278475 e-mail: hlccgolf@aol.com
Parkland course with many varied hazards, including ponds,
a stream and a ditch. 19th-century manor clubhouse. 9-hole
pitch and putt.
Old Course: 18 holes, 6808yds, Par 72, SSS 72.
New Course: 18 holes, 7091yds, Par 72, SSS 74.
Club membership 250.
Visitors   must contact in advance. Societies only for New
                Course.
Societies   must contact in advance.
Green Fees Old course: £17 per 18 holes (£27 weekends).
Cards   ▨▨ ▦▦ ▦▦ ▨▨ ▨
Prof   Norman Greer
Designer   Fred Hawtry
Facilities ⊗ ⅷ by prior arrangement ♿ ▆ ♀ ♨ ☎ ⚐
                ♨ ♐
& Leisure   hard tennis courts, 9 hole pitch and putt (Old
                Course) Japanese bath & jacuzzi (New Course).
Location   On B158 1m S

Hotel   ★★★ 62% Quality Hotel Hatfield, Roehyde
              Way, HATFIELD ☎ 01707 275701 76 ⇆ ↿

GRAVELEY   Map 04 TL22

Chesfield Downs Jack's Hill SG4 7EQ
☎ 01462 482929 Fax 01462 482930
A revolutionary golf course with the emphasis on facilities
for the entire family. Its undulating, open downland course
has an inland links feel. There is a 25-bay floodlit, covered
driving range, a 9-hole Par 3 and many other facilities.
18 holes, 6648yds, Par 71, SSS 72.
Club membership 500.
Visitors   no restrictions.
Societies   must telephone in advance.
Green Fees not confirmed.
Prof   Jane Fernley
Designer   J Gaunt
Facilities ⊗ ⅷ by prior arrangement ♿ ▆ ♀ ♨ ☎ ⚐ ♨
                ♨ ♐ ↿
& Leisure   par3 9 hole course.
Location   Jct 8 of A1, B197 to Graveley

Hotel   L Hotel Ibis, Danestrete, STEVENAGE
              ☎ 01438 779955 98 ⇆ ↿

HARPENDEN   Map 04 TL11

Aldwickbury Park Piggottshill Ln AL5 1AB
☎ 01582 760112 Fax 01582 760113
e-mail: enquiries@aldwickburyparkgolfclub.com
Attractive parkland course with large areas of mature
woodland and good views across the Lee Valley.
18 holes, 6352yds, Par 71, SSS 70, Course record 66.
Club membership 700.
Visitors   may book up to 3 days in advance by telephone.
                May only play after 1pm weekends.
Societies   telephone for brochure, various packages
                available.

Green Fees £22 (£25 weekends).
Cards   ▨▨ ▦▦ ▦▦ ▨▨ ▨
Prof   Simon Plumb
Designer   Ken Brown/Martin Gillett
Facilities ⊗ ⅷ ♿ ▆ ♀ ♨ ☎ ⚐ ♐ ♨ ♐
& Leisure   9 hole par 3 course.
Location   Located just off Wheathampstead Road,
                between Harpenden/Wheathampstead, 10mins
                from junct 9 of M1

Hotel   ★★★ 68% Harpenden House, 18 Southdown
              Rd, HARPENDEN ☎ 01582 449955
              17 ⇆ ↿ Annexe59 ⇆ ↿

Harpenden Hammonds End, Redbourn Ln AL5 2AX
☎ 01582 712580 Fax 01582 712725
e-mail: harpgolf@hammonds.freeservce.com
Gently undulating parkland course, easy walking.
18 holes, 6381yds, Par 70, SSS 70, Course record 67.
Club membership 800.
Visitors   must contact in advance. May not play Thu &
                weekends.
Societies   must apply in writing.
Green Fees not confirmed.
Cards   ▨▨ ▦▦ ▦▦ ▨▨ ▨
Prof   Peter Cherry
Designer   Hawtree & Taylor
Facilities ⊗ ⅷ ♿ ▆ ♀ ♨ ☎ ⚐ ♐ ↿
Location   1m S on B487

Hotel   ★★★ 68% Harpenden House, 18 Southdown
              Rd, HARPENDEN ☎ 01582 449955
              17 ⇆ ↿ Annexe59 ⇆ ↿

Harpenden Common Cravells Rd, East Common AL5 1BL
☎ 01582 715959 Fax 01582 715959
Flat, easy walking, good greens, typical common course.
18 holes, 6214yds, Par 70, SSS 70, Course record 64.
Club membership 710.
Visitors   must contact in advance.
Societies   Thu & Fri only. Must apply in writing.
Green Fees £30 per day; £25 per round(£30 per round
                weekends).
Prof   Danny Fitzsimmons
Designer   K Brown
Facilities ⊗ ⅷ ♿ ▆ ♀ ♨ ☎ ⚐ ♐ ♐
Location   1m S on A1081

Hotel   ★★★ 70% Hanover International Hotel,
              1 Luton Rd, HARPENDEN ☎ 01582 760271
              60 ⇆ ↿

HEMEL HEMPSTEAD   Map 04 TL00

Boxmoor 18 Box Ln, Boxmoor HP3 0DJ
☎ 01442 242434 e-mail: boxmoor90@freeserve.com
Challenging, very hilly, moorland course with sloping
fairways divided by trees. Fine views. Testing holes: 3rd (par
3), 4th (par 4).
9 holes, 4812yds, Par 64, SSS 63, Course record 62.
Club membership 280.
Visitors   may not play on Sun & bank holidays.
                Restricted some Sat.
Societies   must contact in advance.
Green Fees not confirmed.
Facilities ♿ ▆ ♀ ♨
Location   2m SW on B4505

▶

Hotel   ★★ 72% The Two Brewers, The Common, CHIPPERFIELD ☎ 01923 265266   20 ⇌ ͡

Little Hay Box Ln, Bovingdon HP3 0DQ ☎ 01442 833798
Semi-parkland, inland links.
18 holes, 6678yds, Par 72, SSS 72.
Visitors   advisable to contact in advance.
Societies   telephone for details.
Green Fees not confirmed.
Cards   🔲🔲🔲🔲🔲
Prof   D Johnson/M Campbell
Designer   Hawtree
Facilities   ⊗ �𝄞 ⬛ 💼 ♀ ⩍ 🏠 ⛳ ❦ ⁄ ͺ
Location   1.5m SW on B4505 off A41

Hotel   ★★★ 68% Posthouse Hemel Hempstead, Breakspear Way, HEMEL HEMPSTEAD ☎ 0870 400 9041 145 ⇌ ͡

Shendish Manor London Rd, Apsley HP3 0AA
☎ 01442 251806 Fax 01442 230683
18 holes, 5660yds, Par 70, SSS 67.
Location   Just off A4251
Telephone for further details

Hotel   ★★★★ 65% Pendley Manor, Cow Ln, TRING ☎ 01442 891891   74 ⇌ ͡

KNEBWORTH   Map 04 TL22

Knebworth Deards End Ln SG3 6NL
☎ 01438 812752 Fax 01438 815216
Parkland course, easy walking.
18 holes, 6492yds, Par 71, SSS 71, Course record 66.
Club membership 900.
Visitors   must have handicap certificate , but must play with member at weekends.
Societies   Mon, Tue & Thu. Must contact in advance.
Green Fees £30 per day/round.
Cards   🔲🔲🔲🔲🔲
Prof   Garry Parker
Designer   W Park (Jun)
Facilities   ⊗ ⬛ 💼 ♀ ⩍ 🏠 ⛳ ⁄
Location   N side of village off B197

Hotel   ★★★ 61% Posthouse Stevenage, Old London Rd, Broadwater, STEVENAGE ☎ 0870 400 9076 54 ⇌ ͡

LETCHWORTH   Map 04 TL23

Letchworth Letchworth Ln SG6 3NQ
☎ 01462 683203 Fax 01462 484567
Planned more than 50 years ago by Harry Vardon, this adventurous, parkland course is set in a peaceful corner of 'Norman' England. To its variety of natural and artificial hazards is added an unpredictable wind.
18 holes, 6181yds, Par 70, SSS 69, Course record 65.
Club membership 750.
Visitors   with member only at weekends. Must contact in advance and have a handicap certificate.
Societies   Wed, Thu & Fri only, must telephone in advance.
Green Fees £38 per day; £27 per round.
Prof   S Allen

Designer   Harry Vardon
Facilities   ⩍ 🏠 ⁄ ͺ
Location   S side of town centre off A505

Hotel   ★★★ 65% Cromwell Hotel, High St, Old Town, STEVENAGE ☎ 01438 779954   76 ⇌ ͡

LITTLE GADDESDEN   Map 04 SP91

Ashridge HP4 1LY ☎ 01442 842244 Fax 01442 843770
e-mail: info@ashridgegolfclub.ltd.uk
Good parkland course, challenging but fair. Good clubhouse facilities.
18 holes, 6547yds, Par 72, SSS 71, Course record 63.
Club membership 720.
Visitors   must contact in advance , be a member of a recognised club & have handicap certificate, may not play weekends .
Societies   must apply in writing and complete booking form.
Green Fees on application.
Cards   🔲🔲🔲🔲🔲
Prof   Andrew Ainsworth
Designer   Sir G Campbell/C Hutchinson/N Hutchinson
Facilities   ⊗ ⟁ ⬛ 💼 ♀ ⩍ 🏠 ⛳ ⁄ ͺ
Location   5m N of Berkhamsted on the B4506

Hotel   ★★★ 68% Harpenden House, 18 Southdown Rd, HARPENDEN ☎ 01582 449955 17 ⇌ ͡ Annexe59 ⇌ ͡

MUCH HADHAM   Map 05 TL41

Much Hadham Little Hadham Rd SG10 6HD
☎ 01279 843253 Fax 01920 468686
18 holes, 6516yds, Par 71, SSS 71.
Location   1.5m S of A120 fom Little Hadham traffic lights
Telephone for further details

Hotel   ★★★ 60% Roebuck Hotel, Baldock St, WARE ☎ 01920 409955   50 ⇌ ͡

POTTERS BAR   Map 04 TL20

Potters Bar Darkes Ln EN6 1DE
☎ 01707 652020 Fax 01707 655051 e-mail: info@pottersbargolfclub.com
Undulating parkland course with water in play on many holes.
18 holes, 6279yds, Par 71, SSS 70.
Club membership 650.
Visitors   with member only at weekends, Ladies Day Wed morning.
Societies   Mon-Fri & Wed (pm only) by arrangement with Secretary.
Green Fees £25 per round;£35 per day.
Prof   Gary A'Ris/Julian Harding
Designer   James Braid
Facilities   ⊗ ⬛ 💼 ♀ ⩍ 🏠 ⛳ ❦ ⚒ ⁄
Location   1m N of M25 junct 24

Hotel   ★★★ 66% Posthouse South Mimms, SOUTH MIMMS ☎ 0870 400 9072 143 ⇌ ͡

RADLETT   Map 04 TL10

Porters Park Shenley Hill WD7 7AZ
☎ 01923 854127 Fax 01923 855475
e-mail: info@porterspark.fsnet.co.uk
A splendid, undulating parkland course with fine trees
and lush grass. The holes are all different and interesting
- on many accuracy of shot to the green is of paramount
importance.
18 holes, 6313yds, Par 70, SSS 70, Course record 64.
Club membership 1000.
Visitors   must book 24hrs in advance. With member
                 only weekends.
Societies   Wed & Thu only, must apply in writing.
Green Fees   not confirmed.
Prof   David Gleeson
Designer   Braid
Facilities   ⊗ ⫟ ┗ ■ ♀ 凸 ⋔ ⋔ ⏧ ⌀ ⸂
Location   NE side of village off A5183

Hotel   ★★★ 66% Posthouse South Mimms,
                 SOUTH MIMMS ☎ 0870 400 9072
                 143 ⇥ ♟

REDBOURN   Map 04 TL11

Redbourn Kinsbourne Green Ln AL3 7QA
☎ 01582 793493 Fax 01582 794362
e-mail: enquiries@redbourngolfclub.com
Testing parkland course (Five par 4's over 400 yds).
Also 9-hole par 3 course.
Ver Course: 18 holes, 6506yds, Par 70, SSS 71, Course
record 67.
Kingsbourne Course: 9 holes, 1361yds, Par 27.
Club membership 750.
Visitors   must contact up to 3 days in advance for Ver
                 Course. No restrictions for Par 3.
Societies   must telephone in advance.
Green Fees   not confirmed.
Cards   ⊡ ⚍ ⚍ ⚏ ⬚
Prof   Stephen Hunter
Facilities   ⊗ ⫟ ┗ ■ ♀ 凸 凸 ⋔ ⋔ ⏧ ⌀ ⸂
Location   1m N off A5183

Hotel   ★★★ 68% Harpenden House, 18 Southdown
                 Rd, HARPENDEN ☎ 01582 449955
                 17 ⇥ ♟ Annexe59 ⇥ ♟

RICKMANSWORTH   Map 04 TQ09

Moor Park WD3 1QN
☎ 01923 773146 Fax 01923 777109
e-mail: moorparkgolfclub@aol.com
Two parkland courses - High Course is challenging and
will test the best golfer and West Course demands a high
degree of accuracy.
High Golf Course: 18 holes, 6713yds, Par 72, SSS 72,
Course record 63.
West Golf Course: 18 holes, 5815yds, Par 69, SSS 68,
Course record 62.
Club membership 1700.
Visitors   must contact in advance but may not play at
                 weekends, bank holidays or before 1pm on
                 Tue & Thu.
Societies   must contact in advance.
Green Fees High: £60 per round. West: £35 per round.

Cards   ⊡ ⚍ ⚍ ⚏ ⬚
Prof   Lawrence Farmer
Designer   H S Colt
Facilities   ⊗ ┗ ■ ♀ 凸 凸 ⋔ ⋔ ⏧ ⌀ ⸂
& Leisure   hard and grass tennis courts.
Location   Off A404 to Northwood,close to jcnt17&18
                 on M25

Hotel   ★★★ 69% The Bedford Arms Chenies,
                 CHENIES ☎ 01923 283301   10 ⇥ ♟

Rickmansworth Public Course Moor Ln WD3 1QL
☎ 01923 775278
Undulating, municipal parkland course.
18 holes, 4469yds, Par 64, SSS 62.
Club membership 240.
Visitors   must contact the club in advance, 7 day booking.
                 Set of clubs per person.
Societies   must contact in advance.
Green Fees £10 per 18 holes(£14.20 weekends).
Cards   ⊡ ⚍ ⚍ ⚏ ⬚
Prof   Alan Dobbins
Designer   Colt
Facilities   ⊗ ⫟ ┗ ■ ♀ 凸 凸 ⋔ ⋔ ⏧ ⌀
Location   2m S of town off A4145

Hotel   ★★★ 69% The Bedford Arms Chenies,
                 CHENIES ☎ 01923 283301   10 ⇥ ♟

ROYSTON   Map 05 TL34

Barkway Park Nuthampstead Rd, Barkway SG8 8EN
☎ 01763 849070 & 848215
An undulating course criss-crossed by ditches which come
into play on several holes. The challenging par 3 7th features
a long, narrow green with out of bounds close to the right
edge of the green.
18 holes, 6997yds, Par 74, SSS 74.
Club membership 310.
Visitors   must contact in advance, telephone for tee times.
Societies   apply for booking form.
Green Fees not confirmed.
Cards   ⊡ ⚍ ⚍ ⚏
Prof   Jamie Bates
Designer   Vivien Saunders
Facilities   ⊗ ┗ ■ ♀ 凸 凸 ⋔ ⌀
Location   Off B1368 from A10

Hotel   ★★★ 73% Duxford Lodge Hotel, Ickleton Rd,
                 DUXFORD ☎ 01223 836444
                 11 ⇥ ♟ Annexe4 ⇥ ♟

Heydon Grange Golf & Country Club Heydon SG8 7NS
☎ 01763 208988 Fax 01763 208926
e-mail: enquiries@heydon-grange.co.uk
Three 9-hole parkland courses - the Essex, Cambridgeshire
and Hertfordshire - situated in gently rolling countryside.
Courses are playable all year round.
Essex: 9 holes, 3013yds, Par 36, SSS 35, Course record 66.
Cambridgeshire: 9 holes, 3323yds, Par 36, SSS 36.
Hertfordshire: 9 holes, 3180yds, Par 36, SSS 36.
Club membership 250.
Visitors   must contact to book tee times, welcome all
                 times weekends included.
Societies   telephone in advance for booking form.

▶

Green Fees £10 per 9 holes;£12.50 per 18 holes(£12/£17.50 weekends).
Cards ⊠ ▬ ▬ 💳 ▨ 🏧 ▨
Prof Stuart Smith
Designer Cameron Sinclair
Facilities ⊗ ⊪ ♨ ♣ ♀ ⚒ ⌕ 🏌 ✈ ♂ ⚑
Location A505 between Royston/Duxford, off junct 10 on M11

Hotel ★★★ 73% Duxford Lodge Hotel, Ickleton Rd, DUXFORD ☎ 01223 836444 11 ⇄ ⋒ Annexe4 ⇄ ⋒

Kingsway Cambridge Rd, Melbourn SG8 6EY
☎ 01763 262727 Fax 01763 263298
Short and deceptively tricky 9-hole course providing a good test for both beginners and experienced golfers. Out of bounds and strategically placed bunkers come into play on several holes, in particular the tough par 3 7th.
9 holes, 2455yds, Par 33, SSS 32.
Club membership 150.
Visitors welcome.
Societies telephone for details.
Green Fees not confirmed.
Cards ⊠ ▬ ▬ ▨ ▨
Prof Denise Hastings/Mark Sturgess
Facilities ⊗ ♨ ♣ ♀ ⚒ 🏌 ⌕ ♂ ⚑
Location Off the A10

Hotel ★★★ 73% Duxford Lodge Hotel, Ickleton Rd, DUXFORD ☎ 01223 836444 11 ⇄ ⋒ Annexe4 ⇄ ⋒

Royston Baldock Rd SG8 5BG
☎ 01763 242696 Fax 01763 246910
e-mail: roystongolf@btconnect.com
Heathland course on undulating terrain and fine fairways. The 8th, 10th and 15th are the most notable holes on this all weather course.
18 holes, 6052yds, Par 70, SSS 70, Course record 65.
Club membership 850.
Visitors Mon-Fri only subject to availability. Must contact in advance.
Societies by arrangement Mon-Fri.
Green Fees £30 per day; £25 per round.
Cards ⊠ ▬ ▨ ▨ ▨
Prof Sean Clark
Designer Harry Vardon
Facilities ⊗ ♨ ♣ ♀ ⚒ 🏌 ♂
Location 0.5m W of town centre

Hotel ★★★ 73% Duxford Lodge Hotel, Ickleton Rd, DUXFORD ☎ 01223 836444 11 ⇄ ⋒ Annexe4 ⇄ ⋒

ST ALBANS   Map 04 TL10

Abbey View Westminster Lodge Leisure Ctr, Hollywell Hill AL1 2DL ☎ 01727 868227 Fax 01727 863017
e-mail: westminsterlodge/leisureconnection@circanotesdomain
Abbey View is a public golf course designed for beginners, but is sufficiently challenging for experienced golfers who only have time for a short game. There is a resident professional for assistance and lessons.
9 holes, 1383yds, Par 29.
Visitors welcome but no sharing clubs, suitable footwear & wide wheel trolleys.
Societies telephone or write in advance.

Green Fees £5.40 per 9 holes;£7 per 18 holes.
Prof Roddy Watkins
Facilities ⊗ ⊪ ♨ ♣ ♀ ⚒ 🏌 ⌕ ♂
& Leisure hard and grass tennis courts, heated indoor swimming pool, sauna, solarium, gymnasium.
Location Centre of St Albans, off Holywell hill

Hotel ★★ 67% Apples Hotel, 133 London Rd, ST ALBANS ☎ 01727 844111 9 ⇄ ⋒

Batchwood Hall Batchwood Dr AL3 5XA
☎ 01727 844250 Fax 01727 858506
e-mail: batchwood@leisureconnection.co.uk
Municipal parkland course designed by J H Taylor and opened in 1935.
Batchwood Hall Golf Club: 18 holes, 6487yds, Par 71, SSS 71. Club membership 350.
Visitors must contact in advance, in person.
Societies must contact in advance.
Green Fees £10.50(£13.50 weekends).
Cards ⊠ ▬ ▬ ▨ ▨
Prof Mark Flitton
Facilities ⊗ ⊪ ♨ ♣ ♀ ⚒ 🏌 ⌕ ♂
& Leisure hard tennis courts, squash, solarium, gymnasium, Indoor tennis courts.
Location 1m NW off A5183

Hotel ★★★ 77% St Michael's Manor, Fishpool St, ST ALBANS ☎ 01727 864444 23 ⇄ ⋒

Verulam London Rd AL1 1JG
☎ 01727 853327 Fax 01727 812201
e-mail: genman@verulamgolf.co.uk
Easy walking parkland course with fourteen holes having out-of-bounds. Water affects the 12th, 13th and 14th holes. Samuel Ryder was Captain here in 1927 when he began the now celebrated Ryder Cup Competition.
18 holes, 6448yds, Par 72, SSS 71, Course record 67.
Club membership 720.
Visitors must contact pro shop in advance. With member only at weekends.
Societies must contact advance.
Green Fees Mon: £25 per day, £15 per round. Tue-Fri: £35/£25.
Cards ⊠ ▬ ▬ ▨ ▨
Prof Nick Burch
Designer Braid
Facilities ⊗ ⊪ by prior arrangement ♨ ♣ ♀ ⚒ 🏌 ♂
Location 0.5m from St albans town centre on London RdA1081

Hotel ★★★★ 74% Sopwell House Hotel & Country Club, Cottonmill Ln, Sopwell, ST ALBANS ☎ 01727 864477 112 ⇄ ⋒ Annexe16 ⇄ ⋒

SAWBRIDGEWORTH   Map 05 TL41

Manor of Groves Golf & Country Club High Wych CM21 0LA ☎ 01279 722333 Fax 01279 726972
The course is set out over 150 acres of established parkland and rolling countryside and is a true test of golf for the club golfer.
18 holes, 6280yds, Par 71, SSS 70, Course record 63.
Club membership 450.
Visitors telephone bookings preferred, restrictions on Tue, Thu and weekends.
Societies Mon-Fri by prior arrangement, telephone in advance.

▶

Green Fees	£20 per round (£25 weekends).Mon £15.
Cards	▨ ■ ▨ ▨ ▨ ▨
Prof	Craig Laurence
Designer	S Sharer
Facilities	⊗ ⫙ ⍦ ▶ ♀ ⚲ 📦 ⚐ ↘ ⚓ ⛳
Location	1.5m on west side of town

Hotel   ★★★ 73% Swallow Churchgate Hotel, Churchgate St Village, Old Harlow, HARLOW ☎ 01279 420246   85 ⇄ ↾

STANSTEAD ABBOTS   Map 05 TL31

Briggens House Hotel Briggens Park, Stanstead Rd SG12 8LD ☎ 01279 793742 Fax 01279 793685
An attractive 9-hole course set in the grounds of a 80 acres of countryside.
9 holes, 2793yds, Par 36, SSS 69, Course record 31.
Club membership 230.

Visitors	may not play Thu 5-6pm and Sun am. No jeans. Must have own clubs and golf shoes (hire available).
Societies	must contact in advance.
Green Fees	£14 per 18 holes;£10 per 9 holes(£17/£13 weekends).
Cards	▨ ■ ▨ ▨ ▨ ▨
Prof	Alan McGinn
Facilities	⊗ ⫙ ⍦ ▶ ♀ ⚲ 📦 ⚐ ↘ ⚓ ⛳
& Leisure	hard tennis courts, heated outdoor swimming pool, fishing.
Location	Off Stanstead road A414

Hotel   ★★★★ 60% Briggens House Hotel, Stanstead Rd, STANSTEAD ABBOTTS ☎ 01279 829955   54 ⇄ ↾

STEVENAGE   Map 04 TL22

Stevenage Golf Centre Aston Ln SG2 7EL
☎ 01438 880424 & 880223 Fax 01438 880040
Municipal course designed by John Jacobs, with natural water hazards and some wooded areas.
18 holes, 6451yds, Par 72, SSS 71.
Club membership 600.

Visitors	no restrictions.
Societies	must contact 1 week in advance. Deposit required.
Green Fees	not confirmed.
Cards	▨ ■ ▨ ▨ ▨ ▨
Prof	Steve Barker
Designer	John Jacobs
Facilities	⊗ ⫙ ⍦ ▶ ♀ ⚲ 📦 ⚐ ↘ ⚓ ⛳
& Leisure	par3 course.
Location	4m SE off B5169

Hotel   ★★★ 61% Posthouse Stevenage, Old London Rd, Broadwater, STEVENAGE ☎ 0870 400 9076 54 ⇄ ↾

WARE   Map 05 TL31

Chadwell Springs Hertford Rd SG12 9LE
☎ 01920 461447 Fax 01920 466596
Quick drying moorland course on high plateau subject to wind. The first two holes are par 5 and notable.
9 holes, 6418yds, Par 72, SSS 71, Course record 68.
Club membership 650.

Visitors	with member only at weekends.
Societies	bookings accepted, Mon, Wed & Fri only.
Green Fees	£15 (£17 weekends).
Cards	▨ ■ ▨ ▨ ▨ ▨
Prof	Mark Wall
Facilities	⊗ ⫙ ⍦ ▶ ♀ ⚲ 📦 ⛳
Location	0.75m W on A119

Hotel   ★★★ 60% Roebuck Hotel, Baldock St, WARE ☎ 01920 409955   50 ⇄ ↾

MARRIOTT HANBURY MANOR GOLF AND COUNTRY CLUB   See page 143

Whitehill Dane End SG12 0JS
☎ 01920 438495 Fax 01920 438891
e-mail: whitehillgolfcentre@btinternet.com
Undulating course providing a good test for both the average golfer and the low handicapper. Several lakes in challenging positions.
18 holes, 6618yds, Par 72, SSS 72.
Club membership 600.

Visitors	handicap certificate must be produced or competence test taken (free), appropriate clothing must be worn.
Societies	telephone or write for booking form.
Green Fees	not confirmed.
Cards	▨ ■ ▨ ▨ ▨
Prof	David Ling
Facilities	⊗ ⫙ ⍦ ▶ ♀ ⚲ 📦 ⚐ ↘ ⚓ ⛳ ↾

Hotel   ★★★ 60% Roebuck Hotel, Baldock St, WARE ☎ 01920 409955   50 ⇄ ↾

WATFORD   Map 04 TQ19

West Herts Cassiobury Park WD3 3GG
☎ 01923 236484 Fax 01923 222300
The West Herts course is close to Watford but its tree-lined setting is beautiful and tranquil. Set out on a plateau the course is exceedingly dry. It also has a very severe finish with the 17th, a hole of 378 yards, the toughest on the course. The last hole measures over 480 yards.
18 holes, 6400yds, Par 72, SSS 71, Course record 65.
Club membership 700.

Visitors	must contact in advance.
Societies	must telephone in advance and confirm in writing.
Green Fees	£26 per round ;£38 per day(£35 per round weekends).
Cards	▨ ▨ ▨
Prof	Charles Gough
Designer	Tom Morris
Facilities	⊗ ⫙ ⍦ ▶ ♀ ⚲ 📦 ⚐ ↘ ⚓ ⛳
& Leisure	indoor teaching facility.
Location	W side of town centre off A412

AA Hotels that have special arrangements with golf courses are listed at the back of the guide

Marriott Hanbury Manor

Ware, *Hertfordshire*   ☎ 01920 487722   Fax 01920 487692   Map 05 TL31

This PGA European Tour venue has played host to many major championships, most recently it has been a regular venue for the English Open. Golf clinics, tuition, swing analysis and corporate events are available, complemented by the extensive leisure facilities.

The superb parkland course was first built around the family home in 1890, the original Harry Vardon course has since been sympathetically redesigned by Jack Nicklaus II to create something unforgettable. Its cleverly sited trees and several picturesque water features offer a true challenge to anyone who enjoys their golf. The Par 4 13th hole is an interesting dog-leg which requires a mid iron second shot over a lake to a well guarded two tiered green, being stroke index two it could make or break your score.

Visitors with handicap certificate, members guests and hotel residents only. Must contact in advance

Societies must be booked in advance. Mon-Thu only

Green Fees £75 per round as hotel guest

Facilities ⊗ ⫫ 🏌 🍺 ♀ ♨ 🏠 ⛳ 🐾 🛒 🏌 🏌

Leisure tennis, swimming, sauna, solarium, gymnasium

Location Ware SG12 0SD (adjacent to A10. From N just past sign for Thunderidge)

Holes/Par/Course record 18 holes, 7016 yds, Par 72, Course record 61

Championship Course

WHERE TO STAY AND EAT NEARBY

Hotel
WARE

★★★★★ 🌟🌟🌟 73%
Marriott Hanbury Manor Hotel & Country Club
☎ 01920 487722. 134 ⇆ 🏠 Annexe 27 ⇆ 🏠

WELWYN GARDEN CITY   Map 04 TL21

Mill Green Gypsy Ln AL6 4TY
☎ 01707 276900 & 270542 (Pro shop) Fax 01707 276898
The course plays over the second 9 holes around the lakes
and sweeps back through the woods. The first 9 holes are
subject to the prevailing winds. The par 3 9-hole gives a
good test for improving the short game.
18 holes, 6615yds, Par 72, SSS 72, Course record 64.
Club membership 700.
Visitors   must contact in advance by telephone. 3 day
         booking arrangement.
Societies   apply in writing for details.
Green Fees not confirmed.
Cards   🖬 ■ 🖬 💷 🖾 🔊 🕊
Prof   Alan Hall
Designer   Alliss & Clark
Facilities   ⊗ 🏢 🖟 🖢 💡 🛆 🛱 🛡 🐾 🦺 ⌀ 🕻
& Leisure 9 hole par 3 course.
Location   Exit 4 of A1(M), A414 to Mill Green

Hotel   ★★★ 63% Quality Hotel Welwyn, The Link,
           WELWYN ☎ 01438 716911   96 ⇄ 🕊

Panshanger Golf & Squash Complex Old Herns Ln
AL7 2ED ☎ 01707 333350 & 333312 Fax 01707 390010
e-mail: r.preece@welhat.gov.uk
Picturesque, mature course overlooking Mimram Valley.
18 holes, 6347yds, Par 72, SSS 70, Course record 65.
Club membership 400.
Visitors   advisable to book 1 week in advance by
         telephone. Dress code in force.
Societies   telephone for details.
Green Fees not confirmed.
Cards   🖬 🖬 🔊 🕊
Prof   Bryan Lewis/Mick Corlass
Designer   Peter Kirkham
Facilities   ⊗ 🖟 🖢 💡 🛆 🛡 🐾 🦺 ⌀
& Leisure squash.
Location   N side of town centre signposted off B1000

Hotel   ★★★ 63% Quality Hotel Welwyn, The Link,
           WELWYN ☎ 01438 716911   96 ⇄ 🕊

Welwyn Garden City Mannicotts, High Oaks Rd AL8 7BP
☎ 01707 325243 Fax 01707 393213
Undulating parkland course with a ravine. A former course
record holder is Nick Faldo.
18 holes, 6074yds, Par 70, SSS 69, Course record 63.
Club membership 975.
Visitors   must contact in advance but may not play Sun
         am.
Societies   must contact in advance.
Green Fees not confirmed.
Cards   🖬 🖬 🔊 🕊
Prof   Richard May
Facilities   ⊗ 🏢 🖟 🖢 💡 🛆 🛡 🐾 🦺 ⌀
Location   W side of city, exit 6 off A1

Hotel   ★★★ 63% Quality Hotel Welwyn, The Link,
           WELWYN ☎ 01438 716911   96 ⇄ 🕊

Where to stay, where to eat?
Visit the AA internet site
www.theAA.com

WHEATHAMPSTEAD   Map 04 TL11

Mid Herts Lamer Ln, Gustard Wood AL4 8RS
☎ 01582 832242 Fax 01582 834834 e-
mail: secretary@mid-hertsgolfclub.co.uk
Commonland, wooded with heather and gorse-lined
fairways.
18 holes, 6060yds, Par 69, SSS 69.
Club membership 760.
Visitors   may not play Tue, Wed afternoons & weekends.
Societies   must contact in writing/telephone
Green Fees not confirmed.
Prof   Barney Puttick
Facilities   ⊗ 🖟 🖢 💡 🛆 🛡 🛱 ⌀
Location   1m N on B651

Hotel   ★★★ 68% Harpenden House, 18 Southdown
           Rd, HARPENDEN ☎ 01582 449955
           17 ⇄ 🕊 Annexe59 ⇄ 🕊

KENT

ADDINGTON   Map 05 TQ65

West Malling London Rd ME19 5AR
☎ 01732 844785 Fax 01732 844795
Two 18-hole parkland courses.
*Spitfire Course: 18 holes, 6142yds, Par 70, SSS 70, Course
record 67.*
*Hurricane Course: 18 holes, 6281yds, Par 70, SSS 70,
Course record 68.*
Visitors   must contact in advance, may not play weekends
         until 12 noon.
Societies   prior booking required.
Green Fees range from £15-£35 depending on time and day,
                contact pro shop for prices.
Cards   🖬 🖬 🖾 🔊 🕊
Prof   Duncan Lambert
Designer   Max Falkner
Facilities   ⊗ 🏢 by prior arrangement 🖟 🖢 💡 🛆 🛱 🐾
             🦺 ⌀ 🕻
& Leisure gymnasium, jaccuzi.
Location   1m S off A20

Hotel   ★★★ 66% Larkfield Priory Hotel, London Rd,
           Larkfield, MAIDSTONE
           ☎ 01732 846858   52 ⇄ 🕊

ASH   Map 05 TQ66

The London South Ash Manor Estate TN15 7EN
☎ 01474 879899 Fax 01474 879912
e-mail: golf@londongolf.co.uk
Visitors may only play the courses at LGC as guests of
members or prospective members by invitation.The courses,
the Heritage and the International were designed by Jack
Nicklaus: both include a number of lakes, generous fairways
framed with native grasses and many challenging holes. A
state-of-the-art drainage system ensures continuous play.
*Heritage Course: 18 holes, 7208yds, Par 72, SSS 74, Course
record 68.*
International Course: 18 holes, 7005yds, Par 70, SSS 72.
Club membership 600.

▶

Visitors guest of member & prospective members invited by the membership office only.
Societies must write in advance
Green Fees International Course only: £70 per round (£80 per round weekends).
Cards 🖃 ⚏ ⚏ 🖂
Prof Bill Longmuir
Designer Jack Nicklaus
Facilities ⊗ ⅲ ⅃ 🖢 ♥ ♀ ⚎ 🖻 ⚷ ➘ 🛪 ⚷ ⚲
& Leisure sauna.
Location A20, 2m from Brands Hatch

Hotel ★★★ 66% Larkfield Priory Hotel, London Rd, Larkfield, MAIDSTONE ☎ 01732 846858 52 ⇄ 🖝

ASHFORD   Map 05 TR04

Ashford Sandyhurst Ln TN25 4NT
☎ 01233 622655 Fax 01233 622655
Parkland course with good views and easy walking. Narrow fairways and tightly bunkered greens ensure a challenging game.
18 holes, 6263yds, Par 71, SSS 70, Course record 65.
Club membership 650.
Visitors must contact in advance & have handicap certificate.
Societies Tue & Thu only, by arrangement.
Green Fees £38 per day; £28 per round (£35 weekends).
Prof Hugh Sherman
Designer Cotton
Facilities ⚷ 🖻 ⚲
Location 1.5m NW off A20

Hotel ★★★★ 64% Ashford International, Simone Weil Av, ASHFORD ☎ 01233 219988 200 ⇄ 🖝

Homelands Bettergolf Centre Ashford Rd, Kingsnorth TN26 1NJ ☎ 01233 661620 Fax 01233 720553
e-mail: isj@bettergolf.co.uk
Challenging 9-hole course designed by Donald Steel to provide a stern test for experienced golfers and for others to develop their game. With 4 par 3s and 5 par 4s it demands accuracy rather than length. Floodlit driving range.
9 holes, 2205yds, Par 32, SSS 31.
Club membership 400.
Visitors no restrictions, but booking essential for weekend and summer evenings.
Societies prior arrangements are essential.
Green Fees not confirmed.
Prof Tony Bowers
Designer Donald Steel
Facilities ⅃ 🖢 ♀ ⚷ ➘ 🛪 ⚷ ⚲
Location Take exit 10 off M20, follow A2070, course signposted from 2nd rdbt to Kingsnorth

Hotel ★★ 68% Pilgrims Rest Hotel, Canterbury Rd, Kennington, ASHFORD ☎ 01233 636863 34 ⇄ 🖝

Entries with a green background identify courses considered to be particularly interesting

---

BARHAM   Map 05 TR25

Broome Park The Broome Park Estate CT4 6QX
☎ 01227 830728 Fax 01227 832591
e-mail: broomepark@u.genie.co.uk
Championship standard parkland course in a valley, with a 350-year-old mansion clubhouse.
18 holes, 6610yds, Par 72, SSS 72, Course record 66.
Club membership 700.
Visitors advisable to contact in advance, must have handicap certificate, but may not play Sat/Sun mornings.
Societies Mon-Fri and Sat-Sun after 1pm, apply in writing or by telephone.
Green Fees not confirmed.
Cards 🖃 ⚏ ⚏ 🖂
Prof Tienne Britz
Designer Donald Steel
Facilities ⊗ ⅲ ⅃ 🖢 ♥ ♀ ⚎ 🖻 ⚷ ➘ 🛪 ⚷ ⚲
& Leisure hard tennis courts.
Location 1.5m SE on A260

Hotel ★★★ 67% The Chaucer, Ivy Ln, CANTERBURY ☎ 0870 400 8106 42 ⇄ 🖝

BEARSTED   Map 05 TQ85

Bearsted Ware St ME14 4PQ
☎ 01622 738198 Fax 01622 735608
Parkland course with fine views of the North Downs.
18 holes, 6437yds, Par 72, SSS 71.
Club membership 780.
Visitors must have handicap certificate and may not play weekends unless with member. Must contact in advance.
Societies write for reservation forms.
Green Fees £30 per 18 holes; £40 per 36 holes (£35 per 18 holes weekends).
Prof Tim Simpson
Facilities ⊗ ⅲ ⅃ 🖢 ♥ ♀ ⚎ 🖻 ⚲
Location 2.5m E of Maidstone off A20

Hotel ★★★★ 70% Marriott Tudor Park Hotel & Country Club, Ashford Rd, Bearsted, MAIDSTONE ☎ 01622 734334 120 ⇄ 🖝

BIDDENDEN   Map 05 TQ83

Chart Hills Weeks Ln TN27 8JX
☎ 01580 292222 Fax 01580 292233
e-mail: info@charthills.co.uk
Created by Nick Faldo, this huge course of grand design measures 7,000 yards from the back tees. Facilities include a David Leadbetter Golf Academy.
18 holes, 7119yds, Par 72, SSS 74, Course record 66.
Club membership 490.
Visitors may play Tue, Thu, Fri & Sun.
Societies telephone for details.
Green Fees contact for details.
Cards 🖃 ⚏ ⚏ 🖂
Prof Danny French
Designer Nick Faldo
Facilities ⊗ ⅲ ⅃ 🖢 ♥ ♀ ⚎ 🖻 ⚷ ➘ 🛪 ⚷ ⚲
& Leisure sauna, solarium, gymnasium, teaching academy.
Location 1m N of Biddenden off A274

▶

Chart Hills Golf Club

Hotel   ★★🏵 Kennel Holt Hotel, Goudhurst Rd,
              CRANBROOK ☎ 01580 712032   10 ⇥ ⃗

BOROUGH GREEN   Map 05 TQ65

Wrotham Heath Seven Mile Ln TN15 8QZ
☎ 01732 884800 Fax 01732 887370
Heathland woodland course with magnificent views of North
Downs.
18 holes, 5954yds, Par 70, SSS 69, Course record 66.
Club membership 550.
Visitors   weekends with member only.
Societies   Thu & Fri only, by arrangement.
Green Fees   £25 per round.
Cards   ▨
Prof   Harry Dearden
Designer   Donald Steel (part)
Facilities   ⊗ ⅏ ⓛ ♨ ⚲ ⚼ 🖝 ⬧
Location   2.25m E on B2016

Hotel   ★★★ 68% Posthouse Maidstone/Sevenoaks,
              London Rd, Wrotham Heath, WROTHAM
              ☎ 0870 400 9054 106 ⇥ ⃗

BRENCHLEY   Map 05 TQ64

Moatlands Watermans Ln TN12 6ND
☎ 01892 724400 Fax 01892 723300
e-mail: moatlandsgolf@btinternet.com
A rolling parkland course with dramatic views over the
Weald of Kent. The challenging holes are the Par 4 8th with
its tough dogleg, the 10th where there is a wooded copse
with a Victorian bath-house to be avoided and the 14th where
the approach to the green is guarded by oak trees.
18 holes, 6693yds, Par 72, SSS 72, Course record 63.
Club membership 620.

Visitors   must book in advance.
Societies   apply in writing or telephone.
Green Fees   £29 per 18 holes (£39 weekends & bank
                 holidays).
Cards   ▨ ▩ ▦ ▧ ▨ ⬚
Prof   Simon Wood
Designer   T Saito
Facilities   ⊗ ⅏ ⓛ ♨ ⚲ ⚿ 🖝 ⬧ ⬥ ⬧ ⟨
& Leisure   hard tennis courts, heated indoor swimming
                 pool, sauna, gymnasium.
Location   3m N of Brenchley off B2160

Hotel   ★★ 63% Russell Hotel, 80 London Rd,
                 TUNBRIDGE WELLS ☎ 01892 544833
                 19 ⇥ ⃗ Annexe5 ⇥ ⃗

BROADSTAIRS   Map 05 TR36

North Foreland Convent Rd, Kingsgate CT10 3PU
☎ 01843 862140 Fax 01843 862663
e-mail: bpre342845@aol.com
A picturesque course situated where the Thames Estuary
widens towards the sea. North Foreland always seems to
have a breath of tradition of golf's earlier days about it.
Perhaps the ghost of one of its earlier professionals, the
famous Abe Mitchell, still haunts the lovely turf of the
fairways. Walking is easy and the wind is deceptive. The
8th and 17th, both par 4, are testing holes. There is also
an 18 hole approach and putting course.
18 holes, 6430yds, Par 71, SSS 71, Course record 65.
Club membership 1100.
Visitors   for Main course required to book in advance
                 & have handicap certificate. May play
                 afternoons only Mon and Tue, weekends
                 restricted and no visitors Sun morning.
                 Northcliffe course has no restrictions.
Societies   Wed & Fri only, by arrangement.
Green Fees   not confirmed.
Cards   ▨ ▦ ▧ ⬚
Prof   Neil Hansen
Designer   Fowler & Simpson
Facilities   ⊗ ⅏ ⓛ ♨ ⚲ ⚿ 🖝 ⬧ ⬥ ⬧
& Leisure   hard tennis courts.
Location   1.5m N off B2052

Hotel   ★★★ 64% Royal Albion Hotel,
                 Albion St, BROADSTAIRS
                 ☎ 01843 868071   19 ⇥ ⃗

CANTERBURY   Map 05 TR15

Canterbury Scotland Hills, Littlebourne Rd CT1 1TW
☎ 01227 453532 Fax 01227 784277
e-mail: cgc@freeola.com
Undulating parkland course, densely wooded in places, with
elevated tees and challenging drives on several holes.
18 holes, 6249yds, Par 70, SSS 70, Course record 64.
Club membership 650.
Visitors   may play after 9.30am except when
                 competitions being held. Restricted times
                 weekends and bank holidays. Must have
                 handicap certificate.
Societies   by arrangement.
Green Fees   £36 per day, £30 per round; (£36 weekends &
                 bank holidays).
Cards   ▨ ▩ ▦ ▧ ▨ ⬚

▶

Prof Paul Everard
Designer Harry Colt
Facilities ⊗ ⅲ ᄂ ♥ ♀ ♨ 🏠 ✓
Location 1.5m E on A257

Hotel ★★★ 67% The Chaucer, Ivy Ln,
CANTERBURY ☎ 0870 400 8106 42 ⇄ ♠

CHART SUTTON   Map 05 TQ84

The Ridge Chartway St, East Sutton ME17 3DL
☎ 01622 844382
This flat parkland course was designed by Patrick Dawson
around mature orchards to challenge all levels of player. The
par 5, 18th has two lakes to negotiate.
18 holes, 6254yds, Par 71, SSS 70, Course record 68.
Club membership 650.
Visitors weekdays only, must have handicap certificate.
Societies Tue & Thu, by arrangement.
Green Fees not confirmed.
Prof Tim Milford
Designer Tyton Design
Facilities ⊗ ⅲ ᄂ ♥ ♀ ♨ 🏠 ᅲ ⅃ ♨ ✓ ♪
& Leisure solarium, gymnasium.
Location 5m S of Bearsted, off A274

Hotel ★★★★ 70% Marriott Tudor Park Hotel &
Country Club, Ashford Rd, Bearsted,
MAIDSTONE ☎ 01622 734334 120 ⇄ ♠

CRANBROOK   Map 05 TQ73

Executive Golf Club at Cranbrook Golford Rd TN17 4AL
☎ 01580 712833 Fax 01580 714274
Scenic, parkland course with easy terrain, backed by
Hemstead Forest and close to Sissinghurst Castle (1m) and
Bodiam Castle (6m). The course has been transformed over
recent years with the introduction of over 5,000 mature pine
trees. Keeping the ball straight is paramount, a challenging
test of golf for all levels.
18 holes, 6305yds, Par 70, SSS 71, Course record 64.
Club membership 1450.
Visitors welcome weekdays after 8.30 am. weekends
after 11.30 am. Tee reservations may be booked
up to 1 calendar month in advance.
Societies minimum of 12. Write or telephone to book.
Green Fees £25(£30 weekends).
Cards ▭ ▭ ▭ ⅃
Prof Grant Kay
Designer Commander J Harris
Facilities ⊗ ᄂ ♥ ♀ ♨ 🏠 ✓
Location 2m E

Hotel ★★♣♣ Kennel Holt Hotel, Goudhurst Rd,
CRANBROOK ☎ 01580 712032 10 ⇄ ♠

DARTFORD   Map 05 TQ57

Birchwood Park Birchwood Rd, Wilmington DA2 7HJ
☎ 01322 662038 & 660554 Fax 01322 667283
The main course offers highly challenging play and will test
golfers of all abilities. Beginners and those requiring a quick
game or golfers wishing to improve their short game will
appreciate the Orchard course where holes range from 96 to
258yards.
18 holes, 6364yds, Par 71, SSS 70, Course record 64.
Orchard: 9 holes, 1349yds, Par 29.
Club membership 500.

Birchwood Park Golf Centre Ltd

Visitors must contact in advance for Main Course.
Societies telephone for details.
Green Fees not confirmed.
Cards ▭ ▭ ▭ ▭ ⅃
Designer Howard Swann
Facilities ⊗ ⅲ ᄂ ♥ ♀ ♨ 🏠 ᅲ ♪ ♨ ✓ ♪
& Leisure sauna, solarium, gymnasium.
Location B258 between Dartford & Swanley

Hotel ★★★★ 71% Bexleyheath Marriott Hotel,
1 Broadway, BEXLEYHEATH
☎ 020 8298 1000 138 ⇄ ♠

Dartford Heath Ln (Upper), Dartford Heath DA1 2TN
☎ 01322 226455 e-mail: dartfordgolf@hotmail.com
Heathland course.
18 holes, 5914yds, Par 69, SSS 69, Course record 62.
Club membership 700.
Visitors may not play at weekends. Must have a
handicap certificate.
Societies Mon & Fri only by prior arrangement with
Secretary.
Green Fees £30 per 36 holes; £21 per 18 holes.
Prof John Gregory
Designer James Braid
Facilities ⊗ ⅲ ᄂ ♥ ♀ ♨ 🏠 ✓
Hotel ★★★ 64% Posthouse Bexley, Black Prince
Interchange, Southwold Rd, BEXLEY
☎ 0870 400 9006 105 ⇄ ♠

DEAL   Map 05 TR35

Royal Cinque Ports Golf Rd CT14 6RF
☎ 01304 374007 Fax 01304 379530
Famous championship seaside links, windy but with easy
walking. Outward nine is generally considered the easier,
inward nine is longer and includes the renowned 16th,
perhaps the most difficult hole. On a fine day there are
wonderful views across the Channel.
18 holes, 6785yds, Par 72, SSS 72.
Club membership 850.
Visitors restricted Wed mornings, weekends & bank
holidays. Must contact in advance and have
a handicap certificate. Men max 18
handicap; Ladies max 28 handicap.
Societies must contact in advance.
Green Fees not confirmed.
Cards ▭ ▭ ⅃
Prof Andrew Reynolds
Designer James Braid
Facilities ⊗ ⅲ by prior arrangement ᄂ ♥ ♀ ♨ 🏠
ᅲ ♨ ✓ ♪
Location Along seafront at N end of Deal ▶

147

| **Hotel** | ★★★ 68% Dunkerleys Hotel & Restaurant, 19 Beach St, DEAL ☎ 01304 375016 16 ➡ ͡ |

EDENBRIDGE Map 05 TQ44

Edenbridge Golf & Country Club Crouch House Rd TN8 5LQ ☎ 01732 865097 & 867381 Fax 01732 867029
e-mail: david@golf-course-management.com
Two parkland course with water on many holes, quiet with excellent views of rural Kent and Surrey.
Old Course: 18 holes, 6646yds, Par 73, SSS 72.
New Course: 18 holes, 5605yds, Par 67, SSS 68.
Club membership 750.
Visitors must contact in advance for Old Course. All tee times bookable 7 days in advance.
Societies contact in advance.
Green Fees Old Course: £20 (£27.50 weekends); New Course: £12 (£16 weekends).
Prof Mark Whaler
Facilities ⊗ ⓑ 🍽 ♀ ♨ 🏠 ➤ ♨ ⚑ ͡
& Leisure hard tennis courts, gymnasium.
Location 0.75m W of town centre, signposted 'Golf Course'

| **Hotel** | ★★★♨ Gravetye Manor Hotel, EAST GRINSTEAD ☎ 01342 810567 18 ➡ ͡ |

Sweetwoods Park Cowden TN8 7JN
☎ 01342 850729 (Pro shop) & 850942 (Secretary)
Fax 01342 850866
An undulating and mature parkland course with very high quality greens, testing water hazards and fine views across the Weald from four holes. A good challenge off the back tees. Signature holes include the 2nd, 4th and 14th.
18 holes, 6512yds, Par 71, SSS 71, Course record 67.
Club membership 800.
Visitors no restrictions.
Societies Mon-Fri after 9am & Sat pm. Contact for details.
Green Fees £38 per day; £22 per round (£50/£30 weekends).
Cards
Prof Ben Clover
Designer P Strand
Facilities ⊗ ⓑ 🍽 ♀ ♨ 🏠 ➤ ♨ ⚑ ͡
Location 5m E of East Grinstead on the A264

| **Hotel** | ★★★ 64% Woodbury House Hotel, Lewes Rd, EAST GRINSTEAD ☎ 01342 313657 14 ➡ ͡ |

EYNSFORD Map 05 TQ56

Austin Lodge Upper Austin Lodge Rd DA4 0HU
☎ 01322 863000 Fax 01322 862406
A well drained course designed to lie naturally in three secluded valleys in rolling countryside. Over 7000 yds from the medal tees. Practice ground, nets and a putting green add to the features.
18 holes, 6600yds, Par 73, SSS 71, Course record 68.
Club membership 600.
Visitors must contact in advance, may not play until after 1pm on weekends.
Societies telephone for bookings.
Green Fees £20 per round (£25 weekends).

Cards
Prof Paul Edwards
Designer P Bevan
Facilities ⊗ ⓘ ⓑ 🍽 ♀ ♨ 🏠 ➤ ♨ ⚑ ͡
Location 6m S of Dartford

| **Hotel** | ★★★ 66% Brandshatch Place, Fawkham, BRANDS HATCH ☎ 01474 872239 29 ➡ ͡ Annexe12 ➡ ͡ |

FAVERSHAM Map 05 TR06

Boughton Brickfield Ln, Boughton ME13 9AJ
☎ 01227 752277 Fax 01227 752361
Rolling parkland/downland course set in 160 acres of Kent countryside, providing a good test of golf, even for the more accomplished players.
18 holes, 6469yds, Par 72, SSS 71, Course record 68.
Club membership 350.
Visitors Must phone in advance.
Societies telephone for details.
Green Fees not confirmed.
Cards
Prof Trevor Dungate
Designer P Sparks
Facilities ⊗ ⓘ ⓑ 🍽 ♀ ♨ 🏠 ➤ ♨ ⚑ ͡
Location Off junct 7 of M2 - Brenley Corner

| **Hotel** | ★★★★♨ Eastwell Manor, Eastwell Park, Boughton Lees, ASHFORD ☎ 01233 213000 23 ➡ ͡ Annexe39 ➡ ͡ |

Faversham Belmont Park ME13 0HB
☎ 01795 890561 Fax 01795 890760
A beautiful inland course laid out over part of a large estate with pheasants walking the fairways quite tamely. Play follows two heavily wooded valleys but the trees affect only the loose shots going out of bounds. Fine views.
18 holes, 6030yds, Par 70, SSS 69, Course record 63.
Club membership 800.
Visitors must have handicap certificate. With member only at weekends. Contacting the club in advance is advisable.
Societies must contact in advance.
Green Fees not confirmed.
Prof Stuart Rokes
Facilities ⊗ ⓘ ⓑ 🍽 ♀ ♨ 🏠 ➤ ♨ ⚑
Location 3.5m S

| **Hotel** | ★★★★♨ Eastwell Manor, Eastwell Park, Boughton Lees, ASHFORD ☎ 01233 213000 23 ➡ ͡ Annexe39 ➡ ͡ |

FOLKESTONE Map 05 TR23

Etchinghill Canterbury Rd, Etchinghill CT18 8FA
☎ 01303 863863 Fax 01303 863210
18 holes, 6121yds, Par 70, SSS 69, Course record 67.
Location N of M20, access from junct 11 or 12
Telephone for further details

| **Hotel** | ★★★ 70% Clifton Hotel, The Leas, FOLKESTONE ☎ 01303 851231 80 ➡ ͡ |

Etchinghill Golf Course

GILLINGHAM
Map 05 TQ76

Gillingham Woodlands Rd ME7 2AP
☎ 01634 853017 (office) & 855862 (pro)
Fax 01634 574749
Parkland course.
18 holes, 5557yds, Par 69, SSS 67, Course record 64.
Club membership 800.
Visitors   contact in advance, weekends only with member, must have handicap certificate.
Societies   must apply in writing.
Green Fees not confirmed.
Prof   Mark Day
Designer   James Braid/Steel
Facilities   ⊗ 🖿 ☕ ♀ 🛆 🏠 ⚐ ⚘ ⚑
Location   1.5m SE on A2

Hotel   ★★★ 65% Posthouse Rochester, Maidstone Rd, ROCHESTER
☎ 0870 400 9069 145 ⇄ 🐾

GRAVESEND
Map 05 TQ67

Mid Kent Singlewell Rd DA11 7RB
☎ 01474 568035 Fax 01474 564218
A well-maintained downland course with some easy walking and some excellent greens. The first hole is short, but nonetheless a real challenge. The slightest hook and the ball is out of bounds or lost.
18 holes, 6199yds, Par 69, SSS 69, Course record 60.
Club membership 900.
Visitors   must contact in advance & have handicap certificate. May not play weekends.
Societies   Tue only, apply in writing.
Green Fees £30 per day; £20 per round.
Prof   Mark Foreman
Designer   Frank Pennick
Facilities   ⊗ 〗 by prior arrangement 🖿 ☕ ♀ 🛆 🏠 ⚐ ⚘ ⚑
Location   S side of town centre off A227

Hotel   ★★ 67% Clarendon Royal Hotel, Royal Pier Rd, GRAVESEND
☎ 01474 63151 24rm(13 ⇄1 🐾)

Where to stay, where to eat?
Visit the AA internet site
www.theAA.com

Southern Valley Thong Ln, Shorne DA12 4LF
☎ 01474 568568 Fax 01474 360366
All year playing conditions on a course landscaped with gorse, bracken and thorn and designed to enhance the views across the Thames Estuary. The course features undulating greens, large trees and rolling fairways with both the 9th and 18th holes located close to the clubhouse.,
18 holes, 6100yds, Par 69, SSS 69.
Club membership 450.
Visitors   no restrictions.
Societies   must telephone in advance.
Green Fees £15.50 (£18.50 weekends).
Cards   🖳 🖃 🔤 🔼 🗒
Prof   Larry Batchelor
Facilities   ⊗ 〗 🖿 ☕ ♀ 🛆 🏠 ⚐ ⚘ ⚑ ⚑
Location   From A2 junct 4 at top of slip-road turn left into Thong Lane and continue for 1m

Hotel   ★★ 67% Clarendon Royal Hotel, Royal Pier Rd, GRAVESEND
☎ 01474 63151 24rm(13 ⇄1 🐾)

HALSTEAD
Map 05 TQ46

Broke Hill Sevenoaks Rd TN14 7HR
☎ 01959 533225 Fax 01959 532680
Testing downland course featuring 80 bunkers, strategically placed water hazards and good views.
18 holes, 6454yds, Par 72, SSS 71, Course record 69.
Club membership 650.
Visitors   weekdays only. Must book in advance.
Societies   telephone for details.
Green Fees not confirmed.
Cards   🖳 🖃 🔤 🔼 🗒
Prof   Chris West
Designer   David Williams
Facilities   ⊗ 〗 🖿 ☕ ♀ 🛆 🏠 ⚐ ⚘ ⚑ ⚑
& Leisure   sauna.
Location   Off junct 4 of M25, opposite Knockholt railway station

Hotel   ★★★ 68% Donnington Manor, London Rd, Dunton Green, SEVENOAKS
☎ 01732 462681   60 ⇄ 🐾

HAWKHURST
Map 05 TQ73

Hawkhurst High St TN18 4JS ☎ 01580 754074 & 752396
Fax 01580 754074 e-mail: hawkhead@tesco.net
Undulating parkland course.
9 holes, 5751yds, Par 70, SSS 68, Course record 69.
Club membership 500.
Visitors   may play weekdays, weekends after 12 noon subject to availability.
Societies   must apply in advance.
Green Fees £24 per day; £18 per round (£20 per round weekends).
Prof   Tony Collins
Designer   W A Baldock
Facilities   ⊗ 〗 by prior arrangement 🖿 ☕ ♀ 🛆 🏠 ⚐ ⚘ ⚑
& Leisure   squash.
Location   W side of village off A268

Hotel   ★★★ 66% Tudor Court Hotel, Rye Rd, HAWKHURST ☎ 01580 752312   18 ⇄ 🐾

HEADCORN
Map 05 TQ84

Weald of Kent Maidstone Rd TN27 9PT
☎ 01622 891671 Fax 01622 891793
Enjoying delightful views over the Weald of Kent, this pay
and play course features a range of natural hazards, including
lakes, trees, ditches and undulating fairways. A good test to
golfers of every standard.
18 holes, 6240yds, Par 70, SSS 70, Course record 64.
Club membership 450.

Visitors	can book 3 days in advance, smart casual dress no jeans.
Societies	apply in writing or by telephone.
Green Fees	not confirmed.
Cards	💳 💳 💳 💳
Designer	John Millen
Facilities	⊗ ⫟ ⏛ ⬤ ⬤ ⬤ ⬤ 🏌 ⬤ ⬤
Location	Through Leeds village take A274 towards Headcorn, golf course on left

Hotel	★★★★ 70% Marriott Tudor Park Hotel & Country Club, Ashford Rd, Bearsted, MAIDSTONE ☎ 01622 734334 120 ⇄ 🐾

HERNE BAY
Map 05 TR16

Herne Bay Eddington CT6 7PG ☎ 01227 374727
Parkland course with bracing air.
18 holes, 5567yds, Par 68, SSS 68.
Club membership 500.

Visitors	may not play mornings at weekends.
Societies	apply in advance.
Green Fees	not confirmed.
Prof	S Dordoy
Designer	James Braid
Facilities	⬤ ⬤ ⬤ 🏌 ⬤
Location	On A299 at Herne Bay/Canterbury junct

Hotel	★★★ 68% Falstaff Hotel, 8-10 St Dunstans St, Westgate, CANTERBURY ☎ 01227 462138 25 ⇄ 🐾 Annexe22 ⇄ 🐾

HEVER
Map 05 TQ44

Hever Hever Rd, Edenbridge TN8 7NP
☎ 01732 700771 Fax 01732 700775
e-mail: golf@hever.com
This 27-hole parkland course is set in 250 acres with water
hazards and outstanding holes like the Par 3 12th which is
similar to the 12th at Augusta.
27 holes, 6761yds, Par 72, SSS 73, Course record 69.
Club membership 450.

Visitors	May not play before 10.30am weekdays and 11.00am weekends.
Societies	Apply in writing or by phone.
Green Fees	£35 18 holes(£55 weekends & bank holidays).
Cards	💳 💳 💳 💳 💳
Prof	Peter Parks
Designer	Dr Nicholas
Facilities	⊗ ⫟ ⏛ ⬤ ⬤ ⬤ ⬤ 🏌 ⬤ ⬤ ⬤
& Leisure	hard tennis courts, heated indoor swimming pool, sauna, solarium, gymnasium.
Location	10mins from M25, 1 mile past Hever Castle on the right.

Hotel	★★★ 76% The Spa Hotel, Mount Ephraim, TUNBRIDGE WELLS ☎ 01892 520331 71 ⇄ 🐾

HILDENBOROUGH
Map 05 TQ54

Nizels Nizels Ln TN11 9LU
☎ 01732 838926 (Bookings) Fax 01732 833764
18 holes, 6408yds, Par 72, SSS 71, Course record 66.
Location Off B245
Telephone for further details

Hotel	★★★ 66% Rose & Crown Hotel, 125 High St, TONBRIDGE ☎ 01732 357966 49 ⇄ 🐾

HOO
Map 05 TQ77

Deangate Ridge Dux Court Rd ME3 8RZ ☎ 01634 251180
Fax 01634 250537
Parkland, municipal course designed by Fred Hawtree. 18-
hole pitch and putt.
18 holes, 6300yds, Par 71, SSS 70, Course record 65.
Club membership 500.

Visitors	no restrictions.
Societies	please telephone 01634 255370.
Green Fees	not confirmed.
Cards	💳 💳 💳 💳 💳
Prof	Richard Fox
Facilities	⊗ ⫟ ⏛ ⬤ ⬤ ⬤ ⬤ 🏌 ⬤ ⬤ ⬤
& Leisure	hard tennis courts.
Location	4m NE of Rochester off A228

Hotel	★★★ 65% Posthouse Rochester, Maidstone Rd, ROCHESTER ☎ 0870 400 9069 145 ⇄ 🐾

HYTHE
Map 05 TR13

Hythe Imperial Princes Pde CT21 6AE
☎ 01303 267441 Fax 01303 264610
e-mail: hytheimperial@marstonhotels.co.uk
A 9-hole 18 tee links course bounded by the Royal Military
Canal and the English Channel. Although the course is
relatively flat, its aspect offers an interesting and challenging
round to a wide range of golfers
9 holes, 5560yds, Par 68, SSS 66, Course record 62.
Club membership 300.

Visitors	course closed some Sun until 11am for competitions.
Societies	must apply in writing.
Green Fees	not confirmed.
Prof	Gordon Ritchie

▶

Facilities & Leisure ⊗ ∭ 🏔 ☕ ♀ ⌂ 🏠 ☏ 🎣 ➘ ⚷   hard and grass tennis courts, heated indoor swimming pool, squash, sauna, solarium, gymnasium, croquet, snooker, hair & beauty salon.

Location SE side of town

Hotel ★★★★ 77% The Hythe Imperial Hotel, Princes Pde, HYTHE
☎ 01303 267441 100 ⇥ ℝ

Additional hotel ★★★ 73% Stade Court, West Pde, HYTHE
☎ 01303 268263 Fax 01303 261803   42 ⇥ ℝ

Sene Valley Sene CT18 8BL
☎ 01303 268513 (Manager) & 268514 (Pro)
Fax 01303 237513
A two-level downland course which provides interesting golf over an undulating landscape with sea views.
18 holes, 6196yds, Par 71, SSS 70, Course record 61.
Club membership 600.
Visitors must contact professional in advance.
Societies telephone in advance.
Green Fees not confirmed.
Cards ⊡ ▰
Prof Nick Watson
Designer Henry Cotton
Facilities ⊗ ∭ 🏔 ☕ ♀ ⌂ 🏠 ⚷ ☏
Location 1m NE off B2065

Hotel ★★★★ 77% The Hythe Imperial Hotel, Princes Pde, HYTHE
☎ 01303 267441 100 ⇥ ℝ

KINGSDOWN   Map 05 TR34

Walmer & Kingsdown The Leas CT14 8EP
☎ 01304 373256 & 363017 Fax 01304 382336
This course near Deal has through the years been overshadowed by its neighbours at Deal and Sandwich, yet it is a testing circuit with many undulations. The course is famous as being the one on which, in 1964, Assistant Professional, Roger Game became the first golfer in Britain to hole out in one at two successive holes; the 7th and 8th. The course is situated on top of the cliffs, with fine views.
18 holes, 6444yds, Par 72, SSS 71, Course record 66.
Club membership 680.
Visitors must contact in advance. Not before 9.30am weekdays and noon weekends & bank holidays.
Societies apply in advance.
Green Fees not confirmed.
Prof Matthew Paget
Designer James Braid
Facilities ⊗ ∭ 🏔 ☕ ♀ ⌂ 🏠 ☏ ➘ ⚷
Location 1.5m E of Ringwould off A258 Dover-Deal road

Hotel ★★★ 68% Dunkerleys Hotel & Restaurant, 19 Beach St, DEAL
☎ 01304 375016   16 ⇥ ℝ

LAMBERHURST   Map 05 TQ63

Lamberhurst Church Rd TN3 8DT
☎ 01892 890591 Fax 01892 891140
e-mail: pgleeson@lamberhurstgolf.freeserve.co.uk
Parkland course crossing river twice. Fine views.

---

18 holes, 6345yds, Par 72, SSS 70, Course record 65.
Club membership 700.
Visitors may only play after noon weekends unless with member, handicap certificate required.
Societies Tue, Wed & Thu only from Apr-Oct, by arrangement.
Green Fees £35 per day; £25 per round (£40 weekends & bank holidays).
Cards ⊡ ▰ ▰ ▱
Prof Brian Impett
Facilities ⊗ ∭ by prior arrangement 🏔 ☕ ♀ ⌂ 🏠 ☏ ➘ ⚷ ⚷
Location N side of village on B2162

Hotel ★★★ 76% The Spa Hotel, Mount Ephraim, TUNBRIDGE WELLS
☎ 01892 520331   71 ⇥ ℝ

LITTLESTONE   Map 05 TR02

Littlestone St Andrew's Rd TN28 8RB
☎ 01797 363355 Fax 01797 362740
e-mail: secretary@littlestonegolfclub.org.uk
Located in the Romney Marshes, this flattish seaside links course calls for every variety of shot. The 8th, 15th, 16th and 17th are regarded as classics by international golfers. Allowance for wind must always be made. Extensive practice area.
18 holes, 6471yds, Par 71, SSS 72, Course record 67.
Club membership 550.
Visitors must contact in advance, no visitors before 3pm weekends and bank holidays.
Societies must apply in advance.
Green Fees £47 per day; £36 per round (£55/£45 weekends and bank holidays).
Cards ⊡ ▰ ▰ ▱
Prof Stephen Watkins
Designer Laidlaw Purves
Facilities & Leisure ⊗ ∭ 🏔 ☕ ♀ ⌂ 🏠 ☏ ➘ ⚷   hard tennis courts.
Location 1m from New Romney off Littlestone road B2070

Hotel ★★★★ 77% The Hythe Imperial Hotel, Princes Pde, HYTHE
☎ 01303 267441 100 ⇥ ℝ

Romney Warren St Andrews Rd TN28 8RB
☎ 01797 362231 Fax 01797 363511
e-mail: info@romneywarrengolfclub.org.uk
A links style course, normally very dry. Flat providing easy walking and play challenged by sea breezes.
18 holes, 5126yds, Par 67, SSS 65, Course record 69.
Club membership 300.
Visitors contact professional in advance.
Societies contact in advance.
Green Fees £25 per 36 holes; £15 per 18 holes (£30/£20 weekends and bank holidays).
Cards ⊡ ▰ ▰ ▱
Prof Stephen Watkins
Facilities ⊗ ∭ 🏔 ☕ ♀ ⌂ 🏠 ☏ ➘ ⚷
Location N side of Littlestone

Hotel ★★★★ 77% The Hythe Imperial Hotel, Princes Pde, HYTHE
☎ 01303 267441 100 ⇥ ℝ

LYDD   Map 05 TR02

Lydd Romney Rd TN29 9LS
☎ 01797 320808 Fax 01797 321482
e-mail: info@luddgolfclub.co.uk
A links-type course offering some interesting challenges, including a number of eye-catching water hazards, wide fairways and plenty of semi-rough. A good test for experienced golfers and appealing to the complete novice.
18 holes, 6517yds, Par 71, SSS 71, Course record 65.
Club membership 495.

Visitors	contact in advance on 01797 321201.
Societies	telephone in advance.
Green Fees	not confirmed.
Cards	🔲 🔲 🔲
Prof	Andrew Jones
Designer	Mike Smith
Facilities	⊗ �🏌 💪 🍴 🛢 🎒 🏌 🛒 ⛳ ↑
Location	B2075

Hotel	★★★ 62% The George, High St, RYE ☎ 01797 222114 22 ⇔ ↑

MAIDSTONE   Map 05 TQ75

Cobtree Manor Park Chatham Rd, Sandling ME14 3AZ
☎ 01622 753276 Fax 01634 262003
An undulating parkland course with some water hazards.
18 holes, 5611yds, Par 69, SSS 69, Course record 66.
Club membership 500.

Visitors	no restrictions but advisable to telephone in advance on the day.
Societies	Mon-Fri only, by arrangement tel: 01622 751881.
Green Fees	£15 per 18 holes(£18.50 weekends).
Cards	🔲 🔲 🔲 🔲
Prof	Paul Foston
Facilities	⊗ �🏌 💪 🍴 🛢 🎒 🏌 🛒 ⛳
Location	On A229 0.25m N of M20 junc 6

Hotel	★★★ 61% Russell Hotel, 136 Boxley Rd, MAIDSTONE ☎ 01622 692221 42 ⇔ ↑

Leeds Castle Ashford Rd ME17 1PL ☎ 01622 767828
Fax 01622 735616 e-mail: golf@leeds-castle.co.uk

Situated around Leeds Castle, this is one of the most picturesque courses in Britain. Re-designed in the 1980s by Neil Coles, it is a challenging 9-hole course with the added hazard of the Castle moat.
9 holes, 2681yds, Par 33, SSS 33, Course record 30.

Visitors	bookings taken from 6 days in advance.
Societies	must telephone in advance.
Green Fees	£18.50 per 18 holes, £11 per 9 holes (£26/£13 weekends). Green fees include admission to castle and gardens.
Cards	🔲 🔲 🔲
Prof	Steve Purves
Designer	Neil Coles
Facilities	⊗ 💪 🍴 🛢 🎒 🏌 ⛳
& Leisure	Green fees include admission to Leeds Castle's Gardens & Attractions.
Location	On A20 towards Lenham, 4m E of Maidstone via M20 junct 8

Hotel	★★★★ 70% Marriott Tudor Park Hotel & Country Club, Ashford Rd, Bearsted, MAIDSTONE ☎ 01622 734334 120 ⇔ ↑

Marriott Tudor Park Hotel & Country Club Ashford Rd, Bearsted ME14 4NQ ☎ 01622 734334 Fax 01622 735360
The course is set in a 220 acre former deerpark with the pleasant undulating Kent countyside as a backdrop. The natural features of the land have been incorporated into this picturesque course to form a challenge for those of both high and intermediate standard. The Par 5 14th is particularly interesting. It can alter your score dramatically should you gamble with a drive to a narrow fairway. This hole has to be carefully thought out from tee to green depending on the wind direction.
18 holes, 6041yds, Par 70, SSS 69, Course record 64.
Club membership 725.

Visitors	may not play Sat & Sun before noon. Contact pro shop 01622 739412 for bookings.
Societies	please call the Golf Manager.
Green Fees	not confirmed.
Cards	🔲 🔲 🔲 🔲 🔲 🔲
Prof	Nick McNally
Designer	Donald Steel
Facilities	⊗ ⫘ �🏌 💪 🍴 🛢 🎒 🏌 🛒 ⛳
& Leisure	hard tennis courts, heated indoor swimming pool, sauna, solarium, gymnasium, steam room & jacuzzi, golf academy.
Location	On A20, 1.25m W of M20 junct 8

Hotel	★★★★ 70% Marriott Tudor Park Hotel & Country Club, Ashford Rd, Bearsted, MAIDSTONE ☎ 01622 734334 120 ⇔ ↑

> Entries with a green background
> identify courses considered to be
> particularly interesting

RAMSGATE   Map 05 TR36

St Augustine's Cottington Rd, Cliffsend CT12 5JN
☎ 01843 590333 Fax 01843 590444
e-mail: sagc@ic24.net
A comfortably flat course in this famous bracing
Championship area of Kent. Neither as long nor as
difficult as its lordly neighbours, St Augustine's will
nonetheless extend most golfers. Dykes run across the
course.
18 holes, 5254yds, Par 69, SSS 66, Course record 61.
Club membership 670.
Visitors   must contact in advance.
Societies   must contact in advance.
Green Fees   £25 per day; £15 per round (£30/£16.50
                 weekends & bank holidays).
Prof   Derek Scott
Designer   Tom Vardon
Facilities   ⊗ ⫴ ⮶ ⬛ ♀ ⬜ 🏠 ♨ ♂
Location   Off A256 Ramsgate/Sandwich

Hotel   ★★★ 66% San Clu Hotel, Victoria Pde,
                 East Cliff, RAMSGATE
                 ☎ 01843 592345   44 ⇆ 🐾

ROCHESTER   Map 05 TQ76

Rochester & Cobham Park Park Pale ME2 3UL
☎ 01474 823411 Fax 01474 824446
e-mail: rcpgc@talk21.com
A first-rate course of challenging dimensions in
undulating parkland. All holes differ and each requires
accurate drive placing to derive the best advantage. The
clubhouse and course are situated a quarter of a mile
from the western end of the M2.
18 holes, 6596yds, Par 71, SSS 72, Course record 67.
Club membership 720.
Visitors   must contact in advance & have handicap
                 certificate. No visitors weekends.
Societies   apply in advance.
Green Fees   £30 per round.
Prof   Iain Higgins
Designer   Donald Steel
Facilities   ⊗ ⫴ ⮶ ⬛ ♀ ⬜ 🏠 ♨ ♂ ♂
Location   2.5m W on A2

Hotel   ★★★★ 73% Bridgewood Manor Hotel,
                 Bridgewood Roundabout, Walderslade
                 Woods, CHATHAM
                 ☎ 01634 201333 100 ⇆ 🐾

SANDWICH   Map 05 TR35

Prince's Prince's Dr, Sandwich Bay CT13 9QB
☎ 01304 611118 Fax 01304 612000
e-mail: golf@princes-leisure.co.uk
With 27 championship holes, Prince's Golf Club enjoys
a world wide reputation as a traditional links of the finest
quality and is a venue that provides all that is best in
modern links golf. The purpose built clubhouse, located
at the centre of the three loops of nine, can seat 200
diners and offers panoramic views over Sandwich Bay
and the course.
Dunes: 9 holes, 3343yds, Par 36, SSS 36.
Himalayas: 9 holes, 3163yds, Par 35, SSS 35.

Shore: 9 holes, 3347yds, Par 36, SSS 36.
Club membership 250.
Visitors   available all week, must contact in advance.
Societies   welcome all week, please contact in
                 advance.
Green Fees   £45-£60 per 27 holes; £40-£55 per 18 holes
                 (£50-£70/£45-£60 weekends).
Cards   ⊡ ⊞ ⬛ ⬛ ⬛
Prof   Derek Barbour
Designer   (1951 Sir Guy Campbell & J S F Morrison)
Facilities   ⊗ ⫴ ⮶ ⬛ ♀ ⬜ 🏠 ⚑ ♨ ♨ ♂ ♀
& Leisure   snooker.
Location   2m E via toll road, follow signs from
                 Sandwich

Hotel   ★★★ 66% San Clu Hotel, Victoria Pde,
                 East Cliff, RAMSGATE
                 ☎ 01843 592345   44 ⇆ 🐾

SANDWICH   See page 155

SEVENOAKS   Map 05 TQ55

Knole Park Seal Hollow Rd TN15 0HJ
☎ 01732 452150 Fax 01732 463159
The course is set in a majestic park with many fine trees
and deer running loose. It has a wiry turf seemingly
impervious to rain. Certainly a pleasure to play on.
Excellent views of Knole House and the North Downs.
Outstanding greens.
18 holes, 6266yds, Par 70, SSS 70, Course record 62.
Club membership 800.
Visitors   must have a handicap certificate and contact
                 the secretary in advance, may not play at
                 weekends or bank holidays.
Societies   telephone initially.
Green Fees   £46 per 36 holes; £35 per 18 holes.
Cards   ⊡ ⊞ ⬛ ⬛ ⬛
Prof   Phil Sykes
Designer   J A Abercromby
Facilities   ⊗ ⫴ ⮶ ⬛ ♀ ⬜ 🏠 ⚑ ♂ ♂
& Leisure   squash.
Location   SE side of town centre off B2019

Hotel   ★★★ 68% Donnington Manor, London
                 Rd, Dunton Green, SEVENOAKS
                 ☎ 01732 462681   60 ⇆ 🐾

SHEERNESS   Map 05 TQ97

Sheerness Power Station Rd ME12 3AE
☎ 01795 662585 Fax 01795 668100
Semi-links, marshland course, few bunkers, but many ditches
and water hazards.
18 holes, 6460yds, Par 72, SSS 71, Course record 66.
Club membership 650.
Visitors   with member only at weekends.
Societies   weekdays only, book in advance.
Green Fees   £18(£25 weekends).
Prof   L Stanford
Facilities   ⊗ ⫴ by prior arrangement
                 ⮶ ⬛ ♀ ⬜ 🏠 ♨ ♂
Location   1.5m E off A249   ▶

Hotel ★★★★ 73% Bridgewood Manor Hotel,
Bridgewood Roundabout, Walderslade Woods,
CHATHAM ☎ 01634 201333 100 ➡ ➚

SHOREHAM   Map 05 TQ56

Darenth Valley Station Rd TN14 7SA
☎ 01959 522944 & 522922 Fax 01959 525089
Easy walking parkland course in beautiful valley. Testing
12th hole, par 4.
18 holes, 6327yds, Par 72, SSS 71, Course record 64.
Visitors   must book in advance.
Societies   contact in advance.
Green Fees not confirmed.
Cards   ⬛ ⬛ ⬛ ⬛ ⬛
Prof   David J Copsey
Facilities ⊗ ⵉ by prior arrangement ⬛ ⬛ ♀ ⌂ ⬛ ⬀ ✧
& Leisure   fishing.
Location   1m E on A225

Hotel ★★★ 68% Donnington Manor, London Rd,
Dunton Green, SEVENOAKS
☎ 01732 462681 60 ➡ ➚

SITTINGBOURNE   Map 05 TQ96

The Oast Golf Centre Church Rd, Tonge ME9 9AR
☎ 01795 473527 e-mail: range@oastgolf.freeserve.co.uk
A Par 3 Approach course of 9 holes with 18 tees augmented
by a 17-bay floodlit driving range and a putting green.
9 holes, 1664yds, Par 54, SSS 54.
Visitors   no restrictions.
Societies   telephone in advance.
Green Fees £5 per 18 holes(£5 per 9 holes;£7 per 18 holes
                weekends).
Prof   D Chambers
Designer   D Chambers
Facilities ⬛ ⬛ ♀ ⌂ ⬀ ✧ ✧
Location   2m NE, A2 between Bapchild/Teynham

Hotel ★★★★ 73% Bridgewood Manor Hotel,
Bridgewood Roundabout, Walderslade Woods,
CHATHAM ☎ 01634 201333 100 ➡ ➚

Sittingbourne & Milton Regis Wormdale, Newington
ME9 7PX ☎ 01795 842261 Fax 01795 844117
A downland course with pleasant vistas. There are a few
uphill climbs, but the course is far from difficult. The new
back nine holes are very testing.
18 holes, 6291yds, Par 71, SSS 70, Course record 63.
Club membership 670.
Visitors   by prior arrangement or letter of introduction.
                Must contact in advance, may not play at
                weekends.
Societies   Tue & Thu, apply in advance.
Green Fees not confirmed.
Prof   John Hearn
Designer   Donald Steel
Facilities ⊗ ⵉ ⬛ ⬛ ♀ ⌂ ⌂ ⬀ ✧ ✧
Location   Turn off Chestnut Street (old A249) at Danaway

Hotel ★★★★ 73% Bridgewood Manor Hotel,
Bridgewood Roundabout, Walderslade Woods,
CHATHAM ☎ 01634 201333 100 ➡ ➚

Upchurch River Valley Golf Centre Oak Ln, Upchurch
ME9 7AY ☎ 01634 379592 Fax 01634 387784
Undulating parkland course set in picturesque countryside.
Testing water hazards on several holes. Excellent winter
course. The 9-hole course is ideal for beginners and for those
keen to sharpen up their short game.
18 holes, 6237yds, Par 70, SSS 70.
Club membership 541.
Visitors   can play anytime, book for weekend 5 days in
                advance, weekdays 2 days in advance.
Societies   telephone 01634 360626 for details.
Green Fees £11.45(£14.45 weekends).
Cards   ⬛
Prof   Roger Cornwell
Designer   David Smart
Facilities ⊗ ⵉ ⬛ ⬛ ♀ ⌂ ⬛ ➚ ⬀ ✧ ✧
& Leisure   heated outdoor swimming pool.
Location   A2 between Rainham and Newington

Hotel ★★★ 61% Russell Hotel, 136 Boxley Rd,
MAIDSTONE ☎ 01622 692221 42 ➡ ➚

SNODLAND   Map 05 TQ76

Oastpark Malling Rd ME6 5LG
☎ 01634 242661 Fax 01634 240744
A challenging parkland course for golfers of all abilities. The
course has water hazards, orchards and views across the
Valley of Dean.
18 holes, 6173yds, Par 69, SSS 69, Course record 71.
Club membership 300.
Visitors   may book 7 days in advance.
Societies   early booking with deposits required.
Green Fees not confirmed.
Cards   ⬛ ⬛ ⬛ ⬛
Prof   Nathan French
Designer   J D Banks
Facilities ⊗ ⵉ ⬛ ⬛ ♀ ⌂ ⬛ ✧ ✧
Location   Access via junct 4 on M20

Hotel ★★★ 66% Larkfield Priory Hotel, London Rd,
Larkfield, MAIDSTONE
☎ 01732 846858 52 ➡ ➚

TENTERDEN   Map 05 TQ83

Tenterden Woodchurch Rd TN30 7DR
☎ 01580 763987 (sec) & 762409 (shop) Fax 01580 763987
e-mail: tenterden-golf-club@lineone.net
Set in tranquil undulating parkland with beautiful views, the
course is challenging with several difficult holes.
18 holes, 6071yds, Par 70, SSS 69, Course record 61.
Club membership 600.
Visitors   contact secretary. May only play with member
                weekends and bank holidays. Handicap
                certificate required.
Societies   contact secretary, full details on request.
Green Fees not confirmed.
Prof   Kyle Kelsall
Facilities ⊗ ⵉ ⬛ ⬛ ♀ ⌂ ⬛ ➚ ⬀ ✧
Location   0.75m E on B2067

Hotel ★★♨ Kennel Holt Hotel, Goudhurst Rd,
CRANBROOK ☎ 01580 712032 10 ➡ ➚

Royal St George's

Sandwich, *Kent*   ☎ 01304 613090   Fax 01304 611245   Map 05 TR35

This long-established 18-hole championship links course has been the host venue for the Open Championship on 12 occasions, and will be again in 2003. It has been the host venue for the Amateur Championship on 12 occasions, most recently in 1997.

The course itself is the truest links you might find in England, designed by Dr Laidlaw Purves in 1887. Close to the sea, overlooking Pegwell Bay, any kind of wind can make this man-size test even tougher. The sweeping rough at the 1st can be daunting, as can the bunkers and the huge sandhills. Off-sea breezes can become incredible gales and it is possible to find the course virtually unplayable.

Visitors must contact in advance and have a handicap certificate. All golf is two ball golf. May not play at weekends

Societies Mon-Wed, must apply in writing

Green Fees £100 per day; £70 per round

Facilities ⊗ 🍴 (by arrangement)
🍴 ▼ ♀ ♨ 🏠 ⛳ ✐ ♔
Professional (A. Brooks)

Location Sandwich CT13 9PB
(1.5m E of town)

Holes/Par/Course record 18 holes, 6930 yds, Par 70, SSS 74, Course record 63

Championship Course

WHERE TO STAY NEARBY

Hotels
CANTERBURY

★★★68% Falstaff, St Dunstans St.
☎ 01227 462138. 25 (23 ⇄ ♛ 2 ♜)
Annexe 22 ⇄ ♜

★★★67% The Chaucer, Ivy Lane.
☎ 0870 400 8106. 42 ⇄ ♜

★★🌀 68% Canterbury, 71 New Dover Rd.
☎ 01227 450551. 23 (16 ⇄ 7 ♜)

DOVER

★★★70% The Churchill, Dover Waterfront. ☎ 01304 203633.
66 (54 ⇄ ♜ 12 ♜)

★★🌀🌀 75% Wallets Court, West Cliffe, St Margarets-at-Cliffe.
☎ 01304 852424.
3 ⇄ ♜ Annexe 12 (10 ⇄ ♜ 2 ♜)

Restaurant
SANDWICH

🌀 Fishermans Wharf, The Quay.
☎ 01304 613636.

TONBRIDGE
Map 05 TQ54

Poultwood Higham Ln TN11 9QR
☎ 01732 364039 Fax 01732 353781
There are two public 'pay and play' parkland courses in an idyllic woodland setting. The courses are ecologically designed, over predominantly flat land offering challenging hazzards and interesting playing conditions for all standards of golfer.
Course 1: 18 holes, 5569yds, Par 68, SSS 67 or 9 holes, 1281yds, Par 28.
Course 2: 9 holes, 1218yds, Par 28, SSS 28.

Visitors	non registered golfers may book up to 2 days in advance for 18 hole course, or take available tee times, pay and play system on 9 hole.
Societies	apply in advance to the clubhouse manager tel 01732 366180.
Green Fees	not confirmed.
Cards	🖅 🖃 🖅 🖅 ⑨
Prof	Chris Miller
Facilities	⊗ ⪥ 🖩 ⬛ ☕ 𝄞 🏠 ❡ ⚲
& Leisure	squash.
Location	Off A227, 3m N of Tonbridge

Hotel	★★★ 66% Rose & Crown Hotel, 125 High St, TONBRIDGE ☎ 01732 357966 49 ⇔ ⚑

TUNBRIDGE WELLS (ROYAL)
Map 05 TQ53

Nevill Benhall Mill Rd TN2 5JW
☎ 01892 525818 Fax 01892 517861
e-mail: manager@nevillgolfclub.co.uk
The county boundaries of Kent and Sussex run along the northern perimeter of the course. Open undulating ground, well-wooded with some heather and gorse for the first half. The second nine holes slope away from the clubhouse to a valley where a narrow stream hazards two holes.
18 holes, 6349yds, Par 71, SSS 70, Course record 64.
Club membership 900.

Visitors	must contact 48 hours in advance, handicap certificate required, permission from secretary for weekends play.
Societies	must apply in writing one month in advance.
Green Fees	£25 per round;333 per day(£32.50 weekends).
Prof	Paul Huggett
Designer	Henry Cotton
Facilities	⊗ ⪥ by prior arrangement 🖩 ⬛ ☕ 𝄞 🏠 ❡ ⚲
Location	S of Tunbridge Wells, off forest road

Hotel	★★★ 76% The Spa Hotel, Mount Ephraim, TUNBRIDGE WELLS ☎ 01892 520331 71 ⇔ ⚑

Tunbridge Wells Langton Rd TN4 8XH
☎ 01892 523034 Fax 01892 536918
Somewhat hilly, well-bunkered parkland course with lake; trees form natural hazards.
9 holes, 4725yds, Par 65, SSS 62, Course record 59.
Club membership 470.

Visitors	must contact in advance, limited availability weekends.
Societies	weekdays, apply in advance.

Green Fees	£25 per day; £15 per 18 holes; £10 per 9 holes (£25 per 18 holes; £15 per 9 holes weekends).
Cards	🖅 🖃 ⑨
Prof	Mike Barton
Facilities	🖩 ⬛ ☕ 𝄞 🏠 ❡ ⚲
Location	1m W on A264

Hotel	★★★ 76% The Spa Hotel, Mount Ephraim, TUNBRIDGE WELLS ☎ 01892 520331 71 ⇔ ⚑

WESTERHAM
Map 05 TQ45

Parkwood Chestnut Av, Tatsfield TN16 2EG
☎ 01959 577744 & 577177 (pro-shop) Fax 01959 572702
Situated in an area of natural beauty, flanked by an ancient woodland with superb views across Kent and Surrey. An undulating course, tree lined and with some interesting water features. Playable in all weather conditions.

18 holes, 6835yds, Par 72, SSS 72, Course record 66.
Club membership 500.

Visitors	telephone in advance. May not play bank holidays.
Societies	apply in writing/telephone in advance.
Green Fees	not confirmed.
Cards	🖅 🖃 🖅 ⑨
Prof	Nick Terry
Facilities	⊗ ⪥ 🖩 ⬛ ☕ 𝄞 🏠 ❡ ⚲
Location	A25 onto B2024 Croydon Rd which becomes Clarks Lane. At Church Hill junct join Chestnut Av

Hotel	★★★ 68% Donnington Manor, London Rd, Dunton Green, SEVENOAKS ☎ 01732 462681 60 ⇔ ⚑

Westerham Valence Park, Brasted Rd TN16 1LJ
☎ 01959 567100 Fax 01959 567101
e-mail: westerham.golfclub@virgin.net
Originally completely wooded forestry land with thousands of mature pines. The storms of 1987 created natural fairways and the mature landscape makes the course both demanding and spectacular. A clubhouse with first class facilities and magnificent views.
18 holes, 6272yds, Par 72, SSS 72.
Club membership 700.

Visitors	welcome but may not play Sat & Sun am.
Societies	telephone events office for details.
Green Fees	£25 per round(mon-thurs);£30 (fri);£35 (weekends).
Cards	🖅 🖃 🖃 🖅 ⑨
Prof	Ewan Campbell
Designer	D Williams
Facilities	⊗ ⪥ 🖩 ⬛ ☕ 𝄞 🏠 ❡ ⚲ ⚲
Location	A25 between Westerham and Brasted

Hotel	★★★ 68% Donnington Manor, London Rd, Dunton Green, SEVENOAKS ☎ 01732 462681 60 ⇔ ⚑

AA Hotels that have special arrangements with golf courses are listed at the back of the guide

WESTGATE ON SEA   Map 05 TR37

Westgate and Birchington 176 Canterbury Rd CT8 8LT
☎ 01843 831115
A fine blend of inland and seaside holes which provide a
good test of the golfer despite the apparently simple
appearance of the course.
18 holes, 4926yds, Par 64, SSS 64, Course record 60.
Club membership 320.
Visitors   Mon-Sat after 10am, Sun and bank holidays
              after 11am, must contact in advance & have
              handicap certificate, restricted at weekends.
Societies   must contact the secretary.
Green Fees £15 per day (£18 weekends)plus 50p insurance
              cover.
Prof   Roger Game
Facilities   ⊗ ℿ by prior arrangement ⌷ ☰ ♀ ⚘ 🛅 ⚷
Location   E side of town centre off A28

Hotel   ★★★ 64% Royal Albion Hotel, Albion St,
              BROADSTAIRS ☎ 01843 868071   19 ⇌ ☏

WEST KINGSDOWN   Map 05 TQ56

Woodlands Manor Tinkerpot Ln, Otford TN15 6AB
☎ 01959 523806 & 524161 Fax 524398
e-mail: woodlandsgolfclub@hotmail.com
Interesting, challenging & undulating parkland course with
testing 1st, 9th and 15th holes. Set in a designated area of
outstanding natural beauty.
18 holes, 6037yds, Par 69, SSS 68.
Club membership 600.
Visitors   by prior arrangement. May not play weekends
              am, or Tue am.
Societies   apply in advance.
Green Fees £21 per round, £31.50 per day (£27 per round
              weekends).
Cards   ▨ ▰ ▨ ▨ ▨
Prof   Philip Womack
Designer   Lyons/Coles
Facilities   ⊗ ℿ ⌷ ☰ ♀ ⚘ 🛅 ⚷ ☏
Location   2m S off A20 at West Kingsdown

Hotel   ★★★ 68% Posthouse Maidstone/Sevenoaks,
              London Rd, Wrotham Heath, WROTHAM
              ☎ 0870 400 9054 106 ⇌ ☏

WHITSTABLE   Map 05 TR16

Chestfield (Whitstable) 103 Chestfield Rd, Chestfield
CT5 3LU ☎ 01227 794411 & 792243 Fax 01227 794454
e-mail: secretary@chestfield-golfclub.co.uk
Gently undulating parkland course with sea views. The Par 3
3rd is generally played into the wind and the 4th has a
difficult lefthand dogleg.
18 holes, 6200yds, Par 70, SSS 70.
Club membership 650.
Visitors   contact for times.
Societies   must apply in writing/telephone.
Green Fees not confirmed.
Prof   John Brotherton
Designer   D Steel/James Braid
Facilities   ⊗ ℿ ⌷ ☰ ♀ ⚘ 🛅 ❦ ⚷
Location   0.5m S by Chestfield Railway Station

Hotel   ★★★ 67% The Chaucer, Ivy Ln,
             CANTERBURY ☎ 0870 400 8106 42 ⇌ ☏

Whitstable & Seasalter Collingwood Rd CT5 1EB
☎ 01227 272020 Fax 01227 280822
Links course.
9 holes, 5357yds, Par 66, SSS 63, Course record 62.
Club membership 300.
Visitors   weekend play by prior arrangement.
Green Fees £15 per 18 holes.
Facilities   ⌷ ☰ ♀ ⚘
Location   W side of town centre off B2205

Hotel   ★★★ 67% The Chaucer, Ivy Ln,
             CANTERBURY ☎ 0870 400 8106 42 ⇌ ☏

LANCASHIRE

ACCRINGTON   Map 07 SD72

Accrington & District Devon Av, Oswaldtwistle BB5 4LS
☎ 01254 381614 Fax 01254 381614
e-mail: info@accrington-golf-club.fsnet.co.uk
Moorland course with pleasant views of the Pennines and
surrounding areas. The course is a real test for even the best
amateur golfers and has hosted many County matches and
Championships over its 100 plus years history.
18 holes, 6044yds, Par 70, SSS 69, Course record 63.
Club membership 600.
Visitors   must contact in advance, handicap certificate
              required.
Societies   contact in advance.
Green Fees £22 Mon-Thurs; £28 (Fri-Sun & bank holidays).
Prof   Bill Harling
Designer   J Braid
Facilities   ⊗ ℿ ⌷ ☰ ♀ ⚘ 🛅 ❦ ❧ ⚘ ⚷
Location   Mid way between Accrington & Blackburn

Hotel   ★★★★ 65% Dunkenhalgh Hotel, Blackburn
             Rd, Clayton-le-Moors, ACCRINGTON
             ☎ 01254 398021   37 ⇌ ☏ Annexe42 ⇌ ☏

Baxenden & District Top o' th' Meadow, Baxenden
BB5 2EA ☎ 01254 234555 e-mail: baxgolf@hotmail.com
Moorland course with a long par 3 to start.
9 holes, 5740yds, Par 70, SSS 68, Course record 67.
Club membership 340.
Visitors   may not play Sat, Sun and bank holidays except
              with member.
Societies   must contact in advance.
Green Fees not confirmed.
Facilities   ⊗ ℿ ⌷ ☰ ♀ ⚘
Location   1.5m SE off A680

Hotel   ★★★★ 65% Dunkenhalgh Hotel, Blackburn
             Rd, Clayton-le-Moors, ACCRINGTON
             ☎ 01254 398021   37 ⇌ ☏ Annexe42 ⇌ ☏

> Looking for a driving range?
> See the index at the back of the guide

Green Haworth Green Haworth BB5 3SL
☎ 01254 237580 & 382510 Fax 01254 396176
e-mail: golf@greenhaworth.freeserve.co.uk
Moorland course dominated by quarries and difficult in
windy conditions.
9 holes, 5522yds, Par 68, SSS 67, Course record 66.
Club membership 320.
Visitors may not play Sun, Mar-Oct.
Societies apply in writing. Weekdays only before 5pm. Or
contact secretary on above telephone number.
Green Fees £15 per day.
Facilities ⊗ ⅏ 🏠 💷 ♀ ♨
Location 2m S off A680

Hotel ★★★ 63% County Hotel Blackburn, Yew Tree
Dr, Preston New Rd, BLACKBURN
☎ 01254 899988 101 ⇆ 🅿

BACUP   Map 07 SD82

Bacup Maden Rd OL13 8HY
☎ 01706 873170 & 877726 Fax 01706 877726
Moorland course, predominantly flat except climbs to 1st and
10th holes.
9 holes, 6008yds, Par 70, SSS 69.
Club membership 350.
Visitors no restrictions. Club competitions in season on
Sat & some Sun, advisable to contact in
advance.
Societies must contact in writing.
Green Fees not confirmed.
Facilities ♨
Location W side of town off A671

Hotel ★★★ 66% Rosehill House Hotel, Rosehill Av,
BURNLEY ☎ 01282 453931 30 ⇆ 🅿

BARNOLDSWICK   Map 07 SD84

Ghyll Skipton Rd BB18 6JH ☎ 01282 842466
Excellent, parkland course with outstanding views, especially
from the 8th tee where you can see the Three Peaks. Testing
8th hole is an uphill par 4. 11 holes in total 9 in Yorkshire
and 2 in Lancashire.
9 holes, 5790yds, Par 68, SSS 66, Course record 62.
Club membership 345.
Visitors may not play Tue, Fri after 4.30pm & Sun.
Societies must contact in writing.
Green Fees £15 per day (£18 weekends).
Facilities ⅏ by prior arrangement 💷 ♀ ♨
Location 1m NE on B6252

Hotel ★★★ 67% Stirk House Hotel, GISBURN
☎ 01200 445581 40 ⇆ 🅿 Annexe10 ⇆ 🅿

BLACKBURN   Map 07 SD62

Blackburn Beardwood Brow BB2 7AX
☎ 01254 51122 Fax 01254 665578
Parkland course on a high plateau with stream and hills.
Superb views of Lancashire coast and the Pennines.
18 holes, 6144yds, Par 71, SSS 70.
Club membership 550.
Visitors must contact professional in advance.
Societies must contact in advance.
Green Fees £24 per day (£28 weekends & bank holidays).

Prof Alan Rodwell
Facilities ⊗ ⅏ 🏠 💷 ♀ ♨ 🍴 👕 ♂
Location 1.25m NW of town centre off A677

Hotel ★★★ 63% County Hotel Blackburn, Yew Tree
Dr, Preston New Rd, BLACKBURN
☎ 01254 899988 101 ⇆ 🅿

BLACKPOOL   Map 07 SD33

Blackpool North Shore Devonshire Rd FY2 0RD
☎ 01253 352054 Fax 01253 591240
Undulating parkland course.
18 holes, 6432yds, Par 71, SSS 71, Course record 63.
Club membership 900.
Visitors may not play Thu & Sat. Advisable to contact in
advance.
Societies must contact in advance.
Green Fees £30 (£35 weekends & bank holidays).
Prof Brendan Ward
Facilities ⊗ ⅏ 🏠 💷 ♀ ♨ 🍴 👕 ♂
& Leisure Y.
Location on A587 N of town centre

Hotel ★★ 67% Brabyns Hotel, 1-3 Shaftesbury Av,
North Shore, BLACKPOOL
☎ 01253 354263 352163 Fax 01253 352915
22 ⇆ 🅿 Annexe3 ⇆ 🅿

De Vere Blackpool (Herons Reach) East Park Blackpool
FY3 8LL ☎ 01253 766156 & 838866 Fax 01253 798800
e-mail: mechelle.kelso@devere-hotels.com
The course was designed by Peter Alliss and Clive Clarke.
There are 10 man-made lakes and several existing ponds.
Built to a links design, well mounded but fairly easy walking.
Water comes into play on 9 holes, better players can go for
the carry or shorter hitters can take the safe route. The course
provides an excellent and interesting challenge for golfers of
all standards.
18 holes, 6628yds, Par 72, SSS 71, Course record 64.
Club membership 450.

Visitors may book up to 2 weeks in advance tel 01253
766156, (hotel guest/visiting society no limit to
how far in advance bookings can be made).
Handicap essential, etiquette and dress rules
must be adhered to
Societies telephone or write to golf sales office
01253 838866.
Green Fees £40(£45 weekends).
Cards 🆒 ■ ■ 🆒 💷 🆒 ⚙️
Prof Dominik Naughton
Designer Peter Alliss/Clive Clark   ▶

Facilities ⊗ �𝄬 ⯗ ▟ ♀ ⯑ 🏠 ⛴ 🏇 ⛳ ✓ ⟨
& Leisure hard tennis courts, heated indoor swimming
pool, squash, sauna, solarium, gymnasium,
health and beauty facilities.
Location Off A587 adjacent to Stanley Park & Zoo

Hotel ★★★★ 64% De Vere Hotel, East Park Dr,
BLACKPOOL ☎ 01253 838866 164 ⇥ 🏾

Stanley Park Municipal North Park Dr FY3 8LS
☎ 01253 397916 Fax 01253 397916
The golf course, situated in Stanley Park is municipal. The
golf club (Blackpool Park) is private but golfers may use the
clubhouse facilities if playing the course. An abundance of
grassy pits, ponds and open dykes.
18 holes, 6087yds, Par 70, SSS 69, Course record 64.
Club membership 600.
Visitors must apply to Mrs A Hirst, Town Hall, Talbot
Square, Blackpool.
Societies must apply in writing to Mrs A Hirst, Blackpool
Borough Council, Town Hall, Talbot Square,
Blackpool.
Green Fees £11.50 per round(£13.50 weekend & bank
holidays).
Prof Brian Purdie
Designer Mckenzie
Facilities ⊗ ⯑ ⯗ ▟ ♀ ⯑ 🏠 ⯑ ✓
Location 1m E of Blackpool Tower

Hotel ★★★ 60% Savoy Hotel, Queens Promenade,
North Shore, BLACKPOOL
☎ 01253 352561 131 ⇥ 🏾

BURNLEY   Map 07 SD83

Burnley Glen View BB11 3RW
☎ 01282 421045 & 451281 Fax 01282 451281
e-mail: burnleygolf@currantbun.com
Moorland course with hilly surrounds.
18 holes, 5911yds, Par 69, SSS 69, Course record 64.
Club membership 750.
Visitors must contact in advance. May not play on
Saturdays.
Societies must apply in writing.
Green Fees not confirmed.
Prof William Tye
Facilities ⊗ ⯑ ⯗ ▟ ♀ ⯑ 🏠 ✓
Location 1.5m S off A646

Hotel ★★★ 66% Rosehill House Hotel, Rosehill Av,
BURNLEY ☎ 01282 453931 30 ⇥ 🏾

Towneley Towneley Park, Todmorden Rd BB11 3ED
☎ 01282 438473
Parkland course, with other sporting facilities.
18 holes, 5811yds, Par 70, SSS 68, Course record 67.
Club membership 290.
Visitors must contact in advance.
Societies must contact in advance in writing.
Green Fees £10 (£11 weekends & bank holidays).
Facilities ⊗ ⯑ ▟ ♀ ⯑ 🏠 ✓
Location 1m SE of town centre on A671

Hotel ★★★ 74% Oaks Hotel, Colne Rd, Reedley,
BURNLEY ☎ 01282 414141 50 ⇥ 🏾

CHORLEY   Map 07 SD51

Charnock Richard Preston Rd, Charnock Richard PR7 5LE
☎ 01257 470707 Fax 01257 794343
Flat parkland course with plenty of Americanised water
hazards. Signature hole the 6th Par 5 with an island green.
18 holes, 6234yds, Par 71, SSS 70, Course record 68.
Club membership 550.
Visitors strict full dress code, members time 8.30-
9.30pm and 12.00-1.00pm weekdays, telephone
for weekend play.
Societies contact club secretary in writing.
Green Fees £20 per round (£30 weekends); half price
second round.
Cards 📶 💳 💳 ♀
Prof Lee Taylor
Designer Chris Court
Facilities ⊗ ⯑ ⯗ ▟ ♀ ⯑ 🏠 ⯑ ⛳ ✓
Location On the main A49, 0.25m from Camelot Theme
Park

Hotel ★★★ 69% Park Hall Hotel, Park Hall Rd,
Charnock Richard, CHORLEY
☎ 01257 452090 54 ⇥ 🏾 Annexe84 ⇥ 🏾

Chorley Hall o' th' Hill, Heath Charnock PR6 9HX
☎ 01257 480263 Fax 01257 480722
A splendid moorland course with plenty of fresh air. The
well-sited clubhouse affords some good views of the
Lancashire coast and of Angelzarke, a local beauty spot.
Beware of the short 3rd hole with its menacing out-of-
bounds.
18 holes, 6307yds, Par 71, SSS 70, Course record 63.
Club membership 550.
Visitors must contact in advance and may not play
weekends or bank holidays.
Societies must contact in advance. Tue-Fri only.
Green Fees not confirmed.
Prof Gavin Mutch
Designer J A Steer
Facilities ⊗ by prior arrangement ⯗ ▟ ♀ ⯑ 🏠 ⯑
🏇 ✓
Location 2.5m SE on A673

Hotel ★★★ 70% Pines Hotel, 570 Preston Rd,
Clayton-Le-Woods, CHORLEY
☎ 01772 338551 37 ⇥ 🏾

Duxbury Jubilee Park Duxbury Hall Rd PR7 4AT
☎ 01257 265380 Fax 01257 274500
A municipal parkland course set in parkland and mature
woodland. The contours, elevated tees and greens, the
bunkers and the water hazards on several holes give constant
interest and challenge, particularly around the turn when the
woods come into play. The 10th to the 12th offer the hardest
challenges with the 17th not far behind.
18 holes, 6390yds, Par 71, SSS 70.
Club membership 250.
Visitors must contact 6 days in advance via Pro shop.
Societies must contact in advance by letter.
Green Fees £8 per round (£10.50 weekends).
Prof S Middleman
Designer Hawtree & Sons
Facilities ⊗ ▟ ⯑ 🏠 ⯑ ✓
Location 2.5m S off A6

▶

Hotel   Welcome Lodge, Welcome Break, Charnock
Richard - M6, Mill Ln, CHORLEY
☎ 01257 791746 100 ⇄ 🐾

Shaw Hill Hotel Golf & Country Club Preston Rd,
Whittle-Le-Woods PR6 7PP
☎ 01257 269221 Fax 01257 261223
e-mail: info@shaw-hill.co.uk
A fine heavily wooded parkland course designed by one
of Europe's most prominent golf architects and offering
a considerable challenge as well as tranquillity and
scenic charm. Six holes are protected by water and
signature holes are the 8th and the closing 18th played
slightly up-hill to the imposing Club House.
18 holes, 6252yds, Par 72, SSS 70, Course record 65.
Club membership 500.
Visitors   must contact in advance, denims and
trainers not allowed on course or in
clubhouse.
Societies   must telephone in advance.
Green Fees £40 per 18 holes (£30 winter).
Cards   💳 💳 💳 💳 💳 💳
Prof   David Clark
Designer   Harry Vardon
Facilities   ⊗ 🍴 🛏 💪 🍸 🎿 🏡 ⛳ 🏐 🎯 💈 ⚘
& Leisure   heated indoor swimming pool, sauna,
solarium, gymnasium, Beauty salon.
Location   On A6 1.5m N

Hotel   ★★★ 71% Shaw Hill Hotel Golf &
Country Club, Preston Rd, Whittle-le-
Woods, CHORLEY ☎ 01257 269221
26 ⇄ 🐾 Annexe4 ⇄ 🐾

CLITHEROE   Map 07 SD74

Clitheroe Whalley Rd, Pendleton BB7 1PP
☎ 01200 422292 Fax 01200 422292
One of the best inland courses in the country. Clitheroe
is a parkland-type course with water hazards and good
scenic views, particularly on towards Longridge, and
Pendle Hill.
18 holes, 6326yds, Par 71, SSS 71, Course record 67.
Club membership 750.
Visitors   must contact in advance.
Societies   must contact in advance.
Green Fees £33 per day (£39 weekends & bank
holidays).
Prof   John Twissell
Designer   James Braid
Facilities   ⊗ 🍴 🛏 💪 🍸 🎿 🏡 ⛳ ⚘ ⚑
Location   2m S of Clitheroe on Whalley Road

Hotel   ★★ 68% Shireburn Arms Hotel, Whalley
Rd, Hurst Green, CLITHEROE
☎ 01254 826518 18 ⇄ 🐾

COLNE   Map 07 SD84

Colne Law Farm, Skipton Old Rd BB8 7EB
☎ 01282 863391
Moorland course with scenic surroundings.
9 holes, 5961yds, Par 70, SSS 69, Course record 63.
Club membership 356.

Visitors   restricted Thu. Must contact in advance.
Societies   must contact in advance.
Green Fees not confirmed.
Facilities   ⊗ 🍴 🛏 💪 🍸 🎿
Location   1m E off A56

Hotel   ★★★ 67% Stirk House Hotel, GISBURN
☎ 01200 445581 40 ⇄ 🐾 Annexe10 ⇄ 🐾

DARWEN   Map 07 SD62

Darwen Winter Hill BB3 0LB
☎ 01254 701287 (club) & 776370 (pro) Fax 01254 773833
First 9 holes on parkland, the second 9 on moorland.
18 holes, 5863yds, Par 69, SSS 68, Course record 63.
Club membership 600.
Visitors   may not play on Tue or Sat.
Societies   must contact in advance.
Green Fees £30 per day; £25 per round (£40/£30 weekends).
Prof   Wayne Lennon
Facilities   ⊗ 🍴 🛏 💪 🍸 🎿 🏡
Location   1m NW

Hotel   ★★★ 67% Whitehall Hotel, Springbank,
Whitehall, DARWEN ☎ 01254 701595
17 ⇄ 🐾

FLEETWOOD   Map 07 SD34

Fleetwood Princes Way FY7 8AF
☎ 01253 873661 & 773573 Fax 01253 773573
Championship length, flat seaside links where the player
must always be alert to changes of direction or strength
of the wind.
18 holes, 6723yds, Par 72, SSS 72.
Club membership 600.

Visitors   may not play on competition days or Tue.
Societies   must contact in advance. A deposit of £5
per player is required.
Green Fees not confirmed.
Prof   S McLaughlin
Designer   J A Steer
Facilities   ⊗ 🍴 🛏 💪 🍸 🎿 🏡 ⚘
Location   W side of town centre

Hotel   ★★ 67% Brabyns Hotel, 1-3 Shaftesbury
Av, North Shore, BLACKPOOL
☎ 01253 354263 352163
Fax 01253 352915
22 ⇄ 🐾 Annexe3 ⇄ 🐾

GARSTANG　　　　　　　Map 07 SD44

Garstang Country Hotel & Golf Club Garstang Rd,
Bowgreave PR3 1YE ☎ 01995 600100 Fax 01995 600950
e-mail: garstanghotel@btconnect.com
Fairly flat parkland course following the contours of the
Rivers Wyre and Calder and providing a steady test of
ability, especially over the longer back nine. Exceptional
drainage makes the course playable all year round.
18 holes, 6050yds, Par 68, SSS 68.

Visitors	tee times bookable 6 days in advance.
Societies	telephone for availability and confirm in writing.
Green Fees	not confirmed.
Cards	〓 ▨▨ ▨▨ ▨ ▨▨ ▨
Prof	Robert Head
Designer	Richard Bradbeer
Facilities	⊗ ⅷ ᕤ ☕ ♀ ⚲ 🏠 ⚑ ⚐ ♂ ▮
Location	Situated on B6430 1m S of Garstang

GREAT HARWOOD　　　　Map 07 SD73

Great Harwood Harwood Bar, Whalley Rd BB6 7TE
☎ 01254 884391
Flat parkland course with fine views of the Pendle region.
9 holes, 6411yds, Par 73, SSS 71, Course record 68.
Club membership 380.

Visitors	must contact in advance.
Societies	welcome mid-week only, apply in writing.
Green Fees	£16 per day (£22 weekends & bank holidays).
Facilities	ᕤ ☕ ♀ ⚲
Location	E side of town centre on A680

Hotel ★★★★ 65% Dunkenhalgh Hotel, Blackburn
Rd, Clayton-le-Moors, ACCRINGTON
☎ 01254 398021　37 ⇋ ♠ Annexe42 ⇋ ♠

HASLINGDEN　　　　　　Map 07 SD72

Rossendale Ewood Ln Head BB4 6LH ☎ 01706 831339 &
213616 (Pro) Fax 01706 228669 e-mail: rgc@golfers.net
Testing meadowland course, mainly flat, situated on a
plateau with panoramic views.
18 holes, 6293yds, Par 72, Course record 64.
Club membership 700.

Visitors	must contact in advance. Must play with member on Sat.
Societies	must telephone in advance & confirm in writing.
Green Fees	£25.50 (£30.50 Sun).
Prof	Stephen Nicholls
Facilities	⊗ ⅷ ᕤ ☕ ♀ (ex Mon) ⚲ 🏠 ♂
Location	0.5m S off A56

Hotel ★★★ 63% County Hotel Blackburn, Yew Tree
Dr, Preston New Rd, BLACKBURN
☎ 01254 899988 101 ⇋ ♠

HEYSHAM　　　　　　　　Map 07 SD46

Heysham Trumacar Park, Middleton Rd LA3 3JH
☎ 01524 851011 Fax 01524 853030
Seaside parkland course, partly wooded. The 15th is a 459
yard Par 4 hole nearly always played into the prevailing
south west wind.
18 holes, 6266yds, Par 69, SSS 70, Course record 64.
Club membership 1100.

Visitors	book in advance via the professional, restricted at weekends.
Societies	must contact in advance.
Green Fees	£27 per day; £22 per round (£33 per day/round weekends & bank holidays).
Prof	Ryan Done
Designer	Alex Herd
Facilities & Leisure	⊗ ⅷ ᕤ ☕ ♀ ⚲ 🏠 ♂ snooker.
Location	0.75m S off A589

Hotel ★ 58% Clarendon Hotel, Marine Rd West,
West End Promenade, MORECAMBE
☎ 01524 410180 31rm(28 ⇋ ♠)

KNOTT END-ON-SEA　　　Map 07 SD34

Knott End Wyreside FY6 0AA
☎ 01253 810576 Fax 01253 813446
Pleasant, undulating parkland course on banks of River
Wyre. Open to sea breezes.
18 holes, 5789yds, Par 69, SSS 68, Course record 63.
Club membership 500.

Visitors	book via professional up to 7 days in advance.
Societies	must contact in advance.
Green Fees	not confirmed.
Prof	Paul Walker
Designer	Braid
Facilities	⊗ ⅷ ᕤ ☕ ♀ ⚲ 🏠 ♂
Location	W side of village off B5377

Hotel ★★ 67% Brabyns Hotel, 1-3 Shaftesbury Av,
North Shore, BLACKPOOL
☎ 01253 354263 352163 Fax 01253 352915
22 ⇋ ♠ Annexe3 ⇋ ♠

LANCASTER　　　　　　　Map 07 SD46

Lancaster Golf Club Ashton Hall, Ashton-with-
Stodday LA2 0AJ ☎ 01524 751247 Fax 01524 752742
This course is unusual for parkland golf as it is exposed
to the winds coming off the Irish Sea. It is situated on the
Lune estuary and has some natural hazards and easy
walking. There are however several fine holes among
woods near the old clubhouse.
18 holes, 6282yds, Par 71, SSS 71, Course record 66.
Club membership 925.

Visitors	must play with member or resident weekends. Must contact in advance and have a handicap certificate.
Societies	Mon-Fri only. Must contact in advance. Handicap certificate required.
Green Fees	£32 per day.
Cards	〓 ▨▨ ▨ ▨
Prof	David Sutcliffe
Designer	James Braid
Facilities	⊗ ⅷ ᕤ ☕ ♀ ⚲ 🏠 ⚑ ♂
Location	3m S on A588

Hotel ★★★★ 67% Lancaster House Hotel,
Green Ln, Ellel, LANCASTER
☎ 01524 844822　80 ⇋ ♠

Where to stay, where to eat?
Visit the AA internet site
www.theAA.com

Lansil Caton Rd LA1 3PE ☎ 01524 61233
Challenging parkland course.
9 holes, 5523yds, Par 70, SSS 67, Course record 68.
Club membership 375.
Visitors may not play before 1pm on Sun.
Societies weekdays only; must contact in writing.
Green Fees £12 per round.
Facilities 🏋 💺 ♀ 🔥
Location N side of town centre on A683

Hotel ★★★ 67% Posthouse Lancaster, Waterside
Park, Caton Rd, LANCASTER
☎ 0870 400 9047 157 ➡ 🏐

LANGHO   Map 07 SD73

Mytton Fold Hotel & Golf Complex Whalley Rd BB6 8AB
☎ 01254 240662 & 245392 (pro shop) Fax 01254 248119
e-mail: mutton-fold.hotel@virgin.net
The course has panoramic views across the Ribble Valley
and Pendle Hill. Tight fairways and water hazards are
designed to make this a challenging course for any golfer.
18 holes, 6082yds, Par 72, SSS 69, Course record 69.
Club membership 350.
Visitors weekends restricted must contact in advance.
Societies telephone in advance.
Green Fees not confirmed.
Cards 🔲 🔲 🔲 🔲 🔲
Prof Gary P Coope
Designer Frank Hargreaves
Facilities 🏋 🍴 💺 💪 ♀ 🔥 🍴 📷 🍴 🔥
Location On A59 between Langho and Whalley

Hotel ★★★ 70% Northcote Manor, Northcote Rd,
LANGHO ☎ 01254 240555 14 ➡ 🏐

LEYLAND   Map 07 SD52

Leyland Wigan Rd PR5 2UD
☎ 01772 436457 Fax 01772 436457
e-mail: manager@leylandgc.demon.co.uk
Parkland course, fairly flat and usually breezy.
18 holes, 6123yds, Par 69, SSS 70, Course record 64.
Club membership 650.
Visitors must contact in advance. Welcome weekdays,
with member only at weekends.
Societies must contact in advance.
Green Fees £25 per round/day.
Prof Colin Burgess
Facilities 🏋 🍴 💺 💪 ♀ 🔥 📷 🔥 🍴
Location E side of town centre on A49

Hotel ★★★ 70% Pines Hotel, 570 Preston Rd,
Clayton-Le-Woods, CHORLEY
☎ 01772 338551 37 ➡ 🏐

LONGRIDGE   Map 07 SD63

Longridge Fell Barn, Jeffrey Hill PR3 2TU
☎ 01772 783291 Fax 01772 783022
One of the oldest clubs in England. A moorland course with
panoramic views of the Ribble Valley, Trough of Bowland,
The Fylde and Welsh Mountains.
18 holes, 5975yds, Par 70, SSS 69, Course record 65.
Club membership 700.

Visitors welcome. Must contact in advance. Limited play
at weekends Jul-Aug.
Societies welcome by prior arrangement.
Green Fees £20 per day, £15 per round.
Prof Stephen Taylor
Facilities 🏋 🍴 💺 💪 ♀ 🔥 📷 🔥
Location 8m NE of Preston off B6243

Hotel ★★ 68% Shireburn Arms Hotel, Whalley Rd,
Hurst Green, CLITHEROE
☎ 01254 826518 18 ➡ 🏐

LYTHAM ST ANNES   See page 163

LYTHAM ST ANNES   Map 07 SD32

Fairhaven Lytham Hall Park, Ansdell FY8 4JU
☎ 01253 736741 (Secretary) 736976 (Pro)
Fax 01253 731461
A flat, but interesting parkland links course of good standard.
There are natural hazards as well as numerous bunkers and
players need to produce particularly accurate second shots.
An excellent test of golf for all abilities
18 holes, 6883yds, Par 74, SSS 73, Course record 66.
Club membership 750.
Visitors telephone professional in advance.
Societies must contact in advance.
Green Fees not confirmed.
Cards 🔲 🔲 🔲 🔲 🔲
Prof Brian Plucknett
Designer J A Steer
Facilities 🏋 🍴 💺 💪 ♀ 🔥 📷 🔥 🍴
Location E side of town centre off B5261

Hotel ★★★ 63% Bedford Hotel, 307-311 Clifton Dr
South, LYTHAM ST ANNES
☎ 01253 724636 35 ➡ 🏐

Lytham Green Drive Ballam Rd FY8 4LE
☎ 01253 737390 737379 Fax 01253 731350
Pleasant parkland course, ideal for holidaymakers.
18 holes, 6163yds, Par 70, SSS 69, Course record 64.
Visitors must contact in advance,weekend play by
arrangement only.
Societies telephone to book in advance.
Green Fees £35 per day; £25 per round (£35 weekends).
Prof Andrew Lancaster
Designer Steer
Facilities 🏋 🍴 💺 💪 ♀ 🔥 📷 🔥 🍴 🔥
Location E side of town centre off B5259

Hotel ★★★★ 64% Clifton Arms, West Beach,
Lytham, LYTHAM ST ANNES
☎ 01253 739898 48 ➡ 🏐

St Annes Old Links Highbury Rd East FY8 2LD
☎ 01253 723597 Fax 01253 781506
e-mail: sectysaolgc.uk.com
Seaside links, qualifying course for Open Championship;
compact and of very high standard, particularly greens.
Windy, very long 5th, 17th and 18th holes. Famous hole: 9th
(171 yds), par 3. Excellent club facilities.
18 holes, 6616yds, Par 72, SSS 72.
Club membership 950.

▶

Royal Lytham & St Annes

ytham St Annes, *Lancs* ☎ 01253 724206 Fax 01253 780946 Map 07 SD32

The Old Course, founded in 1900, was designed by Willie Park. It is a classic course at just 6308 yards long, with gorse and pine trees, silver birch, heather and immaculate turf. The new course is no less a challenge, created by HS Holt in 1922 it is 6443 yards. There is a long wait for anyone wishing to become a member of this prestigious club, it's location within easy reach of London is an attraction in itself. Visitors playing two rounds will be asked to alternate onto the other course in the afternoon. Short rounds may be played by finishing at the 10th or 13th green on the Old Course, and the 10th or 11th green on the New Course. On Monday one course is designated the two ball course until 3.00pm, check when booking a tee time.

Visitors Mon & Thu (unless guest at Dormy House). Must contact in advance and have a handicap certificate

Societies must apply to Secretary (large groups Thu only)

Green Fees £92 per round (includes lunch)

Facilities ⊗ ⟩⊪ ⦧ ⬛ ⵣ ⟑ 🏠 ✂ ⟨

Location Links Gate, Lytham FY8 3LQ (0.5m E of St Annes town)

Holes/Par/Course record 18 holes, 6334 yds, Par 71, SSS 71

Championship Course

Visitors   may not play on Sat or before 9.15am &
            between noon-2pm weekdays. Sundays by prior
            arrangement only. Handicap certificate
            requested.
Societies   must contact in advance.
Green Fees £38 per day(£48 weekends & bank holidays).
Prof   G Hardiman
Designer   George Lowe
Facilities ⊗ ⅷ ㄴ ♥ ♀ ♨ 슙 ⌀
Location   N side of town centre

Hotel   ★★★ 63% Bedford Hotel, 307-311 Clifton Dr
            South, LYTHAM ST ANNES
            ☎ 01253 724636   35 ⇦ ⋔

MORECAMBE   Map 07 SD46

Morecambe Bare LA4 6AJ
☎ 01524 412841 Fax 01524 400088
e-mail: morecambegolf@btconnect.com
Holiday golf at its most enjoyable. The well-maintained,
wind-affected seaside parkland course is not long but full
of character. Even so the panoramic views across
Morecambe Bay and to the Lake District and Pennines
make concentration difficult. The 4th is a testing hole.
18 holes, 5770yds, Par 67, SSS 69, Course record 69.
Club membership 850.
Visitors   may play from yellow tees, must contact in
            advance.
Societies   must contact in advance.
Green Fees £28 per day; £23 per round (£33/£28
            weekends).
Prof   Simon Fletcher
Designer   Dr Alister Mackenzie
Facilities ⊗ ⅷ ㄴ ♥ ♀ ♨ 슙 ⌀
Location   N side of town centre on A5105

Hotel   ★★★ 65% Elms Hotel, Bare Village,
            MORECAMBE ☎ 01524 411501
            40 ⇦ ⋔

NELSON   Map 07 SD83

Marsden Park Townhouse Rd BB9 8DG ☎ 01282 661912
A semi-parkland course offering panoramic views of
surrounding countryside, set in the foothills of Pendle
Marsden Park, a testing 18 holes for golfers of all abilities.
18 holes, 5813yds, Par 70, SSS 68, Course record 66.
Club membership 298.
Visitors   welcome at any time, advised to book in
            advance at weekends.
Societies   Must contact in writing.
Green Fees not confirmed.
Cards   ▨▨ ▆▆ ▨▨ 🖃
Prof   Martin Ross
Facilities ⊗ ⅷ ㄴ ♥ ♀ ♨ 슙 ⌀
Location   E side of town centre off A56

Hotel   ★★★ 74% Oaks Hotel, Colne Rd, Reedley,
            BURNLEY ☎ 01282 414141   50 ⇦ ⋔

Nelson King's Causeway, Brierfield BB9 0EU
☎ 01282 611834 & 617000 Fax 01282 606226
Moorland course, usually windy, with good views. Testing
8th hole, par 4.
18 holes, 5967yds, Par 70, SSS 69, Course record 63.
Club membership 500.

Visitors   must telephone 01282 617000 in advance, may
            not play before 9.30am or between 12.30-
            1.30pm.
Societies   must contact in advance.
Green Fees £25 per day (£30 weekends & bank holidays).
Prof   Nigel Sumner
Designer   Dr Mackenzie
Facilities ⊗ ⅷ ㄴ ♥ ♀ ♨ 슙 ⌀
Location   Take A682 to Brierfield, left at traffic lights into
            Halifax Road which becomes Kings Causeway

Hotel   ★★★ 74% Oaks Hotel, Colne Rd, Reedley,
            BURNLEY ☎ 01282 414141   50 ⇦ ⋔

ORMSKIRK   Map 07 SD40

Hurlston Hall Hurlston Ln, Southport Rd, Scarisbrick
L40 8HB ☎ 01704 840400 & 841120 (pro shop)
Fax 01704 841404 e-mail: hurlston_hall@btinternet.com
Designed by Donald Steel, this gently undulating course
offers fine views across the Pennines and Bowland Fells.
With generous fairways, large tees and greens, two streams
and seven lakes, it provides a good test of golf for players of
all standards. Luxurious colonial-style clubhouse.
18 holes, 6746yds, Par 72, SSS 72, Course record 66.
Club membership 650.
Visitors   welcome, but may be asked for handicap
            certificate or letter of introduction from own
            club. Preferable to book in advance.
Societies   registered Golf Societies and others approved by
            club, write or telephone for details.
Green Fees not confirmed.
Cards   ▨▨ ▆▆ ▨▨ 🖃 🄼
Prof   Jon Esclapez
Designer   Donald Steel
Facilities ⊗ ⅷ ㄴ ♥ ♀ ♨ 슙 ⌀ 🎣
& Leisure   fishing.
Location   Situated 6m from Southport and 2m from
            Ormskirk along A570

Hotel   ★★★ 67% Beaufort Hotel, High Ln,
            Burscough, ORMSKIRK
            ☎ 01704 892655   20 ⇦ ⋔

Ormskirk Cranes Ln, Lathom L40 5UJ
☎ 01695 572227 Fax 01695 572227
e-mail: secretary@ormskirkgolfclub.mersinet.co.uk
A pleasantly secluded, fairly flat, parkland course with
much heath and silver birch. Accuracy from the tees will
provide an interesting variety of second shots.
18 holes, 6358yds, Par 70, SSS 71, Course record 63.
Club membership 300.
Visitors   restricted Sat.
Societies   must telephone or contact in writing.
Green Fees £45 per day; £35 per round.
Prof   Jack Hammond
Facilities ⊗ ⅷ ㄴ ♥ ♀ ♨ 슙 ⌀
Location   1.5m NE

Hotel   ★★★ 67% Beaufort Hotel, High Ln,
            Burscough, ORMSKIRK
            ☎ 01704 892655   20 ⇦ ⋔

Looking for a driving range?
See the index at the back of the guide

PLEASINGTON   Map 07 SD62

Pleasington BB2 5JF
☎ 01254 202177 Fax 01254 201028
Plunging and rising across lovely parkland and heathland turf this course tests judgement of distance through the air to greens of widely differing levels. The 11th and 4th are testing holes.
18 holes, 6417yds, Par 71, SSS 71.
Club membership 700.

Visitors	may play Mon & Wed-Fri only.
Societies	must contact in advance.
Green Fees	£42 per 2 rounds;£36 per 1 round.
Prof	Ged Furey
Facilities	⊗ ⫟ ⬧ ♥ ♀ ⚍ 🏠 ✐
Location	J3 off M65 follow sign for Blackburn

Hotel   ★★★ 63% County Hotel Blackburn, Yew Tree Dr, Preston New Rd, BLACKBURN ☎ 01254 899988 101 ⇋ ℩

POULTON-LE-FYLDE   Map 07 SD33

Poulton-le-Fylde Breck Rd FY6 7HJ
☎ 01253 892444 Fax 01253 892444
Municipal parkland course, with easy walking.
9 holes, 4454yds, Par 71, SSS 68.
Club membership 200.

Visitors	no restrictions.
Societies	contact in advance by telephone or in writing.
Green Fees	not confirmed.
Cards	▭▭ ▬▬ ▭▭
Prof	Lewis Ware
Designer	E Astbury
Facilities	⊗ ♥ ♀ ⚍ 🏠 🐾 ✐ ℩
& Leisure	heated indoor swimming pool.
Location	N side of town

Hotel   ★★ 67% Brabyns Hotel, 1-3 Shaftesbury Av, North Shore, BLACKPOOL ☎ 01253 354263 352163 Fax 01253 352915 22 ⇋ ℩ Annexe3 ⇋ ℩

PRESTON   Map 07 SD52

Ashton & Lea Tudor Av, Lea PR4 0XA
☎ 01772 726480 & 735282 Fax 01772 735762
e-mail: ashtonleagolf@supanet.com
Fairly flat parkland course with pond and streams, offering pleasant walks and some testing holes for golfers of all standards.
18 holes, 6334yds, Par 71, SSS 70, Course record 65.
Club membership 650.

Visitors	must contact professional on 01772 720374 or secretary on 01772 735282.
Societies	must contact in writing or by telephone.
Green Fees	£23 per round (£25 weekends & bank holidays).
Prof	M Greenough
Designer	J Steer
Facilities	⊗ ⫟ ⬧ ♥ ♀ ⚍ 🏠 ✐
Location	3m W of Preston on A5085

Hotel   ★★★ 62% Posthouse Preston, Ringway, PRESTON ☎ 0870 400 9066 119 ⇋ ℩

Fishwick Hall Glenluce Dr, Farringdon Park PR1 5TD
☎ 01772 798300 & 795870 Fax 01772 704600
Meadowland course overlooking River Ribble. Natural hazards.
18 holes, 6045yds, Par 70, SSS 69, Course record 66.
Club membership 750.

Visitors	advisable to contact in advance.
Societies	must contact in advance.
Green Fees	not confirmed.
Prof	Nick Paranomos
Facilities	⊗ ⫟ ⬧ ♥ ♀ ⚍ 🏠 ✐

Hotel   ★★★ 62% Posthouse Preston, Ringway, PRESTON ☎ 0870 400 9066 119 ⇋ ℩

Ingol Tanterton Hall Rd, Ingol PR2 7BY
☎ 01772 734556 Fax 01772 729815
e-mail: ingol@golfers.net
Long, high course with natural water hazards set in 250 acres of beautiful parkland.
18 holes, 6294yds, Par 72, SSS 70, Course record 68.
Club membership 700.

Visitors	must contact booking office in advance.
Societies	must contact.
Green Fees	Contact office for details.
Cards	▭▭ ▬▬ ▭▭ ▬▬ ▬
Prof	Ryan Grimshaw
Designer	Henry Cotton
Facilities	⊗ ⫟ ⬧ ♥ ♀ ⚍ 🏠 🐾 ✐
& Leisure	squash, Snooker & Pool.
Location	Junct 32 off M6,take slip road to Garstang & Preston A6,then follow signs to Ingol

Hotel   ★★★ 62% Posthouse Preston, Ringway, PRESTON ☎ 0870 400 9066 119 ⇋ ℩

Penwortham Blundell Ln, Penwortham PR1 0AX
☎ 01772 744630 Fax 01772 744630
A progressive golf club set close to the banks of the River Ribble. The course has tree-lined fairways, excellent greens, and provides easy walking. Testing holes include the 178-yd, par 3 third, the 480-yd, par 5 sixth, and the 398-yd par 4 sixteenth.
18 holes, 6056yds, Par 69, SSS 69.
Club membership 975.

Visitors	must contact in advance; restricted Tue & Sat.
Societies	must apply in writing.
Green Fees	not confirmed.
Cards	▭▭ ▬▬ ▭▭ ▬▬ ▬
Facilities	⊗ ⫟ ⬧ ♥ ♀ ⚍ 🏠 ✐
Location	1.5m W of town centre off A59 ▶

| Hotel | ★★★★ 59% Tickled Trout, Preston New Rd, Samlesbury, PRESTON ☎ 01772 877671 72 ⇄ ᶜ |

Preston Fulwood Hall Ln, Fulwood PR2 8DD
☎ 01772 700011 Fax 01772 794234
Pleasant inland golf at this course set in very agreeable parkland. There is a well-balanced selection of holes, undulating amongst groups of trees, and not requiring great length.
18 holes, 6312yds, Par 71, SSS 71.
Club membership 800.

Visitors	may play midweek only. Must contact in advance and have a handicap certificate.
Societies	must contact in writing/telephone.
Green Fees	£32 per day; £27 per round.
Prof	Andrew Greenbank
Designer	James Braid
Facilities	⊗ ⊪ ⧺ ⬛ ♀ ⚖ 🛆 ⁄ ᵗ
Location	N side of town centre

| Hotel | ★★★★ 67% Preston Marriott Hotel, Garstang Rd, Broughton, PRESTON ☎ 01772 864087 150 ⇄ ᶜ |

RISHTON   Map 07 SD73

Rishton Eachill Links, Hawthorn Dr BB1 4HG
☎ 01254 884442 Fax 01254 601205
e-mail: msm@cwcom.net
Undulating moorland course.
9 holes, 6097yds, Par 70, SSS 69, Course record 68.
Club membership 270.

Visitors	must play with member on weekends and bank holidays.
Societies	must contact in writing.
Green Fees	£12 per day.
Designer	Peter Alliss/Dave Thomas
Facilities	⊗ ⊪ ⧺ ⬛ ♀ by arrangement ⚖
Location	S side of town off A678

| Hotel | ★★★★ 65% Dunkenhalgh Hotel, Blackburn Rd, Clayton-le-Moors, ACCRINGTON ☎ 01254 398021 37 ⇄ ᶜ Annexe42 ⇄ ᶜ |

SILVERDALE   Map 07 SD47

Silverdale Redbridge Ln LA5 0SP
☎ 01524 701300 Fax 01524 702074
Difficult heathland course with rock outcrops. Excellent views.
12 holes, 5210yds, Par 69, SSS 64.
Club membership 500.

Visitors	telephone 01524-701300 to book tee.Sun not available April-Sept inclusive.
Societies	must contact in writing.
Green Fees	£15-£18 per round.
Facilities	⊗ ⊪ ⧺ ⬛ ♀ ⚖ 🛆 ⁄
Location	Opposite Silverdale Station

| Hotel | ★★ 65% Royal Station Hotel, Market St, CARNFORTH ☎ 01524 732323 & 733636 Fax 01524 720267 13 ⇄ ᶜ |

UPHOLLAND   Map 07 SD50

Beacon Park Beacon Ln WN8 7RU
☎ 01695 622700 Fax 01695 633066
Undulating/hilly parkland course, designed by Donald Steel, with magnificent view of the Welsh hills. Twenty-four-bay floodlit driving range open 9am-9pm in summer.
18 holes, 6000yds, Par 72, SSS 69, Course record 68.
Club membership 200.

Visitors	may book 6 days in advance.
Societies	must contact in advance.
Green Fees	not confirmed.
Prof	Ray Peters
Designer	Donald Steel
Facilities	⊗ ⊪ by prior arrangement ⧺ by prior arrangement ⬛ ♀ 🛆 ⧫ ⁄ ᵗ
Location	S of Ashurst Beacon Hill

| Hotel | ★★★ 67% Beaufort Hotel, High Ln, Burscough, ORMSKIRK ☎ 01704 892655 20 ⇄ ᶜ |

Dean Wood Lafford Ln WN8 0QZ
☎ 01695 622219 Fax 01695 622245
e-mail: dwgc.fsnet.co.uk
This parkland course has a varied terrain - flat front nine, undulating back nine. Beware the par 4, 11th and 17th holes, which has ruined many a card. If there were a prize for the best maintained course in Lancashire, Dean Wood would be a strong contender.
18 holes, 6179yds, Par 71, SSS 71, Course record 66.
Club membership 800.

Visitors	must play with member Tue, Wed.
Societies	must contact in advance.
Green Fees	£30 (£33 weekends).
Prof	Stuart Danchin
Designer	James Braid
Facilities	⊗ ⊪ ⧺ ⬛ ♀ 🛆 ⧫ ⁄
Location	1m from junct 26 of M6

WHALLEY   Map 07 SD73

Whalley Long Leese Barn, Clerk Hill Rd BB7 9DR
☎ 01254 822236
Parkland course near Pendle Hill, overlooking the Ribble Valley. Superb views. Ninth hole over pond.
9 holes, 6258yds, Par 72, SSS 70, Course record 69.
Club membership 400.

Visitors	must telephone 01254 824766 in advance.
Societies	must apply in writing.
Green Fees	£16 per day (£20 weekends).
Prof	Jamie Hunt
Facilities	⊗ ⊪ ⧺ ⬛ ♀ 🛆 ⧫ ⁄
Location	1m SE off A671

| Hotel | ★★★★ 58% Clarion Hotel & Suites Foxfields, Whalley Rd, Billington, CLITHEROE ☎ 01254 822556 44 ⇄ ᶜ |

AA Hotels that have special arrangements with golf courses are listed at the back of the guide

WHITWORTH · · · · · · · · · · · · · · · · Map 07 SD81

Lobden Lobden Moor OL12 8XJ
☎ 01706 343228 Fax 01706 343228
Moorland course, with hard walking. Windy.
9 holes, 5697yds, Par 70, SSS 68, Course record 66.
Club membership 250.
Visitors May not play Sat.
Societies must apply in writing to Secretary.
Green Fees £12 (£15 weekends & bank holidays).
Facilities ⊗ ⦀ 🏌 💪 ♥ 🏌 ⚐
Location E side of town centre off A671

Hotel ★★★★ 64% Norton Grange Hotel, Manchester Rd, Castleton, ROCHDALE
☎ 01706 630788 51 ➩ 🐾

WILPSHIRE · · · · · · · · · · · · · · · · Map 07 SD63

Wilpshire Whalley Rd BB1 9LF
☎ 01254 248260 Fax 01254 248260
Parkland/moorland course with varied and interesting holes.
Magnificent views of Ribble Valley, the coast and the
Yorkshire Dales.
18 holes, 5971yds, Par 69, SSS 69, Course record 65.
Club membership 500.
Visitors must contact in advance.
Societies must contact by telephone and confirm in writing.
Green Fees not confirmed.
Cards 🔗 📇 💳
Prof Walter Slaven
Designer James Braid
Facilities ⊗ ⦀ 🏌 💪 ♥ 🏌 🏠 🎯 ⚐
Location 2m NE of Blackburn, on A666 towards Clitheroe

Hotel ★★★ 63% County Hotel Blackburn, Yew Tree Dr, Preston New Rd, BLACKBURN
☎ 01254 899988 101 ➩ 🐾

LEICESTERSHIRE

ASHBY-DE-LA-ZOUCH · · · · · · · · Map 08 SK31

Willesley Park Measham Rd LE65 2PF
☎ 01530 414596 Fax 01530 414596
Undulating heathland and parkland course with quick
draining sandy sub-soil.
18 holes, 6304yds, Par 70, SSS 70, Course record 64.
Club membership 600.
Visitors must contact in advance. Restricted weekends. Handicap certificate required.
Societies Wed-Fri only. Must apply in writing.
Green Fees not confirmed.
Prof C J Hancock
Designer J Braid
Facilities ⊗ ⦀ 🏌 💪 ♥ 🏌 🏠 ❧ ⚐
Location SW side of town centre on A453

Hotel ★★ 65% Charnwood Arms Hotel, Beveridge Ln, Bardon Hill, COALVILLE
☎ 01530 813644 34 ➩ 🐾

BIRSTALL · · · · · · · · · · · · · · · · Map 04 SK50

Birstall Station Rd LE4 3BB
☎ 0116 267 4322 Fax 0116 267 4322
Parkland course with trees, shrubs, ponds and ditches.
18 holes, 6222yds, Par 70, SSS 70.
Club membership 650.
Visitors with member only weekends; may not play Tue, Wed & Fri after 9am.
Societies apply in writing.
Green Fees £30 per day; £25 per round.
Prof David Clark
Facilities ⊗ ⦀ 🏌 💪 ♥ 🏌 🏠 ⚐
Location 3m N of Leicester on A6

Hotel ★★ 65% Red Cow, Hinckley Rd, Leicester Forest East, LEICESTER
☎ 0116 238 7878 31 ➩ 🐾

BOTCHESTON · · · · · · · · · · · · · · Map 04 SK40

Forest Hill Markfield Ln LE9 9FJ
☎ 01455 824800 Fax 01455 828522
18 holes, 6039yds, Par 72, SSS 69.
Telephone for further details

Hotel ★★ 66% The Mill On The Soar, Coventry Rd, SUTTON IN THE ELMS
☎ 01455 282419 25 ➩ 🐾

COSBY · · · · · · · · · · · · · · · · · · Map 04 SP59

Cosby Chapel Ln, Broughton Rd LE9 1RG
☎ 0116 286 4759 Fax 0116 286 4484
e-mail: secretary@cosby-golf-club.co.uk
Undulating parkland course with a number of tricky, tight
driving holes. Challenging holes include the par 4 1st with an
unseen meandering brook, the deceptively long par 4 3rd, the
12th from an elevated tee and the hogs back shaped par 3
14th, both affected by the prevailing wind.
18 holes, 6410yds, Par 71, SSS 71, Course record 66.
Club membership 750.
Visitors welcome weekdays before 4pm. May not play at weekends. Recommended to telephone in advance. Handicap certificate required.
Societies Mon-Fri only ,book with secretary.
Green Fees £26 per day; £18 per round.
Prof Martin Wing
Designer Hawtree
Facilities ⊗ ⦀ 🏌 💪 ♥ 🏌 🏠 🎯 ⚐
Location S side of village

Hotel ★★★ 68% Posthouse Leicester, Braunstone Ln East, LEICESTER
☎ 0870 400 9051 0870 4009051
Fax 0116 282 3623 172 ➩ 🐾

EAST GOSCOTE · · · · · · · · · · · · Map 08 SK61

Beedles Lake 170 Broome Ln LE7 3WQ
☎ 0116 260 6759
Fairly flat parkland course, founded in 1992, with an
adjoining lake and well maintained greens.
18 holes, 6625yds, Par 72, SSS 72, Course record 71.
Club membership 400.

▶

Visitors telephone booking required for weekends.
Societies welcome Mon-Fri
Green Fees £10 (£13 weekends & bank holidays).
Prof Sean Byrne
Designer D Tucker
Facilities ⊗ ⅢⅢ ᴸ ⚑ ♀ ♣ 🏠 ⅄ ⚐ ✓ ⏾
& Leisure fishing.
Location Off A46, just N of Leicester through village of Ratcliffe on the Wreake

---

Hotel ★★★ 64% Rothley Court, Westfield Ln, ROTHLEY ☎ 0116 237 4141 13 ⇄ �س Annexe21 ⇄ �س

ENDERBY   Map 04 SP59

Enderby Mill Ln LE9 5HL
☎ 0116 284 9388 Fax 0116 284 9388
A gently undulating 9-hole course at which beginners are especially welcome. The longest hole is the 2nd at 407 yards and there are 5 Par 3's.
9 holes, 2750yds, Par 36, SSS 36.
Club membership 150.
Visitors no restrictions.
Societies must telephone in advance.
Green Fees £5.10 (£6.10 weekends).
Prof Chris D'Araujo
Designer David Lowe
Facilities ♣ 🏠 ⚐ ✦ ✓
& Leisure heated indoor swimming pool, squash, sauna, solarium, gymnasium.
Location 2m S, M1 junct21 on Narborough road. Right turn off roundabout at Foxhunter pub, 0.5m on left

---

Hotel ★★ 67% Charnwood Hotel, 48 Leicester Rd, Narborough, LEICESTER
☎ 0116 286 2218 20 ⇄ �س

HINCKLEY   Map 04 SP49

Hinckley Leicester Rd LE10 3DR
☎ 01455 615124 & 615014 Fax 01455 890841 & 01455 615014 e-mail: proshop@hinckleygolfclub.com
Rolling parkland with lake features, and lined fairways.
18 holes, 6529yds, Par 71, SSS 71, Course record 65.
Club membership 750.
Visitors with member only weekends and bank holidays. Must contact in advance and have a handicap certificate.
Societies Mon,wed must contact in advance.
Green Fees £35 per day; £25 per round.
Cards ▦ ▬▬ ▭ 🎫 ⛛ 🖂
Prof Richard Jones
Designer Southern Golf Ltd
Facilities ⊗ ⅢⅢ ᴸ ⚑ ♀ ♣ 🏠 ✦ ⚒ ✓
& Leisure snooker.
Location 1.5m NE on B4668

Hotel ★★★ 65% Weston Hall Hotel, Weston Ln, Weston in Arden, Bulkington, NUNEATON
☎ 024 76312989 40 ⇄ �س

Where to stay, where to eat?
Visit the AA internet site
www.theAA.com

KETTON   Map 04 SK90

Luffenham Heath PE9 3UU
☎ 01780 720205 Fax 01780 722146
e-mail: jringleby@theluffenhamheathgc.co.uk
This undulating heathland course with low bushes, much gorse and many trees, lies in a conservation area for flora and fauna. From the higher part of the course there is a magnificent view across the Chater Valley. The course places a premium on accuracy with many demanding driving holes, challenging bunkers and well guarded greens. The course is not long but there are several outstanding holes.
18 holes, 6315yds, Par 70, SSS 70, Course record 64.
Club membership 550.
Visitors must contact in advance.
Societies write or telephone in advance.
Green Fees £45 per day; £35 per round.
Cards ▬▬ ▭ 🖂
Prof Ian Burnett
Designer James Braid
Facilities ⊗ ⅢⅢ ᴸ ⚑ ♀ ♣ 🏠 ⚐ ✓
Location 1.5m SW of Ketton by Fosters Railway Bridge on A6121

Hotel ★★★ 76% The George of Stamford, 71 St Martins, STAMFORD
☎ 01780 750750 & 750700 (Res)
Fax 01780 750701 47 ⇄ �س

KIBWORTH   Map 04 SP69

Kibworth Weir Rd, Beauchamp LE8 0LP
☎ 0116 279 2301 Fax 0116 279 6434
Parkland course with easy walking. A brook affects a number of fairways
18 holes, 6333yds, Par 71, SSS 70, Course record 65.
Club membership 700.
Visitors must contact in advance. With member only weekends.
Societies must contact in advance.
Green Fees £30 per day; £23 per round.
Prof Bob Larratt
Facilities ♣ 🏠 ⚐ ✓ ⏾
Location S side of village off A6

Hotel ★★★ 72% Three Swans Hotel, 21 High St, MARKET HARBOROUGH
☎ 01858 466644 18 ⇄ �س Annexe43 ⇄ �س

KIRBY MUXLOE   Map 04 SK50

Kirby Muxloe Station Rd LE9 2EP
☎ 0116 239 3457 Fax 0116 239 3457
Pleasant parkland course with a lake in front of the 17th green and a short 18th.
18 holes, 6351yds, Par 70, SSS 70, Course record 65.
Club membership 870.
Visitors must contact in advance and a handicap certificate is required. No visitors on Tue or at weekends.
Societies must contact in advance.
Green Fees not confirmed.
Prof Bruce Whipham
Facilities ⊗ ⅢⅢ ᴸ ⚑ ♀ ♣ 🏠 ⚐ ✓ ⏾
Location S side of village off B5380

Hotel ★★★ 68% Posthouse Leicester, Braunstone Ln East, LEICESTER
☎ 0870 400 9051 0870 4009051
Fax 0116 282 3623 172 ⇋ ₭

LEICESTER   Map 04 SK50

Humberstone Heights Gypsy Ln LE5 0TB
☎ 0116 276 3680 & 299 5570 (pro) Fax 0116 2995569
Municipal parkland course with 9 hole pitch and putt and 30 bay driving range.
18 holes, 6343yds, Par 70, SSS 70, Course record 66.
Club membership 400.
Visitors must telephone in advance at weekends.
Societies must telephone in advance.
Green Fees contact professional shop.
Cards ▦
Prof Phil Highfield
Designer Hawtry & Sons
Facilities ⊗ ♨ 🍺 ♀ ⚲ 🏠 ⛴ ➤ 🏌 ♂ ₤
Location 2.5m NE of city centre

Hotel ★★★ 74% Belmont House Hotel, De Montfort St, LEICESTER ☎ 0116 254 4773 77 ⇋ ₭

Leicestershire Evington Ln LE5 6DJ
☎ 0116 273 8825 Fax 0116 273 1900
e-mail: theleicestershiregolfclub@hotmail.com
Pleasantly undulating parkland course.
18 holes, 6329yds, Par 68, SSS 71, Course record 63.
Club membership 800.
Visitors must contact in advance. May not play Sat. Must hold a handicap certificate.
Societies must contact in advance.
Green Fees £32 per day; £27 per round (£38/£33 Sun & bank holidays).
Prof Darren Jones
Designer Hawtree
Facilities ⊗ 🎿 ♨ 🍺 ♀ ⚲ 🏠 ♂
Location 2m E of city off A6030

Hotel ★★★ 66% Hermitage Hotel, Wigston Rd, Oadby, LEICESTER ☎ 0116 256 9955 56 ⇋ ₭

Western Scudamore Rd, Braunstone Frith LE3 1UQ
☎ 0116 299 5566 Fax 0116 299 5568
Pleasant, undulating parkland course with open aspect fairways in two loops of nine holes.Not too difficult but a good test of golf off the back nine.
18 holes, 6518yds, Par 72, SSS 71.
Club membership 400.
Visitors must contact in advance.
Societies must contact the professional in advance.
Green Fees not confirmed.
Cards ▦ ▦ ▦ ▦ ▦
Prof Dave Butler
Facilities ⊗ 🎿 ♨ 🍺 ♀ ⚲ 🏠 ⛴ ♂ ₤
Location 1.5m W of city centre off A47

Hotel ★★★ 68% Posthouse Leicester, Braunstone Ln East, LEICESTER
☎ 0870 400 9051 0870 4009051
Fax 0116 282 3623 172 ⇋ ₭

LOUGHBOROUGH   Map 08 SK51

Longcliffe Snell's Nook Ln, Nanpantan LE11 3YA
☎ 01509 239129 Fax 01509 231286
A re-designed course of natural heathland with outcrops of granite forming natural hazards especially on the 1st and 15th. The course is heavily wooded and has much bracken and gorse. There are a number of tight fairways and ponds on the 14th and 15th holes.
18 holes, 6625yds, Par 72, SSS 72, Course record 65.
Club membership 660.

Visitors must contact in advance. With member only at weekends.Handicap certificate required.
Societies telephone for availability, handicap certificate required.
Green Fees £39 per day; £29 per round.
Prof David Mee
Designer Williamson
Facilities ⊗ 🎿 ♨ 🍺 ♀ ⚲ 🏠 ♂
Location 3m SW off B5350

Hotel ★★★ 64% Quality Hotel, New Ashby Rd, LOUGHBOROUGH
☎ 01509 211800 94 ⇋ ₭

LUTTERWORTH   Map 04 SP58

Kilworth Springs South Kilworth Rd, North Kilworth LE17 6HJ ☎ 01858 575082 & 575974 Fax 01858 575078
An 18-hole course of two loops of 9: the front 9 are links style while the back 9 are in parkland with 4 lakes. On a windy day it is a very challenging course and the 6th hole is well deserving of its nickname 'the Devil's Toenail'.
18 holes, 6543yds, Par 72, SSS 71, Course record 66.
Club membership 800.
Visitors welcome subject to availability. May only play after 12am at weekends.
Societies contact in advance.
Green Fees £18 per 18 holes; £11 per 9 holes (£21/£13 weekends).
Cards ▦ ▦ ▦ ▦ ▦
Prof Anders Mankert
Designer Ray Baldwin
Facilities ⊗ 🎿 ♨ 🍺 ♀ ⚲ 🏠 🏌 ♂ ₤
Location 4m E of M1 junc 20, A4304 to Mkt Harborough

Hotel ★★ 71% The Sun Inn, Main St, MARSTON TRUSSELL ☎ 01858 465531 20 ⇋ ₭

Lutterworth Rugby Rd LE17 4HN
☎ 01455 552532 Fax 01455 553586
18 holes, 6226yds, Par 70, SSS 70.
Location 0.5m S on A426
Telephone for further details

Hotel ★★★ 66% Brownsover Hall Hotel,
Brownsover Ln, Old Brownsover, RUGBY
☎ 01788 546100 27 ⇄ ♠ Annexe20 ⇄ ♠

MARKET HARBOROUGH   Map 04 SP78

Market Harborough Oxendon Rd LE16 8NF
☎ 01858 463684 Fax 01858 432906
A parkland course situated close to the town. There are wide-ranging views over the surrounding countryside. Lakes a feature on 4 holes; challenging last 3 holes.
18 holes, 6070yds, Par 70, SSS 69, Course record 63.
Club membership 600.
Visitors must play with member at weekends.
Societies must apply in writing.
Green Fees not confirmed.
Prof Frazer Baxter
Designer H Swan
Facilities ⚒ 🏠 ♂
Location 1m S on A508

Hotel ★★★ 72% Three Swans Hotel, 21 High St,
MARKET HARBOROUGH
☎ 01858 466644 18 ⇄ ♠ Annexe43 ⇄ ♠

Stoke Albany Ashley Rd, Stoke Albany LE16 8PL
☎ 01858 535208 Fax 01858 535505
Parkland course in the picturesque Welland Valley. Affording good views, the course should appeal to the mid-handicap golfer, and provide an interesting test to the more experienced player.
18 holes, 6132yds, Par 71, SSS 69.
Club membership 400.
Visitors welcome at all times.
Societies please telephone secretary.
Green Fees £13 per 18 holes (£18 weekends).
Cards 🟦🟥🟩🟧🔲🔲
Prof Adrian Clifford
Designer Hawtree
Facilities ⊗ ⽊ ⛳ ♥ ♀ ⚒ 🏠 ♂
Location Located N off A427 Market Harborough/Corby Road, follow Stoke Albany 500m towards Ashley village

Hotel ★★★ 72% Three Swans Hotel, 21 High St,
MARKET HARBOROUGH
☎ 01858 466644 18 ⇄ ♠ Annexe43 ⇄ ♠

MELTON MOWBRAY   Map 08 SK71

Melton Mowbray Waltham Rd, Thorpe Arnold LE14 4SD
☎ 01664 562118
Downland but flat course providing easy walking.
18 holes, 6222yds, Par 70, SSS 70, Course record 61.
Club membership 650.
Visitors must contact professional on 01664 569629.
Societies must contact in advance.
Green Fees £20 per round (£23 weekends).
Prof James Hetherington
Facilities ⊗ ⽊ ⛳ ♥ ♀ ⚒ 🏠 ♂
Location 2m NE of Melton Mowbray on A607

Hotel ★★★ 69% Sysonby Knoll Hotel, Asfordby Rd,
MELTON MOWBRAY
☎ 01664 563563 23 ⇄ ♠ Annexe1 ⇄ ♠

OADBY   Map 04 SK60

Glen Gorse Glen Rd LE2 4RF
☎ 0116 271 4159 Fax 0116 271 4159
Fairly flat 18-hole parkland course with some strategically placed mature trees, new saplings and ponds affecting play on 6 holes. Ridge and furrow is a feature of 5 holes.
18 holes, 6648yds, Par 72, SSS 72, Course record 67.
Club membership 600.
Visitors must contact in advance. Must play with member at weekends.
Societies must telephone secretary in advance.
Green Fees £28.50 per day; £24 per round.
Prof Dominic Fitzpatrick
Facilities ⊗ ⽊ ⛳ ♥ ♀ ⚒ 🏠 ♂
& Leisure snooker room.
Location On A6 trunk road between Oadby/Great Glen, 5m S of Leicester city centre

Hotel ★★★ 66% Hermitage Hotel, Wigston Rd,
Oadby, LEICESTER
☎ 0116 256 9955 56 ⇄ ♠

Oadby Leicester Rd LE2 4AJ ☎ 0116 270 9052
Municipal parkland course.
18 holes, 6376yds, Par 72, SSS 70, Course record 60.
Club membership 400.
Visitors no restrictions.
Societies by arrangement contact pro shop.
Green Fees £7.50 per round(£10 weekends).
Prof Alan Kershaw
Facilities ⛳ ♥ ♀ ⚒ 🏠 ♂
Location West of Oadby, off A6

Hotel ★★★ 66% Hermitage Hotel, Wigston Rd,
Oadby, LEICESTER
☎ 0116 256 9955 56 ⇄ ♠

ROTHLEY   Map 08 SK51

Rothley Park Westfield Ln LE7 7LH
☎ 0116 230 2809 Fax 0116 230 2809 e-mail: secretary@rothleypark.co.uk
Parkland course in picturesque situation.
18 holes, 6477yds, Par 71, SSS 71, Course record 67.
Club membership 600.
Visitors must contact professional on 0116 230 3023. Weekends and bankholidays with member only.
Societies apply in writing to secretary.
Green Fees £30 per day; £25 per round.
Prof Andrew Collins
Facilities ⊗ ⽊ ⛳ ♥ ♀ ⚒ 🏠 ♂
Location Off A6 N of Leicester

Hotel ★★★ 64% Rothley Court,
Westfield Ln, ROTHLEY
☎ 0116 237 4141 13 ⇄ ♠ Annexe21 ⇄ ♠

Entries with a green background
identify courses considered to be
particularly interesting

SCRAPTOFT   Map 04 SK60

Scraptoft Beeby Rd LE7 9SJ
☎ 0116 241 8863 Fax 0116 241 8863 e-
mail: info@scraptoft-golf.co.uk
Pleasant, inland country course.
18 holes, 6166yds, Par 70, SSS 70.
Club membership 650.
Visitors with member only weekends. Handicap
certificate required.
Societies apply in writing/telephone.
Green Fees £25 per day; £20 per round.
Prof Simon Wood
Facilities ⊗ ⅷ ╠ ♨ ♀ ♧ 🏠 ⛳ ♂
Location 1m NE

Hotel ★★★ 66% Hermitage Hotel, Wigston Rd,
Oadby, LEICESTER
☎ 0116 256 9955 56 ⇥ ♠

SEAGRAVE   Map 08 SK61

Park Hill Park Hill LE12 7NG
☎ 01509 815454 & 815775 (pro) Fax 01509 816062
e-mail: mail@parkhillgolf.co.uk
A rolling parkland course with tree lined fairways and views
over Charnwood Forest. The opening hole is 420 yards with
a forced water carry 100 yards short of the green. The 10th is
a 610 yard Par 5 against the prevailing wind. The closing
hole is a challenging Par 5 with water protecting both sides
of the green.
18 holes, 7219yds, Par 73, SSS 75, Course record 71.
Club membership 500.

Park Hill
Golf Club
Park Hill, Seagrave, Leicestershire, LE12 7NG
Tel 01509 815454   Fax 01509 816062
E-mail: mail@parkhillgolf.co.uk
www.parkhillgolf.co.uk

Nestled in the heart of Leicestershire,
overlooking the Charnwood Forest and beyond,
Park Hill boasts an 18 hole, Championship
length course, that utilises the lands natural
features to ensure that no two holes are the
same, the combination of water features and
precisely positioned bunkers provide for a
challenging course and excellent playing
conditions all year round.
Our fully licensed Clubhouse is open daily for
meals and refreshments.

Visitors must contact in advance, play after 9am
weekends.
Societies apply in advance.
Green Fees £20 (£24 weekends).
Cards ⬜ 💳 💳 💳 💳 💳
Prof Matthew Ulyett
Facilities ⊗ ⅷ ╠ ♨ ♀ ♧ 🏠 ♂ ⚒ ⛳ ♂
Location 6m N of Leicester off A46 Northbound, follow
signs to Seagrave

Hotel ★★★ 64% Quality Hotel, New Ashby Rd,
LOUGHBOROUGH
☎ 01509 211800 94 ⇥ ♠

ULLESTHORPE   Map 04 SP58

Ullesthorpe Frolesworth Rd LE17 5BZ
☎ 01455 209023 Fax 01455 202537
e-mail: bookings@ullesthorpecourt.co.uk
Set in 130 acres of parkland surrounding a 17th-century
manor house, this championship length course can be very
demanding and offers a challenge to both beginners and
professionals. Excellent leisure facilities. Water plays a part
on 3 holes.
18 holes, 6650yds, Par 72, SSS 72, Course record 67.
Club membership 650.

Visitors must contact in advance. With member only Sat,
no play on Sun.
Societies contact well in advance.
Green Fees £30 per day; £18 per round.
Cards ⬜ 💳 💳 💳 💳 💳
Prof David Bowring
Facilities ⊗ ⅷ ╠ ♨ ♀ ♧ 🏠 ♂ ⛳ ⚒ ♂
& Leisure hard tennis courts, heated indoor swimming
pool, sauna, solarium, gymnasium, Beauty
room, steam room & jaccuzi.
Location 5m Lutterworth junct 20 M1

Hotel ★★★ 67% Ullesthorpe Court Country Hotel &
Golf Club, Frolesworth Rd, ULLESTHORPE
☎ 01455 209023 38 ⇥ ♠

WHETSTONE   Map 04 SP59

Whetstone Cambridge Rd, Cosby LE9 1SJ
☎ 0116 286 1424 Fax 0116 286 1424
Easy to walk, parkland course where accuracy rather than
length is required.
18 holes, 5795yds, Par 68, SSS 68, Course record 63.
Club membership 500.

▶

Visitors must contact in advance, limited times at weekends.
Societies must contact in advance.
Green Fees not confirmed.
Cards ▦▦▦▦▦▦
Prof David Raitt
Designer E Calloway
Facilities ⊗ ⫽ 🏋 💪 ♀ 👤 🏠 ➤ 🏊 ⚐ ⌐
Location 1m S of village

Hotel ★★★ 66% Time Out Hotel & Leisure, Enderby Rd, Blaby, LEICESTER
☎ 0116 278 7898 48 ⇄ ♔

WILSON   Map 08 SK42

Breedon Priory Green Ln DE73 1AT
☎ 01332 863081 Fax 01332 865319
A relatively short and forgiving course set in undulating countryside with magnificent views from several holes.
18 holes, 5777yds, Par 69, SSS 68, Course record 67.
Club membership 779.
Visitors may play any time if tee available, must book for weekends one week in advance.
Societies apply in writing or telephone for booking form.
Green Fees £15.50 (£20.50 weekends).
Cards ▦▦▦
Prof Jim Broughton
Designer David Snell
Facilities ⊗ ⫽ 🏋 💪 ♀ 👤 🏠 ➤ ⚐ ⌐
& Leisure sauna, gymnasium.
Location 4m W of A42/M1 junct 24

Hotel ★★★ 69% The Priest House on the River, Kings Mills, CASTLE DONINGTON
☎ 01332 810649 25 ⇄ ♔ Annexe20 ⇄ ♔

WOODHOUSE EAVES   Map 08 SK51

Charnwood Forest Breakback Ln LE12 8TA
☎ 01509 890259 Fax 01509 890925
Hilly heathland course with hard walking, but no bunkers.
9 holes, 5960yds, Par 69, SSS 69, Course record 64.
Club membership 218.
Visitors must contact in advance, weekends restricted.
Societies Wed & Thu only. Must contact in advance. Mon & Fri by special arrangement.
Green Fees £15 per 9 holes;£20 per 18 holes;£25 per 27 holes;£30 per 36 holes.(£25 per 18 holes weekends & bank holidays).
Designer James Braid
Facilities ⊗ ⫽ 🏋 💪 ♀ 👤 ⚐
Location 3m from junct 22 or 23 of M1

Hotel ★★★★ 70% Quorn Country Hotel, Charnwood House, 66 Leicester Rd, QUORN
☎ 01509 415050 23 ⇄ ♔

Lingdale Joe Moore's Ln LE12 8TF
☎ 01509 890703 Fax 01509 890703
Parkland course located in Charnwood Forest with some hard walking at some holes. The par 3, (3rd) and par 5, (8th) are testing holes. Several holes have water hazards.
18 holes, 6545yds, Par 71, SSS 71, Course record 68.
Club membership 620.

Visitors must contact in advance for play.
Societies must contact in advance.
Green Fees £23 per round;£26 per day(£28/£33 weekends).
Prof Peter Sellears
Designer David Tucker
Facilities ⊗ ⫽ 🏋 💪 ♀ 👤 🏠 ⌐
Location 1.5m S off B5330

Hotel ★★★★ 70% Quorn Country Hotel, Charnwood House, 66 Leicester Rd, QUORN
☎ 01509 415050 23 ⇄ ♔

LINCOLNSHIRE

BELTON   Map 08 SK93

Belton Woods Hotel NG32 2LN
☎ 01476 593200 Fax 01476 574547
e-mail: devere.belton@airtime.co.uk
Two challenging 18-hole courses, a 9-hole Par 3 and a driving range. The Lakes Course has 13 lakes, while The Woodside boasts the third longest hole in Europe at 613 yards. Many leisure facilities.
The Lakes Course: 18 holes, 6831yds, Par 72, SSS 73, Course record 68.
The Woodside Course: 18 holes, 6623yds, Par 73, SSS 72, Course record 67.
Spitfire Course: 9 holes, 1010yds, Par 27, SSS 27.
Club membership 600.
Visitors book tee times in advance with exception of the Spitfire. Dress code in operation.
Societies welcome all week, reservations to be made by telephone or letter.
Green Fees £24 per round (£26 weekend).
Cards ▦▦▦▦▦▦
Prof Steve Sayers
Facilities ⊗ ⫽ 🏋 💪 ♀ 👤 🏠 🏴 🎾 🏊 ⚐ ⌐
& Leisure hard tennis courts, heated indoor swimming pool, squash, sauna, solarium, gymnasium.
Location On A607, 2m N of Grantham

Hotel ★★★★ 77% Belton Woods Hotel, BELTON
☎ 01476 593200 136 ⇄ ♔

BLANKNEY   Map 08 TF06

Blankney LN4 3AZ ☎ 01526 320263 Fax 01526 322521
Open parkland course with mature trees; fairly flat.
18 holes, 6634yds, Par 72, SSS 73, Course record 69.
Club membership 700.
Visitors must contact in advance, may not play Wed mornings, restricted at weekends.
Societies not Wed mornings, booking required.
Green Fees £30 per day; £22 per round (£35/£30 weekends).
Prof Graham Bradley
Designer C Sinclair
Facilities ⊗ ⫽ 🏋 💪 ♀ 👤 🏠 🏴 ➤ ⚐ ⌐
& Leisure snooker.
Location 10m SW on B1188

Hotel ★★ 70% Moor Lodge Hotel, Sleaford Rd, BRANSTON ☎ 01522 791366 24 ⇄ ♔

BOSTON   Map 08 TF34

Boston Cowbridge, Horncastle Rd PE22 7EL
☎ 01205 350589 Fax 01205 350589
Parkland course many water hazards in play on ten holes.
18 holes, 6490yds, Par 72, SSS 71, Course record 69.
Club membership 650.
Visitors evidence of handicap may be requested, contact
in advance for tee time.
Societies apply in writing/telephone.
Green Fees £25 per day; £19 per round (£30/£25 weekends
& bank holidays).
Prof Terry Squires
Facilities ⊗ ⅁ ㄴ ♥ ♀ ㄥ 合 ㎡ ♂
Location 2m N of Boston on B1183

Hotel ★★★ 62% New England Hotel,
49 Wide Bargate, BOSTON
☎ 01205 365255   25 ⇔ ↾

Kirton Holme Holme Rd, Kirton Holme PE20 1SY
☎ 01205 290669
A young parkland course designed for mid to high
handicappers. It is flat but has 2500 young trees, two natural
water course plus water hazards. The 2nd is a challenging,
386yard Par 4 dogleg.
9 holes, 5778yds, Par 70, SSS 68, Course record 69.
Club membership 350.
Visitors no restrictions but booking advisable for
weekends & summer evenings.
Societies by prior arrangement.
Green Fees £8.50 per day; £5 per 9 holes (£9.50/£6
weekends & bank holidays).
Designer D W Welberry
Facilities ⊗ ㄴ ♥ ♀ ㄥ ㎡ ♂
Location 4m W of Boston off A52

Hotel ★★ 63% Comfort Inn, Donnington Rd, Bicker
Bar, BOSTON ☎ 01205 820118   55 ⇔ ↾

BOURNE   Map 08 TF02

Toft Hotel Toft PE10 0JT
☎ 01778 590616 Fax 01778 590264
Parkland course on the verge of the Lincoln Edge. Includes
lake and uses contours of the hills to full effect.
18 holes, 6486yds, Par 72, SSS 71, Course record 63.
Club membership 450.

Visitors advisable to book for weekends
Societies apply in advance by telephone.
Green Fees £20 per round (£25 weekends).
Cards ▱ ▰ ▱ ▰ ⑨

Prof Mark Jackson
Designer Roger Fitton
Facilities ⊗ ⅁ ㄴ ♥ ♀ ㄥ 合 ㎡ �024 ♥ ♣ ♂ ↾
Location On A6121 Bourne/Stamford road

Hotel ★★ 69% Black Horse Inn, Grimsthorpe,
BOURNE ☎ 01778 591247 6 ⇔ ↾

CLEETHORPES   Map 08 TA30

Cleethorpes Kings Rd DN35 0PN ☎ 01472 816110
A mature coastal course founded in 1894. Slight undulations
give variety but the flat landscape makes for easy walking.
The course provides a challenge to all levels of player.
18 holes, 6349yds, Par 70, SSS 70, Course record 67.
Club membership 710.
Visitors restricted Wed afternoons, handicap certificate
preferred, must be a member of a golf club.
Societies Mon, Thu, Fri, Sun only. Must telephone in
advance.
Green Fees £20 per day (£25 weekends & bank holidays).
Prof Paul Davies
Designer Harry Vardon
Facilities ⊗ ⅁ ㄴ ♥ ♀ ㄥ 合 ♂
Location 2 miles SE of Cleethorpes, A180/A46 from W,
A16 from S

Hotel ★★★ 70% Kingsway Hotel, Kingsway,
CLEETHORPES ☎ 01472 601122   49 ⇔ ↾

Tetney Station Rd, Tetney DN36 5HY
☎ 01472 211644 & 811344 Fax 01472 211644
18-hole parkland course set at the foot of the Lincolnshire
Wolds. Noted for its challenging water features.
18 holes, 6100yds, Par 71, SSS 69, Course record 65.
Club membership 450.
Visitors contact in advance.
Societies apply in writing.
Green Fees not confirmed.
Prof Jason Abrams
Designer J S Grant
Facilities ⊗ ⅁ ㄴ ♥ ♀ ㄥ 合 ㎡ ♥ ♣ ♂ ↾
Location 1m off A16 Louth/Grimsby road

Hotel ★★★ 70% Kingsway Hotel, Kingsway,
CLEETHORPES ☎ 01472 601122   49 ⇔ ↾

CROWLE   Map 08 SE71

Hirst Priory *DN17 4BU* ☎ 01724 711619
Traditional flat parkland course. Generous sized greens with
discreet use of water and bunkers.
18 holes, 6283yds, Par 71, SSS 70.
Club membership 380.
Visitors no restrictions.
Societies may only play at weekends after 11am.
Green Fees not confirmed.
Prof Gavin Keeley
Designer David Barter
Facilities ⊗ ⅁ ㄴ ♥ ♀ ㄥ 合 ㎡ ♥ ♣ ♂

Hotel ★★ 71% Belmont Hotel, Horsefair Green,
THORNE ☎ 01405 812320   23 ⇔ ↾

Looking for a driving range?
See the index at the back of the guide

ELSHAM   Map 08 TA01

Elsham Barton Rd DN20 0LS
☎ 01652 680291(Sec) 680432(Pro) Fax 01652 680308
Mature parkland course in a rural setting with a variety of
wild life including many pheasants. Very secluded with easy
walking and a reservoir to maintain irrigation.
18 holes, 6402yds, Par 71, SSS 71, Course record 67.
Club membership 650.
Visitors   with member only weekends & bank holidays.
                  Preferable to contact in advance.
Societies   must apply in writing.
Green Fees   £27 per 36 holes; £18 per 18 holes.
Prof   Stuart Brewer
Facilities   ⊗ ⫪ ⬧ ☕ ♀ ⚲ 🏠 ↘ ⚒ ✗
Location   2m SW of Brigg on B1206

Hotel   ★★★ 68% Hanover International Hotel,
                  Rowland Rd, SCUNTHORPE
                  ☎ 01724 842223   38 ⇄ ☏

GAINSBOROUGH   Map 08 SK88

Gainsborough Thonock DN21 1PZ
☎ 01427 613088 Fax 01427 810172
Thonock Park course, founded in 1894 is an attractive
parkland course with many deciduous trees. Karsten Lakes
course is a championship course designed by Neil Coles. Set
in rolling countryside the lakes and well bunkered greens
provide a true test of golf. Floodlit driving range.
*Thonock Park: 18 holes, 6266yds, Par 72, SSS 70, Course
record 63.*
*Karsten Lakes: 18 holes, 6721yds, Par 72, SSS 72, Course
record 65.*
Club membership 700.
Visitors   Thonock Park: welcome weekdays. Ladies Day
                  Thu morning. Karsten Lakes: welcome 7 days,
                  advance booking available.
Societies   must telephone in advance.
Green Fees   Thonock Park £25 per day, £18 per round.
                  Karsten Lakes £25 per round.
Prof   Stephen Cooper
Designer   Neil Coles
Facilities   ⊗ ⫪ ⬧ ☕ ♀ ⚲ 🏠 ↘ ⚒ ✗
Location   1m N off A159. Signposted off A631

Hotel   ★★★ 64% West Retford Hotel, 24 North Rd,
                  RETFORD ☎ 01777 706333 Annexe62 ⇄ ☏

GEDNEY HILL   Map 08 TF31

Gedney Hill West Drove PE12 0NT
☎ 01406 330922 Fax 01406 330323
e-mail: d.t.h@fsddail.co.uk
Flat parkland course similar to a links course. Made testing
by Fen winds and small greens. Also a 10-bay driving range.
18 holes, 5493yds, Par 70, SSS 66, Course record 67.
Club membership 200.
Visitors   no restrictions.
Societies   telephone in advance.
Green Fees   not confirmed.
Prof   David Hutton
Designer   Monkwise Ltd
Facilities   ⊗ ⫪ ⬧ ☕ ♀ ⚲ 🏠 ⚒ ↘ ✗
Location   5m SE of Spalding

Hotel   ★★ 66% Rose & Crown Hotel, Market Place,
                  WISBECH ☎ 01945 589800   20 ⇄ ☏

GRANTHAM   Map 08 SK93

Belton Park Belton Ln, Londonthorpe Rd NG31 9SH
☎ 01476 567399 Fax 01476 592078
e-mail: greatgolf@beltonpark
Three 9-hole courses set in classic mature parkland of Lord
Brownlow's country seat, Belton House. Gently undulating
with streams, ponds, plenty of trees and beautiful scenery,
including a deer park. Famous holes: 5th, 12th, 16th and
18th. Combine any of the three courses for a testing 18-hole
round.
Brownlow: 18 holes, 6420yds, Par 71, SSS 71,
Course record 64.
Ancaster: 18 holes, 6325yds, Par 70, SSS 70.
Belmont: 18 holes, 6075yds, Par 69, SSS 69.
Club membership 850.
Visitors   contact professional for suitable tee times. No
                  green fees on Tuesday before 3pm.
Societies   apply in advance.
Green Fees   £33 per day, £27 per round (£39/33 weekends).
Cards   💳 💳
Prof   Brian McKee
Designer   Williamson/Allis
Facilities   ⊗ ⫪ ⬧ ☕ ♀ ⚲ 🏠 ⚒ ✗
Location   1.5m NE of Grantham

Hotel   ★★★ 68% Kings Hotel, North Pde,
                  GRANTHAM ☎ 01476 590800   21 ⇄ ☏

Sudbrook Moor Charity St, Carlton Scroop NG32 3AT
☎ 01400 250796
A picturesque 9-hole parkland/meadowland course in a
picturesque valley setting with easy walking.
9 holes, 4811yds, Par 66, SSS 64, Course record 69.
Visitors   telephone in advance.
Green Fees   Summer: £6 per day (£9 weekends); Winter: £5
                  per day (£7 weekends).
Prof   Tim Hutton
Designer   Tim Hutton
Facilities   ⬧ ☕ ♀ ⚲ 🏠 ⚒ ✗
Location   6m NE of Grantham on A607

Hotel   ★★★ 68% Kings Hotel, North Pde,
                  GRANTHAM ☎ 01476 590800   21 ⇄ ☏

GRIMSBY   Map 08 TA21

Grimsby Littlecoates Rd DN34 4LU
☎ 01472 342630 Fax 01472 342630
Undulating parkland course.
18 holes, 6098yds, Par 70, SSS 69, Course record 66.
Club membership 730.
Visitors   contact in advance.
Societies   by prior arrangement with secretary.
Green Fees   not confirmed.
Prof   Richard Smith
Designer   Colt
Facilities   ⊗ ⫪ ⬧ ☕ ♀ ⚲ 🏠 ↘ ⚒ ✗
Location   1m from A180 & 1m from A46

Hotel   ★★★ 64% Humber Royal, Littlecoates Rd,
                  GRIMSBY ☎ 01472 240024   52 ⇄ ☏

The Admiral Rodney Hotel is situated in the Market Town of Horncastle, well known for its many Antique Shops, and has a reputation for friendliness. All bedrooms are en-suite, and the hotel benefits from a full refurbishment. The splendid furnishings and unique decor of the Courtyard Restaurant provides a delightful setting for dinner and the popular Rodney Bar, with it's 'Nautical Theme' serves a selection of Real Ales.
SPECIAL GOLFING BREAKS AVAILABLE WITH LOUTH AND HORNCASTLE GOLF CLUB

North Street, Horncastle, Lincoln LN9 5DX
AA
Telephone: 01507 523131   Fax: 01507 523104
★★
www.admiralrodney.com
10 minutes drive from Woodhall Spa's Famous Courses

HORNCASTLE   Map 08 TF26

Horncastle West Ashby LN9 5PP ☎ 01507 526800
Parkland course with many water hazards and bunkers; very challenging. There is a 25-bay floodlit driving range.
18 holes, 5717yds, Par 70, SSS 68, Course record 71.
Club membership 200.
Visitors   dress code must be adhered to, welcome anytime, may contact in advance.
Societies   apply in writing or telephone in advance.
Green Fees   £20 per day; £15 per round inc bank holidays.
Cards   [cards]
Prof   E C Wright
Designer   E C Wright
Facilities   ⊗ ⅧⅠ ᐟ ᐧ ♥ ♀ ♨ ⋔ ⌀ ᚸ
& Leisure   fishing.
Location   Off A158 Lincoln/Skegness road at Edlington, off A153 at West Ashby

Hotel   ★★ 71% Admiral Rodney Hotel, North St, HORNCASTLE ☎ 01507 523131 31 ⇄ ⋔

IMMINGHAM   Map 08 TA11

Immingham St Andrews Ln, off Church Ln DN40 2EU
☎ 01469 575298 Fax 01469 577636
e-mail: admin@immgc.com
An excellent, flat parkland course noted for its numerous dykes which come into play on most holes.
18 holes, 6215yds, Par 71, SSS 70, Course record 69.
Club membership 700.
Visitors   telephone in advance.
Societies   telephone (am) to arrange date.
Green Fees   not confirmed.
Prof   Nick Harding
Designer   Hawtree & Son
Facilities   ⊗ ⅧⅠ ᐟ ᐧ ♥ ♀ ♨ ᚸ ⋔ ⌀
Location   7m NW off Grimsby

Hotel   ★★ 65% Old Chapel Hotel & Restaurant, 50 Station Rd, Habrough, IMMINGHAM ☎ 01469 572377 14 ⇄ ⋔

LACEBY   Map 08 TA20

Manor Barton St, Laceby Manor DN37 7EA
☎ 01472 873468(shop) & 873469(office)
Fax 01472 276706 e-mail: manorgolf@hotmail.com
The first nine holes played as a parkland course, all the fairways lined with young trees. The second nine are mainly open fairways. The 18th hole green is surrounded by water.
18 holes, 6354yds, Par 71, SSS 70.
Club membership 550.

Visitors   booked tee system at all times, visitors may book 6 days in advance.
Societies   telephone in advance.
Green Fees   £16 per 18 holes.(£18 weekends). Prices under review.
Cards   [cards]
Facilities   ⊗ ᐟ ᐧ ♥ ♀ ♨ ᚸ ⋔ ⌀
& Leisure   fishing.
Location   A18 Barton St - Laceby/Louth

Hotel   ★★★ 64% Humber Royal, Littlecoates Rd, GRIMSBY ☎ 01472 240024 52 ⇄ ⋔

LINCOLN   Map 08 SK97

Canwick Park Canwick Park, Washingborough Rd LN4 1EF ☎ 01522 522166 & 542912 Fax 01522 542912
e-mail: secretary@canwickparkgc.co.uk
Parkland course with views of Lincoln Cathedral. Testing 5th hole (200 yd par 3).
18 holes, 6160yds, Par 70, SSS 69, Course record 65.
Club membership 650.
Visitors   with member only Sat also Sun before 3pm.
Societies   weekdays only by prior arrangement in writing.
Green Fees   £17 per round (£21weeknds).
Prof   S Williamson
Designer   Hawtree & Sons
Facilities   ⊗ ⅧⅠ ᐟ ᐧ ♥ ♀ ♨ ᚸ ᐟ ⋔ ⌀
Location   1m E of Lincoln

Hotel   ★★★ 65% Posthouse Lincoln, Eastgate, LINCOLN ☎ 0870 400 9052 70 ⇄ ⋔

Carholme Carholme Rd LN1 1SE
☎ 01522 523725 Fax 01522 533733
Parkland course where prevailing west winds can add interest. Good views. 1st hole out of bounds left and right of fairway, pond in front of bunkered green at 5th, lateral water hazards across several fairways.
18 holes, 6243yds, Par 71, SSS 70, Course record 69
Club membership 625.
Visitors   must contact in advance. Weekends may not play before 2.30pm.
Societies   apply in writing/telephone in advance.
Green Fees   not confirmed.
Prof   Richard Hunter
Facilities   ⊗ ⅧⅠ ᐟ ᐧ ♥ ♀ ♨ ᚸ ⋔ ⌀
Location   1m W of city centre on A57

Hotel   ★★★ 66% The White Hart, Bailgate, LINCOLN ☎ 0870 400 8117 48 ⇄ ⋔

LOUTH
Map 08 TF38

Louth Crowtree Ln LN11 9LJ
☎ 01507 603681 Fax 01507 608501
Undulating parkland course, fine views in an area of
outstanding natural beauty.
18 holes, 6430yds, Par 72, SSS 71, Course record 64.
Club membership 700.
Visitors   must contact in advance to make sure tee is not
               reserved for competition.
Societies   a booking form will be sent on request.
Green Fees £25 day; £18 per round (£30/£25 weekends).
Cards   💳 💳 💳 💳 💳
Prof   A Blundell
Facilities   ⊗ ⅏ 🐂 ♥ 🏌 🛆 🏠 ⚑ 🐾 🏑 ✓
& Leisure   squash.
Location   W side of Louth between A157/A153

Hotel   ★★★ 69% Beaumont Hotel, 66 Victoria Rd,
               LOUTH ☎ 01507 605005 16 ⇄ ↾

MARKET RASEN
Map 08 TF18

Market Rasen & District Legsby Rd LN8 3DZ
☎ 01673 842319
Picturesque, well-wooded heathland course, easy walking,
breezy with becks forming natural hazards. Good views of
Lincolnshire Wolds.
18 holes, 6045yds, Par 70, SSS 69, Course record 66.
Club membership 600.
Visitors   must play with member at weekends and must
               contact in advance.
Societies   Tue & Fri only; must contact in advance.
Green Fees £25 per day; £18 per round.
Prof   A M Chester
Facilities   ⊗ ⅏ 🐂 ♥ 🏌 🛆 🏠 ✓
Location   1m E, off A46

Hotel   ★★★ 69% Beaumont Hotel, 66 Victoria Rd,
               LOUTH ☎ 01507 605005 16 ⇄ ↾

Market Rasen Race Course (Golf Course) Legsby Rd
LN8 3EA ☎ 01673 843434 Fax 01673 844532
e-mail: marketrasen@rht.net
This is a public course set within the bounds of Market Rasen
race course - the entire racing area is out of bounds. The
longest hole is the 4th at 454yards with the race course
providing a hazard over the whole length of the drive.
9 holes, 2532yds, Par 32.

Visitors   closed racedays apart from evening meetings
               when open until noon.
Societies   telephone in advance to arrange.

Green Fees £4 per 9 holes;£6 per 18 holes(£5/£8 weekends
               & bank holidays).
Designer   Edward Stenton
Facilities   ⚑
Location   1m E of Market Rasen

Hotel   ★★★ 69% Beaumont Hotel, 66 Victoria Rd,
               LOUTH ☎ 01507 605005 16 ⇄ ↾

NORMANBY
Map 08 SE81

Normanby Hall Normanby Park DN15 9HU
☎ 01724 720226 (Pro shop) 853212 (Secretary)
e-mail: secretarydmac1066@aol.com
Well maintained course set in secluded mature parkland.
A challenge to golfers of all abilities.
18 holes, 6561yds, Par 72, SSS 71, Course record 66.
Club membership 850.
Visitors   book in advance by contacting professional.
Societies   must contact in advance: Rachael Lennox,
               01724 297860.
Green Fees £19.50 per day; £12.50 per round (£13.50 per
               round weekends & bank holidays).
Cards   💳 💳 💳
Prof   Christopher Mann
Designer   Hawtree & Son
Facilities   ⊗ ⅏ 🐂 ♥ 🏌 🛆 🏠 ⚑ 🐾 🏑 ✓
Location   3m N of Scunthorpe adj to Normanby Hall on
               B1130

Hotel   ★★★ 67% Menzies Royal Hotel,
               Doncaster Rd, SCUNTHORPE
               ☎ 0870 6003013 33 ⇄ ↾

SCUNTHORPE
Map 08 SE81

Ashby Decoy Burringham Rd DN17 2AB
☎ 01724 866561 Fax 01724 271708
e-mail: ashby.decoy@btclick.com
Pleasant, flat parkland course to satisfy all tastes, yet test the
experienced golfer.
18 holes, 6281yds, Par 71, SSS 71, Course record 66.
Club membership 650.
Visitors   may not play Tue, weekends or bank holidays.
               Handicap certificate required.
Societies   apply in advance.
Green Fees £24 per day; £18 per round.
Prof   A Miller
Facilities   ⊗ ⅏ 🐂 ♥ 🏌 🛆 🏠 🐾 🏑 ✓
Location   2.5m SW on B1450 near Asda Superstore

Hotel   ★★★ 67% Menzies Royal Hotel,
               Doncaster Rd, SCUNTHORPE
               ☎ 0870 6003013 33 ⇄ ↾

Forest Pines - Briggate Lodge Inn Hotel Ermine St,
Broughton DN20 0AQ
☎ 01652 650770 & 650756 Fax 01652 650495
e-mail: enquires@forestpines.co.uk
Set in 185 acres of mature parkland and open heathland and
constructed in a similar design to that of Wentworth or
Sunningdale, Forest Pines offers three challenging 9-hole
courses - Forest, Pines and Beeches. Any combination can be
played. Facilities include a 17-bay driving range and a
spacious clubhouse.
Forest Course: 9 holes, 3291yds, Par 36, SSS 36.
Pines Course: 9 holes, 3591yds, Par 37, SSS 37.

▶

Beeches: 9 holes, 3102yds, Par 35, SSS 35.
Club membership 330.
Visitors   must contact in advance.
Societies   telephone in advance.
Green Fees   £40 per day; £30 per round.
Cards   ▨▨▨ ▨▨ ▨ ▨▨ ▨
Prof   David Edwards
Designer   John Morgan
Facilities   ⊗ ⫝̸ ⮾ ▨ ♎ ☖ ⌂ ⫝̸ ▨ ⤚ ⤸ ♎
& Leisure   heated indoor swimming pool, sauna, solarium,
                 gymnasium.
Location   200yds from junct 4 M180

Forest Pines Golf Club

Hotel   ★★★★ 70% Forest Pines Hotel, Ermine St,
                 Broughton, SCUNTHORPE
                 ☎ 01652 650770 86 ⇆ ♘

Holme Hall Holme Ln, Bottesford DN16 3RF
☎ 01724 862078 Fax 01724 862078
Heathland course with sandy subsoil. Easy walking.
18 holes, 6404yds, Par 71, SSS 71, Course record 65.
Club membership 724.
Visitors   must play with member at weekends & bank
                 holidays. Must contact in advance.
Societies   must contact in advance.
Green Fees   not confirmed.
Prof   Richard McKiernan
Facilities   ⊗ ⫝̸ ⮾ ▨ ♎ ☖ ⌂ ⫝̸ ⤚ ⤸ ♎
Location   3m SE

Hotel   ★★★ 67% Menzies Royal Hotel, Doncaster
                 Rd, SCUNTHORPE
                 ☎ 0870 6003013 33 ⇆ ♘

Kingsway Kingsway DN15 7ER ☎ 01724 840945
9 holes, 1915yds, Par 29, Course record 28.
Location   W side of town centre off A18
Telephone for further details

Hotel   ★★★ 67% Menzies Royal Hotel,
                 Doncaster Rd, SCUNTHORPE
                 ☎ 0870 6003013 33 ⇆ ♘

SKEGNESS   Map 09 TF56

North Shore Hotel & Golf Club North Shore Rd PE25 1DN
☎ 01754 763298 Fax 01754 761902
e-mail: golf@north-shore.co.uk
A half-links, half-parkland course designed by James Braid
in 1910. Easy walking and good sea views.
18 holes, 6200yds, Par 71, SSS 71, Course record 67.
Club membership 450.

North Shore Hotel & Golf Club
Visitors   tee times must be booked if possible.
Societies   write or telephone in advance.
Green Fees   £35 per day; £25 per round (£45/£35 weekends
                 and bank holidays).
Prof   J Cornelius
Designer   James Braid
Facilities   ⊗ ⫝̸ ⮾ ▨ ♎ ☖ ⌂ ⤚ ♎
& Leisure   snooker.
Location   1m N of town centre off A52

Hotel   ★★ 66% North Shore Hotel & Golf Course,
                 North Shore Rd, SKEGNESS
                 ☎ 01754 763298 33 ⇆ ♘ Annexe3 ⇆ ♘

Seacroft Drummond Rd, Seacroft PE25 3AU
☎ 01754 763020 Fax 01754 763020
e-mail: richard@seacroft-golfclub.co.uk
A championship seaside links traditionally laid out with tight
undulations and hogsback fairways. Adjacent to 'Gibraltar
Point Nature Reserve'.
18 holes, 6479yds, Par 71, SSS 71, Course record 66.
Club membership 590.

Visitors   must be a member of an affiliated golf
                 club/society.
Societies   contact in advance.
Green Fees   £35 per day; £26 per round (£40/£31 weekends
                 & bank holidays).Compulsory£1 third party
                 insurance per player per day.
Prof   Robin Lawie
Designer   Tom Dunn/Willie Fernie
Facilities   ⊗ ⫝̸ ⮾ ▨ ♎ ☖ ⌂ ⤚ ♎
Location   S side of town centre

Hotel   ★★★ 64% Crown Hotel, Drummond Rd,
                 Seacroft, SKEGNESS
                 ☎ 01754 610760 27 ⇆ ♘

SLEAFORD   Map 08 TF04

Sleaford Willoughby Rd, South Rauceby NG34 8PL
☎ 01529 488273 Fax 01529 488326
e-mail: sleafordgolfclub@btinternet.com
Inland links-type course, moderately wooded and fairly flat.
18 holes, 6443yds, Par 72, SSS 71, Course record 67.
Club membership 630.
Visitors   contact in advance, may not play Sun in winter.
Societies   telephone enquiry to professional. Written
            confirmation required.
Green Fees £18 per round;£25 per day(£36 round/day
            weekends0.
Prof   James Wilson
Designer   T Williamson
Facilities   ⊗ ⅷ ㄴ ☕ ♥ ♀ 占 合 ⚒ ✆
Location   2m W of Sleaford, off A153

Hotel   ★★★ 68% Kings Hotel, North Pde,
          GRANTHAM ☎ 01476 590800   21 ⇄ ☞

SOUTH KYME   Map 08 TF14

South Kyme Skinners Ln LN4 4AT
☎ 01526 861113 Fax 01526 861113
A challenging fenland course described as an 'Inland links'
with water hazards, trees and fairway hazards.
18 holes, 6568yds, Par 72, SSS 71, Course record 67.
Club membership 425.
Visitors   advisable to telephone in advance for course
            availability.
Societies   telephone for booking form.
Green Fees £15 per round (£18 weekends).
Cards   ▭ ▭
Prof   Peter Chamberlain
Facilities   ⊗ ⅷ ㄴ ☕ ♥ ♀ 占 合 ㏉ ⚒ ✆
Location   Off B1395 in South Kyme village

SPALDING   Map 08 TF22

Spalding Surfleet PE11 4EA
☎ 01775 680386 (office) & 680474 (pro)
Fax 01775 680988
A pretty, well laid-out course in a fenland area. The River
Glen runs beside the 1st, 2nd and 4th holes, and ponds and
lakes are very much in play on the 9th, 10th and 11th holes.
Challenging holes include the river dominated 2nd and the
10th which involves a tight drive and dog-leg left to reach a
raised three-tier green.
18 holes, 6478yds, Par 72, SSS 71, Course record 62.
Club membership 750.
Visitors   must contact in advance. Handicap certificate
            required.
Societies   write to the secretary, Societies on Thu all day
            and Tue pm.
Green Fees £25 per day;£20 per round(£30 per round/day
            weekends & bank holidays).
Prof   John Spencer
Designer   Price/Spencer/Ward
Facilities   ⊗ ⅷ ㄴ ☕ ♥ ♀ 占 合 ㏉ ✆
Location   4m N of Spalding adjacent to A16

Hotel   ★★ 70% Cley Hall Hotel, 22 High St,
          SPALDING ☎ 01775 725157
          4 ⇄ ☞ Annexe8 ⇄ ☞

STAMFORD   Map 08 TF00

Burghley Park St Martins PE9 3JX
☎ 01780 762100 & 753789 Fax 01780 753789
Open parkland course with superb greens, many trees, ponds
and bunkers. Situated in the grounds of Burghley House.
18 holes, 6236yds, Par 70, SSS 70, Course record 64.
Club membership 775.
Visitors   with member only weekends. Must contact in
            advance & have handicap certificate.
Societies   prior arrangement in writing, preferably by 1st
            Dec previous year.
Green Fees not confirmed.
Prof   Glenn Davies
Designer   Rev J Day (1938)
Facilities   ⊗ ⅷ by prior arrangement ㄴ ♥ ♀ 占 合 ㏉
            ⚒ ✆
Location   1m S of town on B1081

Hotel   ★★★ 76% The George of Stamford, 71 St
          Martins, STAMFORD
          ☎ 01780 750750 & 750700 (Res)
          Fax 01780 750701   47 ⇄ ☞

STOKE ROCHFORD   Map 08 SK92

Stoke Rochford NG33 5EW   ☎ 01476 530275
Parkland course designed by C. Turner and extended in 1936
to 18 holes by Major Hotchkin.
18 holes, 6252yds, Par 70, SSS 70, Course record 65.
Club membership 525.
Visitors   must contact Professional in advance. No
            visitors before 9am weekdays, weekends by
            prior arrangement.
Societies   contact one year in advance, in writing.
Green Fees £22 per round(£28 weekends).
Cards   ▭ ▭ ▯
Prof   Angus Dow
Designer   Major Hotchkin
Facilities   ⊗ ⅷ ㄴ ☕ ♥ ♀ 占 合 ㏉ ⅗ ⚒ ✆
Location   Off A1 5m S of Grantham

Hotel   ★★★ 68% Kings Hotel, North Pde,
          GRANTHAM ☎ 01476 590800   21 ⇄ ☞

SUTTON BRIDGE   Map 09 TF42

Sutton Bridge New Rd PE12 9RQ ☎ 01406 350323
Parkland course built around Victorian dock basin, near river
Nene.
9 holes, 5724yds, Par 70, SSS 68.
Club membership 350.
Visitors   may not play competition days, weekends &
            bank holidays, must contact in advance. Must
            have handicap certificate.
Societies   write or telephone in advance.
Green Fees £18 per day.
Prof   D Woolley
Facilities   ⊗ ⅷ ㄴ ☕ ♥ ♀ 占 合 ㏉ ✆
Location   E side of village off A17

Hotel   ★★★ 64% The Duke's Head, Tuesday Market
          Place, KING'S LYNN
          ☎ 01553 774996   71 ⇄ ☞

Woodhall Spa

Woodhall Spa, *Lincs*   ☎ 01526 352511   Fax 01526 351817   Map 08 TF16

e-mail: booking@englishgolfunion.org

The Championship Course at Woodhall Spa, now known as The Hotchkin, is arguably the best inland course in Britain. Golf has been played here for over 100 years and the Hotchkin has hosted most of the top national and international amateur events.

The English Golf Union acquired Woodhall Spa in 1995 to create a centre of excellence. A second course, The Bracken, has been built together with extensive practice facilities including one of Europe's finest short game practice areas. The English Golf Union actively encourages visitors throughout the year to The National Golf Centre to experience these facilities and to enjoy the unique ambience. The Academy aims to coach players of all standards with a special driving range and indoor school with computer/video equipment.

Visitors must contact in advance. Handicap certificate must be produced

Societies must apply by telephone initially

Green Fees Hotchkin Course: £95 per day, £55 per round; Bracken Course: £65 per day, £40 per day

Facilities ⊗ ⋌Ⅱ⊵ 💻 ♀⅄ 🏠 🛒 ⚬ ⌘
Professional (C. C. Elliot)

Location The Broadway LN10 6PU
(NE side of village off B1191)

Holes/Par/Course record Hotchkin: 18 holes, 7080 yds, Par 73, SSS 73, Course record 67. Bracken: 18 holes, 6735 yds, Par 72, SSS 74, Course record 68

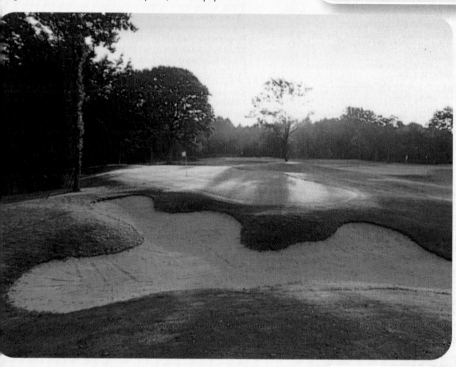

Championship Course

WHERE TO STAY AND EAT NEARBY

Hotels
WOODHALL SPA

★★ 67% Petwood Hotel, Stixwould Rd.
☎ 01526 352411. 50 ⇆ 🐾

★★ 62% Golf Hotel, The Broadway.
☎ 01526 353535. 50 (36 ⇆ 🐾 14 🐾)

★★ 63% Eagle Lodge, The Broadway.
☎ 01526 353231. 23 (15 ⇆ 8 🐾)

Restaurant
HORNCASTLE

◎◎ Magpies, 71-75 East St.
☎ 01507 527004.

SUTTON ON SEA   Map 09 TF58

Sandilands Roman Bank LN12 2RJ
☎ 01507 441432 Fax 01507 441617
Flat links course on the sea shore.
18 holes, 6173yds, Par 71, SSS 68, Course record 59.
Club membership 200.
Visitors   no restrictions.
Societies   telephone in advance.
Green Fees £20 per day; £15 per round (£25/£18 weekends;
                £18 per round bank holidays).
Cards   ▭▭ ▭▭
Facilities ⊗ ⅷ ┗ ♥ ⅴ ᐃ ⸸ ┛ ⟍ ⟍ ⨷ ᛚ
& Leisure   hard and grass tennis courts, gymnasium.
Location   1.5m S off A52

Hotel   ★★★ 66% Grange & Links Hotel, Sea Ln,
            Sandilands, MABLETHORPE
            ☎ 01507 441334   23 ⇌ ╚

TORKSEY   Map 08 SK87

Lincoln LN1 2EG ☎ 01522 718721 Fax 718721
e-mail: lincolngolfclub@btinternet.com
A mature testing inland course on near ideal golfing terrain.
18 holes, 6438yds, Par 71, SSS 71, Course record 65.
Club membership 800.
Visitors   no restrictions, may play at any time.
Societies   Book in advance.
Green Fees £32 per day; £26 per round.
Prof   Ashley Carter
Designer   J H Taylor
Facilities ⊗ ⅷ ┗ ♥ ⅴ ᐃ ┗ ⟍ ⨷ ᛚ
Location   NE side of village, off A156 midway between
                Lincoln & Gainsborough

Hotel   ★★★ 66% The White Hart, Bailgate,
            LINCOLN ☎ 0870 400 8117 48 ⇌ ╚

Millfield Laughterton LN1 2LB
☎ 01427 718255 Fax 01427 718473
e-mail: secretary@millfieldgolfclub.fsnet.co.uk
This golf complex offers a range of facilities to suit every
golfer. The Millfield is designed to suit the more experienced
golfer and follows the natural contours of the landscape. The
Grenville Green is designed for more casual golfers and the
Par 3 is suitable for beginners, family games or for warm-up
and practice play.
*The Millfield: 18 holes, 6004yds, Par 72, SSS 69, Course
record 68.*
The Grenville Green: 18 holes, 4485yds, Par 65.
Visitors   Millfield: shoes must be worn, no jeans etc.
                Grenville Green no restrictions. Par 3 9 hole no
                restrictions.
Societies   telephone in advance.
Green Fees not confirmed.
Prof   Richard Hunter
Designer   C W Watson
Facilities ⊗ ┗ ♥ ⅴ ᐃ ┗ ⟍ ⨷ ᛚ
& Leisure   grass tennis courts.
Location   On A1133 1m N of A57

Hotel   ★★★ 66% The White Hart, Bailgate,
            LINCOLN ☎ 0870 400 8117 48 ⇌ ╚

WOODHALL SPA   Map 08 TF16

Hotel   ★★★ 67% Petwood Hotel, Stixwould Rd,
            WOODHALL SPA
            ☎ 01526 352411   47 ⇌ ╚

WOODHALL SPA   See page 179

WOODTHORPE   Map 09 TF48

Woodthorpe Hall LN13 0DD
☎ 01507 450000 Fax 01507 450000
e-mail: secretary@woodthorpehall.co.uk
Parkland course.
18 holes, 5140yds, Par 67, SSS 65, Course record 68.
Club membership 300.
Visitors   contact in advance .
Societies   Mon-Fri, apply to the secretary at least one
                month prior to visit.
Green Fees £10 per day.
Facilities ⊗ ⅷ ┗ ♥ ⅴ ᛚ
& Leisure   fishing.
Location   3m NNW of Alford on B1373

Hotel   ★★★ 66% Grange & Links Hotel, Sea Ln,
            Sandilands, MABLETHORPE
            ☎ 01507 441334   23 ⇌ ╚

LONDON

Courses within the London Postal District area (ie those
that have London Postcodes - W1, SW1 etc) are listed
here in postal district order commencing East then North,
South and West. Courses outside the London Postal area,
but within Greater London are to be found listed under the
county of **Greater London** in the gazetteer (see page 98).

LONDON

E4 CHINGFORD

Royal Epping Forest Forest Approach, Chingford E4 7AZ
☎ 020 8529 2195 Fax 020 8559 4664
Woodland course. 'Red' garments must be worn.
18 holes, 6342yds, Par 71, SSS 70.
Club membership 400.
Visitors   booking system in operation, telephone
                0208 5295708
Societies   must contact secretary in advance.

▶

Green Fees not confirmed.
Prof A Traynor
Facilities 🍺🏠⛳🏌 🏊
Location 300 yds S of Chingford station

Hotel ★★★ 66% County Hotel Epping Forest, 30 Oak Hill, WOODFORD GREEN
☎ 020 8787 9988 99 ⇆ 🐾

West Essex Bury Rd, Sewardstonebury, Chingford E4 7QL
☎ 020 8529 7558 Fax 020 8524 7870
e-mail: sec@westessexgolfclub.co.uk
Testing parkland course within Epping Forest. Notable holes are 8th (par 5), 16th (par 4), 18th (par 5).
18 holes, 6289yds, Par 71, SSS 70.
Club membership 645.
Visitors must have handicap certificate but may not play on Tue morning, Thu afternoon & weekends.
Societies must contact in advance.
Green Fees £35 per day; £28 per round.
Prof Robert Joyce
Designer James Braid
Facilities ⊗🍴🏠🍺♀👥🏠⛳🏌 🏊 🎯
Location 1.5m N of Chingford station. Access via M25 junct 26

Hotel ★★★ 63% Roebuck Hotel, North End, BUCKHURST HILL
☎ 020 8505 4636 28 ⇆ 🐾

E11 LEYTONSTONE & WANSTEAD

Wanstead Overton Dr, Wanstead E11 2LW
☎ 020 8989 3938 Fax 020 8532 9138
e-mail: wgclub@aol.com
A flat, picturesque parkland course with many trees and shrubs and providing easy walking. The par 3, 16th, involves driving across a lake.
18 holes, 6004yds, Par 69, SSS 69, Course record 62.
Club membership 600.
Visitors must contact in advance and may only play Mon, Tue & Fri.
Societies by prior arrangement.
Green Fees not confirmed.
Prof David Hawkins
Designer James Braid
Facilities ⊗🍴🏠🍺♀👥🏠⛳🏌
& Leisure fishing.
Location From central London A12 NE to Wanstead

Hotel ★★★ 66% County Hotel Epping Forest, 30 Oak Hill, WOODFORD GREEN
☎ 020 8787 9988 99 ⇆ 🐾

N2 EAST FINCHLEY

Hampstead Winnington Rd N2 0TU
☎ 020 8455 0203 Fax 020 8731 6194
Undulating parkland course with many mature trees.
18 holes, 5822yds, Par 68, SSS 68, Course record 64.
Club membership 526.
Visitors restricted Tue and weekends. Contact Professional in advance on 0208 4557089.
members societies only
Green Fees £15 for 9 holes;£30 per 18 holes(£20/£35 weekends & bank holidays).
Prof Peter Brown

Designer Tom Dunn
Facilities ⊗🏠🍺♀👥🏠⛳🏌
Location Off Hampstead Lane

Hotel ★★★ 66% Posthouse Hampstead, 215 Haverstock Hill, LONDON
☎ 0870 400 9037 140 ⇆ 🐾

N6 HIGHGATE

Highgate Denewood Rd N6 4AH
☎ 020 8340 5467 Fax 020 8348 9152
e-mail: secretary @highgategolfclub.freeserve.co.uk
Parkland course.
18 holes, 5985yds, Par 69, SSS 69, Course record 66.
Club membership 700.
Visitors may not play Wed,weekends & bankholidays.
Societies by arrangement.
Green Fees £30 per round;£38 per day.
Prof Robin Turner
Designer Cuthbert Butchart
Facilities ⊗🍴 by prior arrangement 🏠🍺♀👥🏠⛳🏌
Location A1,Bishops Avenue,Hampstead lane,Sheldon Avenue

Hotel ★★★★ 71% London Marriott Hotel Regents Park, 128 King Henry's Rd, LONDON
☎ 020 7722 7711 303 ⇆ 🐾

N9 LOWER EDMONTON

Lee Valley Leisure Lee Valley Leisure Centre, Meridian Way, Edmonton N9 0AS ☎ 020 8803 3611
Tricky municipal parkland course with some narrow fairways and the River Lea providing a natural hazard.
18 holes, 4962yds, Par 66, SSS 64, Course record 66.
Club membership 200.
Visitors may telephone for advance bookings.
Societies must telephone in advance.
Green Fees £11.50 per round(£14.50 weekends).
Prof R Gerken
Facilities 🏠🍺♀👥🏠⛳🏌 🎯
& Leisure heated indoor swimming pool, squash, sauna, solarium, gymnasium.

Hotel ★★ 71% Oak Lodge Hotel, 80 Village Rd, Bush Hill Park, ENFIELD ☎ 020 8360 7082 7 ⇆ 🐾

N14 SOUTHGATE

Trent Park Bramley Rd, Oakwood N14 4XS
☎ 020 8367 4653
Parkland course set in 150 acres of green belt area. Seven holes played across Merryhills brook. Testing holes are 2nd (423 yds) over brook, 190 yds from the tee, and up to plateau green; 7th (463 yds) dog-leg, over brook, par 4.
18 holes, 6381yds, Par 70, SSS 69, Course record 64.
Club membership 700.
Visitors must book in advance.
Societies must telephone in advance.
Green Fees not confirmed.
Prof R Stocker
Designer D McGibbon
Facilities ⊗🍴🏠🍺♀👥🏠⛳🏌 🏊 🎯
Location Opposite Oakwood underground station ▶

Hotel ★★★★**▲▲** 71% West Lodge Park Hotel, Cockfosters Rd, HADLEY WOOD
☎ 020 8216 3900 46 ⇆ ╏▗ Annexe9 ⇆ ╏▗

Hotel ★★ 71% Oak Lodge Hotel, 80 Village Rd, Bush Hill Park, ENFIELD
☎ 020 8360 7082 7 ⇆ ╏▗

N20 WHETSTONE

North Middlesex The Manor House, Friern Barnet Ln, Whetstone N20 0NL
☎ 020 8445 1604 & 020 8445 3060 Fax 020 8445 5023
e-mail: office@northmiddlesexgc.co.uk
Short parkland course renowned for its tricky greens.
18 holes, 5625yds, Par 69, SSS 67, Course record 64.
Club membership 580.
Visitors advisable to contact in advance, contact professional shop. May play at weekends by arrangement or with member.
Societies bookings in advance, winter offers & summer packages by prior arrangement.
Cards ▨ ▨ ▨ ▨ ▨
Prof Freddie George
Designer Willie Park Jnr
Facilities ⊗ ⅲ ⌾ ☟ ⚐ ⌂ 🏠 ⚐ ♂

Hotel ★★★ 75% Edgwarebury Hotel, Barnet Ln, ELSTREE ☎ 020 8953 8227 47 ⇆ ╏▗

South Herts Links Dr, Totteridge N20 8QU
☎ 020 8445 2035 Fax 020 8445 7569
An open undulating parkland course officially in Hertfordshire, but now in a London postal area. It is, perhaps, most famous for the fact that two of the greatest of all British professionals, Harry Vardon and Dai Rees, CBE were professionals at the club. The course is testing, over rolling fairways, especially in the prevailing south-west wind.
18 holes, 6432yds, Par 72, SSS 71, Course record 63.
Club membership 850.
Visitors must be members of recognised golf club & have handicap certificate of 24 or less. May not play at weekends.
Societies Wed-Fri only, must apply in writing.
Green Fees not confirmed.
Prof Bobby Mitchell
Designer Harry Vardon
Facilities ⌂ 🏠 ⚐ ▚ ▟ ♂
Location 2m E of A1 at Apex Corner

Hotel ★★★ 66% Posthouse South Mimms, SOUTH MIMMS ☎ 0870 400 9072 143 ⇆ ╏▗

N21 WINCHMORE HILL

Bush Hill Park Bush Hill, Winchmore Hill N21 2BU
☎ 020 8360 5738 Fax 020 8360 5583
Pleasant parkland course surrounded by trees. Contains a large number of both fairway sandtraps and green side bunkers. Undulating, but not too harsh.
18 holes, 5809yds, Par 70, SSS 68.
Club membership 700.
Visitors may not play Wed mornings or weekends & bank holidays. Handicap certificate required.
Societies by arrangement.
Green Fees not confirmed.
Prof Adrian Andrews
Facilities ⌂ 🏠 ♂
Location 1m S of Enfield

N22 WOOD GREEN

Muswell Hill Rhodes Av, Wood Green N22 7UT
☎ 020 8888 1764 Fax 020 8889 9380
Narrow parkland course featuring numerous water hazards.
18 holes, 6438yds, Par 71, SSS 71, Course record 65.
Club membership 560.
Visitors must contact in advance, restricted weekends.
Societies apply in writing or telephone.
Green Fees £36 per day; £26 per round(£27 weekends).
Prof David Wilton
Designer Braid/Wilson
Facilities ⌂ 🏠 ⚐ ♂
Location Off N Circular Rd at Bounds Green

Hotel ★★★ 66% Raglan Hall Hotel, 8-12 Queens Ave, Muswell Hill, LONDON
☎ 020 8883 9836 46 ⇆ ╏▗

NW4 HENDON Map 04 TQ28

The Metro Golf Centre Barnet Copthall Sports Centre, Gt North Way NW4 1PS
☎ 020 8202 1202 Fax 020 8203 1203
e-mail: golf@metrogolf.btinternet.com
Located just seven miles from London's West End, the Metro Golf Centre represents a new generation of golf facility dedicated to the development of all standards of golfer. Facilities include a 48 bay two-tiered driving range, a testing 9-hole par 3 course with water hazards, pot bunkers and postage stamp greens, a short game practice area, and a Golf Academy offering unique teaching methods.
9 holes, 898yds, Par 27, SSS 27, Course record 24.
Club membership 500.
Visitors welcome any time between 8am-10pm all week for lessons, to play on the course or use driving range.
Societies telephone in advance.
Green Fees not confirmed.
Cards ▨ ▨ ▨ ▨ ▨
Prof Barney Puttick
Designer Cousells
Facilities ⊗ ⅲ ⌾ ☟ ⚐ ⌂ 🏠 ⚐ ♂ ╏
Location Just off A41 and A1 at junct 2 of the M1, within the Barnet Copthall Sporting Complex

Hotel ★★★★ 71% London Marriott Hotel Regents Park, 128 King Henry's Rd, LONDON
☎ 020 7722 7711 303 ⇆ ╏▗

NW7 MILL HILL

Finchley Nether Court, Frith Ln, Mill Hill NW7 1PU
☎ 020 8346 2436 & 8346 5086 Fax 020 8343 4205
e-mail: secretary@finchleygolfclub.co.uk
Easy walking on wooded parkland course.
18 holes, 6411yds, Par 72, SSS 71.
Club membership 500.
Visitors must contact in advance.
Societies must apply in writing.
Green Fees not confirmed.
Prof David Brown

▶

Finchley Golf Club

Designer James Braid
Facilities ⊗ 🛅 🍺 ♀ ⚱ 🏠 ⚓ 🎯 🏌 ⚙
Location Near Mill Hill East Tube Station

Hotel ★★★ 75% Edgwarebury Hotel, Barnet Ln, ELSTREE ☎ 020 8953 8227 47 ⇆ ☏

Hendon Ashley Walk, Devonshire Rd, Mill Hill NW7 1DG
☎ 020 8346 6023 Fax 020 8343 1974
e-mail: hendongolf@talk21.com
Easy walking, parkland course with a good variety of trees, and providing testing golf.
18 holes, 6289yds, Par 70, SSS 70, Course record 68.
Club membership 560.
Visitors Restricted weekends & bank holidays.Must contact professional in advance on 0208 3468990
Societies Tue-Fri. Must contact in advance.
Green Fees £35 per day; £30 per round (£35 weekends & bank holidays).
Cards 〰 〰 〰 〰 🗇
Prof Matt Deal
Designer H S Colt
Facilities ⊗ 🎼 by prior arrangement 🛅 🍺 ♀ ⚱ 🏠 ⚓ ⚙
Location 10 mins from junc 2 of M1 southbound

Hotel ★★★ 75% Edgwarebury Hotel, Barnet Ln, ELSTREE ☎ 020 8953 8227 47 ⇆ ☏

Mill Hill 100 Barnet Way, Mill Hill NW7 3AL
☎ 020 8959 2339 Fax 020 8906 0731
e-mail: davidbeal@dbeal.freeserve.co.uk
Undulating parkland course with tree and shrub lined fairways, water features strongly on holes 2,10 and 17.
18 holes, 6247yds, Par 70, SSS 70, Course record 65.
Club membership 550.

Visitors restricted weekends & bank holidays. Must contact in advance.
Societies must contact in advance.
Green Fees £25 per round;£30 per day(£30 per round weekends & bank holidays).
Cards 〰 〰
Prof David Beal
Designer J F Abercrombie/H S Colt
Facilities ⊗ 🛅 🍺 ♀ ⚱ 🏠 ⚓ 🏌 ⚓ ⚙
& Leisure snooker.
Location On A1 S bound carriageway

Hotel ★★★ 75% Edgwarebury Hotel, Barnet Ln, ELSTREE ☎ 020 8953 8227 47 ⇆ ☏

SE9 ELTHAM

Eltham Warren Bexley Rd, Eltham SE9 2PE
☎ 020 8850 4477 & 8850 1166
e-mail: secretary@elthamwarren.idps.co.uk
Parkland course with narrow fairways and small greens. The course is bounded by the A210 on one side and Eltham Park on the other.
9 holes, 5840yds, Par 69, SSS 68, Course record 63.
Club membership 440.
Visitors may not play at weekends. Must contact in advance and have a handicap certificate.
Societies Thu only. Must book in advance. Deposit required.
Green Fees £25 per day.
Prof Gary Brett
Designer James Braid
Facilities ⊗ 🛅 🍺 ♀ ⚱ 🏠 ⚙
Location 0.5m from Eltham station on A210

Hotel ★★★ 71% Bromley Court Hotel, Bromley Hill, BROMLEY ☎ 020 8461 8600 115 ⇆ ☏

Royal Blackheath Court Rd SE9 5AF
☎ 020 8850 1795 Fax 020 8859 0150
e-mail: info@rbgc.com
A pleasant, parkland course of great character as befits the antiquity of the Club; the clubhouse dates from the 17th century. Many great trees survive and there are two ponds. The 18th requires a pitch to the green over a thick clipped hedge, which also crosses the front of the 1st tee.
18 holes, 6219yds, Par 70, SSS 70, Course record 65.
Club membership 720.
Visitors must contact in advance but may play mid-week only, handicap certificate is required.
Societies must apply in writing.
Green Fees £60 per day; £40 per round.
Cards 〰 〰 🗇
Prof Ian McGregor
Designer James Braid
Facilities ⊗ 🎼 🛅 🍺 ♀ ⚱ 🏠 ⚓ 🏌 ⚓ ⚙
Location From M25 junct 3 take A20 towards London. Turn right at 2nd traffic lights to club 500yds on right

Hotel ★★★ 71% Bromley Court Hotel, Bromley Hill, BROMLEY ☎ 020 8461 8600 115 ⇆ ☏

SE18 WOOLWICH

Shooters Hill Eaglesfield Rd, Shooters Hill SE18 3DA
☎ 020 8854 6368 Fax 020 8854 0469
Hilly and wooded parkland course with good view and
natural hazards.
18 holes, 5721yds, Par 69, SSS 68, Course record 63.
Club membership 900.
Visitors   must have handicap certificate and be a member
                   of a recognised golf club but may not play at
                   weekends, unless with member.
Societies   Tue & Thu only, by arrangement.
Green Fees   £27 per day; £22 per round.
Prof   David Brotherton
Designer   Willie Park
Facilities   ⊗ ⋓ ⅃ ☮ ⅃ ⚲ ☗ ⏚ ⌁
Location   Shooters Hill Rd from Blackheath

Hotel   ★★★ 64% Posthouse Bexley, Black Prince
                   Interchange, Southwold Rd, BEXLEY
                   ☎ 0870 400 9006 105 ⇄ ☏

SE21 DULWICH

Dulwich & Sydenham Hill Grange Ln, College Rd
SE21 7LH ☎ 020 8693 3961 & 8693 8491
Fax 020 8693 2481
Parkland course overlooking London. Hilly with narrow
fairways.
18 holes, 6008yds, Par 69, SSS 69, Course record 63.
Club membership 850.
Visitors   must contact in advance and have a handicap
                   certificate. May not play weekends or bank
                   holidays.
Societies   must telephone in advance & confirm in writing.
Green Fees   £35 per day; £25 per round.
Prof   David Baillie
Designer   H Colt
Facilities   ⊗ ⅃ ☮ ⅃ ⚲ ☗ ⏚ ⌁ ⏚ ⌁

Hotel   ★★★ 71% Bromley Court Hotel, Bromley
                   Hill, BROMLEY ☎ 020 8461 8600 115 ⇄ ☏

SE22 EAST DULWICH

Aquarius Marmora Rd, Honor Oak, Off Forest Hill Rd SE22
0RY ☎ 020 8693 1626
9 holes, 5246yds, Par 66, SSS 66, Course record 66.
Telephone for further details

Hotel   ★★★ 71% Bromley Court Hotel, Bromley
                   Hill, BROMLEY ☎ 020 8461 8600 115 ⇄ ☏

SE28 WOOLWICH

Riverside Fairway Dr, Summerton Way, Thamesmead
SE28 8PP ☎ 020 8310 7975
A delightful undulating course with a mix of mature trees,
new trees and water hazards. The 4th hole is a challenging
515yards down a narrow fairway.
9 holes, 5462yds, Par 70, SSS 66.
Club membership 150.
Visitors   no restrictions.
Societies   book by telephone or in writing.
Green Fees   £7 per 18 holes; £5 per 9 holes (£11/£7
                   weekends).
Cards   ▭ ▭ ▭ ▭ ▧

Prof   Sarah Jarrett
Designer   Heffernan
Facilities   ⊗ ⋓ ☮ ⅃ ⚲ ☗ ⏚ ⌁
Location   Off A2 near Woolwich ferry

Hotel   ★★★ 65% Bardon Lodge Hotel, 15-17
                   Stratheden Rd, Blackheath, LONDON
                   ☎ 020 8853 7000 32 ⇄ ☏

SW15 PUTNEY

Richmond Park Roehampton Gate, Priory Ln
SW15 5JR ☎ 020 8876 1795 Fax 020 8878 1354
e-mail: info@gcm.com
Two public parkland courses.
Princes Course: 18 holes, 5868yds, Par 69, SSS 68,
Course record 64.
Dukes Course: 18 holes, 6036yds, Par 69, SSS 68.
Visitors   must contact in advance or pay and play.
Societies   must contact in advance.
Green Fees   £15 (£18 weekends).
Prof   Stuart Hill & David Bown
Designer   Fred Hawtree
Facilities   ⊗ ⅃ ☮ ⅃ ⚲ ☗ ⏚ ⌁ ⏚ ⌁
Location   Inside Richmond Park Roehampton gate

Hotel   ★★★ 69% The Richmond Hill Hotel,
                   Richmond Hill, RICHMOND UPON
                   THAMES ☎ 020 8940 2247 138 ⇄ ☏

SW18 WANDSWORTH

Central London Golf Centre Burntwood Ln, Wandsworth
SW17 0AT ☎ 020 8871 2468 Fax 020 8874 7447
e-mail: clgc@aol.com
Attractive flat parkland course in the middle of London. The
longest drive is the 430 yard 3rd to one of the course's
superb greens. Well placed bunkers trap the careless shot and
the course rewards the accurate player.
9 holes, 2277yds, Par 62, SSS 62.
Club membership 200.
Visitors   must book tee-times for weekends.
Societies   telephone or write to the manager.
Green Fees   not confirmed.
Cards   ▭ ▭ ▭ ▭ ▧
Prof   Jeremy Robson
Designer   Patrick Tallock
Facilities   ⊗ ⅃ ☮ ⅃ ⚲ ☗ ⏚ ⌁ ⏚
Location   Between Garatt Lane and Trinity Road

Hotel   ★★★★ 75% Cannizaro House, West Side,
                   Wimbledon Common, LONDON
                   ☎ 020 8879 1464 45 ⇄ ☏

SW19 WIMBLEDON

Royal Wimbledon 29 Camp Rd SW19 4UW
☎ 020 8946 2125 Fax 020 8944 8652 e-
mail: secretary@royal-wimbledon-golf.co.uk
A club steeped in the history of the game, it is also of
great age, dating back to 1865. Of sand and heather like
so many of the Surrey courses its 12th hole (par 4) is
rated as the best on the course.
18 holes, 6300yds, Par 70, SSS 70, Course record 66.
Club membership 1050. ▶

Visitors	must be guests of current club member or contact club in advance, weekdays only. Maximum handicap 18 and must be member of recognised club.
Societies	welcome Wed-Thu. Must apply in writing.
Green Fees	£55.
Prof	Hugh Boyle
Designer	H Colt
Facilities	⊗ ⅷ ᴸᴸ ♥ ♀ ⚑ 📠 ↑ ⌀
Hotel	★★★★ 75% Cannizaro House, West Side, Wimbledon Common, LONDON ☎ 020 8879 1464 45 ⇄ ♟

Wimbledon Common 19 Camp Rd SW19 4UW
☎ 020 8946 0294 (Pro shop) 8946 7571 (Sec)
Fax 020 8947 8697 e-mail: secretary@wcgc.co.uk
18 holes, 5438yds, Par 68, SSS 66, Course record 63.
Location 0.5m N of Wimbledon Village
Telephone for further details

Hotel	★★★★ 75% Cannizaro House, West Side, Wimbledon Common, LONDON ☎ 020 8879 1464 45 ⇄ ♟

Wimbledon Park Home Park Rd, Wimbledon SW19 7HR
☎ 020 8946 1250 Fax 020 8944 8688
e-mail: secretary@wpgc.co.uk
Easy walking on parkland course. Sheltered lake provides
hazard on 3 holes.
18 holes, 5465yds, Par 66, SSS 66.
Club membership 700.

Visitors	restricted weekends & bank holidays. Must contact in advance and have handicap certificate or letter of introduction.
Societies	must apply in writing.
Green Fees	£40 per round.
Prof	Dean Wingrove
Designer	Willie Park Jnr
Facilities	⊗ ⅷ by prior arrangement ᴸᴸ ♥ ♀ ⚑ 📠 ⌀
Location	400 yds from Wimbledon Park Station

Hotel	★★★ 69% The Richmond Hill Hotel, Richmond Hill, RICHMOND UPON THAMES ☎ 020 8940 2247 138 ⇄ ♟

W7 HANWELL

Brent Valley 138 Church Rd, Hanwell W7 3BE
☎ 020 8567 1287
18 holes, 5426yds, Par 67, SSS 66.
Telephone for further details

Hotel	★★★ 64% Master Robert Hotel, 366 Great West Rd, HOUNSLOW ☎ 020 8570 6261 Annexe94 ⇄ ♟

AA Hotels that have special
arrangements with golf courses are listed at
the back of the guide

BEBINGTON Map 07 SJ38

Brackenwood Brackenwood Golf Course, Bracken Ln CH63
2LY ☎ 0151 608 3093
Municipal parkland course with easy walking, a very testing
but fair course in a fine rural setting, usually in very good
condition.
18 holes, 6285yds, Par 70, SSS 70, Course record 66.
Club membership 320.

Visitors	must book for weekends one week in advance.
Societies	must telephone in advance.
Green Fees	£7.50 per round.
Prof	Ken Lamb
Facilities	♥ 📠 ↑ ⌀
Location	0.75m N of M53 junc 4 on B5151

Hotel	★★★ 70% Thornton Hall Hotel, Neston Rd, THORNTON HOUGH ☎ 0151 336 3938 5 ⇄ ♟ Annexe58 ⇄ ♟

BIRKENHEAD Map 07 SJ38

Arrowe Park Woodchurch L49 5LW ☎ 0151 677 1527
Pleasant municipal parkland course.
18 holes, 6435yds, Par 72, SSS 71, Course record 66.
Club membership 220.

Visitors	no restrictions, Booking at weekends 1wk in advance.
Societies	must telephone in advance.
Green Fees	not confirmed.
Prof	Colin Disbury
Facilities	⊗ ⅷ ᴸᴸ ♥ ♀ ⚑ 📠 ↑ ⚒ ⌀
& Leisure	tennis courts, pitch & putt.
Location	1m from M53 junc 3 on A551

Hotel	★★★ 69% Bowler Hat Hotel, 2 Talbot Rd, Prenton, BIRKENHEAD ☎ 0151 652 4931 32 ⇄ ♟

Prenton Golf Links Rd, Prenton CH42 8LW
☎ 0151 608 1053 Fax 0151 609 1580
Parkland course with easy walking and views of the Welsh
Hills.
18 holes, 6429yds, Par 71, SSS 71.
Club membership 610.

Visitors	no restrictions.
Societies	must telephone in advance and confirm in writing.
Green Fees	£30 per day (£35 weekends).
Prof	Robin Thompson
Designer	James Braid
Facilities	⊗ ⅷ ᴸᴸ ♥ ♀ ⚑ 📠 ⌀
Location	M53 junct 3 off A552 towards Birkenhead

Hotel	★★★ Riverhill Hotel, Talbot Rd, Prenton, BIRKENHEAD ☎ 0151 653 3773 14 ⇄ ♟

Wirral Ladies 93 Bidston Rd, Oxton CH43 6TS
☎ 0151 652 1255 Fax 0151 653 4323
Heathland course with heather and birch.
18 holes, 4948yds, Par 69, SSS 69.
Club membership 430.

Visitors	may not play before 11am weekends or over Christmas and Easter holidays.
Societies	must telephone in advance. Weekdays only.
Green Fees	£25.50 per round.
Prof	Angus Law
Facilities	⚐🏠𝄞
Location	W side of town centre on B5151

Hotel	★★★ 69% Bowler Hat Hotel, 2 Talbot Rd, Prenton, BIRKENHEAD ☎ 0151 652 4931 32 ⇥ ℟

BLUNDELLSANDS   Map 07 SJ39

West Lancashire Hall Rd West L23 8SZ
☎ 0151 924 1076 Fax 0151 931 4448
e-mail: golf@wlgc.lancastrian.co.uk
Challenging, traditional links with sandy subsoil overlooking the Mersey Estuary. The course provides excellent golf throughout the year. The four short holes are very fine.
18 holes, 6763yds, Par 72, SSS 73, Course record 66.
Club membership 650.

Visitors	must have a handicap certificate. May not play before 9.30am Mon-Fri and on competition days and weekends only after 3.30pm.
Societies	must contact in advance.
Green Fees	£65 per day; £50 per round (£70 per round weekends).
Cards	💳💳💳💳💳
Prof	Tim Hastings
Designer	C K Cotton
Facilities	⊗ 〣 ⅊ 🍴 ⬙ ⚐ 🏠 𝄞
Location	N side of village

BOOTLE   Map 07 SJ39

Bootle 2 Dunnings Bridge Rd L30 2PP
☎ 0151 928 1371 Fax 0151 949 1815
Municipal seaside course, with prevailing north-westerly wind. Testing holes: 5th (200 yds) par 3; 7th (415 yds) par 4.
18 holes, 6362yds, Par 70, SSS 70, Course record 64.
Club membership 380.

Visitors	must contact Golf Shop on 0151 928 1371 not between 9-9.45am Sat and 7.45-12 Sun.
Societies	must apply in writing/telephone in advance.
Green Fees	£6.25 per round (£8 weekends).
Cards	💳💳💳
Prof	Alan Bradshaw
Facilities & Leisure	⊗ ⅊ 🍴 ⬙ ⚐ 🏠 ⚲ 𝄞 fishing.
Location	2m NE on A5036

BROMBOROUGH   Map 07 SJ38

Bromborough Raby Hall Rd CH63 0NW
☎ 0151 334 2155 Fax 0151 334 7300
e-mail: sec@bromborough-golf-club.freeserve.co.uk
Parkland course.
18 holes, 6650yds, Par 72, SSS 73, Course record 67.
Club membership 800.

Visitors	are advised to contact professional on 0151 334 4499 in advance.
Societies	normal society day Wed ; must apply in advance.

Green Fees	£28 per day.
Prof	Geoff Berry
Designer	J Hassall
Facilities	⊗ 〣 ⅊ ⬙ 🍴 ⚐ 🏠 ⚲ 𝄞
Location	0.5m W of Station

Hotel	★★★ 69% Bowler Hat Hotel, 2 Talbot Rd, Prenton, BIRKENHEAD ☎ 0151 652 4931 32 ⇥ ℟

CALDY   Map 07 SJ28

Caldy Links Hey Rd CH48 1NB
☎ 0151 625 5660 Fax 0151 6257394
e-mail: gail@caldygolfclub.fsnet.co.uk
A parkland course situated on the estuary of the River Dee with many of the fairways running parallel to the river. Of Championship length, the course offers excellent golf all year, but is subject to variable winds that noticeably alter the day to day playing of each hole. There are excellent views of North Wales and Snowdonia.
18 holes, 6668yds, Par 72, SSS 72, Course record 68.
Club membership 800.

Visitors	may play on weekdays only by prior arrangement. N ot before 3.30pm Tue or after 12.30pm Wed.
Societies	must telephone in advance.
Green Fees	£42 per day, £37 per round.
Prof	K Jones
Designer	J Braid
Facilities	⊗ 〣 by prior arrangement ⬙ ⅊ ⚐ 🏠 ⚲ 🚲 𝄞
Location	SE side of village, from Caldy rdbt on A540 follow signs to Caldy and golf club

Hotel	★★★ 70% Thornton Hall Hotel, Neston Rd, THORNTON HOUGH ☎ 0151 336 3938 5 ⇥ ℟ Annexe58 ⇥ ℟

EASTHAM   Map 07 SJ38

Eastham Lodge 117 Ferry Rd CH62 0AP
☎ 0151 327 3003 Fax 0151 327 3003
A parkland course with many mature trees, recently upgraded to 18 holes. Most holes have a subtle dogleg to left or right. The 1st hole requires an accurate drive to open up the green which is guarded on the right by a stand of pine trees.
18 holes, 5436yds, Par 68, SSS 66.
Club membership 800.

Visitors	advisable to telephone in advance to check availability, tel 0151 327 3008 professionals shop, start times available up to 2 weeks in advance, with member only at weekends.
Societies	welcome Tue. Must apply in writing.
Green Fees	£22.50 per day/round.
Prof	N Sargent
Designer	Hawtree/D Hemstock
Facilities	⊗ 〣 ⬙ ⅊ 🍴 ⚐ 🏠 𝄞
Location	1.5m N,off A41 to Wirral Metropolitan College & Eastham Country Park

Hotel	★★★ Quality Hotel Chester, Welsh Road/Berwick Rd, Little Sutton, ☎ 0151 339 5121 53 ⇥ ℟

FORMBY   Map 07 SD30

Formby Golf Rd L37 1LQ
☎ 01704 872164 Fax 01704 833028
e-mail: info@formbygolfclub.co.uk
Championship seaside links through sandhills and partly
through pine trees. Partly sheltered from the wind by
high dunes it features firm, springy turf, fast seaside
greens and natural sandy bunkers. Well drained it plays
well throughout the year.
18 holes, 6701yds, Par 72, SSS 72, Course record 65.
Club membership 700.

Visitors	must contact in advance, very limited on Sat & Wed.
Societies	must contact well in advance.
Green Fees	£65 per day/round.
Cards	💳
Prof	Gary Butler
Designer	Park/Colt
Facilities	⊗ ⑴ 🖪 ♥ ♀ 🏖 🏠 ⛳ 🛒 ⛷
Location	N side of town

Formby Ladies Golf Rd L37 1YH
☎ 01704 873493 Fax 01704 873493
Seaside links - one of the few independent ladies clubs in the
country. The course has contrasting hard-hitting holes in flat
country and tricky holes in sandhills and woods.
18 holes, 5374yds, Par 71, SSS 71, Course record 60.
Club membership 570.

Visitors	must contact in advance and may not play Thu or before 11am Sat & Sun.
Societies	must apply in advance. Handicap certificate required.
Green Fees	not confirmed.
Prof	Gary Butler
Facilities	⊗ 🖪 ♥ ♀ 🏖 🏠 ⛷
Location	N side of town

HESWALL   Map 07 SJ28

Heswall Cottage Ln CH60 8PB
☎ 0151 342 1237 Fax 0151 342 1237
A pleasant parkland course in soft undulating country
over-looking the estuary of the River Dee. There are
excellent views of the Welsh hills and coastline, and a
good test of golf. The clubhouse is modern and well-
appointed with good facilities.
18 holes, 6492yds, Par 72, SSS 72, Course record 62.
Club membership 940.

Visitors	must contact in advance.
Societies	must apply in advance.
Green Fees	not confirmed.
Prof	Alan Thompson
Facilities	⊗ ⑴ 🖪 ♥ ♀ 🏖 🏠 ⛷
Location	1m S off A540

Hotel	★★★ 70% Thornton Hall Hotel, Neston Rd, THORNTON HOUGH ☎ 0151 336 3938 5 ⇨ 📢 Annexe58 ⇨ 📢

Where to stay, where to eat?
Visit the AA internet site
www.theAA.com

HOYLAKE   Map 07 SJ28

Hoylake Carr Ln, Municipal Links CH47 4BG
☎ 0151 632 2956
Flat, generally windy semi-links course. Tricky fairways,
with some very deep bunkers.
18 holes, 6313yds, Par 70, SSS 70, Course record 67.
Club membership 303.

Visitors	tee times booked with professional, weekend bookings one week in advance
Societies	must telephone 0151 632 4883 club steward or 0151 632 2956 club professional.
Green Fees	not confirmed.
Cards	💳 💳 💳
Prof	Simon Hooton
Designer	James Braid
Facilities	⊗ ⑴ 🖪 ♥ ♀ 🏖 🏠 ⛳ 🛒 ⛷
Location	SW side of town off A540

Hotel	★★★ 67% Leasowe Castle Hotel, Leasowe Rd, MORETON ☎ 0151 606 9191 47 ⇨ 📢

Royal Liverpool Meols Dr CH47 4AL
☎ 0151 632 3101 & 632 3102 Fax 0151 632 6737
e-mail: sec@royalliverpool-golf.com
A world famous, windswept seaside links course, venue
for ten Open Championships and 18 Amateur
Championships.
18 holes, 6219yds, Par 72, SSS 71.
Club membership 650.

Visitors	must contact in advance & have a handicap certificate. Restricted before 9.30am & between 1-2pm. No play Thu am (ladies day). Limited play weekends (pm only).
Societies	must contact in advance.
Green Fees	£95 per day; £70 per round (£100 per round weekends and bank holidays).
Cards	💳 💳 💳 💳 💳
Prof	John Heggarty
Designer	R Chambers/G Morris
Facilities	⊗ ⑴ 🖪 ♥ ♀ 🏖 🏠 ⛳ ⛷ ⛵
Location	SW side of town on A540

Hotel	★★★ 67% Leasowe Castle Hotel, Leasowe Rd, MORETON ☎ 0151 606 9191 47 ⇨ 📢

HUYTON   Map 07 SJ49

Bowring Roby Rd L36 4HD ☎ 0151 443 0424 489 1901
e-mail: bowringpark@knowsley.gov.uk
Flat parkland course.
Bowring Golf Club: 18 holes, 6082yds, Par 70.

Visitors	no restrictions.
Societies	bookings over the phone and confirmed in writing.
Green Fees	£6.50 per round (£7 weekends & bank holidays).
Facilities	♥ ⛷
Location	On A5080 adjacent M62 junc 5

Hotel	★ 62% Rockland Hotel, View Rd, RAINHILL ☎ 0151 426 4603 11rm(9 ⇨1 📢)

Huyton & Prescot Hurst Park, Huyton Ln L36 1UA
☎ 0151 489 3948 Fax 0151 489 0797
An easy walking, parkland course providing excellent golf.
18 holes, 5779yds, Par 68, SSS 68, Course record 65.
Club membership 700.
Visitors   must contact in advance and be arranged with
                 secretary,
Societies   must apply in writing.
Green Fees available on request..
Prof   John Fisher
Facilities   ⊗ ⫝̸ ᴸᴮ ♨ ♀ ⚲ 🖻 ♂
Location   1.5m NE off B5199

Hotel   ★ 62% Rockland Hotel, View Rd, RAINHILL
                 ☎ 0151 426 4603 11rm(9 ⇆1 ↾)

LIVERPOOL   Map 07 SJ39

Allerton Park Allerton Manor Golf Estate, Allerton Rd
L18 3JT ☎ 0151 428 7490 Fax 428 7490
Parkland course.
18 holes, 5494yds, Par 67, SSS 66.
Visitors   Must book with professional in advance for 18
                 hole course.
Societies   Application in writing to golf professional.
Green Fees £7.10 (£8.10 weekends).
Prof   Barry Large
Facilities   ♨ 🖻 ⋔ ♂
& Leisure   9 hole par 3 course..
Location   5.5m SE of city centre off A562 and B5180

Hotel   ★★★ 65% The Royal Hotel, Marine Ter,
                 Waterloo, LIVERPOOL
                 ☎ 0151 928 2332 25 ⇆ ↾

The Childwall Naylors Rd, Gateacre L27 2YB
☎ 0151 487 0654 Fax 0151 487 0882
e-mail: manager@childwallgc.fsnet.co.uk
Parkland golf is played here over a testing course, where
accuracy from the tee is well-rewarded. The course is
very popular with visiting societies for the clubhouse has
many amenities. Course designed by James Braid.
18 holes, 6425yds, Par 72, SSS 71, Course record 66.
Club membership 650.
Visitors   must contact in advance.
Societies   must apply in writing.
Green Fees not confirmed.
Prof   Nigel M Parr
Designer   James Braid
Facilities   ⊗ ⫝̸ ᴸᴮ ♨ ♀ ⚲ 🖻 ⋔ ♂ ↾
Location   7m E of city centre off B5178

Hotel   ★ 62% Rockland Hotel, View Rd,
                 RAINHILL ☎ 0151 426 4603
                 11rm(9 ⇆1 ↾)

Kirkby-Liverpool Municipal Ingoe Ln, Kirkby L32 4SS
☎ 0151 546 5435
18 holes, 6704yds, Par 72, SSS 72, Course record 68.
Location   7.5m NE of city centre on A506

Telephone for further details
Hotel   ★★★ 65% The Royal Hotel, Marine Ter,
                 Waterloo, LIVERPOOL
                 ☎ 0151 928 2332 25 ⇆ ↾

Lee Park Childwall Valley Rd L27 3YA
☎ 0151 487 3882 Fax 0151 487 3882
Flat parkland course with ponds in places and plenty of trees.
18 holes, 6095yds, Par 72, SSS 69.
Club membership 600.
Visitors   must dress acceptably. Must contact in advance.
Societies   must contact in advance.
Green Fees not confirmed.
Designer   G Cotton
Facilities   ⊗ ⫝̸ ᴸᴮ ♨ ♀ ⚲ ♂
Location   7m E of city centre off B5178

Hotel   ★★★ 64% Everglades Park Hotel, Derby Rd,
                 WIDNES ☎ 0151 495 2040 65 ⇆ ↾

West Derby Yew Tree Ln, West Derby L12 9HQ
☎ 0151 254 1034 Fax 0151 259 0505
e-mail: pmilne@westderbygc.freeserve.co.uk
A parkland course always in first-class condition, and so
giving easy walking. The fairways are well-wooded.
Care must be taken on the first nine holes to avoid the
brook which guards many of the greens. A modern well-
designed clubhouse with many amenities, overlooks the
course.
18 holes, 6277yds, Par 72, SSS 70, Course record 65.
Club membership 550.
Visitors   may not play before 9.30am. May not play
                 weekends and bank holidays.
Societies   may not play on Sat, Sun & bank holidays;
                 must contact in advance.
Green Fees £27 per day.
Prof   Andrew Witherup
Facilities   ⊗ ⫝̸ ᴸᴮ ♨ ♀ ⚲ 🖻 ♂
Location   4.5m E of city centre off A57

Hotel   ★★★ 65% The Royal Hotel, Marine Ter,
                 Waterloo, LIVERPOOL
                 ☎ 0151 928 2332 25 ⇆ ↾

Woolton Doe Park, Speke Rd, Woolton L25 7TZ
☎ 0151 486 2298 Fax 0151 486 1664
Parkland course providing a good round of golf for all
standards. A members' owned course which includes two par
5's and five par 3's.
18 holes, 5717yds, Par 69, SSS 68, Course record 63.
Club membership 700.
Visitors   must contact in advance. Restricted at
                 weekends.
Societies   must contact in advance.
Green Fees £24 (£35 weekends).
Prof   Dave Thompson
Facilities   ⊗ ⫝̸ ᴸᴮ ♨ ♀ ⚲ 🖻 ➘ 🛒
& Leisure   Indoor teaching unit.
Location   7m SE of city centre off A562

Hotel   ★★★ 65% The Royal Hotel, Marine Ter,
                 Waterloo, LIVERPOOL
                 ☎ 0151 928 2332 25 ⇆ ↾

Entries with a green background
identify courses considered to be
particularly interesting

NEWTON-LE-WILLOWS — Map 07 SJ59

Haydock Park Newton Ln WA12 0HX
☎ 01925 228525 Fax 01925 228525
A well-wooded parkland course, close to the well-known racecourse, and always in excellent condition. The pleasant undulating fairways offer some very interesting golf and the 6th, 9th, 11th and 13th holes are particularly testing. The clubhouse is very comfortable.
18 holes, 6043yds, Par 70, SSS 69, Course record 65.
Club membership 560.

Visitors	welcome weekdays except Tue, with member only weekends & bank holidays. Must contact in advance.
Societies	must contact in advance.
Green Fees	£27 per day/round.
Prof	Peter Kenwright
Designer	James Braid
Facilities	⊗ ⅲ ⅂ ▋ ♀ ♨ 🛍 ✐
Location	0.75m NE off A49

Hotel ★★★ 66% Posthouse Haydock, Lodge Ln, HAYDOCK ☎ 0870 400 9039 138 ⇆ 🕾

RAINHILL — Map 07 SJ49

Blundells Hill Blundells Ln L35 6NA
☎ 0151 4309551(secretary) 4300100(pro)
Fax 0151 4265256 e-mail: information@blundellshill.co.uk
Parkland course, with free-draining sandy soil, which allows play throughout the winter.
18 holes, 6256yds, Par 71, SSS 70, Course record 69.
Club membership 600.

Visitors	may not play off white tees.
Societies	telephone for prices and availability.
Green Fees	not confirmed..
Cards	▭ 💳 🅱
Prof	Richard Burbidge
Designer	Steve Marnoch
Facilities	⊗ ⅲ ⅂ ▋ ♀ ♨ 🛍 ⤳ 🚜 ✐ ⚑
& Leisure	pool/snooker.
Location	3 mins from junct 7 (eastbound M62)

Hotel ★ 62% Rockland Hotel, View Rd, RAINHILL ☎ 0151 426 4603 11rm(9 ⇆1 🕾)

Eccleston Park Rainhill Rd L35 4PG
☎ 0151 493 0033 Fax 0151 493 0044
e-mail: epgc@crownsportsplc.com
A tough parkland course designed to test all golfing abilities. Strategically placed water features, bunkers and mounding enhance the beauty and difficulty of this manicured course.
18 holes, 6495yds, Par 70, SSS 70.
Club membership 500.

Visitors	booking 7 days in advance.
Societies	telephone in advance.
Green Fees	£13.50,summer(£18 weekends);£12,winter(£15 weekends).
Cards	▭ 💳 🅱
Prof	Richard Stockdale
Designer	Adas
Facilities	⊗ ⅲ ⅂ ▋ ♀ ♨ 🛍 🚜 ✐
Location	junct 7 M62,follow A57 to Prescot.after hump back bridge immediately turn right at lights,course 1m

Hotel ★ 62% Rockland Hotel, View Rd, RAINHILL ☎ 0151 426 4603 11rm(9 ⇆1 🕾)

ST HELENS — Map 07 SJ59

Grange Park Prescot Rd WA10 3AD
☎ 01744 26318 Fax 01744 26318
e-mail: gpgc@ic24.net
A course of Championship length set in pleasant country surroundings - playing the course it is hard to believe that industrial St Helens lies so close at hand. The course is a fine test of golf and there are many attractive holes liable to challenge all grades.
18 holes, 6446yds, Par 72, SSS 71, Course record 65.
Club membership 730.

Visitors	welcome except Tue, weekends by prior arrangement. Advisable to contact professional in advance (01744 28785)
Societies	apply in writing
Green Fees	£26 per 18-27 holes;£33 per 36 holes(333 weekends).
Prof	Paul Roberts
Designer	James Braid
Facilities	⊗ ⅲ ⅂ ▋ ♀ ♨ 🛍 ✐
Location	1.5m SW on A58

Hotel ★★ 66% Kirkfield Hotel, 2/4 Church St, NEWTON LE WILLOWS ☎ 01925 228196 15 ⇆ 🕾

Houghwood Golf Billinge Hill, Crank Rd, Crank WA11 8RL ☎ 01744 894444 Fax 01744 894754
e-mail: enquiries@houghwoodgolfclub.co.uk
In a perfect setting Houghwood has magnificent panoramic views over Lancashire plain and Welsh Hills. With large USGA greens this undulating course is a superb test of golf for all abilities.
18 holes, 6116yds, Par 70, SSS 69, Course record 68.
Club membership 700.

Visitors	no restrictions but dress code must be adhered to.
Societies	telephone enquiries welcome, deposit secures booking.
Green Fees	£17.50 per round;327.50 per day(£25/£37.50 weekends).
Cards	▭ 💳 🅱 🆅
Prof	Paul Dickenson
Designer	Neville Pearsons
Facilities	⊗ ⅲ ⅂ ▋ ♀ ♨ 🛍 ⤳ 🚜 ✐
& Leisure	indoor golf simulator.
Location	From M6 junct 23 follow A580 to A571 to Billinge

Hotel ★★★ 66% Posthouse Haydock, Lodge Ln, HAYDOCK ☎ 0870 400 9039 138 ⇆ 🕾

Sherdley Park Sherdley Rd WA9 5DE ☎ 01744 813149
Fairly hilly course with ponds in places.
18 holes, 5941yds, Par 70, SSS 69.
Club membership 160.

Visitors	no restrictions.
Green Fees	not confirmed.
Facilities	♨ 🛍 🍴
Location	2m S off A570

▶

Hotel ★★ 66% Kirkfield Hotel, 2/4 Church St, NEWTON LE WILLOWS
☎ 01925 228196 15 ⇋ ⋔

SOUTHPORT Map 07 SD31

The Hesketh Cockle Dick's Ln, off Cambridge Rd
PR9 9QQ ☎ 01704 536897 Fax 01704 539250
e-mail: secretary@heskethgolf.freeserve.co.uk
The Hesketh is the oldest of the six clubs in Southport, founded in 1885. Used as a final qualifying course for the Open Championship.
18 holes, 6572yds, Par 72, SSS 72, Course record 67.
Club membership 600.
Visitors welcome, with handicap certificate, at all time other than Tues am (Ladies) and 12.30-2pm daily. Must contact in advance.
Societies please contact Martyn G Senior in advance.
Green Fees £50 per day; £40 per round(£50 per round weekends & bank holidays).
Prof John Donoghue
Designer J F Morris
Facilities ⊗ ⽊ ⼊ ▄ ♀ ⚲ 🏠 ⚑ ♂
Location 1m NE of town centre off A565

Hotel ★★★ 68% Stutelea Hotel & Leisure Club, Alexandra Rd, SOUTHPORT
☎ 01704 544220 20 ⇋ ⋔

Hillside Hastings Rd, Hillside PR8 2LU
☎ 01704 567169 Fax 01704 563192
Championship links course with natural hazards open to strong wind.
18 holes, 6850yds, Par 72, SSS 74, Course record 66.
Club membership 700.
Visitors welcome except Sat, restricted on Sun & Tue (Ladies Day), must contact in advance through secretary.
Societies must apply to secretary in advance.
Green Fees £65 per day; £50 per round(£65 per day sunday).
Prof Brian Seddon
Designer Hawtree
Facilities ⊗ ⽊ ⼊ ▄ ♀ ⚲ 🏠 ⚑ ♂ ⤳ ⚓ ♂ ⋔
Location 3m S of town centre on A565

Hotel ★★★ 68% Royal Clifton Hotel, Promenade, SOUTHPORT
☎ 01704 533771 110 ⇋ ⋔

SOUTHPORT See page 191

Southport & Ainsdale Bradshaws Ln, Ainsdale
PR8 3LG ☎ 01704 578000 Fax 01704 570896
e-mail: secretary@sandagolfclub.co.uk
'S and A', as it is known in the North is another of the fine Championship courses for which this part of the country is famed. This Club has staged many important events and offers golf of the highest order.
18 holes, 6687yds, Par 72, SSS 73, Course record 62.
Club membership 815.
Visitors welcome except Thu, Sat & Sun am & bank holidays. Must contact club in advance & have handicap certificate.

Societies must apply in advance.
Green Fees £45/£60 per round/day(£60 per round weekends).
Cards ▨▨ ▬▬ 🟦
Prof M Houghton
Designer James Braid
Facilities ⊗ ⽊ ⼊ ▄ ♀ ⚲ 🏠 ⚑ ♂
Location 3m S off A565

Hotel ★★★ 68% Royal Clifton Hotel, Promenade, SOUTHPORT
☎ 01704 533771 110 ⇋ ⋔

Southport Municipal Park Rd West PR9 0JR
☎ 01704 535286
18 holes, 6400yds, Par 70, SSS 69, Course record 67.
Location N side of town centre off A565
Telephone for further details

Hotel ★★★ 68% Royal Clifton Hotel, Promenade, SOUTHPORT ☎ 01704 533771 110 ⇋ ⋔

Southport Old Links Moss Ln, Churchtown PR9 7QS
☎ 01704 228207 Fax 01704 505353
e-mail: secretary@solgc.freeserve.co.uk
Seaside course with tree-lined fairways and easy walking. One of the oldest courses in Southport, Henry Vardon won the 'Leeds Cup' here in 1922.
9 holes, 6244yds, Par 72, SSS 71, Course record 68.
Club membership 450.
Visitors advisable to contact in advance, no play Wed/Sun
Societies apply in writing.
Green Fees £30 per day; £22 per round (£30 per round weekends).
Prof Gary Copeman
Facilities ⊗ ⽊ ⼊ ▄ ♀ ⚲ 🏠 ♂
Location NW side of town centre off A5267

Hotel ★★ 68% Bold Hotel, 585 Lord St, SOUTHPORT
☎ 01704 532578 23rm(9 ⇋11 ⋔)

WALLASEY Map 07 SJ29

Bidston Bidston Link Rd CH44 2HR
☎ 0151 638 3412 Fax 6306650
Parkland course, with westerly winds.
18 holes, 6233yds, Par 70, SSS 70.
Club membership 600.
Visitors must contact in advance and confirm in writing. No play by societies on Sun.
Societies must apply in writing.
Green Fees available on application..
Cards ▨▨ ▬▬ 🟥 🟦
Prof Neil McFallane
Facilities ⊗ ⽊ ⼊ ▄ ♀ ⚲ 🏠 ⤳
Location 0.5m W of M53 junc 1 entrance off A551

Hotel ★★★ 67% Leasowe Castle Hotel, Leasowe Rd, MORETON ☎ 0151 606 9191 47 ⇋ ⋔

Where to stay, where to eat?
Visit the AA internet site
www.theAA.com

The Royal Birkdale

Southport, *Merseyside*   ☎ 01704 567920   Fax 01704 562327   Map 07 SD31

e-mail: royalbirkdalegc@dial.pipex.com

The Royal Birkdale is considered by many to be the ultimate championship venue having hosted every major event in the game including eight Open Championships, two Ryder Cup matches, the Walker Cup, the Curtis Cup and many major amateur events. The Ryder Cup match played here in September 1969 was perhaps the most memorable as for the first time ever a Ryder Cup match was halved. Tony Jacklin's final putt on the 18th green was conceded by Jack Nicklaus to half their game and the match; an unforgettable gesture of sportsmanship.

The club was founded in 1889 by eight golfing enthusiasts who rented a piece of land for a nine hole golf course. In 1897 some 230 acres of sandhills was leased and it is here that the present course stands. The links have been fine-tuned over the years to keep up with developments in equipment, course design and talent, and to provide a severe but fair test. All the greens were re-designed and completely rebuilt between the 1991 and 1998 Open Championships.

Visitors must contact in advance and have a handicap certificate. Not Sat, and restricted on Sun

Societies must apply in advance

Green Fees contact secretary's office

Facilities ⊗ ⅷ (by arrangement)
🄻 ♛ ♀ ♨ 🏠 ⚐ ♂
Professional (Richard Bradbeer)

Location Waterloo Rd, Birkdale, Southport PR8 2LX (1.75m S of town centre on A565)

Holes/Par/Course record
18 holes, 6726 yds, Par 72, SSS 73, Course record 65

Championship Course

191

Leasowe Moreton CH46 3RD
☎ 0151 677 5852 Fax 0151 604 1448
Rather flat, semi-links, seaside course.
18 holes, 6227yds, Par 71, SSS 71.
Club membership 637.
Visitors telephone professional (0151 678 5460).
Handicap certificate required. Not Sat play and
not before noon on Sun.
Societies contact in advance.
Green Fees £25 per 18 holes(£30 sundays).
Cards ▨▨ ▨▨ ▨▨ ▨▨ ▨▨ ▨
Prof Andrew Ayres
Designer John Ball Jnr
Facilities ⊗ ⊪ ▙ ▐ ♀ ⚲ ⚑ ⚐ ⚮ ✓
Location 2m W on A551

Hotel ★★★ 67% Leasowe Castle Hotel, Leasowe Rd,
MORETON ☎ 0151 606 9191 47 ⇄ ↿

Wallasey Bayswater Rd L45 8LA
☎ 0151 691 1024 Fax 0151 638 8988
e-mail: wallaseygc@aol.com
A well-established sporting links, adjacent to the Irish
Sea, with huge sandhills and many classic holes where
the player's skills are often combined with good fortune.
Large, firm greens and fine views but not for the fainthearted.
18 holes, 6607yds, Par 72.
Club membership 605.

Visitors must contact one month in advance.
Societies must apply in writing or telephone.
Green Fees £40 per round:£45 per day(£45/£55
weekends).
Cards ▨
Prof Mike Adams
Designer Tom Morris
Facilities ⊗ ▙ ▐ ♀ ⚲ ⚑ ✓
Location N side of town centre off A554

Hotel ★★★ 70% Grove House Hotel, Grove Rd,
WALLASEY
☎ 0151 639 3947 & 0151 630 4558
Fax 0151 639 0028 14 ⇄ ↿

Warren Grove Rd CH45 0JA ☎ 0151 639 8323
Short, undulating links course with first-class greens and
prevailing winds off the sea.
9 holes, 5854yds, Par 72, SSS 68.
Club membership 150.
Visitors welcome except Sun 7-11am.
Societies contact in advance.

Green Fees not confirmed.
Prof Steve Konrad
Facilities ⚑ ⚐ ✓
Location N side of town centre off A554

Hotel ★★★ 67% Leasowe Castle Hotel, Leasowe Rd,
MORETON ☎ 0151 606 9191 47 ⇄ ↿

NORFOLK

BARNHAM BROOM   Map 05 TG00

Barnham Broom Hotel, Golf, Conference, Leisure
Honingham Rd NR9 4DD
☎ 01603 759393 hotel 759552 golf shop
Fax 01603 758224
e-mail: enquiry@barnhambroomhotel.co.uk
Valley course meanders through the River Yare Valley,
parkland and mature trees. Hill course has wide
fairways, heavily guarded greens and spectacular views.
Valley Course: 18 holes, 6603yds, Par 72, SSS 72.
Hill Course: 18 holes, 6495yds, Par 71, SSS 71.
Club membership 500.
Visitors must contact in advance.
Societies must contact in advance.
Green Fees not confirmed.
Prof P Ballingall
Designer Frank Pennink
Facilities ⊗ ⊪ ▙ ▐ ♀ ⚲ ⚑ ⚐ ⚮ ⛳ ⚑ ⚒ ✓ ↿
& Leisure hard tennis courts, heated indoor swimming
pool, squash, sauna, solarium, gymnasium,
Indoor golf simulator with video analysis,
workshop for club repairs.
Location 1m N, S of A47

Hotel ★★★ 74% Barnham Broom Hotel &
Country Club, BARNHAM BROOM
☎ 01603 759393 52 ⇄ ↿

BAWBURGH   Map 05 TG10

Bawburgh Glen Lodge, Marlingford Rd NR9 3LU
☎ 01603 740404 Fax 01603 740403
e-mail: info@bawburgh.com
Undulating course, mixture of parkland & heathland.
Excellent 18th hole to finish.
*Bawburgh Golf Club 1: 18 holes, 6231yds, Par 70, SSS 70,
Course record 65.*
Bawburgh Golf Club 2: 18 holes, 5968yds, Par 70, SSS 69.
Club membership 700.
Visitors must contact in advance, limited play at
weekends.
Societies must contact in advance.
Green Fees £30 per 36 holes; £22 per 18 holes (£32/£25
weekends).
Prof Chris Potter
Designer Shaun Manser
Facilities ⊗ ▙ ▐ ♀ ⚲ ⚑ ⚮ ⚒ ✓ ↿
Location S of Royal Norfolk Showground, on A47

Hotel ★★★ 72% Park Farm Hotel, HETHERSETT
☎ 01603 810264 5 ⇄ ↿ Annexe42 ⇄ ↿

BRANCASTER   Map 09 TF74

Royal West Norfolk PE31 8AX
☎ 01485 210223 Fax 01485 210087
If you want to see what golf courses were like years ago, then go to the Royal West Norfolk where tradition exudes from both clubhouse and course. Close by the sea, the links are laid out in the grand manner and are characterised by sleepered greens, superb cross-bunkering and salt marshes.
18 holes, 6428yds, Par 71, SSS 71, Course record 66.
Club membership 825.

Visitors	must contact well in advance. Restrictions at weekends and in Aug.
Societies	must contact Secretary in advance.
Green Fees	£60 per round (£70 weekends). Reduced winter rate.
Cards	⊟ ■ ▦ ▣ 𝟻
Prof	S Rayner
Designer	Holcombe-Ingleby
Facilities	⊗ ⅏ ℔ ♥ ♀ ⚲ 🖻 ⛳ ✧
Location	7m E of Hunstanton. In Brancaster village turn N at the beach/Broad Lane junct with A149 for 1m
Hotel	★★ 73% Titchwell Manor Hotel, TITCHWELL ☎ 01485 210221 11rm(7 ⇄ 🟈) Annexe4 ⇄ 🟈

CROMER   Map 09 TG24

Royal Cromer 145 Overstrand Rd NR27 0JH
☎ 01263 512884 Fax 01263 512430
e-mail: general.manager@royal-cromer.com
Seaside course set out on cliff edge, hilly and subject to wind. Challenging upland course with spectacular views out to sea and overlooking town. Strong sea breezes affect the clifftop holes, the most famous being the 14th (the Lighthouse) which has a green in the shadow of the lighthouse.
18 holes, 6508yds, Par 72, SSS 72, Course record 67.
Club membership 700.

Visitors	must contact in advance & have handicap certificate.
Societies	must contact in advance.
Green Fees	£37 per day (£42 weekends). Winter £27 (£32 weekends).
Prof	Lee Patterson
Designer	J H Taylor
Facilities	⊗ ⅏ ℔ ♥ ♀ ⚲ 🖻 ⛳ ✧ ⚒ ✧
Location	1m E on B1159
Hotel	★★ 68% Red Lion, Brook St, CROMER ☎ 01263 514964 12 ⇄ 🟈

DENVER   Map 05 TF60

Ryston Park PE38 0HH
☎ 01366 382133 Fax 01366 383834
Parkland course.
9 holes, 6310yds, Par 70, SSS 70, Course record 66.
Club membership 330.

Visitors	must contact in advance. May not play weekends or bank holidays.
Societies	must apply in writing.
Green Fees	£20 per day/round summer (£15 winter).
Designer	James Braid
Facilities	⊗ ⅏ ℔ ♥ ♀ ⚲ 🖻 ✧
Location	0.5m S on A10
Hotel	★★ 71% Castle Hotel, High St, DOWNHAM MARKET ☎ 01366 384311 12 ⇄ 🟈

DEREHAM   Map 09 TF91

Dereham Quebec Rd NR19 2DS
☎ 01362 695900 Fax 01362 695904
Parkland course.
9 holes, 6225yds, Par 71, SSS 70, Course record 64.
Club membership 480.

Visitors	must contact in advance. Weekends with member only.
Societies	must apply in writing or telephone in advance.
Green Fees	£15 per round, £20 per day.
Prof	Robert Curtis
Facilities	⊗ ⅏ ℔ ♥ ♀ ⚲ 🖻 ✧
Location	N side of town centre off B1110
Hotel	★★★ 74% Barnham Broom Hotel & Country Club, BARNHAM BROOM ☎ 01603 759393 52 ⇄ 🟈

The Norfolk Golf & Country Club Hingham Rd, Reymerston NR9 4QQ
☎ 01362 850297 Fax 01362 850614
The course meanders through more than 200 acres of rolling Norfolk countryside, including ancient ditches, hedging and woodland. Large greens are built to USGA specification.
18 holes, 6609yds, Par 72, SSS 72, Course record 69.
Club membership 400.

Visitors	contact Golf reception for advance bookings.
Societies	apply in writing to the Society Organiser.
Green Fees	£20 per round (£25 weekends).
Cards	⊟ ▦ ▣ 𝟻
Prof	Tony Varney
Facilities	⊗ ⅏ ℔ ♥ ♀ ⚲ 🖻 ⛳ ✧ ⚒ ✧ ⚒
& Leisure	heated indoor swimming pool, sauna, solarium, gymnasium, pitch & putt.
Location	12m W of Norwich, off B1135 ▶

Hotel ★★★ 74% Barnham Broom Hotel & Country
Club, BARNHAM BROOM
☎ 01603 759393 52 ⇄ ⋔

DISS   Map 05 TM18

Diss Stuston IP22 3JB ☎ 01379 641025
Fax 01379 641025
Commonland course with natural hazards.
18 holes, 6238yds, Par 73, SSS 70.
Club membership 750.
Visitors   must contact in advance but may not play
weekends & bank holidays.
Societies   by arrangement.
Green Fees not confirmed.
Prof   N J Taylor
Facilities   ⊗ ⊪ ⅃ ♥ ♀ ⚘ 🏠 ⬆ 🛒 ✐
Location   1.5m SE on B1118

Hotel ★★★ 71% The Cornwallis Country Hotel &
Restaurant, BROME ☎ 01379 870326
11 ⇄ ⋔ Annexe5 ⇄ ⋔

FAKENHAM   Map 09 TF92

Fakenham Gallow Sports Centre, The Race Course
N21 7NY ☎ 01328 863534
A well-wooded 9-hole course.
9 holes, 6174yds, Par 71, SSS 70, Course record 65.
Club membership 460.
Visitors   any time with member, restricted until after
noon weekends.
Societies   apply in writing or telephone.
Green Fees £18 per day (£24 weekends & bank holidays).
Cards   ▭ ▭ 💳 ▭ 📎 💷
Prof   Martyn Clarke PGA
Designer   Cotton(UK)
Facilities   ⊗ ⊪ ⅃ ♥ ♀ ⚘ 🏠 ✐
& Leisure hard tennis courts, squash, indoor bowling.

Hotel ★★ 68% Crown Hotel, Market Place,
FAKENHAM ☎ 01328 851418 12 ⇄ ⋔

FRITTON   Map 05 TG40

Caldecott Hall Golf & Leisure Caldecott Hall, Beccles Rd
NR31 9EY ☎ 01493 488488 Fax 01493 488561
e-mail: caldecotthall@supanet
Facilities at Caldecott Hall include an 18-hole course with
testing dog-leg fairways, a short par 3 9-hole course, a
floodlit driving range, and good practising areas.
Main Course: 18 holes, 6572yards, Par 72, SSS 71.
Par 3: 9 holes, 1503yds, Par 27.
Club membership 500.
Visitors   visitors always welcome, subject to availability.
Societies   arrangements in advance.
Green Fees £20 per day (£25 weekends).
Cards   ▭ ▭ ▭ ▭ 📎 💷
Prof   Syer Shulver
Facilities   ⊗ ⊪ ⅃ ♥ ♀ ⚘ 🏠 ⬆ 🍴 ⛳ ♥ 🛒 ✐ ⟨
& Leisure heated indoor swimming pool.
Location   On the A143 Beccles/Gt Yarmouth road at
Fritton

Caldecott Hall Golf & Leisure

Hotel ★★★ 71% Caldecott Hall Golf & Leisure,
Caldecott Hall, Beccles Rd, FRITTON
☎ 01493 488488 8 ⇄ ⋔

GORLESTON-ON-SEA   Map 05 TG50

Gorleston Warren Rd NR31 6JT
☎ 01493 661911 & 662103 Fax 01493 661911
Cliff top course, the most easterly in the British Isles. One of
the outstanding features of the course is the 7th hole, which
was rescued from the ravages of cliff erosion about 20 years
ago. The green, only eight yards from the cliff edge, is at the
mercy of the prevailing winds and club selection is critical.
18 holes, 6391yds, Par 71, SSS 71, Course record 68.
Club membership 860.
Visitors   advisable to contact in advance, must have
handicap. Dress code in operation.
Societies   must apply in writing.
Green Fees £22 per round/day (£26 weekends).
Prof   Nick Brown
Designer   J H Taylor
Facilities   ⊗ ⊪ ⅃ ♥ ♀ ⚘ 🏠 ⛳ ✐
Location   S side of town centre

Hotel ★★★ 74% Cliff Hotel, Cliffe Hill, Gorleston,
GREAT YARMOUTH
☎ 01493 662179 39 ⇄ ⋔

GREAT YARMOUTH   Map 05 TG50

Great Yarmouth & Caister Beach House, Caister-on-
Sea NR30 5TD ☎ 01493 728699 Fax 01493 728831
e-mail: office@caistergolf.co.uk
This great old club, which celebrated its centenary in
1982, has played its part in the development of the game.
It is a fine old-fashioned links where not many golfers
have bettered the SSS in competitions. The 468-yard 8th
(par 4), is a testing hole and the 7th is an extremely fine
short hole. A feature of the course is a number of
sleepered bunkers, a line of 4 bisecting the 4th.
18 holes, 6330yds, Par 70, SSS 70, Course record 66.
Club membership 720.
Visitors   must contact in advance. Restricted
weekends.
Societies   must apply in writing or telephone.
Green Fees £30 per day (£35 weekends).
Cards   ▭
Prof   James Hill   ▶

Designer	H Colt
Facilities	⊗ ⍕ ⬛ ☰ ♀ ⛳ 🏠 ⚷
Location	0.5m N off A149

| Hotel | ★★★ 68% Imperial Hotel, North Dr, GREAT YARMOUTH ☎ 01493 842000 39 ⇌ 🏠 |

HUNSTANTON   Map 09 TF64

Hunstanton Golf Course Rd PE36 6JQ
☎ 01485 532811 Fax 01485 532319
e-mail: hunstanton.golf@eidosnet.co.uk
A championship links course set among some of the most natural golfing country in East Anglia. Keep out of the numerous bunkers and master the fast greens to play to your handicap - then you only have the wind to contend with! Good playing conditions all year round.
18 holes, 6333yds, Par 72, SSS 70.
Club membership 675.

Visitors	must contact in advance and be a club member with current handicap certificate. Restricted at weekends & may not play bank holiday weekends. Play in two ball format ie singles or foursomes.
Societies	apply in advance.
Green Fees	£55 (£65 weekends). Winter £35 (£45 weekends).
Prof	James Dodds
Designer	James Braid
Facilities	⊗ ⍕ by prior arrangement ⬛ ☰ ♀ ⛳ 🏠 🚩 ⚲ ☖ ⚷
Location	Off A149 in Old Hunstanton Village signposted

| Hotel | ★★ 74% Caley Hall Motel, Old Hunstanton Rd, HUNSTANTON ☎ 01485 533486 Annexe33 ⇌ |

KING'S LYNN   Map 09 TF62

Eagles 39 School Rd, Tilney All Saints PE34 4RS
☎ 01553 827147 Fax 01553 829777
e-mail: shop@eagles-golf-tennis.co.uk
Parkland course with plenty of water hazards and bunkers. Also Par-3 course and floodlit, covered driving range.
9 holes, 4284yds, Par 64, SSS 61, Course record 64.
Club membership 200.

Visitors	must contact in advance.Dress code required.
Societies	must apply in writing.
Green Fees	£11 per 18 holes, £7.50 per 9 holes (£14.50/£8.50 weekends & bank holidays).
Cards	🖃 ▦ 📶 🔘
Prof	Nigel Pickerell
Designer	D W Horn
Facilities	⊗ by prior arrangement ⬛ ☰ ♀ ⛳ 🏠 🚩 ⚷ ⚲
& Leisure	hard tennis courts.
Location	Off A47 at roundabout to Tilney All Saints between Kings Lynn and Wisbech

| Hotel | ★★★ 64% The Duke's Head, Tuesday Market Place, KING'S LYNN ☎ 01553 774996 71 ⇌ 🏠 |

King's Lynn Castle Rising PE31 6BD
☎ 01553 631654 Fax 631036 e-mail: klgc@eidosnet.co.uk
The course is set among silver birch and fir woodland and benefits, especially in the winter from well-drained sandy soil.
18 holes, 6609yds, Par 72, SSS 73, Course record 64.
Club membership 910.

Visitors	must contact in advance.
Societies	apply in writing or by phone in advance.
Green Fees	£40 per day (£50 weekends and bank holidays).
Prof	John Reynolds
Designer	Thomas & Allis
Facilities	⊗ ⍕ ⬛ ☰ ♀ ⛳ 🏠 🚩 ⚷
& Leisure	Snooker.
Location	4m NE off A149

| Hotel | ★★★ 64% The Duke's Head, Tuesday Market Place, KING'S LYNN ☎ 01553 774996 71 ⇌ 🏠 |

MATTISHALL   Map 09 TG01

Mattishall South Green NR20 3JZ ☎ 01362 850111
Mattishall has the distinction of having the longest hole in Norfolk at a very demanding 625yds.
9 holes, 3300mtrs, Par 72, SSS 69.
Club membership 120.

Visitors	no restrictions.
Societies	welcome.
Green Fees	£8 per 9 holes; £15 per 18 holes;£20 all day.
Designer	B Todd
Facilities	☰ ♀ ⛳ 🚩 ⚷
Location	0.75m S of Mattishall Church

| Hotel | ★★★ 74% Barnham Broom Hotel & Country Club, BARNHAM BROOM ☎ 01603 759393 52 ⇌ 🏠 |

MIDDLETON   Map 09 TF61

Middleton Hall Hall Orchards PE32 1RH
☎ 01553 841800 Fax 01553 841800
The setting is one of natural undulations, and mature specimen trees, offering a most attractive environment for the game of golf. The architecturally designed course provides a challenge for the competent golfer, there is also a covered floodlit driving range and practice putting green.
18 holes, 6004yds, Par 71, SSS 69, Course record 71.
Club membership 600.

Visitors	no restrictions.
Societies	must contact in advance.
Green Fees	£30 per day; £25 per round (£35/£30 weekends).
Cards	🖃 ▦ 📶 🔘
Prof	Steve White
Designer	D Scott
Facilities	⊗ ⍕ ⬛ ☰ ♀ ⛳ 🏠 ☖ ⚷ ⚲
Location	4m from King's Lynn on A47

| Hotel | ★★★ 66% Butterfly Hotel, Beveridge Way, Hardwick Narrows, KING'S LYNN ☎ 01553 771707 50 ⇌ 🏠 |

Looking for a driving range?
See the index at the back of the guide

MUNDESLEY   Map 09 TG33

Mundesley Links Rd NR11 8ES
☎ 01263 720279 & 720095 Fax 01263 720279
Parkland course, undulating with panoramic views, short but
competitive. One mile from the sea.
9 holes, 5377yds, Par 68, SSS 66, Course record 64.
Club membership 520.
Visitors   restricted Wed & weekends, also Tue 4-6pm,
              dress regulations, no sharing clubs, golf shoes
              must be worn, prior booking preferred.Handicap
              certificate required.
Societies   must contact one month in advance.
Green Fees   £20 per day; £18 per round (£25 per round
              weekends).
Prof   T G Symmons
Facilities   ⊗ ↗ㄍ by prior arrangement ਓ ♥ ♀ ♨ ☎ ♂ ┞
Location   W side of village off B1159

Hotel   ★★ 68% Red Lion, Brook St, CROMER
              ☎ 01263 514964 12 ⇄ ☞

NORWICH   Map 05 TG20

Costessey Park Old Costessey NR8 5AL
☎ 01603 746333 & 747085 Fax 01603 746185
The course lies in the gently contoured Two River valley,
providing players with a number of holes that bring the river
and man-made lakes into play.
18 holes, 5820yds, Par 71, SSS 68, Course record 68.
Club membership 600.
Visitors   may not play competition days, prior booking
              required for weekends.
Societies   welcome by prior arrangement.
Green Fees   not confirmed.
Prof   Simon Cook
Facilities   ⊗ ↗ㄍ ਓ ♥ ♀ ♨ ☎ ⚐ ↘ ♒ ♂

Hotel   ★★★ 67% Quality Hotel, 2 Barnard Rd,
              Bowthorpe, NORWICH
              ☎ 01603 741161 80 ⇄ ☞

De Vere Dunston Hall Hotel Ipswich Rd NR14 8PQ
☎ 01508 470444 Fax 01508 470689
e-mail: dhreception@devere-hotels.com
Parkland course with water features at many holes. Varied
and challenging woodland setting. Floodlit driving range.
18 holes, 6300yds, Par 71, SSS 70, Course record 70.
Visitors   must book in advance.
Societies   apply in writing or telephone for details.
Green Fees   £25 per round (£30 Fri-Sun).
Cards   ▭▭ ▮▮ ▭▭ ▭▭ ▭▭ ▩ ⑤
Prof   Peter Briggs
Designer   M Shaw
Facilities   ⊗ ↗ㄍ ਓ ♥ ♀ ♨ ☎ ⚐ ♒ ♂ ┞
& Leisure   hard tennis courts, heated indoor swimming
              pool, sauna, solarium, gymnasium.
Location   On A140

Hotel   ★★★★ 66% De Vere Dunston Hall, Ipswich
              Rd, NORWICH ☎ 01508 470444 130 ⇄ ☞

Eaton Newmarket Rd NR4 6SF
☎ 01603 451686 & 452881 Fax 01603 451686
e-mail: lizbovill@eatongolfclub.fsnet.co.uk
An undulating, tree-lined parkland course with excellent
trees. Easy opening par 5 followed by an intimidating par 3
that is well bunkered with deep rough on both sides. The
challenging 17th hole is uphill to a small hidden green and
always needs more club than expected.
18 holes, 6114yds, Par 70, SSS 70, Course record 64.
Club membership 800.
Visitors   restricted before 11.30am weekends. Advised to
              contact in advance.
Societies   must contact in advance.
Green Fees   £30per day (£40 weekends and bank holidays).
Prof   Mark Allen
Facilities   ⊗ ↗ㄍ by prior arrangement ਓ ♥ ♀ ♨ ☎ ♂
Location   1.5m SW of city centre off A11

Hotel   ★★★ 72% Park Farm Hotel, HETHERSETT
              ☎ 01603 810264 5 ⇄ ☞ Annexe42 ⇄ ☞

Marriott Sprowston Manor Hotel & Country Club
Wroxham Rd NR7 8RP
☎ 01603 254290 Fax 01603 788884
e-mail: sprowston.manor@marriotthotels.co.uk

Set in 100 acres of parkland, including an impressive
collection of oak trees which provide a backdrop to many
holes. A very tight course, so accuracy is required for good
golf. The facilities include a 27-bay driving range.
18 holes, 5763yds, Par 70, SSS 68, Course record 63.
Club membership 600.
Visitors   no restrictions. Advisable to book in advance.
Societies   must contact in advance.
Green Fees   £21 per round (£27 weekends).
Cards   ▭▭ ▮▮ ▭▭ ▭▭ ▭▭ ▩ ⑤
Prof   Guy D Ireson
Facilities   ⊗ ↗ㄍ ਓ ♥ ♀ ♨ ☎ ⚐ ↘ ♒ ♂ ┞
& Leisure   heated indoor swimming pool.
Location   4m NE from city centre on A1151

Hotel   ★★★★ 75% Marriott Sprowston Manor Hotel
              & Country Club, Sprowston Park, Wroxham Rd,
              Sprowston, NORWICH ☎ 01603 410871
              94 ⇄ ☞

Royal Norwich Drayton High Rd, Hellesdon NR6 5AH
☎ 01603 429928 & 408459 (Pro) Fax 01603 417945
Undulating mature parkland course complimented with
gorse. Largely unchanged since the alterations carried out by
James Braid in 1924. A challenging test of golf.
18 holes, 6506yds, Par 72, SSS 72, Course record 65.
Club membership 700.

Visitors	must contact in advance. Restricted weekends & bank holidays.
Societies	must contact in advance.
Green Fees	£30 per day (£36 weekends & bank holidays).
Prof	Dean Futter
Designer	James Braid
Facilities	⊗ ⓑ ▆ ♈ 🛆 🛋 🐾 ✐
Location	2.5m NW of city centre on A1067

Hotel	★★★ 67% Quality Hotel, 2 Barnard Rd, Bowthorpe, NORWICH ☎ 01603 741161 80 ⇆ 🐾

Wensum Valley Hotel, Golf & Country Club Beech Av,
Taverham NR8 6HP ☎ 01603 261012 Fax 01603 261664
e-mail: enqs@wensumvalley.co.uk
An undulating, picturesque golf course situated on the side of
a valley. The greens in particular are very undulating and
always give the average golfer a testing time. The 12th hole
from a raised tee provides a blind and windy tee shot and a
very sloping green.
Valley Course: 18 holes, 6172yds, Par 71, SSS 69,
Course record 67.
Wensum Course: 9 holes, 2906yds, Par 70, SSS 68.
Club membership 900.

Visitors	no restrictions but advisable to book tee times at weekends.
Societies	apply in writing or by telephone.
Green Fees	£18 per day.
Cards	🖭 ▆ 💳 🔄 ⑨
Prof	Peter Whittle
Designer	B Todd
Facilities	⊗ ⑪ ⓑ ▆ ♈ 🛆 🛋 ⌇ 🎣 🐾 🛶 ✐ ⑂
& Leisure	heated indoor swimming pool, fishing, sauna, solarium, gymnasium.
Location	5m N of Norwich

Hotel	★★★ 68% Swallow Nelson Hotel, Prince of Wales Rd, NORWICH ☎ 01603 760260 132 ⇆ 🐾

SHERINGHAM   Map 09 TG14

Sheringham Weybourne Rd NR26 8HG
☎ 01263 823488 & 822038 Fax 01263 825189
e-mail: sgc.sec@care4free.net
Splendid cliff-top links with gorse, good 'seaside turf'
and plenty of space. Straight driving is essential for a
low score. The course is close to the shore and can be
very windswept, but offers magnificent views.
18 holes, 6495yds, Par 70, SSS 71, Course record 65.
Club membership 680.

Visitors	must contact in advance & have handicap certificate. Restricted weekends.
Societies	must apply in writing.
Green Fees	£40 per day (£45 weekends & bank holidays).
Prof	M W Jubb
Designer	Tom Dunn
Facilities	⊗ ⑪ ⓑ ▆ ♈ 🛆 🛋 🛶 ✐
Location	W side of town centre on A149

Hotel	★★ 70% Beaumaris Hotel, South St, SHERINGHAM ☎ 01263 822370 21 ⇆ 🐾

SWAFFHAM   Map 05 TF80

Swaffham Cley Rd PE37 8AE ☎ 01760 721621(secretary)
721611(pro) Fax 01760 721621
Heathland course and designated wildlife site.
9 holes, 6252yds, Par 72, SSS 70.
Club membership 400.

Visitors	must contact in advance. With member only at weekends & not before mid day.
Societies	must contact in advance.
Green Fees	£20.
Prof	Peter Field
Facilities	⊗ ⓑ ▆ ♈ 🛆 🛋 ⌇ ✐
Location	1.5m SW

Hotel	★★★ 65% George Hotel, Station Rd, SWAFFHAM ☎ 01760 721238 29 ⇆ 🐾

THETFORD   Map 05 TL88

Feltwell Thor Ave, Feltwell IP26 4AY ☎ 01842 827644
In spite of being an inland links, this 9-hole course is still
open and windy.
9 holes, 6488yds, Par 72, SSS 71, Course record 71.
Club membership 400.

Visitors	dress restriction, no jeans,tracksuits or collarless shirts, golf shoes to be worn.
Societies	apply in writing or telephone in advance.
Green Fees	£15 per day(£24 weekends & bank holidays).
Prof	Neil Mitchell
Facilities	⊗ ⑪ ⓑ ▆ ♈ (closed Mon) 🛆 🛋 ✐
Location	On B1112

Hotel	★★ 65% The Thomas Paine Hotel, White Hart St, THETFORD ☎ 01842 755631 13 ⇆ 🐾

Thetford Brandon Rd IP24 3NE
☎ 01842 752169 Fax 01842 766212
This is a course with a good pedigree. It was laid-out by
a fine golfer, C.H. Mayo, later altered by James Braid
and then again altered by another famous course
designer, Mackenzie Ross. It is a testing heathland
course with a particularly stiff finish.
18 holes, 6849yds, Par 72, SSS 73, Course record 66.
Club membership 850.

Visitors	pre booking advisable, may not play weekends or bank holidays except with member. Handicap certificate required.
Societies	must contact in advance, Wed-Fri only.
Green Fees	£34.
Cards	🖭 ▆ 💳 🔄 ⑨
Prof	Gary Kitley
Designer	James Braid
Facilities	⊗ ⑪ ⓑ ▆ ♈ 🛆 🛋 ⌇ ✐
Location	2m W of Thetford on B1107

Hotel	★★ 65% The Thomas Paine Hotel, White Hart St, THETFORD ☎ 01842 755631 13 ⇆ 🐾

Where to stay, where to eat?
Visit the AA internet site
www.theAA.com

WATTON   Map 05 TF90

Richmond Park Saham Rd IP25 6EA
☎ 01953 881803 Fax 01953 881817
e-mail: info@richmondpark.co.uk
Compact parkland course with mature and young trees.
These together with the Little Wissey river and other water
hazards create an interesting but not daunting challenge.
18 holes, 6289yds, Par 71, SSS 70, Course record 69.
Club membership 600.
Visitors   not before 10.30am weekends & bank holidays.
Societies   must contact in advance.
Green Fees £25 per day; £18 per round (£25 per day/round
           weekends & bank holidays).
Cards   ⬛ ⬛ ⬛ ⬛ ⬛
Prof   Alan Hemsley
Designer   D Jessup/D Scott
Facilities   ⬛ ⬛ ⬛ ⬛ ⬛ ⬛ ⬛
& Leisure   gymnasium.
Location   500yds NW of town centre

Hotel   ★★★ 65% George Hotel, Station Rd,
           SWAFFHAM ☎ 01760 721238   29 ⇆ 🐾

WESTON LONGVILLE   Map 09 TG11

Weston Park NR9 5JW
☎ 01603 872363 Fax 01603 873040
Testing course set in 200 acres of mature parkland with
specimen trees.
18 holes, 6648yds, Par 72, SSS 72, Course record 69.
Club membership 400.

Visitors   must telephone for tee times on 01603 872998.
Societies   must telephone for prices and tee times.
Green Fees £29 per round/£38 per day(£34/£43 weekends).
Prof   Michael Few
Designer   Golf Technology
Facilities   ⬛ ⬛ ⬛ ⬛ ⬛ ⬛ ⬛ ⬛
& Leisure   hard tennis courts.
Location   Off the A1067 Norwich/Fakenham road, 9m
           NW of Norwich

Hotel   ★★★ 67% Quality Hotel, 2 Barnard Rd,
           Bowthorpe, NORWICH
           ☎ 01603 741161   80 ⇆ 🐾

Entries with a green background
identify courses considered to be
particularly interesting

WEST RUNTON   Map 09 TG14

Links Country Park Hotel & Golf Club NR27 9QH
☎ 01263 838215 Fax 01263 838264
e-mail: sales@links-hotel.co.uk
Parkland course 500 yds from the sea, with superb views
overlooking West Runton. The hotel offers extensive leisure
facilities.
9 holes, 4842yds, Par 66, SSS 64.
Club membership 300.
Visitors   restrictions weekends.
Societies   must telephone in advance.
Green Fees £25 per day (£30 weekends & bank holidays).
Cards   ⬛ ⬛ ⬛ ⬛ ⬛
Prof   Andrew Collison
Designer   J.H Taylor
Facilities   ⬛ ⬛ ⬛ ⬛ ⬛ ⬛ ⬛ ⬛ ⬛ ⬛ ⬛
& Leisure   hard tennis courts, heated indoor swimming
           pool, sauna, solarium.
Location   S side of village off A149

Hotel   ★★ 70% Beaumaris Hotel, South St,
           SHERINGHAM ☎ 01263 822370   21 ⇆ 🐾

NORTHAMPTONSHIRE

CHACOMBE   Map 04 SP44

Cherwell Edge OX17 2EN
☎ 01295 711591 Fax 01295 712404
Parkland course. The front nine is short and tight with mature
trees. The back nine is longer and more open.
18 holes, 5947yds, Par 70, SSS 68, Course record 64.
Club membership 500.

Visitors   no restrictions but golf shoes to be worn (can be
           hired) and tidy appearance expected.
Societies   must apply in advance.
Green Fees £16 per 18 holes (£20 weekends).
Cards   ⬛ ⬛ ⬛ ⬛ ⬛
Prof   Joe Kingston
Designer   R Davies
Facilities   ⬛ ⬛ ⬛ ⬛ ⬛ ⬛ ⬛ ⬛ ⬛ ⬛ ⬛
Location   Exit M40 junct 11, 0.5m S off B4525

Hotel   ★★★ 68% Whately Hall, Banbury Cross,
           BANBURY ☎ 0870 400 8104 72 ⇆ 🐾

COLD ASHBY · · · · · · · · · · · · Map 04 SP67

Cold Ashby Stanford Rd NN6 6EP
☎ 01604 740548 Fax 01604 740548
e-mail: coldashby.golfclub@virgin.net
Undulating parkland course, nicely matured, with superb
views. The 27 holes consist of three loops of nine which can
be interlinked with each other. All three loops have their own
challenge and any combination of two loops will give an
excellent course. The start of the Elkington loop offers 5
holes of scenic beauty and testing golf and the 3rd on the
Winwick loop is a 200-yard par 3 from a magnificent plateau
tee.
*Ashby-Elkington: 18 holes, 6308yds, Par 72, SSS 70, Course
record 69.*
*Elkington-Winwick: 18 holes, 6250yds, Par 70, SSS 70,
Course record 69.*
*Winwick-Ashby: 18 holes, 6004yds, Par 70, SSS 69, Course
record 66.*
Club membership 700.
Visitors start time must be reserved at weekends.
Societies must contact in advance.
Green Fees £12.50 per 18 holes (£15 weekends).
Cards 🖭 🖩 🖾 🗐
Prof Shane Rose
Designer David Croxton
Facilities ⊗ ⫙ 🖫 🍺 ♀ 🛆 🖻 ⫟ 🐾 🚲 ♂
Location Close to junct 1 A14 & junct 18 M1 midway
between Rugby, Leicester & Northampton

Hotel ★★★ 64% Posthouse Northampton/Rugby,
CRICK ☎ 0870 400 9059 88 ⇋ 🏲

COLLINGTREE · · · · · · · · · · · Map 04 SP75

Collingtree Park Windingbrook Ln NN4 0XN
☎ 01604 700000 & 701202 Fax 01604 702600
e-mail: info@collingtreeparkgolf.com
Superb 18-hole resort course designed by former U.S.
and British Open champion Johnny Miller. The
American style course has water hazards on 10 holes
with a spectacular par 5 18th Island Green.The Golf
Academy includes a driving range, practice holes, indoor
video teaching room.
18 holes, 6776yds, Par 72, SSS 72, Course record 66.
Visitors must contact in advance & have handicap
certificate.
Societies contact in advance.
Green Fees £17.50 per 18 holes; £9 per 9
holes(£23/12weekends).
Cards 🖭 🖩 🖾 🗐 🖾 🗐
Prof Geoff Pook/Henry Bareham
Designer Johnny Miller
Facilities ⊗ ⫙ 🖫 🍺 ♀ 🛆 🖻 ⫟ 🐾 🚲 ♂ ♟
& Leisure fishing, 3 hole Academy. indoor teaching
room.
Location M1-junc 15 on A508 to Northampton

Hotel ★★★★ 69% Northampton Marriott Hotel,
Eagle Dr, NORTHAMPTON
☎ 01604 768700 120 ⇋ 🏲

CORBY · · · · · · · · · · · · · · · · Map 04 SP88

Corby Public Stamford Rd, Weldon NN17 3JH
☎ 01536 260756 Fax 01536 260756
Municipal course laid out on made-up quarry ground and
open to prevailing wind. Wet in winter. Played over by Priors
Hall Club.
18 holes, 6677yds, Par 72, SSS 72.
Club membership 600.
Visitors are advised to book in advance.
Societies must contact in advance.
Green Fees £9.85 (£12.70 weekends).
Prof Jeff Bradbrook
Designer F Hawtree
Facilities ⊗ ⫙ 🖫 🍺 ♀ 🛆 🖻 ⫟ 🐾 🚲 ♂
Location 4m NE on A43

Hotel ★★★ 67% The Talbot, New St, OUNDLE
☎ 01832 273621 39 ⇋ 🏲

DAVENTRY · · · · · · · · · · · · · Map 04 SP56

Daventry & District Norton Rd NN11 5LS
☎ 01327 702829
A hilly course with hard walking.
9 holes, 5812yds, Par 69, SSS 68, Course record 68.
Club membership 310.
Visitors no visitors before 11.30am Sun mornings.
Societies contact the club secretary.
Green Fees £10 per round (£15 weekends & bank holidays).
Facilities ⊗ by prior arrangement ⫙ by prior arrangement
🖫 by prior arrangement 🍺 ♀ 🛆 🖻
Location 0.5m NE

Hotel ★★★★ 62% Hanover International Hotel &
Club, Sedgemoor Way, DAVENTRY
☎ 01327 307000 138 ⇋ 🏲

FARTHINGSTONE · · · · · · · · Map 04 SP65

Farthingstone Hotel & Golf Course NN12 8AH
☎ 01327 361533 & 361291 Fax 01327 361645
e-mail: bookings@farthingstone.co.uk
A mature and challenging course set in picturesque
countryside.
18 holes, 6299yds, Par 70, SSS 70, Course record 68.
Club membership 500.
Visitors must contact in advance.
Societies must contact in advance.
Green Fees £18 holes from £15 (from £20 weekends).
Cards 🖭 🖩 🖾 🗐
Prof Greg Lunn
Designer Don Donaldson
Facilities ⊗ ⫙ 🖫 🍺 ♀ 🛆 🖻 ⫟ 🖾 🐾 🚲 ♂
& Leisure squash, Snooker room.
Location 1m W

Hotel ★★ 64% Globe Hotel, High St, WEEDON
☎ 01327 340336 15 ⇋ 🏲 Annexe3 ⇋ 🏲

Looking for a driving range?
See the index at the back of the guide

AA Hotels that have special
arrangements with golf courses are listed at
the back of the guide

★★★★ HELLIDON LAKES
HOTEL, GOLF & COUNTRY CLUB

Situated in 220 acres of beautiful countryside, Hellidon lakes has a
spectacular 27 hole championship course meandering through scenic lakes and valleys -
a haven of peace and tranquillity yet only 20 minutes from the M1, M40, M6 and A14 as
well as major rail links. Leisure facilities include a putting green, fishing, tennis, 4 lanes
of ten pin bowling, indoor golf simulator, heated indoor swimming pool, 55 station gym
and health studio with beauty therapists, sunbed, steam room and spa bath. 71
bedrooms with private bathrooms, award winning restaurant, bistro and bar.

2 NIGHT BREAKS - SOCIETY & CORPORATE DAYS - CONFERENCES - BANQUETS - WEDDINGS

www.marstonhotels.com

HELLIDON LAKES, HELLIDON, DAVENTRY, NORTHANTS NN11 6GG TEL: 01327 262550 FAX: 01327 262559

HELLIDON   Map 04 SP55

Hellidon Lakes Hotel & Country Club NN11 6GG
☎ 01327 262550 Fax 01327 262559
e-mail: stay@hellidon.demon.co.uk
Spectacular parkland course designed by David Snell.
18 holes, 6691yds, Par 72, SSS 72.
Club membership 500.
Visitors   18 hole course; must contact in advance & have
               handicap certificate at weekends. 9 hole; open to
               beginners.
Societies   must telephone in advance.
Green Fees not confirmed.
Cards   💳 💳 💳 💳 💳 💳
Prof   Gary Wills
Designer   D Snell
Facilities ⊗ 🎿 ⅃ 🍺 ⅄ 🏖 🍴 🏌 🛥 ♨ ⚒
& Leisure hard tennis courts, heated indoor swimming
               pool, fishing, solarium, gymnasium, golf
               simulator, ten pin bowling.
Location   0.5m off A361 between Daventry & Banbury

Hotel   ★★★★ 67% Hellidon Lakes Hotel & Country
               Club, HELLIDON ☎ 01327 262550 71 ⇆ 🐾

KETTERING   Map 04 SP87

Kettering Headlands NN15 6XA
☎ 01536 511104 Fax 01536 511104
e-mail: kgc@ukgateway.net.
A very pleasant, mainly flat meadowland course with easy
walking.
18 holes, 6081yds, Par 69, SSS 69, Course record 64.
Club membership 700.
Visitors   welcome but with member only weekends &
               bank holidays.
Societies   Wed & Fri only, apply in writing.
Green Fees not confirmed.
Prof   Kevin Theobald
Designer   Tom Morris
Facilities ⊗ 🎿 ⅃ 🍺 ⅄ 🏖 🍴 ⚒
Location   S side of town centre

Hotel   ★★★★ 72% Kettering Park Hotel, Kettering
               Parkway, KETTERING
               ☎ 01536 416666 119 ⇆ 🐾

NORTHAMPTON   Map 04 SP76

Brampton Heath Sandy Ln, Church Brampton NN6 8AX
☎ 01604 843939 Fax 01604 843885
e-mail: slawrence@bhgc.co.uk
Appealing to both the novice and experienced golfer, this
beautiful, well drained heathland course affords panoramic
views over Northampton.
18 holes, 6366yds, Par 71, SSS 70, Course record 67.
Club membership 500.
Visitors   advisable to book especially for weekends, may
               book up to 8 days in advance.
Societies   write or telephone for details.
Green Fees £13 per 18 holes; £7.80 per 9 holes (£17/£10.20
               weekends & bank holidays).
Cards   💳 💳 💳 💳 💳
Prof   Richard Hudson
Designer   D Snell
Facilities ⊗ 🎿 ⅃ 🍺 ⅄ 🏖 🍴 🏌 🛥 ♨ ⚒ ⚑
Location   Signposted off old A50 Kingsthorpe to Welford
               road, 2m N of Kingsthorpe

Hotel   ★★★ 69% Lime Trees Hotel, 8 Langham
               Place, Barrack Rd, NORTHAMPTON
               ☎ 01604 632188 27 ⇆ 🐾

Delapre Golf Complex Eagle Dr, Nene Valley Way
NN4 7DU ☎ 01604 764036 Fax 01604 706378
e-mail: ruth@delapre.northampton.gov.uk
Rolling parkland course, part of municipal golf complex,
which includes two 9-hole, par 3 courses, pitch-and-putt and
40 bay floodlit driving-range.
*Main Course: 18 holes, 6269yds, Par 70, SSS 70,
Course record 66.*
Hardingstone Course: 9 holes, 2109yds, Par 32, SSS 32.
Club membership 900.
Visitors   no restrictions but advance booking advised for
               weekends.
Societies   must book and pay full green fees 2 weeks in
               advance.
Green Fees £10 per 18 holes; £7 per 9 holes (£14/£9
               weekends).
Cards   💳 💳 💳 💳 💳
Prof   John Corby
Designer   John Jacobs/John Corby
Facilities ⊗ 🎿 ⅃ 🍺 ⅄ 🏖 🍴 🏌 ⚒ ⚑
Location   2m SE

Hotel   ★★★ 64% Quality Hotel Northampton,
               Ashley Way, Weston Favell,
               NORTHAMPTON ☎ 01604 739955
               31 ⇆ 🐾 Annexe35 ⇆ 🐾

> Entries with a green background
> identify courses considered to be
> particularly interesting

Kingsthorpe Kingsley Rd NN2 7BU
☎ 01604 710610 Fax 01604 710610
A compact, undulating parkland course set within the town
boundary. Not a long course but the undulating terrain
provides a suitable challenge for golfers of all standards.
Whilst not a hilly course, the valley that runs through it
ensures plenty of sloping lies. The 18th hole is claimed to be
the longest 400yds in the county when played into wind and
is amongst the finest finishing holes in the area.
18 holes, 5918yds, Par 69, SSS 69, Course record 63.
Club membership 600.
Visitors   must contact in advance and have handicap
certificate. With member only weekends.
Societies   must contact in advance.
Green Fees £25 per day.
Prof   Paul Armstrong
Designer   Mr Alison
Facilities   ⊗ ⅧⅢ ⅃ ♥ ♀ ♨ 🏠 ⌑
Location   N side of town centre on A5095 between the
Racecourse and Kingsthorpe

Hotel   ★★★ 64% Quality Hotel Northampton, Ashley
Way, Weston Favell, NORTHAMPTON
☎ 01604 739955   31 ⇄ 🎇 Annexe35 ⇄ 🎇

Northampton Harlestone NN7 4EF
☎ 01604 845155 Fax 01604 820262
Parkland course with water in play on three holes.
18 holes, 6615yds, Par 72, SSS 72, Course record 67.
Club membership 750.
Visitors   must contact in advance and have handicap
certificate. With member only at weekends, no
visitors on Wed.
Societies   must contact in advance.
Green Fees not confirmed.
Cards   🖭 ▆▆ 🖚 🖾 🎇 ⌑
Prof   Kevin Dickens
Designer   Sinclair Steel
Facilities   ⊗ ⅧⅢ ⅃ ♥ ♀ ♨ 🏠 ⌑
Location   NW of town centre on A428

Hotel   ★★★ 69% Lime Trees Hotel, 8 Langham
Place, Barrack Rd, NORTHAMPTON
☎ 01604 632188   27 ⇄ 🎇

Northamptonshire County Golf Ln, Church Brampton
NN6 8AZ   ☎ 01604 843025 Fax 01604 843463
A fine, traditional championship golf course situated on
undulating heathland with areas of gorse, heather and
extensive coniferous and deciduous woodland. A river and a
railway line pass through the course.
18 holes, 6505yds, Par 70, SSS 72, Course record 65.
Club membership 750.
Visitors   restricted weekends. May not play on bank
holidays. Must contact in advance and have a
handicap certificate.
Societies   Wed/Thu only, must contact in advance.
Green Fees £45 per day.
Prof   Tim Rouse
Designer   H S Colt
Facilities   ⊗ ⅧⅢ ⅃ ♥ ♀ ♨ 🏠 ⌑ 🥪 ⌑ ℓ
Location   5m NW of Northampton, off A5199

Hotel   ★★★ 64% Quality Hotel Northampton, Ashley
Way, Weston Favell, NORTHAMPTON
☎ 01604 739955   31 ⇄ 🎇 Annexe35 ⇄ 🎇

Overstone Park Billing Ln NN6 0AP
☎ 01604 647666 Fax 01604 642635
e-mail: steph@overstonepark.co.uk
A testing parkland course, gently undulating within
panoramic views of local stately home. Excellent drainage
and fine greens make the course great all year round. Water
comes into play on three holes.
18 holes, 6602yds, Par 72, SSS 72, Course record 69.
Club membership 500.
Visitors   contact in advance, only after 2pm at weekends.
Societies   write or telephone.
Green Fees not confirmed.
Cards   🖭 ▆▆ 🖚 🎇 ⌑
Prof   Brain Mudge
Designer   Donald Steel
Facilities   ⊗ ⅧⅢ ⅃ ♥ ♀ ♨ 🏠 🥪 🥢 ⌑
& Leisure   hard tennis courts, heated indoor swimming
pool, fishing, sauna, solarium, gymnasium.
Location   Exit M1 junct15, follow A45 to Billing
Aquadrone turn off, course is 2m on Gt Billing
Way

Hotel   ★★★ 69% Lime Trees Hotel, 8 Langham
Place, Barrack Rd, NORTHAMPTON
☎ 01604 632188   27 ⇄ 🎇

OUNDLE   Map 04 TL08

Oundle Benefield Rd PE8 4EZ
☎ 01832 273267 (Gen Manager) Fax 01832 273267
e-mail: office@oundlegolfclub.fsnet.co.uk
Undulating parkland course, shortish but difficult. A small
brook affects some of the approaches to the greens.
18 holes, 6235yds, Par 72, SSS 70, Course record 68.
Club membership 600.
Visitors   may not play Tue (Ladies Day) or before
10.30am weekends unless with member.
Societies   must apply in advance.
Green Fees £25.50 (£35.50 weekends).
Prof   Richard Keys
Facilities   ⊗ ⅧⅢ ⅃ ♥ ♀ ♨ 🏠 🥪 ⌑
Location   1m W on A427

Hotel   ★★★ 67% The Talbot, New St, OUNDLE
☎ 01832 273621   39 ⇄ 🎇

STAVERTON   Map 04 SP56

Staverton Park Staverton Park NN11 6JT
☎ 01327 302000
18 holes, 6661yds, Par 71, SSS 72, Course record 65.
Location   0.75m NE of Staverton on A425
Telephone for further details

Hotel   ★★★★ 62% Hanover International Hotel &
Club, Sedgemoor Way, DAVENTRY
☎ 01327 307000 138 ⇄ 🎇

WELLINGBOROUGH   Map 04 SP86

Rushden Kimbolton Rd, Chelveston NN9 6AN
☎ 01933 418511
Parkland course with brook running through the middle.
10 holes, 6335yds, Par 71, SSS 70, Course record 68.
Club membership 400.

▶

Visitors may not play Wed afternoon. With member only weekends.
Societies must apply in writing.
Green Fees not confirmed.
Facilities ⊗ 〗 🝙 ♣ ♀ ⅄
Location 2m E of Higham Ferrers on Kimbolton Rd

Hotel ★★★ 65% Menzies Hind Hotel, Sheep St, WELLINGBOROUGH
☎ 0870 6003013 34 ⇆ ╠

Wellingborough Great Harrowden Hall NN9 5AD
☎ 01933 677234 Fax 01933 679379
An undulating parkland course with many trees. The 514-yd, 14th is a testing hole. The clubhouse is a stately home.
18 holes, 6617yds, Par 72, SSS 72, Course record 68.
Club membership 820.
Visitors may not play at weekends & bank holidays or Tue between 10am and 2.30pm.
Societies must apply in writing.
Green Fees £40 per day; £30 per round.
Prof David Clifford
Designer Hawtree
Facilities ⊗ 〗 🝙 ♣ ♀ ⅄ 🏠 ⟍ 🏌 ⚌
& Leisure outdoor swimming pool.
Location 2m N on A509

Hotel ★★★ 65% Menzies Hind Hotel, Sheep St, WELLINGBOROUGH
☎ 0870 6003013 34 ⇆ ╠

WHITTLEBURY Map 04 SP64

Whittlebury Park Golf & Country Club NN12 8XW
☎ 01327 858092 Fax 01327 858009
The 36 holes incorporate three loops of tournament-standard nines plus a short course. The 1905 Course is a reconstruction of the original parkland course built at the turn of the century, the Royal Whittlewood is a lakeland course playing around copses and the Grand Prix, next to Silverstone Motor Racing circuit has a strong links feel playing over gently undulating grassland with challenging lake features.
Grand Prix: 9 holes, 3339yds, Par 36, SSS 36.
Royal Whittlewood: 9 holes, 3323yds, Par 36, SSS 36.
1905: 9 holes, 3256yds, Par 36, SSS 36.
Club membership 400.
Visitors must contact in advance.
Societies telephone 01327 858092 in advance.
Green Fees not confirmed.
Designer Cameron Sinclair
Facilities ⊗ 🝙 ♣ ♀ ⅄ 🏠 🏌 ⟍ ⚌ 🏌 ⟍
Location A413 Buckingham Road

Hotel ★★★ 65% Buckingham Four Pillars Hotel, Buckingham Ring Rd South, BUCKINGHAM
☎ 01280 822622 70 ⇆ ╠

AA Hotels that have special arrangements with golf courses are listed at the back of the guide

---

NORTHUMBERLAND

ALLENDALE Map 12 NY85

Allendale High Studdon, Allenheads Rd NE47 9DH
☎ 01434 683926 & 682809 Fax 01434 683668
e-mail: pmason@aol.com
Challenging and hilly parkland course set 1000 feet above sea level with superb views of Allendale. New club house.
18 holes, 4541yds, Par 66, SSS 62, Course record 69.
Club membership 270.
Visitors may not play Aug bank holiday until after 3pm.
Societies must apply in writing to Secretary.
Green Fees not confirmed.
Facilities 🝙 ♣ ♀ ⅄
Location 1.5m S on B6295

Hotel ★★★ 68% Beaumont Hotel, Beaumont St, HEXHAM ☎ 01434 602331 25 ⇆ ╠

ALNMOUTH Map 12 NU21

Alnmouth Foxton Hall NE66 3BE
☎ 01665 830231 Fax 01665 830922
e-mail: alnmouthgolfclub.com
Coastal course with pleasant views.
18 holes, 6429yds, Par 69, SSS 69, Course record 64.
Club membership 800.
Visitors Fri, weekends & bank holidays. Must contact in advance.
Societies Mon-Thu only..
Green Fees £30 per day.
Cards ▨▨ ▨▨ ▨▨ ▨ ▨
Prof Linzi Hardy
Designer H S Colt
Facilities ⊗ 🝙 by prior arrangement 🝙 ♣ ♀ ⅄ 🏠 🏌 🏠 ⟍ ⚌ ⚌ 🏌
& Leisure snooker room.
Location 1m NE. 4m E of Alnwick

Hotel ★★★ 60% White Swan Hotel, Bondgate Within, ALNWICK
☎ 01665 602109 58 ⇆ ╠

Alnmouth Village Marine Rd NE66 2RZ ☎ 01665 830370
Fax 01665 602096 e-mail: bill@billmaclean.fsnet.co.uk
Seaside course with part coastal view.
9 holes, 6090yds, Par 70, SSS 70, Course record 63.
Club membership 480.
Visitors may not play before 11am on competition days.
Societies must contact in advance.
Green Fees £15 (£20 weekends & bank holidays).
Facilities ⅄
Location E side of village

Hotel ★★★ 60% White Swan Hotel, Bondgate Within, ALNWICK
☎ 01665 602109 58 ⇆ ╠

ALNWICK Map 12 NU11

Alnwick Swansfield Park NE66 1AT ☎ 01665 602632
Parkland course offering a fair test of golfing skills.
18 holes, 6284yds, Par 70, SSS 70, Course record 66.
Club membership 500.

Visitors	some restrictions on competition days.
Societies	must contact secretary in advance.
Green Fees	£25 per day; £20 per round (£25 per round/day weekends & bank holidays).
Designer	Rochester
Facilities	⊗ ⊞ ⅃ ▮ ⚑ ♀ ♨ ⚘
Location	S side of town

| Hotel | ★★★ 60% White Swan Hotel, Bondgate Within, ALNWICK ☎ 01665 602109 58 ⇄ ⚑ |

BAMBURGH　　　　　　　　　　Map 12 NU13

Bamburgh Castle The Club House, 40 The Wynding NE69 7DE ☎ 01668 214378 (club) & 214321 (sec) Fax 01668 214607
e-mail: bamburghcastlegolfclub@hotmail.com
Superb coastal course with excellent greens that are both fast and true, natural hazards of heather and whin bushes abound. Magnificent views of Farne Islands, Holy Island, Lindisfarne Castle, Bamburgh Castle and Cheviot Hils.
18 holes, 5621yds, Par 68, SSS 67, Course record 64.
Club membership 785.

Visitors	must contact in advance. Restricted weekends, bank holidays and competition days.
Societies	apply in writing. Weekdays & Sun only.
Green Fees	summer £30 per day; £25 per round (£35/£30 weekends & bank holidays). Reduced rates winter.
Cards	🖾 🖭 🖭 📇 🖵
Designer	George Rochester
Facilities	⊗ ⊞ ⅃ ▮ ⚑ ♀ ♨ ⚘ ♨ ⚘
Location	6m E of A1 via B1341 or B1342

| Hotel | ★★ 66% Lord Crewe Arms, Front St, BAMBURGH ☎ 01668 214243 18rm(17 ⇄ ⚑) |

BEDLINGTON　　　　　　　　　Map 12 NZ28

Bedlingtonshire Acorn Bank NE22 6AA
☎ 01670 822457 822087
Meadowland/parkland course with easy walking. Under certain conditions the wind can be a distinct hazard.
18 holes, 6813yards, Par 73, SSS 73, Course record 64.
Club membership 770.

Visitors	may not play before 9.30am weekdays or before 10.30am weekends and bank holidays.
Societies	contact the professional in writing or telephone.
Green Fees	not confirmed.
Prof	Marcus Webb
Designer	Frank Pennink
Facilities	⊗ ⊞ by prior arrangement ⅃ ▮ ⚑ ♀ ⚘
Location	1m SW on A1068

| Hotel | ★★★★ 63% Holiday Inn, Great North Rd, SEATON BURN ☎ 0191 201 9988 150 ⇄ ⚑ |

Where to stay, where to eat?
Visit the AA internet site
www.theAA.com

BELFORD　　　　　　　　　　　Map 12 NU13

Belford South Rd NE70 7DP
☎ 01668 213433 Fax 01668 213919
An east coast parkland course. Crosswinds affect the 4th but the compensation is spectacular views over Holy Island.
9 holes, 3152yds, Par 72, SSS 70, Course record 72.
Club membership 200.

Visitors	not before 10am Sun.
Societies	must contact in advance.
Green Fees	£17 per day; £14 per 18 holes; £10 per 9 holes (£22/£17/£11 weekends & bank holidays).
Designer	Nigel Williams
Facilities	⊗ ⊞ ⅃ ▮ ⚑ ♀ ♨ ⚘ ⚑ ⚘ ⚘
Location	Just off A1, midway between Alnwick & Berwick on Tweed

| Hotel | ★★★ 69% Blue Bell Hotel, Market Place, BELFORD ☎ 01668 213543 17 ⇄ ⚑ |

BELLINGHAM　　　　　　　　　Map 12 NY88

Bellingham Boggle Hole NE48 2DT
☎ 01434 220530 (Secretary) Fax 01434 220160
e-mail: secretary_bellinghamgc@hotmail.com
This highly regarded 18-hole golf course is situated between Hadrian's Wall and the Scottish Border. A rolling parkland course with many natural hazards. There is a mixture of testing par threes, long par fives and tricky par fours.
18 holes, 6093yds, Par 70, SSS 70, Course record 70.
Club membership 550.

Visitors	welcome all week, advisable to contact in advance as starting sheet in operation.
Societies	must contact in advance.
Green Fees	£20 per day/round (£25 per day/round weekends).
Designer	E Johnson/I Wilson
Facilities	⊗ by prior arrangement ⊞ by prior arrangement ⅃ ▮ ⚑ ♀ ♨ ⚘ ⚘ ⚘
Location	N side of village on B6320

| Hotel | ★★ 67% Riverdale Hall Hotel, BELLINGHAM ☎ 01434 220254 20 ⇄ ⚑ |

BERWICK-UPON-TWEED　　　　Map 12 NT95

Berwick-upon-Tweed (Goswick) Goswick TD15 2RW
☎ 01289 387256 Fax 01289 387334
e-mail: goswickgc@btconnect.com
Natural seaside links course, with undulating fairways, elevated tees and good greens.
18 holes, 6465yds, Par 72, SSS 71, Course record 69.
Club membership 600.

Visitors	must contact in advance for weekends, advisable at other times.
Societies	must telephone in advance (apply in writing Apr-Sep).
Green Fees	£30 per day; £25 per round (£30/£40 weekends).
Cards	🖾 🖭 🖭 📇 🖵
Prof	Paul Terras
Designer	James Braid
Facilities	⊗ ⊞ ⅃ ▮ ⚑ ♀ ♨ ⚘ ⚑ ⚘ ⚘ ⚘
Location	6m S off A1

▶

Visitors are welcomed at

Berwick-upon-Tweed (Goswick) Golf Club

Signposted off the A1, south of Berwick, only 10 minutes from the centre.
The club is open all year to non-members
Anytime weekdays. Bookings weekends. Bar. Service/Catering. Residents Pro
Secretary Mr D. Wilkinson (01289) 387256　　　Email: goswickgc@btconnect.com
Membership available　　　　　　　　　　　　www.goswicklinksgc.co.uk
Paul Terras, Goswick Golf Club Pro Shop
Golf Club Repairs ★ Tuition ★ Sales Tel: 01289 387380

Hotel　★★★ 69%　Blue Bell Hotel, Market Place,
BELFORD ☎ 01668 213543　17 ⇄ ʀ

Magdalene Fields Magdalene Fields TD15 1NE
☎ 01289 306384 & 306130 Fax 01289 306384
e-mail: mfgc@firefly.club24.co.uk
Seaside course with natural hazards formed by sea bays. All
holes open to winds. Testing 8th hole over bay (par 3).
18 holes, 6407yds, Par 72, SSS 71, Course record 65.
Club membership 400.
Visitors　must contact in advance for weekend play.
Societies　must contact in advance.
Green Fees £17 per round (£19 weekends).
Designer　Willie Park
Facilities　⊗ 〉Ⅲ ↳ ♨ ♀ ♬ 🏌 ♣ ⌀
Location　0.5m on E side of town centre

Hotel　★★★♨♨ 71% Tillmouth Park Country House
Hotel, CORNHILL-ON-TWEED
☎ 01890 882255　12 ⇄ ʀ Annexe2 ⇄ ʀ

BLYTH　　　　　　　　　　　　　　　Map 12 NZ38

Blyth New Delaval, Newsham NE24 4DB
☎ 01670 540110 (sec) & 356514 (pro)
Fax 01670 540134 e-mail: blythgc@lineone.net
Course built over old colliery. Parkland with water hazards.
18 holes, 6456yds, Par 72, SSS 71, Course record 65.
Club membership 860.
Visitors　with member only after 3pm & at weekends
before 3pm. Must contact in advance.
Societies　apply in writing/telephone.
Green Fees £24 per day; £19 per round (£25 per round
weekends).
Prof　　Andrew Brown
Designer　Hamilton Stutt
Facilities　⊗ ↳ ♨ ♀ ♬ ♣ ⌀
Location　6m N of Whitley Bay

Hotel　★★★ 65% Windsor Hotel, South Pde,
WHITLEY BAY ☎ 0191 251 8888 70 ⇄ ʀ

CRAMLINGTON　　　　　　　　　　Map 12 NZ27

Arcot Hall NE23 7QP
☎ 0191 236 2794 Fax 0191 217 0370
A wooded parkland course, reasonably flat.
18 holes, 6380yds, Par 70, SSS 70, Course record 65.
Club membership 695.
Visitors　must contact in advance. May not play
weekends.　　　　　　　　　　*continued*

Societies　must contact in advance.
Green Fees £26 per day (£30 weekends).
Prof　　John Metcalfe
Designer　James Braid
Facilities　⊗ 〉Ⅲ ↳ ♨ ♀ ♬ ♣ 🏌 ⌀
Location　2m SW off A1

Hotel　★★★★ 63% Holiday Inn, Great North Rd,
SEATON BURN ☎ 0191 201 9988 150 ⇄ ʀ

EMBLETON　　　　　　　　　　　　Map 12 NU22

Dunstanburgh Castle NE66 3XQ
☎ 01665 576562 Fax 01665 576562
e-mail: enquiries@dunstanburgh.com
Rolling links designed by James Braid, adjacent to the
beautiful Embleton Bay. Historic Dunstansburgh Castle is at
one end of the course and a National Trust lake and bird
sanctuary at the other. Superb views.
18 holes, 6298yds, Par 70, SSS 69, Course record 69.
Club membership 385.
Visitors　advisable to contact in advance at weekends and
holiday periods.
Societies　must contact in advance.
Green Fees £16 per day (£26 per day; £20 per round
weekends).
Designer　James Braid
Facilities　⊗ 〉Ⅲ ↳ ♨ ♀ ♬ ♣ 🏌 ⌀
Location　7m NE of Alnwick off A1

Hotel　★★ 70% Dunstanburgh Castle Hotel,
EMBLETON ☎ 01665 576111　17 ⇄ ʀ

GREENHEAD　　　　　　　　　　　Map 12 NY66

Haltwhistle Walend Farm CA6 7HN
☎ 016977 47367 & 01434 344000 (sec) Fax 01434 344311
Interesting course with panoramic views of Northumberland
National Park. The 515yard Par 5 14th hole is a real test of
golf skill, played from the highest point of the course through
an undulating fairway to a viciously sloping green. The
188yard Par 3 now the 1st hole, played uphill, is particularly
difficult playing into the prevailing west wind.
18 holes, 5522yds, Par 69, SSS 67, Course record 70.
Club membership 391.
Visitors　no visitors Sun mornings.
Societies　apply in writing to: Hon Secretary, John
Gilbertson, Parkhead Farmhouse, Bardon Mill,
Northumberland NE47 7JS.
Green Fees £12 per day (£15 weekends).
Facilities　⊗ 〉Ⅲ ↳ ♨ ♀ ♬
Location　N on A69 past Haltwhistle on Gilsland Road

Hotel   ★★★🏅 Farlam Hall Hotel, Hallbankgate,
BRAMPTON ☎ 016977 46234
11 ⇄ ʰ Annexe1 ⇄ ʰ

HEXHAM   Map 12 NY96

De Vere Slaley Hall, Golf Resort & Spa Slaley NE47 0BY
☎ 01434 673154 Fax 01434 673152
e-mail: slaley.hall@devere-hotels.com
Measuring 7073yds from the championship tees, this Dave
Thomas designed course incorporates forest, parkland and
moorland with an abundance of lakes and streams. The
challenging par 4 9th (452yds) is played over water through a
narrow avenue of towering trees and dense rhododendrons.
An official PGA European Tour venue and hosts the
COMPAQ European Grand Prix. The Priestman course
designed by PGA Chairman, Neil Coles of equal length
and standard as the Hunting course. Opened in spring 1999
the Priestman is situated in 280 acres on the western side of
the estate, giving panoramic views over the Tyne Valley.
*Hunting Course: 18 holes, 7073yds, Par 72, SSS 74, Course
record 65.*
*Priestman Course: 18 holes, 7010yds, Par 72, SSS 72,
Course record 67.*
Club membership 350.
Visitors   must contact in advance, times subject to
availability.
Societies   apply in writing to bookings co-ordinator, small
groups 8 or less may book by telephone.
Green Fees Hunting Course: £60 per round; Priestman
Course: £40 per round.
Cards   ⊞ ▬ 🏧 💳 📠 🔳 🗔
Prof   Gordon Robinson
Designer   Dave Thomas/Neil Coles
Facilities   ⊗ ⋔ ᴸᵇ 🝙 ♀ ⚒ 🏠 ⚴ 🏹 ➤ ⚓ ✐ ⚑
& Leisure   heated indoor swimming pool, fishing, sauna,
solarium, gymnasium.
Location   8m S of Hexham off A68

Hotel   ★★★★ 71% De Vere Slaley Hall, Slaley,
HEXHAM ☎ 01434 673350 139 ⇄ ʰ

Hexham Spital Park NE46 3RZ
☎ 01434 603072 Fax 01434 601865
e-mail: hexham.golf.club@talk21.com
A very pretty well drained parkland course with
interesting natural contours. Exquisite views from parts
of the course, of the Tyne valley below. As good a
parkland course as any in the North of England.
18 holes, 6000yds, Par 70, SSS 68, Course record 64.
Club membership 700.
Visitors   advance booking advisable.
Societies   welcome weekdays, contact in advance.
Green Fees £40 per day; £30 per round (£40 per round
weekends).
Cards   ⊞ ▬ 🏧 💳 🔳 🗔
Prof   Martin Forster
Designer   Vardon/Caird
Facilities   ⊗ ⋔ ᴸᵇ 🝙 ♀ ⚴ 🏠 ⚒ 🏹 ✐
& Leisure   squash.
Location   1m NW on B6531

Hotel   ★★★ 68% Beaumont Hotel, Beaumont St,
HEXHAM ☎ 01434 602331 25 ⇄ ʰ

THE BEAUMONT HOTEL,
Hexham, Northumberland
NE46 3LT
Tel: (01434) 602331
Email: Beaumont.hotel@btinternet.com
www.beaumont-hotel.co.uk
The perfect base for 3 of the North East's finest
Golf Courses: Slaley, Hexham
& Matfen Hall.
25 Bedrooms, with full facilities, excellent food
and choice of bars make a wonderful 'Golfing
Hotel'. Special Golf Rates on Request

AA ★★★   Best Western

LONGHORSLEY   Map 12 NZ19

Linden Hall NE65 8XF
☎ 01670 500011 Fax 01670 500001
e-mail: golf@lindenhall.co.uk
Set within the picturesque Linden Hall Estate, with views of
the Cheviot Hills and the Northumberland coast, this newly
established course features mature woodland and several
burns and lakes.
18 holes, 6846yds, Par 72, SSS 73.
Club membership 240.
Visitors   must book in advance.
Societies   must be of reasonable standard of play, observe
dress code & etiquette, preferably have handicap
certificate.
Green Fees £33 per day; £20 per 18 holes (£40/£25
weekends).
Cards   ⊞ ▬ 🏧 💳 🔳 🗔
Prof   David Curry
Designer   Jonathan Gaunt
Facilities   ⊗ ⋔ ᴸᵇ 🝙 ♀ ⚴ 🏠 ⚒ 🏹 ➤ ⚓ ✐ ⚑
& Leisure   hard tennis courts, heated indoor swimming
pool, sauna, solarium, gymnasium.
Location   From A1 N/S take A697 to Coldstream, approx
4m to Longhorsley, Linden Hall 0.5m past
village

Hotel   ★★★ 70% Linden Hall Hotel, Health Spa &
Golf Course, LONGHORSLEY
☎ 01670 500000 50 ⇄ ʰ

MATFEN Map 12 NZ07

Matfen Hall NE20 0RH
☎ 01661 886400 (bookings) Fax 01661 886055
e-mail: david@matfenhall.com
An 18-hole parkland course set in beautiful countryside with many natural and man-made hazards. Also a challenging 9-hole par 3 course and a driving range.
18 holes, 6516yds, Par 72, SSS 71, Course record 67.
Club membership 500.
Visitors contact in advance, restricted on weekends between 8-10am.
Societies telephone for details.
Green Fees £35 per day; £25 per round (£40/£30 weekends).
Cards 🔲 ■ ■ 🔲 🔲 🔲
Prof John Harrison
Facilities ⊗ ⅷ ⅃ ⅃ 🖤 ♀ ♨ 🍽 ↘ 🚜 ♂ ☍
Location Just off B6318 Military road 15m W of Newcastle

Hotel ★★ 66% Angel Inn, Main St, CORBRIDGE
☎ 01434 632119 5 ⇄ 🐾

MORPETH Map 12 NZ28

Morpeth The Clubhouse NE61 2BT
☎ 01670 504942 Fax 01670 504918
Parkland course with views of the Cheviots. Venue for 2000 County Match Play Championship.
18 holes, 6206yds, Par 71, SSS 69, Course record 65.
Club membership 700.
Visitors restricted weekends & bank holidays. Must contact in advance and have a handicap certificate.
Societies apply in writing.
Green Fees not confirmed.
Prof Martin Jackson
Designer Harry Vardon
Facilities ⊗ ⅷ ⅃ ⅃ 🖤 ♀ ♨ 🍽 ↘ ♂
Location S side of town centre on A197

Hotel ★★★ 70% Linden Hall Hotel, Health Spa & Golf Course, LONGHORSLEY
☎ 01670 500000 50 ⇄ 🐾

NEWBIGGIN-BY-THE-SEA Map 12 NZ38

Newbiggin-by-the-Sea Prospect Place NE64 6DW
☎ 01670 817344 Fax 01670 520236
Seaside-links course.
18 holes, 6452yds, Par 72, SSS 71, Course record 65.
Club membership 620.
Visitors must contact professional on arrival and may not play before 10am.
Societies must apply in writing.
Green Fees £16 per day (£22 weekends and bank holidays).
Prof Marcus Webb
Facilities ⊗ ⅷ ⅃ ⅃ 🖤 ♀ ♨ 🍽 ↘ 🚜 ♂
& Leisure snooker.
Location N side of town

Hotel ★★★ 70% Linden Hall Hotel, Health Spa & Golf Course, LONGHORSLEY
☎ 01670 500000 50 ⇄ 🐾

PONTELAND Map 12 NZ17

Ponteland 53 Bell Villas NE20 9BD
☎ 01661 822689 Fax 01661 860077
Open parkland course offering testing golf and good views.
18 holes, 6524yds, Par 72, SSS 71, Course record 66.
Club membership 720.
Visitors with member only Fri, weekends & bank holidays.
Societies welcome Tue & Thu only. Must contact in advance.
Green Fees not confirmed.
Cards 🔲
Prof Alan Robson-Crosby
Designer Harry Fernie
Facilities ⊗ ⅷ ⅃ ⅃ 🖤 ♀ ♨ 🍽 ♂
Location 0.5m E on A696

Hotel ★★★ 66% Novotel Newcastle upon Tyne, Ponteland Rd, Kenton, NEWCASTLE UPON TYNE
☎ 0191 214 0303 126 ⇄ 🐾

PRUDHOE Map 12 NZ06

Prudhoe Eastwood Park NE42 5DX
☎ 01661 832466 Fax 01661 830710
Parkland course with natural hazards and easy walking along undulating fairways.
18 holes, 5812yds, Par 69, SSS 69, Course record 60.
Club membership 700.
Visitors must contact in advance. Weekends after 4.30pm
Societies must contact in writing.
Green Fees £20 (£25 weekends).
Prof John Crawford
Facilities ⊗ ⅷ ⅃ ⅃ 🖤 ♀ ♨ 🍽
Location E side of town centre off A695

Hotel ★★★ 69% Gibside Arms Hotel, Front St, WHICKHAM
☎ 0191 488 9292 45 ⇄ 🐾

ROTHBURY Map 12 NU00

Rothbury Old Race Course NE65 7TR
☎ 01669 620718 & 621271
Very flat parkland course alongside the River Coquet.
9 holes, 5681yds, Par 68, SSS 67, Course record 65.
Club membership 320.
Visitors weekends by arrangement only.
Societies must contact secretary in advance.
Green Fees £11 per day (£16 weekends & bank holidays).
Designer J Radcliffe
Facilities ⅃ 🖤 ♀ ♨
Location SW side of town off B6342

Hotel ★★★ 60% White Swan Hotel, Bondgate Within, ALNWICK
☎ 01665 602109 58 ⇄ 🐾

> Entries with a green background
> identify courses considered to be
> particularly interesting

SEAHOUSES   Map 12 NU23

Seahouses Beadnell Rd NE68 7XT
☎ 01665 720794 Fax 01665 721994
Typical links course with many hazards, including the
famous 10th, 'Logans Loch', water hole.
18 holes, 5516yds, Par 67, SSS 67, Course record 63.
Club membership 750.
Visitors   must contact in advance.
Societies   must contact in advance. May not play Sun.
Green Fees £18 per day (£25 weekends & bank holidays).
Facilities   ⊗ ⫿ ⅊ ♨ ⅊ ♧ ∂
Location   S side of village on B1340

Hotel   ★★ 69% Bamburgh Castle Hotel,
SEAHOUSES ☎ 01665 720283   20 ⇌ ♞

STOCKSFIELD   Map 12 NZ06

Stocksfield New Ridley Rd NE43 7RE
☎ 01661 843041 Fax 01661 843046
e-mail: info@sgcgolf.co.uk
Challenging course: parkland (9 holes), woodland (9 holes).
Some elevated greens and water hazards.
18 holes, 5978yds, Par 70, SSS 70, Course record 63.
Club membership 550.
Visitors   welcome except Wed am & Sat until 4pm,
          unless accompanied by a member.
Societies   must contact in advance.
Green Fees £30 per day; £25 per round (£30 weekends &
          bank holidays).
Prof   David Mather
Designer   Pennick
Facilities   ⊗ ⫿ by prior arrangement ⅊ ♨ ⅊ ♧ ⌂ ⚐ ∂
& Leisure   snooker.
Location   Hexham to Newcastle A695,1.5malong New
          Ridley Rd at Esso Station

Hotel   ★★★ 68% Beaumont Hotel, Beaumont St,
HEXHAM ☎ 01434 602331   25 ⇌ ♞

SWARLAND   Map 12 NU10

Swarland Hall Coast View NE65 9JG
☎ 01670 787010
Parkland course set in mature woodland. There are seven Par
4 holes in excess of 400 yards.
18 holes, 6628yds, Par 72, SSS 72.
Club membership 400.
Visitors   restricted on competition days. Advisable to
          contact in advance.
Societies   apply in advance.
Green Fees not confirmed.
Cards   ▦ ▬ ▣ ▨ ▰ ▨
Prof   Graham cant
Facilities   ⊗ ⫿ ⅊ ♨ ⅊ ♧ ⌂ ⚐ ♥ ⚒ ∂
Location   Approx 1m W of A1

Hotel   ★★★ 70% Linden Hall Hotel, Health Spa &
Golf Course, LONGHORSLEY
☎ 01670 500000   50 ⇌ ♞

Looking for a driving range?
See the index at the back of the guide

WARKWORTH   Map 12 NU20

Warkworth The Links NE65 0SW ☎ 01665 711596
Seaside links course, with good views and alternative tees for
the back nine.
9 holes, 5870yds, Par 70, SSS 68, Course record 66.
Club membership 470.
Visitors   welcome except Tue & Sat.
Societies   must contact in advance.
Green Fees £12 per day (£20 Sun & bank holidays).
Designer   T Morris
Facilities   ⊗ ⅊ ♨ ⅊ ♨
Location   0.5m E of village off A1068

Hotel   ★★★ 60% White Swan Hotel, Bondgate
Within, ALNWICK
☎ 01665 602109   58 ⇌ ♞

WOOLER   Map 12 NT92

Wooler Dod Law, Doddington NE71 6EA
☎ 01668 282135
Hilltop, moorland course with spectacular views over the
Glendale valley. Nine greens played from 18 tees. A very
challenging course when windy with one Par 5 of 580 yards.
The course is much under used during the week so is always
available.
9 holes, 6358yds, Par 72, SSS 70, Course record 71.
Club membership 300.
Visitors   normally no restrictions.
Societies   by prior arrangement with secretary.
Green Fees £10 per day(£15 weekends).
Facilities   ⊗ by prior arrangement ⫿ by prior arrangement
          ⅊ by prior arrangement ♨ ⅊ ♧ ♥ ⚒ ∂
Location   At Doddington on B6525 Wooler/Berwick Rd

Hotel   ★★★ 69% Blue Bell Hotel, Market Place,
BELFORD ☎ 01668 213543   17 ⇌ ♞

NOTTINGHAMSHIRE

CALVERTON   Map 08 SK64

Ramsdale Park Golf Centre Oxton Rd NG14 6NU
☎ 0115 965 5600 Fax 0115 965 4105
The High course is a challenging and comprehensive test for
any standard of golf. A relatively flat front nine is followed
by an undulating back nine that is renowned as one of the
best 9 holes of golf in the county. The Low course is an 18
hole Par 3 course gaining a reputation as one of the best in
the country. Hole lengths vary from 100 to 207yds.
*High Course: 18 holes, 6546yds, Par 71, SSS 71, Course
record 70.*
Low Course: 18 holes, 2844yds, Par 54, SSS 54.
Club membership 400.
Visitors   may book up to 7 days in advance.
Societies   welcome midweek, apply in writing or
          telephone.
Green Fees High Course: £15 (weekends £18.50. Low
Course: £8 (weekends £8.70).
Cards   ▦ ▬ ▰ ▨
Prof   Robert Macey   ▶

Designer   Hawtree
Facilities   ⊗ ⨎ 🛏 ♨ ♀ ⚲ 🏠 ⚐ 🍴 ❧ ⚘ 🛇 ⚑
Location   8m NE of Nottingham, off B6386

Hotel   ★★★ 66% Westminster Hotel, 312 Mansfield Rd, Carrington, NOTTINGHAM ☎ 0115 955 5000 72 ⇆ 🏕

Springwater Moor Ln NG14 6FZ ☎ 0115 965 2129
18 holes, 6224yds, Par 71, SSS 70.
Location   300yds on the left from the turning to Calverton off A6097
Telephone for further details

Hotel   ★★★ 66% Westminster Hotel, 312 Mansfield Rd, Carrington, NOTTINGHAM ☎ 0115 955 5000 72 ⇆ 🏕

EAST LEAKE   Map 08 SK52

Rushcliffe Stocking Ln LE12 5RL
☎ 01509 852959 Fax 01509 852688
e-mail: rushcliffegc@netscapeonline.co.uk
Hilly, tree-lined and picturesque parkland course.
18 holes, 6013yds, Par 70, SSS 69, Course record 63.
Club membership 700.
Visitors   welcome but may not play Tue and restricted weekends & bank holidays 9.30-11am & 3-4.30pm.
Societies   must apply in advance.
Green Fees   £25(£30 weekends).
Prof   Chris Hall
Facilities   ⊗ ⨎ 🛏 ♨ ♀ ⚲ 🏠 🛇

Hotel   ★★★ 73% Best Western Yew Lodge Hotel, Packington Hill, KEGWORTH ☎ 01509 672518 64 ⇆ 🏕

HUCKNALL   Map 08 SK54

Leen Valley Golf Centre Wigwam Ln NG15 7TA
☎ 0115 964 2037 Fax 0115 964 2724
e-mail: leen-jackbarker@btinternet.com
An interesting and challenging parkland course, featuring several lakes, the River Leen and the Baker Brook. Suitable for all standards of golfers.
18 holes, 6233yds, Par 72, SSS 70.
Club membership 750.
Visitors   tee times can be booked in advance and are advisable for Fri, Sat & Sun.
Societies   by arrangement.
Green Fees   available on application.
Cards   💳 💳 💳 💳 🌀
Prof   John Lines
Designer   Tom Hodgetts
Facilities   ⊗ ⨎ 🛏 ♨ ♀ ⚲ 🏠 🛇
& Leisure   9 hole par 3 course.
Location   0.5m from Hucknall Town Centre, follow signs for railway station and turn right into Wigwam Lane

Hotel   ★★★ 65% Bestwood Lodge, Bestwood Country Park, Arnold, NOTTINGHAM ☎ 0115 920 3011 39 ⇆ 🏕

KEYWORTH   Map 08 SK63

Stanton on the Wolds Golf Rd, Stanton-on-the-Wolds NG12 5BH ☎ 0115 937 4885 & 937 2044 Fax 0115 937 4885
Parkland course, fairly flat with stream running through four holes.
18 holes, 6437yds, Par 73, SSS 71, Course record 67.
Club membership 705.
Visitors   must contact in advance. Must play with member at weekends and may not play Tue.
Societies   must apply in writing.
Green Fees   not confirmed.
Prof   Nick Hernon
Designer   Tom Williamson
Facilities   ⊗ ⨎ by prior arrangement 🛏 ♨ ♀ ⚲ 🏠 🛇
Location   E side of village

Hotel   ★★ 65% Rufford Hotel, 53 Melton Rd, West Bridgford, NOTTINGHAM ☎ 0115 981 4202 34 ⇆ 🏕

KIRKBY IN ASHFIELD   Map 08 SK55

Notts Derby Rd NG17 7QR
☎ 01623 753225 Fax 01623 753655
e-mail: nottsgolfclub@yahoo.co.uk
Undulating heathland Championship course.
18 holes, 7030yds, Par 72, SSS 75, Course record 64.
Club membership 450.
Visitors   must contact in advance & have handicap certificate. With member only weekends & bank holidays.
Societies   must apply in advance.
Green Fees   £65 per day; £45 per round.
Prof   Alasdair Thomas
Designer   Willie Park
Facilities   ⊗ ⨎ 🛏 ♨ ♀ ⚲ 🏠 ⚐ 🍴 ❧ ⚘ 🛇 ⚑
Location   2M SE Mansfield off A611

Hotel   ★★★★ 68% Swallow Hotel, Carter Ln East, SOUTH NORMANTON ☎ 01773 812000 158 ⇆ 🏕

LONG EATON   Map 08 SK43

Trent Lock Golf Centre Lock Ln, Sawley NG10 2FY
☎ 0115 946 4398 Fax 0115 946 1183
Main course has two par 5, five par 3 and eleven par 4 holes, plus water features and three holes adjacent to the river. A challenging test of golf. A 24 bay floodlit golf range is available.
Main Course: 18 holes, 5717yds, Par 69, SSS 68, Course record 73.
9 hole: 9 holes, 2911yds, Par 36.
Club membership 500.
Visitors   no restriction Mon-Fri am but booking system 12pm Fri-closing Sun. May play 9 hole course at any time.
Societies   apply in writing or telephone in advance.
Green Fees   not confirmed.
Prof   M Taylor
Designer   E McCausland
Facilities   ⚲ 🏠 ❧ ⚘ 🛇 ⚑

Hotel   ★★★ 66% Novotel Nottingham, Bostock Ln, LONG EATON ☎ 0115 946 5111 108 ⇆ 🏕

MANSFIELD   Map 08 SK56

Sherwood Forest Eakring Rd NG18 3EW
☎ 01623 626689 Fax 01623 420412
e-mail: sherwood@forest43.freeserve.co.uk
As the name suggests, the Forest is the main feature of this natural heathland course with its heather, silver birch and pine trees. The homeward nine holes are particularly testing. The 11th to the 14th are notable par 4 holes on this well-bunkered course designed by the great James Braid.
18 holes, 6698yds, Par 71, SSS 73, Course record 64.
Club membership 750.

Visitors	weekdays only by prior arrangement with the Secretary.
Societies	by arrangement with the Secretary.
Green Fees	£55 per day; £40 per round.
Prof	Ken Hall
Designer	W S Colt/James Braid
Facilities	⊗ ⌇ⅢⅢ ⌇⊑ ♥ ♀ ⚲ ⌂ ♂
& Leisure	snooker.
Location	E of Mansfield

Hotel   ★★ 66% Pine Lodge Hotel, 281-283 Nottingham Rd, MANSFIELD
☎ 01623 622308   20 ⇆ ✿

MANSFIELD WOODHOUSE   Map 08 SK56

Mansfield Woodhouse Leeming Ln North NG19 9EU
☎ 01623 623521
Easy walking on heathland.
9 holes, 2446yds, Par 68, SSS 64.
Club membership 130.

Visitors	no restrictions.
Societies	must contact by telephone.
Green Fees	not confirmed.
Prof	Leslie Highfield
Designer	A Highfield & F Horfman
Facilities	⊗ ⌇ⅢⅢ ⌇⊑ ♥ ♀ ⌂ ♂
Location	N side of town centre off A60

Hotel   ★★ 66% Pine Lodge Hotel, 281-283 Nottingham Rd, MANSFIELD
☎ 01623 622308   20 ⇆ ✿

NEWARK-ON-TRENT   Map 08 SK75

Newark Coddington NG24 2QX
☎ 01636 626282 Fax 01636 626497
Wooded, parkland course in secluded situation with easy walking.
18 holes, 6444yds, Par 71, SSS 71, Course record 66.
Club membership 600.

Visitors	must contact in advance and have handicap certificate. May not play Tue (Ladies Day).
Societies	must contact in advance.
Green Fees	£28 per day;£23 per round (£28 per round weekend).
Prof	P A Lockley
Designer	T Williamson
Facilities	⊗ ⌇ⅢⅢ ⌇⊑ ⚲ ⌂ ♂
& Leisure	snooker.
Location	4m E of Newark on Sleaford Road(A17)

Hotel   ★★ 68% The Grange Hotel, 73 London Rd, NEWARK ☎ 01636 703399
10 ⇆ ✿ Annexe5 ⇆ ✿

NOTTINGHAM   Map 08 SK53

Beeston Fields Old Dr, Wollaton Rd, Beeston NG9 3DD
☎ 0115 925 7062 Fax 0115 925 4280
Parkland course with sandy subsoil and wide, tree-lined fairways. The par 3, 14th has elevated tee and small bunker-guarded green.
18 holes, 6402yds, Par 71, SSS 71, Course record 64.
Club membership 600.

Visitors	must contact professional on 0115 922 0872 for availability.
Societies	must apply in advance.
Green Fees	£36 per 36 holes; £26 per round(£31 per round weekends & bank holidays0.
Prof	Alun Wardle
Designer	Tom Williamson
Facilities	⊗ ⌇ⅢⅢ by prior arrangement ⌇⊑ ♥ ♀ ⚲ ⌂ ♂ ♂
Location	400mtrs SW off A52 Nottingham/Derby road

Hotel   ★★★ 66% Posthouse Nottingham/Derby, Bostocks Ln, SANDIACRE
☎ 0870 400 9062 93 ⇆ ✿

Bramcote Hills Thoresby Rd, off Derby Rd, Bramcote NG9 3EP ☎ 0115 928 1880
A Pay and Play, 18-hole Par 3 course, a great challenge.
18 holes, 1500yds, Par 54.

Visitors	no restrictions.
Societies	telephone in advance.
Green Fees	not confirmed..
Facilities	♥ ♂
Location	Off A52 Derby rd

Hotel   ★★★ 63% Posthouse Nottingham City, St James's St, NOTTINGHAM
☎ 0870 400 9061 160 ⇆ ✿

Bulwell Forest Hucknall Rd, Bulwell NG6 9LQ
☎ 0115 976 3172 (pro shop)
Municipal heathland course with many natural hazards. Very tight fairways and subject to wind. 5 challenging par 3's. Excellent drainage.
18 holes, 5616yds, Par 68, SSS 67, Course record 62.
Club membership 350.

Visitors	restricted weekends. Contact pro shop 24hours in advance.
Societies	must apply in advance.
Green Fees	£16 per day; £11 per round.
Cards	▦ ▦ ▦ ▦ ▦ ▦
Prof	Lee Rawlings
Facilities	⊗ ⌇⊑ ♥ ♀ ⚲ ⌂ ♂ ♂
& Leisure	hard tennis courts.
Location	3m from junct 26 on M1. 4m NW of city centre on A611

Hotel   ★★★ 65% Nottingham Gateway, Nuthall Rd, Cinderhill, NOTTINGHAM
☎ 0115 979 4949 107 ⇆ ✿

Where to stay, where to eat?
Visit the AA internet site
www.theAA.com

Chilwell Manor Meadow Ln, Chilwell NG9 5AE
☎ 0115 925 8958 Fax 0115 922 0575
Flat parkland course.
18 holes, 6379yds, Par 70, SSS 70, Course record 66.
Club membership 750.
Visitors with member only weekends. Must contact in
advance and have a handicap certificate.
Societies welcome Mon, must apply in advance.
Green Fees £20 per round.
Cards 🖃
Prof Paul Wilson
Designer Tom Williamson
Facilities ⊗ ⅲ ⓛ ⛳ ♀ ⅄ 🖻 ∂
Location 4m SW on A6005

Hotel ★★ 64% Europa Hotel, 20-22 Derby Rd,
LONG EATON ☎ 0115 972 8481 15 ⇆ ⋔

Edwalton Municipal Wellin Ln, Edwalton NG12 4AS
☎ 0115 923 4775
Gently sloping, 9-hole parkland course. Also 9-hole Par 3
and large practice ground.
9 holes, 3336yds, Par 72, SSS 72, Course record 71.
Club membership 900.
Visitors booking system in operation.
Societies prior booking necessary.
Green Fees not confirmed.
Cards 🖃 ▰ ▰ 🗓
Prof John Staples
Facilities ⊗ ⓛ ⛳ ♀ ⅄ 🖻 ∂
Location S of Nottingham, off A606

Hotel ★★ 65% Rufford Hotel, 53 Melton Rd, West
Bridgford, NOTTINGHAM
☎ 0115 981 4202 34 ⇆ ⋔

Mapperley Central Av, Plains Rd, Mapperley NG3 5RH
☎ 0115 955 6672 Fax 0115 955 6670
Hilly meadowland course but with easy walking.
18 holes, 6303yds, Par 71, SSS 70, Course record 68.
Club membership 650.
Visitors must contact in advance. May not play Tue or Sat.
Societies must telephone in advance.
Green Fees £20 per day; £15 per round (£25/£20 weekends
& bank holidays).
Designer John Mason
Facilities ⊗ ⅲ ⓛ ⛳ ♀ ⅄ 🖻 ∂
& Leisure pool room.
Location 3m NE of city centre off B684

Hotel ★★★ 63% Posthouse Nottingham City, St
James's St, NOTTINGHAM
☎ 0870 400 9061 160 ⇆ ⋔

Nottingham City Lawton Dr, Bulwell NG6 8BL
☎ 0115 927 6916 & 927 2767 Fax 0115 927 6916
A pleasant municipal parkland course on the city outskirts.
18 holes, 6218yds, Par 69, SSS 70, Course record 65.
Club membership 425.
Visitors restricted Sat 7am-3pm. Contact Professional in
advance.
Societies welcome, contact professional.
Green Fees on request.
Cards 🖃 ▰ ▰ 🗓
Prof Cyril Jepson
Designer H Braid
Facilities ⊗ ⅲ ⓛ ⛳ ♀ ⅄ 🖻 ∂
Location 4m NW of city centre off A6002

Wollaton Park Limetree Av, Wollaton Park NG8 1BT
☎ 0115 978 7574 Fax 0115 970 0736
A pleasant, fairly level course set in a park close to the
centre of Nottingham, with red and fallow deer herds.
The fairways are tree-lined. The 502-yd dog-leg 15th is a
notable hole. The stately home - Wollaton Hall - is
situated in the park.
18 holes, 6445yds, Par 71, SSS 71, Course record 64.
Club membership 700.
Visitors may not play Wed or competition days.
Societies must apply in advance.
Green Fees £38 per day;£27.50 per round(£43/£32.50
weekends).
Prof John Lower
Designer W Williamson
Facilities ⊗ ⅲ ⓛ ⛳ ♀ ⅄ 🖻 ∂
Location 2.5m W of city centre off A52

Hotel ★★★ 59% Swans Hotel & Restaurant,
84-90 Radcliffe Rd, West Bridgford,
NOTTINGHAM
☎ 0115 981 4042 30 ⇆ ⋔

OLLERTON Map 08 SK66

Rufford Park Golf Centre Rufford Ln, Rufford NG22 9DG
☎ 01623 825253 Fax 01623 825254
e-mail: ruffordgolf@btconnect.com
Rufford Park is noted for its pictuesque 18 holes with its
especially challenging Par 3's. From the unique 173yard Par
3 17th over water to the riverside 596yard 13th, the course
offers everything the golfer needs from beginner to
professional.
18 holes, 6173yds, Par 70, SSS 69, Course record 67.
Club membership 650. ▶

Visitors are advised to book in advance. Unable to play weekend mornings.
Societies society packages on request, need to be booked in advance.
Green Fees £15 per round (£20 weekends).
Cards ▨▩▨▨▨▨▨
Prof John Vaughan/James Thompson
Designer David Hemstock
Facilities ⊗ℳ♭☐♥♀♣☐ℐ☆∂ʼ
Location S Of Ollerton off A614. Take the 'Rufford Mill' turn

Hotel ★★★ 67% Clumber Park Hotel, Clumber Park, WORKSOP ☎ 01623 835333 48 ⇆ ♠

OXTON   Map 08 SK65

Oakmere Park Oaks Ln NG25 0RH ☎ 0115 965 3545 Fax 0115 965 5628 e-mail: oakmerepark@ukgolf.net
Set in rolling parkland in the heart of picturesque Robin Hood country. The par 4 (16th) and par 5 (1st) are notable. Twenty-bay floodlit driving range.
Admirals: 18 holes, 6617yds, Par 72, SSS 72.
Commanders: 9 holes, 6407yds, Par 72, SSS 72.
Club membership 450.
Visitors correct golf attire required, please book for weekends.
Societies please apply in writing or telephone.
Green Fees Admirals: £18 per round (£25 weekends). Commanders: £6 per 9 holes (£8 weekends).
Cards ▨▩▨▨▨
Prof Daryl St-John Jones
Designer Frank Pennick
Facilities ⊗ℳ♭☐♥♀♣☐☆∂ʼ
Location 1m NW off A6097

Hotel ★★★ 66% Westminster Hotel, 312 Mansfield Rd, Carrington, NOTTINGHAM ☎ 0115 955 5000 72 ⇆ ♠

RADCLIFFE-ON-TRENT   Map 08 SK63

Cotgrave Place Golf & Country Club Main Rd, Stragglethorpe, Nr Cotgrave Village NG12 3HB
☎ 0115 933 3344 Fax 0115 933 4567
e-mail: cotgrave@americangolf.com
The course now offers 36 holes of championship golf. The front nine of the Open Course are placed around a beautiful lake, man made ponds and the Grantham Canal. The back nine is set in magnificent parkland with mature trees and wide fairways. Masters has an opening nine set amongst hedgerows and coppices. The huge greens with their interesting shapes are a particularly challenging test of nerve. The par 5, 17th hole is one of the toughest in the country.
Open course: 18 holes, 6303yds, Par 71, SSS 70.
Masters course: 18 holes, 5887yds, Par 69, SSS 68.
Club membership 750.
Visitors must contact, can book 1 week in advance.
Societies telephone in advance.
Green Fees £16/£17 (£20-£25 weekends).
Cards ▨▨▨▨▨▨▨
Prof Robert Smith
Facilities ⊗ℳ♭☐♥♀♣☐☆∂ʼ
Location Off A52, 6 miles from Nottingham

Hotel ★★★♨♨ 69% Langar Hall, LANGAR ☎ 01949 860559 12rm(11 ⇆ ♠)

Radcliffe-on-Trent Dewberry Ln, Cropwell Rd NG12 2JH
☎ 0115 933 3000 Fax 0115 911 6991
e-mail: les.rotgc@talk21.com
Fairly flat, parkland course with three good finishing holes: 16th (427 yds) par 4; 17th (180 yds) through spinney, par 3; 18th (331 yds) dog-leg par 4. Excellent views.
18 holes, 6381yds, Par 70, SSS 71, Course record 64.
Club membership 670.
Visitors must contact in advance,societies only on Wed.
Societies welcome Wed. Must contact in advance.
Green Fees £23 per day (£28 weekends).
Prof Robert Ellis
Designer Tom Williamson
Facilities ⊗ℳ♭☐♥♀♣☐ℐ☆∂
Location Take the A52 to Nottingham, turn L at 2nd set of traffic lights, 400yds on left

Hotel ★★★ 59% Swans Hotel & Restaurant, 84-90 Radcliffe Rd, West Bridgford, NOTTINGHAM ☎ 0115 981 4042 30 ⇆ ♠

RETFORD   Map 08 SK78

Retford Brecks Rd, Ordsall DN22 7UA
☎ 01777 860682 (Secretary) & 703733 (Pro)
Fax 01777 710412
A wooded, parkland course.
18 holes, 6409yds, Par 72, SSS 72, Course record 67.
Club membership 700.
Visitors advisable to contact in advance, with member only at weekends and holidays.
Societies apply in writing or telephone. Not welcome Tue morning or bank holidays, limited availability weekends.
Green Fees not confirmed.
Prof Craig Morris
Designer Tom Williamson
Facilities ⊗ℳ♭☐♥♀♣☐ℐ☆∂
Location 1.5m S A620, between Worksop & Gainsborough

Hotel ★★★ 64% West Retford Hotel, 24 North Rd, RETFORD ☎ 01777 706333 Annexe62 ⇆ ♠

RUDDINGTON   Map 08 SK53

Ruddington Grange Wilford Rd NG11 6NB
☎ 0115 984 6141 Fax 0115 9405165
e-mail: info@ruddingtongrange.com
Undulating parkland course with water hazards on 12 holes.
18 holes, 6543yds, Par 72, SSS 72, Course record 69.
Club membership 650.
Visitors a handicap certificate is required, tee time must be booked in advance. Play may be restricted Sat & Wed mornings.
Societies must contact in advance.
Green Fees not confirmed..
Prof Robert Simpson
Designer E MacAusland
Facilities ⊗ℳ♭☐♥♀♣☐☆∂
Location 5m S of Nottingham, A60 to Ruddington

Hotel ★★★ 59% Swans Hotel & Restaurant, 84-90 Radcliffe Rd, West Bridgford, NOTTINGHAM ☎ 0115 981 4042 30 ⇆ ♠

SERLBY   Map 08 SK68

Serlby Park DN10 6BA ☏ 01777 818268
Parkland course.
11 holes, 5325yds, Par 66, SSS 66, Course record 63.
Club membership 250.
Visitors   must be introduced by and play with member.
Societies   apply in writing before 31 Dec for following
               year.
Green Fees £10 (£15 weekends & bank holidays).
Designer   Viscount Galway
Facilities   ⊗ ⽊ ⽥ ⛳ ⌾ ⽥ ⛳
Location   E side of village off A638

Hotel   ★★★ 69% Charnwood Hotel, Sheffield Rd,
               BLYTH ☏ 01909 591610 34 ⇌ ⽊

SUTTON IN ASHFIELD   Map 08 SK45

Coxmoor Coxmoor Rd NG17 5LF
☏ 01623 557359 Fax 01623 557359
e-mail: coxmoor@freeuk.com
Undulating moorland/heathland course with easy
walking and excellent views. The clubhouse is
traditional with a well-equipped games room. The course
lies adjacent to Forestry Commission land over which
there are several footpaths and extensive views.
18 holes, 6571yds, Par 73, SSS 72, Course record 65.
Club membership 700.
Visitors   must play with member weekends & bank
               holidays. Must contact in advance.
Societies   must apply in advance.
Green Fees £35 per 18 holes; £45 per 27/36 holes.
Prof   David Ridley
Facilities   ⊗ ⽊ ⽥ ⛳ ⽥ ⛳ ⌾
& Leisure   snooker.
Location   2m SE off A611. 4m from junct 27 on M1

Hotel   ★★★★ 68% Swallow Hotel, Carter Ln
               East, SOUTH NORMANTON
               ☏ 01773 812000 158 ⇌ ⽊

WORKSOP   Map 08 SK57

Bondhay Golf & Country Club Bondhay Ln, Whitwell
S80 3EH ☏ 01909 723608 Fax 01909 720226
The wind usually plays quite an active role in making this
pleasantly undulating course testing. Signatures holes are the
10th which requires a 2nd shot over water into a basin of
trees; the 11th comes back over the same expanse of water
and requires a mid to short iron to a long, narrow green; the
18th is a Par 5 with a lake right in lay up distance - the
dilemma is whether to lay up short or go for the carry. The
par 3's are generally island like in design, requiring accuracy
to avoid the protective bunker features.
Devonshire Course: 18 holes, 6705yds, Par 72, SSS 71,
Course record 67.
Family Course: 9 holes, 1118yds, Par 27, Course record 24.
Club membership 400.
Visitors   must contact in advance.
Societies   must telephone in advance.
Green Fees Summer: £16 (£21 weekends) Winter: £14 (£18
               weekends).
Cards   ▨ ▨ ▨ ▨ ▨
Prof   Michael Ramsden
Designer   Donald Steel

Facilities   ⊗ ⽊ ⽥ ⽥ ⽥ ⛳ ⽥ ⛳ ⌾ ⽥ ⛳ ⽥
& Leisure   fishing.
Location   5m W of Worksop, off A619

Hotel   ★★★ 64% Sitwell Arms Hotel, Station Rd,
               RENISHAW ☏ 01246 435226 30 ⇌ ⽊

Kilton Forest Blyth Rd S81 0TL ☏ 01909 486563
Slightly undulating, parkland course on the north edge of
Sherwood Forest. Includes three ponds. Excellent conditions
all the year round.
18 holes, 6424yds, Par 72, SSS 71, Course record 68.
Club membership 320.
Visitors   must contact in advance. May not play at
               weekends before 10am.
Societies   must contact in advance.
Green Fees not confirmed.
Prof   Stuart Betteridge
Facilities   ⊗ ⽊ ⽥ ⛳ ⽥ ⛳ ⌾ ⽥ ⛳ ⽥
& Leisure   bowling.
Location   1m NE of town centre on B6045

Hotel   ★★★ 66% Lion Hotel, 112 Bridge St,
               WORKSOP ☏ 01909 477925 32 ⇌ ⽊

Lindrick Lindrick Common S81 8BH
☏ 01909 475282 Fax 01909 488685
Heathland course with some trees and masses of gorse.
18 holes, 6486yds, Par 71, SSS 72, Course record 65.
Club membership 490.
Visitors   must contact in advance. Restricted Tue &
               weekends. Handicap certificate required.
Societies   welcome except Tue (am) & weekends by
               prior arrangement with the Secretary.
Green Fees £48 per day weekdays (£48 per round
               weekends).
Prof   John R King
Facilities   ⊗ ⽊ ⽥ ⽥ ⛳ ⽥ ⽥ ⌾
& Leisure   buggies for disabled only.
Location   4m NW on A57

Hotel   ★★★ 66% Lion Hotel, 112 Bridge St,
               WORKSOP ☏ 01909 477925 32 ⇌ ⽊

Worksop Windmill Ln S80 2SQ
☏ 01909 472696 & 477731 Fax 01909 477731
Adjacent to Clumber Park this course has a heathland-type
terrain, with gorse, broom, oak and birch trees. Fast, true
greens, dry all year round.
18 holes, 6660yds, Par 72, SSS 73.
Club membership 600.
Visitors   by arrangement with professional
               tel: 01909 477732.
Societies   must apply in advance.
Green Fees not confirmed.
Prof   C Weatherhead
Facilities   ⽥ ⽥ ⽥ ⽥ ⌾
& Leisure   snooker.
Location   Off A57 Ringroad, B6034 to Edwinstowe

Hotel   ★★★ 67% Clumber Park Hotel, Clumber Park,
               WORKSOP ☏ 01623 835333 48 ⇌ ⽊

Looking for a driving range?
See the index at the back of the guide

OXFORDSHIRE

ABINGDON   Map 04 SU49

Drayton Park Steventon Rd, Drayton Village OX14 4LA
☎ 01235 550607 (Pro Shop) & 528989 (Secretary)
Fax 01235 525731
Set in the heart of the Oxfordshire countryside, an 18-hole parkland course designed by Hawtree. Five lakes and sand based greens.
18 holes, 5500yds, Par 67, SSS 67.
Club membership 500.
Visitors   may phone to book, must have golf shoes, no jeans or tracksuits.
Societies   contact in advance.
Green Fees not confirmed.
Prof   Martin Morbey
Designer   Hawtree
Facilities   ⊗ ⑪ ㋿ ♚ ♀ ♨ 🏠 🛥 🚜 ✍ ♻
& Leisure   9 hole par 3 course.
Location   Between Oxford & Newbury,off A34 at Didcot

Hotel   ★★★ 66% The Upper Reaches, Thames St, ABINGDON ☎ 0870 400 8101 31 ⇄ 🐾

BANBURY   Map 04 SP44

Rye Hill Milcombe OX15 4RU
☎ 01295 721818 Fax 01295 720089
Well drained course features wide fairways, large undulating greens, water hazards on the 10th, and fine views of the surrounding countryside.
18 holes, 6919yds, Par 72, SSS 73, Course record 71.
Club membership 400.
Visitors   must book in advance, especially at weekends. May not play Sat before 11am.
Societies   telephone for details of Packages available.
Green Fees £15 per round (£20 weekends).
Cards   🌐 🟥 🟦 🟨 🟢
Prof   Tony Pennock
Facilities   ⊗ ㋿ ♚ ♀ ♨ 🏠 🛥 🚜 ✍
& Leisure   fishing, 3 hole par 3 academy.
Location   Junct 11 M40. A361 towards Chipping Norton, signed 1m out of Bloxham

Hotel   ★★★ 70% Banbury House, Oxford Rd, BANBURY ☎ 01295 259361   63 ⇄ 🐾

BURFORD   Map 04 SP21

Burford Swindon Rd OX18 4JG
☎ 01993 822583 Fax 01993 822801
Parkland with mature, treelined fairways and high quality greens.
18 holes, 6414yds, Par 71, SSS 71, Course record 64.
Club membership 750.
Visitors   must contact in advance. May not play weekends.
Societies   apply in writing.
Green Fees not confirmed.
Prof   Michael Ridge
Designer   John H Turner
Facilities   ⊗ ⑪ ㋿ ♚ ♀ ♨ 🏠 🛥 ✍
Location   0.5m S off A361

Hotel   ★★ 63% Golden Pheasant Hotel, 91 High St, BURFORD ☎ 01993 823223 12rm(11 ⇄ 🐾)

CHESTERTON   Map 04 SP52

Bicester Golf & Country Club OX26 1TE
☎ 018695 241204
Laid out over one-time farmland. Well-bunkered, and water hazards increase the difficulty of the course.
18 holes, 6229yds, Par 71, SSS 70, Course record 68.
Club membership 400.
Visitors   may pre-book upto 7 days ahead.
Societies   by appointment and in advance
Green Fees £25 per day; £15 per round (£30/£20 weekends).
Prof   J Wilkshire
Designer   R Stagg
Facilities   ⊗ ⑪ by prior arrangement ㋿ ♚ ♀ ♨ 🏠 ✍
Location   0.5m W off A4095, 1m E of B430 at Weston-on-the-Green

Hotel   ★★ 70% Jersey Arms Hotel, BICESTER ☎ 01869 343234 & 343505
                Fax 01869 343565 6 ⇄ Annexe14rm(10 ⇄)

CHIPPING NORTON   Map 04 SP32

Chipping Norton Southcombe OX7 5QH
☎ 01608 642383 Fax 01608 645422
Downland course situated at 800 feet above sea level, its undulations providing a good walk. On a limestone base, the course dries quickly in wet conditions. The opening few holes provide a good test of golf made more difficult when the prevailing wind makes the player use the extremes of the course.
18 holes, 6241yds, Par 71, SSS 70, Course record 62.
Club membership 900.
Visitors   with member only at weekends & bank holidays.
Societies   telephone in advance.
Green Fees £27 weekdays.
Prof   Derek Craik
Facilities   ⊗ ⑪ ㋿ ♚ ♀ ♨ 🏠 🛥 🚜 ✍
Location   1.5m E on A44

Hotel   ★★★ 73% The Mill House Hotel & Restaurant, KINGHAM ☎ 01608 658188   21 ⇄ 🐾 Annexe2 ⇄

Lyneham Lyneham OX7 6QQ
☎ 01993 831841 Fax 01993 831775
Lyneham was designed to use the natural features. It is set in 170 acres on the fringe of the Cotswolds and blends superbly with its surroundings. Lakes and streams enhance the challenge of the course with water coming into play on 8 of the 18 holes. All greens are sand based, built to USGA specification.
18 holes, 6669yds, Par 72, SSS 72, Course record 67.
Club membership 725.
Visitors   must contact in advance.
Societies   apply in advance.
Green Fees not confirmed.
Prof   Richard Jefferies
Designer   D G Carpenter
Facilities   ⊗ ⑪ ㋿ ♚ ♀ ♨ 🏠 🛥 🚜 ✍ ♻
Location   Off A361, between Burford/Chipping Norton

▶

Hotel ★★★ 73% The Mill House Hotel &
Restaurant, KINGHAM
☎ 01608 658188 21 ⇆ ♟ Annexe2 ⇆

DIDCOT   Map 04 SU59

Hadden Hill Wallingford Rd OX11 9BJ
☎ 01235 510410 Fax 01235 511260
e-mail: info@haddenhillgolf.co.uk
A challenging course on undulating terrain with excellent
drainage so visitors can be sure of playing no matter what the
weather conditions have been. Two loops of nine holes.
18 holes, 6563yds, Par 71, SSS 71, Course record 65.
Club membership 400.
Visitors telephone to book tee times.
Societies telephone to arrange times & dates & receive
booking form.
Green Fees £24 per day; £14 per 18 holes; £8.50 per 9 holes
(£30/£19.50/£10weekends).
Prof Adrian Waters
Designer Michael V Morley
Facilities ⊗ ⌇ ⬧ ■ ♥ ♀ ⚘ 🖰 ✲ ♦ ⚙ ⚑
Location On A4130 1m E of Didcot

Hotel ★★★ 64% Abingdon Four Pillars Hotel,
Marcham Rd, ABINGDON
☎ 01235 553456 62 ⇆ ♟

FARINGDON   Map 04 SU29

Carswell Carswell SN7 8PU
☎ 01367 870422 Fax 01367 870592
An attractive course set in undulating wooded countryside
close to Faringdon. Mature trees, five lakes and well placed
bunkers add interest to the course. Floodlit driving range.
18 holes, 6133yds, Par 72, SSS 70.
Club membership 750.
Visitors must book 8 days in advance, no earlier for tee
time.
Societies on weekdays only telephone to check
availability, deposit required,
Green Fees £16 per round (£25 weekends).
Cards 🔲 🔲 🔲 🔲
Prof Steve Parker
Facilities ⊗ ⌇ ⬧ ■ ♥ ♀ ⚘ 🖰 ⚒ ♦ ⚙ ⚑
& Leisure sauna, solarium, gymnasium.
Location Just off the A420 between Oxford and Swindon

Hotel ★★★ 73% Sudbury House Hotel &
Conference Centre, London St, FARINGDON
☎ 01367 241272 49 ⇆ ♟

FRILFORD   Map 04 SU49

Frilford Heath OX13 5NW
☎ 01865 390864 Fax 01865 390823
e-mail: secretary@frilfordheath.co.uk
54 holes in three distinctive layouts of significantly
differing character. The Green course is a fully mature
heathland course of some 6000 yards. The Red course is
of championship length at 6800 yards with a parkland
flavour and a marked degree of challenge. The Blue
course is of modern design, and at 6728 yards, it
incorporates water hazards and large shallow sand traps.

*Red Course: 18 holes, 6884yds, Par 73, SSS 73, Course
record 68.*
Green Course: 18 holes, 6006yds, Par 69, SSS 69.
Blue Course: 18 holes, 6728yds, Par 72, SSS 72.
Club membership 1300.
Visitors contact in advance. Handicap certificates
required.
Societies apply in advance.
Green Fees £50 per day/round(£65 weekends & bank
holidays).
Prof Derek Craik
Designer J Taylor/D Cotton/S Gidman
Facilities ⊗ ⌇ ⬧ ■ ♥ ♀ ⚘ 🖰 ✲ ♦ ⚙ ⚑
Location 3m W of Abingdon off A338 Oxford-
Wantage road

Hotel ★★★ 64% Abingdon Four Pillars Hotel,
Marcham Rd, ABINGDON
☎ 01235 553456 62 ⇆ ♟

HENLEY-ON-THAMES   Map 04 SU78

Aspect Park Remenham Hill RG9 3EH ☎ 01491 578306
18 holes, 6643yds, Par 72, SSS 72.
Telephone for further details

Hotel ★★★ 71% Red Lion Hotel, Hart St,
HENLEY-ON-THAMES
☎ 01491 572161 26 ⇆ ♟

Badgemore Park Badgemore RG9 4NR
☎ 01491 572206 Fax 01491 576899
e-mail: info@badgemorepark.com
Mature parkland course with easy walking. The 13th is a
very difficult par 3 hole played over a valley to a narrow
green and accuracy off the tee is essential.
18 holes, 6129yds, Par 69, SSS 69, Course record 64.
Club membership 600.

Visitors check for availability by contacting professional
shop on 01491 574175. 48 hrs booking
minimum for weekend play. Tue mornings, lady
members only.
Societies contact the Club Secretary to book.
Green Fees £19 per round (£30 weekends & bank holidays).
Cards 🔲 🔲 🔲 🔲
Prof Jonathan Dunn
Designer Robert Sandow
Facilities ⊗ ⌇ by prior arrangement ⬧ ■ ♥ ♀ ⚘ 🖰 ✲ ♦
♦ ⚙ ⚑
Location From Henley take B290 to Rotherfield Greys
Club, 1.5m on right   ▶

Hotel   ★★★ 71% Red Lion Hotel, Hart St,
HENLEY-ON-THAMES
☎ 01491 572161   26 ⇄ ♠

Henley Harpsden RG9 4HG
☎ 01491 575742 Fax 01491 412179
e-mail: henleygolfclub@btinternet.com
Undulating parkland course, with adjoining woodlands.
18 holes, 6329yds, Par 70, SSS 70, Course record 63.
Club membership 800.
Visitors   must contact in advance. Weekend only with a
member.
Societies   Wed & Thu, apply in writing.
Green Fees £30.
Prof   Mark Howell
Designer   James Braid
Facilities ⊗ ⅷ ⅊ ♨ ⅊ 🛆 🏠 ✓
Location   1.25m S off A4155

Hotel   ★★★ 71% Red Lion Hotel, Hart St,
HENLEY-ON-THAMES
☎ 01491 572161   26 ⇄ ♠

HORTON-CUM-STUDLEY   Map 04 SP51

Studley Wood The Straight Mile OX33 1BF
☎ 01865 351122 & 351144 Fax 01865 351166
e-mail: admin@swgc.co.uk.
Woodland course set in a former deer park with twelve lakes
and specimen oak trees providing challenging natural hazards
on almost all the holes.
18 holes, 6811yds, Par 73, SSS 73, Course record 65.
Club membership 700.
Visitors   must play to handicap standard, tee times
booked up to 4 days in advance.
Societies   contact secretary for details.
Green Fees £30 per round; £16 per 9 holes (£40 per round
weekends and bank holidays).
Cards 🔲 🔲 🔲 🔲 🔲
Prof   Tony Williams
Designer   Simon Gidman
Facilities ⊗ ⅷ ⅊ ♨ ⅊ 🛆 🏠 ✓
Location   4m from Oxford follow signs for Horton-cum-
Studley from Headington rdbt on Oxford
ringroad

Hotel   ★★★♨ 77% Studley Priory Hotel,
HORTON-CUM-STUDLEY
☎ 01865 351203 & 351254
Fax 01865 351613   18 ⇄ ♠

KIRTLINGTON   Map 04 SP41

Kirtlington OX5 3JY
☎ 01869 351133 Fax 01869 351143
A five year old inland links type course with challenging
greens. The course incorporates many mature natural features
and boasts 102 bunkers and a 'bye-hole', the 110 yard par 3
19th when an extra hole is required to determine a winner.
18 holes, 6107yds, Par 70, SSS 69.
Club membership 400.
Visitors   must book for weekends and advisable to book
for wekdays. Must contact in advance.
Societies   contact for Society packages.
Green Fees £17 per 18 holes (£22 weekends & bank
holidays).

Cards 🔲 🔲 🔲 🔲 🔲 🔲
Designer   Graham Webster
Facilities ⊗ ⅊ ♨ ⅊ 🛆 🏠 ⅷ ✓
Location   on A4095 just outside village of Kirtlington

Hotel   ★★★ 67% Weston Manor Hotel, WESTON-
ON-THE-GREEN ☎ 01869 350621
15 ⇄ ♠ Annexe20 ⇄ ♠

MILTON COMMON   Map 04 SP60

The Oxfordshire Rycote Ln OX9 2PU
☎ 01844 278300 Fax 01844 278003
Designed by Rees Jones, The Oxfordshire is considered
to be one of the most exciting courses in the country.
With four man-made lakes and 135 bunkers, it is a
magnificent test of shot-making where almost every hole
deserves special mention. Unfortunately it is only open
to members and their guests.
18 holes, 7187yds, Par 72, SSS 76, Course record 64.
Club membership 750.
Visitors   members guests only.
Green Fees not confirmed..
Cards 🔲 🔲 🔲 🔲 🔲
Prof   Neil Pike
Designer   Rees Jones
Facilities 🛆 🏠 ⅷ ⅊ 🏠 ✓
Location   1.5m from junct 7, M40 on A329

Hotel   ★★★ 76% Spread Eagle Hotel,
Cornmarket, THAME
☎ 01844 213661   33 ⇄ ♠

NUFFIELD   Map 04 SU68

Huntercombe RG9 5SL
☎ 01491 641207 Fax 01491 642060
18 holes, 6301yds, Par 70, SSS 70, Course record 63.
Location   N off A423
Telephone for further details

Hotel   ★★★ 65% Shillingford Bridge Hotel,
Shillingford, WALLINGFORD
☎ 01865 858567   34 ⇄ ♠ Annexe8 ⇄ ♠

OXFORD   Map 04 SP50

North Oxford Banbury Rd OX2 8EZ
☎ 01865 554924 Fax 01865 515921
Gently undulating parkland course.
18 holes, 5736yds, Par 67, SSS 67, Course record 62.
Club membership 700.
Visitors   at weekends & bank holidays may only play
after 4pm.
Societies   must contact in advance.
Green Fees not confirmed.
Prof   Robert Harris
Facilities ⊗ ⅷ ⅊ ♨ ⅊ 🛆 🏠 ⅷ ✓
Location   3m N of city centre on A423

Hotel   ★★★ 66% The Oxford Hotel, Godstow Rd,
Wolvercote Roundabout, OXFORD
☎ 01865 489988 173 ⇄ ♠

Southfield Hill Top Rd OX4 1PF
☎ 01865 242158 Fax 01865 242158
e-mail: southfieldgolfclub@btinternet.com
Home of the City, University and Ladies Clubs, and
well-known to graduates throughout the world. A
challenging course, in varied parkland setting, providing
a real test for players.
18 holes, 6328yds, Par 70, SSS 70, Course record 61.
Club membership 850.
Visitors   with member only at weekends.
Societies   must apply in writing.
Green Fees not confirmed.
Cards   🔳🔳
Prof   Tony Rees
Designer   H S Colt
Facilities ⊗ 🞰 ⓑ 💺 ♀ ⚲ 🏠 ⛳ 🏌 🚜 ⚘
Location 1.5m SE of city centre off B480

Hotel   ★★★ 65% Eastgate Hotel, The High,
           Merton St, OXFORD
           ☎ 0870 400 8201 64 ⇆ 🐾

SHRIVENHAM   Map 04 SU28

Shrivenham Park Penny Hooks SN6 8EX
☎ 01793 783853 Fax 01793 782999
An undulating course with excellent drainage, providing a
good challenge for all standards of golfer.
18 holes, 5769yds, Par 69, SSS 69, Course record 64.
Club membership 350.
Visitors   phone in advance.
Societies   phone for details.
Green Fees not confirmed.
Cards   🔳🔳 🔳 🔳 🔳
Prof   Jamie McArthur
Designer   Gordon Cox
Facilities ⊗ 🞰 ⓑ 💺 ♀ ⚲ 🏠 ⛳ 🚜 ⚘
Location 0.5m NE of town centre

Hotel   ★★★ 73% Sudbury House Hotel &
           Conference Centre, London St, FARINGDON
           ☎ 01367 241272 49 ⇆ 🐾

TADMARTON   Map 04 SP33

Tadmarton Heath OX15 5HL
☎ 01608 737278 Fax 01608 730548
A mixture of heath and sandy land, the course, which is
open to strong winds, incorporates the site of an old
Roman encampment. The clubhouse is an old farm
building with a 'holy well' from which the greens are
watered. The 7th is a testing hole over water.
18 holes, 5917yds, Par 69, SSS 69, Course record 63.
Club membership 600.
Visitors   weekday by appointment, with member
           only at weekends.
Societies   by arrangement with club office.
Green Fees £33 summer;£25 winter.
Prof   Tom Jones
Designer   Col Hutchinson
Facilities ⊗ ⓑ 💺 ♀ ⚲ 🏠 ⛳ 🚜 ⚘ ⓛ
& Leisure fishing.
Location 1m SW of Lower Tadmarton off B4035,
           4m from Banbury

Hotel   ★★★ 70% Banbury House, Oxford Rd,
           BANBURY ☎ 01295 259361 63 ⇆ 🐾

WALLINGFORD   Map 04 SU68

Springs Hotel Wallingford Rd, North Stoke OX10 6BE
☎ 01491 827310 Fax 01491 827312
e-mail: info@thespringshotel.co.uk
133 acres of park land, bordered by the river Thames, within
which lie three lakes and challenging wetland areas. The
course has traditional features like a double green and
sleepered bunker with sleepered lake edges of the typical
American design.
18 holes, 6470yds, Par 72, SSS 71, Course record 67.
Club membership 570.
Visitors   handicap certificate required. Must book in
           advance. Dress code must be adhered to.
Societies   apply in writing,telephone/e-mail.
Green Fees £37 per day; £26 per round;16.50 per 9
           holes(£45/£33/£19 weekends & bank holidays).
Cards   🔳 🔳 🔳 🔳 🔳 🔳
Prof   Leigh Atkins
Designer   Brian Hugget
Facilities ⊗ 🞰 ⓑ 💺 ♀ ⚲ 🏠 ⛳ 🏌 🍴 🚜 ⚘
& Leisure heated outdoor swimming pool, fishing, sauna.
Location 15 miles SE of Oxford & 12.5 miles NW of
           Reading.

Hotel   ★★★ 72% Springs Hotel, Wallingford Rd,
           North Stoke, WALLINGFORD
           ☎ 01491 836687 31 ⇆ 🐾

WATERSTOCK   Map 04 SP60

Waterstock Thame Rd OX33 1HT
☎ 01844 338093 Fax 01844 338036
A 6,500yard course designed by Donald Steel with USGA
greens and tees fully computer irrigated. Four Par 3's facing
North, South, East and West. A brook and hidden lake affect
six holes, with doglegs being 4th and 10th holes. Five Par 5's
on the course, making it a challenge for players of all
standards.
18 holes, 6535yds, Par 73, SSS 71, Course record 68.
Club membership 500.
Visitors   no restrictions.
Societies   apply in writing or telephone.
Green Fees not confirmed.
Prof   Julian Goodman
Designer   Donald Steel
Facilities ⚲ 🏠 ⛳ 🏌 🚜 ⚘ ⓛ
& Leisure fishing.
Location On junc 8 of M40

Hotel   ★★★ 76% Spread Eagle Hotel, Cornmarket,
           THAME ☎ 01844 213661 33 ⇆ 🐾

WITNEY   Map 04 SP31

Witney Lakes Downs Rd OX8 5SY
☎ 01993 893011 Fax 01993 778866
e-mail: resort@witney-lakes.co.uk
A lakeland style course with 5 large lakes coming into play
on 8 holes. An excellent test of golf that will use every club
in your bag.
18 holes, 6700yds, Par 71, Course record 67.
Club membership 400.

▶

Visitors may pre-book 5 days in advance,weekends after 10.30 am
Societies telephone or write in advance.
Green Fees £16(£22 weekends).
Cards ⊡ 🖭 🏧 📇 💳
Prof Adam Souter
Designer Simon Gidman
Facilities ⊗ ⨉ ⬛ 💺 ♥ ♀ ♤ 🏠 🍴 🛒 🚴 🏌 ⚑
& Leisure heated indoor swimming pool, sauna, solarium, gymnasium.
Location 2m W of Witney town centre, off B4047 Witney/Burford road

Hotel ★★★ *70%* Witney Four Pillars Hotel, Ducklington Ln, WITNEY ☎ 01993 779777 83 ⇆ 🏲

RUTLAND

GREAT CASTERTON Map 08 TF00

Rutland County PE9 4AQ
☎ 01780 460330 Fax 01780 460437
Inland links-style course with gently rolling fairways, large tees and greens. Playable all year round due to good drainage.
18 holes, 6401yds, Par 71, SSS 71, Course record 64.
Club membership 650.
Visitors must book in advance at the shop, tel 01780 460239.
Societies contact office by phone, must be booked in advance.
Green Fees £30 per day, £20 per round (£35/25 weekends).
Cards ⊡ 🖭 🏧 📇 💳 🟦
Prof James Darroch
Designer Cameron Sinclair
Facilities ⊗ ⨉ ⬛ 💺 ♥ ♀ ♤ 🏠 🍴 🛒 🚴 🏌 ⚑
Location 2m N of Stamford on A1

Hotel ★★ *67%* The White Horse Inn, Main St, EMPINGHAM ☎ 01780 460221 & 460521 Fax 01780 460521 4 ⇆ 🏲 Annexe9 ⇆ 🏲

GREETHAM Map 08 SK91

Greetham Valley Wood Ln LE15 7NP
☎ 01780 460004 Fax 01780 460623
e-mail: GVGC@rutnet.co.uk
Set in 260 acres, including mature woodland, undulating natural valley, and water hazards. The complex comprises 2x18 hole courses The Lakes and The Valley. A luxurious clubhouse, 9 hole par 3, floodlit driving range and teaching academy.
Lakes: 18 holes, 6779yds, Par 72, SSS 72, Course record 68.
Valley: 18 holes, 5595yds, Par 68, SSS 67.
Club membership 1000.
Visitors must contact in advance.
Societies must contact in advance.
Green Fees £32 per day; £24 per 18 holes (£35/£28 weekends).
Cards ⊡ 🖭 🏧 📇 💳
Prof John Pengelly
Designer F E Hinch

Facilities ⊗ ⨉ ⬛ 💺 ♥ ♀ ♤ 🏠 🍴 🛒 🚴 🏌 ⚑
& Leisure bowls green 9 hole par 3.
Location Take the B668 Oakham road off the A1 and follow signs to the course which are clearly marked

Hotel ★★★ *72%* Barnsdale Lodge Hotel, The Avenue, Rutland Water, North Shore, OAKHAM ☎ 01572 724678 45 ⇆ 🏲

SHROPSHIRE

BRIDGNORTH Map 07 SO79

Bridgnorth Stanley Ln WV16 4SF
☎ 01746 763315 Fax 01746 761381
A pleasant course laid-out on parkland on the bank of the River Severn.
18 holes, 6673yds, Par 73, SSS 73, Course record 65.
Club membership 725.
Visitors must contact in advance but may not play on Wed. Restricted weekends.
Societies must contact in writing.
Green Fees £24 per round; £30 per 36 holes (£30/£34 weekends & bank holidays).
Prof Paul Hinton
Facilities ⊗ ⨉ ⬛ 💺 ♥ ♀ ♤ 🏠 🛒 ⚑
& Leisure fishing.
Location 1m N off B4373, 0.5m from town centre

Hotel ★★ *63%* Falcon Hotel, Saint John St, Lowtown, BRIDGNORTH ☎ 01746 763134 12 ⇆ 🏲

CHURCH STRETTON Map 07 SO49

Church Stretton Trevor Hill SY6 6JH
☎ 01694 722281 Fax 01694 722633
Hillside course designed by James Braid on the lower slopes of the Long Mynd.
18 holes, 5020yds, Par 66, SSS 65, Course record 63.
Club membership 450.
Visitors Tee reserved for members Sat 9-10.30 & 1-2.30, Sun prior to 10.30 & 1-2.30 (summer).
Societies must contact in advance.
Green Fees £18 per day/round (£26 weekends & bank holidays).
Prof J Townsend
Designer James Braid
Facilities ⊗ ⨉ ⬛ 💺 ♥ ♀ ♤ 🏠
Location W of the town. From Cardington Valley drive up Trevor Hill, a steep, winding road

Hotel ★★ *70%* Mynd House Hotel, Ludlow Rd, Little Stretton, CHURCH STRETTON ☎ 01694 722212 7 ⇆ 🏲

AA Hotels that have special arrangements with golf courses are listed at the back of the guide

CLEOBURY MORTIMER — Map 07 SO67

Cleobury Mortimer Wyre Common DY14 8HQ
☎ 01299 271112 Fax 01299 271468
e-mail: cleoburygolfclub.com
Well designed 27-hole parkland course set in undulating countryside with fine views from all holes, and offering an interesting challenge to golfers of all abilities.
Foxes Run: 9 holes, 2980yds, Par 34, SSS 34.
Badgers Sett: 9 holes, 3271yds, Par 36, SSS 36.
Deer Park: 9 holes, 3167yds, Par 35, SSS 35.
Club membership 650.
Visitors advisable to book in advance, handicap certificate may be required at weekends.
Societies write or telephone in advance.
Green Fees £30 per day; £20 per 18 holes (£36/£24 weekends & bank holidays).
Cards 🖼🖼🖼🖼
Prof Jon Jones/Martin Payne
Designer E.G.U
Facilities ⊗⏐🏌️🍴♀⛳🏠🐾🥢♂🥤
& Leisure fishing.
Location 10m W of Kidderminster on A4117 1m N of Cleobury Mortimer, off B4201

Hotel ★★ 66% The Redfern Hotel, CLEOBURY MORTIMER ☎ 01299 270395 5 ➡ ⟨ Annexe6rm(5 ➡ ⟨)

HIGHLEY — Map 07 SO78

Severn Meadows WV16 6HZ ☎ 01746 862212
9 holes, 5258yds, Par 68, SSS 67.
Telephone for further details

Hotel ★★★★ 66% Mill Hotel & Restaurant, ALVELEY ☎ 01746 780437 21 ➡ ⟨

LILLESHALL — Map 07 SJ71

Lilleshall Hall TF10 9AS ☎ 01952 603840 & 604776
Fax 01952 604776
Heavily-wooded parkland course. Easy walking.
18 holes, 5906yds, Par 68, SSS 68, Course record 65.
Club membership 650.
Visitors must contact in advance and play with member at weekends.
Societies must apply in writing by Dec for the following year.
Green Fees £20 per 18 holes. Prices under review.
Prof Stuart McKane
Designer H S Colt
Facilities ⊗⏐🏌️🍴♀⛳🏠♂
Location 3m SE

Hotel ★★ 68% White House Hotel, Wellington Rd, Muxton, TELFORD ☎ 01952 604276 & 603603 Fax 01952 670336 32 ➡ ⟨

Where to stay, where to eat?
Visit the AA internet site
www.theAA.com

LUDLOW — Map 07 SO57

Ludlow Bromfield SY8 2BT
☎ 01584 856366 Fax 01584 856366
e-mail: ludlowgolfclub@talk21.com
A long-established heathland course in the middle of the racecourse. Very flat, quick drying, with broom and gorse-lined fairways.
18 holes, 6277yds, Par 70, SSS 70, Course record 65.
Club membership 700.
Visitors advisable to contact in advance.
Societies apply in advance.
Green Fees £24 per day; £18 per round.
Prof Russell Price
Facilities ⊗⏐🏌️🍴♀⛳🏠♂♂
Location 1m N of Ludlow, off A49

Hotel ★★★ 64% The Feathers at Ludlow, Bull Ring, LUDLOW ☎ 01584 875261 40 ➡ ⟨

MARKET DRAYTON — Map 07 SJ63

Market Drayton Sutton Ln TF9 2HX
☎ 01630 652266 Fax 01630 652266
e-mail: marketdraytongc@btinternet.com
Parkland course in quiet, picturesque surroundings providing a good test of golf. Bungalow on course is made available for golfing holidays.
18 holes, 6290yds, Par 71, SSS 71, Course record 69.
Club membership 600.
Visitors may not play on Sun; must play with member on Sat. Must contact in advance.
Societies welcome Mon,Wed,Thu & Fri, must contact in advance.
Green Fees £24 per round (£16 winter).
Prof Russell Clewes
Facilities ⊗⏐🏌️🍴♀⛳🏠♂
Location 1m SW

Hotel ★★★♨ 65% Goldstone Hall, Goldstone, MARKET DRAYTON ☎ 01630 661202 & 661487 Fax 01630 661585 8 ➡ ⟨

MEOLE BRACE — Map 07 SJ41

Meole Brace Otely Rd SY2 6QQ ☎ 01743 364050
9 holes, 5830yds, Par 68, SSS 68, Course record 66.
Location NE side of village off A49
Telephone for further details

Hotel ★★★ 64% The Lion, Wyle Cop, SHREWSBURY ☎ 01743 353107 59 ➡ ⟨

OSWESTRY — Map 07 SJ22

Mile End Mile End, Old Shrewsbury Rd SY11 4JE
☎ 01691 671246 Fax 01691 670580
e-mail: mileendgc@aol.com
A gently undulating parkland-type course boasting challenging holes for all standards of golfing ability. Longest hole is par 5 14th at 540yds. A number of water features need to be negotiated including two large ponds on the 3rd and 17th. The course is set in 140 acres, ensuring all holes are sufficiently isolated.
▶

18 holes, 6194yds, Par 71, SSS 69, Course record 69.
Club membership 550.
Visitors   welcome at all times please telephone in
             advance to check availability.
Societies must contact in advance, information available.
Green Fees £22 per day; £15 per round (£28/£20 weekends).
Prof   Scott Carpenter
Designer   Price/Gough
Facilities ⊗ ⓑ ♣ ♀ ⚲ 🏠 ♂ ℓ
Location   1m SE of Oswestry, just off A5

Hotel   ★★★ 70% Wynnstay Hotel, Church St,
             OSWESTRY ☎ 01691 655261   29 ⇄ ♠

Oswestry Aston Park SY11 4JJ
☎ 01691 610535 Fax 01691 610535
Parkland course laid-out on undulating ground.
18 holes, 6024yds, Par 70, SSS 69, Course record 62.
Club membership 960.
Visitors   must contact in advance. Must have a handicap
             certificate or play with member.
Societies must contact in advance.
Green Fees £28 per day, £23 per round (£36/£31 weekends
             & bank holidays).
Prof   David Skelton
Designer   James Braid
Facilities ⊗ �𝄞 ⓑ ♣ ♀ ⚲ 🏠 ♂
Location   2m SE on A5

Hotel   ★★★ 70% Wynnstay Hotel, Church St,
             OSWESTRY ☎ 01691 655261   29 ⇄ ♠

PANT   Map 07 SJ22

Llanymynech SY10 8LB ☎ 01691 830983
Upland course on the site of an early Iron Age/Roman
hillfort with far-reaching views. 15 holes in Wales 3 holes in
England, drive off in Wales putt out in England on 4th hole.
18 holes, 6114yds, Par 70, SSS 69, Course record 65.
Club membership 700.
Visitors   prior contact advisable, some weekends
             restricted.
Societies must contact Secretary.
Green Fees £25 per day; £20 per round (£25 per round
             weekends).
Prof   Andrew P Griffiths
Facilities ⊗ �𝄞 ⓑ ♣ ♀ ⚲ 🏠 ♂
Location   6m S of Oswestry on A483. In village of Pant
             turn at Cross Guns Inn

Hotel   ★★★ 70% Wynnstay Hotel, Church St,
             OSWESTRY ☎ 01691 655261   29 ⇄ ♠

SHIFNAL   Map 07 SJ70

Shifnal Decker Hill TF11 8QL
☎ 01952 460330 Fax 01952 460330
Well-wooded parkland course. Walking is easy and an
attractive country mansion serves as the clubhouse.
18 holes, 6468yds, Par 71, SSS 71, Course record 65.
Club membership 700.
Visitors   must contact in advance, may not play at
             weekends or on Thursdays.
Societies must contact in advance.
Green Fees not confirmed.
Cards   🖩 🖩 🖩 🖩 🖩 🖩
Prof   Justin Flanagan

Designer   Pennick
Facilities ⊗ ⟆ ⓑ ♣ ♀ ⚲ 🏠 ♂
Location   1m N of Shifnal, off B4379

Hotel   ★★★★ 63% Park House Hotel, Park St,
             SHIFNAL ☎ 01952 460128
             38 ⇄ ♠ Annexe16 ⇄ ♠

SHREWSBURY   Map 07 SJ41

Arscott Arscott, Pontesbury SY5 0XP
☎ 01743 860114 Fax 01743 860114
At 365 feet above sea level, the views from Arscott Golf
Club, of the hills of south Shropshire and Wales are superb.
Arscott is a new course, set in mature parkland with water
features and holes demanding all sorts of club choice. A
challenge to all golfers both high and low handicap.
18 holes, 6178yds, Par 70, SSS 69, Course record 68.
Club membership 480.
Visitors   most times available by prior arrangement.
Societies apply in writing or telephone for tee reservation.
Green Fees £22 per day; £16 per round (£25/£20
             weekends)reductions in winter..
Designer   M Hamer
Facilities ⊗ ⟆ ⓑ ♣ ♀ ⚲ 🏠 ⚓ ♂
& Leisure fishing.
Location   Off A488, S of Shrewsbury 3m from A5

Hotel   ★★★ 64% The Lion, Wyle Cop,
             SHREWSBURY ☎ 01743 353107   59 ⇄ ♠

Shrewsbury Condover SY5 7BL
☎ 01743 872976, 872977 (sec) & 874581 (pro)
Fax 01743 874647 e-mail: pseal@talk21.com
Parkland course. First nine flat, second undulating with good
views of the Long Mynd Range. Several holes with water
features. Fast putting surfaces.
18 holes, 6300yds, Par 70, SSS 70.
Club membership 872.
Visitors   must contact in advance, weekend restrictions
             and have a handicap certificate.
Societies must contact in writing.
Green Fees not confirmed..
Prof   Peter Seal
Facilities ⊗ ⟆ ⓑ ♣ ♀ ⚲ 🏠 ⚓ ♂ ℓ
Location   4m S off A49

Hotel   ★★★ 71% Prince Rupert Hotel, Butcher Row,
             SHREWSBURY ☎ 01743 499955   70 ⇄ ♠

TELFORD   Map 07 SJ60

The Shropshire Granville Park, Muxton TF2 8PQ
☎ 01952 677800 Fax 01952 677622
e-mail: golf@theshropshire.co.uk
Designed by Martin Hawtree this 27 hole course comprises 3
loops of 9. Each course has an abundance of lakes and water
hazards making club selection a vital part of the round.
Championship tees are available by pre-arrangement for the
low handicap player.
Blue: 9 holes, 3286yds, Par 35, SSS 35.
Silver: 9 holes, 3303yds, Par 36, SSS 36.
Gold: 9 holes, 3334yds, Par 36, SSS 36.
Club membership 400.

▶

Visitors recommended to book 7 days in advance.
Societies must book in advance.
Green Fees £18 per 18 holes; £11per 9 holes
(£22/£12weekends).
Cards 🖨 💳 🖼 💳 🔲 💳
Prof Steve Marr
Designer Martin Hawtree
Facilities ⊗ �𝄫 🛅 💶 ♀ ᚼ 🏠 ♦ ⚒ ♣ (
Location From M54/A5 take B5060 towards Donnington.
Take 3rd exit at Granville rdbt and continue

Hotel ★★★ 63% Telford Golf & Country Club,
Great Hay Dr, Sutton Heights, TELFORD
☎ 01952 429977 96 ⇆ 🐾

Telford Golf & Country Club Great Hay Dr, Sutton
Heights TF7 4DT ☎ 01952 429977 Fax 01952 586602
Rolling parkland course with easy walking. Five lakes and
large sand traps are hazards to the fine greens.
18 holes, 6761yds, Par 72, SSS 72, Course record 66.
Club membership 450.
Visitors must book in advance, be a competent golfer
and abide by dress regulations.
Societies must telephone in advance 01952 429977
Green Fees £25 per round(£30 weekends).
Cards 🖨 💳 🖼 💳 🔲 💳
Prof Daniel Bateman
Designer Harris/Griffiths
Facilities ⊗ �𝄫 🛅 💶 ♀ ᚼ 🏠 🚩 ♦ ⚒ ♣ (
& Leisure heated indoor swimming pool, squash, sauna,
solarium, gymnasium, snooker,pool,steam room
& beauty &masseur treatments..
Location 4m S of town centre off A442

Hotel ★★★ 63% Telford Golf & Country Club,
Great Hay Dr, Sutton Heights, TELFORD
☎ 01952 429977 96 ⇆ 🐾

WELLINGTON   Map 07 SJ61

Wrekin Ercall Woods, Golf Links Ln TF6 5BX
☎ 01952 244032 Fax 01952 252906
Downland course with some hard walking but superb views.
18 holes, 5570yds, Par 67, SSS 66, Course record 64.
Club membership 675.

Visitors must contact in advance. Limited weekends &
bank holidays.
Societies must apply in writing/telephone.
Green Fees £28 per day; £20 per round (£28 weekends &
bank holidays).
Prof K Housden
Facilities ⊗ ⍀ 🛅 💶 ♀ 🏠 ✎
Location Off junct 7 of M54,1.25m S off B5061

Hotel ★★★★ 65% Buckatree Hall Hotel,
The Wrekin, Wellington, TELFORD
☎ 01952 641821 60 ⇆ 🐾

WESTON-UNDER-REDCASTLE   Map 07 SJ52

Hawkstone Park Hotel SY4 5UY
☎ 01939 200611 Fax 01939 200311
e-mail: info@hawkstone.co.uk
The Hawkstone Course plays through the English
Heritage designated Grade I landscape of the historic
park and follies providing a beautiful, tranquil yet
dramatic back drop to a round of golf. The Windmill
Course utilises many American style features and
extensive water hazards and is a challenging alternative.
Hawkstone Course: 18 holes, 6491yds, Par 72, SSS 71,
Course record 65.
Windmill Course: 18 holes, 6476yds, Par 72, SSS 72,
Course record 64.
Academy Course: 6 holes, 741yds, Par 18, SSS 18.
Club membership 650.

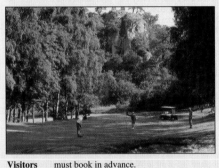

Visitors must book in advance.
Societies must contact in advance by telephone.
Green Fees not confirmed.
Cards 🖨 💳 🖼 💳 🔲 💳
Prof Paul Wesselingh
Designer B Huggett
Facilities ⊗ ⍀ 🛅 💶 ♀ 🏠 🚩 ♦ ⚒ ♣ (
& Leisure 6 hole, par 3 course..
Location N side of village 0.75m E of A49

WHITCHURCH.   Map 07 SJ54

Hill Valley Terrick Rd SY13 4JZ
☎ 01948 663584 & 667788 Fax 01948 665927
e-mail: info@hillvalley.co.uk
Two testing parkland courses ideally suited to the club
and scratch golfer alike. The Emerald, cleverly designed
by Peter Alliss and Dave Thomas, has fairways that
thread their way through 160 acres of trees, lakes and
streams to American-style greens trapped by sand and
water. Shorter Sapphire with smaller greens requiring
accurate approach shots.
Emerald: 18 holes, 6628yds, Par 73, SSS 72, Course
record 64.
Sapphire: 18 holes, 4800yds, Par 66, SSS 64.
Club membership 600.
Visitors must contact in advance, deposit required.
Societies must contact in advance; a deposit will be
required.   ▶

Green Fees	not confirmed.
Cards	⊟ 🔲 🔳 📶 🔲
Prof	A R Minshall & Clive Burgess
Designer	Peter Alliss/Dave Thomas
Facilities	⊗ ⑪ ⅄ ♥ ♀ ⚲ 🏠 🍴 🛏 ↘ ⚒ 🏌 ↾
& Leisure	sauna, solarium, gymnasium.
Location	1m N. Follow signs from Bypass
Hotel	★★ 69% Crown Hotel & Restaurant, High St, NANTWICH ☎ 01270 625283 18 ⇥ ↾

WORFIELD   Map 07 SO79

Worfield Roughton WV15 5HE
☎ 01746 716372 Fax 01746 716302
This undulating course with good-sized greens, well placed bunkers and 3 lakes, rated highly in a golf magazine survey. All year round golf based on sandy soil.
18 holes, 6801yds, Par 73, SSS 73, Course record 68.
Club membership 500.

Visitors	must contact in advance, weekends only after 2pm.
Societies	contact in advance.
Green Fees	not confirmed.
Cards	⊟ 🔲 🔳 📶 🔲
Prof	Steve Russell
Designer	T Williams
Facilities	⊗ ⑪ ⅄ ♥ ♀ ⚲ 🏠 ↘ ⚒ ⚒
Location	3m W of Bridgnorth, off A454
Hotel	★★★ Old Vicarage Hotel, BRIDGWORTH ☎ 01746 716497 & 0800 0968010 Fax 01746 716552 10 ⇥ ↾ Annexe4 ⇥ ↾

SOMERSET

BACKWELL   Map 03 ST46

Tall Pines Cooks Bridle Path, Downside BS48 3DJ
☎ 01275 472076 Fax 01275 474869
Parkland course with views over the Bristol Channel.
18 holes, 6049yds, Par 70, SSS 69.
Club membership 500.

Visitors	no green fees before 11am unless by prior arrangement. Must book in advance at weekends and may not play before noon.
Societies	prior arrangement by telephone for details.
Green Fees	£16 per round.
Prof	Alex Murray
Designer	T Murray
Facilities	⊗ ⑪ ⅄ ♥ ♀ ⚲ 🏠 ↘ ⚒ ⚒
Location	Adjacent to Bristol Airport, 1m off A38
Hotel	★★★ 66% Beachlands Hotel, 17 Uphill Rd North, WESTON-SUPER-MARE ☎ 01934 621401 24 ⇥ ↾

Looking for a driving range?
See the index at the back of the guide

BATH   Map 03 ST76

Bath Sham Castle, North Rd BA2 6JG
☎ 01225 463834 Fax 01225 331027
e-mail: enquiries@bathgolfclub.org.uk
Considered to be one of the finest courses in the west, this is the site of Bath's oldest golf club. An interesting course situated on high ground overlooking the city and with splendid views over the surrounding countryside. The rocky ground supports good quality turf and there are many good holes. The 17th is a dog-leg right past, or over the corner of an out-of-bounds wall, and thence on to an undulating green.
18 holes, 6442yds, Par 71, SSS 71, Course record 66.
Club membership 750.

Visitors	advisable to contact in advance. Handicap certificates required.
Societies	Wed & Fri by prior arrangement.
Green Fees	£32 per day; £27 per round (£38/£33 weekends & bank holidays).
Prof	Peter J Hancox
Designer	Colt & others
Facilities	⊗ ⑪ ⅄ ♥ ♀ ⚲ 🏠 🍴 ⚒
Location	1.5m SE city centre off A36
Hotel	★★★ 70% The Francis, Queen Square, BATH ☎ 0870 400 8223 94 ⇥ ↾

Entry Hill BA2 5NA ☎ 01225 834248
9 holes, 2065yds, Par 33, SSS 30.
Club membership 300.

Visitors	advisable to book in advance, must wear golf shoes or training shoes.
Societies	bookings required in advance.
Green Fees	not confirmed.
Prof	Tim Tapley
Facilities	♥ ⚲ 🏠 🍴 ⚒
Location	Off A367

Lansdown Lansdown BA1 9BT
☎ 01225 422138 Fax 01225 339252
A flat parkland course situated 800 feet above sea level, providing a challenge to both low and high handicap golfers.
18 holes, 6316yds, Par 71, SSS 70, Course record 65.
Club membership 700.

Visitors	must contact in advance to ascertain availability and have a handicap certificate.
Societies	apply in writing or telephone in advance.
Green Fees	not confirmed.
Cards	⊟ 🔲 🔳 📶 🔲
Prof	Terry Mercer
Designer	C A Whitcombe
Facilities	⊗ ⑪ ⅄ ♥ ♀ ⚲ 🏠 ⚒ ↾
Location	6m SW of exit 18 of M4
Hotel	★★★ 68% Pratt's Hotel, South Pde, BATH ☎ 01225 460441 46 ⇥ ↾

BRIDGWATER   Map 03 ST23

Cannington Cannington College, Cannington TA5 2LS
☎ 01278 655050 Fax 01278 655055
Nine hole golf course with 18 tees of 'links-like' appearance, designed by Martin Hawtree of Oxford. The 4th hole is a challenging 464yard Par 4, slightly up hill and into the prevailing wind.

▶

9 holes, 6072yds, Par 68, SSS 70.
Club membership 240.
Visitors pay & play anytime ex Wed evening.
Societies apply in writing.
Green Fees not confirmed.
Prof Ron Macrow
Designer Martin Hawtree
Facilities ⛳🏌️🚶⛳🏌️
& Leisure Cycle hire.
Location 4m NW of Bridgwater of A39

Hotel ★★ 66% Friarn Court Hotel, 37 St Mary St, BRIDGWATER ☎ 01278 452859 16 ⇄ 🐾

BURNHAM-ON-SEA Map 03 ST34

Brean Coast Rd, Brean Sands TA8 2QY
☎ 01278 752111(pro shop) Fax 01278 752111
e-mail: admin@holidayunity.demon.co.uk.
Level and open moorland course with water hazards.
Facilities of 'Brean Leisure Park' adjoining.
18 holes, 5715yds, Par 69, SSS 68, Course record 66.
Club membership 350.

Visitors may not play on Sat & Sun before 11.30am. Book in advance through professional.
Societies contact office or professional in advance.
Green Fees not confirmed.
Cards 💳💳
Prof David Haines
Facilities ⊗🏌️🚶⛳🏌️⛳🏌️🚶🏌️
& Leisure heated indoor plus outdoor swimming pool, fishing, fun park with 30 rides/attractions..
Location 4m from junct 22 M5 on coast road

Hotel ★★🏌️ 70% Batch Country Hotel, Batch Ln, LYMPSHAM ☎ 01934 750371 10 ⇄ 🐾

Burnham & Berrow St Christopher's Way TA8 2PE
☎ 01278 785760 Fax 01278 795440
e-mail: secretary@burnhamandberrowgc.2-golf.com
Natural championship links course with panoramic views of the Somerset hills sweeping across the famed reed beds and the Bristol channel with the islands of Steepholm and Flatholm against the background of the Welsh coast line.
Championship Course: 18 holes, 6606yds, Par 71, SSS 73, Course record 66.
Channel Course: 9 holes, 6120yds, Par 70, SSS 69.
Club membership 900.
Visitors must contact in advance & have handicap certificate (22 or under gentlemen, 30 or under ladies) to play on the Championship course.

Societies telephone in advance.
Green Fees Championship Course: £40 (£60 weekends); Channel Course £12.
Prof Mark Crowther-Smith
Facilities ⊗🏌️🚶⛳🏌️🚶⛳🏌️🚶🏌️
Location 1m N of town on B3140

Hotel ★★ 68% Woodlands Country House Hotel, Hill Ln, BRENT KNOLL ☎ 01278 760232 8 ⇄ 🐾

CHARD Map 03 ST30

Windwhistle Golf, Squash & Country Club Cricket St Thomas TA20 4DG ☎ 01460 30231 Fax 01460 30055
Parkland course at 735 ft above sea level with outstanding views over the Somerset Levels to the Bristol Channel and South Wales.
East/West Course: 18 holes, 6470yds, Par 71, SSS 68, Course record 69.
Club membership 500.
Visitors must contact in advance.
Societies by prior arrangement.
Green Fees £16 per round/day (£20 weekends).
Cards 💳💳💳💳
Prof Duncan Driver
Designer Braid & Taylor
Facilities ⊗🏌️🚶⛳🏌️🚶⛳🏌️
& Leisure squash.
Location 3m E of Chard on A30

Hotel ★★★ 66% Shrubbery Hotel, ILMINSTER ☎ 01460 52108 14 ⇄ 🐾

CLEVEDON Map 03 ST47

Clevedon Castle Rd, Walton St Mary BS21 7AA
☎ 01275 874057 Fax 01275 341228
e-mail: clevedongc.sec@virgin.net
Situated on the cliff-top overlooking the Severn estuary and with distant views of the Welsh coast. Excellent parkland course in first-class condition overlooking the Severn estuary. Magnificent scenery and some tremendous 'drop' holes.
18 holes, 6117yds, Par 70, SSS 69, Course record 65.
Club membership 750.
Visitors must contact in advance. No play Wed morning.
Societies not bank holidays, telephone or apply in writing.
Green Fees £25 per day (£40 weekends).
Prof Robert Scanlan
Designer S Herd
Facilities ⊗🏌️🚶⛳🏌️🚶⛳🏌️
Location 1m NE of town centre

Hotel ★★★ 65% Walton Park Hotel, Wellington Ter, CLEVEDON ☎ 01275 874253 40 ⇄ 🐾

CONGRESBURY Map 03 ST46

Mendip Spring Honeyhall Ln BS49 5JT
☎ 01934 852322 Fax 01934 853021
e-mail: mendipspring@lineone.net
Set in peaceful countryside with the Mendip Hills as a backdrop, this 18-hole course includes lakes and numerous ▶

water hazards covering some 12 acres of the course. The 12th is an island green surrounded by water and there are long drives on the 7th and 13th. The 9-hole Lakeside course is an easy walking course, mainly par 4. Floodlit driving range.
Brinsea Course: 18 holes, 6334yds, Par 71, SSS 70, Course record 64.
Lakeside: 9 holes, 2392yds, Par 34, SSS 66.
Club membership 445.

Visitors	must contact in advance for Brinsea course and handicap certificate required for weekends. Lakeside is play & pay anytime.
Societies	Booking in advance by arrangement.
Green Fees	not confirmed.
Cards	🔲 🔳 🔲 🔲 🔲
Prof	John Blackburn & Robert Moss
Facilities	⊗ ⫿ ⓛ 🏌 ♀ ⩍ 🏠 ⸙ ❨ 🐾 ⛳ 🏌 ❩
Location	8m E of Weston-Super-Mare between A370 and A38

Hotel	★★★♨ 74% Daneswood House Hotel, Cuck Hill, SHIPHAM ☎ 01934 843145 & 843945 Fax 01934 843824 14 ⇌ ❨ Annexe3 ⇌ ❨

ENMORE   Map 03 ST23

Enmore Park TA5 2AN
☎ 01278 671481 & 671519 Fax 01278 671740
e-mail: golfclub@enmore.fsnet.co.uk
Hilly, parkland course with water features on foothills of Quantocks. Wooded countryside and views of Quantocks and Mendips. 1st and 10th are testing holes.
18 holes, 6406yds, Par 71, SSS 71, Course record 66.
Club membership 750.

Visitors	phone professional for details, must have handicap certificate for weekends.
Societies	must contact in advance.
Green Fees	£30 per day; £20 per round (£30 per round weekends& bank holidays).
Cards	🔲 🔳 🔲
Prof	Nigel Wixon
Designer	Hawtree
Facilities	⊗ ⫿ ⓛ 🏌 ♀ ⩍ 🏠 ⸙ ❨ 🐾 ⛳ 🏌
Location	A39 to Minehead, at first set of lights turn left to Spaxton, then 1.5m to reservoir and turn left

Hotel	★★★ 73% Walnut Tree Hotel, North Petherton, BRIDGWATER ☎ 01278 662255 32 ⇌

FARRINGTON GURNEY   Map 03 ST65

Farrington Marsh Ln BS39 6TS
☎ 01761 241274 (office) & 241787 (pro)
Fax 01761 241274
USGA spec greens on both challenging 9 and 18 hole courses. Newly completed 18 hole course with computerised irrigation, six lakes, four tees per hole and excellent views. Testing holes include the 12th (282yds) with the green set behind a lake at the base of a 100ft drop, and the 17th which is played between two lakes.
Executive Course: 9 holes, 3022yds, Par 54, SSS 53, Course record 54.
Main Course: 18 holes, 6316yds, Par 72, SSS 71, Course record 66.
Club membership 750.

Visitors	must book starting times at weekends.
Societies	welcome except for weekends & bank holidays, telephone or write in advance.
Green Fees	not confirmed.
Prof	Peter Thompson
Designer	Peter Thompson
Facilities	⊗ ⫿ ⓛ 🏌 ♀ ⩍ 🏠 ⸙ ❨ 🐾 ⛳ 🏌 ❩
& Leisure	sauna, video teaching studio.

Hotel	★★★ 70% Centurion Hotel, Charlton Ln, MIDSOMER NORTON ☎ 01761 417711 44 ⇌ ❨

FROME   Map 03 ST74

Frome Golf Centre Critchill Manor BA11 4LJ
☎ 01373 453410 Fax 01373 453410
Attractive parkland course, founded in 1993, situated in a picturesque valley just outside the town, complete with practice areas and a driving range.
18 holes, 5466yds, Par 69, SSS 67, Course record 64.
Club membership 360.

Visitors	no restrictions.
Societies	telephone in advance.
Green Fees	ring clubhouse for details.
Prof	Murdock McEwen
Facilities	⊗ ⓛ 🏌 ♀ ⩍ 🏠 ⸙ ❨
Location	A361 Frome/Shepton Mallet, at Nunney Catch rdbt through Nunney, course on left before Frome

Hotel	★★ 65% The George at Nunney, 11 Church St, NUNNEY ☎ 01373 836458 9rm(8 ⇌ ❨)

Orchardleigh BA11 2PH ☎ 01373 454200 & 454206
Fax 01373 454202
Originally designed by Ryder Cup golfer, Brian Huggett, as two returning nines through mature parkland. Five lakes bring water into play on seven holes.
18 holes, 6831yds, Par 72, SSS 73, Course record 70.
Club membership 500.

Visitors	no visitors before 11am at weekends.
Societies	apply in writing or telephone in advance.
Green Fees	£20 per round (£27.50 weekends & bank holidays).
Cards	🔲 🔳 🔲 🔲 🔲
Designer	Brian Huggett
Facilities	⊗ ⫿ ⓛ 🏌 ♀ ⩍ 🏠 ⸙ ❨ 🛏 ⛳ 🏌 ❩
& Leisure	fishing.
Location	1m W of Frome on the A362

Hotel	★★ 65% The George at Nunney, 11 Church St, NUNNEY ☎ 01373 836458 9rm(8 ⇌ ❨)

GURNEY SLADE   Map 03 ST64

Mendip BA3 4UT ☎ 01749 840570 Fax 01749 841439
e-mail: mendipgolfclub@lineone.net
Undulating downland course offering an interesting test of golf on superb fairways and extensive views over the surrounding countryside.
18 holes, 6383yds, Par 71, SSS 71, Course record 65.
Club membership 900.

Visitors	Handicap certificates required for play at weekends and bank holidays.
Societies	by arrangement with secretary.

▶

223

Green Fees £26 per day; £21 per round (£31 per day weekends).
Prof Adrian Marsh
Designer C K Cotton
Facilities ⊗ ℐ ⅃ ᒪ ♨ ♀ ⚲ ♙ ⚐ ✔ ✆
Location 1.5m S off A37

Hotel ★★★ 70% Centurion Hotel, Charlton Ln, MIDSOMER NORTON
☎ 01761 417711 44 ⊨ ⏴

KEYNSHAM   Map 03 ST66

Stockwood Vale Stockwood Ln BS31 2ER
☎ 0117 986 6505 Fax 0117 986 8974
e-mail: stockwoodvalegc@netscapeonline.co.uk
Undulating and challenging public course in a beautiful setting with interesting well bunkered holes, in particular the beautiful and challenging 5th and 13th holes.
18 holes, 6031yds, Par 71, SSS 69.
Club membership 600.
Visitors no restrictions, but must reserve a start time.
Societies telephone in advance.
Green Fees £15 (£17 weekends).
Cards ⊞ ⚏ 🏧 ➡ ⚐
Prof John Richards
Facilities ⊗ ℐ ⅃ ᒪ ♨ ♀ ⚲ ♙ ✆ ✝
Location Off Hicks Gate on A4

Guesthouse ◆◆◆◆ Grasmere Court Hotel, 22-24 Bath Rd, KEYNSHAM ☎ 0117 986 2662 16 ⊨ ⏴

LANGPORT   Map 03 ST42

Long Sutton Long Sutton TA10 9JU
☎ 01458 241017 Fax 01458 241022
Gentle, undulating, Pay and Play course.
18 holes, 6367yds, Par 71, SSS 70, Course record 71.
Club membership 600.
Visitors advisable to phone in advance.
Societies telephone in advance.
Green Fees £16 (£20 weekends).
Cards ⊞ 🏧 ➡ ⚐
Prof Andrew Hayes
Designer Patrick Dawson
Facilities ⊗ ℐ ⅃ ᒪ ♨ ♀ ⚲ ♙ ✔ ⚥ ♙ ✆ ✝
Location 10m NW of Yeovil off A372

Hotel ★★★ 71% The Hollies, Bower Hinton, MARTOCK ☎ 01935 822232 Annexe32 ⊨ ⏴

LONG ASHTON   Map 03 ST57

Long Ashton The Clubhouse, Clarken Coombe BS41 9DW
☎ 01275 392229 Fax 01275 394395
e-mail: secretary@longashtongolfclub
Wooded parkland course with fine turf, wonderful views of Bristol and surrounding areas and a spacious practice area. Good testing holes, especially the back nine, in prevailing south-west winds. The short second hole (126yds) cut from an old quarry and played over a road can ruin many a card! Good drainage ensures pleasant winter golf. Two extra holes have been added, giving a variety of course.
Ashton Course: 18 holes, 6077yds, Par 70, SSS 70.
Coombe Course: 18 holes, 6381, Par 71, SSS 71.
Club membership 700.

Visitors with recognised handicap certificate.
Societies must contact the secretary in advance.
Green Fees not confirmed.
Cards ⊞ 🏧 ➡ ⚐
Prof Denis Scanlan
Designer J H Taylor
Facilities ⊗ ℐ ⅃ ᒪ ♨ ♀ ⚲ ♙ ✆
Location 0.5m N on B3128

Hotel ★★★ 66% Redwood Lodge Hotel, Beggar Bush Ln, Failand, BRISTOL
☎ 01275 393901 112 ⊨ ⏴

Woodspring Golf & Country Club Yanley Ln BS18 9LR
☎ 01275 394378 Fax 01275 394473
Set in 180 acres of undulating heathland featuring superb natural water hazards, protected greens and a rising landscape. Designed by Peter Alliss and Clive Clark and laid out by Donald Steel, the course has three individual 9-hole courses, the Avon, Severn & Brunel. The 9th hole on the Brunel course is a feature hole here, with an elevated tee shot over a natural gorge. In undulating hills south of Bristol, long carries to tight fairways, elevated island tees and difficult approaches to greens make the most of the 27 holes.
Avon Course: 9 holes, 2960yds, Par 35, SSS 34.
Brunel Course: 9 holes, 3320yds, Par 37, SSS 35.
Severn Course: 9 holes, 3267yds, Par 36, SSS 35.
Club membership 960.
Visitors must contact in advance, weekends may be limited to play after midday. Dress codes must be adhered to.
Societies must contact Kevin Pitts in advance.
Green Fees not confirmed.
Cards ⊞ ⚏ 🏧 ➡ ⚐ ➡ ⚐
Prof Nigel Beer
Designer Clarke/Alliss/Steel
Facilities ⊗ ℐ ⅃ ᒪ ♨ ♀ ⚲ ♙ ✔ ⚥ ✆ ✝
& Leisure sauna.
Location Off A38 Bridgewater Road

Hotel ★★★ 66% Redwood Lodge Hotel, Beggar Bush Ln, Failand, BRISTOL
☎ 01275 393901 112 ⊨ ⏴

MIDSOMER NORTON   Map 03 ST65

Fosseway Golf Course Charlton Ln BA3 4BD
☎ 01761 412214 Fax 01761 418357
e-mail: centurion@centurionhotel.co.uk
Very attractive tree-lined parkland course, not demanding but with lovely views towards the Mendip Hills.
9 holes, 4565yds, Par 69, SSS 61.
Club membership 300.
Visitors may not play on Wed evenings, Sun mornings & competitions days.
Societies apply in writing or telephone.
Green Fees £15 per day.
Cards ⊞ 🏧 ⚐
Designer C K Cotton/F Pennink
Facilities ⊗ ℐ ⅃ ᒪ ♨ ♀ ⚲ ♙ ⊠ ✆
& Leisure heated indoor swimming pool, sauna, gymnasium.
Location SE of town centre off A367

Hotel ★★★ 70% Centurion Hotel, Charlton Ln, MIDSOMER NORTON
☎ 01761 417711 44 ⊨ ⏴

MINEHEAD   Map 03 SS94

Minehead & West Somerset The Warren TA24 5SJ
☎ 01643 702057 Fax 01643 705095
Flat seaside links, very exposed to wind, with good turf
set on a shingle bank. The last five holes adjacent to the
beach are testing. The 215-yard 18th is wedged between
the beach and the club buildings and provides a good
finish.
18 holes, 6228yds, Par 71, SSS 71, Course record 65.
Club membership 620.
Visitors   must contact secretary in advance.
Societies   telephone in advance.
Green Fees   £24.50 (£27.50 weekends).
Cards   [card symbols]
Prof   Ian Read
Facilities   ⊗ ⅏ ▯ ☂ ♀ ♁ 🏠 ⛳ ➤ ⌁
Location   E end of esplanade

Hotel   ★★ 76% Channel House Hotel, Church
                  Path, MINEHEAD
                  ☎ 01643 703229 8 ⊟ ☏

SALTFORD   Map 03 ST66

Saltford Golf Club Ln BS31 3AA ☎ 01225 872043
Parkland course with easy walking and panoramic views
over the Avon Valley. The par 4, 2nd and 13th are notable.
18 holes, 6081yds, Par 71, SSS 71.
Club membership 800.
Visitors   must contact in advance & have handicap
                  certificate.
Societies   must telephone in advance.
Green Fees   not confirmed.
Prof   Dudley Millinstead
Designer   Harry Vardon
Facilities   ⚶ 🏠 ⛳ ➤ ⌁ ⌁
Location   S side of village

Hotel   ★★★ 77% Hunstrete House Hotel,
                  HUNSTRETE ☎ 01761 490490   22 ⊟ ☏

SOMERTON   Map 03 ST42

Wheathill Wheathill TA11 7HG
☎ 01963 240667 Fax 01963 240230
18 holes, 5362yds, Par 68, SSS 66.
Location   5m E of Somerton off B3153
Telephone for further details

Hotel   ★★★ 60% Wessex Hotel, High St, STREET
                  ☎ 01458 443383   50 ⊟ ☏

TAUNTON   Map 03 ST22

Oake Manor Oake TA4 1BA
☎ 01823 461993 Fax 01823 461995
e-mail: golf@oakemanor.co.uk
A parkland/lakeland course situated in breathtaking Somerset
countryside with views of the Quantock, Blackdown and
Brendon Hills. Ten holes feature water hazards such as lakes,
cascades and a trout stream. The 15th hole (Par 5, 476yds) is
bounded by water all down the left with a carry over another
lake on to an island green. The course is challenging yet
great fun for all standards of golfer.

18 holes, 6109yds, Par 70, SSS 69.
Club membership 600.
Visitors   no restrictions but visitors must book start times
                  in order to avoid disapointment.phone 01823
                  461993.
Societies   contact professional Russell Gardner by
                  telephone.
Green Fees   £18 per round (£25 weekends).
Cards   [card symbols]
Prof   Russell Gardner
Designer   Adrian Stiff
Facilities   ⊗ ⅏ ▯ ☂ ♀ ♁ 🏠 ⛳ ⌁ ⌁
Location   Exit M5 junct 26, take A38 towards Taunton
                  and follow signs to Oake

Oake Manor Golf Club

Hotel   ★★★ 71% Rumwell Manor Hotel, Rumwell,
                  TAUNTON ☎ 01823 461902
                  10 ⊟ ☏ Annexe10 ⊟ ☏

Taunton & Pickeridge Corfe TA3 7BY
☎ 01823 421537 Fax 01823 421742
e-mail: sec@taunt-pickgolfclub.sagehost.co.uk
Downland course with extensive views.
18 holes, 5927yds, Par 69, SSS 68, Course record 63.
Club membership 600.
Visitors   must have a handicap certificate
Societies   must telephone in advance.
Green Fees   £26 per day; £22 per round (£30 weekends).
Prof   Gary Milne
Facilities   ⚶ 🏠 ⌁
Location   4m S off B3170

Hotel   ★★★ 75% The Mount Somerset Hotel,
                  Henlade, TAUNTON
                  ☎ 01823 442500   11 ⊟ ☏

Taunton Vale Creech Heathfield TA3 5EY
☎ 01823 412220 Fax 01823 413583
An 18 hole and a 9 hole golf course in a parkland complex
occupying 156 acres in the Vale of Taunton. Complex
includes a floodlit driving range.
*Charlton Course: 18 holes, 6167yds, Par 70, SSS 69, Course
record 65.*
Durston Course: 9 holes, 2004yds, Par 64, SSS 60.
Club membership 670.
Visitors   telephone booking essential. Must contact
                  Professional on 01823 412880
Societies   must book in advance.
Green Fees   not confirmed.
Prof   Martin Keitch
Designer   John Payne
Facilities   ⊗ ⅏ ▯ ☂ ♀ ♁ 🏠 ⛳ ➤ ⌁ ⌁
Location   Off A361 between juncts 24 & 25 on M5 ▶

Hotel ★★★ 75% The Mount Somerset Hotel, Henlade, TAUNTON
☎ 01823 442500 11 ⇆ ľ

Vivary Park Municipal Fons George TA1 3JU
☎ 01823 333875 Fax 01823 352713
e-mail: vivary.golf.course@tauntondeane.gov.uk
A parkland course, tight and narrow with ponds.
18 holes, 4620yds, Par 63, SSS 63, Course record 59.
Club membership 700.
Visitors may play anytime except weekends before 9am, bookings can be made 8 days in advance.
Societies apply in writing.
Green Fees £8.40 per round.
Prof Mike Steadman
Designer W H Fowler
Facilities ⊗ ⅷ ⓑ ♥ ♀ ♧ 盒 ☝ ♂
& Leisure hard tennis courts.
Location S side of town centre off A38

Hotel ★★ 64% Falcon Hotel, Henlade, TAUNTON
☎ 01823 442502 11 ⇆ ľ

WEDMORE Map 03 ST44

Isle of Wedmore Lineage BS28 4QT
☎ 01934 713649 (Office) 712452 (Pro)
Fax 01934 713696
Gentle undulating course designed to maintain natural environment. Existing woodland and hedgerow enhanced by new planting. Magnificent panoramic views of Cheddar Valley and Glastonbury Tor.
18 holes, 6006yds, Par 70, SSS 69, Course record 70.
Club membership 620.
Visitors telephone professional in advance. Not before 9.30am weekends.
Societies weekdays telephone in advance,weekends subject to competitions.
Green Fees £18 per round (£22 weekends) reductions in winter.
Cards ▦ 🟥 🟥 🟥 🟦 ▨
Prof Graham Coombe
Designer Terry Murray
Facilities ⊗ ⅷ ⓑ ♥ ♀ ♧ 盒 ☝ ⊞ ⏚ ♂
Location Off B3139 between Wells & Burnham-on-Sea

Hotel ★★★ 69% Swan Hotel, Sadler St, WELLS
☎ 01749 836300 35 ⇆ ľ

WELLS Map 03 ST54

Wells (Somerset) East Horrington Rd BA5 3DS
☎ 01749 675005 Fax 01749 675005
e-mail: secretary@wellsgolfclub99.freeserve.co.uk
Beautiful wooded course with wonderful views. The prevailing SW wind complicates the 448-yd, 3rd.
18 holes, 6015yds, Par 70, SSS 69, Course record 66.
Club membership 700.
Visitors must contact in advance & have handicap certificate weekends. Tee times restricted at weekends to after 9.30pm
Societies must apply in advance.
Green Fees not confirmed.
Prof Adrian Bishop
Facilities ⊗ ⓑ ♥ ♧ 盒 ☝ ♦ ⏚ ♂ ℓ
Location 1.5m E off B3139

Hotel ★★★ 69% Swan Hotel, Sadler St, WELLS
☎ 01749 836300 35 ⇆ ľ

WESTON-SUPER-MARE Map 03 ST36

Weston-Super-Mare Uphill Rd North BS23 4NQ
☎ 01934 626968 & 633360(pro) Fax 01934 621360
e-mail: karen@wsmgolfclub.fsnet.co.uk
A compact and interesting layout with the opening hole adjacent to the beach. The sandy, links-type course is slightly undulating and has beautifully maintained turf and greens. The 15th is a testing 455-yard, par 4.
18 holes, 6300yds, Par 70, SSS 70, Course record 65.
Club membership 778.
Visitors must have handicap certificate to play.
Societies apply in writing or telephone.
Green Fees £35 per day;£24 per round(£45/£35 weekends & bank holidays).
Prof Mike Laband
Designer T Dunne/Dr Mackenzie
Facilities ⊗ ⅷ ⓑ ♥ ♀ ♧ 盒 ♂
Location S side of town centre off A370

Hotel ★★★ 66% Beachlands Hotel, 17 Uphill Rd North, WESTON-SUPER-MARE
☎ 01934 621401 24 ⇆ ľ

Worlebury Monks Hill BS22 9SX
☎ 01934 625789 Fax 01934 621935
e-mail: secretary@worleburygc.co.uk
Situated on the ridge of Worlebury Hill, this seaside course offers fairly easy walking and extensive views of the Severn estuary and Wales.
18 holes, 5963yds, Par 70, SSS 69, Course record 66.
Club membership 650.
Visitors must be recognised golfers, handicap certificate or proof of club membership may be required.
Societies apply in writing or telephone in advance.
Green Fees not confirmed.
Prof Gary Marks
Designer H Vardon
Facilities ⊗ ⅷ ⓑ ♥ ♀ ♧ 盒 ♂
Location 2m NE off A370

Hotel ★★★ 66% Beachlands Hotel, 17 Uphill Rd North, WESTON-SUPER-MARE
☎ 01934 621401 24 ⇆ ľ

YEOVIL Map 03 ST51

Yeovil Sherborne Rd BA21 5BW
☎ 01935 422965 Fax 01935 411283
e-mail: yeovilgolfclub@yeovilgc.fsnet.co.uk
On the Old Course the opener lies by the River Yeo before the gentle climb to high downs with good views. The outstanding 14th and 15th holes present a challenge, being below the player with a deep railway cutting on the left of the green. The 1st on the Newton Course is played over the river which then leads to a challenging but scenic golf course.
Old Course: 18 holes, 6144yds, Par 72, SSS 70, Course record 64.
Newton Course: 9 holes, 4891yds, Par 68, SSS 65, Course record 63.
Club membership 1000.   ▶

Visitors	must contact in advance. Members only before 9.30am and 12.30-2. Handicap certificate required for Old Course.
Societies	telephone in advance.
Green Fees	Old Course: £30 per day; £25 per round (£40 weekends). Newton Course: £15 per round (£18 weekends).
Cards	💳 🔤 🔣 ⬜
Prof	Geoff Kite
Designer	Fowler & Allison
Facilities	⊗ ⅲ ╚ ⬛ ♀ ⚐ 🏠 ⛤ 𝄐 ⌇
Location	1m E on A30
Hotel	★★★ 71% Yeovil Court Hotel, West Coker Rd, YEOVIL ☎ 01935 863746 15 ⇔ 𝄐 Annexe15 ⇔ 𝄐

STAFFORDSHIRE

BROCTON   Map 07 SJ91

Brocton Hall ST17 0TH
☎ 01785 661901 Fax 01785 661591
Parkland course with gentle slopes in places, easy walking.
18 holes, 6064yds, Par 69, SSS 69, Course record 66.
Club membership 665.

Visitors	not competition days. Must contact in advance.
Societies	must apply in advance.
Green Fees	£33 per day (£40 weekends & bank holidays).
Prof	R G Johnson
Designer	Harry Vardon
Facilities	⊗ ⅲ ╚ ⬛ ♀ ⚐ 🏠 ⛤ ⬸ ⛏ 𝄐
Location	NW side of village off A34
Hotel	★★★ 65% Garth Hotel, Wolverhampton Rd, Moss Pit, STAFFORD ☎ 01785 256124 60 ⇔ 𝄐

BURTON-UPON-TRENT   Map 07 SK22

Branston Burton Rd, Branston DE14 3DP
☎ 01283 512211 Fax 01283 566984
Flat semi-parkland course, adjacent to River Trent, on undulating ground with natural water hazards on 13 holes. A new 9 hole course is under construction.
18 holes, 6697yds, Par 72, SSS 72, Course record 65.
Club membership 800.

Visitors	may not play before noon or at weekends. Must contact in advance.
Societies	must telephone in advance.
Green Fees	Mon-Thu £38 per 27/36 holes; £28 per 9/18 holes (Fri-Sun £40 per 9/18 holes).
Cards	💳 🔤 🔣 ⬜
Prof	Jacob Sture
Designer	G Ramshall
Facilities & Leisure	⊗ ⅲ ╚ ⬛ ♀ ⚐ 🏠 ⬸ ⛏ ⌇ heated indoor swimming pool, sauna, solarium, gymnasium.
Location	1.5m SW on A5121
Hotel	★★★ 68% Ye Olde Dog & Partridge Hotel, High St, TUTBURY ☎ 01283 813030 6 ⇔ 𝄐 Annexe14 ⇔ 𝄐

Burton-upon-Trent 43 Ashby Rd East DE15 0PS
☎ 01283 544551 Fax 01283 544551
e-mail: burtongolfclub@talk21.com
Undulating parkland course with trees a major feature. There are testing par 3s at 10th and 12th. The 18th has a lake on the approach to the green.
18 holes, 6579yds, Par 71, SSS 71, Course record 64.
Club membership 650.

Visitors	must contact in advance and have a handicap certificate.
Societies	must contact in advance.
Green Fees	£38 per day; £28 per round (£40/£32 weekends).
Prof	Gary Stafford
Designer	H S Colt
Facilities	⊗ ⅲ ╚ ⬛ ♀ ⚐ 🏠 ⛤ 𝄐
Location	3m E on A511

Guesthouse ♦♦♦♦ Edgecote Hotel, 179 Ashby Rd, BURTON UPON TRENT ☎ 01283 568966 11rm(5 𝄐)

Craythorne Craythorne Rd, Stretton DE13 0AZ
☎ 01283 564329 Fax 01283 511908
e-mail: admin@craythorne.co.uk
A relatively short and challenging parkland course with tight fairways and views of the Trent Valley. Excellent greens. Suits all standards but particularly good for society players. The course is now settled and in good condition after major refurbishments.
18 holes, 5525yds, Par 68, SSS 67, Course record 66.
Club membership 500.

Visitors	must contact in advance.
Societies	apply in writing or telephone for details.
Green Fees	£22 per round (£28 weekends & bank holidays).
Cards	💳 🔤 🔣 ⬜
Prof	Steve Hadfield
Facilities	⊗ ⅲ ╚ ⬛ ♀ ⚐ 🏠 ⛤ 𝄐 ⌇
Location	Off A38 through Stretton village

Guesthouse ♦♦♦♦ Edgecote Hotel, 179 Ashby Rd, BURTON UPON TRENT ☎ 01283 568966 11rm(5 𝄐)

Hoar Cross Hall Health Spa Golf Academy Hoar Cross DE13 8QS ☎ 01283 575671
Telephone for further details

CANNOCK   Map 07 SJ91

Beau Desert Rugeley Rd, Hazelslade WS12 5PJ
☎ 01543 422626 Fax 01543 451137
Heathland course surrounded by a forest.
18 holes, 6310yds, Par 70, SSS 71, Course record 64.
Club membership 500.

Visitors	are advised to contact professional in advance.
Societies	must contact in advance.
Green Fees	not confirmed.
Prof	Barrie Stevens
Designer	Herbert Fowler
Facilities	⊗ ⅲ ╚ ⬛ ♀ ⚐ 🏠 ⛤ 𝄐 ⌇
Location	0.5m NE of village
Hotel	★★★ Roman Way Hotel, Watling St, Hatherton, CANNOCK ☎ 01543 572121 56 ⇔ 𝄐

Cannock Park Stafford Rd WS11 2AL
☎ 01543 578850 Fax 01543 578850
e-mail: david.dunk@18global.co.uk
Part of a large leisure centre, this parkland-type course plays alongside Cannock Chase. Good drainage, open all year.
18 holes, 5149yds, Par 67, SSS 65.
Club membership 250.
Visitors   telephone pro shop on 01543 578850 to book in advance.
Societies   please telephone in advance.
Green Fees   £9 weekdays (£11 weekends).
Prof   David Dunk
Designer   John Mainland
Facilities   ⊗ ⅢⅡ ⓑ ♥ ♀ ⚘ ♨ ☞ ♂
& Leisure   hard tennis courts, heated indoor swimming pool, sauna, solarium, gymnasium.
Location   0.5m N of town centre on A34

Hotel   ★★★ Roman Way Hotel, Watling St,
                 Hatherton, CANNOCK
                 ☎ 01543 572121   56 ⇆ ⋔

ENVILLE   Map 07 SO88

Enville Highgate Common DY7 5BN
☎ 01384 872074 (Office) Fax 01384 873396
e-mail: enville@egolfclub.freeserve.co.uk
Easy walking on two fairly flat woodland/heathland courses - the 'Highgate' and the 'Lodge'.
Highgate Course: 18 holes, 6556yds, Par 72, SSS 72, Course record 65.
Lodge Course: 18 holes, 6290yds, Par 70, SSS 70.
Club membership 900.
Visitors   must play with member at weekends.
Societies   phone initially for details.
Green Fees   £40 per 36 holes; £35 per 27 holes; £30 per 18 holes.
Prof   Sean Power
Facilities   ⊗ ⅢⅡ ⓑ ♥ ♀ ⚘ ♨ ♥ ⚙
Location   From Stourbridge take A458 towards Bridgnorth, after 4.5m turn right. Golf club signposted

Hotel   ★★★★ 66% Mill Hotel & Restaurant,
                 ALVELEY ☎ 01746 780437   21 ⇆ ⋔

GOLDENHILL   Map 07 SJ85

Goldenhill Mobberley Rd ST6 5SS
☎ 01782 234200 Fax 01782 234303
Rolling parkland course with water features on six of the back nine holes.
18 holes, 5957yds, Par 71, SSS 69.
Club membership 300.
Visitors   advisable to contact in advance.
Societies   must apply in writing or telephone.
Green Fees   not confirmed.
Facilities   ⊗ ⅢⅡ ⓑ ♥ ♀ ⚘ ♨ ☞ ♂
Location   On A50, 4m N of Stoke

Hotel   ★★★ 71% Manor House Hotel, Audley Rd,
                 ALSAGER ☎ 01270 884000   57 ⇆ ⋔

Looking for a driving range?
See the index at the back of the guide

HIMLEY   Map 07 SO89

Himley Hall Golf Centre Log Cabin, Himley Hall Park
DY3 4DF ☎ 01902 895207
Parkland course set in grounds of Himley Hall Park, with lovely views. Large practice area including a pitch-and-putt.
9 holes, 6215yds, Par 72, SSS 70, Course record 65.
Club membership 200.
Visitors   restricted weekends.
Green Fees   £6.00 per 9 holes; £8.50 per 18 holes.
Prof   Jeremy Nichols
Designer   A Baker
Facilities   ⓑ ♥ ⚘ ♂
Location   0.5m E on B4176

Hotel   ★★★ 63% Himley Country Hotel, School Rd,
                 HIMLEY ☎ 01902 896716   73 ⇆ ⋔

LEEK   Map 07 SJ95

Leek Birchall, Cheddleton Rd ST13 5RE
☎ 01538 384779 Fax 01538 384535
Undulating, challenging mainly parkland course, reputedly one of the best in the area.
18 holes, 6218yds, Par 70, SSS 70, Course record 63.
Club membership 750.
Visitors   must contact Professional in advance.
Societies   must apply in advance.
Green Fees   £24 (£30 weekends).
Prof   Peter A Stubbs
Facilities   ⊗ ⅢⅡ ⓑ ♥ ♀ ⚘ ♨ ♂
Location   0.75m S on A520

Hotel   ★★★ 69% George Hotel, Swan Square,
                 Burslem, STOKE-ON-TRENT
                 ☎ 01782 577544   39 ⇆ ⋔

Westwood (Leek) Newcastle Rd ST13 7AA
☎ 01538 398385 & 398897 (Prof) Fax 01538 382485
A challenging moorland/parkland course set in beautiful open countryside with an undulating front nine. The back nine is more open and longer with the River Churnet coming into play on several holes.
18 holes, 6207yds, Par 70, SSS 69, Course record 66.
Club membership 700.
Visitors   must book in advance.
Societies   apply by phone or in writing.
Green Fees   £18(£20 weekends).
Prof   Neale Hyde
Facilities   ⊗ ⅢⅡ ⓑ ♥ ♀ ⚘ ♨ ☞ ♂
Location   On A53, S of Leek

Hotel   ★★★ 69% George Hotel, Swan Square,
                 Burslem, STOKE-ON-TRENT
                 ☎ 01782 577544   39 ⇆ ⋔

LICHFIELD   Map 07 SK10

Seedy Mill Elmhurst WS13 8HE
☎ 01543 417333 Fax 01543 418098
e-mail: s.dixon@clubhaus.com
A 27 hole course in picturesque parkland scenery. Numerous holes crossed by meandering mill streams. Undulating greens defended by hazards lie in wait for the practised approach. Well appointed clubhouse.
18 holes, 6308yds, Par 72, SSS 70, Course record 68.
Club membership 1200.   ▶

Visitors	must contact at least 3 days in advance, weekend time restrictions.
Societies	apply in writing or telephone.
Green Fees	not confirmed.
Cards	🖃 🔳 🔳 🔳 💷
Prof	Chris Stanley
Designer	Hawtree & Son
Facilities	⊗ ⫙ ♿ ☕ ♀ ⚲ 🏠 ⛟ 🛒 ℓ ſ
Location	At Elmhurst, 2m N of Lichfield, off A515
Hotel	★★★ 68% Little Barrow Hotel, Beacon St, LICHFIELD ☎ 01543 414500 24 ⇆ ſ

Whittington Heath Tamworth Rd WS14 9PW
☎ 01543 432317 Fax 01543 432317
18 magnificent holes winding their way through heathland and trees, presenting a good test for the serious golfer. Leaving the fairway can be severely punished. The dog-legs are most tempting, inviting the golfer to chance his arm. Local knowledge is a definite advantage. Clear views of the famous three spires of Lichfield Cathedral.
18 holes, 6490yds, Par 70, SSS 71, Course record 64.
Club membership 660.

Visitors	must contact in advance. May not play at weekends. Handicap certificate required.
Societies	welcome Wed & Thu, must apply in writing.
Green Fees	£40 per 36 holes, £35 per 27 holes, £30 per 18 holes.
Cards	🖃 🔳 🔳 🔳 💷
Prof	Adrian Sadler
Designer	Colt
Facilities	⊗ ⫙ ♿ ☕ ♀ ⚲ 🏠
Location	2.5m SE on A51 Lichfield-Tamworth road
Hotel	★★★ 68% Little Barrow Hotel, Beacon St, LICHFIELD ☎ 01543 414500 24 ⇆ ſ

NEWCASTLE-UNDER-LYME   Map 07 SJ84

Keele Golf Club Newcastle Rd, Keele ST5 5AB
☎ 01782 627596
Open course on the side of a hill without maturing trees.
18 holes, 6396yds, Par 71, SSS 70, Course record 64.
Club membership 200.

Visitors	must contact in advance.
Societies	by prior arrangement to Newcastle-under-Lyme Borough Council, Civic Offices, Merrial St, Newcastle-Under-Lyme, Staffs.
Green Fees	not confirmed.
Prof	Colin Smith
Facilities	⊗ ⫙ ♿ ☕ ♀ ⚲ 🏠 ℓ ſ
Location	2m W on A525
Hotel	★★★ 67% Posthouse Stoke on Trent, Clayton Rd, NEWCASTLE-UNDER-LYME ☎ 0870 400 9077 119 ⇆ ſ

Newcastle-Under-Lyme Whitmore Rd ST5 2QB
☎ 01782 617006
Parkland course.
18 holes, 6404yds, Par 72, SSS 71.
Club membership 600.

Visitors	must contact in advance. With member only weekends.

Societies	must contact in advance.
Green Fees	not confirmed.
Prof	Paul Symonds
Facilities	♿ ☕ ♀ ⚲ 🏠 ⛟ ℓ
Location	1m SW on A53
Hotel	★★ 62% Comfort Inn, Liverpool Rd, Cross Heath, NEWCASTLE-UNDER-LYME ☎ 01782 717000 43 ⇆ ſ Annexe24 ⇆ ſ

Wolstanton Dimsdale Old Hall, Hassam Pde, Wolstanton ST5 9DR ☎ 01782 622413 (Sec) & 616995
A challenging undulating suburban course incorporating 6 difficult Par 3 holes. The 6th hole (Par 3) is 233yds from the Medal Tee.
18 holes, 5807yds, Par 68, SSS 68, Course record 63.
Club membership 700.

Visitors	must contact in advance. May not play Tue (Ladies Day). With member only at weekends & bank holidays.
Societies	must contact in advance.
Green Fees	£25 per day.
Cards	🖃 🔳 🔳 🔳 💷
Prof	Simon Arnold
Facilities	⊗ ⫙ ♿ ☕ ♀ ⚲ 🏠 ℓ
Location	1.5m from town centre. Turn off A34 nr MacDonalds
Hotel	★★★ 67% Posthouse Stoke on Trent, Clayton Rd, NEWCASTLE-UNDER-LYME ☎ 0870 400 9077 119 ⇆ ſ

ONNELEY   Map 07 SJ74

Onneley CW3 5QF ☎ 01782 750577
A tight, picturesque, hillside parkland course. An ideal test for the short game.
13 holes, 5781yds, Par 70, SSS 68.
Club membership 410.

Visitors	welcome except during competitions, but may not play on Sun and with member only Sat and bank holidays.
Societies	packages available apply in writing to secretary.
Green Fees	£20 per day.
Facilities	⊗ ⫙ by prior arrangement ♿ ☕ ♀ ⚲
Location	2m from Woore on A525
Hotel	★★ Wheatsheaf Inn at Onneley, Barhill Rd, ONNELEY ☎ 01782 751581 6 ſ

PATTINGHAM   Map 07 SO89

Patshull Park Hotel Golf & Country Club WV6 7IIR
☎ 01902 700100 Fax 01902 700874
e-mail: sales@patshull-park.co.uk
Picturesque course set in 280 acres of glorious Capability Brown landscaped parkland. Designed by John Jacobs, the course meanders alongside trout fishing lakes. Water comes into play alongside the 3rd hole and there is a challenging drive over water on the 13th. Wellingtonia and cedar trees prove an obstacle to wayward drives off several holes. The 12th is the toughest hole on the course and the tee shot is vital, anything wayward and the trees block out the second to the green.
18 holes, 6400yds, Par 72, SSS 71, Course record 64.
Club membership 330.

▶

Patshull Park Hotel Golf & Country Club

Visitors must contact in advance.
Societies must contact in advance.
Green Fees £30 per 18 holes (£40 weekends & bank holidays).
Cards 🗂️ 🟥 🟦 💳 🟦 🟢
Prof Richard Bissell
Designer John Jacobs
Facilities ⊗ ⏳ 🍴 🍺 🏌️ 🛍️ 🏠 ⛳ 🐎 🏌️ ♂
& Leisure heated indoor swimming pool, fishing, sauna, solarium, gymnasium.
Location 1.5m W of pattingham at Pattingham Church take the Patshull Rd ,Golf club on right

Hotel ★★★ 67% Patshull Park Hotel Golf & Country Club, Patshull Park, PATTINGHAM
☎ 01902 700100 49 ⇔ ℉

PERTON   Map 07 SO89

Perton Park Wrottesley Park Rd WV6 7HL
☎ 01902 380103 & 380073 Fax 01902 326219
Challenging inland links style course set in the picturesque Staffordshire countryside.
18 holes, 6520yds, Par 72, SSS 72, Course record 61.
Club membership 500.
Visitors must book in advance.
Societies must telephone in advance.
Green Fees £12 per round (£18 weekends & bank holidays).
Cards 🗂️ 🟥
Prof Jeremy Harrold
Facilities ⊗ ⏳ 🍴 🍺 🏌️ 🛍️ 🏠 ⛳ 🐎 ♂ ℉
& Leisure hard tennis courts.
Location 6m W of Wolverhampton, off A454

Hotel ★★ Ely House Hotel, 53 Tettenhall Rd, WOLVERHAMPTON
☎ 01902 311311 19 ⇔ ℉

STAFFORD   Map 07 SJ92

Stafford Castle Newport Rd ST16 1BP ☎ 01785 223821
Parkland type course built around Stafford Castle.
9 holes, 6382yds, Par 71, SSS 70, Course record 68.
Club membership 400.
Visitors must contact in advance. May not play Sun morning.
Societies must apply in writing or by telephone.
Green Fees £16 per day (£20 weekends).
Facilities ⊗ ⏳ 🍴 🍺 🏌️
Location SW side of town centre off A518

Hotel ★★★ 65% Garth Hotel, Wolverhampton Rd, Moss Pit, STAFFORD
☎ 01785 256124 60 ⇔ ℉

STOKE-ON-TRENT   Map 07 SJ84

Burslem Wood Farm, High Ln, Tunstall ST6 7JT
☎ 01782 837006
On the outskirts of Tunstall, a moorland course with hard walking.
9 holes, 5354yds, Par 66, SSS 66, Course record 66.
Club membership 250.
Visitors except Sun & with member only Sat & bank holidays.
Societies must telephone in advance.
Green Fees not confirmed.
Facilities ⊗ ⏳ 🍴 🍺 🏌️ 🍴
Location 4m N of city centre on B5049

Hotel ★★★ 69% George Hotel, Swan Square, Burslem, STOKE-ON-TRENT
☎ 01782 577544 39 ⇔ ℉

Greenway Hall Stanley Rd, Stockton Brook ST9 9LJ
☎ 01782 503158
18 holes, 5678yds, Par 68, SSS 67.
Location 5m NE off A53
Telephone for further details

Hotel ★★★ 69% George Hotel, Swan Square, Burslem, STOKE-ON-TRENT
☎ 01782 577544 39 ⇔ ℉

Trentham 14 Barlaston Old Rd, Trentham ST4 8HB
☎ 01782 658109 Fax 01782 644024
e-mail: secretary@trenthamgolf.org
Parkland course. The par 3, 4th is a testing hole reached through a copse of trees.
18 holes, 6644yds, Par 72, SSS 72, Course record 67.
Club membership 600.
Visitors must contact in advance.
Societies must contact in advance.
Green Fees £40 per round (£50 weekends & bank holidays).
Cards 🗂️ 🟥 🟢
Prof Sandy Wilson
Designer Colt & Alison
Facilities ⊗ ⏳ 🍴 🍺 🏌️ 🏠 ⛳ 🐎 ♂ ℉
& Leisure squash.
Location 3m S off A5035

Hotel ★★★ 66% Haydon House Hotel, Haydon St, Basford, STOKE-ON-TRENT
☎ 01782 711311 17 ⇔ ℉ Annexe6 ⇔ ℉

Trentham Park Trentham Park ST4 8AE
☎ 01782 658800 Fax 01782 658800
Fine woodland course. Set in established parkland with many challenging and interesting holes.
18 holes, 6425yds, Par 71, SSS 71, Course record 67.
Club membership 850.
Visitors must contact in advance.
Societies Wed & Fri, must apply in advance.
Green Fees £25 per day;£22.50 per round(£30 per day).
Prof Brian Rimmer
Facilities ⊗ ⏳ 🍴 🍺 🏌️ 🏠 ⛳ 🐎 ♂
Location Adjacent to Trentham Gardens, off A34 3m S of Newcastle-under-Lyme   ▶

Hotel ★★★ 67% Posthouse Stoke on Trent, Clayton Rd, NEWCASTLE-UNDER-LYME ☎ 0870 400 9077 119 ⇆ ↟

STONE   Map 07 SJ93

Barlaston Meaford Rd ST15 8UX
☎ 01782 372795 & 372867 Fax 01782 372867
Picturesque meadowland course designed by Peter Alliss.
18 holes, 5800yds, Par 69, SSS 68.
Club membership 650.
Visitors   may not play before 10am or after 4pm Fridays, weekends and bank holidays.
Societies   telephone or apply in writing.
Green Fees not confirmed.
Prof   Ian Rogers
Designer   Peter Alliss
Facilities   ⊗ ⓑ ⓛ ♥ ♀ ⚲ ⌂ ℓ

Hotel ★★★ 68% Stone House Hotel, Stafford Rd, STONE ☎ 01785 815531   50 ⇆ ↟

Izaak Walton Eccleshall Rd, Cold Norton ST15 0NS
☎ 01785 760900
A gently undulating meadowland course with streams and ponds as features.
18 holes, 6281yds, Par 72, SSS 72, Course record 72.
Club membership 400.
Visitors   must contact in advance for weekends play.
Societies   must telephone in advance.
Green Fees £15 per round:£20 per day (£20/28 weekends).
Prof   Julie Brown
Facilities   ⊗ ⓜ ⓑ ⓛ ♥ ♀ ⚲ ⌂ ℓ ⏵
Location   On B5026 between Stone & Eccleshall

Hotel ★★★ 68% Stone House Hotel, Stafford Rd, STONE ☎ 01785 815531   50 ⇆ ↟

Stone Filleybrooks ST15 0NB ☎ 01785 813103
9-hole parkland course with easy walking and 18 different tees.
9 holes, 6299yds, Par 71, SSS 70, Course record 67.
Club membership 310.
Visitors   with member only weekends & bank holidays.
Societies   must apply in writing.
Green Fees £15 per day/round.
Facilities   ⊗ ⓜ ⓑ ⓛ ♥ ♀ ⚲ ℓ
Location   0.5m W on A34

Hotel ★★★ 68% Stone House Hotel, Stafford Rd, STONE ☎ 01785 815531   50 ⇆ ↟

TAMWORTH   Map 07 SK20

Drayton Park Drayton Park, Fazeley B78 3TN
☎ 01827 251139 Fax 01827 284035
Parkland course designed by James Braid. Club established since 1897.
18 holes, 6214yds, Par 71, SSS 71, Course record 62.
Club membership 450.
Visitors   with member only weekends. Must book in advance (call either professional or secretary).
Societies   must apply in writing.
Green Fees not confirmed.
Prof   M W Passmore
Designer   James Braid

Facilities   ⊗ ⓜ ⓑ ⓛ ♥ ♀ ⚲ ⌂ ℓ
Location   2m S on A4091, next to Drayton Manor Leisure Park

Hotel ★★★★ 75% The De Vere Belfry, WISHAW ☎ 01675 470301 324 ⇆ ↟

Tamworth Municipal Eagle Dr, Amington B77 4EG
☎ 01827 709303 Fax 01827 709304
First-class municipal, parkland course and a good test of golf.
18 holes, 6605yds, Par 73, SSS 72, Course record 63.
Club membership 600.
Visitors   must book in advance at weekends.
Societies   must contact in advance.
Green Fees £15.50 per 18 holes.
Cards   ▭▭ 🗓
Prof   Aynsley Hill
Designer   Hawtree & Son
Facilities   ⊗ ⓜ ⓑ ⓛ ♥ ♀ ⚲ ⌂ ⚑ ⚒ ℓ ⏴
Location   2.5m E off B5000

Hotel ★★ 63% Angel Croft Hotel, Beacon St, LICHFIELD ☎ 01543 258737 10rm(3 ⇆5 ↟) Annexe8 ⇆ ↟

UTTOXETER   Map 07 SK03

Manor Leese Hill, Kingstone ST14 8QT
☎ 01889 563234 Fax 01889 563234
e-mail: ant-foulds@bigfoot.com
A short but tough course set in the heart of the Staffordshire countryside with fine views of the surrounding area.
18 holes, 6060yds, Par 71, SSS 69, Course record 67.
Club membership 400.
Visitors   must contact in advance.
Societies   must telephone in advance.
Green Fees £10 (£15 weekends).
Cards   ▭▭ ▬ ▭▬ 🗓
Designer   Various
Facilities   ⊗ ⓜ ⓑ ♥ ♀ ⚲ ⌂ ⏵ ⚒ ℓ ⏴
& Leisure fishing.
Location   2m from Uttoxeter on A518 towards Stafford

Hotel ★★★ 68% Stone House Hotel, Stafford Rd, STONE ☎ 01785 815531   50 ⇆ ↟

Uttoxeter Wood Ln ST14 8JR
☎ 01889 564884 (Pro) & 566552 (Office)
Fax 01889 567501 e-mail: uttoxetergolfclub@talk21.com
Undulating, challenging course with spectacular views adjacent to the racecourse.
18 holes, 5710yds, Par 70, SSS 69, Course record 66.
Club membership 900.
Visitors   restricted weekends and competition days. Advisable to check availability during peak periods.
Societies   must book in advance.
Green Fees £20 per round:£30 per day(£30 per round weekends & bank holidays).
Prof   Adam McCandless
Designer   G Rothera
Facilities   ⊗ ⓜ ⓑ ⓛ ♥ ♀ ⚲ ⌂ ℓ
Location   Close to A50, 0.5m beyond main entrance to racecourse

Hotel ★★★ 68% Stone House Hotel, Stafford Rd, STONE ☎ 01785 815531   50 ⇆ ↟

WESTON   Map 07 SJ92

Ingestre Park ST18 0RE
☎ 01889 270845 Fax 01889 270845
Parkland course set in the grounds of Ingestre Hall, former home of the Earl of Shrewsbury, with mature trees and pleasant views.
18 holes, 6268yds, Par 70, SSS 70, Course record 67.
Club membership 750.
Visitors   with member only weekends & bank holidays. Must play before 3.30pm weekdays. Advance booking preferred. Handicap certificate required.
Societies   must apply in advance.
Green Fees £30 per day; £25 per round.
Prof   Danny Scullion
Designer   Hawtree
Facilities   ⊗ 〕🐴 🍴 ♀ 🛆 🏡 ➤ ⚒ ✐
Location   2m SE off A51

Hotel   ★★★ 66% Tillington Hall Hotel, Eccleshall Rd, STAFFORD ☎ 01785 253531 91 ⇆ ↾

WHISTON   Map 07 SK04

Whiston Hall Whiston Hall ST10 2HZ ☎ 01538 266260
A challenging 18-hole course in scenic countryside, incorporating many natural obstacles and providing a test for all golfing abilities.
18 holes, 5742yds, Par 71, SSS 69, Course record 70.
Club membership 400.
Visitors   reasonable dress on the course. Must telephone in advance at weekends.
Societies   phone for details.
Green Fees not confirmed.
Designer   T Cooper
Facilities   ⊗ 〕🐴 🍴 ♀ 🛆 ✐
& Leisure   fishing, snooker.
Location   Off A52, between Stoke-on-Trent and Ashbourne

Hotel   ★★★ 69% George Hotel, Swan Square, Burslem, STOKE-ON-TRENT ☎ 01782 577544 39 ⇆ ↾

SUFFOLK

ALDEBURGH   Map 05 TM45

Aldeburgh Saxmundham Rd IP15 5PE
☎ 01728 452890 Fax 01728 452937
e-mail: info@aldeburghgolfclub.co.uk
Fine heathland golf course providing a varied and interesting challenge for the handicap golfer. Additional 9 hole course suitable for golfing holiday makers.
18 holes, 6330yds, Par 68, SSS 71, Course record 65.
River Course: 9 holes, 4228yds, Par 64, SSS 61, Course record 62.
Club membership 850.
Visitors   must contact in advance and have a handicap certificate. 2 ball/foursomes only.
Societies   must contact in advance.

Green Fees £45 per day, Mon-Fri, £35 after noon (£60 weekends, £40 after noon).
Prof   Keith Preston
Designer   various
Facilities   ⊗ 🐴 🍴 ♀ 🛆 🏡 ➤ ✐
Location   1m W of Aldeburgh on A1094

Hotel   ★★★ 74% Wentworth Hotel, Wentworth Rd, ALDEBURGH ☎ 01728 452312 30rm(24 ⇆4 ↾) Annexe7 ⇆ ↾

BECCLES   Map 05 TM49

Beccles The Common NR34 9YN
☎ 01502 712244
Common course with gorse bushes, no water hazards or bunkers.
9 holes, 2779yds, Par 68, SSS 67.
Club membership 175.
Visitors   no restrictions.
Societies   must telephone in advance.
Green Fees £5 per round (£10 weekends).
Facilities   ♀ 🛆 🏡 ✐
Location   NE side of town

Hotel   ★★★ 65% Hotel Hatfield, The Esplanade, LOWESTOFT ☎ 01502 565337 33 ⇆ ↾

WENTWORTH
HOTEL ★★★
Aldeburgh, Suffolk
Tel: (01728) 452312 Fax: (01728) 454343
E-mail: wentworth.hotel@anglianet.co.uk
Website: www.wentworth-aldeburgh.com

The Hotel has the comfort and style of a Country House. Two comfortable lounges, with open fires and antique furniture, provide ample space to relax. Each individually decorated bedroom, many with sea views, is equipped with a colour television, radio, hairdryer and tea making facilities. The Restaurant serves a variety of fresh produce whilst a light lunch can be chosen from the Bar menu, eaten outside in the sunken terrace garden. Aldeburgh is timeless and unhurried. There are quality shops, two excellent golf courses within a short distance from the hotel, long walks and some of the best birdwatching at Minsmere Bird reserve. Music and the Arts can be heard at the Internationally famous Snape Malting Concert hall. Lastly, there are miles of beach to sit upon and watch the sea!

BUNGAY

Map 05 TM38

Bungay & Waveney Valley Outney Common NR35 1DS
☎ 01986 892337 Fax 01986 892222
Heathland course partly comprising Neolithic stone
workings, easy walking.
18 holes, 6044yds, Par 69, SSS 69, Course record 64.
Club membership 730.
Visitors   should contact in advance. With member only
              weekends & bank holidays.
Societies   must contact in advance.
Green Fees   £24 per round; £30 per day.
Cards   [symbols]
Prof   Nigel Whyte
Designer   James Braid
Facilities   [symbols]
Location   0.5m NW on A143

Hotel   ★★★ 65% Hotel Hatfield, The Esplanade,
              LOWESTOFT ☎ 01502 565337   33 [symbols]

BURY ST EDMUNDS

Map 05 TL86

Bury St Edmunds Tut Hill IP28 6LG
☎ 01284 755979 Fax 01284 763288
e-mail: bury.golf@talk21.com
Undulating parkland course with easy walking and attractive
short holes, but quite long. 9 hole course made up of 5 Par
3's and 4x4.
18 holes, 6669yds, Par 72, SSS 72, Course record 68.
9 holes, 2217yds, Par 62, SSS 62.
Club membership 850.
Visitors   with member only at weekends for 18 hole
              course.
Societies   must apply in writing.
Green Fees   18 hole course: £30 per day ; £25 per round. 9
              hole course: £12 per round (£15 weekends).
Cards   [symbols]
Prof   Mark Jillings
Designer   Ted Ray
Facilities   [symbols] by prior arrangement [symbols]
Location   2m NW on B1106 off A14

Hotel   ★★★ 71% Angel Hotel, Angel Hill, BURY
              ST EDMUNDS ☎ 01284 714000   64 [symbols]

The Suffolk Golf & Country Club Fornham St Genevieve
IP28 6JQ ☎ 01284 706777 Fax 01284 706721
A classic parkland course with the river Lark running
through it, which comes into play regularly.
*The Genevieve Course: 18 holes, 6345yds, Par 72, SSS 71,
Course record 70.*
Club membership 600
Visitors   contact golf reception, bookings up to 1 week in
              advance.
Societies   apply in writing to the General Manager.
Green Fees   £25 per round (£30 weekends).
Cards   [symbols]
Prof   Steve Hall
Facilities   [symbols]
& Leisure   heated indoor swimming pool, sauna, solarium,
              gymnasium.
Location   Off the A14 onto the B1106 to Fornham

Hotel   ★★★₤₤ 70% Ravenwood Hall Hotel,
              Rougham, BURY ST EDMUNDS
              ☎ 01359 270345 7 [symbols] Annexe7 [symbols]

CRETINGHAM

Map 05 TM26

Cretingham IP13 7BA
☎ 01728 685275 Fax 01728 685037
9 holes, 4552yds, Par 66, SSS 64, Course record 61.
Location   2m from A1120 at Earl Soham
Telephone for further details

Hotel   ★★ 65% Cedars Hotel, Needham Rd,
              STOWMARKET ☎ 01449 612668   25 [symbols]

FELIXSTOWE

Map 05 TM33

Felixstowe Ferry Ferry Rd IP11 9RY
☎ 01394 286834 Fax 01394 273679
Seaside links course, pleasant views, easy walking. Testing
491-yd, 7th hole. 9 hole course now open.
*Martello Course: 18 holes, 6272yds, Par 72, SSS 70, Course
record 66.*
Club membership 900.
Visitors   may not play weekends on Martello Course.
Societies   Tue, Wed & Fri.
Green Fees   £30 per day (£20 after 2pm).
Prof   Ian MacPherson
Designer   Henry Cotton
Facilities   [symbols] by prior arrangement [symbols]
Location   NE side of town centre. Signposted from A14

Hotel   ★★ 70% Waverley Hotel, 2 Wolsey Gardens,
              FELIXSTOWE ☎ 01394 282811   19 [symbols]

FLEMPTON

Map 05 TL86

Flempton IP28 6EQ ☎ 01284 728291
Breckland course.
9 holes, 6240yds, Par 70, SSS 70.
Club membership 300.
Visitors   must contact in advance and produce handicap
              certificate. With member only weekends & bank
              holidays.
Societies   limited to small societies - must apply in
              writing.
Green Fees   not confirmed.
Prof   Mark Jillings
Designer   J H Taylor
Facilities   [symbols]
Location   0.5m W on A1101

Hotel   ★★★ 70% The Priory Hotel, Tollgate, BURY
              ST EDMUNDS ☎ 01284 766181
              9 [symbols] Annexe30 [symbols]

HALESWORTH

Map 05 TM37

Halesworth Bramfield Rd IP19 9XA
☎ 01986 875567 Fax 01986 874565
A 27-hole professionally designed parkland complex of one
18 hole membership course and a 9 hole pay and play.
18 holes, 6580yds, Par 72, SSS 72, Course record 71.
9 holes, 2398yds, Par 33, SSS 33.
Club membership 700.
Visitors   visitors welcome at all times except for Sunday
              before noon on the 18 hole course. Handicap
              certificate required for 18 hole course.
Societies   telephone for booking form.
Green Fees   not confirmed.

Prof	Richard Whyte
Designer	J W Johnson
Facilities	⊗ ⟦ 🏠 🍴 ♀ 👤 🏠 ⚑ 🏌 🚃 🏌 (
Location	0.75m S of town, signposted on left of A144 road to Bramfield

Hotel	★★★ 71% Swan Hotel, Market Place, SOUTHWOLD ☎ 01502 722186 26rm(25 ⇄ ↑) Annexe17 ⇄ ↑

HAVERHILL   Map 05 TL64

Haverhill Coupals Rd CB9 7UW
☎ 01440 761951 Fax 01440 761951
e-mail: haverhillgolf@coupalsroad.fsnet.co.uk
An 18 hole course lying across two valleys in pleasant parkland. The front nine with undulating fairways is complimented by a saucer shaped back nine, bisected by the River Stour, presenting a challenge to golfers of all standards.
18 holes, 5898yds, Par 70, SSS 69, Course record 67.
Club membership 767.

Visitors	telephone to check for club competitions.
Societies	must contact in advance. Tue & Thu only.
Green Fees	£20 per 18 holes (£25 weekends).
Cards	💳 🔳 🔳 💳 🔳 🎏
Prof	Simon Mayfield
Designer	P Pilgrem/C Lawrie
Facilities	⊗ ⟦ 🏠 ♀ 👤 🏠 🍴 🏌
Location	1m SE off A1017

Hotel	★★ 72% Four Seasons Hotel, Walden Rd, THAXTED ☎ 01371 830129 9 ⇄ ↑

HINTLESHAM   Map 05 TM04

Hintlesham Hall IP8 3NS
☎ 01473 652761 Fax 01473 652750
Magnificent championship length course blending harmoniously with the ancient parkland surrounding this exclusive hotel. The 6630yd parkland course was designed by Hawtree and Son, one of the oldest established firms of golf course architects in the world. The course is fair but challenging for low and high handicappers alike. Hotel offers beautiful accommodation, excellent cuisine and many facilities.
18 holes, 6638yds, Par 72, SSS 72, Course record 67.
Club membership 470.

Visitors	must contact 48 hours in advance.
Societies	must telephone in advance.
Green Fees	£30(£38 weekends & bank holidays).
Cards	💳 🔳 🔳 💳 🎏

Prof	Alastair Spink
Designer	Hawtree & Sons
Facilities	⊗ ⟦ 🏠 ♀ 👤 🏠 🍴 🏌 🚃 🏌
& Leisure	hard tennis courts, heated outdoor swimming pool, sauna, gymnasium.
Location	In village on A1071

Hotel	★★★★♨ Hintlesham Hall Hotel, HINTLESHAM ☎ 01473 652334 & 652268 Fax 01473 652463 33 ⇄ ↑

IPSWICH   Map 05 TM14

Alnesbourne Priory Priory Park IP10 0JT
☎ 01473 727393 Fax 01473 278372
e-mail: PrioryParkIpswich@msn.com
A fabulous outlook facing due south across the River Orwell is one of the many good features of this course set in woodland. All holes run among trees with some fairways requiring straight shots. The 8th green is on saltings by the river.
9 holes, 1700yds, Par 29.
Club membership 30.

Visitors	closed on Tuesday. Closed 8 Jan-01 Mar.
Societies	Tue only, telephone in advance.
Green Fees	£10 (£11 Sat; £12 Sun & bank holidays).
Facilities	⊗ ⟦ 🏠 ♀ 👤 🍴
Location	3m SE, off A14

Hotel	★★★ 69% Courtyard by Marriott Ipswich, The Havens, Ransomes Europark, IPSWICH ☎ 01473 272244 60 ⇄ ↑

Fynn Valley IP6 9JA ☎ 01473 785267 Fax 01473 785632
e-mail: enquiries@fynn-valley.co.uk
Undulating parkland course plus Par-3 nine-hole and driving range.
18 holes, 6310yds, Par 70, SSS 71, Course record 67.
Club membership 700.

Visitors	members only Sun until noon.
Societies	must apply in advance.
Green Fees	from £15 per 18 holes.
Cards	💳 🔳 🔳 🎏
Prof	Kelvin Vince
Designer	Tony Tyrrell
Facilities	⊗ ⟦ 🏠 ♀ 👤 🏠 🚃 🏌 (
& Leisure	Par 3 course.
Location	2m N of Ipswich on B1077

Hotel	★★★ 65% Novotel Ipswich, Greyfriars Rd, IPSWICH ☎ 01473 232400 100 ⇄ ↑

Ipswich Purdis Heath IP3 8UQ
☎ 01473 728941 Fax 01473 715236 e-mail: mail@ipswichgolfclub.com
Many golfers are suprised when they hear that Ipswich has, at Purdis Heath, a first-class golf course. In some ways it resembles some of Surrey's better courses; a beautiful heathland course with two lakes and easy walking.
18 holes, 6435yds, Par 71, SSS 71, Course record 64 or 9 holes, 1930yds, Par 31.
Club membership 850.

▶

Visitors	must contact in advance & have a handicap certificate for 18 hole course.
Societies	must contact in advance.
Green Fees	£40 per day; £25 per round,for 18 hole course (£43/£30 weekends & bank holidays). 9 hole course £10 per day (£12.50 weekends & bank holidays).
Cards	▦ 🎫 ⬛ ⛏ ▨
Prof	Stephen Whymark
Designer	James Braid
Facilities	⊗ ⓛ ⬛ ♈ ⚽ 🏠 ⌀
Location	E side of town centre off A1156
Hotel	★★★ 71% Marlborough Hotel, Henley Rd, IPSWICH ☎ 01473 226789 22 ⇆ ☞

Rushmere Rushmere Heath IP4 5QQ
☎ 01473 725648 Fax 01473 725648
e-mail: rushmeregolfclub@talk21.com
Heathland course with gorse and prevailing winds. Testing 5th hole - dog leg, 419 yards (par 4).
18 holes, 6262yds, Par 70, SSS 70, Course record 66.
Club membership 770.

Visitors	not before 2.30pm weekends & bank holidays. Must have a handicap certificate. Must contact in advance.
Societies	weekdays (ex Wed) by arrangement.
Green Fees	£25 per round/day.
Prof	N T J McNeill
Facilities	⚽ 🏠 ⌀
Location	Off A12 N of Ipswich. Signposted
Hotel	★★★ 71% Marlborough Hotel, Henley Rd, IPSWICH ☎ 01473 226789 22 ⇆ ☞

LOWESTOFT Map 05 TM59

Rookery Park Carlton Colville NR33 8HJ
☎ 01502 560380 Fax 01502 560380
Parkland course with a 9-hole, Par 3 adjacent.
18 holes, 6714yds, Par 72, SSS 72.
Club membership 1000.

Visitors	must have handicap certificate.
Societies	by arrangement.
Green Fees	not confirmed.
Prof	Martin Elsworthy
Designer	C D Lawrie
Facilities	⊗ ⫿ ⓛ ⬛ ♈ 🏠 ⌀
Location	3.5m SW on A146
Hotel	★★★ 65% Hotel Hatfield, The Esplanade, LOWESTOFT ☎ 01502 565337 33 ⇆ ☞

NEWMARKET Map 05 TL66

Links Cambridge Rd CB8 0TG
☎ 01638 663000 Fax 01638 661476
Gently undulating parkland.
18 holes, 6582yds, Par 72, SSS 71, Course record 66 or , Par 72.
Club membership 780.

Visitors	must have handicap certificate, may not play Sun before 11.30am.
Societies	telephone secretary in advance.
Green Fees	£32 (£36 weekends & bank holidays).

Prof	John Sharkey
Designer	Col. Hotchkin
Facilities	⊗ ⫿ ⓛ ⬛ ♈ ⚽ 🏠 ⌀
Location	1m SW on A1034
Hotel	★★★ 68% Heath Court Hotel, Moulton Rd, NEWMARKET ☎ 01638 667171 41 ⇆ ☞

NEWTON Map 05 TL94

Newton Green Newton Green CO10 0QN
☎ 01787 377217 & 377501 Fax 01787 377549
Flat, 18-hole course with lake.
18 holes, 5960yds, Par 69, SSS 68.
Club membership 640.

Visitors	must contact in advance but may not play on Tue or Sat & Sun before 12.30.
Societies	apply in advance.
Green Fees	not confirmed.
Prof	Tim Cooper
Facilities	⊗ ⫿ ⓛ ⬛ ♈ ⚽ 🏠 ⌀
Location	W side of village on A134
Hotel	★★★ 67% The Bull, Hall St, LONG MELFORD ☎ 01787 378494 25 ⇆ ☞

RAYDON Map 05 TM03

Brett Vale Noakes Rd IP7 5LR
☎ 01473 310718 Fax 01473 312270
Brett Vale course takes you through a nature reserve and on lakeside walks, affording views over Dedham Vale. The excellent fairways demand an accurate tee and good approach shots. 1, 2, 3, 8, 10 and 15 are all affected by crosswinds, but once in the valley it is much more sheltered. Although only 5,797 yards the course is testing and interesting at all levels of golf.
18 holes, 5797yds, Par 70, SSS 69, Course record 65.
Club membership 600.

Visitors	must book tee times and wear appropriate clothing.
Societies	apply in writing or telephone.
Green Fees	£20 (£25 weekends & bank holidays).
Cards	▦ 🎫 ⬛ ⛏ ▨
Prof	Robert Taylor
Designer	Howard Smith
Facilities & Leisure	⊗ ⫿ ⓛ ⬛ ♈ ⚽ 🏠 ⌖ ⛏ ⛴ ⚒ ⌀ ☘ fishing.
Location	B1070 at Raydon, 2m from A12
Hotel	★★★⭐ Maison Talbooth, Stratford Rd, DEDHAM ☎ 01206 322367 10 ⇆ ☞

SOUTHWOLD Map 05 TM57

Southwold The Common IP18 6TB
☎ 01502 723234 & 723248
Commonland course with 4-acre practice ground and panoramic views of the sea.
9 holes, 6052yds, Par 70, SSS 69, Course record 67.
Club membership 450.

Visitors	restricted on competition days (Ladies-Wed, Gents-Sun).
Societies	must contact in advance.
Green Fees	£18 (£20 weekends & bank holidays).
Prof	Brian Allen ▶

Facilities   ⊗ ᕲ ♥ ♀ ♣ 🏠 ⛳ ⚑ ✓
Location   From A12 - B1140 to Southwold

Hotel   ★★★ 71% Swan Hotel, Market Place, SOUTHWOLD ☎ 01502 722186 26rm(25 ⇔ ℝ) Annexe17 ⇔ ℝ

STOWMARKET   Map 05 TM05

Stowmarket Lower Rd, Onehouse IP14 3DA
☎ 01449 736473 Fax 01449 736826 e-mail: mail@stowmarketgc.sagehost.co.uk
Parkland course.
18 holes, 6107yds, Par 69, SSS 69, Course record 66.
Club membership 630.
Visitors must contact in advance.
Societies Thu or Fri, by arrangement.
Green Fees £31 per day; £25 per round(£43/£31 weekends).
Prof Duncan Burl
Facilities ⊗ ᕲ ᕲ ♥ ♀ ♣ 🏠 ⛳ ⚒ ✓ ℂ
Location 2.5m SW off B1115

Hotel   ★★ 65% Cedars Hotel, Needham Rd, STOWMARKET ☎ 01449 612668 25 ⇔ ℝ

THORPENESS   Map 05 TM45

Thorpeness Golf Club & Hotel IP16 4NH
☎ 01728 452176 Fax 01728 453868
e-mail: info@thorpeness.co.uk
The holes of this moorland course are pleasantly varied with several quite difficult par 4's. Natural hazards abound. The 15th, with its sharp left dog-leg, is one of the best holes. Designed by James Braid.
Thorpeness Golf Club & Hotel: 18 holes, 6271yds, Par 69, SSS 71, Course record 66.
Club membership 329.
Visitors contact in advance.
Societies telephone in advance, deposit required.
Green Fees £32 per day (£37 weekends & bank holidays).
Cards 🔲 🔲 🔲 🔲
Prof Frank Hill
Designer James Braid
Facilities ⊗ ᕲ ᕲ ♥ ♀ ♣ 🏠 ⛳ ✦ ⚒ ✓
& Leisure hard tennis courts, snooker room.
Location W side of village off B1353

Hotel   ★★★ 74% White Lion Hotel, Market Cross Place, ALDEBURGH ☎ 01728 452720 38 ⇔ ℝ

WALDRINGFIELD   Map 05 TM24

Waldringfield Heath Newbourne Rd IP12 4PT
☎ 01473 736768 Fax 01473 736436
Easy walking heathland course with long drives on 1st and 13th (590yds) and some ponds.
18 holes, 6141yds, Par 71, SSS 69, Course record 67.
Club membership 630.
Visitors welcome Mon-Fri, weekends & bank holidays after noon.
Societies weekdays by arrangement.
Green Fees not confirmed.
Prof Robin Mann
Designer Phillip Pilgrem

Facilities   ⊗ ᕲ ᕲ ♥ ♀ ♣ 🏠 ⚒ ⚑ ✓
Location   3m NE of Ipswich off old A12

Hotel   ★★★ 76% Seckford Hall Hotel, WOODBRIDGE ☎ 01394 385678 22 ⇔ ℝ Annexe10 ⇔ ℝ

WOODBRIDGE   Map 05 TM24

Seckford Seckford Hall Rd, Great Bealings IP13 6NT
☎ 01394 388000 Fax 01394 382818 e-mail: seckfordgolfclub@btinternet.com
A challenging course interspersed with young tree plantations, numerous bunkers, water hazards and undulating fairways, providing a tough test for all levels of golfer. The testing 18th is almost completely surrounded by water.
18 holes, 5303yds, Par 68, SSS 66, Course record 65.
Club membership 400.
Visitors telephone in advance for tee times.
Societies telephone in advance. Computerised booking system.
Green Fees not confirmed.
Cards 🔲 🔲 🔲 🔲 🔲 🔲
Prof Simon Jay
Designer J Johnson
Facilities ⊗ ᕲ ᕲ ♥ ♀ ♣ 🏠 ⚑ ⚒ ⚒ ✓ ℂ
& Leisure heated indoor swimming pool, fishing, sauna, solarium, gymnasium.
Location 3m W of Woodbridge, 0ff A12

Hotel   ★★★ 76% Seckford Hall Hotel, WOODBRIDGE ☎ 01394 385678 22 ⇔ ℝ Annexe10 ⇔ ℝ

Ufford Park Hotel Golf & Leisure Yarmouth Rd, Ufford IP12 1QW ☎ 01394 383555 & 382836 Fax 01394 383582 e-mail: uffordparkltd@btinternet.com
The 18-hole Par 71 course is set in ancient parkland has many natural features including 11 water hazards retained from the original parkland. Free draining making it playable all year. There is also an extensive hotel and leisure complex beside the course.
18 holes, 6325yds, Par 71, SSS 71, Course record 65.
Club membership 320.
Visitors must book tee time from golf shop 01394 382836. Must adhere to dress code. Handicap certificates required for Sat/Sun mornings.
Societies telephone or fax in advance to book tee time.
Green Fees £25 per day; £18 per round (£30/£20 weekends).
Cards 🔲 🔲 🔲 🔲
Prof Stuart Robertson
Designer Phil Pilgrim
Facilities ⊗ ᕲ ᕲ ♥ ♀ ♣ 🏠 ⚑ ⚒ ⚒ ✓ ℂ
& Leisure heated indoor swimming pool, fishing, sauna, solarium, gymnasium.
Location Just off A12, on the B1438

Hotel   ★★★ 70% Ufford Park Hotel Golf & Leisure, Yarmouth Rd, Ufford, IPSWICH / WOODBRIDGE ☎ 01394 383555 42 ⇔ ℝ Annexe8 ⇔ ℝ

Where to stay, where to eat?
Visit the AA internet site
www.theAA.com

Woodbridge Bromeswell Heath IP12 2PF
☎ 01394 382038 Fax 01394 382392
e-mail: woodbridgegc@anglianet.co.uk
A beautiful course, one of the best in East Anglia. It is
situated on high ground and in different seasons present
golfers with a great variety of colour. Some say that of
the many good holes the 16th is the best.
18 holes, 6299yds, Par 70, SSS 70, Course record 64.
Forest Course: 9 holes, 3191yds, Par 70, SSS 70.
Club membership 900.
Visitors	Main Course: must contact in advance, handicap certificate required, with member only weekends. Forest Course: open all days and no handicap certificate required.
Societies	by prior telephone call or in writing.
Green Fees	Main Course: £33 per day/round. Forest Course: £16 per day/round.
Prof	Adrian Hubert
Designer	Davie Grant
Facilities	⊗ 〗ⅢⅢ ⬥ 🍺 ♀ ⚲ 🏠 ♂
Location	2.5m NE off A1152

Hotel	★★★♨ 76% Seckford Hall Hotel, WOODBRIDGE ☎ 01394 385678 22 ⇆ 🝙 Annexe10 ⇆ 🝙

WORLINGTON — Map 05 TL67

Royal Worlington & Newmarket IP28 8SD
☎ 01638 712216 Fax 01638 717787
Inland 'links' course. Favourite 9-hole course of many
golf writers.
9 holes, 3105yds, Par 35, SSS 70, Course record 67.
Club membership 325.
Visitors	with member only at weekends. Must contact in advance and have a handicap certificate.
Societies	must apply in writing.
Green Fees	not confirmed.
Prof	Malcolm Hawkins
Designer	Tom Dunn
Facilities	⊗ ⬥ 🍺 ♀ ⚲ 🏠 ♂
Location	0.5m SE

Hotel	★★★ 76% Riverside Hotel, Mill St, MILDENHALL ☎ 01638 717274 17 ⇆ 🝙 Annexe4 ⇆ 🝙

SURREY

ADDLESTONE — Map 04 TQ06

New Zealand Woodham Ln KT15 3QD
☎ 01932 345049 Fax 01932 342891
e-mail: roger.marrett@nzgc.org,
Heathland course set in trees and heather.
18 holes, 6012yds, Par 68, SSS 69, Course record 66.
Club membership 320.
Visitors	must contact in advance.
Societies	telephone initially.
Green Fees	available on application.

Prof	Vic Elvidge
Designer	Muir Fergusson/Simpson
Facilities	⊗ ⬥ 🍺 ♀ ⚲ 🏠 ⚙ ♂ 🛒 ♂
Location	1.5m E of Woking

Hotel	★★★ 67% The Ship, Monument Green, WEYBRIDGE ☎ 01932 848364 39 ⇆ 🝙

ASHFORD — Map 04 TQ07

Ashford Manor Fordbridge Rd TW15 3RT
☎ 01784 424644 Fax 01784 424649
Tree lined parkland course, looks easy but is difficult.
18 holes, 6352yds, Par 70, SSS 70, Course record 64.
Club membership 700.
Visitors	advisable to telephone in advance, handicap certificate required, with member only at weekends but may not play competition days.
Societies	welcome weekdays, except Thu am, must contact in advance.
Green Fees	£35 per day, £30 per round (weekdays only).
Prof	Mike Finney
Facilities	⊗ 〗ⅢⅢ ⬥ 🍺 ♀ ⚲ 🏠 ♂
Location	2m E of Staines via A308 Staines by-pass

Hotel	★★★ 69% The Thames Lodge, Thames St, STAINES ☎ 0870 400 8121 78 ⇆ 🝙

BAGSHOT — Map 04 SU96

Pennyhill Park Hotel & Country Club London Rd
GU19 5EU ☎ 01276 471774 Fax 01276 473217
e-mail: pennyhillpark@msn.com
A nine-hole course set in 11.4 acres of beautiful parkland. It
is challenging to even the most experienced golfer.
9 holes, 2095yds, Par 32, SSS 32.
Club membership 100.

Visitors	prior booking must be made. telephone in advance.
Green Fees	not confirmed.
Cards	💳 💳 💳 💳
Facilities	⊗ 〗ⅢⅢ ⬥ 🍺 ♀ ⚲ 🏠 ♂
& Leisure	hard tennis courts, heated outdoor swimming pool, fishing, gymnasium.
Location	Off A30 between Camberley and Bagshot

Hotel	★★★★★ 72% Pennyhill Park Hotel & Country Club, London Rd, BAGSHOT ☎ 01276 471774 26 ⇆ 🝙 Annexe97 ⇆ 🝙

Windlesham Grove End GU19 5HY
☎ 01276 452220 Fax 01276 452290
A parkland course with many demanding Par 4 holes over 400 yards. Thoughtfully designed by Tommy Horton.
18 holes, 6650yds, Par 72, SSS 72, Course record 69.
Club membership 800.
Visitors   handicap certificate required, contact in advance.
Societies apply in advance.
Green Fees not confirmed.
Cards   ▨ ▆ ▨ ▨
Prof   Lee Mucklow/Alan Barber
Designer Tommy Horton
Facilities ⊗ ℔ ▆ ♀ ☆ ⌂ 🛈 ♪ 𝄢 ♐ ┇
Location Junct of A30/A322

Hotel   ★★★★★ 72% Pennyhill Park Hotel & Country Club, London Rd, BAGSHOT
☎ 01276 471774 26 ⇋ ↾ Annexe97 ⇋ ↾

BANSTEAD   Map 04 TQ25

Banstead Downs Burdon Ln, Belmont, Sutton SM2 7DD
☎ 020 8642 2284 Fax 020 8642 5252
e-mail: bdgc@ukonline.co.uk
A natural downland course set on a site of botanic interest. A challenging 18 holes with narrow fairways and tight lies.
18 holes, 6194yds, Par 69, SSS 69, Course record 64.
Club membership 902.
Visitors   must book in advance and have handicap certificate or letter of introduction. With member only weekends.
Societies Thu, by prior arrangement
Green Fees not confirmed.
Prof   Robert Dickman
Designer J H Taylor/James Braid
Facilities ⊗ ℻ by prior arrangement ℔ ▆ ♀ ☆ ⌂ ♪
Location 1.5m N on A217

Hotel   ★★ 63% Thatched House Hotel, 135 Cheam Rd, Sutton ☎ 020 8642 3131
32rm(29 ⇋ ↾) Annexe5rm

Cuddington Banstead Rd SM7 1RD ☎ 020 8393 0952
Fax 020 8786 7025 e-mail: cuddingtongc@aol.com
Parkland course with easy walking and good views.
18 holes, 6595yds, Par 71, SSS 71, Course record 67.
Club membership 694.
Visitors   must contact in advance and have a handicap certificate or letter of introduction.
Societies welcome Thu, must apply in advance.
Green Fees £35 weekday (£45 weekends).
Prof   Mark Warner
Designer H S Colt
Facilities ⊗ ℻ ♀ ☆ ⌂ 🛈 ♪ ♐
Location N of Banstead station on A2022

Hotel   ★★ 63% Thatched House Hotel, 135 Cheam Rd, Sutton ☎ 020 8642 3131
32rm(29 ⇋ ↾) Annexe5rm

BRAMLEY   Map 04 TQ04

Bramley GU5 0AL ☎ 01483 892696 Fax 01483 894673
e-mail: secretary@bramleygolfclub.co.uk
Parkland course, from the high ground picturesque views of the Wey Valley on one side and the Hog's Back. Full on course irrigation system with three reservoirs on the course.

18 holes, 5990yds, Par 69, SSS 69, Course record 63.
Club membership 850.
Visitors   may not play Tue am (Ladies Morning) and must play with member at weekends & bank holidays. Must contact secretary on 01483 892696.
Societies must telephone the secretary in advance.
Green Fees £35 per day; £28 per round.
Prof   Gary Peddie
Designer James Braid
Facilities ⊗ ℻ ℔ ▆ ♀ ☆ ⌂ 🛈 ♪ 𝄢 ♐ ┇
Location 3m S of Guildford on A281

Hotel   ★★★ 69% Posthouse Guildford, Egerton Rd, GUILDFORD ☎ 0870 400 9036 162 ⇋ ↾

BROOKWOOD   Map 04 SU95

West Hill Bagshot Rd GU24 0BH
☎ 01483 474365 Fax 01483 474252
e-mail: secretary@westhill-golfclub.co.uk
Set in the Surrey landscape of heath, heather and tree lined fairways. An interesting and challenging course with subtle greens and a stream which affects play on seven holes. Drives on the fairway must be precisely placed and many of the greens are subtly contoured and putts can never be taken for granted.
18 holes, 6368yds, Par 69, SSS 70, Course record 62.
Club membership 500.
Visitors   must contact in advance & have handicap certificate, may not play weekends & bank holidays.
Societies weekdays only (ex Wed). Telephone in advance.
Green Fees £60 per day; £45 per round.
Cards   ▨ ▆ ▨ ▨ ▨ ▨
Prof   John A Clements
Designer C Butchart/W Parke
Facilities ⊗ ℔ ▆ ♀ ☆ ⌂ 🛈 ♪ 𝄢 ♐
Location E side of village on A322

Hotel   ★★★★★ 72% Pennyhill Park Hotel & Country Club, London Rd, BAGSHOT
☎ 01276 471774
26 ⇋ ↾ Annexe97 ⇋ ↾

CAMBERLEY   Map 04 SU86

Camberley Heath Golf Dr GU15 1JG ☎ 01276 23258
Fax 01276 692505 e-mail: camberleyheathgolfclub.co.uk
One of the great 'heath and heather' courses so frequently associated with Surrey. Several very good short holes - especially the 8th. The 10th is a difficult and interesting par 4, as also is the 17th, where the drive must be held well to the left as perdition lurks on the right. A fairway irrigation system has been installed.
18 holes, 6147yds, Par 72, SSS 70, Course record 65.
Club membership 600.
Visitors   may not play at weekends. Must contact in advance.
Societies must apply in advance.
Green Fees £48 per round.
Cards   ▨ ▆ ▨ ▨ ▨ ▨ ▨   ▶

Camberley Heath Golf Club

Prof Glen Ralph
Designer Harry S Colt
Facilities ⊗ ⓑ 🍺 ♀ 🛆 📷 ⛳ 🏌 🚜 ✎ ᛊ
Location 1.25m SE of town centre off A325

Hotel ★★★★★ 72% Pennyhill Park Hotel & Country Club, London Rd, BAGSHOT ☎ 01276 471774 26 ⇆ ⍅ Annexe97 ⇆ ⍅

Pine Ridge Old Bisley Rd, Frimley GU16 9NX
☎ 01276 675444 & 20770 Fax 01276 678837
e-mail: enquiry@pineridgegolf.co.uk
Pay and play heathland course cut through a pine forest with challenging par 3s, deceptively demanding par 4s and several bird[ie par 5s. Easy walking, but gently undulating. Good corporate or society packages.
18 holes, 6458yds, Par 72, SSS 71, Course record 67.
Club membership 400.
Visitors no jeans or trainers,necessary to book for weekends.
Societies apply in advance by writing/telephone, packages available to suit.
Green Fees £21.50per round (£27.50 weekends & Bank holidays).
Cards 💳 ⍺
Prof Peter Sefton
Designer Clive D Smith
Facilities ⊗ ⫛ ⓑ 🍺 ♀ 🛆 📷 ⛳ 🏌 🚜 ✎ ᛊ
& Leisure ten pin bowling.
Location Just off B3015, near A30

Hotel ★★★ 71% Frimley Hall, Lime Av, CAMBERLEY ☎ 0870 400 8224 86 ⇆ ⍅

CATERHAM   Map 05 TQ35

Happy Valley Rook Ln, Chaldon CR3 5AA
☎ 01883 344555 Fax 01883 344422
e-mail: cgm.wells@virgin.net
Opened in May 1999, this technically challenging course is set in beautiful countryside and features fully irrigated greens and fairways. It also has large practice area.
18 holes, 6858yds, Par 72, SSS 73, Course record 73.
Club membership 750.
Visitors may play weekdays and weekends and can book in advance.
Societies apply in writing/telephone in advance.
Green Fees £18 per round (winter includes breakfast). £25 per round weekends and bank holidays.

Cards 💳 💳 💳 💳 ⍺
Prof David Kent
Designer David Williams
Facilities ⊗ ⫛ ⓑ 🍺 ♀ 🛆 📷 ⛳ 🏌 🚜 ✎ ᛊ
Location M25 junct 7/M23 junct 6/A22

Hotel ★★★★ 77% Coulsdon Manor, Coulsdon Court Rd, Coulsdon, CROYDON ☎ 020 8668 0414 35 ⇆ ⍅

CHERTSEY   Map 04 TQ06

Laleham Laleham Reach KT16 8RP
☎ 01932 564211 Fax 01932 564448
e-mail: sec@laleham-golf.co.uk
Well-bunkered parkland/meadowland course.
18 holes, 6204yds, Par 70, SSS 70.
Club membership 600.
Visitors members guests only at weekends.
Societies must contact in writing/telephone.
Green Fees £27 per day; £20 per round.
Prof Hogan Stott
Facilities ⊗ ⫛ ⓑ 🍺 ♀ 🛆 📷 ✎
Location M25 junct 11/A320 to Thorpe Park, at roundabout take exit to Penton Mauna and follow signs to club

Hotel ★★★ 69% The Thames Lodge, Thames St, STAINES ☎ 0870 400 8121 78 ⇆ ⍅

CHIDDINGFOLD   Map 04 SU93

Chiddingfold Petworth Rd GU8 4SL
☎ 01428 685888 Fax 01428 685939
With panoramic views across the Surrey Downs, this challenging course offers a unique combination of lakes, mature woodland and wildlife.
18 holes, 5501yds, Par 70, SSS 67.
Club membership 325.
Visitors telephone bookings up to one week in advance.
Societies prior telephone booking required.
Green Fees not confirmed.
Cards 💳 💳 💳 💳 ⍺
Prof Paul Creamer
Designer Johnathan Gaunt
Facilities ⊗ ⫛ ⓑ 🍺 ♀ 🛆 📷 ⛳ 🏌 🚜 ✎ ᛊ
Location A283

Hotel ★★★★ 65% Lythe Hill Hotel, Petworth Rd, HASLEMERE ☎ 01428 651251 41 ⇆ ⍅

CHIPSTEAD   Map 04 TQ25

Chipstead How Ln CR5 3LN
☎ 01737 555781 Fax 01737 555404
Hilly parkland course, hard walking, good views. Testing 18th hole.
18 holes, 5491yds, Par 68, SSS 67, Course record 61.
Club membership 650.
Visitors must contact in advance. May not play weekends or Tue mornings.
Societies must apply in writing.
Green Fees £40 per day; £30 per round.
Prof Gary Torbett
Facilities ⊗ ⫛ ⓑ 🍺 ♀ 🛆 📷 ⛳ 🏌 🚜 ✎ ᛊ
Location 0.5m N of village ▶

Hotel ★★★★ 70% Selsdon Park Hotel, Addington Rd, Sanderstead, SOUTH CROYDON ☎ 020 8657 8811 204 ⇄ ♥

CHOBHAM Map 04 SU96

Chobham Chobham Rd, Knaphill GU21 2TZ ☎ 01276 855584 Fax 01276 855663
Designed by Peter Allis and Clive Clark, Chobham course sits among mature oaks and tree nurseries offering tree-lined fairways, together with six man-made lakes.
18 holes, 5959yds, Par 69, SSS 67, Course record 67.
Club membership 750.
Visitors booking in advance essential.
Societies by prior arrangement.
Green Fees not confirmed.
Cards 🖸🖸🖸🖸🖸🖸
Prof Tim Coombes
Designer Peter Alliss/Clive Clark
Facilities ⊗ ⊪ by prior arrangement 🝙 🝙 ♀ 🝙 🝙 ∥
Location A3046 between Chobham and Knaphill

Hotel ★★★ 63% Falcon Hotel, 68 Farnborough Rd, FARNBOROUGH ☎ 01252 545378 30 ⇄ ♥

COBHAM Map 04 TQ16

Silvermere Redhill Rd KT11 1EF ☎ 01932 866007 Fax 01932 868259
Parkland course with many very tight holes through woodland, 17th has 170-yd carry over the lake. 18th played to a new island green. Driving range.
18 holes, 6700yds, Par 73.
Club membership 740.
Visitors may not play at weekends until 1pm. Must contact in advance.
Societies must contact by telephone.
Green Fees not confirmed.
Prof Doug McClelland
Facilities ⊗ ⊪ 🝙 🝙 ♀ 🝙 🝙 🝙 ∥
& Leisure fishing.
Location 2.25m NW off A245

Hotel ★★★★ 69% Woodlands Park Hotel, Woodlands Ln, STOKE D'ABERNON ☎ 01372 843933 59 ⇄ ♥

CRANLEIGH Map 04 TQ03

Fernfell Golf & Country Club Barhatch Ln GU6 7NG ☎ 01483 268855 Fax 01483 267251
Scenic woodland/parkland course at the base of the Surrey hills, easy walking. Clubhouse in 400-year-old barn.
18 holes, 5648yds, Par 68, SSS 67, Course record 64.
Club membership 1000.
Visitors welcome weekdays but restricted Thu am. For weekends contact professional shop in advance on 01483 277188
Societies telephone in advance.
Green Fees £32 per day, £25 per round (£27 per round weekends & bank holidays).
Cards 🖸🖸🖸🖸🖸
Prof Trevor Longmuir
Facilities ⊗ 🝙 🝙 ♀ 🝙 🝙 🝙 🝙 ∥
& Leisure hard tennis courts, heated indoor swimming pool, sauna, gymnasium.

Location Off A281 Guildford to Horsham road, signposted Cranleigh

Hotel ★★★ 63% Gatton Manor Hotel Golf & Country Club, Standon Ln, OCKLEY ☎ 01306 627555 18 ⇄ ♥

Wildwood Country Club Horsham Rd, Alfold, Cranleigh GU6 8JE ☎ 01403 753255 Fax 01403 752005
Parkland with stands of old oaks dominating several holes, a stream fed by a natural spring winds through a series of lakes and ponds. The greens are smooth, undulating and large. The 5th and 16th are the most challenging holes.
18 holes, 6655yds, Par 72, SSS 73, Course record 65.
Club membership 400.
Visitors welcome subject to availability & booking.
Societies apply in writing or telephone for enquiries.
Green Fees not confirmed.
Cards 🖸🖸🖸🖸🖸🖸
Prof Simon Andrews/Dean Mara
Designer Hawtree & Sons
Facilities ⊗ ⊪ 🝙 🝙 ♀ 🝙 🝙 🝙 🝙 ∥ ∥
& Leisure fishing.
Location Off A281, approx 9m S of Guildford

Hotel ★★★ 66% Hurtwood Inn Hotel, Walking Bottom, PEASLAKE ☎ 01306 730851 9 ⇄ ♥ Annexe8 ⇄ ♥

CROYDON

For other golf courses in the area, please see Greater London.

DORKING Map 04 TQ14

Betchworth Park Reigate Rd RH4 1NZ ☎ 01306 882052 Fax 01306 877462
e-mail: manager@betchworthpark.golfagent.co.uk
Parkland course, with hard walking on southern ridge of Boxhill.
18 holes, 6266yds, Par 69, SSS 70, Course record 64.
Club membership 725.
Visitors weekend play Sun pm only. Must contact in advance.
Societies apply in writing/telephone/fax.
Green Fees £34 all day (£27 pm); Sundays £45 pm only.
Prof Tocher
Designer H Colt
Facilities ⊗ ⊪ 🝙 🝙 ♀ 🝙 🝙 🝙 ∥
Location 1m E on A25

Hotel ★★★ 64% The White Horse, High St, DORKING ☎ 0870 400 8282 37 ⇄ ♥ Annexe32 ⇄ ♥

Dorking Chart Park, Deepdene Av RH5 4BX ☎ 01306 886917 e-mail: dorkinggolfclub@ukgateway.net
Undulating parkland course, easy slopes, wind-sheltered. Testing holes: 5th 'Tom's Puddle' (par 4); 7th 'Rest and Be Thankful' (par 4); 9th 'Double Decker' (par 4).
9 holes, 5120yds, Par 66, SSS 65, Course record 62.
Club membership 392.
Visitors may not play Wed am and with member only weekends & bank holidays. Contact in advance.
Societies Tue & Thu, telephone in advance.
Green Fees not confirmed.

▶

Prof Paul Napier
Designer J Braid/Others
Facilities ⊗ ⓑ ▆ ♀ ⚐ 🝙 🏌 ❀ 🏌 ✧
Location 1m S on A24

Hotel ★★★★ 67% The Burford Bridge, Burford Bridge, Box Hill, DORKING ☎ 0870 400 8283 57 ➪ ☏

EAST HORSLEY　　　　　　　　Map 04 TQ05

Drift The Drift, Off Forest Rd KT24 5HD
☎ 01483 284641 & 284772(shop) Fax 01483 284642
Woodland course with secluded fairways and picturesque setting. A challenging course that punishes the wayward shot.
18 holes, 6424yds, Par 73, SSS 72, Course record 68.
Club membership 730.
Visitors book in advance to the pro shop, Mon-Fri only, except bank holidays.
Societies Mon-Fri, telephone in advance.
Green Fees not confirmed.
Cards 🖅 🖅 🖅 🖅 🈂
Prof Liam Greasley/Alan Brennan
Designer Robert Sandow
Facilities ⊗ ⓑ ▆ ♀ ⚐ 🝙 🏌 ❀ 🏌 ✧ ☏
Location 1.5m N off B2039

Hotel ★★ 62% Bookham Grange Hotel, Little Bookham Common, Bookham, LEATHERHEAD ☎ 01372 452742　27 ➪ ☏

EFFINGHAM　　　　　　　　　Map 04 TQ15

Effingham Guildford Rd KT24 5PZ
☎ 01372 452203 Fax 01372 459959
e-mail: secretary@effinghamgolfclub.freeserve.co.uk
Easy-walking downland course laid out on 270-acres with tree-lined fairways. It is one of the longest of the Surrey courses with wide subtle greens that provide a provocative but by no means exhausting challenge. Fine views.
18 holes, 6524yds, Par 71, SSS 71, Course record 64.
Club membership 800.
Visitors contact in advance. With member only weekends & bank holidays.
Societies Wed, Thu & Fri only and must book in advance.
Green Fees not confirmed.
Prof Steve Hoatson
Designer H S Colt
Facilities ⊗ ⓑ ▆ ♀ ⚐ 🝙 🏌 ❀ 🏌 ✧ ☏
& Leisure hard tennis courts.
Location W side of village on A246

Hotel ★★ 62% Bookham Grange Hotel, Little Bookham Common, Bookham, LEATHERHEAD ☎ 01372 452742　27 ➪ ☏

Entries with a green background
identify courses considered to be
particularly interesting

ENTON GREEN　　　　　　　　Map 04 SU94

West Surrey GU8 5AF
☎ 01483 421275 Fax 01483 41519
e-mail: westsurreygolfclub@btinternet.com
A good parkland-type course in rolling, well-wooded setting. Some fairways are tight with straight driving at a premium. The 17th is a testing hole with a long hill walk.
18 holes, 6300yds, Par 71, SSS 70, Course record 65.
Club membership 600.
Visitors must contact in advance and have a handicap certificate.
Societies must apply in writing. All players to have a handicap.
Green Fees £39 per day; £27 per round (£48/36 weekends).
Prof Alister Tawse
Designer Herbert Fowler
Facilities ⊗ 🝙 ⓑ ▆ ♀ ⚐ 🝙 ✧ ☏
Location S side of village

Hotel ★★★ 65% The Bush Hotel, The Borough, FARNHAM ☎ 0870 400 8225 83 ➪ ☏

EPSOM　　　　　　　　　　　Map 04 TQ26

Epsom Longdown Ln South KT17 4JR
☎ 01372 721666 Fax 01372 817183
Traditional downland course with many mature trees and fast undulating greens. Thought must be given to every shot to play to ones handicap.
18 holes, 5701yds, Par 69, SSS 68, Course record 62.
Club membership 800.
Visitors available any day except Tue, Sat & Sun till 12.00 hrs.
Societies telephone 01372 721666.
Green Fees £26/£30 per round.
Cards 🖅 🖅 🖅 🖅 🖅 🈂
Prof Ron Goudie
Designer Willie Dunne
Facilities ⊗ 🝙 ⓑ ▆ ♀ ⚐ 🝙 ✧
Location SE side of town centre on B288

Hotel ★★★★ 69% Woodlands Park Hotel, Woodlands Ln, STOKE D'ABERNON ☎ 01372 843933　59 ➪ ☏

Horton Park Golf & Country Club Hook Rd KT19 8QG
☎ 020 8393 8400 & 8394 2626 Fax 020 8394 1369
e-mail: hortonparkgc@aol.com
Parkland course in picturesque surroundings within a country park with a natural lake. The course offers a challenge to all golfers with dog-legs, water hazards and the 10th at 160yds with an island green. There is also a separate full length Par 3 9 hole course.
Millennium: 18 holes, 6257yds, Par 71, SSS 70.
Club membership 450.
Visitors must book for weekends, recommended booking for midweek. Dress code in force.
Societies must telephone in advance to play at weekends & bank holidays.
Green Fees £18 summer;£15 winter.
Cards 🖅 🖅 🈂
Prof Martyn Hirst
Designer Dr Peter Nicholson
Facilities ⊗ 🝙 ⓑ ▆ ♀ ⚐ 🝙 🏌 ❀ 🏌 ✧ ☏　▶

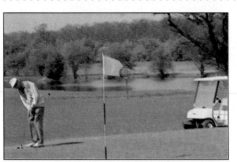

Horton Park Country Club

Hotel ★★★★ 69% Woodlands Park Hotel,
Woodlands Ln, STOKE D'ABERNON
☎ 01372 843933 59 ⇌ ↱

ESHER   Map 04 TQ16

Moore Place Portsmouth Rd KT10 9LN
☎ 01372 463533
Public course on attractive, undulating parkland laid out
some 60 years ago by Harry Vardon. Examples of most of
the trees that will survive in the UK are to be found on the
course. Testing short holes at 2nd, 3rd and 9th.
9 holes, 2078yds, Par 33, SSS 30, Course record 28.
Club membership 150.
Visitors   no restrictions.
Societies   must contact in advance.
Green Fees   £6.30(£8 weekends & bank holidays).
Prof   Nick Gadd
Designer   Harry Vardon/David Allen
Facilities   ⊗ ⫯Ⅲ ⓛ ☕ ♀ ⚑ 🏌 ⚐
Location   0.5m from town centre on A307

Hotel ★★★ 67% The Ship, Monument Green,
WEYBRIDGE
☎ 01932 848364 39 ⇌ ↱

Thames Ditton & Esher Portsmouth Rd KT10 9AL
☎ 020 8398 1551
Commonland course with public right of way across the
course. Although the course is not long, accuracy is essential
and wayward shots are normally punished.
18 holes, 5149yds, Par 66, SSS 65, Course record 63.
Club membership 250.
Visitors   may not play on Sun mornings. Advisable to
telephone for availability.
Societies   must contact in advance.
Green Fees   not confirmed.
Cards   ⬛ ⬛ ⚐
Prof   Mark Rodbard
Facilities   ⊗ ⫯Ⅲ by prior arrangement ⓛ ☕ ♀ ⚑ ⚐
Location   1m NE on A307

Hotel ★★ 63% Haven Hotel, Portsmouth Rd,
ESHER ☎ 020 8398 0023
16 ⇌ ↱ Annexe4 ⇌ ↱

Where to stay, where to eat?
Visit the AA internet site
www.theAA.com

FARLEIGH   Map 05 TQ36

Farleigh Court Old Farleigh Rd CR6 9PX
☎ 0188362 7711 & 7733 Fax 0188362 7722
e-mail: fcgc@fbd-uk.u-net.com
The course occupies 350 acres of land and is surrounded by a
bird sanctuary and natural woodlands. The course designer
has instinctively utilised the two valleys which the land
incorporates to make the course interesting and challenging.
Members: 18 holes, 6414yds, Par 72, SSS 71.
Pay & Play: 9 holes, 3281yds, Par 36.
Club membership 450.
Visitors   may not play Members course before 10am at
weekends.
Societies   welcome, please and ask for Society Co
ordinator.
Green Fees   not confirmed.
Cards   ⬛ ⬛ ⬛ ⬛ ⬛ ⬛ ⚐
Prof   S Graham
Designer   John Jacobs
Facilities   ⊗ ⫯Ⅲ ⓛ ☕ ♀ ⚑ ⚑ 🏌 ⚐ ⚐ ⚐
& Leisure   sauna.
Location   1.5m from Selsdon

Hotel ★★★★ 70% Selsdon Park Hotel, Addington
Rd, Sanderstead, SOUTH CROYDON
☎ 020 8657 8811 204 ⇌ ↱

FARNHAM   Map 04 SU84

Blacknest Binsted GU34 4QL
☎ 01420 22888 Fax 01420 22001
Privately owned pay and play golf centre catering for all ages
and levels of abilities. Facilities include a 15-bay driving
range, gymnasium and a challenging 18-hole course
featuring water on 14 holes.
18 holes, 6019yds, Par 69, SSS 69, Course record 65.
Club membership 450.
Visitors   welcome at all times but should telephone for
tee times especially weekends. No denims or
collarless shirts.
Societies   prior arrangements necessary telephone or write.
Green Fees   not confirmed.
Cards   ⬛ ⬛ ⬛ ⬛ ⬛ ⚐
Prof   Ian Benson
Designer   Mr Nicholson
Facilities   ⊗ ⫯Ⅲ by prior arrangement ⓛ ☕ ♀ ⚑
⚐ 🏌 ⚐ ⚐
& Leisure   sauna, solarium, gymnasium.
Location   0.5m S of A31 at Bentley

Hotel ★★★⚑⚑ 59% Farnham House Hotel, Alton Rd,
FARNHAM ☎ 01252 716908 25 ⇌ ↱

Farnham The Sands GU10 1PX ☎ 01252 782109
Fax 01252 781185 e-mail: info@farnhamgolfclub.com
A mixture of meadowland and heath with quick drying
sandy subsoil. Several of the earlier holes have
interesting features, the finishing holes rather less.
18 holes, 6325yds, Par 72, SSS 70, Course record 66.
Club membership 700.
Visitors   must contact in advance. Must be member
of recognised club & have handicap
certificate. With member only weekends.
Societies   must apply in writing.   ▶

Green Fees £35 per 18 holes;£40 per 36 holes..
Prof   Grahame Cowlishaw
Facilities ⊗ ⑂ by prior arrangement ⓑ ♨ ♀ ⚐
           🍴 ✐

Location   3m E off A31

Hotel   ★★★ 65% The Bush Hotel, The Borough,
           FARNHAM ☎ 0870 400 8225 83 ⇆ 🐾

Farnham Park Folly Hill, Farnham Park GU9 0AU
☎ 01252 715216
Pay & Play parkland course in Farnham Park.
9 holes, 1163yds, Par 27, SSS 50, Course record 50.
Visitors   pay and play everyday.
Societies telephone in advance.
Green Fees not confirmed.
Cards   ▭ ▬ ▭
Prof   Peter Chapman
Designer   Henry Cotton
Facilities ⊗ ⑂ ⓑ ♨ ♀ 🍴 ⚐
Location   N side of town centre on A287, adjacent to
           Farnham Castle

Hotel   ★★★ 65% The Bush Hotel, The Borough,
           FARNHAM ☎ 0870 400 8225 83 ⇆ 🐾

GODALMING   Map 04 SU94

Broadwater Park Guildford Rd, Farncombe GU7 3BU
☎ 01483 429955 Fax 01483 429955
A Par-3 public course with floodlit driving range.
9 holes, 1287yds, Par 54, SSS 50.
Club membership 160.
Visitors   must book for weekends & bank holidays.
Societies telephone in advance.
Green Fees not confirmed..
Prof   Kevin D Milton
Designer   Kevin Milton
Facilities ⓑ ♨ ♀ 🍴 ⚐ ✐ ⚑
Location   4m SW of Guildford

Hotel   ★★★ 75% The Angel Posting House and
           Livery, 91 High St, GUILDFORD
           ☎ 01483 564555 11 ⇆ 🐾 Annexe10 ⇆ 🐾

Hurtmore Hurtmore Rd, Hurtmore GU7 2RN
☎ 01483 426492 Fax 01483 426121
A Peter Alliss/Clive Clark Pay and Play course with seven
lakes and 85 bunkers. The 15th hole is the longest at 537yds.
Played mainly into the wind there are 10 bunkers to
negotiate. The 3rd hole at 448yds stroke Index 1 is a real test.
A dogleg right around a lake and 9 bunkers makes this hole
worthy of its stroke index.
18 holes, 5530yds, Par 70, SSS 67, Course record 66.
Club membership 200.
Visitors   book by telephone up to 7 days in advance.
Societies telephone in advance.
Green Fees £12 per 18 holes (£16 weekends).
Cards   ▭ ▬ ▭ ▭ ▭ ▭
Prof   Maxine Burton
Designer   Peter Alliss/Clive Clark
Facilities ⊗ ⓑ ♨ ♀ ⚐ 🍴 ✐
& Leisure practice nets.
Location   5m S of Guildford on the A3

Hotel   ★★★ 75% The Angel Posting House and
           Livery, 91 High St, GUILDFORD
           ☎ 01483 564555 11 ⇆ 🐾 Annexe10 ⇆ 🐾

Shillinglee Park Chiddingfold GU8 4TA
☎ 01428 653237 & 708158 Fax 01428 644391
Manicured parkland course with many natural features
including seven ponds. The 4th and 7th are the signature
holes requiring tee shots and second shots over ponds, to
well-guarded greens.
9 holes, 5032yds, Par 64, SSS 64, Course record 65.
Club membership 400.
Visitors   restricted Sat, Tue and Thu morning, advisable
           to book any other time.
Societies apply for details.
Green Fees not confirmed.
Cards   ▭ ▬ ▭ ▭ ▭
Prof   David Parkinson
Designer   Roger Mace
Facilities ⊗ ⑂ by prior arrangement ⓑ ♨ ♀ ⚐ 🍴 ⚑
           🥤 ✐
Location   5m S of Godalming, off A283

Hotel   ★★★★ 65% Lythe Hill Hotel, Petworth Rd,
           HASLEMERE ☎ 01428 651251 41 ⇆ 🐾

GUILDFORD   Map 04 SU94

Guildford High Path Rd, Merrow GU1 2HL
☎ 01483 563941 Fax 01483 453228
The course is on typical Surrey downland bordered by
attractive woodlands. Situated on chalk, it is
acknowledged to be one of the best all-weather courses
in the area, and the oldest course in Surrey. The holes
provide an interesting variety of play, an invigorating
experience.
18 holes, 6090yds, Par 69, SSS 70, Course record 65.
Club membership 700.
Visitors   must contact in advance. With member only
           weekends & bank holidays.
Societies welcome Mon-Fri. Must apply in advance.
Green Fees £40 per day; £30 per round.
Prof   P G Hollington
Designer   J H Taylor/Hawtree
Facilities ⊗ ⑂ ⓑ ♨ ♀ ⚐ 🍴 ⚑ ✖ ✐
Location   E side of town centre off A246

Hotel   ★★★ 70% The Manor, Newlands Corner,
           GUILDFORD ☎ 01483 222624 45 ⇆ 🐾

Merrist Wood Coombe Ln, Worplesdon GU3 3PE
☎ 01483 884045 Fax 01483 884047
e-mail: mwgc@merristwood-golfclub.co.uk
More parkland than heathland, Merrist Wood has a bit of
everything. Water comes into play on five holes, the
bunkering is fierce, the greens slope and the back nine has
plenty of trees. Two holes stand out especially: the
picturesque par 3 11th with a tee shot through the trees and
the dastardly par 4 17th, including a 210yd carry over a lake
and ditches either side of the green.
18 holes, 6600yds, Par 72, SSS 71, Course record 69.
Club membership 650.
Visitors   must contact in advance, at weekends only after
           11am, subject to availability.
Societies apply in writing.

                                                        ▶

243

Green Fees £50 per day; £29.50 per round (£39 per round weekends).
Cards 🔲🔲🔲🔲🔲
Prof Andrew Kirk
Designer David Williams
Facilities ⊗ �𝍢 🛆 ⬛ ♀ ⚲ 🏠 🔨 ♂ ⌕
Location 3m out of Guildford on A323 to Aldershot

Hotel ★★★ 75% The Angel Posting House and Livery, 91 High St, GUILDFORD ☎ 01483 564555 11 ⇄ ↑ Annexe10 ⇄ ↑

Milford Station Ln, Milford GU8 5HS
☎ 01483 419200 Fax 01483 419199
e-mail: milford@americangolf.uk.com
A Peter Alliss/Clive Clark designed course. The design has cleverly incorporated a demanding course within an existing woodland and meadow area.
18 holes, 5960yds, Par 69, SSS 68, Course record 64.
Club membership 750.
Visitors must contact in advance, tee booking system, telephone 01483 416291 up to 1 week in advance. May not play weekends until 12 noon.
Societies telephone in advance.
Green Fees £22.50 per 18 holes (£27.50 weekends).
Cards 🔲🔲🔲🔲🔲🔲
Prof Nick English
Designer Peter Alliss
Facilities ⊗ ⟊ 🛆 ⬛ ♀ ⚲ 🏠 ↑ ➤ 🔨 ♂
Location 6m SW Guildford, leave A3 at Milford, A3100 to Enton

Hotel ★★★ 75% The Angel Posting House and Livery, 91 High St, GUILDFORD ☎ 01483 564555 11 ⇄ ↑ Annexe10 ⇄ ↑

Roker Park Rokers Farm, Aldershot Rd GU3 3PB
☎ 01483 236677 Fax 01483 232324
A Pay and Play 9-hole parkland course. A challenging course with two Par 5 holes.
9 holes, 3037yds, Par 36, SSS 72.
Club membership 200.
Visitors no restrictions, pay & play, phone for reservations.
Societies prior arrangement with deposit at least 14 days before, minimum 12 persons.
Green Fees not confirmed..
Prof Kevin Warn
Designer W V Roker
Facilities ⊗ ⟊ 🛆 ⬛ ♀ ⚲ 🏠 ↑ ➤ 🔨 ♂ ⌕
Location A323, 3m from Guildford

Hotel ★★★ 75% The Angel Posting House and Livery, 91 High St, GUILDFORD ☎ 01483 564555 11 ⇄ ↑ Annexe10 ⇄ ↑

HINDHEAD   Map 04 SU83

Hindhead Churt Rd GU26 6HX
☎ 01428 604614 Fax 01428 608508
An excellent example of a Surrey heath-and-heather course, and most picturesque. Players must be prepared for some hard walking. The first nine fairways follow narrow valleys requiring straight hitting; the second nine are much less restricted.
18 holes, 6356yds, Par 70, SSS 70, Course record 63.
Club membership 770.

Visitors must contact in advance and have a handicap certificate.
Societies Wed & Thu only, contact in advance
Green Fees £47 per day; £36 per round (£57/£46 weekends & bank holidays).
Prof Neil Ogilvy
Designer J H Taylor
Facilities ⊗ ⟊ 🛆 ⬛ ♀ ⚲ 🏠 ↑ ♂ ⌕
Location 1.5m NW of Hindhead on A287

Hotel ★★★★ 65% Lythe Hill Hotel, Petworth Rd, HASLEMERE ☎ 01428 651251 41 ⇄ ↑

KINGSWOOD   Map 04 TQ25

Kingswood Sandy Ln KT20 6NE ☎ 01737 832188
Flat parkland course, easy walking.
18 holes, 6880yds, Par 72, SSS 73.
Club membership 700.
Visitors must contact professional at least 24 hrs in advance. May not play weekend mornings.
Societies must apply in advance.
Green Fees not confirmed.
Cards 🔲🔲🔲🔲🔲🔲
Prof James Dodds
Designer James Braid
Facilities ⊗ ⟊ 🛆 ⬛ ♀ ⚲ 🏠 ↑ ➤ 🔨 ♂ ⌕
& Leisure squash.
Location 0.5m S of village off A217

Hotel ★★★ 66% Reigate Manor Hotel, Reigate Hill, REIGATE ☎ 01737 240125 50 ⇄ ↑

LEATHERHEAD   Map 04 TQ15

Leatherhead Kingston Rd KT22 0EE
☎ 01372 843966 & 843956 Fax 01372 842241
e-mail: secretary@lgc-golf.co.uk
Undulating parkland course with tree lined fairways and strategically placed bunkers. Easy walking.
18 holes, 6203yds, Par 71, SSS 70, Course record 67.
Club membership 630.
Visitors telephone pro shop 01372 843956 up to 21 days in advance. May not play before 1pm weekends.
Societies telephone in advance.
Green Fees not confirmed.
Cards 🔲🔲🔲🔲🔲🔲
Prof Simon Norman
Facilities ⊗ ⟊ 🛆 ⬛ ♀ ⚲ 🏠 ↑ 🔨 ♂
Location 0.25m from junct 9 of M25, on A243

Hotel ★★★★ 69% Woodlands Park Hotel, Woodlands Ln, STOKE D'ABERNON ☎ 01372 843933 59 ⇄ ↑

Pachesham Park Golf Complex Oaklawn Rd KT22 0BT
☎ 01372 843453 Fax 01372 844076
e-mail: philktaylor@hotmail.com
A 9-hole undulating parkland course playing out over 18 holes at 5,618yds, starting with 5 shorter but tight holes followed by 4 longer more open but testing to finish.
9 holes, 2805yds, Par 70, SSS 67, Course record 67.
Club membership 250.

▶

Visitors book 2 days in advance by phone. May play weekends
Societies apply in advance.
Green Fees £15 per 18 holes; £9 per 9 holes (£18/£10.50 weekends & bank holidays).
Cards
Prof Philip Taylor
Designer Phil Taylor
Facilities ⊗ ⅲ by prior arrangement ㄴ ♥ ⴹ ⼂ 🍴 ⵏ ⌀ 𝄐
Location off A244, 0.5m from M25 junct 9

Hotel ★★★★ 69% Woodlands Park Hotel, Woodlands Ln, STOKE D'ABERNON
☎ 01372 843933   59 ⇆ ℝ

Tyrrells Wood The Drive KT22 8QP
☎ 01372 376025 Fax 01372 360836
Parkland course with easy walking.
18 holes, 6282yds, Par 71, SSS 70, Course record 65.
Club membership 700.
Visitors must contact in advance. Restricted weekends.
Societies must apply in advance.
Green Fees £34 per round weekdays.
Prof Simon Defoy
Designer James Braid
Facilities ⊗ ⅲ ㄴ ♥ ⴹ ⼂ 🍴 ⵏ ⌀
Location 2m SE of town, off A24

Hotel ★★★★ 67% The Burford Bridge, Burford Bridge, Box Hill, DORKING
☎ 0870 400 8283 57 ⇆ ℝ

LIMPSFIELD   Map 05 TQ45

Limpsfield Chart Westerham Rd RH8 0SL
☎ 01883 723405 & 722106
Tight heathland course set in National Trust land, well wooded.
9 holes, 5718yds, Par 70, SSS 68, Course record 64.
Club membership 300.
Visitors with member only or by appointment weekends & not before 3.30pm Thu (Ladies Day).
Societies must apply in advance.
Green Fees £18(£20 weekends).
Facilities ♥ ⴹ ⼂
& Leisure putting green, practice area.
Location 1m E on A25 from M25 junct 6

Hotel ★★★ 68% Donnington Manor, London Rd, Dunton Green, SEVENOAKS
☎ 01732 462681   60 ⇆ ℝ

LINGFIELD   Map 05 TQ34

Lingfield Park Lingfield Rd, Racecourse Rd RH7 6PQ
☎ 01342 834602 Fax 01342 834602
e-mail: cmorley@lingfieldpark.co.uk
Difficult and challenging, tree-lined parkland course set in 210 acres of beautiful Surrey countryside with water features and 60 bunkers.
18 holes, 6473yds, Par 71, SSS 72, Course record 69.
Club membership 700.
Visitors must be accompanied by member on Sat & Sun. Advisable to telephone first.
Societies must telephone in advance.
Green Fees £38 (£50 weekends).

Cards
Prof Christopher Morley
Facilities ⊗ ⅲ ㄴ ♥ ⴹ ⼂ 🍴 ⵏ ⌀ 𝄐
& Leisure squash, sauna, solarium, gymnasium.
Location Jcnt 6 off M25 follow signs to racecourse

Hotel ★★★ 64% Woodbury House Hotel, Lewes Rd, EAST GRINSTEAD
☎ 01342 313657   14 ⇆ ℝ

NEWDIGATE   Map 04 TQ14

Rusper Rusper Rd RH5 5BX
☎ 01293 871871 (shop) & 871456 (office)
Fax 01293 871456
Course set in mature woodland. The opening two holes give the golfer an encouraging start with the following holes demanding accurate play through the trees. The 5th hole is a challenging Par 5 from the back tee with a gentle dogleg tempting the golfer to take a shortcut. Play is from two sets of tees to 2 pin positions, giving the golfer alternative holes on the second nine.
9 holes, 6218yds, Par 71, SSS 69, Course record 67.
Club membership 220.
Visitors welcome but telephone to reserve time, some restrictions if competitions being played.
Societies telephone in advance for details.
Green Fees £8 per 9 holes;£11.50 per 18 holes(£10/£15.50 weekends).
Cards
Prof Janice Arnold
Designer A Blunden
Facilities ⊗ ⅲ ㄴ ♥ ⴹ ⼂ 🍴 ⵏ ⌀ 𝄐
Location Between Newdigate/Rusper, off A24

Hotel ★★★★ 67% The Burford Bridge, Burford Bridge, Box Hill, DORKING
☎ 0870 400 8283 57 ⇆ ℝ

OCKLEY   Map 04 TQ14

Gatton Manor Hotel Golf & Country Club Standon Ln
RH5 5PQ ☎ 01306 627555 Fax 01306 627713
e-mail: gattonmanor@enterprise.net
Undulating parkland course through woods and over many challenging water holes.
18 holes, 6629yds, Par 72, SSS 72, Course record 68.
Club membership 300.

Visitors may book up to 10 days in advance. Restricted Sun (am). Tee times to be booked through professional 01306 627557
Societies must apply in advance.

245

Green Fees £40 per day; £23 per 18 holes (£30 per round weekends).
Cards ⊟⊟ ▦ ▦ ▣ ▥ ▩ ▢
Prof Rae Sargent
Designer Henry Cotton
Facilities ⊗ ⫪ ⅃ ▆ ♖ ♀ ⚑ ⚐ ☂ ▱ ◥ ⚘ ⚔ ⚵ ♭
& Leisure grass tennis courts, fishing, sauna, solarium, gymnasium.
Location 1.5m SW off A29

Hotel ★★★ 63% Gatton Manor Hotel Golf & Country Club, Standon Ln, OCKLEY ☎ 01306 627555   18 ⇄ ☈

OTTERSHAW   Map 04 TQ06

Foxhills Stonehill Rd KT16 0EL ☎ 01932 872050 Fax 01932 875200 e-mail: events@foxhills.co.uk
A pair of parkland courses designed in the grand manner with three championship courses. One course is tree-lined, the other, as well as trees, has massive bunkers and artificial lakes which contribute to the interest. Both courses offer testing golf and they finish on the same long 'double green'. Par 3 'Manor' course also available.
The Bernard Hunt Course: 18 holes, 6734yds, Par 73, SSS 72.
Longcross Course: 18 holes.
Manor Course: 9 holes.
Visitors contact sales office to reserve times. Restricted before noon weekends.
Societies welcome Mon-Fri, must apply in advance.
Green Fees £65(£75 weekend).
Cards ⊟⊟ ▦ ▦ ▣ ▩ ▢
Prof B Hunt/A Good/R Summerscales
Designer F W Hawtree
Facilities ⊗ ⫪ ⅃ ▆ ♖ ♀ ⚑ ⚐ ☂ ▱ ◥ ⚘ ⚔ ⚵ ♭
& Leisure hard tennis courts, outdoor and indoor heated swimming pools, squash, sauna, solarium, gymnasium.
Location 1m NW

Hotel ★★★ 65% The Crown Hotel, 7 London St, CHERTSEY ☎ 01932 564657 Annexe30 ⇄ ☈

PIRBRIGHT   Map 04 SU95

Goal Farm Gole Rd GU24 0PZ
☎ 01483 473183 & 473205
Beautiful lanscaped parkland 'Pay and Play' course with excellent greens.
9 holes, 1273yds, Par 54, SSS 48, Course record 50.
Club membership 300.
Visitors may not play on Sat before 4pm or Thu before 2pm.
Societies telephone in advance.
Green Fees not confirmed.
Designer Bill Cox
Facilities ⅃ ▆ ♀ ⚐ ☂ ⚑ ⚐
Location 1.5m NW on B3012

Hotel ★★★ 68% Posthouse Farnborough, Lynchford Rd, FARNBOROUGH ☎ 0870 400 9029 143 ⇄ ☈

PUTTENHAM   Map 04 SU94

Puttenham Heath Rd GU3 1AL
☎ 01483 810498 Fax 01483 810988
Picturesque tree-lined heathland course offering testing golf, easy walking.
18 holes, 6211yds, Par 71, SSS 70.
Club membership 650.
Visitors weekdays by prior arrangment tel: 01483 810498, with member only weekends & public holidays.
Societies apply in advance to secretary.
Green Fees £35 per day; £25 per round.
Cards ⊟⊟ ▦
Prof Gary Simmons
Facilities ⊗ ⅃ ▆ ♖ ♀ ⚐ ☂ ⚘ ♭
Location 1m SE on B3000

Hotel ★★★ 65% The Bush Hotel, The Borough, FARNHAM ☎ 0870 400 8225 83 ⇄ ☈

REDHILL   Map 04 TQ25

Redhill & Reigate Clarence Rd, Pendelton Rd RH1 6LB
☎ 01737 240777 Fax 01737 242117
Flat well wooded parkland course.
18 holes, 5272yds, Par 68, SSS 66, Course record 65.
Club membership 600.
Visitors may not play before 11am weekends. Must contact in advance.
Societies must apply in writing.
Green Fees £15 (£25 weekends & bank holidays)per 18 holes.
Prof Warren Pike
Designer James Braid
Facilities ⊗ ⅃ ▆ ♖ ♀ ⚐ ☂ ⚘ ♭
Location 1m S on A23

Hotel ★★★ 66% Reigate Manor Hotel, Reigate Hill, REIGATE ☎ 01737 240125   50 ⇄ ☈

REIGATE   Map 04 TQ25

Reigate Heath Flanchford Rd RH2 8QR
☎ 01737 242610 & 226793 Fax 01737 226793
Gorse, heather, pine and birch trees abound on this popular 9-hole heathland course. Sandy soil gives all year round play even in the wettest winters. Clubhouse enjoys panoramic views of the North Downs and Leith Hill.
9 holes, 5658yds, Par 67, SSS 67, Course record 65.
Club membership 550.
Visitors with member only weekends & bank holidays. Must contact in advance.
Societies must apply in writing.
Green Fees £30 per day; £15-£20 per round.
Prof Barry Davies
Facilities ⊗ ⫪ by prior arrangement ⅃ ▆ ♖ ♀ ⚐ ☂ ⚘
Location 1.5m W off A25

Hotel ★★★ 66% Reigate Manor Hotel, Reigate Hill, REIGATE ☎ 01737 240125   50 ⇄ ☈

Looking for a driving range?
See the index at the back of the guide

Wentworth Club

Virginia Water, *Surrey*   ☎ 01344 842201   Fax 01344 842804   Map 04 TQ06

e-mail: reception@wentworthclub.com

Wentworth Club, the home of the Volvo PGA and Cisco World Match Play Championships, is a very special venue for any sporting, business or social occasion. The West Course (7047 yards) is familiar to millions of television viewers who have followed the championships here. There are two other 18-hole courses, The East Course (6188 yards) and The Edinburgh Course (7004 yards) as well as a 9-hole Par 3 executive course. The courses are Surrey heathland with woodland of pine, oak and birch trees.

The Club is renowned for its fine English food and the superb new Tennis and Health facility, which include a holistic Spa. The centre opened in January 1999 and has 13 outdoor tennis courts with 4 different playing surfaces, a 25m indoor pool and further extensive leisure facilities.

Visitors must contact in advance and have a handicap certificate (men max 24, ladies max 32). May not play weekends

Societies contact in advance in writing

Green Fees West Course: £200 per round; East Course: £105 per round; Edinburgh Course: £135 per round Nov-May, lower rates apply.

Facilities ⊗ ⫟ 🗼 🍴 ♀ ⅄ 🏠 ⚐ 🎣 🛒 ⛳ ♠

Professional (David Rennie)

Leisure tennis, squash, swimming, sauna, solarium, gymnasium

Location Wentworth Drive GU25 4LS (main gate directly opposite turning for A329 on main A30)

Holes/Par/Course record 54 holes.

West Course: 18 holes, 7047 yds, Par 73, SSS 74, Course record 63
East Course: 18 holes, 6201 yds, Par 68, SSS 70, Course record 62
Edinburgh: 18 holes, 7004 yds, Par 72, SSS 74, Course record 67

Championship Course

WHERE TO STAY AND EAT NEARBY

Hotels

ASCOT

★★★★⑥ 68% The Royal Berkshire, London Rd, Sunninghill. ☎ 01344 623322.
63 ⇋ ⋔

★★★★ 64% The Berystede, Bagshot Rd, Sunninghill. ☎ 0870 400 8111.
90 (89 ⇋ ⋔ 1 ⋔)

BAGSHOT

★★★★★⑥⑥⑥ 72% Pennyhill Park, London Rd. ☎ 01276 471774.
26 ⇋ ⋔ Annexe 97 ⇋ ⋔

EGHAM

★★★★⑥⑥ 73% Runnymede Hotel & Spa, Windsor Rd. ☎ 01784 436171.
180 ⇋ ⋔

Restaurant

BRAY

⑥⑥⑥⑥ Waterside Inn, Ferry Rd.
☎ 01628 620691

Reigate Hill Gatton Bottom RH2 0TU
☎ 01737 645577 Fax 01737 642650
Championship standard course with fully irrigated tees and greens. Feature holes include the 5th which is divided by four bunkers and the par 5 14th involving a tricky second shot across a lake. Very good short holes at 8th and 12th with panoramic views from the tees.
18 holes, 6175yds, Par 72, SSS 70, Course record 75.
Club membership 550.
Visitors   must contact in advance to book tee time, may not play weekends until 12 noon.
Societies   welcome Mon-Fri but must book in advance.
Green Fees   not confirmed.
Cards   ▨▨ ▆ ▨▨ ▨ ▨▨ ▨▨ ▨
Prof   Martin Platts
Designer   David Williams
Facilities   ⊗ �&▮ ▮ ▯ ⚑ ⛳ ▮ ▮ ⚡ ⚷
Location   1m from junct 8 of M25

Hotel   ★★★ 63% Bridge House Hotel, Reigate Hill, REIGATE ☎ 01737 246801 & 244821 Fax 01737 223756   39 ⇄ ⏸

SHEPPERTON   Map 04 TQ06

American Golf at Sunbury Charlton Ln TW17 8QA
☎ 01932 771414 Fax 01932 789300
e-mail: sunbury@americangolf.uk.com
27 holes of golf catering for all standards of golfer.
Sunbury Golf Course: 18 holes, 5103yds, Par 68, SSS 65, Course record 60.
Academy: 9 holes, 2444yds, Par 33, SSS 32.
Club membership 600.
Visitors   no restrictions.
Societies   advance booking necessary.
Green Fees   £14 per 18 holes; £8 per 9 holes (£20/£10 wekends).
Cards   ▨▨ ▆ ▨▨ ▨▨ ▨
Prof   Alistair Hardaway
Facilities   ⊗ ▮ ▮ ▯ ⚑ ⛳ ▮ ▮ ⚡ ⚷
Location   Off junct 1 of the M3

Hotel   ★★★ 69% The Thames Lodge, Thames St, STAINES ☎ 0870 400 8121 78 ⇄ ⏸

SUTTON GREEN   Map 04 TQ05

Sutton Green New Ln GU4 7QF
☎ 01483 747898 Fax 01483 750289
Set in the Surrey countryside, a challenging course with many water features. Excellent year round conditions with fairway watering. Many testing holes with water surrounding greens and fairways, making accuracy a premium.
18 holes, 6350yds, Par 71, SSS 70, Course record 67.
Club membership 550.
Visitors   must contact in advance,play after 2pm weekends
Societies   Mon-Fri. Call for details.
Green Fees   not confirmed.
Prof   Paul Tedder
Designer   David Walker/Laura Davies
Facilities   ⊗ ⫝ ▮ ▮ ▯ ⚑ ⛳ ▮ ▮ ⚡
Location   Off A320 between Woking & Guildford

Hotel   ★★★★★ 72% Pennyhill Park Hotel & Country Club, London Rd, BAGSHOT ☎ 01276 471774   26 ⇄ ⏸ Annexe97 ⇄ ⏸

TANDRIDGE   Map 05 TQ35

Tandridge RH8 9NQ
☎ 01883 712274 Fax 01883 730537
A parkland course with two loops of 9 holes from the clubhouse. The first 9 is relatively flat. The second 9 undulates and reveals several outstanding views of the North Downs and the South.
18 holes, 6250yds, Par 70, SSS 70, Course record 66.
Club membership 750.
Visitors   must contact in advance. May play Mon, Wed, Thu
Societies   Mon, Wed & Thu, apply in advance.
Green Fees   not confirmed.
Prof   Chris Evans
Designer   H S Colt
Facilities   ⊗ ▮ ▮ ▯ ⚑ ⛳ ▮ ⚡
Location   2m SE junc 6 M25, 1.5m E of Godstone on A25

Hotel   ★★★★ 71% Nutfield Priory, Nutfield, REDHILL ☎ 01737 824400   60 ⇄ ⏸

TILFORD   Map 04 SU84

Hankley Common The Club House GU10 2DD
☎ 01252 792493 Fax 01252 795699
A natural heathland course subject to wind. Greens are first rate. The 18th, a long par 4, is most challenging, the green being beyond a deep chasm which traps any but the perfect second shot. The 7th is a spectacular one-shotter.
18 holes, 6438yds, Par 71, SSS 71.
Club membership 700.
Visitors   handicap certificate required, restricted to afternoons at weekends.
Societies   apply in writing.
Green Fees   £65 per day; £50 per round (£65 per round wekends).
Cards   ▨▨ ▨▨ ▨ ▨▨ ▨
Prof   Peter Stow
Facilities   ⊗ ⫝ ▮ ▮ ▯ ⚑ ⛳ ⚡
Location   0.75m SE of Tilford

Hotel   ★★★ 65% The Bush Hotel, The Borough, FARNHAM ☎ 0870 400 8225 83 ⇄ ⏸

VIRGINIA WATER   Map 04 TQ06

VIRGINIA WATER See page 247

WALTON-ON-THAMES   Map 04 TQ16

Burhill Burwood Rd KT12 4BL
☎ 01932 227345 Fax 01932 267159
A relatively short and easy parkland course with some truly magnificent trees. The 18th is a splendid par 4 requiring a well-placed drive and a long firm second. This course is always in immaculate condition.
18 holes, 6479yds, Par 70, SSS 71, Course record 65.
Club membership 1000.

▶

Walton Heath

Walton on the Hill, *Surrey* ☎ 01737 812380 Fax 01737 814225 Map 04 TQ25

Walton Heath is famous for staging the Ryder Cup and the European Open Championships. Once owned by the News of the World Newspaper; MPs, Lords and members of the press would be invited down to Walton Heath by Sir Elmsley Carr, who was one of the first to employ a lady as Secretary and Manager of a well-known championship course.

The courses were designed in 1903 by Herbert Fowler, he used natural hollows and channels for drainage so the fairways dry out quickly. The Old Course is popular with visitors however the New Course is very challenging requiring subtle shots to get the ball near the hole. Straying from the fairway brings its punishment with gorse, bracken and heather to test the most patient golfer.

Visitors limited play weekends. Must contact in advance and have a handicap certificate or letter of introduction

Societies must contact in advance

Green Fees from £65-£85 per round

Facilities ⊗ ⅃ ▆ ♀ ⅄ 🏠 ⚐ ⚑
Professional (Ken MacPherson)

Location Deans Lane, Tadworth KT20 7TP (SE side of village, off B2032)

Holes/Par/Course record 36 holes. Old course: 18 holes, 6801 yds, Par 72, SSS 73, Course record 65. New course: 18 holes, 6613 yds, Par 72, SSS 72 Course record 67

Championship Course

Visitors	may not play Fri-Sun unless introduced by member. Must contact in advance.
Societies	apply in writing.
Green Fees	£60 per 18 holes;£80 per 36 holes.
Cards	▨
Prof	Lee Johnson
Designer	Willie Park
Facilities	⊗ ⅲ ᨈ ⬛ ♀ ⚘ 🏠 ⚮ (
& Leisure	squash.
Location	2m S
Hotel	★★★ 67% The Ship, Monument Green, WEYBRIDGE ☎ 01932 848364 39 ⇋ ℞

WALTON-ON-THE-HILL   Map 04 TQ25

WALTON-ON-THE-HILL See page 249

WEST BYFLEET   Map 04 TQ06

West Byfleet Sheerwater Rd KT14 6AA
☎ 01932 343433 Fax 01932 340667
An attractive course set against a background of woodland and gorse. The 13th is the famous 'pond' shot with a water hazard and two bunkers fronting the green. No less than six holes of 420 yards or more.
18 holes, 6211yds, Par 70, SSS 70.
Club membership 600.

Visitors	must contact professional in advance, only with member at weekends. Restricted Thu (Ladies Day).
Societies	must apply in writing.
Green Fees	not confirmed.
Prof	David Regan
Designer	C S Butchart
Facilities	⊗ ⅲ ᨈ ⬛ ♀ ⚘ 🏠 ⚙ ➘ ⚰ ⚮ (
Location	W side of village on A245
Hotel	★★★ 70% The Manor, Newlands Corner, GUILDFORD ☎ 01483 222624 45 ⇋ ℞

WEST CLANDON   Map 04 TQ05

Clandon Regis Epsom Rd GU4 7TT
☎ 01483 224888 Fax 01483 211781
e-mail: office@crgc.freeserve.co.uk
High quality parkland course with challenging lake holes on the back nine. European Tour specification tees and greens.
18 holes, 6419yds, Par 72, SSS 71, Course record 66.
Club membership 700.

Visitors	contact in advance. Afternoon only at weekends & bank holidays.
Societies	telephone in advance.
Green Fees	not confirmed..
Cards	▨ ▨ ▨ ▨ ▨
Prof	Steve Lloyd
Designer	David Williams
Facilities	⊗ ⅲ ᨈ ⬛ ♀ ⚘ 🏠 ⚮ (
& Leisure	sauna.
Location	From A246 Leatherhead direction
Hotel	★★★ 70% The Manor, Newlands Corner, GUILDFORD ☎ 01483 222624 45 ⇋ ℞

WEST END   Map 04 SU96

Windlemere Windlesham Rd GU24 5LS ☎ 01276 858727
A parkland course, undulating in parts with natural water hazards. There is also a floodlit driving range.
9 holes, 2673yds, Par 34, SSS 33, Course record 30.

Visitors	no restrictions.
Societies	advisable to contact in advance.
Green Fees	£9 per 9 holes;£16 per 18 holes(£10.50/£18 wekends).
Cards	▨ ▨ ▨ ▨ ▨
Prof	David Thomas
Designer	Clive Smith
Facilities	ᨈ ⬛ ♀ ⚘ 🏠 ⚮ ⚙ (
Location	N side of village at junct of A319/A322
Hotel	★★★★★ 72% Pennyhill Park Hotel & Country Club, London Rd, BAGSHOT ☎ 01276 471774 26 ⇋ ℞ Annexe97 ⇋ ℞

WEYBRIDGE   Map 04 TQ06

St George's Hill Golf Club Rd, St George's Hill KT13 0NL ☎ 01932 847758 Fax 01932 821564
e-mail: admin@stgeorgeshillgolfclub.co.uk
Comparable and similar to Wentworth, a feature of this course is the number of long and difficult par 4s. To score well it is necessary to place the drive - and long driving pays handsomely. Walking is hard on this undulating, heavily wooded course with plentiful heather and rhododendrons.
Red & Blue: 18 holes, 6569yds, Par 70, SSS 71, Course record 64.
Green: 9 holes, 2897yds, Par 35.
Club membership 600.

Visitors	must contact in advance and have a handicap certificate. Visitors may only play Wed-Fri.
Societies	apply in writing
Green Fees	£90 per day; £65 per round..
Prof	A C Rattue
Designer	H S Colt
Facilities	⊗ ᨈ ⬛ ♀ ⚘ 🏠 ⚮ ⚙
Location	2m S off B374
Hotel	★★★ 67% The Ship, Monument Green, WEYBRIDGE ☎ 01932 848364 39 ⇋ ℞

WOKING   Map 04 TQ05

Hoebridge Golf Centre Old Woking Rd GU22 8JH
☎ 01483 722611 Fax 01483 740369
e-mail: info@hoebridge.co.uk
Three public courses set in parkland on Surrey sand belt. 36-bay floodlit driving range.
Main Course: 18 holes, 6536yds, Par 72, SSS 71, Course record 68.
Shey Course: 9 holes, 2294yds, Par 33.
Maybury Course: 18 holes, 2230yds, Par 54.
Club membership 600.

Visitors	welcome every day, course and reservation desk open dawn to dusk. Credit card reservations 6 days in advance.
Societies	Mon-Fri only, telephone in advance

▶

Green Fees Main course: £17.50 per round(£21 weekends). Shey:£9(£10weekends). Maybury;£7.20(£8 weekends).
Cards 🖃 🖃 🖃 💳
Prof Tim Powell
Designer John Jacobs
Facilities ⊗ ⫴ ⅃ ⅃ ⦿ ⦿ ⊕ ⅃ ⦿ ⦿ ⦿ ⦿
& Leisure snooker.
Location On B382 Old Woking to West Byfleet road

Hotel ★★★★★ 72% Pennyhill Park Hotel & Country Club, London Rd, BAGSHOT ☎ 01276 471774 26 ⇄ ⦿ Annexe97 ⇄ ⦿

Pyrford Warren Ln, Pyrford GU22 8XR
☎ 01483 723555 Fax 01483 729777
e-mail: pyrford@americangolf.uk.com
This inland links style course was designed by Peter Alliss and Clive Clark. Set between Surrey woodlands, the fairways weave between 23 acres of water courses while the greens and tees are connected by rustic bridges. The signature hole is the Par 5 9th at 595 yards, with a dogleg and final approach over water and a sand shelf.
18 holes, 6230yds, Par 72, SSS 70, Course record 64.
Club membership 600.
Visitors must book in advance.
Societies must contact in advance.
Green Fees £38 (£52 weekends & bank holidays).
Cards 🖃 🖃 🖃 💳
Prof Nicholas Sharratt
Designer Peter Allis & Clive Clark
Facilities ⊗ ⫴ ⅃ ⅃ ⦿ ⦿ ⊕ ⅃ ⦿ ⦿ ⦿ ⦿
Location Off A3 Ripley to Pyrford

Hotel ★★★★★ 72% Pennyhill Park Hotel & Country Club, London Rd, BAGSHOT ☎ 01276 471774 26 ⇄ ⦿ Annexe97 ⇄ ⦿

Traditions Pyrford Rd, Pyrford GU22 8UE
☎ 01932 350355 Fax 01932 350234
Situated in the heart of the Surrey countryside with a mature setting which includes various woodland and water features. A course with many challenges which can be enjoyed by golfers of all levels and experience.
18 holes, 6304yds, Par 71, SSS 70, Course record 67.
Club membership 400.
Visitors no restrictions.
Societies telephone in advance.
Green Fees not confirmed.
Cards 🖃 🖃 💳 🖃 💳
Prof Darren Brewer
Designer Peter Allis
Facilities ⊗ ⫴ ⅃ ⅃ ⦿ ⦿ ⊕ ⅃ ⦿ ⦿
Location Off A3 through Wisley village

Hotel ★★★★★ 72% Pennyhill Park Hotel & Country Club, London Rd, BAGSHOT ☎ 01276 471774 26 ⇄ ⦿ Annexe97 ⇄ ⦿

Woking Pond Rd, Hook Heath GU22 0JZ
☎ 01483 760053 Fax 01483 772441
An 18-hole course on Surrey heathland with few changes from the original course designed in 1892 by Tom Dunn. Bernard Darwin a past Captain and President has written 'the beauty of Woking is that there is something distinctive about every hole...'.
18 holes, 6340yds, Par 70, SSS 70, Course record 65.
Club membership 550.

Visitors must contact secretary at least 7 days prior to playing. No visitors weekends & bank holidays.
Societies telephone intially then confirm in writing, normally 12 months notice.
Green Fees £58 per day/round.
Prof Carl Bianco
Designer Tom Dunn
Facilities ⊗ ⫴ ⅃ ⅃ ⦿ ⦿ ⊕ ⅃ ⦿ ⦿
Location W of town centre in area of St Johns/Hook Heath

Hotel ★★★★★ 72% Pennyhill Park Hotel & Country Club, London Rd, BAGSHOT ☎ 01276 471774 26 ⇄ ⦿ Annexe97 ⇄ ⦿

Worplesdon Heath House Rd GU22 0RA
☎ 01483 472277
The scene of the celebrated mixed-foursomes competition. Accurate driving is essential on this heathland course. The short 10th across a lake from tee to green is a notable hole, and the 18th provides a wonderfully challenging par-4 finish.
18 holes, 6440yds, Par 71, SSS 71, Course record 64.
Club membership 590.
Visitors must play with member at weekends & bank holidays. Must contact in advance and have a handicap certificate.
Societies must contact in writing.
Green Fees £65 per day; £48 per round.
Cards 🖃 🖃 🖃 💳
Prof J Christine
Facilities ⊗ ⅃ ⅃ ⦿ ⦿ ⊕ ⅃ ⦿
Location 6m N of Guildford, off A322

Hotel ★★★★★ 72% Pennyhill Park Hotel & Country Club, London Rd, BAGSHOT ☎ 01276 471774 26 ⇄ ⦿ Annexe97 ⇄ ⦿

WOLDINGHAM   Map 05 TQ35

Duke's Dene Slines New Rd CR3 7HA
☎ 01883 653501 Fax 01883 653502
Located in Halliloo Valley and designed by the American architect Bradford Benz, this pleasant course utilises all the contours and features of the valley.
18 holes, 6393yds, Par 71, SSS 70.
Club membership 744.
Visitors tee times should be booked in advance with pro shop. Weekends available after noon for visitors.
Societies telephone to book.
Green Fees not confirmed.
Cards 🖃 ■ 🖃 🖃 💳
Prof Paul Thornley
Designer Bradford Benz
Facilities ⊗ ⫴ by prior arrangement ⅃ ⦿ ⅃ ⦿ ⦿ ⦿ ⦿

Hotel ★★★ 68% Donnington Manor, London Rd, Dunton Green, SEVENOAKS ☎ 01732 462681 60 ⇄ ⦿

North Downs Northdown Rd CR3 7AA
☎ 01883 652057 Fax 01883 652832
e-mail: info@northdownsgolfclub.co.uk
Downland course, 850 ft above sea-level, with several testing holes and magnificent views.
18 holes, 5843yds, Par 69, SSS 68, Course record 65.
Club membership 550.

Visitors	must play with member at weekends and bank holidays. Must contact in advance.
Societies	must telephone in advance and confirm in writing.
Green Fees	£30 per day;£20 per round(£15 per day weekends).
Prof	M Homewood
Designer	Pennink
Facilities	⊗ ﹚ℿ ﹢ ☕ ♀ ♨ 🏠 🛒 ⚌
Location	0.75m S of Woldingham village

Hotel	★★★ 68% Donnington Manor, London Rd, Dunton Green, SEVENOAKS ☎ 01732 462681 60 ⇄ ⓕ

SUSSEX, EAST

BEXHILL Map 05 TQ70

Cooden Beach Cooden Sea Rd TN39 4TR
☎ 01424 842040 & 843938 (Pro Shop)
Fax 01424 842040 e-mail: cbgc@btconnect.com
The course is close by the sea, but is not real links in character. Despite that, it is dry and plays well throughout the year. There are some excellent holes such as the 4th, played to a built-up green, the short 12th, and three good holes to finish. There are added ponds which make the player think more about tee shots and shots to the green.
18 holes, 6500yds, Par 72, SSS 71, Course record 67.
Club membership 730.

Visitors	must have a handicap certificate. Restricted at weekends. Book in advance with professional 01424 843938.
Societies	must contact in advance by telephoning secretary.
Green Fees	£32 per day/round (£35 weekends).
Cards	💳 💳
Prof	Jeffrey Sim
Designer	W Herbert Fowler
Facilities	⊗ ﹢ ☕ ♀ ♨ 🏠 🛒 ⚌
Location	2m W on A259

Hotel	★★★ 71% Lansdowne Hotel, King Edward's Pde, EASTBOURNE ☎ 01323 725174 112 ⇄ ⓕ

Highwoods Ellerslie Ln TN39 4LJ
☎ 01424 212625 Fax 01424 216866
Undulating course.
18 holes, 6218yds, Par 70, SSS 70.
Club membership 750.

Visitors	must play with member on Sun. Must contact in advance and have an introduction from own club. Handicap required.

Societies	advance notice advised.
Green Fees	£28 per day; £22 per round.
Prof	Mike Andrews
Designer	J H Taylor
Facilities	⊗ ﹚ℿ ﹢ ☕ ♀ ♨ 🏠 ⚌
Location	1.5m NW

BRIGHTON & HOVE Map 04 TQ30

Brighton & Hove Devils Dyke Rd BN1 8YJ
☎ 01273 556482 Fax 01273 554247
e-mail: bhgolf@lineone.net
Testing 9 hole course with glorious views over the Downs and the sea. Famous drop hole par 3.
9 holes, 5704yds, Par 68, SSS 68, Course record 65.
Club membership 300.

Visitors	must contact in advance, restricted play Wed, Fri & weekends.
Societies	must contact secretary in advance.
Green Fees	£15 per 18 holes (£25 weekends).
Prof	Phil Bonsall
Designer	James Braid
Facilities	⊗ ﹚ℿ ﹢ ☕ ♀ ♨ 🏠 🛒 ⚌ 🛒 ⚌
Location	4m NW

Hotel	★★ 63% St Catherines Lodge Hotel, Seafront, Kingsway, HOVE ☎ 01273 778181 40 ⇄ ⓕ

Dyke Devils Dyke, Dyke Rd BN1 8YJ
☎ 01273 857296(office) & 857260(pro shop)
Fax 01273 857078
e-mail: secretary@dykegolfclub.org.uk
This downland course has some glorious views both towards the sea and inland. The best hole on the course is probably the 17th; it is one of those teasing short holes of just over 200 yards, and is played across a gully to a high green.
18 holes, 6611yds, Par 72, SSS 72, Course record 66.
Club membership 750.

Visitors	advisable to contact in advance. May not play before noon on Sun.
Societies	apply by telephone or in writing.
Green Fees	phone for fees.
Prof	Richard Arnold
Designer	Fred Hawtree
Facilities	⊗ ﹚ℿ ﹢ ☕ ♀ ♨ 🏠 🛒 ⚌ 🛒 ⚌
Location	4m N of Brighton, between A23 & A27

Hotel	★★ 63% St Catherines Lodge Hotel, Seafront, Kingsway, HOVE ☎ 01273 778181 40 ⇄ ⓕ

East Brighton Roedean Rd BN2 5RA
☎ 01273 604838 Fax 01273 680277
Undulating downland course, overlooking the sea with extensive views.
18 holes, 6346yds, Par 72, SSS 70, Course record 62.
Club membership 650.

Visitors	contact in advance & may only play weekends after 11am.
Societies	must contact in advance, handicap certificate required.
Green Fees	£25 per round (£30 weekends & bank holidays).
Cards	💳 💳 💳 💳 💳
Prof	Mark Stuart-William
Designer	James Braid ▶

Facilities ⊗ ⫴ 🏒 ⚑ ♀ 🛆 🏠 ⛳ 🚗 ✔

Location 2m E of Palace Pier, overlooking marina

Hotel ★★★ 64% Quality Hotel Brighton, West St,
BRIGHTON ☎ 01273 220033 138 ⇄ 🏮

Hollingbury Park Ditchling Rd BN1 7HS
☎ 01273 552010 (sec) & 500086 (res) Fax 01273 552010/6
e-mail: graemecrompton@sussexgolfcentre.fsnet.co.uk
Municipal course in hilly situation on the Downs,
overlooking the sea.
18 holes, 6500yds, Par 72, SSS 71, Course record 65.
Club membership 300.
Visitors must contact in advance.
Societies telephone the secretary for details.
Green Fees not confirmed.
Prof Graeme Crompton
Facilities ⚑ ♀ 🛆 🏠 ⛳ 🚗 🚗 ✔
Location 2m N of town centre

Hotel ★★★ 64% Quality Hotel Brighton, West St,
BRIGHTON ☎ 01273 220033 138 ⇄ 🏮

Waterhall Saddlescombe Rd BN1 8YN ☎ 01273 508658
Hilly downland course with hard walking and open to the
wind. Private club playing over municipal course.
18 holes, 5773yds, Par 69, SSS 68, Course record 66.
Club membership 300.
Visitors must contact in advance. Restricted tee times Sat
and Sun am.
Societies must contact the secretary in writing or
telephone.
Green Fees not confirmed.
Prof Paul Charman
Facilities ⊗ ⫴ 🏒 ⚑ ♀ 🛆 🏠 ⛳ ✔
Location 2m NE from A27

Hotel ★★ 63% St Catherines Lodge Hotel, Seafront,
Kingsway, HOVE ☎ 01273 778181 40 ⇄ 🏮

West Hove Church Farm, Hangleton BN3 8AN
☎ 01273 419738 & 413494 (pro) Fax 01273 439988
e-mail: info@westhovegolfclub.co.uk
A downland course designed by Hawtree & Sons.
18 holes, 6216yds, Par 71, SSS 70, Course record 65.
Club membership 600.
Visitors tee times by arrangement.
Societies by arrangement, telephone, write or e-mail.
Green Fees £22 per round (£27 weekends).
Prof Darren Cook
Designer Hawtree & Sons
Facilities ⊗ ⫴ by prior arrangement 🏒 ⚑ ♀ 🛆 🏠 ⛳ 🦢
🚗 ✔ 🏮
Location Easy access from A27, N of Brighton

Hotel ★★ 63% St Catherines Lodge Hotel, Seafront,
Kingsway, HOVE ☎ 01273 778181 40 ⇄ 🏮

CROWBOROUGH   Map 05 TQ53

Crowborough Beacon Beacon Rd TN6 1UJ
☎ 01892 661511 Fax 01892 667339
e-mail: cbgc@eastsx.fsnet.co.uk
Standing some 800 feet above sea level, this is a testing
heathland course, with panoramic views of the South
Downs, Eastbourne and even the sea on a clear day.
18 holes, 6279yds, Par 71, SSS 70, Course record 66.
Club membership 700.

Visitors must contact in advance & have handicap
certificate but may only play at weekends
& bank holidays after 2.30pm.
Societies telephone or apply in writing to secretary.
Green Fees £40 per day; £27.50 per round (£32.50 per
round weekends & bank holidays after
2.30pm).
Prof D C Newnham
Facilities ⊗ 🏒 ⚑ ♀ 🛆 🏠 ⛳ ✔
Location 1m SW on A26

Hotel ★★★ 76% The Spa Hotel, Mount
Ephraim, TUNBRIDGE WELLS
☎ 01892 520331 71 ⇄ 🏮

Dewlands Manor Cottage Hill, Rotherfield TN6 3JN
☎ 01892 852266 Fax 01892 853015
A beautifully kept compact meadowland course. The short
par 4 4th can be played by the brave by launching a driver
over the trees, the 7th requires accurate driving on a tight
fairway and the final two holes are sweeping par 5s travelling
parallel to each other, a small stream guarding the front of
the 9th green.   ▶

9 holes, 3186yds, Par 36, SSS 70.
Visitors	must telephone in advance.
Societies	telephone for availability.
Green Fees	18 holes £24; 9 holes £13 (£15/£28 weekends).
Cards	▨ ▨ ▨ ▨ ▨
Prof	Nick Godin
Designer	R M & N M Godin
Facilities	⊗ ⓑ ▆ �ⵗ ⵣ ⋒ ⵝ ⵧ ⵙ ⵔ ⵑ
& Leisure	indoor teaching facilities with computer analysis..
Location	0.5m S of Rotherfield

Inn	◆◆◆◆ Plough & Horses Inn, Walshes Rd, CROWBOROUGH ☎ 01892 652614 8 ⇄ ℝ

DITCHLING   Map 05 TQ31

Mid Sussex Spatham Ln BN6 8XJ
☎ 01273 846567 Fax 01273 845767
e-mail: msgc@fastnet.co.uk
Mature parkland course with many trees, water hazards, strategically placed bunkers and superbly contoured greens. The 14th hole, a spectacular par 5, demands accurate shotmaking to avoid the various hazards along its length.
18 holes, 6462yds, Par 71, SSS 71, Course record 65.
Club membership 600.
Visitors	telephone in advance to book tee times. After 12.30pm at weekends.
Societies	advance booking required.
Green Fees	£25.
Cards	▨ ▨ ▨ ▨ ▨
Prof	Chris Connell
Designer	David Williams
Facilities	⊗ ⑪ ⓑ ▆ ⵗ ⵣ ⋒ ⵝ ⵧ ⵙ ⵔ ⵑ ⵒ
Location	1m E of Ditchling village

Hotel	★★★ 76% Shelleys Hotel, High St, LEWES ☎ 01273 472361 19 ⇄ ℝ

EASTBOURNE   Map 05 TV69

Eastbourne Downs East Dean Rd BN20 8ES
☎ 01323 720827 Fax 01323 412506
This downland course has spectacular views over the South Downs and Channel. Situated in an area of outstanding natural beauty approximately 1 mile behind Beachy Head.
18 holes, 6601yds, Par 72, SSS 72, Course record 70.
Club membership 650.
Visitors	a handicap certificate is required for weekends. Visitors may not play before 9.15am weekdays and before 11am weekends except by arrangement.
Societies	contact secretary in advance for details.
Green Fees	£23 per day; £18 per round (£30/£25 weekends).
Cards	▨ ▨
Prof	T Marshall
Designer	J H Taylor
Facilities	⊗ ⑪ ⓑ ▆ ⵗ ⵣ ⋒ ⵝ ⵒ
Location	0.5m W of town centre on A259

Hotel	★★★ 71% Lansdowne Hotel, King Edward's Pde, EASTBOURNE ☎ 01323 725174 112 ⇄ ℝ

Royal Eastbourne Paradise Dr BN20 8BP
☎ 01323 729738 Fax 01323 729738
A famous club which celebrated its centenary in 1987. The course plays longer than it measures. Testing holes are the 8th, a par 3 played to a high green and the 16th, a par 5 righthand dogleg.
Devonshire Course: 18 holes, 6107yds, Par 70, SSS 69, Course record 62.
Hartington Course: 9 holes, 2147yds, Par 64, SSS 61.
Club membership 800.
Visitors	must contact in advance, may not play weekends except by arrangement. Handicap certificate required for Devonshire course.
Societies	must apply in advance.
Green Fees	Devonshire: £22 per day (£27.50 weekends & bank holidays); Hartington: £14 per day.
Prof	Richard Wooller
Designer	Arthur Mayhewe
Facilities	⊗ ⓑ ▆ ⵗ ⵣ ⋒ ⵝ ⵧ ⵙ ⵔ ⵑ
Location	0.5m W of town centre

Hotel	★★★ 71% Lansdowne Hotel, King Edward's Pde, EASTBOURNE ☎ 01323 725174 112 ⇄ ℝ

Willingdon Southdown Rd, Willingdon BN20 9AA
☎ 01323 410981 Fax 01323 411510
e-mail: secretary@wgc.demon.co.uk
Unique, hilly downland course set in oyster-shaped amphitheatre.
18 holes, 6118yds, Par 69, SSS 69.
Club membership 570.
Visitors	no restrictions.
Societies	apply in advance.

▶

7 Courses to choose from!
Any 2 days - 18 January - 31 December 2002
Your break includes 2 days' free golf (up to 36 holes each day on the same course), accommodation, full English breakfast, light lunch at the golf club, with a 4 course Dinner and coffee at the hotel. Guaranteed tee-off times. Handicap certificates required.

All our 112 rooms are en suite with every modern facility inc. Satellite TV. Sky Sports TV in public room.

The cost of your golf break from 18 Jan-28 Feb £145: 1-31 Mar £154: 1 Apr-31 May £162: 1 Jun-30 Sep £174: 1 Oct-31 Dec £156.

You may, subject to availability, play at a selection of 7 golf clubs (all 18-hole) in this lovely area.

Please write or telephone for our Golfing Break folder.

Lansdowne Hotel   AA ★★★
King Edward's Parade · Eastbourne BN21 4EE
Tel: (01323) 725174   Fax: (01323) 739721

Green Fees £25 per day; £18 per round (£28/20 weekends).
Winter £14 per day/round (£16 weekends).
Cards ⊟ 🎫
Prof Troy Moore
Designer J Taylor/Dr Mackenzie
Facilities ⊗ 🏠 🍺 ♀ 🛠 🏪 ↑ ⤢ ⤨ ♂
Location 0.5m N of town centre off A22

Hotel ★★★ 61% Wish Tower Hotel, King Edward's
Pde, EASTBOURNE
☎ 01323 722676 56 ⇄ ℟

FOREST ROW   Map 05 TQ43

Ashdown Forest Golf Hotel Chapel Ln RH18 5BB
☎ 01342 824866 Fax 01342 824869
e-mail: enquiries@ashgolf.co.uk
A natural undulating heathland and woodland course cut out
of the Ashdown Forest. No sand bunkers, just equally testing
heather dunes with the 14th hole regarded as the best. The
hotel specialises in catering for golf breaks and societies.
West Course: 18 holes, 5606yds, Par 68, SSS 67.
Club membership 180.
Visitors must contact in advance, bookings up to 6 days
in advance. Prepayment required.
Societies must telephone in advance.
Green Fees not confirmed.
Cards ⊟ 🎫 📶 🏧 📶 🎫
Prof Martyn Landsborough
Facilities ⊗ 🏮 🏠 🍺 ♀ 🛠 🏪 ↑ ⤨ ♂
Location 4m S of East Grinstead off A22 & B2110

Royal Ashdown Forest Chapel Ln RH18 5LR
☎ 01342 822018 Fax 01342 825211
e-mail: office@royalashdown.co.uk
Old Course on undulating heathland. No bunkers. Long
carries off the tees and magnificent views over the
Forest. Not a course for the high handicapper. West
Course on natural heathland. No bunkers.
*Old Course: 18 holes, 6477yds, Par 72, SSS 71, Course
record 67.*
West Course: 18 holes, 5606yds, Par 68, SSS 67.
Club membership 450.
Visitors restricted weekends & Tue. Must have a
handicap certificate on Old Course. No
restrictions on West Course.
Societies must contact in advance.
Green Fees not confirmed.
Cards ⊟ 🎫
Prof Martyn Landsborough
Facilities ⊗ 🏠 🍺 ♀ 🛠 🏪 ↑ ⤢ ⤨ ♂
Location SE side of Forest Row village, off B2110

Hotel ★★★ 64% Woodbury House Hotel, Lewes
Rd, EAST GRINSTEAD
☎ 01342 313657 14 ⇄ ℟

HAILSHAM   Map 05 TQ50

Wellshurst Golf & Country Club North St,
Hellingly BN27 4EE
☎ 01435 813456(pro shop) & 813636(office)
Fax 01435 812444 e-mail: info@wellshurst.com
There are outstanding views of the South Downs and the
Weald Valley from this 18-hole, well-manicured, undulating
course. There are varied features and some water hazards. A

practice sand bunker, putting green and driving range are
available to improve your golf. The clubhouse and leisure
facilities are open to visitors.
18 holes, 5771yds, Par 70, SSS 68, Course record 64.
Club membership 360.
Visitors no restrictions but advisable to book.
Societies telephone in advance to book tee times.
Green Fees £16 per 18 holes; £12 per 9 holes (£20/£15
weekends & bank holidays).
Cards 🎫 🏧 🔲
Prof Mark Jarvis
Designer The Golf Corporation
Facilities ⊗ 🏮 🏠 🍺 ♀ 🛠 🏪 ↑ ⤢ ↑ ⤨ ♂ ℟
& Leisure sauna, solarium, gymnasium.
Location 2.5m N of Hailsham, on A267

Hotel ★★ 69% The Olde Forge Hotel & Restaurant,
Magham Down, HAILSHAM
☎ 01323 842893 7 ⇄ ℟

HASTINGS & ST LEONARDS   Map 05 TQ80

Hastings Beauport Park Estate, St Leonards TN38 0TA
☎ 01424 852981
18 holes, 6248yds, Par 71, SSS 70, Course record 70.
Location 3m N of Hastings on A2100
Telephone for further details

Hotel ★★★⚓ Beauport Park Hotel, Battle Rd,
HASTINGS ☎ 01424 851222 25 ⇄ ℟

The Beauport Park Hotel
Hastings, Sussex TN38 8EA ★★★
Telephone: 01424 851222
Fax: 01424 852465

A Georgian country house hotel set in 38 acres of
parkland with its own swimming pool, tennis
courts, putting green, badminton lawn, French
boules, outdoor chess, croquet lawn and country
walks. Candle-lit restaurant and open log fires.
Adjacent to an 18 hole and 9 hole golf course,
floodlight driving range and riding stables.
Convenient for East Sussex National Golf Course –
and many other interesting courses.

Luxurious golf lodge now available.

Special Golfing Breaks inclusive of green
fees all year. Please send for our colour
brochure and tariff.

HEATHFIELD
Map 05 TQ52

Horam Park Chiddingly Rd, Horam TN21 0JJ
☎ 01435 813477 Fax 01435 813677
e-mail: angie@horamgolf.freeserve.co.uk
A pretty woodland course with lakes.
9 holes, 6237yds, Par 70, SSS 68, Course record 64.
Club membership 450.
Visitors   contact for tee times.
Societies   prior booking required.
Green Fees   £15 per 18 holes; £10 per 9 holes (£16/£10.50 weekends).
Cards   ▨ ▬ ▭ ▦ ▧ ▨
Prof   Giles Velvick
Designer   Glen Johnson
Facilities   ⊗ ⽊ ⽥ ⽦ ▼ ♀ ⽕ ⽥ ⼳ ⼲ ⼱ ⽄ ⼳
& Leisure   pitch & putt.
Location   Off A267 Hailsham-Heathfield

Hotel   ★★★ 65% Boship Farm Hotel, Lower Dicker, HAILSHAM
☎ 01323 844826 Annexe47 ⇥ ⽨

HOLTYE
Map 05 TQ43

Holtye TN8 7ED
☎ 01342 850635 & 850576 Fax 01342 850576
e-mail: j.p.holmes@holtyegolfclub.fsnet.co.uk
Undulating forest/heathland course with tree-lined fairways providing testing golf. Different tees on back nine.
9 holes, 5325yds, Par 66, SSS 66, Course record 62.
Club membership 400.
Visitors   may not play mornings Wed-Thu & weekends.
Societies   Tue & Fri by arrangement.
Green Fees   not confirmed.
Prof   Kevin Hinton
Facilities   ⽦ ▼ ♀ ⼳ ⽥ ⼳
Location   4m E of East Grinstead and 6m W of Tunbridge Wells on A264

Hotel   ★★★ 64% Woodbury House Hotel, Lewes Rd, EAST GRINSTEAD
☎ 01342 313657 14 ⇥ ⽨

LEWES
Map 05 TQ41

Lewes Chapel Hill BN7 2BB ☎ 01273 483474 & 473245
Downland course. Fine views.
18 holes, 6220yds, Par 71, SSS 70, Course record 64.
Club membership 680.
Visitors   may not play at weekends before 2pm. Bookings taken up to 7 days in advance.
Societies   must contact in advance.
Green Fees   not confirmed.
Prof   Paul Dobson
Designer   Jack Rowe
Facilities   ⊗ ⽊ by prior arrangement ⽦ ▼ ♀ ⼳ ⽥ ⼲ ⼱ ⼳
Location   E side of town centre

Hotel   ★★★ 63% White Hart Hotel, 55 High St, LEWES ☎ 01273 476694
23 ⇥ ⽨ Annexe29 ⇥ ⽨

NEWHAVEN
Map 05 TQ40

Peacehaven Brighton Rd BN9 9UH
☎ 01273 512571 & 514049 Fax 01273 512571
Downland course, sometimes windy. Testing holes: 1st (par 3), 4th (par 4), 9th (par 3), 10th (par 3), 18th (par 3).
Attractive views over the Sussex Downs, the River Ouse and Newhaven Harbour.
9 holes, 5488yds, Par 70, SSS 67, Course record 65.
Club membership 270.
Visitors   may not play before 11am weekends.
Societies   telephone in advance.
Green Fees   £12 per 18 holes; £9 per 9 holes (£18/£12 weekends).
Cards   ▨ ▬ ▦ ▧ ▨
Prof   Ian Pearson
Designer   James Braid
Facilities   ⽦ ▼ ♀ ⼳ ⽥ ⼳
Location   0.75m W of Newhaven on A259

Hotel   ★★★ 67% The Star Inn, ALFRISTON
☎ 0870 400 8102 37 ⇥ ⽨

RYE
Map 05 TQ92

Rye New Lydd Rd, Camber TN31 7QS
☎ 01797 225241 Fax 01797 225460
e-mail: ryelinks@btclick.com
Unique links course with superb undulating greens set amongst ridges of sand dunes alongside Rye Harbour. Fine views over Romney Marsh and towards Fairlight and Dungeness.
Old Course: 18 holes, 6317yds, Par 68, SSS 71, Course record 64.
Jubilee Course: 9 holes, 3109yds, Par 71, SSS 70.
Club membership 1100.
Visitors   must be invited/introduced by a member.
Green Fees   not confirmed.
Prof   Michael Lee
Designer   H S Colt
Facilities   ⊗ ▼ ♀ ⼳ ⽥ ⼲ ⽥ ⼳
Location   2.75m SE off A259

Hotel   ★★★ 62% The George, High St, RYE
☎ 01797 222114 22 ⇥ ⽨

SEAFORD
Map 05 TV49

Seaford Firle Rd, East Blatchington BN25 2JD
☎ 01323 892442 Fax 01323 894113
e-mail: secretary@seafordgolfclub.co.uk
The great H Taylor did not perhaps design as many courses as his friend and rival, James Braid, but Seaford's original design was Taylor's. It is a splendid downland course with magnificent views and some fine holes.
18 holes, 6551yds, Par 69, SSS 71.
Club membership 600.
Visitors   must contact in advance.
Societies   must contact in advance.
Green Fees   £27 per 18 holes.
Cards   ▨ ▬ ▦ ▧
Prof   David Mills/Clay Morris
Designer   J H Taylor
Facilities   ⊗ ⽊ ⽦ ▼ ♀ ⼳ ⽥ ⼲ ⼱ ⼳ ⼳
Location   Turn inland at war memorial off A259 ▶

East Sussex National

Uckfield, *East Sussex*   ☎ 01825 880088 | Fax 01825 880066 | Map 05 TQ42

e-mail: golf@eastsussexnational.co.uk

East Sussex National offers two huge courses ideal for big-hitting professionals. The European Open has been staged here and it is home to the European Headquarters of the David Leadbetter Golf Academy, with indoor or outdoor video analysis. Bob Cupp designed the courses using 'bent' grass from tee to green, resulting in an American-style course to test everyone. The greens on both the East and West courses are immaculately maintained, the West course is reserved for members and their guests, but visitors are welcomed on the other course.

The entrance seems daunting for first-time visitors unprepared for the vast car park, huge red-brick clubhouse and suspended corridor from the reception area through to the well-stocked professional's shop.

Visitors contact Advance Reservations 01825 880230

Societies contact Advance Reservations 01825 880230

Green Fees £55 per round (£60 weekends)

Facilities ⊗ ⵄ ⌕ ☕ ⚑ ⌂ ⛳ ⅄ ⛴ ⚐ ꝑ
Professional (Sarah Machennan). Golf Academy

Leisure tennis, swimming, sauna, solarium

Location Little Horsted TN22 5ES (2m S of Uckfield on A22)

Holes/Par/Course record 36 holes. East Course: 18 holes, 7138 yds, Par 72, SSS 74, Course record 63 West Course: 18 holes, 7154 yds, Par 72, SSS 74,

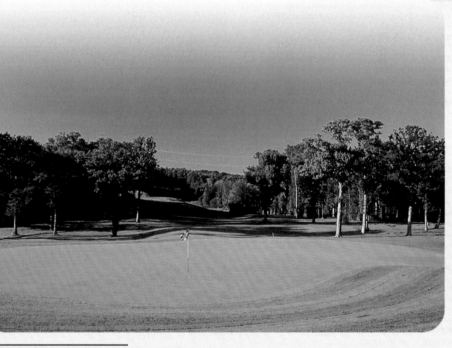

Championship Course

WHERE TO STAY

Hotels

UCKFIELD

★★★★⑥ 71% Buxted Park Country House Hotel, Buxted.
☎ 01825 732711. 44 ⇌ ↟

★★★⑥⑥ ♨ 78% Horsted Place, Little Horsted. ☎ 01825 750581.
17 ⇌ ↟

NEWICK

★★★⑥⑥ 81%
Newick Park Country Estate
☎ 01825 723633. 13 (9 ⇌ ↟4 ↟)

Hotel	★★★ 67% The Star Inn, ALFRISTON ☎ 0870 400 8102 37 ⇄ ♜

Seaford Head Southdown Rd BN25 4JS
☎ 01323 890139 & 894843
18 holes, 5848yds, Par 71, SSS 68, Course record 63.
Telephone for further details

Hotel	★★★ 67% Deans Place, Seaford Rd, ALFRISTON ☎ 01323 870248　36 ⇄ ♜

SEDLESCOMBE　　　　　　　　　Map 05 TQ71

Sedlescombe Kent St TN33 0SD
☎ 01424 871700 Fax 01424 871712
e-mail: golf@golfschool.co.uk
Situated in the beautiful Sussex countryside. The natural water and tree line adds to the beauty as well as making it an enjoyable round of golf.
18 holes, 6269yds, Par 72, SSS 70.
Club membership 300.
Visitors　　please telephone and reserve tee times.No jeans or tracksuits allowed,golf shoes must be worn on the course.Hire shoes available.
Societies　　please telephone to reserve tee times.
Green Fees　£16 per 18 holes; £10 per 9 holes (£20/£12 weekends).
Cards　　　🖃🖃🖃🖃 🔟
Prof　　　James Andrews
Facilities　⊗ �ℳ ⓛ ♥ ⚑ ♨ 🏠 ♈ 🚗 🧴 ♨ 🌣 ℓ
& Leisure　gymnasium.
Location　　A21, 4m N of Hastings

Hotel	★★★ 68% Brickwall Hotel, The Green, SEDLESCOMBE ☎ 01424 870253　26 ⇄ ♜

TICEHURST　　　　　　　　　　Map 05 TQ63

Dale Hill Hotel & Golf Club TN5 7DQ
☎ 01580 200112 Fax 01580 201249
e-mail: info@dalehill.co.uk
Picturesque course with woodland, water and gently undulating fairways. Hotel and leisure centre within grounds.
Dale Hill: 18 holes, 6106yds, Par 70, SSS 69.
Ian Woosnam: 18 holes, 6512yds, Par 71, SSS 71.
Club membership 950.
Visitors　　booking only 7 days in advance, may not play at weekends.
Societies　　must contact in advance.
Green Fees　Dale Hill:£30;Ian Woosnam:£55,both includes buggy..
Cards　　　🖃🖃🖃🖃🖃 🔟
Prof　　　PGA approved pro
Designer　Ian Woosnam
Facilities　⊗ ⅏ ⓛ ♥ ⚑ ♨ 🏠 ♈ 🚗 🧴 ♨ 🌣 ℓ
& Leisure　heated indoor swimming pool, sauna, gymnasium.
Location　　N side of village off B2087

Hotel	★★★★ 68% Dale Hill Hotel & Golf Club, TICEHURST ☎ 01580 200112　26 ⇄ ♜

UCKFIELD　　　　　　　　　　Map 05 TQ42

UCKFIELD See page 257

Piltdown Piltdown TN22 3XB
☎ 01825 722033 Fax 01825 724192
Natural heathland course with much heather and gorse. No bunkers, easy walking, fine views.
18 holes, 6070yds, Par 68, SSS 69, Course record 67.
Club membership 400.
Visitors　　must telephone pro shop in advance 01825 722389 and have a handicap certificate. Play on Tue, Thu and weekends is restricted.
Societies　　must contact in writing.
Green Fees　£33 per 18 holes.
Prof　　　Jason Partridge
Facilities　⊗ ⅏ ⓛ ♥ ⚑ ♨ 🏠 ♈ 🧴 🚗 🌣 ℓ
Location　　Between Newick & Maresfield off A272, club signposted

Hotel	★★★ 78% Horsted Place, Little Horsted, UCKFIELD ☎ 01825 750581　17 ⇄ ♜

SUSSEX, WEST

ANGMERING　　　　　　　　　Map 04 TQ00

Ham Manor BN16 4JE
☎ 01903 783288 Fax 01903 850886
Two miles from the sea, this parkland course has fine springy turf and provides an interesting test in two loops of nine holes each.
18 holes, 6267yds, Par 70, SSS 70, Course record 64.
Club membership 780.
Visitors　　must have a handicap certificate. Telephone pro shop in advance 01903 783732.
Societies　　telephone for details
Green Fees　not confirmed.
Prof　　　Simon Buckley
Designer　Harry Colt
Facilities　⚖ 🏠 🌣
Location　　Off A259

Guest-house	♦♦♦♦ Kenmore Guest House, Claigmar Rd, RUSTINGTON ☎ 01903 784634 7rm(1 ⇄5 ♜)

ARUNDEL　　　　　　　　　　Map 04 TQ00

Avisford Park Yapton Ln, Walberton BN18 0LS
☎ 01243 554611 Fax 01243 555580
A 18 hole course enjoying a country hotel complex setting. The course opens with a real challenge as there is out of bounds water and tree hazards the whole length of this 414yard drive.
18 holes, 5703yds, Par 68, SSS 66.
Club membership 100.
Visitors　　must contact in advance for weekend play.
Societies　　apply in writing or telephone.
Green Fees　not confirmed.
Cards　　　🖃🖃🖃🖃🖃 🔟　　　　　　　　▶

Prof	Richard Beach
Facilities	⊗ 𝄆 ⬛ ♀ ⚱ 🏠 ⛳ 🏌 🛒 ✎
& Leisure	hard tennis courts, outdoor and indoor heated swimming pools.
Location	Off A27, towards Yapton
Hotel	★★★ 66% Norfolk Arms Hotel, High St, ARUNDEL ☎ 01903 882101 21 ⇄ Annexe13 ⇄

BOGNOR REGIS　　　　　　　　　Map 04 SZ99

Bognor Regis Downview Rd, Felpham PO22 8JD
☎ 01243 821929 (Secretary) Fax 01243 860719
e-mail: secretary@bognorgoflclub.co.uk
This flattish, well tree lined, parkland course has more variety than is to be found on some other South Coast courses. The club is also known far and wide for its enterprise in creating a social atmosphere. The course is open to the prevailing wind and the River Rife and many water ditches need negotiation.
18 holes, 6238yds, Par 70, SSS 70, Course record 64.
Club membership 700.

Visitors	handicap certificate required. Must contact in advance (pro shop 01243 865209).
Societies	phone initially.
Green Fees	not confirmed.
Prof	Stephen Bassil
Designer	James Braid
Facilities	⊗ 𝄆 𝄆 ⬛ ♀ ⚱ 🏠 ❧ 🛒 ✎
Location	0.5m N at Felpham traffic lights on A259
Hotel	★★ 69% Aldwick Hotel, Aldwick Rd, Aldwick, BOGNOR REGIS ☎ 01243 821945　20 ⇄ 🐾

BURGESS HILL　　　　　　　　　Map 04 TQ31

Burgess Hill Cuckfield Rd RH15 8RE
☎ 01444 258585 Fax 247318
e-mail: golfacademy@skynow.net
Opened May 1998, an academy course bordered by a tributary of the River Adur. Facilities available for public use include a floodlit driving range and a large sweeping putting green.
9 holes, 1250yds, Par 27.

Visitors	None.
Societies	contact in advance.
Green Fees	not confirmed.
Prof	Mark Collins
Designer	Donald Steel
Facilities	⊗ 𝄆 𝄆 ⬛ ♀ ⚱ 🏠 ⛳ ✎ ⟡
& Leisure	pitching & chipping green.
Location	N of town on B2036
Hotel	★★★⚜ 79% Ockenden Manor, Ockenden Ln, CUCKFIELD ☎ 01444 416111　22 ⇄ 🐾

CHICHESTER　　　　　　　　　Map 04 SU80

Chichester Hunston Village PO20 6AX
☎ 01243 533833 Fax 01243 539922
e-mail· chigolfclub@mistral.co.uk
Set amongst lush farmland, the Tower course has four lakes which bring water into play on seven holes. Also the Florida-style Cathedral and a 9-hole par 3 and a floodlit driving range.

Tower Course: 18 holes, 6175yds, Par 72, SSS 69, Course record 67.
Cathedral Course: 18 holes, 6461yds, Par 72, SSS 71, Course record 65.
Club membership 600.

Visitors	a strict dress code is in operation. Must contact in advance. Tee reservations up to 7 days in advance on 01243 533833.
Societies	must contact in advance.
Green Fees	not confirmed.
Cards	💳 💳 💳 💳 💳 💳
Prof	John Slinger
Designer	Philip Saunders
Facilities	⊗ 𝄆 𝄆 ⬛ ♀ ⚱ 🏠 ⛳ 🛒 ✎ ⟡
& Leisure	mini golf and par 3 course..
Location	3m S of Chichester, on B2145 at Hunston
Hotel	★★★ 68% The Ship Hotel, North St, CHICHESTER ☎ 01243 778000　36 ⇄ 🐾

COPTHORNE　　　　　　　　　Map 05 TQ33

Copthorne Borers Arms Rd RH10 3LL
☎ 01342 712033 & 712058 Fax 01342 717682
e-mail: info@copthornegolfclub.co.uk
Despite it having been in existence since 1892, this club remains one of the lesser known Sussex courses. It is hard to know why because it is most attractive with plenty of trees and much variety
18 holes, 6505yds, Par 71, SSS 71, Course record 67.
Club membership 550.

Visitors	advised to contact in advance, may not play weekends before 1pm.
Societies	must contact in advance.
Green Fees	£30 per round; £38 per day.
Cards	💳 💳 💳
Prof	Joe Burrell
Designer	James Braid
Facilities	⊗ 𝄆 ⬛ ♀ ⚱ 🏠 ⛳ ✎
Location	E side of village junc 10 of M23 off A264
Hotel	★★★★ 70% Copthorne Hotel London Gatwick, Copthorne Way, COPTHORNE ☎ 01342 348800 & 348888 Fax 01342 348833 227 ⇄ 🐾

Effingham Park The Copthorne Effingham Park, Hotel, West Park Rd RH10 3EU ☎ 01342 716528 Fax 716039
9 holes, 1822yds, Par 30, SSS 57, Course record 28.

Location	2m E on B2028

Telephone for further details

Hotel ★★★★ 65% Copthorne Hotel Effingham Park
Gatwick, West Park Rd, COPTHORNE
☎ 01342 714994 122 ⇌ ↑

CRAWLEY   Map 04 TQ23

Cottesmore Buchan Hill, Pease Pottage RH11 9AT
☎ 01293 528256 Fax 01293 522819 e-
mail: cottesmore@americangolf.uk.com
Founded in 1974, the Griffin Course is a fine test of golfing
skill with fairways lined by silver birch, pine, oak and
rhododendrons. 4 holes have lakes as hazards.
*Griffin Course: 18 holes, 6248yds, Par 71, SSS 70, Course
record 67.*
Visitors   dress code applies. Advisable to contact in
                  advance.
Societies   must telephone in advance.
Green Fees   not confirmed.
Prof   Calum J Callan
Designer   Michael J Rogerson
Facilities   ⊗ ⊪ ┗ ➡ ♀ ♔ 🏠 ⌂ ♈ ➘ 🛆 ♂
& Leisure   hard tennis courts, heated indoor swimming
                  pool, sauna, solarium, gymnasium.
Location   3m SW 1m W of M23 junc 11

Hotel ★★★ Alexander House Hotel, East St,
TURNERS HILL ☎ 01342 714914 15 ⇌ ↑

Ifield Golf & Country Club Rusper Rd, Ifield RH11 0LN
☎ 01293 520222 Fax 01293 612973
Parkland course.
18 holes, 6330yds, Par 70, SSS 70, Course record 64.
Club membership 750.
Visitors   must contact professional in advance. Must be
                  guest of member at weekends.
Societies   apply in advance.
Green Fees   £33 per day; £23 per round weekdays.
Prof   Jonathan Earl
Designer   Bernard Darwin
Facilities   ⊗ ⊪ ┗ ➡ ♀ 🛆 🏠 ➘ 🛆 ♂
& Leisure   squash.
Location   1m W side of town centre off A23

Hotel ★★★ Alexander House Hotel, East St,
TURNERS HILL ☎ 01342 714914 15 ⇌ ↑

Tilgate Forest Golf Centre Titmus Dr RH10 5EU
☎ 01293 530103 Fax 523478
Designed by former Ryder Cup players Neil Coles and Brian
Huggett, the course has been carefully cut through a silver
birch and pine forest. It is possibly one of the most beautiful
public courses in the country. The 17th is a treacherous Par 5
demanding an uphill third shot to a green surrounded by
rhododendrons.
18 holes, 6359yds, Par 71, SSS 70, Course record 69.
Club membership 200.
Visitors   public course, pay & play at all times.
Societies   telephone in advance for details.
Green Fees   £13 per 18 holes (£18 weekends& bank
                  holidays).
Cards   ▦ ▮ ▦ ▦ 🆑
Prof   Sean Trussell
Designer   Neil Coles/Brian Huggett

Facilities   ⊗ ⊪ ┗ ➡ ♀ 🛆 🏠 ⌂ ♈ ♂ ₵
& Leisure   par 3 nine hole course.
Location   2 miles east of Crawley town centre

Hotel ★★★ Alexander House Hotel, East St,
TURNERS HILL ☎ 01342 714914 15 ⇌ ↑

GOODWOOD   Map 04 SU80

Goodwood Kennel Hill PO18 0PN
☎ 01243 774968 Fax 01243 781741
Downland course designed by the master architect,
James Braid. Many notable holes, particularly the
finishing ones: 17 down an avenue of beech trees and 18
along in front of the terrace. Superb views of the downs
and the coast.
18 holes, 6434yds, Par 72, SSS 71.
Club membership 930.
Visitors   must have handicap certificate
Societies   Wed & Thu, telephone secretary in advance.
Green Fees   not confirmed..
Prof   Keith MacDonald
Designer   J Braid
Facilities   ⊗ ⊪ ┗ ➡ ♀ 🛆 🏠 ⌂ ♈ ➘ 🛆 ♂
Location   3m NE of Chichester off A27

Hotel ★★★★ 72% Marriott Goodwood Park
Hotel & Country Club, GOODWOOD
☎ 01243 775537 94 ⇌ ↑

Marriott Goodwood Park Hotel & Country Club
PO18 0QB ☎ 01243 775537 Fax 01243 520120
A parkland course set within the 12,000 acre Goodwood
estate.
18 holes, 6579yds, Par 72, SSS 71, Course record 68.
Club membership 700.

Visitors   must hold a current handicap certificate.
Societies   telephone or write.
Green Fees   £28 per round (£35 weekends & bank holidays).
Cards   ▦ ▮ ▦ ▦ 🆑
Prof   Adrian Wratting
Designer   Donald Steele
Facilities   ⊗ ⊪ ┗ ➡ ♀ 🛆 🏠 ⌂ ♈ ⌂ ➘ 🛆 ♂ ₵
& Leisure   hard tennis courts, heated indoor swimming
                  pool, sauna, solarium, gymnasium.
Location   3m N of Chichester, in the grounds of
                  Goodwood House

Hotel ★★★★ 72% Marriott Goodwood Park Hotel &
Country Club, GOODWOOD
☎ 01243 775537 94 ⇌ ↑

HASSOCKS   Map 04 TQ31

Hassocks London Rd BN6 9NA
☎ 01273 846630 & 846990 Fax 01273 846070
e-mail: jaki@hassocksgc.fsnet.co.uk
Set against the backdrop of the South Downs, Hassocks is an 18 hole par 70 course designed and contoured to blend naturally with the surrounding countryside. A friendly and relaxed course, appealing to golfers of all ages and abilities.
18 holes, 5754yds, Par 70, SSS 68, Course record 70.
Club membership 400.
Visitors   phone Pro. Shop in advance,01273 846990.
Societies   apply in writing or telephone in advance.
Green Fees £14.25 per 18 holes (£17.50 weekends and bank holidays).
Cards   ▨▨▨▨▨
Prof   Charles Ledger
Designer   Paul Wright
Facilities   ⊗ ▚ ♥ ♀ ⚐ ㋡ ↟ ♣ ◿ ◊
Location   On the A273 between Burgess Hill and Hassocks

Hotel   ★★★ 62% The Hickstead Hotel, Jobs Ln, Bolney, HICKSTEAD
☎ 01444 248023   50 ⇌ ㏌

HAYWARDS HEATH   Map 05 TQ32

Haywards Heath High Beech Ln RH16 1SL
☎ 01444 414457 Fax 01444 458319
Pleasant parkland course with several challenging par 4s and 3s.
18 holes, 6216yds, Par 71, SSS 70, Course record 66.
Club membership 770.
Visitors   must have a handicap certificate. Must contact in advance.
Societies   Wed & Thu only by prior arrangement with the secretary.
Green Fees £26 per 18 holes (£35 weekends).
Prof   Michael Henning
Facilities   ⊗ ▚ ♥ ♀ ⚐ ◿ ♣
Location   1.25m N off B2028

Hotel   ★★★♨ 79% Ockenden Manor, Ockenden Ln, CUCKFIELD ☎ 01444 416111   22 ⇌ ㏌

Paxhill Park East Mascalls Ln, Lindfield RH16 2QN
☎ 01444 484467 Fax 01444 482709
e-mail: johnbowen@paxhillpark.fsnet.co.uk
A relatively flat parkland course designed by Patrick Tallack.
Water hazard on 5th, 13th and 14th holes,
18 holes, 6117yds, Par 70, SSS 69, Course record 67.
Club membership 320.
Visitors   welcome but may not play weekend and some weekday mornings.
Societies   must contact in advance.
Green Fees not confirmed..
Cards   ▨▨▨▨▨
Prof   Paul Lyons
Designer   P Tallack
Facilities   ⊗ ▚ ♥ ♀ ⚐ ㋡ ◿ ♣
& Leisure   snooker.

Hotel   ★★★♨ 79% Ockenden Manor, Ockenden Ln, CUCKFIELD ☎ 01444 416111   22 ⇌ ㏌

HORSHAM   Map 04 TQ13

See also **Slinfold**

Horsham Worthing Rd RH13 7AX
☎ 01403 271525 Fax 01403 274528
A short but challenging course with six Par 4's and three Par 3's, two of which are played across water. Designed for beginners and intermediates but also challenges better players with a standard scratch of six below par.
9 holes, 4122yds, Par 33, SSS 30, Course record 55.
Club membership 280.
Visitors   no restrictions.
Societies   apply in advance.
Green Fees £9 per 18 holes; £7 per 9 holes (£11/£8 weekends).
Cards   ▨▨▨▨▨▨
Prof   Alister Fitt
Facilities   ⊗ ᾿⑁ ▚ ♥ ♀ ⚐ ㋡ ◿ ♣
& Leisure   solarium, gymnasium.
Location   Off A24 rdbt, between Horsham/Southwater, by garage on B2237

Hotel   ★★ 67% Ye Olde King's Head Hotel, Carfax, HORSHAM ☎ 01403 253126 42rm(41 ⇌ ㏌)

HURSTPIERPOINT   Map 04 TQ21

Singing Hills Albourne BN6 9EB
☎ 01273 835353 Fax 01273 835444
Three distinct nines (Lake, River & Valley) can be combined to make a truly varied game. Gently undulating fairways and spectacular waterholes make Singing Hills a test of accurate shotmaking. The opening 2 holes of the River nine have long drives, while the second hole on the Lake course is an Island green where the tee is also protected by two bunkers. The Valley Course demand long, accurate tee shots.
Lake: 9 holes, 3253yds, Par 35, SSS 35.
River: 9 holes, 2861yds, Par 34, SSS 34.
Valley: 9 holes, 3362yds, Par 36, SSS 34.
Club membership 390.
Visitors   no restrictions, but strict dress code observed.
Societies   apply in advance.
Green Fees not confirmed..
Prof   Wallace Street
Designer   M R M Sandow
Facilities   ⊗ ᾿⑁ ▚ ♥ ♀ ⚐ ㋡ ◿ ♣
Location   Off A23, on B2117

Hotel   ★★★ 62% The Hickstead Hotel, Jobs Ln, Bolney, HICKSTEAD
☎ 01444 248023   50 ⇌ ㏌

LITTLEHAMPTON   Map 04 TQ00

Littlehampton 170 Rope Walk, Riverside West BN17 5DL ☎ 01903 717170 Fax 726629
e-mail: lgc@talk21.com
A delightful seaside links in an equally delightful setting - and the only links course in the area.
18 holes, 6226yds, Par 70, SSS 70.
Club membership 500.
Visitors   may not book tee times, contact Pro Shop for availability on 01903 716369.
Societies   welcome weekdays, must apply in advance.

Green Fees	£33 per 36 holes, £23 per 18 holes.
Prof	Guy McQuitty
Designer	Hawtree
Facilities	⊗ Ⅲ ⅃ ▲ ☕ ♀ ⚲ ☖ ♨ ∅
Location	1m W of Littlehampton off A259

Hotel	★★★ 76% Bailiffscourt Hotel, CLIMPING ☎ 01903 723511 9 ⇄ ♙ Annexe22 ⇄ ♙

LOWER BEEDING   Map 04 TQ22

Mannings Heath Hotel Winterpit Ln RH13 6LY
☎ 01403 891191 Fax 01403 891499
An 8 hole practice course and a driving range, designed as an
executive course for beginners and those who find if difficult
to play a full 18 holes. It is very popular.
9 holes, 1529yds, Par 31.
Club membership 150.

Visitors	phone for details.
Societies	telephone in advance.
Green Fees	by arrangement..
Cards	🟰 🟰 🟰 🟰 🟰 🟰
Prof	Jim Debenham
Facilities	⊗ Ⅲ⅃ ▲ ☕ ♀ ⚲ ⅋ 🞛
& Leisure	fishing.
Location	Located off the A281 south of Horsham

Hotel	★★★★⚘South Lodge Hotel, Brighton Rd, LOWER BEEDING ☎ 01403 891711 Fax 01403 891766 41 ⇄

SOUTH LODGE HOTEL & CAMELLIA RESTAURANT

AA
⊛⊛⊛
★★★★

MANNINGS HEATH GOLF CLUB
South Lodge Hotel & Camellia Restaurant is a fine Victorian
Country House set in 93 acres of secluded wooded parkland
with views over the South Downs. It has 41 individually
designed luxurious bedrooms and also offers fine dining.
Our Sister property *Mannings Heath Golf Club* is just a 5
minute drive away and offers excellent golf with its
Two 18 Hole Championship Courses.
The Golf Club was founded in 1905 as a private members' Club,
which over the past 90 years has evolved and matured. We are
pleased to be able to offer our very special
Golfing Break
5 course Camellia Menu Dinner, Luxury Accommodation,
Traditional English Country House Breakfast and a Round of
Golf from
£240.00 (double/twin) £205.00 (single)
inclusive of VAT @17.5%
For reservations, please contact our Sales Department at
South Lodge Hotel & Camellia Restaurant
Brighton Road, Lower Beeding,
near Horsham, West Sussex RH13 6PS.
Telephone: (01403) 891711 Fax: (01403) 891766
E-mail: enquiries@southlodgehotel.co.uk
http://www.exclusivehotels.co.uk

MANNINGS HEATH   Map 04 TQ22

Mannings Heath Fullers, Hammerpond Rd RH13 6PG
☎ 01403 210228 Fax 01403 270974
e-mail: manningsheathclubandvenue@msn.com
The waterfall course meanders up hill and down dale
over heathland with streams affecting 10 of the holes.
Wooded valleys protect the course from strong winds.
Famous holes at 10th (the 'Waterfall', par 3), and 11th
(the 'Valley', par 4). The Kingfisher course winds its
way over the Downs with extensive views. Skirted by
mature woodland, many holes requiring accurate ball
positioning in order to score well.
*Waterfall: 18 holes, 6378yds, Par 71, SSS 70, Course
record 66.*
Kingfisher: 18 holes, 6217yds, SSS 70.
Club membership 700.

Visitors	may book up to 28 days in advance.
Societies	must contact in advance.
Green Fees	£38 per 18 holes(£45 weekends).
Cards	🟰 🟰 🟰 🟰
Prof	Clive Tucker
Designer	David Williams
Facilities	⊗ Ⅲ⅃ ▲ ☕ ♀ ⚲ ☕ ⅋ ♨ ⚲ ∅ ♛
& Leisure	hard tennis courts, fishing, sauna, chipping practice area.
Location	M23 junct 11, take A281 from Horsham or Brighton. Club on N side of village

Hotel	★★★★⚘ South Lodge Hotel, Brighton Rd, LOWER BEEDING ☎ 01403 891711 41 ⇄

MIDHURST   Map 04 SU82

Cowdray Park Petworth Rd GU29 0BB
☎ 01730 813599 Fax 01730 815900
e-mail: cowdray-golf@lineone.net
Undulating parkland course with scenic views of surrounding
countryside, including Elizabethan ruins. The course is
situated in a National Park originally designed by Capability
Brown in the 18th century.
18 holes, 6212yds, Par 70, SSS 70, Course record 66.
Club membership 720.

Visitors	advised to contact in advance. Handicap certificate required.
Societies	apply in writing/telephone/e-mail/fax.
Green Fees	£40 per day; £30 per 18 holes (£30/£25 winter).
Cards	🟰 🟰 🟰 🟰
Prof	Richard Gough
Designer	Jack White
Facilities	⊗ Ⅲ⅃ ▲ ☕ ♀ ⚲ ☕ ♨ ⚲ ∅
Location	1m E of Midhurst on A272

Hotel	★★★ 74% Spread Eagle Hotel and Health Spa, South St, MIDHURST ☎ 01730 816911 35 ⇄ ♙ Annexe4 ♙

PULBOROUGH   Map 04 TQ01

West Sussex Golf Club Ln, Wiggonholt RH20 2EN
☎ 01798 872563 Fax 01798 872033
Heathland course.
18 holes, 6223yds, Par 68, SSS 70, Course record 61.
Club membership 850.   ▶

Visitors	must contact in advance, may not play weekends except by prior agreement of the secretary, and on Fri except with a member.
Societies	Wed & Thu only, apply in writing.
Green Fees	£57.50 per day;£47.50 per 18 holes(£62.50/£52.50 weekends & bank holidays).
Prof	Tim Packham
Designer	Campbell/Hutcheson
Facilities	⊗ ⌊ ♥ ♀ ⚲ 🏠 🖈 ⚒ ⚙ ┇
Location	1.5m E of Pulborough off A283
Hotel	★★★ 67% Roundabout Hotel, Monkmead Ln, WEST CHILTINGTON ☎ 01798 813838 23 ⇆ 🍴

PYECOMBE   Map 04 TQ21

Pyecombe Clayton Hill BN45 7FF
☎ 01273 845372 Fax 01273 843338
Typical downland course on the inland side of the South Downs. Picturesque with magnificent views.
18 holes, 6278yds, Par 71, SSS 70, Course record 67.
Club membership 700.

Visitors	must contact in advance and may only play after 9.15am weekdays and after 2.15pm weekends
Societies	telephone secretary in advance.
Green Fees	£25 per round (£30 weekends & bank holidays).
Prof	C R White
Facilities	⊗ ⫞ by prior arrangement ⌊ ♥ ♀ ⚲ 🏠 🖈 ⚙
Location	E side of village on A273
Hotel	★★★ 64% Courtlands Hotel, 15-27 The Drive, HOVE ☎ 01273 731055 60 ⇆ 🍴 Annexe7 ⇆ 🍴

SELSEY   Map 04 SZ89

Selsey Golf Links Ln PO20 9DR
☎ 01243 602203 Fax 01243 602722
e-mail: selsey.cc@talk21.com
Fairly difficult seaside course, exposed to wind and has natural ditches.
9 holes, 5834yds, Par 68, SSS 68, Course record 64.
Club membership 360.

Visitors	must contact in advance.
Societies	must contact in advance in writing
Green Fees	£12 per 18 holes;£17 per day(£15/£20 weekends).
Prof	Peter Grindley
Designer	J H Taylor
Facilities	⊗ ⫞ ⌊ ♥ ♀ ⚲ 🏠 ⚙
& Leisure	hard tennis courts.
Location	1m N off B2145
Hotel	★★★ 68% The Ship Hotel, North St, CHICHESTER ☎ 01243 778000 36 ⇆ 🍴

SLINFOLD   Map 04 TQ13

Slinfold Park Golf & Country Club Stane St RH13 7RE
☎ 01403 791555 Fax 01403 791465
e-mail: info@slinfoldpark.co.uk
Slinfold course enjoys splendid views among mature trees. The 10th tee is spectacularly located on the centre of one of

the two large landscaped lakes. The 166-yard 16th has water running in front of of the tee and everything sloping towards it!
Championship Course: 18 holes, 6407yds, Par 72, SSS 71, Course record 64.
Academy Course: 9 holes, 1315yds, Par 28.
Club membership 611.

Visitors	book 7 days in advance, restricted weekends and bank holidays.
Societies	advance booking required, weekends and bank holidays not available.
Green Fees	£25 per 18 holes(£30 weekends).
Cards	▭ ▭ ▭ ▭ 🟦
Prof	T Clingan
Designer	John Fortune
Facilities	⊗ ⫞ ⌊ ♥ ♀ ⚲ 🏠 🖈 ⚒ ⚙ ┇
Location	4m W on the A29
Hotel	★★★ 66% Hurtwood Inn Hotel, Walking Bottom, PEASLAKE ☎ 01306 730851 9 ⇆ 🍴 Annexe8 ⇆ 🍴

WEST CHILTINGTON   Map 04 TQ01

West Chiltington Broadford Bridge Rd RH20 2YA
☎ 01798 812115 (bookings) & 813574 Fax 01798 812631
The Main Course is situated on gently undulating, well-drained greens and offers panoramic views of the Sussex Downs. Three large double greens provide an interesting feature to this course. Also 9-hole short course and 13-bay driving range.
Windmill: 18 holes, 5888yds, Par 70, SSS 69, Course record 66 or 9 holes, 1360yds, Par 28.

Visitors	book tee times in advance.
Societies	by prior arrangement.
Green Fees	£15(£17.50 weekend).
Cards	▭ ▭ ▭ 🟦
Prof	Barrie Aram/Ian Williams
Designer	Brian Barnes
Facilities	⊗ ⫞ ⌊ ♥ ♀ ⚲ 🏠 🖈 ⚙ ┇
Location	On N side of village
Hotel	★★★ 67% Roundabout Hotel, Monkmead Ln, WEST CHILTINGTON ☎ 01798 813838 23 ⇆ 🍴

WORTHING   Map 04 TQ10

Hill Barn Municipal Hill Barn Ln BN14 9QE
☎ 01903 237301
Downland course with views of both Isle of Wight and Brighton.
18 holes, 6224yds, Par 70, SSS 70.
Club membership 1000.

Visitors	no restrictions, but advisable to book tee times, 7 days in advance.
Societies	must telephone in advance.
Green Fees	not confirmed.
Cards	▭ ▭ ▭ ▭ 🟦
Prof	S Blanshard
Designer	Fred Hawtree
Facilities	⊗ ⫞ ⌊ ♥ ♀ ⚲ 🏠 🖈 ⚒ ⚙
Location	N side of town at junct of A24/A27
Hotel	★★★ 65% Findon Manor Hotel, High St, Findon, WORTHING ☎ 01903 872733 11 ⇆ 🍴

Worthing Links Rd BN14 9QZ
☎ 01903 260801 Fax 01903 694664
e-mail: worthinggolf@pavilion.co.uk
The Upper Course, short and tricky with entrancing views, will provide good entertainment. Lower Course is considered to be one of the best downland courses in the country.
Lower Course: 18 holes, 6530yds, Par 71, SSS 72, Course record 62.
Upper Course: 18 holes, 5243yds, Par 66, SSS 66.
Club membership 1200.
Visitors   advisable to contact in advance, not weekends during summer.
Societies   contact in advance.
Green Fees   £38 per day;£32 per round(Lower);£22(Upper).
Prof   Stephen Rolley
Designer   H S Colt
Facilities   ⊗ ⅢⅢ ᒪ ⲙ ♀ ⳩ 🖻 ⵢ ⳹ ⳩ ⳩ (
Location   N side of town centre off A27

Hotel   ★★★ 71% Ardington Hotel,
             Steyne Gardens, WORTHING
             ☎ 01903 230451 45 ⇄ ℟

TYNE & WEAR

BACKWORTH   Map 12 NZ37

Backworth The Hall NE27 0AH ☎ 0191 268 1048
Parkland course with easy walking, natural hazards and good scenery.
9 holes, 5930yds, Par 71, SSS 69, Course record 63.
Club membership 480.
Visitors   visitors may not play Tue (Ladies Day) & weekend mornings. Play limited Sat/Sun during Apr-Sep. Must contact in advance.
Societies   apply in writing to secretary.
Green Fees   £12 per round; £16 per day (£16 weekends & bank holidays).
Facilities   ⊗ ⅢⅢ by prior arrangement ᒪ ⲙ ♀ ⳩
& Leisure   bowling green.
Location   W side of town on B1322

Hotel   ★★★★ 63% Holiday Inn, Great North Rd,
             SEATON BURN ☎ 0191 201 9988 150 ⇄ ℟

BIRTLEY   Map 12 NZ25

Birtley Birtley Ln DH3 2LR ☎ 0191 410 2207
Parkland course.
9 holes, 5662yds, Par 67, SSS 67, Course record 63.
Club membership 270.
Visitors   must play with member at weekends & bank holidays.
Societies   apply in writing, must contact 1 month in advance in summer.
Green Fees   £12 per round/day.
Facilities   ⲙ ⳩
Hotel   ★★★ 67% Posthouse Newcastle/Washington,
             Emerson District 5, WASHINGTON
             ☎ 0870 400 9084 138 ⇄ ℟

BOLDON   Map 12 NZ36

Boldon Dipe Ln, East Boldon NE36 0PQ
☎ 0191 536 5360 & 0191 536 4182 Fax 0191 537 2270
Parkland links course, easy walking, distant sea views.
18 holes, 6362yds, Par 72, SSS 70, Course record 67.
Club membership 700.
Visitors   may not play after 3.30pm at weekends & bank holidays.
Societies   must contact in advance.
Green Fees   not confirmed.
Designer   Harry Varden
Facilities   ⊗ ⅢⅢ ᒪ ⲙ ♀ ⳩ 🖻 ⵢ ⳹ ⳩ (
& Leisure   snooker.
Location   S side of village off A184

Hotel   ★★★ 68% Quality Hotel, Witney Way,
             Boldon, SUNDERLAND
             ☎ 0191 519 1999 82 ⇄ ℟

CHOPWELL   Map 12 NZ15

Garesfield NE17 7AP
☎ 01207 561309 Fax 01207 561309 e-mail: information@garesfieldgc.fsbusiness.co.uk
Undulating parkland course with good views and picturesque woodland surroundings.
18 holes, 6458yds, Par 72, SSS 71, Course record 68.
Club membership 746.
Visitors   weekends after 4.30pm only, unless with member. Must contact in advance.
Societies   must contact secretary in advance. May play Sun only and max of 24 players.
Green Fees   £18 per day, £16 per round weekdays.
Prof   David Race
Designer   Harry Fernie
Facilities   ⊗ ⅢⅢ ᒪ ⲙ ♀ ⳩ 🖻 ⵢ ⳹ ⳩
Location   From A1 take A694 to Rowlands Gill. Turn right (signed Ryton) to High Spen. Turn left for Chopwell

Hotel   ★★★ 61% Quality Hotel Newcastle, Newgate St, NEWCASTLE UPON TYNE
             ☎ 0191 232 5025 93 ⇄ ℟

FELLING   Map 12 NZ26

Heworth Gingling Gate, Heworth NE10 8XY
☎ 0191 469 4424(club house)
Fairly flat, parkland course.
18 holes, 6437yds, Par 71, SSS 71.
Club membership 800.
Visitors   may not play Sat & before 10am Sun, Apr-Sep.
Societies   must apply in writing.
Green Fees   £15 per day.
Facilities   ⊗ ⅢⅢ ᒪ ⲙ ♀ ⳩
Location   On A195, 0.5m NW of junc with A1(M)

Hotel   ★★★ 67% Posthouse Newcastle/Washington,
             Emerson District 5, WASHINGTON
             ☎ 0870 400 9084 138 ⇄ ℟

> Entries with a green background identify courses considered to be particularly interesting

GATESHEAD   Map 12 NZ26

Ravensworth Moss Heaps, Wrekenton NE9 7UU
☎ 0191 487 2843
18 holes, 5966yds, Par 69, SSS 69.
Location   3m SE off A6127
Telephone for further details

Hotel   ★★★ 67% Swallow Hotel, High West St,
GATESHEAD ☎ 0191 477 1105 103 ⇆ ♞

GOSFORTH   Map 12 NZ26

Gosforth Broadway East NE3 5ER
☎ 0191 285 3495 Fax 0191 284 6274
Parkland course with natural water hazards, easy walking.
18 holes, 6024yds, Par 69, SSS 68, Course record 65.
Club membership 500.
Visitors   must contact in advance. Restricted play on
             competition days.
Societies   telephone in advance.
Green Fees not confirmed..
Prof   G Garland
Facilities ⊗ ⫙ ᴸ ♥ ♀ ♨ 🏠 ⌀
Location   N side of town centre off A6125

Hotel   ★★★★ 78% Newcastle Marriott Hotel,
Gosforth Park, High Gosforth Park, Gosforth,
NEWCASTLE UPON TYNE
☎ 0191 236 4111 178 ⇆ ♞

Parklands Gosforth Park Golfing Complex, High Gosforth
Park NE3 5HQ ☎ 0191 236 4867 & 236 4480
Parklands course is set in pleasant parkland with challenging
shots around and sometimes over attractive water hazards.
The first 9 holes are easier but the second 9 test even the
most experienced golfer.
18 holes, 6060yds, Par 71, SSS 69, Course record 66.
Club membership 600.
Visitors   a daily start sheet operates with bookings taken
             from 4.30pm the previous day during weekdays,
             and from 8am Fri & Sat for weekends.
Societies   by prior arrangement with club secretary.
Green Fees £15 per 18 holes (£18 weekends & bank
             holidays).
Prof   Brian Rumney
Facilities ⊗ ⫙ ᴸ ♥ ♀ ♨ 🏠 ⌀ ℓ
Location   3m N, at the end A1 Western by Pass

Hotel   ★★★★ 78% Newcastle Marriott Hotel,
Gosforth Park, High Gosforth Park, Gosforth,
NEWCASTLE UPON TYNE
☎ 0191 236 4111 178 ⇆ ♞

HOUGHTON-LE-SPRING   Map 12 NZ35

Elemore Elemore Ln, Hetton-le-Hole DH5 0QB
☎ 0191 517 3061 Fax 0191 517 3054
Elmore course tests a players ability in all aspects of the
game, with drives over water as well as wedges. The greens
are firm all year round and there are well positioned bunkers.
18 holes, 5947yds, Par 69, Course record 68.
Club membership 100.
Visitors   no restrictions. Phone to avoid society days.
Societies   apply in writing, telephone enquiries welcome.
Green Fees not confirmed.

Designer   J Gaunt
Facilities ⊗ ᴸ ♥ ♀ ♨ 🏠 ⍟ ➤ 🛒 ⌀
Location   4m S of Houghton-Le-Spring on the A182

Hotel   ★★ 66% Chilton Lodge Country Pub & Hotel,
Black Boy Rd, Chilton Moor, Fencehouses,
HOUGHTON-LE-SPRING
☎ 0191 385 2694 25 ⇆ ♞

Houghton-le-Spring Copt Hill DH5 8LU
☎ 0191 584 1198 & 584 0048
Hilly, downland course with natural slope hazards.
18 holes, 6443yds, Par 72, SSS 71, Course record 64.
Club membership 600.
Visitors   may not play on Sun until 4pm.
Societies   must contact secretary in advance.
Green Fees not confirmed.
Prof   Kevin Gow
Facilities ⊗ ⫙ ᴸ ♥ ♀ ♨ 🏠
Location   0.5m E on B1404

Hotel   ★★ 66% Chilton Lodge Country Pub & Hotel,
Black Boy Rd, Chilton Moor, Fencehouses,
HOUGHTON-LE-SPRING
☎ 0191 385 2694 25 ⇆ ♞

NEWCASTLE UPON TYNE   Map 12 NZ26

City of Newcastle Three Mile Bridge NE3 2DR
☎ 0191 285 1775 Fax 0191 2840700
A well-manicured parkland course in the Newcastle suburbs.
18 holes, 6528yds, Par 72, SSS 71, Course record 64.
Club membership 560.
Visitors   no restrictions but advisable to telephone first.
Societies   telephone in advance
Green Fees £24 per day (£28 weekends & bank holidays).
Prof   Steve McKenna
Designer   Harry Vardon
Facilities ⊗ ⫙ ᴸ ♥ ♀ ♨ 🏠 ⍟ ⌀
Location   3m N on B1318

Hotel   ★★★ 63% The Caledonian Hotel, Newcastle,
64 Osborne Rd, Jesmond, NEWCASTLE
UPON TYNE ☎ 0191 281 7881 89 ⇆ ♞

Newcastle United Ponteland Rd, Cowgate NE5 3JW
☎ 0191 286 9998 Fax 0191 286 4323
Moorland course with natural hazards.
18 holes, 6617yds, Par 72, SSS 72, Course record 68.
Club membership 600.
Visitors   must play with member at weekends.
Societies   must contact in writing.
Green Fees not confirmed.
Facilities ⊗ ᴸ ♥ ♀ ♨ 🏠 ⍟ ⌀
Location   1.25m NW of city centre off A6127

Hotel   ★★★ 66% Swallow Imperial Hotel, Jesmond
Rd, NEWCASTLE UPON TYNE
☎ 0191 281 5511 122 ⇆ ♞

Northumberland High Gosforth Park NE3 5HT
☎ 0191 236 2498 Fax 0191 236 2498
Many golf courses have been sited inside racecourses,
although not so many survive today. One which does is
the Northumberland Club's course at High Gosforth
Park. Naturally the course is flat but there are plenty of ▶

mounds and other hazards to make it a fine test of golf. It should be said that not all the holes are within the confines of the racecourse, but both inside and out there are some good holes. This is a Championship course.
18 holes, 6629yds, Par 72, SSS 72, Course record 65.
Club membership 580.

Visitors	may not play at weekends or competition days. Must contact in advance.
Societies	must apply in writing.
Green Fees	£45 per day; £35 per round.
Designer	Colt/Braid
Facilities	⊗ ⊪ ⅃ ⅃ ☕ ⏅ ⟲
Location	4m N of city centre off A1
Hotel	★★★★ 78% Newcastle Marriott Hotel, Gosforth Park, High Gosforth Park, Gosforth, NEWCASTLE UPON TYNE ☎ 0191 236 4111 178 ⊒ ꧁

Westerhope Whorlton Grance, Westerhope NE5 1PP
☎ 0191 286 7636 Fax 0191 2146287
Attractive parkland course with tree-lined fairways, and easy walking. Good open views towards the airport.
18 holes, 6444yds, Par 72, SSS 71, Course record 64.
Club membership 778.

Visitors	with member only at weekends and bank holidays.Must contact in advance.
Societies	must contact Secretary in advance.
Green Fees	£18 per 18 holes.
Cards	⊞ ⬛ ⬛
Prof	Nigel Brown
Facilities	⊗ ⊪ ⅃ ⅃ ☕ ⏅ ⟲ ❦ ⟲ ⏅ ⟲
Location	4.5m NW of city centre off B6324
Hotel	★★★★ 78% Newcastle Marriott Hotel, Gosforth Park, High Gosforth Park, Gosforth, NEWCASTLE UPON TYNE ☎ 0191 236 4111 178 ⊒ ꧁

RYTON   Map 12 NZ16

Ryton Clara Vale NE40 3TD
☎ 0191 413 3737 Fax 0191 413 1642
e-mail: secretary@rytongolfclub.co.uk
Parkland course.
18 holes, 5950yds, Par 70, SSS 69, Course record 67.
Club membership 600.

Visitors	with member only at weekends.
Societies	apply in advance.
Green Fees	not confirmed.
Facilities	⊗ ⊪ ⅃ ⅃ ☕ ⏅
Location	NW side of town off A695
Hotel	★★★ 69% Gibside Arms Hotel, Front St, WHICKHAM ☎ 0191 488 9292 45 ⊒ ꧁

Tyneside Westfield Ln NE40 3QE
☎ 0191 413 2742 Fax 0191 413 2742
Open parkland course, water hazard, hilly, practice area.
18 holes, 6042yds, Par 70, SSS 69, Course record 65.
Club membership 900.

Visitors	must contact in advance to play at weekends (after 3pm)
Societies	must apply in advance.
Green Fees	£25 per day; £20 per round.

Cards	⊞ ⬛ ⟲
Prof	Malcolm Gunn
Designer	H S Colt
Facilities	⊗ ⊪ ⅃ ⅃ ☕ ⏅ ☕ ⟲
Location	NW side of town off A695
Hotel	★★★ 69% Gibside Arms Hotel, Front St, WHICKHAM ☎ 0191 488 9292 45 ⊒ ꧁

SOUTH SHIELDS   Map 12 NZ36

South Shields Cleadon Hills NE34 8EG
☎ 0191 456 8942 Fax 0191 456 8942
e-mail: thesecretary@south-shields-golf.freeserve.co.uk
A slightly undulating downland course on a limestone base ensuring good conditions underfoot. Open to strong winds, the course is testing but fair. There are fine views of the coastline.
18 holes, 6264yds, Par 71, SSS 70, Course record 64.
Club membership 750.

Visitors	must contact in advance.
Societies	by arrangement.
Green Fees	£20 per day (£25 weekends & bank holidays).
Prof	Gary Parsons
Designer	McKenzie-Braid
Facilities	⊗ ⊪ ⅃ ⅃ ☕ ⏅ ☕
Location	SE side of town centre off A1300
Hotel	★★★ 65% Sea Hotel, Sea Rd, SOUTH SHIELDS ☎ 0191 427 0999 32 ⊒ ꧁

Whitburn Lizard Ln NE34 7AF ☎ 0191 529 4944 (Sec)
& 529 2144 (club) Fax 0191 529 4944
Parkland course.
18 holes, 5899yds, Par 69, SSS 68, Course record 64.
Club membership 700.

Visitors	restricted weekends & Tue. Contact professional in advance.
Societies	must apply in writing to secretary
Green Fees	£20 per day (£25 weekends & bank holidays).
Prof	David Stephenson
Designer	Colt, Alison & Morrison
Facilities	⊗ ⊪ ⅃ ⅃ ☕ ⏅ ☕ ⟲
Location	2.5m SE off A183
Hotel	★★★★ 67% Swallow Hotel, Queen's Pde, Seaburn, SUNDERLAND ☎ 0191 529 2041 98 ⊒ ꧁

SUNDERLAND   Map 12 NZ35

Ryhope Leechmore Way, Ryhope SR2 0DH
☎ 0191 523 7333
A municipal course.
18 holes, 4601yds, Par 65, SSS 63.
Club membership 350.

Visitors	no restrictions.
Societies	apply in writing, telephone enquiries welcome.
Green Fees	not confirmed.
Facilities	⅃ ⏅ ☕ ❦
Location	3.5m S of city centre
Hotel	★★★★ 67% Swallow Hotel, Queen's Pde, Seaburn, SUNDERLAND ☎ 0191 529 2041 98 ⊒ ꧁

Wearside Coxgreen SR4 9JT
☎ 0191 534 2518 Fax 0191 5346186
Open, undulating parkland course rolling down to the
River Wear and beneath the shadow of the famous
Penshaw Monument. Built on the lines of an Athenian
temple it is a well-known landmark. Two ravines cross
the course presenting a variety of challenging holes.
18 holes, 6373yds, Par 71, SSS 74, Course record 63.
Club membership 648.
Visitors   may not play before 9.30am, between
                12.30-1.30 or after 4pm.
Societies   must apply in writing.
Green Fees   £26 (£33 weekends).
Prof   Doug Brolls
Facilities   ⊗ ⽵ 🅱 ⛳ ♀ 🏌 🏪 ♂
Location   3.5m W off A183

Hotel   ★★★★ 67% Swallow Hotel, Queen's Pde,
                Seaburn, SUNDERLAND
                ☎ 0191 529 2041 98 ⇆ ☏

TYNEMOUTH   Map 12 NZ36

Tynemouth Spital Dene NE30 2ER
☎ 0191 257 4578 Fax 0191 259 5193
Well-drained parkland course, easy walking.
18 holes, 6359yds, Par 70, SSS 71, Course record 66.
Club membership 800.
Visitors   must play with member weekends & bank
                holidays.
Societies   must contact in writing.
Green Fees   £25 per day; £20 per round(£25 per round
                weekends & bank holidays).
Cards   🖃 🖃 🖃 🖃 🖃
Prof   J P McKenna
Designer   Willie Park
Facilities   ⊗ ⽵ 🅱 ⛳ ♀ 🏌 🏪 🏌 ♂
Location   0.5m W

Hotel   ★★★ 68% Grand Hotel,
                Grand Pde, TYNEMOUTH
                ☎ 0191 293 6666 Annexe45 ⇆ ☏

WALLSEND   Map 12 NZ26

Wallsend Rheydt Av, Bigges Main NE28 8SU
☎ 0191 262 1973
Parkland course.
18 holes, 6608yds, Par 72, SSS 72, Course record 66.
Club membership 655.
Visitors   may not play before 12.30pm weekends. Must
                book in advance
Societies   must apply in writing.
Green Fees   £14.50 per round(£16.50 weekends).
Prof   Ken Phillips
Designer   A Snowball
Facilities   🅱 ⛳ ♀ 🏌 🏪 🏌 ♂ ☏
Location   NW side of town centre off A193

Hotel   ★★★ 66% Swallow Imperial Hotel, Jesmond
                Rd, NEWCASTLE UPON TYNE
                ☎ 0191 281 5511 122 ⇆ ☏

> Looking for a driving range?
> See the index at the back of the guide

WASHINGTON   Map 12 NZ25

George Washington Hotel Golf & Country Club Stone
Cellar Rd, High Usworth, District 12 NE37 1PH
☎ 0191 402 9988 & 417 8346 Fax 0191 4151166
e-mail: georgewashington@corushotel.com
Championship-standard course. Also a 9-hole (par 3) course,
putting green and 21-bay floodlit driving range.
18 holes, 6604yds, Par 73, SSS 72, Course record 68.
Club membership 500.
Visitors   must contact in advance. May not play before
                10am or between noon & 2pm at weekends.
Societies   book in advance.
Green Fees   £30 per day; £20 per round.
Cards   🖃 🖃 🖃 🖃
Prof   David Patterson
Designer   Eric Watson
Facilities   ⊗ ⽵ 🅱 ⛳ ♀ 🏌 🏪 🏌 🏪 ❧ 🏌 ♂ ☏
& Leisure   heated indoor swimming pool, squash, sauna,
                solarium, gymnasium, 9 hole par 3 course.
Location   From A195 signed Washington North take last
                exit on rdbt, then right at mini-rdbt

Hotel   ★★★ 65% George Washington Golf &
                Country Club, Stone Cellar Rd, District 12,
                High Usworth, WASHINGTON
                ☎ 0191 402 9988 103 ⇆ ☏

WHICKHAM   Map 12 NZ26

Whickham Hollinside Park, Fellside Rd NE16 5BA
☎ 0191 488 1576 Fax 0191 488 1576
Undulating parkland course with attractive panoramic views.
18 holes, 5878yds, Par 68, SSS 68, Course record 61.
Club membership 660.
Visitors   must contact Professional in advance.
Societies   by arrangement.
Green Fees   not confirmed.
Prof   Graeme Lisle
Facilities   ⊗ ⽵ by prior arrangement 🅱 ⛳ ♀ 🏌 🏪 🏌 ♂
Location   1.5m S

Hotel   ★★★ 67% Swallow Hotel, High West St,
                GATESHEAD ☎ 0191 477 1105 103 ⇆ ☏

WHITLEY BAY   Map 12 NZ37

Whitley Bay Claremont Rd NE26 3UF
☎ 0191 252 0180 Fax 0191 297 0030
An 18-hole links type course, close to the sea, with a stream
running through the undulating terrain.
18 holes, 6579yds, Par 71, SSS 71, Course record 66.
Club membership 800.
Visitors   may not play Sat, telephone for Sun play.
                Advisable to contact in advance.
Societies   telephone initially.
Green Fees   £33 per day; £22 per round(£35 per round
                sundays).
Prof   Gary Shipley
Facilities   ⊗ ⽵ 🅱 ⛳ ♀ 🏌 🏪 🏌 ♂
Location   NW side of town centre off A1148

Hotel   ★★★ 65% Windsor Hotel, South Pde,
                WHITLEY BAY ☎ 0191 251 8888 70 ⇆ ☏

WARWICKSHIRE

Hotel   ★★★ 64% The Brandon Hall, Main St, BRANDON ☎ 0870 400 8105 60 ⇆ ⭍

ATHERSTONE   Map 04 SP39

Atherstone The Outwoods, Coleshill Rd CV9 2RL
☎ 01827 713110 Fax 01827 715686
Scenic parkland course, established in 1894 and laid out on hilly ground.
18 holes, 6006yds, Par 72, SSS 70, Course record 68.
Club membership 495.
Visitors   handicap certificate required. With member only weekends and bank holidays but not Sun. Also with holder of handicap certificate.by permission of Club Secretary.
Societies   contact in advance.
Green Fees £13 per day Mondays (£17 Tues-Fri).
Designer   Hawtree & Gaunt Mornoch
Facilities   ⊗ ⫟ ⏳ ⬛ ♥ ♀ ⚲ ⚓
Location   0.5m S on B4116

Hotel   ★★ 75% Chapel House Hotel, Friar's Gate, ATHERSTONE ☎ 01827 718949   14 ⇆ ⭍

BIDFORD-ON-AVON   Map 04 SP15

Bidford Grange Stratford Rd B50 4LY
☎ 01789 490319 Fax 01789 490998
Designed by Howard Swan & Paul Tillman, this very long, championship standard course is built to represent a links course and is fully irrigated. There are water hazards on the first 7 holes, and particularly challenging holes on the 16th (223yds,par 3), 8th (600yds, par 5) and an uphill par 4 at the 13th.
18 holes, 7233yds, Par 72, SSS 74, Course record 66.
Club membership 200.
Visitors   Telephone for tee reservations.
Societies   apply in writing or phone, minimum 12.
Green Fees £12 per 18 holes;£18 per 18 holes(£10/£15 weekends).
Cards   ⊞ ▆ ▆ ▆ ▆ ⑨
Prof   Simon Leahy
Facilities   ⊗ ⫟ ⏳ ⬛ ♥ ♀ ⚲ ⬟ ⚑ ⊨ ➤ ⚓ ⬧ ⚘
& Leisure fishing.
Location   4m W of Stratford upon Avon, B439

Hotel   ★★★ 75% Salford Hall Hotel, ABBOT'S SALFORD ☎ 01386 871300
14 ⇆ ⭍ Annexe19 ⇆ ⭍

BRANDON   Map 04 SP47

City of Coventry-Brandon Wood Brandon Ln, Wolston CV8 3GQ ☎ 024 76543141 Fax 024 76545108
Municipal parkland course surrounded by fields and bounded by River Avon on east side. Floodlit driving range.
18 holes, 6610yds, Par 72, SSS 71, Course record 68.
Club membership 500.
Visitors   telephone for details, advance booking recommended.
Societies   telephone secretary for details
Green Fees £9.70 per round (£12.90 weekends).
Cards   ⊞ ▆ ▆ ▆ ▆ ⑨
Prof   Chris Gledhill
Facilities   ⊗ ⏳ ⬛ ♥ ♀ ⚲ ⬟ ⚑ ⚓ ⬧ ⚘
Location   Off A45 southbound

COLESHILL   Map 04 SP28

Maxstoke Park Castle Ln B46 2RD
☎ 01675 466743 Fax 01675 466743
Parkland course with easy walking. Numerous trees and a lake form natural hazards.
18 holes, 6442yds, Par 71, SSS 71, Course record 64.
Club membership 720.
Visitors   with member only at weekends & bank holidays.
Societies   contact in advance.
Green Fees £27.50 per 18 holes.
Prof   Neil McEwan
Designer   various
Facilities   ⊗ ⫟ ⏳ ⬛ ♥ ♀ ⚲ ⬟ ⚑ ⚘
Location   3m NE of Coleshill on B4114 turn right for Maxstoke then 1m on right

Hotel   ★★★ 65% Grimstock Country House Hotel, Gilson Rd, Gilson, COLESHILL
☎ 01675 462121 & 462161
Fax 01675 467646   44 ⇆ ⭍

HENLEY-IN-ARDEN   Map 04 SP16

Henley Golf & Country Club Birmingham Rd B95 5QA
☎ 01564 793715 Fax 01564 795754
e-mail: professional@henleygcc
This improving course is maturing well and provides a good golfing challenge for all handicaps. All facilities recently upgraded.
18 holes, 6933yds, Par 73, SSS 73.
Club membership 675.
Visitors   may book up to 7 days in advance.
Societies   apply in writing or telephone in advance.
Green Fees not confirmed.
Cards   ▆ ▆ ⑨
Prof   Simon Edwin
Designer   N Selwyn Smith
Facilities   ⊗ ⫟ ⏳ ⬛ ♥ ♀ ⚲ ⬟ ⚑ ⊨ ⬧ ⚘ ⚑
& Leisure hard tennis courts, 9 hole par 3 course.
Location   On the left hand side of the Birmingham road, just N of Henley-in-Arden

Hotel   ★★★ 66% Quality Hotel, Pool Bank, Southcrest, REDDITCH
☎ 01527 541511   73 ⇆ ⭍

KENILWORTH   Map 04 SP27

Kenilworth Crewe Ln CV8 2EA
☎ 01926 858517 Fax 01926 864453
Parkland course in open hilly situation. Club founded in 1889.
18 holes, 6400yds, Par 73, SSS 71, Course record 62.
Club membership 755.
Visitors   must contact in advance.
Societies   apply in writing.
Green Fees £38.
Cards   ⊞ ▆ ▆ ⑨ ▆ ▆ ⑨
Prof   Steve Yates
Designer   Hawtree

▶

268

Facilities ⊗)Ⅲ 🛉 ⚑ ⚑ ⚐ 🏠 ⚑ ⚐ ⚑ ⚑
& Leisure Par 3 chipping green.
Location 0.5m NE

Hotel ★★ 69% Clarendon House Hotel, Old High St, KENILWORTH ☎ 01926 857668 30 ⇋ 🛈

LEA MARSTON   Map 04 SP29

Lea Marston Hotel & Leisure Complex Haunch Ln
B76 0BY ☎ 01675 470468 & 470707 Fax 01675 470871
e-mail: leamarstonhotel@btinternet.com

The Marston Lakes course was completed in June 2000 and opened in Spring 2001. The layout includes many water and sand hazards through undulating parkland. Whilst short by modern standards, it is a good test for even low handicap players, requiring virtually everything in the bag. Tees and greens have been built to championship course specifications. ▶

Lea Marston Hotel & Leisure Complex

With its newly opened beautiful Marston Lakes course, Lea Marston is a superb venue for a relaxing golf break. The new course flows across undulating parkland, featuring many beautifully designed water and sand hazards, creating an enjoyable test for golfers of all abilities. There is also a magnificent Par 3 Academy course, floodlit driving range, indoor Smart Golf Simulator and putting green. Guests can also enjoy complimentary use of the Health Club, including indoor swimming pool, sauna, and steam room.

**Haunch Lane, Lea Marston, Sutton Coldfield, Warwickshire B76 0BY
Tel:01675 470468 Fax: 01675470871
www.leamarstonhotel.co.uk
e-mail: info@leamarstonhotel.co.uk**

Marston Lakes: 9 holes, 2059yds, Par 31, SSS 30.
Club membership 200.
Visitors book in advance and dress code applies.
Societies must telephone in advance.
Green Fees not confirmed.
Cards 💳 ▬ ▬ 💳 📇 ▬ 🐷
Prof Andrew Stokes & Darren Lewis
Designer Mark Jones
Facilities ⊗)Ⅲ 🛉 ⚑ ⚐ ⚑ 🏠 ⚑ ⚑ ⚐ ⚑ ⚑
& Leisure hard tennis courts, heated indoor swimming pool, sauna, solarium, gymnasium, 9 hole par 3 course smart golf simulator.
Location From M42 take the A4091 to Kingsbury. Turn right after 1 mile and golf club is 300yds on the right

Hotel ★★★ 72% Lea Marston Hotel & Leisure Complex, Haunch Ln, LEA MARSTON ☎ 01675 470468 83 ⇋ 🛈

LEAMINGTON SPA   Map 04 SP36

Leamington & County Golf Ln, Whitnash CV31 2QA
☎ 01926 425961 Fax 01926 425961
Undulating parkland course with extensive views.
18 holes, 6488yds, Par 71, SSS 71, Course record 65.
Club membership 802.
Visitors must contact in advance.
Societies telephone in advance.
Green Fees not confirmed.
Prof Julian Mellor
Designer H S Colt
Facilities ⚑ 🏠 ⚑ ⚑ ⚐
Location S side of town centre

Hotel ★★★ 58% Manor House Hotel, Avenue Rd, LEAMINGTON SPA ☎ 01926 423251 53 ⇋ 🛈

Newbold Comyn Newbold Ter East CV32 4EW
☎ 01926 421157
Municipal parkland course with hilly front nine. The par 4, 9th is a 467-yd testing hole. The back 9 holes are rather flat but include two par 5's.
18 holes, 6315yds, Par 70, SSS 70, Course record 70.
Club membership 280.
Visitors no restrictions.
Societies apply to professional.
Green Fees not confirmed.
Prof Ricky Carvell
Facilities ⊗)Ⅲ 🛉 ⚑ ⚑ ⚐ 🏠 ⚑ ⚐
& Leisure heated indoor swimming pool, gymnasium.
Location 0.75m E of town centre off B4099

Hotel ★★★ 58% Manor House Hotel, Avenue Rd, LEAMINGTON SPA ☎ 01926 423251 53 ⇋ 🛈

LEEK WOOTTON   Map 04 SP26

The Warwickshire CV35 7QT
☎ 01926 408409 Fax 01926 498911
This is an unusual championship standard course. Designed by Karl Litten, the 36 holes are laid out as four interchangeable loops of 9 holes to create six contrasting yet superb courses in a parkland and woodland setting. ▶

South East Course: 18 holes, 7000yds, Par 72, SSS 72,
Course record 68.
North West Course: 18 holes, 7421yds, Par 74, SSS 73,
Course record 70.
Club membership 1150.

The Warwickshire

Visitors	can book up to 7 days in advance.
Societies	apply to sales office for details.
Green Fees	£35(£45 weekends).
Cards	⊞ 🖾 📼 🖾 🖸
Prof	Danny Peck
Designer	Karl Litten
Facilities	⊗ ⫴ ᒧᕇ ᕐ ᖙ ᒧ ᗰ ☆ ⚄ ↝ ⚒ ⸿ ↆ
Location	1m from Kenilworth on B4115

Hotel	★★★★ 65% Chesford Grange Hotel, Chesford Bridge, KENILWORTH ☎ 01926 859331 145 ➯ 🖻 Annexe9 ➯ 🖻

NUNEATON   Map 04 SP39

Nuneaton Golf Dr, Whitestone CV11 6QF
☎ 024 7634 7810 Fax 024 7632 7563
Undulating parkland and woodland course with Silver Birch lining the fairways. Easy walking.
18 holes, 6429yds, Par 71, SSS 71.
Club membership 700.

Visitors	must produce evidence of membership of a recognised golf club or society, with member only at weekends.
Societies	apply in writing.
Green Fees	not confirmed.
Prof	Steven Bainbridge
Facilities	ᒧ ᗰ ⚒ ⸿
Location	2m SE off B4114

Hotel	★★★ 65% Weston Hall Hotel, Weston Ln, Weston in Arden, Bulkington, NUNEATON ☎ 024 76312989 40 ➯ 🖻

Oakridge Arley Ln, Ansley Village CV10 9PH
☎ 01676 541389 & 540542 Fax 01676 542709
e-mail: admin@oakridgegolf.fsnet.co.uk
There are a number of water hazards on the back nine which add to the natural beauty of the countryside. The undulating course is affected by winter cross winds on several holes. Overall it will certainly test golfing skills.
18 holes, 6242yds, Par 71, SSS 70.
Club membership 500.

Visitors	contact in advance, with members only at weekends.
Societies	apply in writing or telephone in advance.
Green Fees	£15 per round.

Cards	⊞ 🖾 📼 🖾 🖸
Designer	Algy Jayes
Facilities	⊗ ⫴ ᒧᕇ ᕐ ᖙ ᒧ ᗰ ☆ ⚄ ↝ ⚒ ⸿
Location	4m W

Hotel	★★★ 65% Weston Hall Hotel, Weston Ln, Weston in Arden, Bulkington, NUNEATON ☎ 024 76312989 40 ➯ 🖻

Purley Chase Pipers Ln, Ridge Ln CV10 0RB
☎ 024 7639 3118 Fax 024 7639 8015
e-mail: enquiries@purleychase.co.uk
Meadowland course with tricky water hazards on eight holes and undulating greens. 13-bay driving range.
18 holes, 6772yds, Par 72, SSS 72, Course record 64.
Club membership 650.

Visitors	welcome weekends after 12 noon and mon-fri.
Societies	telephone for provisional booking (Mon-Fri only).
Green Fees	£15 per 18 holes.
Cards	⊞ 🖾 🖸
Prof	Gary Carver
Facilities	⊗ ⫴ ᒧᕇ ᕐ ᖙ ᒧ ᗰ ↝ ⚒ ⸿ ↆ
Location	2m NW off B4114

Hotel	★★★ 65% Weston Hall Hotel, Weston Ln, Weston in Arden, Bulkington, NUNEATON ☎ 024 76312989 40 ➯ 🖻

RUGBY   Map 04 SP57

Rugby Clifton Rd CV21 3RD
☎ 01788 542306 (Sec) 575134 (Pro) Fax 01788 542306
Parkland course with brook running through the middle and crossed by a viaduct.
18 holes, 5457yds, Par 68, SSS 67, Course record 62.
Club membership 700.

Visitors	weekends & bank holidays with member only.
Societies	apply in writing.
Green Fees	£20 per day.
Prof	Nat Summers
Facilities	⊗ ⫴ ᒧᕇ ᕐ ᖙ ᒧ ᗰ ☆ ↝ ⸿
Location	1m NE on B5414

Hotel	★★★ 58% Grosvenor Hotel Rugby, 81-87 Clifton Rd, RUGBY ☎ 01788 535686 26 ➯ 🖻

Whitefields Hotel Golf & Country Club Coventry Rd, Thurlaston CV23 9JR ☎ 01788 815555 Fax 01788 817777
Whitefields has superb natural drainage. There are many water features and the 13th has a stunnning dogleg 442yard Par 4 with a superb view across Draycote Water. The 16th is completely surrounded by water and is particularly difficult.
18 holes, 6223yds, Par 71, SSS 70, Course record 66.
Club membership 400.

Visitors	advisable to book unless hotel guest, available 7 days, contact secretary on 01788 815555.
Societies	contact secretary in advance.
Green Fees	not confirmed.
Cards	⊞ 🖾 📼 ᖶ 🖾 🖸
Prof	Darren Price
Designer	Reg Mason
Facilities	⊗ ⫴ ᒧᕇ ᕐ ᖙ ᒧ ᗰ ☆ ⊞ ↝ ⚒ ⸿ ↆ
Location	Junct of M45 where it meets the A45 Coventry road, near Dunchurch

▶

The De Vere Belfry

Wishaw, *Warwickshire*   ☎ 01675 470301   Fax 01675 470178   Map 07 SP19

e-mail: enquiries@thebelfry.com

The Belfry is unique as the only venue to have staged the biggest golf event in the world, The Ryder Cup Matches, an unprecedented 4 times, most recently in 2001. The Brabazon is regarded throughout the world as a great championship course with some of the most demanding holes in golf; world famous holes like the 10th (Ballesteros's Hole) and the 18th with its dangerous lakes and its amphitheatre around the final green. These remained intact during the £2.4million redevelopment in 1998 which made the course even more testing.

Alternatively, you can pit your wits against a new legend in the making, The PGA National Course, which has won plaudits from near and far. The Dave Thomas designed course has been used for professional competition and is already established as one of Britain's leading courses. For those who like their golf a little easier or like to get back into the swing gently, The Derby is ideal and can be played by golfers of any standard.

The Bel Air night club, The De Vere Club leisure centre and The Aqua Spa with its fire and ice bio-thermal treatments offer unique experiences away from the golf course.

Visitors Handicap certificate is required for the Brabazon & PGA courses; 24 or better for gentlemen, 32 or better for ladies & juniors. Reservations 24 hrs in advance for non - residents

Societies must telephone in advance

Green Fees Brabazon £95 per round, PGA £60, Derby £30, lower rates Nov-Mar. 🔲 ▣ ▣ ▣ ▣ 🔲 🔳

Facilities ⊗ ⑈ ⿹ ⿹ ♀⛛ 🏠 ⿹ ⤶ ⿹ ⿹ ⿹
Professional (P. McGovern)

Leisure tennis, squash, swimming, sauna, solarium, gymnasium

Location Wishaw. Sutton Coldfield B76 9PR (exit J9 M42, 4m E on A446)

Holes/Par/Course record Brabazon: 18 holes, 6724 yds, Par 72, SSS 71
Derby: 18 holes, 6057 yds, Par 69, SSS 69
PGA: 18 holes, 6639 yds, Par 71, SSS 70

Championship Course

Whitefields Hotel Golf & Country Club

Hotel ★★ 64% Whitefields Hotel Golf & Country Club, Coventry Rd, Thurlaston, RUGBY ☎ 01788 521800 & 522393 Fax 01788 521695 34 ⇄ ♛

STONELEIGH   Map 04 SP37

Stoneleigh Deer Park The Clubhouse, The Old Deer Park, Coventry Rd CV8 3DR
☎ 024 76639991 &76639912 Fax 024 76511533
Parkland course in old deer park with many mature trees. The River Avon meanders through the course and comes into play on 4 holes. Also 9-hole course.
Tantara Course: 18 holes, 6023yds, Par 71, SSS 69.
Avon Course: 9 holes, 1251yds, Par 27.
Club membership 800.
Visitors must contact in advance.
Societies by prior arrangement.
Green Fees £16 per 18 holes(£25 weekends).
Cards 📇 💳 📇 📇 🈺
Prof Matt McGuire
Facilities ⊗ �🝙 ⌱ 🍺 ♀ ⚲ 🏠 ᛉ ⚓ ⚸
Location 3m NE of Kenilworth

Hotel ★★★★ 65% De Montfort Hotel, The Square, KENILWORTH ☎ 01926 855944 104 ⇄ ♛

STRATFORD-UPON-AVON   Map 04 SP25

Stratford Oaks Bearley Rd, Snitterfield CV37 0EZ
☎ 01789 731980 Fax 01789 731981
e-mail: stratford.oaks@virgin.net
American styled, level parkland course with some water features designed by Howard Swann.
18 holes, 6100yds, Par 71, SSS 69, Course record 66.
Club membership 655.
Visitors contact in advance.
Societies telephone in advance.
Green Fees £20 per round (£25 weekends).
Cards 📇 💳 📇 📇 🈺
Prof Andrew Dunbar
Designer H Swann
Facilities ⊗ �🝙 ⌱ 🍺 ♀ ⚲ 🏠 ᛉ ⚸ ⚓
Location 4m N of Stratford-upon-Avon

Hotel ★★★★ 71% Stratford Manor, Warwick Rd, STRATFORD-UPON-AVON ☎ 01789 731173 104 ⇄ ♛

Stratford-upon-Avon Tiddington Rd CV37 7BA
☎ 01789 205749 Fax 414909
e-mail: sec@stratfordgolf.co.uk
Beautiful parkland course. The par 3, 16th is tricky and the par 5, 17th and 18th, provide a tough end.
18 holes, 6311yds, Par 72, SSS 70, Course record 63.
Club membership 750.
Visitors may not play before 11.00am weekends. Phone in advance.
Societies must apply in advance. Tues & Thurs only.
Green Fees not confirmed.
Prof D Sutherland
Designer Taylor
Facilities ⊗ �🝙 ⌱ 🍺 ♀ ⚲ 🏠 ᛉ ⚓ ⚸
Location 0.75m E on B4086

Hotel ★★★★ 66% The Alveston Manor, Clopton Bridge, STRATFORD-UPON-AVON ☎ 0870 400 8181 114 ⇄ ♛

Welcombe Hotel Warwick Rd CV37 0NR
☎ 01789 295252 Fax 01789 414666
e-mail: sales@welcombe.co.uk
Wooded parkland course of great character and boasting superb views of the River Avon, Stratford and the Cotswolds. Set within the hotel's 157-acre estate, it has two lakes and water features.
18 holes, 6274yds, Par 70, SSS 70, Course record 64.
Visitors must contact in advance.
Societies booking via Hotel.
Green Fees £40 per round (£50 weekends).
Cards
Prof Carl Mason
Designer Thomas Macauley   ▶

Facilities	⊗ 〣 ⅃ ♨ ♀ ⌂ ☗ ☗ ⚑ ⚓ ⟋ ⌀
& Leisure	hard tennis courts, fishing, solarium, gymnasium.
Location	1.5m NE off A46

Hotel	★★★★ 74% Welcombe Hotel and Golf Course, Warwick Rd, STRATFORD-UPON-AVON ☎ 01789 295252 64 ⇄ 🐾

TANWORTH-IN-ARDEN   Map 07 SP17

Ladbrook Park Poolhead Ln B94 5ED
☎ 01564 742264 Fax 01564 742909
Parkland course lined with trees.
18 holes, 6427yds, Par 71, SSS 71, Course record 65.
Club membership 700.

Visitors	welcome weekdays, with member at weekends. Must contact in advance & have handicap certificate.
Societies	apply in advance.
Green Fees	£40 per 36 holes, £32 per 28 holes, £25 per 18 holes.
Cards	▱ ▰ ▨ ▱
Prof	Richard Mountford
Designer	H S Colt
Facilities	⊗ 〣 ⅃ ♨ ♀ ⌂ ☗ ☗ ⟋
Location	2.5m SE of M42 junct 3

Hotel	★★★🍴 Nuthurst Grange Country House Hotel, Nuthurst Grange Ln, HOCKLEY HEATH ☎ 01564 783972 15 ⇄ 🐾

UPPER BRAILES   Map 04 SP33

Brailes Sutton Ln, Lower Brailes OX15 5BB
☎ 01608 685336 Fax 01608 685205
e-mail: office@brailes-golf-club.co.uk
Undulating meadowland on 130 acres of Cotswold countryside. Sutton brook passes through the course and is crossed 5 times.The Par 5 17th offers the most spectacular view of three counties from the tee. Challenging Par 3 short holes.
18 holes, 6311yds, Par 71, SSS 70, Course record 67.
Club membership 430.

Visitors	advance telephone advisable to 01608 685633.
Societies	telephone or write for information to the secretary.
Green Fees	not confirmed.
Prof	Steve Hutchinson
Designer	B A Hull
Facilities	⊗ 〣 ⅃ ♨ ♀ ⌂ ☗ ☗ ⚓ ⟋
Location	4m E of Shipston-on-Stour, on B4035

Inn	♦♦♦♦ The Red Lion Hotel, Main St, Long Compton, SHIPSTON ON STOUR ☎ 01608 684221 5 ⇄ 🐾

WARWICK   Map 04 SP26

Warwick The Racecourse CV34 6HW ☎ 01926 494316
Parkland course with easy walking. Driving range with floodlit bays.
9 holes, 2682yds, Par 34, SSS 66, Course record 67.
Club membership 150.

Visitors	must contact in advance. May not play Sun before 12.30pm

Societies	contact in advance.
Green Fees	£5 per 9 holes (£5.50 weekends).
Prof	Phil Sharp
Designer	D G Dunkley
Facilities	♀ ♀ ⌂ ☗ ⟋ ⌀
Location	W side of town centre

Hotel	★★ 64% Warwick Arms Hotel, 17 High St, WARWICK ☎ 01926 492759 35 ⇄ 🐾

WISHAW   Map 07 SP19

WISHAW   See page 271

WEST MIDLANDS

ALDRIDGE   Map 07 SK00

Druids Heath Stonnall Rd WS9 8JZ
☎ 01922 455595 (Office) & 459523 (Prof)
Testing, undulating heathland course.
18 holes, 6659yds, Par 72, SSS 73.
Club membership 590.

Visitors	contact in advance recommended. Weekend play permitted after 2pm.
Societies	phone initially.
Green Fees	not confirmed.
Prof	Glenn Williams
Facilities	⊗ 〣 ⅃ ♨ ♀ ♀ ⌂ ⟋
& Leisure	snooker.
Location	NE side of town centre off A454

Hotel	★★★ 76% The Fairlawns at Aldridge, 178 Little Aston Rd, Aldridge, WALSALL ☎ 01922 455122 50 ⇄ 🐾

BIRMINGHAM   Map 07 SP08

Brandhall Heron Rd, Oldbury, Warley B68 8AQ
☎ 0121 552 2195
Municipal parkland course, easy walking, good hazards.
Testing holes: 1st-502 yds (par 5); 10th-455 yds dog-leg (par 5).
18 holes, 5734yds, Par 70, SSS 68, Course record 66.

Visitors	restricted weekends. Telephone for tee times (access to clubhouse on payment of small entrance fee and subject to prior arrangement).
Societies	by arrangement, apply in writing
Green Fees	not confirmed.
Cards	▱ ▰
Prof	Carl Yates
Facilities	⊗ ⅃ ♀ ⌂ ☗ ⟋
Location	5.5m W of Birmingham city centre off A4123

Hotel	★★★ 67% Posthouse Birmingham Great Barr, Chapel Ln, Great Barr, BIRMINGHAM ☎ 0870 400 9009 192 ⇄ 🐾

Cocks Moors Woods Alcester Rd South, Kings Heath B14
4ER ☎ 0121 464 3584 Fax 0121 441 1305
Although quite short this tree-lined, parkland course has well
maintained greens and offers a good test of golf.
18 holes, 5769yds, Par 69, SSS 68.
Club membership 400.
Visitors   no restrictions.
Societies   must contact in advance.
Green Fees £11 per round weekends.
Prof   Steve Ellis
Facilities   ⊗ ⽇ ⮕ ⮕ ⽷ ⽷ ⽷ ⽷
& Leisure   heated indoor swimming pool, solarium,
                gymnasium.
Location   5m S of city centre on A435

Hotel   ★★★ 64% Posthouse Birmingham City,
                Smallbrook Queensway, BIRMINGHAM
                ☎ 0870 400 9008 280 ⇄

Edgbaston Church Rd, Edgbaston B15 3TB
☎ 0121 454 1736 Fax 0121 454 2395
e-mail: secretary@edgbastongc.co.uk
Set in 144 acres of woodland, lake and parkland, two
miles from the centre of Birmingham, this delightful
course utilises the wealth of natural features to provide a
series of testing and adventurous holes set in the
traditional double loop that starts directly in front of the
Clubhouse, an imposing Georgian mansion.
18 holes, 6106yds, Par 69, SSS 69, Course record 63.
Club membership 970.
Visitors   recommended to contact in advance through
                golf reservations, must have handicap
                certificate. Most weekends pm.
Societies   must apply in writing.
Green Fees £50 per day; £40 per 18 holes (weekends
                pm £50 per 18 holes).
Prof   Jamie Cundy
Designer   H S Colt
Facilities   ⊗ ⽇ ⮕ ⮕ ⽷ ⽷ ⽷ ⽷ ⽷ ⽷ ⽷
Location   2m S of city centre on B4217 off A38

Hotel   ★★★ 63% Plough & Harrow,
                135 Hagley Rd, EDGBASTON
                ☎ 0121 454 4111 44 ⇄

Great Barr Chapel Ln, Great Barr B43 7BA
☎ 0121 357 5270
Parkland course with easy walking. Pleasant views of Barr
Beacon National Park.
18 holes, 6523yds, Par 72, SSS 72, Course record 67.
Club membership 600.
Visitors   no visitors at weekends.
Societies   must contact in writing.
Green Fees £36 per day; £30 per 18 holes.
Prof   Richard Spragg
Facilities   ⊗ by prior arrangement ⽇ by prior arrangement
                ⽷ ⽷ ⽷ ⽷ ⽷
Location   6m N of city centre off A 34

Hotel   ★★★ 67% Posthouse Birmingham Great Barr,
                Chapel Ln, Great Barr, BIRMINGHAM
                ☎ 0870 400 9009 192 ⇄

Handsworth 11 Sunningdale Close, Handsworth Wood B20
1NP ☎ 0121 554 0599 & 554 3387 Fax 0121 554 3387
Undulating parkland course with some tight fairways but
subject to wind.
18 holes, 6267yds, Par 70, SSS 70, Course record 65.
Club membership 800.
Visitors   restricted weekends, bank holidays & Xmas.
                Must contact in advance and have a handicap
                certificate.
Societies   must contact in advance.
Green Fees £35 per day..
Prof   Lee Bashford
Facilities   ⊗ ⽇ ⮕ ⮕ ⽷ ⽷ ⽷
& Leisure   squash.
Location   3.5m NW of city centre off A4040

Hotel   ★★ 65% Sheriden House Hotel, 82
                Handsworth Wood Rd, Handsworth Wood,
                BIRMINGHAM ☎ 0121 554 2185 &
                0121 523 5960 Fax 0121 551 4761 11 ⇄

Harborne 40 Tennal Rd, Harborne B32 2JE
☎ 0121 427 3058
Parkland course in hilly situation, with brook running
through.
18 holes, 6230yds, Par 70, SSS 70, Course record 65.
Club membership 655.
Visitors   must have handicap certificate, contact in
                advance, may not play weekends except with
                member, Ladies have priority Tue.
Societies   Mon, Wed-Fri apply to secretary, by phone or
                letter.
Green Fees £35 per day; £30 per round.
Prof   Alan Quarterman
Designer   Harry Colt
Facilities   ⊗ ⽇ ⮕ ⮕ ⽷ ⽷ ⽷ ⽷
Location   3.5 m SW of city centre off A4040

Hotel   ★★★ 63% Plough & Harrow, 135 Hagley Rd,
                EDGBASTON ☎ 0121 454 4111 44 ⇄

Harborne Church Farm Vicarage Rd, Harborne B17 0SN
☎ 0121 427 1204 Fax 0121 428 3126
Parkland course with water hazards and easy walking. Some
holes might prove difficult.
9 holes, 4882yds, Par 66, SSS 64, Course record 62.
Club membership 200.
Visitors   must contact in advance.
Societies   must telephone in advance.
Green Fees contact for details.
Cards   ▦ ▦ ▦ ▦ ▦ ▦
Prof   Paul Johnson
Facilities   ⊗ ⽇ ⮕ ⮕ ⽷ ⽷ ⽷
& Leisure   practice net.
Location   3.5m SW of city centre off A4040

Hotel   ★★★ 63% Plough & Harrow, 135 Hagley Rd,
                EDGBASTON ☎ 0121 454 4111 44 ⇄

Hatchford Brook Coventry Rd, Sheldon B26 3PY
☎ 0121 743 9821 Fax 0121 743 3420
e-mail: idt@hbgc.freeserve.co.uk
Fairly flat, municipal parkland course.
18 holes, 6155yds, Par 69, SSS 69.
Club membership 450.
Visitors   are restricted early Sat & Sun.
Societies   must contact in advance.

▶

Green Fees not confirmed.
Prof Mark Hampton
Facilities ⊗ ⓑ ☖ 丛 🏠 ⛳ ℓ
Location 6m E of city centre on A45

Hotel ★★★ 65% Posthouse Birmingham Airport, Coventry Rd, BIRMINGHAM ☎ 0870 400 9007 141 ⇆ ☏

Hilltop Park Ln, Handsworth B21 8LJ ☎ 0121 554 4463
A good test of golf with interesting layout, undulating fairways and large greens, located in the Sandwell Valley conservation area.
18 holes, 6208yds, Par 71, SSS 70.
Club membership 400.
Visitors no restrictions but booking necessary.
Societies Mon-Fri, telephone Professional in advance.
Green Fees £9.50 per 18 holes (£11 weekends).
Prof Kevin Highfield
Designer Hawtree
Facilities ⊗ ⑪ ⓑ ☖ 丛 🏠 ⛳ ℓ
Location On A41, 1m from junct 1 M5

Hotel ★★ 65% Sheriden House Hotel, 82 Handsworth Wood Rd, Handsworth Wood, BIRMINGHAM ☎ 0121 554 2185 & 0121 523 5960 Fax 0121 551 4761 11 ⇆ ☏

Lickey Hills Rosehill, Rednal B45 8RR
☎ 0121 453 3159 Fax 0121 457 8779
18 holes, 5835yds, Par 68, SSS 68.
Location 10m SW of city centre on B4096
Telephone for further details

Hotel ★★ 68% Norwood Hotel, 87-89 Bunbury Rd, Northfield, BIRMINGHAM ☎ 0121 411 2202 18 ⇆ ☏

Moseley Springfield Rd, Kings Heath B14 7DX
☎ 0121 444 2115 Fax 0121 441 4662
e-mail: admin@mosgolf.freeserve.co.uk
Parkland course with a lake, pond and stream to provide natural hazards. The par-3, 4th goes through a cutting in woodland to a tree and garden-lined amphitheatre, and the par-4, 5th entails a drive over a lake to a dog-leg fairway.
18 holes, 6315yds, Par 70, SSS 71, Course record 63.
Club membership 600.
Visitors may only play by prior arrangement, weekdays excluding bank holidays.
Societies by prior arrangement.
Green Fees £37 per day.
Prof Gary Edge
Designer various
Facilities ⊗ ⑪ ⓑ ☖ ♀ 丛 🏠 ℓ
Location 4m S of city centre on B4146 off A435

Hotel ★★ 68% Norwood Hotel, 87-89 Bunbury Rd, Northfield, BIRMINGHAM ☎ 0121 411 2202 18 ⇆ ☏

North Worcestershire Frankley Beeches Rd, Northfield B31 5LP ☎ 0121 475 1047 Fax 0121 476 8681
Designed by James Braid and established in 1907, this is a mature parkland course. Tree plantations rather than heavy rough are the main hazards.
18 holes, 5959yds, Par 69, SSS 68, Course record 64.
Club membership 600.

Visitors by prior arrangement with professional. Must play with member at weekends. All visitors must have an official CONGU handicap.
Societies apply in advance in writing or by telephone to the professional tel: 0121 475 5721.
Green Fees not confirmed.
Prof Finley Clarke
Designer James Braid
Facilities 丛 🏠 ⛳ ℓ
Location 7m SW of Birmingham city centre, off A38

Hotel ★★ 68% Norwood Hotel, 87-89 Bunbury Rd, Northfield, BIRMINGHAM ☎ 0121 411 2202 18 ⇆ ☏

Warley Woods The Pavilion, Lightswood Hill, Warley B67 5ED ☎ 0121 429 2440 & 6862619(secretary) Fax 0121 434 4430
Municipal parkland course in Warley Woods. New out of bounds areas and bunkers have tightened the course considerably with further improvement following tree planting.
9 holes, 5346yds, Par 68, SSS 66, Course record 64.
Club membership 200.
Visitors must contact in advance. Linc card system for easier booking.
Societies booking advised, times very limited for large parties.
Green Fees £11 per 18 holes; reductions midweek.
Cards ▱ ▱ ▱
Prof David Owen
Facilities ⊗ ☖ 丛 🏠 ⛳ ℓ
Location 4m W of city centre off A456

Hotel ★★★ 63% Plough & Harrow, 135 Hagley Rd, EDGBASTON ☎ 0121 454 4111 44 ⇆ ☏

COVENTRY   Map 04 SP37

Ansty Golf Centre Brinklow Rd, Ansty CV7 9JH
☎ 024 76621341 Fax 024 76602671
18-hole Pay and Play course of two 9-hole loops. Membership competitions for handicaps. Driving range and putting green.
18 holes, 6079yds, Par 71, SSS 68, Course record 66.
Club membership 400.
Visitors no restrictions.
Societies welcome, telephone in advance.
Green Fees £6 per holes; £10 per 18 holes (£8/£14 weekends & bank holidays).
Cards ▱ ▱ ▱
Prof Craig Philips
Designer David Morgan
Facilities ⊗ ⑪ by prior arrangement ⓑ ☖ ♀ 丛 🏠 ⛳ ➤ 🛒 ℓ ⚑
Location 1m from jct 2 M6/M69

Hotel ★★★ 62% Novotel Coventry, Wilsons Ln, COVENTRY ☎ 024 7636 5000 98 ⇆ ☏

Coventry St Martins Rd, Finham Park CV3 6RJ
☎ 024 76414152 Fax 024 76690131
The scene of several major professional events, this undulating parkland course has a great deal of quality. More than that, it usually plays its length, and thus scoring is never easy, as many professionals have found to their cost. ▶

18 holes, 6601yds, Par 73, SSS 73, Course record 66.
Club membership 500.

Visitors	must contact in advance. May not play at weekends and bank holidays.
Societies	must apply in writing/telephone.
Green Fees	£35 per day.
Cards	🖩 📠 🖩 📠
Prof	Philip Weaver
Designer	Vardon Bros/Hawtree
Facilities	⊗ ⊪ ⓑ ⛴ ♀ ♨ 🏠 ✐
Location	3m S of city centre on B4113, 2m from jct of A45/A46

Hotel	★★★ 69% Hylands Hotel, Warwick Rd, COVENTRY ☎ 024 7650 1600 61 ⇄ ⁍

Coventry Hearsall Beechwood Av CV5 6DF
☎ 024 76713470 Fax 024 76691534
Parkland course with fairly easy walking. A brook provides an interesting hazard.
18 holes, 6005yds, Par 70, SSS 69.
Club membership 650.

Visitors	with member only at weekends.
Societies	apply in writing to secretary.
Green Fees	not confirmed..
Prof	Mike Tarn
Facilities	♨ 🏠 ❦ ✐
Location	1.5m SW of city centre off A429

Hotel	★★★ 69% Hylands Hotel, Warwick Rd, COVENTRY ☎ 024 7650 1600 61 ⇄ ⁍

Windmill Village Hotel Golf & Leisure Club Birmingham Rd, Allesley CV5 9AL ☎ 024 76404040 Fax 024 76404042
e-mail: windmillvillage@compuserve.co.uk
An attractive 18-hole course over rolling parkland with plenty of trees and two lakes that demand shots over open water. Four challenging Par 5 holes. Good leisure facilities.
18 holes, 5213yds, Par 70, SSS 67, Course record 66.
Club membership 600.

Visitors	must contact in advance. Pre-payment required at peak times. May not play weekends 7-10am.
Societies	telephone for booking form.
Green Fees	not confirmed.
Cards	🖩 📠 🖩 📠 📠
Prof	Robert Hunter
Designer	Robert Hunter
Facilities	⊗ ⊪ ⓑ ⛴ ♀ ♨ 🏠 ⛴ ❦ ✐ ❧ ♨ ✐
& Leisure	hard tennis courts, heated indoor swimming pool, fishing, sauna, solarium, gymnasium, beauty suite.
Location	On A45 W of Coventry

Hotel	★★★ Brooklands Grange Hotel & Restaurant, Holyhead Rd, COVENTRY ☎ 024 7660 1601 30 ⇄ ⁍

DUDLEY   Map 07 SO99

Dudley Turner's Hill, Rowley Regis, Warley B65 9DP
☎ 01384 233877 Fax 01384 233177
Fairly hilly parkland course.
18 holes, 5714yds, Par 69, SSS 68.
Club membership 550.

Visitors	must contact in advance, may not play at weekends.

Societies	must contact in advance.
Green Fees	not confirmed.
Cards	🖩 ■ 🖩
Prof	Guy Dean
Facilities	⊗ ⊪ ⓑ ⛴ ♀ ♨ 🏠 ✐
Location	2m S of town centre off B4171

Hotel	★★★ 63% Himley Country Hotel, School Rd, HIMLEY ☎ 01902 896716 73 ⇄ ⁍

Swindon Bridgnorth Rd, Swindon DY3 4PU
☎ 01902 897031 & 895226 Fax 01902 326219
Attractive undulating woodland/parkland course, with spectacular views.
Old Course: 18 holes, 6091yds, Par 71, SSS 69.
New Course: 9 holes, 1135yds, Par 27.
Club membership 700.

Visitors	must contact in advance.
Societies	must apply in writing.
Green Fees	£18 per round (£27 weekends & bank holidays).
Cards	🖩 ■
Prof	Phil Lester
Facilities	⊗ ⊪ ⓑ ⛴ ♀ ♨ 🏠 ♨ ✐ ⁍
& Leisure	fishing.
Location	On B4176, 3m from A449 at Himley

Hotel	★★★ 63% Himley Country Hotel, School Rd, HIMLEY ☎ 01902 896716 73 ⇄ ⁍

HALESOWEN   Map 07 SO98

Halesowen The Leasowes, Leasowes Ln B62 8QF
☎ 0121 501 3606 Fax 0121 501 3606
e-mail: halesowen-gc@msn.com
Parkland course in convenient position within the only Grade I listed park in the Midlands.
18 holes, 5754yds, Par 69, SSS 69, Course record 66.
Club membership 625.

Visitors	welcome weekdays, may only play weekends & bank holidays with member unless previously agreed.
Societies	must apply in writing/telephone.
Green Fees	£30 per day; £25 per round.
Prof	Jon Nicholas
Facilities	⊗ ⊪ ⓑ ⛴ ♀ ♨ 🏠 ⛴ ✐
Location	1m E junct 3 M5, Leasowes Lane off Manor Lane

Hotel	★★ 66% Cedars Hotel, Mason Rd, KIDDERMINSTER ☎ 01562 515595 21 ⇄ ⁍

KNOWLE   Map 07 SP17

Copt Heath 1220 Warwick Rd B93 9LN
☎ 01564 772650 Fax 01564 771022
Flat parkland course designed by H. Vardon.
18 holes, 6517yds, Par 71, SSS 71, Course record 64.
Club membership 700.

Visitors	must contact in advance and possess official handicap certificate. May not play weekends & bank holidays.
Societies	must contact in advance.
Green Fees	£40 per day.
Prof	Brian J Barton
Designer	H Vardon

Facilities ⊗ 🍽 🛒 💺 🏌 🏖 🏠 🖐 🚃 🏌 🏌

Location On A4141, 0.50m S of junct 5 of M42

Hotel ★★★★ 66% Swallow St John's Hotel, 651 Warwick Rd, SOLIHULL ☎ 0121 711 3000 178 ⇥ 🏠

MERIDEN　　　　　　　　　　　　Map 04 SP28

MARRIOTT FOREST OF ARDEN HOTEL & COUNTRY CLUB See page 279

North Warwickshire Hampton Ln CV7 7LL
☎ 01676 522259 Fax 01676 522464
Parkland course with easy walking.
9 holes, 6390yds, Par 72, SSS 71, Course record 65.
Club membership 425.
Visitors must contact in advance. Must play with member at weekends.
Societies must apply in writing to secretary.
Green Fees £18.
Prof Andrew Bownes
Facilities ⊗ by prior arrangement 🍽 by prior arrangement 🛒 💺 🏌 🏖 🏠 🏌
Location 1m SW on B4102

Hotel ★★★ 74% Manor Hotel, Main Rd, MERIDEN ☎ 01676 522735 114 ⇥ 🏠

Stonebridge Golf Centre Somers Rd CV7 7PL
☎ 01676 522442 Fax 01676 522447
The course is set in the beautiful landscape of the Packington estate, with mature shrubs and trees. Water features are incorporated to provide an excellent variety for a wide range of golfing abilities.
18 holes, 6240yds, Par 70, SSS 70, Course record 70.
Club membership 400.
Visitors advisable to book in advance, booking up to 9 days in advance.
Societies apply in writing or telephone in advance.
Green Fees £14.50(£16.50 weekends & bank holidays).
Cards 💳 ▬▬ ▬▬ 💳 ▬▬ 🔌 💲
Prof Robert Grier
Designer Mark Jones
Facilities ⊗ 🍽 🛒 💺 🏌 🏖 🏠 🏌 🖐 🚃 🏌 🏌
& Leisure fishing.

Hotel ★★★ 74% Manor Hotel, Main Rd, MERIDEN ☎ 01676 522735 114 ⇥ 🏠

SEDGLEY　　　　　　　　　　　　Map 07 SO99

Sedgley Golf Centre Sandyfields Rd DY3 3DL
☎ 01902 880503
Public Pay and Play course. Undulating contours and mature trees with extensive views over surrounding countryside.
9 holes, 3147yds, Par 72, SSS 70.
Club membership 150.
Visitors booking advisable for weekends.
Societies must contact in advance.
Green Fees £6.50 per 9 holes;£8.50 per 18 holes..
Prof Garry Mercer
Designer W G Cox
Facilities 💺 🏖 🖐 🚃 🏌 🏌
Location 0.5m from town centre off A463

Hotel ★★★ 63% Himley Country Hotel, School Rd, HIMLEY ☎ 01902 896716 73 ⇥ 🏠

SOLIHULL　　　　　　　　　　　　Map 07 SP17

Olton Mirfield Rd B91 1JH
☎ 0121 704 1936 & 0121 705 1083 Fax 0121 711 2010
18 holes, 6265yds, Par 69, SSS 71, Course record 63.
Location Exit M42 junct 5 and take A41 for 1.5m
Telephone for further details

Hotel ★★★★ 66% Swallow St John's Hotel, 651 Warwick Rd, SOLIHULL ☎ 0121 711 3000 178 ⇥ 🏠

Robin Hood St Bernards Rd B92 7DJ
☎ 0121 706 0061 Fax 0121 706 0061
e-mail: robin.hood.golf.club@dial.pipex.com
Pleasant parkland course with easy walking and open to good views.Tree lined fairways and varied holes, culminating in two excellent finishing holes. Modern clubhouse.
18 holes, 6635yds, Par 72, SSS 72, Course record 68.
Club membership 650.
Visitors must contact in advance. With member only at weekends.
Societies must contact in advance.
Green Fees not confirmed.
Prof Alan Harvey
Designer H S Colt
Facilities ⊗ 🍽 🛒 💺 🏌 🏖 🏠 🖐 🏌 🏌
Location 2m W off B4025

Hotel ★★★★ 66% Swallow St John's Hotel, 651 Warwick Rd, SOLIHULL ☎ 0121 711 3000 178 ⇥ 🏠

Shirley Stratford Rd, Monkpath, Shirley B90 4EW
☎ 0121 744 6001 Fax 0121 745 8220
e-mail: shirleygolfclub@btclick.com
Fairly flat parkland course.
18 holes, 6510yds, Par 72, SSS 71.
Club membership 600.
Visitors may not play bank holidays & with member only at weekends. Handicap certificate is required.
Societies only on Thu, must contact in advance.
Green Fees £25 per 18 holes;£30 per 27 holes;£35 per 36 holes.
Prof S Bottrill
Facilities ⊗ 🍽 🛒 💺 🏌 🏖 🏠 🏌
Location 0.5m N of junct 4 M42 on A34

Hotel ★★★ 66% Regency Hotel, Stratford Rd, Shirley, SOLIHULL ☎ 0121 745 6119 112 ⇥ 🏠

STOURBRIDGE　　　　　　　　　　Map 07 SO98

Hagley Golf & Country Club Wassell Grove, Hagley DY9 9JW ☎ 01562 883701 Fax 01562 887518
Undulating parkland course set beneath the Clent Hills; there are superb views. Testing 15th, par 5, 557 yards.
18 holes, 6353yds, Par 72, SSS 72, Course record 66.
Club membership 700.
Visitors welcome weekdays but restricted Wed (Ladies Day) & with member only at weekends.
Societies Mon-Fri only, must apply in writing.
Green Fees not confirmed.

▶

Prof Iain Clark
Designer Garratt & Co
Facilities ⊗ ⫟ ⑂ 🏌 💷 ♀ ⚐ 🏠 𝄪
& Leisure squash.
Location 1m E of Hagley off A456. 2m from junct 3 0n M5

Hotel ★★ 66% Cedars Hotel, Mason Rd, KIDDERMINSTER
☎ 01562 515595 21 ⇆ ♜

Stourbridge Worcester Ln, Pedmore DY8 2RB
☎ 01384 395566 Fax 01384 444660
e-mail: secretary@stourbridge-golf-club.co.uk
Parkland course.
18 holes, 6231yds, Par 70, SSS 69, Course record 67.
Club membership 865.
Visitors contact secretary, no casual visitors weekends. Ladies day Wednesday.
Societies must apply in writing/by e-mail.
Green Fees £30 per round;£37.50 per day.
Prof M Male
Facilities ⊗ ⫟ ⑂ 🏌 💷 ♀ ⚐ 🏠 𝄪
Location 2m from town centre

Hotel ★★ 66% Cedars Hotel, Mason Rd, KIDDERMINSTER
☎ 01562 515595 21 ⇆ ♜

SUTTON COLDFIELD   Map 07 SP19

Boldmere Monmouth Dr B73 6JL
☎ 0121 354 3379 Fax 0121 355 4534
Established municipal course with 10 par 3s and a lake coming into play on the 16th and 18th holes.
18 holes, 4493yds, Par 63, SSS 62, Course record 57.
Club membership 300.
Visitors must contact in advance.
Societies midweek only, apply in writing.
Green Fees not confirmed.
Prof Trevor Short
Facilities ⊗ ⑂ 🏌 💷 ⚐ 🏠 𝄪 𝄪
Location Adjacent to Sutton Park

Hotel ★★★ 74% Moor Hall Hotel, Moor Hall Dr, Four Oaks, SUTTON COLDFIELD
☎ 0121 308 3751 74 ⇆ ♜

Little Aston Streetly B74 3AN ☎ 0121 353 2942
Fax 0121 580 8387 e-mail: manager@littleastongolf.co.uk
Parkland course.
18 holes, 6670yds, Par 72, SSS 73, Course record 64.
Club membership 350.
Visitors must contact in advance & may not play on Saturdays.
Societies must apply in writing.
Green Fees £60 per day;£50 per 18 holes.
Cards ▦▦ ▦▦ ▦
Prof John Anderson
Designer H Vardon
Facilities ⊗ ⫟ ⑂ 🏌 💷 ♀ ⚐ 🏠 𝄪
Location 3.5m NW of Sutton Coldfield off A454

Hotel ★★★ 74% Moor Hall Hotel, Moor Hall Dr, Four Oaks, SUTTON COLDFIELD
☎ 0121 308 3751 74 ⇆ ♜

Moor Hall Moor Hall Dr B75 6LN
☎ 0121 308 6130 Fax 0121 308 6130
Parkland course. The 14th is a notable hole.
18 holes, 6249yds, Par 70, SSS 70.
Club membership 600.
Visitors must contact in advance. With member only weekends & bank holidays.
Societies must apply in writing.
Green Fees not confirmed.
Prof Alan Partridge
Designer Hawtree & Taylor
Facilities ⊗ ⫟ ⑂ 🏌 💷 ♀ ⚐ 🏠 𝄪 𝄪
Location 2.5m N of town centre off A453

Hotel ★★★ 74% Moor Hall Hotel, Moor Hall Dr, Four Oaks, SUTTON COLDFIELD
☎ 0121 308 3751 74 ⇆ ♜

Pype Hayes Eachel Hurst Rd, Walmley B76 1EP
☎ 0121 351 1014 Fax 0121 313 0206
Attractive, fairly flat course with excellent greens.
18 holes, 5927yds, Par 71, SSS 69.
Club membership 400.
Visitors phone professional in advance.
Societies contact professional in advance.
Green Fees not confirmed.
Cards ▦▦ ▦
Prof James Bayliss
Designer Bobby Jones
Facilities ⊗ ⫟ ⑂ 🏌 💷 🏠 𝄪 𝄪
Location 2.5m S off B4148

Hotel ★★★ 67% Marston Farm Hotel, Bodymoor Heath, SUTTON COLDFIELD
☎ 01827 872133 37 ⇆ ♜

Sutton Coldfield 110 Thornhill Rd, Streetly B74 3ER
☎ 0121 353 9633 Fax 0121 353 5503
A fine natural, all-weather, heathland course, with tight fairways, gorse, heather and trees. A good challenge for all standards of golfer.
18 holes, 6541yds, Par 72, SSS 71, Course record 65.
Club membership 600.
Visitors must contact in advance. Restricted at weekends and bank holidays.
Societies must apply in writing.
Green Fees £35 per day;£25 per round(£35 weeekends & bank holidays).
Prof Jerry Hayes
Designer D McKenzie
Facilities ⊗ ⫟ ⑂ 🏌 💷 ♀ ⚐ 🏠 𝄪
Location 3m NW on B4138

Hotel ★★★ 74% Moor Hall Hotel, Moor Hall Dr, Four Oaks, SUTTON COLDFIELD
☎ 0121 308 3751 74 ⇆ ♜

Walmley Brooks Rd, Wylde Green B72 1HR
☎ 0121 373 0029 & 377 7272 Fax 0121 377 7272
Pleasant parkland course with many trees. The hazards are not difficult.
18 holes, 6585yds, Par 72, SSS 72, Course record 67.
Club membership 650.
Visitors must contact in advance. Weekends may only play as guest of member.
Societies must contact in advance.
Green Fees £35 per day; £30 per round.

Marriott Forest of Arden

Meriden, *Warwickshire*   ☎ 01676 522335   Fax 01676 523711   Map 04 SP28

This is one of the finest golf destinations in the UK, with a range of facilities to impress every golfer. The jewel in the crown is the Arden course, one of the country's most spectacular challenges and host to a succession of international tournaments, including the British Masters and English Open.

The shorter Aylesford course offers a varied and enjoyable challenge which golfers of all abilities will find rewarding. Golf events are a speciality and there is a Golf Academy as well as extensive leisure facilities.

Visitors ring to book in advance

Societies by arrangement

Green Fees Arden Course £65 per round (£75 weekends); Aylesford £40 per round (£45 weekends)

Facilities ⊗ ⅢⅬ ♥ 🍴 ⚐ 🎯 ↑ 🏹 🛺 ♂ 𝄞 Professional (Damien Tudor)

Leisure tennis, swimming, fishing, sauna, solarium, gymnasium

Location Maxstoke Lane, Meriden CV7 7HR (1m SW of Meriden on B4102)

Holes/Par/Course record Arden Course: 18 holes, 6718 yds, Par 72, SSS 73, Course record 62 Aylesford Course: 18 holes, 6525 yds, Par 71, SSS 72

WHERE TO STAY AND EAT NEARBY

Hotels
MERIDEN

★★★★◉ 72%
Marriott Forest of Arden Hotel & Country Club, Maxstoke Ln.
☎ 01676 522335. 214 🛏 🌲

★★★◉◉ 74%
Manor Hotel, Main Rd.
☎ 01676 522735. 114 🛏 🌲

Championship Course

Prof C J Wicketts
Facilities ⊗ ℍ ℡ ♥ ♀ ♣ 🏠 ⚑ ✈
Location 2m S off A5127

Hotel ★★★ 67% Marston Farm Hotel, Bodymoor Heath, SUTTON COLDFIELD ☎ 01827 872133 37 ⇆ ☞

WALSALL   Map 07 SP09

Bloxwich Stafford Rd, Bloxwich WS3 3PQ
☎ 01922 476593 Fax 01922 493449
e-mail: bloxwich.golf-club@virgin.net
Undulating parkland course with natural hazards and subject to strong north wind.
18 holes, 6257yds, Par 71, SSS 71, Course record 68.
Club membership 650.
Visitors may not play at weekends.
Societies must contact in advance.
Green Fees £25 per day; £20 per round.
Prof Richard J Dance
Facilities ⊗ ℍ ℡ ♥ ♀ ♣ 🏠 ✈
Location 3m N of town centre on A34

Hotel ★★★ 76% The Fairlawns at Aldridge, 178 Little Aston Rd, Aldridge, WALSALL ☎ 01922 455122 50 ⇆ ☞

Calderfields Aldridge Rd WS4 2JS
☎ 01922 632243 Fax 01922 638787
Parkland course with lake.
18 holes, 6509yds, Par 73, SSS 71.
Club membership 526.
Visitors no restrictions.
Societies telephone 01922 632243 in advance.
Green Fees not confirmed.
Prof David Williams
Designer Roy Winter
Facilities ⊗ ℍ ℡ ♥ ♀ ♣ 🏠 ⚑ ❧ ⚒ ✈ ▸
& Leisure fishing.
Location On A454

Hotel ★★★ 76% The Fairlawns at Aldridge, 178 Little Aston Rd, Aldridge, WALSALL ☎ 01922 455122 50 ⇆ ☞

Walsall The Broadway WS1 3EY
☎ 01922 613512 Fax 01922 616460
Well-wooded parkland course with easy walking.
18 holes, 6300yds, Par 70, SSS 70, Course record 65.
Club membership 600.
Visitors must contact in advance. May not play weekends & bank holidays.
Societies must apply in writing.
Green Fees £33 per 18 holes;£40 per day.
Prof Richard Lambert
Designer McKenzie
Facilities ⊗ ℍ ℡ ♥ ♀ ♣ 🏠 ✈
Location 1m S of town centre off A34

Hotel ★★★ 63% The Boundary Hotel, Birmingham Rd, WALSALL ☎ 01922 633609 95 ⇆ ☞

AA Hotels that have special arrangements with golf courses are listed at the back of the guide

WEST BROMWICH   Map 07 SP09

Dartmouth Vale St B71 4DW
☎ 0121 588 2131 Fax 0121 588 2131
Meadowland course with undulating but easy walking. The 617 yd (par 5) first hole is something of a challenge.
9 holes, 6060yds, Par 71, SSS 71, Course record 66.
Club membership 350.
Visitors with member only at weekends. May not play bank holidays or medal weekends.
Societies must apply in writing/telephone.
Green Fees not confirmed.
Prof Guy Dean
Facilities ⊗ ℍ ℡ ♥ ♀ ♣ 🏠 ⚑ ✈
Location E side of town centre off A4041

Hotel Express by Holiday Inn Oldbury, Bickley Park, OLDBURY ☎ 0121 511 0000 109 ☞

Sandwell Park Birmingham Rd B71 4JJ
☎ 0121 553 4637 Fax 0121 525 1651 e-mail: secretary@sandwellparkgolfclub.co.uk
Undulating wooded heathland course situated in the Sandwell Valley.
18 holes, 6468yds, Par 71, SSS 73, Course record 65.
Club membership 550.

Visitors must contact in advance. May not play at weekends.
Societies must contact in advance.
Green Fees £36 per 27/36 holes;£31 per 18 holes.
Prof Nigel Wylie
Designer H S Colt
Facilities ⊗ ℍ ℡ ♥ ♀ ♣ 🏠 ✈
& Leisure practice chipping area.
Location On A41, 200yds from juct 1 of the M5

WOLVERHAMPTON   Map 07 SO99

Oxley Park Stafford Rd, Bushbury WV10 6DE
☎ 01902 425892 Fax 01902 712241
Rolling parkland course with trees, bunkers and water hazards.
18 holes, 6226yds, Par 71, SSS 70, Course record 68.
Club membership 550.
Visitors must contact in advance.
Societies must contact in advance.
Green Fees not confirmed.
Prof Les Burlison
Designer H S Colt

Facilities ⊗ ☓ by prior arrangement ⓑ ♣ ♀ ⚘
🍴 ⛟ ✐
& Leisure snooker.
Location N of town centre off A449

Hotel ★★ Ely House Hotel, 53 Tettenhall Rd,
WOLVERHAMPTON
☎ 01902 311311 19 ⇆ 🐾

Penn Penn Common, Penn WV4 5JN
☎ 01902 341142 Fax 01902 620504
e-mail: penn-golf.freeserve.co.uk
Heathland course just outside the town.
18 holes, 6462yds, Par 70, SSS 71, Course record 68.
Club membership 650.
Visitors must play with member at weekends.
Societies must contact in advance.
Green Fees £25 per day; £20 per round.
Prof A Briscoe
Facilities ⚘ 🍴 ⚑ ✐
Location SW side of town centre off A449

Hotel ★★★ 66% Quality Hotel Wolverhampton,
Penn Rd, WOLVERHAMPTON
☎ 01902 429216 66 ⇆ 🐾 Annexe26 ⇆ 🐾

South Staffordshire Danescourt Rd, Tettenhall WV6 9BQ
☎ 01902 751065 Fax 01902 741753
A parkland course.
18 holes, 6513yds, Par 71, SSS 71, Course record 67.
Club membership 500.
Visitors must contact in advance but may not play
weekends & before 2pm Tue.
Societies must apply in writing.
Green Fees not confirmed.
Prof Mark Sparrow
Designer Harry Vardon
Facilities ⊗ ☓ ⓑ ♣ ♀ ⚘ 🍴 ⛟ ✐
Location 3m NW off A41

Hotel ★★ Ely House Hotel, 53 Tettenhall Rd,
WOLVERHAMPTON ☎ 01902 311311
19 ⇆ 🐾

Three Hammers Short Course Old Stafford Rd,
Coven WV10 7PP ☎ 01902 790940
18 holes, 1438yds, Par 54, SSS 54, Course record 43.
Location On A449 N of junct 2 M54
Telephone for further details

Hotel ★★★ Roman Way Hotel, Watling St,
Hatherton, CANNOCK ☎ 01543 572121
56 ⇆ 🐾

Wergs Keepers Ln, Tettenhall WV6 8UA
☎ 01902 742225 Fax 01902 744748
Open parkland course with gently undulating fairways.
18 holes, 6949yds, Par 72, SSS 73.
Club membership 250.
Visitors are advised to contact in advance.
Societies must contact in advance.
Green Fees £15 per day;£9 per 9 holes(£20/£11 weekends &
bank holidays).
Cards 🔲 🔲 🔲
Designer C W Moseley
Facilities ⊗ by prior arrangement ⓑ ♣ ♀ ⚘
🍴 ⚘ ⛟ ✐

Location From Wolverhampton take A41 towards
Newport for 2.5m then R for 0.5m then R again

Hotel ★★ Ely House Hotel, 53 Tettenhall Rd,
WOLVERHAMPTON
☎ 01902 311311 19 ⇆ 🐾

WIGHT, ISLE OF

COWES   Map 04 SZ49

Cowes Crossfield Av PO31 8HN
☎ 01983 292303 (secretary)
Fairly level, tight parkland course with difficult par 3s and
Solent views.
9 holes, 5934yds, Par 70, SSS 68, Course record 66.
Club membership 300.
Visitors restricted Thu & Sun mornings.
Societies Mon-Wed, must contact in advance.
Green Fees £15 per day/round (£18 weekends).
Designer Hamilton-Stutt
Facilities ⚘ ⚑ ✐
Location NW side of town, next to Cows High School

Hotel ★★★ 66% New Holmwood Hotel, Queens Rd,
Egypt Point, COWES
☎ 01983 292508 25 ⇆ 🐾

EAST COWES   Map 04 SZ59

Osborne Osborne House Estate PO32 6JX
☎ 01983 295421
Undulating parkland course in the grounds of Osborne
House. Quiet and peaceful situation.
9 holes, 6418yds, Par 70, SSS 70, Course record 71.
Club membership 450.
Visitors may not play Tue before 1pm, weekends before
noon & bank holidays before 11am.
Societies telephone initially.
Green Fees £18 per day (£20 weekends & bank holidays).
Facilities ⊗ ☓ ⓑ ♣ ♀ ⚘ 🍴 ⚑ ✐
Location E side of town centre off A3021

Hotel ★★★ 66% New Holmwood Hotel, Queens Rd,
Egypt Point, COWES
☎ 01983 292508 25 ⇆ 🐾

FRESHWATER   Map 04 SZ38

Freshwater Bay Afton Down PO40 9TZ
☎ 01983 752955 Fax 01983 756704
e-mail: fbgc_iow@yahoo.co.uk
A downland/seaside links with wide fairways and spectacular
coastal views of the Solent and Channel.
18 holes, 5725yds, Par 69, SSS 68.
Club membership 450.
Visitors may play daily after 9.30 ex Thu & Sun (10.30).
Societies apply to secretary.
Green Fees not confirmed.
Designer J H Taylor
Facilities ⊗ ☓ ⓑ ♣ ♀ ⚘ ⚑ ✐
Location 0.5m E of village off A3055

▶

281

| Hotel | ★★★ 66% Sentry Mead Hotel, Madeira Rd, TOTLAND BAY ☎ 01983 753212 14 ⇆ ⁕ |

| Hotel | ★★ 67% Cygnet Hotel, 58 Carter St, SANDOWN ☎ 01983 402930 45rm(44 ⇆ ⁕) |

NEWPORT   Map 04 SZ58

Newport St George's Down, Shide PO30 2JB
☎ 01983 525076
Downland course, fine views.
9 holes, 5710yds, Par 68, SSS 68.
Club membership 350.
Visitors   may not play Wed noon-3.30pm or before 3pm Sat & noon Sun.
Societies   contact Secretary in advance.
Green Fees not confirmed.
Facilities ☕♀⚥🏠⚐
Location   1.5m S off A3020

| Hotel | ★★★ 66% New Holmwood Hotel, Queens Rd, Egypt Point, COWES ☎ 01983 292508 25 ⇆ ⁕ |

RYDE   Map 04 SZ59

Ryde Binstead Rd PO33 3NF
☎ 01983 614809 Fax 01983 567418
e-mail: secretary@rydegolfclub.freeserve.co.uk
Downland course with wide views over the Solent.
9 holes, 5287yds, Par 66, SSS 66, Course record 65.
Club membership 500.
Visitors   may not play Wed afternoons, Sun mornings or before 10.30am Sat.
Societies   must contact in writing.
Green Fees £15 per day/round (£20 weekends & bank holidays).
Cards   ▭
Designer   Hamilton-Stutt
Facilities ⊗ ⅃ ♥ ♀ ⚥ 🏠 ⚐ ✐
Location   1m W on A3054

| Hotel | ★★ 70% Biskra Beach Hotel & Restaurant, 17 Saint Thomas's St, RYDE ☎ 01983 567913 14 ⇆ ⁕ |

SANDOWN   Map 04 SZ58

Shanklin & Sandown The Fairway, Lake PO36 9PR
☎ 01983 403217 (office) & 404424 (pro)
Fax 01983 403217 (office)/404424 (pro)
Heathland course with some hilly holes. Mostly sandy base but some clay makes it generally playable all year.
18 holes, 6063yds, Par 70, SSS 69, Course record 64.
Club membership 640.
Visitors   must contact in advance & have handicap certificate. May not play before noon Sat or 9.30am Sun.
Societies   apply in writing.
Green Fees £25 (£30 weekends & bank holidays).
Cards   ▭ ▭ ▭ ▭
Prof   Peter Hammond
Designer   Braid
Facilities ⊗ ⅃ ⅃ ♥ ♀ ⚥ 🏠 ⚐ ✐
Location   From Sandown drive towards Shanklin past Heights Leisure Centre after 200yds R into Fairway for 1m

VENTNOR   Map 04 SZ57

Ventnor Steephill Down Rd PO38 1BP ☎ 01983 853326
Downland course subject to wind. Fine seascapes.
12 holes, 5767yds, Par 70, SSS 68.
Club membership 297.
Visitors   may not play Fri noon-3pm or Sun mornings.
Societies   telephone initially.
Green Fees not confirmed.
Facilities ⚥ ⚐ ✐
Location   1m NW off B3327

| Hotel | ★★★★ 70% The Royal Hotel, Belgrave Rd, VENTNOR ☎ 01983 852186 55 ⇆ ⁕ |

BISHOPS CANNINGS   Map 04 SU06

North Wilts SN10 2LP
☎ 01380 860627 Fax 01380 860877
High, downland course with fine views.
18 holes, 6401yds, Par 71, SSS 70, Course record 65.
Club membership 800.
Visitors   a handicap certificate is required at weekends.
Societies   must book in advance.
Green Fees £30 per day; £21 per round (£24 per round weekends).
Cards   ▭ ▭ ▭ ▭
Prof   Graham Laing
Facilities ⊗ ⅃ ⅃ ♥ ♀ ⚥ 🏠 ⚐ ⚒ ✐
Location   2m NW

| Hotel | ★★★ 64% Bear Hotel, Market Place, DEVIZES ☎ 01380 722444 24 ⇆ ⁕ |

CALNE   Map 03 ST97

Bowood Golf & Country Club Derry Hill SN11 9PQ
☎ 01249 822228 Fax 01249 822218
e-mail: enquiries@bowood-estate.co.uk
Designed by Dave Thomas and set in a magnificent Grade I listed 'Capability Brown' park, this course provides a fine test for golfers and hosts the European Challenge Tour Championship. There are fine practice and teaching facilities and accommodation is available, along with conference facilities in the historic clubhouse.
18 holes, 6890yds, Par 72, SSS 73, Course record 63.
Club membership 500.
Visitors   welcome except before noon on Sat and Sun. Advisable to book.
Societies   booking by telephone.
Green Fees not confirmed.
Cards   ▭ ▭ ▭ ▭ ▭ ▭
Prof   Max Taylor
Designer   Dave Thomas
Facilities ⊗ ⅃ ⅃ ♥ ♀ ⚥ 🏠 ⚐ ⚒ ⚒ ✐ ⚓
& Leisure   Bowood House and Gardens.

▶

Location M4 junct 17 off A4 between Chippenham & Calne

Bowood Golf & Country Club

Hotel ★★★ 64% Lansdowne Strand Hotel, The Strand, CALNE ☎ 01249 812488
21 ⇆ ꜝ Annexe5 ⇆ ꜝ

CASTLE COMBE   Map 03 ST87

Manor House SN14 7JW
☎ 01249 782982 Fax 01249 782992
e-mail: manorhousegolfclubatcastlecombe@msn.com
Set in one of the finest locations in England, this 18-hole Peter Alliss/Clive Clark course was designed to marry neatly with the surrounding conservation area. Many mature trees have been used to great effect giving individuality and challenge to every shot. There are spectacular holes at the 17th & 18th with lakes and waterfalls making them memorable.
18 holes, 6286yds, Par 72, SSS 71.
Club membership 450.

Visitors must have a handicap certificate and must contact in advance.
Societies contact in advance.
Green Fees £60 per day; £40 per round (£80/£50 Fri-Sun).
Cards [card symbols]
Prof Peter Green
Designer Peter Alliss/Clive Clark
Facilities ⊗ ⍾ ⅃ 🍴 ♀ ⚘ 🏠 🎣 🛵 ♂ ꜝ
& Leisure hard tennis courts, heated outdoor swimming pool, fishing, sauna, snooker.
Location On B4039, 5m NW of Chippenham

Hotel ★★★★♨ Manor House Hotel, CASTLE COMBE ☎ 01249 782206
21 ⇆ ꜝ Annexe25 ⇆ ꜝ

CHAPMANSLADE   Map 03 ST84

Thoulstone Park BA13 4AQ
☎ 01373 832825 Fax 01373 832821
A rolling parkland course with natural lakes and mature trees. Hole 7, stroke index 1 has a second shot over a large lake to the green so a straight drive is essential.
18 holes, 6161yds, Par 71, SSS 69.
Club membership 500.
Visitors restricted Sat & Sun mornings. Dress code applies.
Societies telephone in advance.
Green Fees not confirmed.
Prof Tony Isaac
Facilities ⊗ ⅃ 🍴 ♀ ⚘ 🏠 ꜝ ♂ ꜝ
Location On A36 between Bath/Warminster

Hotel ★★ 69% Woolpack Inn, BECKINGTON ☎ 01373 831244 12 ⇆ ꜝ

CHIPPENHAM   Map 03 ST97

Chippenham Malmesbury Rd SN15 5LT
☎ 01249 652040 Fax 01249 446681
Easy walking on downland course. Testing holes at 1st and 15th.
18 holes, 5559yds, Par 69, SSS 67, Course record 64.
Club membership 650.
Visitors must contact in advance.
Societies must contact in writing.
Green Fees £20 per day/round (£25 weekends & bank holidays).
Prof Bill Creamer
Facilities ⅃ ♀ ⚘ 🏠 ꜝ ♂
Location M4 junct 17, 1m N of Chippenham beside A350

Hotel ★★★★♨ Manor House Hotel, CASTLE COMBE ☎ 01249 782206
21 ⇆ ꜝ Annexe25 ⇆ ꜝ

CRICKLADE   Map 04 SU09

Cricklade Hotel & Country Club Common Hill SN6 6HA
☎ 01793 750751 Fax 01793 751767
e-mail: jane@cricklidehotel.fsnet.co.uk
A challenging 9-hole course with undulating greens and beautiful views. Par 3 6th (128yds) signature hole from an elevated tee to a green protected by a deep pot bunker.
9 holes, 1830yds, Par 62, SSS 57.
Club membership 170.
Visitors may not play weekends or bank holidays unless accompanied by a member. Must contact in advance.
Societies apply in writing.
Green Fees not confirmed.
Cards [card symbols]
Prof Ian Bolt
Designer Ian Bolt/Colin Smith
Facilities ⊗ ⍾ ⅃ 🍴 ♀ ⚘ 🏠 ꜝ ♂
& Leisure hard tennis courts, heated indoor swimming pool, solarium, gymnasium.
Location On the B4040 out of Cricklade, towards Malmesbury

Hotel ★★★ 67% Stanton House Hotel, The Avenue, Stanton Fitzwarren, SWINDON ☎ 01793 861777 86 ⇆ ꜝ

ERLESTOKE   Map 03 ST95

Erlestoke Sands SN10 5UB
☎ 01380 831069 Fax 01380 831284
e-mail: erlestokesands@europe.com
The course is set on the lower slopes of Salisbury Plain with distant views to the Cotswolds and Marlborough Downs. The 7th plunges from an elevated three-tiered tee, high in the woods, to a large green with a spectacular backdrop of a meandering river and hills. The course was built to suit every standard of golfer from the novice to the very low handicapper and its two tiers offer lakes and rolling downland.
18 holes, 6406yds, Par 73, SSS 71, Course record 69. Club membership 720.
Visitors   phone for tee booking in advance 01380 830300. Dress rules apply.
Societies   must book in advance.
Green Fees £25 per day; £18 per round (£35/£25 weekends and bank holidays). Mon only £15 per round..
Cards   🖃 💳 🔟
Prof   Michael Waters
Designer   Adrian Stiff
Facilities   ⊗ ⅏ 🖫 💺 ♀ 📤 🖻 ☏ 🏌 ⚒ ⚙ ♟
Location   On B3098 Devizes/Westbury road

Hotel   ★★★ 64% Bear Hotel, Market Place, DEVIZES ☎ 01380 722444   24 ⇆ 🏮

GREAT DURNFORD   Map 04 SU13

High Post SP4 6AT
☎ 01722 782356 Fax 01722 782674
e-mail: highpostgolfclub@lineone.net
An interesting downland course on Wiltshire chalk with good turf and splendid views over the southern area of Salisbury Plain. The par 3, 17th and the two-shot 18th require good judgement. The course is noted for quality of its greens and year round playability.
18 holes, 6305yds, Par 70, SSS 70, Course record 64. Club membership 600.
Visitors   a handicap certificate is required at weekends & bank holidays. Telephone professional in advance 01722 782219.
Societies   apply by telephone to manager.
Green Fees £37 per day; £28 per round (£45/£35 weekends).
Prof   Ian Welding
Designer   Hawtree & Ptrs
Facilities   ⊗ ⅏ 🖫 💺 ♀ 📤 🖻 ⚙ ♟
Location   1.75m SE on A345

Hotel   ★★★ 65% Rose & Crown Hotel, Harnham Rd, Harnham, SALISBURY ☎ 01722 399955   28 ⇆ 🏮

HIGHWORTH   Map 04 SU29

Highworth Community Golf Centre Swindon Rd SN6 7SJ
☎ 01793 766014 Fax 01793 766014
Public downland course, situated in a high position affording good views of the Wiltshire Downs.
9 holes, 3120yds, Par 35, SSS 35, Course record 29. Club membership 150.
Visitors   no restrictions.
Societies   advisable to contact in advance.

Green Fees £13 per 18 holes; £7.90 per 9 holes.
Prof   Geoff Robins
Designer   T Watt/ B Sandry/D Lang
Facilities   💺 📤 🖻 🏌 ⚙
Location   Off A361 Swindon to Lechlade

Hotel   ★★★ 73% Sudbury House Hotel & Conference Centre, London St, FARINGDON ☎ 01367 241272   49 ⇆ 🏮

Wrag Barn Golf & Country Club Shrivenham Rd
SN6 7QQ ☎ 01793 861327 Fax 01793 861325
e-mail: info@wragbarn.com
Listed in 'Golf's Best Top 100 UK Courses'. An outstanding course for golfers of all abilities.
18 holes, 6700yds, Par 72, SSS 71, Course record 65. Club membership 600.
Visitors   no restrictions but may not play before noon at weekends.
Societies   contact in advance.
Green Fees £35 per day; £25 per round (£30 per round Fri-Sun).
Prof   Barry Loughrey
Designer   Hawtree
Facilities   ⊗ 🖫 💺 ♀ 📤 🖻 🏌 ⚒ ⚙ ♟
Location   On B4000 Shrivenham Road out of Highworth. Follow signs

Hotel   ★★★ 67% Stanton House Hotel, The Avenue, Stanton Fitzwarren, SWINDON ☎ 01793 861777   86 ⇆ 🏮

KINGSDOWN   Map 03 ST86

Kingsdown SN13 8BS
☎ 01225 742530 Fax 01225 743472
Fairly flat, open downland course with very sparse tree cover but surrounding wood.
18 holes, 6445yds, Par 72, SSS 71, Course record 64. Club membership 650.
Visitors   welcome except at weekends. Must contact in advance & have a handicap certificate.
Societies   apply by letter.
Green Fees £24 per day.
Prof   Andrew Butler
Facilities   ⊗ ⅏ 🖫 💺 ♀ 📤 🖻 🏌 ⚙
Location   W side of village,between Corsham & Bath

Hotel   ★★★★ Lucknam Park, COLERNE ☎ 01225 742777   23 ⇆ 🏮 Annexe18 ⇆ 🏮

LANDFORD   Map 04 SU21

Hamptworth Golf & Country Club Hamptworth Rd, Hamptworth SP5 2DU ☎ 01794 390155 Fax 01794 390022
e-mail: info@hamptworthgolf.co.uk
Hamptworth enjoys ancient woodland and an abundance of wildlife in a beautiful setting on the edge of the New Forest. The 14th is one of its most challenging holes having a narrow fairway guarded by established forest oaks. The 2nd is a dogleg of 543yds and plays differently all year.
18 holes, 6516yds, Par 72, SSS 71, Course record 68. Club membership 450.
Visitors   telephone to check availability.
Societies   write or telephone in advance.
Green Fees not confirmed.
Cards   🖃 💳 🔟 🔟

▶

Prof   Phil Stevens
Designer   Philip Sanders/Brian Pierson
Facilities   Ⓧ ⍴ ⌂ ♨ ♀ ⚐ 🏠 🎯 ♣ ✎ ⚐
& Leisure   gymnasium, croquet lawns.
Location   1m NW, A36/B3079

Hotel   ★★★ 71% Bartley Lodge, Lyndhurst Rd,
CADNAM ☎ 023 8081 2248 31 ⇆ ♋

MARLBOROUGH   Map 04 SU16

Marlborough The Common SN8 1DU
☎ 01672 512147 Fax 01672 513164
Downland course with extensive views over the Og valley
and Marlborough Downs.
18 holes, 6491yds, Par 72, SSS 71, Course record 61.
Club membership 900.
Visitors   restricted at certain times; must have a handicap
certificate at weekends. Must contact in
advance.
Societies   must contact in advance.
Green Fees £33 per day; £25 per round (£40/£30 weekends).
Cards   ▦ ▦ ▦ ▦ ▦
Prof   S Amor
Facilities   Ⓧ ⍴ ⌂ ♨ ♀ ⚐ 🏠 ♣ 🎯 ✎
Location   N side of town centre on A346

Hotel   ★★★ 68% The Castle & Ball, High St,
MARLBOROUGH
☎ 01672 515201 34 ⇆ ♋

OAKSEY   Map 03 ST99

Oaksey Park Golf & Leisure SN16 9SB
☎ 01666 577995 Fax 01666 577174
9 holes, 3100yds, Par 70, SSS 69, Course record 66.
Location   On B road connecting A419 & A429, on
outskirts of village of Oaksey. S of Cirencester
Telephone for further details

Hotel   ★★★ 68% Stratton House Hotel, Gloucester
Rd, CIRENCESTER
☎ 01285 651761 41 ⇆ ♋

OGBOURNE ST GEORGE   Map 04 SU27

Ogbourne Downs SN8 1TB
☎ 01672 841327 Fax 01672 841327
Downland turf and magnificent greens. Wind and slopes
make this one of the most challenging courses in Wiltshire.
Extensive views.
18 holes, 6353yds, Par 71, SSS 70, Course record 65.
Club membership 890.
Visitors   phone in advance. Handicap certificate required.
Societies   must apply for booking form in advance.
Green Fees not confirmed..
Cards   ⚐
Prof   Colin Harraway
Designer   J H Taylor
Facilities   Ⓧ ⍴ ⌂ ♨ ♀ ⚐ 🏠 ♣ 🎯 ✎ ⚐
Location   N side of village on A346

Hotel   ★★★ 72% Ivy House Hotel, High St,
MARLBOROUGH
☎ 01672 515333 28 ⇆ ♋

SALISBURY   Map 04 SU12

Salisbury & South Wilts Netherhampton SP2 8PR
☎ 01722 742645 Fax 01722 742645
e-mail: mail@salisburygolf.co.uk
Gently undulating and well drained parkland courses in
country setting with panoramic views of the cathedral and
surrounding country. A 27 hole course played in various
configurations.
*Main Course: 18 holes, 6485yds, Par 71, SSS 71, Course
record 61.*
Bibury Course: 9 holes, 2837yds, Par 34.
Club membership 1150.
Visitors   advisable to telephone in advance.
Societies   telephone,write or e-mail for information park.
Green Fees Main Course £25 per round;£30 per
day(£40/£55 weekends & bank holidays)Bibury
Course £9 per 9 holes;£12 per 18 holes(£12/£15
weekends & bank holidays).
Prof   John Cave/Geraldine Teschner
Designer   J H Taylor/S Gidman
Facilities   Ⓧ ⍴ ⌂ ♨ ♀ ⚐ 🏠 ♣ 🎯 ✎
Location   2m SW of Salisbury,on A3094

Hotel   ★★★ 65% Rose & Crown Hotel, Harnham Rd,
Harnham, SALISBURY
☎ 01722 399955 28 ⇆ ♋

SWINDON   Map 04 SU18

Broome Manor Golf Complex Pipers Way SN3 1RG
☎ 01793 532403 Fax 01793 433255
Two courses and a 34-bay floodlit driving range. Parkland
with water hazards, open fairways and short cut rough.
Walking is easy on gentle slopes.
18 holes, 6283yds, Par 71, SSS 70, Course record 62.
Broom Manor Golf complex: 9 holes, Par 33.
Club membership 800.
Visitors   pre-booking advised for 18 hole course,
payment of green fee is required at the time of
booking by credit card.
Societies   must be prebooked.
Green Fees £13 per round; £7.90 per 9 holes.
Cards   ▦ ▦ ▦ ▦ ▦ ⚐
Prof   Barry Sandry
Designer   Hawtree
Facilities   Ⓧ ⍴ ⌂ ♨ ♀ ⚐ 🏠 🎯 ✎ ⚐
Location   1.75m SE of town centre off B4006

Hotel   ★★★★ 65% Swindon Marriott Hotel, Pipers
Way, SWINDON ☎ 01793 512121 153 ⇆ ♋

TIDWORTH   Map 04 SU24

Tidworth Garrison Bulford Rd SP9 7AF
☎ 01980 842301 Fax 01980 842301
A breezy, dry downland course with lovely turf, fine
trees and views over Salisbury Plain and the surrounding
area. The 4th and 12th holes are notable. The 565-yard
14th, going down towards the clubhouse, gives the big
hitter a chance to let fly.
18 holes, 6320yds, Par 70, SSS 70, Course record 63.
Club membership 850.
Visitors   must contact in advance, weekend & bank
holiday bookings may not be made until
Thursday prior. ▶

Societies	Tue & Thu, bookings required 12-18 months in advance.
Green Fees	£27.50 per day(£35 weekends).
Prof	Terry Gosden
Designer	Donald Steel
Facilities	⊗)Ⅲ ┗ ♥ ♀ ⚐ ⛤ ⛳ ⛴ ∅
Location	W side of village off A338

Hotel	★★★ 63% Quality Hotel Andover, Micheldever Rd, ANDOVER ☎ 01264 369111 13 ⇔ ┌ Annexe36 ⇔ ┌

TOLLARD ROYAL   Map 03 ST91

Rushmore Park Golf Club SP5 5QB ☎ 01725 516326
Peaceful and testing parkland course situated on Cranborne Chase with far-reaching views. An undulating course with avenues of trees and well drained greens.
18 holes, 6100yds, Par 71, SSS 69.
Club membership 385.

Visitors	Must book in advance. Strict dress code enforced.
Societies	welcome by appointment.
Green Fees	not confirmed.
Cards	▭ ▭ ▭
Prof	Sean McDonagh
Designer	David Pottage/John Jacobs Developments
Facilities	⊗)Ⅲ by prior arrangement ┗ ♥ ♀ ⚐ ⛤ ⛳ ∅
Location	16m SW of Salisbury, entrance off the B3081 between Sixpenny Handley and Tollard Royal

Hotel	★★★ 67% Royal Chase Hotel, Royal Chase Roundabout, SHAFTESBURY ☎ 01747 853355 35 ⇔ ┌

UPAVON   Map 04 SU15

Upavon Douglas Av SN9 6BQ
☎ 01980 630787 & 630281 Fax 01980 630787
Downland course set on sides of infamous valley, with some wind affecting play. Includes a par 5 of 602 yards and finishing hole of 170 yards across a ravine.
18 holes, 6402yds, Par 71, SSS 71, Course record 69.
Club membership 600.

Visitors	must contact in advance and may not play before noon at weekends.
Societies	telephone in advance.
Green Fees	£24 per day; £18 per round (£20 per round weekends).
Cards	▭ ▭ ▭ ▭
Prof	Richard Blake
Designer	Richard Blake
Facilities	⊗)Ⅲ by prior arrangement ┗ ♥ ♀ ⚐ ⛤ ⛳ ⛴ ∅
& Leisure	hard tennis courts.
Location	1.5m SE of Upavon on A342 Andover road

Hotel	★★★ 64% Bear Hotel, Market Place, DEVIZES ☎ 01380 722444 24 ⇔ ┌

Looking for a driving range?
See the index at the back of the guide

WARMINSTER   Map 03 ST84

West Wilts Elm Hill BA12 0AU ☎ 01985 213133
Fax 01985 219809
A hilltop course among the Wiltshire downs on downland turf. Free draining, short, but a very good test of accurate iron play. Excellent greens and clubhouse facilities.
18 holes, 5709yds, Par 70, SSS 68, Course record 62.
Club membership 650.

Visitors	must contact in advance. Handicap certificate required.
Societies	apply by letter.
Green Fees	£20 per round (£25 weekends & bank holidays).
Prof	Andrew Lamb
Designer	J H Taylor
Facilities	⊗)Ⅲ ┗ ♥ ♀ ⚐ ⛤ ⛳ ∅
Location	N side of town centre off A350

Hotel	★★★★ 74% Bishopstrow House, WARMINSTER ☎ 01985 212312 32 ⇔ ┌

WOOTTON BASSETT   Map 04 SU08

Brinkworth Longmans Farm, Brinkworth SN15 5DG
☎ 01666 510277
Fairly long and open course with ditches and water hazards on the 2nd and 18th holes. Several testing par 3s with crosswinds and three long and tricky par 5s, notably the 4th, 8th and 14th holes.
18 holes, 5884yds, Par 70, SSS 70.
Club membership 100.

Visitors	welcome any time no contact needed.
Societies	telephone in advance or apply in writing.
Green Fees	not confirmed.
Designer	Jullian Sheppard
Facilities	┗ ♥ ♀ ⚐ ⛤ ⛳ ∅
Location	Just off B4042 between Malmesbury/Wootton Bassett

Hotel	★★★ 74% Marsh Farm Hotel, Coped Hall, WOOTTON BASSETT ☎ 01793 848044 11 ⇔ ┌ Annexe27 ⇔ ┌

Wiltshire Vastern SN4 7PB
☎ 01793 849999 Fax 01793 849988
e-mail: wiltsgc@btinternet.com
A Peter Alliss/Clive Clark design set in rolling Wiltshire downland countryside. A number of lakes add a challenge for both low and high handicappers.
18 holes, 6522yds, Par 72, SSS 71.
Club membership 800.

Visitors	must contact in advance.
Societies	contact in advance.
Green Fees	not confirmed.
Cards	▭ ▭ ▭ ▭
Prof	Andy Gray
Designer	Peter Allis & Clive Clark
Facilities	⊗)Ⅲ ┗ ♥ ♀ ⚐ ⛤ ⛳ ⛵ ⛴ ∅ ┌
Location	Leave M4 at junc 16, on A3102

Hotel	★★★ 74% Marsh Farm Hotel, Coped Hall, WOOTTON BASSETT ☎ 01793 848044 11 ⇔ ┌ Annexe27 ⇔ ┌

WORCESTERSHIRE

ALVECHURCH   Map 07 SP07

Kings Norton Brockhill Ln, Weatheroak B48 7ED
☎ 01564 826706 & 826789 Fax 01564 826955 e-mail: golf@kingsnortongc.demon.co.uk
A 27 hole Championship venue, 18 hole course 7000yds par 72 plus 12 hole par 3 course. Parkland with water hazards.
Weatheroak: 18 holes, 6748yds, Par 72, SSS 72, Course record 65.
Brockhill: 18 holes, 6648yds, Par 72, SSS 72.
Wythall: 18 holes, 6612yds, Par 72, SSS 72.
Club membership 1000.

Visitors	must contact in advance. No visitors at weekends.
Societies	must telephone in advance.
Green Fees	£37 per day; £31 per round.
Cards	〓 〓 〓 〓 〓
Prof	Kevin Hayward
Designer	F Hawtree
Facilities	⊗ ⽉ ㉨ ▼ ♀ ♨ 🏠 ⛳ ❧ 🏌 𝄢
Location	M42 junct3, off A435
Hotel	★★★★ 65% Hanover International Hotel & Club, Kidderminster Rd, BROMSGROVE ☎ 01527 576600 114 ⇄ 🐾

BEWDLEY   Map 07 SO77

Little Lakes Golf and Country Club Lye Head DY12 2UZ
☎ 01299 266385 Fax 01299 266178
e-mail: info@littlelakes.co.uk
A pleasant undulating 18 hole parkland course. A challenging test of golf with stunning views of the Worcestershire countryside.
18 holes, 5644yds, Par 69, SSS 68, Course record 63.
Club membership 400.

Visitors	advisable to telephone in advance.
Societies	must telephone in advance.
Green Fees	£15 per day (£20 per round weekends and bank holidays).
Cards	〓 〓 〓 〓
Prof	Mark A Laing
Designer	M Laing
Facilities	⊗ by prior arrangement ⽉ by prior arrangement ㉨ by prior arrangement ▼ by prior arrangement ♀ ♨ 🏠 ❧ 🏌 𝄢
& Leisure	hard tennis courts, heated outdoor swimming pool, fishing.
Location	2.25m W off A456
Hotel	★★ 63% The George Hotel, Load St, BEWDLEY ☎ 01299 402117 11 ⇄ 🐾

Wharton Park Longbank DY12 2QW
☎ 01299 405222 & 405163 Fax 01299 405121
18-hole championship-standard course in 140 acres of countryside. Some long Par 5s eg the 9th (594yds) as well as superb par 3 holes at 3rd, 10th, 15th make this a very challenging course.
18 holes, 6603yds, Par 72, SSS 71, Course record 66.
Club membership 500.

Visitors	must contact in advance. May not play weekend mornings.
Societies	prior booking required.
Green Fees	£27.50 per day; £20 per round (£25 weekends & bank holidays).
Cards	〓 〓 〓 〓 〓
Prof	Angus Hoare
Designer	Harold Swan
Facilities	⊗ ⽉ ㉨ ▼ ♀ ♨ 🏠 ❧ 🏌 𝄢
Location	Off A456 Bewdley bypass
Hotel	★★ 63% The George Hotel, Load St, BEWDLEY ☎ 01299 402117 11 ⇄ 🐾

BISHAMPTON   Map 03 SO95

Vale Golf Club Hill Furze Rd WR10 2LZ
☎ 01386 462781 Fax 01386 462597
e-mail: tvgcc@crownsportsplc
This course offers an American-style layout, with large greens, trees and bunkers and several water hazards. Its rolling fairways provide a testing round, as well as superb views of the Malvern Hills. Picturesque and peaceful.
International Course: 18 holes, 7174yds, Par 74, SSS 74, Course record 72.
Lenches Course: 9 holes, 5518yds, Par 70, SSS 66.
Club membership 650.

Visitors	booking up to one week in advance. Some weekend restrictions on International course.
Societies	must apply in advance. Some weekend restrictions.
Green Fees	International: £20 per round (£25 weekends) Lenchese: £10 per round.
Cards	〓 〓 〓 〓
Prof	Caroline Griffiths
Designer	Bob Sandon
Facilities	⊗ ⽉ ㉨ ▼ ♀ ♨ 🏠 ❧ 🏌 𝄢
Location	Signposted off A4538, between Evesham & Worcester
Hotel	★★ 66% The Chequers Inn, Chequers Ln, FLADBURY ☎ 01386 860276 & 860527 Fax 01386 861286 8 ⇄ 🐾

BLAKEDOWN   Map 07 SO87

Churchill and Blakedown Churchill Ln DY10 3NB
☎ 01562 700018 & 700200
Pleasant course on hilltop with extensive views.
9 holes, 6488yds, Par 72, SSS 71.
Club membership 400.

Visitors	with member only weekends & bank holidays. Handicap certificate required.
Societies	by arrangement through secretary.
Green Fees	£20 per 18 holes.
Facilities	⊗ ⽉ ㉨ ▼ ♀ ♨ 🏠 𝄢
Location	W side of village off A456
Hotel	★★★★ 67% Stone Manor Hotel, Stone, KIDDERMINSTER ☎ 01562 777555 52 ⇄ 🐾 Annexe5 ⇄ 🐾

Where to stay, where to eat?
Visit the AA internet site
www.theAA.com

BROADWAY   Map 04 SP03

Broadway Willersey Hill WR12 7LG
☎ 01386 853683 Fax 01386 858643
At the edge of the Cotswolds this downland course lies at an
altitude of 900 ft above sea level, with extensive views.
Natural contours and man made hazards mean that drives
have to be placed, approaches carefully judged and the
greens expertly read.
18 holes, 5970yds, Par 72, SSS 70, Course record 65.
Club membership 850.
Visitors   may not play Sat between Apr-Sep before 3pm.
                 Restricted play Sun. Must contact in advance.
Societies   Wed-Fri, must contact in advance.
Green Fees   £37 per day; £30 per round (£37 weekends &
                 bank holidays).
Cards   ▦ ▤ ▦ 🖩
Prof   Martyn Freeman
Designer   James Braid
Facilities   ⊗ ⫲ ⬥ 🍺 ♀ 🛆 🛍 ⛳ ⬥ 🛒 ⬧
Location   1.5m E on A44

Hotel   ★★★ 76% Dormy House Hotel, Willersey
                 Hill, BROADWAY ☎ 01386 852711
                 25 ⇆ ⧍ Annexe23 ⇆

BROMSGROVE   Map 07 SO97

Blackwell Agmore Rd, Blackwell B60 1PY
☎ 0121 445 1994 Fax 0121 445 4911
Pleasantly undulating parkland with a variety of trees. Laid
out in two 9-hole loops.
18 holes, 6230yds, Par 70, SSS 71.
Club membership 365.
Visitors   must contact in advance, must have handicap
                 certificate, may not play at weekends,
Societies   must contact in advance.
Green Fees   £50 per 18 holes (£60 per 27/36 holes).
Prof   Nigel Blake
Designer   Harry Colt
Facilities   ⊗ by prior arrangement ⫲ by prior arrangement
                 🍺 ♀ 🛆 🛍 ⛳ 🛒 ⬧
Location   2m W of Alvechurch

Hotel   ★★★★ 65% Hanover International Hotel &
                 Club, Kidderminster Rd, BROMSGROVE
                 ☎ 01527 576600 114 ⇆ ⧍

Bromsgrove Golf Centre Stratford Rd B60 1LD
☎ 01527 575886 & 570505 Fax 01527 570964
e-mail: enquiries@bromsgrovegolf.f9.co.uk
Gently undulating parkland course with large contoured
greens, generous tee surfaces and superb views over
Worcestershire. Tricky par 3 16th across a lake. Also 41 bay
floodlit driving range, floodlit practice bunker and clubhouse
with conference facilities.
18 holes, 5880yds, Par 68, SSS 68.
Club membership 900.
Visitors   dress restriction, no T-shirts, jeans, tracksuits
                 etc. 7 day booking facilities available.
Societies   packages available, apply in writing or
                 telephone.
Green Fees   £8.50 per 9 holes; £14.50 per 18 holes
                 (£11.50/£19weekends & bank holidays).

Bromsgrove Golf Centre

Cards   ▦ ▤ ▦ 🖩
Prof   Graeme Long/James Stratham
Designer   Hawtree & Son
Facilities   ⊗ ⫲ ⬥ 🍺 ♀ 🛆 🛍 ⛳ 🛒 ⬧ ⧍
Location   1m from Bromsgrove town centre at junct of
                 A38/A448

Hotel   ★★★★ 65% Hanover International Hotel &
                 Club, Kidderminster Rd, BROMSGROVE
                 ☎ 01527 576600 114 ⇆ ⧍

DROITWICH   Map 03 SO86

Droitwich Ford Ln WR9 0BQ
☎ 01905 774344 Fax 01905 797290
Undulating parkland course.
18 holes, 5976yds, Par 70, SSS 69, Course record 62.
Club membership 732.
Visitors   with member only weekends & bank holidays.
Societies   must apply by telephone and letter.
Green Fees   £26 per day/round.
Prof   C Thompson
Designer   J Braid/G Franks
Facilities   ⊗ ⫲ ⬥ 🍺 ♀ 🛆 🛍 ⬧
& Leisure   snooker.
Location   Off A38 Droitwich to Bromsgrove road,
                 midway between Droitwich and M5 junct 5

Hotel   ★★★★ 67% Chateau Impney Hotel,
                 DROITWICH SPA ☎ 01905 774411
                 67 ⇆ ⧍ Annexe53 ⇆ ⧍

Gaudet Luce Middle Ln, Hadzor WR9 7DP
☎ 01905 796375 Fax 01905 797245
e-mail: info@gaudet-luce.co.uk
A challenging 18-hole course with two contrasting 9-hole
loops. The front nine are long and fairly open, the back nine
are tight and compact requiring good positional and approach
play. Water features on several holes.
18 holes, 5887yds, Par 70, SSS 68.
Club membership 500.
Visitors   welcome, advisable to telephone in advance,
                 proper golfing attire required at all times.
Societies   telephone for details.
Green Fees   prices available from professional shop by
                 telephone.
Cards   ▦ ▤ ▦ 🖩
Prof   Phil Cundy
Designer   M A Laing
Facilities   ⊗ ⫲ ⬥ 🍺 ♀ 🛆 🛍 🛒 ⬧
Location   M5 junct 5, left at Tagwell road into Middle
                 Lane, 1st driveway on left to clubhouse   ▶

Hotel   ★★★★ 67% Chateau Impney Hotel, DROITWICH SPA ☎ 01905 774411 67 ⇄ ❦ Annexe53 ⇄ ❦

Ombersley Bishops Wood Rd, Lineholt, Ombersley WR9 0LE ☎ 01905 620747 Fax 01905 620047
Undulating course in beautiful countryside high above the edge of the Severn Valley. Covered driving range and putting green.
18 holes, 6139yds, Par 72, SSS 69, Course record 67.
Club membership 750.
Visitors   suitable dress expected, no jeans, shirts must have a collar.
Societies   telephone in advance.
Green Fees not confirmed.
Cards   💳
Prof   Graham Glenister
Designer   David Morgan
Facilities   ⊗ ⅏ ⓛ ♥ ♀ ♨ 🍴 🔾 ➴ ⚒ ♂ ᛣ
Location   3m W of Droitwich, off A449. At Mitre Oak pub, take A4025 to Stourport, signposted 400yds on left

Hotel   ★★★★ 65% Raven Hotel, Victoria Square, DROITWICH SPA ☎ 01905 772224 72 ⇄ ❦

FLADBURY   Map 03 SO94

Evesham Craycombe Links, Old Worcester Rd WR10 2QS ☎ 01386 860395 Fax 861356 e-mail: eveshamgolfclub@talk21.com
Parkland, heavily wooded, with the River Avon running alongside 5th and 14th holes. Good views. Nine greens played from eighteen different tees.
9 holes, 6415yds, Par 72, Course record 65.
Club membership 450.
Visitors   must contact in advance, and have a handicap certificate.
Societies   must apply by in advance by phone or writing.
Green Fees £20.
Prof   Dan Cummins
Facilities   ⊗ ⅏ ⓛ ♥ ♀ ♨ 🍴 🔾
Location   0.75m N on A4538

Hotel   ★★★ 71% The Evesham Hotel, Coopers Ln, Off Waterside, EVESHAM ☎ 01386 765566 & 0800 716969 (Res) Fax 01386 765443   39 ⇄ ❦ Annexe1 ⇄ ❦

HOLLYWOOD   Map 07 SP07

Gay Hill Hollywood Ln B47 5PP ☎ 0121 430 8544 & 474 6001 (pro) Fax 0121 436 7796
A meadowland course, some 7 miles from Birmingham.
18 holes, 6406yds, Par 72, SSS 72, Course record 64.
Club membership 740.
Visitors   must contact in advance. No visitors at weekends or bank holidays
Societies   telephone in advance.
Green Fees £28.50.
Prof   Andrew Potter
Facilities   ⊗ ⅏ ⓛ ♥ ♀ ♨ 🍴 🔾
Location   N side of village

Hotel   ★★★ 66% Regency Hotel, Stratford Rd, Shirley, SOLIHULL ☎ 0121 745 6119 112 ⇄ ❦

KIDDERMINSTER   Map 07 SO87

Habberley Low Trimpley DY11 5RG ☎ 01562 745756 Fax 01562 745756
Very hilly, wooded parkland course.
9 holes, 5401yds, Par 69, Course record 62.
Club membership 230.
Visitors   may only play weekends with a member, weekdays by prior arrangement.
Societies   telephone initially.
Green Fees £10 per round.
Facilities   ⊗ ⅏ ⓛ ♥ ♀ ♨
Location   2m NW of Kidderminster

Hotel   ★★★★ 67% Stone Manor Hotel, Stone, KIDDERMINSTER ☎ 01562 777555 52 ⇄ ❦ Annexe5 ⇄ ❦

Kidderminster Russell Rd DY10 3HT ☎ 01562 822303 Fax 01562 827866
e-mail: kidderminstergolfclub@hotmail.com
Parkland course with natural hazards and some easy walking.
18 holes, 6405yds, Par 72, SSS 71, Course record 65.
Club membership 860.
Visitors   with member only weekends & bank holidays. Must have a handicap certificate.
Societies   Thu only, apply in advance.
Green Fees £40 per day; £30 per round.
Prof   Nick Underwood
Facilities   ⊗ ⅏ ⓛ ♥ ♀ ♨ 🍴 🔾
Location   0.5m SE of town centre, signposted off A449

Hotel   ★★★★ 67% Stone Manor Hotel, Stone, KIDDERMINSTER ☎ 01562 777555 52 ⇄ ❦ Annexe5 ⇄ ❦

Wyre Forest Zortech Av DY11 7EX ☎ 01299 822682 Fax 01299 879433
Making full use of the existing contours, this interesting and challenging course is bounded by woodland and gives extensive views over the surrounding area. Well drained fairways and greens.
18 holes, 5790yds, Par 70, SSS 68, Course record 68.
Club membership 397.
Visitors   must telephone in advance.
Societies   brochure on request, deposit secures date, write or telephone.
Green Fees not confirmed.
Prof   Simon Price
Facilities   ♨ 🍴 🔾 ➴ ⚒ 🔾 ᛣ
Location   Approx half way between Kidderminster/Stourport, on the A451

Hotel   ★★★★ 71% Menzies Stourport Manor, Hartlebury Rd, STOURPORT-ON-SEVERN ☎ 0870 6003013   68 ⇄ ❦

AA Hotels that have special arrangements with golf courses are listed at the back of the guide

---

MALVERN WELLS Map 03 SO74

Worcestershire Wood Farm, Wood Farm Rd WR14 4PP
☎ 01684 575992 Fax 01684 575992 e-
mail: wgolf@talk21.com
Fairly easy walking on windy downland course with trees,
ditches and other natural hazards. Outstanding views of
Malvern Hills and Severn Valley. 17th hole (par 5) is
approached over a small lake.
18 holes, 6500yds, Par 71, SSS 72.
Club membership 750.

Visitors	handicap certificate required.
Societies	Apply in advance by telephone.
Green Fees	not confirmed.
Prof	Richard Lewis
Designer	J H Taylor
Facilities	⊗ ℳ ㄴ 里 ♀ ♨ 🏠 ♨ ✐
Location	2m S of Gt Malvern on B4209

Hotel ★★★♨ 74% The Cottage in the Wood Hotel,
Holywell Rd, Malvern Wells, MALVERN
☎ 01684 575859 8 ⇄ ♜ Annexe12 ⇄ ♜

REDDITCH Map 07 SP06

Abbey Hotel Golf & Country Club Dagnell End Rd
B98 7BD ☎ 01527 406500 (golf shop) Fax 01527 584112
Young parkland course with rolling fairways. A Site of
Special Scientific Interest, the course includes two fishing
lakes and is pleasant to play.
18 holes, 6561yds, Par 72, SSS 72.
Club membership 700.

Visitors	must contact in advance.
Societies	must apply in writing.

Green Fees not confirmed.
Prof S Edwards
Facilities ⊗ ℳ ㄴ 里 ♀ ♨ 🏠 ♨ 🏡 ♨ ♨ ✐ ⑂
& Leisure heated indoor swimming pool, fishing, sauna,
solarium, gymnasium.
Location 1.25m N off A441 on B4101

Hotel ★★★ 72% The Abbey Hotel Golf & Country
Club, Hither Green Ln, Dagnel End Rd,
Bordesley, REDDITCH
☎ 01527 406600 38 ⇄ ♜

Pitcheroak Plymouth Rd B97 4PB
☎ 01527 541054 Fax 01527 65216
Woodland course, hilly in places. There is also a putting
green and a practice ground.
9 holes, 4561yds, Par 65, SSS 62.
Club membership 200.

Visitors	no restrictions.
Societies	telephone to book.

Green Fees not confirmed.
Cards 🟦 🟥 🟥 🟥 🟦 🟦
Prof David Stewart
Facilities ⊗ ℳ ㄴ 里 ♀ ♨ 🏠 ♨ ✐
Location SW side of town centre off A448

Hotel ★★★ 66% Quality Hotel, Pool Bank,
Southcrest, REDDITCH
☎ 01527 541511 73 ⇄ ♜

Looking for a driving range?
See the index at the back of the guide

Set amidst a beautiful undulating
landscape in North Worcestershire.
The course offers a variety of
challenges from wooded areas to
water. Early in your round but
many holes offer welcome relief
with their spacious fairways.
A £4 million extension programme was
completed in September 2001 making the Abbey
the ideal venue to stay and play. All guests have
complimentary use of the new health club which
includes swimming pool and gymnasium.

**Hither Green Lane, Dagnell End Road,
Redditch, Worcestershire B98 9BE
Tel: 01528 406600 Fax: 01527 406514
www.theabbeyhotel.co.uk**

Redditch Lower Grinsty, Green Ln, Callow Hill B97 5PJ
☎ 01527 5430799(sec) & 546372(pro) Fax 01527 547413
Parkland course, the hazards including woods, ditches and
large ponds. The par 4, 14th is a testing hole.
18 holes, 6671yds, Par 72, SSS 72, Course record 68.
Club membership 650.
Visitors   with member only weekends & bank holidays,
                no visitors on competition days, advisable to
                telephone in advance.
Societies   apply in writing to secretary.
Green Fees £28 per round;£35 per day.
Prof   David Down
Designer   F Pennick
Facilities ⊗ ⫲ ⌱ ⯐ 🍴 ♀ ⯑ 🛈 ⦶ 🏌 ⟋
Location   2m SW

Hotel   ★★★ 66% Quality Hotel, Pool Bank,
                Southcrest, REDDITCH
                ☎ 01527 541511   73 ⇥ ⟋

TENBURY WELLS   Map 07 SO56

Cadmore Lodge Hotel & Country Club St Michaels,
Berrington Green WR15 8TQ
☎ 01584 810044 Fax 01584 810044
e-mail: info@cadmorelodge.demon.co.uk
A picturesque 9-hole course in a brook valley. Challenging
holes include the 1st and 6th over the lake, 8th over the
valley and 9th over hedges.
9 holes, 5132yds, Par 68, SSS 65.
Club membership 200.

Visitors   no restrictions but check availability.
Societies   telephone in advance.
Green Fees £10 per day(£14 weekends).
Cards   ▦ ▬ ▭ 🝙 📇 ⦿
Facilities ⊗ ⫲ ⌱ ⯐ ♀ ⟑ 🛈 ⟋
& Leisure   hard tennis courts, heated indoor swimming
                pool, fishing, sauna, gymnasium, pool table.
Location   From Tenbury take A4112 to Leominster, after
                approx 2m turn right for Berrington, 0.75 on left

---

Hotel   ★★ 66% Cadmore Lodge Hotel & Country
                Club, Berrington Green, St Michaels,
                TENBURY WELLS
                ☎ 01584 810044   14 ⇥ ⟋

WORCESTER   Map 03 SO85

Bank House Hotel Golf & Country Club Bransford
WR6 5JD ☎ 01886 833551 Fax 01886 832461
The Bransford course is designed as a 'Florida' style course
with fairways weaving between water courses, 13 lakes and
sculptured mounds with colouful plant displays. The 6,204yd
course has doglegs, island greens and tight fairways to
challenge all standards of player. The 10th, 16th and 18th
(The Devil's Elbow) are particularly tricky.
Bransford Course: 18 holes, 6204yds, Par 72, SSS 71,
Course record 65.
Club membership 380.

Visitors   all tee times must be booked, no play before
                9.30am.
Societies   contact the golf secretary, all tee times must be
                booked in advance.
Green Fees not confirmed.
Cards   ▦ ▬ ▭ 🝙 📇 ▧ ⦿
Prof   Craig George
Designer   Bob Sandow
Facilities ⊗ ⫲ ⌱ ⯐ ♀ ⯑ 🛈 ⟑ 🏌 ♀ ⦶ 🏌 ⟋ ⟋
& Leisure   outdoor swimming pool, sauna, solarium,
                gymnasium, spa pool.
Location   3m S of Worcester, A4103

Hotel   ★★★ 70% Bank House Hotel Golf & Country
                Club, Bransford, WORCESTER
                ☎ 01886 833551   68 ⇥ ⟋

Worcester Golf & Country Club Boughton Park WR2 4EZ
☎ 01905 422555 Fax 01905 749090
Fine parkland course with many trees, a lake, and views of
the Malvern Hills.
18 holes, 6251yds, Par 70, SSS 70, Course record 67.
Club membership 1000.
Visitors   must contact professional in advance. May not
                play at weekends
Societies   telephone in advance.
Green Fees not confirmed.
Prof   Colin Colenso
Designer   Dr A Mackenzie
Facilities ⊗ by prior arrangement ⫲ by prior arrangement
                ⌱ ⯐ ♀ ⯑ 🛈 ⟋
& Leisure   hard and grass tennis courts, squash.
Location   1.5m from city centre on A4103

Hotel   ★★★ 62% The Gifford Hotel, High St,
                WORCESTER ☎ 01905 726262 103 ⇥ ⟋

WYTHALL   Map 07 SP07

Fulford Heath Tanners Green Ln B47 6BH
☎ 01564 824758 Fax 01564 822629
A mature parkland course encompassing two classic par
threes. The 11th, a mere 149 yards, shoots from an elevated
tee through a channel of trees to a well protected green. The
16th, a 166 yard par 3, elevated green, demands a 140 yard
carry over an imposing lake.
18 holes, 6179yds, Par 70, SSS 70, Course record 66.
Club membership 750.
Visitors   with member only weekend & bank holidays.
             Handicap certificate required.
Societies   must apply in advance.
Green Fees £35.
Prof   Mike Herbert
Designer   Braid/Hawtree
Facilities   ⊗ 〗 ⤓ ⚊ ♀ ⚏ 🕏 ⚑
Location   1m SE off A435

Hotel   ★★★★ 66% Swallow St John's Hotel, 651
             Warwick Rd, SOLIHULL
             ☎ 0121 711 3000 178 ⇆ ⬧

YORKSHIRE, EAST RIDING OF

AUGHTON   Map 08 SE73

Oaks Aughton Common YO42 4PW
☎ 01757 288577 & 288007 Fax 01757 289029
e-mail: oaksgolfclub@hotmail.com
Built amongst mature woodland and six lakes in the
picturesque Derwent Ings and further enhanced by thousands
of specimen trees. Greens are built with substantial
moulding.
The Oaks: 18 holes, 6743yds, Par 72, SSS 72.
Club membership 680.
Visitors   weekdays only.
Societies   may play weekdays. Telephone in advance.
Green Fees £22 per round.
Cards   ⊟ ⬛ ⬛ ⬛ ⬛ ⬛
Prof   Joe Townhill
Designer   Julian Covey
Facilities   ⊗ 〗 ⤓ ⚊ ♀ ⚏ ⬧ ✈ ⚏ ⚑ ⛾
& Leisure   3 self-catering cottages with own putting greens.
Location   1m N of Bubwith on B1228

Hotel   ★★★ 75% The Parsonage Country House
             Hotel, York Rd, ESCRICK
             ☎ 01904 728111   12 ⇆ ⬧ Annexe9 ⇆ ⬧

BEVERLEY   Map 08 TA03

Beverley & East Riding The Westwood HU17 8RG
☎ 01482 868757 Fax 01482 868757
Picturesque parkland course with some hard walking and
natural hazards - trees and gorse bushes. Also cattle (spring
to autumn); horse-riders are an occasional hazard in the early
morning.
Westwood: 18 holes, 6127yds, Par 69, SSS 69,
Course record 65.
Club membership 530.

Visitors   must contact in advance.
Societies   telephone 01482 868757, then written
             confirmation.
Green Fees £17 per day; £13 per round (£22/£17 weekends).
Prof   Alex Ashby
Facilities   ⊗ 〗 ⤓ ⚊ ♀ ⚏ 🕏 ⚑ ⚑
Location   1m SW on B1230

Hotel   ★★★ 67% Beverley Arms Hotel, North Bar
             Within, BEVERLEY
             ☎ 01482 869241   56 ⇆ ⬧

BRANDESBURTON   Map 08 TA14

Hainsworth Park Burton Holme YO25 8RT
☎ 01964 542362 Fax 01964 542362
A parkland course with easy walking.
18 holes, 6435yds, Par 71, SSS 71.
Club membership 500.
Visitors   contact in advance.
Societies   telephone initially.
Green Fees not confirmed.
Cards   ⊟ ⬛ ⬛ ⬛ ⬛
Prof   Paul Binnington
Facilities   ⊗ 〗 ⤓ ⚊ ♀ ⚏ ⬧ ⚑ ⬧ ✈ ⚏ ⚑
& Leisure   grass tennis courts, fishing.
Location   SW side of village on A165

Hotel   ★★ 68% Burton Lodge Hotel,
             BRANDESBURTON
             ☎ 01964 542847 7 ⇆ ⬧ Annexe2 ⇆ ⬧

BRIDLINGTON   Map 08 TA16

Bridlington Belvedere Rd YO15 3NA
☎ 01262 606367 Fax 01262 606367
Clifftop, seaside course, windy at times, with hazards of
bunkers, ponds, ditches and trees.
18 holes, 6638yds, Par 72, SSS 72, Course record 66.
Club membership 600.
Visitors   must contact in advance, professional 01262
             674721 limited at weekends.
Societies   telephone bookings in advance.
Green Fees £18 per round,£25 per day (£28 per round
             weekends).
Prof   Anthony Howarth
Designer   James Braid
Facilities   ⊗ 〗 ⤓ ⚊ ♀ ⚏ ⬧ ⚑ ⬧ ✈ ⚏ ⚑
Location   1m S off A165

Hotel   ★★★ 69% Revelstoke Hotel, 1-3 Flamborough
             Rd, BRIDLINGTON
             ☎ 01262 672362   25 ⇆ ⬧

Bridlington Links Flamborough Rd, Marton YO15 1DW
☎ 01262 401584 Fax 01262 401702
Main: 18 holes, 6719yds, Par 72, SSS 72, Course record 70.
Location   On the B1255 between Bridlington and
              Flamborough
Telephone for further details

Hotel   ★★★ 67% Expanse Hotel, North Marine Dr,
              BRIDLINGTON ☎ 01262 675347 48 ⇌ ⋔

BROUGH   Map 08 SE92

Brough Cave Rd HU15 1HB
☎ 01482 667291 Fax 01482 669873
e-mail: gt@brough-golfclub.co.uk
Parkland course, where accurate positioning of the tee ball is
required for good scoring.
18 holes, 6075yds, Par 68, SSS 69, Course record 64.
Club membership 700.
Visitors   must have handicap certificate and contact in
              advance.
Societies   apply by letter.
Green Fees   £30 per round; £40 per day(£40/£50 weekends
              & bank holidays).
Prof   Gordon Townhill
Facilities   ⊗ ⽊ ⌄ ♥ ♀ ⚲ 🏠 ⊤ ∮
Location   0.5m N

Hotel   ★★★ 62% The Humber Crown Hotel, Ferriby
              High Rd, NORTH FERRIBY
              ☎ 01482 645212 95 ⇌ ⋔

COTTINGHAM   Map 08 TA03

Cottingham Woodhill Way HU16 5RZ
☎ 01482 846030 Fax 01482 845932
e-mail: jane@cottinghamgolf.totalserve.co.uk
Gently undulating parkland course incorporating many
natural features, including lateral water hazards, several
ponds on the approach to greens, and rolling fairways.
18 holes, 6459yds, Par 72, SSS 71, Course record 66.
Club membership 600.
Visitors   may book by telephone in advance, times
              available weekdays and weekends.
Societies   deposit required and confirmation in writing.
              After 2pm weekends.
Green Fees   £16 per round (£24 weekends & bank holidays).
Cards   ▨ ▨▨ ⨾
Prof   Chris Gray
Designer   Terry Litten
Facilities   ⊗ ⽊ ⌄ ♥ ♀ ⚲ 🏠 ⊤ ∮ ₵
& Leisure   heated indoor swimming pool, sauna,
              gymnasium.
Location   4m from A63/M62 on A164. Turn off to
              Cottingham on B1233, in 100yds turn left into
              Woodhill Way

Hotel   ★★ 68% The Rowley Manor Hotel, Rowley
              Rd, LITTLE WEIGHTON
              ☎ 01482 848248 16 ⇌ ⋔

Entries with a green background
identify courses considered to be
particularly interesting

DRIFFIELD (GREAT)   Map 08 TA05

Driffield Sunderlandwick YO25 9AD
☎ 01377 253116 Fax 01377 240599
An easy walking, mature parkland course set within the
beautiful Sunderlandwick Estate.
18 holes, 6215yds, Par 70, SSS 69, Course record 67.
Club membership 693.
Visitors   must book in advance and adhere to club dress
              rule.
Societies   apply in writing or telephone.
Green Fees   not confirmed.
Prof   Dennis Taylor
Facilities   ⊗ ⽊ ⌄ ♥ ♀ ⚲ 🏠 ∮
& Leisure   fishing.
Location   2m S off A164

Hotel   ★★★ 71% Bell Hotel, 46 Market Place,
              DRIFFIELD ☎ 01377 256661 16 ⇌ ⋔

FLAMBOROUGH   Map 08 TA27

Flamborough Head Lighthouse Rd YO15 1AR
☎ 01262 850333 & 850417 & 850683
Fax 01262 850279 e-mail: fhgc@cwcom.net
Undulating seaside course.
18 holes, 5976yds, Par 70, SSS 69, Course record 70.
Club membership 500.
Visitors   welcome but may not play; before 1pm Sun,
              Wed between 10.30 & 1.30, Sat between 11.30
              & 12.30.
Societies   must contact in advance.
Green Fees   £18 per day; £15 per round (£20 per round
              weekends & bank holidays).
Facilities   ⊗ ⽊ ⌄ ♥ ♀ ⚲ 🏠 ⚲ ∮
Location   2m E off B1259

Hotel   ★★ 65% Flaneburg Hotel & Restaurant,
              North Marine Rd, FLAMBOROUGH
              ☎ 01262 850284 13 ⋔

HESSLE   Map 08 TA02

Hessle Westfield Rd, Raywell HU16 5YL
☎ 01482 650171 & 650190 (Prof) Fax 01482 652679
Well-wooded downland course with easy walking. The
greens, conforming to USGA specification, are large and
undulating with excellent drainage, enabling play throughout
the year.
18 holes, 6604yds, Par 72, SSS 72, Course record 68.
Club membership 720.
Visitors   not Tue between 9-1 and may not play before
              11am on Sat & Sun.
Societies   by prior arrangement.
Green Fees   not confirmed.
Prof   Grahame Fieldsend
Designer   D Thomas/P Allis
Facilities   ⊗ ⽊ ⌄ ♥ ♀ ⚲ 🏠 ∮
Location   3m SW of Cottingham

Hotel   ★★★ 62% The Humber Crown Hotel, Ferriby
              High Rd, NORTH FERRIBY
              ☎ 01482 645212 95 ⇌ ⋔

HORNSEA   Map 08 TA14

Hornsea Rolston Rd HU18 1XG
☎ 01964 532020 Fax 01964 532020
Flat, parkland course with good greens.
18 holes, 6685yds, Par 72, SSS 72, Course record 66.
Club membership 600.
Visitors   with member only at weekends until 3pm. Must
               contact in advance.
Societies   contact Secretary in advance.
Green Fees   £30 per day; £22 per round.
Prof   Stretton Wright
Facilities   ⊗ ⓑ ♥ ♀ ⚲ 🍴 ⛳ ♐ ∅
Location   1m S on B1242, follow signs for Hornsea
               Freeport

Hotel   ★★★ 67% Beverley Arms Hotel, North Bar
               Within, BEVERLEY
               ☎ 01482 869241   56 ⇌ ☞

HULL   Map 08 TA02

Ganstead Park Longdales Ln, Coniston HU11 4LB
☎ 01482 817754 Fax 01482 817754
e-mail: secretary@gansteadpark
Parkland course, easy walking, with water features.
18 holes, 6801yds, Par 72, SSS 73, Course record 62.
Club membership 500.
Visitors   contact in advance.
Societies   telephone in advance.
Green Fees   £24 per day; £18 per round; (£26 per round
               weekends).
Prof   Michael J Smee
Designer   P Green
Facilities   ⊗ ⫰ ⓑ ♥ ♀ ⚲ 🍴 ⛳ ♐ ↘ ♣ ∅
Location   6m NE on A165

Hotel   ★★★ 65% Quality Hotel Hull, 170 Ferensway,
               HULL ☎ 01482 325087 155 ⇌ ☞

Hull The Hall, 27 Packman Ln HU10 7TJ
☎ 01482 658919 Fax 01482 658919
Parkland course.
18 holes, 6242yds, Par 70, SSS 70.
Club membership 840.
Visitors   only weekdays. Contact professional 01482
               653074.
Societies   Mon Tue Thu & Fri by prior arrangement.
Green Fees   £32 per day; £26.50 per round.
Prof   David Jagger
Designer   James Braid
Facilities   ⊗ ⫰ ⓑ ♥ ♀ ⚲ 🍴 ∅
Location   5m W of city centre off A164

Hotel   ★★★ 72% Willerby Manor Hotel, Well Ln,
               WILLERBY ☎ 01482 652616   51 ⇌ ☞

Springhead Park Willerby Rd HU5 5JE ☎ 01482 656309
Municipal parkland course with tight, tree-lined, undulating
fairways.
18 holes, 6402yds, Par 71, SSS 71.
Club membership 667.
Visitors   welcome ex Sun (tee reserved).
Green Fees   not confirmed.
Prof   Barry Herrington
Facilities   ⓑ ⛳
Location   5m W off A164

Hotel   ★★★ 72% Willerby Manor Hotel, Well Ln,
               WILLERBY ☎ 01482 652616   51 ⇌ ☞

Sutton Park Salthouse Rd HU8 9HF
☎ 01482 374242 Fax 01482 701428
Municipal parkland course.
18 holes, 6251yds, Par 70, SSS 69, Course record 67.
Club membership 300.
Visitors   no restrictions.
Societies   prior arrangement via club, telephone and
               confirm in writing.
Green Fees   not confirmed.
Prof   To be appointed
Facilities   ⊗ by prior arrangement ⫰ by prior arrangement
               ⓑ ♥ ♀ ⚲ 🍴 ♐ ∅
Location   3m NE on B1237 off A165

Hotel   ★★★ 65% Quality Hotel Hull, 170 Ferensway,
               HULL ☎ 01482 325087 155 ⇌ ☞

SOUTH CAVE   Map 08 SE93

Cave Castle Hotel & Country Club Church Hill,
South Cave HU15 2EU
☎ 01430 421286 & 422245 Fax 01430 421118
An undulating meadow and parkland course at the foot of the
Wolds, with superb views. Golf breaks are available.
18 holes, 6500yds, Par 73, SSS 72, Course record 71.
Club membership 450.
Visitors   must contact in advance, may not play before
               11am weekends/bank holidays.
Societies   by arrangement with Manager.
Green Fees   £15 (£20 weekends & bank holidays).
Cards   ▨▨ ▨▨ ▨
Prof   Stephen MacKinder
Designer   Mrs N Freling
Facilities   ⊗ ⫰ ⓑ ♥ ♀ ⚲ 🍴 ⛳ ♐ 🏊 ↘ ♣ ∅
& Leisure   heated indoor swimming pool, fishing, sauna,
               solarium, gymnasium.
Location   1m from A63

Hotel   ★★★ 62% The Humber Crown Hotel, Ferriby
               High Rd, NORTH FERRIBY
               ☎ 01482 645212   95 ⇌ ☞

WITHERNSEA   Map 08 TA32

Withernsea Chesnut Av HU19 2PG ☎ 01964 612078
Exposed seaside links with narrow, undulating fairways,
bunkers and small greens.
9 holes, 5907yds, Par 72, SSS 69.
Club membership 300.
Visitors   with member only at weekends before 3pm.
Societies   apply in writing/telephone
Green Fees   not confirmed.
Prof   Graham Harrison
Facilities   ⊗ ⫰ ⓑ ♥ ♀ ⚲ 🍴
Location   S side of town centre off A1033

Hotel   ★★★ 65% Quality Hotel Hull, 170 Ferensway,
               HULL ☎ 01482 325087 155 ⇌ ☞

Where to stay, where to eat?
Visit the AA internet site
www.theAA.com

YORKSHIRE, NORTH

### ALDWARK									Map 08 SE46

Aldwark Manor YO61 1UF
☎ 01347 838353 Fax 01347 830007
An easy walking, scenic 18-hole parkland course with holes both sides of the River Ure. The course surrounds the Victorian Aldwark Manor Golf Hotel. A warm welcome to society and corporate days.
18 holes, 6171yds, Par 71, SSS 70, Course record 69.
Club membership 400.

Visitors		must contact in advance, restricted weekends.
Societies	must telephone in advance.
Green Fees	£30 per day; £25 per round (£35/£30 weekends & bank holiday.
Cards		🃏 💳 💳 💳 💳 💳
Prof		Phil Harrison
Facilities	⊗ ⅷ � ⅐ ⅐ ♨ 🝙 🝙 ⚲ ⚷ ⚷
& Leisure	heated indoor swimming pool, fishing, sauna, gymnasium.
Location	5m SE of Boroughbridge off A1, 12m NW of York off A19

Hotel		★★★ 69% Aldwark Manor Hotel, Golf & Country Club, ALDWARK
			☎ 01347 838146 & 838251 Fax 01347 838867
			25 ➩ ℟ Annexe3rm(2 ➩ ℟)
			See advertisement on page 302

### BEDALE									Map 08 SE28

Bedale Leyburn Rd DL8 1EZ
☎ 01677 422451 Fax 01677 427143
e-mail: bedalegolfclub@aol.com
Secluded parkland course with many trees and water features. A quiet, testing course ideal for beginners and the more adept golfer.
18 holes, 6610yds, Par 72, SSS 72, Course record 68.
Club membership 600.
Visitors		welcome when course is free, contact Manager to book.
Societies	must apply in advance.
Green Fees	£20 per day (£30 weekends & bank holidays).
Prof		Tony Johnson
Facilities	⊗ ⅷ ⅐ ⅐ ♨ 🝙 ⚲ ⚷ ⚷
Location	0.25 N of town on A684

Hotel		★ 69% Buck Inn, THORNTON WATLASS
			☎ 01677 422461 7rm(5 ➩ ℟)

### BENTHAM									Map 07 SD66

Bentham Robin Ln LA2 7AG ☎ 01524 262455
Moorland course with glorious views.
9 holes, 5760yds, Par 70, SSS 69, Course record 69.
Club membership 480.
Visitors		no restrictions.
Societies	must apply in advance.
Green Fees	£15 per day.
Facilities	⊗ ⅷ ⅐ ⅐ ♨ ⚲
Location	N side of High Bentham

Guesthouse Ferncliffe Country Guest House, 55 Main St, INGLETON ☎ 015242 42405 5 ℟

### CATTERICK GARRISON						Map 08 SE29

Catterick Leyburn Rd DL9 3QE
☎ 01748 833268 Fax 01748 833268
Scenic parkland/moorland course of Championship standard, with good views of the Pennines and Cleveland hills. Testing 1st and 6th holes.
18 holes, 6329yds, Par 71, SSS 70, Course record 68.
Club membership 700.
Visitors		tee reservation system in operation telephone professional shop 01748 833671. May not play before 10am Tue/Thu/weekends and bank holidays.
Societies	by arrangement.
Green Fees	£27 per day; £24 per round (£33 day/round weekends and bank holidays).
Prof		Andy Marshall
Designer	Arthur Day
Facilities	⊗ ⅷ ⅐ ⅐ ♨ 🝙 ⚲ ⚷ 🝙 ⚷ ⚷
Location	0.5m W of Catterick Garrison Centre

Hotel		★★ 68% King's Head Hotel, Market Place, RICHMOND ☎ 01748 850220
			26 ➩ ℟ Annexe4 ➩ ℟

### COPMANTHORPE							Map 08 SE54

Pike Hills Tadcaster Rd YO23 3UW
☎ 01904 700797 Fax 01904 700797
Parkland course surrounding nature reserve. Level terrain.
18 holes, 6146yds, Par 71, SSS 70, Course record 67.
Club membership 750.
Visitors		welcome weekdays, with member only weekends & bank holidays.
Societies	must apply in advance.
Green Fees	£26 per day; £20 per round.
Prof		Ian Gradwell
Facilities	⊗ ⅷ ⅐ ⅐ ♨ 🝙 ⚲ 🝙 ⚷ ⚷
Location	3m SW of York on A64

Hotel		★★★★ 64% Swallow Hotel, Tadcaster Rd, YORK ☎ 01904 701000 112 ➩ ℟

### EASINGWOLD								Map 08 SE56

Easingwold Stillington Rd YO61 3ET
☎ 01347 821964 (Prof) & 822474 (Sec) Fax 01347 822474
e-mail: brian@easingwold-golf-club.fsnet.co.uk
Parkland course with easy walking. Trees are a major feature and on six holes water hazards come into play.
18 holes, 6627yds, Par 72, SSS 72, Course record 67.
Club membership 750.

▶

Visitors	prior enquiry essential.
Societies	prior application in writing essential.
Green Fees	£30 per day; £25 per round (£30 weekends).
Prof	John Hughes
Designer	Hawtree
Facilities	⊗)Ⅲ ╚ ■ ♀ ⚐ ☎ ⚒ ♂ ↯ (
Location	1m S of Easingwold, 12m N of York

Hotel	★★ 67% George Hotel, Market Place, EASINGWOLD ☎ 01347 821698 15 ⇆

FILEY   Map 08 TA18

Filey West Av YO14 9BQ
☎ 01723 513293 Fax 01723 514952
Parkland course with good views. Stream runs through course. Testing 9th and 13th holes.
18 holes, 6112yds, Par 70, SSS 69, Course record 64.
Club membership 900.

Visitors	must telephone to reserve tee time.
Societies	contact by telephone.
Green Fees	not confirmed.
Prof	Gary Hutchinson
Designer	Braid
Facilities	⊗)Ⅲ ╚ ■ ♀ ⚐ ☎ ↯ ➤ ⚒ ♂
Location	0.5m S of Filey

Hotel	★★ 68% Wrangham House Hotel, 10 Stonegate, HUNMANBY ☎ 01723 891333 8 ⇆ ░ Annexe4 ⇆ ░

GANTON   Map 08 SE97

Ganton YO12 4PA
☎ 01944 710329 Fax 01944 710922
Championship course, heathland, gorse-lined fairways and heavily bunkered; variable winds. The opening holes make full use of the contours of the land and the approach to the second demands the finest touch. The fourth is considered as one of the best holes on the outward half with its shot across a valley to a plateau green, the surrounding gorse punishing anything less than a perfect shot.
18 holes, 6734yds, Par 72, SSS 73, Course record 65.
Club membership 500.

Visitors	by prior arrangement. Restricted play at weekends.
Societies	prior arrangement in writing.
Green Fees	£55 per round/day (£65 weekends & bank holidays).
Cards	☷ ▆ ▣ ▩ ▩
Prof	Gary Brown
Designer	Dunn/Vardon/Braid/Colt
Facilities	⚐ ☎ ↯ ➤ ⚒ ♂
Location	11m SW of Scarborough on A64

Hotel	★★★ 63% East Ayton Lodge Country House, Moor Ln, Forge Valley, EAST AYTON ☎ 01723 864227 11 ⇆ ░ Annexe20 ⇆ ░

AA Hotels that have special arrangements with golf courses are listed at the back of the guide

---

HARROGATE   Map 08 SE35

Harrogate Forest Ln Head, Starbeck HG2 7TF
☎ 01423 862999 Fax 01423 860073
e-mail: hon.secretary@harrogate-gc.co.uk
One of Yorkshire's oldest and best courses was designed in 1897 by 'Sandy' Herd. A perfect example of golf architecture, its greens and fairways offer an interesting but fair challenge. The undulating parkland course once formed part of the ancient Forest of Knaresborough. Excellent clubhouse.
18 holes, 6241yds, Par 69, SSS 70, Course record 64.
Club membership 650.

Visitors	advisable to contact professional in advance, weekend play limited.
Societies	must contact in writing or intially by telephone.
Green Fees	£35 per day; £30 per round (£40 day/round weekend).
Cards	☷ ▆ ▣ ▩ ▩ ▩ ▩
Prof	Paul Johnson
Designer	Sandy Herd
Facilities	⊗)Ⅲ ╚ ■ ♀ ⚐ ☎ ⚒ ♂
& Leisure	snooker.
Location	2.25m N on A59

Hotel	★★ 71% The White House, 10 Park Pde, HARROGATE ☎ 01423 501388 10 ⇆ ░

Oakdale Oakdale Glen HG1 2LN
☎ 01423 567162 & 567188 Fax 01423 536030
A pleasant, undulating parkland course which provides a good test of golf for the low handicap player without intimidating the less proficient. A special feature is an attractive stream which comes in to play on four holes. Excellent views from the clubhouse which has good facilities.
18 holes, 6456yds, Par 71, SSS 71, Course record 61.
Club membership 1034.

Visitors	no party bookings weekends.
Societies	telephone followed by letter.
Green Fees	£27 per 18 holes; £40 per day (£32 per 18 holes weekends & bank holidays).
Prof	Clive Dell
Designer	Dr McKenzie
Facilities	⊗ ╚ ■ ♀ ⚐ ☎ ↯ ⚒ ♂
Location	N side of town centre off A61

Hotel	★★★ 71% Grants Hotel, 3-13 Swan Rd, HARROGATE ☎ 01423 560666 42 ⇆ ░

Rudding Park Hotel and Golf Rudding Park, Follifoot HG3 1JH ☎ 01423 872100 Fax 01423 873400
e-mail: sales@ruddingpark.com
The course provides panoramic views over the surrounding countryside and good drainage makes it playable for most of the year. Societies are particularly welcome.
Rudding Park Hotel& Golf: 18 holes, 6871yds, Par 72, SSS 73, Course record 65.
Club membership 329.

Visitors	handicap certificate required, tee reservation available 7 days in advance.
Societies	apply by telephone in advance.

▶

Green Fees £30 per day; £19.50 per 18 holes (£40/£23 weekends).
Cards ⬚⬚⬚⬚⬚⬚
Prof M & N Moore/P Jones
Designer Martin Hawtree
Facilities ⊗⏐▦▯▮♀⛉🏠⛳🏌🛒⚮♀
& Leisure heated outdoor swimming pool.
Location 2m SE of Harrogate town centre, off A658 follow brown tourist signs

Rudding Park House & Hotel

Hotel ★★★★ 78% Rudding Park House & Hotel, Rudding Park, Follifoot, HARROGATE ☎ 01423 871350 50 ⇄ ☏

HOWDEN   Map 08 SE72

Boothferry Park Spaldington Ln DN14 7NG
☎ 01430 430364 Fax 01430 430567
Pleasant meadowland course in the Vale of York with interesting natural dykes creating extra challenge on some holes. The par 3 5th over water will test your nerve.
18 holes, 6651yds, Par 73, SSS 72, Course record 64.
Club membership 500.
Visitors must contact in advance, tee times bookable.
Societies must contact for booking form.
Green Fees £10(£15 weekends).
Prof Nigel Bundy
Designer Donald Steel
Facilities ⊗⏐▦▯▮♀⛉🏠⛳🛒⚮♀
Location 2.5m N of Howden off B1228

Hotel ★★ 71% Clifton Hotel, 155 Boothferry Rd, GOOLE ☎ 01405 761336 9rm(8 ⇄ ☏)

KIRKBYMOORSIDE   Map 08 SE68

Kirkbymoorside Manor Vale YO62 6EG
☎ 01751 431525 Fax 01751 433190
e-mail: info@kirkbymoorsidegolf.co.uk
Hilly parkland course with narrow fairways, gorse and hawthorn bushes. Beautiful views.
18 holes, 6101yds, Par 69, SSS 69, Course record 65.
Club membership 650.
Visitors are advised to contact in advance, may not play before 9.30 or between 12.30-1.30.
Societies must apply in advance.
Green Fees £20 per day (£27 weekends).
Cards ⬚⬚⬚⬚
Prof Chris Tyson

Facilities ⊗⏐▦▯▮♀⛉🏠⛳♀
& Leisure gymnasium.
Location N side of village

Hotel ★★ 65% George & Dragon Hotel, 17 Market Place, KIRKBYMOORSIDE ☎ 01751 433334 11 ⇄ ☏ Annexe7 ⇄ ☏

KNARESBOROUGH   Map 08 SE35

Knaresborough Boroughbridge Rd HG5 0QQ
☎ 01423 862690 Fax 01423 869345
Undulating parkland course with mature trees and two water features in attractive rural setting.
18 holes, 6433yds, Par 70, SSS 71, Course record 67.
Club membership 802.
Visitors restricted start times summer weekends.
Societies apply by telephone or letter, no bookings for Sat, Sun or Tue.
Green Fees not confirmed.
Prof Gary J Vickers
Designer Hawtree
Facilities ⊗⏐▦▯▮♀⛉🏠⛳♀
Location 1.25 N on A6055

Hotel ★★★ 69% Dower House Hotel, Bond End, KNARESBOROUGH ☎ 01423 863302 28 ⇄ ☏ Annexe3 ⇄ ☏

MALTON   Map 08 SE77

Malton & Norton Welham Park, Norton YO17 9QE
☎ 01653 697912 Fax 01653 697912
e-mail: maltonandnorton@golfcl.fsnet.co.uk
Parkland course, consisting of 3 nine hole loops, with panoramic views of the moors. Very testing 1st hole (564 yds dog-leg, left).
Welham Course: 18 holes, 6456yds, Par 72, SSS 71.
Park Course: 18 holes, 6242yds, Par 72, SSS 70.
Derwent Course: 18 holes, 6286yds, Par 72, SSS 70.
Club membership 825.
Visitors anytime except during competitions.
Societies telephone and confirm in writing.
Green Fees £24 per day/round (£30 weekends & bank holidays).
Cards ⬚⬚⬚⬚
Prof S Robinson
Facilities ⊗⏐▦▯▮♀⛉🏠⛳♀
Location Approx 20m E of York/0.75m of Malton

Hotel ★★★♨ 72% Burythorpe House Hotel, Burythorpe, MALTON ☎ 01653 658200 11 ⇄ ☏ Annexe5 ⇄ ☏

MASHAM   Map 08 SE28

Masham Burnholme, Swinton Rd HG4 4HT
☎ 01765 688054 Fax 01765 688054
Flat parkland course crossed by River Burn, which comes into play on several holes.
9 holes, 6068yds, Par 70, SSS 69, Course record 73.
Club membership 327.
Visitors must play with member at weekends & bank holidays.
Societies write or telephone well in advance.
Green Fees not confirmed.

▶

Facilities ⊗ by prior arrangement ⅏ by prior arrangement
    ⓑ by prior arrangement ♥ by prior
    arrangement ♀ ⅄
Location 8m from junction of B6267 off A1 signposted
    Thirsk/Masham. Then 1m SW off A6108

Hotel ★ 69% Buck Inn, THORNTON WATLASS
    ☎ 01677 422461 7rm(5 ➼ ☏)

MIDDLESBROUGH   Map 08 NZ41

Middlesbrough Brass Castle Ln, Marton TS8 9EE
☎ 01642 311515 Fax 01642 319607
e-mail: golf@brass45.fsbusiness.co.uk
Undulating parkland course, prevailing winds. Testing 6th,
12th and 15th holes.
18 holes, 6278yds, Par 70, SSS 70, Course record 63.
Club membership 960.
Visitors restricted Tue & Sat.
Societies Wed, Thu & Fri only. Must contact the club in
    advance.
Green Fees £32(£37 weekends & bank holidays).
Prof Don Jones
Designer Baird
Facilities ⊗ ⅏ ⓑ ♥ ♀ ⅄ ⓐ ➹ ♨ ⌀
& Leisure snooker table.
Location 4m S off A172

Hotel ★★★ 71% Parkmore Hotel, 636 Yarm Rd,
    Eaglescliffe, STOCKTON-ON-TEES
    ☎ 01642 786815 55 ⇌ ☏

Middlesbrough Municipal Ladgate Ln TS5 7YZ
☎ 01642 315533 Fax 01642 300726
Parkland course with good views. The front nine holes have
wide fairways and large, often well-guarded greens while the
back nine demand shots over tree-lined water hazards and
narrow entrances to subtly contoured greens. Driving range.
18 holes, 6333yds, Par 71, SSS 70, Course record 67.
Club membership 630.
Visitors book on the day weekdays, 7days in advance for
    weekends & bank holidays.
Societies apply in writing giving at least 2 weeks in
    advance.
Green Fees not confirmed.
Prof Alan Hope
Designer Shuttleworth
Facilities ⓑ ♥ ♀ ⅄ ⓐ ➹ ♨ ⌀ ⌀ ⓣ
Location 2m S of Middlesbrough on the A174

Hotel ★★★ 71% Parkmore Hotel, 636 Yarm Rd,
    Eaglescliffe, STOCKTON-ON-TEES
    ☎ 01642 786815 55 ⇌ ☏

NORTHALLERTON   Map 08 SE39

Romanby Yafforth Rd DL7 0PE
☎ 01609 779988 Fax 01609 779084
e-mail: grant@romanbygolf.co.uk
Set in natural undulating terrain with the River Wiske
meandering through the course it offers a testing round of
golf for all abilities. In addition to the river, two lakes come
into play on the 2nd, 5th and 11th holes. 12-bay floodlit
driving range.
18 holes, 6663yds, Par 72, SSS 72, Course record 72.
Club membership 575.

Visitors welcome everyday please book tee time in
    advance.
Societies contact Grant McDonnell for details, tel 01609
    778855.
Green Fees not confirmed.
Cards ⊞ ⏍ ⏍ ⏍ ⌀
Prof Tim Jenkins
Designer Will Adamson
Facilities ⊗ ⅏ ⓑ ♥ ♀ ⅄ ⓐ ⌀ ➹ ♨ ⌀ ⓣ
& Leisure 6 hole par 3 academy course.
Location On the main Northallerton/Richmond road
    B6271, 1m W of Northallerton

Hotel ★★ 64% The Golden Lion, High St,
    NORTHALLERTON
    ☎ 01609 777411 25 ⇌ ☏

PANNAL   Map 08 SE35

Pannal Follifoot Rd HG3 1ES
☎ 01423 872628 Fax 01423 870043
e-mail: pannelgolfclub@btconnect.com
Fine championship course. Moorland turf but well-
wooded with trees closely involved with play.
18 holes, 6622yds, Par 72, SSS 72, Course record 62.
Club membership 780.
Visitors preferable to contact in advance, weekends
    limited.
Societies apply in advance.
Green Fees £50 per 36 holes; £40 per round (£50 per
    round weekends & bank holidays).
Cards ⊞ ⏍ ⏍ ⏍ ⌀
Prof David Padgett
Designer Sandy Herd
Facilities ⊗ ⅏ ⓑ ♥ ♀ ⅄ ⓐ ➹ ⌀ ⓣ
& Leisure snooker.
Location E side of village off A61

Hotel ★★★ 65% The Imperial, Prospect Place,
    HARROGATE ☎ 01423 565071
    83 ⇌ ☏

RAVENSCAR   Map 08 NZ90

Raven Hall Hotel Golf Course YO13 0ET
☎ 01723 870353 Fax 01723 870072
Opened by the Earl of Cranbrook in 1898, this 9-hole clifftop
course is sloping and with good quality small greens.
Because of its clifftop position it is subject to strong winds
which make it great fun to play, especially the 6th hole.
9 holes, 1894yds, Par 32, SSS 32.
Club membership 120.
Visitors must contact in advance, busy at weekends,
    spikes essential, no jeans/T shirts.
Societies telephone in advance.
Green Fees not confirmed.
Cards ⊞ ⏍ ⏍ ⌀
Facilities ⊗ ⅏ ⓑ ♥ ♀ ⌀ ☷
& Leisure hard tennis courts, heated indoor plus outdoor
    swimming pool, sauna.
Location Situated on cliff top

Hotel ★★★ 65% Raven Hall Country House Hotel &
    Golf Course, RAVENSCAR
    ☎ 01723 870353 53 ⇌ ☏

REDCAR   Map 08 NZ62

Cleveland Queen St TS10 1BT
☎ 01642 471798 Fax 01642 471798
e-mail: peterfletcher@clevelandgolf.fa.co.uk
The oldest golf club in Yorkshire playing over the only links
championship course in Yorkshire. A true test of traditional
golf, especially when windy. Flat seaside links with easy
walking.
18 holes, 6700yds, Par 72, SSS 72, Course record 67.
Club membership 820.
Visitors   advisable to book in advance.
Societies   initially telephone for details.
Green Fees £22 per day; £20 per round (£26/£22 weekends).
Prof   Stephen Wynn
Facilities   ⊗ ⅷ ╚ 🍺 ♀ ♨ 🏠
Location   8m E of Middlesborough, at N end of Redcar

Hotel   ★★★♨ 72% Grinkle Park Hotel,
               EASINGTON ☎ 01287 640515   20 ⇆ 🐾

Wilton Wilton TS10 4QY
☎ 01642 465265 (Secretary) & 452730 (Prof)
Fax 01642 465463
Parkland course with some fine views.
18 holes, 6126yds, Par 70, SSS 69, Course record 64.
Club membership 750.
Visitors   telephone professional 01642 452730 to check
               availability, no visitors Saturday, Ladies
               competition have priority Tuesday, tee off 10am
               or later.
Societies   must telephone secretary in advance.
Green Fees not confirmed.
Prof   P D Smillie
Facilities   ⊗ ⅷ by prior arrangement ╚ 🍺 ♀ ♨ 🏠
& Leisure   snooker.
Location   3m W of Redcar, on A174

Hotel   ★★★♨ 72% Grinkle Park Hotel,
               EASINGTON ☎ 01287 640515   20 ⇆ 🐾

RICHMOND   Map 07 NZ10

Richmond Bend Hagg DL10 5EX
☎ 01748 823231(Secretary)
Undulating parkland course. Ideal to play 27 holes, not too
testing but very interesting.
18 holes, 5769yds, Par 70, SSS 68, Course record 63.
Club membership 600.
Visitors   may not play before 3.30am on Sun.
Societies   must contact in writing or telephone 01748
               822457.
Green Fees £22 per day, £20 per round (£30/25 weekends).
Prof   Paul Jackson

Designer   P Pennink
Facilities   ⊗ ⅷ ╚ 🍺 ♀ ♨ 🏠 ⛳ 🏌 🏇 ✓
Location   0.75m N

Hotel   ★★ 68% King's Head Hotel, Market Place,
               RICHMOND ☎ 01748 850220
               26 ⇆ 🐾 Annexe4 ⇆ 🐾

RIPON   Map 08 SE37

Ripon City Palace Rd HG4 3HH
☎ 01765 603640 Fax 01765 692880
e-mail: office@ripongolf.com
Moderate walking on undulating parkland course; two testing
par 3's at 5th and 16th.
18 holes, 6084yds, Par 70, SSS 69, Course record 66.
Club membership 750.
Visitors   book with professional. No play
               Saturdays,limited play Sundays.
Societies   contact in writing or telephone.
Green Fees £20 (£30 weekends & bank holidays).
Prof   S T Davis
Designer   H Varden
Facilities   ⊗ ╚ 🍺 ♀ ♨ 🏠 ⛳ 🏇 🏌 ✓
Location   1m NW on A6108

Hotel   ★★★ 69% Ripon Spa Hotel, Park St, RIPON
               ☎ 01765 602172   40 ⇆ 🐾

SALTBURN-BY-THE-SEA   Map 08 NZ62

Hunley Hall Golf Club & Hotel Ings Ln, Brotton
TS12 2QQ ☎ 01287 676216 Fax 01287 678250
e-mail: enquiries@hunleyhall.co.uk
A picturesque 27 hole coastal course a providing a good test
of golf for all abilities.
*Morgans: 18 holes, 6918yds, Par 73, SSS 73, Course record
67.*
Millennium: 18 holes, 5948yds, Par 68, SSS 68.
Jubilee: 18 holes, 6292yds, Par 71, SSS 70.
Club membership 500.
Visitors   tee off times must be reserved in advance, times
               available between 9.30-11.30am and after 1pm.
Societies   telephone for information and availability.
Green Fees £20 per day (£30 weekends & Bank holidays).
Cards   💳 🔲 🔲 🔲 🔲 💳
Prof   Andrew Brook
Designer   John Morgan
Facilities   ⊗ ⅷ ╚ 🍺 ♀ ♨ 🏠 ⛳ 🏌 🏇 🏇 🏌 ✓ ♺
Location   From A174 in Brotton take St margarets
               Way,700 yds to club

Hotel   ★★★♨ 72% Grinkle Park Hotel,
               EASINGTON ☎ 01287 640515   20 ⇆ 🐾

Hunley Hall Golf Club & Hotel
Modern hotel situated amid rolling countryside by the
Heritage Coast with unrivalled panoramic views and
overlooking our own 27 hole golf course. The course
incorporates lakes and ponds to provide exciting and
challenging courses giving players of all levels and abilities a
rewarding and enjoyable game.
Golf breaks from £138.00 including two nights D,B&B and
three days unlimited mid-week golf.
For reservations/enquiries please call 01287 676216   Fax: 01287 678250
E-mail: enquiries@hunleyhall.co.uk   website www.hunleyhall.co.uk
BROTTON, SALTBURN, NORTH YORKSHIRE TS12 2QQ

Saltburn by the Sea Hob Hill, Guisborough Rd TS12 1NJ
☎ 01287 622812 Fax 01287 625988
Undulating meadowland course surrounded by woodland.
Particularly attractive in autumn. There are fine views of the
Cleveland Hills and of Tees Bay.
18 holes, 5846yds, Par 70, SSS 68, Course record 62.
Club membership 900.

Visitors	telephone in advance, no visitors on Saturday.
Societies	apply in writing.
Green Fees	£22 (£28 weekends) per day.prices under review.
Prof	Mike Nutter
Designer	J Braid
Facilities	⬛ 💺 ♀ ♨ 📠 ⌀
Location	0.5m out of Saltburn on Guisborough road

Hotel   ★★★♨ 72% Grinkle Park Hotel,
EASINGTON ☎ 01287 640515   20 ⇆ 🐾

SCARBOROUGH   Map 08 TA08

Scarborough North Cliff North Cliff Av YO12 6PP
☎ 01723 360786 Fax 01723 362134
Seaside parkland course begining on cliff top overlooking
bay and castle. Good views.
18 holes, 6425yds, Par 71, SSS 71, Course record 66.
Club membership 895.

Visitors	must be member of a club with handicap certificate. May not play before 10.30am Sun.
Societies	prior booking with secretary for parties of 8-40.
Green Fees	not confirmed.
Prof	Simon N Deller
Designer	James Braid
Facilities	⊗ ⏸ ⬛ 💺 ♀ ♨ 📠 ⛳ ↘ ⌀
Location	2m N of town centre off A165

Hotel   ★★★ 65% Esplanade Hotel, Belmont Rd,
SCARBOROUGH ☎ 01723 360382   73 ⇆ 🐾

Scarborough South Cliff Deepdale Av YO11 2UE
☎ 01723 374737
18 holes, 6039yds, Par 70, SSS 69, Course record 66.
Location   1m S on A165
Telephone for further details

Hotel   ★★ 65% Bradley Court Hotel, Filey Rd, South
Cliff, SCARBOROUGH
☎ 01723 360476   40 ⇆ 🐾

SELBY   Map 08 SE63

Selby Brayton Barff YO8 9LD   ☎ 01757 228622
e-mail: selbygolfclub@hotmail.com
Mainly flat, links-type course; prevailing SW wind. Testing
holes including the 3rd, 7th and 16th.
18 holes, 6374yds, Par 71, SSS 71, Course record 63.
Club membership 840.

Visitors	contact professional on 01757 228785, members and guests only at weekends.
Societies	welcome Mon-Fri, must apply in advance.
Green Fees	£30 per day; £25 per round.
Prof	Andrew Smith
Designer	J Taylor & Hawtree
Facilities	⊗ ⏸ ⬛ 💺 ♀ ♨ 📠 ⛳ ⌀
Location	Off A19 at Brayton

Hotel   ★★★♨ Monk Fryston Hall Hotel, MONK
FRYSTON ☎ 01977 682369   30 ⇆ 🐾

SETTLE   Map 07 SD86

Settle Buckhaw Brow, Giggleswick BD24 0DH
☎ 01729 825288 Fax 01729 825288
Picturesque parkland course with stream affecting play on
four holes.
9 holes, 5414yds, Par 68, SSS 66, Course record 59.
Club membership 380.

Visitors	may not play before 4pm on Sun.
Societies	apply in writing or telephone 4 weeks in advance.
Green Fees	not confirmed.
Designer	Tom Vardon
Facilities	♨
Location	1m N on A65

Inn   ◆◆◆ Golden Lion, 5 Duke St, SETTLE
☎ 01729 822203 14rm(1 ⇆4 🐾)

SKIPTON   Map 07 SD95

Skipton Off North West By-Pass BD23 3LF
☎ 01756 795657 Fax 01756 796665
e-mail: enquiries@skiptongolfclub.co.uk
Undulating parkland course with some water hazards and
panoramic views.
18 holes, 6049yds, Par 70, SSS 69, Course record 67.
Club membership 800.

Visitors	welcome by prior arrangement,may not play weekends
Societies	must apply in writing.
Green Fees	£24 per day (£26 weekends).
Prof	Peter Robinson
Facilities	⊗ ⏸ ⬛ 💺 ♀ ♨ 📠 ⛳ ⌀
& Leisure	snooker.
Location	1m N of Skipton on A59

Hotel   ★★★ The Devonshire Arms Country House
Hotel, BOLTON ABBEY
☎ 01756 710441   41 ⇆ 🐾

TADCASTER   Map 08 SE44

Cocksford Cocksford, Stutton LS24 9NG
☎ 01937 834253 Fax 01937 834253
e-mail: enquiries@cocksfordgolfclub.freeserve.co.uk
The course is set on undulating meadowland with the famous
Cock Beck featuring on 8 of the original 18 holes. Whatever
combination you choose the course is relatively short
featuring a number of drivable par 4s, but beware, danger
surrounds many of the greens!
Old Course: 18 holes, 5570yds, Par 71, SSS 69, Course record 65.
Plews Course: 18 holes, 5559yds, Par 70, SSS 68.
Quarry Hills Course: 18 holes, 4951yds, Par 67, SSS 65.
Club membership 450.

Visitors	welcome, contact pro shop.
Societies	telephone the secretary.
Green Fees	not confirmed.
Prof	Graham Thompson
Facilities	⊗ ⏸ ⬛ 💺 ♀ ♨ 📠 ⛳ ⌀
Location	Between York & Leeds, adjacent to the village of Stutton

▶

Hotel ★★★♨ 73% Wood Hall Hotel, Trip Ln, Linton, WETHERBY
☎ 01937 587271   36 ⇆ ⚑ Annexe6 ⇆ ⚑

Scathingwell Scathingwell LS24 9PF
☎ 01937 557864 (pro) 557878 (club) Fax 01937 557909
Testing water hazards and well placed bunkers and trees provide a challenging test of golf for all handicaps at this scenic parkland course, located 4 miles south of Tadcaster.
18 holes, 6771yds, Par 72, SSS 72.
Club membership 500.
Visitors   dress code must be adhered to. May play anytime midweek and Sundays,after 2.00pm Saturdays.
Societies   golf packages available, book one month in advance.
Green Fees available on request..
Prof   Steve Footman
Facilities ⊗ 〤 ▣ ♥ ♀ ♨ 🏠 ✂
Location 4m S of Tadcaster on the A162 Tadcaster/Ferrybridge road, approx 2m from the A1

Hotel ★★★ 77% Hazlewood Castle, Paradise Ln, Hazlewood, TADCASTER
☎ 01937 535353 9 ⇆ ⚑ Annexe12 ⇆ ⚑

THIRSK   Map 08 SE48

Thirsk & Northallerton Thornton-le-Street YO7 4AB
☎ 01845 522170 & 525115 Fax 01845 525115
The course has good views of the nearby Hambleton Hills. Testing course, mainly flat land.
18 holes, 6514yds, Par 72, SSS 71.
Club membership 500.
Visitors   must telephone in advance, and have handicap certificate. No play Sun unless with member.
Societies   must apply in writing.
Green Fees £25 per day; £20 per round (£30/£25 weekend & bank holidays).
Prof   Robert Garner
Designer ADAS
Facilities ⊗ 〤 ▣ ♥ ♀ ♨ 🏠 ⚑ ⚒ ✂
Location 2m N on A168

Hotel ★★ 62% Three Tuns Hotel, Market Place, THIRSK ☎ 01845 523124   10 ⇆ ⚑

WHITBY   Map 08 NZ81

Whitby Low Straggleton, Sandsend Rd YO21 3SR
☎ 01947 600660 Fax 01947 600660
e-mail: whitby-golf-club@compuserve.com
Seaside course with 4 holes along cliff tops and over ravines. Good views and fresh sea breeze.
18 holes, 6134yds, Par 71, Course record 66.
Club membership 800.
Visitors   may not play on competition days, parties must contact in advance.
Societies   must contact in writing.
Green Fees £22 per day (£28 weekends).
Prof   Tony Mason
Facilities ⊗ 〤 ▣ ♥ ♀ ♨ 🏠 ⚑ ✂
Location 1.5m NW on A174

Hotel ★★ 67% White House Hotel, Upgang Ln, West Cliff, WHITBY ☎ 01947 600469   10 ⇆ ⚑

YORK   Map 08 SE65

Forest of Galtres Moorlands Rd, Skelton YO32 2RF
☎ 01904 766198 Fax 01904 769400
Level parkland course in the heart of the ancient Forest of Galtres with mature oak trees and interesting water features coming into play on the 6th, 14th and 17th holes. Views towards York Minster.
18 holes, 6312yds, Par 72, SSS 70, Course record 67.
Club membership 450.
Visitors   telephone to book, may play anytime.
Societies   not Sat, booking system, telephone for forms.
Green Fees £23 per day; £18 per round (£30/£25 weekends & bank holidays).
Prof   Phil Bradley
Designer Simon Gidman
Facilities ⊗ 〤 by prior arrangement ▣ ♥ ♀ ♨ 🏠 ⚑ ✂
Location 0.5m from the York ring road B1237, just off A19 Thirsk road through the village of Skelton

Hotel ★★ 70% Beechwood Close Hotel, 19 Shipton Rd, Clifton, YORK
☎ 01904 658378   14 ⇆ ⚑

Forest Park Stockton-on-the-Forest YO32 9UW
☎ 01904 400425 & 400688 Fax 01904 400717
A parkland/meadowland course with natural features including a stream and mature and new trees.
Old Foss Course: 18 holes, 6600yds, Par 71, SSS 72, Course record 73.
The West Course: 9 holes, 3186yds, Par 70, SSS 70.
Club membership 600.
Visitors   welcome, subject to tee availability. Advisable to contact club in advance.
Societies   by prior arrangement.
Green Fees not confirmed.
Cards   ▤ ▤ ▣ ♀
Facilities ⊗ ▣ ♥ ♀ ♨ 🏠 ⚑ ✂ ✂
Location 4m NE of York, 1.5m from end of A64, York bypass

Hotel ★★★ 72% York Pavilion Hotel, 45 Main St, Fulford, YORK ☎ 01904 622099   57 ⇆ ⚑

Fulford Heslington Ln YO10 5DY
☎ 01904 413579 Fax 01904 416918
e-mail: info@fulfordgolfclub.co.uk
A flat, parkland/moorland course well-known for the superb quality of its turf, particularly the greens, and now famous as the venue for some of the best golf tournaments in the British Isles, in past years.
18 holes, 6775yds, Par 72, SSS 72, Course record 62.
Club membership 775.
Visitors   must contact in advance.
Societies   not Tue am, book with the manager.
Green Fees £48 per day; £37 per round (£48 weekends & bank holidays).
Prof   Bryan Hessay
Designer Dr Mckenzie
Facilities ⊗ 〤 ▣ ♥ ♀ ♨ 🏠 ⚑ ✂ ✂
Location 2m S of York off A19

Hotel ★★★★ 64% Swallow Hotel, Tadcaster Rd, YORK ☎ 01904 701000 112 ⇆ ⚑

ALDWARK MANOR
HOTEL, GOLF & COUNTRY CLUB
Aldwark, Near Alne, York, Y061 1UF
Golf Phone 01347 838353   Facsimile 01347 838007
www.aldwarkmanor.co.uk
AA   <http://www.aldwarkmanor.co.uk>
reception@aldwarkmanor

Hidden away in the heart of the North Yorkshire Countryside yet within easy reach of historic York, Harrogate, Yorkshire Dales and Moors. This 28-bedroom Victorian Manor house has 28 en-suite bedrooms, surrounded by a challenging 18-hole golf course set in mature parkland. Our recently opened Health Spa provides the latest in leisure facilities with highly trained therapist providing Decleor treatments.

Heworth Muncaster House, Muncastergate YO31 9JY
☎ 01904 422389 Fax 01904 426156
12-hole parkland course, easy walking. Holes 3, 7 and 9 played twice from different tees.
12 holes, 6141yds, Par 70, SSS 69, Course record 68.
Club membership 550.
Visitors   advisable to telephone the professional in advance, no catering Mondays
Societies   apply in writing/telephone professional 01904 422389
Green Fees £18 per day; £14 per round (£20/£18 weekends).
Prof   Stephen Burdett
Designer   B Cheal
Facilities   ⊗ ⅢL ≞ ⌇ℒⓈ 🏠 ⛳ ⋞
Location   1.5m NE of city centre on A1036

Hotel   ★★★ 67% Monkbar Hotel, St Maurices Rd, YORK ☎ 01904 638086   99 ⇥ ⋔

Swallow Hall Crockey Hill YO19 4SG
☎ 01904 448889 Fax 01904 448219
e-mail: jtscores@hotmail.com
A small 18-hole, Par 3 course with 2 par 4s. Attached to a caravan park and holiday cottages.
18 holes, 3600yds, Par 56, SSS 56, Course record 58.
Club membership 100.
Visitors   no restrictions.
Societies   must telephone in advance.
Green Fees £8 per 18 holes; £4 per 9 holes (£10/£5 weekends &bank holidays).
Designer   Brian Henry
Facilities   ⊗ ⅢL ≞ ⌇ℒⓈ ⋔ 🍴 🏌 ⋞ ⌇
& Leisure hard tennis courts.
Location   Off A19, signposted to Wheldrake

Hotel   ★★★ 72% York Pavilion Hotel, 45 Main St, Fulford, YORK ☎ 01904 622099   57 ⇥ ⋔

York Lords Moor Ln, Strensall YO32 5XF
☎ 01904 491840 (Sec) 490304 (Pro) Fax 01904 491852
A pleasant, well-designed, heathland course with easy walking. The course is of good length but being flat the going does not tire. The course is well bunkered with excellent greens and there are two testing pond holes.
18 holes, 6301yds, Par 70, SSS 70, Course record 66.
Club membership 700.
Visitors   with member only weekends, must contact in advance.
Societies   more than 16 contact secretary, under 16 contact professional.
Green Fees £30 per 18 holes;£35 per 27 holes;£40 per 36 holes(£40 per 18 holes;£45 per 27 holes weekends).
Prof   A P Hoyles

Designer   J H Taylor
Facilities   ⊗ ⅢL ≞ ⌇ℒⓈ 🏠 ⋞
Location   6m NE, E of Strensall village

Hotel   ★★★ 75% Dean Court Hotel, Duncombe Place, YORK ☎ 01904 625082   40 ⇥ ⋔

BARNSLEY   Map 08 SE30

Barnsley Wakefield Rd, Staincross S75 6JZ
☎ 01226 382856 Fax 01226 382856
Undulating municipal parkland course with easy walking apart from last 4 holes. Testing 8th and 18th holes.
18 holes, 5951yds, Par 69, SSS 69, Course record 64.
Club membership 450.
Visitors   booking advisable, telephone professional on 01226 380358.
Societies   by arrangement,contact club professional at 01226 380358
Green Fees £9 per round.
Prof   Shaun Wyke
Facilities   ⊗ by prior arrangement Ⅲ by prior arrangement L by prior arrangement ≞ ⌇ℒⓈ 🏠 ⋞ ⋞
Location   3m N on A61

Hotel   ★★★ 72% Ardsley House Hotel & Health Club, Doncaster Rd, Ardsley, BARNSLEY ☎ 01226 309955   74 ⇥ ⋔

Sandhill Middlecliffe Ln, Little Houghton S72 0HW
☎ 01226 753444 Fax 01226 753444
The course is reasonably flat with generously wide fairways laid out between and amongst 25 acres of newly planted woodlands. Holes of note are the 4th which is a 311 yard Par 4 to a horseshoe green around a 9-foot deep bunker; the 7th Par 3 to blind reverse Mackenzie Green and the 11th 416 yard Par 4 dogleg where the brave can take on the out of bounds.
18 holes, 6257yds, Par 71, SSS 70, Course record 69.
Club membership 375.
Visitors   welcome by prior booking.
Societies   telephone for availability, write to confirm.
Green Fees not confirmed.
Cards   ▱▱ ▱▱ ▱▱ ▱▱ ▱
Designer   John Royston
Facilities   ⊗ L ≞ ⌇ℒⓈ 🏠 ⌇
Location   5m E of Barnsley, off A635

                                            ▶

Hotel ★★★ 72% Ardsley House Hotel & Health Club, Doncaster Rd, Ardsley, BARNSLEY
☎ 01226 309955 74 ⇄ ↟

BAWTRY Map 08 SK69

Austerfield Park Cross Ln, Austerfield DN10 6RF
☎ 01302 710841 Fax 01302 710850
e-mail: apgc@aol.com
Long moorland course with postage stamp 8th and testing 618-yd 7th. Driving range and Par 3 attached.
18 holes, 6900yds, Par 73, SSS 73, Course record 69.
Club membership 500.
Visitors welcome weekdays, after 10am weekends.
Societies must contact in advance.
Green Fees not confirmed.
Cards 🖃 💳
Prof Darran Roberts
Facilities ⊗ ⅊ ⅃ ☕ ♀ ♨ 🛒 ➤ ⬆ 🏌 ⚒ ⍿
Location 2m from Bawtry on A614

Hotel ★★★ 63% The Crown Hotel, High St, BAWTRY ☎ 01302 710341 57 ⇄ ↟

CONISBROUGH Map 08 SK59

Crookhill Park Municipal Carr Ln DN12 2BE
☎ 01709 862979
18 holes, 5849yds, Par 70, SSS 68, Course record 64.
Location 1.5m SE on B6094
Telephone for further details

Hotel ★★★ 64% Danum Hotel, High St, DONCASTER ☎ 01302 342261 66 ⇄ ↟

DONCASTER Map 08 SE50

Doncaster 278 Bawtry Rd, Bessacarr DN4 7PD
☎ 01302 868316 & 865994 Fax 01302 865994 e-mail: doncastergolf@aol.com
Pleasant undulating heathland course with wooded surroundings. Quick drying, ideal all year round course.
18 holes, 6220yds, Par 69, SSS 70, Course record 66.
Club membership 500.
Visitors must contact in advance for both weekdays and weekends.
Societies must contact in advance.
Green Fees £33 per day; £27.50 per round (£33 weekends pm only).
Prof Graham Bailey
Designer Mackenzie/Hawtree
Facilities ⊗ ⅊ ⅃ ☕ ♀ ♨ 🛒 ➤ ⬆ ⍿
Location 4m SE on A638

Hotel ★★★ 72% Mount Pleasant Hotel, Great North Rd, ROSSINGTON ☎ 01302 868696 & 868219 Fax 01302 865130 42 ⇄ ↟

Doncaster Town Moor Bawtry Rd, Belle Vue DN4 5HU
☎ 01302 535286 & 533167 Fax 01302 533778
Easy walking, but testing, heathland course with good true greens. Friendly club. Notable hole is 11th (par 4), 464 yds. Situated in centre of racecourse.
18 holes, 6072yds, Par 69, SSS 69, Course record 66.
Club membership 520.

Societies must contact in advance.
Green Fees not confirmed.
Prof Steven Shaw
Facilities ⊗ ⅊ ⅃ ☕ ♀ ♨ 🛒 ⍿
Location 1.5m E,at racecourse,on A638

Hotel ★★★ 64% Danum Hotel, High St, DONCASTER ☎ 01302 342261 66 ⇄ ↟

Owston Park Owston Ln, Owston DN6 8EF
☎ 01302 330821 e-mail: will@owstonpark.fsnet.co.uk
A flat easy walking course surrounded by woodland. A lot of mature trees and a few ditches in play. A practice putting green and chipping area.
9 holes, 2866yds, Par 35, SSS 70.
Visitors no restrictions.
Societies telephone in advance.
Green Fees £4.25 per 9 holes (£4.50 weekends).
Cards 🖃 💳 🖃 💳 🖃 💳
Prof Mike Parker
Designer M Parker
Facilities ♀ ♨ 🛒 🏌 ⍿
Location 5m N of Doncaster off A19

Hotel ★★★ 64% Danum Hotel, High St, DONCASTER ☎ 01302 342261 66 ⇄ ↟

Thornhurst Park Holme Ln, Owston DN5 0LR
☎ 01302 337799 Fax 01302 721495
Surrounded by Owston Wood, this scenic parkland course has numerous strategically placed bunkers, and a lake comes into play at the 7th and 8th holes.
18 holes, 6490yds, Par 72, SSS 72, Course record 72.
Club membership 160.
Visitors must wear trousers, shirt with collar and golf shoes, can contact 2 days in advance.
Societies telephone or write in advance.
Green Fees £10 per 18 holes; £5 per 9 holes (£12/£6 weekends & bank holidays).
Prof Kevin Pearce
Facilities ⊗ ⅊ ⅃ ☕ ♀ ♨ 🛒 ➤ ⍿
Location On the A19 between Bentley/Askern, easy access from M62 and A1 (M)

Hotel ★★★ 64% Danum Hotel, High St, DONCASTER ☎ 01302 342261 66 ⇄ ↟

Wheatley Armthorpe Rd DN2 5QB
☎ 01302 831655 & 834085 Fax 01302 834085
Fairly flat well-bunkered, lake-holed, parkland course. Well-drained, in excellent condition all year round.
18 holes, 6405yds, Par 71, SSS 71, Course record 64.
Club membership 600.
Visitors telephone in advance. Must contact in advance
Societies must contact professional in advance.
Green Fees not confirmed.
Cards 🖃 💳 🖃 💳
Prof Steven Fox
Designer George Duncan
Facilities ⊗ ⅊ ⅃ ☕ ♀ ♨ 🛒 ⍿
Location NE side of town centre off A18

Hotel ★★★ 67% Regent Hotel, Regent Square, DONCASTER ☎ 01302 364180 50 ⇄ ↟

Looking for a driving range?
See the index at the back of the guide

HATFIELD   Map 08 SE60

Kings Wood Thorne Rd DN7 6EP ☎ 01405 741343
A flat course with ditches that come into play on several
holes, especially on the testing back nine. Notable holes are
the 12th par 4, 16th and par 5 18th. Water is a prominent
feature with several large lakes strategically placed.
18 holes, 6002yds, Par 70, SSS 69, Course record 69.
Club membership 100.
Visitors   visitors are welcome any time.
Societies   or telephone in advance.
Green Fees £7 per 18 holes;£4 per 9 holse(£8/£4.50
                weekends).
Cards   🖳 🖳 🖳 🖳 🖳
Prof   Jonathan Drury
Designer   John Hunt
Facilities 🍺 🏠 ⛳ ✓
Location   2m SW of junct 1 of M180, take A614 to
                Thorne, then Thorne road to Hatfield

Hotel   ★★ 71% Belmont Hotel, Horsefair Green,
                THORNE ☎ 01405 812320 23 ➡ ℝ

HICKLETON   Map 08 SE40

Hickleton Lidgett Ln DN5 7BE
☎ 01709 896081 Fax 01709 896083 e-
mail: hickleton@hickletongolfclub.freeserve.co.uk
Undulating, picturesque parkland course designed by Neil
Coles and Brian Huggett offering a good test of golf.
18 holes, 6434yds, Par 71, SSS 71, Course record 68.
Club membership 625.
Visitors   weekdays after 9am & weekends after 2.30pm.
                Must contact in advance.
Societies   must contact in advance.
Green Fees £24 per day, £20 per round (£27 per day
                weekends & bank holidays).
Prof   Paul J Audsley
Designer   Huggett/Coles
Facilities 🖳 🖳 🖳 🖳 🖳 🖳 🖳
Location   0.5m W on B6411

Hotel   ★★★ 64% Danum Hotel, High St,
                DONCASTER ☎ 01302 342261 66 ➡ ℝ

HIGH GREEN   Map 08 SK39

Tankersley Park S35 4LG
☎ 0114 246 8247 Fax 0114 245 7818
Rolling parkland course that demands accuracy rather than
length. Lush fairways. A good test of golf.
18 holes, 6212yds, Par 69, SSS 70, Course record 64.
Club membership 634.
Visitors   must contact in advance.
Societies   must apply in writing.
Green Fees £34 per day; £26 per round.
Cards   🖳 🖳 🖳 🖳 🖳
Prof   Ian Kirk
Designer   Hawtree
Facilities 🖳 🖳 🖳 🖳 🖳 🖳 🖳
Location   Off A61/M1 onto A616, Stocksbridge bypass

Hotel   ★★★ 69% Tankersley Manor, Church Ln,
                TANKERSLEY ☎ 01226 744700 70 ➡ ℝ

RAWMARSH   Map 08 SK49

Wath Abdy Ln S62 7SJ
☎ 01709 872149 & 878609 (office) Fax 01709 878609
e-mail: wathgolf@aol.com
Parkland course, not easy in spite of its length; 17th hole (par
3) is a difficult 244yds with narrow driving area.
18 holes, 5857yds, Par 68, SSS 68.
Club membership 550.
Visitors   must play with member at weekends. Must
                contact in advance and have a handicap
                certificate.
Societies   must contact in writing, may not play at
                weekends.
Green Fees not confirmed.
Prof   Chris Bassett
Facilities 🖳 🖳 🖳 🖳 🖳 🖳 🖳
Location   2.5m N off A633

Hotel   ★★★ 59% Carlton Park Hotel, 102/104
                Moorgate Rd, ROTHERHAM
                ☎ 01709 849955 76 ➡ ℝ

ROTHERHAM   Map 08 SK49

Grange Park Upper Wortley Rd S61 2SJ
☎ 01709 559497 e-mail: crowncourt@bun.com
Parkland/meadowland course, with panoramic views
especially from the back nine. The golf is testing, particularly
at the 1st, 4th and 18th holes (par 4), and 8th, 12th and 15th
(par 5).
18 holes, 6421yds, Par 71, SSS 71, Course record 65.
Club membership 214.
Visitors   no restrictions.
Societies   apply in writing to professional.
Green Fees £10.50 per 18 holes(£11.50 weekends).
Prof   Eric Clark
Designer   Fred Hawtree
Facilities 🖳 🖳 🖳 🖳 🖳 🖳 🖳 🖳 🖳
Location   3m NW off A629

Hotel   ★★★ 69% Tankersley Manor, Church Ln,
                TANKERSLEY ☎ 01226 744700 70 ➡ ℝ

Phoenix Pavilion Ln, Brinsworth S60 5PA
☎ 01709 363864 & 382624 Fax 01709 363788
Undulating meadowland course with variable wind.
18 holes, 6182yds, Par 71, SSS 69, Course record 65.
Club membership 1100.
Visitors   must contact in advance.
Societies   must apply in writing.
Green Fees not confirmed.
Prof   M Roberts
Designer   C K Cotton
Facilities 🖳 🖳 🖳 🖳 🖳 🖳 🖳
& Leisure   hard tennis courts, squash, fishing, gymnasium.
Location   SW side of town centre off A630

Hotel   ★★★ 59% Carlton Park Hotel, 102/104
                Moorgate Rd, ROTHERHAM
                ☎ 01709 849955 76 ➡ ℝ

Rotherham Golf Club Ltd Thrybergh Park, Doncaster Rd,
Thrybergh S65 4NU ☎ 01709 859500 Fax 01709 859517
Parkland course with easy walking along tree-lined fairways.
18 holes, 6324yds, Par 70, SSS 70, Course record 65.
Club membership 500. ▶

Visitors	must contact in advance.
Societies	must contact secretary in advance.
Green Fees	£35 per day; £30 per round (£37 round or day weekends).
Prof	Simon Thornhill
Facilities	⊗ ⅲ ⓑ ⚑ ♀ ⚐ 🕭 📣 🏌 ✓
Location	3.5m E on A630

Hotel	★★★ 68% Elton Hotel, Main St, Bramley, ROTHERHAM ☎ 01709 545681 13 ⇆ ⚑ Annexe16 ⇆ ⚑

Sitwell Park Shrogswood Rd S60 4BY
☎ 01709 541046 Fax 01709 703637
Parkland course with easy walking.
18 holes, 6229yds, Par 71, SSS 70, Course record 61.
Club membership 450.

Visitors	must contact in advance. May not play on Sat.
Societies	must contact in advance.
Green Fees	£28 per day; £24 per round (£32/£28 weekends & bank holidays).
Prof	Nic Taylor
Designer	A MacKenzie
Facilities	⊗ ⅲ ⓑ ⚑ ♀ ⚐ 🕭 📣 🏌 ✓

Hotel	★★★★ 62% Hellaby Hall Hotel, Old Hellaby Ln, Hellaby, ROTHERHAM ☎ 01709 702701 52 ⇆ ⚑

SHEFFIELD   Map 08 SK38

Abbeydale Twentywell Ln, Dore S17 4QA
☎ 0114 236 0763 Fax 2360762
e-mail: abbeygolf@compuserve.com
Parkland course, well-kept and wooded. Testing hole: 12th, par 3.
18 holes, 6407yds, Par 72, SSS 71, Course record 64.
Club membership 640.

Societies	larger groups must apply in writing, smaller groups by telephone.
Green Fees	£40 per day;£30 per round(£45 per round/day weekends,£35 after 2.30pm).
Prof	Nigel Perry
Designer	Herbert Fowler
Facilities	⊗ ⅲ ⓑ ⚑ ♀ ⚐ 🕭 📣 🏌 ✓
Location	4m SW of city centre off A621

Hotel	★★★ 71% Beauchief Hotel, 161 Abbeydale Rd South, SHEFFIELD ☎ 0114 262 0500 50 ⇆ ⚑

Beauchief Public Abbey Ln S8 0DB ☎ 0114 236 7274
Municipal course with natural water hazards. The rolling land looks west to the Pennines and a 12th-century abbey adorns the course.
18 holes, 5452yds, Par 67, SSS 66, Course record 65.
Club membership 450.

Visitors	are advised to book in advance in summer.
Societies	telephone pro-shop for advice.
Green Fees	£8 per round(£11 weekends).
Prof	A Highfield
Facilities	⊗ ⓑ ⚑ ♀ ⚐ 🕭 📣 ✓
Location	4m SW of city centre off A621

Hotel	★★★ 71% Beauchief Hotel, 161 Abbeydale Rd South, SHEFFIELD ☎ 0114 262 0500 50 ⇆ ⚑

Birley Wood Birley Ln S12 3BP ☎ 0114 264 7262
Undulating meadowland course with well-varied features, easy walking and good views. Practice range and putting green.
18 holes, 5100yds, Par 66, SSS 65, Course record 64.
Club membership 300.

Visitors	apply in advance.
Societies	apply in advance.
Green Fees	not confirmed.
Prof	Peter Ball
Facilities	♀ ⚐ 📣
Location	4.5m SE of city centre off A616

Hotel	★★★ 65% Mosborough Hall Hotel, High St, Mosborough, SHEFFIELD ☎ 0114 248 4353 23 ⇆ ⚑

Concord Park Shiregreen Ln S5 6AE ☎ 0114 257 7378
Hilly municipal parkland course with some fairways wood-flanked, good views, often windy. Seven par 3 holes.
18 holes, 4872yds, Par 67, SSS 64, Course record 57.
Club membership 150.

Visitors	no restrictions.
Societies	pay & play
Green Fees	£8 per 18 holes.
Prof	W Allcroft
Facilities	⊗ ⓑ ⚑ ♀ ⚐ 🕭 📣 🏌 🏍 ✓ ⓣ
& Leisure	hard tennis courts, heated indoor swimming pool, squash, gymnasium.
Location	3.5m N of city centre on B6086 off A6135

Hotel	★★★ 61% Posthouse Sheffield, Manchester Rd, Broomhill, SHEFFIELD ☎ 0870 400 9071 136 ⇆ ⚑

Dore & Totley Bradway Rd, Bradway S17 4QR
☎ 0114 236 0492
Flat parkland course.
18 holes, 6265yds, Par 70, SSS 70, Course record 65.
Club membership 580.

Visitors	must contact in advance a handicap certificate may be requested, may not play weekends.
Societies	must apply in writing.
Green Fees	not confirmed.
Prof	Gregg Roberts
Facilities	⊗ ⅲ ⓑ ⚑ ♀ ⚐ 🕭 ✓
Location	7m S of city centre on B6054 off A61

Hotel	★★★ 61% Posthouse Sheffield, Manchester Rd, Broomhill, SHEFFIELD ☎ 0870 400 9071 136 ⇆ ⚑

Hallamshire Golf Club Ltd Sandygate S10 4LA
☎ 0114 230 2153 Fax 0114 230 2153
Situated on a shelf of land at a height of 850 ft.
Magnificent views to the west. Moorland turf, long carries over ravine. Good natural drainage.
18 holes, 6359yds, Par 71, SSS 71, Course record 63.
Club membership 600.

Visitors	contact professional in advance. Tees reserved for members 8-9.30 and noon-1.30.
Societies	parties of 12+ should book in advance with secretary.
Green Fees	not confirmed.
Cards	🟦 🟦
Prof	G R Tickell ▶

Designer	Various
Facilities	⊗) III ६ ☕ ♀ ⚐ 📠 ⛳ ⚘
Location	Off A57 at Crosspool onto Sandygate Rd, clubhouse 0.75m on right

Hotel	★★★ 61% Posthouse Sheffield, Mancheater Rd, Broomhill, SHEFFIELD ☎ 0870 400 9071 136 ⇄ 📠

Hillsborough Worrall Rd S6 4BE
☎ 0114 234 9151 (Secretary) & 233 2666 (Pro)
Fax 0114 234 9151
e-mail: admin@hillsboroughgolfclub.co.uk
Beautiful moorland/woodland course 500 ft above sea-level, reasonable walking. Challenging first four holes into a prevailing wind and a tight, testing 14th hole.
18 holes, 6216yards, Par 71, SSS 70, Course record 64.
Club membership 650.

Visitors	contact professional in advance. May not play Tue (Ladies Day), Thu and weekends before 2pm without prior arrangement.
Societies	must apply in writing to secretary.
Green Fees	£30 per day (£35 per day weekends).
Prof	Lewis Horsman
Facilities	⊗) III ६ ☕ ♀ ⚐ 📠 ⛳ 🛒 ⚘ ⛴
Location	3m NW of city centre off A616

Hotel	★★★ 65% Menzies Rutland Hotel, 452 Glossop Rd, SHEFFIELD ☎ 0870 6003013 63 ⇄ 📠 Annexe13 ⇄ 📠

Lees Hall Hemsworth Rd, Norton S8 8LL
☎ 0114 255 4402
18 holes, 6171yds, Par 71, SSS 70, Course record 63.

Location	3.5m S of city centre off A6102

Telephone for further details

Hotel	★★★ 61% Posthouse Sheffield, Manchester Rd, Broomhill, SHEFFIELD ☎ 0870 400 9071 136 ⇄ 📠

Rother Valley Golf Centre Mansfield Rd, Wales Bar
S26 5PQ ☎ 0114 247 3000 Fax 0114 247 6000
e-mail: rother@jack-barker.co.uk
The challenging Blue Monster parkland course features a variety of water hazards. Notable holes include the 7th, with its island green fronted by water and dominated by bunkers to the rear. Lookout for the water on the par 5 18th.
18 holes, 6602yds, Par 72, SSS 72, Course record 70.
Club membership 500.

Visitors	2 days in advance booking format.
Societies	apply in writing or telephone in advance.
Green Fees	not confirmed.
Cards	⬚⬚ ⬚⬚ ⬚⬚ ⬚
Prof	Jason Ripley
Designer	Michael Shattock & Mark Roe
Facilities	⊗) III ६ ☕ ♀ ⚐ 📠 ⛳ 🛒 ⚘ ⛴
Location	Off junct 31 of the M1, follow signs to Rother Valley Country Park

Hotel	★★★ 65% Mosborough Hall Hotel, High St, Mosborough, SHEFFIELD ☎ 0114 248 4353 23 ⇄ 📠

Tinsley Park Municipal Golf High Hazels Park,
Darnall S9 4PE
☎ 0114 2037435
e-mail: tinsleyparkgc@hotmail.com
Undulating meadowland course with plenty of trees and rough. A test for all categories of golfer.
18 holes, 6064yds, Par 70, SSS 68, Course record 66.
Club membership 250.

Visitors	prior booking essential.
Societies	apply to professional shop on 0114 2037435
Green Fees	not confirmed..
Cards	⬚⬚ ⬚
Prof	A P Highfield
Facilities	⊗) III ६ ☕ ♀ ⚐ 📠 ⛳ ⚘
& Leisure	hard tennis courts.
Location	4m E of city centre off A630

Hotel	★★★ 65% Mosborough Hall Hotel, High St, Mosborough, SHEFFIELD ☎ 0114 248 4353 23 ⇄ 📠

SILKSTONE   Map 08 SE20

Silkstone Field Head, Elmhirst Ln S75 4LD
☎ 01226 790328 Fax 01226 792653
Parkland/downland course, fine views over the Pennines.
Testing golf.
18 holes, 6069yds, Par 70, SSS 70, Course record 64.
Club membership 530.

Visitors	with member only at weekends.
Societies	contact in advance.
Green Fees	£28 per day; £22 per round.
Prof	Kevin Guy
Facilities	⊗) III ६ ☕ ♀ ⚐ 📠 ⛴ 🛒 ⚘
Location	1m E off A628

Hotel	★★★ 72% Ardsley House Hotel & Health Club, Doncaster Rd, Ardsley, BARNSLEY ☎ 01226 309955 74 ⇄ 📠

STOCKSBRIDGE   Map 08 SK29

Stocksbridge & District 30 Royd Ln, Townend,
Deepcar S36 2RZ ☎ 0114 288 2003 (office) &
288 2779 (pro) Fax 0114 2882003
Hilly moorland course.
18 holes, 5200yds, Par 65, SSS 65, Course record 60.
Club membership 470.

Visitors	contact the professional.
Societies	apply to secretary.
Green Fees	not confirmed.
Prof	Timothy Brookes
Designer	Dave Thomas
Facilities	⊗) III ६ ☕ ♀ ⚐ 📠 ⚘
Location	S side of town centre

Hotel	★★★ 61% Posthouse Sheffield, Manchester Rd, Broomhill, SHEFFIELD ☎ 0870 400 9071 136 ⇄ 📠

AA Hotels that have special
arrangements with golf courses are listed at
the back of the guide

THORNE   Map 08 SE61

Thorne Kirton Ln DN8 5RJ
☎ 01405 812084 Fax 01405 741899
Picturesque parkland course with 6000 newly planted trees.
Water hazards on 11th, 14th & 18th holes.
18 holes, 5366yds, Par 68, SSS 66, Course record 62.
Club membership 300.
Visitors   no restrictions.
Societies   telephone in advance.
Green Fees £9 per round (£10 weekends & bank holidays).
Cards   ⊞ ▦ ▩ ▨
Prof   Edward Highfield
Designer   R D Highfield
Facilities   ⊗ ⅊ ⅃ ▐ ♀ ⚐ ⌂ ⚑ ⌲ ⚒ ✂
Location   8m E of Doncaster

Hotel   ★★ 71% Belmont Hotel, Horsefair Green,
                 THORNE ☎ 01405 812320 23 ⇥ ↾

WORTLEY   Map 08 SK39

Wortley Hermit Hill Ln S35 7DF
☎ 0114 288 8469 Fax 0114 288 8469
Well-wooded, undulating parkland course sheltered from
prevailing wind.
18 holes, 6028yds, Par 69, SSS 68, Course record 62.
Club membership 510.
Visitors   may not play between 11.30am and 1pm. Must
                 contact professional in advance and hold a
                 handicap certificate.
Societies   telephone in advance and confirm in writing
                 with deposit.
Green Fees £28(£32 weekends).
Cards   ⊞ ▦
Prof   Ian Kirk
Facilities   ⊗ ⅊ ⅃ ▐ ♀ ⚐ ⌂ ⚑ ✂
Location   0.5m NE of village off A629

Hotel   ★★★ 61% Posthouse Sheffield, Mancheater
                 Rd, Broomhill, SHEFFIELD
                 ☎ 0870 400 9071 136 ⇥ ↾

YORKSHIRE, WEST

ALWOODLEY   Map 08 SE24

Alwoodley Wigton Ln LS17 8SA
☎ 0113 268 1680 Fax 0113 293 9458
e-mail: julie@alwoodleygolfclub.freeserve.co.uk
A fine heathland course with length, trees and abundant
heather. Many attractive situations - together a severe
test of golf.
18 holes, 6666yds, Par 72, SSS 72.
Club membership 460.
Visitors   must contact Secretary in advance.
Societies   must apply in advance.
Green Fees £55 per day/round (£75 weekends & bank
                 holidays).
Cards   ⊞ ▦ ▩ ▨
Prof   John R Green
Designer   Dr Alistair Mackenzie

Facilities   ⊗ ⅊ ⅃ ▐ ♀ ⚐ ⌂ ⚑ ✂
Location   5m N off A61

Hotel   ★★★ 68% The Merrion, Merrion Centre,
                 LEEDS ☎ 0113 243 9191 109 ⇥ ↾

BAILDON   Map 07 SE13

Baildon Moorgate BD17 5PP
☎ 01274 584266 Fax 01274 530551
e-mail: sec@baildongolfclub.freeserve.co.uk
Moorland course set out in links style with outward front
nine looping back to clubhouse. Panoramic views with
testing short holes in prevailing winds.
18 holes, 6225yds, Par 70, SSS 70, Course record 63.
Club membership 750.
Visitors   contact in advance, restricted Tue & weekends.
Societies   large numbers apply in writing, small numbers
                 check with the professional.
Green Fees £16 per day (£20 weekends & bank holidays;
                 £10 after 3pm).
Prof   Richard Masters
Designer   Tom Morris
Facilities   ⊗ ⅊ ⅃ ▐ ♀ ⚐ ⌂ ⚑ ✂
& Leisure   snooker tables.
Location   3m N of Bradford, off A6038

Hotel   ★★★★ 70% Marriott Hollins Hall Hotel &
                 Country Club, Hollins Hill, Baildon, SHIPLEY
                 ☎ 01274 530053 122 ⇥ ↾

BINGLEY   Map 07 SE13

Bingley St Ives Golf Club House, St Ives Estate, Harden
BD16 1AT ☎ 01274 562436 Fax 01274 511788
Parkland/moorland course.
18 holes, 6485yds, Par 71, SSS 71, Course record 69.
Club membership 450.

Visitors   contact professional on 01274 562506, no green
                 fees Sat.
Societies   telephone in advance, the professional 01274
                 562506.
Green Fees £30 per day; £25 per round (£35/£30 weekends).
Cards   ⊞ ▦ ▩ ▨
Prof   Ray Firth
Designer   Alastair Mackenzie
Facilities   ⊗ ⅊ ⅃ ▐ ♀ ⚐ ⌂ ⚒ ✂
Location   0.75m W off B6429

Hotel   ★★ 66% Dalesgate Hotel, 406 Skipton Rd,
                 Utley, KEIGHLEY ☎ 01535 664930 20 ⇥ ↾

Shipley Beckfoot Ln BD16 1LX
☎ 01274 568652 (Secretary) & 563674 (Pro)
Fax 01274 567739 e-mail: office@shipleygc.co.uk
Well established parkland course, founded in 1922, featuring
6 good par 3's
18 holes, 6235yds, Par 71, SSS 70, Course record 65.
Club membership 600.
Visitors   may play Mon, Wed-Fri & Sun, but Tue only
           after 2.30pm & Sat after 4pm.
Societies   initial enquiry by phone to professional 01274
           563674 and or by letter.
Green Fees Mon £22 per round/day; Tue-Fri £32 per day,
           £25 per day (£35/£28 Sun and bank holidays).
Cards   💳💳💳💳
Prof   J R Parry
Designer   Colt, Allison, Mackenzie, Braid
Facilities   ⊗〒🍴♨♀⚘🚻🏌🎯✎
Location   6m N of Bradford on A650

Hotel   ★★ 66% Dalesgate Hotel, 406 Skipton Rd,
           Utley, KEIGHLEY
           ☎ 01535 664930   20 ⇄ 🐾

BRADFORD   Map 07 SE13

Bradford Moor Scarr Hall, Pollard Ln BD2 4RW
☎ 01274 771716 & 771693
Moorland course with tricky undulating greens.
9 holes, 5900yds, Par 70, SSS 68, Course record 65.
Club membership 330.
Visitors   no visitors at weekends except with member.
Societies   can book starting times by application in
           writing.
Green Fees £10 before 1.30pm, thereafter £12.
Facilities   ♀♨🚻✎
Location   2m NE of city centre off A658

Hotel   ★★ 68% Park Drive Hotel, 12 Park Dr,
           BRADFORD ☎ 01274 480194   11 ⇄ 🐾

Clayton Thornton View Rd, Clayton BD14 6JX
☎ 01274 880047
Parkland course, difficult in windy conditions.
9 holes, 5407yds, Par 68, SSS 67.
Club membership 300.
Visitors   may not play before 4pm on Sun.
Societies   apply in writing to the Secretary or Captain.
Green Fees £10 per round (£12 weekends & bank holidays).
Cards   💳💳💳💳
Facilities   ⊗〒🍴♨♀♨
Location   2.5m SW of city centre on A647

Hotel   ★★★ Novotel Bradford, 6 Roydsdale Way,
           Euroway Estate, BRADFORD
           ☎ 01274 683683 127 ⇄ 🐾

East Bierley South View Rd, East Bierley BD4 6PP
☎ 01274 681023 Fax 01274 683666
e-mail: rjwelch@hotmail.com
Hilly moorland course with narrow fairways. Two par 3
holes over 200 yds.
9 holes, 4700yds, Par 64, SSS 63, Course record 59.
Club membership 300.
Visitors   restricted Sat (am), Sun & Mon evening. Must
           contact in advance.
Societies   must apply in writing.
Green Fees not confirmed.

Facilities   ⊗🍴♨♀♨
Location   4m SE of city centre off A650

Hotel   ★★★ Novotel Bradford, 6 Roydsdale Way,
           Euroway Estate, BRADFORD
           ☎ 01274 683683 127 ⇄ 🐾

Headley Headley Ln, Thornton BD13 3LX
☎ 01274 833481 Fax 01274 833481
Hilly moorland course, short but very testing, windy, fine
views.
9 holes, 5140yds, Par 65, SSS 65, Course record 57.
Club membership 443.
Visitors   must contact in advance.
Societies   must contact in advance.
Green Fees £25 per day; £15 per round.
Facilities   ⊗〒🍴♨♀♨
Location   4m W of city centre off B6145 at Thornton

Hotel   ★★ 68% Park Drive Hotel, 12 Park Dr,
           BRADFORD ☎ 01274 480194   11 ⇄ 🐾

Queensbury Brighouse Rd, Queensbury BD13 1QF
☎ 01274 882155 & 816864
Undulating woodland/parkland course.
9 holes, 5024yds, Par 66, SSS 65, Course record 63.
Club membership 380.
Visitors   preferable to telephone in advance, restricted at
           weekends.
Societies   apply in writing.
Green Fees £15 per 18 holes (weekends phone first).
Prof   David Delaney
Designer   Jonathan Gaunt
Facilities   ⊗〒🍴♨♀♨🚻✎
Location   4m from Bradford on A647

Hotel   ★★ 68% Park Drive Hotel, 12 Park Dr,
           BRADFORD ☎ 01274 480194   11 ⇄ 🐾

South Bradford Pearson Rd, Odsal BD6 1BH
☎ 01274 673346 (pro shop)
Hilly course with good greens, trees and ditches. Interesting
short 2nd hole (par 3) 200 yds, well-bunkered and played
from an elevated tee.
9 holes, 6068yds, Par 70, SSS 68, Course record 65.
Club membership 300.
Visitors   must contact professional in advance. Weekends
           contact for availability. Tuesday Ladies Day.
Societies   must apply in writing to the secretary.
Green Fees £16 per day (£24 weekends).
Cards   💳💳
Prof   Paul Cooke
Facilities   ⊗〒🍴♨♀♨🚻✎
Location   2m S of city centre off A638

Hotel   ★★★ Novotel Bradford, 6 Roydsdale Way,
           Euroway Estate, BRADFORD
           ☎ 01274 683683 127 ⇄ 🐾

West Bowling Newall Hall, Rooley Ln BD5 8LB
☎ 01274 393207 (office) & 728036 (pro)
Fax 01274 393207
Undulating, tree-lined parkland course. Testing hole: 'the
Coffin' short par 3, very narrow.
18 holes, 5769yds, Par 69, SSS 67, Course record 65.
Club membership 500.
Visitors   must apply in writing, very limited at weekends.
Societies   must apply in writing/telephone in advance. ▶

Green Fees £24 per day; £20 per round (£30 per round weekends & bank holidays).
Prof Ian A Marshall
Facilities ⊗ ⽶ ⽫ ⽒ ♀ ⽬ ⽾ ⽿
Location Corner of M606 & A638 (east)

Hotel ★★★★ 63% Cedar Court Hotel Bradford, Mayo Av, Off Rooley Ln, BRADFORD ☎ 01274 406606 & 406601 Fax 01274 406600 131 ⇄ ⽰

West Bradford Chellow Grange Rd BD9 6NP
☎ 01274 542767 Fax 01274 482079
Parkland course, windy, especially 3rd, 4th, 5th and 6th holes. Hilly but not hard.
18 holes, 5741yds, Par 69, SSS 68.
Club membership 440.
Visitors restricted Sat & Sun. Tuesday is Ladies day, can play if available, advisable to telephone 01274 542102 to reserve a time.
Societies must contact in advance.
Green Fees £21 per day/round.
Prof Nigel M Barber
Facilities ⽒ ⽬ ⽾
Location W side of city centre off B6144

Hotel ★★★★ 70% Marriott Hollins Hall Hotel & Country Club, Hollins Hill, Baildon, SHIPLEY ☎ 01274 530053 122 ⇄ ⽰

BRIGHOUSE   Map 07 SE12

Willow Valley Golf & Country Club Highmoor Ln, Clifton HD6 4JB ☎ 01274 878624 Fax 01274 852805
e-mail: julian@wrgc.co.uk
A championship length 18-hole course offering a unique golfing experience, featuring island greens, shaped fairways and bunkers, and multiple teeing areas. The 9-hole course offers an exciting challenge to less experienced golfers.
South: 18 holes, Par 72, SSS 74, Course record 69.
Fountain: 9 holes, 3184yds, Par 62, SSS 60.
Club membership 350.
Visitors tee times may be booked by phone on payment of green fee by credit/debit card.
Societies telephone in advance for availability and booking form.
Green Fees South: £23 (£26 weekends & bank holidays). Fountain £6.50 (£7.50 weekends & bank holidays).
Cards 💳 💳 💳 💳 💳
Prof Julian Haworth
Designer Jonathan Gaunt
Facilities ⊗ ⽶ ⽫ ⽒ ♀ ⽬ ⽾ ⽿ ⽦ ⽾ ⽿
& Leisure 3 hole academy course.
Location Junct 25 of M62 follow A644 towards Brighouse, at small rdbt turn right, A643, course is 2m on righ

Hotel ★★ 71% Healds Hall Hotel, Leeds Rd, Liversedge, DEWSBURY ☎ 01924 409112 24 ⇄ ⽰

CLECKHEATON   Map 08 SE12

Cleckheaton & District Bradford Rd BD19 6BU
☎ 01274 851266 Fax 01274 871382
e-mail: info@cleckheatongolf.fsnet.co.uk
Parkland course with gentle hills.
18 holes, 5769yds, Par 71, SSS 68.
Club membership 550.
Visitors parties must arrange in advance, not weekends.
Societies weekdays only; must contact in advance.
Green Fees not confirmed.
Prof Mike Ingham
Facilities ⊗ ⽶ ⽫ ⽒ ♀ ⽬ ⽾ ⽿
Location 1.5m NW on A638 junc 26 M62

Hotel ★★★ Gomersal Park Hotel, Moor Ln, GOMERSAL ☎ 01274 869386 52 ⇄ ⽰

DEWSBURY   Map 08 SE22

Hanging Heaton White Cross Rd WF12 7DT
☎ 01924 461606 Fax 01924 430100
Arable land course, easy walking, fine views. Testing 4th hole (par 3).
9 holes, 5836yds, Par 69, SSS 68.
Club membership 500.
Visitors must play with member at weekends & bank holidays. Must contact in advance.
Societies must telephone in advance.
Green Fees £16 per day.
Prof Gareth Moore
Facilities ⊗ ⽶ ⽫ ⽒ ♀ ⽬ ⽾
Location 0.75m NE off A653

Hotel ★★ 71% Healds Hall Hotel, Leeds Rd, Liversedge, DEWSBURY ☎ 01924 409112 24 ⇄ ⽰

ELLAND   Map 07 SE12

Elland Hammerstones, Leach Ln HX5 0TA
☎ 01422 372505 & 374886 (pro)
Parkland course.
9 holes, 2815yds, Par 66, SSS 67, Course record 64.
Club membership 450.
Visitors welcome.
Societies must contact in writing.
Green Fees not confirmed.
Prof N Krzywicki
Facilities ⊗ ⽶ ⽫ ⽒ ♀ ⽬ ⽾ ⽿
Location 1m SW

Hotel ★★★ 67% The Rock Inn Hotel, Holywell Green, HALIFAX ☎ 01422 379721 30 ⇄ ⽰

FENAY BRIDGE   Map 08 SE11

Woodsome Hall HD8 0LQ
☎ 01484 602739 Fax 01484 608260
A parkland course with good views and an historic clubhouse.
18 holes, 6096yds, Par 70, SSS 69, Course record 67.
Club membership 800.

▶

Visitors must contact in advance. Jacket and tie required in all rooms except casual bar.
Societies must apply in writing.
Green Fees £40 per day, £30 per round (£50/£40 weekends & bank holidays).
Prof M Higginbotton
Facilities ⊗ ⅏ ⅃ ♨ ♀ ⚘ 🏠 ⚷
Location 1.5m SW off A629

Hotel ★★★ 65% Bagden Hall, Wakefield Rd, Scissett, HUDDERSFIELD
☎ 01484 865330 17 ⇄ ⋔

GARFORTH   Map 08 SE43

Garforth Long Ln LS25 2DS
☎ 0113 286 2021 Fax 0113 286 3308
Parkland course with fine views, easy walking.
18 holes, 6005yds, Par 69, SSS 69.
Club membership 500.
Visitors must contact in advance and have handicap certificate. With member only weekends & bank holidays.
Societies must apply in advance.
Green Fees not confirmed.
Prof Ken Findlater
Facilities ⊗ ⅏ ⅃ ♨ ♀ ⚘ 🏠 ⚷ ♩
Location 1m N

Hotel ★★★ 70% Milford Lodge Hotel, A1 Great North Rd, Peckfield, LEEDS
☎ 01977 681800 47 ⇄ ⋔

GUISELEY   Map 08 SE14

Bradford (Hawksworth) Hawksworth Ln LS20 8NP
☎ 01943 875570 & 873719 (Pro) Fax 01943 875570
Moorland course with eight par 4 holes of 360 yds or more. The course is a venue for county championship events.
18 holes, 6259yds, Par 71, SSS 71, Course record 66.
Club membership 650.
Visitors must have a handicap certificate and contact in advance. May not play Sat.
Societies make prior arrangements with manager.
Green Fees £35 per day; £30 per round(£40/£35 weekends & bank holidays).
Prof Sydney Weldon
Designer W H Fowler
Facilities ⊗ ⅏ ⅃ ♨ ♀ ⚘ 🏠 ⚷
Location SW side of town centre off A6038

Hotel ★★★★ 70% Marriott Hollins Hall Hotel & Country Club, Hollins Hill, Baildon, SHIPLEY
☎ 01274 530053 122 ⇄ ⋔

HALIFAX   Map 07 SE02

Halifax Union Ln, Ogden HX2 8XR
☎ 01422 244171 Fax 01422 241459
Hilly moorland course crossed by streams, natural hazards, and offering fine views. Testing 172-yd 17th (par3).
18 holes, 6037yds, Par 70, SSS 70, Course record 63.
Club membership 700.
Visitors contact professional for tee times, 01422 240047. Limited play weekend.
Societies contact secretary for dates.
Green Fees £20 per round(£30 weekends).

Prof Michael Allison
Designer A Herd/J Braid
Facilities ⊗ ⅏ ⅃ ♨ ♀ ⚘ 🏠 ⚷ ⚷
Location A629 Halifax/Keighley, 4 miles from Halifax

Hotel ★★★ 76% Holdsworth House Hotel, Holdsworth, HALIFAX
☎ 01422 240024 40 ⇄ ⋔

Lightcliffe Knowle Top Rd, Lightcliffe HX3 8SW
☎ 01422 202459 204081
Heathland course.
9 holes, 5388mtrs, Par 68, SSS 68.
Club membership 460.
Visitors Must contact in advance.
Societies Must apply in writing.
Green Fees not confirmed.
Prof Robert Kershaw
Facilities ⊗ ⅏ ⅃ ♨ ♀ ⚘ 🏠 ⚷
Location 3.5m E on A58

Hotel ★★★ 76% Holdsworth House Hotel, Holdsworth, HALIFAX
☎ 01422 240024 40 ⇄ ⋔

West End Paddock Ln, Highroad Well HX2 0NT
☎ 01422 341878 Fax 01422 341878
Semi-moorland course. Tree lined. Two ponds.
18 holes, 5951yds, Par 69, SSS 69, Course record 62.
Club membership 560.
Visitors contact in advance.
Societies must apply in writing to Secretary.
Green Fees £26 per day; £21 per round (£31/£26 sunday).
Prof David Rishworth
Facilities ⊗ ⅏ ⅃ ♨ ♀ ⚘ 🏠 ⚷
Location W side of town centre off A646

Hotel ★★★ 76% Holdsworth House Hotel, Holdsworth, HALIFAX
☎ 01422 240024 40 ⇄ ⋔

HEBDEN BRIDGE   Map 07 SD92

Hebden Bridge Mount Skip, Wadsworth HX7 8PH
☎ 01422 842896 & 842732
Moorland course with splendid views.
9 holes, 5242yds, Par 68, SSS 67, Course record 61.
Club membership 300.
Visitors weekends after 4pm only.
Societies contact in advance.
Green Fees £12 (£15 weekends).
Facilities ⊗ by prior arrangement ⅏ by prior arrangement ⅃ by prior arrangement ♨ by prior arrangement ⚘
Location 1.5m E off A6033

Hotel ★★★ 66% Carlton Hotel, Albert St, HEBDEN BRIDGE ☎ 01422 844400 16 ⇄ ⋔

HOLYWELL GREEN   Map 07 SE01

Halifax Bradley Hall HX4 9AN ☎ 01422 374108
Moorland/parkland course, tightened by tree planting, easy walking.
18 holes, 6138yds, Par 70, SSS 70, Course record 65.
Club membership 500.

▶

Visitors contact in advance.
Societies must apply in advance.
Green Fees £18 per round (£28 weekends).
Prof Peter Wood
Facilities ⊗ ⅏ ℍ ☕ ♥ ♀ ⚲ 🛍 ⚘
Location S on A6112

Hotel ★★★ 67% The Rock Inn Hotel, Holywell Green, HALIFAX
☎ 01422 379721 30 ⇌ ℞

HUDDERSFIELD   Map 07 SE11

Bagden Hall Hotel & Golf Course Wakefield Rd, Scissett HD8 9LE ☎ 01484 864839 Fax 01484 861001
e-mail: info@bagdenhall.demon.co.uk.
Well maintained tree-lined course set in idyllic surroundings and offering a challenging test of golf for all levels of handicap. Lake guarded greens require pin-point accuracy.
9 holes, 3002yds, Par 56, SSS 55, Course record 60.
Club membership 200.
Visitors anytime.
Societies company day packages available, telephone Director of golf.
Green Fees £9 per 18 holes (£13 weekends).
Cards ▭ ▬ ▬ ▨ ▨
Prof Iain Darren
Designer F O'Donnell/R Brathwaite
Facilities ⊗ ⅏ ℍ ☕ ♥ ♀ ⚲ 🛍 ⛳ ⚘ ⚘
Location A636 Wakefield-Denby Dale

Hotel ★★★ 65% Bagden Hall, Wakefield Rd, Scissett, HUDDERSFIELD
☎ 01484 865330 17 ⇌ ℞

Bradley Park Off Bradley Rd HD2 1PZ
☎ 01484 223772 Fax 01484 451613
Parkland course, challenging with good mix of long and short holes. Also 14-bay floodlit driving range and 9-hole par 3 course, ideal for beginners. Superb views.
18 holes, 6284yds, Par 70, SSS 70, Course record 65.
Club membership 300.
Visitors may book by phone for weekends and bank holidays from the preceeding Thu. No restrictions on other days.
Societies welcome midweek, apply in writing to professional.
Green Fees £12.50(£14.50 weekends).
Cards ▭ ▬ ▬ ▨ ▨
Prof Parnell E Reilly
Designer Cotton/Pennick/Lowire & Ptnrs
Facilities ⊗ ⅏ ℍ ☕ ♥ ♀ ⚲ 🛍 ⛳ ⚘ ⚘ ⚘
& Leisure 9 hole par 3 course.
Location 2.5m from junct 25 of M62

Hotel ★★★ 65% The George Hotel, St George's Square, HUDDERSFIELD
☎ 01484 515444 60 ⇌ ℞

Crosland Heath Felk Stile Rd, Crosland Heath HD4 7AF
☎ 01484 653216
Moorland course with fine views over valley.
18 holes, 6007yds, Par 70, SSS 70.
Club membership 550.
Visitors welcome, but advisable to check with professional. May not play Sat.
Societies must telephone in advance.
Green Fees not confirmed.

Prof James Coverley
Facilities ⊗ ⅏ ℍ ☕ ♥ ♀ ⚲ 🛍 ⚘
Location SW off A62

Hotel ★★★ 65% The George Hotel, St George's Square, HUDDERSFIELD
☎ 01484 515444 60 ⇌ ℞

Huddersfield Fixby Hall, Lightridge Rd, Fixby HD2 2EP
☎ 01484 426203 Fax 01484 424623
e-mail: secretary@huddersfield-golf.co.uk
A testing heathland course of championship standard laid out in 1891.
18 holes, 6432yds, Par 71, SSS 71, Course record 64.
Club membership 759.
Visitors must book tee times with professional.
Societies welcome Mon & Wed-Fri, prior arrangement required.
Green Fees £47 per 36 holes; £37 per 18 holes (£57/£47 weekends and bank holidays).
Prof Paul Carman
Facilities ⊗ ⅏ ℍ ☕ ♥ ♀ ⚲ 🛍 ⚘ ⚘ ⚘
Location 2m N off A641

Hotel ★★★ 65% The George Hotel, St George's Square, HUDDERSFIELD
☎ 01484 515444 60 ⇌ ℞

Longley Park Maple St, Off Somerset Rd HD5 9AX
☎ 01484 422304
Lowland course, surrounded by mature woodland.
9 holes, 5212yds, Par 66, SSS 66, Course record 61.
Club membership 440.
Visitors by arrangement with professional, must have handicap certificate, restricted Thu & weekends. No catering Mon.
Societies must apply in writing to secretary.
Green Fees not confirmed.
Prof Nick Leeming
Facilities ⊗ ⅏ ℍ ☕ ♥ ♀ ⚲ 🛍 ⚘ ⚘
Location 0.5m SE of town centre off A629

Hotel ★★★ 65% The George Hotel, St George's Square, HUDDERSFIELD
☎ 01484 515444 60 ⇌ ℞

ILKLEY   Map 07 SE14

Ben Rhydding High Wood, Ben Rhydding LS29 8SB
☎ 01943 608759
Moorland/parkland course with splendid views over the Wharfe valley.
9 holes, 4611yds, Par 65, SSS 63, Course record 64.
Club membership 290.
Visitors contact in advance. May only play at weekend as guest of member.
Societies advance notice in writing. In view of limited resources requests considered by monthly committee meeting.
Green Fees £12 per day (£17 weekends & bank holidays).
Designer William Dell
Facilities ♀ ⚲
Location SE side of town

Hotel ★★★ 70% Rombalds Hotel & Restaurant, 11 West View, Wells Rd, ILKLEY
☎ 01943 603201 15 ⇌ ℞

Ilkley Nesfield Rd, Myddleton LS29 0BE
☎ 01943 600214 Fax 01943 816130
e-mail: ilkley.golf.club@talk21.com
This beautiful parkland course is situated in Wharfedale and the Wharfe is a hazard on each of the first seven holes. In fact, the 3rd is laid out entirely on an island in the middle of the river.
18 holes, 5953yds, Par 69, SSS 70, Course record 66.
Club membership 450.
Visitors advisable to contact in advance.
Societies apply in writing.
Green Fees £37 per day (£42 weekends & bank holidays).
Prof John L Hammond
Facilities ⊗ ⅷ Ⅼ ☡ ♀ ♨ 🖻 🕈 ⚑
& Leisure fishing.
Location W side of town centre off A65

Hotel ★★★ 70% Rombalds Hotel & Restaurant, 11 West View, Wells Rd, ILKLEY
☎ 01943 603201   15 ⇋ ♠

KEIGHLEY   Map 07 SE04

Branshaw Branshaw Moor, Oakworth BD22 7ES
☎ 01535 643235 (sec) & 647441 (pro) Fax 01535 648011
Picturesque moorland course with fairly narrow fairways and good greens. Extensive views.
18 holes, 6000yds, Par 69, SSS 69, Course record 64.
Club membership 500.
Visitors welcome most times, restrictions at weekends advisable to ring.
Societies apply in writing to Professional.
Green Fees £20 per day (£30 weekends & bank holidays).
Prof Mark Tyler
Designer James Braid
Facilities ⊗ ⅷ Ⅼ ♀ ♨ 🖻 ⚑
Location 2m SW on B6149

Hotel ★★ 66% Dalesgate Hotel, 406 Skipton Rd, Utley, KEIGHLEY
☎ 01535 664930   20 ⇋ ♠

Keighley Howden Park, Utley BD20 6DH
☎ 01535 604778 Fax 01535 604833
e-mail: golf@keighleygolfclub.fsnet.co.uk
Parkland course with good views down the Aire Valley.
18 holes, 6141yds, Par 69, SSS 70, Course record 64.
Club membership 600.
Visitors restricted Sat & Sun. Must contact in advance.Ladies day on Tuesday.
Societies must apply in advance.
Green Fees summer; £31 per day, £27 per 18 holes (£37/£31 weekends & bank holidays). Winter; £18 per 18 holes (£22 weekends & bank holidays).
Prof Mike Bradley
Facilities ⊗ ⅷ Ⅼ ♀ ♨ 🖻 ⚑
Location 1m NW of town centre off B6143,turn north at Roebuck pub

Hotel ★★ 66% Dalesgate Hotel, 406 Skipton Rd, Utley, KEIGHLEY
☎ 01535 664930   20 ⇋ ♠

LEEDS   Map 08 SE33

Brandon Holywell Ln, Shadwell LS17 8EZ
☎ 0113 273 7471
An 18-hole links type course enjoying varying degrees of rough, water and sand hazards.
18 holes, 4000yds, Par 63.
Visitors pay & play course booking not usually necessary.
Societies telephone or write in advance.
Green Fees £6.50 per 18 holes;£4.50 per 9 holes(£7.50/£5.50 weekends).
Prof Carl Robinson
Designer William Binner
Facilities Ⅼ ♀ ♨ ⚑
Location From Leeds-Wetherby Rd turn left to Shadwell left again up Main St, right at Red Lion Pub

Hotel ★★★ 80% Haley's Hotel & Restaurant, Shire Oak Rd, Headingley, LEEDS
☎ 0113 278 4446 22 ⇋ ♠ Annexe7 ⇋ ♠

Cookridge Hall Golf & Country Club Cookridge Ln LS16 7NL ☎ 0113 2300641 Fax 0113 2857115
American-style course designed by Karl Litten. Expect plenty of water hazards, tees for all standards. Large bunkers and fairways between mounds and young trees.
Cookridge Hall: 18 holes, 6497yds, Par 72, SSS 72.
Club membership 600.
Visitors must contact in advance. Strict dress code applies. Soft spikes policy.
Societies telephone in advance.
Green Fees £25(£30 weekends).
Cards 🖻 🖭 🖭 🖭 🖭
Prof Mark Pearson
Designer Karl Liiten
Facilities ⊗ ⅷ Ⅼ ♀ ♨ 🖻 🕈 ⚑ ⚑
& Leisure heated indoor swimming pool, sauna, solarium, gymnasium, health and fitness club.
Location On Otley Old Road, off A660, 3m N of Leeds

Hotel ★★★ 80% Haley's Hotel & Restaurant, Shire Oak Rd, Headingley, LEEDS
☎ 0113 278 4446 22 ⇋ ♠ Annexe7 ⇋ ♠

Gotts Park Armley Ridge Rd LS12 2QX ☎ 0113 231 1896 & 231 0492 e-mail: mgil.mg@talk21.com
18 holes, 4960yds, Par 65, SSS 64, Course record 63.
Location 3m W of city centre off A647
Telephone for further details

Hotel ★★★★ 69% Le Meridien Queen's, City Square, LEEDS
☎ 0113 243 1323 & 0870 4008696
Fax 0113 242 5154 199 ⇋ ♠

Headingley Back Church Ln, Adel LS16 8DW
☎ 0113 267 9573 Fax 0113 281 7334
An undulating course with a wealth of natural features offering fine views from higher ground. Its most striking hazard is the famous ravine at the 18th. Leeds's oldest course, founded in 1892.
18 holes, 6298yds, Par 69, SSS 70, Course record 64.
Club membership 700.
Visitors must contact in advance, restricted at weekends.
Societies must telephone in advance and confirm in writing.

▶

Green Fees £35 per day; £30 per round (£40 per day/round weekends & bank holidays).
Prof Steven Foster
Designer Dr Mackenzie
Facilities ⊗ ⅲ ᴸ ☕ ♀ ⚲ 🏠 ⛳ ✐
Location 5.5m N of city centre off A660

Hotel ★★★ 70% Posthouse Bramhope, Leeds Rd, BRAMHOPE ☎ 0113 284 2911 124 ⇆ ☏

Horsforth Layton Rise, Layton Rd, Horsforth LS18 5EX
☎ 0113 258 6819 & 258 5200(pro) Fax 0113 258 6819
Moorland/parkland course overlooking airport.
18 holes, 6243yds, Par 71, SSS 70, Course record 65.
Club membership 750.
Visitors restricted Sat & with member only Sun.
Societies must apply in writing.
Green Fees not confirmed..
Prof Dean Stokes/Simon Booth
Facilities ⚲ 🏠 ✐
Location 6.5m NW of city centre off A65

Hotel ★★★ 70% Posthouse Bramhope, Leeds Rd, BRAMHOPE ☎ 0113 284 2911 124 ⇆ ☏

Leeds Elmete Ln LS8 2LJ
☎ 0113 265 8775 Fax 0113 232 3369
e-mail: leedsgccobble@btconnect.com
Parkland course with pleasant views.
18 holes, 6097yds, Par 69, SSS 69, Course record 63.
Club membership 600.
Visitors with member only weekends.weekends. Must book in advance with member only,weekdays Must book in advance weekdays.
Societies must apply in writing.
Green Fees £27 per round/£32 per day.
Prof Simon Longster
Facilities ⊗ ⅲ ᴸ ☕ ♀ ⚲ 🏠 ⛳ ☍ ✐
Location 5m NE of city centre on A6120 off A58

Hotel ★★★ 80% Haley's Hotel & Restaurant, Shire Oak Rd, Headingley, LEEDS ☎ 0113 278 4446 22 ⇆ ☏ Annexe7 ⇆ ☏

Leeds Golf Centre Wike Ridge Ln, Shadwell LS17 9JW
☎ 0113 288 6000 Fax 0113 288 6185
Two courses - the 18-hole Wike Ridge, a traditional heathland course designed by Donald Steel. The sand-based greens are constructed to USGA specification and there are an excellent variety of holes with some very challenging Par 5's. The 12-hole Oaks is complemented by a floodlit driving range and other practice facilities. The course is the home of the Leeds Golf Academy.
Wike Ridge Course. 18 holes, 6482yds, Par 72, SSS 71.
Oaks: 12 holes, 1610yds, Par 36.
Club membership 500.
Visitors no restrictions, telephone booking advisable.
Societies tee reservation available in advance.
Green Fees £14.50(£16.50 weekends).
Cards ▦ ▬ ▬ ▦ ▦ ▨
Prof Neil Harvey
Designer Donald Steel
Facilities ⊗ ⅲ ᴸ ☕ ♀ ⚲ 🏠 ☍ ☍ ✐ ♐
Location 5m N,take A58 course on N side of Shadwell

Hotel ★★★ 80% Haley's Hotel & Restaurant, Shire Oak Rd, Headingley, LEEDS ☎ 0113 278 4446 22 ⇆ ☏ Annexe7 ⇆ ☏

Middleton Park Municipal Middleton Park, Middleton
LS10 3TN ☎ 0113 270 0449 & 270 9506
Parkland course.
18 holes, 5263yds, Par 68, SSS 66, Course record 63.
Club membership 320.
Visitors may only use the club 6 times in one year, club only open weekends.
Green Fees prices under review.
Prof Jim Pape
Facilities ᴸ ♀ ⚲ 🏠 ⛳
Location 3m S off A653

Hotel ★★★★ 69% Le Meridien Queen's, City Square, LEEDS
☎ 0113 243 1323 & 0870 4008696
Fax 0113 242 5154 199 ⇆ ☏

Moor Allerton Coal Rd, Wike LS17 9NH
☎ 0113 266 1154 Fax 0113 237 1124
e-mail: pat@mooorallerton.demon.co.uk
The Moor Allerton Club, established in 1923, has 27 holes set in 220 acres of undulating parkland, with testing water hazards and magnificent views extending across the Vale of York. The Championship Course was designed by Robert Trent Jones, the famous American course architect, and provides a challenge to both high and low handicapped golfers.
Lakes Course: 18 holes, 6470yds, Par 71, SSS 72.
Blackmoor Course: 18 holes, 6673yds, Par 71, SSS 73.
High Course: 18 holes, 6841yds, Par 72, SSS 74.
Club membership 1200.

Visitors contact professional (0113 266 5209).
Societies must apply in advance.
Green Fees £50 per day; £45 per round (£83/£72 weekends).
Cards ▦ ▬ ▨
Prof Richard Lane
Designer Robert Trent Jones
Facilities ⊗ ⅲ ᴸ ☕ ♀ ⚲ 🏠 ⛳ ☍ ☍ ✐ ♐
& Leisure sauna.
Location 5.5m N of city centre on A61

Hotel ★★★ 68% The Merrion, Merrion Centre, LEEDS ☎ 0113 243 9191 109 ⇆ ☏

Moortown Harrogate Rd, Alwoodley LS17 7DB
☎ 0113 268 6521 Fax 0113 268 0986
e-mail: moortown-gc.co.uk
Championship course, tough but fair. Springy moorland turf, natural hazards of heather, gorse and streams, cunningly placed bunkers and immaculate greens. Original home of Ryder Cup in 1929. ▶

18 holes, 6782yds, Par 72, SSS 73, Course record 66.
Club membership 566.
Visitors   must contact in advance.
Societies   apply in writing in advance.
Green Fees not confirmed.
Prof   Bryon Hutchinson
Designer   A McKenzie
Facilities   ⊗ ⫼ ⓘ ⓘ ⚑ ⓘ ☒ ↘ ⚒ ⊘
Location   6m N of city centre on A61

Hotel   ★★★ 68% The Merrion, Merrion Centre,
                 LEEDS ☎ 0113 243 9191 109 ⇄ ⚑

Oulton Park Rothwell LS26 8EX
☎ 0113 282 3152 Fax 0113 282 6290
27-hole championship-length municipal course. Although
municipal, a dress rule is applied. 22-bay floodlit driving
range. Two tier putting. Host to the City of Leeds Cup (PGA)
each July.
Hall Course: 9 holes, 3286yds, Par 36, SSS 36.
Park Course: 9 holes, 3184yds, Par 35, SSS 35.
Royds Course: 9 holes, 3169yds, Par 35, SSS 35.
Club membership 450.
Visitors   must apply up to 5 days in advance. Dress code
                 in operation.
Societies   Mon-Fri. Must contact in advance.
Green Fees not confirmed.
Cards   ⊟ ▦ ▦ ▨ ▨
Prof   Stephen Gromett
Designer   Dave Thomas
Facilities   ⊗ ⫼ ⓘ ⓘ ⚑ ⓘ ☒ ⚑ ⓘ ↘ ⊘ ⎰
& Leisure   heated indoor swimming pool, squash, fishing,
                 sauna, solarium, gymnasium.
Location   Junc 30 on M62

Hotel   ★★★★★ 63% Oulton Hall Hotel,
                 Rothwell Ln, Oulton, LEEDS
                 ☎ 0113 282 1000 152 ⇄ ⚑

Roundhay Park Ln LS8 2EJ ☎ 0113 266 2695
Attractive municipal parkland course, natural hazards, easy
walking.
9 holes, 5223yds, Par 70, SSS 65, Course record 61.
Club membership 250.
Visitors   must contact professional at all times.
Societies   telephone or write to the professional.
Green Fees not confirmed.
Prof   James Pape
Facilities   ⓘ ☒ ⚑ ⓘ ⊘
Location   4m NE of city centre off A58

Hotel   ★★★ 80% Haley's Hotel & Restaurant, Shire
                 Oak Rd, Headingley, LEEDS
                 ☎ 0113 278 4446 22 ⇄ ⚑ Annexe7 ⇄ ⚑

Sand Moor Alwoodley Ln LS17 7DJ
☎ 0113 268 5180 Fax 0113 268 5180
A beautiful, undulating course overlooking Lord
Harewood's estate and the Eccup Reservoir. The course
is wooded with some holes adjacent to water. The 12th is
perhaps the most difficult where the fairway falls away
towards the reservoir.
18 holes, 6429yds, Par 71, SSS 71, Course record 63.
Club membership 553.
Visitors   restricted weekends & bank holidays.
Societies   must apply in advance.
Green Fees not confirmed.

Prof   Peter Tupling
Designer   Dr A Mackenzie
Facilities   ⊗ ⫼ ⓘ ⓘ ⚑ ⓘ ☒ ⚑ ⓘ ⊘
Location   5m N of city centre off A61

Hotel   ★★★ 70% Posthouse Bramhope, Leeds
                 Rd, BRAMHOPE
                 ☎ 0113 284 2911 124 ⇄ ⚑

South Leeds Gipsy Ln, Beeston LS11 5TU
☎ 0113 277 1676 & 270 2598 (pro)
e-mail: johneal.sec@slgc.freeserve.co.uk
Parkland course, windy, hard walking, good views.
18 holes, 5769yds, Par 69, SSS 68, Course record 64.
Club membership 500.
Visitors   welcome weekdays except competition time,
                 may not play weekends.
Societies   must apply in advance.
Green Fees £18(£26 weekends & bank holidays).
Prof   Mike Lewis
Facilities   ⊗ ⫼ ⓘ ⓘ ⚑ ⓘ ☒ ⚑ ⊘
Location   3m S of city centre off A653

Hotel   ★★★★ 69% Le Meridien Queen's, City
                 Square, LEEDS
                 ☎ 0113 243 1323 & 0870 4008696
                 Fax 0113 242 5154 199 ⇄ ⚑

Temple Newsam Temple-Newsam Rd LS15 0LN
☎ 0113 264 5624
Two parkland courses. Testing long 13th (563 yds) on
second course.
Lord Irwin: 18 holes, 6460yds, Par 68, SSS 71,
Course record 66.
Lady Dorothy: 18 holes, 6299yds, Par 70, SSS 70,
Course record 67.
Club membership 520.
Visitors   no restrictions.
Societies   must apply in advance in writing.
Green Fees not confirmed.
Prof   Alan Swaine
Facilities   ⊗ ⫼ by prior arrangement ☒ ⚑ ⓘ ⚑ ⓘ ⊘
Location   3.5m E of city centre off A63

Hotel   ★★★ 80% Haley's Hotel & Restaurant, Shire
                 Oak Rd, Headingley, LEEDS
                 ☎ 0113 278 4446 22 ⇄ ⚑ Annexe7 ⇄ ⚑

MARSDEN   Map 07 SE01

Marsden Mount Rd, Hemplow HD7 6NN
☎ 01484 844253
Moorland course with good views, natural hazards, windy.
9 holes, 5702yds, Par 68, SSS 68, Course record 63.
Club membership 200.
Visitors   must play with member at weekends but not
                 before 4pm Sat.
Societies   Mon-Fri; must contact in advance.
Green Fees £10 per round(£15 bank holidays).
Prof   Nick Krzywicki
Designer   Dr McKenzie
Facilities   ⊗ ⫼ ⓘ ⓘ ☒ ⚑ ⓘ
& Leisure   hard tennis courts.
Location   S side off A62   ▶

Hotel   ★★★ 64% Briar Court Hotel, Halifax Rd, Birchencliffe, HUDDERSFIELD
☎ 01484 519902   48 ⇥ ☏

MELTHAM   Map 07 SE01

Meltham Thick Hollins Hall HD7 3DQ
☎ 01484 850227 Fax 01484 850227
e-mail: meltham@thegolfcourse.co.uk
Parkland course with good views. Testing 548 yd, 13th hole (Par 5).
18 holes, 6379yds, Par 71, SSS 70, Course record 67.
Club membership 680.
Visitors   may not play Sat & Wed (Ladies Day), desirable to contact professional in advance.
Societies   apply in writing/telephone.Application form on website.
Green Fees £27 per day; £22 per round (£32/£27 weekends & bank holidays).
Prof   Paul Davies
Designer   Alex Herd
Facilities   ⊗ ⫼ ⯮ ⯑ ♀ ⛛ ⛿ ⛳ ⌁
Location   SE side of village off B6107

Hotel   ★★★ 65% The George Hotel, St George's Square, HUDDERSFIELD
☎ 01484 515444   60 ⇥ ☏

MIRFIELD   Map 08 SE21

Dewsbury District Sands Ln WF14 8HJ
☎ 01924 492399 & 496030 Fax 01924 492399
Heathland/parkland course with panoramic views and hard walking. Ponds in middle of 3rd fairway, left of 5th green and 17th green.
18 holes, 6360yds, Par 71, SSS 71.
Club membership 600.
Visitors   At weekends only after 2.30pm on Sundays.Telephone in advance.
Societies   telephone bookings.
Green Fees £22.50 per day; £17.50 per round (£22.50 per round Sun).
Prof   Nigel P Hirst
Designer   Old Tom Morris/ Peter Alliss
Facilities   ⊗ ⫼ by prior arrangement ⯮ ⯑ ♀ ⛛ ⛿ ⛳ ⌁
& Leisure   snooker tables.
Location   Off A644, 6m from junct 25 on M62

Hotel   ★★★ 65% The George Hotel, St George's Square, HUDDERSFIELD
☎ 01484 515444   60 ⇥ ☏

MORLEY   Map 08 SE22

Howley Hall Scotchman Ln LS27 0NX
☎ 01924 478417 & 350102 (Prof) Fax 01924 350104
e-mail: office@howleyhall.co.uk
Parkland course with easy walking and superb views of the Pennines and Calder Valley.
18 holes, 6346yds, Par 71, SSS 71, Course record 66.
Club membership 700.
Visitors   play from yellow markers. May not play Sat.
Societies   contact for details.
Green Fees £30 per day; £27.50 per 18 holes(£38 weekends & bank holidays).
Prof   Gary Watkinson

Facilities   ⊗ ⫼ ⯮ ⯑ ♀ ⛛ ⛿ ⛳ ⌁ ⌂ ⌁
Location   1.5m S on B6123

Hotel   ★★ 70% Alder House Hotel, Towngate Rd, Healey Ln, BATLEY
☎ 01924 444777   20 ⇥ ☏

NORMANTON   Map 08 SE32

Normanton Snydale Rd WF6 1PN
☎ 01924 892943 Fax 01924 220134
9 holes, 5288yds, Par 66, SSS 66.
Location   0.5m SE on B6133
Telephone for further details

Hotel   ★★★ 64% Chasley Hotel, Queen St, WAKEFIELD ☎ 01924 372111   64 ⇥ ☏

OSSETT   Map 08 SE22

Low Laithes Parkmill Ln, Flushdyke WF5 9AP
☎ 01924 274667 & 266067 Fax 01924 266067
Testing parkland course.
18 holes, 6463yds, Par 72, SSS 71, Course record 65.
Club membership 600.
Visitors   may not play before 9.30am and 12.30-1.30 weekdays and before 10am and 12-2 weekends/bank holidays.
Societies   by prior arrangement.
Green Fees not confirmed.
Prof   Paul Browning
Designer   Dr Mackenzie
Facilities   ⊗ ⫼ ⯮ ⯑ ♀ ⛛ ⛿ ⛳ ⌁
Location   Leave M1 at jct 40 then signposted on Dewsbury road 0.5m from M1

Hotel   ★★★ 64% Posthouse Northampton/Rugby, CRICK ☎ 0870 400 9059 88 ⇥ ☏

OTLEY   Map 08 SE24

Otley Off West Busk Ln LS21 3NG
☎ 01943 465329 Fax 01943 850387
e-mail: office@otley-golfclub.co.uk
An expansive course with magnificent views across Wharfedale. It is well-wooded with streams crossing the fairway. The 4th is a fine hole which generally needs two woods to reach the plateau green. The 17th is a good short hole.
18 holes, 6225yds, Par 70, SSS 70, Course record 65.
Club membership 700.
Visitors   telephone to check tee time. May not play Tue morning or Sat.
Societies   telephone enquiries welcome, bookings in writing.
Green Fees £35 per 36 holes; £28 per 18/27 holes (£41/35 weekends and bank holidays).
Prof   Steven Tomkinson
Facilities   ⊗ ⫼ ⯮ ⯑ ♀ ⛛ ⛿ ⛳ ⌁
Location   1m W of Otley off A6038

Hotel   ★★★ 70% Posthouse Bramhope, Leeds Rd, BRAMHOPE
☎ 0113 284 2911 124 ⇥ ☏

OUTLANE   Map 07 SE01

Outlane Slack Ln, Off New Hey Rd HD3 3YL
☎ 01422 311789 & 374762 Fax 01422 311789
18 hole moorland course with undulating fairways. Four par 3 holes with an 8th hole of 249 yards and a 15th regarded as the hardest par 3 in Yorkshire. The three par 5's may be reachable on a good day in 2 strokes but in adverse conditions will take more than three. Smaller than average greens on some holes, which makes for accurate second shots.
18 holes, 6015yds, Par 71, SSS 70, Course record 66.
Club membership 600.
Visitors   telephone in advance, must be correctly equipped and attired. No play Sat, limited Sun morning.
Societies   apply in writing.
Green Fees £18 (£28 weekends & bank holidays reduced rate after 1.30pm Sun).
Prof   David Chapman
Facilities   ⊗ ∭ ⅃ ■ ♀ ⚲ 🏠 ☂ ♂
Location   S side of village off A640

Hotel   ★★★ 69% Old Golf House Hotel, New Hey Rd, Outlane, HUDDERSFIELD
☎ 01422 379311   52 ⇆ ☏

PONTEFRACT   Map 08 SE42

Mid Yorkshire Havercroft Ln, Darrington WF8 3BP
☎ 01977 704522 Fax 01977 600823
An 18-hole championship-standard course opened in 1993, and widely considered to be one of the finest new courses in Yorkshire.
18 holes, 6500yds, Par 72, SSS 71, Course record 68.
Club membership 500.
Visitors   tee times bookable by telephone, visitors after 12 noon at weekends.
Societies   apply in writing to the secretary.
Green Fees £18 per round(£25 weekends).
Cards   ▦ ▭ ⑨
Prof   Alistair Cobbett
Designer   Steve Marnoch
Facilities   ⊗ ∭ ⅃ ■ ♀ ⚲ 🏠 ☂ ⤢ 🚜 ♂ ꝉ
Location   On the A1, 0.5m south intersection of A1/M62

Hotel   ★★★ 71% Wentbridge House Hotel, WENTBRIDGE, ☎ 01977 620444
14 ⇆ ☏ Annexe4 ⇆ ☏

Pontefract & District Park Ln WF8 4QS ☎ 01977 792241
Fax 01977 792241 e-mail: pdgc@cwcom.net
Undulating parkland course, some elevated tees.
18 holes, 6227yds, Par 72, SSS 70.
Club membership 800.
Visitors   welcome except Wed & weekends, advisable to contact in advance.
Societies   welcome except Wed & weekends.
Green Fees £25 per day/round(£32 weekends).
Prof   Nick Newman
Designer   A McKenzie
Facilities   ⊗ ∭ ⅃ ■ ♀ ⚲ 🏠 ♂
Location   1.5m W on B6134

Hotel   ★★★ 71% Wentbridge House Hotel, WENTBRIDGE, ☎ 01977 620444
14 ⇆ ☏ Annexe4 ⇆ ☏

PUDSEY   Map 08 SE23

Calverley Woodhall Ln LS28 5QY
☎ 0113 256 9244 Fax 0113 256 4362
Parkland course on gently undulating terrain where accurate approach shots are rewarded to small greens.
18 holes, 5590yds, Par 68, SSS 67, Course record 64.
Club membership 565.
Visitors   advisable to book 18 hole course in advance and may not play Sun morning. 9 hole course, pay and play at all times.
Societies   contact in writing or telephone.
Green Fees £21 per day; £15 per round (£20 weekends); £6 per 18 holes. Short course.
Prof   Derek Johnson
Facilities   ⊗ ∭ ⅃ ■ ♀ ⚲ 🏠 ☂ 🚜 ♂
Location   Signposted Calverley from A647 Leeds/Bradford road

Hotel   ★★ 68% Park Drive Hotel, 12 Park Dr, BRADFORD ☎ 01274 480194   11 ⇆ ☏

Fulneck LS28 8NT ☎ 0113 256 5191
Picturesque parkland course.
9 holes, 5456yds, Par 66, SSS 67, Course record 65.
Club membership 250.
Visitors   with member only weekends & bank holidays.
Societies   must apply in writing.
Green Fees not confirmed.
Facilities   ⚲
Location   Pudsey, between Leeds/Bradford

Hotel   ★★★ Novotel Bradford, 6 Roydsdale Way, Euroway Estate, BRADFORD
☎ 01274 683683 127 ⇆ ☏

Woodhall Hills Calverley LS28 5UN ☎ 0113 255 4594
Meadowland course, prevailing SW winds, fairly hard walking. Testing holes: 8th, 377 yd (par 4); 14th, 206 yd (par 3).
18 holes, 6296yds, Par 71, SSS 70, Course record 63.
Club membership 570.
Visitors   any day advise manager/professional in advance, Sat after 16.30; Sun after 9.30am.
Societies   telephone in advance.
Green Fees £20.50(£25 weekends).
Prof   Warren Lockett
Facilities   ⊗ ∭ ⅃ ■ ♀ ⚲ 🏠 ♂
Location   1m NW off A647

Hotel   ★★ 68% Park Drive Hotel, 12 Park Dr, BRADFORD ☎ 01274 480194   11 ⇆ ☏

RAWDON   Map 08 SE23

Rawdon Golf & Lawn Tennis Club Buckstone Dr LS19 6BD ☎ 0113 250 6040
Undulating parkland course.
9 holes, 5980yds, Par 72, SSS 69, Course record 65.
Club membership 600.
Visitors   must contact in advance & have handicap certificate. With member only.
Societies   must contact in advance.
Green Fees £10(£11 weekends).
Facilities   ⊗ ∭ ⅃ ■ ♀ ⚲ 🏠 ♂
& Leisure   hard and grass tennis courts.
Location   Nw of Leeds off A65   ▶

Hotel ★★★ 67% Apperley Manor, Apperley Ln, Apperley Bridge, BRADFORD ☎ 0113 250 5626 13 ⇆ ⟁

RIDDLESDEN   Map 07 SE04

Riddlesden Howden Rough BD20 5QN ☎ 01535 602148
Undulating moorland course with prevailing west winds, some hard walking and beautiful views. Ten par 3 holes and spectacular 6th and 15th holes played over old quarry sites.
18 holes, 4295yds, Par 63, SSS 61.
Club membership 350.
Visitors restricted before 2pm weekends.
Societies apply by telephone or in writing.
Green Fees £16 per round/day(£21 weekends & bank holidays).
Facilities ⊗ ⟨ ⟩ ▯ ☭ ♀ ⟁
Location 1m NW

Hotel ★★ 66% Dalesgate Hotel, 406 Skipton Rd, Utley, KEIGHLEY
☎ 01535 664930 20 ⇆ ⟁

SCARCROFT   Map 08 SE34

Scarcroft Syke Ln LS14 3BQ
☎ 0113 289 2311 Fax 0113 289 3835
e-mail: sge@cwcomm.net
Undulating parkland course with prevailing west wind and easy walking.
18 holes, 6426yds, Par 71, SSS 69.
Club membership 667.
Visitors must contact in advance.Handicap certificate required.
Societies must contact in advance.
Green Fees £38 per day; £30 per round (£40 per round weekends).
Cards ▦ ▦ ▦ ▦ ▩ ▨
Prof Darren Tear
Designer Charles Mackenzie
Facilities ⊗ ⟨ ⟩ ▯ ☭ ♀ ⟁ ⎕ ⌁ ⟋
Location 0.5m N of village off A58

Hotel ★★★ 68% The Merrion, Merrion Centre, LEEDS ☎ 0113 243 9191 109 ⇆ ⟁

SHIPLEY   Map 07 SE13

Marriott Hollins Hall Hotel & Country Club
Hollins Hill, Otley Rd BD17 7QW
☎ 01274 534212 & 534211 Fax 01274 534220
Set in natural heathland amongst the beautiful Yorkshire moors and dales. The course is majestic, challenging and classically designed in the spirit of the game.
18 holes, 6671yds, Par 71, SSS 71, Course record 70.
Club membership 350.
Visitors must contact in advance - 10 days max.
Societies telephone in advance 01274 530053.
Green Fees £30 per round;£45 per day(£40 per round weekends).
Cards ▦ ▦ ▦ ▩ ▨
Designer Ross McMurray
Facilities ⊗ ⟨ ⟩ ▯ ☭ ♀ ⟁ ⎕ ⌁ ⟌ ⟍ ⟋ ⎿
& Leisure heated indoor swimming pool, sauna, solarium, gymnasium.
Location 3m N on the A6038 Otley road

Marriott-Hollins Hall

Hotel ★★★★ 70% Marriott Hollins Hall Hotel & Country Club, Hollins Hill, Baildon, SHIPLEY ☎ 01274 530053 122 ⇆ ⟁

Northcliffe High Bank Ln BD18 4LJ ☎ 01274 596731
Fax 01274 596731 e-mail: northcliffe@bigfoot.com
Parkland course with magnificent views of moors. Testing 1st hole (18th green 100 feet below tee).
18 holes, 6104yds, Par 71, SSS 69, Course record 64.
Club membership 700.
Visitors no restrictions.
Societies book via secretary in advance, weekdays only.
Green Fees £20 per round (£25 weekend and bank holidays).
Prof M Hillas
Designer James Braid
Facilities ⊗ ⟨ ⟩ ▯ ☭ ♀ ⟁ ⎕ ⌁ ⟍ ⟋
Location 1.25m SW of Shipley, off A650

Hotel ★★★★ 70% Marriott Hollins Hall Hotel & Country Club, Hollins Hill, Baildon, SHIPLEY ☎ 01274 530053 122 ⇆ ⟁

SILSDEN   Map 07 SE04

Silsden Brunthwaite Ln, Brunthwaite BD20 0ND
☎ 01535 652998 Fax 01535 654273
e-mail: info@silsdengolfclub.co.uk
Tight downland course which can be windy. Good views of the Aire Valley. A new clubhouse offers day-long facilities and the course is currently being redesigned.
18 holes, 5259yds, Par 67, SSS 66, Course record 62.
Club membership 350.
Visitors telephone in advance for weekend bookings.
Societies telephone in advance or apply in writing.
Green Fees not confirmed.
Facilities ⊗ ⟨ ⟩ ▯ ☭ ♀ ⟁
Location entering Silsden from direction of Aire Valley trunk road, turn immediately right after canal bridge

Hotel ★★ 66% Dalesgate Hotel, 406 Skipton Rd, Utley, KEIGHLEY
☎ 01535 664930 20 ⇆ ⟁

> AA Hotels that have special arrangements with golf courses are listed at the back of the guide

SOWERBY
Map 07 SE02

Ryburn The Shaw, Norland HX6 3QP
☎ 01422 831355
Moorland course, easy walking.
9 holes, 4984yds, Par 66, SSS 64, Course record 64.
Club membership 200.
Visitors must contact in advance.
Societies apply in writing.
Green Fees not confirmed.
Facilities ⊗ ⅊Ⅲ ⅃ ⅃ ⅄ ⅄ ⅄
Location 1m S of Sowerby Bridge off A58

Hotel ★★★ 67% The Rock Inn Hotel, Holywell
Green, HALIFAX
☎ 01422 379721 30 ⇆ ♠

TODMORDEN
Map 07 SD92

Todmorden Rive Rocks, Cross Stone Rd OL14 8RD
☎ 01706 812986
Pleasant moorland course.
9 holes, 5902yds, Par 68, SSS 68, Course record 67.
Club membership 240.
Visitors restricted Thu & weekends. Advisable to contact
in advance.
Societies must apply in writing.
Green Fees not confirmed.
Facilities ⊗ by prior arrangement ⅊Ⅲ by prior arrangement
⅃ ⅄ ⅄
Location NE off A646

Hotel ★★★ 66% Carlton Hotel, Albert St, HEBDEN
BRIDGE ☎ 01422 844400 16 ⇆ ♠

WAKEFIELD
Map 08 SE32

City of Wakefield Horbury Rd WF2 8QS
☎ 01924 360282
Mature, level parkland course.
18 holes, 6319yds, Par 72, SSS 70, Course record 67.
Club membership 600.
Visitors restricted weekends.
Societies must apply in advance to stewardess 01924
367242.
Green Fees not confirmed.
Prof Roger Holland
Designer J S F Morrison
Facilities ⊗ ⅊Ⅲ ⅃ ⅃ ⅄ ⅄ ⅄
Location 1.5m W of city centre on A642

Hotel ★★★ 68% Posthouse Wakefield, Queen's Dr,
Ossett, WAKEFIELD
☎ 0870 400 9082 99 ⇆ ♠

Painthorpe House Painthorpe Ln, Painthorpe, Crigglestone
WF4 3HE ☎ 01924 274527 & 255083 Fax 01924 252022
Undulating meadowland course, easy walking.
9 holes, 4544yds, Par 62, SSS 62, Course record 63.
Club membership 150.
Visitors pay and play Mon-Sat, after 2.30pm on Sun.
Societies must telephone in advance.
Green Fees £5 per 18 holes(£6 weekends).
Cards ▨
Facilities ⊗ ⅊Ⅲ ⅃ ⅃ ⅄ ⅄
Location 2m S off A636, 0.5m from jct 39 M1

Hotel ★★★ 68% Posthouse Wakefield, Queen's Dr,
Ossett, WAKEFIELD
☎ 0870 400 9082 99 ⇆ ♠

Wakefield Woodthorpe Ln, Sandal WF2 6JH
☎ 01924 258778 (sec) & 255380 (pro) Fax 01924 242752
A well-sheltered meadowland/heath course with easy
walking and good views.
18 holes, 6653yds, Par 72, SSS 72, Course record 66.
Club membership 540.
Visitors contact must be made in advance. Visitors Wed,
Thu and Fri only.
Societies must apply in writing.
Green Fees £27 per round;£32 per day(£40 weekends).
Prof Ian M Wright
Designer A McKenzie/S Herd
Facilities ⊗ ⅊Ⅲ ⅃ ⅃ ⅄ ⅄ ⅄ ⅄
Location 3m S of Wakefield, off A61

Hotel ★★★ 68% Posthouse Wakefield, Queen's Dr,
Ossett, WAKEFIELD
☎ 0870 400 9082 99 ⇆ ♠

WETHERBY
Map 08 SE44

Wetherby Linton Ln LS22 4JF
☎ 01937 580089 Fax 01937 581915
Parkland course with fine views.
18 holes, 6235yds, Par 71, SSS 70, Course record 63.
Club membership 650.
Visitors may not play Mon & Tues morning.
Societies apply in writing or telephone in advance.
Green Fees not confirmed.
Prof Mark Daubney
Facilities ⊗ ⅊Ⅲ ⅃ ⅃ ⅄ ⅄ ⅄ ⅄ ⅄ ⅄ ⅄
Location 1m W off A661

Hotel ★★★♨ 73% Wood Hall Hotel, Trip Ln,
Linton, WETHERBY
☎ 01937 587271 36 ⇆ ♠ Annexe6 ⇆ ♠

WIKE
Map 08 SE34

The Village Golf Course Backstone Gill Ln LS17 9JU
☎ 0113 273 7471
A 9 hole pay and play course in an elevated position enjoying
long panoramic views. The holes are par 3, 4 and 5's and
include water hazards and shaped large greens.
9 holes, 5200yds, Par 72, SSS 68, Course record 66.
Visitors smart casual wear
Societies contact in advance by letter/telephone
Green Fees £10 per 18 holes; per 9 holes (£12/£8
weekends and bak holidays)n.
Designer B & D Hemines
Facilities ⊗ ⅊Ⅲ ⅃ ⅃ ⅄ ⅄
& Leisure fishing.
Location signposted, 1m off A61, 2m off A58

Hotel ★★ 69% Aragon Hotel, 250 Stainbeck Ln,
LEEDS ☎ 0113 275 9306 12 ⇆ ♠

> Entries with a green background
> identify courses considered to be
> particularly interesting

CHANNEL ISLANDS

ALDERNEY

ALDERNEY   Map 16

Alderney Route des Carrieres GY9 3YD ☎ 01481 822835
Undulating seaside course with sea on all sides and offering
magnificent views from its high tees and greens. Course
designed by Frank Pennink.
9 holes, 5006yds, Par 64, SSS 65, Course record 65.
Club membership 400.
Visitors   may not play before 10am at weekends.
                Advisable to contact in advance.
Societies   must contact in advance.
Green Fees £20 per day (£25 weekends & bank holidays).
Cards   ▨ 🔳 📇 ▨
Facilities ⊗ by prior arrangement ⊾ ⬛ ♀ ♨ 🏠 ⚐ ♂
Location   1m E of St Annes

GUERNSEY

L'ANCRESSE VALE   Map 16

Royal Guernsey GY3 5BY
☎ 01481 246523 Fax 01481 243960
e-mail: r-g-g-c@lineone.net
Not quite as old as its neighbour Royal Jersey, Royal
Guernsey is a sporting course which was re-designed
after World War II by Mackenzie Ross, who has many
fine courses to his credit. It is a pleasant links, well-
maintained, and administered by the States of Guernsey
in the form of the States Tourist Committee. The 8th
hole, a good par 4, requires an accurate second shot to
the green set amongst the gorse and thick rough. The
18th, with lively turns, needs a strong shot to reach the
green well down below. The course is windy, with hard
walking. There is a junior section.
18 holes, 6215yds, Par 70, SSS 70, Course record 64.
Club membership 934.
Visitors   must have a handicap certificate; may not
                play on Thu, Sat afternoons & Sun.
Green Fees £36 per day.
Prof   Norman Wood
Designer   Mackenzie Ross
Facilities ⊗ ⅲ ⊾ ⬛ ♀ ♨ 🏠 ⚐ ♂ ⚘
Location   3m N of St Peter Port

Hotel   ★★★★ 68% St Pierre Park Hotel, Rohais,
                ST PETER PORT
                ☎ 01481 728282 132 ⇥ ♠

ST PETER PORT   Map 16

St Pierre Park Golf Club Rohais GY1 1FD
☎ 01481 728282 Fax 01481 712041 e-mail: stppark@itl.net
Par 3 parkland course with delightful setting, with lakes,
streams and many tricky holes.
9 holes, 2610yds, Par 54, SSS 50, Course record 52.
Club membership 200.

Visitors   must book tee times. Strict dress code, contact
                club in advance for datails.
Societies   must contact in advance.
Green Fees not confirmed.
Cards   ▨ 🔳 📇 ▨ ▨
Prof   Roy Corbet
Designer   Jacklin
Facilities ⊗ ⅲ ⊾ ⬛ ♀ ♨ 🏠 ⚐ ♂ ♂ ♂ ♂
& Leisure   hard tennis courts, heated indoor swimming
                pool, sauna, solarium, gymnasium.
Location   1m W off Rohais Rd

Hotel   ★★★★ 68% St Pierre Park Hotel, Rohais,
                ST PETER PORT ☎ 01481 728282 132 ⇥ ♠

JERSEY

GROUVILLE   Map 16

Royal Jersey Le Chemin au Greves JE3 9BD
☎ 01534 854416 Fax 01534 854684
A seaside links, historic because of its age: its centenary
was celebrated in 1978. It is also famous for the fact that
Britain's greatest golfer, Harry Vardon, was born in a
little cottage on the edge of the course and learned his
golf here.
18 holes, 6100yds, Par 70, SSS 70, Course record 63.
Club membership 1209.
Visitors   restricted to 10am-noon & 2pm-4pm Mon-
                Fri & after 2.30pm weekends & bank
                holidays.
Societies   welcome Mon-Fri. Must apply in writing.
Green Fees £45 per round.
Cards   ▨ 🔳 📇 ▨ ▨
Prof   David Morgan
Facilities ⊗ ⅲ ⊾ ⬛ ♀ ♨ 🏠 ⚐ ♂ ⚘ ♂
Location   4m E of St Helier off coast rd

Hotel   ★★★ 66% Old Court House Hotel,
                GOREY ☎ 01534 854444 58 ⇥ ♠

LA MOYE   Map 16

La Moye La Route Orange JE3 8GQ
☎ 01534 743401 Fax 01534 747289
Seaside championship links course (venue for the Jersey
Seniors Open) situated in an exposed position on the
south western corner of the island overlooking St Ouens
Bay. Offers spectacular views, two start points, full
course all year - no temporary greens.
18 holes, 6664yds, Par 72, SSS 72, Course record 68.
Club membership 1300.
Visitors   must contact course ranger in advance
                01534 747166. Visitors may play after
                2.30pm weekends and bank holidays.
Societies   apply in writing.
Green Fees £45 per round (£50 weekends & bank
                holidays).
Cards   ▨ 🔳 📇 ▨
Prof   Mike Deeley
Designer   James Braid

                                          ▶

Facilities	⊗ ⫻ ▙ ▆ ♀ ⚘ 🏠 ⛳ ♨ ✓ ⎛
Location	W side of village off A13

Hotel	★★★★ 78% The Atlantic Hotel, Le Mont de la Pulente, ST BRELADE ☎ 01534 744101 50 ⇆ 🐾

ST CLEMENT   Map 16

St Clement Jersey Recreation Grounds JE2 6PN
☎ 01534 21938
Very tight moorland course. Holes cross over fairways, impossible to play to scratch. Suitable for middle to high handicaps.
9 holes, 2244yds, Par 30.
Club membership 500.
Green Fees not confirmed.
Facilities ⚘
& Leisure hard tennis courts.
Location E side of St Helier on A5

Hotel   ★★★★🏊 Longueville Manor Hotel, ST SAVIOUR ☎ 01534 725501   32 ⇆ 🐾

ST OUEN   Map 16

Les Mielles Golf & Country Club JE3 7FQ
☎ 01534 482787 Fax 01534 485414
e-mail: lmgolfcc@itl.net
Challenging seaside parkland course with bent grass greens, dwarf rye fairways and picturesque ponds situated in the Island's largest conservation area within St Ouen's Bay.
18 holes, 6713yds, Par 70, SSS 68, Course record 59.
Club membership 1500.
Visitors welcome all times, prior booking recommended.
Societies write in advance to avoid disappointment.
Green Fees not confirmed.
Cards ▭ ▬ ▭ ▭ ▭
Prof Lee Elstone/Wayne Osmand
Designer J Le Brun/R Whitehead
Facilities ⊗ ⫻ ▙ ▆ ♀ ⚘ 🏠 ⛳ ♨ 🛒 ✓ ⎛
Location Centre of St Ouen's Bay

Hotel   ★★★ 69% Mermaid Hotel, ST PETER ☎ 01534 741255   68 ⇆ 🐾

ISLE OF MAN

CASTLETOWN   Map 06 SC26

Castletown Golf Links Fort Island, Derbyhaven IM9 1UA
☎ 01624 822201 & 822211 (pro shop) Fax 01624 824633
e-mail: fowlds@enterprise.net
Set on the Langness Peninsula, this superb Championship course is surrounded on three sides by the sea, and holds many surprises from its Championship tees. The hotel offers many leisure facilities.
18 holes, 6750yds, Par 72, SSS 72, Course record 64.
Club membership 600.
Visitors contact in advance. Sat reserved for hotel residents and club members. Ladies only Wed morning
Societies must telephone in advance.
Green Fees £30 (£35 weekends).
Cards ▭ ▬ ▭ ▭ ▭ ▭

Castletown Golf Links

Prof Murray Crowe
Designer McKenzie Ross
Facilities ⊗ ⫻ ▙ ▆ ♀ ⚘ 🏠 ⛳ ♨ 🛒 ✓ ⎛
& Leisure heated indoor swimming pool, sauna.

Hotel   ★★★ 68% Castletown Golf Links Hotel, Fort Island, CASTLETOWN ☎ 01624 822201   58 ⇆ 🐾

DOUGLAS   Map 06 SC37

Douglas Pulrose Park IM2 1AE ☎ 01624 661558
Hilly, parkland and moorland course under the control of Douglas Corporation.
18 holes, 5937yds, Par 69, SSS 69, Course record 62.
Club membership 330.
Visitors no restrictions.
Societies telephone to book tee time.
Green Fees £10 per round(£12 weekends).
Designer Dr A Mackenzie
Facilities ▙ ▆ ♀ ⚘ ♨ ✓
Location 1m W off A1

Hotel   ★★★ 67% The Empress Hotel, Central Promenade, DOUGLAS ☎ 01624 661155 102 ⇆ 🐾

Mount Murray Hotel & Country Club Mount Murray, Santon IM4 2HT ☎ 01624 661111 Fax 01624 611116
e-mail: hotel@enterprise.net
A challenging course with many natural features, lakes, streams etc. Six Par 5's, five Par 3's and the rest Par 4. Fine views over the whole island.
18 holes, 6664yds, Par 73, SSS 73, Course record 69.
Club membership 378.

Visitors must contact in advance. Visitors may not play before 9.30am weekends
Societies telephone in advance.   ▶

Green Fees £10 per 9 holes(£12.50 weekends);£20 per 18
holes (£25 weekends).
Cards 🖼️ 🖼️ 🖼️ 🖼️ 🖼️ 🖼️
Prof Andrew Dyson
Designer Bingley Sports Research
Facilities ⊗ ⅶ ⅄ 🍽️ ♀ ⚘ 🏠 🎯 🛶 👜 🦅 ♟️
& Leisure hard tennis courts, heated indoor swimming
pool, squash, sauna, solarium, gymnasium.
Location Located on main road 5m from Douglas towards
airport

Hotel ★★★★ 68% Mount Murray Hotel & Country
Club, Santon, DOUGLAS
☎ 01624 661111 90 ⇌ 🐾

ONCHAN   Map 06 SC47

King Edward Bay Golf & Country Club Howstrake,
Groudle Rd IM3 2JR ☎ 01624 672709
Club plays over King Edward Bay course. Hilly seaside links
course with natural hazards and good views.
18 holes, 5485yds, Par 67, SSS 65, Course record 62.
Club membership 370.
Visitors must have a handicap certificate.
Societies must contact in advance.
Green Fees not confirmed.
Prof Donald Jones
Designer Tom Morris
Facilities ⊗ ⅶ ⅄ 🍽️ ♀ ⚘ 🏠 🎯 🛶 ♟️
Location E side of town off A11

Hotel ★★★★ 69% Sefton Hotel, Harris Promenade,
DOUGLAS ☎ 01624 645500 104 ⇌ 🐾

PEEL   Map 06 SC28

Peel Rheast Ln IM5 1BG
☎ 01624 842227 & 843456 Fax 01624 843456
e-mail: lcullen@peelgolfclub.idps.co.uk
Moorland course, with natural hazards and easy walking.
Good views. 11th hole is a par 4, dog-leg.
18 holes, 5850yds, Par 69, SSS 69, Course record 69.
Club membership 856.
Visitors must contact in advance. Limited availability
weekends.
Societies apply in writing/telephone
Green Fees £18 per day (£25 weekends & bank holidays).
Cards 🖼️ 🖼️ 🖼️ 🖼️ 🖼️
Prof Murray Crowe
Designer Robert Braide
Facilities ⊗ ⅶ by prior arrangement ⅄ 🍽️ ♀ ⚘
🏠 🎯 🦅 ♟️
& Leisure snooker.
Location SE side of town centre on A1

Hotel ★★★ 67% The Empress Hotel, Central
Promenade, DOUGLAS
☎ 01624 661155 102 ⇌ 🐾

PORT ERIN   Map 06 SC16

Rowany Rowany Dr IM9 6LN ☎ 01624 834108 or 834072
Fax 01624 834072
Undulating seaside course with testing later holes.
18 holes, 5840yds, Par 70, SSS 69, Course record 66.
Club membership 550.
Visitors must contact in advance.
Societies telephone in advance.
Green Fees £14 per round(£18 weekends).
Designer G Lowe
Facilities ⊗ ⅶ by prior arrangement ⅄ 🍽️ ♀ ⚘ 🏠 🎯 🦅
♟️
Location N side of village off A32

Hotel ★★★ 67% Cherry Orchard Hotel, Bridson St,
PORT ERIN ☎ 01624 833811 32 ⇌ 🐾

PORT ST MARY   Map 06 SC26

Port St Mary Kallow Point Rd ☎ 01624 834932
Slightly hilly course with beautiful scenic views over Port St
Mary and the Irish Sea.
9 holes, 5418yds, Par 68, SSS 67, Course record 62.
Club membership 324.
Visitors anytime except between 8-10.30am weekends.
Societies contact for details.
Green Fees not confirmed.
Cards 🖼️ 🖼️ 🖼️
Designer George Duncan
Facilities ⊗ ⅶ ⅄ 🍽️ ♀ ⚘ 🎯 🛶 ♟️
& Leisure hard tennis courts, Croquet lawn.
Location Signposted on entering Port St Mary

Hotel ★★★ 67% Cherry Orchard Hotel, Bridson St,
PORT ERIN ☎ 01624 833811 32 ⇌ 🐾

RAMSEY   Map 06 SC49

Ramsey Brookfield IM8 2AH ☎ 01624 812244
Fax 01624 815833 e-mail: ramsey.golfclub@iofm.net
Parkland course, with easy walking. Windy. Good views.
Testing holes: 1st, par 5; 18th, par 3.
18 holes, 5960yds, Par 70, SSS 69, Course record 63.
Club membership 1000.
Visitors contact in advance, visitors may not play before
10am weekdays.
Societies must apply in advance.
Green Fees £22 per day(£25 per round weekends).
Cards 🖼️ 🖼️
Prof Calum Wilson
Designer James Braid
Facilities ⊗ ⅶ ⅄ 🍽️ ♀ ⚘ 🏠 🎯 ♟️
Location SW side of town

Hotel ★★★ 67% The Empress Hotel, Central
Promenade, DOUGLAS
☎ 01624 661155 102 ⇌ 🐾

AA Hotels that have special
arrangements with golf courses are listed at
the back of the guide

Where to stay, where to eat?
Visit the AA internet site
www.theAA.com

Scotland

ABERDEEN CITY

ABERDEEN   Map 15 NJ90

Auchmill Bonnyview Rd, West Heatheryfold AB16 7FQ
☎ 01224 714577 Fax 01224 648693
This course is definitely not for beginners - the fairways are tree-lined and very tight on most holes. Three holes are quite hilly and although the remainder is flat there are nice views over Aberdeen. The course is not recommended for anyone over 22 handicap unless they have plenty of golf balls!
18 holes, 5123metres, Par 68, SSS 67, Course record 67.
Club membership 300.
Visitors members have priority Sat & Wed for club competitions.
Societies apply in writing to Art and Recreation Dept, Aberdeen City Council.
Green Fees not confirmed.
Designer Neil Coles/Brian Hugget
Facilities ⊗ ⨶ ⑂ 𝄞 ⌣
Location Outskirts Aberdeen, A96 Aberdeen/Inverness

Hotel ★★★ 64% The Craighaar, Waterton Rd, Bankhead, ABERDEEN
☎ 01224 712275   55 ⇆ ſ⁓

Balnagask St Fitticks Rd AB11 3QT
☎ 01224 876407 Fax 01224 648693
Links course. Used by the Nigg Bay Club.
18 holes, 5986yds, Par 70, SSS 69.
Visitors book in person on day of play.
Societies apply to council tel 01224 522000.
Green Fees not confirmed.
Facilities ⊗ ⨶ ⑂ 𝄞 ⌣
& Leisure 9 hole pitch & putt course.
Location 2m E of city centre

Hotel ★★★ 67% Maryculter House Hotel, South Deeside Rd, Maryculter, ABERDEEN
☎ 01224 732124   23 ⇆ ſ⁓

Deeside Golf Rd, Bieldside AB15 9DL
☎ 01224 869457 Fax 01224 869457
An interesting riverside course with several tree-lined fairways. A stream comes into play at 9 of the 18 holes on the main course.
18 holes, 5971yds, Par 71, SSS 69, Course record 63.
Club membership 900.
Visitors must contact in advance, may not play competition days.
Societies apply in writing.
Green Fees £35 (£45 weekends).
Prof Frank J Coutts
Facilities ⊗ ⨶ ⑂ 𝄞 ⌣
Location 3m W of city centre off A93

Hotel ★★★★ 73% Ardoe House, South Deeside Rd, Blairs, ABERDEEN
☎ 01224 860600 112 ⇆ ſ⁓

Hazelhead Public Hazelhead AB1 8BD
☎ 01224 321830 Fax 01224 648693
Both No 1 and No 2 courses are tree-lined. The 9 hole course is open but surrounded by trees.
No 1 Course: 18 holes, 6211yds, Par 70, SSS 70.
No 2 Course: 18 holes, 5742yds, Par 67, SSS 67.

Visitors no restrictions.
Societies must contact in advance.
Green Fees not confirmed.
Prof A Smith/G Taylor/C Nelson
Facilities ⌣ ⓐ 𝄞 ⌣
& Leisure 9 hole pitch & putt course.
Location 4m W of city centre off A944

Hotel ★★★★ 73% Ardoe House, South Deeside Rd, Blairs, ABERDEEN
☎ 01224 860600 112 ⇆ ſ⁓

Kings Links AB24 1RZ
☎ 01224 632269 Fax 01224 648693
A typical links course with no tree lines and plenty of bunkers.The 14th hole is tricky - a long par 4 with a raised green and not much fairway round the green. The course is playable all year. Nearby there is a 6-hole course. The Bon Accord Club, Caledonian Club and Northern Club play over this course.
18 holes, 6384yds, Par 72, SSS 71.
Visitors contact starters box on 01224 632269 regarding booking of tee times.
Societies write to the Arts & Recreation Dept, St Nicholas House, Broad Street, Aberdeen.
Green Fees not confirmed.
Facilities ⌣
Location 0.75m NE of city centre

Hotel ★★★ 65% Grampian Hotel, Stirling St, ABERDEEN ☎ 01224 589101   49 ⇆ ſ⁓

Murcar Bridge of Don AB23 8BD
☎ 01224 704354 Fax 01224 704354
Murcar: 18 holes, 6287yds, Par 71, SSS 71, Course record 65.
Strabathie: 9 holes, 2680yds, Par 35, SSS 35.
Location 5m NE of city centre off A92
Telephone for further details

Hotel ★★★ 64% The Craighaar, Waterton Rd, Bankhead, ABERDEEN
☎ 01224 712275   55 ⇆ ſ⁓

Royal Aberdeen Links Rd, Balgownie, Bridge of Don AB23 8AT ☎ 01224 702571 Fax 01224 826591
Championship links course with undulating dunes. Windy, easy walking.
Balgownie Course: 18 holes, 6372yds, Par 71, SSS 71, Course record 63.
Silverburn Course: 18 holes, 4066yds, Par 60, SSS 60.
Club membership 500.
Visitors times for visitors 10-11.30am and 2-3.30pm weekdays, after 3.30pm weekends. Must contact in advance.
Societies apply in writing.
Green Fees £60 per round;£85 per day(£70 per round weekends).
Cards ▣▣ ▣▣
Prof Ronnie MacAskill
Designer Baird & Simpson
Facilities ⊗ ⑂ 𝄞 ⌣ ⓐ 𝄞 ⌣
Location 2.5m N of city centre off A92

Hotel ★★★ 65% Grampian Hotel, Stirling St, ABERDEEN ☎ 01224 589101   49 ⇆ ſ⁓

Westhill Westhill Heights, Westhill AB32 6RY
☎ 01224 742567 & 740159 Fax 01224 749124 &
01224 740159 e-mail: WGolfclub@aol.com
A highland course.
18 holes, 5921yds, Par 69, SSS 69, Course record 65.
Club membership 808.
Visitors   welcome except Saturdays.
Societies   telephone in advance.
Green Fees £14 per round;£20 per day(£20/£25 weekends).
Cards   ⊡ ▦ ▧ ▨
Prof   George Bruce
Designer   Charles Lawrie
Facilities   ⊗ ⅷ ⌙ ♥ ♀ ⚐ ⌂ ⌦ ✓
Location   7m NW of city centre off A944

Hotel   ★★★ 69% Westhill Hotel, Westhill,
                      ABERDEEN ☎ 01224 740388   38 ⇆ ♖

PETERCULTER   Map 15 NJ80

Peterculter Oldtown, Burnside Rd AB14 0LN
☎ 01224 734994(shop) & 735245(office)
Fax 01224 735580 e-mail: info@petercultergolfclub.co.uk
The course is a tight Par 68 (from Yellow tees) with a
beautiful Par 2 2nd and two Par 5 holes in excess of 500
yards. Surrounded by wonderful scenery and bordered by the
River Dee, there is a variety of birds, deer and foxes on the
course, which also has superb views up the Dee Valley.
18 holes, 5947yds, Par 68, SSS 68, Course record 64.
Club membership 1035.
Visitors   contact 3 days in advance, welcome between
                      9am-4pm weekdays.9.30am-6pm weekends.
Societies   contact up to 7 days in advance.
Green Fees £16 per round;£22 per day(£20/£26 weekends).
Cards   ⊡ ▦ ▧ ▨
Prof   Dean Vannet
Designer   Greens of Scotland
Facilities   ⊗ ⅷ ⌙ ♥ ♀ ⚐ ⌂ ⌦ ✓
Location   On A93

Hotel   ★★★ 69% Westhill Hotel, Westhill,
                      ABERDEEN ☎ 01224 740388   38 ⇆ ♖

ABERDEENSHIRE

ABOYNE   Map 15 NO59

Aboyne Formaston Park AB34 5HP
☎ 013398 86328 Fax 013398 87592
Beautiful parkland with outstanding views. Two lochs on
course.
18 holes, 5975yds, Par 68, SSS 69, Course record 62.
Club membership 930.
Visitors   no restrictions. Advisable to contact in advance.
Societies   prior booking essential.
Green Fees not confirmed.
Cards   ⊡ ▦ ▨
Prof   Innes Wright
Facilities   ⊗ ⅷ ⌙ ♥ ♀ ⚐ ⌂ ⌦ ✓
Location   E side of village, N of A93

Hotel   ★★ 70% Loch Kinord Hotel, Ballater Rd,
                      Dinnet, BALLATER ☎ 013398 85229 11rm(9
                      ⇆ ♖)

ALFORD   Map 15 NJ51

Alford Montgarrie Rd AB33 8AE
☎ 019755 62178 Fax 019755 62178
e-mail: golf@alford.co.uk
A flat parkland course in scenic countryside. Divided into
sections by a road, a narrow-gauge railway and a burn.
18 holes, 5483yds, Par 69, SSS 65, Course record 64.
Club membership 600.
Visitors   advisable to contact in advance.
Societies   telephone/e-mail in advance.
Green Fees £19 per day; £13 per round (£26/£20 weekends).
Cards   ⊡ ▦
Facilities   ⊗ ⅷ ⌙ ♥ ♀ ⚐ ⌂ ⌦ ✓
Location   In the centre of the village on A944

AUCHENBLAE   Map 15 NO77

Auchenblae AB30 1WQ ☎ 01561 320002
Picturesque, small, undulating parkland course offering good
views.
9 holes, 2226yds, Par 33, SSS 32, Course record 62.
Club membership 450.
Visitors   restricted Wed & Fri evenings but telephone to
                      confirm.
Societies   must telephone in advance.
Green Fees £9.50 per day(£12 weekends).
Designer   Robin Hiseman
Facilities   ♥ ⚐ ✓
& Leisure   grass tennis courts.
Location   0.5m NE

Hotel   ★★ 66% County Hotel & Leisure Club,
                      Arduthie Rd, STONEHAVEN
                      ☎ 01569 764386   14 ⇆ ♖

BALLATER   Map 15 NO39

Ballater Victoria Rd AB35 5QX
☎ 013397 55567 Fax 013397 55057
e-mail: ballater@ifb.co.uk
Heather covered course with testing long holes and beautiful
scenery.
18 holes, 5638yds, Par 67, SSS 67, Course record 62.
Club membership 750.
Visitors   advisable to contact in advance.
Societies   prior booking recommended.
Green Fees not confirmed.
Cards   ⊡ ▦ ▧ ▨
Prof   Bill Yule
Facilities   ⊗ ⅷ ⌙ ♥ ♀ ⚐ ⌂ ⌦ ⚘ ⚒ ✓
& Leisure   hard tennis courts, fishing, snooker.
Location   W side of town

Hotel   ★★★ 76% Darroch Learg Hotel,
                      Braemar Rd, BALLATER
                      ☎ 013397 55443 13 ⇆ ♖ Annexe5 ⇆ ♖

┌──────────────────────────────────────┐
│   Looking for a driving range?   │
│   See the index at the back of the guide   │
└──────────────────────────────────────┘

BANCHORY   Map 15 NO69

Banchory Kinneskie Rd AB31 5TA
☎ 01330 822365 Fax 01330 822491
Sheltered parkland course situated beside the River Dee, with
easy walking and woodland scenery. 12th and 13th holes are
testing.
18 holes, 5781yds, Par 69, SSS 68, Course record 65.
Club membership 975.
Visitors   must contact in advance, telephone for details on
            01330 822447
Societies   must book in advance.
Green Fees £25 per day, £18 per round (£21 per round
            weekends).
Cards   ▨▨
Prof   David Naylor
Facilities   ⊗ ⅲ ㄥ ▥ ♀ ♨ 🏠 ⛳ ⚲ ♠ ⚘ ⚟
Location   A93, 300 yds from W end of High St

Hotel   ★★★♨♨ 74% Banchory Lodge Hotel,
            BANCHORY ☎ 01330 822625 22 ⇄ 🐾

BANFF   Map 15 NJ66

Duff House Royal The Barnyards AB45 3SX
☎ 01261 812062 Fax 01261 812224
e-mail: duff-house-royal@btinternet.com
Well-manicured flat parkland, bounded by woodlands and
River Deveron. Well bunkered and renowned for its large,
two-tier greens.
18 holes, 6161yds, Par 68, SSS 70, Course record 63.
Club membership 1000.
Visitors   telephone professional in advance, handicap
            certificate is preferred. Restrictions at weekends
            due to members medal play.
Societies   must apply in writing.
Green Fees £24 per day; £18 per round (£30/£25 weekends).
Cards   ▨
Prof   Bob Strachan
Designer   Dr McKenzie
Facilities   ⊗ ⅲ ㄥ ▥ ♀ ♨ 🏠 ⚲ ⚟
Location   0.5m S on A98

Hotel   ★★★ 67% Banff Springs Hotel, Golden
            Knowes Rd, BANFF
            ☎ 01261 812881 31 ⇄ 🐾

BRAEMAR   Map 15 NO19

Braemar Cluniebank Rd AB35 5XX
☎ 013397 41618 Fax 013397 41400
Flat course, set amid beautiful countryside on Royal Deeside,
with River Clunie running through several holes. The 2nd
hole is one of the most testing in the area.
18 holes, 5000yds, Par 65, SSS 64, Course record 59.
Club membership 450.
Visitors   are advised to book 24 hours in advance to play
            at weekends. Tee reserved until 12.30 on Sat for
            members only.
Societies   must contact secretary in advance 01224
            704471.
Green Fees £20 per day;£15 per round(£26/£18 weekends).
Designer   Joe Anderson
Facilities   ⊗ ⅲ ㄥ ▥ ♀ ♨ 🏠 ⛳ ⚟
Location   0.5m S

Hotel   ★★★ 67% The Invercauld Arms, BRAEMAR
            ☎ 013397 41605 68 ⇄ 🐾

CRUDEN BAY   Map 15 NK03

Cruden Bay Aulton Rd AB42 0NN
☎ 01779 812285 Fax 01779 812945
e-mail: cbaygc@aol.com
A typical links course which epitomizes the old
fashioned style of rugged links golf. The drives require
accuracy with bunkers and protecting greens, blind holes
and undulating greens. The 10th provides a panoramic
view of half the back nine down at beach level, and to
the east can be seen the outline of the spectacular ruin of
Slains Castle (featured in Bram Stoker's Dracula). The
figure eight design of the course is quite unusual.
Main Course: 18 holes, 6395yds, Par 70, SSS 72, Course
record 65.
St Olaf Course: 9 holes, 5106yds, Par 64, SSS 65.
Club membership 1100.
Visitors   welcome on weekdays, at weekends only
            when there are no competitions, advisable
            to contact for details.
Societies   weekdays only telephone in advance.
Green Fees £50 per round;£70 per day(£60 per round
            weekends).
Cards   ▨▨ ▨▨ ▨▨ ▨▨ ▨
Prof   Robbie Stewart
Designer   Thomas Simpson
Facilities   ⊗ ⅲ ㄥ ▥ ♀ ♨ 🏠 ⛳ ⚲ ⚟ ▯
Location   SW side of village on A975

Hotel   ★★ 69% Red House Hotel, Aulton Rd,
            CRUDEN BAY
            ☎ 01779 812215 6rm(5 ⇄ 🐾)

ELLON   Map 15 NJ93

McDonald Hospital Rd AB41 9AW
☎ 01358 720576 Fax 01358 720001
e-mail: mcdonald.golf@virgin.net
Tight, parkland course with streams and a pond.
18 holes, 5986yds, Par 70, SSS 69.
Club membership 710.
Visitors advisable to book in advance
Societies telephone in advance.
Green Fees not confirmed.
Prof Ronnie Urquhart
Facilities ⊗ ⍵ ⓛ ☕ ♈ ♉ ☖ ☞ ℰ
Location 0.25m N on A948

Hotel ★★ 72% Udny Arms Hotel, Main St,
NEWBURGH ☎ 01358 789444 26 ⇆ ↑

FRASERBURGH   Map 15 NJ96

Fraserburgh AB43 8TL
☎ 01346 516616 Fax 01346 516616
e-mail: fburghgolf@aol.com
Testing seaside course, natural links. An extremely scenic
course, surrounded and protected by substantial sand dunes.
*Corbie: 18 holes, 6278yds, Par 70, SSS 70, Course record
65.*
Rosehill: 9 holes, 2400yds, Par 66, SSS 66.
Club membership 650.
Visitors no restrictions but advised to check availability.
Societies must contact in advance.
Green Fees not confirmed.
Designer James Braid
Facilities ⊗ ⍵ ⓛ ☕ ♈ ♉ ☖ ☞ ℰ
& Leisure Various open competitions throughout the year.
Location 1m SE on B9033

Hotel ★★★★ 64% Waterside Inn, Fraserburgh Rd,
PETERHEAD ☎ 01779 471121
69 ⇆ ↑ Annexe40 ⇆ ↑

HUNTLY   Map 15 NJ53

Huntly Cooper Park AB54 4SH ☎ 01466 792643
18 holes, 5399yds, Par 67, SSS 66.
Location N side of Huntly, turn off A96 at bypass
roundabout
Telephone for further details

INSCH   Map 15 NJ62

Insch Golf Ter AB52 6JY
☎ 01464 820363 Fax 01464 820363
A challenging 18 hole course, a mixture of flat undulating
parkland, with trees, stream and pond.
18 holes, 5500yds, Par 70, SSS 67.
Club membership 400.
Visitors restricted during club competitions and Tee
times, ie Mon - Ladies night, Tue - Mens night,
Wed - juniors, telephone clubhouse 01464
820363 for information. Pre-booking is advised.
Societies apply in writing or telephone, bookings
accepted.
Green Fees not confirmed.

Designer Greens of Scotland
Facilities ⊗ by prior arrangement ⍵ by prior arrangement
ⓛ ☕ ♈ ♉ ☖ ℰ
Location A96

Hotel ★★ Lodge Hotel, OLD RAYNE
☎ 01464 851205 Annexe6 ⇆ ↑

INVERALLOCHY   Map 15 NK06

Inverallochy Whitelink AB43 8XY ☎ 01346 582000
Seaside links course with natural hazards, tricky par 3s and
easy walking.
18 holes, 5351yds, Par 66, SSS 66, Course record 57.
Club membership 600.
Visitors restricted at weekends and competition days,
contact for availability.
Societies apply in writing/telephone in advance.
Green Fees £12 per 18 holes;£15 per day(£15/£20
weekends).
Facilities ⊗ ⍵ ⓛ ☕ ♈ ♉ ☖
Location E side of village off B9107

Hotel ★★★★ 64% Waterside Inn, Fraserburgh Rd,
PETERHEAD ☎ 01779 471121
69 ⇆ ↑ Annexe40 ⇆ ↑

INVERURIE   Map 15 NJ72

Inverurie Blackhall Rd AB51 5JB
☎ 01467 624080 Fax 01467 621051
e-mail: administrator@inveruriegc.co.uk
Parkland course, part of which is through wooded area.
18 holes, 5711yds, Par 69, SSS 68, Course record 64.
Club membership 750.
Visitors book tee time through shop up to 24 hrs in
advance 01467 620193.
Societies telephone administrator.
Green Fees £18 per day; £14 per round (£24/£18 weekends).
Cards 💳 🏧 💳 💳 💳 💳
Prof Mark Lees
Facilities ⊗ ⍵ ⓛ ☕ ♈ ♉ ☖ ☞ ℰ
Location E side of town off A96

Hotel ★★★ 67% Strathburn Hotel, Burghmuir Dr,
INVERURIE ☎ 01467 624422 25 ⇆ ↑

KEMNAY   Map 15 NJ71

Kemnay Monymusk Rd AB51 5RA
☎ 01467 642225 shop & 643746 office Fax 01467 643746
Undulating parkland course with superb views. A stream
crosses four holes.
18 holes, 6342yds, Par 71, SSS 71, Course record 67.
Club membership 800.
Visitors telephone shop for booking.
Societies must telephone in advance.
Green Fees £24 per day;£18 per round(£28/£22 weekends).
Prof Ronnie McDonald
Designer Greens of Scotland
Facilities ⊗ ⍵ ⓛ ☕ ♈ ♉ ☖ ☞ ☜ ℰ
Location W side of village on B993

Hotel ★★★ 69% Westhill Hotel, Westhill,
ABERDEEN ☎ 01224 740388 38 ↵ ↑

KINTORE   Map 15 NJ71

Kintore Balbithan AB51 0UR
☎ 01467 632631 Fax 01467 632631
The course covers a large area of ground from the Don
Basin, near the clubhouse, to mature woodland at the far
perimeter. One of the main attractions is the excellent
drainage which results in very few days of lost play.
18 holes, 6019yds, Par 70, SSS 69, Course record 62.
Club membership 700.
Visitors   during season booking system is in operation &
                  slots for visitors are available. Other times can
                  be booked 24 hours in advance.
Societies   apply in writing or telephone.
Green Fees £18 per day; £13 per round (£24/£19 weekends).
Facilities ⊗ ⫴ ⮭ 🛢 ♀ 👤 🏌
Location   1m from village centre on B977

Hotel   ★★ 66% Torryburn Hotel, School Rd,
                  KINTORE ☎ 01467 632269 9rm(8 🛌)

MACDUFF   Map 15 NJ76

Royal Tarlair Buchan St AB44 1TA ☎ 01261 832897
Fax 01261 833455 e-mail: info@royaltarlair.co.uk
Seaside clifftop course, can be windy. Testing 13th, 'Clivet'
(par 3).
18 holes, 5866yds, Par 71, SSS 68, Course record 62.
Club membership 520.
Visitors   no restrictions.
Societies   apply in writing.
Green Fees not confirmed.
Facilities ⊗ ⫴ ⮭ 🛢 ♀ 👤 🏠 🏌
Location   0.75m E off A98

Hotel   ★★★ 67% Banff Springs Hotel, Golden
                  Knowes Rd, BANFF ☎ 01261 812881
                  31 ⇆ 🛌

NEWBURGH ON YTHAN   Map 15 NJ92

Newburgh on Ythan Beach Rd AB41 6BE
☎ 01358 789058
e-mail: secretary@newburgh-on-ythan.co.uk
This seaside course was founded in 1888 and is adjacent to a
bird sanctuary. Testing 550-yd dog leg (par 5).
18 holes, 6162yds, Par 72, SSS 70, Course record 68.
Club membership 800.
Visitors   must contact in advance, may not play Sat am.
Societies   apply in advance.
Green Fees £21 per day; £16 per round (£26/£21 weekends).
Cards 💳 💳 💳 💳
Facilities ⊗ ⫴ ⮭ 🛢 ♀ 👤 🏠 🏌
& Leisure   hard tennis courts.
Location   E side of village on A975

Hotel   ★★ 72% Udny Arms Hotel, Main St,
                  NEWBURGH ☎ 01358 789444 26 ⇆ 🛌

AA Hotels that have special
arrangements with golf courses are listed at
the back of the guide

NEWMACHAR   Map 15 NJ81

Newmachar Swailend AB21 7UU
☎ 01651 863002 Fax 01651 863055
e-mail: newmachargolfclub@compuserve.com
Hawkshill is a championship-standard parkland course
designed by Dave Thomas. Several lakes affect five of the
holes and there are well developed birch and Scots pine trees.
Swailend is a parkland course designed by Dave Thomas and
opened in 1997. It provides a test all of its own with some
well positioned bunkering and testing greens.
*Hawkshill Course: 18 holes, 6623yds, Par 72, SSS 74,
Course record 67.*
*Swailend Course: 18 holes, 6338yds, Par 72, SSS 71, Course
record 67.*
Club membership 900.
Visitors   contact in advance & must have handicap
                  certificate for Hawkshill course.
Societies   apply in writing.
Green Fees from £15 per round.
Cards 💳 💳 💳 💳
Prof   Gordon Simpson
Designer   Dave Thomas/Peter Allis
Facilities ⊗ ⫴ ⮭ 🛢 ♀ 👤 🏠 🏌 🚩 🥤 🛒 🏌 ♣
Location   2m N of Dyce, off A947

Hotel   ★★★ 67% Strathburn Hotel, Burghmuir Dr,
                  INVERURIE ☎ 01467 624422 25 ⇆ 🛌

OLDMELDRUM   Map 15 NJ82

Old Meldrum Kirk Brae AB51 0DJ
☎ 01651 872648 Fax 01651 873555
Parkland course with tree-lined fairways and superb views.
Challenging 196 yard, Par 3, 11th over two ponds to a green
surrounded by bunkers.
18 holes, 5988yds, Par 70, SSS 69, Course record 66.
Club membership 700.
Visitors   may not play during Club competitions.
Societies   apply in writing to secretary
Green Fees £14 per day/round (£24 per day; £20 per round
                  weekends).
Prof   Hamish Love
Designer   Various
Facilities ⊗ ⫴ ⮭ 🛢 ♀ 👤 🏠 🏌 🏌
Location   E side of village off A947

Hotel   ★★★ 67% Strathburn Hotel, Burghmuir Dr,
                  INVERURIE ☎ 01467 624422 25 ⇆ 🛌

PETERHEAD   Map 15 NK14

Peterhead Craigewan Links, Riverside Dr AB42 1LT
☎ 01779 472149 & 480725 Fax 01779 480725
e-mail: phdgc@freenetname.co.uk
The Old Course is a natural links course bounded by the sea
and the River Ugie. Varying conditions of play depending on
wind and weather. The New Course is more of a parkland
course.
*Old Course: 18 holes, 6173yds, Par 70, SSS 71, Course
record 64.*
New Course: 9 holes, 2228yds, Par 31.
Club membership 650.
Visitors   welcome any day apart from Saturdays,
                  restricted times on the Old Course. Telephone
                  for details.   ▶

Societies   apply in writing, restricted availablility on
                 Saturdays
Green Fees £18(£22 weekends).
Cards   ▨
Designer   W Park/ L Auchterconie/J Braid
Facilities   ⊗ �𝄃 ᄂ 🍺 ♀ 🏌 ⚑ ⚲
Location   N side of town centre off A90

Hotel   ★★★★ 64% Waterside Inn, Fraserburgh Rd,
                 PETERHEAD ☎ 01779 471121
                 69 ⇄ 🅟 Annexe40 ⇄ 🅟

PORTLETHEN   Map 15 NO99

Portlethen Badentoy Rd AB12 4YA
☎ 01224 782575 & 781090 Fax 01224 781090
Set in pleasant parkland, this new course features mature
trees and a stream which affects a number of holes.
18 holes, 6707yds, Par 72, SSS 72, Course record 63.
Club membership 1000.
Visitors   may not play Sat. Contact in advance.
Societies   apply in advance.
Green Fees not confirmed.
Cards   ⊟ ▨ ⬛ ▨ ⊘
Prof   Muriel Thomson
Designer   Cameron Sinclair
Facilities   ⊗ �𝄃 ᄂ 🍺 ♀ 🏌 🏠 ⚑ ⚲ ✦ ⚲
Location   Off A90 S of Aberdeen

Hotel   ★★ 66% County Hotel & Leisure Club,
                 Arduthie Rd, STONEHAVEN
                 ☎ 01569 764386 14 ⇄ 🅟

STONEHAVEN   Map 15 NO88

Stonehaven Cowie AB39 3RH
☎ 01569 762124 Fax 01569 765973
Challenging meadowland course overlooking sea with three
gullies and splendid views.
18 holes, 5103yds, Par 66, SSS 65, Course record 61.
Club membership 850.
Visitors   prefer prior booking, may not play before 4pm
                 Sat.
Societies   telephone or fax in advance to W A Donald.
Green Fees £18 per day;£14 per round(£25/£18 weekends).
Cards   ⊟ ▨ ⬛ ▨ ⊘
Designer   C Simpson
Facilities   ⊗ �𝄃 ᄂ 🍺 ♀ 🏌 🏠 ⚑ ⚲
& Leisure   snooker.
Location   1m N off A92

Hotel   ★★ 66% County Hotel & Leisure Club,
                 Arduthie Rd, STONEHAVEN
                 ☎ 01569 764386 14 ⇄ 🅟

TARLAND   Map 15 NJ40

Tarland Aberdeen Rd AB34 4TB
☎ 013398 81000 Fax 013398 81000
Difficult upland course, but easy walking. Some spectacular
holes, mainly 4th (par 4) and 5th (par 3) and fine scenery.
9 holes, 5888yds, Par 67, SSS 68, Course record 65.
Club membership 406.
Visitors   must contact in advance.
Societies   must telephone in advance.
Green Fees £14 per day (£18 weekends).
Designer   Tom Morris

Facilities   ⊗ �𝄃 ᄂ 🍺 ♀ 🏌 ⚲
Location   E side of village off B9119

Hotel   ★★ 70% Loch Kinord Hotel, Ballater Rd,
                 Dinnet, BALLATER
                 ☎ 013398 85229 11rm(9 ⇄ 🅟)

TORPHINS   Map 15 NJ60

Torphins Bog Rd AB31 4JU
☎ 013398 82115 & 82402 (Sec) Fax 013398 82402
e-mail: stuart@macgregor5.fsnet.co.uk
Heathland/parkland course built on a hill with views of the
Cairngorms.
9 holes, 4800yds, Par 64, SSS 64, Course record 63.
Club membership 380.
Visitors   Restricted on competition days (alternate Sat
                 and Sun).No visitors on Tuesday evenings.
Societies   apply in advance.
Green Fees £12(£14 weekends)£7 per 9 holes.
Facilities   ⊗ ᄂ 🍺 ⚲
Location   0.25m W of village off A980

Hotel   ★★★ 78% Tor-na-Coille Hotel, BANCHORY
                 ☎ 01330 822242 22 ⇄ 🅟

TURRIFF   Map 15 NJ74

Turriff Rosehall AB53 4HD
☎ 01888 562982 Fax 01888 568050
e-mail: grace@turriffgolf.sol.co.uk
A well-maintained parkland course alongside the River
Deveron in picturesque surroundings. 6th and 12th
particularly challenging in a testing course.
18 holes, 6107yds, Par 70, SSS 69, Course record 64.
Club membership 894.
Visitors   may not play before 10am weekends. Must
                 contact in advance.
Societies   apply in writing to the secretary.
Green Fees £22 per day; £18 per round (£28/£22 weekends).
Prof   Robin Smith
Facilities   ⊗ �𝄃 ᄂ 🍺 ♀ 🏌 🏠 ⚲
Location   1m W off B9024

Hotel   ★★★ 67% Banff Springs Hotel, Golden
                 Knowes Rd, BANFF
                 ☎ 01261 812881 31 ⇄ 🅟

ANGUS

ARBROATH   Map 12 NO64

Arbroath Elliot DD11 2PE
☎ 01241 872069 Fax 01241 875837 e-
mail: golfshop@fsmail.net
Municipal seaside links course, with bunkers guarding
greens. Played upon by Arbroath Artisan Club.
18 holes, 6185yds, Par 70, SSS 69, Course record 64.
Club membership 550.
Visitors   contact professional 01241 875837.
Societies   contact professional 01241 875837.
Green Fees £18 per round;£24 per day(£24/£32 weekends).

▶

329

Prof	Lindsay Ewart
Designer	Braid
Facilities	⊗ ⫪ ⓛ ⬛ ♀ ⛰ 🏠 ⛳ ♂
Location	2m SW on A92

LETHAM GRANGE RESORT HOTEL

★★★★

Colliston by
Arbroath
Angus DD11 4RL
Tel: 01241 890373 Fax: 01241 890725
E-mail: lethamgrange@sol.co.uk

Situated in the heart of Angus countryside with many sporting and leisure pursuits on the estate, Letham Grange offers a tranquil oasis in which to recharge.

The main house is a beautifully restored Victorian mansion and the Golf Estate rooms set in the grounds offer a good quality. Friendly, efficient staff serving a mix of Scottish and French cuisine.

Taste of Scotland Recommended

Hotel Seaforth

Hotel ★★ 65% Hotel Seaforth, Dundee Rd,
ARBROATH ☎ 01241 872232 19 ⇆ ╠

Letham Grange Colliston DD11 4RL
☎ 01241 890373 & 809377 Fax 01241 890725
e-mail: lethamgrange@sol.co.uk
Often referred to as the 'Augusta of Scotland', the Old Course provides championship standards in spectacular surroundings with attractive lochs and burns. The Glens Course is less arduous and shorter using many natural features of the estate.
Old Course: 18 holes, 6632yds, Par 73, SSS 73, Course record 68.
Glens Course: 18 holes, 5528yds, Par 68, SSS 68, Course record 63.
Club membership 850.

Visitors	no visitors weekends before 9.30am, Old Course before 10am Tue & Glens Course before 10am Fri.
Societies	telephone in advance.
Green Fees	not confirmed.
Cards	⬛⬛⬛⬛⬛⬛
Prof	Steven Moir
Designer	G K Smith/Donald Steel
Facilities	⊗ ⫪ ⓛ ⬛ ♀ ⛰ 🏠 ⛳ 🏨 ➘ ⚒ ♂
Location	4m N on A933

Hotel ★★★★ 64% The Letham Grange Mansion House Hotel, Colliston, ARBROATH
☎ 01241 890373 19 ⇆ ╠ Annexe22 ⇆ ╠

BARRY
Map 12 NO53

Panmure Burnside Rd DD7 7RT
☎ 01241 855120 Fax 01241 859737
e-mail: secretary@panmuregolfclub.co.uk
A nerve-testing, adventurous course set amongst sandhills - its hazards belie the quiet nature of the opening holes. This tight links has been used as a qualifying course for the Open Championship, and features Ben Hogan's favourite hole, the dog-leg 6th, which heralds the toughest stretch, around the turn.
18 holes, 6317yds, Par 70, SSS 71, Course record 62.
Club membership 700.

Visitors	may not play Sat. Parties of 5 or more must contact in advance.

Societies	must contact secretary in advance.
Green Fees	not confirmed.
Cards	⬛⬛⬛⬛
Prof	Neil Mackintosh
Facilities	⊗ ⫪ ⓛ ⬛ ♀ ⛰ 🏠 ⛳ ⚒ ♂ ⚑
Location	S side of village off A930

Hotel	★★ 68% Carnoustie Links Hotel, Links Pde, CARNOUSTIE ☎ 01241 853273 7 ⇆ ╠

BRECHIN
Map 15 NO56

Brechin Trinity DD9 7PD
☎ 01356 622383 Fax 01356 626925
Rolling parkland course, with easy walking and good views of Strathmore Valley and Grampian Mountains.
18 holes, 6092yds, Par 72, SSS 70, Course record 66.
Club membership 850.

Visitors	contact Professional on 01356 625270 in advance. Restricted weekends.
Societies	must contact club steward in advance.
Green Fees	£25 per day; £17 per round (£30/£22 weekends).
Prof	Stephen Rennie
Designer	James Braid (partly)
Facilities	⊗ ⫪ ⓛ ⬛ ♀ ⛰ 🏠 ⛳ ➘ ⚒ ♂
& Leisure	squash.
Location	1m N on B966

▶

Carnoustie Golf Links

Carnoustie, *Angus*   ☎ 01241 853789   Fax 01241 852720   Map 12 NO53

e-mail: (bookings) kirsty@carnoustiegolflinks.co.uk

This Championship Course has been voted the top course in Britain by many golfing greats and described as Scotland's ultimate golfing challenge. The course developed from origins in the 1560s; James Braid added new bunkers, greens and tees in the 1920s. The Open Championship first came to the course in 1931 and Carnoustie recently returned to prominence as the host of the Scottish Open in 1995 and 1996 and the venue for the 1999 Open Championship.

The Burnside Course (6020 yards) is enclosed on three sides by the Championship Course and has been used for Open Championship qualifying rounds. The Buddon Course (5400 yards) has been extensively remodelled making it ideal for mid to high handicappers.

Visitors must contact in advance, Sat after 2pm, Sun after 11.30am. Must have handicap certificate for championship course

Societies must contact in advance

Green Fees £75 per round 🍴 🍺 🍴 🔲 💷 📶 🚬 📀

Facilities ⊗ ⊞ ⅏ ⅊ ♙ 🍴 ⚐ 🏠 ⚲

Professional (Lee Vannet)

Leisure swimming, sauna, solarium, gym

Location Links Parade, Carnoustie DD7 7JE (SW side of town, off A930)

Holes/Par/Course record 54 holes Championship Course: 18 holes, 6936 yds, Par 72, SSS 75, Course record 64
Burnside Course: 18 holes, 6020 yds, Par 68, SSS 69
Buddon Links: 18 holes, 5420 yds, Par 66, SSS 68

Championship Course

WHERE TO STAY AND EAT NEARBY

Hotels
ARBROATH

★★ 65% Hotel Seaforth, Dundee Rd.
☎ 01241 872232. 19 (18 🛏 1 🛏)

CARNOUSTIE

★★ 67% Carlogie House, Carlogie Rd.
☎ 01241 853185.
12 (2 🛏 🐾 10 🐾) Annexe 4 🐾

★★ 68% Carnoustie Links, Links Pde.
☎ 01241 853273. 7 (3 🛏 🐾 4 🐾)

Restaurant
CARNOUSTIE

◉ 11 Park Avenue. ☎ 01241 853336.

Northern Hotel

Hotel ★★ 64% Northern Hotel, 2/4 Clerk St, BRECHIN ☎ 01356 625505 16 ⇔ ♠

CARNOUSTIE Map 12 NO53

CARNOUSTIE See page 331

EDZELL Map 15 NO66

Edzell High St DD9 7TF
☎ 01356 647283 (Secretary) Fax 01356 648094
e-mail: secretary@edzellgolfclub.demon.co.uk
This delightful course is situated in the foothills of the Scottish Highlands and provides good golf as well as conveying to everyone who plays there a feeling of peace and quiet. The village of Edzell is one of the most picturesque in Scotland.
18 holes, 6348yds, Par 71, SSS 71, Course record 62.
Club membership 750.
Visitors may not play 4.45-6.15 weekdays & 7.30-10, 12-2 weekends. Not before 2pm on 1st Sat each month.
Societies must contact secretary at least 14 days in advance.
Green Fees £33 per day; £23 per round (£43/£29 weekends).
Cards ⊟ ▒ 🗒
Prof A J Webster
Designer Bob Simpson
Facilities ⊗ 〗 ⤸ ▐ ♀ ⚐ 🏌 ⬢ 🛉 🛒 ❨
Location S side of village on B966

Hotel ★★★ 64% Glenesk Hotel, High St, EDZELL ☎ 01356 648319 24 ⇔ ♠

FORFAR Map 15 NO45

Forfar Cunninghill, Arbroath Rd DD8 2RL
☎ 01307 463773 Fax 01307 468495
e-mail: forfargolfclub@uku.co.uk
Moorland course with wooded, undulating fairways and fine views.
18 holes, 6066yds, Par 69, SSS 70, Course record 61.
Club membership 850.
Visitors may not play before 2.30pm Sat.Advance booking required.
Societies must contact in advance.

Green Fees £25 per day; £20 per round (£30/£25 weekends).
Cards ⊟ ▒ 🗒 🗒 🗒 ▒ 🗒
Prof Peter McNiven
Designer James Braid
Facilities ⊗ 〗 ⤸ ▐ ♀ ⬢ 🛉 🏌 ❨
Location 1.5m E of Forfar on A932

Hotel ★★★⤴ 68% Idvies House Hotel, Letham, FORFAR ☎ 01307 818787 11 ⇔ ♠

KIRRIEMUIR Map 15 NO35

Kirriemuir Shielhill Rd, Northmuir DD8 4LN
☎ 01575 573317 Fax 01575 574608
Parkland and heathland course set at the foot of the Angus glens, with good view.
18 holes, 5553yds, Par 68, SSS 67, Course record 62.
Club membership 750.
Visitors must play with member at weekends.
Societies must apply in advance, may not play weekends.
Green Fees £26 per day; £20 per round(£32/£25 weekends).
Cards ⊟ ▒ 🗒
Prof Karyn Dallas
Designer James Braid
Facilities ⊗ 〗 ⤸ ▐ ♀ ⬢ 🛉 🏌 ❨
Location 1m N off B955

Hotel ★★★⤴ 68% Idvies House Hotel, Letham, FORFAR ☎ 01307 818787 11 ⇔ ♠

MONIFIETH Map 12 NO43

Monifieth Princes St DD5 4AW
☎ 01382 532767 (Medal) & 532967 (Ashludie)
Fax 01382 535553
The chief of the two courses at Monifieth is the Medal Course. It has been one of the qualifying venues for the Open Championship on more than one occasion. A seaside links, but divided from the sand dunes by a railway which provides the principal hazard for the first few holes. The 10th hole is outstanding, the 17th is excellent and there is a delightful finishing hole. The other course here is the Ashludie, and both are played over by a number of clubs who share the links.
Medal Course: 18 holes, 6655yds, Par 71, SSS 72, Course record 63.
Ashludie Course: 18 holes, 5123yds, Par 68, SSS 66.
Club membership 1750.
Visitors must contact in advance. Restricted to after 2pm Sat, 10am Sun & after 9.30pm Mon-Fri.
Societies must contact in advance by telephone or writing to Medal Starter's Box, Princes St, Monifieth.
Green Fees not confirmed.
Prof Ian McLeod
Facilities ⊗ 〗 by prior arrangement ⤸ ▐ ♀ ⬢ 🛉 🏌 ❨
Location NE side of town on A930

Hotel ★★ 67% Carlogie House Hotel, Carlogie Rd, CARNOUSTIE ☎ 01241 853185 12 ⇔ ♠ Annexe4 ♠

Looking for a driving range?
See the index at the back of the guide

Two links courses: MEDAL COURSE (Par 71, SSS72) BROOMFIELD COURSE (Par 66, SSS 63)
AN INVITATION TO COME AND PLAY OUR HISTORIC LINKS WHICH WAS A FINAL QUALIFYING COURSE FOR THE OPEN IN 1999.
RANKED FIFTH OLDEST IN THE WORLD
VISITORS VERY WELCOME
Individual Round and Day Tickets Available on Both Courses All Visitors and Parties Very Welcome.

Special packages available including catering and in conjunction with local hotels
Enquiries to:　Mrs M Stewart, Secretary,
Montrose Links Trust, Traill Drive,
Montrose, Angus DD10 8SW.
Tel: 01674 672932
Fax: 01674 671800

Additional hotel	★★★ 71% Links Hotel, Mid Links, MONTROSE ☎ 01674 671000 Fax 01674 672698 25 ⇆ ☜

ARGYLL & BUTE

CARDROSS　　　　　　　　　　Map 10 NS37

Cardross Main Rd G82 5LB
☎ 01389 841754 Fax 01389 842162
e-mail: golf@cardross.com
Undulating parkland course, testing with good views.
18 holes, 6469yds, Par 71, SSS 72, Course record 64.
Club membership 800.
Visitors　　　may not play at weekends unless introduced by member. Contact professional in advance 01359 841350.
Societies　　must contact in writing.
Green Fees　£40 per day; £28 per round.
Cards　　　　💳 💳
Prof　　　　　Robert Farrell
Designer　　James Braid
Facilities　　⊗ ⅊ ⅊ ⅊ ⅊ ⅊ ⅊ ⅊ ⅊ ⅊
Location　　In centre of village on A814

Hotel　　　★★★★★ 66% Cameron House Hotel, BALLOCH ☎ 01389 755565　96 ⇆ ☜

MONTROSE　　　　　　　　　Map 15 NO75

Montrose Links Trust Traill Dr DD10 8SW
☎ 01674 672932 Fax 01674 671800
e-mail: secretary@montrosegolf.co.uk
The links at Montrose like many others in Scotland are on commonland and are shared by three clubs. The Medal course at Montrose - the fifth oldest in the world - is typical of Scottish seaside links, with narrow, undulating fairways and problems from the first hole to the last. The Broomfield course is flatter and easier.
Medal Course: 18 holes, 6495yds, Par 71, SSS 72, Course record 63.
Broomfield Course: 18 holes, 4800yds, Par 66, SSS 63.
Club membership 1300.
Visitors　　　may not play on the Medal Course on Sat before 2.30pm & before 10am on Sun. Must have a handicap certificate for Medal Course. Contact in advance. No restrictions on Broomfield Course. Must contact in advance.
Societies　　must contact secretary in advance.
Green Fees　Medal: £38 per day; £28 per round (£48/£32 weekends). Broomfield: £12 per round.
Cards　　　　💳 💳 💳 💳 💳
Prof　　　　　Kevin Stables
Designer　　W Park/Tom Morris
Facilities　　⊗ ⅊ ⅊ ⅊ ⅊ ⅊ ⅊ ⅊ ⅊ ⅊
Location　　NE side of town off A92

Hotel　　　★★★ 65% Montrose Park Hotel, 61 John St, MONTROSE ☎ 01674 663400　54 ⇆ ☜ Annexe5 ☜

CARRADALE　　　　　　　　　Map 10 NR83

Carradale PA28 6RY ☎ 01583 431378
Pleasant seaside course built on a promontory overlooking the Isle of Arran. Natural terrain and small greens are the most difficult natural hazards. Described as the most sporting 9-hole course in Scotland. Testing 7th hole (240 yds), par 3. Beware of wild goats in summer.
9 holes, 2358yds, Par 65, SSS 64, Course record 66.
Club membership 320.
Visitors　　　no restrictions,advisable to contact at weekends during summer months.
Societies　　contact in advance.
Green Fees　£10 per day.
Facilities　　⅊ ⅊
Location　　S side of village, on B842

Hotel　　　★★ 68% Seafield Hotel, Kilkerran Rd, CAMPBELTOWN ☎ 01586 554385 3 ⇆ ☜ Annexe6 ☜

DALMALLY　　　　　　　　　Map 10 NN12

Dalmally Old Saw Mill PA33 1AE ☎ 01838 200370
A 9-hole flat parkland course bounded by the River Orchy and surrounded by mountains. Many water hazards and bunkers.
9 holes, 2257yds, Par 64, SSS 63, Course record 64.
Club membership 100.
Visitors　　　no visitors on Sun between 9-10 & 1-2.
Societies　　telephone in advance.
Green Fees　£10 per day/round.
Designer　　MacFarlane Barrow Co

Facilities   ⊗ by prior arrangement 🏴 by prior arrangement
🍺 by prior arrangement ♀ by arrangement ⚐
⛳ ♂

Location   On A85, 1.5m W of Dalmally

Hotel   ★★ 60% Polfearn Hotel, TAYNUILT
☎ 01866 822251 14 ⇆ 🎋

DUNOON   Map 10 NS17

Cowal Ardenslate Rd PA23 8LT
☎ 01369 705673 Fax 01369 705673
e-mail: Info@cowalgolfclub.co.uk
Moorland course. Panoramic views of Clyde Estuary and
surrounding hills.
18 holes, 6063yds, Par 70, SSS 70, Course record 63.
Club membership 900.
Visitors   advisable to book in advance.
Societies   must telephone in advance.
Green Fees £36 per day/£23 per round(£45/£33 weekends).
Prof   Russell Weir
Designer   James Braid
Facilities   ⊗ 川 🏴 🍺 ♀ ⚐ 🏠 ⛳ ♂
Location   1m N

Hotel   ★★ 76% Enmore Hotel, Marine Pde, Kirn,
DUNOON ☎ 01369 702230 10 ⇆ 🎋

ERISKA   Map 10 NM94

Isle of Eriska PA37 1SD
☎ 01631 720371 Fax 01631 720531
e-mail: gc@eriska-hotel.co.uk
This remote and most beautiful 6-hole course, set around the
owner's hotel, is gradually being upgraded to a testing 9-hole
challenge, complete with stunning views.
6 holes, 1588yds, Par 22.
Club membership 40.
Visitors   contact in advance.
Green Fees not confirmed.
Cards   💳 💳 💳 💳 🔲
Designer   H Swan
Facilities   ⊗ 🍺 ⚐ ⛳ 🛏 ⚐ ♂ ♭
& Leisure   hard tennis courts, heated indoor swimming
pool, sauna, gymnasium.
Location   A828 Connel/Fort William, signposted 4m from
North of Benderloch village

Hotel   ★★★★🏊 Isle of Eriska, Eriska, Ledaig, BY
OBAN ☎ 01631 720371 17 ⇆ 🎋

GIGHA ISLAND   Map 10 NR64

Gigha PA41 7AA
☎ 01583 505287 & 01583 505254 Fax 01583 505244
A 9-hole course with scenic views of the Sound of Gigha and
Kintyre. Ideal for the keen or occasional golfer.
9 holes, 5042yds, Par 66, SSS 65.
Club membership 40.
Visitors   no restrictions.
Societies   telephone for details.
Green Fees £10 per day/round.
Designer   Members
Facilities   ⚐
Location   0.5m from ferry terminal beside main road

HELENSBURGH   Map 10 NS28

Helensburgh 25 East Abercromby St G84 9HZ
☎ 01436 674173 Fax 01436 671170
Sporting moorland course with superb views of Loch
Lomond and River Clyde.
18 holes, 6104yds, Par 69, SSS 70, Course record 64.
Club membership 880.
Visitors   may not play at weekends.
Societies   weekdays only, must contact in writing.
Green Fees £32 per day; £20 per round.
Prof   David Fotheringham
Designer   Old Tom Morris
Facilities   ⊗ 川 🏴 🍺 ♀ ⚐ 🏠 ♂
Location   NE side of town off B832

Hotel   ★★★★★ 66% Cameron House Hotel,
BALLOCH ☎ 01389 755565 96 ⇆ 🎋

INNELLAN   Map 10 NS17

Innellan Knockamillie Rd PA23 7SG
☎ 01369 830242 & 702573
Situated above the village of Innellan, this undulating hilltop
course has extensive views of the Firth of Clyde.
9 holes, 4683yds, Par 64, SSS 64, Course record 63.
Club membership 199.
Visitors   welcome but may not play after 5pm on
Mondays.
Societies   telephone initially.
Green Fees not confirmed.
Facilities   🏴 🍺 ♀ ⛳
Location   4m S of Dunoon

Hotel   ★★ 70% Royal Marine Hotel, Hunters Quay,
DUNOON ☎ 01369 705810
28 ⇆ 🎋 Annexe10 ⇆ 🎋

INVERARAY   Map 10 NN00

Inveraray North Cromalt PA32 8XT ☎ 01499 302140
Testing parkland course with beautiful views overlooking
Loch Fyne.
9 holes, 5790yds, Par 70, SSS 68, Course record 69.
Club membership 178.
Visitors   no restrictions.
Societies   write or telephone to the secretary.
Green Fees not confirmed.
Facilities   ⚐
Location   1m S of Inveraray

LOCHGILPHEAD   Map 10 NR88

Lochgilphead Blarbuie Rd PA31 8LE
☎ 01546 602340
A varied course with short but interesting holes. Some
elevated greens and tees and some tight fairways.
9 holes, 2242yds, Par 64, SSS 63, Course record 54.
Club membership 250.
Visitors   restricted during weekend club competitions.
Societies   apply in advance, restricted wekends.
Green Fees £12 per 18 holes.
Designer   Dr I McCamond
Facilities   🏴 🍺 ♀ ⚐ 🏠 ♂
Location   Adjacent to the hospital. Signposted from the
village.   ▶

Hotel   ★★ 62% The Stag Hotel, Argyll St,
LOCHGILPHEAD ☎ 01546 602496 17 ➡ ♠

LUSS   Map 10 NS39

Loch Lomond Rossdhu House G83 8NT
☎ 01436 655555 Fax 01436 655500
e-mail: info@lochlomond.com
This exclusive club is strictly members only and getting
to play here is notoriously difficult. Nick Faldo called it
the finest new course in Europe and others have given it
similar accolades. It was designed by two Americans,
Jay Morrish and Tom Weiskopf and was founded in
1993. There is a putting green, practice area and driving
range. The clubhouse used to be the home of the chiefs
of Clan Colquhoun. We are told that it boasts a Chinese
Drawing Room with portraits in oil and beautiful
ceilings. There are conference facilities as well as a gym
and private fishing.
18 holes, 7060yds, Par 71, Course record 62.
Visitors   strictly members only.
no visitors strictly private.
Green Fees not confirmed.
Prof   Colin Campbell
Designer   Tom Weiskopf
Facilities   ⛳ 🏨 🗞 ✆
& Leisure fishing, gymnasium.
Location   Off A82 at Luss

Hotel   ★★★★★ 66% Cameron House Hotel,
BALLOCH ☎ 01389 755565 96 ➡ ♠

MACHRIHANISH   Map 10 NR62

Machrihanish PA28 6PT
☎ 01586 810213 Fax 01586 810221
e-mail: machrihanishgolf@ic24.net
Magnificent seaside links of championship status. The
1st hole is the famous drive across the Atlantic. Sandy
soil allows for play all year round. Large greens, easy
walking, windy. Fishing.
18 holes, 6225yds, Par 70, SSS 71.
Club membership 1200.
Visitors   no restrictions.
Societies   apply in writing.
Green Fees £50 per day; £30 per round (£60/£40 Sat).
Cards   🖃 🖃 🖃 🖃
Prof   Ken Campbell
Designer   Tom Morris
Facilities   ⊗ 🏨 🗞 ♣ ♀ ♨ ✆
Location   5m W of Campbeltown on B843

Hotel   ★★ 68% Seafield Hotel, Kilkerran Rd,
CAMPBELTOWN
☎ 01586 554385 3 ➡ ♠ Annexe6 ♠

OBAN   Map 10 NM83

Glencruitten Glencruitten Rd PA34 4PU
☎ 01631 564604
There is plenty of space and considerable variety of hole
on this downland course - popular with holidaymakers.
In a beautiful, isolated situation, the course is hilly and
testing, particularly the 1st and 12th, par 4's, and 10th
and 15th, par 3's.

18 holes, 4452yds, Par 61, SSS 63, Course record 55.
Club membership 500.
Visitors   restricted Thu & weekends.
Societies   must contact in writing.
Green Fees £16 per day/round.
Designer   James Braid
Facilities   ⊗ 🏨 🗞 🗞 ♀ ♣ 🏨 ♨ ✆
Location   NE side of town centre off A816

Hotel   ★★ 61% Caledonian Hotel, Station
Square, OBAN
☎ 01631 563133 70 ➡ ♠

SOUTHEND   Map 10 NR60

Dunaverty PA28 6RW
☎ 01586 830677 Fax 01586 830677
e-mail: dunavertygc@aol.com
Undulating, seaside course with spectacular views of Ireland
and the Ayrshire coast.
18 holes, 4799yds, Par 66, SSS 63, Course record 59.
Club membership 400.
Visitors   limited Sat, contact in advance.
Societies   apply in advance.
Green Fees £14 per round;£21 per day(£16/£24 weekends).
Facilities   ⊗ 🏨 🗞 🗞 ♣ 🏨 ♨ ✆
& Leisure fishing.
Location   10m S of Campbeltown on B842

Hotel   ★★ 68% Seafield Hotel, Kilkerran Rd,
CAMPBELTOWN
☎ 01586 554385 3 ➡ ♠ Annexe6 ♠

TARBERT   Map 10 NR86

Tarbert PA29 6XX ☎ 01546 606896
Beautiful moorland course. Four fairways crossed by
streams.
9 holes, 4460yds, Par 66, SSS 63, Course record 62.
Visitors   may not play Sat pm.
Societies   apply in writing.
Green Fees £10 per day.
Location   N1m W on B8024

Hotel   ★★★👬 71% Stonefield Castle Hotel,
TARBERT ☎ 01880 820836 33 ➡ ♠

TIGHNABRUAICH   Map 10 NR97

Kyles of Bute PA21 2EE ☎ 01700 811603
Moorland course which is hilly and exposed to wind. Fine
mountain and sea views.
9 holes, 4778yds, Par 66, SSS 64, Course record 62.
Club membership 150.
Visitors   may not play Wed 6pm or Sun am.
Societies   telephone in advance.
Green Fees £8 per day/round(£10 weekends).
Facilities   ♣ ♨ ✆
Location   1.25m S off B8000

Hotel   ★★ 73% Royal Hotel, Shore Rd,
TIGHNABRUAICH
☎ 01700 811239 11 ➡ ♠

CITY OF EDINBURGH

EDINBURGH Map 11 NT27

Baberton 50 Baberton Av, Juniper Green EH14 5DU
☎ 0131 453 4911 Fax 0131 453 4678
e-mail: babertongolfclub@btinternet.com
Parkland course.
18 holes, 6129yds, Par 69, SSS 70, Course record 64.
Club membership 900.
Visitors   may not play at weekends or after 3.30pm
            weekdays. Contact in advance.
Societies   must contact in advance.
Green Fees £22 per round;£32 per day(£25 per round
            weekends).
Prof   Ken Kelly
Designer   Willie Park Jnr
Facilities ⊗ ⅲ ╘ 🍴 ♀ ⚘ 🏠 🏌 ⚐
Location   5m W of city centre off A70

Hotel   ★★★★ 62% Swallow Royal Scot Hotel, 111
            Glasgow Rd, EDINBURGH
            ☎ 0131 334 9191 245 ⇄ ☛

Braid Hills Braid Hills Approach EH10 6JZ
☎ 0131 447 6666 Fax 0131 557 5170
Municipal heathland course with superb views of Edinburgh
and the Firth of Forth, quite challenging.
Course No 1: 18 holes, 5390yds, Par 70, SSS 68.
Course No 2: 18 holes, 4602yds, Par 65.

Visitors   two courses Braids 1 & Braids 2 operate from
            Apr-Sep, one course only during winter. Braids
            1 is closed on Sun.
Societies   telephone 0131 557 5457 or apply in writing to
            Edinburgh Leisure, 23 Waterloo Place,
            Edinburgh EH1 3BH
Green Fees not confirmed.
Designer   Peter McEwan & Bob Ferguson

Facilities ♿ 🏌 ⚐
Location   2.5m S of city centre off A702

Hotel   ★★★ 70% Braid Hills Hotel, 134 Braid Rd,
            EDINBURGH ☎ 0131 447 8888 68 ⇄ ☛

Bruntsfield Links Golfing Society 32 Barnton Av EH4 6JH
☎ 0131 336 1479 Fax 0131 336 5538
Mature parkland course with magnificent views over the
Firth of Forth and to the west. Greens and fairways are
generally immaculate. Challenging for all categories of
handicap.
18 holes, 6407yds, Par 71, SSS 71, Course record 67.
Club membership 1100.
Visitors   must telephone in advance. 0131 336 4050 or
            0131 336 1479
Societies   apply in writing.
Green Fees £55 per day; £40 per round (£60/£45 weekends).
Cards   ▦ ▦▦ 🔲
Prof   Brian Mackenzie
Designer   Willie Park Jr,A Mackenzle,hawtree
Facilities ⊗ ⅲ ╘ ♀ ⚘ 🏠 🏌 🏌 ⚐ ☚
Location   4m NW of city centre off A90

Hotel   ★★★ The Barnton, Queensferry Rd, Barnton,
            EDINBURGH ☎ 0131 339 1144 50 ⇄ ☛

Carrick Knowe Carrick Knowe, Glendevon Park EH12 5UZ
☎ 0131 337 1096 & 557 5457(bookings)
Fax 0131 557 5170
Flat parkland course. Played over by two clubs, Carrick
Knowe and Carrick Vale.
18 holes, 5697yds, Par 70, SSS 69.
Visitors   may be restricted at weekends.
Societies   telephone 0131 557 5457 or write to Edinburgh
            Leisure, 23 Waterloo Place EH1 3BH.
Green Fees not confirmed.
Facilities ♿ 🏌 ⚐
Location   3m W of city centre, S of A8

Hotel   ★★★ 73% Posthouse Premier Edinburgh,
            Corstorphine Rd, EDINBURGH
            ☎ 0870 400 9026 303 ⇄ ☛

Craigentinny Fillyside Rd EH7 6RG
☎ 0131 554 7501 & 557 5457(bookings)
Fax 0131 557 5170
To the north east of Edinburgh, Craigentinny course is
between Leith and Portobello. It is generally flat although
there are some hillocks with gentle slopes. The famous
Arthur's Seat dominates the southern skyline.
18 holes, 5205yds, Par 67, SSS 65.
Visitors   must contact in advance.
Societies   telephone 0131 557 5457 or apply in writing to:
            Edinburgh Leisure, 23 Waterloo Place
            EH1 3BH.
                                                    ▶

Marriott Dalmahoy Hotel

Kirknewton, *Edinburgh*   ☎ 0131 3358010   Fax 0131 3353577   Map 11 NT27

The Championship East Course has hosted many major events including the Solheim Cup, The Scottish Seniors Open Championship and the PGA Championship of Scotland. The greens are large with immaculate putting surfaces and many of the long par 4 holes offer a serious challenge to the golfer. The short holes are well bunkered and the 15th hole in particular, known as the 'Wee Wrecker' will test your nerve and skill.

The shorter West Course offers a different test with small greens requiring accuracy from the player's short game, however, the finishing holes with the Gogar Burn meandering through the fairway creates a tough finale. Training and leisure facilities are extensive with corporate events catered for.

Visitors welcome Mon-Fri, weekend by application. Call in advance to book tee times, subject to availability

Societies telephone or write for details

Green Fees telephone for current fees ⊞ ▦ ▬ ▣ 🗐

Facilities ⊗ 🎱 ▤ 🍺 ♀△ 🏠 ⛏ 🎣 ✂ ⚑

Professional (Neal Graham)

Leisure tennis, swimming, sauna, solarium, gymnasium

Location Kirknewton EH27 8EB (7m W of city centre on A71)

Holes/Par/Course record East Course: 18 holes, 6648 yds, Par 72, SSS 72, Course record 62

West Course: 18 holes, 5168 yds, Par 68, SSS 66

Championship Course

WHERE TO STAY AND EAT NEARBY

Hotels

KIRKNEWTON

★★★★◉◉ 74% Marriott Dalmahoy Hotel & Country Club
☎ 0131 333 1845.
43 ⇄ 🛏 Annexe 172 ⇄ 🛏

EDINBURGH

★★★★ 62% Swallow Royal Scot, 111

Glasgow Rd. ☎ 0131 334 9191.
245 ⇄ 🛏

UPHALL

★★★★◉◉ 67% Houstoun House Hotel & Country Club EH52 6JS.
☎ 01506 853831. 25 ⇄ 🛏
Annexe 47 ⇄ 🛏

Restaurant

LINLITHGOW

◉◉ Livingston's Restaurant, 52 High St.
☎ 01506 846565

Green Fees £9.20 per round before 4pm; £11 after 4pm & weekends.
Facilities ⌂ ⛳ ✓
Location NE side of city, between Leith & Portobello

Hotel ★★★ 66% Kings Manor, 100 Milton Rd East, EDINBURGH ☎ 0131 669 0444 66 ⇌ ⁂

Craigmillar Park 1 Observatory Rd EH9 3HG
☎ 0131 667 0047
Parkland course, with good views.
18 holes, 5851yds, Par 70, SSS 69, Course record 63.
Club membership 750.
Visitors must contact in advance, welcome Monday-Friday and Sunday afternoons
Societies must contact in writing.
Green Fees not confirmed.
Prof B McGhee
Designer James Braid
Facilities ⊗ ⊞ ⏚ ⚑ ♀ ⌂ ⛳ ✓
Location 2m S of city centre off A7

Hotel ★★ 68% Allison House Hotel, 15/17 Mayfield Gardens, EDINBURGH ☎ 0131 667 8049 23rm(21 ⁂)

Duddingston Duddingston Rd West EH15 3QD
☎ 0131 661 7688 Fax 0131 652 6057
Parkland course with burn as a natural hazard. Testing 11th hole. Easy walking and windy.
18 holes, 6647yds, Par 71, SSS 71.
Club membership 700.
Visitors may not play at weekends.
Societies Tue & Thu only. Must contact in advance.
Green Fees not confirmed.
Cards ▦ ⬇
Prof Alastair McLean
Designer Willie Park Jnr
Facilities ⊗ ⊞ ⏚ ⚑ ♀ ⌂ ⛳ ✓
Location 2.5m SE of city centre off A1

Hotel ★★ 67% Salisbury View Hotel, 64 Dalkeith Rd, EDINBURGH ☎ 0131 667 1133 8 ⁂

Kingsknowe 326 Lanark Rd EH14 2JD
☎ 0131 441 1145 (Secretary) & 441 1144 (Club)
Fax 0131 441 2079 e-mail: kingsknowe.golfclub@virgin.net
Hilly parkland course with prevailing SW winds.
18 holes, 5979yds, Par 69, SSS 69, Course record 63.
Club membership 800.
Visitors contact in advance and subject to availability of tee times.
Societies apply in writing or telephone secretary.
Green Fees £30 per day; £20 per round.
Prof Chris Morris
Designer A Herd/James Braid
Facilities ⊗ ⊞ ⏚ ⚑ ♀ ⌂ ✓
Location 4m SW of city centre on A70

Hotel ★★★ 75% Bruntsfield Hotel, 69/74 Bruntsfield Place, EDINBURGH ☎ 0131 229 1393 75 ⇌ ⁂

Where to stay, where to eat?
Visit the AA internet site
www.theAA.com

Liberton 297 Gilmerton Rd EH16 5UJ
☎ 0131 664 3009 (sec) & 664 1056 (pro)
Fax 0131 666 0853
Undulating, wooded parkland course.
18 holes, 5306yds, Par 67, SSS 67, Course record 61.
Club membership 675.
Visitors must contact in advance.
Societies must contact in writing.
Green Fees not confirmed.
Cards ▦
Prof Iain Seath
Facilities ⊗ ⊞ ⏚ ⚑ ♀ ⌂ ⛳ ✓
Location 3m SE of city centre on A7

Hotel ★★★ 74% Dalhousie Castle And Spa, Bonnyrigg, EDINBURGH
☎ 01875 820153 27 ⇌ ⁂ Annexe5 ⁂

Lothianburn 106A Biggar Rd, Fairmilehead EH10 7DU
☎ 0131 445 2206 & 0131 445 5067
Hillside course with a 'T' shaped wooded-area, situated in the Pentland foothills. Testing in windy conditions. Fine views of Edinburgh and the Lothians.
18 holes, 5662yds, Par 71, SSS 68, Course record 66.
Club membership 850.
Visitors weekends after 3.30pm contact professional, weekdays up to 4pm.
Societies apply to the secretary or telephone in the first instance.
Green Fees £22.50 per day; £16.50 per round (£27.50/£22.50 weekends).
Prof Kurt Mungall
Designer J Braid (re-designed 1928)
Facilities ⊗ ⊞ ⏚ ⚑ ♀ ⌂ ⛳ ✓
Location 4.5m S of city centre on A702

Hotel ★★★ 70% Braid Hills Hotel, 134 Braid Rd, EDINBURGH ☎ 0131 447 8888 68 ⇌ ⁂

EDINBURGH See page 337

EDINBURGH Map 11 NT27

Merchants of Edinburgh 10 Craighill Gardens EH10 5PY
☎ 0131 447 1219
Testing hill course with fine views over the city and the surrounding countryside.
18 holes, 4889yds, Par 65, SSS 64, Course record 59.
Club membership 900.
Visitors must contact Secretary or Professional in advance.
Societies must contact secretary in writing.
Green Fees not confirmed.
Prof Neil Colquhoun
Designer R G Ross
Facilities ⊗ ⊞ ⏚ ⚑ ♀ ⌂ ⛳ ✓
Location 2m SW of city centre off A702

Hotel ★★★ 70% Braid Hills Hotel, 134 Braid Rd, EDINBURGH ☎ 0131 447 8888 68 ⇌ ⁂

Mortonhall 231 Braid Rd EH10 6PB
☎ 0131 447 6974 Fax 0131 447 8712
Moorland/parkland course with views over Edinburgh.
18 holes, 6502yds, Par 72, SSS 72, Course record 66.
Club membership 525.
▶

Visitors advisable to contact by phone.
Societies may not play at weekends. Must contact in writing.
Green Fees not confirmed.
Cards ▦
Prof Douglas Horn
Designer James Braid/F Hawtree
Facilities ⊗ ⅃ ♨ ♀ 🏔 🏠 ⚑ ✐
Location 3m S of city centre off A702

Hotel ★★★ 70% Braid Hills Hotel, 134 Braid Rd, EDINBURGH ☎ 0131 447 8888 68 ⇌ ⋔

Murrayfield 43 Murrayfield Rd EH12 6EU
☎ 0131 337 3478 Fax 0131 313 0721
Parkland course on the side of Corstorphine Hill, with fine views.
18 holes, 5725yds, Par 70, SSS 69.
Club membership 815.
Visitors contact in advance, may not play at weekends.
Societies apply in writing
Green Fees £35 per day; £30 per round.
Prof J J Fisher
Facilities ⊗ ⅃ ♨ ♀ 🏔 🏠 ⚑ ✐
Location 2m W of city centre off A8

Hotel ★★★ 73% Posthouse Premier Edinburgh, Corstorphine Rd, EDINBURGH ☎ 0870 400 9026 303 ⇌ ⋔

Portobello Stanley St EH15 1JJ
☎ 0131 669 4361 & 557 5457(bookings)
Fax 0131 557 5170
Public parkland course, easy walking.
9 holes, 2252yds, Par 32, SSS 32.
Visitors advanced booking recommended. Contact Edinburgh Leisure.
Societies contact in advance, telephone 0131 557 5457 or write to Edinburgh Leisure, 23 Waterloo Place EH1 3BH.
Green Fees not confirmed.
Facilities 🏠 ⚑ ✐
Location 3m E of city centre off A1

Hotel ★★★ 66% Kings Manor, 100 Milton Rd East, EDINBURGH ☎ 0131 669 0444 66 ⇌ ⋔

Prestonfield 6 Priestfield Rd North EH16 5HS
☎ 0131 667 9665 Fax 0131 667 9665
Parkland course with beautiful views.
18 holes, 6212yds, Par 70, SSS 70, Course record 66.
Club membership 850.
Visitors contact secretary in advance. May not play Sat before 10.30am or between 12pm-1.30pm & Sun before 11.30am.
Societies must contact secretary.
Green Fees £30 per day; £20 per round (£40/£30 weekends).
Cards ▦ 🖃
Prof John Macfarlane
Designer James Braid
Facilities ⊗ 〕Ⅲ ⅃ ♨ ♀ 🏔 🏠 ⚑ 🛒 ✐
Location 1.5m S of city centre off A68

Hotel ★★ 67% Salisbury View Hotel, 64 Dalkeith Rd, EDINBURGH ☎ 0131 667 1133 8 ⋔

Looking for a driving range?
See the index at the back of the guide

Ravelston 24 Ravelston Dykes Rd EH4 3NZ
☎ 0131 315 2486 Fax 0131 315 2486
Parkland course.
9 holes, 5230yds, Par 66, SSS 65, Course record 64.
Club membership 610.
Visitors must contact in advance but may not play at weekends & bank holidays.
Green Fees £15 per round.
Designer James Braid
Facilities ⅃ ♨ 🏔
Location 3m W of city centre off A90

Hotel ★★★ 73% Posthouse Premier Edinburgh, Corstorphine Rd, EDINBURGH ☎ 0870 400 9026 303 ⇌ ⋔

Royal Burgess 181 Whitehouse Rd, Barnton EH4 6BY
☎ 0131 339 2075 Fax 0131 339 3712
e-mail: secretary@royalburgess.co.uk
No mention of golf clubs would be complete without mention of the Royal Burgess, which was instituted in 1735, thus being the oldest golfing society in the world. Its course is a pleasant parkland, and one with very much variety. A club which all those interested in the history of the game should visit.
18 holes, 6111yds, Par 68, SSS 69.
Club membership 620.
Visitors must contact in advance. Gentlemen only.
Societies must contact in advance.
Green Fees £55 per day; £42 per round.
Cards 🖃 ▬ 🖃 ▦ 🖃
Prof George Yuille
Designer Tom Morris
Facilities ⊗ ⅃ ♨ ♀ 🏔 🏠 ⚑ ✐
Location 5m W of city centre off A90

Hotel ★★★ The Barnton, Queensferry Rd, Barnton, EDINBURGH ☎ 0131 339 1144 50 ⇌ ⋔

Silverknowes Silverknowes, Parkway EH4 5ET
☎ 0131 336 3843 & 557 5457(bookings)
Fax 0131 557 5170
Public links course on coast overlooking the Firth of Forth with magnificent views.
18 holes, 6070yds, Par 71, SSS 70.
Visitors advanced booking recommended in summer, contact Edinburgh Leisure.
Societies telephone 0131 557 5457 or apply in writing to: Edinburgh Leisure, 23 Waterloo Place, Edinburgh EH1 3BH.
Green Fees not confirmed.
Facilities 🏠 ⚑ ✐
Location 4m NW of city centre, easy access from city by-pass

Hotel ★★★ The Barnton, Queensferry Rd, Barnton, EDINBURGH ☎ 0131 339 1144 50 ⇌ ⋔

Swanston 111 Swanston Rd, Fairmilehead EH10 7DS
☎ 0131 445 2239
Hillside course with steep climb at 12th & 13th holes.
18 holes, 5024yds, Par 66, SSS 65, Course record 63.
Club membership 600.
Visitors contact in advance. Weekends restricted.
Societies must contact in advance. ▶

Green Fees not confirmed.
Prof Ian Taylor
Designer Herbert More
Facilities ⓧ ⫙ ⬛ ⬛ ♀ ⚘ 🏠 ⚐ ⚒ ✓
Location 4m S of city centre off B701

Hotel ★★★ 70% Braid Hills Hotel, 134 Braid Rd, EDINBURGH ☎ 0131 447 8888 68 ⇌ ⏸

Torphin Hill Torphin Rd, Colinton EH13 0PG
☎ 0131 441 1100 Fax 0131 441 7166
e-mail: info@torphinhillgc.saefhost.co.uk
Beautiful hillside, heathland course, with fine views of
Edinburgh and the Forth Estuary.
18 holes, 4580mtrs, Par 67, SSS 66, Course record 63.
Club membership 550.
Visitors must contact in advance, limited access Sat & Sun (only after 2pm)
Societies must contact in advance.
Green Fees £14 per round;£20 per day(£20 per round weekends).
Cards ▦
Prof Jamie Browne
Facilities ⓧ ⫙ ⬛ ⬛ ♀ ⚘ 🏠 ⚒
Location 5m SW of city centre S of A720

Hotel ★★★ 70% Braid Hills Hotel, 134 Braid Rd, EDINBURGH ☎ 0131 447 8888 68 ⇌ ⏸

Turnhouse 154 Turnhouse Rd EH12 0AD
☎ 0131 339 1014
Hilly, parkland/heathland course, good views over the
Pentland Hills and Forth Valley.
18 holes, 6171yds, Par 69, SSS 70, Course record 62.
Club membership 800.
Visitors with member only at weekends, and no visitors Wed or Medal days. Must contact professional in advance.
Societies must contact in writing.
Green Fees £25 per 18 holes;£33 per day.
Prof John Murray
Designer J Braid
Facilities ⓧ ⫙ ⬛ ⬛ ♀ ⚘ 🏠 ⚒ ✓
Location 6m W of city centre N of A8

Hotel ★★★ The Barnton, Queensferry Rd, Barnton, EDINBURGH ☎ 0131 339 1144 50 ⇌ ⏸

RATHO   Map 11 NT17

Ratho Park EH28 8NX
☎ 0131 335 0069 & 335 0068 Fax 0131 333 1752
Flat parkland course.
18 holes, 5900yds, Par 69, SSS 68, Course record 62.
Club membership 850.
Visitors must contact in advance.
Societies must contact in writing. Only able to play Tue-Thu
Green Fees £35 per day £25 per round (£35 per round weekends).
Prof Alan Pate
Designer James Braid
Facilities ⓧ ⫙ ⬛ ⬛ ♀ ⚘ 🏠 ⚒ ✓
Location 0.75m E, N of A71

Hotel ★★★ 73% Posthouse Premier Edinburgh, Corstorphine Rd, EDINBURGH ☎ 0870 400 9026 303 ⇌ ⏸

SOUTH QUEENSFERRY   Map 11 NT17

Dundas Parks Dundas Estate EH30 9PQ
☎ 0131 319 1347 Fax 0131 319 1347
e-mail: christine.wood@euphony.net
Parkland course situated on the estate of Dundas Castle, with
excellent views. For 18 holes, the 9 are played twice.
9 holes, 6024yds, Par 70, SSS 69, Course record 64.
Club membership 500.
Visitors must contact in advance. May not play at weekends.
Societies must contact in writing.
Green Fees £10.
Facilities ⚘
Location 0.5m S on A8000

Hotel ★★★ 61% Forth Bridges Hotel, 1 Ferrymuir Gait, SOUTH QUEENSFERRY ☎ 0131 469 9955 108 ⇌ ⏸

CITY OF GLASGOW

GLASGOW   Map 11 NS56

Alexandra Alexandra Park, Alexandra Pde G31 8SE
☎ 0141 556 1294
Parkland course, hilly with some woodland. Many bunkers
and a barrier of trees between 1st and 9th fairway. Work
currently in progress to alter greens and improve course.
9 holes, 2800yds, Par 31, Course record 25.
Club membership 85.
Visitors no restrictions.
Societies telephone 24 hrs in advance or by writing one week in advance.
Green Fees £3.70 per round.
Designer G McArthur
Facilities ⚘
& Leisure bowling green.
Location 2m E of city centre off M8/A8

Cowglen Barrhead Rd G43 1AU
☎ 0141 632 0556 Fax 01505 503000
Undulating and challenging parkland course with good views
over the Clyde valley to the Campsie Hills. Club and line
selection is most important on many holes due to the
strategic placing of copses on the course.
18 holes, 6079yds, Par 69, SSS 69, Course record 63.
Club membership 805.
Visitors play on shorter course. Must contact in advance and have a handicap certificate. No visitors Tue, Fri and weekends.
Societies must be booked in writing through the secretary.
Green Fees not confirmed.
Prof John McTear
Designer David Adams/James Braid
Facilities ⓧ ⫙ ⬛ ⬛ ♀ ⚘ 🏠 ⏸
Location 4.5m SW of city centre on B762

Hotel ★★★ 71% Dalmeny Park Country House Hotel, Lochlibo Rd, BARRHEAD ☎ 0141 881 9211 20 ⇌ ⏸

Haggs Castle 70 Dumbreck Rd, Dumbreck G41 4SN
☎ 0141 427 1157 Fax 0141 427 1157
Wooded, parkland course where Scottish National
Championships and the Glasgow and Scottish Open have
been held. Quite difficult.
18 holes, 6419yds, Par 71, SSS 71, Course record 68.
Club membership 900.
Visitors   may not play at weekends. Must contact in
             advance.
Societies   apply in writing.
Green Fees   not confirmed.
Cards   [icons]
Prof   Jim McAlister
Designer   James Baird
Facilities   ⊗ ↗↿ ㄴ ☕ ♀ ♨ 🏠 ⚑ ♦ ♣ ♂
Location   2.5m SW of city centre on B768

Hotel   ★★★ 68% Swallow Hotel, 517 Paisley Rd
             West, GLASGOW
             ☎ 0141 427 3146 117 ⇆ ♙

Kirkhill Greenless Rd, Cambuslang G72 8YN
☎ 0141 641 8499 Fax 0141 641 8499
Meadowland course designed by James Braid.
18 holes, 6030yds, Par 70, SSS 70, Course record 63.
Club membership 650.
Visitors   must play with member at weekends.
Societies   must contact in advance.
Green Fees   £20 per round;£25 per day.
Prof   Duncan Williamson
Designer   J Braid
Facilities   ⊗ ↗↿ ㄴ ☕ ♀ ♨ 🏠 ♣
Location   5m SE of city centre off A749

Hotel   ★★★ 63% Stuart Hotel, 2 Cornwall Way,
             Town Centre, EAST KILBRIDE
             ☎ 013552 21161 38 ⇆ ♙

Knightswood Lincoln Av G13 5QZ ☎ 0141 959 6358
Flat parkland course within easy reach of city. Two dog-legs.
9 holes, 5586yds, Par 68, SSS 67.
Club membership 40.
Visitors   reserved tee Wed and Fri am bookings 1 day in
             advance, no other restrictions.
Societies   welcome, must book 1 day in advance.
Green Fees   £7.20 per 18 holes.
Facilities   ♨
Location   4m W of city centre off A82

Hotel   ★★★ 68% Jurys Glasgow Hotel, Great
             Western Rd, GLASGOW
             ☎ 0141 334 8161 136 ⇆ ♙

Lethamhill 1240 Cumbernauld Rd, Millerston G33 1AH
☎ 0141 770 6220 Fax 1041 770 0520
Municipal parkland course.
18 holes, 5859yds, Par 70, SSS 69.
Visitors   must contact in advance.
Societies   must contact in advance.
Green Fees   not confirmed.
Facilities   ♨
Location   3m NE of city centre on A80

Hotel   ★★★★ 72% Millennium Hotel Glasgow,
             George Square, GLASGOW
             ☎ 0141 332 6711 117 ⇆ ♙

Linn Park Simshill Rd G44 5EP ☎ 0141 633 0377
Municipal parkland course with six par 3's in outward half.
18 holes, 4952yds, Par 65, SSS 65, Course record 61.
Visitors   must contact in advance.
Societies   advance booking in writing
Green Fees   not confirmed.
Facilities   ♨
Location   4m S of city centre off B766

Hotel   ★★★ 70% Bruce Hotel, Cornwall St, EAST
             KILBRIDE ☎ 01355 229771 65 ⇆ ♙

Pollok 90 Barrhead Rd G43 1BG
☎ 0141 632 4351 & 632 1080 Fax 0141 649 1398
Parkland course with woods and river.
18 holes, 6254yds, Par 71, SSS 70, Course record 62.
Club membership 620.
Visitors   Members only until 2pm weekends. Must
             contact in advance. Ladies only as part of
             visiting parties
Societies   must contact in writing.
Green Fees   £42 per day; £32 per round(£50/£40 weekends).
Designer   James Braid
Facilities   ⊗ ↗↿ by prior arrangement ㄴ ☕ ♀ ♨
Location   4m SW of city centre on A762

Hotel   ★★★ 60% The Tinto Firs, 470 Kilmarnock Rd,
             GLASGOW ☎ 0141 637 2353 27 ⇆ ♙

Williamwood Clarkston Rd G44 3YR
☎ 0141 637 1783 Fax 0141 571 0166
Undulating parkland course with mature woodlands.
18 holes, 5878yds, Par 68, SSS 69, Course record 61.
Club membership 800.
Visitors   apply in writing to secretary, no weekend play.
Societies   midweek bookings only, apply in writing to
             secretary.
Green Fees   £37 per day; £27 per round.
Cards   [icons]
Prof   Stewart Marshall
Designer   James Braid
Facilities   ⊗ ↗↿ ㄴ ☕ ♀ ♨ 🏠 ♂
Location   5m S of city centre on B767

ALLOA   Map 11 NS89

Alloa Schawpark, Sauchie FK10 3AX
☎ 01259 724476 Fax 01259 724476
Undulating, wooded parkland course, situated under the
Ochil hills, scenery and playing conditions are exceptional.
18 holes, 6229yds, Par 69, SSS 71, Course record 63.
Club membership 910.
Visitors   7 day booking system through professional.
             Advised to book especially at weekends.
Societies   apply in writing/telephone.
Green Fees   £24 per round;£34 per day(£28/£38 weekends).
Cards   [icons]
Prof   Bill Bennett
Designer   James Braid
Facilities   ⊗ ↗↿ ㄴ ☕ ♀ ♨ 🏠 ⚑ ♦ ♣ ♂
Location   1.5m NE on A908   ▶

Hotel   ★★ 69% Terraces Hotel, 4 Melville Ter,
STIRLING ☎ 01786 472268 17 ⇄ ⸙

Braehead Cambus FK10 2NT ☎ 01259 725766
Attactive parkland course at the foot of the Ochil Hills, and
offering spectacular views.
18 holes, 6086yds, Par 70, SSS 69, Course record 64.
Club membership 800.
Visitors   advisable to telephone in advance.
Societies   must contact the clubhouse manager in advance
tel 01259 725766.
Green Fees £24.50 per day; £18.50 per round
(£32.50/£24.50 weekends).
Cards   ▨ ▬ ▱
Prof   David Boyce
Designer   Robert Tait
Facilities ⊗ ⅶ ⬛ ⬛ ⚡ ♀ ⚖ ⬛ ⚐ ◥ ⚓ ⚘ ♂
Location   1m W on A907

Hotel   ★★ 69% Terraces Hotel, 4 Melville Ter,
STIRLING ☎ 01786 472268 17 ⇄ ⸙

ALVA   Map 11 NS89

Alva Beauclerc St FK12 5LD ☎ 01259 760431
A 9-hole course at the foot of the Ochil Hills which gives it
its characteristic sloping fairways and fast greens.
9 holes, 2423yds, Par 66, SSS 64, Course record 63.
Club membership 318.
Visitors   may not play during medal competitions or Thu
evening (Ladies night).
Societies   apply in writing or telephone in advance.
Green Fees not confirmed.
Facilities ⬛ ⬛ ♀ ⚖
Location   7m from Stirling,A91 Stirling/St Andrews rd

DOLLAR   Map 11 NS99

Dollar Brewlands House FK14 7EA
☎ 01259 742400 Fax 01259 743497
e-mail: dollargc@brewlandshouse.freeserve.co.uk
Compact hillside course with magnificent views along the
Ochil Hills.
18 holes, 5242yds, Par 69, SSS 66, Course record 62.
Club membership 450.
Visitors   weekdays course available but restricted Wed
ladies day, weekends advised to contact in
advance.
Societies   write or telephone in advance.
Green Fees £17.50 per day; £13.50 per round (£22
day/round weekends).
Designer   Ben Sayers
Facilities ⊗ ⅶ ⬛ ⬛ ⚡ ♀ ⚖ ◥ ♂
Location   0.5m N off A91

Hotel   ★★★ 69% Royal Hotel, Henderson St,
BRIDGE OF ALLAN
☎ 01786 832284 32 ⇄ ⸙

MUCKHART   Map 11 NO00

Muckhart FK14 7JH ☎ 01259 781423
Fax 01259 781544
Scenic heathland/downland course.
*Muckhart Course: 18 holes, 6034yds, Par 71, SSS 70, Course
record 65.*
Naemoor Course: 9 holes.
Club membership 750.
Visitors   telephone to book - 01259 781423 or
professional 01259 781493.Correct attire to be
worn at all times.
Societies   booking by prior arrangement.
Green Fees £25 per day; £23 per 27 holes; £17 per round
(£35/£32/£25 weekends).
Cards   ▨ ▬ ▱
Prof   Keith Salmoni
Facilities ⊗ ⅶ ⬛ ⬛ ⚡ ♀ ⚖ ⬛ ♂
Location   SW of village off A91

Hotel   ★★★ 66% Gartwhinzean Hotel, POWMILL
☎ 01577 840595 23 ⇄ ⸙

TILLICOULTRY   Map 11 NS99

Tillicoultry Alva Rd FK13 6BL
☎ 01259 750124 Fax 01259 750124
e-mail: tillygc@stirling.co.uk
Parkland course at foot of the Ochil Hills entailing some hard
walking.
9 holes, 4904metres, Par 68, SSS 66, Course record 61.
Club membership 400.
Visitors   must contact in advance.
Societies   apply to the secretary.
Green Fees not confirmed.
Facilities ⬛ ⬛ ♀ ⚖
Location   A91, 9m E of Stirling

DUMFRIES & GALLOWAY

CASTLE DOUGLAS   Map 11 NX76

Castle Douglas Abercromby Rd DG7 1BB
☎ 01556 502801 or 502099
Parkland course, one severe hill.
9 holes, 2704yds, Par 68, SSS 66.
Club membership 500.
Societies   apply by writing to secretary.
Green Fees not confirmed.
Facilities ⊗ ⬛ ⬛ ⚡ ♀ ⚖ ⬛ ⚐ ♂
Location   W side of town

Hotel   ★★ 66% Imperial Hotel, 35 King St, CASTLE
DOUGLAS ☎ 01556 502086 12 ⇄ ⸙

Entries with a green background
identify courses considered to be
particularly interesting

AA Hotels that have special
arrangements with golf courses are listed at
the back of the guide

COLVEND   Map 11 NX85

Colvend Sandyhills DG5 4PY
☎ 01556 630398 & 610878 (Sec) Fax 01556 630495
Picturesque and challenging course on Solway coast. Superb views.
18 holes, 5220yds, Par 68, SSS 67, Course record 64.
Club membership 490.

Visitors	restricted Apr-Sep on Tue, 1st tee reserved for weekly Medal 1-1.30 & 4-6pm and some weekends for open competitions.
Societies	must telephone in advance.
Green Fees	£20 per day.
Designer	Allis & Thomas
Facilities	⊗ ⅷ ﴾ ☕ ♥ 오 ﻼ ᛆ ⑀ ᕈ ♨ ✄
Location	6m from Dalbeattie on A710 Solway Coast Rd

Hotel ★★ 68% Clonyard House Hotel, COLVEND
☎ 01556 630372 15 ⇆ ﹙

CUMMERTREES   Map 11 NY16

Powfoot DG12 5QE
☎ 01461 700276 Fax 01461 700276
This British Championship Course is on the Solway Firth, playing at this delightfully compact semi-links seaside course is a scenic treat. Lovely holes include the 2nd, the 8th and the 11th, also 9th with World War II bomb crater.
18 holes, 6283yds, Par 71, SSS 70, Course record 63.
Club membership 950.

Visitors	contact in advance. May not play before 9am between 11am-1pm and after 3.30pm wekdays, no visitors Sat or before 1pm Sun.
Societies	must book in advance.
Green Fees	£31 per day; £24 per round(£35/£26 bank holiday)£26 Sundays.
Cards	▦ ▣
Prof	Gareth Dick
Designer	J Braid
Facilities	⊗ ⅷ ☕ ♥ 오 ᛆ ᕈ ✄
Location	0.5m off B724

Hotel ★★ 70% Powfoot Golf Hotel, Links Av,
POWFOOT ☎ 01461 700254 18 ⇆ ﹙

DALBEATTIE   Map 11 NX86

Dalbeattie Off Maxwell Park DG5 4JR
☎ 01556 610682
This 9 hole course provides an excellent challenge for golfers of all abilities. There are a few gentle slopes to negotiate but compensated by fine views along the Urr Valley. The 363 yard 4th hole is a memorable par 4. A good straight drive is required to the corner of the course where a right angle dog-leg is taken for a pitch to a smallish green.
9 holes, 5710yds, Par 68, SSS 68.
Club membership 300.

Visitors	club competitions Mon, Wed and Thu, visitors requested not to play after 5pm.
Societies	apply in writing to Secretary or telephone 01556 610311/611760.
Green Fees	£15 per day/round.
Facilities	ᛆ
Location	Signposted off B794

Hotel ★★ 65% King's Arms Hotel, St Andrew's St,
CASTLE DOUGLAS
☎ 01556 502626 10rm(9 ⇆ ﹙)

DUMFRIES   Map 11 NX97

Dumfries & County Nunfield, Edinburgh Rd DG1 1JX
☎ 01387 253585 Fax 01387 253585
Parkland course alongside River Nith, with views over the Queensberry Hills.
Nunfield: 18 holes, 5928yds, Par 69, SSS 69, Course record 63.
Club membership 800.

Visitors	must contact in advance but may not play Saturdays and during competitions on Sundays
Societies	apply in writing.
Green Fees	£26 per day/round.
Prof	Stuart Syme
Designer	William Fernie
Facilities	⊗ ⅷ ☕ ♥ 오 ᛆ 🏠 ᕈ ♨ ✄
Location	1m NE of Dumfries on A701

Hotel ★★★ 68% Station Hotel, 49 Lovers Walk,
DUMFRIES ☎ 01387 254316 32 ⇆ ﹙

Dumfries & Galloway 2 Laurieston Av DG2 7NY
☎ 01387 263848 Fax 01387 263848
e-mail: joe@golfclub.fsnet.co.uk
Parkland course.
18 holes, 6309yds, Par 70, SSS 71.
Club membership 800.

Visitors	may not play on competition days.Must contact in advance. No visitors on Saturdays during season. Some Sundays not available.
Societies	apply in writing.
Green Fees	£26 per day/round (£32 weekends).
Prof	Joe Fergusson
Designer	W Fernie
Facilities	⊗ ⅷ ☕ ♥ 오 ᛆ 🏠 ᕈ ✄
Location	W side of town centre on A75

Hotel ★★★ 69% Cairndale Hotel & Leisure Club,
English St, DUMFRIES
☎ 01387 254111 91 ⇆ ﹙

GATEHOUSE-OF-FLEET   Map 11 NX55

Gatehouse Laurieston Rd DG7 2BE
☎ 01644 450260 Fax 01644 450260
Set against a background of rolling hills with scenic views of Fleet Bay and the Solway Firth.
9 holes, 2521yds, Par 66, SSS 66, Course record 62.
Club membership 370.

Visitors	restricted Sun before 11.30am.
Societies	telephone in advance.
Green Fees	£10 per day.
Designer	Tom Fernie
Facilities	ᛆ
Location	0.25m N of town

Hotel ★★★ 64% Murray Arms Hotel,
GATEHOUSE OF FLEET
☎ 01557 814207
12 ⇆ ﹙ Annexe1 ⇆ ﹙   ▶

Cally Palace

★★★★   GATEHOUSE OF FLEET,   AA ROSETTE
        SOUTH WEST SCOTLAND   FOR FOOD

The Cally Palace has its own private
18 hole golf course, exclusive to hotel
guests. Spacious lounges, large
conservatory, indoor swimming pool,
jacuzzi, sauna and billiards room
compliment the Cally facilities. There
are excellent golf packages available.

Tel 01557 814 341

FOR LATEST NEWS AND SEASONAL OFFERS VISIT
www.callypalace.co.uk

Additional ★★★★♨ 69% Cally Palace Hotel,
hotel   GATEHOUSE OF FLEET
             ☎ 01557 814341
             Fax 01557 814522   55 ⇄ ⚑

GLENLUCE   Map 10 NX15

Wigtownshire County Mains of Park DG8 0NN
☎ 01581 300420 e-mail: wgc@glenluce.org.uk
Seaside links course on the shores of Luce Bay, easy walking
but affected by winds. The 12th hole, a dogleg with out of
bounds to the right, is named after the course's designer,
Gordon Cunningham.
18 holes, 5843yds, Par 70, SSS 68, Course record 67.
Club membership 450.
Visitors   may play any day by prior arrangement ex
                competition days.
Societies   must contact in advance.
Green Fees   £25 per day; £19per round (£27/£21 weekends).
Designer   W Gordon Cunningham
Facilities   ⊗ ⵊ ⓛ ⓜ ♀ ⌂ ☗ ⵏ ↘ ⚒ ✐
Location   1.5m W off A75, 200 yds off A75 on shores of
                Luce Bay

Hotel   ★★★★ 68% North West Castle Hotel,
                STRANRAER
                ☎ 01776 704413
                70 ⇄ ⚑ Annexe3 ⇄ ⚑

Looking for a driving range?
See the index at the back of the guide

GRETNA   Map 11 NY36

Gretna Kirtle View DG16 5HD
☎ 01461 338464 Fax 01461 337362 e-
mail: georgebirnie@aol.co.uk
A nice parkland course on gentle hills. It offers a good test of
skill.
9 holes, 3214yds, Par 72, SSS 71, Course record 71.
Club membership 250.
Visitors   no restrictions.
Societies   telephone in advance.
Green Fees   £5 per 9 holes;£10 per day.
Designer   N Williams
Facilities   ⚒ ⵏ ✐ ⚑
Location   0.5m W of Gretna on B721,signposted

Hotel   ★★ 68% Solway Lodge Hotel, Annan Rd,
                GRETNA ☎ 01461 338266
                3 ⇄ ⚑ Annexe7 ⇄ ⚑

KIRKCUDBRIGHT   Map 11 NX65

Brighouse Bay Brighouse Bay, Borgue DG6 4TS
☎ 01557 870409 Fax 01557 870409
e-mail: golfandleisure@brighouse-bay.co.uk
A beautifully situated scenic maritime course on free
draining coastal grassland and playable all year. Making use
of many natural features - water, gullies and rocks - it
provides a testing challenge to golfers of all handicaps.
18 holes, 6602yds, Par 74, SSS 73.
Club membership 170.
Visitors   pay as you play - payment at adjacent Golf &
                Leisure Club. Phoning in advance
                recommended. Parties over 8 must book in
                advance.
Societies   prior arrangement necessary.
Green Fees   not confirmed.
Cards   🟥 🟥 🟥 🟦 🟩
Designer   D Gray
Facilities   ⊗ ⵊ ⓛ ⓜ ♀ ⌂ ☗ ⵏ ⍜ ↘ ⚒ ✐ ⚑
& Leisure   heated indoor swimming pool, fishing, solarium,
                gymnasium.
Location   3m S of Borgue off B727

Hotel   ★★★ 72% Selkirk Arms Hotel, Old High St,
                KIRKCUDBRIGHT ☎ 01557 330402
                13 ⇄ ⚑ Annexe3 ⇄ ⚑

Kirkcudbright Stirling Crescent DG6 4EZ
☎ 01557 330314
Parkland course. Hilly, with good views over the Harbour
town of Kirkcudbright and the Dee Estuary.
18 holes, 5739yds, Par 69, SSS 69, Course record 63.
Club membership 500.
Visitors   advisable to contact in advance.
Societies   contact in advance.
Green Fees   not confirmed.
Facilities   ⊗ ⵊ ⓛ ⓜ ♀ ⌂ ⵏ ↘ ⚒ ✐
Location   NE side of town off A711

Hotel   ★★★ 72% Selkirk Arms Hotel, Old High St,
                KIRKCUDBRIGHT ☎ 01557 330402
                13 ⇄ ⚑ Annexe3 ⇄ ⚑

LANGHOLM   Map 11 NY38

Langholm Whiteside DG13 0JR
☎ 013873 80673 & 81247 e-
mail: golf@langholmgolfclub.co.uk
Hillside course with fine views, easy to medium walking.
9 holes, 6180yds, Par 70, SSS 70, Course record 65.
Club membership 200.
Visitors   restricted Sat & Sun.
Societies   apply in writing to secretary.
Green Fees £10 per day.
Facilities   ⊗ by prior arrangement ⃝ℿ by prior arrangement
             ⓑ by prior arrangement ♀
Location   E side of village off A7

Guesthouse ♦♦♦ The Reivers Rest, 81 High St,
LANGHOLM ☎ 01387 381343 5 ⇔ r̂

LOCHMABEN   Map 11 NY08

Lochmaben Castlehillgate DG11 1NT ☎ 01387 810552
Attractive parkland course surrounding the Kirk Loch,
excellent views on this well maintained course.
18 holes, 5357yds, Par 67, SSS 66, Course record 62.
Club membership 850.
Visitors   advised to contact in advance,01387 810552.
Societies   must contact in advance,on .01387-810552
Green Fees £22 per day; £18 per round (£28/£22 weekends).
Designer   James Braid
Facilities   ⊗ ⃝ℿ ⓑ ▼ ♀ ⌂ ⏚ ⚲
& Leisure   fishing.
Location   S side of village off A709

Hotel   ★★★ 72% The Dryfesdale Country House
Hotel, Dryfrbridge, LOCKERBIE
☎ 01576 202427   15 ⇔ r̂

LOCKERBIE   Map 11 NY18

Lockerbie Corrie Rd DG11 2ND
☎ 01576 203363 Fax 01576 203363
Parkland course with fine views and featuring the only pond
hole in Dumfriesshire. Pond comes into play at 3 holes.
18 holes, 5614yds, Par 68, SSS 67, Course record 64.
Club membership 620.
Visitors   restricted Sun. Advisable to book in advance.
Societies   must contact secretary in advance.
Green Fees £20 per day; £16 per round (£20 round
               weekends)£25 per day Sat.
Designer   James Braid
Facilities   ⊗ ⓑ ▼ ♀ ⌂ ⚲ ⚲
Location   E side of town centre off B7068

Hotel   ★★★ 72% The Dryfesdale Country House
Hotel, Dryfrbridge, LOCKERBIE
☎ 01576 202427   15 ⇔ r̂

MOFFAT   Map 11 NT00

Moffat Coatshill DG10 9SB
☎ 01683 220020 Fax 01683 220020
Scenic moorland course overlooking the town, with
panoramic views of southern uplands.
18 holes, 5218yds, Par 69, SSS 67, Course record 60.
Club membership 350.

Visitors   advised to contact in advance, no visitors after
              12 noon on Wed.
Societies   apply in writing/telephone the clubmaster.
Green Fees not confirmed.
Designer   Ben Sayers
Facilities   ⊗ ⓑ ▼ ♀ ⌂ ⌂ ⚲ ⚲
& Leisure   snooker.
Location   From A74 1m on A701 to Moffat, course
              signposted

Hotel   ★★★ 74% Moffat House Hotel, High St,
MOFFAT ☎ 01683 220039   21 ⇔ r̂

MONREITH   Map 10 NX34

St Medan DG8 8NJ ☎ 01988 700358
Links course with panoramic views of the Solway and Isle of
Man.
9 holes, 4608yds, Par 64, SSS 63, Course record 60.
Club membership 300.
Visitors   no restrictions.
Societies   apply in advance by telephone or writing
Green Fees not confirmed.
Designer   James Braid
Facilities   ⊗ ⃝ℿ ⓑ ▼ ♀ ⌂ ⚲
Location   1m SE off A747

Hotel   ★★★⚬⚬ 66% Corsemalzie House Hotel,
PORT WILLIAM ☎ 01988 860254   14 ⇔ r̂

NEW GALLOWAY   Map 11 NX67

New Galloway High St DG7 3RN
☎ 01644 420737 & 450685 Fax 01644 450685
Set on the edge of the Galloway Hills and overlooking Loch
Ken, the course has excellent tees and first class greens. The
course rises through the first two fairways to a plateau with
all round views that many think unsurpassed.
9 holes, 5006yds, Par 68, SSS 67, Course record 63.
Club membership 350.
Visitors   restricted on Sun (competition days). All visitors
              play off yellow markers. Contact Secretary in
              advance. Smart/casual dress.
Societies   contact secretary in advance.
Green Fees £12.50 per day.
Designer   James Braid
Facilities   ⓑ ▼ ♀ ⌂ ⚲
Location   S side of town on A762

Hotel   ★★ 70% Douglas Arms, King St,
CASTLE DOUGLAS
☎ 01556 502231   24 ⇔ r̂

NEWTON STEWART   Map 10 NX46

Newton Stewart Kirroughtree Av, Minnigaff DG8 6PF
☎ 01671 402172 Fax 01671 402172
Parkland course in picturesque setting. A good test for all
standards of golfers with a variety of shots required.
18 holes, 5903yds, Par 69, SSS 70, Course record 66.
Club membership 380.
Visitors   must contact in advance.
Societies   must contact in advance.
Green Fees £21/£22 per 18 holes.
Facilities   ⊗ ⓑ ▼ ♀ ⌂ ⌂ ⚲ ⏚ ⚲
Location   0.5m N of town centre   ▶

Hotel   ★★ 70% Creebridge House Hotel, NEWTON STEWART ☎ 01671 402121 19 ⇄ ☏

Hotel   ★★ 68% Clonyard House Hotel, COLVEND ☎ 01556 630372 15 ⇄ ☏

PORTPATRICK   Map 10 NX05

Portpatrick Golf Course Rd DG9 8TB
☎ 01776 810273 Fax 01776 810811
Seaside links-type course, set on cliffs overlooking the Irish Sea, with magnificent views.
Dunskey Course: 18 holes, 5908yds, Par 70, SSS 67, Course record 63.
Dinvin Course: 9 holes, 1504yds, Par 27, SSS 27, Course record 23.
Club membership 750.

Visitors	must contact in advance. £5 deposit required
Societies	must contact in advance.
Green Fees	Dunskey: £33 per day; £22 per round (£38/£27 weekends) Dinvin:£9 per round;£13 per day.
Cards	⊟ 🗓 🗓 🗓
Designer	Charles Hunter
Facilities	⊗ ⫻ ⭡ ♥ ♀ ⚘ 🗓 ⛳ ⬩ 🏌 ⬩ ∅
Location	On entering village fork right at War Memorial, 300yds signposted

Hotel   ★★★ 73% Fernhill Hotel, Heugh Rd, PORTPATRICK ☎ 01776 810220
14 ⇄ ☏ Annexe9 ⇄ ☏

SANQUHAR   Map 11 NS70

Sanquhar Euchan Golf Course, Blackaddie Rd DG4 6JZ
☎ 01659 50577 & 66095 e-mail: douglas@nithb.freeserve.co.uk
Parkland course, fine views, easy walking. A good test for all standards of golfer.
9 holes, 5594yds, Par 70, SSS 68, Course record 66.
Club membership 200.

Visitors	no restrictions.
Societies	must pre-book.
Green Fees	£12 per day (£15 weekends).
Designer	Willie Fernie
Facilities & Leisure	♀ ⚘ snooker,pool..
Location	0.5m SW off A76

Hotel   ★★ 67% Blackaddie House Hotel, Blackaddie Rd, SANQUHAR ☎ 01659 50270 9 ⇄ ☏

SOUTHERNESS   Map 11 NX95

Southerness DG2 8AZ
☎ 01387 880677 Fax 01387 880644
e-mail: admin@southernessgc.sol.co.uk
Natural links, Championship course with panoramic views. Heather and bracken abound.
18 holes, 6566yds, Par 69, SSS 73, Course record 65.
Club membership 830.

Visitors	must have handicap certificate and contact in advance. May only play from yellow markers.
Societies	must contact in advance.
Green Fees	£35 per day (£45 per day weekends & bank holidays).
Cards	⊟ 🗓
Designer	McKenzie Ross
Facilities	⊗ ⫻ ⭡ ♥ ♀ ⚘ ∅
Location	3.5m S of Kirkbean off A710

Hotel   ★★ 68% Clonyard House Hotel, COLVEND ☎ 01556 630372 15 ⇄ ☏

STRANRAER   Map 10 NX06

Stranraer Creachmore by Stranraer DG9 0LF
☎ 01776 870245 Fax 01776 870445
Parkland course with beautiful view of Loch Ryan.
18 holes, 6308yds, Par 70, SSS 72, Course record 66.
Club membership 700.

Visitors	must contact in advance. Members times reserved throughout year.
Societies	must telephone in advance.
Green Fees	£20 per round;£26 per 27 holes;£30 per 36 holes(£25/£31/£35 weekends).
Cards	⊟ 🗓 🗓
Designer	James Braid
Facilities	⊗ ⫻ ⭡ ♥ ♀ ⚘ 🗓 ⛳ ⬩ 🏌 ⬩ ∅
Location	2.5m NW on A718

Hotel   ★★★★ 68% North West Castle Hotel, STRANRAER ☎ 01776 704413
70 ⇄ ☏ Annexe3 ⇄ ☏

THORNHILL   Map 11 NX89

Thornhill Blacknest DG3 5DW ☎ 01848 330546
Moorland/parkland course with fine views over the southern uplands.
18 holes, 6011yds, Par 71, SSS 70, Course record 67.
Club membership 700.

Visitors	apply in advance, restricted competition days.
Societies	apply in writing.
Green Fees	not confirmed.
Prof	James Davidson
Facilities	⊗ ⫻ ⭡ ♥ ♀ ⚘ 🗓 ∅
Location	1m E of town off A76

Hotel   ★★ 73% Trigony House Hotel, Closeburn, THORNHILL ☎ 01848 331211 8 ⇄ ☏

WIGTOWN   Map 10 NX45

Wigtown & Bladnoch Lightlands Ter DG8 9EF
☎ 01988 403354
Slightly hilly parkland course with fine views over Wigtown Bay to Galloway Hills.
9 holes, 5462yds, Par 68, SSS 67, Course record 62.
Club membership 150.

Visitors	advisable to contact in advance for weekend play. Course closed to visitors during open competitions.
Societies	contact secretary in advance.
Green Fees	£10 per 9 holes;£15 per 18 holes;£20 per day;£50 per week.
Designer	W Muir
Facilities	⚘
Location	SW on A714

Hotel   ★★ 70% Creebridge House Hotel, NEWTON STEWART ☎ 01671 402121 19 ⇄ ☏

> Entries with a green background identify courses considered to be particularly interesting

DUNDEE CITY

EAST AYRSHIRE

DUNDEE   Map 11 NO43

Caird Park Mains Loan DD4 9BX
☎ 01382 438871 Fax 01382 434601
A pay-as-you-play course situated in extensive parkland in the heart of the Carnoustie countryside. A reasonably easy start belies the difficulty of the middle section (holes 7-13) and the back nine cross the Gelly Burn four times.
18 holes, 6280yds, Par 72, SSS 69, Course record 67.
Club membership 1600.
Visitors   no restrictions.
Societies   must contact in advance 01382 438871.
Green Fees £28 per round day; £17 per round.
Prof   J Black
Facilities   ⓑ ♥ ♀ ♨ 🖬 ⛳ 🧳 ⚑
Location   From Kingsway (A90) take Forfar Road, turn left onto Claverhouse Road, 1st left into Caird Park

Hotel   ★★★ 70% Swallow Hotel, Kingsway West, Invergowrie, DUNDEE
                 ☎ 01382 641122 107 ⇌ ⏴

Camperdown Camperdown Park, Coupar Angus Rd DD2 4TF ☎ 01382 432688
A beautiful course located within the Camperdown Country Park with undulating, tree lined fairways. Testing golf for players of all abilities.
18 holes, 6548yds, Par 71, SSS 72.
Club membership 1600.
Visitors   telephone in advance to be assured of a tee time.
Societies   must contact in advance.
Green Fees £28 per day; £17 per round.
Prof   Roddy Brown
Facilities   ⓧ ⫼ ⓑ ♥ ♀ ♨ 🖬
& Leisure   hard tennis courts.
Location   Kingsway (A90), turn off at Coupar Angus Road (A923) then turn left into Camperdown Park

Hotel   ★★ 70% The Shaftesbury, 1 Hyndford St, DUNDEE ☎ 01382 669216 12 ⇌ ⏴

Downfield Turnberry Av DD2 3QP
☎ 01382 825595 Fax 01382 813111
e-mail: downfieldgc@ukonline.co.uk
A 1999 Open Qualifying venue. A course with championship credentials providing an enjoyable test for all golfers.
18 holes, 6803yds, Par 73, SSS 73, Course record 65.
Club membership 750.
Visitors   must contact in advance, no visitors at weekends.
Societies   must contact in advance.
Green Fees £45 per day; £31 per round.
Cards   ▦ ▦ ▦ ▦ 🖸
Prof   Kenny Hutton
Designer   C K Cotton
Facilities   ⓧ ⫼ ⓑ ♥ ♀ ♨ 🖬 ⛳ 🧳 ☟ ⚑
Location   N of city centre off A923

Hotel   ★★ 70% The Shaftesbury, 1 Hyndford St, DUNDEE ☎ 01382 669216 12 ⇌ ⏴

GALSTON   Map 11 NS53

Loudoun Edinburgh Rd KA4 8PA
☎ 01563 821993 & 820551 Fax 01563 820011
e-mail: secretary@loudgowf.sol.co.uk
Pleasant, fairly flat parkland course with many mature trees.
18 holes, 5773yds, Par 68, SSS 68, Course record 61.
Club membership 750.
Visitors   must contact in advance. Weekdays only, must play with member at weekends/public holidays
Societies   telephone in advance.
Green Fees £30 per day; £20 per round.
Facilities   ⓧ ⫼ ⓑ ♥ ♀ ♨ 🖬 ⚑
Location   NE side of town on A71

Hotel   ★★★ 70% Strathaven Hotel, Hamilton Rd, STRATHAVEN ☎ 01357 521778 22 ⇌ ⏴

KILMARNOCK   Map 10 NS43

Annanhill Irvine Rd KA1 2RT ☎ 01563 521644
Municipal, tree-lined parkland course played over by private clubs.
18 holes, 6269yds, Par 71, SSS 70, Course record 66.
Club membership 394.
Visitors   must book at starters office,01563-521512.
Societies   apply in writing.
Green Fees on application.
Designer   Jack McLean
Facilities   ♨
Location   1m N on A71

Hotel   ★★★ 65% Annfield House Hotel, 6 Castle St, IRVINE ☎ 01294 278903 9 ⇌ ⏴
Additional   ★★★ 75% Montgreenan Mansion House
hotel   Hotel, Montgreenan Estate, KILWINNING
                 ☎ 01294 557733 Fax 01294 850397 21 ⇌ ⏴

Caprington Ayr Rd KA1 4UW
☎ 01563 523702 & 521915 (Gen Enq)
Municipal parkland course.
18 holes, 5810yds, Par 68, SSS 68.
Club membership 400.
Visitors   may not play on Sat.
Societies   must contact in advance.
Green Fees on application.
Facilities   ♨ 🖬 ⚑
Location   1.5m S on B7038

MAUCHLINE   Map 11 NS42

Ballochmyle Catrine Rd KA5 6LE
☎ 01290 550469 Fax 01290 550469
Wooded parkland course.
18 holes, 5972yds, Par 70, SSS 69, Course record 64.
Club membership 730.
Visitors   welcome. May not play Sat.
Societies   apply in writing.
Green Fees £30 per day; £20 per round (£35/£25 Sun).
Cards   ▦ ▦ 🖸
Facilities   ⓧ ⫼ ⓑ ♥ ♀ ♨ 🖬 ⚑
Location   1m SE on B705   ▶

Hotel   ★★★ 60% Quality Hotel Ayr, Burns Statue
             Square, AYR ☎ 01292 263268 74 ⇌ ⬤

NEW CUMNOCK   Map 11 NS61

New Cumnock Lochhill, Cumnock Rd KA18 4PN
☎ 01290 338848
Parkland course.
9 holes, 5176yds, Par 68, SSS 68, Course record 63.
Club membership 280.
Visitors   restricted on Sun competition days. After 4 pm
             only
Societies   apply in writing.
Green Fees   £8 per day/round..
Designer   Willie Fernie
Facilities   ⊗ ⌇ ⮡ ♥ ♀ ⅄ ⬤
& Leisure   fishing.
Location   0.75m N on A76

Hotel   ★★ 67% Blackaddie House Hotel, Blackaddie
             Rd, SANQUHAR ☎ 01659 50270 9 ⇌ ⬤

PATNA   Map 10 NS41

Doon Valley Hillside Park KA6 7JT ☎ 01292 531607
Established parkland course located on an undulating
hillside.
9 holes, 5886yds, Par 70, SSS 69, Course record 56.
Club membership 100.
Visitors   no restrictions mid week, advisable to contact in
             advance for weekends.
Societies   telephone to arrange.
Green Fees   £10 per round; £15 per day.
Facilities   ⅄
& Leisure   fishing.
Location   10m S of Ayr on the A713

Hotel   ★★ Ladyburn, MAYBOLE
             ☎ 01655 740585 8rm(4 ⇌ 3 ⬤)

EAST DUNBARTONSHIRE

BALMORE   Map 11 NS57

Balmore Golf Course Rd G64 4AW
☎ 01360 620284 Fax 01360 620284
Parkland course with fine views.
18 holes, 5530yds, Par 66, SSS 67, Course record 63.
Club membership 700.
Visitors   must contact in advance and be accompanied by
             member, may not play at weekends
Societies   apply in writing.
Green Fees   £35 per day; £25 per round.
Prof   David Pirie
Designer   James Braid
Facilities   ⊗ ⌇ ⮡ ♥ ♀ ⅄ ⬤ ⚐
Location   N off A807

Hotel   ★★★ 64% Patio Hotel, 1 South Av, Clydebank
             Business Park, CLYDEBANK
             ☎ 0141 951 1133 82 ⇌ ⬤

BEARSDEN   Map 11 NS57

Bearsden Thorn Rd G61 4BP ☎ 0141 942 2351
Parkland course, with 16 greens and 11 teeing grounds. Easy
walking and views over city.
9 holes, 6014yds, Par 68, SSS 69, Course record 67.
Club membership 600.
Visitors   must be accompanied by and play with member.
Societies   apply by writing.
Green Fees   £15 per 18 holes.
Facilities   ⊗ ⌇ ⮡ ♥ ♀ ⅄
Location   1m W off A809

Hotel   ★★★ 64% Patio Hotel, 1 South Av, Clydebank
             Business Park, CLYDEBANK
             ☎ 0141 951 1133 82 ⇌ ⬤

Douglas Park Hillfoot G61 2TJ
☎ 0141 942 2220 (Clubhouse) 942 0985 (Secretary) Fax 01
41 942 0985
Parkland course with wide variety of holes.
18 holes, 5962yds, Par 69, SSS 69.
Club membership 900.
Visitors   must be accompanied by member and must
             contact in advance, Wednesdays and Thursdays
             for visiting parties only.
Societies   Wed & Thu. Must telephone in advance.
Green Fees   £30 per day; £22 per round.
Prof   David Scott
Designer   Willie Fernie
Facilities   ⊗ ⌇ by prior arrangement ⮡ ♥ ♀ ⅄ ⬤ ⚐
             ⚐
Location   E side of town on A81

Hotel   ★★★ 64% Patio Hotel, 1 South Av, Clydebank
             Business Park, CLYDEBANK
             ☎ 0141 951 1133 82 ⇌ ⬤

Windyhill Baljaffray Rd G61 4QQ
☎ 0141 942 2349 Fax 0141 942 5874 e-
mail: secretary@windyhill.co.uk
Interesting parkland/moorland course with panoramic views
of Glasgow and beyond; testing 12th hole.
18 holes, 6254yds, Par 71, SSS 70, Course record 64.
Club membership 800.
Visitors   may not play at weekends. Must contact
             professional in advance. Must have a handicap
             certificate.
Societies   must apply in writing.
Green Fees   £30 per day; £20 per round.
Prof   Chris Duffy
Designer   James Braid
Facilities   ⊗ ⌇ ⮡ ♥ ♀ ⅄ ⬤ ⚐ ⚐
Location   2m NW off B8050

Hotel   ★★★ 64% Patio Hotel, 1 South Av, Clydebank
             Business Park, CLYDEBANK
             ☎ 0141 951 1133 82 ⇌ ⬤

BISHOPBRIGGS   Map 11 NS67

Bishopbriggs Brackenbrae Rd G64 2DX
☎ 0141 772 1810 772 8938 Fax 7622532 e-
mail: bgcsecretary@dial.pipex.com
Parkland course with views to Campsie Hills.
18 holes, 6041yds, Par 69, SSS 69, Course record 63.
Club membership 800.

▶

Visitors   Must contact in advance. May not play at
                weekends.
Societies   apply in writing in advance.
Green Fees not confirmed.
Designer   James Braid
Facilities ⊗ ⅏ ⅃ ♥ ♀ ⚎ 🏠
Location   0.5m NW off A803

Hotel   ★★★ 64% Patio Hotel, 1 South Av, Clydebank
                Business Park, CLYDEBANK
                ☎ 0141 951 1133 82 ⇄ 🐾

Cawder Cadder Rd G64 3QD
☎ 0141 772 7101 Fax 0141 772 4463
Two parkland courses; Cawder Course is hilly, with 5th, 9th,
10th, 11th-testing holes. Keir Course is flat.
Cawder Course: 18 holes, 6295yds, Par 70, SSS 71.
Keir Course: 18 holes, 5877yds, Par 68, SSS 68.
Club membership 1150.
Visitors   must contact in advance & may play on
                weekdays only.
Societies   must contact in writing, not on Bank Holidays
Green Fees not confirmed.
Cards   ▩ ▬ ▧ ▨
Prof   Ken Stavely
Designer   James Braid
Facilities ⊗ ⅏ ⅃ ♥ ♀ ⚎ 🏠 ⚐ ✎
Location   1m NE off A803

Hotel   ★★★ 64% Patio Hotel, 1 South Av, Clydebank
                Business Park, CLYDEBANK
                ☎ 0141 951 1133 82 ⇄ 🐾

Littlehill Auchinairn Rd G64 1UT ☎ 0141 772 1916
Municipal parkland course.
18 holes, 6240yds, Par 70, SSS 70.
Visitors   must contact in advance.
Societies   advance bookings required in writing
Green Fees not confirmed.
Facilities ♥ ⚎
Location   3m NE of Glasgow city centre on A803

KIRKINTILLOCH   Map 11 NS67

Hayston Campsie Rd G66 1RN
☎ 0141 776 1244 & 775 0723 (Sec) Fax 0141 7769030
An undulating, tree-lined course with a sandy subsoil.
18 holes, 6042yds, Par 70, SSS 70, Course record 60.
Club membership 800.
Visitors   must apply in advance, may not play weekends.
Societies   Tue & Thu, apply in writing
Green Fees £30 per day; £20 per round
Prof   Steven Barnett
Designer   James Braid
Facilities ⊗ ⅏ ⅃ ♥ ♀ ⚎ 🏠 ✎
Location   1m NW off A803

Hotel   ★★★★ 66% Westerwood Hotel Golf &
                Country Club, 1 St Andrews Dr, Westerwood,
                CUMBERNAULD ☎ 01236 457171 49 ⇄ 🐾

Kirkintilloch Campsie Rd G66 1RN ☎ 0141 776 1256
Parkland course in rural setting.
18 holes, 5860yds, Par 70, SSS 68.
Club membership 650.
Visitors   must be introduced by member.
Societies   apply in writing.
Green Fees on application to secretary.

Designer   James Braid
Facilities ⊗ ⅏ ⅃ ♥ ♀ ⚎ 🏠
Location   1m NW off A803

Hotel   ★★★★ 66% Westerwood Hotel Golf &
                Country Club, 1 St Andrews Dr, Westerwood,
                CUMBERNAULD ☎ 01236 457171 49 ⇄ 🐾

LENNOXTOWN   Map 11 NS67

Campsie Crow Rd G66 7HX ☎ 01360 310244
Scenic hillside course.
18 holes, 5507yds, Par 70, SSS 68, Course record 69.
Club membership 620.
Visitors   preferred weekdays. Weendens only by prior
                arrangment, contact professional 01360 310920.
Societies   wrtten application.
Green Fees not confirmed..
Prof   Mark Brennan
Designer   W Auchterlonie
Facilities ⊗ ⅏ ⅃ ♥ ♀ ⚎ 🏠 ⚐
Location   0.5m N on B822

Hotel   ★★★★ 66% Westerwood Hotel Golf &
                Country Club, 1 St Andrews Dr,
                Westerwood, CUMBERNAULD
                ☎ 01236 457171 49 ⇄ 🐾

LENZIE   Map 11 NS67

Lenzie 19 Crosshill Rd G66 5DA
☎ 0141 776 1535 & 812 3018
Fax 0141 777 7748 or 0141 812 3018
e-mail: scottdavidson@lenziegolfclub.demon.co.uk
Pleasant parkland course.
18 holes, 5984yds, Par 69, SSS 69, Course record 64.
Club membership 890.
Visitors   must contact in advance.
Societies   apply in writing/telephone in advance.
Green Fees £30 per day; £24 per round.
Prof   Jim McCallum
Facilities ⊗ ⅏ ⅃ ♥ ♀ ⚎ 🏠 ⚘ ✎
Location   N of Glasgow, approx 15 mins from Glasgow
                city centre, Kirkintilloch turn off M80

Hotel   ★★★★ 66% Westerwood Hotel Golf &
                Country Club, 1 St Andrews Dr,
                Westerwood, CUMBERNAULD
                ☎ 01236 457171 49 ⇄ 🐾

MILNGAVIE   Map 11 NS57

Clober Craigton Rd G62 7HP ☎ 0141 956 1685
Parkland course. Testing 5th hole, par 3.
18 holes, 4824yds, Par 66, SSS 65, Course record 61.
Club membership 600.
Visitors   may not play after 4pm Mon-Fri. Must play with
                member weekends and bank holidays.
Societies   must contact in advance.
Green Fees £16 per round.
Prof   C Elliott
Facilities ⊗ ⅏ ⅃ ♥ ♀ ⚎ 🏠 ✎
Location   NW side of town

Hotel   ★★★ 64% Patio Hotel, 1 South Av, Clydebank
                Business Park, CLYDEBANK
                ☎ 0141 951 1133 82 ⇄ 🐾

Designer   James Braid
Facilities ⊗ ⅏ ⅃ ♥ ♀ ⚎ 🏠
Location   1m NW off A803

Hotel   ★★★★ 66% Westerwood Hotel Golf &
                Country Club, 1 St Andrews Dr, Westerwood,
                CUMBERNAULD ☎ 01236 457171 49 ⇄ 🐾

Esporta, Dougalston Strathblane G62 8HJ
☎ 0141 955 2404 & 955 2434 Fax 0141 955 2406
A golf course of tremendous character set in 400 acres dotted
with drumlins, lakes and criss-crossed by streams and
ditches. One of the toughest tests of golf in the west of
Scotland.
18 holes, 6225yds, Par 71, SSS 72, Course record 68.
Club membership 800.
Visitors	contact in advance. May not play on Sat, tee times may be booked 3 days in advance.Sun-Fri all subject to availability of tee times.
Societies	weekdays only.
Green Fees	£20 per round (£35 weekends).£25 Sunday.
Cards	⊞ ▬ ▣
Prof	Craig Everett
Designer	Commander Harris
Facilities	⊗ ⅈ ≞ ♨ ♀ ⚐ 🛆 ⌂ ⛾ ✀
& Leisure	heated indoor swimming pool, sauna, solarium, gymnasium.
Location	NE side of town on A81

Hotel   ★★★ 64% Patio Hotel, 1 South Av, Clydebank
        Business Park, CLYDEBANK
        ☎ 0141 951 1133 82 ⇋ ☏

Hilton Park Auldmarroch Estate, Stockiemuir Rd G62 7HB
☎ 0141 956 4657 Fax 0141 956 4657
e-mail: info@hiltonparkgolfclub.fsnet.co.uk
Moorland courses set amidst magnificent scenery.
Hilton Course: 18 holes, 6054yds, Par 70, SSS 70, Course record 65.
Allander Course: 18 holes, 5487yards, Par 69, SSS 67, Course record 65.
Club membership 1200.
Visitors	must contact in advance but may not play at weekends.
Societies	apply in advance to secretary.
Green Fees	on application.
Prof	W McCondichie
Designer	James Braid
Facilities	⊗ ⅈ ≞ ♨ ♀ 🛆 ⌂ ⛾ ➘ ✀
Location	3m NW of Milngavie, on A809

Hotel   ★★★ 64% Patio Hotel, 1 South Av, Clydebank
        Business Park, CLYDEBANK
        ☎ 0141 951 1133 82 ⇋ ☏

Milngavie Laighpark G62 8EP
☎ 0141 956 1619 Fax 0141 956 4252
Very scenic moorland course, which plays its full length,
challenging SSS, testing 1st hole followed by many others.
18 holes, 5818yds, Par 68, SSS 68, Course record 59.
Club membership 700.
Visitors	must contact in advance, may not play weekends.
Societies	apply in writing.
Green Fees	not confirmed.
Designer	The Auchterlonie Brothers
Facilities	⊗ ⅈ ≞ ♨ ♀ 🛆
Location	1.25m N

Hotel   ★★★ 64% Patio Hotel, 1 South Av, Clydebank
        Business Park, CLYDEBANK
        ☎ 0141 951 1133 82 ⇋ ☏

EAST LOTHIAN

ABERLADY   Map 12 NT47

Kilspindie EH32 0QD
☎ 01875 870358 Fax 01875 870358
Traditional Scottish seaside course, short but tight and well-
bunkered. Situated on the shores of the river Forth. Testing
holes: 2nd, 3rd, 4th and 7th. A new 6200 yard par 71 links
course opens in mid 2000.
Kilspindie: 18 holes, 5480yds, Par 69, SSS 66, Course record 59.
Club membership 750.
Visitors	must contact in advance, prefered days for visitors Mon-Fri,but some tee times available at weekends.
Societies	contact secretary in advance.
Green Fees	£40 per day; £25 per round (£50/£30 weekends).
Prof	Graham J Sked
Designer	Various
Facilities	⊗ ⅈ ≞ ♨ ♀ 🛆 ⌂ ⛾ ✀
Location	N side of village off A198, private road access located at Eastern end of village of Aberlady

Hotel   ★★★🏮 Greywalls Hotel, Muirfield,
        GULLANE ☎ 01620 842144
        17 ⇋ ☏ Annexe5 ⇋ ☏

Luffness New EH32 0QA
☎ 01620 843114 & 843336 Fax 01620 842933
Links course, National Final Qualifying Course for Open
Championship.
18 holes, 6122yds, Par 69, SSS 70, Course record 62.
Club membership 700.
Visitors	must contact in advance but may not play at weekends & bank holidays.
Societies	telephone for application form.
Green Fees	not confirmed.
Designer	Tom Morris
Facilities	⊗ ⅈ ≞ ♨ ♀ 🛆 ⌂ ✀
Location	1m E on A198

Hotel   ★★★🏮 Greywalls Hotel, Muirfield,
        GULLANE ☎ 01620 842144
        17 ⇋ ☏ Annexe5 ⇋ ☏

BROXBURN   Map 11 NT07

Niddry Castle Castle Rd, Winchburgh EH52 6RQ
☎ 01506 891097
A 9-hole parkland course. While not very long, it requires
accurate golf to score well.
9 holes, 5615yds, Par 70, SSS 67, Course record 64.
Club membership 600.
Visitors	advisable to contact at weekends, restricted during competition time.
Societies	must contact in advance.
Green Fees	£12 per 9 holes;£23 per 18 holes.
Facilities	ⅈ ≞ ♨ ♀ 🛆
Location	9m W of Edinburgh on B9080

Hotel   ★★★ 61% Forth Bridges Hotel, 1 Ferrymuir
        Gait, SOUTH QUEENSFERRY
        ☎ 0131 469 9955 108 ⇋ ☏

DUNBAR   Map 12 NT67

Dunbar East Links EH42 1LL
☎ 01368 862317 Fax 01368 865202
Another of Scotland's old links. It is said that it was some Dunbar members who first took the game of golf to the North of England. A natural links course on a narrow strip of land, following the contours of the sea shore, there is a wall bordering one side and the shore on the other side making this quite a challenging course for all levels of player. The wind, if blowing from the sea, is a problem.
18 holes, 6406yds, Par 71, SSS 71, Course record 64.
Club membership 1000.
Visitors   may not play Thu, between 12.30-2 weekdays, 12-2 weekends or before 9.30am any day.
Societies   telephone in advance.
Green Fees £40 per day; £30 per round (£45/£35 weekends).
Cards   〓 〓 〓 〓 〓 〓
Prof   Jacky Montgomery
Designer   Tom Morris
Facilities   ⊗ ⅷ ⅂ ☕ ♀ △ 🏠 ⚲ ♂
Location   0.5m E off A1087

Hotel   ★★ 67% Bayswell Hotel, Bayswell Park, DUNBAR ☎ 01368 862225   18 ⇄ ✿

Winterfield North Rd EH42 1AU
☎ 01368 863562 Fax 01368 863562
Seaside course with superb views.
18 holes, 5155yds, Par 65, SSS 64, Course record 61.
Club membership 350.
Visitors   contact in advance.weekends from 10am-12 noon & 2pm-4pm
Societies   must arrange in advance through professional
Green Fees £20 per day; £14.50 per round (£25/£16.50 weekends).
Prof   Kevin Phillips
Facilities   ⊗ ⅷ ⅂ ☕ ♀ △ 🏠 ⚲ ♂
Location   W side of town off A1087

Hotel   ★★ 67% Bayswell Hotel, Bayswell Park, DUNBAR ☎ 01368 862225   18 ⇄ ✿

GIFFORD   Map 12 NT56

Gifford Edinburgh Rd EH41 4JE ☎ 01620 810267
Parkland course, with easy walking.
9 holes, 6243yds, Par 71, SSS 70, Course record 69.
Club membership 600.

Visitors   may not play on the 1st Sun of the month during Apr-Oct. Telephone Starter on 01620 810 591 to book tee times.
Societies   telephone in advance.
Green Fees £13 per 18 holes; £10 per 9 holes.
Designer   W Wood
Facilities   ♀ △ ♂
Location   1m SW off B6355

Inn   ♦♦♦ Goblin Ha', GIFFORD
☎ 01620 810244 7rm(6 ⇄ ✿)

GULLANE   Map 12 NT48

Gullane West Links Rd EH31 2BB
☎ 01620 842255 Fax 01620 842327
e-mail: bookings@gullonegolfclub.com
Gullane is a delightful village and one of Scotland's great golf centres. Gullane club was formed in 1882. There are three Gullane courses and the No 1 is of championship standard. It differs from most Scottish courses in as much as it is of the upland links type and really quite hilly. The first tee is literally in the village. The views from the top of the course are magnificent and stretch far and wide in every direction - in fact, it is said that 14 counties can be seen from the highest spot.
Course No 1: 18 holes, 6466yds, Par 71, SSS 72, Course record 66.
Course No 2: 18 holes, 6244yds, Par 71, SSS 70.
Course No 3: 18 holes, 5252yds, Par 68, SSS 66.
Club membership 1200.
Visitors   advance booking recommended.
Societies   advance booking advised.
Green Fees Course no 1: £90 per day; £60 per round (£75 per round weekends). Course no 2: £40 per day; £28 per round (£50/£33 weekends). Course no 3 £25 per day; £16 per round (£33/£22 weekends).
Cards   〓 〓 〓 〓 〓
Prof   Jimmy Hume
Designer   Various
Facilities   ⊗ ⅷ ⅂ ☕ ♀ △ 🏠 ⚲ 🏌 ⚑ ♂ ↾
Location   At west end of village on A198

Hotel   ★★★♨♨ Greywalls Hotel, Muirfield, GULLANE ☎ 01620 842144 17 ⇄ ✿ Annexe5 ⇄ ✿

GULLANE   Map 12 NT48

GULLANE See page 353

HADDINGTON   Map 12 NT57

Haddington Amisfield Park EH41 4PT
☎ 01620 Fax 01620 822727 e-mail: hadd.golg1@tesco.net
Silghtly undulating parkland course, within the grounds of a former country estate.
18 holes, 6317yds, Par 71, SSS 70, Course record 68.
Club membership 650.
Visitors   may not play between 7am-10am & noon-2pm at weekends. Must contact in advance.
Societies   must contact in advance; deposits required.
Green Fees £28 per day; £20 per round (£34/£25 weekends).
Prof   John Sandilands   ▶

Facilities ⊗ ⅷ ⅃ ⅃ ♥ ♀ ⚘ ⅃ ⚐ ⅃ ♥ ⚓ ♂
Location E side off A613 off A1,17 miles E of Edinburgh

Hotel ★★★↟↟ Greywalls Hotel, Muirfield,
GULLANE ☏ 01620 842144
17 ⇆ ♞ Annexe5 ⇆ ♞

LONGNIDDRY   Map 12 NT47

Longniddry Links Rd EH32 0NL
☏ 01875 852141 & 01875 852228 Fax 01875 853371
Undulating seaside links and partial parkland course.
One of the numerous courses which stretch east from
Edinburgh right to Dunbar. The inward half is more open
than the wooded outward half, but can be difficult in
prevailing west wind. No par 5s.
18 holes, 6260yds, Par 68, SSS 70, Course record 63.
Club membership 1140.
Visitors may book tee times up to 7 days in advance,
but deposit required.may not play on
competition days.
Societies Mon-Thu, apply in writing, handicap
certificate required.
Green Fees £45 per day; £32 per round (£40 per round
weekends).
Cards ▦▦ ▦▦
Prof John Gray
Designer H S Colt
Facilities ⊗ ⅷ ⅃ ♥ ♀ ⚘ ⅃ ⚐ ⅃ ♥ ⚓ ♂
Location N side of village off A198

Hotel ★★★↟↟ Greywalls Hotel, Muirfield,
GULLANE ☏ 01620 842144
17 ⇆ ♞ Annexe5 ⇆ ♞

MUSSELBURGH   Map 11 NT37

Musselburgh Monktonhall EH21 6SA ☏ 0131 665 2005
Testing parkland course with natural hazards including trees
and a burn, easy walking.
18 holes, 6725yds, Par 71, SSS 73, Course record 65.
Club membership 1000.
Visitors must contact in advance.
Societies must contact in advance.
Green Fees £30 per day; £20 per round (£35/£25 weekends).
Prof Fraser Mann
Designer James Braid
Facilities ⊗ ⅷ ⅃ ♥ ♀ ⚘ ⅃ ⚐ ⅃ ♥ ⚓ ♂
Location 1m S on B6415

Guesthouse ♦♦♦♦ Arden House, 26 Linkfield Rd,
Musselburgh, EDINBURGH
☏ 0131 665 0663 & 07957 867512
Fax 0131 665 0663 4 ⇆ ♞

Musselburgh Links, The Old Golf Course
The Starter's Hut, Balcarres Rd EH21 7SB
☏ 0131 665 5438 (Starter) 665 4861(secretary)
Fax 0131 665 5438 e-mail: info@musselburgholdlinks.co.uk
This course is steeped in the history and tradition of golf.
Mary Queen of Scots reputedly played this 9 hole links
course in 1567, but documentary evidence dates back to
1672.
9 holes, 2808yds, Par 34, SSS 34.
Visitors must book in advance
Societies must contact in advance.

Green Fees £8 per 9 holes.
Facilities ♥ ⚘ ♂
Location 1m E of town off A1

Guesthouse ♦♦♦♦ Arden House, 26 Linkfield Rd,
Musselburgh, EDINBURGH
☏ 0131 665 0663 & 07957 867512
Fax 0131 665 0663 4 ⇆ ♞

NORTH BERWICK   Map 12 NT58

Glen East Links, Tantallon Ter EH39 4LE
☏ 01620 892726 Fax 01620 895447 e-
mail: secretary@glen.gowf.net
An interesting course with a good variety of holes. The views
of the town, the Firth of Forth and the Bass Rock are
breathtaking.
18 holes, 6043yds, Par 69, SSS 69, Course record 64.
Club membership 650.
Visitors booking advisable.
Societies advance booking recommended.
Green Fees not confirmed.
Designer Ben Sayers/James Braid
Facilities ⊗ ⅷ ⅃ ♥ ♀ ⚘ ⅃ ⚐ ♂
Location 1m E of B198

Hotel ★★ 64% Nether Abbey Hotel, 20 Dirleton Av,
NORTH BERWICK
☏ 01620 892802 14 ⇆ ♞

North Berwick Beach Rd EH39 4BB
☏ 01620 892135 Fax 01620 893274
e-mail: northberwickgc@aol.com
Another of East Lothian's famous courses, the links at
North Berwick is still popular. A classic championship
links, it has many hazards including the beach, streams,
bunkers, light rough and low walls. The great hole on the
course is the 15th, the famous 'Redan'. Used by both the
Tantallon and Bass Rock Golf Clubs.
*West Links: 18 holes, 6420yds, Par 71, SSS 71, Course
record 64.*
Club membership 730.
Visitors must contact in advance 01620 892135
(beyond 7 days) or 01620 892666 (within 7
days).
Societies must contact in advance.
Green Fees £60 per day; £40 per round (£80/£60
weekends).
Cards ▦▦ ▦▦ ▦▦ ▦▦ ▦
Prof D Huish
Facilities ⊗ ⅷ ⅃ ♥ ♀ ⚘ ⅃ ⚐ ♂
Location W side of town on A198

Hotel ★★★ 65% The Marine, Cromwell Rd,
NORTH BERWICK
☏ 0870 400 8129 83 ⇆ ♞

Whitekirk Whitekirk EH39 5PR
☏ 01620 870300 Fax 01620 870330
e-mail: golf@whitekirk.u-net.com
Scenic coastal course with lush green fairways, gorse
covered rocky banks and stunning views. Natural water
hazards and strong sea breezes make this well designed
course a good test of golf.
18 holes, 6526yds, Par 72, SSS 72, Course record 64.
Club membership 400.   ▶

(Honourable Company of Edinburgh Golfers) *Muirfield*

Gullane, *East Lothian*   ☎ 01620 842123   Fax 01620 842977   Map 12 NT48

The course at Muirfield was designed by Old Tom Morris in 1891 and is generally considered to be one of the top ten courses in the world. The club itself has an excellent pedigree, it was founded in 1744, making it just ten years older than the Royal & Ancient but not as old as Royal Blackheath.

Muirfield has staged some outstanding Open Championships, perhaps one of the most memorable was in 1972 when Lee Trevino the defending champion seemed to be losing his grip, until a spectacular shot brought him back to beat Tony Jacklin, who subsequently never won an Open again.

Visitors Tue & Thu only. Must contact in advance and have a handicap certificate, 18 gentlemen, 24 ladies.

Societies Tue & Thu with handicap limits (18 gentlemen, 24 ladies). Must be mmbers of recognised golf course. Up to 12 in a group

Green Fees £110 per day, £85 per round

Facilities ⊗ ▆ ♀ ♨ ⚐ ♂

Location Muirfield, Gullane EH31 2EG (NE side of village)

Holes/Par/Course record 18 holes, 6801 yds, Par 70, SSS 73, Course record 63

Championship Course

WHERE TO STAY AND EAT NEARBY

Hotels

DIRLETON

★★★@ 71% The Open Arms.
☎ 01620 850241. 10 (7 ⇌ 1 ⇌ 3 ♜)

GULLANE

★★★@@ ♨♨ Greywalls, Muirfield.
☎ 01620 842144. 17 (16 ⇌ ♜ 1 ⇌)
Annexe 5 (4 ⇌ ♜ 1 ⇌)

NORTH BERWICK

★★★ 65% The Marine, Cromwell Rd.
☎ 0870 400 8129. 83 ⇌ ♜

★★ 64% Nether Abbey, 20 Dirleton Ave.
☎ 01620 892802. 14 (10 ⇌ ♜ 4 ♜)

Visitors   no restrictions.
Societies   apply in writing or telephone.
Green Fees   £30 per day, £20 per round (£40/£25 weekends).
Cards   ▭▭ ▭▭ ▭▭ ▶◀ ▱
Prof   Paul Wardell
Designer   Cameron Sinclair
Facilities   ⊗ ⫘ ⅃ ☂ ♀ ⚲ ⸗ ✄ ♏ ☄ ✓ ⌀
Location   3m off the main A1 Edinburgh/Berwick-upon-
                 Tweed road A198 North Berwick

Hotel   ★★ 64% Nether Abbey Hotel, 20 Dirleton Av,
                 NORTH BERWICK
                 ☎ 01620 892802   14 ⇋ ⋔

PRESTONPANS   Map 11 NT37

Royal Musselburgh Prestongrange House EH32 9RP
☎ 01875 810276 Fax 01875 810276
e-mail: royalmusselburgh@btinternet.com
Tree-lined parkland course overlooking Firth of Forth. Well
maintained and providing an excellent challenge.
18 holes, 6237yds, Par 70, SSS 70, Course record 64.
Club membership 1000.
Visitors   must contact professional in advance, restricted
                 Fri afternoons & weekends.
Societies   should contact in advance through Management
                 secretary
Green Fees   £35 per 36 holes:£22 per 18 holes(£35 per 18
                 holes weekends).
Prof   John Henderson
Designer   James Braid
Facilities   ⊗ ⫘ ⅃ ☂ ♀ ⚲ ✉ ⸗ ☄ ⌀
Location   W side of town centre on B1361 Prestonpans to
                 North Berwick rd

Guesthouse ◆◆◆◆ Arden House, 26 Linkfield Rd,
               Musselburgh, EDINBURGH
               ☎ 0131 665 0663 & 07957 867512
               Fax 0131 665 0663 4 ⇋ ⋔

EAST RENFREWSHIRE

BARRHEAD   Map 11 NS45

Fereneze Fereneze Av G78 1HJ
☎ 0141 881 1519 Fax 0141 887 1103
Hilly moorland course, with a good view at the end of a hard
climb to the 3rd, then levels out.
18 holes, 5821yds, Par 70, SSS 68, Course record 66.
Club membership 700.
Visitors   must contact in advance but may not play at
                 weekends.
Societies   apply in writing.
Green Fees   not confirmed.
Prof   Stuart Kerr
Facilities   ⊗ ⫘ ⅃ ☂ ♀ ⚲ ✉ ⸗
Location   NW side of town off B774

Hotel   ★★★ 71% Dalmeny Park Country House
                 Hotel, Lochlibo Rd, BARRHEAD
                 ☎ 0141 881 9211 20 ⇋ ⋔

CLARKSTON   Map 11 NS55

Cathcart Castle Mearns Rd G76 7YL
☎ 0141 638 9449 Fax 0141 638 1201
Tree-lined parkland course, with undulating terrain.
18 holes, 5832yds, Par 68, SSS 68.
Club membership 995.
Visitors   by prior arrangement with professional, must
                 have a handicap certificate from own club.
Societies   Tue & Thu only; must apply in writing.
Green Fees   not confirmed.
Prof   Stephen Duncan
Facilities   ⊗ ⫘ ⅃ ☂ ♀ ⚲ ✉ ♏ ⌀
Location   0.75m SW off A726

EAGLESHAM   Map 11 NS55

Bonnyton Kirktonmoor Rd G76 0QA
☎ 01355 302781 Fax 01355 303151
Dramatic moorland course offering spectacular views
beautiful countryside as far as snow-capped Ben Lomond.
Tree-lined fairways, plateau greens, natural burns and well
situated bunkers and a unique variety of holes offer golfers
both challenge and reward.
18 holes, 6255yds, Par 72, SSS 71.
Club membership 960.
Visitors   welcome Mon & Thu. Must contact in advance.
Societies   must telephone in advance.
Green Fees   £38 per day.
Prof   Kendal McWade
Facilities   ⊗ ⫘ ⅃ ☂ ♀ ⚲ ✉ ⸗ ☄ ⌀
Location   0.25m SW off B764

Hotel   ★★★ 70% Bruce Hotel, Cornwall St, EAST
                 KILBRIDE ☎ 01355 229771 65 ⇋ ⋔

NEWTON MEARNS   Map 11 NS55

East Renfrewshire Pilmuir G77 6RT
☎ 01355 500256 Fax 01355 500323
Undulating moorland with loch; prevailing SW wind.
18 holes, 6097yds, Par 70, SSS 70, Course record 63.
Club membership 900.
Visitors   must contact professional in advance
Societies   Tues & Thur only, must contact in advance.
Green Fees   £40 per day; £30 per round.
Prof   Stewart Russell
Designer   James Braid
Facilities   ⊗ ⫘ ⅃ ☂ ♀ ⚲ ✉ ⌀
Location   3m SW off Newton Mearns on A77

Hotel   ★★★ 71% Dalmeny Park Country House
                 Hotel, Lochlibo Rd, BARRHEAD
                 ☎ 0141 881 9211 20 ⇋ ⋔

Eastwood Muirshield, Loganswell G77 6RX
☎ 01355 500285
An undulating moorland course situated in a scenic setting.
18 holes, 5864yds, Par 68, SSS 69, Course record 62.
Club membership 900.
Visitors   contact in advance. No visitors at weekends.
Societies   must contact in advance.
Green Fees   £30 per day; £24 per round.
Prof   Allan McGinness
Designer   Theodore Moone
Facilities   ⊗ ⫘ ⅃ ☂ ♀ ⚲ ✉ ⌀
Location   2.5m S of Newton Mearns, on A77   ▶

Hotel   ★★★ 71% Dalmeny Park Country House Hotel, Lochlibo Rd, BARRHEAD
☎ 0141 881 9211 20 ⇆ 🏿

Whitecraigs 72 Ayr Rd G46 6SW
☎ 0141 639 4530 & 0141 639 2140 pro
Fax 0141 639 4530 e-mail: wcraigsgc@aol.com
Beautiful parkland course only twenty minutes from the centre of Glasgow.
18 holes, 6230yds, Par 70, SSS 70, Course record 63.
Club membership 1078.
Visitors   must contact professional in advance and have a handicap certificate.
Societies   apply in advance.
Green Fees £50 per day inc tea/coffee, high tea & sandwiches; £37 per round inc tea/coffee & high tea.
Prof   Alistair Forrow
Facilities   ⊗ ⫼ ⮱ ☕ ♀ ♨ 🏠 ⛾ ⛿
Location   1.5m NE on A77

Hotel   ★★★ 71% Dalmeny Park Country House Hotel, Lochlibo Rd, BARRHEAD
☎ 0141 881 9211 20 ⇆ 🏿

UPLAWMOOR   Map 10 NS45

Caldwell G78 4AU
☎ 01505 850366 (Secretary) & 850616 (Pro)
Fax 01505 850604
Parkland course.
18 holes, 6294yds, Par 71, SSS 70, Course record 63.
Club membership 600.
Visitors   must be with member at weekends & bank holidays. Must contact professional in advance.
Societies   writing to Secretary.
Green Fees £40 per day; £30 per round.
Prof   Stephen Forbes
Designer   W. Fernie
Facilities   ⊗ ⫼ ⮱ ☕ ♀ ♨ 🏠 ⛿
Location   0.5m SW A736

Hotel   ★★★ 71% Dalmeny Park Country House Hotel, Lochlibo Rd, BARRHEAD
☎ 0141 881 9211 20 ⇆ 🏿

FALKIRK

FALKIRK   Map 11 NS88

Falkirk Carmuirs, 136 Stirling Rd, Camelon FK2 7YP
☎ 01324 611061 (club) Fax 01324 639573 (Sec)
e-mail: carmuirs.fgc@virgin.net
Parkland course with trees, gorse and streams.
18 holes, 6230yds, Par 71, SSS 70, Course record 66.
Club membership 800.
Visitors   telephone starter 01324 612219, visiting parties may not play Sat.
Societies   telephone 01324 612219 in advance.
Green Fees £25 per day; £15 per round (£35 per day Sun).
Cards   🔲 🔲 🔲 🔲
Designer   James Braid

Facilities   ⊗ ⫼ ⮱ ☕ ♀ ♨ 🏠 ⛿
Location   1.5m W on A9

Hotel   ★★★★ 70% Inchyra Grange Hotel, Grange Rd, POLMONT ☎ 01324 711911 109 ⇆ 🏿

LARBERT   Map 11 NS88

Falkirk Tryst 86 Burnhead Rd FK5 4BD
☎ 01324 562054 & 562415
Links-type course, fairly level with trees and broom, well-bunkered. Winds can affect play.
18 holes, 6053yds, Par 70, SSS 69, Course record 62.
Club membership 850.
Visitors   must contact in advance no play at weekends.
Societies   visitors welcome Mon-Fri must book or telephone.
Green Fees £27 per day; £18 per round.
Prof   Steven Dunsmore
Facilities   ⊗ ⮱ ☕ ♀ ♨ 🏠 ⛾ ⛿
Location   On A88 between A9 and A905

Hotel   ★★★★ 70% Inchyra Grange Hotel, Grange Rd, POLMONT ☎ 01324 711911 109 ⇆ 🏿

Glenbervie Clubhouse Stirling Rd FK5 4SJ
☎ 01324 562605 Fax 01324 551054
Parkland course with good views.
Glenbervie: 18 holes, 6423yds, Par 71, SSS 71, Course record 64.
Club membership 600.
Visitors   Mon to Fri till 4pm, parties Tues & Thurs only
Societies   Tue & Thu only. Apply in writing.
Green Fees £30 per round;£40 per day.
Cards   🔲 🔲
Prof   John Chillas
Designer   James Braid
Facilities   ⊗ ⮱ ☕ ♀ ♨ 🏠 ⛿
Location   2m NW on A9

Hotel   ★★★★ 70% Inchyra Grange Hotel, Grange Rd, POLMONT ☎ 01324 711911 109 ⇆ 🏿

POLMONT   Map 11 NS97

Grangemouth Polmont Hill FK2 0YE
☎ 01324 503840 Fax 01324 503841
Windy parkland course. Testing holes: 3rd, 4th (par 4's); 5th (par 5); 7th (par 3) 216 yds over reservoir (elevated green); 8th, 9th, 18th (par 4's).
18 holes, 6314yds, Par 71, SSS 71, Course record 65.
Club membership 700.
Visitors   must contact 24 hours in advance.Must have own golf shoes and clubs.
Societies   must contact in writing.
Green Fees £14 (£17.50 weekends & bank holidays).
Prof   Greg McFarlane
Facilities   ⊗ ⫼ ⮱ ☕ ♀ ♨ 🏠 ⛿
Location   On unclass rd 0.5m N of M9 junc 4

Hotel   ★★★★ 70% Inchyra Grange Hotel, Grange Rd, POLMONT ☎ 01324 711911 109 ⇆ 🏿

AA Hotels that have special arrangements with golf courses are listed at the back of the guide

Polmont Manuelrigg, Maddiston FK2 0LS
☎ 01324 711277 Fax 01324 712504
Parkland course, hilly with few bunkers. Views of the River
Forth and Ochil Hills.
9 holes, 3073yds, Par 72, SSS 69, Course record 66.
Club membership 300.
Visitors   no visitors on Sat from Apr-Sep, Mon-Fri must
            tee of before 5pm.
Societies   apply in writing to club secretary.
Green Fees £8 per round (£15Sun).
Facilities ⊗ ⍊ ⅃ ▆ ♀ ⚒
Location   A805 from Falkirk, 1st right after fire brigade
            headquarters

Hotel   ★★★★ 70% Inchyra Grange Hotel, Grange
            Rd, POLMONT ☎ 01324 711911 109 ⇄ ↾

FIFE

ABERDOUR   Map 11 NT18

Aberdour Seaside Place KY3 0TX
☎ 01383 860080 Fax 01383 860050
e-mail: aberdourgc@aol.com
Parkland course with lovely views over Firth of Forth.
18 holes, 5460yds, Par 67, SSS 66, Course record 63.
Club membership 800.
Visitors   must contact in advance, may not play
            Saturdays.
Societies   telephone or write to secretary in advance
Green Fees £28 per day; £17 per round (£35 per round
            Sundays).
Prof   Gordon McCallum
Facilities ⊗ ⍊ ⅃ ▆ ♀ ⚒ ⌂ ↾ ➤ ✓
Location   S side of village

Hotel   ★★ 68% Woodside Hotel, High St,
            ABERDOUR ☎ 01383 860328 20 ⇄ ↾

ANSTRUTHER   Map 12 NO50

Anstruther Marsfield, Shore Rd KY10 3DZ
☎ 01333 310956 Fax 01333 312283
Seaside links course with some excellent par 3 holes; always
in good condition.
9 holes, 2266mtrs, Par 62, SSS 63, Course record 59.
Club membership 550.
Visitors   advised to phone in advance.
Societies   welcome except Jun-Aug. Must apply in
            writing.
Green Fees £12 per 18 holes; £8 per 9 holes (£16/£10
            weekends).
Designer   Tom Morris
Facilities ⅃ ▆ ♀ ⚒ ✓
Location   SW off A917

Hotel   ★★ 64% Smugglers Inn, High St East,
            ANSTRUTHER ☎ 01333 310506 9 ⇄ ↾

BURNTISLAND   Map 11 NT28

Burntisland Golf House Club Dodhead, Kirkcaldy Rd
KY3 9LQ ☎ 01592 874093 (Manager) & 872116 (Pro)
Fax 01592 874093 e-mail: wktbghc@aol.com

A lush, testing course offering magnificent views over the
Forth Estuary.
18 holes, 5965yds, Par 70, SSS 70, Course record 62.
Club membership 800.
Visitors   weekend play may be restricted. Book by
            telephoning professional or manager.
Societies   apply in writing to manager.
Green Fees £25 per day; £17 per round (£37/£25 weekends).
Cards   ▨▨ ▨▨ ▨▨ ▨ ▨
Prof   Paul Wytrazek
Designer   Willie Park Jnr
Facilities ⊗ ⍊ ⅃ ▆ ♀ ⚒ ⌂ ↾ ➤ ➤ ✓ ↾
Location   1m E on B923

Hotel   ★★ 67% Inchview Hotel, 69 Kinghorn Rd,
            BURNTISLAND ☎ 01592 872239 12 ⇄ ↾

CARDENDEN   Map 11 NT29

Auchterderran Woodend Rd KY5 0NH ☎ 01592 721579
9 holes, 5250yds, Par 66, SSS 66, Course record 63.
Location   N end Cardendon, Kirkcaldy/Glenrothes road
Telephone for further details

Hotel   ★★★ 67% Dean Park Hotel, Chapel Level,
            KIRKCALDY ☎ 01592 261635
            34 ⇄ ↾ Annexe12 ⇄ ↾

COWDENBEATH   Map 11 NT19

Cowdenbeath Seco Place KY4 8PD ☎ 01383 511918
A parkland-based 9-hole golf course.
*Dora Course: 18 holes, 6201yds, Par 70, SSS 70, Course
record 68.*
Club membership 250.
Visitors   no restrictions.
Societies   Apply in advance by phone or write to secretary.
Green Fees £11.50 per round;£15.50 per 36 holes
            (£15.50/£22 weekends).
Facilities ⊗ ⅃ ▆ ♀ ⚒ ✓
Location   Turn off A92 into Cowdenbeath. Take 2nd right
            and follow signs to course.

Hotel   ★★ 68% Woodside Hotel, High St,
            ABERDOUR ☎ 01383 860328 20 ⇄ ↾

CRAIL   Map 12 NO60

Crail Golfing Society Balcomie Clubhouse,
Fifeness KY10 3XN
☎ 01333 450686 & 450960 Fax 01333 450416
e-mail: crailgolfs@aol.com

Perched on the edge of the North Sea on the very point
of the golfing county of Fife, the Crail Golfing Society's
course at Balcomie is picturesque and sporting. And here
again golf history has been made for Crail Golfing
Society began its life in 1786. The course is highly
thought of by students of the game both for its testing
holes and the standard of its greens. Craighead Links has
panoramic seascape and country views. With wide
sweeping fairways and large greens it is a testing but fair
challenge, be warned there are hungry bunkers a plenty!
This second links at Fifeness is set to join Balcomie as
one of Scotlands's 'must play' courses.
Balcomie Links: 18 holes, 5922yds, Par 69, SSS 69,
Course record 64.
Craighead Links: 18 holes, 6700yds, Par 71, SSS 73,
Course record 69.
Club membership 1735.
Visitors   must contact in advance, restricted 10am-
              noon & 2-4.30pm.
Societies   must contact in advance, as much notice as
              possible for weekend play.
Green Fees £38per day; £25 per round (£48/£30
              weekends).
Cards   ▭ ▭ ▭ ▭ ▭ ▭
Prof   Graeme Lennie
Designer   Tom Morris
Facilities ⓧ ⅷ ᗺ ᗭ ♀ ᗢ 📇 ᛎ ᖚ ᙏ ᗉ
Location   2m NE off A917

Hotel   ★★ 64% Balcomie Links Hotel, Balcomie
              Rd, CRAIL ☎ 01333 450237
              15rm(13 ⇆ ᛊ)

Additional ♦♦♦♦ The Spindrift, Pittenweem Rd,
Guesthouse ANSTRUTHER ☎ 01333 310573
              Fax 01333 310573 8 ⇆ ᛊ

CUPAR   Map 11 NO31

Cupar Hilltarvit KY15 5JT ☎ 01334 653549
e-mail: secretary@cupargolfclub.freeserve.co.uk
Hilly parkland course with fine views over north east Fife.
5th/14th hole is most difficult - uphill and into the prevailing
wind.
9 holes, 5074yds, Par 68, SSS 65, Course record 61.
Club membership 400.
Visitors   welcome except Sat.
Societies   must contact in advance.
Green Fees £15 per day.
Designer   Allan Robertson
Facilities ⓧ ⅷ ᗺ ᗭ ♀ ᗢ ᛎ ᖚ ᗉ
Location   0.75m S off A92

Hotel   ★★ 69% Eden House Hotel, 2 Pitscottie Rd,
              CUPAR ☎ 01334 652510
              9 ⇆ ᛊ Annexe2 ⇆ ᛊ

DUNFERMLINE   Map 11 NT08

Canmore Venturefair Av KY12 0PE
☎ 01383 724969 728416
Parkland course with excellent turf, ideal for 36 hole play,
suitable all ages - a good test of golf.
18 holes, 5376yds, Par 67, SSS 66, Course record 61.
Club membership 710.
Visitors   Sat not usually available. Limited Sun. Must
              contact Professional in advance.
Societies   apply in writing to secretary.
Green Fees £20 per day: £15 per round (£30/£20 weekends).
Prof   Jim McKinnon
Designer   Ben Sayers & others
Facilities ⓧ ⅷ ᗺ ᗭ ♀ ᗢ 📇 ᗉ
Location   1m N on A823

Hotel   ★★★ 65% King Malcolm, Queensferry Rd,
              DUNFERMLINE
              ☎ 01383 722611 48 ⇆ ᛊ

Dunfermline Pitfirrane, Crossford KY12 8QW
☎ 01383 723534 & 729061 e-mail: pitfirrane@aol.com
Gently undulating parkland course with interesting contours.
Five Par 5's, Five Par 3's. No water hazards.
18 holes, 6121yds, Par 72, SSS 70, Course record 65.
Club membership 950.
Visitors   may not play weekends. Contact to check times.
Societies   must contact in advance.
Green Fees £31 per day; £21 per round.
Prof   Steve Craig
Designer   J R Stutt
Facilities ⓧ ⅷ ᗺ ᗭ ♀ ᗢ 📇 ᗉ
Location   2m W of Dunfermline on A994

Hotel   ★★★ 65% King Malcolm, Queensferry Rd,
              DUNFERMLINE
              ☎ 01383 722611 48 ⇆ ᛊ

Pitreavie Queensferry Rd KY11 8PR
☎ 01383 722591 Fax 01383 722591
Picturesque woodland course with panoramic view of the
River Forth Valley. Testing golf.
18 holes, 6086yds, Par 70, SSS 69, Course record 64.
Club membership 700.
Visitors   welcome except for competition days.
Societies   must write or telephone in advance.
Green Fees £26.50 per day:£19.50 per round(£38.50/£24.50
weekends).
Prof   Paul Brookes
Designer   Dr Alaistair McKenzie
Facilities   ⊗)Ⅲ ﹏ ♥ ♀ ⚏ 🖅 📻 ✄
Location   SE side of town on A823

Hotel   ★★★ 65% King Malcolm, Queensferry Rd,
DUNFERMLINE ☎ 01383 722611 48 ⇄ ℟

ELIE   Map 12 NO40

Golf House Club KY9 1AS
☎ 01333 330301 Fax 01333 330895
One of Scotland's most delightful holiday courses with
panoramic views over the Firth of Forth. Some of the
holes out towards the rocky coastline are splendid. This
is the course which has produced many good
professionals, including the immortal James Braid.
18 holes, 6273yds, Par 70, SSS 70, Course record 62.
Club membership 600.
Visitors   advisable to contact in advance, limited
availability Sat May-Sep and no visitors
Sun May-Sep, ballot in operation for tee
times during July and August.
Societies   must contact in advance.
Green Fees £50 per day; £38 per round (£60/£48
weekends).
Cards   ▦ ▰ ▦ ◪
Prof   Robin Wilson
Designer   James Braid
Facilities   ⊗)Ⅲ ﹏ ♥ ♀ ⚏ 🖅 📻 ✄ ℓ
& Leisure   hard tennis courts.
Location   W side of village off A917

Hotel   ★★★ 65% The Golf Hotel, Bank St, ELIE
☎ 01333 330209 22 ⇄ ℟

FALKLAND   Map 11 NO20

Falkland The Myre KY15 7AA ☎ 01337 857404
A flat, well kept course with excellent greens and views of
East Lomond Hill and Falkland Palace.
9 holes, 5216yds, Par 68, SSS 65, Course record 62.
Club membership 300.
Visitors   parties must make prior arrangements, please
check availability at weekends.
Societies   must contact in advance.
Green Fees not confirmed.
Facilities   ⊗ by prior arrangement)Ⅲ by prior arrangement
﹏ ♥ ♀ ⚏ ✄
Location   N side of town on A912

Hotel   ★★ 67% Lomond Hills Hotel, Parliament
Square, FREUCHIE
☎ 01337 857329 & 857498
Fax 01337 858180 24 ⇄ ℟

GLENROTHES   Map 11 NO20

Glenrothes Golf Course Rd KY6 2LA
☎ 01592 754561
Mature parkland, challenging back nine with burn crossing
4 fairways. Wide fairways offer opportunities for long hitters
and birdy chances for those with good short game.
18 holes, 6444yds, Par 71, SSS 71, Course record 67.
Club membership 750.
Visitors   no restrictions except for some times at
weekends . Bookings for parties can be made in
advance.
Societies   write to secretary.
Green Fees not confirmed.
Designer   J R Stutt
Facilities   ⊗)Ⅲ ﹏ ♥ ♀ ⚏
Location   W side of town off B921

Hotel   ★★★★⚑ Balbirnie House, Balbirnie Park,
MARKINCH
☎ 01592 610066 30 ⇄ ℟

KINCARDINE   Map 11 NS98

Tulliallan Alloa Rd FK10 4BB
☎ 01259 730798 Fax 01259 730798
Pleasant parkland course with easily negotiable slopes, a
meandering burn and scenic views.
18 holes, 5965yds, Par 69, SSS 69, Course record 63.
Club membership 600.
Visitors   restricted at weekends, must contact
professional shop.
Societies   may not play on Sat; must contact in advance.
Green Fees £28.50 per day, £16 per round (£38/£20
weekends).
Prof   Steven Kelly
Facilities   ⊗)Ⅲ ﹏ ♥ ♀ ⚏ 🖅 📻 ✄
Location   1m NW on A977

Hotel   ★★★ 68% Dall Lodge Country House Hotel,
Main St, KILLIN
☎ 01567 820217 10 ⇄ ℟

KINGHORN   Map 11 NT28

Kinghorn Macduff Cres KY3 9RE
☎ 01592 890345 & 890978
Municipal course, 300 ft above sea level with views over
Firth of Forth and North Sea. Undulating and quite testing.
Facilities shared by Kinghorn Ladies.
18 holes, 5269yds, Par 65, SSS 67, Course record 62.
Club membership 190.
Visitors   may not play between 7.30am-10.30am &
12pm-3pm Sat.
Societies   must contact in writing.
Green Fees £14 (£18 weekends).
Designer   Tom Morris
Facilities   ⚏
Location   S side of town on A921

Hotel   ★★★ 67% Dean Park Hotel, Chapel Level,
KIRKCALDY ☎ 01592 261635
34 ⇄ ℟ Annexe12 ⇄ ℟

KIRKCALDY   Map 11 NT29

Dunnikier Park Dunnikier Way KY1 3LP
☎ 01592 261599
Parkland, rolling fairways, not heavily bunkered, views of
Firth of Forth.
18 holes, 6036metres, Par 72, SSS 72, Course record 65.
Club membership 720.
Visitors   visitors must contact course starter in person.
Societies   apply in writing.
Green Fees not confirmed.
Prof   Gregor Whyte
Designer   R Stutt
Facilities   ⊗ ⅷ ▚ 🝙 ♀ 🛆 🖻 🚜 ◯
Location   2m N on B981

Hotel   ★★★ 67% Dean Park Hotel, Chapel Level,
                KIRKCALDY ☎ 01592 261635
                34 ⇄ 🐾 Annexe12 ⇄ 🐾

Kirkcaldy Balwearie Rd KY2 5LT
☎ 01592 205240 & 203258 (Pro Shop) Fax 01592 205240
e-mail: enquiries@kirkcaldygolfclub.sol.co.uk
Challenging parkland course in rural setting, with beautiful
views. On-course watering ensures good conditions all
season.
18 holes, 6004yds, Par 71, SSS 69, Course record 65.
Club membership 822.
Visitors   limited play Sat. Advised to contact pro-shop
                01592 203258.
Societies   apply in writing/telephone.
Green Fees £22 per round;£28 per day(£28/£36 weekends).
Prof   Anthony Caira
Designer   Tom Morris
Facilities   ⊗ ⅷ ▚ 🝙 ♀ 🛆 🖻 🏌 🐾 🚜 ◯
Location   SW side of town off A910

Hotel   ★★★ 67% Dean Park Hotel, Chapel Level,
                KIRKCALDY ☎ 01592 261635
                34 ⇄ 🐾 Annexe12 ⇄ 🐾

LADYBANK   Map 11 NO30

Ladybank Annsmuir KY15 7RA
☎ 01337 830814 Fax 01337 831505
e-mail: ladybankgc@aol.com
Picturesque parkland/heathland course, popular with visitors.
Qualifying course for the British Open.
18 holes, 6601yds, Par 71, SSS 72, Course record 63.
Club membership 1000.
Visitors   advance booking essential.
Societies   must telephone or write in advance.
Green Fees £45 per day; £35 per round (£40 per round
                weekends).
Cards   💳 ▮▮
Prof   Martin Gray
Designer   Tom Morris
Facilities   ⊗ ⅷ ▚ 🝙 ♀ 🛆 🖻 🏌 🐾 🚜 ◯
Location   Take Kirkcardy Rd for 0.5miles,at A91/A92
                intersection.

Hotel   ★★★ 65% Fernie Castle, Letham, CUPAR
                ☎ 01337 810381   20 ⇄ 🐾

LESLIE   Map 11 NO20

Leslie Balsillie Laws KY6 3EZ ☎ 01592 620040
Challenging parkland course.
9 holes, 4686yds, Par 63, SSS 64, Course record 63.
Club membership 230.
Visitors   contact secretary in writing.
Societies   letter to the Secretary.
Green Fees not confirmed.
Designer   Tom Morris
Facilities   ▚ ♀ 🛆
Location   N side of town off A911

Hotel   ★★★ 59% Balgeddie House Hotel, Balgeddie
                Way, GLENROTHES
                ☎ 01592 742511   19 ⇄ 🐾

LEUCHARS   Map 12 NO42

Drumoig Hotel & Golf Course Drumoig KY16 0BE
☎ 01382 541800 Fax 01382 542211
e-mail: drumoig@sol.co.uk
A developing but challenging young championship course.
Set in a parkland environment, the course is links like in
places. Features include Whinstone Quarries and views over
to St Andrews and Carnoustie. Water features are
demanding, especially on the 9th where the fairway runs
between Drumoig's two mini lochs.
18 holes, 6784yds, Par 71, SSS 72.
Club membership 200.
Visitors   advisable to telephone in advance.
Societies   telephone in advance.
Green Fees £25 per round ; £45 per day (£30/£55
                weekends).
Cards   💳 ▮▮ 🝙 💳 📇 🝙
Facilities   ⊗ ⅷ ▚ 🝙 ♀ 🛆 🏌 🛏 🚜 ◯ ♭
& Leisure   Scottish National Golf Centre in grounds.
Location   On the A914 between St Andrews and Dundee

Hotel   ★★★ 69% Drumoig Golf Hotel, Drumoig,
                LEUCHARS ☎ 01382 541800
                5 ⇄ 🐾 Annexe24 ⇄ 🐾

St Michaels KY16 0DX
☎ 01334 839365 & 838666 Fax 01334 838666
e-mail: stmichaelsgc@btclick.com
Parkland course with open views over Fife and Tayside. The
undulating course weaves its way through tree plantations.
The short Par 4 17th, parallel to the railway and over a pond
to a stepped green, poses an interesting challenge.
18 holes, 5802yds, Par 70, SSS 68, Course record 67.
Club membership 550.
Visitors   may not play on Sun before noon.
Societies   must apply in writing, limited weekends
Green Fees £28 per day; £20 per round (£30/£22 weekends).
Cards   💳 ▮▮ 🝙 🝙
Facilities   ⊗ ⅷ by prior arrangement ▚ 🝙 ♀ 🛆 ◯
Location   NW side of village on A919

Hotel   ★★ 69% Eden House Hotel, 2 Pitscottie Rd,
                CUPAR ☎ 01334 652510
                9 ⇄ 🐾 Annexe2 ⇄ 🐾

LEVEN   Map 11 NO30

Leven Links The Promenade KY8 4HS
☎ 01333 428859 & 421390 Fax 01333 428859
Leven has the classic ingredients which make up a golf
links in Scotland; undulating fairways with hills and
hallows, out of bounds and a 'burn' or stream. A top
class championship links course used for British Open
final qualifying stages, it has fine views over Largo Bay.
18 holes, 6436yds, Par 71, SSS 70, Course record 62.
Club membership 1000.
Visitors   contact in advance. Limited availability Fri
              pm & Sat, contact for these times no more
              than 5 days in advance.
Societies   apply in advance.
Green Fees not confirmed.
Designer   Tom Morris
Facilities   ⊗ ⫴ ﹅ ☕ ♀ ⚐ 🏠 ✦ ♂
Hotel   ★★★ 75% Old Manor Hotel, Leven Rd,
             LUNDIN LINKS ☎ 01333 320368
             24 ⇄ ﹖

Scoonie North Links KY8 4SP
☎ 01333 423437(Starter) & 307007 (Club)
e-mail: manager@scooniegc.fsnet.co.uk
A pleasant inland links course suitable for all ages.
18 holes, 4979mtrs, Par 67, SSS 65, Course record 63.
Club membership 200.
Visitors   no restrictions.
Societies   apply in writing.
Green Fees not confirmed.
Facilities   ⊗ ⫴ ﹅ ☕ ♀ ⚑

Hotel   ★★★ 75% Old Manor Hotel, Leven Rd,
             LUNDIN LINKS ☎ 01333 320368 24 ⇄ ﹖

LOCHGELLY   Map 11 NT19

Lochgelly Cartmore Rd KY5 9PB ☎ 01592 780174
Parkland course with easy walking and often windy.
18 holes, 5491yds, Par 68, SSS 67, Course record 63.
Club membership 650.
Visitors   no restrictions, parties must book in advance by
             writing.
Societies   must apply in writing.
Green Fees £23 per day; £14 per round (£29/£20 weekends).
Prof   Martin Goldie
Designer   Ian Marchbanks
Facilities   ⊗ ⫴ ﹅ ☕ ♀ ⚑ 🏠 ♂
Location   W side of town off A910

Hotel   ★★★ 67% Dean Park Hotel, Chapel Level,
             KIRKCALDY ☎ 01592 261635
             34 ⇄ ﹖ Annexe12 ⇄ ﹖

Lochore Meadows Lochore Meadows Country Park,
Crosshill, Lochgelly KY5 8BA
☎ 01592 414300 Fax 01592 414345
Lochside course with natural stream running through, and
woodland nearby. Country park offers many leisure facilities.
9 holes, 5554yds, Par 72, SSS 71. Club membership 240.
Visitors   no restrictions.
Societies   must contact in advance.
Green Fees £7.50 per 18 holes; £4.50 per 9 holes (£10/£6.50
             weekends & bank holidays).
Facilities   ⊗ ﹅ ☕ ⚑

& Leisure outdoor swimming pool, fishing.
Location   2m N off B920

Hotel   ★★★ 73% Green Hotel, 2 The Muirs,
             KINROSS ☎ 01577 863467 46 ⇄ ﹖

LUNDIN LINKS   Map 12 NO40

Lundin Golf Rd KY8 6BA
☎ 01333 320202 Fax 01333 329743
e-mail: secretary@lundingolfclub.co.uk
The Leven Links and the course of the Lundin Club
adjoin each other. The course is part seaside and part
inland. The holes are excellent but those which are
described as seaside holes have a very different nature
from the inland style ones. The par 3 14th looks
seawards across the Firth of Forth towards Edinburgh
and the old railway line defines out of bounds at several
holes. A number of burns snake across the fairways.
18 holes, 6394yds, Par 71, SSS 71, Course record 63.
Club membership 820.
Visitors   visitors welcome weekdays 9-3.30 (3pm
             Fridays) and Sat after 2.30pm, no vistors
             Sun. Book well in advance.
Societies   book well in advance by telephoning
             Secretary (mornings).
Green Fees £40 per day; £32 per round. Sat pm £40.
Cards   ▭▭ ▬▬ 🖰
Prof   David Webster
Designer   James Braid
Facilities   ⊗ ⫴ ﹅ ☕ ♀ ⚑ 🏠 ♂
Location   W side of village off A915

Hotel   ★★★ 75% Old Manor Hotel, Leven Rd,
             LUNDIN LINKS ☎ 01333 320368 24 ⇄ ﹖

Lundin Ladies Woodielea Rd KY8 6AR
☎ 01333 320832
Short, lowland course with Roman stones on the second
fairway, and coastal views.
9 holes, 2365yds, Par 68, SSS 67, Course record 67.
Club membership 350.
Visitors   contact in advance. Competition days Wed and
             some weekends.
Societies   telephone secretary.
Green Fees not confirmed.
Designer   James Braid
Facilities   ☕ ♀ ♂
Location   W side of village off A915

Hotel   ★★★ 75% Old Manor Hotel, Leven Rd,
             LUNDIN LINKS ☎ 01333 320368 24 ⇄ ﹖

St Andrews Links

t Andrews, *Fife*   ☎ 01334 466666   Fax 01334 479555 Map 12 NO51

e-mail: linkstrust@standrews.org.uk

Golf was first played here around 1400AD and the Old Course is acknowledged world-wide as the Home of Golf. The Old has played host to the greatest golfers in the vorld and many of golf's most dramatic moments. The course is in average 6566 yards long from the medal tees.

The New Course (6604 yards) opened in 1895, having been aid out by Old Tom Morris. The Jubilee opened in 1897, the hampionship Jubilee Course is 6805 yards long from the medal ees. A shorter version of the Jubilee Course is also available, nown as the Bronze Course, measuring 5674 yards. There is no andicap limit for the shorter course and it is best for ower/middle handicap golfers.

The Eden opened in 1914 and is recommended for middle to igh handicap golfers. The Strathtyrum has a shorter, less testing ayout best for high handicap golfers. The Balgove nine hole ourse, upgraded and re-opened in 1993, is best for beginners nd children.

Visitors must book in advance and have handicap certificate. Old Course closed Sun and booking at least 1 year in advance

Societies must book at least a month in advance

Green Fees Old Course £85; New Course £42; Jubilee £37; Eden £28; Strathtyrum £18; Balgove £10 (9 holes) 📷 🍴🍽🅿🚫

Facilities ⊗ 🍴🛍🍺♀👥🏠🚩🐕 🛒✏🍸

Location Pilmour House, St Andrews KY16 9SF (NW of town, off A91)

Holes/Par/Course record Old Course: 18 holes, 6566 yds, Par 72, SSS 72, Course record 67
New (West Sands Rd): 18 holes, 6604 yds, Par 71, SSS 71
Jubilee (West Sands Rd): 18 holes, 6805 yds, Par 72, SSS 72
Eden (Dundee Rd): 18 holes, 6162 yds, Par 70, SSS 70
Strathtyrum: 18 holes, 5094 yds, Par 69, SSS 69

Championship Course

HERE TO STAY AND EAT NEARBY

tels

ENFARG

★ 65% Glenfarg, Main St.
01577 830241. 16 (5 ⇄ 🛏 11 🛏)

ST ANDREWS

★★★★★🏵🏵 74% Old Course Hotel, Golf Resort & Spa, Old Station Rd. ☎ 01334 474371. 146 ⇄ 🛏

★★★🏵🏵 77% St Andrews Golf, 40 The Scores. ☎ 01334 472611. 22 (20 ⇄ 🛏 2 🛏)

★★★ 66% Scores, 76 The Scores.
☎ 01334 472451. 30 (28 ⇄ 🛏 2 🛏)

Restaurant

CUPAR

🏵🏵🏵 Ostlers Close, Bonnygate.
☎ 01334 655574

MARKINCH   Map 11 NO20

Balbirnie Park Balbirnie Park KY7 6NR
☎ 01592 612095 & 752006 (tee times) Fax 01592 612383
A fine example of the best in traditional parkland design,
with natural contours the inspiration behind the layout.
18 holes, 6214yds, Par 71, SSS 70, Course record 62.
Club membership 900.
Visitors   must contact in advance. Numbers restricted
            weekends and visitors must play from yellow
            tees, smart but casual dress code.
Societies   booking forms sent out on request by asst
            secretary.
Green Fees £33 per day; £25 per round (£40/£30 weekends).
Cards   📇 💳 💰 🖃
Prof   Craig Donnelly
Facilities   ⚒ 🏠 ⛳ 🍴 ▣ ♦ 🚜 ⁄
Location   2m E of Glenrothes

Hotel   ★★★★🏵 Balbirnie House, Balbirnie Park,
            MARKINCH ☎ 01592 610066 30 ⇄ 🏝

ST ANDREWS   Map 12 NO51

British Golf Museum
☎ 01334 460046 (situated opposite Royal & Ancient
Golf Club)
The museum which tells the history of golf from its origins to
the present day, is of interest to golfers and non-golfers alike.
Themed galleries and interactive displays explore the history
of the major championships and the lives of the famous
players, and trace the development of golfing equipment.
An audio-visual theatre shows historic golfing moments
Open: Etr-mid Oct, daily 9.30am-5.30pm (mid Oct-Etr
Thu-Mon 11am-3pm, closed Tue & Wed.
Admission: There is a charge.
☎ for details.

Dukes Course Craigtoun KY16 8NS ☎ 01334 474371
Fax 01334 479456 e-mail: jkelly@oldcoursehotel.co.uk
Blending the characteristics of a links course with an
inland course, Dukes offers rolling fairways, undulating
greens and a testing woodland section, and magnificent
views over St Andrews Bay towards Carnoustie.
18 holes, 6749yds, Par 72, SSS 73, Course record 71.
Club membership 500.
Visitors   booking should be in advance to avoid
            disappointment through the hotel resort
            reservations team.
Societies   apply in writing or fax in advance.
Green Fees from £35-£75 per round.

Cards   📇 ■ 💳 💰 🖃 🗂
Prof   John Kelly
Designer Peter Thomson
Facilities   ⊗ ⚒ 🏠 💰 ⛳ 🍴 🏠 ♦ 🚜 ⁄
& Leisure heated indoor swimming pool, sauna,
            solarium, gymnasium, computer swing
            analyses.
Location   Follow M90 from Edinburgh onto A91 to
            Cupar then to St Andrew turning off for
            Strathkiness

Hotel   ★★★★★ 74% The Old Course Hotel Golf
            Resort & Spa, ST ANDREWS
            ☎ 01334 474371 146 ⇄ 🏝

The Glenfarg Hotel & Restaurant
Additional ★★ 67% The Glenfarg Hotel & Restaurant,
hotel   Main St, GLENFARG ☎ 01577 830241
            Fax 01577 830665 17rm(16 ⇄ 🏝)
Additional ♦♦♦♦ Riverview Guest House, Edenside,
Guesthouse ST ANDREWS ☎ 01334 838009
            Fax 01334 839944 7 🏝

ST ANDREWS
Map 12 NO51

Hotel ★★★★♨ Balbirnie House, Balbirnie Park, MARKINCH ☎ 01592 610066 30 ⇄ 🐾

ST ANDREWS See page 361

SALINE
Map 11 NT09

Saline Kinneddar Hill KY12 9LT ☎ 01383 852591
Hillside parkland course with excellent turf and panoramic view of the Forth Valley.
9 holes, 5302yds, Par 68, SSS 66, Course record 62.
Club membership 400.
Visitors advisable to contact in advance and may not play Sat, some restrictions Sun.
Societies contact in advance.
Green Fees £9 per day (£11 Sun).
Facilities ⊗ �𝄂 🏐 🍵 ♀ 🛝 ℓ
Location Junct 4 of M90, 0.5m E at junc B913/914

Hotel ★★★ 65% King Malcolm, Queensferry Rd, DUNFERMLINE ☎ 01383 722611 48 ⇄ 🐾

TAYPORT
Map 12 NO42

Scotscraig Golf Rd DD6 9DZ
☎ 01382 552515 Fax 01382 553130
e-mail: scotscraig@scottishgolf.com
A rather tight course on downland-type turf with an abundance of gorse. The sheltered position of this Open qualifying course ensures good weather throughout the year.
18 holes, 6550yds, Par 71, SSS 72, Course record 67.
Club membership 850.
Visitors restricted at weekends and weekdays, contact in advance.
Societies advance booking.
Green Fees £35 per day (£40 weekends).
Cards 💳 ▒▒▒ 🗒
Prof S J Campbell
Designer James Braid
Facilities ⊗ ⟨⊪ 🏐 💺 ♀ 🛝 🏬 🍴 📦 🛝 ℓ
Location S side of village off B945

Hotel ★★★ 68% Sandford Country House Hotel, Newton Hill, Wormit, DUNDEE ☎ 01382 541802 16 ⇄ 🐾

THORNTON
Map 11 NT29

Thornton Station Rd KY1 4DW
☎ 01592 771111 Fax 01592 774955
e-mail: johntgc@ic24.net
A relatively flat, lightly tree-lined, parkland course bounded on three sides by a river which comes into play at holes 14-16.
18 holes, 6155yds, Par 70, SSS 69, Course record 64.
Club membership 700.
Visitors restricted at weekends before 10am & between 12.30-2pm, also Tue 1-1.30 & Thu 9-10. Booking in advance recommended.
Societies apply in advance.
Green Fees £27 per day; £17 per round (£35/£25 weekends).
Facilities ⊗ ⟨⊪ 🏐 💺 ♀ 🛝 ℓ
Location 1m E of town off A92

HIGHLAND

ALNESS
Map 14 NH66

Alness Ardross Rd IV17 0QA ☎ 01349 883877
e-mail: info@alnessgolfclub.co.uk
A testing, parkland course with beautiful views over the Cromarty Firth and the Black Isle. An additional 9 holes have been developed, four holes run alongside the Averon river making the course more scenic and interesting.
18 holes, 4886yds, Par 67, SSS 64, Course record 62.
Club membership 300.
Visitors telephone in advance for weekend play, parties must telephone for booking
Societies must contact in advance.
Green Fees £13 per round:£16 per day(£15/318 weekends).
Facilities 🏐 💺 ♀ 🛝 🍴 ℓ
& Leisure fishing.
Location 0.5m N off A9

Hotel ★★★ 72% Morangie House Hotel, Morangie Rd, TAIN ☎ 01862 892281 26 ⇄ 🐾

ARISAIG
Map 13 NM68

Traigh Traigh PH39 4NT
☎ 01687 450337 Fax 01678 450293
According to at least one newspaper Traigh is 'probably the most beautifully sited nine-hole golf course in the world'. Whether that is true or not, Traigh lies by the sea alongside sandy beaches with views to Skye and the Inner Hebrides. The feature of the course is a line of grassy hills, originally sand dunes, that rise to some 60 feet.
9 holes, 2456yds, Par 68, SSS 65, Course record 67.
Club membership 150.
Visitors no restrictions.
Societies contact in advance.
Green Fees £12 per day.
Designer John Salvesen 1994
Facilities 💺 📦 🍴 ℓ
Location On A830 6 miles S of Mallaig,2Miles N of Arisaig

Hotel ★★ 68% Arisaig Hotel, ARISAIG ☎ 01687 450210 13 ⇄ 🐾

BOAT OF GARTEN
Map 14 NH91

Boat of Garten PH24 3BQ
☎ 01479 831282 Fax 01479 831523
e-mail: boatgolf@enterprise.net
This heathland course was cut out from a silver birch forest though the fairways are adequately wide. There are natural hazards of broom and heather, good views and walking is easy. A round provides great variety.
18 holes, 5866yds, Par 69, SSS 69, Course record 67.
Club membership 650.

▶

Visitors	must contact in advance. Handicap certificate required. Play restricted to 10am-4pm weekends & 9.20am-7pm weekdays
Societies	must telephone in advance.
Green Fees	£28 per day; £23 per round (£33/£28 weekends).
Cards	🔲🔲🔲🔲🔲
Designer	James Braid
Facilities	⊗ 🗒 🕿 💺 🍴 👥 🏠 ⛳ 🏌 🛒 🏌
& Leisure	hard tennis courts.
Location	E side of village

Boat Hotel

Hotel	★★★ 70% Boat Hotel, BOAT OF GARTEN ☎ 01479 831258 32 ⇥ 🏠

BONAR BRIDGE   Map 14 NH69

Bonar Bridge-Ardgay Migdale Rd IV24 3EJ
☎ 01863 766375 Fax 01863 766738
e-mail: secbbagc@aol.com
Wooded moorland course with picturesque views of hills and loch.
9 holes, 5284yds, Par 68, SSS 66.
Club membership 250.

Visitors	no restrictions.
Societies	apply in writing.
Green Fees	not confirmed.
Facilities	💺 🏌 ⛳
Location	0.5m E

Guesthouse ♦♦♦ Kyle House, Dornoch Rd, BONAR BRIDGE ☎ 01863 766360 6rm(3 ⇥ 🏠)

BRORA   Map 14 NC90

Brora Golf Rd KW9 6QS
☎ 01408 621417 Fax 01408 622157
e-mail: secretary@broragolf.co.uk
Typical seaside links with little rough and fine views. Some testing holes.
18 holes, 6110yds, Par 69, SSS 69, Course record 61.
Club membership 704.

Visitors	advisable to book in advance May-Oct.
Societies	advisable to book in advance.
Green Fees	£25 per round (£30 weekends).
Cards	🔲🔲
Designer	James Braid
Facilities	⊗ 🗒 🕿 💺 🍴 🏠 ⛳ 🏌
Location	E side of village. Follow signs to Beach Car Park

Hotel	★★★ 67% The Links Hotel, Golf Rd, BRORA ☎ 01408 621225 23 ⇥ 🏠

CARRBRIDGE   Map 14 NH92

Carrbridge Inverness Rd PH23 3AU ☎ 01479 841623
e-mail: enquiries@carrbridgegolf
Short but challenging part-parkland, part-moorland course with magnificent views of the Cairngorms.
9 holes, 5402yds, Par 71, SSS 68, Course record 64.
Club membership 650.

Visitors	during May-Sep, course not open to visitors after 5pm Wed & before 4pm most Sun.
Societies	small parties welcome, apply in writing.
Green Fees	£12-£13 per day; £15 weekends (reductions after 6pm).
Facilities	💺 🏌 🏌 ⛳
Location	N side of village

Hotel	★★★ 68% Dalrachney Lodge Hotel, CARRBRIDGE ☎ 01479 841252 11 ⇥ 🏠

DORNOCH   Map 14 NH78

The Carnegie Club Skibo Castle IV25 3RQ
☎ 01862 894600 Fax 01862 894601
e-mail: skibo@carnegieclubs.com
Set within the grounds of an enchanting castle, with the sea on three sides and the hills of Sutherland and Ross-shire all around, this splendid course enjoys a magnificent position. Although not long by modern standards, strong and fickle winds will test even the most experienced golfer. Excellent leisure facilities.
18 holes, 6403yds, Par 71, SSS 71.
Club membership 550.

Visitors	weekdays only by written application to the secretary. Tee times between 11am & 12pm.
Societies	by prior arrangement
Green Fees	not confirmed.
Prof	David Thomson
Designer	J Sutherland/Donald Steel
Facilities	⊗ by prior arrangement 💺 🍴 🏠 🏌 📮 ⛳ 🏌
& Leisure	hard tennis courts, heated indoor swimming pool, fishing, sauna, solarium, gymnasium.
Location	Off A9 3m before Dornoch

Hotel	★★ 65% Burghfield House Hotel, DORNOCH ☎ 01862 810212 13 ⇥ 🏠 Annexe15 ⇥ 🏠

Royal Dornoch Golf Rd IV25 3LW
☎ 01862 810219 Fax 01862 810792
e-mail: rdgc@royaldornoch.com
Very challenging seaside championship links, designed by Tom Morris and John Sutherland.
Championship: 18 holes, 6514yds, Par 70, SSS 73, Course record 62.
Struie Course: 18 holes, 5438yds, Par 69, SSS 66.
Club membership 1550.

Visitors	must have a handicap of 24 for gentlemen (ladies 39) on Championship Course. Must contact in advance.
Societies	must apply in advance.

▶

Royal Dornoch Golf Club

Green Fees Championship course: £45-£60 per round (£50-£70 Sundays). Struie course: £12-25 per day; £9-18 per round.
Cards
Prof A Skinner
Designer Tom Morris
Facilities ⊗ ⅻ ⅋ ⬛ ♀ ⌂ 🗐 ⛟ ✵ 🥢 ♂
& Leisure hard tennis courts.
Location E side of town

Hotel ★★★ 68% Royal Golf Hotel, The First Tee, Grange Rd, DORNOCH
☎ 01862 810283 25 ⇆ ⋒ Annexe8rm

DURNESS   Map 14 NC46

Durness Balnakeil IV27 4PG
☎ 01971 511364 Fax 01971 511205
A 9-hole course set in tremendous scenery overlooking Balnakeil Bay. Part links and part inland with water hazards. Off alternative tees for second 9 holes giving surprising variety. Tremendous last hole played across the sea to the green over 100 yards away.
9 holes, 5555yds, Par 70, SSS 67, Course record 69.
Club membership 150.
Visitors restricted 10am-12.30pm on Sun during Jun-Sep.
Societies must telephone in advance 01971 511364 (ex Sun).
Green Fees £15 per day.
Designer F Keith
Facilities ⊗ ⬛ ⌂ ⛟ ♂
& Leisure fishing.
Location 1m W of village overlooking Balnakeil Bay

Guesthouse ◆◆◆◆ Port-Na-Con House, Loch Eriboll, LAIRG ☎ 01971 511367 3 ⇆ ⋒

FORT AUGUSTUS   Map 14 NH30

Fort Augustus Markethill PH32 4DP
☎ 01320 366660 366309
Moorland course, with narrow fairways and good views. Bordered by the tree-lined Caledonian Canal to the north and heather clad hills to the south.
9 holes, 5454yds, Par 67, SSS 67, Course record 67.
Club membership 170.
Visitors may not play Sat 1.30-4 & occasional Sun.
Societies telephone in advance.
Green Fees £10 per day.
Designer Colt
Facilities ♀ ⌂ ⛟ ♂
Location 1m SW on A82

FORTROSE   Map 14 NH75

Fortrose & Rosemarkie Ness Rd East IV10 8SE
☎ 01381 620529 Fax 01381 621328
e-mail: secretary@fortrosegolfclub.co.uk
Seaside links course, set on a peninsula with sea on three sides. Easy walking, good views. Designed by James Braid; the club was formed in 1888.
18 holes, 5875yds, Par 71, SSS 69, Course record 64.
Club membership 770.
Visitors restricted 8.45-10.15am & 1-2.15pm then 4.45-6.30pm.
Societies must telephone in advance.
Green Fees £32 per day; £21per round (£37/£26 weekends).
Cards
Designer James Braid
Facilities ⊗ ⬛ ⬛ ♀ ⌂ 🗐 ⛟ ♂
Location E side of town centre

FORT WILLIAM   Map 14 NN17

Fort William Torlundy PH33 7SN ☎ 01397 704464
Spectacular moorland location looking onto the cliffs of Ben Nevis. Tees and greens are in excellent condition following and major drainage improvements to the fairways.
18 holes, 6500yds, Par 72, SSS 71, Course record 67.
Club membership 420.
Visitors no restrictions.
Societies must contact in writing.
Green Fees £20 per day; £17 per round.
Cards
Designer Hamilton Stutt
Facilities ⬛ ⬛ ♀ ⌂ ⛟ ♂
Location 3m NE on A82

Hotel ★★★ 71% Moorings Hotel, Banavie, FORT WILLIAM ☎ 01397 772797 27 ⇆ ⋒

GAIRLOCH   Map 14 NG87

Gairloch IV21 2BE ☎ 01445 712407 Fax 01445 712407
e-mail: secreatry@gairlochgc.freeserve.co.uk
Fine seaside links course running along Gairloch Sands with good views over the sea to Skye. In windy conditions each hole is affected. The par 5 eighth hole is described by one of Scotlands teaching professionals as one of the best natural par 5's in the country.
9 holes, 4514yds, Par 63, SSS 64, Course record 64.
Club membership 275.
Visitors must be competent golfer and member of a recognised club.
Societies apply in writing to secretary.
Green Fees not confirmed.
Cards
Designer Capt Burgess
Facilities ⬛ ♀ ⌂ 🗐 ⛟ ♂
Location 1m S on A832

Hotel ★★★ 67% Creag Mor Hotel, Charleston, GAIRLOCH ☎ 01445 712068 17 ⇆ ⋒

Entries with a green background
identify courses considered to be
particularly interesting

GOLSPIE · Map 14 NH89

Golspie Ferry Rd KW10 6ST
☎ 01408 633266 Fax 01408 633393
Founded in 1889, Golspie's seaside course offers easy walking and natural hazards including beach heather and whins. Spectacular scenery.
18 holes, 5890yds, Par 68, SSS 68, Course record 64.
Club membership 300.
Visitors contact in advance.
Societies contact in advance.
Green Fees £25 per day; £30 per round.
Cards ▭
Designer James Braid
Facilities ⊗ ℳ by prior arrangement ⓑ ♨ ♀ ♨ 🏠 ⚑ ♂
Location 0.5m S off A9

Hotel ★★★ 67% The Links Hotel, Golf Rd, BRORA
☎ 01408 621225 23 ⇆ ⋔

GRANTOWN-ON-SPEY · Map 14 NJ02

Grantown-on-Spey Golf Course Rd PH26 3HY
☎ 01479 872079 (Apr-Oct) Fax 01479 873725
e-mail: secretary@grantownonspeygolfclub.co
Parkland and woodland course. Part easy walking, remainder hilly. The 7th to 13th really sorts out the golfers.
18 holes, 5710yds, Par 70, SSS 68, Course record 60.
Club membership 800.
Visitors advisable to contact in advance. No visitors before 10am weekends.
Societies clubhouse open Apr-Oct, apply in advance to secretary.
Green Fees £20 per day (£25 weekends); £10 evening round..
Cards ▭ ■ ▭ ▤ ☒ ▨
Designer A Brown/W Park/J Braid
Facilities ⊗ ℳ by prior arrangement ⓑ ♨ ♀ ♨ 🏠 ⚑ ♦ ♨ ♂
Location NE side of town centre

Hotel ★★ 77% Culdearn House Hotel, Woodlands Ter, GRANTOWN ON SPEY
☎ 01479 872106 9 ⇆ ⋔

HELMSDALE · Map 14 ND01

Helmsdale Golf Rd KW8 6JA ☎ 01431 821650
Sheltered, undulating course following the line of the Helmsdale River.
9 holes, 1860yds, Par 62, SSS 61.
Club membership 90.
Visitors no restrictions.
Societies apply in writing.
Green Fees not confirmed.
Facilities ♨
Location NW side of town on A896

Hotel ★★★ 67% The Links Hotel, Golf Rd, BRORA
☎ 01408 621225 23 ⇆ ⋔

INVERGORDON · Map 14 NH76

Invergordon King George St IV18 0BD ☎ 01349 852715
Fairly easy but windy 18-hole parkland course, with woodland, wide fairways and good views over Cromarty Firth. Very good greens and a fair challenge, especially if the wind is from the west.
18 holes, 6030yds, Par 69, SSS 69, Course record 65.
Club membership 240.
Visitors visitors advised to avoid Tue & Thu 4.30-6, Mon & Wed 5-6 and Sat 8.30-10 & 1-2pm.
Societies must contact in advance, call 01349 852715.
Green Fees £20 per day; £15 per round.
Designer A Rae
Facilities ⓑ ♨ ♀ ♨ ⚑ ♂
Location W side of town centre on B817

Hotel ★★★ 72% Morangie House Hotel, Morangie Rd, TAIN ☎ 01862 892281 26 ⇆ ⋔

INVERNESS · Map 14 NH64

Inverness Culcabock IV2 3XQ
☎ 01463 239882 Fax 01463 239882
e-mail: igc@freeuk.com
Fairly flat parkland course with burn running through it. Windy in winter. The 14th is one of the most difficult Par 4's in the north of Scotland.
18 holes, 6226yds, Par 69, SSS 70, Course record 62.
Club membership 1100.
Visitors restricted at weekends.Prior booking required.Handicap certificate required.
Societies must telephone in advance.
Green Fees £29 per round;£39 per day.
Cards ▭ ▭ ▤ ☒ ▨
Prof Alistair P Thomson
Facilities ⊗ ℳ ⓑ ♨ ♀ ♨ 🏠 ⚑ ♂
Location 1 mile from town centre on Culcabock road.

Hotel ★★★★ 71% Inverness Marriott Hotel, Culcabock Rd, INVERNESS
☎ 01463 237166 76 ⇆ ⋔ Annexe6 ⇆ ⋔

Loch Ness Fairways Leisure, Castle Heather IV2 6AA
☎ 01463 713335 Fax 01463 712695
e-mail: info@golflochness.com
Challenging parkland course with superb views over Inverness, the Beauly Firth and the Black Isle.
18 holes, 6772yds, Par 73, SSS 72, Course record 71.
Club membership 580.
Societies telephone for details.
Green Fees £20 per day (£25 weekends).
Cards ▭ ■ ▭ ☒ ▨
Prof Martin Piggot
Designer Caddies
Facilities ⊗ ℳ ⓑ ♨ ♀ ♨ 🏠 ⚑ ♦ ♨ ♂ ⍭
Location SW outskirts of Inverness, along new bypass

Hotel ★★★ 66% Loch Ness House Hotel, Glenurquhart Rd, INVERNESS
☎ 01463 231248 22 ⇆ ⋔

AA Hotels that have special arrangements with golf courses are listed at the back of the guide

Looking for a driving range?
See the index at the back of the guide

Torvean Glenurquhart Rd IV3 8JN
☎ 01463 711434 (Starter) & 225651 (Secretary)
Fax 01463 225651
Municipal parkland course, easy walking, good views.
18 holes, 5784yds, Par 69, SSS 68, Course record 64.
Club membership 400.
Visitors   Advance booking advisable especially at
                  weekends.
Societies   advance bookings through The Highland
                  Council, Town House, Inverness.
Green Fees   £18 per day; £13.50 per round; (£20/£16
                  weekends).
Designer   Hamilton
Facilities   ⓑ ⓦ ⓠ ⓐ ⓣ ⓕ ⓖ
Location   1.5m SW on A82

Hotel   ★★★ 66% Loch Ness House Hotel,
                  Glenurquhart Rd, INVERNESS
                  ☎ 01463 231248   22 ⇄ ⓡ

KINGUSSIE   Map 14 NH70

Kingussie Gynack Rd PH21 1LR
☎ 01540 661600 Fax 01540 662066
e-mail: kinggolf@globalnet.co.uk
Hilly upland course with natural hazards and magnificent
views. Stands about 1000ft above sea level at its highest
point, and the River Gynack, which runs through the course,
comes into play on five holes.
18 holes, 5500yds, Par 67, SSS 68, Course record 63.
Club membership 800.
Visitors   advisable to book in advance.
Societies   must contact in advance.
Green Fees   £20 per day; £18 per round (£25/£20 weekends).
Designer   Vardon/Herd
Facilities   ⓑ ⓦ ⓠ ⓐ ⓣ ⓦ ⓖ
Location   0.25m N off A86

Hotel   ★★ 74% The Scot House Hotel, Newtonmore
                  Rd, KINGUSSIE ☎ 01540 661351 9 ⇄ ⓡ

LOCHCARRON   Map 14 NG83

Lochcarron East End IV54 8YU ☎ 01520 766211
Seaside links course with some parkland with an interesting
2nd hole. A short course but great accuracy is required.
9 holes, 1789yds, Par 62, SSS 60, Course record 60.
Club membership 130.
Visitors   restricted Sat 2-5pm.
Societies   welcome but restricted Sat 2-5pm.
Green Fees   £40 per week; £10 per day.
Facilities   ⓕ
Location   By A896,1 mile E of Lochcarron village

Hotel   ★★ 68% Lochcarron Hotel, Main St,
                  LOCHCARRON ☎ 01520 722226
                  10rm(9 ⇄ ⓡ)

LYBSTER   Map 15 ND23

Lybster Main St KW3 6AE ☎ 01593 721308
Picturesque, short heathland course, easy walking.
9 holes, 1896yds, Par 62, SSS 61, Course record 59.
Club membership 140.
Visitors   no restrictions.
Societies   must contact in advance.

Green Fees £8 per day.
Facilities   ⓐ ⓕ
Location   E side of village

Hotel   ★★ 67% Mackay's Hotel, Union St, WICK
                  ☎ 01955 602323 27rm(19 ⇄ ⓡ)

MUIR OF ORD   Map 14 NH55

Muir of Ord Great North Rd IV6 7SX
☎ 01463 870825 Fax 01463 871867
e-mail: muirgolf@supanet.com-email
Old established (1875), heathland course with tight fairways
and easy walking. Testing 13th, 'Castle Hill' (par 3).
18 holes, 5596yds, Par 68, SSS 68, Course record 61.
Club membership 730.
Visitors   may not play during competitions. Booking
                  required for weekends.
Societies   write to secretary or telephone golf shop on
                  01463 871311.
Green Fees   not confirmed.
Designer   James Braid
Facilities   ⓧ by prior arrangement ⓜ by prior arrangement
                  ⓑ ⓦ ⓠ ⓐ ⓣ ⓕ ⓥ ⓦ ⓖ
Location   S side of village on A862

Hotel   ★★★ 72% Priory Hotel, The Square,
                  BEAULY ☎ 01463 782309   34 ⇄ ⓡ

NAIRN   Map 14 NH85

Nairn Seabank Rd IV12 4HB
☎ 01667 453208 Fax 01667 456328
e-mail: secretary@nairngolfclub.prestel.co.uk
Championship, seaside links founded in 1887 and
created from a wilderness of heather and whin. Designed
by Archie Simpson, old Tom Morris and James Braid.
Opening holes stretch out along the shoreline with the
turn for home at the 10th. Regularly chosen for national
championships.
18 holes, 6452yds, Par 71, SSS 73, Course record 65.
Newton: 9 holes, 3542yds, Par 58, SSS 57.
Club membership 1150.
Visitors   book in advance through secretary, may not
                  play between 8-11.00 am & 12-2.30 pm (Fri
                  & Sat).
Societies   subject to availability bookings through
                  secretary's office.
Green Fees   £70 per round.
Cards   ⬛ ⬛ ⬛ ⬛
Prof   Robin P Fyfe
Designer   A Simpson/Old Tom Morris/James Braid
Facilities   ⓧ ⓜ ⓑ ⓦ ⓠ ⓐ ⓣ ⓕ ⓖ ⓣ
& Leisure   snooker.
Location   16m E of Inverness on A96

Hotel   ★★★★ 67% Golf View Hotel & Leisure
                  Club, Seabank Rd, NAIRN
                  ☎ 01667 452301   48 ⇄ ⓡ

Nairn Dunbar Lochloy Rd IV12 5AE
☎ 01667 452741 Fax 01667 456897
Links course with sea views and testing gorse-and whin-lined
fairways. Testing hole: 'Long Peter' (527 yds).
18 holes, 6720yds, Par 72, SSS 73.
Club membership 700.

▶

Visitors April-Oct only. Weekends restricted, contact in advance.
Societies must contact in advance.
Green Fees not confirmed.
Cards ▭▭
Prof David Torrance
Facilities ⊗ ⅏ ⅃ ☕ ▮ ♀ ⚴ ☖ ⚲ ⚑ ⚸
Location E side of town off A96

Hotel ★★ 66% Alton Burn Hotel, Alton Burn Rd, NAIRN ☎ 01667 452051
19rm(14 ⇆3 🐾) Annexe7 ⇆ 🐾

NETHY BRIDGE   Map 14 NJ02

Abernethy PH25 3EB ☎ 01479 821305
Traditional Highland course featuring a mixture of undulating parkland and moorland.
9 holes, 2551yds, Par 66, SSS 66.
Club membership 480.
Visitors contact in advance.
Societies must contact in advance.
Green Fees £13 per day (£16 weekends).
Facilities ⊗ ⅃ ▮ ⚴ ⚑ ⚸
Location N side of village on B970

Hotel ★★★ 73% Muckrach Lodge Hotel, DULNAIN BRIDGE
☎ 01479 851257 9 ⇆ 🐾 Annexe4 ⇆ 🐾

NEWTONMORE   Map 14 NN79

Newtonmore Golf Course Rd PH20 1AT
☎ 01540 673328 & 673878 Fax 01540 673878
Inland course beside the River Spey. Beautiful views and easy walking. Testing 17th hole (par 3).
18 holes, 6029yds, Par 70, SSS 69, Course record 68.
Club membership 420.
Visitors contact in advance.
Societies apply in writing to secretary.
Green Fees not confirmed.
Prof Robert Henderson
Facilities ⊗ ⅏ ⅃ ▮ ♀ ⚴ ☖ ⚲ ⚑ ⚸
Location E side of town off A9

Hotel ★★ 74% The Scot House Hotel, Newtonmore Rd, KINGUSSIE ☎ 01540 661351 9 ⇆ 🐾

REAY   Map 14 NC96

Reay KW14 7RE ☎ 01847 811288 Fax 01847 894189
e-mail: info@reaygolfclub.co.uk
Picturesque seaside links with natural hazards, following the contours of Sandside Bay. Tight and testing.
18 holes, 5831yds, Par 69, SSS 69, Course record 64.
Club membership 368.
Visitors restricted competition days
Societies apply to the secretary in advance.
Green Fees £15 per day/round (£45 per week).
Designer Braid
Facilities ⊗ ⅏ by prior arrangement ⅃ by prior arrangement ▮ ♀ ⚴ ⚑ ⚸
& Leisure see web site.
Location 0.5m E off A836

STRATHPEFFER   Map 14 NH45

Strathpeffer Spa IV14 9AS
☎ 01997 421219 & 421011 Fax 01997 421011
e-mail: mail@strathpeffergolf.co.uk
Upland course with many natural hazards (only 3 sand bunkers), hard walking and fine views. Testing 3rd hole (par 3) across loch.
18 holes, 4792yds, Par 65, SSS 64, Course record 60.
Club membership 500.
Visitors advisable to contact in advance.
Societies apply in writing.
Green Fees £21 per day; £15 per round.
Cards ▭▭
Designer Willie Park/Tom Morris
Facilities ⅃ ▮ ♀ ⚴ ☖ ⚑ ⚸
Location 0.25m N of village off A834

Hotel ★★ 70% Achilty Hotel, CONTIN ☎ 01997 421355 8 ⇆ 🐾 Annexe4 ⇆ 🐾

TAIN   Map 14 NH78

Tain Chapel Rd IV19 1JE
☎ 01862 892314 Fax 01862 892099 e-mail: tgc@cali.co.uk
Heathland/links course with river affecting 3 holes; easy walking, fine views.
18 holes, 6404yds, Par 70, SSS 71, Course record 68.
Club membership 500.
Visitors no restrictions.
Societies must book in advance.
Green Fees £30 per round; £36 per day (£36/£46 weekends).
Cards ▭▭ ▭▭ ▭▭ ◪
Designer Tom Morris
Facilities ⊗ ⅏ ⅃ ☕ ▮ ♀ ⚴ ☖ ⚲ ⚑ ⚸ ⚴ ⚸
Location E side of town centre off B9174

Hotel ★★★ 72% Morangie House Hotel, Morangie Rd, TAIN ☎ 01862 892281 26 ⇆ 🐾

THURSO   Map 15 ND16

Thurso Newlands of Geise KW14 7XD ☎ 01847 893807
Parkland course, windy, but with fine views of Dunnet Head and the Orkney Islands.
18 holes, 5853yds, Par 69, SSS 69, Course record 63.
Club membership 230.
Visitors may not play 9-10.30 Sat or 1-1.30 Sat.
Societies apply in advance.
Green Fees £15 per day(May-Sep); £8 per day(Oct-April).
Designer W S Stewart
Facilities ⅃ ▮ ♀ ⚴ ⚑
Location 2m SW of Thurso on B874

Hotel ★★★ 63% Royal Hotel, Traill St, THURSO ☎ 01847 893191 102 ⇆ 🐾

WICK   Map 15 ND35

Wick Reiss KW1 4RW
☎ 01955 602726 Fax 01955 604418
e-mail: info@wickgolfclub.co.uk
Typical seaside links course, fairly flat, easy walking. 9 holes straight out and straight back. Normally breezy.
18 holes, 5976yds, Par 69, SSS 70, Course record 63.
Club membership 352.

▶

Visitors no restrictions.
Societies apply in writing or telephone in advance.
Green Fees £20 per day.
Designer James Braid
Facilities ⓑ ⬤ ♀ ⚲ ⚑ ✂
Location 3.5m N off A9

Hotel ★★ 67% Mackay's Hotel, Union St, WICK
☎ 01955 602323 27rm(19 ⇆ ↾)

INVERCLYDE

GOUROCK   Map 10 NS27

Gourock Cowal View PA19 1HD
☎ 01475 631001 Fax 01475 631001
18 holes, 6512yds, Par 73, SSS 73, Course record 64.
Location SW side of town off A770
Telephone for further details

Hotel L Howard Johnson Greenock, Cartsburn,
GREENOCK ☎ 01475 786666

GREENOCK   Map 10 NS27

Greenock Forsyth St PA16 8RE
☎ 01475 720793 Fax 01475 791912
Testing moorland course with panoramic views of Clyde
Estuary.
18 holes, 5838yds, Par 69, SSS 69.
Club membership 700.
Visitors may not play Sat. Must contact in advance and
have a handicap certificate.
Societies must telephone in advance.
Green Fees not confirmed.
Prof Stewart Russell
Designer James Braid
Facilities ⓧ ⍫ ⓑ ⬤ ♀ ⚲ ✂
Location SW side of town off A770

Hotel Howard Johnson Greenock, Cartsburn,
GREENOCK ☎ 01475 786666

Greenock Whinhill Beith Rd PA16 9LN
☎ 01475 724694 evenings & weekends only
18 holes, 5504yds, Par 68, SSS 68, Course record 64.
Location 1.5m SW off B7054
Telephone for further details

Hotel Howard Johnson Greenock, Cartsburn,
GREENOCK ☎ 01475 786666

KILMACOLM   Map 10 NS36

Kilmacolm Porterfield Rd PA13 4PD
☎ 01505 872139 Fax 01505 874007
e-mail: secretary@kilmacolmgolf.sagehost.co.uk
Moorland course, easy walking, fine views. Testing 7th, 13th
and 14th holes.
18 holes, 5961yds, Par 69, SSS 69, Course record 64.
Club membership 850.
Visitors must contact in advance, visitors welcome
Tuesday, Wednesday & Thursday.

Societies apply in writing.
Green Fees not confirmed.
Prof Iain Nicholson
Designer Willie Campbell
Facilities ⚲ 🍴 ⚲ ✂
Location SE side of town off A761

Hotel ★★★★♨ 67% Gleddoch House Hotel,
LANGBANK ☎ 01475 540711 39 ⇆ ↾

PORT GLASGOW   Map 10 NS37

Port Glasgow Devol Rd PA14 5XE
☎ 01475 704181 & 791214 (Sec)
A moorland course set on a hilltop overlooking the Clyde,
with magnificent views to the Cowal hills.
18 holes, 5712yds, Par 68, SSS 68.
Club membership 390.
Visitors may not play on Sat. By prior arrangement or
with member Sun.
Societies apply in writing.
Green Fees £20 per day; £15 per round.
Cards 💳 💳 🗾
Facilities ⓧ ⍫ ⓑ ⚲ 🍴
Location 1m S

Hotel ★★★★♨ 67% Gleddoch House Hotel,
LANGBANK ☎ 01475 540711 39 ⇆ ↾

MIDLOTHIAN

BONNYRIGG   Map 11 NT36

Broomieknowe 36 Golf Course Rd EH19 2HZ
☎ 0131 663 9317 Fax 0131 663 2152
Easy walking mature parkland course laid out by Ben Sayers
and extended by James Braid. Elevated site with excellent
views.
18 holes, 6150yds, Par 70, SSS 70, Course record 65.
Visitors must contact in advance.
Societies contact for details.
Green Fees not confirmed.
Prof Mark Patchett
Designer Ben Sayers/Hawtree
Facilities ⓧ ⍫ ⓑ ⬤ ♀ ⚲ 🍴 ⚑ ✂
Location 0.5m NE off B704

Hotel ★★★ 74% Dalhousie Castle And Spa,
Bonnyrigg, EDINBURGH
☎ 01875 820153 27 ⇆ ↾ Annexe5 ↾

DALKEITH   Map 11 NT36

Newbattle Abbey Rd EH22 3AD
☎ 0131 663 2123 & 0131 663 1819 Fax 0131 654 1810
Undulating parkland course on three levels, surrounded by
woods.
18 holes, 6025yds, Par 69, SSS 70, Course record 61.
Club membership 700.
Visitors Mon-Fri ex public holidays, before 4pm.
Societies welcome weekdays ex public holidays, before
4pm.

▶

Green Fees £27 per day; £18 per round.
Prof Scott McDonald
Designer S Colt
Facilities ⊗ 〼 🏠 🍷 ♀ ⚐ 🏚 ⛳ ✓
Location SW side of town off A68

Hotel ★★★ 74% Dalhousie Castle And Spa,
Bonnyrigg, EDINBURGH
☎ 01875 820153   27 ⇌ 🏠 Annexe5 🏠

GOREBRIDGE   Map 11 NT36

Vogrie Vogrie Estate Country Park EH23 4NU
☎ 01875 821716
A 9-hole municipal course located within a country park. The wide fairways are particularly suited to beginners.
9 holes, 2530yds, Par 33.
Visitors book by telephone 24 hrs in advance.
Green Fees not confirmed.
Facilities 🍷 ⚐
Location Off B6372

PENICUIK   Map 11 NT25

Glencorse Milton Bridge EH26 0RD
☎ 01968 677189 Fax 01968 674399
Picturesque parkland course with burn affecting ten holes. Testing 5th hole (237 yds) par 3.
18 holes, 5217yds, Par 64, SSS 66, Course record 60.
Club membership 700.

Visitors contact secretary, unable to play during club competitions
Societies contact secretary for details.
Green Fees not confirmed.
Prof Cliffe Jones
Designer Willie Park
Facilities ⊗ 〼 🏠 🍷 ♀ ⚐ 🏚 ⛳ ✓ 🍷
Location 9m S of Edinburgh on A701 Pebbles Road. 1.5m N of Penicuik on A701

Hotel ★★ 65% Roslin Glen Hotel, 2 Penicuik Rd,
ROSLIN ☎ 0131 440 2029 7 ⇌ 🏠

Entries with a green background identify courses considered to be particularly interesting

---

MORAY

BUCKIE   Map 15 NJ46

Buckpool Barhill Rd, Buckpool AB56 1DU
☎ 01542 832236 Fax 01542 832236
Links course with superlative view over Moray Firth, easy walking.
18 holes, 6257yds, Par 70, SSS 70, Course record 64.
Club membership 430.
Visitors parties please apply in advance.
Societies apply in advance.
Green Fees £20 per day; £15 per round (£25/£20 weekends).
Facilities ⊗ 〼 🏠 🍷 ♀ ⚐ ✓
& Leisure squash, snooker.
Location Off A98

Hotel ★★ 67% Mill House Hotel, Tynet, BUCKIE
☎ 01542 850233   15 ⇌ 🏠

Strathlene Portessie AB56 2DJ ☎ 01542 831798
Raised seaside links course with magnificent view. A special feature of the course is approach shots to raised greens (holes 4,5,6 & 13).
18 holes, 5980yds, Par 69, SSS 69, Course record 65.
Club membership 370.
Visitors booking essential at weekends.
Societies telephone for Mon-Fri & apply in writing for weekends.
Green Fees not confirmed.
Facilities ⊗ 🏠 🍷 ♀ ⚐ ✓
Location 2m E of Buckie on A942

Hotel ★★ 67% Mill House Hotel, Tynet, BUCKIE
☎ 01542 850233   15 ⇌ 🏠

CULLEN   Map 15 NJ56

Cullen The Links AB56 4WB ☎ 01542 840685
Fax 01542 841977 e-mail: cullengolfclub@btinternet.com
Interesting course on two levels with rocks and ravines offering some challenging holes. Spectacular scenery.
18 holes, 4610yds, Par 63, SSS 62, Course record 58.
Club membership 600.
Visitors no restrictions but during summer club medal matches given preference on Mon/Wed/Sat.
Societies advance applications advisable.
Green Fees £18 per day; £12 per round (£22/£16 weekends).
Designer Tom Morris/Charlie Neaves
Facilities ⊗ 〼 🏠 🍷 ♀ ⚐ ✓
Location 0.5m W off A98

Hotel ★★ 67% Mill House Hotel, Tynet, BUCKIE
☎ 01542 850233   15 ⇌ 🏠

DUFFTOWN   Map 15 NJ33

Dufftown Methercluny, Tomintoul Rd AB55 4BS
☎ 01340 820325 Fax 01340 820325
e-mail: marion_dufftowngolfclub@yahoo.com
A short and undulating inland course with spectacular views. Highest hole over 1200 ft above sea level.
18 holes, 5308yds, Par 67, SSS 67, Course record 64.
Club membership 250.

▶

Visitors	tee reserved Tue & Wed 4.30-6.30 & Sun 7.30-9 & 12.30-2. Prior booking recommended.
Societies	apply in writing or by telephone
Green Fees	£15 per day; £12 per round.
Cards	▨▨
Designer	Members
Facilities	⊗ by prior arrangement ⵏ by prior arrangement ⌾ ⛳ ♀ ⚲ ⚑ ⚲
Location	0.75m SW off B9009

Hotel	★★★ 76% Craigellachie Hotel, CRAIGELLACHIE ☎ 01340 881204 26 ⇔ ☽

ELGIN   Map 15 NJ26

Elgin Hardhillock, Birnie Rd, New Elgin IV30 8SX
☎ 01343 542338 Fax 01343 542341
e-mail: secretary@elgingolfclub.com
Possibly the finest inland course in the north of Scotland, with undulating greens and compact holes that demand the highest accuracy. There are thirteen par 4's and one par 5 hole on its parkland layout.
18 holes, 6163yds, Par 68, SSS 69, Course record 63.
Club membership 1000.

Visitors	must contact in advance, weekend play only by prior arrangement.
Societies	telephone secretary for details.
Green Fees	£30 per day; £24 per round.
Prof	Kevin Stables
Designer	John Macpherson
Facilities	⊗ ⵏ ⛳ ♀ ⚲ 🛍 ⚑ ⚲ ⚲
Location	1m S on A941

Hotel	★★★ 76% Mansion House Hotel, The Haugh, ELGIN ☎ 01343 548811 23 ⇔ ☽

FORRES   Map 14 NJ05

Forres Muiryshade IV36 2RD
☎ 01309 672250 Fax 01309 672250
e-mail: sandy@forresgolfclub.fsnet.co.uk
An all-year parkland course laid on light, well-drained soil in wooded countryside. Walking is easy despite some hilly holes. A test for the best golfers.
18 holes, 6240yds, Par 70, SSS 70, Course record 60.
Club membership 1000.

Visitors	welcome although club competitions take priority. Weekends may be restricted in summer.
Societies	advised to telephone 2-3 weeks in advance.
Green Fees	£19 per round;£27 per day.
Cards	▨▨
Prof	Sandy Aird
Designer	James Braid/Willie Park
Facilities	⚲ 🛍 ⚑ ⚲ ⚲ ⚲
Location	SE side of town centre off B9010

Hotel	★★★ 66% Ramnee Hotel, Victoria Rd, FORRES ☎ 01309 672410 20 ⇔ ☽

GARMOUTH   Map 15 NJ36

Garmouth & Kingston Spey St IV32 7NJ
☎ 01343 870388 Fax 01343 870388
e-mail: garmouthgolfclub@aol.com
Seaside course with several parkland holes and tidal waters. Naturally flat and suitable for the elderly.
18 holes, 5905yds, Par 69, SSS 69, Course record 66.
Club membership 560.

Visitors	must contact in advance.
Societies	advisable to phone in advance.
Green Fees	£18 per day; £16 per round (£25/£22 weekends).
Designer	George Smith
Facilities	⊗ ⵏ ⛳ ♀ ⚲ ⚑ ⚲
& Leisure	fishing.
Location	In village on B9015

Hotel	★★★ 76% Mansion House Hotel, The Haugh, ELGIN ☎ 01343 548811 23 ⇔ ☽

HOPEMAN   Map 15 NJ16

Hopeman Clubhouse IV30 5YA
☎ 01343 830578 Fax 01343 830152
e-mail: hopemangc@aol.com
Links-type course with beautiful views over the Moray Firth. The 12th hole, called the Priescach, is a short hole with a drop of 100 feet from tee to green. It can require anything from a wedge to a wood depending on the wind.
18 holes, 5590yds, Par 68, SSS 67.
Club membership 700.

Visitors	must contact in advance, restricted tee times at weekend and between 12:45-1:45 weekdays
Societies	contact in advance.
Green Fees	£13 per round(£18 weekends).
Facilities	⊗ ⵏ ⛳ ♀ ⚲ 🛍 ⚲ ⚲
Location	E side of village off B9040

Hotel	★★★ 76% Mansion House Hotel, The Haugh, ELGIN ☎ 01343 548811 23 ⇔ ☽

KEITH   Map 15 NJ45

Keith Fife Park AB55 5DF
☎ 01542 882469 Fax 01542 888176
Parkland course, with natural hazards over first 9 holes. Testing 7th hole, 232 yds, par 3.
18 holes, 5767yds, Par 69, SSS 68.
Club membership 500.

Visitors	no restrictions except competitions.
Societies	by arrangement with outings secretary (01542 886114)
Green Fees	not confirmed.
Facilities	♀ ⚲ ⚲
Location	NW side of town centre off A96, onto B9014 and first right

Hotel	★★★ 76% Craigellachie Hotel, CRAIGELLACHIE ☎ 01340 881204 26 ⇔ ☽

Looking for a driving range?
See the index at the back of the guide

Where to stay, where to eat?
Visit the AA internet site
www.theAA.com

LOSSIEMOUTH   Map 15 NJ27

Moray IV31 6QS
☎ 01343 812018 Fax 01343 815102
e-mail: secretary@moraygolf.co.uk
Two fine Scottish Championship links courses, known as
Old and New (Moray), and situated on the Moray Firth
where the weather is unusually mild.
*Old Course: 18 holes, 6643yds, Par 71, SSS 73, Course
record 65.*
*New Course: 18 holes, 6004yds, Par 69, SSS 69, Course
record 62.*
Club membership 1550.
Visitors   must contact in advance 01343 812018
                 Secretary.
Societies   Contact in advance.
Green Fees not confirmed.
Cards   ▨▨ ▨▨ ▨▨ 🌐 ▨
Prof   Alistair Thomson
Designer   Tom Morris
Facilities   ⊗ ◗Ⅲ ⓑ ▞ 𝄞 △ 🍴 ⏁ ◊
Location   N side of town

Hotel   ★★★ 76% Mansion House Hotel, The
                 Haugh, ELGIN
                 ☎ 01343 548811   23 ⇋ ♞

ROTHES   Map 15 NJ24

Rothes Blackhall AB38 7AN
☎ 01340 831443 (evenings) Fax 01340 831443
e-mail: rothesgolfclub@netscapeonline.co.uk
A hilly course on an elevated site overlooking the remains of
Rothes castle and the Spey valley. The 2nd fairway and most
of the 3rd are sheltered by woodland. The ground alongside
the 5th & 6th falls away steeply.
9 holes, 4972yds, Par 68, SSS 64.
Club membership 350.
Visitors   course reserved Mon 5-6.30 & Tue 5-
                 7.30.Telephone to confirm bookings.
Societies   apply in writing to secretary.
Green Fees £12 (£15 weekends).
Designer   John Souter
Facilities   △
Location   9m S of Elgin on A941

Hotel   ★★★ 76% Craigellachie Hotel,
                 CRAIGELLACHIE
                 ☎ 01340 881204   26 ⇋ ♞

SPEY BAY   Map 15 NJ36

Spey Bay IV32 7PJ ☎ 01343 820424
Fax 01343 829282 e-mail: info@speybay.com
Seaside links course over gently undulating banks and well-
drained ground. Good views along Moray coast. Driving
range.
18 holes, 6182yds, Par 70, SSS 69, Course record 65.
Club membership 350.
Visitors   telephone for details (especially for Sun)
Societies   book by telephone.
Green Fees £25 per round (£27 weekends).
Cards   ▨▨ ▨▨ ▨
Designer   Ben Sayers
Facilities   ⊗ ◗Ⅲ ⓑ ▞ 𝄞 △ 🍴 ⏁ ◊ ♘ ◊ ⏁
& Leisure   hard tennis courts.

Location   4.5m N of Fochabers on B9104

Hotel   ★★ 67% Mill House Hotel, Tynet, BUCKIE
                 ☎ 01542 850233   15 ⇋ ♞

NORTH AYRSHIRE

BEITH   Map 10 NS35

Beith Threewood Rd KA15 2JR
☎ 01505 503166 & 506814 Fax 01505 506814
Hilly course, with panoramic views over 7 counties.
18 holes, 5616yds, Par 68, SSS 68.
Club membership 420.
Visitors   contact for details.
Societies   apply in writing to secretary at least 1 month in
                 advance.
Green Fees not confirmed.
Designer   Members
Facilities   ⊗ ◗Ⅲ ⓑ ▞ 𝄞 △
Location   1.5m NE off A737

Hotel   ★★★ 67% Bowfield Hotel & Country Club,
                 HOWWOOD ☎ 01505 705225   23 ⇋ ♞

GREAT CUMBRAE ISLAND   Map 10 NS15
(MILLPORT)

Millport Golf Rd KA28 OHB
☎ 01475 530305 (Prof) & 530311 (Club)
Fax 01475 530306 e-mail: secretary@millportgolfclub.co.uk
Pleasantly situated on the west side of Cumbrae looking over
Bute to Arran and the Mull of Kintyre. Exposure means
conditions may vary according to wind strength and
direction. A typical seaside resort course welcoming visitors.
18 holes, 5828yds, Par 68, SSS 69, Course record 64.
Club membership 525.
Visitors   advisable to phone and book tee times especially
                 in summer months.
Societies   telephone or write in advance.
Green Fees £25 per day; £20 per round (£30/£25 weekends
                 & bank holidays).
Cards   ▨▨ ▨
Prof   William Haldane Lee
Designer   James Braid
Facilities   ⊗ ◗Ⅲ ⓑ ▞ 𝄞 △ ⏁ ◊
Location   Approx 4m from ferry slip

Hotel   ★★★ 74% Brisbane House, 14 Greenock Rd,
                 Esplanade, LARGS
                 ☎ 01475 687200   23 ⇋ ♞

IRVINE   Map 10 NS33

Glasgow Gailes KA11 5AE
☎ 0141 942 2011 Fax 0141 942 0770
e-mail: secretary@glasgow-golf.com
A lovely seaside links. The turf of the fairways and all
the greens is truly glorious and provides tireless play.
Established in 1882, and is a qualifying course for the
Open Championship.   ▶

Glasgow Gailes: 18 holes, 6539yds, Par 71, SSS 72,
Course record 63.
Club membership 1200.
Visitors prior booking through secretary reccomended, no visitors before 2.30pm Sat & Sun.
Societies initial contact by telephone.
Green Fees £50 per day; £42 per round (£55 per round weekends).
Cards ▨ ▧▧ ▨▨ ▨
Prof J Steven
Designer W Park Jnr
Facilities ⊗ ⅲ by prior arrangement ⅃ ☕ ♀ ⚑ ♠ ☂ ⚓ ✆
Location 2m S off A737

Irvine Bogside KA12 8SN ☎ 01294 275979
Testing links course; only two short holes.
18 holes, 6400yds, Par 71, SSS 73, Course record 65.
Club membership 450.
Societies are welcome weekdays and pm weekends, telephone in advance.
Green Fees not confirmed.
Prof Keith Erskine
Designer James Braid
Facilities ♠ ⚑ ✆ ⚓
Location N side of town off A737

Hotel ★★★ 75% Montgreenan Mansion House Hotel, Montgreenan Estate, KILWINNING ☎ 01294 557733 21 ⇆ ☏

Irvine Ravenspark 13 Kidsneuk Ln KA12 8SR
☎ 01294 271293
e-mail: secretary@irvine-ravenspark-golfclub.org.uk
Parkland course.
18 holes, 6702yds, Par 71, SSS 71, Course record 65.
Club membership 600.
Visitors may not play Sat before 2pm.
Societies not allowed Sat, contact club steward in advance.
Green Fees not confirmed.
Prof Peter Bond
Facilities ⊗ ⅲ ⅃ ☕ ♀ ♠ ⚑ ✆
Location N side of town on A737

Hotel ★★★ 75% Montgreenan Mansion House Hotel, Montgreenan Estate, KILWINNING ☎ 01294 557733 21 ⇆ ☏

Western Gailes Gailes by Irvine KA11 5AE
☎ 01294 311649 Fax 01294 312312
e-mail: enquiries@westerngailes.com
A magnificent seaside links with glorious turf and wonderful greens. The view is open across the Firth of Clyde to the neighbouring islands. It is a well-balanced course crossed by 3 burns. There are 2 par 5's, the 6th and 14th, and the 11th is a testing 445-yd, par 4, dog-leg.
18 holes, 6639yds, Par 71, SSS 73, Course record 65.
Visitors welcome Mon, Wed, Fri. Must contact in advance and have a handicap certificate. Limited number of times on Sundays-at discretion of clubhouse Manager.
Societies Mon/Wed/Fri, must contact in advance.

Green Fees £95 per day; £75 per round (£85 per round Sun).
Cards ▨ ▧▧ ▨▨ ▨
Facilities ⊗ ⅲ by prior arrangement ⅃ ☕ ♀ ♠ ⚓ ✆
Location 2m S off A737

Hotel ★★★ 75% Montgreenan Mansion House Hotel, Montgreenan Estate, KILWINNING ☎ 01294 557733 21 ⇆ ☏

KILBIRNIE Map 10 NS35

Kilbirnie Place Largs Rd KA25 7AT ☎ 01505 684444
Easy walking parkland course.
18 holes, 5543yds, Par 69, SSS 67, Course record 65.
Club membership 578.
Visitors must contact in advance, may not play Sat or on competition days.
Societies must apply in writing in advance.
Green Fees £12 per round, £29 per day (£18/£38 Sun).
Facilities ⊗ ⅲ ⅃ ☕ ♀ ♠
Location 1m W on A760

Hotel ★★★ 72% Priory House Hotel, Broomfields, LARGS ☎ 01475 686460 21 ⇆ ☏

LARGS Map 10 NS25

Largs Irvine Rd KA30 8EU
☎ 01475 673594 Fax 01475 673594
e-mail: secretary@largsgolfclub.co.uk
A parkland, tree-lined course with views to the Clyde coast and Arran Isles.
18 holes, 6115yds, Par 70, SSS 71, Course record 63.
Club membership 850.
Visitors may not play competition days. Other times by arrangement with secretary.
Societies apply in writing.
Green Fees £30 per round;£40 per day(£30/40 per round weekends.
Prof Kenneth Docherty
Designer H Stutt
Facilities ⊗ ⅲ ⅃ ☕ ♀ ♠ ⚑ ✆
Location 1m S of town centre on A78

Hotel ★★★ 72% Priory House Hotel, Broomfields, LARGS ☎ 01475 686460 21 ⇆ ☏

Routenburn Routenburn Rd KA30 8QA ☎ 01475 673230
18 holes, 5675yds, Par 68, SSS 68.
Location 1m N off A78
Telephone for further details

Hotel ★★ 69% Willowbank Hotel, 96 Greenock Rd, LARGS ☎ 01475 672311 675435 Fax 01475 689027 30 ⇆ ☏

SKELMORLIE Map 10 NS16

Skelmorlie Beithglass PA17 5ES ☎ 01475 520152
Parkland/moorland course with magnificent views over Firth of Clyde. Designed by James Braid.
18 holes, 5030yds, Par 65, SSS 65.
Club membership 450.

▶

Visitors no visitors before 3pm Sat.
Societies apply by telephone.
Green Fees not confirmed.
Designer James Braid
Facilities ⊗ by prior arrangement 〗Ⅲ by prior arrangement
🝙 by prior arrangement ☗ ♀ ♨ ⚲
& Leisure fishing.
Location E side of village off A78

Hotel ★★ 69% Willowbank Hotel, 96 Greenock Rd,
LARGS ☎ 01475 672311 675435
Fax 01475 689027   30 ⇔ 🐾

STEVENSTON   Map 10 NS24

Ardeer Greenhead KA20 4LB
☎ 01294 464542 & 465316 Fax 01294 465316
e-mail: peter@ardeergolfclub.netlineuk.net
Parkland course with natural hazards.
18 holes, 6401yds, Par 72, SSS 72, Course record 66.
Club membership 650.
Visitors may not play Sat.
Societies must contact in advance.
Green Fees not confirmed.
Designer Stutt
Facilities ⊗ 〗Ⅲ 🝙 ☗ ♀ ♨ 🍴 ⚲
Location 0.5m N off A78

Hotel ★★★ 75% Montgreenan Mansion House
Hotel, Montgreenan Estate, KILWINNING
☎ 01294 557733   21 ⇔ 🐾

WEST KILBRIDE   Map 10 NS24

West Kilbride 33-35 Fullerton Dr, Seamill KA23 9HT
☎ 01294 823911 Fax 01294 829573
e-mail: golf@westkilbridegolfclub.com
Seaside links course on Firth of Clyde, with fine views of
Isle of Arran from every hole.
18 holes, 5974yds, Par 70, SSS 70, Course record 63.
Club membership 840.
Visitors may not play at weekends or bank holidays,
must contact in advance.
Societies Tue & Thu only; must contact in advance.
Green Fees £27 per round(after 1.30pm);£38 per day..
Prof Graham Ross
Designer James Braid
Facilities ⊗ 〗Ⅲ 🝙 ☗ ♀ ♨ 🍴 🍴 ⚲
Location W side of town off A78

Hotel ★★★ 72% Priory House Hotel, Broomfields,
LARGS ☎ 01475 686460   21 ⇔ 🐾

AIRDRIE   Map 11 NS76

Airdrie Rochsoles ML6 0PQ ☎ 01236 762195
Picturesque parkland course with good views.
18 holes, 6004yds, Par 69, SSS 69, Course record 63.
Club membership 450.
Visitors must contact in advance. With member only
weekends & bank holidays.

Societies apply in writing.
Green Fees not confirmed.
Prof G Monks
Designer J Braid
Facilities ⊗ 〗Ⅲ 🝙 ☗ ♀ ♨ 🍴 ⚲
Location 1m N on B802

Hotel ★★★★ 66% Westerwood Hotel Golf &
Country Club, 1 St Andrews Dr, Westerwood,
CUMBERNAULD ☎ 01236 457171   49 ⇔ 🐾

Easter Moffat Mansion House, Station Rd, Plains ML6 8NP
☎ 01236 842878 Fax 01236 842904
e-mail: gordonmiller@emgc.freeserve.co.uk
Moorland/parkland course.
18 holes, 6221yds, Par 72, SSS 70, Course record 66.
Club membership 500.
Visitors may only play on weekdays.
Societies must contact in advance.
Green Fees £30 per day; £20 per round.
Prof Graham King
Facilities ⊗ 〗Ⅲ 🝙 ☗ ♀ ♨ 🍴 ⚲
Location 2m E of Airdrie on A89

Hotel ★★★★ 66% Westerwood Hotel Golf &
Country Club, 1 St Andrews Dr, Westerwood,
CUMBERNAULD ☎ 01236 457171   49 ⇔ 🐾

BELLSHILL   Map 11 NS76

Bellshill Community Rd, Orbiston ML4 2RZ
☎ 01698 745124 Fax 01698 292576
Parkland course.
18 holes, 6264yds, Par 71, SSS 70.
Club membership 500.
Visitors apply in writing in advance, may not play on
competition Sat & Sun.
Societies apply in writing in advance.
Green Fees £20 per day(£25 weekends).
Facilities ⊗ 〗Ⅲ 🝙 ☗ ♀ ♨
Location 1m SE off A721

Hotel ★★ 68% Redstones Hotel, 8-10 Glasgow Rd,
UDDINGSTON ☎ 01698 813774 & 814843
Fax 01698 815319   14 ⇔ 🐾

COATBRIDGE   Map 11 NS76

Drumpellier Drumpellier Av ML5 1RX
☎ 01236 424139 Fax 01236 428723
Parkland course.
18 holes, 6227yds, Par 71, SSS 70, Course record 60.
Club membership 827.
Visitors must contact in advance, may not play
weekends.
Societies apply in advance.
Green Fees not confirmed.
Prof David Ross
Designer W Fernie
Facilities ⊗ 〗Ⅲ 🝙 ☗ ♀ ♨ 🍴 🍴 ⚲
Location 0.75m W off A89

Hotel ★★★ 67% Bothwell Bridge Hotel, 89 Main St,
BOTHWELL ☎ 01698 852246   90 ⇔ 🐾

CUMBERNAULD   Map 11 NS77

Dullatur 1A Glen Douglas Dr G68 0DW
☎ 01236 723230 Fax 01236 727271
Dullatur Carrickstone is a parkland course, with natural hazards and wind. Dullatur Antonine, designed by Dave Thomas, is a modern course,
Carrickstone: 18 holes, 6204yds, Par 70, SSS 70, Course record 68.
Antonine: 18 holes, 5875yds, Par 69, SSS 68.
Club membership 700.
Visitors   telephone for availability.
Societies   must apply in writing to secretary.
Green Fees £20 per round;£30 per day(£25/£35 weekends).
Cards   🔲 🔲
Prof   Duncan Sinclair
Designer   James Braid
Facilities   ⊗ ⫙ 🛅 ♥ ♀ 🏖 🏠 ♦ 🏌 ♂
& Leisure   hard tennis courts, sauna, solarium, gymnasium, bowling green.
Location   1.5m N of A80 at Cumbernauld

Hotel   ★★★★ 66% Westerwood Hotel Golf & Country Club, 1 St Andrews Dr, Westerwood, CUMBERNAULD ☎ 01236 457171   49 🛏 🐾

Palacerigg Palacerigg Country Park G67 3HU
☎ 01236 734969 & 721461 Fax 01236 721461
e-mail: palacerigg-golfclub@lineone.net
Well wooded parkland course.
18 holes, 6444yds, Par 72, SSS 71, Course record 65.
Club membership 350.
Visitors   anytime except club competitions, advance booking advisable.
Societies   apply in writing to the Secretary.
Green Fees £7.90 per round;£10 per day(£10 per round weekends).
Designer   Henry Cotton
Facilities   ⊗ ⫙ 🛅 ♥ ♀ 🏖 🏠
Location   2m S of Cumbernauld on Palacerigg road off Lenziemill road B8054

Hotel   ★★★★ 66% Westerwood Hotel Golf & Country Club, 1 St Andrews Dr, Westerwood, CUMBERNAULD ☎ 01236 457171   49 🛏 🐾

Westerwood Hotel Golf & Country Club 1 St Andrews Dr, Westerwood G68 0EW
☎ 01236 725281 Fax 01236 725281
e-mail: westerwood@mortonhotels.com

Undulating parkland/woodland course designed by Dave Thomas and Seve Ballesteros. Holes meander through silver birch, firs, heaths and heathers, and the spectacular 15th,

'The Waterfall', has its green set against a 40ft rockface. Buggie track. Hotel facilities.
18 holes, 6616yds, Par 72, SSS 72, Course record 65.
Club membership 1000.
Visitors   advised to book in advance.
Societies   all bookings in advance to 01236 725281.
Green Fees not confirmed.
Cards   🔲 🔲 🔲 🔲 🔲
Prof   Alan Tait
Designer   Seve Ballesteros/Dave Thomas
Facilities   ⊗ ⫙ 🛅 ♥ ♀ 🏖 🏠 🏌 🐾 ♦ ♂ ♂ (
& Leisure   hard tennis courts, heated indoor swimming pool, solarium, gymnasium, Beauty salon.
Location   Adjacent to A80, 14m from Glasgow City Centre

Hotel   ★★★★ 66% Westerwood Hotel Golf & Country Club, 1 St Andrews Dr, Westerwood, CUMBERNAULD ☎ 01236 457171   49 🛏 🐾

GARTCOSH   Map 11 NS66

Mount Ellen Johnston Rd G69 8EY
☎ 01236 872277 Fax 01236 872249
Downland course with 73 bunkers. Testing hole: 10th ('Bedlay'), 156 yds, par 3.
18 holes, 5525yds, Par 68, SSS 67, Course record 67.
Club membership 500.
Visitors   may play Mon-Fri 9am-4pm. Must contact in advance.
Societies   must contact in advance.
Green Fees not confirmed.
Prof   Iain Bilsborough
Facilities   🛅 ♥ ♀ 🏖 🏠 🐾 ♦ ♂
Location   0.75m N off A752

Hotel   ★★★★ 72% Millennium Hotel Glasgow, George Square, GLASGOW ☎ 0141 332 6711 117 🛏 🐾

KILSYTH   Map 11 NS77

Kilsyth Lennox Tak Ma Doon Rd G65 0RS
☎ 01236 824115 Fax 01236 823089
18 holes, 5912yds, Par 70, SSS 70, Course record 66.
Location   N side of town off A803
Telephone for further details

Hotel   ★★★★ 66% Westerwood Hotel Golf & Country Club, 1 St Andrews Dr, Westerwood, CUMBERNAULD ☎ 01236 457171   49 🛏 🐾

MOTHERWELL   Map 11 NS75

Colville Park New Jerviston House, Jerviston Estate, Merry St ML1 4UG ☎ 01698 265779 (pro) Fax 01698 230418
Parkland course. First nine, tree-lined, second nine, more exposed. Testing 10th hole par 3, 16th hole par 4.
18 holes, 6250yds, Par 71, SSS 70, Course record 63.
Club membership 875.
Visitors   must contact in advance in writing. Smart dress code.
Societies   apply in writing.
Green Fees £20 per day.
Prof   John Currict
Designer   James Braid

▶

Facilities ⊗ ⫘ ⛭ ⚑ ♀ ⚤ 📖
Location 1.25m NE on A723 from Motherwell town centre

Hotel ★★★ 67% Bothwell Bridge Hotel, 89 Main St, BOTHWELL ☎ 01698 852246 90 ⇥ ⟨

MUIRHEAD   Map 11 NS66

Crow Wood Garnkirk House, Cumbernauld Rd G69 9JF
☎ 0141 779 4954 Fax 0141 779 9148
e-mail: crowwood@golfclub.golfagent.co.uk
Parkland course.
18 holes, 6261yds, Par 71, SSS 71, Course record 62.
Club membership 800.
Visitors must contact in advance but may not play weekends, bank holidays or competition days.
Societies apply in advance.
Green Fees not confirmed.
Prof Brian Moffat
Designer James Braid
Facilities ⊗ ⫘ ⛭ ⚑ ♀ ⚤ 📖 ✧
& Leisure snooker,pool.
Location 6 miles from Glasgow city centre

Hotel ★★★ 73% Malmaison, 278 West George St, GLASGOW ☎ 0141 572 1000 72 ⇥ ⟨

SHOTTS   Map 11 NS86

Shotts Blairhead ML7 5BJ
☎ 01501 822658 Fax 01501 822650
Moorland course with fine panoramic views. A good test for all abilities.
18 holes, 6205yds, Par 70, SSS 70, Course record 63.
Club membership 800.
Visitors visitors by arrangement on Sun.
Societies apply in writing.
Green Fees not confirmed.
Prof John Strachan
Designer James Braid
Facilities ⊗ ⫘ ⛭ ⚑ ♀ ⚤ 📖 ♦ ✧
Location 2m from M8 off Benhar Road

Hotel ★★★ 65% The Hilcroft Hotel, East Main St, WHITBURN ☎ 01501 740818 31 ⇥ ⟨

WISHAW   Map 11 NS75

Wishaw 55 Cleland Rd ML2 7PH
☎ 01698 372869 (Sec) & 357480 (admin)
Parkland course with many tree-lined areas. Bunkers protect 17 of the 18 greens.
18 holes, 6073yds, Par 69, SSS 69, Course record 64.
Club membership 984.
Visitors must contact secretary in advance. May not play Sat but may play alternate Sun.
Societies apply in writing.
Green Fees not confirmed.
Prof Stuart Adair
Designer James Braid
Facilities ⊗ ⫘ ⛭ ⚑ ♀ ⚤ 📖 ♦ ✧
Location NW side of town off A721

Hotel ★★★ 71% Popinjay Hotel, Lanark Rd, ROSEBANK ☎ 01555 860441 38 ⇥ ⟨

PERTH & KINROSS

ABERFELDY   Map 14 NN84

Aberfeldy Taybridge Rd PH15 2BH
☎ 01887 820535 Fax 01887 820535
e-mail: abergc@supanet.com.uk
Founded in 1895, this flat, parkland course is situated by River Tay near the famous Wade Bridge and Black Watch Monument and enjoys some splendid scenery. The new layout will test the keen golfer.
18 holes, 5283yds, Par 68, SSS 66, Course record 67.
Club membership 300.
Visitors are advised to book in advance especially at weekends.
Societies must contact in advance.
Green Fees £25 per day; £15 per round (£28/£20 weekends).
Cards ▭▭ ▭ ▨
Designer Soutars
Facilities ⊗ ⫘ ⛭ ⚑ ♀ ⚤ 📖 ⚐ ♠ ✧
Location N side of town centre

Hotel ★★⚤ 72% Guinach House Hotel, "By The Birks", Urlar Rd, ABERFELDY ☎ 01887 820251 7 ⇥ ⟨

ALYTH   Map 15 NO24

Alyth Pitcrocknie PH11 8HF
☎ 01828 632268 Fax 01828 633491
e-mail: mansec@alythgolf.freeserve.co.uk
Windy, heathland course with easy walking.
18 holes, 6205yds, Par 71, SSS 71, Course record 65.
Club membership 1000.
Visitors advance booking advisable, handicap certificate required and dress etiquette must be observed.
Societies must telephone in advance.
Green Fees not confirmed.
Prof Tom Melville
Designer James Braid
Facilities ⊗ ⫘ ⛭ ⚑ ♀ ⚤ 📖 ⚐ ♦ ♠ ✧ ⟨
Location 1m E on B954

Hotel ★★★ 61% Angus Hotel, 46 Wellmeadow, BLAIRGOWRIE ☎ 01250 872455 81 ⇥ ⟨

Strathmore Golf Centre Leroch PH11 8NZ
☎ 01828 633322 Fax 01828 633533
e-mail: enquiries@strathmoregolf.com
The Rannaleroch course is set on rolling parkland and heath with splendid views over Strathmore. The course is laid out in two loops of nine which both start and finish at the clubhouse. Among the challenging holes is the 480yard 5th with a 180yard carry over water from a high tee position (a cop out route available!). The nine hole Leitfie Links has been specially designed with beginners, juniors and older golfers in mind.
Rannaleroch Course: 18 holes, 6454yds, Par 72, SSS 72, Course record 68.
Leitfie Links: 9 holes, 1719yds, Par 29, SSS 29.
Club membership 400.
Visitors no restrictions, advised to book in advance.
Societies phone enquiry recommended.
Green Fees Rannaleroch: £30 per day; £20 per round; £11 per 9 holes (£37.50/£25/£13 weekends) Leitfie links;£8 per day(£10 weekends). ▶

Strathmore Golf Centre

Cards 🏧 💳 💳 🖊
Prof Colin Smith
Designer John Salvesen
Facilities ⊗ ⅲ ⅃ ☕ 🍴 👤 🏠 ⚐ 🚜 🔫 ⚓
Location 2m SE of Alyth, off B954 at Meigle onto A926

Hotel ★★ 73% Altamount House Hotel, Coupar
Angus Rd, BLAIRGOWRIE
☎ 01250 873512 7 ⇄ 🀫

AUCHTERARDER   Map 11 NN91

Auchterarder Orchil Rd PH3 1LS
☎ 01764 662804 (Secretary) 663711(pro)
Fax 01764 662804(sec),663711(pro)
Parkland course with easy walking.
18 holes, 5775yds, Par 69, SSS 68, Course record 61.
Club membership 765.
Visitors must contact professional/secretary in advance.
Societies must contact in advance.
Green Fees £30 per day; £20 per round (£40/£25 weekends).
Prof Gavin Baxter
Designer Ben Sayers
Facilities ⊗ ⅲ ⅃ ☕ 🍴 👤 🏠 ⚐ 🔫
Location 0.75m SW on A824

Hotel ★★★★★ The Gleneagles Hotel,
AUCHTERARDER
☎ 01764 662231 216 ⇄ 🀫

AUCHTERARDER   Map 11 NN91

AUCHTERARDER See page 379

BLAIR ATHOLL   Map 14 NN86

Blair Atholl Invertilt Rd PH18 5TG
☎ 01796 481407 Fax 01796 481292
Parkland course, river runs alongside 3 holes, easy walking.
9 holes, 5816yds, Par 70, SSS 68, Course record 65.
Club membership 460.
Visitors apply in advance to avoid competition times.
Societies apply in writing.
Green Fees not confirmed.
Designer Morriss
Facilities ⅃ ☕ 🍴 👤 ⚐ 🔫
Location 0.5m S off B8079

Hotel ★★ 70% Atholl Arms Hotel,
Old North Rd, BLAIR ATHOLL
☎ 01796 481205 30 ⇄ 🀫

BLAIRGOWRIE   Map 15 NO14

Blairgowrie Rosemount PH10 6LG
☎ 01250 872622 Fax 01250 875451
e-mail: admin@blairgowrie-golf.co.uk
Two 18-hole heathland courses, also a 9-hole course.
Rosemount Course: 18 holes, 6229yds, Par 72, SSS 73, Course record 64.
Lansdowne Course: 18 holes, 6802yds, Par 72, SSS 73, Course record 67.
Wee Course: 9 holes, 4704yds, Par 64, SSS 63.
Club membership 1550.
Visitors must contact in advance & have handicap certificate, restricted Wed, Fri & weekends.
Societies must contact in advance.
Green Fees £60 per day for all courses. Rosemount:£50 per round(£55 weekends)Lansdowne:£40 per round(£45 weekends).
Cards 🏧 💳 💳 🖊
Prof Charles Dernie
Designer J Braid/P Allis/D Thomas/Old Tom Morris
Facilities ⊗ ⅲ ⅃ ☕ 🍴 👤 🏠 ⚐ 🦢 🚜 🔫
Location Off A93 Rosemount

Hotel ★★★🍴 Kinloch House Hotel,
BLAIRGOWRIE
☎ 01250 884237 20 ⇄ 🀫

Looking for a driving range?
See the index at the back of the guide

KINLOCH HOUSE HOTEL

AA ★★★ 🌟🌟🌟

By Blairgowrie, Perthshire, PH10 6SG
Telephone: Blairgowrie (01250) 884 237 Fax: (01250) 884 333
Kinloch House is an award winning, family run, Country house hotel in the heart of
Sporting Perthshire. Located approximately 1½ hours from Glasgow, Edinburgh,
Inverness and Aberdeen, the hotel has 30 golf courses within an hour's drive,
including many Championship ones. Full drying facilities for clothes and equipment
are available, we would be delighted to help plan your golf and book your tee times.
Please write or telephone for a brochure *David and Sarah Shentall*

COMRIE
Map 11 NN72

Comrie Laggan Braes PH6 2LR ☎ 01764 670055
Scenic highland course with two tricky par 3 holes.
9 holes, 6040yds, Par 70, SSS 70, Course record 62.
Club membership 350.
Visitors apply in advance (for party bookings)
Societies must contact in advance.
Green Fees £15 per day(£20 per round weekends).
Designer Col. Williamson
Facilities ⊗ ☲ ♨ ☆ ⚑ ⚐ ⌀
& Leisure fishing.
Location E side of village off A85

Guesthouse ♦♦♦ Mossgiel Guest House, Burrell St,
COMRIE ☎ 01764 670567 3 ☞

CRIEFF
Map 11 NN82

Crieff Ferntower, Perth Rd PH7 3LR
☎ 01764 652909 Fax 01764 655096
This course is what you might call 'up and down' but the
turf is beautiful and the highland air fresh and
invigorating. There are views from the course over
Strathearn. Of the two courses the Ferntower is the more
challenging. Both parkland, the Dornock has one water
hazard.
Ferntower Course: 18 holes, 6427yds, Par 71, SSS 72,
Course record 65.
Dornock Course: 9 holes, 2372yds, Par 32.
Club membership 720.

Visitors must contact professional in advance.
Societies must contact professional in advance.
Green Fees Ferntower;£25 per round(£34
weekends)Dornock:£12 per 18 holes.
Cards ▤▤ ▰▰▱ ▨
Prof David Murchie
Designer James Braid
Facilities ⊗ �川 ㄴ ☲ ♀ ♨ 🖴 ⚑ ↘ ⚒ ⌀ ⎰
Location 0.5m NE on A85

Hotel ★★ 65% Locke's Acre Hotel, 7 Comrie
Rd, CRIEFF ☎ 01764 652526 7rm(4 ☞)

AA Hotels that have special
arrangements with golf courses are listed at
the back of the guide

DUNKELD
Map 11 NO04

Dunkeld & Birnam Fungarth PH8 0HU
☎ 01350 727524 Fax 01350 728660
Interesting heathland course with spectacular views of
surrounding countryside.
18 holes, 5508yds, Par 70, SSS 67.
Club membership 500.
Visitors must contact in advance at weekends,public
holidays,or large parties during the week.
Societies apply in writing/telephone.
Green Fees £25 per day; £18 per round (£30/£21 weekends
& bank holidays).
Designer D A Tod
Facilities ⊗ 川 ㄴ ☲ ♀ ♨ 🖴 ⚑ ⌀
Location 1m N of village on A923

Hotel ★★★★♨♨ Kinnaird, Kinnaird Estate,
DUNKELD ☎ 01796 482440 9 ⇄ ☞

DUNNING
Map 11 NO01

Dunning Rollo Park PH2 0RH ☎ 01764 684747
Parkland course with a series of stone built bridges crossing a
burn meandering over a large part of the course.
9 holes, 4836yds, Par 66, SSS 63, Course record 62.
Club membership 580.
Visitors Gents competitions Saturday, Ladies Tue, other
than that no restrictions.
Societies must contact in advance in writing.
Green Fees £14 per 18 holes.
Facilities ☲ ♨
Location 1.5m off A9, 4m N of Auchterarder

Hotel ★★★ 68% Lovat Hotel, 90 Glasgow Rd,
PERTH ☎ 01738 636555 30 ⇄ ☞

Whitemoss Whitemoss Rd PH2 0QX
☎ 01738 730300 Fax 01738 730300
18 holes, 5595yds, Par 68, SSS 68, Course record 63.
Location Turn off A9 at Whitemoss Road junct, 3m N of
Gleneagles
Telephone for further details

Hotel ★★ 77% Cairn Lodge, Orchil Rd,
AUCHTERARDER
☎ 01764 662634 & 662431
Fax 01764 664866 11 ⇄ ☞

The Gleneagles Hotel

uchterarder, *Perth & Kinross*   ☎ 01764 662231 Fax 01764 662134   Map 11 NN91

e-mail: resort.sales@gleneagles.com

he Monarch's Course, designed by Jack Nicklaus and launched in style in May 1993, boasts an American/Scottish layout with many water hazards, elevated tees and raised ontoured greens. The King's Course with its abundance of eather, gorse, raised greens and plateau tees, is set within the alley of Strathearn with the Grampian mountains spectacularly in iew to the north. The shorter Queen's course, with its Scots Pine ned fairways and water hazards, is set within a softer landscape nd considered an easier test of golf.

You can improve your game at The Golf Academy at Gleneagles, /here the philosophy is that golf should be fun and fun in golf omes from playing better. Other pursuits on offer include horse- ding, carriage-driving, shooting, fishing, falconry and purpose- uilt 4x4 off-road courses.

Visitors advance booking essential, 8 weeks notice. Full payment in advance is required to secure fee times.
Societies contact for details. Full payment in advance is required to secure fee times.
Green Fees Visitors £75-£100, reductions for residents.
Facilities ⊗ ⟩�𝕀⅃ ᒪ ♥ ♀ ⚲ 🏠 ⓕ ⅄ 🛥 ♫ (
Golf Academy
Leisure tennis, squash, swimming, sauna, solarium, gymnasium, riding, shooting, fishing
Location Auchterarder PH3 1NF (2m SW of A823)
Holes/Par/Course record 63 holes.
Kings: 18 holes, 6471 yds, Par 70, SSS 73 Course Rec 60
Queens: 18 holes, 5965 yds, Par 68, SSS 70 Course Rec 62
Monarch: 18 holes, 6551 yds, Par 72, SSS 73 Course Rec 63

Championship Course

WHERE TO STAY NEARBY

Hotels
AUCHTERARDER

★★★★★⊛⊛ The Gleneagles Hotel
☎ 01764 662231. 216 ⇆ ℟

★★★⊛⊛ ▲▲ 81%
Auchterarder House
☎ 01764 663646. 15 ⇆ ℟

★★⊛⊛ 77%
Cairn Lodge, Orchil Rd
☎ 01764 662634.
11 (8 ⇆ ℟ 3 ℟)

GLENSHEE (SPITTAL OF)   Map 15 NO16

Dalmunzie Dalmunzie Estate PH10 7QG ☎ 01250 885226
Fax 01250 885225 e-mail: dalmunzie@aol.com
Well maintained Highland course with difficult walking.
Testing short course with small but good greens.
9 holes, 2099yds, Par 30, SSS 30.
Club membership 78.
Visitors   restricted Sun 10.30-11.30am.
Societies   advance contact preferred.
Green Fees £10.50 per day.
Designer   Alistair Campbell
Facilities   ⊗ ⅷ ᴸ ♨ ᵀ ⌂
& Leisure   hard tennis courts, fishing.
Location   2m NW of Spittal of Glenshee

Hotel   ★★♨♨ 69% Dalmunzie House Hotel,
                  SPITTAL OF GLENSHEE
                  ☎ 01250 885224 18rm(16 ⇄ 🐾)

KENMORE   Map 14 NN74

Kenmore PH15 2HN ☎ 01887 830226 Fax 01887 830211
e-mail: golf@taymouth.co.uk
Testing course in mildly undulating natural terrain. Beautiful
views in tranquil setting by Loch Tay.
9 holes, 6052yds, Par 70, SSS 69, Course record 69.
Club membership 200.
Visitors   advance booking advisable.
Societies   telephone in advance.
Green Fees £13 per 18 holes; £9 per 9 holes;£17 per day
                  (£14/£10/£18 weekends).
Cards   ══ ══
Designer   Robin Menzies
Facilities   ⊗ ⅷ ᴸ ♨ ♀ ᴧ ⌂ ᵀ ⌂ ⦆ ⛏ ⋌
& Leisure   fishing.
Location   On A827, beside Kenmore Bridge

Hotel   ★★★ 66% Kenmore Hotel, The Square,
                  KENMORE ☎ 01887 830205
                  27 ⇄ 🐾 Annexe15 ⇄ 🐾

Taymouth Castle Taymouth Castle Estate PH15 2NT
☎ 01887 830228 Fax 01887 830830 e-
mail: taymouth@fishingnet.com
Parkland course set amidst beautiful mountain and loch
scenery. Easy walking. Fishing.
18 holes, 6066yds, Par 69, SSS 69, Course record 62.
Club membership 250.
Visitors   parties must book in advance to avoid busy
                  times.
Societies   should contact in advance.
Green Fees not confirmed.
Prof   Alex Marshall
Designer   James Braid
Facilities   ⊗ ⅷ ᴸ ♨ ♀ ᴧ ⌂ ᵀ ⌂ ⦆ ⛏ ⋌
& Leisure   hard tennis courts, fishing.
Location   1m E on A827, 5m W of Aberfeldy

Hotel   ★★★ 66% Kenmore Hotel, The Square,
                  KENMORE ☎ 01887 830205
                  27 ⇄ 🐾 Annexe15 ⇄ 🐾

KINROSS   Map 11 NO10

Green Hotel 2 The Muirs KY13 8AS
☎ 01577 863407 Fax 01577 863180 e-mail: golf@green-
hotel.com
Two interesting and picturesque parkland courses, with easy
walking.
Red Course: 18 holes, 6256yds, Par 73, SSS 71.
Blue Course: 18 holes, 6438yds, Par 72, SSS 72.
Club membership 600.
Visitors   Large parties should contact in advance.
Societies   must contact in advance.
Green Fees £27 per day, £17 per round (£37/27 weekends).
Cards   ══ ══ ══ ⓪
Prof   Stuart Geraghty
Designer   Sir David Montgomery
Facilities   ⊗ ⅷ ᴸ ♨ ♀ ᴧ ⌂ ᵀ ⌂ ⦆ ⋌
& Leisure   hard tennis courts, heated indoor swimming
                  pool, squash, fishing, sauna, 4 sheet curling
                  rink..
Location   NE side of town on B996

Hotel   ★★★ 73% Green Hotel, 2 The Muirs,
                  KINROSS ☎ 01577 863467 46 ⇄ 🐾

MILNATHORT   Map 11 NO10

Milnathort South St KY13 9XA ☎ 01577 864069 e-
mail: milnathortgolf@ukgateway.net
Undulating inland course with lush fairways and excellent
greens for most of the year. Strategically placed copses of
trees require accurate tee shots. Different tees and greens for
some holes will make for more interesting play.   ▶

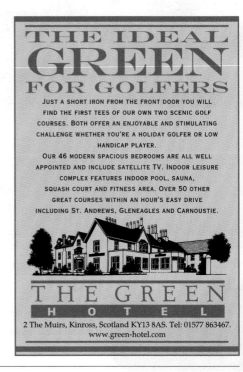

THE IDEAL
GREEN
FOR GOLFERS

JUST A SHORT IRON FROM THE FRONT DOOR YOU WILL
FIND THE FIRST TEES OF OUR OWN TWO SCENIC GOLF
COURSES. BOTH OFFER AN ENJOYABLE AND STIMULATING
CHALLENGE WHETHER YOU'RE A HOLIDAY GOLFER OR LOW
HANDICAP PLAYER.
OUR 46 MODERN SPACIOUS BEDROOMS ARE ALL WELL
APPOINTED AND INCLUDE SATELLITE TV. INDOOR LEISURE
COMPLEX FEATURES INDOOR POOL, SAUNA,
SQUASH COURT AND FITNESS AREA. OVER 50 OTHER
GREAT COURSES WITHIN AN HOUR'S EASY DRIVE
INCLUDING ST. ANDREWS, GLENEAGLES AND CARNOUSTIE.

THE GREEN
H O T E L

2 The Muirs, Kinross, Scotland KY13 8AS. Tel: 01577 863467.
www.green-hotel.com

9 holes, 5969yds, Par 71, SSS 69, Course record 65.
Club membership 575.
Visitors   no restrictions.
Societies   advisable to book in advance.
Green Fees £18 per day; £12 per round (£20/£14 weekends).
Facilities ⊗ ⫼ by prior arrangement ⅃ ♨ ♀ ⚲
Location   S side of town on A922

Hotel   ★★ 67% The Glenfarg Hotel & Restaurant,
Main St, GLENFARG
☎ 01577 830241 17rm(16 ⇄ ℟)

MUTHILL   Map 11 NN81

Muthill Peat Rd PH5 2DA
☎ 01764 681523 Fax 01764 681557
e-mail: muthillgolf@lineone.net
Parkland course with fine views. Not too hilly, narrow
fairways and small well bunkered greens.
9 holes, 4700yds, Par 66, SSS 63, Course record 61.
Club membership 420.
Visitors   no restrictions.
Societies   book in advance.
Green Fees £15 per round; £10 per 9 holes (£16 per round
weekends).
Designer Members
Facilities ⊗ ⫼ ⅃ ♨ ⚲ ⏻ ⚘
Location   W side of village off A822

Hotel   ★★ 65% Locke's Acre Hotel, 7 Comrie Rd,
CRIEFF ☎ 01764 652526 7rm(4 ℟)

PERTH   Map 11 NO12

Craigie Hill Cherrybank PH2 0NE
☎ 01738 620829 & 622644 Fax 01738 620829
Slightly hilly, parkland course. Good views over Perth.
18 holes, 5386yds, Par 66, SSS 67, Course record 60.
Club membership 600.
Visitors   no access Sat. Telephone up to 3 days in
advance.
Societies   must contact in writing.May not play on
Saturdays.
Green Fees £30 per day; £18 per round (£30/£25 Sun).
Prof   Ian Muir
Designer Fernie/Anderson
Facilities ⊗ ⫼ ⅃ ♨ ♀ ⚲ ⏻ ⚘ ⚘
Location   1m SW of city centre off A952

Hotel   ★★★ 67% Queens Hotel, Leonard St, PERTH
☎ 01738 442222 51 ⇄ ℟

King James VI Moncreiffe Island PH2 8NR
☎ 01738 445132 (Secretary) Fax 01738 445132
Parkland course, situated on island in the middle of River
Tay. Easy walking.
18 holes, 6038yds, Par 70, SSS 69, Course record 62.
Club membership 650.
Visitors   visitors restricted on competition days. Must
contact professional in advance for bookings.
May not play Sat.
Societies   book by telephone.
Green Fees not confirmed.
Prof   Andrew Crerar
Designer Tom Morris
Facilities ⊗ ⅃ ♨ ♀ ⚲ ⏻ ⚘ ⚘
Location   SE side of city centre

Hotel   ★★★ 67% Queens Hotel, Leonard St, PERTH
☎ 01738 442222 51 ⇄ ℟

Murrayshall Country House Hotel Murrayshall, Scone
PH2 7PH ☎ 01738 552784 & 551171 Fax 01738 552595
Set within 350 acres of undulating parkland, Murrayshall
now offers 36 holes of outstanding golf. The original
championship course is set out within the the parkland estate
and the Lyndoch is a woodland style course full of natural
features. Many of the fairways are lined by majestic tall trees
whilst white sand bunkers and water hazards, with natural
stone bridges, protect the generous greens.
Murrayshall Course: 18 holes, 6441yds, Par 73, SSS 72.
Lyndoch Course: 18 holes, 5800yds, Par 69.
Club membership 350.
Visitors   telephone in advance.
Societies   telephone in advance.
Green Fees not confirmed.
Cards   ⬛ ⬛ ⬛ ⬛ ⬛ ⬛
Prof   Alan Reid
Designer Hamilton Stutt
Facilities ⊗ ⫼ ⅃ ♨ ♀ ⚲ ⏻ ⚘ ⚘ ⚘ ⚘ ⚘
& Leisure hard tennis courts, sauna, gymnasium.
Location   E side of village off A94

Hotel   ★★★ 76% Murrayshall Country House Hotel
& Golf Course, New Scone, PERTH
☎ 01738 551171 27 ⇄ ℟ Annexe14 ⇄ ℟

North Inch North Inch, off Hay St PH1 5PH
☎ 01738 636481
An enjoyable short and often testing course incorporating
mature trees, open parkland with fine views and attractive
riverside. ▶

18 holes, 5401yds, Par 65.
Club membership 476.
Visitors advisable to telephone in advance.
Societies apply in writing.
Green Fees not confirmed.
Designer Tom Morris
Facilities ⊗ ⅢⅢ 🝖 💺 ♀ 🛆 ∂
& Leisure squash, gymnasium.
Location N of City

Hotel ★★★ 67% Queens Hotel, Leonard St, PERTH
☎ 01738 442222 51 ⇄ 🝖

PITLOCHRY   Map 14 NN95

Pitlochry PH16 5QY
☎ 01796 472792 Fax 01796 473599
A varied and interesting heathland course with fine
views and posing many problems. Its SSS permits few
errors in its achievement.
18 holes, 5811yds, Par 69, SSS 69, Course record 63.
Club membership 500.
Visitors Must book times in advance.
Societies must contact in advance.
Green Fees £26 per day, £18 per round (£32/£21
weekends).
Cards 🖃 ▨ ▨ 🖭
Prof George Hampton
Designer Willy Fernie
Facilities ⊗ 💺 💺 ♀ 🛆 🏠 🍴 🐾 ∂
Location N side of town off A924

Hotel ★★★ 76% Pine Trees Hotel, Strathview
Ter, PITLOCHRY
☎ 01796 472121 19 ⇄ 🝖

ST FILLANS   Map 11 NN62

St Fillans South Loch Earn Rd PH6 2NJ ☎ 01764 685312
Fairly flat, beautiful parkland course. Beside the river Earn
and set amongst the Perthshire hills. Wonderfully rich in
flora, animal and bird life.
9 holes, 5896yds, Par 68, SSS 67, Course record 73.
Club membership 400.
Visitors advisable to contact in advance.
Societies Apr-Oct, apply to starter.
Green Fees not confirmed.
Designer W Auchterlonie
Facilities ⊗ ⅢⅢ 💺 💺 🛆 🍴 🐾 🐦 ∂
Location E side of village off A85

Hotel ★★★ 67% The Four Seasons Hotel, Loch
Earn, ST FILLANS
☎ 01764 685333 12 ⇄ 🝖 Annexe6 ⇄ 🝖

STRATHTAY   Map 14 NN95

Strathtay Lyon Cottage PH9 0PG ☎ 01887 840211
A wooded mainly hilly course with pleasing panoramic
views. 5th hole 'Spion Kop' is especially difficult. It is steep,
with heavy rough on both sides of the hilly fairway and an
unsighted green on the back of the hill which is affected by
winds.
9 holes, 4082yds, Par 63, SSS 63, Course record 61.
Club membership 260.

Visitors restricted May-Sep; Sun 12.30-5pm & Mon 6-
8pm. Also some Wed & Thu evenings.
Societies in writing/telephone Secretary.
Green Fees not confirmed.
Facilities 🛆
Location Eastern end of minor rd to Weem, off A827

Hotel ★★🏅 72% Guinach House Hotel, "By The
Birks", Urlar Rd, ABERFELDY
☎ 01887 820251 7 ⇄ 🝖

RENFREWSHIRE

BISHOPTON   Map 10 NS47

Erskine PA7 5PH ☎ 01505 862302
Parkland course.
18 holes, 6287yds, Par 71, SSS 70.
Club membership 700.
Visitors introduced by member or by prior arrangement.
Societies apply in writing.
Green Fees not confirmed.
Prof Peter Thomson
Facilities ⊗ ⅢⅢ 💺 💺 ♀ 🛆 🏠 🚜 ∂
Location 0.75 NE off B815

Hotel ★★★ 66% The Erskine Bridge Hotel, North
Barr, ERSKINE ☎ 0141 812 0123 177 ⇄ 🝖

BRIDGE OF WEIR   Map 10 NS36

Ranfurly Castle The Clubhouse, Golf Rd PA11 3HN
☎ 01505 612609 Fax 01505 610406
e-mail: ranfurlycastle@lineone.net
A highly challenging, 240 acre, picturesque moorland course.
18 holes, 6284yds, Par 70, SSS 71, Course record 65.
Club membership 825.
Visitors golf club members on weekdays only.
Societies Tue only, apply in writing.
Green Fees not confirmed.
Prof Tom Eckford
Designer A Kirkcaldy/W Auchterlomie
Facilities ⊗ ⅢⅢ 💺 💺 ♀ 🛆 🏠 🍴 🚜 ∂
Location 5m NW of Johnstone

Hotel ★★★ 67% Bowfield Hotel & Country Club,
HOWWOOD ☎ 01505 705225 23 ⇄ 🝖

JOHNSTONE   Map 10 NS46

Cochrane Castle Scott Av, Craigston PA5 0HF
☎ 01505 320146 Fax 01505 325338
Fairly hilly parkland course,wooded with two small streams
running through it.
18 holes, 6223yds, Par 71, SSS 71, Course record 65.
Club membership 721.
Visitors contact professional for booking, may play at
weekends if introduced by a member.
Societies apply in writing.
Green Fees £30 per day; £22per round.
Prof Jason Boyd
Designer J Hunter

▶

Facilities ⊗ ⍲ ⓑ ♥ ♀ ⚐ ⛢ ✐
Location 1m from Johnstone town centre, off Beith Rd

Hotel ★★★ 69% Lynnhurst Hotel, Park Rd, JOHNSTONE ☎ 01505 324331 & 324600 Fax 01505 324219 21 ⇋ ♙

Elderslie 63 Main Rd, Elderslie PA5 9AZ
☎ 01505 323956 Fax 01505 340346
e-mail: anneanderson@eldersliegolfclub.freeserve.co.uk
Parkland course, undulating, with good views.
18 holes, 6175yds, Par 70, SSS 70, Course record 61.
Club membership 940.
Visitors may not play at weekends & bank holidays. Must contact club in advance and preferably have a handicap certificate.
Societies must telephone in advance.
Green Fees not confirmed.
Prof Richard Bowman
Designer J Braid
Facilities ⊗ ⍲ ⓑ ♥ ♀ ⚐ ⛢ ✎ ✐
Location E side of town on A737

Hotel ★★★ 69% Lynnhurst Hotel, Park Rd, JOHNSTONE ☎ 01505 324331 & 324600 Fax 01505 324219 21 ⇋ ♙

LANGBANK   Map 10 NS37

Gleddoch Golf and Country Club PA14 6YE
☎ 01475 540304 Fax 01475 540201
Parkland and heathland course with other sporting facilities available to temporary members. Good views over Firth of Clyde.
18 holes, 6330yds, Par 71, SSS 71, Course record 64.
Club membership 600.
Visitors must contact in advance.
Societies must contact in advance.
Green Fees From £30 per round.
Cards 💳 💳 💳 📇
Prof Keith Campbell
Designer Hamilton Strutt
Facilities ⊗ ⍲ ⓑ ♥ ♀ ⚐ ⛢ ✎ ✐ ✐ ⛏ ✐
& Leisure heated indoor swimming pool.
Location B789-Old Greenock Road

Hotel ★★★★♨ 67% Gleddoch House Hotel, LANGBANK ☎ 01475 540711 39 ⇋ ♙

LOCHWINNOCH   Map 10 NS35

Lochwinnoch Burnfoot Rd PA12 4AN
☎ 01505 842153 & 01505 843029 Fax 01505 843668
18 holes, 6243yds, Par 71, SSS 71, Course record 63.
Location W side of town off A760, between Johnstone & Beith, off A737 on Largs road A760
Telephone for further details

Hotel ★★★ 67% Bowfield Hotel & Country Club, HOWWOOD ☎ 01505 705225 23 ⇋ ♙

PAISLEY   Map 11 NS46

Barshaw Barshaw Park PA1 3TJ ☎ 0141 889 2908
Municipal parkland course.
18 holes, 5703yds, Par 68, SSS 67, Course record 63.
Club membership 100.

Visitors no restrictions.
Societies by prior arrangement with Parks Manager, Renfrewshire Council, Enviorment House, Bridge Street, Paisley PA3 2AB.
Green Fees £8 per round.
Designer J R Stutt
Facilities ⚐ ✐
Location 1m E off A737

Hotel ★★★ 69% Glynhill Hotel & Leisure Club, Paisley Rd, RENFREW ☎ 0141 886 5555 & 885 1111 Fax 0141 885 2838 125 ⇋ ♙

Paisley Braehead PA2 8TZ
☎ 0141 884 3903 884 4114 Fax 0141 884 3903
e-mail: paisleygc@onetel.net.uk
Moorland course with good views, which suits all handicaps. The course has been designed in two loops of nine holes. Holes feature trees and gorse.
18 holes, 6215yds, Par 71, SSS 72.
Club membership 850.
Visitors must have handicap certificate. May not play weekends or public holidays, or after 4pm weekdays.
Societies handicaps certificate essential. Groups over 12 must apply in writing, smaller groups may phone in advance.
Green Fees £32 per day; £24 per round.
Prof Gordon Stewart
Facilities ⊗ ⍲ ⓑ ♥ ♀ ⚐ ⛢ ✎ ✐
Location S side of town off B774

Hotel ★★★ 69% Glynhill Hotel & Leisure Club, Paisley Rd, RENFREW ☎ 0141 886 5555 & 885 1111 Fax 0141 885 2838 125 ⇋ ♙

Ralston Strathmore Av, Ralston PA1 3DT
☎ 0141 882 1349 Fax 0141 883 9837
Parkland course.
18 holes, 6071yds, Par 71, SSS 69, Course record 62.
Club membership 750.
Visitors Mon-Fri only and must be accompanied by member.
Societies written notice required
Green Fees not confirmed.
Cards 💳 💳 📇
Prof Colin Munro
Designer J Braid
Facilities ⊗ ⍲ ⓑ ♥ ♀ ⚐ ⛢ ✐
Location 2m E off A737

Hotel ★★★ 68% Swallow Hotel, 517 Paisley Rd West, GLASGOW ☎ 0141 427 3146 117 ⇋ ♙

RENFREW   Map 11 NS46

Renfrew Blythswood Estate, Inchinnan Rd PA4 9EG
☎ 0141 886 6692 Fax 0141 886 1808
e-mail: secretary@renfrew.scottishgolf.com
Tree-lined parkland course.
18 holes, 6818yds, Par 72, SSS 73, Course record 65.
Club membership 800.
Visitors restricted to Mon, Tue & Thu, apply in advance.
Societies apply in writing in advance.
Green Fees £35 per day; £25 per round.   ▶

Designer Commander Harris
Facilities ⊗ �川 ㄥ ☕ ♀ ⚑ 📱 ✓
Location 0.75m W off A8

Hotel ★★★ 69% Glynhill Hotel & Leisure Club,
Paisley Rd, RENFREW
☎ 0141 886 5555 & 885 1111
Fax 0141 885 2838 125 ⇆ ↱

SCOTTISH BORDERS

COLDSTREAM   Map 12 NT83

Hirsel Kelso Rd TD12 4NJ
☎ 01890 882678 & 882233 Fax 01890 882233
18 holes, 6092yds, Par 70, SSS 70, Course record 65.
Location At W end of Coldstream on A697
Telephone for further details

Hotel ★★★♨ 71% Tillmouth Park Country House
Hotel, CORNHILL-ON-TWEED
☎ 01890 882255 12 ⇆ ↱ Annexe2 ⇆ ↱

DUNS   Map 12 NT75

Duns Hardens Rd TD11 3NR
☎ 01361 882717 (Sec) & 882194 (Clubhouse)
e-mail: aeccduns@btinternet.com
Interesting upland course, with natural hazards of water and
hilly slopes. Views south to the Cheviot Hills. A burn comes
into play at 7 of the holes.
18 holes, 6209yds, Par 70, SSS 70.
Club membership 520.
Visitors welcome except competition days and Mon, Tue
and Wed after 4pm. Advisable to contact in
advance Apr-Oct.
Societies write or telephone the secretary in advance for
booking details.
Green Fees £19 per day; £16 per round (£24/£19 weekends).
Designer A H Scott
Facilities ⊗ �川 ㄥ ☕ ♀ ⚑ ✓
Location 1m W off A6105

Hotel ★★★ 66% Marshall Meadows Country House
Hotel, BERWICK-UPON-TWEED
☎ 01289 331133 19 ⇆ ↱

EYEMOUTH   Map 12 NT96

Eyemouth Gunsgreen Hill TD14 5SF
☎ 01890 750551 & 750004 (Starter)
e-mail: eyemouth@globalnet.co.uk
A superb course set on the East Berwickshire coast,
containing interesting and challenging holes. The clubhouse
overlooks the picturesque fishing village of Eyemouth and
provides panoramic views over the course and North Sea.
18 holes, 6520yds, Par 72, SSS 72, Course record 66.
Club membership 400.
Visitors May play at any time by arrangement.Some
competition restrictions on saturday & sunday
mornings.Telephone pro shop.
Societies apply in writing or telephone.

Green Fees £28 per day; £20 per 18 holes (£35/£25
weekends).
Cards 🖃 ■ 🖃 💳
Prof Paul Terras, Tony McLeman
Designer J R Bain
Facilities ⊗ ㄥ ☕ ♀ ⚑ 🏠 ✈ ↘ ✓
Location E side of town, 8m N of Berwick and 2m off A1

Hotel ★★★ 66% Marshall Meadows Country House
Hotel, BERWICK-UPON-TWEED
☎ 01289 331133 19 ⇆ ↱

GALASHIELS   Map 12 NT43

Galashiels Ladhope Recreation Ground TD1 2NJ
☎ 01896 753724
Hillside course, superb views from the top; 10th hole very
steep.
18 holes, 5185yds, Par 67, SSS 66, Course record 61.
Club membership 311.
Visitors must contact the secretary in advance especially
for weekends.
Societies arrangements with secretary especially for
weekends.
Green Fees not confirmed.
Designer James Braid
Facilities ⊗ by prior arrangement �川 by prior arrangement
ㄥ by prior arrangement ☕ by prior
arrangement ⚑ ✓
Location N side of town centre off A7

Hotel ★★★ 66% Kingsknowes Hotel, Selkirk Rd,
GALASHIELS ☎ 01896 758375 11 ⇆ ↱

Torwoodlee Edinburgh Rd TD1 2NE ☎ 01896 752260
Parkland course with natural hazards designed by Willie Park
with a new extension by John Garner, provides a good test
for all abilities of play.
18 holes, 6200yds, Par 70, SSS 69, Course record 68.
Club membership 550.
Visitors restricted Thu - ladies day and Sat - mens
competitions.
Societies letter to secretary.
Green Fees £27 per day; £20 per round (£30/£25 weekends).
Cards 🖃 🖃 💳
Prof R Elliot
Designer Willie Park
Facilities ⊗ �川 ㄥ ☕ ♀ ⚑ 🏠 ↘ ⚓ ✓
Location 1.75m NW off A7

Hotel ★★★ 66% Kingsknowes Hotel, Selkirk Rd,
GALASHIELS ☎ 01896 758375 11 ⇆ ↱

HAWICK   Map 12 NT51

Hawick Vertish Hill TD9 0NY ☎ 01450 372293
Hill course with good views.
18 holes, 5929yds, Par 68, SSS 69, Course record 63.
Club membership 600.
Visitors must contact in advance. Course busy Sat until
3pm. 1st tee off time for visitors on Sun
10.30pm.
Societies write or telephone for booking arrangement.
Green Fees £26 per day; £21 per round.
Facilities ⊗ �川 ㄥ ☕ ♀ ⚑ 🏠 ✓
Location SW side of town

▶

Hotel   ★★ 66% Kirklands Hotel, West Stewart Place, HAWICK ☎ 01450 372263 5 ⇄ ☏

INNERLEITHEN   Map 11 NT33

Innerleithen Leithen Water, Leithen Rd EH44 6NL
☎ 01896 830951
Moorland course, with easy walking. Burns and rivers are natural hazards. Testing 5th hole (100 yds) par 3.
9 holes, 6066yds, Par 70, SSS 69, Course record 65.
Club membership 280.
Visitors advisable to check for availability for weekends.
Societies by prior booking.
Green Fees not confirmed.
Designer Willie Park
Facilities ⓑ ☕ ♀ △
Location 1.5m N on B709

Hotel   ★★★ 73% Peebles Hydro Hotel, PEEBLES ☎ 01721 720602 133 ⇄ ☏

JEDBURGH   Map 12 NT62

Jedburgh Dunion Rd TD8 6DQ
☎ 01835 863587 & 862360
Undulating parkland course, windy, with young trees.
9 holes, 5760yds, Par 68, SSS 67, Course record 62.
Club membership 320.
Visitors weekend restrictions.Weekdays prior to 6pm.
Societies must contact at least one month in advance.
Green Fees £16 per round/day.
Designer William Park
Facilities ⓧ ⫟ ⓑ ☕ ♀ △ ⛏
Location 1m W on B6358

Hotel   ★★ 66% Kirklands Hotel, West Stewart Place, HAWICK ☎ 01450 372263 5 ⇄ ☏

KELSO   Map 12 NT73

Kelso Racecourse Rd TD5 7SL ☎ 01573 223009
Parkland course. Easy walking.
18 holes, 6046yds, Par 70, SSS 69, Course record 64.
Club membership 500.
Visitors advisable to telephone in advance.
Societies apply in writing.
Green Fees not confirmed.
Designer James Braid
Facilities ⓧ ⫟ ⓑ ☕ ♀ △ 🍴 ⛏ ⌁
Location N side of town centre off B6461

Hotel   ★★★ 63% Cross Keys Hotel, 36-37 The Square, KELSO ☎ 01573 223303 27 ⇄ ☏

Roxburghe Heiton TD5 8JZ
☎ 01573 450333 Fax 01573 450611
e-mail: golf@roxburghe.net
Opened in 1996 and designed by Dave Thomas, this undulating course is set in 200 acres of mature parkland. Deep challenging bunkers, rolling greens and dramatic water hazards, including the River Teviot, provide a good test for all golfing abilities.
Roxburghe Golf Course: 18 holes, 6925yds, Par 72, SSS 74, Course record 66.
Club membership 310.

Visitors dress code (smart casual, no jeans, no training shoes).
Societies please telephone in advance, a number of packages available.
Green Fees £60 per day, £40 per round.
Cards 🪙 ▆▆ 🟦 📇 🎴 🍎
Prof Gordon Niven
Designer Dave Thomas
Facilities ⓧ ⫟ ⓑ ☕ ♀ △ 🏠 🍴 🏡 ⛏ ⌁ ⌁
& Leisure hard tennis courts, fishing, Clay pigeon shooting,falconry,archery,health & beauty suite.
Location 5m E of Jedburgh on A698, 2m W of Kelso on A698

Hotel   ★★★⛳ 74% The Roxburghe Hotel & Golf Course, Heiton, KELSO ☎ 01573 450331 16 ⇄ ☏ Annexe6 ⇄ ☏

LAUDER   Map 12 NT54

Lauder Galashiels Rd TD2 6RS ☎ 01578 722240
e-mail: laudergc@aol.com
Inland course and practice area on gently sloping hill with stunning views of the Lauderdale district.
9 holes, 3001yds, Par 72, SSS 69, Course record 66.
Club membership 350.
Visitors restricted Wed 4.30-5.30pm and Sun before noon.
Societies telephone in advance.
Green Fees £10 per day.
Designer Willie Park Jnr
Facilities △
Location On Galashiels Rd, off A68, 0.5m from Lauder ▶

Hotel   ★★ 68% Lauderdale Hotel, 1 Edinburgh Rd,
LAUDER ☎ 01578 722231 9 ➡ ✦

MELROSE   Map 12 NT53

Melrose Dingleton TD6 9HS ☎ 01896 822855
Undulating tree-lined fairways with spendid views. Many
bunkers.
9 holes, 5579yds, Par 70, SSS 68, Course record 61.
Club membership 380.
Visitors   competitions all Sats and many Suns Apr-Oct,
ladies priority Tue, junior priority Wed am in
holidays.
Societies   apply in writing.
Green Fees not confirmed.
Designer   James Braid
Facilities ⊗ by prior arrangement ⫶ by prior arrangement
⬓ by prior arrangement ⧈ ⌂
Location   Off A68, S side of town centre on B6359

Hotel   ★★★ 66% Burt's Hotel, The Square,
MELROSE ☎ 01896 822285 20 ➡ ✦

MINTO   Map 12 NT52

Minto TD9 8SH ☎ 01450 870220 Fax 01450 870126
e-mail: mintogolfclub.freeserve.co.uk
Pleasant, undulating parkland course featuring mature trees
and panoramic views of Scottish Border country. Short but
quite testing.
18 holes, 5542yds, Par 69, SSS 67, Course record 63.
Club membership 650.
Visitors   advisable to telephone in advance, and essential
for weekends.
Societies   contact in advance.
Green Fees not confirmed.
Cards   ▦ ■ ▦ ▨ ▨
Facilities ⊗ ⫶ ⬓ ⬛ ⌂ ⧈ ⧈ ⌂
Location   5m from Hawick, 1.25m off A698 at Denholm

Hotel   ★★ 66% Kirklands Hotel, West Stewart Place,
HAWICK ☎ 01450 372263 5 ➡ ✦

NEWCASTLETON   Map 12 NY48

Newcastleton Holm Hill TD9 0QD ☎ 01387 375257
Hilly course with scenic views over the Liddesdale Valley
and Newcastleton.
9 holes, 5503yds, Par 69, SSS 70, Course record 69.
Club membership 100.
Visitors   contact the Secretary in advance.
Societies   contact by telephone or in writing in advance.
Green Fees £10 per day.
Designer   J Shade
Facilities ⌂ ⧈
& Leisure   fishing.
Location   W side of village

Hotel   ★★★ 65% Garden House Hotel, Sarkfoot Rd,
GRETNA ☎ 01461 337621 21 ➡ ✦

PEEBLES   Map 11 NT24

Peebles Kirkland St EH45 8EU
☎ 01721 720197 Fax 01721 724441
e-mail: secretary@peeblesgolfclub.co.uk
Parkland course with fine views.
18 holes, 6160yds, Par 70, SSS 70, Course record 63.
Club membership 750.
Visitors   advisable to ring for information on availability,
no visitors on Sat.
Societies   apply by telephone or in writing in advance.
Green Fees £30 per day; £27 per round (£35/£25 weekends).
Cards   ▦ ▦ ▨
Prof   Craig Imlah
Designer   H S Colt
Facilities ⊗ ⫶ ⬓ ⬛ ⌂ ⧈ ⌂ ⧈ ➤ ⧈ ⌂
Location   W side of town centre off A72

Hotel   ★★★ 73% Peebles Hydro Hotel, PEEBLES
☎ 01721 720602 133 ➡ ✦

ST BOSWELLS   Map 12 NT53

St Boswells Braeheads TD6 0DE ☎ 01835 823527
Attractive parkland course by the banks of the River Tweed;
easy walking.
9 holes, 5274yds, Par 66.
Club membership 320.
Visitors   contact in advance.
Societies   booking by writing to secretary.
Green Fees £15 per round/day.
Designer   W Park
Facilities ⫶ by prior arrangement ⬛ ⌂ ⌂
& Leisure   fishing.
Location   500yds off A68 east end of village

Hotel   ★★★★⚑ 76% Dryburgh Abbey Hotel,
ST BOSWELLS ☎ 01835 822261
37 ➡ ✦ Annexe1 ➡ ✦

SELKIRK   Map 12 NT42

Selkirk Selkirk Hill TD7 4NW ☎ 01750 20621
Pleasant moorland course set around Selkirk Hill. Unrivalled
views.
9 holes, 5620yds, Par 68, SSS 67, Course record 61.
Club membership 364.
Visitors   contact in advance, may not play Mon evening,
competition/match days.
Societies   must telephone in advance.
Green Fees £16 per day.
Facilities ⊗ by prior arrangement ⬓ by prior arrangement
⬛ by prior arrangement ⌂ ⧈ ⌂
Location   1m S on A7

Hotel   ★★★ 66% Burt's Hotel, The Square,
MELROSE ☎ 01896 822285 20 ➡ ✦

Entries with a green background
identify courses considered to be
particularly interesting

Where to stay, where to eat?
Visit the AA internet site
www.theAA.com

Royal Troon

Troon, *South Ayrshire* ☎ 01292 311555 Fax 01292 318204 Map 10 NS33

e-mail: bookings@royaltroon.com

Troon was founded in 1878 with just 5 holes on linksland, in its first decade it grew from 5 holes to 6, then 12, and finally 18 holes. It became Royal Troon in 1978 on the occasion of its 100th anniversary.

Royal Troon has been one of the venues of the Open Championship in Western Scotland since 1923. Troon's reputation is based on its combination of rough and sandy hills, bunkers, and a severity of finish that has diminished the championship hopes of many. The most successful players have relied on an equal blend of finesse and power. The British Open Championship has been played at Royal Troon in 1923, 1950, 1962, 1973, 1982, 1989 and 1997. It is recommended that you apply to the course in advance for full visitor information.

Visitors must play Mon, Tue and Thu only. Must write in advance and have a letter of introduction from own club and a handicap certificate of under 20. Ladies and under 18s may only play on the Portland

Green Fees £135 per day, 1 round each Old Course and Portland Course plus lunch. £95 per 2 rounds of Portland plus lunch ⊟ ▦ ▨ ▨

Facilities ⊗ ▥ ▣ ▨ ♀⚲ ⛾ 🏠 ⚐ ⚑ 𝑓
Professional (R. B. Anderson)

Location Craigend Rd, Troon KA10 6EP (S side of town on B749)

Holes/Par/Course record 36 holes. Old Course: 18 holes, 6641 yds, Par 71, SSS 73, Course record 64
Portland: 18 holes, 6289 yds, Par 71, SSS 71, Course record 65

Championship Course

WHERE TO STAY NEARBY

Hotels
TROON

★★★ 66% Marine, Crosbie Rd.
☎ 01292 314444. 74 ⇆ ℟

★★★▩▩▩ 🛄 Lochgreen House, Monktenhill Rd, Southwood.
☎ 01292 313343. 7 ⇆ ℟ Annexe 8 ⇆ ℟

★★★▩▩ 75% Highgrove House, Old Loans Rd. ☎ 01292 312511.
9 (7 ⇆ ℟ 2 ▩)

★★★▩▩ 74% Piersland House, Craigend Rd. ☎ 01292 314747.
15 (9 ⇆ 6 ▩) Annexe 13 ⇆ ℟

Restaurant
TROON

▩ Cellars, 147 Templehill.
☎ 01292 317448.

WEST LINTON — Map 11 NT15

Rutherford Castle Golf Club EH46 7AS
☎ 01968 661 233 Fax 01968 661 233
e-mail: info@ruth-castlegc.co.uk
Undulating parkland set beneath the Pentland hills. With many challenging holes. A good test for the better player whilst offering great enjoyment to the average player.
18 holes, 6525yds, Par 72, SSS 71.
Club membership 360.
Visitors telephone booking anytime.
Societies application form forwarded on request.
Green Fees £15 per round (£25 weekends).
Prof Martin Brown
Designer Bryan Moore
Facilities 🅱 ♥ ♀ ⚘ 🏠 🚜 ✐
& Leisure fishing.
Location S of Edinburgh city bypass (A720) on A702 towards Carlisle

Hotel ★★★ 73% Peebles Hydro Hotel, PEEBLES
☎ 01721 720602 133 ⇄ ✿

West Linton EH46 7HN ☎ 01968 660256 & 660970
Moorland course with beautiful views of Pentland Hills.
18 holes, 6132yds, Par 69, SSS 70, Course record 63.
Club membership 800.
Visitors weekdays anytime, weekends not before 1pm. Contact Professional.
Societies contact the secretary by telephone.
Green Fees £30 per day; £20 per round (£30 per round weekends).
Prof Ian Wright
Designer Millar/Braid/Fraser
Facilities ⊗ ⅲ 🅱 ♥ ♀ ⚘ 🏠 🚜 ✐
Location NW side of village off A702

Hotel ★★★ 73% Peebles Hydro Hotel, PEEBLES
☎ 01721 720602 133 ⇄ ✿

SOUTH AYRSHIRE

AYR — Map 10 NS32

Belleisle Belleisle Park KA7 4DU
☎ 01292 441258 Fax 01292 442632
Parkland course with beautiful sea views. First-class conditions.
Belleisle Course: 18 holes, 6431yds, Par 71, SSS 72, Course record 63.
Seafield Course: 18 holes, 5498yds, Par 68, SSS 66.
Club membership 2400.
Visitors advised to contact in advance, telephone to book.
Societies advised to contact in advance, telephone 01292 441258.
Green Fees £18per round (£25 weekends).
Cards 💳 💳 💳 💳 💳
Prof David Gemmell
Designer James Braid
Facilities ⊗ ⅲ 🅱 ♥ ♀ ⚘ 🏠 ✐ ⛳ ✐
Location 2m S of Ayr on Coastal Road

Hotel ★★★ 60% Quality Hotel Ayr, Burns Statue Square, AYR ☎ 01292 263268 74 ⇄ ✿

Dalmilling Westwood Av KA8 0QY
☎ 01292 263893 Fax 01292 610543
Meadowland course, with easy walking.
18 holes, 5724yds, Par 69, SSS 68, Course record 61.
Club membership 260.
Visitors must contact in advance.
Societies must contact in advance.
Green Fees £12 per round (£16 weekends).
Cards 💳 💳 💳 💳 💳
Prof Philip Cheyney
Facilities ⚘ 🏠 ⛳ ✐
Location 1.5m E of town centre off A77

Hotel ★★★ 60% Quality Hotel Ayr, Burns Statue Square, AYR ☎ 01292 263268 74 ⇄ ✿

BARASSIE — Map 10 NS33

Kilmarnock (Barassie) 29 Hillhouse Rd KA10 6SY
☎ 01292 313920 Fax 01292 313920 & 313824
e-mail: secretarykbgc@lineone.net
The club now has a 27 hole layout. Magnificent seaside links, relatively flat with much heather and small, undulating greens.
18 holes, 6817yds, Par 72, SSS 74, Course record 63.
9 hole course: 9 holes, 2888yds, Par 34.
Club membership 600.
Visitors with member only Wed & weekends. May not play Fri am. Contact secretary in advance.
Societies must telephone in advance and confirm in writing.
Green Fees £60 per 36 holes; £50 per 27 holes; £40 per 18 holes;.
Cards 💳 💳 💳 💳 💳
Prof Gregor Howie
Designer Theodore Moone
Facilities ⊗ ⅲ 🅱 ♥ ♀ ⚘ 🏠 ⛳ ✐
Location E side of village on B746, 2m N of Troon

Hotel ★★★★ 62% Marine Hotel, Crosbie Rd, TROON ☎ 01292 314444 74 ⇄ ✿

GIRVAN — Map 10 NX19

Brunston Castle Golf Course Rd, Dailly KA26 9GD
☎ 01465 811471 Fax 01465 811545
e-mail: golf@brunstoncastle.co.uk
Sheltered inland parkland course. A championship design by Donald Steel, the course is bisected by the River Girvan and shaped to incorporate all the natural surroundings. Lined with mature trees and incorporating a number of water features in addition to the river.
Burns: 18 holes, 6662yds, Par 72, SSS 72, Course record 63.
Club membership 400.
Visitors reserved for members at weekends 8-10 & 12.30-1.30. Must contact in advance.
Societies telephone 01465 811471 to book.
Green Fees £15 per 9 holes;£26 per 18 holes;£38 per 27 holes;£40 per 36 holes(£16/£30/£42/£45 weekends).
Cards 💳 💳 💳 💳
Prof Stephen Forbes

▶

Turnberry Golf Courses

Turnberry, *South Ayrshire*   ☎ 01655 331000   Fax 01655 331706   Map 10 NS20

e-mail: turnberry@westin.com

The renowned Westin Turnberry Hotel is magnificently situated overlooking its two championship golf courses, with views towards the Mull of Kintyre and the Isle of Arran.

Golf at Turnberry began in 1906. The Ailsa course was developed by the Glasgow and South Western Railway Company and continued to prosper until the outbreak of war in 1914 and again in 1939. Golf course architect Mackenzie Ross was given the task of rebuilding the courses and 1951 the transformation was complete.

The Ailsa course is ranked number three in the UK and twenty-one in the world. The Colin Montgomerie Links Golf Academy opened in April 2000, featuring 12 driving bays, 4 short game bays, 2 dedicated teaching rooms and a group teaching room.

Visitors golf courses for residents of hotel only

Societies contact in advance as courses are for residents of the hotel only

Green Fees fees on application 🖥 📷 💳 📠 🖳 📡

Facilities ⊗ 📶 ⓑ ☕ ♀🚶 🏠 ⛳ ✂ ⓕ
Professional (Brian Gunson) Golf Academy

Leisure tennis, squash, swimming, sauna, solarium, gymnasium

Location Turnberry KA26 9LT (15m SW of Ayr on A77)

Holes/Par/Course record 36 holes. Ailsa Course: 18 holes, 6440 yds, Par 69, SSS 72, Course record 63
Kintyre Course: 18 holes, 6481 yds, Par 72.

WHERE TO STAY NEARBY

Hotel
TURNBERRY

★★★★★ The Westin Turnberry Hotel.
☎ 01655 331000. 132 ⇆ 🐾 Annexe 89 ⇆ 🐾

Championship Course

Designer Donald Steel
Facilities ⊗ ⅶ ⓛ ♨ ♀ ♨ 🏠 ⚐ ⚑ ⚓ ∅ ⚙
Location 6m SE of Turnberry, 5m E of Girvan

Hotel ★★★ 77% Malin Court, TURNBERRY
☎ 01655 331457 18 ⇆ ♞

Girvan Golf Course Rd KA26 9HW
☎ 01465 714346 Fax 01465 714272
Municipal seaside and parkland course. Testing 17th hole
(223-yds) uphill, par 3. Good views.
18 holes, 5098yds, Par 64, SSS 65, Course record 61.
Club membership 175.
Visitors telephone to book.
Societies book in advance
Green Fees £12 per round(£16 weekends).
Cards ▱ ▰ ▱ ▱
Designer D Kinnell/J Braid
Facilities ⊗ ⅶ ⓛ ♨ ♀ ♨ ∅
Location N side of town off A77

Hotel ★★★ 77% Malin Court, TURNBERRY
☎ 01655 331457 18 ⇆ ♞

MAYBOLE   Map 10 NS20

Maybole Municipal Memorial Park KA19 7DX
☎ 01655 889770
Hilly parkland course.
9 holes, 2635yds, Par 33, SSS 65, Course record 64.
Club membership 100.
Visitors no restrictions, telephone to check,pay as you
play course.
Societies must contact in advance.
Green Fees £6 per round (£8 weekends).
Leisure heated indoor swimming pool, bowling green.
Location Off A77 S of town

Hotel ★★ Ladyburn, MAYBOLE
☎ 01655 740585 8rm(4 ⇆3 ♞)

PRESTWICK   Map 10 NS32

Prestwick 2 Links Rd KA9 1QG
☎ 01292 477404 Fax 01292 477255
Seaside links with natural hazards, tight fairways and
difficult fast undulating greens.
18 holes, 6544yds, Par 71, SSS 73, Course record 67.
Club membership 575.
Visitors restricted Thu; may not play at weekends.
Must contact in advance and have a
handicap certificate.
Societies must contact in writing.
Green Fees £120 per day; £80 per round.
Cards ▱ ▰ ▱
Prof F C Rennie
Designer Tom Morris
Facilities ⊗ ⓛ ♨ ♀ ♨ 🏠 ⚐ ∅
Location In town centre off A79

Hotel ★★★ 66% Parkstone Hotel, Esplanade,
PRESTWICK ☎ 01292 477286 22 ⇆ ♞

Prestwick St Cuthbert East Rd KA9 2SX
☎ 01292 477101 Fax 01292 671730
e-mail: prestwick.stcuthbert@virgin.net
Parkland course with easy walking, natural hazards and
sometimes windy.
18 holes, 6470yds, Par 71, SSS 71, Course record 64.
Club membership 880.
Visitors must contact in advance but may not play at
weekends & bank holidays.
Societies Mon-Fri, apply in writing.
Green Fees £32 per day; £24 per round.
Designer Stutt & Co
Facilities ⊗ ⅶ ⓛ ♨ ♀ ♨ ∅
Location 0.5m E of town centre off A77

Hotel ★★★ 66% Parkstone Hotel, Esplanade,
PRESTWICK ☎ 01292 477286 22 ⇆ ♞

Prestwick St Nicholas Grangemuir Rd KA9 1SN
☎ 01292 477608 Fax 01292 473900
Seaside links course with whins, heather and tight fairways.
It provides easy walking and has an unrestricted view of the
Firth of Clyde.
18 holes, 5952yds, Par 69, SSS 69, Course record 63.
Club membership 750.
Visitors except Sat, Sun am. Must contact in advance.
Societies must contact in advance.
Green Fees £50.50 per day;£30.50 per round(£35.50
Sundays).
Cards ▱ ▰ ▱ ▱
Designer Charles Hunter
Facilities ⊗ ⅶ ⓛ ♨ ♀ ♨ 🏠 ⚐ ∅
Location S side of town off A79

Hotel ★★★ 66% Parkstone Hotel, Esplanade,
PRESTWICK ☎ 01292 477286 22 ⇆ ♞

TROON   Map 10 NS33

TROON See page 387

Troon Municipal Harling Dr KA10 6NE
☎ 01292 312464 Fax 01292 312578
Lochgreen Course: 18 holes, 6820yds, Par 74, SSS 73.
Darley Course: 18 holes, 6360yds, Par 71, SSS 63.
Fullarton Course: 18 holes, 4870yds, Par 72, SSS 72.
Location 100yds from railway station
Telephone for further details

Hotel ★★★★ 62% Marine Hotel, Crosbie Rd,
TROON ☎ 01292 314444 74 ⇆ ♞

TURNBERRY   Map 10 NS20

TURNBERRY See page 389

Looking for a driving range?
See the index at the back of the guide

AA Hotels that have special
arrangements with golf courses are listed at
the back of the guide

SOUTH LANARKSHIRE

BIGGAR   Map 11 NT03

Biggar The Park, Broughton Rd ML12 6AH
☎ 01899 220618(club) & 220319(course)
Flat parkland course, easy walking and fine views.
18 holes, 5600yds, Par 68, SSS 67, Course record 61.
Club membership 240.
Visitors   Must contact in advance. Smart casual wear required.
Societies   must book in advance, observe dress code.
Green Fees prices under review.
Designer   W Park Jnr
Facilities   ⊗ ⅷ ⅊ ⯊ ♥ ♀ ⯊ ♣ ✿
& Leisure   hard tennis courts, boating.
Location   S side of town

Hotel   ★★★♨ 73% Shieldhill Castle, Quothquan, BIGGAR ☎ 01899 220035   16 ⇄ ⋔

BOTHWELL   Map 11 NS75

Bothwell Castle Blantyre Rd G71 8PJ
☎ 01698 853177 Fax 01698 854052
Flattish tree lined parkland course in residential area.
18 holes, 6200yds, Par 71, SSS 70, Course record 63.
Club membership 1000.
Visitors   may only play Mon-Fri 9.30-10.30am & 2-3pm.
Societies   (Tues only, apply in writing)
Green Fees not confirmed.
Prof   Alan McCloskey
Facilities   ⊗ ⅷ ⅊ ⯊ ♥ ♀ ⯊ ♣ ✿
Location   NW of village off B7071

Hotel   ★★★ 67% Bothwell Bridge Hotel, 89 Main St, BOTHWELL ☎ 01698 852246   90 ⇄ ⋔

BURNSIDE   Map 11 NS65

Blairbeth Fernbrae Av, Fernhill G73 4SF
☎ 0141 634 3355
Parkland course.
18 holes, 5518yds, Par 70, SSS 68, Course record 64.
Club membership 600.
Visitors   must contact in advance & may not play weekends.
Societies   apply in advance.
Green Fees £21 per day; £18 per round.
Facilities   ⊗ ⅷ ⅊ ⯊ ♥ ♀ ⯊
Location   2m S of Rutherglen off Burnside road

Hotel   ★★★ 64% Kings Park Hotel, Mill St, RUTHERGLEN ☎ 0141 647 5491 26 ⇄ ⋔

Cathkin Braes Cathkin Rd G73 4SE
☎ 0141 634 6605 Fax 0141 630 9186 e-mail: golf@cathkinbraes.freeserve.co.uk
Moorland course, prevailing westerly wind, small loch hazard at 5th hole.
18 holes, 6208yds, Par 71, SSS 71, Course record 64.
Club membership 920.
Visitors   must contact in advance & have handicap certificate but may not play at weekends.
Societies   apply in writing.

Green Fees £35 per day; £25 per round.
Prof   Stephen Bree
Designer   James Braid
Facilities   ⊗ ⅷ ⅊ ⯊ ♥ ♀ ⯊ ♣ ✿ ♠ ✿
Location   1m S on B759

CARLUKE   Map 11 NS85

Carluke Mauldslie Rd, Hallcraig ML8 5HG
☎ 01555 770574 & 771070 e-mail: admin.carlukegolf@supanet.com
Parkland course with views over the Clyde Valley. Testing 11th hole, par 3.
18 holes, 5853yds, Par 70, SSS 68, Course record 63.
Club membership 750.
Visitors   must contact in advance & may not play weekends and bank holidays.
Societies   prior arrangement required.
Green Fees £28 per day; £23 per round.
Prof   Richard Forrest
Facilities   ⊗ ⅷ ⅊ ⯊ ♥ ♀ ⯊ ♣ ✿
Location   1m W off A73

Hotel   ★★★ 71% Popinjay Hotel, Lanark Rd, ROSEBANK ☎ 01555 860441   38 ⇄ ⋔

CARNWATH   Map 11 NS94

Carnwath 1 Main St ML11 8JX
☎ 01555 840251 Fax 01555 841070
Picturesque parkland course slightly hilly, with small greens calling for accuracy. Panoramic views.
18 holes, 5222yds, Par 66, SSS 66, Course record 63.
Club membership 584.
Visitors   restricted after 5pm, no visitors Sat.
Societies   apply in writing or telephone.
Green Fees £25 per day; £15 per round (£30/£20 Sun & bank holidays).
Facilities   ⊗ ⅷ ⅊ ⯊ ♥ ♀ ⯊ ♣ ✿
Location   W side of village on A70

Hotel   ★★★ 63% Cartland Bridge Hotel, Glasgow Rd, LANARK ☎ 01555 664426   18 ⇄ ⋔

EAST KILBRIDE   Map 11 NS65

East Kilbride Chapelside Rd, Nerston G74 4PF
☎ 01355 247728
Parkland course of variable topography. Generous fairways and greens but a challenging test of golf.
18 holes, 6419yds, Par 71, SSS 71, Course record 64.
Club membership 850.
Visitors   by appointment.
Societies   must telephone in advance & submit formal application.
Green Fees not confirmed.
Prof   Willy Walker
Facilities   ⯊ ♣ ✿ ♠ ✿
Location   0.5m N off A749

Hotel   ★★★ 70% Bruce Hotel, Cornwall St, EAST KILBRIDE ☎ 01355 229771   65 ⇄ ⋔

> Entries with a green background
> identify courses considered to be
> particularly interesting

Torrance House Calderglen Country Park, Strathaven Rd
G75 0QZ ☎ 01355 248638 Fax 01355 570916
A mature parkland course.
18 holes, 6476yds, Par 72, SSS 69, Course record 71.
Club membership 1000.
Visitors welcome, may book up to six days in advance.
Societies Mon-Fri. Apply in writing to John Dunlop,
South Lanarkshire Council, Civic Centre, East
Kilbride.
Green Fees not confirmed.
Facilities ⊗ Ⅲ ⓑ ⬛ ♀ ♨ 🐦 ⛳ 🔗
Location 1.5m SE of Kilbride on A726

Hotel ★★★ 70% Bruce Hotel, Cornwall St, EAST
KILBRIDE ☎ 01355 229771 65 ⇔ ✦

HAMILTON   Map 11 NS75

Hamilton Carlisle Rd, Ferniegair ML3 7UE
☎ 01698 459537
Beautiful parkland course.
18 holes, 6243yds, Par 70, SSS 71, Course record 62.
Visitors must contact in advance, may not play
weekends.
Societies apply in writing.
Green Fees not confirmed.
Prof Maurice Moir
Designer James Braid
Facilities ⊗ Ⅲⓑⓑ⬛♀♨⛳🔗
Location 1.5m SE on A72

Hotel Express by Holiday Inn, Hamilton Rd,
HAMILTON ☎ 01698 858585 120 ✦

Strathclyde Park Mote Hill ML3 6BY ☎ 01698 429350
Municipal wooded parkland course with views into the
Strathclyde Park sailing loch.
9 holes, 3128yds, Par 36, SSS 70, Course record 64.
Club membership 240.
Visitors telephone, same day booking system in
operation. May book up to 1 week in advance in
summer months.
Societies must contact in advance on above telephone
number, for prior booking.
Green Fees £3.40 per 9 holes.
Prof William Walker
Facilities ♨ 🏠 ✦
Location N side of town off B7071

Hotel Express by Holiday Inn, Hamilton Rd,
HAMILTON ☎ 01698 858585 120 ✦

LANARK   Map 11 NS84

Lanark The Moor, Whitelees Rd ML11 7RX
☎ 01555 663219 & 661456 Fax 01555 663219
e-mail: lanarkgolfclub@talk21.com
The address of the club, 'The Moor', gives some
indication as to the kind of golf to be found there. Golf
has been played at Lanark for well over a century and the
Club dates from 1851.
Old Course: 18 holes, Par 70, SSS 71, Course record 62.
Wee Course: 9 holes, 1489yds, Par 28.
Club membership 880.

Visitors booking advisable, no visitors weekends.
Societies apply in advance.
Green Fees £40 per day; £26 per round.
Prof Alan White
Designer Tom Morris
Facilities ⊗ Ⅲⓑⓑ⬛♀♨🏠🐦♨⛳🔗
Location E side of town centre off A73

Hotel ★★★ 63% Cartland Bridge Hotel,
Glasgow Rd, LANARK
☎ 01555 664426 18 ⇔ ✦

LARKHALL   Map 11 NS75

Larkhall Burnhead Rd ML9 3AA ☎ 01698 889597
Small, inland parkland course.
9 holes, 6234yds, Par 70, SSS 70, Course record 69.
Club membership 250.
Visitors restricted Tue & Sat.
Green Fees not confirmed.
Facilities ⬛ ♀
Location E side of town on B7019

Hotel ★★★ 71% Popinjay Hotel, Lanark Rd,
ROSEBANK ☎ 01555 860441 38 ⇔ ✦

LEADHILLS   Map 11 NS81

Leadhills ML12 6XR ☎ 01659 74456
A testing, hilly course with high winds. At 1500ft above sea
level it is the highest golf course in Scotland.
9 holes, 4354yds, Par 66, SSS 64.
Club membership 80.
Visitors groups must contact in advance.
Societies must contact in advance.
Green Fees not confirmed.
Location E side of village off B797

Hotel ★★ 67% Blackaddie House Hotel, Blackaddie
Rd, SANQUHAR ☎ 01659 50270 9 ⇔ ✦

LESMAHAGOW   Map 11 NS83

Holland Bush Acretophead ML11 0JS
☎ 01555 893484 & 893646 Fax 01555 893984 e-
mail: mail@hollandbushgolfclub.co.uk
Fairly difficult, tree-lined municipal parkland and moorland
course. 1st half is relatively flat, while 2nd half is hilly.
18 holes, 6246yds, Par 71, SSS 70, Course record 63.
Club membership 400.
Visitors contact shop on 01555 893646 for times etc.
Societies contact shop on 01555 893646 in advance.
Green Fees £8.40 per round;£16.80 per day(£9.80/£19.60
weekends).
Designer J Lawson/K Pate
Facilities ⊗ Ⅲⓑⓑ⬛♀♨🏠🐦⛳🔗
Location 2-3m S of Lesmahagow on the Lesmahagow-
Coalburn Road

Hotel ★★★ 70% Strathaven Hotel, Hamilton Rd,
STRATHAVEN ☎ 01357 521778 22 ⇔ ✦

RIGSIDE   Map 11 NS83

Douglas Water Ayr Rd ML11 9NP ☎ 01555 880361
A 9-hole course with good variety and some hills and
spectacular views. An interesting course with a challenging
longest hole of 564 yards but, overall, not too testing for
average golfers.
9 holes, 5890yds, Par 72, SSS 69, Course record 64.
Club membership 250.
Visitors   no restrictions weekdays or Sun, competitions
                 on Sat normal restrictions.
Societies   apply in writing/telephone in advance.
Green Fees   not confirmed.
Facilities   ♥ ♀ ⚲
Location   Ayr road A70

Hotel   ★★★ 63% Cartland Bridge Hotel, Glasgow
                 Rd, LANARK ☎ 01555 664426 18 ⇄ ↾

STRATHAVEN   Map 11 NS64

Strathaven Glasgow Rd ML10 6NL
☎ 01357 520421 Fax 01357 520539 e-
mail: manager@strathavengolfclub.fsbusiness.co.uk
Gently undulating, tree-lined, Championship parkland course
with panoramic views over town and Avon valley.
18 holes, 6250yds, Par 71, SSS 71, Course record 65.
Club membership 950.
Visitors   welcome weekdays up to 4pm only. May not
                 play at weekends. Must contact in advance.
Societies   apply in writing to general manager.
Green Fees   £35 per day; £25 per round.
Prof   Matt McCrorie
Designer   Willie Fernie/J Stutt
Facilities   ⊗ ⅏ ℄ ♥ ♀ ⚲ 🏠 ⚑ ♦ ♂
Location   NE side of town on A726

Hotel   ★★★ 70% Strathaven Hotel, Hamilton Rd,
                 STRATHAVEN ☎ 01357 521778 22 ⇄ ↾

UDDINGSTON   Map 11 NS66

Calderbraes 57 Roundknowe Rd G71 7TS
☎ 01698 813425
Parkland course with good view of Clyde Valley. Testing 4th
hole (par 4), hard uphill.
9 holes, 5046yds, Par 66, SSS 67, Course record 65.
Club membership 230.
Visitors   weekdays before 5pm.
Societies   welcome
Green Fees   £18 per day.
Facilities   ⊗ ⅏ ℄ ♥ ♀ ⚲
Location   1.5m NW off A74

Hotel   ★★ 68% Redstones Hotel, 8-10 Glasgow Rd,
                 UDDINGSTON ☎ 01698 813774 & 814843
                 Fax 01698 815319 14 ⇄ ↾

> AA Hotels that have special
> arrangements with golf courses are listed at
> the back of the guide

STIRLING

ABERFOYLE   Map 11 NN50

Aberfoyle Braeval FK8 3UY ☎ 01877 382493
Scenic heathland course with mountain views.
18 holes, 5210yds, Par 66, SSS 66.
Club membership 665.
Visitors   weekend restrictions.
Societies   must contact in advance.
Green Fees   £15 per round;£20 per day(£20/£28 weekends).
Facilities   ⊗ ⅏ ℄ ♥ ♀ ⚲ ♂
Location   1m E on A81

Hotel   ★★★★ 64% Forest Hills Hotel, Kinlochard,
                 ABERFOYLE ☎ 01877 387277 56 ⇄ ↾

BANNOCKBURN   Map 11 NS89

Brucefields Family Golfing Centre Pirnhall Rd
FK7 8EH ☎ 01786 818184 Fax 01786 817770
Gently rolling parkland with fine views. Most holes can
be played without too much difficulty with the exception
of the 2nd which is a long and tricky par 4 and the 6th, a
par 3 which requires exact club selection and a straight
shot.
Main Course: 9 holes, 2513yds, Par 68, SSS 68.
Visitors   no restrictions
Societies   apply in writing.
Green Fees   £14 per 18 holes, £8 per 9 holes (£16/£9
                 weekends).
Cards   🖃 🖃 🖃 🖃 🖃
Designer   Souters Sportsturf
Facilities   ⊗ ⅏ ℄ ♥ ♀ ⚲ 🏠 ⚑ ♂ ↾
& Leisure   golf academy.
Location   Exit at interchange of M80/M9 (junct 9),
                 from roundabout take A91, 1st left at sign
                 for Brucefields

Hotel   ★★ 69% Terraces Hotel, 4 Melville Ter,
                 STIRLING ☎ 01786 472268 17 ⇄ ↾

BRIDGE OF ALLAN   Map 11 NS79

Bridge of Allan Sunnylaw FK9 4LY ☎ 01786 832332
Parkland course, very hilly with good views of Stirling
Castle and beyond to the Trossachs. Testing 1st hole, 221 yds
(par 3) uphill 6 ft wall 25 yds before green.
9 holes, 4932yds, Par 66, SSS 65, Course record 59.
Club membership 400.
Visitors   restricted Sat.
Societies   must contact in advance.
Green Fees   not confirmed.
Designer   Tom Morris
Facilities   ⚲ ♂
Location   0.5m N off A9

Hotel   ★★★ 69% Royal Hotel, Henderson St,
                 BRIDGE OF ALLAN
                 ☎ 01786 832284 32 ⇄ ↾

CALLANDER   Map 11 NN60

Callander Aveland Rd FK17 8EN
☎ 01877 330090 & 330975 Fax 01877 330062 e-mail: callandergc@nextcall.net
Challenging parkland course with tight fairways and a number of interesting holes. Designed by Tom Morris Snr and overlooked by the Trossachs.
18 holes, 5115yds, Par 66, SSS 66, Course record 61.
Club membership 600.
Visitors   prior booking 24-48 hrs is advised in the playing season. Handicap certificate Wed/Sun.
Societies   write or telephone for booking form.
Green Fees £26 per day; £18 per round (£31/£26 weekends).
Prof   Allan Martin
Designer   Morris/Fernie
Facilities   ⊗ ⵂ ⅃ ▐ ♀ 丄 🖻 ⫟ ♂
Location   E side of town off A84

Hotel   ★★★♨ 75% Roman Camp Country House Hotel, CALLANDER
☎ 01877 330003   14 ⇄ ♣

DRYMEN   Map 11 NS48

Buchanan Castle G63 0HY
☎ 01360 660307 Fax 01360 870382
e-mail: buchanancastle@sol.co.uk
Parkland course, with easy walking and good views. Owned by the Duke of Montrose.
18 holes, 6059yds, Par 70, SSS 69.
Club membership 830.
Visitors   must contact professional on 01360 660330 in advance.
Societies   must contact in advance.
Green Fees £40 per day; £30 per round.
Cards   🟥
Prof   Keith Baxter
Designer   James Braid
Facilities   丄 🖻 ⫟ ♂
Location   1m W

Hotel   ★★★ 65% Winnock Hotel, The Square, DRYMEN ☎ 01360 660245   48 ⇄ ♣

DUNBLANE   Map 11 NN70

Dunblane New Golf Club Perth Rd FK15 0LJ
☎ 01786 821521 Fax 01786 821522
Well maintained parkland course, with reasonably hard walking. Testing 6th and 9th holes.
18 holes, 5536yds, Par 69, SSS 67.
Club membership 1000.
Visitors   may play 9.30am-noon & 2.30-4pm Mon-Fri. Must contact in advance.
Societies   welcome Mon, Wed-Fri, contact in advance.
Green Fees not confirmed.
Prof   Bob Jamieson
Facilities   ⊗ ⵂ ⅃ ▐ ♀ 丄 🖻 ⫟ ♂
Location   E side of town on A9

Hotel   ★★★♨ Cromlix House Hotel, Kinbuck, Nr DUNBLANE ☎ 01786 822125   14 ⇄ ♣

KILLIN   Map 11 NN53

Killin FK21 8TX ☎ 01567 820312
Parkland course with good views. Glorious setting.
9 holes, 2600yds, Par 66, SSS 65, Course record 61.
Club membership 250.
Visitors   may not play competition days, parties must book in advance.
Societies   previous record of courses visited required. Apply in writing or telephone in advance.
Green Fees not confirmed.
Designer   John Duncan
Facilities   ⊗ ⵂ ⅃ ▐ ♀ 丄 🖻 ⫟ ⅄ ⊿ ♂
Location   1m N on A827

Hotel   ★★★ 68% Dall Lodge Country House Hotel, Main St, KILLIN ☎ 01567 820217   10 ⇄ ♣

STIRLING   Map 11 NS79

Stirling Queens Rd FK8 3AA
☎ 01786 464098 Fax 01786 450748
Undulating parkland course with magnificent views of Stirling Castle and the Grampian Mountains. Testing 15th, 'Cotton's Fancy', 384 yds (par 4).
18 holes, 6438yds, Par 72, SSS 71, Course record 64.
Club membership 1100.
Visitors   may reserve tee off times mid week 9-4.30pm. At weekends tee off times may be reserved on day of play subject to availability.
Societies   must apply in writing or telephone.
Green Fees not confirmed.
Cards   🟥🟥 🟪
Prof   Ian Collins
Designer   James Braid/Henry Cotton
Facilities   ⊗ ⵂ ⅃ ▐ ♀ 丄 🖻 ⫟ ♂ ꜀
Location   W side of town on B8051

Hotel   ★★ 69% Terraces Hotel, 4 Melville Ter, STIRLING ☎ 01786 472268   17 ⇄ ♣

Entries with a green background
identify courses considered to be
particularly interesting

WEST DUNBARTONSHIRE

BONHILL   Map 10 NS37

Vale of Leven North Field Rd G83 9ET ☎ 01389 752351
Hilly moorland course, tricky with many natural hazards -
gorse, burns, trees. Overlooks Loch Lomond.
18 holes, 5162yds, Par 67, SSS 66, Course record 61.
Club membership 640.
Visitors	may not play Sat.
Societies	apply to the secretary.
Green Fees	£25 per day; £18 per round (£30/£20weekends).
Prof	Bary Campbell
Facilities	⊗ 川 ७ ■ ♀ ঌ 🖆 ⛳ ∅
Location	E side of town off A813

Hotel	★★★★★ 66% Cameron House Hotel, BALLOCH ☎ 01389 755565 96 ⇄ 🏻

CLYDEBANK   Map 11 NS56

Clydebank & District Glasgow Rd, Hardgate G81 5QY
☎ 01389 383831 & 383833 Fax 01389 383831
An undulating parkland course established in 1905
overlooking Clydebank.
18 holes, 5823yds, Par 68, SSS 68, Course record 64.
Club membership 889.
Visitors	round only, weekdays only and no bank holidays. Must tee off before 4.30pm. Apply to professional 01389 383835
Societies	must apply in writing.
Green Fees	£15 per round.
Prof	Paul Jamieson
Designer	Members
Facilities	ঌ 🖆 ∅
Location	2m E of Erskine Bridge

Hotel	★★★ 64% Patio Hotel, 1 South Av, Clydebank Business Park, CLYDEBANK ☎ 0141 951 1133 82 ⇄ 🏻

Dalmuir Municipal Overtoun Rd, Dalmuir G81 3RE
☎ 0141 952 6372
Hilly, compact parkland course with tough finishing holes.
18 holes, 5349yds, Par 67, SSS 66, Course record 63.
Visitors	contact in advance.
Societies	contact in advance.
Green Fees	not confirmed.
Prof	Stewart Savage
Facilities	■ ঌ 🖆 ⛳ ∅
Location	2m NW of town centre

Hotel	★★★ 64% Patio Hotel, 1 South Av, Clydebank Business Park, CLYDEBANK ☎ 0141 951 1133 82 ⇄ 🏻

DUMBARTON   Map 10 NS37

Dumbarton Broadmeadow G82 2BQ
☎ 01389 732830 Fax 01389 765995
Flat parkland course.
18 holes, 5992yds, Par 71, SSS 69, Course record 64.
Club membership 700.
Visitors	may play Mon, Thu & Fri only.
Societies	must apply in writing to Secretary.

Green Fees not confirmed.
Facilities	⊗ 川 ७ ■ ♀ ঌ
Location	0.25m N off A814

Guesthouse ♦♦♦♦♦ Kirkton House, Darleith Rd,
CARDROSS ☎ 01389 841951 6 ⇄ 🏻

WEST LOTHIAN

BATHGATE   Map 11 NS96

Bathgate Edinburgh Rd EH48 1BA
☎ 01506 630553 & 652232 Fax 01506 636775
e-mail: bathgate.golfclub@lineone.net
Moorland course. Easy walking. Testing 11th hole, par 3.
18 holes, 6328yds, Par 71, SSS 70, Course record 58.
Club membership 900.
Visitors	casual visitors welcome other than on competition days. Handicap certificate advisable.
Societies	apply in writing.
Green Fees	£22 per day; £17 per round (£33 per day weekends).
Prof	Sandy Strachan
Designer	W Park
Facilities	⊗ 川 ७ ■ ♀ ঌ 🖆 ⛳ 🏑 🛺 ∅
Location	E side of town off A89

Hotel	★★★ 65% The Hilcroft Hotel, East Main St, WHITBURN ☎ 01501 740818 31 ⇄ 🏻

FAULDHOUSE   Map 11 NS96

Greenburn 6 Greenburn Rd EH47 9HJ ☎ 01501 770292
e-mail: secretary@greenburngolfclub.fsnet.co.uk
Exposed rolling course with sparse tree cover. Water hazards
from a pond and a burn.
18 holes, 6045yds, Par 71, SSS 70, Course record 65.
Club membership 900.
Visitors	contact in advance for details.
Societies	by prior arrangement.
Green Fees	£17 per round;£25 per day(£20/£30 weekends).
Prof	Malcolm Leighton
Facilities	⊗ 川 ७ ■ ♀ ঌ 🖆 ∅
Location	3m SW of Whitburn

Hotel	★★★ 65% The Hilcroft Hotel, East Main St, WHITBURN ☎ 01501 740818 31 ⇄ 🏻

LINLITHGOW   Map 11 NS97

Linlithgow Braehead EH49 6QF
☎ 01506 842585 (Secretary) & 844356 (Pro)
Fax 01506 842764 e-mail: info@linlithgowgolf.co.uk
Slightly hilly parkland course in beautiful setting.
18 holes, 5800yds, Par 70, SSS 68, Course record 64.
Club membership 450.
Visitors	may not play Sat.
Societies	must contact in writing.
Green Fees	£25 per day; £20 per round (£30/£25 Sunday).
Cards	🔲 ■ 🔲
Prof	Steven Rosie

▶

Designer   R Simpson of Carnoustie
Facilities   ⊗ ⫴ ⮝ ♥ ♀ ♨ ☗ ⌇ ❦ ♂
Location   1m S off Bathgate Road off A803

Hotel   ★★★★ 70% Inchyra Grange Hotel, Grange Rd, POLMONT ☎ 01324 711911 109 ⇆ ℿ

West Lothian Airngath Hill EH49 7RH
☎ 01506 826030 Fax 01506 826030
Hilly parkland course with superb views of River Forth.
18 holes, 6228yds, Par 71, SSS 71.
Club membership 800.
Visitors   weekends by arrangement. Advisable to contact in high season.
Societies   apply in writing.
Green Fees   not confirmed.
Cards   ▦ ▦ ▯
Prof   Colin Gillies
Designer   Fraser Middleton
Facilities   ⊗ ⮝ ♥ ♀ ♨ ☗ ⌇ ♂
Location   1m S off A706

Hotel   ★★★★ 70% Inchyra Grange Hotel, Grange Rd, POLMONT ☎ 01324 711911 109 ⇆ ℿ

LIVINGSTON   Map 11 NT06

Deer Park Golf & Country Club Golfcourse Rd EH54 9EG
☎ 01506 431037 Fax 01506 435608
e-mail: deerpark@dial.pipek.com
Long testing course, fairly flat, championship standard.
18 holes, 6688yds, Par 72, SSS 72, Course record 65.
Club membership 650.
Visitors   proper golfing attire to be worn, must book in advance, Sun after 10am.
Societies   telephone or write
Green Fees   not confirmed.
Cards   ▦ ▬ ▦ ▦ ▦ ▯
Prof   Brian Dunbar
Designer   Alliss/Thomas
Facilities   ⊗ ⫴ ⮝ ♥ ♀ ♨ ☗ ⌇ ❦ ⚓ ♂
& Leisure   heated indoor swimming pool, squash, sauna, solarium, gymnasium.
Location   N side of town off A809

Hotel   ★★★ 67% Cairn Hotel, Blackburn Rd, BATHGATE ☎ 01506 633366 61 ⇆ ℿ

Pumpherston Drumshoreland Rd, Pumpherston EH53 0LH
☎ 01506 432869
Undulating parkland course with testing 6th hole (par 4), and view of Pentland Hills.
9 holes, 4950yds, Par 66, SSS 64, Course record 64.
Club membership 440.
Visitors   must be accompanied by a member.
Societies   apply in writing to the secretary.
Green Fees   not confirmed.
Facilities   ⊗ ⮝ ♥ ♀ ♨
Location   1m E of Livingston between A71 & A89

Hotel   ★★★ 67% Cairn Hotel, Blackburn Rd, BATHGATE ☎ 01506 633366 61 ⇆ ℿ

UPHALL   Map 11 NT07

Uphall EH52 6JT ☎ 01506 856404 Fax 01506 855358
18 holes, 5588yds, Par 69, SSS 67, Course record 62.
Location   W side of village on A899
Telephone for further details

Hotel   ★★★★ 67% Houstoun House Hotel and Country Club, UPHALL
☎ 01506 853831 25 ⇆ ℿ Annexe47 ⇆ ℿ

WEST CALDER   Map 11 NT06

Harburn EH55 8RS
☎ 01506 871131 & 871256 Fax 01506 870286
Moorland, reasonably flat.
18 holes, 5921yds, Par 69, SSS 69, Course record 62.
Club membership 870.

Visitors   contact secretary.
Societies   contact by telephone.
Green Fees   £25 per day; £18 per round (£29/£21 Fri, £34/£23 weekends).
Prof   Stephen Mills
Facilities   ⊗ ⫴ ⮝ ♥ ♀ ♨ ☗ ⌇ ❦ ⚓ ♂
Location   2m S on B7008

Hotel   ★★★ 65% The Hilcroft Hotel, East Main St, WHITBURN ☎ 01501 740818 31 ⇆ ℿ

WHITBURN   Map 11 NS96

Polkemmet Country Park EH47 0AD ☎ 01501 743905
Public parkland course surrounded by mature woodland and rhododendron bushes. 15-bay floodlit driving range.
9 holes, 2969mtrs, Par 37.
Visitors   no restrictions.
Green Fees   £4.75(£5.55 weekends & bank holidays).
Facilities   ♂ ℾ
Location   2m W on B7066

Hotel   ★★★ 65% The Hilcroft Hotel, East Main St, WHITBURN ☎ 01501 740818 31 ⇆ ℿ

Where to stay, where to eat?
Visit the AA internet site
www.theAA.com

ARRAN, ISLE OF

BLACKWATERFOOT   Map 10 NR82

Shiskine Shore Rd KA27 8HA
☎ 01770 860226 Fax 01770 860205
e-mail: info@shiskinegolf.com
Unique 12-hole links course with gorgeous outlook to the Mull of Kintyre.
12 holes, 2990yds, Par 42, SSS 42, Course record 38.
Club membership 670.
Visitors   must contact in advance.
Societies   must contact in writing in advance. Jul and Aug no parties.
Green Fees £20 per day; £13 per round (£24/£16 weekends & bank holidays).
Designer   Fernie of Troon
Facilities   ⊗ ⓑ ☕ 🛆 🏠 🍴 ♣ ⌕
& Leisure hard tennis courts, bowling green.
Location   W side of village off A841

Hotel   ★★♨ Kilmichael Country House Hotel, Glen Cloy, BRODICK ☎ 01770 302219
4 ⇔ ⌂ Annexe3 ⇔ ⌂

BRODICK   Map 10 NS03

Brodick KA27 8DL
☎ 01770 302349 & 302513 Fax 01770 302349
Short seaside course, very flat.
18 holes, 4736yds, Par 65, SSS 64, Course record 60.
Club membership 611.
Visitors   must contact in advance but may not play at competition times.
Societies   must contact secretary in writing/telephone.
Green Fees £25 per day; £18 per round (£30/£22 weekends & bank holidays).
Prof   Peter McCalla
Facilities   ⊗ �𝄞 ⓑ ☕ ♀ 🛆 🏠 ♣ ⌕
Location   N side of village, 0.5m N of Brodick Ferry Terminal

Hotel   ★★★ 75% Auchrannie Country House Hotel, BRODICK ☎ 01770 302234 28 ⇔ ⌂

LAMLASH   Map 10 NS03

Lamlash KA27 8JU
☎ 01770 600296 & 600196 (Starter) Fax 01770 600296
Undulating heathland course with magnificent views of the mountains and sea.
18 holes, 4640yds, Par 64, SSS 64, Course record 60.
Club membership 480.
Visitors   book in advance by letter
Societies   must contact in writing.
Green Fees £16 per day; £12 per round after 4pm (£20 weekends).
Cards   💳
Designer   Auchterlonie
Facilities   ⊗ ⟨ ⓑ ☕ ♀ 🛆 🏠 🍴 ⚑ ♣ ⌕
Location   0.75m N of Lamlash on A841. 3m S of Brodick Ferry Terminal

Hotel   ★★★ 75% Auchrannie Country House Hotel, BRODICK ☎ 01770 302234 28 ⇔ ⌂

LOCHRANZA   Map 10 NR95

Lochranza KA27 8HL
☎ 01770 830273 Fax 01770 830600
e-mail: office@lochgolf.demon.co.uk
This course is mainly on the level, set amid spectacular scenery where the fairways are grazed by wild red deer, while overhead buzzards and golden eagles may be seen. There are water hazards including the river which is lined by mature trees. The final three holes, nicknamed the Bermuda Triangle, provide an absorbing finish right to the 18th hole - a 530 yard dogleg through trees and over the river. The large greens are played off 18 tees.
18 holes, 5033mtrs, Par 70, SSS 67, Course record 72.
Club membership 40.
Visitors   no restrictions; course closed Nov-mid Apr.
Societies   advance booking preferred.
Green Fees £13 per 18 holes;£8.50 per 9 holes;£18 per day.
Designer   re laid 1991 I Robertson
Facilities   ☕ 🛆 🏠 🍴 ⌕
Location   Main road, Lochranza village.

Hotel   ★★♨ Kilmichael Country House Hotel, Glen Cloy, BRODICK ☎ 01770 302219
4 ⇔ ⌂ Annexe3 ⇔ ⌂

MACHRIE   Map 10 NR83

Machrie Bay KA27 8DZ ☎ 01770 850232
Fairly flat seaside course. Designed at turn of century by William Fernie.
9 holes, 4400yds, Par 66, SSS 62, Course record 70.
Club membership 315.
Visitors   no restrictions.
Societies   write in advance.
Green Fees not confirmed.
Designer   W Fernie
Facilities   ⊗ ☕ 🛆 🍴 ⌕
& Leisure hard tennis courts.
Location   9m W of Brodick via String Rd

Hotel   ★★♨ Kilmichael Country House Hotel, Glen Cloy, BRODICK ☎ 01770 302219 4 ⇔ ⌂ Annexe3 ⇔ ⌂

SANNOX   Map 10 NS04

Corrie KA27 8JD ☎ 01770 810223 & 600403
A heathland course on the coast with beautiful mountain scenery. An upward climb to 6th hole, then a descent from the 7th. All these holes are subject to strong winds in bad weather.
9 holes, 1948yds, Par 62, SSS 61, Course record 56.
Club membership 300.
Visitors   welcome except Sat pm and first Thu afternoon of the month.
Societies   maximum size of party 12, apply in advance.
Green Fees £10 per day.
Facilities   ⊗ ⟨ ☕ 🛆
Location   6m N of A841

Hotel   ★★★ 75% Auchrannie Country House Hotel, BRODICK ☎ 01770 302234 28 ⇔ ⌂

397

WHITING BAY   Map 10 NS02

Whiting Bay KA27 8QT ☎ 01770 700487
Heathland course.
18 holes, 4405yds, Par 63, SSS 63, Course record 59.
Club membership 350.
Visitors   tee reserved 8.45-9.30am, also Sun 11.45-1pm.
Societies   apply by telephone and confirm in writing with deposit.
Green Fees £18 per day; £14 per round.
Facilities   ⊗ ╠ ♥ ♀ ♨ 🖨 ⛳ ↘ 🏌 ♂
Location   NW side of village off A841

Hotel   ★★🏩 Kilmichael Country House Hotel, Glen Cloy, BRODICK ☎ 01770 302219
4 ⇄ ♠ Annexe3 ⇄ ♠

BUTE, ISLE OF

KINGARTH   Map 10 NS05

Bute Sithean, Academy Rd, Rothesay PA20 0BG
☎ 01700 504369
Flat seaside course with good fenced greens and fine views.
9 holes, 2361mtrs, Par 68, SSS 64, Course record 65.
Club membership 210.
Visitors   restricted Sat until after 11.30am.
Societies   apply in advance.
Green Fees £8 per day.
Facilities   ♨
Location   From Rothesay pier 6m on A845

Hotel   ★★ 73% Royal Hotel, Shore Rd, TIGHNABRUAICH
☎ 01700 811239   11 ⇄ ♠

PORT BANNATYNE   Map 10 NS06

Port Bannatyne Bannatyne Mains Rd PA20 0PH
☎ 01700 502009 504544
Seaside hill course with panoramic views. Difficult hole: 4th (par 3).
13 holes, 5085yds, Par 68, SSS 65, Course record 63.
Club membership 200.
Societies   must telephone in advance.
Green Fees not confirmed.
Designer   Peter Morrison
Facilities   ♨
Location   W side of village off A886

Hotel   ★★ 73% Royal Hotel, Shore Rd, TIGHNABRUAICH
☎ 01700 811239   11 ⇄ ♠

AA Hotels that have special arrangements with golf courses are listed at the back of the guide

ROTHESAY   Map 10 NS06

Rothesay Canada Hill PA20 9HN
☎ 01700 503554 Fax 01700 503554
A scenic island course designed by James Braid and Ben Sayers. The course is fairly hilly, with views of the Firth of Clyde, Rothesay Bay or the Kyles of Bute from every hole. Winds are a regular feature which makes the two par 5 holes extremely challenging.
18 holes, 5395yds, Par 69, SSS 66, Course record 62.
Club membership 400.
Visitors   pre-booking essential for weekends, telephone professional 01700 503554.
Societies   contact in advance, booking essential at weekends.
Green Fees £15 per day; £10 per round (£25/£19 weekends).
Cards   ⊡ ■ ⬛ 🆔 ▣ 💳 ▨ ▢
Prof   James M Dougal
Designer   James Braid & Ben Sayers
Facilities   ⊗ �𝕀 ╠ ♥ ♀ ♨ 🖨 ↘ 🏌 ♂
Location   2 min drive from main ferry terminal

Hotel   ★★ 73% Royal Hotel, Shore Rd, TIGHNABRUAICH
☎ 01700 811239   11 ⇄ ♠

COLONSAY, ISLE OF

SCALASAIG   Map 10 NR39

Colonsay Machrins Farm PA61 7YP
☎ 01951 200364 Fax 01951 200312
e-mail: golf@machrin.free-online.co.uk
Traditional links course on natural machair (hard wearing short grass), challenging, primitive. Colonsay Hotel, 2 miles away, is the headquarters of the club, offering accommodation and facilities.
18 holes, 4775yds, Par 72, SSS 72.
Club membership 200.
Visitors   no restrictions.
Societies   apply in writing.
Green Fees not confirmed.
Facilities   🏌
Location   2m W on A870

Hotel   ★★ 70% Isle of Colonsay Hotel, SCALASAIG ☎ 01951 200316 11rm(9 ⇄ ♠)

ISLAY, ISLE OF

PORT ELLEN   Map 10 NR34

Machrie Hotel Machrie PA42 7AN
☎ 01496 302310 Fax 01496 302404 e-mail: machrie@machrie.com
Championship links course opened in 1891, where golf's first £100 Open Championship was played in 1901. Fine turf and many blind holes. Par 4.
18 holes, 6226yds, Par 71, SSS 71, Course record 65.
Club membership 340.   ▶

Visitors	no restrictions.
Societies	apply in writing or telephone.
Green Fees	£40 per day;£30 per round.
Cards	⊟ ■ ▰ ▦ ▧ ▨
Designer	W Campbell
Facilities	⊗)Ⅲ ዄ ♨ ♀ ♁ 🏠 ⚑ 🍴 🕭 ｢
& Leisure	fishing, snooker, table tennis.
Location	4m N off A846

Hotel	★★ 60% Lochside Hotel, 19 Shore St, BOWMORE ☎ 01496 810244 8 ⇆ ⮐

LEWIS, ISLE OF

STORNOWAY   Map 13 NB43

Stornoway Lady Lever Park HS2 0XP
☎ 01851 702240 e-mail: admin@stornowaygolfclub.co.uk
A short but tricky undulating parkland course set in grounds
of Lews Castle with fine views over the Minch to the
mainland. The clubhouse has recently been rebuilt and
improved.
18 holes, 5252yds, Par 68, SSS 67, Course record 62.
Club membership 450.

Visitors	no golf on Sun.
Societies	apply in writing.
Green Fees	£45 per week; £20 per day; £15 per round.
Facilities	ዄ ♨ ♀ ♁ 🏠 ⚑ 🕭
Location	0.5m from town centre off A857

Hotel	★★★ 66% Cabarfeidh Hotel, STORNOWAY ☎ 01851 702604 46 ⇆ ⮐

MULL, ISLE OF

CRAIGNURE   Map 10 NM73

Craignure Scallastle PA65 6PB
☎ 01680 812487 & 812416 Fax 01680 300402
A natural links course designed round the estuary of the
Scallastle Burn that flows into the Sound of Mull.
Completely re designed in 1978/9. Continual improvements
such as 5 new tees in 1998 have provided 18 teeing areas for
the 9 hole layout.
9 holes, 5233yds, Par 69, SSS 66, Course record 72.
Club membership 100.

Visitors	may not play on competition days, contact for fixture list.
Societies	write to the secretary 10 days in advance.
Green Fees	not confirmed.
Facilities	♁ 🕭
Location	1.5m N of Craignure A849

TOBERMORY   Map 13 NM55

Tobermory PA75 6PG
☎ 01688 302338 Fax 01688 302140
e-mail: tobgolf@fsmail.net
A beautifully maintained hilltop course with superb views
over the Sound of Mull. Testing 7th hole (par 3). Often
described as the best 9 hole course in Scotland.
9 holes, 4890yds, Par 64, SSS 64, Course record 65.
Club membership 150.

Visitors	no restrictions except competition days.
Societies	preferable to contact in advance.
Green Fees	£13 per day.
Designer	David Adams
Facilities	ዄ ♨ ♀ ♁ 🕭
Location	0.5m N off A848

Hotel	★★★♨ 76% Druimard Country House Hotel, DERVAIG ☎ 01688 400345 & 400291 Fax 01688 400345 5 ⇆ ⮐ Annexe2 ⇆ ⮐

ORKNEY

KIRKWALL   Map 16 HY41

Orkney Grainbank KW15 1RB ☎ 01856 872457
18 holes, 5411yds, Par 70, SSS 67, Course record 65.

Location	0.5m W off A965

Telephone for further details

STROMNESS   Map 16 HY20

Stromness Ness KW16 3DW ☎ 01856 850772
Testing parkland/seaside course with easy walking. Beautiful
holiday course with magnificent views of Scapa Flow.
18 holes, 4762yds, Par 65, SSS 63, Course record 61.
Club membership 350.

Visitors	no restrictions except during major competitions.
Societies	no restrictions.
Green Fees	£15 per day.
Facilities	⊗ ዄ ♀ ♁ 🕭
& Leisure	hard tennis courts, Bowling.
Location	S side of town centre off A965

WESTRAY   Map 16 HY44

Westray Rosevale KW17 2DH ☎ 01857 677373
Interesting, picturesque seaside course, easy walking.
9 holes, 2405yds, Par 33.
Club membership 60.

Green Fees	not confirmed.
Facilities	🕭
Location	1m NW of Pierowall off B9066

Looking for a driving range?
See the index at the back of the guide

Entries with a green background
identify courses considered to be
particularly interesting

SHETLAND

LERWICK   Map 16 HU44

Shetland PO Box 18, Dale ZE2 9SB
☎ 01595 840369 Fax 840369
e-mail: clubhousemanager@shetlandgolfclub.co.uk
Challenging moorland course, hard walking. A burn runs the
full length of the course and provides a natural hazard.
Testing holes include the 3rd (par 4), 5th (par 4).
*Dale Course: 18 holes, 5776yds, Par 68, SSS 68, Course
record 67.*
Club membership 430.
Visitors   advisable to contact in advance.
Societies   Apply in writing or telephone in advance.
Green Fees   not confirmed.
Designer   Fraser Middleton
Facilities   🅱 💺 🏌 ⚐ 🛒 &
Location   4m N on A970

Hotel   ★★★ 68% Lerwick Hotel, 15 South Rd,
                 LERWICK ☎ 01595 692166   35 ⇄ 🅜

WHALSAY, ISLAND OF   Map 16 HU56

Whalsay Skaw Taing ZE2 9AA
☎ 01806 566450 & 566481 & 566705
The most northerly golf course in Britain, with a large part of
it running round the coastline, offering spectacular holes in
an exposed but highly scenic setting. There are no cut
fairways as yet, these are defined by marker posts, with
preferred lies in operation all year round.
18 holes, 6009yds, Par 70, SSS 68, Course record 65.
Club membership 205.
Visitors   contact in advance for weekend play.
Societies   telephone in advance.
Green Fees   not confirmed.
Facilities   🅱 💺 🏌 ⚐
Location   Whalsay Island

Hotel   ★★ 64% The Baltasound Hotel, UNST
                 ☎ 01957 711334 8rm(6 ⇄ 🅜) Annexe17 ⇄ 🅜

SKYE, ISLE OF

SCONSER   Map 13 NG53

Isle of Skye IV48 8TD ☎ 01478 613004
e-mail: isleofskye.golfclub@btinternet.com
Seaside course with spectacular views. 9 holes with 18 tees.
Suitable for golfers of all abilities.
18 holes, 4677yds, Par 66, SSS 64, Course record 62.
Club membership 250.
Visitors   no restrictions.
Societies   apply in advance.
Green Fees   £15 per day.
Facilities   ⊗ 🅱 💺 ⚐ 🛒 &
Location   A87 between Broadford and Portree

Hotel   ★★ 73% Rosedale Hotel, Beaumont Crescent,
                 PORTREE ☎ 01478 613131
                 20 ⇄ 🅜 Annexe3 ⇄ 🅜

SKEABOST BRIDGE   Map 13 NG44

Skeabost Skeabost House Hotel IV51 9NR
☎ 01470 532202
Short woodland and seaside course featuring some very tight
fairways and greens.
9 holes, 3056yds, Par 62, SSS 60, Course record 58.
Club membership 80.
Societies   contact in advance.
Green Fees   £12 per 18 holes.
Cards   💳 💳 🅾
Designer   John Stuart
Facilities   ⊗ �🍽 🅱 💺 🏌 🧺 🛒 🛒 🛏 &
& Leisure   fishing.
Hotel   ★★★ 76% Cuillin Hills Hotel, PORTREE
                 ☎ 01478 612003   21 ⇄ 🅜 Annexe9 ⇄ 🅜

SOUTH UIST

ASKERNISH   Map 13 NF72

Askernish Lochboisdale PA81 5SY ☎ 01878 700298
e-mail: askernish.golf.club@cwcom.net
Golfers play on machair (hard-wearing short grass), close to
the Atlantic shore. Excellent views from all tees with
constantly changing conditions.
18 holes, 5042yds, Par 68, SSS 67, Course record 64.
Club membership 45.
Visitors   no restrictions.
Societies   welcome.
Green Fees   not confirmed.
Designer   Tom Morris
Facilities   🛒
Location   5m NW of Lochboisdale off A865

Wales

WALES

ANGLESEY, ISLE OF

AMLWCH   Map 06 SH49

Bull Bay LL68 9RY ☎ 01407 830960 Fax 01407 832612
e-mail: secretary@bullbaygolf.freeserve.co.uk
Wales's northernmost course, Bull Bay is a pleasant coastal,
heathland course with natural rock, gorse and wind hazards.
Views from several tees across Irish Sea to the Isle of Man,
and across Anglesey to Snowdonia.
18 holes, 6217yds, Par 70, SSS 70, Course record 60.
Club membership 700.
Visitors   advisable to contact in advance.
Societies   advance booking essential.
Green Fees   £20 per day(£25 weekends & bank holidays).
Prof   John Burns
Designer   W H Fowler
Facilities   ⊗ ⅷ ⅼ ♥ ♀ ⅄ 📠 ☂ 🏌 ⚒ ♂
Location   1m W of Amlwch on A5025

Hotel   ★★ 66% Trecastell Hotel, Bull Bay,
                 AMLWCH ☎ 01407 830651 13rm(11 ⇄ ↑)

BEAUMARIS   Map 06 SH67

Baron Hill LL58 8YW
☎ 01248 810231 Fax 01248 810231
e-mail: baronhill@line1.net
Undulating course with natural hazards of rock and gorse.
Testing 3rd and 4th holes (par 4's). Hole 5/14 plays into the
prevailing wind with an elevated tee across two streams. The
hole is between two gorse covered mounds.
9 holes, 5062mtrs, Par 68, SSS 69, Course record 62.
Club membership 400.
Visitors   ladies have priority on Tue am & club
                 competitions Sun.
Societies   apply in writing to secretary.
Green Fees   £13 per day;£40 per week.
Facilities   ⊗ ⅼ ♥ ♀ ⅄ ♂
Location   Take A545 from Menai Bridge to Beaumaris,
                 course signed on approach to town

Hotel   ★★ 75% Ye Olde Bulls Head Inn, Castle St,
                 BEAUMARIS ☎ 01248 810329
                 14 ⇄ ↑ Annexe1 ⇄ ↑

Looking for a driving range?
See the index at the back of the guide

AA Hotels that have special
arrangements with golf courses are listed at
the back of the guide

HOLYHEAD   Map 06 SH28

Holyhead Lon Garreg Fawr, Trearddur Bay LL65 2YL
☎ 01407 763279 Fax 01407 763279
Treeless, undulating seaside course which provides a
varied and testing game, particularly in a south wind.
The fairways are bordered by gorse, heather and rugged
outcrops of rock. Accuracy from most tees is paramount
as there are 43 fairway and greenside bunkers and lakes.
Designed by James Braid. Indoor driving range.
18 holes, 6058yds, Par 70, SSS 70, Course record 64.
Club membership 1200.
Visitors   must contact in advance.
Societies   must contact in advance.
Green Fees   £25 per day; £19 per round (£29/£25
                 weekends & bank holidays).
Cards   ▭ ▭
Prof   Stephen Elliot

Designer   James Braid
Facilities   ⅄ 📠 ☂ 🏌 ⚒ ♂ ☂
Location   1.25m S on B4545

Hotel   ★★★ 71% Trearddur Bay Hotel,
                 TREARDDUR BAY
                 ☎ 01407 860301 37 ⇄ ↑

LLANGEFNI   Map 06 SH47

Llangefni (Public) Clai Rd LL77 7LJ
☎ 01248 722193 Fax 01248 750156
9 holes, 1342yds, Par 28, SSS 28.
Location   1.5m off A5
Telephone for further details

Hotel   ★★ 66% Anglesey Arms, MENAI BRIDGE
                 ☎ 01248 712305 16 ⇄ ↑

RHOSNEIGR   Map 06 SH37

Anglesey Station Rd LL64 5QX
☎ 01407 811202 Fax 01407 811202
Links course, low and fairly level with sand dunes and tidal
river.
18 holes, 6300yds, Par 68, SSS 68.
Club membership 500.
Visitors   phone in advance, some times are reserved for
                 members. Dress restrictions.
Societies   telephone & confirm in writing.
Green Fees   not confirmed.
Prof   Paul Lovell
Designer   H Hilton
Facilities   ⊗ ⅷ ⅼ ♥ ♀ ⅄ 📠 ♂
Location   NE side of village on A4080

Hotel   ★★★ 71% Trearddur Bay Hotel,
                 TREARDDUR BAY
                 ☎ 01407 860301 37 ⇄ ↑

Entries with a green background
identify courses considered to be
particularly interesting

BLAENAU GWENT

NANTYGLO
Map 03 SO11

West Monmouthshire Golf Rd, Winchestown NP23 4QT
☎ 01495 310233
Established in 1906, this mountain and heathland course was officially designated in 1994 by the Guiness Book of Record as being the highest above sea level, with the 14th tee at a height of 1513ft. The course has plenty of picturesque views, hard walking and natural hazards. Testing 3rd hole, par 5, and 7th hole, par 4.
18 holes, 6013yds, Par 71, SSS 69, Course record 65.
Club membership 350.

Visitors	welcome, must be guest of member for play on Sun.
Societies	apply in writing or contact golf shop 01495 313052.
Green Fees	not confirmed.
Facilities	⚲ 🏠 🍴
Location	0.25m W off A467

Hotel	★★ 70% Pantrhiwgoch Hotel & Riverside Restaurant, Brecon Rd, ABERGAVENNY ☎ 01873 810550 18 ⇆ ♙

TREDEGAR
Map 03 SO10

Tredegar and Rhymney Cwmtysswg, Rhymney NP2 3BQ
☎ 01685 840743 (club) & 843400 (office)
e-mail: golfclub@tredegarandrhymney.fsnet.co.uk
Mountain course with lovely views. The course is being developed into an 18 hole course.
9 holes, 5504yds, Par 68, SSS 68, Course record 69.
Club membership 194.

Visitors	cannot play Sun before 12.
Societies	must contact in advance.
Green Fees	£10 per day.
Facilities	⚲
Location	1.75m SW on B4256

Hotel	★★★ 69% Tregenna Hotel, Park Ter, MERTHYR TYDFIL ☎ 01685 723627 & 382055 Fax 01685 721951 24 ⇆ ♙

BRIDGEND

BRIDGEND
Map 03 SS97

Coed-Y-Mwstwr The Clubhouse, Coychurch CF35 6AF
☎ 01656 862121 & 864 934 Fax 01656 864934
Challenging holes on this 12-hole course include the par 3 3rd (180yds) involving a drive across a lake and the par 4 5th (448yds) which is subject to strong prevailing winds.
12 holes, 6144yds, Par 70, SSS 70, Course record 71.
Club membership 260.

Visitors	must have handicap certificate, advisable to contact in advance. May only play Sat if with member.

Societies	by prior application.
Green Fees	not confirmed.
Cards	⚋ ▦ 🗐
Designer	Chapman/Warren
Facilities	⊗ 🍴 🐚 🍸 ♀ ⚲ 🏠 ⚘
& Leisure	pool table.
Location	1m out of Coychurch, turn at village garage. 2m W of junct 35 on M4

Hotel	★★★ 76% Coed-Y-Mwstwr Hotel, Coychurch, BRIDGEND ☎ 01656 860621 23 ⇆ ♙

Southerndown Ewenny CF32 0QP
☎ 01656 880476 Fax 01656 880317
e-mail: southerndowngolf@btconnect.com
Downland-links championship course with rolling fairways and fast greens. The par-3 5th is played across a valley and the 18th, with its split level fairway, is a demanding finishing hole. Superb views.
18 holes, 6441yds, Par 70, SSS 72, Course record 64.
Club membership 710.

Visitors	must contact in advance & have handicap certificate.
Societies	by arrangement with secretary.
Green Fees	£25(£35 weekends).
Prof	D G McMonagle
Designer	W Fernie
Facilities	⊗ 🍴 🐚 🍸 ♀ ⚲ 🏠 🐾 ⚘ ⚘ ♟
Location	3m SW of Bridgend on B4524

Hotel	★★★ 69% Heronston Hotel, Ewenny Rd, BRIDGEND ☎ 01656 668811 69 ⇆ ♙ Annexe6 ⇆ ♙

MAESTEG
Map 03 SS89

Maesteg Mount Pleasant, Neath Rd CF34 9PR
☎ 01656 734106 & 732037 Fax 01656 734106
Reasonably flat hill-top course with scenic views.
18 holes, 5929yds, Par 70, SSS 69, Course record 69.
Club membership 789.

Visitors	must be a member of a recognised golf club & have a handicap certificate.
Societies	apply in writing.
Green Fees	not confirmed.
Prof	Chris Riley
Designer	James Braid
Facilities	🐚 🍸 ♀ ⚲ 🏠 ⚘ ⚘
Location	0.5m W off B4282

Hotel	★★★ 67% Aberavon Beach Hotel, PORT TALBOT ☎ 01639 884949 52 ⇆

PENCOED
Map 03 SS98

St Mary's Hotel Golf & Country Club St Mary Hill CF35 5EA ☎ 01656 861100 Fax 01656 863400
A parkland course with many American style features. The Par 3 10th called 'Alcatraz' has a well deserved reputation.
St Mary's Course: 18 holes, 5291yds, Par 69, SSS 66, Course record 68.
Sevenoaks Course: 9 holes, 2426yds, Par 35.
Club membership 830.

▶

★ ★ ★
St. Mary's Hotel, Golf & Country Club

A luxury country hotel converted from a 17th century farmhouse, we offer elegance and comfort with first class friendly service. Set in picturesque surroundings on a privately owned 150 acre 27 hole golf complex 2 mins from M4, making it the perfect location for business or pleasure.

- 18 hole St Mary's Course
- 9 hole Sevenoaks Course
- 15 bay floodlit driving range
- Tennis court and practice area
- Bars
- Restaurant

All rooms fitted with:
- Whirlpool baths
- Satellite TV
- Coffee & tea facilities
- Direct dial telephone

Golf, Equestrian and Weekend Breaks available.

Please call us for a brochure and sample for yourselves "The Magic of St. Mary's".

St. Mary's Golf Club Ltd. St. Mary's Hill Pencoed, South Glamorgan CF35 5EA.
Hotel Reservation: Tel: (01656) 861100 Fax: (01656) 863400

Visitors	St. Mary's Course: must contact in advance, handicap certificate not required between 9-4 Mon-Fri, after 1pm weekends. Seven Oaks: no restrictions
Societies	telephone Kay Brazell.
Green Fees	not confirmed.
Cards	
Prof	John Peters
Facilities & Leisure	hard tennis courts.
Location	5m from junct 35 of M4

Hotel ★★★ 73% St Mary's Hotel & Country Club, St Marys Golf Club, PENCOED
☎ 01656 861100 & 860280
Fax 01656 863400 24 ⇌ ↾

PORTHCAWL   Map 03 SS87

Royal Porthcawl CF36 3UW
☎ 01656 782251 Fax 01656 771687
This championship-standard heathland/downland links course is always in sight of the sea. With holes facing every point of the compass, the golfer is always tested by the wind and the course has hosted many major tournaments.
18 holes, 6406yds, Par 72, SSS 74, Course record 65.
Club membership 800.

Visitors	must contact in advanced & produce handicap certificate limit men 20, ladies 30. Restricted at weekends & bank holidays.
Societies	apply in writing.
Green Fees	not confirmed.
Cards	

Prof	Peter Evans
Designer	Charles Gibson
Facilities	
Location	1.5m NW of town centre

Hotel ★★★ 64% Seabank Hotel, The Promenade, PORTHCAWL
☎ 01656 782261 65 ⇌ ↾

PYLE   Map 03 SS88

Pyle & Kenfig Waun-Y-Mer CF33 4PU
☎ 01656 783093 Fax 01656 772822
Links and downland course, with sand-dunes. Easy walking. Often windy.
18 holes, 6688yds, Par 71, SSS 73, Course record 68.
Club membership 1080.

Visitors	by arrangement midweek, guests of members only at weekends.
Societies	for large numbers apply in writing, small numbers telephone booking accepted.
Green Fees	not confirmed.
Cards	
Prof	Robert Evans
Designer	Colt
Facilities	
Location	S side of Pyle off A4229. Access via junct 37 on M4

Hotel ★★★ 64% Seabank Hotel, The Promenade, PORTHCAWL ☎ 01656 782261 65 ⇌ ↾

CAERPHILLY

BARGOED   Map 03 ST19

Bargoed Heolddu CF81 9GF
☎ 01443 830143 & 836411 (Prof)
e-mail: bargoedgc@barbox.net
Mountain parkland course, challenging par 70 course with
panoramic views.
18 holes, 6049yds, Par 70, SSS 70, Course record 64.
Club membership 600.
Visitors   must contact professional in advance, must play
               with member at weekends.
Societies   must contact in advance.
Green Fees £18 per round.
Prof   B Hunter
Facilities   🏌 🍴 🍸 🏌 🛍 ✓
Location   NW side of town

Hotel   ★★★ 67% Maes Manor Hotel,
               BLACKWOOD ☎ 01495 224551 & 220011
               Fax 01495 228217 8 ⇄ Annexe14 ⇄

BLACKWOOD   Map 03 ST19

Blackwood Cwmgelli NP2 1EL
☎ 01495 222121 (Office) & 223152 (Club)
Heathland course with sand bunkers. Undulating, with hard
walking. Testing 2nd hole par 4. Good views.
9 holes, 5332yds, Par 67, Course record 62.
Club membership 310.
Visitors   contact club or turn up and pay greens staff, may
               not play at weekends & bank holidays unless
               with member. Must be members of recognised
               golf club.
Societies   by prior arrangement for members of a
               recognised golf club.
Green Fees not confirmed.
Facilities   ⊗ 🏌 🍴 🍸 🏌
Location   0.25m N of Blackwood, off A4048

Hotel   ★★★ 67% Maes Manor Hotel,
               BLACKWOOD ☎ 01495 224551 & 220011
               Fax 01495 228217 8 ⇄ Annexe14 ⇄

CAERPHILLY   Map 03 ST18

Caerphilly Penchapel, Mountain Rd CF83 1HJ
☎ 029 20883481 & 20863441 Fax 029 20863441
Undulating mountain course with woodland affording good
views especially from 10th hole, 700 ft above sea level.
13 holes, 5944yds, Par 71, SSS 70.
Club membership 700.
Visitors   telephone in advance, must produce a current
               handicap certificate or letter from club secretary,
               may not play at weekends except with member,
               no visitors bank holidays.
Societies   apply in writing in advance to the secretary.
Green Fees £20 per round.
Prof   Joel Hill
Facilities   🏌 🍴 🍸 🏌 🛍 ✓
Location   0.5m S on A469

Hotel   ★★★ 74% Manor Parc Country Hotel &
               Restaurant, Thornhill Rd, Thornhill, CARDIFF
               ☎ 029 2069 3723 12 ⇄ 🐾

Mountain Lakes & Castell Heights Blaengwynlais
CF83 1NG ☎ 029 20861128 & 20886666
Fax 029 20863243 e-mail: sales@golfclub.co.uk
The 9-hole Castell Heights course within the Mountain Lakes
complex was established in 1982 on a 45-acre site. In 1988 a
further 18-hole course, Mountain Lakes was designed by Bob
Sandow to take advantage of 160-acres of mountain
heathland, combining both mountain top golf and parkland.
Most holes are tree lined and there are 20 'lakes' as hazards.
Host of major PGA tournaments.
Mountain Lakes Course: 18 holes, 6046mtrs, Par 74, SSS 73,
Course record 69.
Castell Heights Course: 9 holes, 2751mtrs, Par 35, SSS 32,
Course record 32.
Club membership 500.
Societies   written or telephone notice in advance.
Green Fees not confirmed.
Cards   💳 💳 💳 💳 💳
Prof   Sion Bebb
Designer   Bob Sandow
Facilities   ⊗ 🏌 🏌 🍴 🍸 🏌 🛍 🏌 🐾 🎣 🏊 ✓ 🎯
Location   Near Black Cock Inn, Caerphilly
               Mountain,junct 32 M4

Hotel   ★★★ 74% Manor Parc Country Hotel &
               Restaurant, Thornhill Rd, Thornhill, CARDIFF
               ☎ 029 2069 3723 12 ⇄ 🐾

Virginia Park Golf Club Virginia Park CF83 3SW
☎ 024 20863919 & 20585368
9 holes, 2566yds, Par 33.
Location   Off Pontyewindy Rd
Telephone for further details

Hotel   ★★★ 74% Manor Parc Country Hotel &
               Restaurant, Thornhill Rd, Thornhill, CARDIFF
               ☎ 029 2069 3723 12 ⇄ 🐾

MAESYCWMMER   Map 03 ST19

Bryn Meadows Golf & Country Hotel Mr G Mayo CF82
7FN ☎ 01495 225590 or 224103 Fax 01495 228272
e-mail: information@brynmeadows.co.uk
A heavily wooded parkland course with panoramic views of
the Brecon Beacons.
18 holes, 6132yds, Par 72, SSS 69, Course record 68.
Club membership 540.
Visitors   may not play Sun mornings. Must contact in
               advance.
Societies   Mon-Fri
Green Fees £15 per 18 holes(£25 weekends & bank
               holidays).
Cards   💳 💳 💳 💳 💳
Prof   Bruce Hunter
Designer   Mayo/Jeffries
Facilities   ⊗ 🏌 🏌 🍴 🍸 🏌 🛍 🏌 🐾 🎣 🏊 ✓ 🎯
& Leisure   heated indoor swimming pool, sauna, solarium,
               gymnasium.
Location   On the A4048 Blackwood to Ystrad Mynach rd

▶

Hotel ★★★ 67% Maes Manor Hotel,
BLACKWOOD ☎ 01495 224551 & 220011
Fax 01495 228217 8 ⇆ Annexe14 ⇆

NELSON

Map 03 ST19

Whitehall The Pavilion CF46 6ST ☎ 01443 740245
Hilltop course. Testing 4th hole (225 yds) par 3, and 6th hole
(402 yds) par 4. Pleasant views.
9 holes, 5666yds, Par 69, SSS 68, Course record 63.
Club membership 300.
Visitors must be a member of a recognised golf club &
have a handicap certificate. Must contact in
advance to play at weekends.
Societies must contact in writing 4 weeks in advance.
Green Fees £15 per round.
Facilities ㎏ ♥ ♀ ㏒
& Leisure snooker.
Location Turn off A470 to Nelson and take A4054 S

Hotel ★★★ 69% Llechwen Hall Hotel, Llanfabon,
PONTYPRIDD ☎ 01443 742050 & 743020
Fax 01443 742189 12 ⇆ ⋔ Annexe8 ⇆ ⋔

OAKDALE

Map 03 ST19

Oakdale Llwynon Ln NP12 0NF ☎ 01495 220044 220440
9 holes, 1344yds, Par 28, Course record 27.
Visitors no restrictions pay & play.
Societies
Green Fees not confirmed.
Designer Ian Goodenough
Facilities ㎏ ♥ ♀ ㏒ ☆ ⍲ ⤳ ♂ ⌀
& Leisure fishing, Snooker tables..
Location Situated off the B4251 to Portllanfraith Road at
Oakdale.

CARDIFF

CARDIFF

Map 03 ST17

Cardiff Sherborne Av, Cyncoed CF2 6SJ
☎ 029 20753320 Fax 029 20680011
Parkland course, where trees form natural hazards.
Interesting variety of holes, mostly bunkered. A stream flows
through course and comes into play on 9 separate holes.
18 holes, 6016yds, Par 70, SSS 70, Course record 66.
Club membership 900.
Visitors Must contact in advance.
Societies Thu only, pre-booking essential.
Green Fees not confirmed.
Prof Terry Hanson
Facilities ⊗ ⍝ ㎏ ♥ ♀ ㏒ ⍟ ⌀
& Leisure snooker.
Location 3m N of city centre

Hotel ★★★ 70% Posthouse Cardiff, Pentwyn Rd,
Pentwyn, CARDIFF
☎ 0870 400 8141 142 ⇆ ⋔

Cottrell Park Cottrell Park, St Nicholas CF5 6SJ
☎ 01446 781781 Fax 01446 781187
e-mail: admin@cottrell-park.co.uk
Two well designed courses, opened in 1996, set in undulating
parkland with mature trees and spectacular views, especially
from the par 35 9-hole course. An enjoyable yet testing game
of golf for players of all abilities.
*Mackintosh: 18 holes, 6110yds, Par 72, SSS 71, Course
record 65.*
Button: 9 holes, 2660yds, Par 70, SSS 67, Course record 27.
Club membership 1050.
Visitors Should have a valid handicap certificate,or be a
member of a golf club.
Societies welcome on Mon-Fri.
Green Fees not confirmed.
Cards ⊟ ▆ ▩ ▨
Prof Steve Birch
Designer MRM Sandow
Facilities ⊗ ⍝ ㎏ ♥ ♀ ㏒ ☆ ⍲ ⌘ ⤳ ♂ ⌀ ⍑
Location M4 junct 33 to Culverhouse Cross A48 to
Cowbridge, through St Nicholas on right hand
side

Hotel ★★★★ 70% Copthorne Cardiff-Caerdydd,
Copthorne Way, Culverhouse Cross, CARDIFF
☎ 029 2059 9100 135 ⇆ ⋔

Llanishen Cwm Lisvane CF4 5UD
☎ 029 20755078 Fax 029 20755078
Mountain course, with hard walking overlooking the Bristol
Channel.
18 holes, 5327yds, Par 68, SSS 67, Course record 63.
Club membership 900.
Visitors must play with member at weekends & bank
holidays. Must contact in advance.
Societies contact in advance.
Green Fees £30 per 18 holes.
Prof Adrian Jones
Facilities ⊗ ⍝ ㎏ ♥ ♀ ㏒ ⍟ ⌀
Location 5m N of city centre off A469

Hotel ★★★ 70% Posthouse Cardiff, Pentwyn Rd,
Pentwyn, CARDIFF
☎ 0870 400 8141 142 ⇆ ⋔

Peterstone Peterstone, Wentloog CF3 2TN
☎ 01633 680009 Fax 01633 680563 e-mail: peterstone-
lakes@yahoo.com
Parkland course with abundant water features and several
long drives (15th, 601yds).
Peterstone Golf Club: 18 holes, 6555yds, Par 72.
Club membership 600.
Visitors contact in advance for tee times.
Societies telephone enquiries welcome.
Green Fees not confirmed.
Cards ⊟ ▆ ▩
Designer Bob Sandow
Facilities ⊗ ⍝ ㎏ ♥ ♀ ㏒ ⌘ ⍜ ⤳ ♂ ⌀
Location 3m from Castleton off A48

Hotel ★★★ 72% St Mellons Hotel & Country Club,
Castleton, CARDIFF
☎ 01633 680355 21 ⇆ ⋔ Annexe20 ⇆ ⋔

Radyr The Clubhouse, Drysgol Rd, Radyr CF15 8BS
☎ 029 20842408 Fax 029 20843914
e-mail: themanager@radyrgolfclub.sagehost.co.uk
Parkland course which can be windy. Good views. Venue for
many county and national championships.
18 holes, 6031yds, Par 69, SSS 70, Course record 62.
Club membership 920.
Visitors	must play with member at weekends,or by special arrangement with club office.
Societies	must contact in advance.
Green Fees	£38 per day.
Cards	〰 📇 🏧 💳 💷
Prof	Robert Butterworth
Designer	Colt
Facilities	⊗ �𝄫 🖦 ☕ ♀ 🏕 🛎 ⛳ ➤ 🛒 ✐
& Leisure	Table tennis, snooker room.
Location	M4 junct32, 4.5m NW of city centre off A4119
Hotel	★★★ 74% Manor Parc Country Hotel & Restaurant, Thornhill Rd, Thornhill, CARDIFF ☎ 029 2069 3723 12 ⇋ ♜

St Mellons St Mellons CF3 2XS
☎ 01633 680408 Fax 01633 681219
This parkland course comprises quite a few par-3 holes
and provides some testing golf. It is indeed a challenge
to the single handicap golfer.
18 holes, 6275yds, Par 70, SSS 70, Course record 63.
Club membership 700.
Visitors	must contact in advance. With member only at weekends.
Societies	must contact in advance.
Green Fees	£32 per round/day.
Prof	Barry Thomas
Facilities	⊗ ⟁ 🖦 ☕ ♀ 🏕 🛎 ➤ 🛒 ✐
Location	5m NE off A48
Hotel	★★★ 72% St Mellons Hotel & Country Club, Castleton, CARDIFF ☎ 01633 680355 21 ⇋ ♜ Annexe20 ⇋ ♜

Whitchurch Pantmawr Rd, Whitchurch CF14 7TD
☎ 029 20620985 (Sec) Fax 029 20529860
Well manicured parkland course, slightly undulating, with
fine views over the city centre and the Bristol Channel
beyond.
18 holes, 6321yds, Par 71, SSS 70, Course record 62.
Club membership 750.
Visitors	may not play on competition days, contact secretary/professional in advance.
Societies	Thu only. Must contact in advance.
Green Fees	£30 per day (£40 weekends & bank holidays).
Prof	Eddie Clark
Designer	F Johns
Facilities	⊗ ⟁ 🖦 ☕ ♀ 🏕 🛎 ⛳ ✐
Location	4m N of city centre on A470, near junct 32 off M4
Hotel	★★★ 74% Manor Parc Country Hotel & Restaurant, Thornhill Rd, Thornhill, CARDIFF ☎ 029 2069 3723 12 ⇋ ♜

CREIGIAU (CREIYIAU)   Map 03 ST08

Creigiau Llantwit Rd CF15 9WN
☎ 029 20890263 Fax 20890706
Downland course, with small greens and many interesting
water hazards.
18 holes, 6063yds, Par 70.
Club membership 1300.
Visitors	must contact in advance
Societies	Deposit required.Apply by telephone or writing.
Green Fees	£30 per 18 holes.
Cards	〰 📇 🏧 💳 💷
Prof	Iain Luntz
Facilities	⊗ ⟁ 🖦 ☕ ♀ 🏕 🛎 ⛳ ✐
Location	6m NW of Cardiff on A4119
Hotel	★★★★ 69% Miskin Manor Hotel, Groes Faen, Pontyclun, MISKIN ☎ 01443 224204 35 ⇋ ♜ Annexe11 ⇋ ♜

AMMANFORD   Map 03 SN61

Glynhir Glynhir Rd, Llandybie SA18 2TF
☎ 01269 850472 & 851365 Fax 01269 851365
e-mail: glynhir.golfclub@virgin.net
Parkland course with good views, latter holes close to Upper
Loughor River. The 14th is a 394-yd dog leg.
18 holes, Par 69, SSS 70, Course record 66.
Club membership 700.
Visitors	no visitors Sun. Contact professional in advance (01269 851010).
Societies	welcome weekdays only. Contact in advance.
Green Fees	£16(£22 weekends).
Prof	Duncan Prior
Designer	F Hawtree
Facilities	⊗ ⟁ 🖦 ☕ ♀ 🏕 🛎 ⛳ ✐
Location	2m N of Ammanford
Hotel	★★ 68% Mill at Glynhir, Glyn-Hir, Llandybie, AMMANFORD ☎ 01269 850672 11 ⇋ ♜

BURRY PORT   Map 02 SN40

Ashburnham Cliffe Ter SA16 0HN
☎ 01554 832269 & 833846
18 holes, 6916yds, Par 72, SSS 74, Course record 70.
Location 5m W of Llanelli, A484 road
Telephone for further details
Hotel	★★ 69% Ashburnham Hotel, Ashburnham Rd, Pembrey, LLANELLI ☎ 01554 834343 & 834455 Fax 01554 834483 12 ⇋ ♜

Where to stay, where to eat?
Visit the AA internet site
www.theAA.com

407

CARMARTHEN   Map 02 SN42

Carmarthen Blaenycoed Rd SA33 6EH ☎ 01267 281588
Hilltop course with good views.
18 holes, 6245yds, Par 71, SSS 71, Course record 66.
Club membership 700.
Visitors   must have a handicap certificate, telephone for
               times at weekends.
Societies   apply in writing minimum of ten days in
               advance.
Green Fees   not confirmed.
Prof   Pat Gillis
Designer   J H Taylor
Facilities   ⊗ ⅲ ᇈ ♥ ♀ ♨ 🏠 🏌 ♦ 𝄢
Location   4m N of town

Hotel   ★★ 63% Falcon Hotel, Lammas St,
               CARMARTHEN ☎ 01267 234959 & 237152
               Fax 01267 221277   14 ⇆ ♠

Derllys Court Llysonnen Rd SA33 5DT
☎ 01267 211575 Fax 01267 211575
e-mail: derllys@hotmail.com
Gently undulating parkland course with challenging par 3s
(5th and 8th) and a testing par 5 involving a shot across a
lake.
9 holes, 2859yds, Par 35, SSS 66, Course record 33.
Club membership 60.
Visitors   welcome at all times.
Societies   telephone in advance.
Green Fees   not confirmed.
Cards   ▭ ▭ ▭ ▭ ▭ ▭
Designer   Peter Johnson
Facilities   ⊗ ⅲ ᇈ ♥ ♀ ♨ 🏠 🏌 🎣 𝄢
Location   Just off A40 between Carmarthen/St Clears

Hotel   ★★ 63% Falcon Hotel, Lammas St,
               CARMARTHEN ☎ 01267 234959 & 237152
               Fax 01267 221277   14 ⇆ ♠

KIDWELLY   Map 02 SN40

Glyn Abbey Trimsaran SA17 4LB
☎ 01554 810278 Fax 01554 810889
e-mail: glynabbey@aol.com
In the Gwendraeth valley, a 18-hole parkland course with
greens well protected by the planting of 35,000 trees.
18 holes, 6173yds, Par 70, SSS 70, Course record 68.
Club membership 200.
Visitors   telephone booking advisable.
Societies   must contact in advance.
Green Fees   £12 per round (£15 weekends).
Prof   Neil Evans
Designer   Hawtree
Facilities   ⊗ ⅲ ᇈ ♥ ♀ ♨ 🏠 🏌 🎣 ♦ 🎣 𝄢 ⎰
& Leisure   gymnasium.
Location   4.5m W of Llanelli

Hotel   ★★ 69% Ashburnham Hotel, Ashburnham Rd,
               Pembrey, LLANELLI
               ☎ 01554 834343 & 834455
               Fax 01554 834483   12 ⇆ ♠

CEREDIGION

ABERYSTWYTH   Map 06 SN58

Aberystwyth Brynymor Rd SY23 2HY
☎ 01970 615104 Fax 01970 626622
e-mail: aberystwythgolf@talk21.com
Undulating meadowland course. Testing holes: 16th (The
Loop) par 3; 17th, par 4; 18th, par 3. Good views over
Cardigan Bay.
18 holes, 6109yds, Par 70, SSS 70, Course record 67.
Club membership 400.
Visitors   must contact in advance.
Societies   write or telephone in advance.
Green Fees   £18.50 per round (£25 weekends & bank
               holidays).
Cards   ▭ ▭ ▭ ▭ ▭ ▭
Designer   Harry Vardon
Facilities   ⊗ ⅲ ᇈ ♥ ♀ ♨ 🏠 𝄢
Location   N side of town

Hotel   ★★★ 70% Belle Vue Royal Hotel, Marine Ter,
               ABERYSTWYTH ☎ 01970 617558   34 ⇆ ♠

BORTH   Map 06 SN69

Borth & Ynyslas SY24 5JS
☎ 01970 871202 Fax 01970 871202
e-mail: secretary@borthgolf.co.uk
Seaside links, over 100 years old, with strong winds at times
although part of the course is sheltered amongst the dunes.
Some narrow fairways and plenty of natural hazards.
18 holes, 6116yds, Par 70, SSS 70, Course record 65.
Club membership 550.
Visitors   must contact in advance, may play weekends
               ring to check no competitions in progress.
Societies   telephone in advance.
Green Fees   not confirmed.
Prof   J G Lewis
Facilities   ⊗ ᇈ ♥ ♀ ♨ 🏠 🏌 ⎰ 𝄢
Location   0.5m N on B4353

Hotel   ★★★★♨ Ynyshir Hall, EGLWYSFACH
               ☎ 01654 781209 8 ⇆ ♠ Annexe2 ⇆ ♠

CARDIGAN   Map 02 SN14

Cardigan Gwbert-on-Sea SA43 1PR
☎ 01239 621775 & 612035 Fax 01239 621775
e-mail: golf@cardigan.fsnet.co.uk
A links course, very dry in winter, with wide fairways, light
rough and gorse. Every hole overlooks the sea.
18 holes, 6687yds, Par 72, SSS 73, Course record 68.
Club membership 600.
Visitors   may not play between 1-2pm. Handicap
               certificate preferred. Contact in advance
Societies   must telephone in advance.
Green Fees   £20 per day (£25 weekends & bank holidays).
Cards   ▭ ▭ ▭ ▭ ▭
Prof   Colin Parsons
Designer   Hawtree
Facilities   ⊗ ⅲ ᇈ ♥ ♀ ♨ 🏠 🏌 ♦ 🎣 𝄢
& Leisure   squash.
Location   3m N off A487

▶

Hotel ★★★ 67% Cliff Hotel, GWBERT-ON-SEA
☎ 01239 613241 70 ⇄ ⦅

GWBERT-ON-SEA   Map 02 SN15

Cliff Hotel SA43 1PP ☎ 01239 613241 Fax 01239 615391
This is a short course with 2 Par 4's and the remainder are
challenging Par 3's. Particularly interesting holes are played
across the sea on to a small island.
9 holes, 1545yds, Par 29.

Visitors   telephone to book in advance.
Societies   telephone in advance.
Green Fees not confirmed.
Cards   ▭ ▭ ▣
Facilities ⛴ 🏠 ⚑ 🎯 ⚑ ♂
& Leisure   heated outdoor swimming pool, squash, fishing,
                sauna, solarium, gymnasium.
Hotel   ★★★ 67% Cliff Hotel, GWBERT-ON-SEA
                ☎ 01239 613241 70 ⇄ ⦅

LLANDYSSUL   Map 02 SN44

Saron Saron SA44 5EL ☎ 01559 370705
Set in 50 acres of mature parkland with large trees and
magnificent Teifi Valley views. Numerous water hazards and
bunkers.
9 holes, 2400yds, Par 32, Course record 34.
Visitors   may play at all times no arrangements required.
Societies   telephone for details.
Green Fees £8 per 18 holes, £6 per 9 holes.
Designer   Adas
Facilities ⚑ 🎯 ♂
& Leisure   fishing.
Location   Off A484 at Saron

Hotel   ★★ 73% Ty Mawr Country Hotel &
                Restaurant, BRECHFA
                ☎ 01267 202332 5rm(4 ⇄ ⦅)

LLANGYBI   Map 02 SN65

Cilgwyn SA48 8NN ☎ 01570 493286
Picturesque parkland course in secluded valley, with natural
hazards of ponds, stream and woodland.
9 holes, 5309yds, Par 68, SSS 66, Course record 66.
Club membership 300.
Visitors   no restrictions, apart from Sun when advisable
                to telephone.
Societies   apply in advance by letter or telephone.

Green Fees not confirmed.
Designer   Sandor
Facilities ⊗ by prior arrangement)Ⅲ by prior arrangement
                ℔ by prior arrangement ▇ ♀ ⅄ 🏠 ♂
Location   5m N of Lampeter on A485

Hotel   ★★★ 68% Falcondale Mansion, LAMPETER
                ☎ 01570 422910 19 ⇄ ⦅

LLANRHYSTUD   Map 06 SN56

Penrhos Golf & Country Club SY23 5AY
☎ 01974 202999 Fax 01974 202100
e-mail: info@penrhosgolf.co.uk
Beautifully scenic course incorporating lakes and spectacular
coastal and inland views. Many leisure facilities.
Penrhos: 18 holes, 6641yds, Par 72, SSS 73,
Course record 71.
Academy: 9 holes, 1827yds, Par 31.
Club membership 300.
Visitors   must telephone, no jeans allowed on main
                course.
Societies   must telephone in advance.
Green Fees £18/£25 per day(£24/£32 weekends).
Cards   ▭ ▭ ▭ ▭ ▣
Prof   Paul Diamond
Designer   Jim Walters
Facilities ⊗)Ⅲ ℔ ▇ ♀ ⅄ 🏠 ⚑ 🎯 ⛴ ♜ ⚓ ♂ ⚑
& Leisure   hard tennis courts, heated indoor swimming
                pool, sauna, solarium, gymnasium, bowling
                green.
Location   Turn off A487 onto B4337 in Llanrhystud.
                Course 0.25m on left

Hotel   ★★★▲▲ 75% Conrah Hotel, Ffosrhydygaled,
                Chancery, ABERYSTWYTH
                ☎ 01970 617941 11 ⇄ ⦅ Annexe6 ⇄ ⦅

CONWY

ABERGELE   Map 06 SH97

Abergele Tan-y-Gopa Rd LL22 8DS
☎ 01745 824034 Fax 01745 824034
A beautiful parkland course with views of the Irish Sea and
Gwrych Castle. There are splendid finishing holes, a testing
par 5, 16th; a 185 yd, 17th to an elevated green, and a superb
par 5 18th with out of bounds just behind the green.
18 holes, 6520yds, Par 72, SSS 71, Course record 66.
Club membership 1250.
Visitors   must contact in advance. Limited play
                weekends.
Societies   must contact in advance.
Green Fees not confirmed.
Prof   Iain R Runcie
Designer   Hawtree
Facilities ⊗)Ⅲ ℔ ▇ ♀ ⅄ 🏠 ♂
Location   0.5m W off A547/A55

Hotel   ★★★ 65% Kinmel Manor Hotel, St Georges
                Rd, ABERGELE ☎ 01745 832014 51 ⇄ ⦅

BETWS-Y-COED   Map 06 SH75

Betws-y-Coed LL24 0AL ☎ 01690 710556
Attractive flat meadowland course set between two rivers in
Snowdonia National Park.
9 holes, 4996yds, Par 64, SSS 63, Course record 63.
Club membership 350.
Visitors advisable to contact in advance.
Societies must telephone in advance.
Green Fees not confirmed.
Facilities ⊗ ⅷ ⅼ ♥ ♀ ♧ ∂
Location NE side of village off A5

Hotel ★★★ 70% The Royal Oak Hotel, Holyhead
Rd, BETWS-Y-COED
☎ 01690 710219 26 ⇌ ⋒

COLWYN BAY   Map 06 SH87

Old Colwyn Woodland Av, Old Colwyn LL29 9NL
☎ 01492 515581 e-mail: oldcolwyngolfclub.co.uk
Hilly, meadowland course with sheep and cattle grazing on it
in parts.
9 holes, 5243yds, Par 68, SSS 66, Course record 63.
Club membership 267.
Visitors welcome ex Sat. Contact in advance.
Societies must contact in advance.
Green Fees £10 per day (£15 weekends & bank holidays).
Designer James Braid
Facilities ⅼ ♀ ♧
Location E side of town centre on B5383

Hotel ★★★ 64% Hopeside Hotel, 63-67 Prince's Dr,
West End, COLWYN BAY
☎ 01492 533244 18 ⇌ ⋒

CONWY   Map 06 SH77

Conwy (Caernarvonshire) Beacons Way, Morfa
LL32 8ER ☎ 01492 592423 Fax 01492 593363
Founded in 1890, Conwy has hosted national and
international championships since 1898. Set among
sandhills, possessing true links greens and a profusion of
gorse on the latter holes, especially the 16th, 17th and
18th. This course provides the visitor with real golfing
enjoyment against a background of stunning beauty.
18 holes, 6647yds, Par 72, SSS 72, Course record 69.
Club membership 1050.
Visitors advisable to contact secretary in advance.
Limited play weekends.
Societies must contact in advance.
Green Fees £30 per day; £25 per round (£37/£32
weekends & bank holidays).
Prof Peter Lees
Facilities ⊗ ⅷ ⅼ ♥ ♀ ♧ ➔ ⋒ ☇ ♣ ∂
Location 1m W of town centre on A55

Hotel ★★★ 73% The Groes Inn, Tyn-y-Groes,
CONWY ☎ 01492 650545 14 ⇌ ⋒

AA Hotels that have special
arrangements with golf courses are listed at
the back of the guide

LLANDUDNO   Map 06 SH78

Llandudno (Maesdu) Hospital Rd LL30 1HU
☎ 01492 876450 Fax 01492 871570
Part links, part parkland, this championship course starts
and finishes on one side of the main road, the remaining
holes, more seaside in nature, being played on the other
side. The holes are pleasantly undulating and present a
pretty picture when the gorse is in bloom. Often windy,
this varied and testing course is not for beginners.
18 holes, 6545yds, Par 72, SSS 72, Course record 65.
Club membership 1045.
Visitors must book in advance.
Societies must apply in advance to secretary.
Green Fees £25 per day, £20 per round after 1pm
(£30/£25 weekends & bank holidays).
Prof Simon Boulden
Facilities ⊗ ⅷ ⅼ ♥ ♀ ♧ ➔ ⋒ ☇ ♣ ∂
& Leisure snooker.
Location S side of town centre on A546

Hotel ★★★ 68% Imperial Hotel, The
Promenade, LLANDUDNO
☎ 01492 877466 100 ⇌ ⋒

North Wales 72 Bryniau Rd, West Shore LL30 2DZ
☎ 01492 875325 Fax 01492 873355
e-mail: nwgc@northwales.uk.com
Challenging seaside links with superb views of Anglesey
and Snowdonia.
18 holes, 6247yds, Par 71, SSS 71, Course record 65.
Club membership 683.
Visitors must contact in advance.
Societies must contact in advance.
Green Fees £18 per round;£25 per day(£23/£35
weekends).
Cards 🔲 🔲 🔲
Prof Richard Bradbury
Designer Tancred Cummins
Facilities ⊗ ⅷ ⅼ ♥ ♀ ♧ ➔ ⋒ ☇ ♣ ∂
& Leisure snooker.
Location W side of town on A546

Hotel ★★ St Tudno Hotel and Restaurant, The
Promenade, LLANDUDNO
☎ 01492 874411 19 ⇌ ⋒

Rhos-on-Sea Penrhyn Bay LL30 3PU
☎ 01492 548115 (Prof) & 549641 (clubhouse)
Fax 01492 549100
Seaside course, with easy walking and panoramic views.
18 holes, 6064yds, Par 69, SSS 69, Course record 68.
Club membership 400.
Visitors advised to telephone beforehand to guarantee tee
times.
Societies booking essential, telephone in advance.
Green Fees £20 per day(£28 weekends).
Prof Mike Macara
Designer J J Simpson
Facilities ⊗ ⅷ ⅼ ♥ ♀ ♧ ➔ ⋒ ∂
Location 0.5m W of LLandudno, off the A55

Hotel ★★★ 64% Hopeside Hotel, 63-67 Prince's
Dr, West End, COLWYN BAY
☎ 01492 533244 18 ⇌ ⋒

LLANFAIRFECHAN   Map 06 SH67

Llanfairfechan Llannerch Rd LL33 0ES
☎ 01248 680144 & 680524
Hillside course with panoramic views of coast.
9 holes, 3119yds, Par 54, SSS 57, Course record 53.
Club membership 176.
Visitors   contact in advance, booking necessary at
                weekends.
Societies   apply in writing.
Green Fees £10 per day.
Facilities ♀ ♨
Location   W side of town on A55

Hotel   ★★ 67% Castle Bank Hotel, Mount Pleasant,
                CONWY ☎ 01492 593888 9 ♠

PENMAENMAWR   Map 06 SH77

Penmaenmawr Conway Old Rd LL34 6RD
☎ 01492 623330 Fax 01492 622105
Hilly course with magnificent views across the bay to
Llandudno and Anglesey. Dry-stone wall natural hazards.
9 holes, 5350yds, Par 67, SSS 66, Course record 62.
Club membership 600.
Visitors   advisable to contact in advance. May not play
                Sat.
Societies   must contact in advance.
Green Fees not confirmed.
Facilities ⊗ ⊮ ⅃ ♥ ♀ ♨ ♂
Location   1.5m NE off A55

Hotel   ★★★ 66% The Castle Hotel, High St,
                CONWY ☎ 01492 592324 29 ⇄ ♠

DENBIGHSHIRE

BODELWYDDAN   Map 06 SJ07

Kimnel Park LL18 5SR
☎ 01745 833548 Fax 01745 833544
Flat parkland pay and play course that is suitable for
beginners.
9 holes, 3100, Par 58, SSS 58.
Visitors   no restrictions.
Societies   telephone for details.
Green Fees not confirmed.
Prof   Peter Stebbings
Designer   Peter Stebbings
Facilities ⅃ ♥ ♨ ♂ ♂ ♠
& Leisure   golf academy.

Hotel   ★★★ 67% Oriel House Hotel, Upper Denbigh
                Rd, ST ASAPH ☎ 01745 582716 19 ⇄ ♠

DENBIGH   Map 06 SJ06

Bryn Morfydd Hotel Llanrhaedr LL16 4NP
☎ 01745 890280 Fax 01745 890488
In a beautiful setting in the Vale of Clwyd, the original 9
hole Duchess course was designed by Peter Alliss in 1982. In
1992, the 18-hole Dukes course was completed: a parkland
course designed to encourage use of finesse in play.

Dukes Course: 18 holes, 5650yds, Par 70, SSS 67,
Course record 74.
Duchess Course: 9 holes, 2098yds, Par 27.
Club membership 200.
Visitors   must book in advance, good standards of dress
                apply.
Societies   apply in writing.
Green Fees £15 per 18 holes (£20 weekends); Duchess £5
                per round.
Cards   ⊡ ⬛ ⬛ ⬛ ☑
Prof   Ivor Jones
Designer   Peter Allis/Duncan Muirhead
Facilities ⊮ ⅃ ♥ ♀ ♨ ♂ ♂ ♂ ♨ ♂
Location   On A525 between Denbigh and Ruthin

Denbigh Henllan Rd LL16 5AA
☎ 01745 814159 Fax 814888
e-mail: secretary@denbighgolfclub.fsbusiness.co.uk
Parkland course, giving a testing and varied game. Good
views.
18 holes, 5712yds, Par 69, SSS 68, Course record 64.
Club membership 725.
Visitors   must contact in advance.
Societies   apply in writing.
Green Fees £24 (£30 weekends & bank holidays).
Prof   Mike Jones
Designer   John Stockton
Facilities ⊗ ⊮ ⅃ ♥ ♀ ♨ ♂ ♂
Location   1.5m NW on B5382

Hotel   ★★★ 67% Oriel House Hotel, Upper Denbigh
                Rd, ST ASAPH ☎ 01745 582716 19 ⇄ ♠

LLANGOLLEN   Map 07 SJ24

Vale of Llangollen Holyhead Rd LL20 7PR
☎ 01978 860906 Fax 01978 860906
Parkland course, set in superb scenery by the River Dee.
18 holes, 6656yds, Par 72, SSS 73, Course record 66.
Club membership 800.
Visitors   must contact in advance. Restricted club
                competition days. Handicap certificate required.
Societies   apply in writing to the secretary.
Green Fees £20 per round (£25 weekends).
Cards   ⊡ ⬛ ⬛ ⬛ ☑
Prof   David Vaughan
Facilities ⊗ ⊮ ⅃ ♥ ♀ ♨ ♂ ♂
Location   1.5m E on A5

Hotel   ★★★♨ 66% Bryn Howel Hotel & Restaurant,
                LLANGOLLEN ☎ 01978 860331 36 ⇄ ♠

PRESTATYN   Map 06 SJ08

Prestatyn Marine Rd East LL19 7HS
☎ 01745 854320 Fax 01745 888327
e-mail: manager@prestatyngc.co.uk
Very flat seaside links exposed to stiff breeze. Testing holes:
9th, par 4, bounded on 3 sides by water; 10th, par 4; 16th, par
4.
18 holes, 6564yds, Par 72, SSS 72, Course record 66.
Club membership 710.
Visitors   welcome except Sat & Tue mornings. Must
                contact in advance.
Societies   prior booking required.
Green Fees £22/£27 per day.
Prof   Malcolm Staton   ▶

411

Designer S Collins
Facilities ⊗ ⫿ 🄻 🖵 ♀ ♨ 🏠 ⚐ ✦
& Leisure snooker.
Location 0.5m N off A548

Hotel ★★ 60% Hotel Marina, Marine Dr, RHYL
☎ 01745 342371 29 ⇄ 🐾

St Melyd The Paddock, Meliden Rd LL19 8NB
☎ 01745 854405 Fax 01745 856908
e-mail: info@stmelydgolf.co.uk
Parkland course with good views of mountains and Irish Sea.
Testing 1st hole (423 yds) par 4. 18 tees.
9 holes, 5829yds, Par 68, SSS 68, Course record 65.
Club membership 400.
Visitors must contact in advance.
Societies must telephone in advance.
Green Fees £18(£22 weekends & bank holidays).reductions
in winter..
Prof Richard Hughes
Facilities ⊗ ⫿ 🄻 🖵 ♀ ♨ 🏠
& Leisure snooker.
Location 0.5m S on A547

Hotel ★★ 60% Hotel Marina, Marine Dr, RHYL
☎ 01745 342371 29 ⇄ 🐾

RHUDDLAN   Map 06 SJ07

Rhuddlan Meliden Rd LL18 6LB
☎ 01745 590217 (Sec) & 590898(Pro) Fax 01745 590472
e-mail: golf@rhuddlangolfclub.fsnet.co.uk
Attractive, gently undulating parkland course with good
views. Well bunkered with trees and water hazards. The 476
yard 8th and 431 yard 11th require both length and accuracy.
The clubhouse has been refurbished.
18 holes, 6471yds, Par 71, SSS 71, Course record 66.
Club membership 1060.
Visitors must contact in advance. Sun with member only.
Societies telephone to book reservation.
Green Fees £26 per day; £20 per round (£30/£25 Fri)£30 per
round Sat.
Cards 💳 🟥 🟦 🟩
Prof Andrew Carr
Designer Hawtree & Son
Facilities ⊗ ⫿ 🄻 🖵 ♀ ♨ 🏠 ⚐ ♣ 🚜 ✦
Location E side of town on A547

Hotel ★★★ 65% Kinmel Manor Hotel, St Georges
Rd, ABERGELE ☎ 01745 832014 51 ⇄ 🐾

RHYL   Map 06 SJ08

Rhyl Coast Rd LL18 3RE
☎ 01745 353171 Fax 01745 353171
e-mail: rhylgolfclub@hotmail.com
Seaside course.
9 holes, 6220yds, Par 70, SSS 70, Course record 65.
Club membership 600.
Visitors must contact in advance. Limited availability at
weekends due to club competitions.
Societies must contact in advance/see web site
Green Fees See website for fees.
Prof Tim Leah
Designer James Braid
Facilities ⊗ ⫿ 🄻 🖵 ♀ ♨ 🏠 ⚐ ♣ 🚜 ✦
Location 1m E on A548

Hotel ★★ 60% Hotel Marina, Marine Dr, RHYL
☎ 01745 342371 29 ⇄ 🐾

RUTHIN   Map 06 SJ15

Ruthin-Pwllglas Pwllglas LL15 2PE
☎ 01978 790692 Fax 01978 790692
Hilly parkland course in elevated position with panoramic
views. Stiff climb to 3rd and 9th holes.
10 holes, 5362yds, Par 66, SSS 66.
Club membership 380.
Visitors welcome except for competition days.
Societies apply in writing or telephone.
Green Fees £15 per 18 holes.
Prof M Jones
Facilities ⊗ by prior arrangement ♀ ♨
Location 2.5m S off A494

Hotel ★★★ 68% Ruthin Castle, RUTHIN
☎ 01824 702664 58 ⇄ 🐾

ST ASAPH   Map 06 SJ07

Llannerch Park North Wales Golf Range, Llannerch Park
LL17 0BD ☎ 01745 730805
9 holes, 1587yds, Par 30.
Visitors pay & play.
Societies telephone in advance.
Green Fees £3 per round.
Designer B Williams
Facilities 🖵 🏠 ⚐ 🍴
Location 200yds S off A525

BRYNFORD   Map 07 SJ17

Holywell Brynford CH8 8LQ
☎ 01352 713937 & 710040 Fax 01352 713937
e-mail: holywell_golf_club@lineone.net
Links type course on well drained mountain turf, with
bracken and gorse flanking undulating fairways. 720 ft above
sea level.
18 holes, 6100yds, Par 70, SSS 70, Course record 67.
Club membership 505.
Visitors advisable to book in advance particularly for
weekends.
Societies by prior arrangement with the secretary.
Green Fees £16 per 18 holes(£23 weekends).
Prof Matt Parsleyr
Facilities ⊗ ⫿ 🄻 🖵 ♀ ♨ 🏠 🚜 ✦
Location 1.25m SW off B5121

Hotel ★★ 67% Stamford Gate Hotel, Halkyn Rd,
HOLYWELL ☎ 01352 712942 12 ⇄ 🐾

Entries with a green background
identify courses considered to be
particularly interesting

CAERWYS   Map 06 SJ17

Caerwys Nine Of Clubs CH7 5AQ ☎ 01352 720692
9 holes, 3080yds, Par 60, Course record 61.
Location   1.5m SW of A55, midway between St Asaph
             and Holywell
Telephone for further details

Hotel   ★★ 65% Bryn Awel Hotel, Denbigh Rd,
             MOLD ☎ 01352 758622
             7 ⇌ ♠ Annexe10 ⇌ ♠

FLINT   Map 07 SJ27

Flint Cornist Park CH6 5HJ
☎ 01244 812974 Fax 01244 811885
e-mail: owens.trave@ukonline.co.uk
Parkland course incorporating woods and streams. Excellent
views of Dee estuary and the Welsh hills.
9 holes, 6984yds, Par 69, SSS 69, Course record 65.
Club membership 260.
Visitors   must contact in advance, not Sun.
Societies   not weekends.
Green Fees £10 per day.
Designer   H G Griffith
Facilities   ⊗ ⓛ ♥ ♀ ♨
Location   1m W

HAWARDEN   Map 07 SJ36

Hawarden Groomsdale Ln CH5 3EH
☎ 01244 531447 & 520809
18 holes, 5842yds, Par 69, SSS 69.
Location   W side of town off B5125
Telephone for further details

Hotel   ★★★ 66% The Gateway To Wales Hotel,
            Welsh Rd, Sealand, Deeside, CHESTER
            ☎ 01244 830332 39 ⇌ ♠

MOLD   Map 07 SJ26

Old Padeswood Station Ln, Padeswood CH7 4JL
☎ 01244 547401 & 547701 Fax 01244 545082
Situated in the beautiful Alyn Valley, half on flat parkland
and half undulating. Striking mountain views.
18 holes, 6685yds, Par 72, SSS 72, Course record 66.
Club membership 600.
Visitors   welcome, subject to tee availability.
Societies   telephone in advance.
Green Fees £20 per round;£25 per day (f25 per round
           Sundays & bank holidays).
Prof   Tony Davies
Designer   Jeffries
Facilities   ⊗ ⋔ ⓛ ♥ ♀ ♨ 🏠 ⛳ ⚓ ✎
Location   3m SE off A5118

Hotel   ★★ 65% Bryn Awel Hotel, Denbigh Rd,
             MOLD ☎ 01352 758622
             7 ⇌ ♠ Annexe10 ⇌ ♠

Padeswood & Buckley The Caia, Station Ln, Padeswood
CH7 4JD ☎ 01244 550537 Fax 01244 541600
e-mail: padeswoodgc@compuserve.com
Gently undulating parkland course, with natural hazards and
good views of the Welsh Hills.
18 holes, 5982yds, Par 70, SSS 69.
Club membership 700.
Visitors   weekdays only, contact secretary in advance.
Societies   apply in writing.
Green Fees not confirmed.
Prof   David Ashton
Designer   Williams Partnership
Facilities   ⊗ ⋔ ⓛ ♥ ♀ ♨ 🏠 ⛳ ⚓ ✎ ♪
& Leisure snooker.
Location   3m SE off A5118

Hotel   ★★ 65% Bryn Awel Hotel, Denbigh Rd,
             MOLD ☎ 01352 758622
             7 ⇌ ♠ Annexe10 ⇌ ♠

NORTHOP   Map 07 SJ26

Northop Country Park CH7 6WA
☎ 01352 840440 Fax 01352 840445
e-mail: northop@stdavidshotel.co.uk
Designed by former British Ryder Cup captain, John Jacobs,
the parkland course gives the impression of having been
established for many years. No two holes are the same and
designed to allow all year play.
18 holes, 6750yds, Par 72, SSS 73, Course record 64.
Club membership 500.

Visitors   must contact in advance and have own
           equipment.
Societies   apply in writing or by telephone in advance.
Green Fees on application.
Cards   ▭ ▬ ▭ ▱
Prof   Matthew Pritchard
Designer   John Jacobs
Facilities   ⊗ ⋔ ⓛ ♥ ♀ ♨ 🏠 ⛳ ⚓ ✎ ♪
& Leisure hard tennis courts, sauna, gymnasium.
Location   150 yds from Connahs Quay turnoff on A55

Hotel   ★★★★ 72% De Vere St Davids Park, St
             Davids Park, EWLOE
             ☎ 01244 520800 145 ⇌ ♠

Where to stay, where to eat?
Visit the AA internet site
www.theAA.com

AA Hotels that have special
arrangements with golf courses are listed at
the back of the guide

PANTYMWYN   Map 07 SJ16

Mold Cilcain Rd CH7 5EH
☎ 01352 740318 & 741513 Fax 01352 741517
e-mail: moldgolfclub@tesco.net
Meadowland course with some hard walking and natural
hazards. Fine views.
18 holes, 5512yds, Par 67, SSS 67, Course record 63.
Club membership 700.
Visitors   contact in advance. Restricted play at weekends
Societies provisional booking by telephone.
Green Fees £18 (£25 per day, £20 per round weekends).
Prof   Mark Jordan
Designer   Hawtree
Facilities ⊗ 〲 ⓛ ⬛ ♀ ⚖ 🏠 ⚑ 🏌 🛒 ✒
Location   E side of village

Hotel   ★★ 65% Bryn Awel Hotel, Denbigh Rd,
               MOLD ☎ 01352 758622
               7 ⇆ 🐾 Annexe10 ⇆ 🐾

Entries with a green background
identify courses considered to be
particularly interesting

GWYNEDD

ABERDYFI   Map 06 SN69

ABERDYFI See page 415

ABERSOCH   Map 06 SH32

Abersoch LL53 7EY
☎ 01758 712622(shop) 712636(office)
Fax 01758 712777
e-mail: admin@abersochgolf.co.uk
Seaside links, with five parkland holes.
18 holes, 5819yds, Par 69, SSS 68, Course record 66.
Club membership 650.
Visitors   must contact in advance. Competition days Sun
               & Thu.
Societies must apply in advance.
Green Fees £18 per round (£20 weekends).
Prof   A D Jones
Designer   Harry Vardon
Facilities ⊗ 〲 ⓛ ⬛ ♀ ⚖ 🏠 ⚑ 🏌 🛒 ✒ ℓ
Location   S side of village

Hotel   ★★★ 76% Neigwl Hotel, Lon Sarn Bach,
               ABERSOCH
               ☎ 01758 712363 7 ⇆ 🐾 Annexe2 ⇆

Aberdovey Golf Course

Aberdyfi, *Gwynedd*   ☎ 01654 767493   Fax 01654 767027   Map 06 SN69

Golf was first played at Aberdovey in 1886, with the club founded in 1892. The links has since developed to become one of the finest championship courses in Wales. The club has hosted many prestigious events over the years and is popular with golfing societies and clubs who regularly return here.

Golfers can enjoy spectacular view from the course, which has all the characteristics of a true seaside links. Fine holes include the 3rd, the 11th and a good short hole at the 12th.

The late Bernard Darwin, former President and Captain of the club, was also golf correspondent for The Times. Many of his writings feature the course and he was a major contributor to its success. Darwin would easily recognise the course if he were to play it today, it remains in his words 'the course that my soul loves best of all the courses in the world'.

In 1995 the old clubhouse was destroyed by fire, however with the help of a lottery grant it was rebuilt. The fine new clubhouse which now graces the course was opened by HRH the Duke of York in 1998.

Visitors visitors welcome, handicap certificate required, must contact in advance, restrictions at weekends

Societies prior arrangement essential.

Green Fees Apr-Oct: weekday £42 per day, £30 per round; weekend £48 per day, £35 per round. Nov-Jan: weekday £24, weekend £26 (per day or round).

Facilities ⊗ ⅢI ⓛ ♥ ♀⚑ 🏠 ⚒ ⛟ ♂
Professional (John Davies)

Location 0.5m W on A493.

Holes/Par/Course record Holes/par/course record 18 holes, 6445 yds Par 71 SSS 71, Course record 66

WHERE TO STAY AND EAT NEARBY

ABERDYFI

Hotels and Restaurants
★★★ 71% Trefeddian Hotel, Aberdyfi LL35 0NA.
☎ 01654 767213. 59 (40 ⇄ 🐾 16 ⇄ 3 🐾)

★★ⓖ 72% Penhelig Arms Hotel & Restaurant, Aberdyfi LL35 OLT ☎ 01654 767215.
10 (6 ⇄ 4 🐾) Annexe 4 ⇄ 🐾

Championship Course

BALA   Map 06 SH93

Bala Penlan LL23 7YD
☎ 01678 520359 & 521361 Fax 01678 521361
Upland course with natural hazards. All holes except first
and last affected by wind. First hole is a most challenging
par3. Irrigated greens and good views of surrounding
countryside.
10 holes, 4962yds, Par 66, SSS 64, Course record 64.
Club membership 229.
Visitors   book in advance at weekends. Parties of more
                 than 4 people contact the secretary in advance.
Societies   must contact in advance.
Green Fees not confirmed.
Prof   A R Davies
Facilities   🏌 by prior arrangement ♀ ⚒ 🏠 ⛳ ⚐
Location   0.5m SW off A494

Hotel   ★★ 65% Plas Coch Hotel, High St, BALA
             ☎ 01678 520309 10 ⇄ 🐾

BANGOR   Map 06 SH57

St Deiniol Penybryn LL57 1PX ☎ 01248 353098
Elevated parkland course with panoramic views of
Snowdonia, Menai Straits, and Anglesey.
18 holes, 5068mtrs, Par 68, SSS 67, Course record 61.
Club membership 300.
Visitors   must contact in advance.
Societies   must contact in advance.
Green Fees £14 per day (£18 weekends).
Cards   💳 🎫 💳 🎫 🐾 🖩
Designer   James Braid
Facilities   ⊗ ⵇ 🏌 ♀ ♀ ⚒ 🏠 ⛳ ⚐
Location   E side of town centre off A5122

Hotel   ★★ 66% Anglesey Arms, MENAI BRIDGE
             ☎ 01248 712305 16 ⇄ 🐾

CAERNARFON   Map 06 SH46

Caernarfon Llanfaglan LL54 5RP
☎ 01286 673783 & 678359 Fax 01286 672535
e-mail: caerngc@talk21.com
Parkland course with gentle gradients.
Caernarfon Golf Club: 18 holes, 5891yds, Par 69, SSS 68,
Course record 64.
Club membership 730.
Visitors   must contact in advance.
Societies   must apply in advance, in writing or by
               telephone.
Green Fees £18 per day; £15 per round Mon: £15/£10
              (£23/£20 weekends).
Cards   💳 🎫 💳 🐾 🖩
Prof   Aled Owen
Facilities   ⊗ ⵇ 🏌 ♀ ♀ ⚒ 🏠 ⛳ ⚐
Location   1.75m SW

Hotel   ★★★ 68% Celtic Royal Hotel, Bangor St,
             CAERNARFON ☎ 01286 674477 110 ⇄ 🐾

Looking for a driving range?
See the index at the back of the guide

CRICCIETH   Map 06 SH43

Criccieth Ednyfed Hill LL52 0PH ☎ 01766 522154
18 holes, 5787yds, Par 69, SSS 68.
Location   1m NE
Telephone for further details

Hotel   ★★★🏌🏌 72% Bron Eifion Country House
             Hotel, CRICCIETH
             ☎ 01766 522385 19 ⇄ 🐾

DOLGELLAU   Map 06 SH71

Dolgellau Hengwrt Estate, Pencefn Rd LL40 2ES
☎ 01341 422603 Fax 01341 422603
e-mail: dolgellaugolfclub@hengwrt.fsnet.co.uk
Undulating parkland course. Good views of mountains and
Mawddach estuary.
9 holes, 4671yds, Par 66, SSS 63, Course record 62.
Club membership 150.
Visitors   no restrictions
Societies   must contact in advance.
Green Fees £15 per day (£20 weekends).
Cards   💳 🎫 💳 🎫 🐾 🖩
Designer   Jack Jones
Facilities   ⊗ ⵇ 🏌 ♀ ♀ ⚒ ⛳ ⚐
Location   0.5m N, near to Town Bridge

Hotel   ★★★🏌🏌 71% Plas Dolmelynllyn, Ganllwyd,
             DOLGELLAU ☎ 01341 440273 10 ⇄ 🐾

HARLECH   Map 06 SH53

Royal St Davids LL46 2UB
☎ 01766 780361 Fax 01766 781110
e-mail: secretsry@royalstdavids.co.uk
Championship links, with easy walking and natural
hazards.
18 holes, 6427yds, Par 69, SSS 72.
Club membership 800.
Visitors   pre booking essential, must hold current
             handicap certificate.
Societies   telephone secretary in advance. Handicap
             certificates required.
Green Fees £30 per round;£40 per day(£27.50/£33
              weekends). reductions in winter..
Cards   💳 🎫 💳 🐾 🖩
Prof   John Barnett
Facilities   ⊗ ⵇ 🏌 ♀ ♀ ⚒ 🏠 🍴 🛺 ⚐
Location   W side of town on A496

Hotel   ★★ 62% Ty Mawr Hotel, LLANBEDR
             ☎ 01341 241440 10 ⇄ 🐾

MORFA NEFYN   Map 06 SH24

Nefyn & District LL53 6DA
☎ 01758 720966 Fax 01758 720476
e-mail: nefyngolf@tesco.net
A 27-hole course played as two separate 18's, Nefyn is a
cliff top links where you never lose sight of the sea. A
well-maintained course which will be a very tough test
for the serious golfer, is still user friendly for the casual
visitor. Every hole has a different challenge and the old
13th fairway is approximately 30 yards acrross   ▶

---

from sea-to-sea. The course has an added bonus of a pub on the beach roughly halfway round for those whose golf may need some bolstering!

Old Course: 18 holes, 6201yds, Par 71, SSS 71, Course record 67.

New Course: 18 holes, 6317yds, Par 71, SSS 71, Course record 66.

Club membership 800.

Visitors	advisable to contact in advance.
Societies	apply by telephone.
Green Fees	£33 per day, £26 per round (£38/£31 weekends & bank holiday).
Cards	⊞ ▬ ▬ 🏧 🗗
Prof	John Froom
Designer	James Braid
Facilities	⊗ ⅲ ⅃ ♨ ♀ ⚘ 🏠 ⚐ ⚓ ⚒ ⚘
Location	0.75m NW
Hotel	★★ 78% Plas Bodegroes, Nefyn Rd, PWLLHELI ☎ 01758 612363 9 ⇄ 🐾 Annexe2 ⇄ 🐾

PORTHMADOG   Map 06 SH53

Porthmadog Morfa Bychan LL49 9UU
☎ 01766 514124 Fax 01766 514638
e-mail: secretary@porthmadog-golf-club.co.uk
Seaside links, very interesting but with easy walking and good views.

18 holes, 6363yds, Par 71, SSS 71.

Club membership 900.

Visitors	must contact in advance. Handicap certificate required.
Societies	apply by telephone initially.
Green Fees	not confirmed.
Prof	Peter L Bright
Designer	James Braid
Facilities	⊗ ⅲ ⅃ ♨ ♀ ⚘ 🏠 ⚐ ⚘
& Leisure	snooker.
Location	1.5m SW
Hotel	★★★⚞ 72% Bron Eifion Country House Hotel, CRICCIETH ☎ 01766 522385 19 ⇄ 🐾

PWLLHELI   Map 06 SH33

Pwllheli Golf Rd LL53 5PS ☎ 01758 701644
18 holes, 6091yds, Par 69, SSS 69, Course record 66.
Location   0.5m SW off A497
Telephone for further details

Hotel	★★ 78% Plas Bodegroes, Nefyn Rd, PWLLHELI ☎ 01758 612363 9 ⇄ 🐾 Annexe2 ⇄ 🐾

AA Hotels that have special arrangements with golf courses are listed at the back of the guide

MERTHYR TYDFIL   Map 03 SO00

Merthyr Tydfil Cilsanws Mountain, Cefn Coed CF48 2NU
☎ 01685 723308
Mountain-top course with good views. Requires accuracy off the tee.

18 holes, 5625yds, Par 69, SSS 68, Course record 65.

Club membership 210.

Visitors	may not play on Sun.
Societies	by prior arrangement.
Green Fees	£10 per round/day(£15 weekends).
Designer	V Price/R Mathias
Facilities	⊗ by prior arrangement ⅲ by prior arrangement ⅃ by prior arrangement ♨ by prior arrangement ♀ ⚘
Location	Off A470 at Cefn Coed
Hotel	★★★ 74% Nant Ddu Lodge Hotel, Cwm Taf, Nant Ddu, MERTHYR TYDFIL ☎ 01685 379111 12 ⇄ 🐾 Annexe10 ⇄ 🐾

Morlais Castle Pant, Dowlais CF48 2UY
☎ 01685 722822 Fax 01685 388700
Beautiful moorland course overlooking National Park with excellent views of Brecon Beacons and surrounding countryside. The interesting layout of the course makes for a testing game.

18 holes, 6320yds, Par 71, SSS 71, Course record 64.

Club membership 600.

Visitors	must contact in advance for weekends.
Societies	apply in writing.
Green Fees	£16(£20 weekends & bank holidays).
Prof	H Jarrett
Designer	James Braid
Facilities	⊗ ⅲ ⅃ ♨ ♀ ⚘ 🏠 ⚐ ⚓ ⚘
Location	2.5m N off A465. Follow signs for Mountain Railway. Course entrance opposite railway car park
Hotel	★★★ 74% Nant Ddu Lodge Hotel, Cwm Taf, Nant Ddu, MERTHYR TYDFIL ☎ 01685 379111 12 ⇄ 🐾 Annexe10 ⇄ 🐾

ABERGAVENNY   Map 03 SO21

Monmouthshire Gypsy Ln, LLanfoist NP7 9HE
☎ 01873 852606 Fax 01873 852606
This parkland course is very picturesque, with the beautifully wooded River Usk running alongside. There are a number of par 3 holes and a testing par 4 at the 15th.

18 holes, 5806yds, Par 70, SSS 69, Course record 65.

Club membership 700.

Visitors	must play with member at weekends. Must contact in advance & have handicap certificate.
Societies	must confirm in writing. ▶

Green Fees	£25 per day (£30 weekends & bank holidays).
Prof	B Edwards
Designer	James Braid
Facilities	⊗ ⅷ by prior arrangement 🏌 ♟ ♀ ⌂ 🏠 ⛳ ♿
Location	2m S off B4269

Hotel	★★ 70% Pantrhiwgoch Hotel & Riverside Restaurant, Brecon Rd, ABERGAVENNY ☎ 01873 810550 18 ⇄ ♞

Wernddu Golf Centre Old Ross Rd NP7 8NG
☎ 01873 856223 Fax 01873 852177
e-mail: wernddugolfclub.co.uk
A parkland course with magnificent views, wind hazards on several holes in certain conditions and water hazards on four holes. There is a 26 bay floodlit driving range.
18 holes, 5403yds, Par 68, SSS 67, Course record 64.
Club membership 550.
Visitors advisable to book in advance.
Societies telephone in advance.
Green Fees £15 per round.
Cards 💳 💳 💳 💳
Prof Alan Ashmead
Designer G Watkins
Facilities ⊗ 🏌 ♟ ♀ ⌂ 🏠 ⛳ ♿
Location 1.5m NE on B4521

Hotel	★★★ 66% Llansantffraed Court Hotel, Llanvihangel Gobion, ABERGAVENNY ☎ 01873 840678 21 ⇄ ♞

BETTWS NEWYDD   Map 03 SO30

Alice Springs NP15 1JY
☎ 01873 880244 & 880708 Fax 01873 880838
Two 18-hole undulating parkland courses set back to back with magnificent views of the Usk Valley. The Queen's course has testing 7th and 15th holes.
Monow Course: 18 holes, 5544yds, Par 69, SSS 69.
Usk Course: 18 holes, 5934, Par 70, SSS 70.
Club membership 500.
Visitors should contact the club in advance for weekend play.
Societies must telephone in advance.
Green Fees £15 per round (£17 weekends & bank holidays).
Cards 💳 💳 💳
Prof Mike Davies
Designer Keith R Morgan
Facilities ⊗ ⅷ by prior arrangement 🏌 ♟ ♀ ⌂ 🏠 ⛳ ♿ ♞ ♿ ⛳
Location N of Usk on B4598 towards Abergavenny

Hotel	★★★ 72% Three Salmons Hotel, Porthycarne St, USK ☎ 01291 672133 10 ⇄ ♞ Annexe14 ⇄ ♞

CAERWENT   Map 03 ST49

Dewstow NP26 5AH ☎ 01291 430444 Fax 01291 425816
Two picturesque parkland courses with easy walking and spectacular views over the Severn estuary towards Bristol. Testing holes include the Par three 7th, Valley Course, which is approached over water, some 50 feet lower than the tee,

and the Par four 15th, Park Course, which has a 50ft totem pole in the middle of the fairway, a unique feature. There is also a 26-bay floodlit driving range.
Valley Course: 18 holes, 6141yds, Par 72, SSS 70, Course record 68.
Park Course: 18 holes, 6200yds, Par 69, SSS 69, Course record 67.
Club membership 950.
Visitors may book 4 days in advance (six days in advance in winter).
Societies apply in writing or telephone for details.
Green Fees £15 (£18 weekends).
Cards 💳 💳 💳 💳 💳
Prof Jonathan Skuse
Facilities ⊗ ⅷ 🏌 ♟ ♀ ⌂ 🏠 ⛳ ♞ ♿ ♿ ♿
Location 0.5m S of A48 at Caerwent

Hotel	★★★ 63% George Hotel, Moor St, CHEPSTOW ☎ 01291 625363 14 ⇄ ♞

CHEPSTOW   Map 03 ST59

CHEPSTOW See page 419

Shirenewton Shirenewton NP16 6RL
☎ 01291 641642 Fax 01291 641472
Parkland course with magnificent views over the Severn estuary and extending to the Devon coastline.
18 holes, 6605yds, Par 72, SSS 72.
Club membership 350.
Visitors welcome, advisable to reserve tee times, must book at weekends
Societies apply in writing/telephone.
Green Fees telephone for rates..
Cards 💳 💳
Prof Lee Pagett
Facilities ⊗ ⅷ 🏌 ♟ ♀ ⌂ 🏠 ⛳ ♞ ♿ ♿ ♿
Location Junct 2 of M48 off A48 at Crick

Hotel	★★ 66% Beaufort Hotel, Beaufort Square, CHEPSTOW ☎ 01291 622497 18 ⇄ ♞

MONMOUTH   Map 03 SO51

Monmouth Leasebrook Ln NP25 3SN
☎ 01600 712212 (clubhouse) & 772399 (sec)
Fax 01600 772399 e-mail: sec.mongc@barbox.net
Parkland course in scenic setting. High, undulating land with good views.
18 holes, 5698yds, Par 69, SSS 69, Course record 68.
Club membership 600.
Visitors advisable to contact in advance, bank holidays only with member.
advance notice advisable, write or telephone secretary.
Green Fees £20 per day; £16 per round (£20 per round weekends).
Facilities ⊗ ⅷ 🏌 ♟ ♀ ⌂ 🏠 ⛳ ♞ ♿ ♿ ♿
Location 1.5m NE off A40

Hotel	★★ 66% Riverside Hotel, Cinderhill St, MONMOUTH ☎ 01600 715577 & 713236 Fax 01600 712668 17 ⇄ ♞

Looking for a driving range?
See the index at the back of the guide

Marriott St Pierre

Chepstow, *Monmouthshire*   ☎ 01291 625261   Fax 01291 629975   Map 03 ST59

Beautiful and challenging, the Old Course is one of the finest golf courses in the country and in recent years has played host to many major championships and staged the old Dunlop Masters. Among the many hazards the lake at the short 18th hole is particularly fearsome.

St Pierre is more than just a championship golfing venue. The Mathern presents its own challenges to experienced and weekend players alike, even the novice golfer can enjoy a game here. The hotel has teaching professionals as well as hire of clubs and equipment. A new 13 bay driving range was added in late 1998.

Visitors booking in advance, not less than 10 days notice, unless hotel resident.
Societies advance reservation required
Green Fees Old Course: £50 per round; Mathern Course: £35 per round
Facilities ⊗ ⋇ ⅃ ♨ ♥ ♀ ⌺ 🍴 ⛳ ⚐ ⟰ ∅ 🛈
Professional (Craig Dun)
Leisure tennis, swimming, sauna, solarium, gymnasium
Location St Pierre Park, Chepstow NP16 6YA (3m SW of town off A48)
Holes/Par/Course record Old Course: 18 holes, 6,700 yards, Par 71, SSS 73, Course Record 64. Mathern Course 18 holes, 5732 yds, Par 68, SSS 68

WHERE TO STAY AND EAT NEARBY

Hotels
CHEPSTOW

★★★★ 71% Marriott St Pierre Hotel & Country Club
☎ 01291 625261, 148 ⇆ 🐾

★★★ 61% The Old Course, Newport Road
☎ 01291 626261 31 ⇆ 🐾

★★ 70% Castle View, 16 Bridge St.
☎ 01291 620349 9(8 ⇆ 1 🐾) Annexe 4 ⇆

★★★ 63% The George Hotel, Moor St
☎ 01291 625363 14 ⇆ 🐾

TINTERN

★★ ⊛ 73% Parva Farmhouse Hotel
☎ 01291 689411 9(7 ⇆ 2 🐾)

★★ ⊛ 70% Royal George Hotel
☎ 01291 689205 2 ⇆ 🐾
Annexe 14 ⇆ 🐾

WHITEBROOK

★★ ⊛⊛ 70%
The Crown at Whitebrook
☎ 01600 860254 10 ⇆ 🐾

Restaurant
CHEPSTOW

⊛⊛ Wye Knot, The Bank
☎ 01291 622929

Championship Course

Rolls of Monmouth The Hendre NP25 5HG
☎ 01600 715353 Fax 01600 713115
A hilly and challenging parkland course encompassing several lakes and ponds and surrounded by woodland. Set within a beautiful private estate complete with listed mansion and panoramic views towards the Black Mountains. The short 4th has a lake beyond the green and both the 17th and 18th holes are magnificent holes with which to end your round.
18 holes, 6733yds, Par 72, SSS 73, Course record 69.
Club membership 147.
Visitors   must telephone in advance.
Societies   must contact in advance.
Green Fees £34 per day (£38 weekends).
Cards   🔲🔲🔲🔲🔲
Facilities   ⊗⍏🏌️♨️🍴♨️🧍‍♂️🏠⚑♣
Location   4m W on B4233

Hotel   ★★ 66% Riverside Hotel, Cinderhill St, MONMOUTH ☎ 01600 715577 & 713236 Fax 01600 712668   17 ⇄ 🏮

RAGLAN   Map 03 SO40

Raglan Parc Parc Lodge, Station Rd NP5 2ER
☎ 01291 690077
18 holes, 6604yds, Par 72, SSS 73, Course record 67.
Location   Off junct of A449/A40
Telephone for further details

Hotel   ★★★ 66% Llansantffraed Court Hotel, Llanvihangel Gobion, ABERGAVENNY ☎ 01873 840678   21 ⇄ 🏮

NEATH PORT TALBOT

GLYNNEATH   Map 03 SN80

Glynneath Pen-y-graig, Pontneathvaughan SA11 5UH
☎ 01639 720452 & 720872 Fax 01639 720452
Attractive hillside golf overlooking the Vale of Neath in the foothills of the Brecon Beacons National Park. Reasonably level farmland/wooded course.
18 holes, 5707yds, Par 69, SSS 68, Course record 63.
Club membership 665.
Visitors   restricted starting times at weekend.
Societies   must contact in advance.
Green Fees £17 per day (£22 weekends).
Designer   Cotton/Pennick/Lawrie
Facilities   ⊗⍏🏌️♨️🍴♨️🧍‍♂️🏠⚑♣
Location   2m NE off Glynneath on B4242

Hotel   ★★ 65% Castle Hotel, The Parade, NEATH ☎ 01639 641119 & 643581 Fax 01639 641624   29 ⇄ 🏮

Where to stay, where to eat?
Visit the AA internet site
www.theAA.com

MARGAM   Map 03 SS78

Lakeside Water St SA13 2PA ☎ 01639 899959
A parkland course with bunkers and natural hazards. Eight Par 4's and ten Par 3's.
18 holes, 4550yds, Par 63, SSS 63, Course record 65.
Club membership 250.
Visitors   no restrictions.
Societies   apply in advance by letter or telephone.
Green Fees £9.50 per 18 holes.
Cards   🔲🔲
Prof   Mathew Wootton
Designer   Matthew Wootton
Facilities   ⊗⍏🏌️♨️🍴♨️🧍‍♂️🏠⚑♣
Location   Off junct 38 of M4

Hotel   ★★★ 67% Aberavon Beach Hotel, PORT TALBOT ☎ 01639 884949   52 ⇄

NEATH   Map 03 SS79

Earlswood Jersey Marine SA10 6JP ☎ 01792 321578
Earlswood is a hillside course offering spectacular scenic views over Swansea Bay. The terrain is gently undulating downs with natural hazards and is designed to appeal to both the new and the experienced golfer.
18 holes, 5084yds, Par 68, SSS 68.
Visitors   no restrictions.
Societies   advisable to contact in advance.
Green Fees £8 per round;£12 per day.
Prof   Mike Day
Designer   Gorvett Estates
Facilities   🏌️♨️🍴♨️🧍‍♂️🏠⚑♣
Location   Approx 4m E of Swansea, off A483

Hotel   ★★ 65% Castle Hotel, The Parade, NEATH ☎ 01639 641119 & 643581 Fax 01639 641624   29 ⇄ 🏮

Neath Cadoxton SA10 8AH
☎ 01639 643615 (clubhouse) & 632759 (secretary)
Mountain course, with spectacular views. Testing holes: 10th par 4; 12th par 5; 15th par 4.
18 holes, 6492yds, Par 72, SSS 72, Course record 66.
Club membership 700.
Visitors   with member only at weekends & bank holidays.
Societies   should either telephone or write in advance.
Green Fees not confirmed.
Prof   M Bennett
Designer   James Braid   ▶

Facilities ⊗)Ⅲ 🖳 💺 ♀ ⚲ 🏠 ⛳ 🖊
& Leisure snooker.
Location 2m NE off A4230

Hotel ★★ 65% Castle Hotel, The Parade, NEATH
☎ 01639 641119 & 643581
Fax 01639 641624   29 ⇆ 🕻

Swansea Bay Jersey Marine SA10 6JP
☎ 01792 812198 & 814153
Fairly level seaside links with part-sand dunes.
18 holes, 6605yds, Par 72, SSS 72.
Club membership 500.
Visitors welcome.
Societies telephone enquiry or letter stating requirements.
Green Fees £16 per round (£22 weekends & bank holidays).
Prof Mike Day
Facilities ⊗)Ⅲ 🖳 💺 ♀ ⚲ 🏠 ⛳ 🖊
Location 4m E of Swansea off A483

Hotel ★★ 65% Castle Hotel, The Parade, NEATH
☎ 01639 641119 & 643581
Fax 01639 641624   29 ⇆ 🕻

PONTARDAWE   Map 03 SN70

Pontardawe Cefn Llan SA8 4SH
☎ 01792 863118 Fax 01792 830041
Meadowland course situated on plateau 600 ft above sea-level with good views over Bristol Channel and Brecon Beacons.
18 holes, 6038yds, Par 70, SSS 70, Course record 64.
Club membership 500.
Visitors must contact in advance, but may not play on weekends.
Societies apply in writing.
Green Fees £22 per day.
Prof Gary Hopkins
Facilities ⊗)Ⅲ 🖳 💺 ♀ ⚲ 🏠 🖊
Location N side of town centre M4 junc 45 off A4067

PORT TALBOT   Map 03 SS78

British Steel Port Talbot Sports & Social Club,
Margam SA13 2NF ☎ 01639 793194
A 9 hole course with two lakes. All the holes are affected by crosswinds and the 7th, Par 3, is alongside a deep stream, so is very tight.
9 holes, 4726yds, Par 62, SSS 63, Course record 60.
Club membership 250.
Visitors contact in advance, may not play at weekends.
Societies by prior arrangement
Green Fees not confirmed.
Facilities ⚲
& Leisure hard tennis courts, fishing.

Hotel ★★★ 67% Aberavon Beach Hotel, PORT
TALBOT ☎ 01639 884949   52 ⇆

> AA Hotels that have special
> arrangements with golf courses are listed at
> the back of the guide

CAERLEON   Map 03 ST39

Caerleon NP6 1AY ☎ 01633 420342
Parkland course.
9 holes, 2900yds, Par 34, SSS 34, Course record 29.
Club membership 148.
Visitors play is allowed on all days, contact for details.
Societies telephone 01633 420342.
Green Fees not confirmed.
Prof Chris Jones
Designer Steel
Facilities ⊗)Ⅲ 🖳 💺 ♀ ⚲ 🏠 ⛳ 🖊 🍸
Location 3m from M4 turn off for Caerleon

Hotel ★★★★★ 75% The Celtic Manor Resort,
Coldra Woods, NEWPORT
☎ 01633 413000 400 ⇆ 🕻

LLANWERN   Map 03 ST38

Llanwern Tennyson Av NP18 2DY
☎ 01633 412029 Fax 01633 412029
e-mail: llanwerngc@hotmail.com
Parkland Course.
18 holes, 6177yds, Par 70, SSS 69, Course record 66.
Club membership 650.
Visitors welcome, but with member only at weekends.
Societies telephone and confirm in writing.
Green Fees £20 per round(£25 weekends).
Prof Stephen Price
Facilities ⊗)Ⅲ 🖳 💺 ♀ ⚲ 🏠
Location 0.5m S off A455

Hotel ★★★★★ 75% The Celtic Manor Resort,
Coldra Woods, NEWPORT
☎ 01633 413000 400 ⇆ 🕻

NEWPORT   Map 03 ST38

Celtic Manor Resort Coldra Woods NP6 2YA
☎ 01633 410255 & 410260 Fax 01633 410269
e-mail: jholland@celtic-manor.com
Three different courses - Wentwood Hills combines hilly landscapes and links-like features. Roman Road has a long and wide front nine, the back nine weaves its way through ravines, lakes and streams beside the Usk valley. Coldra Woods is a scenic short course and is a challenging test of accuracy
Roman Road: 18 holes, 6495yds, Par 69, SSS 72, Course record 68.
Coldra Woods: 18 holes, 3807yds, Par 59, SSS 61.
Wentwood Hills: 18 holes, 7097yds, Par 72, SSS 75.
Club membership 400.
Visitors may play subject to availability, must book in advance
Societies telephone with details in advance.
Green Fees not confirmed.
Cards 🟥 ▬ 🟦 ▬ 🔲
Prof Chris Baron
Designer Robert Trent Jones
Facilities ⊗)Ⅲ 🖳 💺 ♀ ⚲ 🏠 ⛳ 🏊 🏌 🛶 🖊 🍸
& Leisure heated indoor swimming pool, sauna, solarium, gymnasium.
▶

Location   Off junct 24 on M4, midway between Bristol & Cardiff, take A48 to Newport,turn R after 300 metres

Hotel   ★★★★★ 75% The Celtic Manor Resort, Coldra Woods, NEWPORT
☎ 01633 413000 400 ⇆ ↾

Newport Great Oak, Rogerstone NP10 9FX
☎ 01633 892643 Fax 01633 896676
e-mail: newportgolfclub.gwent@cuphony.net
An undulating parkland course, in an ideal situation on an inland plateau 300ft above sea level with fine views over the surrounding wooded countryside. There are no blind holes, but plenty of natural hazards and bunkers.
18 holes, 6460yds, Par 72, SSS 71, Course record 63.
Club membership 800.
Visitors   must contact in advance, handicap certificate required. Not on Sat, limited time Sun.
Societies   must contact in writing or telephone
Green Fees   £30 per day;£25 per round(£40 per day Sun).
Prof   Paul Mayo
Designer   W Fernie
Facilities   ⊗ ⅷ ⅃ ♭ ▟ ♀ ♨ 🏠 ⅃ ♒ ♂
Location   1m NW of junct 27 on M4 on B4591 just beyond 'Promotive' Garage

Hotel   ★★★★★ 75% The Celtic Manor Resort, Coldra Woods, NEWPORT
☎ 01633 413000 400 ⇆ ↾

Parc Church Ln, Coedkernew NP10 8TU
☎ 01633 680933 Fax 01633 681011
A challenging but enjoyable 18-hole course with water hazards and accompanying wildlife. The 38-bay driving range is floodlit until 10pm.
18 holes, 5619yds, Par 70, SSS 68, Course record 71.
Club membership 400.
Visitors   must contact in advance 01633 680933.
Societies   telephone in advance.
Green Fees   not confirmed.
Prof   B Thomas/D Griffiths
Designer   B Thomas/T F Hicks
Facilities   ⊗ ⅷ ⅃ ♭ ▟ ♀ ♨ 🏠 ♒ ♖ ♂ ✔ ♂
Location   3m SW of Newport, off A48

Hotel   ★★★ 66% The Kings Hotel, High St, NEWPORT ☎ 01633 842020 61 ⇆ ↾

Tredegar Park Parc-y-Brain Rd, Rogerstone NP10 9TG
☎ 01633 894433 Fax 01633 897152
A new course completed in 1999 with two balanced halves, mostly in view from the clubhouse. A rolling, open course with fine scenic views.
18 holes, 6150yds, Par 72, SSS 72.
Club membership 750.
Visitors   must be a member of a golf club affiliated to a national golf union, please contact in advance.
Societies   apply to secretary.
Green Fees   not confirmed.
Cards   ▭▭ ▰▰
Prof   M L Morgan
Designer   R Sandow

Facilities   ⊗ ⅷ ⅃ ♭ ▟ ♀ ♨ 🏠 ♒ ♂
Location   N of M4, Junct 27, B4591, club signposted from here

Hotel   ★★★ 66% The Kings Hotel, High St, NEWPORT ☎ 01633 842020 61 ⇆ ↾

HAVERFORDWEST   Map 02 SM91

Haverfordwest Arnolds Down SA61 2XQ
☎ 01437 764523 & 768409 Fax 01437 764143
Fairly flat parkland course, a good challenge for golfers of all handicaps. Set in attractive surroundings with fine views over the Preseli Hills.
18 holes, 5966yds, Par 70, SSS 69, Course record 58.
Club membership 770.
Visitors   restricted at weekends.
Societies   apply in writing or telephone for booking form.
Green Fees   £19 per round (£22 weekends).
Cards   ▭▭ ▰▰ ▭▰ ▰▰ ▱
Prof   Alex Pile
Facilities   ⊗ ⅷ ⅃ ♭ ▟ ♀ ♨ 🏠 ♒ ♖ ♂ ♂
Location   1m E on A40

Hotel   ★★ 67% Hotel Mariners, Mariners Square, HAVERFORDWEST
☎ 01437 763353 28 ⇆ ↾

LETTERSTON   Map 02 SM92

Priskilly Forest Castlemorris SA62 5EH
☎ 01348 840276 Fax 01348 840276
e-mail: jevans@priskilly-forest.co.uk
Testing parkland course surrounded by rhododendrons. Beautiful panoramic views. Challenging dog-leg 4th with hazards both sides.
9 holes, 5874yds, Par 70, SSS 68, Course record 76.
Club membership 70.
Visitors   advance booking advisable at weekends during summer.
Societies   telephone in advance.
Green Fees   not confirmed.
Prof   S Parsons
Designer   J Walters
Facilities   ⊗ ⅃ ♭ ▟ ♀ ♨ 🏠 ♒ ♖ 🏠 ♒ ♖ ♂
& Leisure   fishing.
Location   Off B4331 between Letterston and Mathry

Hotel   ★★ 61% Abergwaun Hotel, The Market Square, FISHGUARD
☎ 01348 872077 10 ⇆ ↾

MILFORD HAVEN   Map 02 SM90

Milford Haven Woodbine House, Hubberston SA73 3RX
☎ 01646 697762 Fax 01646 697870
e-mail: enquires@mhgc.co.uk
Parkland course with excellent greens and views of the Milford Haven waterway.
18 holes, 6030yds, Par 71, SSS 70.
Club membership 650.   ▶

Visitors   no restrictions, advisable to contact in advance.
Societies   telephone to book.
Green Fees not confirmed.
Cards   🖃 🖃 🖃 🖃
Prof   Dylan Williams
Facilities   ⊗ 🏊 🏌 💺 ♀ 🏖 🏠 ⚑ ➤ ⛳ 🏌
Location   1.5m W of M.Haven

Hotel   ★★★ 67% Cleddau Bridge Hotel,
Essex Rd, PEMBROKE DOCK
☎ 01646 685961 & 0800 279 4055
Fax 01646 685746   24 ⇄ ℯ

NEWPORT (PEMBROKESHIRE)   Map 02 SN03

Newport (Pemb) The Golf Club SA42 0NR
☎ 01239 820244 Fax 01239 820244
Seaside links course, with easy walking and good view of the
Preselli Hills and Newport Bay.
9 holes, 5815yds, Par 70, SSS 68, Course record 64.
Club membership 350.
Visitors   telephone in advance.
Societies   must telephone in advance.
Green Fees not confirmed.
Prof   Colin Parsons
Designer   James Baird
Facilities   ⊗ 🏊 🏌 💺 ♀ 🏖 🏠 ⚑ 🏒 ➤ 🏌 ⛳
Location   1.25m N

Hotel   ★★ 68% Trewern Arms, NEVERN
☎ 01239 820395   10 ⇄ ℯ

PEMBROKE DOCK   Map 02 SM90

South Pembrokeshire Military Rd SA72 6SE
☎ 01646 621453
Parkland course overlooking the Cleddau River.
18 holes, 6100yds, Par 71, SSS 70, Course record 65.
Club membership 350.
Visitors   must contact in advance, especially during
season.
Societies   apply in advance.
Green Fees not confirmed.
Designer   Committee
Facilities   ⊗ 🏊 🏌 💺 ♀ 🏖 ⚑
Location   SW side of town centre off B4322

Hotel   ★★ 61% Old Kings Arms, Main St,
PEMBROKE ☎ 01646 683611   21 ⇄ ℯ

ST DAVID'S   Map 02 SM72

St David's City Whitesands Bay SA62 6HR
☎ 01437 720572 & 721751
Links course with alternative tees for 18 holes. Panoramic
views of St David's Head, Ramsey Island and Whitesands
Bay. The course is playable all year.
9 holes, 6117yds, Par 70, SSS 70, Course record 68.
Club membership 200.
Visitors   prior booking with secretary is encouraged but
no always necessary, please check for
weekends, Ladies Day Fri pm.
Societies   book with the secretary in advance.
Green Fees not confirmed.
Facilities   🏌 💺 ⛳
Location   2m W overlooking Whitesands Bay

Hotel   ★★★ Warpool Court Hotel, ST DAVID'S
☎ 01437 720300   25 ⇄ ℯ

TENBY   Map 02 SN10

Tenby The Burrows SA70 7NP
☎ 01834 844447 Fax 01834 844447
The oldest club in Wales, this fine old seaside links, with
sea views and natural hazards provides good golf all the
year round.
18 holes, 6224yds, Par 69, SSS 71.
Club membership 800.
Visitors   subject to competition & tee reservation.
Must produce handicap certificate.
Societies   must apply in advance.
Green Fees not confirmed.
Prof   Mark Hawkey
Designer   James Braid
Facilities   ⊗ 🏊 🏌 💺 ♀ 🏖 🏠 ⚑ 🏌 ⛳
Location   Close to railway station in the town

Hotel   ★★★ 74% Atlantic Hotel, The Esplanade,
TENBY ☎ 01834 842881 & 844176
Fax 01834 842881 ex 256 42 ⇄ ℯ

Trefloyne Trefloyne Park, Penally SA70 7RG
☎ 01834 842165 Fax 01834 842165
Idyllic parkland course with backdrop of mature mixed
woodlands and distant views of Tenby, Carmarthen bay and
Caldey Island. Opened in 1996, natural features and hazards
such as the Old Quarry make for exciting and challenging
golf.
18 holes, 6635yds, Par 71, SSS 73.
Club membership 263.
Visitors   must contact in advance, must play a reasonable
standard of golf and adhere to golf etiiquette and
dress code of club.
Societies   must book in advance by telephone or in
writing.
Green Fees not confirmed.
Cards   🖃 🖃 🖃 🖃 🖃
Prof   Steven Laidler
Designer   F H Gillman
Facilities   ⊗ 🏌 💺 ♀ 🏖 🏠 ⚑ ➤ 🚜 ⛳
& Leisure   lessons by PGA Professional.
Location   Within Trefloyne Park, just west of Tenby

Hotel   ★★★ 66% Fourcroft Hotel, North Beach,
TENBY ☎ 01834 842886   45 ⇄ ℯ

POWYS

BRECON   Map 03 SO02

Brecon Newton Park LD3 8PA ☎ 01874 622004
Parkland course, with easy walking. Natural hazards include
two rivers on its boundary. Good river and mountain scenery.
9 holes, 5256yds, Par 66, SSS 66, Course record 61.
Club membership 360.

▶

Visitors advisable to contact in advance, limited availability at weekends.
Societies apply in writing.
Green Fees £10 per day.
Designer James Braid
Facilities ⊗ 🄱 ☕ ♀ ⚒
Location 0.75m W of town centre on A40

Hotel ★★ 70% Best Western Castle of Brecon Hotel, Castle Square, BRECON
☎ 01874 624611   30 ⇥ 🄵 Annexe12 🄵

Cradoc Penoyre Park, Cradoc LD3 9LP
☎ 01874 623658 Fax 01874 611711
e-mail: secretary@cradoc.co.uk
Parkland with wooded areas, ponds and spectacular views over the Brecon Beacons. Challenging golf.
18 holes, 6331yds, Par 72, SSS 72, Course record 65.
Club membership 700.
Visitors must contact secretary in advance. Limited availability on Sundays
Societies apply in writing or telephone in advance to secretary.
Green Fees £20 per day (£25 weekends & bank holidays).
Cards ▭ ▬ 🄳
Prof Richard Davies
Designer C K Cotton
Facilities ⊗ 🍽 🄱 ☕ ♀ ⚒ 🄴 🔧 ➤ 𝄞 ⚒
Location 2m N on B4520

Hotel ★★ 70% Best Western Castle of Brecon Hotel, Castle Square, BRECON
☎ 01874 624611   30 ⇥ 🄵 Annexe12 🄵

BUILTH WELLS   Map 03 SO05

Builth Wells Golf Links Rd LD2 3NF
☎ 01982 553296 Fax 01982 551064
e-mail: builthwellsgolfclub@btinternet.com
Well guarded greens and a stream running thorough the centre of the course add interest to this 18-hole undulating parkland course. The clubhouse is a converted 16th-century Welsh long house.
18 holes, 5386yds, Par 66, SSS 67, Course record 63.
Club membership 380.
Visitors contact secretary. Handicap certificate perferred.
Societies by prior arrangement.
Green Fees £21 per day; £16 per round (£27/£22 weekends & bank holidays).
Prof Simon Edwards
Facilities ⊗ 🍽 🄱 ☕ ♀ ⚒ 🄴 🔧 𝄞
Location N of A483

Hotel ★★ 68% Pencerrig Gardens Hotel, Llandrindod Rd, BUILTH WELLS
☎ 01982 553226   20 ⇥ 🄵

CAERSWS   Map 06 SO09

Mid-Wales Golf Centre SY17 5SB
☎ 01686 688303 Fax 01686 688303
A 9-hole, Par 3 course with sand bunkers and three ponds.
9 holes, 2554yds, Par 54, SSS 54.
Club membership 95.
Visitors welcome, restricted during competitions on Sun am.
Societies telephone in advance.

Green Fees £6 per 18 holes; £4 per 9 holes (£8/£5 weekends & bank holidays).
Designer Jim Walters
Facilities 🄱 ☕ ♀ ⚒ 🄴 🔧 𝄞 ⚒
Location 0.75m off A470 out of Caersws

HAY-ON-WYE   Map 03 SO24

Summerhill Hereford Rd, Clifford HR3 5EW
☎ 01497 820451
9 holes, 2929yds, Par 70, SSS 67.
Location B4350 Whitney toll bridge road
Telephone for further details

Hotel ★★★ 66% The Swan-at-Hay Hotel, Church St, HAY-ON-WYE ☎ 01497 821188
16 ⇥ 🄵 Annexe3 ⇥ 🄵

KNIGHTON   Map 07 SO27

Knighton Ffrydd Wood LD7 1DB ☎ 01547 528646
Upland course with some hard walking. Fine views over the Welsh/English border.
9 holes, 5362yds, Par 68, SSS 66, Course record 65.
Club membership 150.
Visitors may not play on Sun until after 4.30pm.
Societies telephone in advance
Green Fees £10 per day (£12 weekends & bank holidays).
Designer Harry Vardon
Facilities ⊗ 🄱 ☕ ♀ ⚒
Location 0.5m S off B4355

Hotel ★★★ 63% The Knighton Hotel, Broad St, KNIGHTON ☎ 01547 520530   15 ⇥ 🄵

LLANDRINDOD WELLS   Map 03 SO06

Llandrindod Wells The Clubhouse LD1 5NY
☎ 01597 823873 (sec) & 822247 (shop) Fax 01597 823873
An upland links course, designed by Harry Vardon, with easy walking and panoramic views. One of the highest courses in Wales. (1,100 ft above sea level).
18 holes, 5759yds, Par 69, SSS 69, Course record 65.
Club membership 430.
Visitors no restrictions.
Societies must telephone in advance.
Green Fees £20 per day, £15 per round (£25/£20 weekends).
Designer H Vardon
Facilities ⊗ 🍽 🄱 ☕ ♀ ⚒ 🄴 🔧 ➤ 🏌 𝄞
Location 1m SE off A483

Hotel ★★★ Hotel Metropole, Temple St, LLANDRINDOD WELLS
☎ 01597 823700 121 ⇥ 🄵

LLANGATTOCK   Map 03 SO21

Old Rectory NP8 1PH
☎ 01873 810373 Fax 018373 810373
Sheltered course with easy walking.
9 holes, 2200yds, Par 54, SSS 59, Course record 53.
Club membership 80.
Visitors no play Sun mornings, telephone for information.
Societies telephone for booking.
Green Fees not confirmed.

Facilities & Leisure	⊗)Ⅲ ᛒ ❤ ♀ ⚷ ⚶ ♥ outdoor swimming pool.
Location	SW of village

Hotel ★★★ 71% Gliffaes Country House Hotel, CRICKHOWELL
☎ 01874 730371 & 0800 146719 (Freephone)
Fax 01874 730463   19 ⇌ ⋔ Annexe3 ⇌ ⋔

LLANIDLOES   Map 06 SN98

St Idloes Penrallt SY18 6LG   ☎ 01686 412559
9 holes, 5540yds, Par 66, SSS 66, Course record 61.
Location   1m N off B4569
Telephone for further details

MACHYNLLETH   Map 06 SH70

Machynlleth Ffordd Drenewydd SY20 8UH
☎ 01654 702000
Lowland course with mostly natural hazards.
9 holes, 5726yds, Par 68, SSS 68, Course record 65.
Club membership 250.
Visitors   Thur ladies day, Sun morning mens competition.
Societies   telephone in advance.
Green Fees £12(£15 weekends & bank holidays).
Designer   James Braid
Facilities   ⊗ ᛒ ♀ ⚷ ⚶ ♥ ⚷
Location   0.5m E off A489

Hotel ★★ 63% Wynnstay Hotel, Maengwyn St, MACHYNLLETH
☎ 01654 702941   23 ⇌ ⋔

NEWTOWN   Map 06 SO19

St Giles Pool Rd SY16 3AJ
☎ 01686 625844 Fax 01686 625844
Inland country course with easy walking. Testing 2nd hole, par 3, and 4th hole, par 4. River Severn skirts four holes.
9 holes, 6012yds, Par 70, SSS 70, Course record 67.
Club membership 350.
Visitors   advisable to contact in advance.
Societies   must contact in advance.
Green Fees £12.50 per day (£15 weekends & bank holidays).
Prof   D P Owen
Facilities   ⊗)Ⅲ ᛒ ❤ ♀ ⚷ ⚶ ⚷ ⚷
& Leisure   fishing.
Location   0.5m NE on A483

WELSHPOOL   Map 07 SJ20

Welshpool Golfa Hill SY21 9AQ   ☎ 01938 850249
e-mail: welshpool.golfclub@virginnet.co.uk
Undulating, hilly, heathland course with bracing air. Testing holes are 2nd (par 5), 14th (par 3), 17th (par 3) and a memorable 18th.
18 holes, 5708yds, Par 70, SSS 68, Course record 68.
Club membership 400.
Visitors   must book in advance, restricted some weekends.
Societies   must book in advance.
Green Fees £12.50 per day (£20.50 weekend & bank

---

holiday in summer; £15.50 weekend & bank holiday in winter).
Designer   James Braid
Facilities   ⊗)Ⅲ ᛒ ❤ ♀ ⚷ ⚶ ⚷
Location   3m W off A458

Hotel ★★★ 68% Royal Oak Hotel, WELSHPOOL
☎ 01938 552217   24 ⇌ ⋔

ABERDARE   Map 03 SO00

Aberdare Abernant CF44 0RY
☎ 01685 872797 Fax 01685 872797
Mountain course with parkland features overlooking Brecon Beacons.
18 holes, 5875yds, Par 69, SSS 69, Course record 64.
Club membership 550.
Visitors   must have handicap certificate. May play weekends by prior arrangment with secretary/Manager.
Societies   apply in writing in advance to the secretary.
Green Fees £14 per day (£20 weekends & bank holidays).
Prof   A Palmer
Facilities   ⊗)Ⅲ ᛒ ❤ ♀ ⚷ ⚶ ⚷
Location   A470 to Abercynon, take A4059 to Aberdare. Follow sign to hospital, 400 yds on right

Hotel ★★★ 69% Tregenna Hotel, Park Ter, MERTHYR TYDFIL
☎ 01685 723627 & 382055
Fax 01685 721951   24 ⇌ ⋔

MOUNTAIN ASH   Map 03 ST09

Mountain Ash Cefnpennar CF45 4DT
☎ 01443 479459 Fax 01443 479459
Mountain course on heathland with panoramic views of the Brecon Beacons.
18 holes, 5553yds, Par 69, SSS 67, Course record 63.
Club membership 600.
Visitors   contact in advance for details.
Societies   must contact in writing.
Green Fees £15 per round/day(£20 weekends).
Prof   Marcus Wills
Facilities   ⊗)Ⅲ ᛒ ❤ ♀ ⚷ ⚶ ⚷
Location   1m NW off A4059

Hotel ★★★ 69% Tregenna Hotel, Park Ter, MERTHYR TYDFIL
☎ 01685 723627 & 382055
Fax 01685 721951   24 ⇌ ⋔

PENRHYS   Map 03 ST09

Rhondda Golf Club House CF43 3PW
☎ 01443 441384 Fax 01443 441384 e-mail: rhondda@btinternet.com
Mountain course with good views.
18 holes, 6205yds, Par 70, SSS 71, Course record 67.
Club membership 600.
Visitors   contact secretary for weekend play.   ▶

Societies contact for details.
Green Fees £15 (£20 weekends & bank holidays).
Cards ⬜⬜ ⬛⬛ ⬜⬜ 🔲
Prof G A Bebb
Facilities ⊗ �𝕀 ⬛ 🍺 ♀ ⚒ 🏠 ⛟ 🚜 ⟋ ⦅
Location 0.5m W off B4512

Hotel ★★★ 67% Heritage Park Hotel, Coed Cae Rd,
Trehafod, PONTYPRIDD
☎ 01443 687057 44 ⇆ ⋔

PONTYPRIDD   Map 03 ST09

Pontypridd Ty Gwyn Rd CF37 4DJ
☎ 01443 409904 Fax 01443 491622
Well-wooded mountain course with springy turf. Good views
of the Rhondda Valleys and coast.
18 holes, 5721yds, Par 69, SSS 68.
Club membership 850.
Visitors must contact in advance. Must play with
member on weekends & bank holidays. Must
have a handicap certificate.
Societies weekdays only. Must contact in advance.
Green Fees not confirmed.
Prof Wade Walters
Facilities ⊗ ⟋ ⬛ ⚒ 🏠 ⛟ 🚜 ⟋
Location E side of town centre off A470

Hotel ★★★ 67% Heritage Park Hotel, Coed Cae Rd,
Trehafod, PONTYPRIDD
☎ 01443 687057 44 ⇆ ⋔

TALBOT GREEN   Map 03 ST08

Llantrisant & Pontyclun Off Ely Valley Rd CF72 8AL
☎ 01443 228169 Fax 01443 224601
Parkland course.
18 holes, 5328yds, Par 68, SSS 66.
Club membership 600.
Visitors must have handicap certificate, must contact in
advance, not at weekends
Societies telephone in advance
Green Fees £15 per day.
Prof Mark Phillips
Facilities ⊗ ⟋ ⬛ 🍺 ♀ ⚒ 🏠 ⛟ ⟋

Hotel ★★★★ 69% Miskin Manor Hotel,
Groes Faen, Pontyclun, MISKIN
☎ 01443 224204 35 ⇆ ⋔ Annexe11 ⇆ ⋔

PONTYCLUN   Map 03 ST08

Vale of Glamorgan Hotel Golf & Country Club Hensol Park
CF72 8JY ☎ 01443 222221 Fax 01443 222220
Two courses set in 200 acres of glorious countryside with
views over Hensol Park lake and castle. The 18-hole par 72
Lake Course features towering trees, bunkers and water on
ten holes. The signature hole, the 12th, has an island green
reached via a stone bridge. The club is also home to the
Welsh Golf Academy.
Lake: 18 holes, 6507yds, Par 72, SSS 71.
Hensol: 9 holes, 3115yds, Par 72, SSS 71.
Club membership 1100.
Visitors must have a handicap certificate and may only
play with member at weekends.
Societies apply in writing.
Green Fees not confirmed.

Cards ⬜⬜ ⬛⬛ ⬜⬜ 🔲 ⬜⬜ 🔲 🔲
Prof Peter Johnson
Designer Peter Johnson
Facilities ⊗ ⟋ ⬛ 🍺 ♀ ⚒ 🏠 ⛟ 🚜 ⟋ ⦅
& Leisure hard tennis courts, heated indoor swimming
pool, squash, fishing, sauna, solarium,
gymnasium, many facilities in process of being
built.
Location 2 mins from junct 34 of M4

Hotel ★★★★ 70% Vale of Glamorgan Hotel Golf &
Country Club, Hensol Park, HENSOL
☎ 01443 667800 143rm

SWANSEA

CLYDACH   Map 03 SN60

Inco SA6 5PQ ☎ 01792 843336
Flat meadowland course to be extended to 18 holes.
18 holes, 6064yds, Par 70, SSS 69.
Club membership 450.
Visitors no restrictions.
Societies must contact in advance.
Green Fees not confirmed.
Facilities ⊗ ⬛ 🍺 ♀ ⚒
Location 0.75m SE on B4291

PONTLLIW   Map 02 SS69

Allt-y-Graban Allt-y-Grabam Rd SA4 1DT
☎ 01792 885757
A challenging parkland course with fine panoramic views,
opened in 1993.It is a 9-hole course but with plans for 12
holes. There are 6 par-4 holes and 3 par-3 holes. The 6th is
a challenging hole with a blind tee shot into the valley and a
dogleg to the left onto an elevated green.
9 holes, 2210yds, Par 66, SSS 66, Course record 63.
Club membership 158.
Visitors no restrictions.
Societies telephone in advance.
Green Fees not confirmed..
Designer F G Thomas
Facilities ⬛ 🍺 ♀ ⚒ ⛟ ⟋
Location From junct 47 on M4 take A48 towards
Pontardulais. Turn left after Glamorgan Arms

Hotel ★★★ 65% Posthouse Swansea, The Kingsway
Circle, SWANSEA ☎ 0870 400 9078 99 ⇆ ⋔

SOUTHGATE   Map 02 SS58

Pennard 2 Southgate Rd SA3 2BT
☎ 01792 233131 & 233451 Fax 01792 234797
Undulating, cliff-top seaside links with good coastal views.
18 holes, 6265yds, Par 71, SSS 72, Course record 69.
Club membership 1020.
Visitors advisable to contact Professional in advance.
Societies by prior arrangement, telephone in advance.
Green Fees £27 per 18 holes(£35 weekends & bank
holidays).
Prof M V Bennett
Designer James Braid

▶

426

Facilities ⊗ ⍫ ⍩ ♥ ♀ ⚲ ⌂ ⚲ ✓
Location 8m W of Swansea by A4067 and B4436

Hotel ★★♨ Fairyhill, REYNOLDSTON
☎ 01792 390139 8 ⇆ ⊮

SWANSEA   Map 03 SS69

Clyne 120 Owls Lodge Ln, The Mayals, Blackpyl SA3 5DP
☎ 01792 401989 Fax 01792 401078
e-mail: clynegolfclub@supanet.com
Challenging moorland course with excellent greens and
scenic views of Swansea Bay and The Gower.
18 holes, 6334yds, Par 70, SSS 71, Course record 64.
Club membership 900.
Visitors   must be member of a club with handicap
certificate. Groups over 8 advised to book in
advance.
Societies must contact in advance.
Green Fees not confirmed.
Prof   Jonathan Clenett
Designer   H S Colt & Harries
Facilities ⊗ ⍫ ⍩ ♥ ♀ ⚲ ⌂ ⚲ ✓ ⎓
Location   3.5m SW on B4436 off A4067

Hotel ★★★ 70% Langland Court, Langland
Court Rd, LANGLAND
☎ 01792 361545   14 ⇆ ⊮ Annexe5 ⇆ ⊮

Langland Bay Langland Bay SA3 4QR
☎ 01792 361721 Fax 01792 361082
e-mail: golf@langlandbay.sagehost.co.uk
Parkland course overlooking Gower coast. The par 4, 6th is
an uphill dog-leg open to the wind, and the par 3, 16th (151
yds) is aptly named 'Death or Glory'.
18 holes, 5857yds, Par 70, SSS 69.
Club membership 850.

Visitors   no restrictions. Tue is Ladies Day. No societies
at weekends
Societies must telephone in advance.
Green Fees £28 (£30 weekends).
Prof   Mark Evans
Designer   Henry Cotton
Facilities ⊗ ⍫ ⍩ ♥ ♀ ⚲ ⌂ ⚲ ✓
Location   6m W on A4067

Hotel ★★★ 70% Langland Court, Langland Court
Rd, LANGLAND ☎ 01792 361545
14 ⇆ ⊮ Annexe5 ⇆ ⊮

Morriston 160 Clasemont Rd SA6 6AJ
☎ 01792 796528 Fax 01792 796528
Pleasant parkland course with a very difficult Par 3 15th
hole.
18 holes, 5891yds, Par 68, SSS 68, Course record 61.
Club membership 700.
Visitors   may not play Sat. Must contact in advance.
Societies apply in writing.
Green Fees £18 per day (£30 weekends).
Prof   D A Rees
Facilities ⊗ ⍫ ⍩ ♥ ♀ ⚲ ⌂ ✓
Location   5m N of Swansea on A48.
1m E of junct 46 of M4

THREE CROSSES   Map 02 SS59

Gower Cefn Goleu SA4 3HS
☎ 01792 872480 (Off) 879905 (Pro) Fax 01792 872480
Set in attractive rolling countryside, this Donald Steel
designed course provides good strategic hazards, including
trees, water and bunkers, outstanding views and a
challenging game of golf.
18 holes, 6441yds, Par 71, SSS 72, Course record 70.
Club membership 500.
Visitors   tee booking upto 7 days in advance, reservations
recommended, some weekend vacancies, dress
code and course etiquette must be observed.
Societies by prior notice for established golfers.
Green Fees £15(£17 week ends & bank holidays).
Cards   💳 💳 💳 💳 💳
Prof   Alan Williamson
Designer   Donald Steel
Facilities ⊗ ⍫ ⍩ ♥ ♀ ⚲ ⌂ ❧ ⚒ ✓
Location   Sign posted from the village of Three Crosses

Hotel ★★ 74% Beaumont Hotel, 72-73 Walter Rd,
SWANSEA ☎ 01792 643956 16 ⇆ ⊮

UPPER KILLAY   Map 02 SS59

Fairwood Park Blackhills Ln SA2 7JN
☎ 01792 203648 Fax 01792 297849
Parkland championship course on the beautiful Gower
Peninsula.
18 holes, 6754yds, Par 72, SSS 72, Course record 68.
Club membership 720.
Visitors   welcome except when championship or club
matches are being held. Must contact in
advance.
Societies must contact in advance.
Green Fees £25 per day (£30 weekends & bank holidays).
Prof   Gary Hughes
Designer   Hawtree
Facilities ⊗ ⍫ ⍩ ♥ ♀ ⚲ ⌂ ⚲ ❧ ⚒ ✓
Location   1.5m S off A4118

Hotel ★★ 74% Windsor Lodge Hotel, Mount
Pleasant, SWANSEA
☎ 01792 642158 & 652744
Fax 01792 648996 18 ⇆ ⊮

> Entries with a green background
> identify courses considered to be
> particularly interesting

TORFAEN

CWMBRAN   Map 03 ST29

Green Meadow Golf & Country Club Treherbert Rd,
Croesyceiliog NP44 2BZ
☎ 01633 869321 & 862626 Fax 01633 868430
Undulating parkland course with panoramic views. The 2nd
hole is played partly down hill with the front half of the
green enclosed with water; the 13th is exposed to winds with
large mature trees along righthand side of green.
18 holes, 6029yds, Par 70, SSS 70, Course record 66.
Club membership 400.
Visitors by prior arrangement advised especially at
weekends, tel 01633 862626. Correct standard
of dress compulsory.
Societies telephone for brochure, Golf Shop 01633
862626.
Green Fees Mon: £14 Tues-Fri; £17 (£19 weekends)per 18
holes.
Cards 🖃 🖃 🖃
Prof Peter Stebbings
Designer Peter Richardson
Facilities ⊗ ⊪ ﾑ ♥ ♀ △ 🖻 ➤ 🏌 ♂ ₵
& Leisure hard tennis courts.
Location 5m N of junct 26 M4, off A4042 from Cardiff

Hotel ★★★★ 61% Parkway Hotel, Cwmbran Dr,
CWMBRAN ☎ 01633 871199   70 ⇄ ↾

Pontnewydd Maesgwyn Farm, West Pontnewydd NP44 1AB
☎ 01633 482170
10 holes, 5353yds, Par 68, SSS 67, Course record 63.
Location N side of town centre
Telephone for further details

Hotel ★★★★ 61% Parkway Hotel, Cwmbran Dr,
CWMBRAN ☎ 01633 871199   70 ⇄ ↾

PONTYPOOL   Map 03 SO20

Pontypool Lasgarn Ln, Trevethin NP4 8TR
☎ 01495 763655
Undulating, mountain course with magnificent views.
18 holes, 6046yds, Par 69, SSS 69, Course record 64.
Club membership 638.
Visitors must have a handicap certificate, restricted
availability at weekends, advisable to call in
advance.
Societies apply in writing or by phone, deposit payable.
Green Fees £20 per day.
Prof James Howard
Facilities ⊗ ⊪ ﾑ ♥ ♀ △ 🖻 ➤ 🏌 ♂
Location 1.5m N off A4043

Hotel ★★ 68% Mill at Glynhir, Glyn-Hir, Llandybie,
AMMANFORD ☎ 01269 850672   11 ⇄ ↾

Woodlake Park Golf & Country Club Glascoed NP4 0TE
☎ 01291 673933 Fax 01291 673811
e-mail: golf@woodlake.co.uk
Undulating parkland course with magnificent views over
Llandegfedd Reservoir. Superb green constructed to USGA
specification. Holes 4, 7 & 16 are Par 3's which are
particularly challenging. Holes 6 & 17 are long Par 4's which
can be wind affected.

18 holes, 6278yds, Par 71, SSS 72, Course record 67.
Club membership 450.
Visitors book in advance.
Societies telephone or write for society package.
Green Fees £20 per 18 holes(£25 weekends).
Prof Adrian Pritchard
Facilities ⊗ ⊪ ﾑ ♥ ♀ △ 🖻 ➤ 🏌 ♂
& Leisure fishing.
Location Overlooking Llandegfedd Reservoir

Hotel ★★ 68% Mill at Glynhir, Glyn-Hir, Llandybie,
AMMANFORD ☎ 01269 850672   11 ⇄ ↾

VALE OF GLAMORGAN

BARRY   Map 03 ST16

Brynhill Port Rd CF62 8PN
☎ 01446 720277 Fax 01446 740422
e-mail: gershenson@lineone.net
Meadowland course with some hard walking. Prevailing west
wind.
18 holes, 6336yds, Par 72, SSS 71.
Club membership 750.
Visitors must contact in advance. May not play on Sun.
Societies phone secretary for details.
Green Fees not confirmed.
Prof Peter Fountain
Facilities ⊗ ⊪ ﾑ ♥ ♀ △ 🖻 ♂
Location 1.25m N on B4050

Hotel ★★★ 65% Mount Sorrel Hotel, Porthkerry Rd,
BARRY ☎ 01446 740069   43 ⇄ ↾

RAF St Athan St Athan CF62 4WA
☎ 01446 797186 & 751043 Fax 01446 751862
This is a very windy course with wind straight off the sea to
make all holes interesting. Further interest is added by this
being a very tight course with lots of trees. Beware of low
flying RAF jets.
9 holes, 6480yds, Par 72, SSS 72.
Club membership 450.
Visitors contact in advance, Sun mornings club
competitions only.
Societies apply in advance.
Green Fees not confirmed.
Facilities ⊗ ﾑ ♥ ♀ △ 🖻
Location Between Barry & Llantwit Major

Hotel ★★★▲▲ 77% Egerton Grey Country House
Hotel, Porthkerry, BARRY
☎ 01446 711666   10 ⇄ ↾

St Andrews Major Argae Ln, Coldbrook Rd East,
Cadoxton CF63 1BL ☎ 01446 722227
A new 9-hole, Pay and Play course with 6 Par 4s, 1 par5 and
2 par3s. Further extensions planned.
9 holes, 3000yds, Par 70, SSS 68.
Club membership 520.

Visitors must contact in advance.
Societies telephone in advance.
Green Fees not confirmed.
Designer Richard Hurd
Facilities ⓑ ☕ ♀ ⚐ 🛍 ⚑ ✐
Location Off Barry new link road, Coldbrook Road East

Hotel ★★★✿✿ 77% Egerton Grey Country House Hotel, Porthkerry, BARRY
☎ 01446 711666 10 ⇄ 🏨

DINAS POWIS   Map 03 ST17

Dinas Powis High Walls Av CF64 4AJ
☎ 029 20512727 Fax 029 20512727
Parkland/downland course with views over the Bristol Channel and the seaside resort of Barry.
18 holes, 5486yds, Par 67, SSS 67, Course record 60.
Club membership 550.
Visitors must contact in advance (call G Bennett 02920 513682)
Societies telephone in advance.
Green Fees £15 (£20 weekends).
Prof Gareth Bennett
Facilities ⊗ ⽊ ⓑ ☕ ♀ ⚐ 🛍 ➘ ⚙ ✐
Location NW side of village

Hotel ★★★ 65% Mount Sorrel Hotel, Porthkerry Rd, BARRY ☎ 01446 740069 43 ⇄ 🏨

PENARTH   Map 03 ST17

Glamorganshire Lavernock Rd CF64 5UP
☎ 029 20701185 Fax 029 20701185
Parkland course, overlooking the Bristol Channel.
18 holes, 6181yds, Par 70, SSS 70, Course record 64.
Club membership 1000.
Visitors contact professional in advance.
Societies must contact in advance.
Green Fees not confirmed.
Prof Andrew Kerr-Smith
Designer James Braid
Facilities ⊗ ⽊ ⓑ ☕ ♀ ⚐ 🛍 ⚑ ➘ ⚙ ✐ ⓣ
Location S side of town centre on B4267

Hotel ★★★ 65% Mount Sorrel Hotel, Porthkerry Rd, BARRY ☎ 01446 740069 43 ⇄ 🏨

WENVOE   Map 03 ST17

Wenvoe Castle CF5 6BE ☎ 029 20594371
18 holes, 6422yds, Par 72, SSS 71, Course record 64.
Location 1m S off A4050
Telephone for further details

Hotel ★★★✿✿ 77% Egerton Grey Country House Hotel, Porthkerry, BARRY
☎ 01446 711666 10 ⇄ 🏨

AA Hotels that have special arrangements with golf courses are listed at the back of the guide

WREXHAM

CHIRK   Map 07 SJ23

Chirk Golf Club LL14 5AD
☎ 01691 774407 & 0800 7318598 Fax 01691 773878
e-mail: fiona.barnes@lineone.net
Overlooked by the National Trust's Chirk Castle, is a championship-standard 18-hole course with a 664 yard, par 5 at the 9th - one of the longest in Europe. Also a 9-hole course, driving range and golf academy.
Manor Course: 18 holes, 7045yds, Par 72, SSS 73, Course record 72.
Club membership 750.
Visitors advisable to contact in advance. May not play in members preferred tee times 7-10am daily.
Societies must telephone for provisonal booking.
Green Fees not confirmed.
Cards ▨ ▥ ▨ 🖾
Prof Mark Maddison
Facilities ⊗ ⽊ ⓑ ☕ ♀ ⚐ 🛍 ⚑ ➘ ⚙ ✐ ⓣ
& Leisure squash, fishing.
Location 5m N of Oswestry

Hotel ★★★ 66% Moreton Park Lodge, Moreton Park, Gledrid, CHIRK
☎ 01691 776666 46 ⇄ 🏨

EYTON   Map 07 SJ34

Plassey LL13 0SP ☎ 01978 780028
Pleasant 9-hole course set in naturally contoured parkland with water hazards. It is within Plassey Leisure Park and Craft Centre and all park facilities are available to golfers.
9 holes, 2379yds, Par 32, SSS 32.
Club membership 166.
Visitors must contact in advance.
Societies telephone then confirm in writing.
Green Fees not confirmed.
Designer Welsh Golf Union
Facilities ⓑ ☕ ♀ ⚐ 🛍 ⚑ ✐
Location 2.5m off A483 Chester/Oswestry

Hotel ★★★ 67% Cross Lanes Hotel & Restaurant, Cross Lanes, Bangor Rd, Marchwiel, WREXHAM ☎ 01978 780555 16 ⇄ 🏨

RUABON   Map 07 SJ34

Penycae Ruabon Rd, Penycae LL14 1TP ☎ 01978 810108
An architecturally designed and built 9-hole parkland course offering a challenge for players of all standards. After a lazy Par 4 start the second Par 3 is wooded to one side and guarded by water on the other. The 6th, a 317yds Par 4 makes a very difficult approach to the green. The 7th is another Par 3 , elevated and wooded to one side. The 8th crosses water twice as the river meanders down the fairway.
9 holes, 2140yds, Par 64, SSS 62, Course record 62.
Club membership 200.
Visitors advisable to book in advance.
Societies telephone or write in advance.
Green Fees not confirmed.
Designer John Day
Facilities ⊗ ⓑ ☕ ♀ ⚐ 🛍 ⚑ ✐
Location 1m off A5

Hotel ★★★ 66% Moreton Park Lodge, Moreton Park, Gledrid, CHIRK
☎ 01691 776666 46 ⇄ ⚑

WREXHAM   Map 07 SJ35

Clays Farm Golf Centre Bryn Estyn Rd, Llan-y-Pwll LL13 9UB ☎ 01978 661406 Fax 01978 661417
e-mail: claysgolf@tinyworld.co.uk
Gently undulating parkland course in a rural setting with views of the Welsh mountains and noted for the difficulty of its par 3s.
18 holes, 5908yds, Par 69, SSS 69, Course record 64.
Club membership 420.
Visitors   must contact in advance.
Societies   prior arrangement in writing.
Green Fees not confirmed.
Cards   ▮▮▬▮ ▮▮ ▮▬▮ ▮▮
Prof   David Larvin
Designer   R D Jones
Facilities   ⛳ 🏠 ⛴ ↖ 🛒 ✎ ⏰
Location   Off A534

Hotel ★★★♨ 66% Llwyn Onn Hall Hotel, Cefn Rd, WREXHAM ☎ 01978 261225 13 ⇄ ⚑

Wrexham Holt Rd LL13 9SB
☎ 01978 351476 Fax 01978 364268
Inland, sandy course with easy walking. Testing dog-legged 7th hole (par 4), and short 14th hole (par 3) with full carry to green.
18 holes, 6233yds, Par 70, SSS 70, Course record 64.
Club membership 600.
Visitors   may not play competition days, and are advised to contact in advance. A handicap certificate is required.
Societies   welcome Mon & Wed-Fri. Apply in writing
Green Fees £22 (£27 weekends).
Prof   Paul Williams
Designer   James Braid
Facilities   ⊗ �🍴 ⛴ ⛴ ⚷ ↖ 🏠 🛒 ✎
Location   2m NE on A534

Hotel ★★★♨ 66% Llwyn Onn Hall Hotel, Cefn Rd, WREXHAM ☎ 01978 261225 13 ⇄ ⚑

On 1 January 2002, Euro banknotes and coins will come into circulation throughout the Republic of Ireland. There will be a dual circulation period, during which Irish pound notes and coins will begin to be withdrawn. As we went to press, this dual circulation period was expected to end on 9 February 2002, and certainly before 30 June 2002, after which Irish notes and coins will no longer be legal tender. Prices in the guide are shown in Irish Punts (IEP) as prices in Euros were not available at the time of publication (IEP1 = 1.27 Euros).

Ireland

NORTHERN IRELAND

CO ANTRIM

ANTRIM Map 01 D5

Massereene 51 Lough Rd BT41 4DQ
☎ 028 94428096 Fax 028 94487661
The first nine holes are parkland, while the second, adjacent to the shore of Lough Neagh, have more of a links character with sandy ground.
18 holes, 6602yds, Par 72, SSS 72, Course record 63.
Club membership 969.
Visitors   must contact in advance.
Societies   book in advance.
Green Fees £12.50 per 9 holes(£15 weekends);£25 per 18 holes(£30 weekends).
Cards   [symbols]
Prof   Jim Smyth
Designer   F Hawtree
Facilities [symbols]
Location   1m SW of town

Hotel   ★★★★72% Galgorm Manor, BALLYMENA ☎ 028 2588 1001 24 [symbols]

BALLYCASTLE Map 01 D6

Ballycastle Cushendall Rd BT54 6QP
☎ 028 20762536 Fax 028 20769909
An unusual mixture of terrain beside the sea, with magnificent views from all parts. The first five holes are inland type; the middle holes on the Warren are links type and the rest, on high ground, are heath type.
18 holes, 5406mtrs, Par 71, SSS 70, Course record 64.
Club membership 920.
Visitors   are welcome during the week.
Societies   apply in writing.
Green Fees £20 per round (£30 weekends & bank holidays).
Prof   Ian McLaughlin
Facilities [symbols]
Location   Between Portrush & Cushendall (A2)

BALLYCLARE Map 01 D5

Ballyclare 23 Springdale Rd BT39 9JW
☎ 028 93322696 Fax 028 93322696
Parkland course with lots of trees and shrubs and water hazards provided by the river, streams and lakes.
18 holes, 5745mtrs, Par 71, SSS 71, Course record 66.
Club membership 580.
Visitors   must contact in advance.
Societies   must contact in advance.
Green Fees £16 per round (£22 weekends & bank holidays).
Prof   Alan Johnston
Designer   T McCauley
Facilities [symbols]
Location   1.5m N

Hotel   ★★★ 64% Lansdowne Court Hotel, 657 Antrim Rd, BELFAST ☎ 028 9077 3317 25 [symbols]

Greenacres 153 Ballyrobert Rd BT39 9RT
☎ 028 93354111 Fax 028 93354166
Designed and built into the rolling Co. Antrim countryside, and with the addition of lakes at five of the holes, provides a challenge for both the seasoned golfer and the higher handicapped player.
18 holes, 5819yds, Par 71, SSS 69.
Club membership 440.
Visitors   may not play Sat mornings.
Societies   apply in writing.
Green Fees £12 Mon-Thur;£16 Fri (£18 weekends & bank holidays).
Cards   [symbols]
Prof   Ken Reivie
Facilities [symbols]
Location   6miles from Belfast city center

Hotel   ★★★ 66% Adair Arms Hotel, 1 Ballymoney Rd, BALLYMENA ☎ 028 2565 3674 44 [symbols]

BALLYGALLY Map 01 D5

Cairndhu 192 Coast Rd BT40 2QG
☎ 028 28583324 Fax 028 28583324
e-mail: cairndhu@globalgolf.com
Built on a hilly headland, this course is both testing and scenic, with wonderful coastal views. The 3rd hole has a carry of 180 yds over a headland to the fairway.
18 holes, 5611mtrs, Par 70, SSS 69, Course record 64.
Club membership 905.
Visitors   may not play on Sat.
Societies   must apply in writing.
Green Fees £20 Mon-Fri (£25 Sat & Sun).
Cards   [symbols]
Prof   Robert Walker
Designer   Mr Morrison
Facilities [symbols]
Location   4m N of Larne on coast road

Hotel   ★★★ 69% Londonderry Arms Hotel, 20 Harbour Rd, CARNLOUGH ☎ 028 2888 5255 35 [symbols]

BALLYMENA Map 01 D5

Ballymena 128 Raceview Rd BT42 4HY ☎ 028 25861487
18 holes, 5299mtrs, Par 68, SSS 67, Course record 64.
Location   2m E on A42
Telephone for further details

Hotel   ★★★★ 72% Galgorm Manor, BALLYMENA ☎ 028 2588 1001 24 [symbols]

Galgorm Castle Golf & Country Club Galgorm Rd BT42 1HL ☎ 028 25646161 Fax 028 25651151
e-mail: golf@galgormcastle.co.uk
18 hole championship course set in 220 acres of mature parkland in the grounds of a historic castle. The course is bordered by two rivers which come into play and includes five lakes. A course of outstanding beauty offering a challenge to both the novice and low handicapped golfer.
18 holes, 6736yds, Par 72, SSS 72, Course record 68.
Club membership 400.
Visitors   ring to book times.
Societies   telephone in advance to book tee time.
Green Fees £30 per day; £20 per round (£38/£25 weekends).

Cards ⬚⬚ ⬚⬚ 🗿
Prof Lesley Callen
Designer Simon Gidman
Facilities ⊗ ⅿ 🕒 ⬛ 🍴 ⚘ 🏌 ⛳ ➴ ☂ 🚶 ♪ ⛴ ⌇ 🎇
& Leisure fishing, PGA staffed Academy.
Location 1m S of Ballymena on A42

Hotel ★★★★ 72% Galgorm Manor, BALLYMENA
🕿 028 2588 1001 24 ⇆ 📻

CARRICKFERGUS   Map 01 D5

Carrickfergus 25 North Rd BT38 8LP
🕿 028 93363713 Fax 028 93363023
Parkland course, fairly level but nevertheless demanding, with a notorious water hazard at the 1st. Well maintained, with an interesting in-course riverway and presenting fine views across Belfast Lough.
18 holes, 5768yds, Par 68, SSS 68.
Club membership 850.
Visitors restrictions at weekends.
Societies must contact in advance.
Green Fees not confirmed.
Cards ⬚⬚ ⬚⬚ 🂱 🗿
Prof Mark Johnstonnson
Facilities ⊗ ⅿ 🕒 ⬛ 🍴 ⚘ 🏌 ⌇
Location 9m NE of Belfast on A2

Hotel ★★ 66% Dobbins Inn, 6-8 High St, CARRICKFERGUS
🕿 028 9335 1905 15 ⇆ 📻

Greenisland 156 Upper Rd, Greenisland BT38 8RW
🕿 028 90862236
A parkland course nestling at the foot of Knockagh Hill with scenic views over Belfast Lough.
9 holes, 5536mtrs, Par 71, SSS 68.
Club membership 740.
Visitors contact club in advance. Play restricted Sat and Thu.
Societies by prior arrangement.
Green Fees not confirmed.
Facilities ⊗ ⅿ 🕒 ⬛ 🍴 ⚘
Location N of Belfast, close to Carrickfergus

Hotel ★★ 66% Dobbins Inn, 6-8 High St, CARRICKFERGUS
🕿 028 9335 1905 15 ⇆ 📻

CUSHENDALL   Map 01 D6

Cushendall 21 Shore Rd BT44 0NG 🕿 028 21771318
e-mail: cdda@antrim-glems.demon.co.uk
Scenic course with spectacular views over the Sea of Moyle and Red Bay to the Mull of Kintyre. The River Dall winds through the course, coming into play in seven of the nine holes.
9 holes, 4386mtrs, Par 66, SSS 63, Course record 62.
Club membership 834.
Visitors Ladies day Thursday, time sheet at weekends.
Societies must contact in writing.
Green Fees not confirmed.
Designer D Delargy
Facilities 🕒 ⬛ 🍴 ⚘

Hotel ★★★ 69% Londonderry Arms Hotel, 20 Harbour Rd, CARNLOUGH
🕿 028 2888 5255 35 ⇆ 📻

LARNE   Map 01 D5

Larne 54 Ferris Bay Rd, Islandmagee BT40 3RT
🕿 028 93382228 Fax 028 93382088
An exposed part links, part heathland course offering a good test, particularly on the last three holes along the sea shore.
9 holes, 6686yds, Par 70, SSS 70, Course record 64.
Club membership 430.
Visitors may not play on Sat.
Societies apply in writing or telephone in advance.
Green Fees not confirmed.
Designer G L Bailie
Facilities ⊗ ⅿ 🕒 ⬛ 🍴 ⚘
Location 6m N of Whitehead on Browns Bay rd

Hotel ★★★ 69% Londonderry Arms Hotel, 20 Harbour Rd, CARNLOUGH
🕿 028 2888 5255 35 ⇆ 📻

LISBURN   Map 01 D5

Aberdelghy Bell's Ln, Lambeg BT27 4QH
🕿 028 92662738 Fax 028 92603432
This parkland course, extended to 18 holes in 1997, has no bunkers. The hardest hole on the course is the 340metre 3rd, a dog leg through trees to a green guarded by water. The par-3 12th high on the hill and the 14th hole over the dam provide a challenge. The par-4 15th hole is a long dog leg.
18 holes, 4139mtrs, Par 66, SSS 62, Course record 64.
Club membership 200.
Visitors restricted Sat 7.15am-1pm. Ring in advance for Sun.
Societies telephone in advance.
Green Fees £8 per 18 holes (£10 weekends & bank holidays).
Cards ⬚⬚ ⬚⬚ ⬚⬚ 🂱 🗿
Prof Ian Murdoch
Designer Alec Blair
Facilities ⬛ 🍴 ⚘ 🏌 ⌇
Location 1.5m N of Lisburn off A1

Hotel ★★ 57% Balmoral Hotel, Blacks Rd, Dunmurry, BELFAST
🕿 028 9030 1234 44 ⇆ 📻

Lisburn 68 Eglantine Rd BT27 5RQ
🕿 028 92677216 Fax 92603608
e-mail: lisburngolfclub@aol.com
Meadowland course, fairly level, with plenty of trees and shrubs. Challenging last three holes.
18 holes, 6647yds, Par 72, SSS 72, Course record 67.
Club membership 1200.
Visitors must play with member on Sun. Must tee off before 3pm weekdays unless with a member.
Societies must apply in writing.
Green Fees £25 per day (£30 weekends & bank holidays).
Prof Blake Campbell
Designer Hawtree
Facilities ⊗ ⅿ 🕒 ⬛ 🍴 ⚘ 🏌 ➴ ☂ ⌇
Location 2m from town on A1

Hotel ★★ 57% Balmoral Hotel, Blacks Rd, Dunmurry, BELFAST
🕿 028 9030 1234 44 ⇆ 📻

MAZE   Map 01 D5

Down Royal Park Dunygarton Rd BT27 5RT
☎ 028 92621339 Fax 028 92621339
The 9-hole Valley course and the 18-hole Down Royal Park
are easy walking, undulating heathland courses. Down
Royal's 2nd hole is 628yards and thought to be among the
best par 5 holes in Ireland.
*Down Royal Park Course: 18 holes, 6824yds, Par 72, SSS
72, Course record 69.*
Valley Course: 9 holes, 2019, Par 33.
Club membership 80.
Visitors   no restrictions, except dress code.
Societies   reservations in advance.
Green Fees   £17 (£24 weekends)..
Prof   C J Calder MNCF
Facilities   ⊗ by prior arrangement ⋓ �ℍ ⬛ ♀ ⚲ 🛅 ⛽ 🏌
                  ⚑ 🛒 🖋 ⟨
Location   Inside Down Royal Race Course

Hotel   ★★★ 66% White Gables Hotel,
                  14 Dromore Rd, HILLSBOROUGH
                  ☎ 028 9268 2755 31 ⇆ 🐾

NEWTOWNABBEY   Map 01 D5

Ballyearl Golf & Leisure Centre 585 Doagh Rd,
Mossley BT36 5RZ ☎ 028 90848287 Fax 028 90844896
9 holes, 2520yds, Par 27.
Visitors   no restrictions.
Societies   telephone in advance.
Green Fees   not confirmed.
Cards   ▦ ▬ 🖵
Prof   Richard Johnston
Designer   V Lathery
Facilities   ⬛ ⚲ 🛅 ⛽ ⟨
& Leisure   squash, solarium, gymnasium, Theatre and arts
                  centre.

Mallusk Antrim Rd BT36 ☎ 028 90843799
9 holes, 4444yds, Par 62, SSS 62, Course record 62.
Telephone for further details

PORTBALLINTRAE   Map 01 C6

Bushfoot 50 Bushfoot Rd, Portballintrae BT57 8RR
☎ 028 20731317 Fax 028 20731852
A seaside links course with superb views in an area of
outstanding beauty. A challenging par-3 7th is ringed by
bunkers with out-of-bounds beyond, while the 3rd has a blind
approach. Also a putting green and pitch & putt course.
9 holes, 5914yds, Par 70, SSS 67, Course record 68.
Club membership 850.
Visitors   must contact in advance.
Societies   must contact in advance.
Green Fees   £15/£20 per 18 holes;£7/£9 per 9 holes..
Facilities   ⊗ ⋓ ℍ ⬛ ♀ ⚲ ⛽ 🖋
Location   Off Ballaghmore rd

Hotel   ★★★ 71% The Royal Court Hotel,
                  233 Ballybogey Rd, PORTRUSH
                  ☎ 028 7082 2236 18 ⇆ 🐾

PORTRUSH   Map 01 C6

PORTRUSH See page 435

WHITEHEAD   Map 01 D5

Bentra Municipal Slaughterford Rd BT38 9TG
☎ 028 93378996
A well matured course designed with the experienced golfer
and novice in mind with wide fairways and some particularly
long holes.
9 holes, 2885mtrs, Par 37, SSS 35.
Visitors   no restrictions.
Societies   contact in advance.
Green Fees   £7.70 per 18 holes (£11 weekends & bank
                  holidays).
Facilities   ⬛ 🛅 ⛽ 🖋 ⟨

Hotel   ★★ 66% Dobbins Inn, 6-8 High St,
                  CARRICKFERGUS
                  ☎ 028 9335 1905 15 ⇆ 🐾

Whitehead McCrae's Brae BT38 9NZ
☎ 028 93370820 & 93370822 Fax 028 93370825
e-mail: robin@whiteheadgc.fsnet.co.uk
Undulating parkland course with magnificent sea views.
18 holes, 6050yds, Par 69, SSS 69, Course record 67.
Club membership 962.
Visitors   may not play on Sat. Must play with member on
                  Sun.
Societies   must contact in advance.
Green Fees   £16 per round.
Prof   Colin Farr
Designer   A B Armstrong
Facilities   ℍ ⬛ ♀ ⚲ 🛅
Location   1m from town

Hotel   ★★ 66% Dobbins Inn, 6-8 High St,
                  CARRICKFERGUS
                  ☎ 028 9335 1905 15 ⇆ 🐾

CO ARMAGH

ARMAGH   Map 01 C5

County Armagh The Demesne, Newry Rd BT60 1EN
☎ 028 37525861 Fax 028 37525861
Mature parkland course with excellent views of Armagh city
and its surroundings.
18 holes, 6212yds, Par 70, SSS 69, Course record 63.
Club membership 1000.
Visitors   time sheet operates at weekends. Must contact in
                  advance.
Societies   must contact in advance.
Green Fees   not confirmed.
Prof   Alan Rankin
Facilities   ⊗ ⋓ ℍ ⬛ ♀ ⚲ 🛅 🖋 ⟨
Location   On the Newry road

Hotel   The Cohannon Inn, 212 Ballynakilly Rd,
                  DUNGANNON ☎ 028 8772 4488 50 ⇆ 🐾

Royal Portrush

Portrush, *Co Antrim*   ☎ 028 70822311   Fax 028 70823139   Map 01 D4

e-mail: rpgc@dnet.co.uk

This course, designed by Harry S Colt, is considered among the six best in the UK. Founded in 1888, it was the venue of the first professional golf event held in Ireland, in 1895, where Sandy Herd beat Harry Vardon in the final.

It is spectacular, breathtaking, but one of the tightest driving tests known to man. On a clear day, you have a fine view of Islay and the Paps of Jura from the 3rd tee and the Giant's Causeway from the 5th. While the greens have to be 'read' from the start, there are fairways up and down valleys, and holes called Calamity Corner and Purgatory for good reason! The second hole - Giant's Grave, is 509 yards, there is an even longer hole at the 17th.

Visitors must contact in advance, have a letter of introduction from their own club and a handicap certificate. Restricted Wed & Fri pm, Sat & Sun am on Dunluce Links.

Societies must apply in writing

Green Fees Dunluce £80-£90, Valley £30-£35

Facilities ⊗ ⋙ ⓛ ☕ ♀⌂ 🏠 ⚑ ✎
Professional (Gary McNeill)

Location Dunluce Rd, Portrush BT56 8JQ (0.5m from Portrush, on main road to Bushmills)

Holes/Par/Course record 45 holes.
Dunluce Links: 18 holes, 6641 yds, Par 72, SSS 73
Valley Links: 18 holes, 6054 yds, Par 70, SSS 72

Championship Course

LURGAN   Map 01 D5

Craigavon Golf & Ski Centre Turmoyra Ln, Silverwood
BT66 6NG ☎ 028 38326606 Fax 028 38347272
e-mail: geoffcoupland@craigavon.gov.uk
Parkland course with a lake and stream providing water
hazards.
18 holes, 6496yds, Par 72, SSS 72.
Club membership 400.
Visitors restricted Sat am.
Societies telephone in advance.
Green Fees £13 per round (£16.50 weekends & bank
      holidays).
Cards ▨ ▨ ▨
Facilities ⊗ ☕ 🏌 ⛳ 🥤 ⊺
& Leisure gymnasium, Ski slope.
Location 2m N at Silverwood off the M1

Lurgan The Demesne BT67 9BN
☎ 028 38322087 Fax 028 38316166
Testing parkland course bordering Lurgan Park Lake with a
need for accurate shots. Drains well in wet weather and suits
a long straight hitter.
18 holes, 6257yds, Par 70, SSS 70, Course record 66.
Club membership 856.
Visitors may not play Sat, contact in advance.
Societies must contact in advance, not Sat.
Green Fees £15 per round (£20 weekends & bank holidays).
Prof Des Paul
Designer A Pennink
Facilities ⊗ ☕ 🏌 ☕ ⚐ 🥤 🏠 ⊺
Location 0.5m from town centre near Lurgan Park

Hotel ★★ 57% Balmoral Hotel, Blacks Rd,
      Dunmurry, BELFAST
      ☎ 028 9030 1234 44 ⇄ 🐾

PORTADOWN   Map 01 D5

Portadown 192 Gilford Rd BT63 5LF
☎ 028 38355356 Fax 028 38355356
Well wooded parkland course on the banks of the River
Bann, which features among the water hazards.
18 holes, 5649mtrs, Par 70, SSS 70, Course record 65.
Club membership 981.
Visitors may not play on Tue & Sat.
Societies apply in writing.
Green Fees not confirmed.
Prof Paul Stevenson
Facilities ⊗ ☕ 🏌 ☕ ⚐ 🥤 🏠 ⊺
& Leisure squash.
Location SE via A59

Hotel The Cohannon Inn, 212 Ballynakilly Rd,
      DUNGANNON ☎ 028 8772 4488 50 ⇄ 🐾

TANDRAGEE   Map 01 D5

Tandragee Markethill Rd BT62 2ER ☎ 028 38841272
Fax 028 38840664 e-mail: office@tandragee.co.uk
Pleasant parkland course, the signature hole is the demanding
par 4 11th known as 'The Wall Hole', the real strength of
Tandragee is in the short holes.
18 holes, 5747mtrs, Par 71, SSS 70, Course record 65.
Club membership 1340.

Visitors contact in advance. Ladies day Thur, after
      3.30pm Sat & Sun.
Societies must contact in advance.
Green Fees £15 per round (£20 weekends & bank holidays).
Prof Paul Stevenson
Designer John Stone
Facilities ⊗ ☕ 🏌 ☕ ⚐ 🥤 🏠 ⊺ 🏓 ⊘
& Leisure sauna, gymnasium, sonnker tables, indoor
      bowls..
Location On B3 out of Tandragee towards Markethill

Farmhouse ◆◆◆◆ Brook Lodge Farmhouse, 79 Old
      Ballynahinch Rd, Cargacroy, LISBURN
      ☎ 028 92638454 6rm(4 🐾)

CO BELFAST

BELFAST   Map 01 D5

See also The Royal Belfast, Holywood, Co Down.

Balmoral 518 Lisburn Rd BT9 6GX
☎ 028 90381514 Fax 028 90666759
Parkland course, mainly level, with tree-lined fairways and a
stream providing a water hazard.
18 holes, 6276yds, Par 69, SSS 70, Course record 64.
Club membership 912.
Visitors may not play Sat or Sun before 2.30pm.
Societies Mon & Thu. Must contact in advance.
Green Fees not confirmed.
Prof Geoff Bleakley
Facilities 🥤 🏠 ⊺ ⊘
Location 2m S next to Kings Hall

Hotel ★★ 57% Balmoral Hotel, Blacks Rd,
      Dunmurry, BELFAST
      ☎ 028 9030 1234 44 ⇄ 🐾

Cliftonville 44 Westland Rd BT14 6NH
☎ 028 90744158 & 90746595
e-mail: cliftonvillegolfclub@golfagent.co.uk
Parkland course with rivers bisecting two fairways.
9 holes, 6242yds, Par 70, SSS 70, Course record 65.
Club membership 430.
Visitors may not play: after 5pm unless with member,
      on Sat or on Sun mornings.
Societies must contact in writing.
Green Fees £14 per day(£17 weekends).
Prof Robert Hutton
Facilities 🥤 🏠 ⊘
Location Between Cavehill Rd & Cliftonville Circus

Hotel ★★★ 64% Lansdowne Court Hotel,
      657 Antrim Rd, BELFAST
      ☎ 028 9077 3317 25 ⇄ 🐾

Dunmurry 91 Dunmurry Ln, Dunmurry BT17 9JS
☎ 028 90610834 Fax 028 90602540
Maturing very nicely, this tricky parkland course has several
memorable holes which call for skilful shots.
18 holes, 5832yds, Par 69, SSS 69, Course record 64.
Club membership 900.

▶

Visitors	telephone in advance. May only play Sat after 5pm, restricted Fri (Ladies Day).
Societies	must contact in writing.
Green Fees	£20 per round.
Prof	John Dolan
Facilities	⛳ 🏠 ⛳ ✓

Hotel	★★ 57% Balmoral Hotel, Blacks Rd, Dunmurry, BELFAST ☎ 028 9030 1234 44 ⇆ ☏

Fortwilliam Downview Ave BT15 4EZ
☎ 028 90370770 (Office) & 90770980 (Pro)
Fax 028 90781891
Parkland course in most attractive surroundings. The course is bisected by a lane.
18 holes, 5789yds, Par 70, SSS 68, Course record 65.
Club membership 1000.

Visitors	contact professional in advance.
Societies	must contact in advance.
Green Fees	£22 (£29 weekends).
Cards	💳 💳 💳 💳
Prof	Peter Hanna
Facilities	⊗ �🍽 🛏 🍺 ♀ ⛳ 🏠 ⛳ ✓
Location	Off Antrim road

Hotel	★★★ 64% Lansdowne Court Hotel, 657 Antrim Rd, BELFAST ☎ 028 9077 3317 25 ⇆ ☏

Malone 240 Upper Malone Rd, Dunmurry BT17 9LB
☎ 028 90612758 (Office) & 90614917 (Pro)
Fax 028 90431394
e-mail: manager@malonegolfclub.co.uk
Two parkland courses, extremely attractive with a large lake, mature trees and flowering shrubs and bordered by the River Lagan. Very well maintained and offering a challenging round.
Main Course: 18 holes, 6599yds, Par 71, SSS 71.
Edenderry: 9 holes, 6320yds, Par 72, SSS 70.
Club membership 1300.

Visitors	advisable to contact pro-shop in advance. Main Course: Unable to play Sat,before 3pm,Sun morning or Tues.
Societies	apply in writing or fax to club manager. Large group normally Mon & Thu only.
Green Fees	Main Course: £35 per day (£40 weekends); Edenberry: £15 per day (£18 weekends).
Cards	💳 💳 💳 💳
Prof	Michael McGee
Designer	C K Cotton
Facilities	⊗ �🍽 🛏 🍺 ♀ ⛳ 🏠 ⛳ 🛒 ✓
& Leisure	squash, fishing, Outdoor bowling green..
Location	4.5m S opposite Lady Dixon Park

Hotel	★★ 57% Balmoral Hotel, Blacks Rd, Dunmurry, BELFAST ☎ 028 9030 1234 44 ⇆ ☏

Mount Ober Golf & Country Club 24 Ballymaconaghy Rd BT8 6SB ☎ 028 90401811 & 90795666 Fax 028 90705862
Inland parkland course which is a great test of golf for all handicaps.
18 holes, 5419yds, Par 67, SSS 66, Course record 67.
Club membership 400.

Visitors	must contact in advance at weekends & bank holidays, may play Sat after 3.30pm and Sun after 10.30am.
Societies	book by telephone or fax.
Green Fees	£13 (£15 weekends).
Cards	💳 💳
Prof	Geoff Loughrey/Steve Rourke
Facilities	⊗ �🍽 🛏 🍺 ♀ ⛳ 🏠 ⛳ 🐕 ✓ ℓ
& Leisure	ski slopes, American billiards hall.
Location	Off Saintfield Road

Hotel	★★★ 69% The Crescent Townhouse, 13 Lower Crescent, BELFAST ☎ 028 9032 3349 11 ⇆ ☏

Ormeau 50 Park Rd BT7 2FX
☎ 028 90640700 Fax 028 90646250
e-mail: ormeau.golfclub@virgin.net
Parkland.
9 holes, 2688yds, Par 68, SSS 66.
Club membership 520.

Visitors	welcome weekdays except Tue after 2pm. May play Sat after 5.30pm & Sun by arrangement.
Societies	contact in advance.
Green Fees	£12 (£15 weekends).
Prof	Mr B Wilson
Facilities	⊗ �🍽 🛏 🍺 ♀ ⛳ 🏠 ⛳ ✓
Location	S of city centre between Ravenhill & Ormeau roads

Shandon Park 73 Shandon Park BT5 6NY
☎ 028 90401856
18 holes, 6261yds, Par 70, SSS 70.
Location Off Knock road
Telephone for further details

Hotel	★★★ 69% The Crescent Townhouse, 13 Lower Crescent, BELFAST ☎ 028 9032 3349 11 ⇆ ☏

DUNDONALD   Map 01 D5

Knock Summerfield BT16 2QX
☎ 028 90483251 & 90482249 Fax 028 90483251
Parkland course with huge trees, deep bunkers and a river cutting across several fairways. This is a hard but fair course and will test the best of golfers.
18 holes, 6435yds, Par 70, SSS 71, Course record 66.
Club membership 920.

Visitors	with member only on Sat, Mon & Thu are Society Days, Tue is Ladies Day, advisable to contact in advance.
Societies	must contact in advance.
Green Fees	£20 per day (£25 weekends & bank holidays).
Prof	Gordon Fairweather
Designer	Colt, Allison & McKenzie
Facilities	⊗ �🍽 🛏 🍺 ♀ ⛳ 🏠 ⛳ 🐕 🛒 ✓
Location	5miles E of Belfast

Hotel	★★★ 72% Old Inn, 15 Main St, CRAWFORDSBURN ☎ 028 9185 3255 33 ⇆ ☏

Looking for a driving range?
See the index at the back of the guide

NEWTOWNBREDA   Map 01 D5

The Belvoir Park 73 Church Rd BT8 7AN
☎ 028 90491693 Fax 028 90646113
This undulating parkland course is not strenuous to walk, but is certainly a test of your golf, with tree-lined fairways and a particularly challenging finish at the final four holes.
18 holes, 6516yds, Par 71, SSS 71, Course record 65.
Club membership 1000.
Visitors   must contact in advance, may not play Sat.
Societies   must contact in writing.
Green Fees £33 per day (£38 weekends & bank holidays).
Cards   〰️ 🔳 🈂️
Prof   Maurice Kelly
Designer   H Holt
Facilities   ⊗ ℳ ⅃ ♨ ♀ ⚘ 🏠 ⛳ 🏌 🛒 🏌
Location   2m from city centre off Saintfield/Newcastle rd

Hotel   ★★★ 70% Clandeboye Lodge Hotel, 10 Estate Rd, Clandeboye, BANGOR
☎ 028 9185 2500 43 ⇆ ⌧

CO DOWN

ARDGLASS   Map 01 D5

Ardglass Castle Place BT30 7TP
☎ 028 44841219 Fax 028 44841841
e-mail: golfclub@ardglass.force9.co.uk
A scenic cliff-top seaside course with spectacular views and some memorable holes.
18 holes, 5498mtrs, Par 70, SSS 69, Course record 65.
Club membership 800.
Visitors   must contact in advance.
Societies   must contact in advance, welcome weekdays & restricted times Sun.
Green Fees £15(£12.50 weekends).
Cards   〰️ 🔳 🔳 🔳 🔳 🈂️ 🈂️
Prof   Philip Farrell
Designer   David Jones
Facilities   ⊗ ℳ ⅃ ♨ ♀ ⚘ 🏠 ⛳ 🛒 🏌
Location   7m from Downpatrick on the B1

Hotel   ★★ 64% Enniskeen House Hotel, 98 Bryansford Rd, NEWCASTLE
☎ 028 4372 2392 12 ⇆ ⌧

ARDMILLAN   Map 01 D5

Mahee Island Mahee Island, Comber BT23 6EP
☎ 028 97541234
An undulating parkland course, almost surrounded by water, with magnificent views of Strangford Lough and its islands, with Scrabo Tower in the background. The first professional here was Fred Daly (1933-4) who became British Open Champion in 1947.
9 holes, 5590yds, Par 68, SSS 68, Course record 63.
Club membership 600.

Visitors   may not play on Wed after 5pm or Sat before 5pm.
Societies   contact in advance.
Green Fees £10 per 18 holes (£15 weekends).
Designer   Mr Robinson
Facilities   ⊗ by prior arrangement ℳ by prior arrangement ⅃ by prior arrangement ♀ by prior arrangement ⚘ 🏠 ⛳ 🏌
Location   Off Comber/Killyleagh road to the left 0.5m from Comber

Hotel   ★★★ 70% Clandeboye Lodge Hotel, 10 Estate Rd, Clandeboye, BANGOR
☎ 028 9185 2500 43 ⇆ ⌧

BALLYNAHINCH   Map 01 D5

Spa 20 Grove Rd BT24 8PN
☎ 028 97562365 Fax 028 97564158
Parkland course with tree-lined fairways and scenic views of the Mourne Mountains.
18 holes, 6003mtrs, Par 72, SSS 72, Course record 66.
Club membership 907.

Visitors   must contact in advance. No play on Sat.
Societies   must contact in advance.
Green Fees £15 per round (£20 weekends & bank holidays).
Designer   F Ainsworth
Facilities   ⊗ ℳ ⅃ ♨ ♀ ⚘ 🏠 ⛳ 🛒 🏌
Location   1m S on the Grove Rd

Hotel   ★★ 64% Enniskeen House Hotel, 98 Bryansford Rd, NEWCASTLE
☎ 028 4372 2392 12 ⇆ ⌧

BANBRIDGE   Map 01 D5

Banbridge 116 Huntly Rd BT32 3UR
☎ 028 40662211 Fax 028 40669400
e-mail: info@banbridge-golf.freeserve.co.uk
A picturesque course with excellent views of the Mourne mountains. The holes are not long, but are tricky.
18 holes, 5003mtrs, Par 69, SSS 67, Course record 61.
Club membership 700.
Visitors   may not play Sat or before 11am on Sun. Ladies Day Tue.
Societies   must contact in writing.
Green Fees £15 per day (£20 weekends).
Designer   F Ainsworth
Facilities   ⊗ ℳ ⅃ ♨ ♀ ⚘ 🏠 🏌 ⌧
Location   0.5m along Huntly road

▶

Hotel ★★★ 66% White Gables Hotel,
14 Dromore Rd, HILLSBOROUGH
☎ 028 9268 2755 31 ⇆ ☞

BANGOR Map 01 D5

Bangor Broadway BT20 4RH
☎ 028 91270922 Fax 028 91453394
Undulating parkland course in the town. It is well maintained and pleasant and offers a challenging round, particularly at the 5th.
18 holes, 6410yds, Par 71, SSS 71, Course record 62.
Club membership 1147.
Visitors may not play Sat & weekdays 1-2.
Societies must contact in advance, Mon/Wed by telephone, Fri by letter.
Green Fees £20 (£25 Sun & bank holidays).
Prof Michael Bannon
Designer James Braid
Facilities ⊗ ⅷ ⅂ ⅃ ♥ ♀ ⅄ 🏠 ⚑ ⛳ ♂
Location 1m from town on Donaghadee Road

Hotel ★★★ 60% Royal Hotel, Seafront, BANGOR
☎ 028 9127 1866 50 ⇆ ☞

Blackwood Golf Centre 150 Crawfordsburn Rd,
Clandeboye BT19 1GB
☎ 028 91852706 Fax 028 91853785
The golf centre is a pay and play development with a computerised booking system for the 18-hole championship-standard Hamilton course. The course is built on mature woodland with man-made lakes that come into play on 5 holes. The Temple course is an 18-hole Par 3 course with holes ranging from the 75yd 1st to the 185yd 10th, which has a lake on the right of the green. Banked by gorse with streams crossing throughout, this Par 3 course is no pushover.
Hamilton Course: 18 holes, 6392yds, Par 71, SSS 70, Course record 62.
Temple Course: 18 holes, 2492yds, Par 54.
Visitors pay as you play, computerised booking system for the Hamilton Course, bookable 7 days in advance.
Societies telephone in advance.
Green Fees Hamilton: £16 per round; £9 per 9 holes (£22/£12 weekends). Temple: £9 per round; £6 per 9 holes (£11/£8 weekends).
Cards 〰 ▬ 〰
Prof Debbie Hanna
Designer Simon Gidman
Facilities ⊗ ⅂ ♥ ♀ ⅄ ⚑ ♂ ſ
Location 2m from Bangor, off A2 to Belfast

Hotel ★★★ 70% Clandeboye Lodge Hotel,
10 Estate Rd, Clandeboye, BANGOR
☎ 028 9185 2500 43 ⇆ ☞

Carnalea Station Rd BT19 1EZ
☎ 028 91270368 Fax 028 91273989
A scenic course on the shores of Belfast Lough.
18 holes, 5647yds, Par 69, SSS 67, Course record 63.
Club membership 1354.
Visitors restricted Sat.
Societies must contact in advance.
Green Fees £16 (£20 sun & bank holidays).
Prof Tom Loughran
Facilities ⊗ ⅷ ⅂ ♀ ⅄ 🏠 ⚑ ♂

Location 2m W adjacent to railway station

Hotel ★★★ 72% Old Inn, 15 Main St,
CRAWFORDSBURN
☎ 028 9185 3255 33 ⇆ ☞

Clandeboye Tower Rd, Conlig, Newtownards BT23 3PN
☎ 91271767 Fax 028 91473711
e-mail: clandeboyegolf@dnet.co.uk
Parkland/heathland courses. The Dufferin is the championship course and offers a tough challenge demanding extreme accuracy, with its mass of gorse, bracken and strategically placed trees that flank every hole. The slightest error will be punished. The Ava compliments the Dufferin perfectly. Accuracy is also the key with a notable 2nd hole.
Dufferin Course: 18 holes, 6469yds, Par 71, SSS 71.
Ava Course: 18 holes, 5465yds, Par 70, SSS 68.
Club membership 1450.

Visitors must contact in advance,weekends after 2.30pm.
Societies Mon-Wed, Fri & after 3pm Sat & Sun. Must contact in advance.
Green Fees Dufferin: £27.50 per round (£33 weekends & bank holidays); Ava: £22 per round (£27.50 weekends & bank holidays).
Cards ▬
Prof Peter Gregory
Designer William Robinson
Facilities ⊗ ⅷ ⅂ ♥ ♀ ⅄ 🏠 ⚑ ♂ ⛳ ♂
Location 2m S on A1 between Bangor & Newtownards

Hotel ★★★ 60% Royal Hotel, Seafront, BANGOR
☎ 028 9127 1866 50 ⇆ ☞

Helen's Bay Golf Rd, Helen's Bay BT19 1TL
☎ 028 91852815 & 91852601
Fax 028 91852815
A parkland course on the shores of Belfast Lough with panoramic views along the Antrim coast. The 4th hole Par 3 is particularly challenging as the green is screened by high trees.
9 holes, 5161mtrs, Par 68, SSS 67.
Club membership 750.
Visitors welcome Sun, Mon, Wed, Thu (before 1.30pm), Fri (after 11.30am during Jul & Aug) & Sat after 6pm. Book in advance with secretary.
Societies welcome Sun, Mon, Wed, Thu (before 1.30pm), Fri & Sat after 6pm. Telephone secretary in advance.
Green Fees £15 per day(Mon-Thu);£6(Sat);£17.50 (Fri,Sun & bank holidays).
Facilities ⊗ ⅷ ⅂ ♥ ♀ ⅄ ♂
Location A2 from Belfast ▶

Hotel	★★★ 72% Old Inn, 15 Main St, CRAWFORDSBURN ☎ 028 9185 3255 33 ⇌ ☏

Hotel	★★★ 72% Old Inn, 15 Main St, CRAWFORDSBURN ☎ 028 9185 3255 33 ⇌ ☏

CARRYDUFF   Map 01 D5

Rockmount 28 Drumalig Rd, Carryduff BT8 8EQ
☎ 028 90812279 Fax 020 90815851
e-mail: rockmountgc@btconnect.com
A demanding 18-hole course set in open parkland with mature trees, several streams, and a tricky lake at the 11th hole. Panoramic views.
18 holes, 6373yds, Par 71, SSS 71, Course record 68.
Club membership 700.
Visitors   welcome except for Sat or Wed afternoon.
Societies welcome except for Wed & Sat, book by
              telephone.
Green Fees £20 (£24 Sun).
Cards   💳 💳 🔲
Designer   Robert Patterson
Facilities ⊗ ⅧⒽ ▮ ♥ ♀ ⏦ 🏠 ❯ ♣ 🛒 ♂
Location   10m S of Belfast

Hotel	★★ 57% Balmoral Hotel, Blacks Rd, Dunmurry, BELFAST ☎ 028 9030 1234 44 ⇌ ☏

CLOUGHEY   Map 01 D5

Kirkistown Castle 142 Main Rd, Cloughey BT22 1JA
☎ 028 42771233 Fax 028 42771699
e-mail: kirkistown@aol.com
A seaside semi-links popular with visiting golfers because of its quiet location. The course is exceptionally dry and remains open when others in the area have to close. The Par 4 10th is particularly distinctive with a long drive and a slight dogleg to a raised green with a gorse covered motte waiting for the wayward approach shot.
18 holes, 6167yds, Par 69, SSS 70, Course record 65.
Club membership 948.
Visitors   must contact in advance, restricted weekends.
Societies contact in writing or by phone.
Green Fees £18.75 (£25.75 weekends).
Prof   Jonathan Peden
Designer   James Braid
Facilities ⊗ Ⅷ Ⓛ ▮ ▄ ♀ ⏦ 🏠 ❯ ♂
Location   16m from Newtownards on the A2

Hotel	★★★ 72% Old Inn, 15 Main St, CRAWFORDSBURN ☎ 028 9185 3255 33 ⇌ ☏

DONAGHADEE   Map 01 D5

Donaghadee Warren Rd BT21 0PQ
☎ 028 91883624 Fax 028 91888891
Undulating seaside course, part links, part parkland, requiring a certain amount of concentration. Splendid views.
18 holes, 5570mtrs, Par 71, SSS 69, Course record 64.
Club membership 1160.
Visitors   contact in advance.
Societies write in advance.
Green Fees £22 (£25 Sun).
Prof   Gordon Drew
Facilities ⊗ Ⅷ Ⓛ ▮ ▄ ♀ ⏦ 🏠 ❯ ♣ 🛒 ♂
Location   5 miles S Bangor on Coast Rd

DOWNPATRICK   Map 01 D5

Bright Castle 14 Coniamstown Rd, Bright BT30 8LU
☎ 028 44841319
Parkland course in elevated position with views of the Mountains of Mourne. A good challenge for the energetic golfer.
18 holes, 7300yds, Par 74, SSS 74, Course record 69.
Club membership 60.
Visitors   no restrictions.
Societies must contact in advance.
Green Fees not confirmed.
Designer   Mr Ennis
Facilities ⊗ Ⓛ ▮ ▄ ♀ 🛒 ♂
Location   5m S

Hotel	★★ 64% Enniskeen House Hotel, 98 Bryansford Rd, NEWCASTLE ☎ 028 4372 2392 12 ⇌ ☏

Downpatrick 43 Saul Rd BT30 6PA
☎ 028 44615947 Fax 028 44617502
e-mail: info@downpatrickgolfclub.com
This undulating parkland course provides a good challenge.
18 holes, 6100yds, Par 70, SSS 69, Course record 66.
Club membership 960.
Visitors   must contact in advance.
Societies must telephone in advance.
Green Fees £15 per day (£25 weekends & bank holidays).
Cards   💳 💳
Designer   Hawtree & Son
Facilities ⊗ Ⅷ Ⓛ ▮ ▄ ♀ 🏠 ❯ ♣ 🛒 ♂
& Leisure snooker.
Location   1.5m from town centre

Hotel	★★ 64% Enniskeen House Hotel, 98 Bryansford Rd, NEWCASTLE ☎ 028 4372 2392 12 ⇌ ☏

HOLYWOOD   Map 01 D5

Holywood Nuns Walk, Demesne Rd BT18 9LE
☎ 028 90423135 Fax 028 90425040
e-mail: mail@holywoodgolfclub.co.uk
Hilly parkland course with some fine views and providing an interesting game. Several feature holes, including the short 6th "Nuns Walk" and the treacherous 12th "White House".
18 holes, 5480mtrs, Par 69, SSS 68, Course record 64.
Club membership 1100.
Visitors   must contact in advance.Tee closed 1.30-2.15
              for members,member only saturdays.
Societies must contact in writing.
Green Fees £16(£21 sun & bank holidays).
Cards   🔲
Prof   Paul Gray
Facilities ⊗ Ⅷ Ⓛ ▮ ▄ ♀ 🏠 ❯ ♣ 🛒 ♂ ☕
Location   Just outside Belfast, off the Bangor dual carriageway, behind the town of Holywood

Hotel	★★★ 72% Old Inn, 15 Main St, CRAWFORDSBURN ☎ 028 9185 3255 33 ⇌ ☏

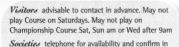

Royal County Down

Newcastle, *Co Down*   ☎ 028 43723314   Fax 028 43726281   Map 01 D5

e-mail: royal.co.down@virgin.net

The Championship Course is consistently rated among the world's top ten courses. Laid out beneath the imperious gaze of the Mountains of Mourne, the course enjoys a magnificent stage-like setting as it stretches out along the shores of Dundrum Bay. As well as being one of the world's most beautiful courses, it is also one of the most challenging, with great swathes of heather and gorse lining fairways that tumble beneath vast sand hills, and wild tussocky faced bunkers defending small subtly contoured greens.

The Annesley Links offers a less formidable, yet extremely characterful game played against the same incomparable backcloth. Recently substantially revised under the direction of Donald Steel, the course begins quite benignly before charging headlong into the dunes. Several charming, and one or two teasing holes have been carved out amid the gorse, heather and bracken.

Visitors advisable to contact in advance. May not play Course on Saturdays. May not play on Championship Course Sat, Sun am or Wed after 9am

Societies telephone for availability and confirm in writing

Green Fees Championship £80 per round (£90 weekends); Annesley £17 per round (£25 weekends)

Facilities ⊗ ⓑ 🍷 ⓨ ⓧ 🏠 ⓨⓕ ⓓ
Professional (Kevan Whitson)

Location Newcastle BT33 0AN
(30m S of Belfast via A24)

Holes/Par/Course record 36 holes.
Championship Course: 18 holes, 7037 yds, Par 71, SSS 74, Course record 66
Annesley Course: 18 holes, 4681 yds, Par 66, SSS 63

Situated thirty miles south of Belfast and fringed by the impressive sweep of Dundrum Bay, Newcastle is where, in the immortal words of Percy French, 'the Mountains of Mourn sweep down to the sea'.

Championship Course

The Royal Belfast Station Rd, Craigavad BT18 0BP
☎ 028 90428165 Fax 028 90421404
e-mail: royalbelfastgc@btclick.com
On the shores of Belfast Lough, this attractive course consists of wooded parkland on undulating terrain which provides a pleasant, challenging game.
18 holes, 6185yds, Par 70, SSS 69.
Club membership 1200.
Visitors   may not play on Wed or Sat before 4.30pm; must be accompanied by a member or present a letter of introduction from their own golf club. Must contact in advance.
Societies   must contact in writing.
Green Fees   £40 per round (£50 weekends).
Cards   ▨ ▨ ▨ ▨
Prof   Chris Spence
Designer   H C Colt
Facilities   ⊗ ⅷ ⓛ ☗ ♀ ♨ 🏌 ➔ ♨ ✓
& Leisure   hard tennis courts, squash.
Location   2m E on A2

Hotel   ★★★ 72% Old Inn, 15 Main St, CRAWFORDSBURN
☎ 028 9185 3255 33 ➩ ♞

KILKEEL   Map 01 D5

Kilkeel Mourne Park BT34 4LB
☎ 028 41765095 & 41762296 Fax 028 41765579
e-mail: kilkeelgolfclub@tinyonline.co.uk
Picturesquely situated at the foot of the Mourne Mountains. Eleven holes have tree-lined fairways with the remainder in open parkland. The 13th hole is testing and a well positioned tee shot is essential.
18 holes, 6615yds, Par 72, SSS 72, Course record 69.
Club membership 750.
Visitors   contact in advance for weekend play.
Societies   must contact in advance.
Green Fees   £18 per round (£22 weekends).
Designer   Babington/Hackett
Facilities   ⊗ ⅷ ⓛ ☗ ♀ ♨ 🏌 ➔ ♨ ✓ 🏌
Location   3m from Kilkeel on Newry road

Hotel   ★★ 64% Enniskeen House Hotel, 98 Bryansford Rd, NEWCASTLE
☎ 028 4372 2392 12 ➩ ♞

KILLYLEAGH   Map 01 D5

Ringdufferin Golf Course 31 Ringdufferin Rd, Toye BT30 9PH ☎ 028 44828812 Fax 028 44828812
The course overlooks Strangford Lough.
18 holes, 4652mtrs, Par 68, SSS 66.
Club membership 300.
Visitors   contact in advance on Saturdays.
Societies   apply in writing/telephone in advance.
Green Fees   not confirmed.
Prof   Mark Lavery
Designer   Frank Ainsworth
Facilities   ⊗ ⓛ ☗ ♀ ♨ 🏌 ♨ ✓ 🏌
& Leisure   fishing.
Location   2m N of Killyleagh

Hotel   ★★★ 66% Portaferry Hotel, 10 The Strand, PORTAFERRY ☎ 028 4272 8231 14 ➩ ♞

MAGHERALIN   Map 01 D5

Edenmore Edenmore House, 70 Drumnabreeze Rd BT67 0RH ☎ 028 92611310 Fax 92613310
e-mail: edenmoregc@aol.com
Set in mature parkland with gently rolling slopes. The front nine holes provide an interesting contrast to the back nine with more open play involved. Many new paths and features have been recently added.
18 holes, 6244yds, Par 71, SSS 70, Course record 70.
Club membership 350.
Visitors   telephone in advance, may not play until after 2pm Sat.
Societies   telephone in advance.
Green Fees   £13 per round;£18 per day;£7 per 9 holes(£15/£20/£8 weekends & bank holidays).
Cards   ▨ ▨ ▨ ▨
Designer   F Ainsworth
Facilities   ⊗ ♨ ♨ ☗ 🏌 ➔ ♨ ✓
Location   20 miles SW of Belfast

Hotel   ★★★ 72% Old Inn, 15 Main St, CRAWFORDSBURN
☎ 028 9185 3255 33 ➩ ♞

NEWCASTLE   Map 01 D5

NEWCASTLE See page 441

NEWRY   Map 01 D5

Newry 11 Forkhill Rd BT35 8LZ
☎ 028 30263871 Fax 028 30263871
18 holes, 3000mtrs, Par 53, SSS 52, Course record 51.
Location   1m from Newry just off the main Dublin road
Telephone for further details

Hotel   ★★ 64% Enniskeen House Hotel, 98 Bryansford Rd, NEWCASTLE ☎ 028 4372 2392 12 ➩ ♞

NEWTOWNARDS   Map 01 D5

Scrabo 233 Scrabo Rd BT23 4SL
☎ 028 91812355 Fax 028 91822919
e-mail: scrabogc@compuserve.com
Hilly and picturesque, this course offers a good test of golf for golfers of all abilities. It benefits from good drainage and remains dry and playable most of the year.
18 holes, 5722mtrs, Par 71, SSS 71, Course record 65.
Club membership 1002.
Visitors   may not play on Saturdays. Contact in advance.
Societies   must contact in advance.
Green Fees   not confirmed.
Prof   Paul McCrystal
Facilities   ⊗ ⅷ ⓛ ☗ ♀ ♨ ♨ ✓
Location   Borders of Newtownards on the Ards Peninsula, follow signs for Scrabo Country Park

Hotel   ★★★ 70% Clandeboye Lodge Hotel, 10 Estate Rd, Clandeboye, BANGOR
☎ 028 9185 2500 43 ➩ ♞

WARRENPOINT   Map 01 D5

Warrenpoint Lower Dromore Rd BT34 3LN
☎ 028 41753695 Fax 028 41752918
e-mail: warrenpointgolfclub@talk21.com
Parkland course with marvellous views and a need for
accurate shots.
18 holes, 6108yds, Par 71, SSS 70, Course record 61.
Club membership 1385.
Visitors   must contact in advance.
Societies   must contact in advance.
Green Fees £20 per round (£27 weekends & bank holidays).
Cards   🔳🔳 💳
Prof   Nigel Shaw
Designer   Tom Craddock/Pat Ruddy
Facilities   ⊗ 🏇 🏌 💺 🍴 🛎 🏠 ⛳ ♂
& Leisure   squash.
Location   1m W

Hotel   ★★ 64% Enniskeen House Hotel,
98 Bryansford Rd, NEWCASTLE ☎ 028 4372
2392 12 ⇌ ♠

CO FERMANAGH

ENNISKILLEN   Map 01 C5

Ashwoods Golf Centre Sligo Rd BT74 7JY
☎ 028 66325321 & 66322908 Fax 028 66329411
Only 1 mile from Lough Erne, this course is open
meadowland. It has been well planted with many young
trees.
14 holes, 1930yds, Par 42.
Visitors   no restrictions.
Societies   must book in advance.
Green Fees £6.
Cards   🔳 🔳 🔳 💳
Prof   Pat Trainor
Designer   P Loughran
Facilities   ⊗ 🏇 by prior arrangement 🏌 💺 🛎 🍴 🏠
♂ ⛳
Location   1.5m W

Hotel   ★★★★ 68% Killyhevlin Hotel,
ENNISKILLEN ☎ 028 6632 3481 43 ⇌ ♠

Castle Hume Castle Hume, Belleek Rd BT93 7ED
☎ 028 66327077 Fax 028 66327076
Castle Hulme is a particularly scenic and challenging course.
Set in undulating parkland with large rolling greens, rivers,
lakes and water hazards all in play on a championship
standard course.
18 holes, 5770mtrs, Par 72, SSS 70, Course record 69.
Club membership 350.
Visitors   may play any time subject to advance
arrangement.
Societies   telephone in advance.
Green Fees £15 per round (£20 weekends & bank holidays).
Cards   🔳 🔳
Designer   B Browne
Facilities   ⊗ 🏇 🏌 💺 🍴 🛎 🏠 🏇 🛎 ⛳ ♂ ⛳
& Leisure   fishing.
Location   4m from Enniskillen on the Belleek/Donegal
Road

Hotel   ★★★★ 68% Killyhevlin Hotel,
ENNISKILLEN ☎ 028 6632 3481 43 ⇌ ♠

Enniskillen Castlecoole BT74 6HZ
☎ 028 66325250 Fax 028 66326510
e-mail: enniskillen.golf@btclick.com
Tree lined parkland course offering panoramic views of
Enniskillen town and the surrounding lakeland area. Situated
beside the National Trust's Castlecoole Estate.
18 holes, 6189yds, Par 71, SSS 69, Course record 67.
Club membership 460.
Visitors   restricted Tue and weekends. Contact Hon
Secretaryor bar steward.
Societies   must contact club steward in advance by
telephone or writing.
Green Fees £15 per day (£18 weekends & bank holidays).
Facilities   ⊗ by prior arrangement 🏇 by prior arrangement
🏌 💺 🍴 🛎 🏠 🏇 ♂
Location   1m E

Hotel   ★★★★ 68% Killyhevlin Hotel,
ENNISKILLEN ☎ 028 6632 3481 43 ⇌ ♠

CO LONDONDERRY

AGHADOWEY   Map 01 C6

Brown Trout Golf & Country Inn 209 Agivey Rd
BT51 4AD ☎ 028 70868209 Fax 028 70868878
e-mail: bill@browntroutinn.com
A challenging course with two par 5s. During the course of
the 9 holes, players have to negotiate water 7 times and all
the fairways are lined with densely packed fir trees.
9 holes, 5510yds, Par 70, SSS 68, Course record 64.
Club membership 150.
Visitors   no restrictions.
Societies   must contact by telephone, restricted tee-off
times Sun.
Green Fees £10 (£15 weekends & bank holidays).
Cards   🔳 🔳 🔳 💳 🔳 💳
Prof   Ken Revie
Designer   Bill O'Hara Snr
Facilities   ⊗ 🏇 🏌 💺 🍴 🛎 🏠 🏇 ♂
& Leisure   fishing, gymnasium.
Location   Junc of A54 & B66, 7m S of Coleraine

Hotel   ★★ 71% Brown Trout Golf & Country Inn,
209 Agivey Rd, AGHADOWEY
☎ 028 7086 8209 15 ⇌ ♠

CASTLEDAWSON   Map 01 C5

Moyola Park 15 Curran Rd BT45 8DG
☎ 028 79468468 & 79468830 (Prof) Fax 028 79468626
e-mail: golf@moyola-park-n-ireland.freeserve.co.uk
Parkland course with some difficult shots, calling for length
and accuracy. The Moyola River provides a water hazard at
the 8th. Newly designed par 3, demands good shot placement
to a green on an island in the Moyola river, players
capabilities will be tested by the undulating green.
18 holes, 6522yds, Par 71, SSS 70, Course record 67.
Club membership 1000.

▶

Visitors   contact professional in advance, G.U.I. dress code applies, Ladies day Wednesday, Sat & Sun after 1.30pm, book in advance to avoid disappointment.
Societies   must contact in advance, preferably in writing
Green Fees   £20 per day (£30 weekends & bank holidays).
Cards ▨
Prof   Vivian Teague
Designer   Don Patterson
Facilities ⊗ 〕ⅢⅢ 🏌 💼 ♀ ⚑ 👜 🗙 🏌 ⚓ 🗙
Location   Take sign for Castledawson. Golf Club signposted

Hotel   ★★★★ 72% Galgorm Manor, BALLYMENA
            ☎ 028 2588 1001 24 ⇔ ☞

CASTLEROCK   Map 01 C6

Castlerock 65 Circular Rd BT51 4TJ ☎ 028 70848314
Fax 028 70849440 e-mail: castlerock18@hotmail.com
A most exhilarating course with three superb par 4s, four testing short holes and five par 5s. After an uphill start, the hazards are many, including the river and a railway, and both judgement and accuracy are called for. A challenge in calm weather, any trouble from the elements will test your golf to the limits.
Mussenden Course: 18 holes, 6499yds, Par 73, SSS 72, Course record 64.
Bann Course: 9 holes, 2938yds, Par 34, SSS 33.
Club membership 1120.
Visitors   contact in advance, limited number of places at weekends. Must be members of a recognised club.
Societies   must contact in advance.
Green Fees   £30 per round;£45 per round(£55 per round weekends).
Cards ▨ ▨ 🗙
Prof   Robert Kelly
Designer   Ben Sayers
Facilities ⊗ 〕ⅢⅢ 🏌 💼 ♀ ⚑ 🗙 🏌 🗙
Location   6m from Coleraine on A2

Hotel   ★★★ 56% Causeway Coast Hotel,
            36 Ballyreagh Rd, PORTRUSH
            ☎ 028 70822435   21 ⇔ ☞

KILREA   Map 01 C5

Kilrea Drumagarner Rd BT51 5TB ☎ 028 25821048
A relatively short undulating inland course with tight fairways and small greens. The opening hole is a long par 3, particularly into the wind.
9 holes, 4514yds, Par 62, SSS 62, Course record 61.
Club membership 300.
Visitors   welcome but restricted Tue pm, Wed pm during summer and Sat all year.
Societies   contact D P Clarke (Sec), 37 Townhill Rd, Portglenone, Co Antrim BT44 8AD.
Green Fees not confirmed.
Facilities ⚑
Location   0.5m outside village of Kilrea on Drumagarner Road

Hotel   ★★ 71% Brown Trout Golf & Country Inn,
            209 Agivey Rd, AGHADOWEY
            ☎ 028 7086 8209 15 ⇔ ☞

LIMAVADY   Map 01 C6

Benone 53 Benone Ave BT49 0LQ
☎ 028 77750555 Fax 77750919
Benone Golf Course: 9 holes, 1334mtrs, Par 27.
Club membership 300.
Visitors   no restrictions.
Societies
Green Fees not confirmed.
Prof   Ken Revie
Facilities ⊗ 〕ⅢⅢ 💼 ♀ 🏌 🗙
& Leisure   hard tennis courts, heated outdoor swimming pool.
Location   Between Coleraine/Limavady on A2

Radisson Roe Park Hotel & Golf Resort Roe Park
BT49 9LB ☎ 028 77722222 Fax 028 77722313
A parkland course opened in 1992 on an historic Georgian estate. The course surrounds the original buildings and a driving range has been created in the old walled garden. Final holes 15-18 are particularly memorable with water, trees, out-of-bounds, etc to provide a testing finish.
18 holes, 6318yds, Par 70, SSS 35.
Club membership 500.
Visitors   advance booking recommended. Handicap certificate required. May not play before 10.30am at weekends.
Societies   contact in advance.
Green Fees not confirmed.
Cards ▨ ▨ ▨ ▨ ▨ ▨ 🗙
Prof   Seamus Duffy
Designer   Frank Ainsworth
Facilities ⊗ 〕ⅢⅢ 🏌 💼 ♀ ⚑ 👜 🗙 🏌 🗙 ⚓ 🗙 🗙
& Leisure   heated indoor swimming pool, fishing, sauna, solarium, gymnasium, indoor golf academy.
Location   Just outside Limavady on A2 Ballykelly/Londonderry road

Hotel   ★★★★ 69% Radisson Roe Park Hotel & Golf Resort, LIMAVADY
            ☎ 028 7772 2222 64 ⇔ ☞

LONDONDERRY   Map 01 C5

City of Derry 49 Victoria Rd BT47 2PU
☎ 028 71346369 Fax 028 71310008
e-mail: cityofderry@aol.com
Two parkland courses on undulating parkland with good views and lots of trees. The 9-hole course will particularly suit novices.
Prehen Course: 18 holes, 6406yds, Par 71, SSS 71, Course record 68.
Dunhugh Course: 9 holes, 2354yds, Par 66, SSS 66.
Club membership 823.
Visitors   must make a booking to play on Prehen Course at weekends or before 4.30pm on weekdays.
Societies   must contact in advance.
Green Fees £20 per 18 holes-Prehen(£8 Dunhugh).
Cards ▨
Prof   Michael Doherty
Facilities ⊗ 〕ⅢⅢ 🏌 💼 ♀ ⚑ 💼 🗙
Location   2m S

Hotel   ★★★ 68% Trinity Hotel, 22-24 Strand Rd,
            DERRY CITY ☎ 028 7127 1271 40 ⇔ ☞

Foyle International Golf Centre 12 Alder Rd BT48 8DB
☎ 028 71352222 Fax 028 71353967
e-mail: mail@foylegolf.club24.co.uk
Foyle International boasts a championship course, a 9 hole par 3 course and a driving range. It is a fine test of golf with water coming into play on the 3rd, 10th and 11th holes. The 6th green overlooks the Amelia Earhart centre.
18 holes, 6678yds, Par 72, SSS 71, Course record 70.
Club membership 320.
Visitors   welcome any time, no restrictions.
Societies   booking up to 12 months in advance with deposit.
Green Fees £12 per round (£15 weekends & bank holidays)..
Cards   🖦 ▱🗝 🖾 🖉
Prof   Kieran McLaughlin
Designer   Frank Ainsworth
Facilities   ⊗ 🍴 ﹗ ﹗ ♀ 🕂 🖿 ⚲ ↘ ✓ ℓ
& Leisure   9 hole par 3 course..
Location   1.5m from Foyle Bridge driving torwards Moville

Hotel   ★★★ 68% Trinity Hotel, 22-24 Strand Rd, DERRY CITY ☎ 028 7127 1271 40 ⇄ 🐾

PORTSTEWART   Map 01 C6

Portstewart 117 Strand Rd BT55 7PG
Strand Course: 18 holes, 6784yds, Par 72, SSS 72.
Old Course: 18 holes, 4733yds, Par 64, SSS 62.
3: 9 holes, 2622yds, Par 32.
Telephone for further details

Hotel   ★★★ 56% Causeway Coast Hotel, 36 Ballyreagh Rd, PORTRUSH ☎ 028 70822435 21 ⇄ 🐾

CO TYRONE

COOKSTOWN   Map 01 C5

Killymoon 200 Killymoon Rd BT80 8TW
☎ 028 86763762 & 86762254 Fax 028 867 63762
Parkland course on elevated, well drained land.
18 holes, 5481mtrs, Par 70, SSS 69, Course record 64.
Club membership 950.
Visitors   booking essential through proshop on 016487 63460.Must contact in advance,have a golf handicap and play after 3.30pm saturdays.
Societies   must contact in advance.
Green Fees £10 per 9 holes;£18 per 18 holes;£28 per day(£22 weekends).
Prof   Gary Chambers
Facilities   ⊗ 🍴 🖦 ﹗ ♀ 🕂 🖿 ✓
& Leisure   snooker & pool.

Guesthouse ◆◆◆◆◆ Grange Lodge, 7 Grange Rd, DUNGANNON ☎ 028 87784212 5 ⇄ 🐾

Looking for a driving range?
See the index at the back of the guide

DUNGANNON   Map 01 C5

Dungannon 34 Springfield Ln BT70 1QX
☎ 028 87722098 or 87727338 Fax 028 87727338
Parkland course with five par 3s and tree-lined fairways.
18 holes, 6046yds, Par 72, SSS 69, Course record 62.
Club membership 600.
Visitors   contact in advance, may not play before 3.30pm Sat and Sun.Handicap certificate required.
Societies   apply in writing to secretary.
Green Fees £18(£22 weekends & bank holidays).
Designer   Sam Bacon
Facilities   ⊗ 🍴 ﹗ ♀ 🕂 🖿 ↘ ✓
Location   0.5m outside town on Donaghmore road

Hotel   The Cohannon Inn, 212 Ballynakilly Rd, DUNGANNON ☎ 028 8772 4488 50 ⇄ 🐾

FINTONA   Map 01 C5

Fintona Ecclesville Demesne, 1 Kiln St BT78 2BJ
☎ 028 82841480 & 82840777 (office) Fax 028 82841480
Attractive 9-hole parkland course with a notable water hazard - a trout stream that meanders through the course causing many problems for badly executed shots.
9 holes, 5765mtrs, Par 72, SSS 70.
Club membership 400.
Visitors   advised to contact in advance at weekends.
Societies   apply in writing well in advance, weekends not advisable as competitions played.
Green Fees £15 per 18 holes.
Prof   Paul Leonard
Facilities   ⊗ 🍴 🖦 by prior arrangement ﹗ ♀ 🕂
Location   8m S of Omagh

Hotel   ★★ 66% Mahons Hotel, Mill St, IRVINESTOWN ☎ 028 6862 1656 18 ⇄ 🐾

NEWTOWNSTEWART   Map 01 C5

Newtownstewart 38 Golf Course Rd BT78 4HU
☎ 028 81661466 & 81662242 (pro shop)
Fax 028 81662506
Parkland course bisected by a stream. Deer and pheasant are present on the course.
18 holes, 5468mtrs, Par 70, SSS 69, Course record 65.
Club membership 700.
Visitors   contact club secretary in advance.
Societies   must contact secretary in advance.
Green Fees £12 per day (£17 weekends & bank holidays).
Designer   Frank Pennick
Facilities   🕂 🖿 ↘ 🐾 ✓
Location   2m SW on B84

Hotel   ★★★ 68% Trinity Hotel, 22-24 Strand Rd, DERRY CITY ☎ 028 7127 1271 40 ⇄ 🐾

OMAGH   Map 01 C5

Omagh 83a Dublin Rd BT78 1HQ
☎ 028 82243160 Fax 028 82243160
Undulating parkland course beside the River Drumnagh, with the river coming into play on 4 of the holes.
18 holes, 5683mtrs, Par 71, SSS 70.
Club membership 850.

▶

Visitors	play restricted Sat, no need to contact unless large numbers.
Societies	must contact in advance.
Green Fees	not confirmed.
Designer	Dun Patterson
Facilities	⊗ by prior arrangement ⋙ by prior arrangement ☕ by prior arrangement ♨ ♀ ⚲
Location	On S outskirts of town

Hotel	★★★ 68% Trinity Hotel, 22-24 Strand Rd, DERRY CITY ☎ 028 7127 1271 40 ⇆ ↟

STRABANE   Map 01 C5

Strabane Ballycolman Rd ☎ 028 71382271 & 71382007
18 holes, 5537mtrs, Par 69, SSS 69, Course record 62.
Telephone for further details

Hotel	★★★ 68% Trinity Hotel, 22-24 Strand Rd, DERRY CITY ☎ 028 7127 1271 40 ⇆ ↟

REPUBLIC OF IRELAND

CO CARLOW

BORRIS   Map 01 C3

Borris Deerpark ☎ 0503 73310 Fax 0503 73750
Testing parkland course with tree-lined fairways situated within the McMorrough Kavanagh Estate at the foot of Mount Leinster.
9 holes, 6120mtrs, Par 70, SSS 70, Course record 66.
Club membership 600.

Visitors	advisable to contact in advance, weekends very restricted.
Societies	applications in writing.
Green Fees	IEP14.
Facilities	⊗ ⋙ ☕ ♨ ♀ ⚲ ⚘

Hotel	★★★★⚑ Mount Juliet Hotel, THOMASTOWN ☎ 056 73000 32 ⇆ ↟ Annexe27 ⇆ ↟

CARLOW   Map 01 C3

Carlow Deerpark ☎ 0503 31695 Fax 0503 40065
e-mail: carlowgolfclub@tinet.ie
Created in 1922 to a design by Tom Simpson, this testing and enjoyable course is set in a wild deer park, with beautiful dry terrain and a varied character. With sandy sub-soil, the course is playable all year round. There are water hazards at the 2nd, 10th and 11th and only two par 5s, both offering genuine birdie opportunities.
18 holes, 5974mtrs, Par 70, SSS 69, Course record 62.
Club membership 1200.

Visitors	are welcome, although play is limited on Tue and difficult on Sat & Sun. Must contact in advance.
Societies	must book in advance.
Green Fees	not confirmed.
Cards	💳 💳
Prof	Andrew Gilbert

Designer	Tom Simpson
Facilities	⊗ ⋙ ☕ ♨ ♀ ⚲ ☕ ↟ ♨ ⚘
Location	2m N of Carlow on N9

Hotel	★★★ 72% Dolmen Hotel, Kilkenny Rd, CARLOW ☎ 0503 42002 40 ⇆ ↟ Annexe12 ↟

TULLOW   Map 01 C3

Mount Wolseley Hotel, Golf & Country Club
☎ 0503 51674 Fax 0503 52123
A magnificent setting, a few hundred yards from the banks of the river Slaney with its mature trees and lakes set against the backdrop of the East Carlow and Wicklow mountains. There are no easy holes, with wide landing areas the only concession to demanding approach shots to almost every green. There is water in play on eleven holes, with the eleventh, an all water carry off the tee of 207 yards.
18 holes, 6300yds, Par 72, SSS 70, Course record 68.
Club membership 350.

Visitors	must contact in advance.
Societies	must contact in advance.
Green Fees	IEP35 per round(IEP40 weekends).
Cards	💳 💳
Prof	Jimmy Bolger
Designer	Christy O'Connor
Facilities	⊗ ⋙ ☕ ♨ ♀ ⚲ ☕ ↟ ♨ ⚘ ♨ ⚲ ⚘
& Leisure	heated indoor swimming pool, sauna, solarium, gymnasium.
Hotel	★★★ 72% Dolmen Hotel, Kilkenny Rd, CARLOW ☎ 0503 42002 40 ⇆ ↟ Annexe12 ↟

CO CAVAN

BALLYCONNELL   Map 01 C4

Slieve Russell Hotel Golf & Country Club
☎ 049 9526444 & 9526458 Fax 049 9526640
e-mail: slieve-russell@quinn-hotels.com
An 18-hole course opened in 1992 and rapidly establishing itself as one of the finest parkland courses in the country. A 9-hole course was recently opened to complement it. On the main course, the 2nd plays across water while the 16th has water surrounding the green. The course finishes with a 519 yard, Par 5 18th.
18 holes, 6650yds, Par 72, SSS 72, Course record 65.
Club membership 900.

Visitors	must book in advance for Saturdays.
Societies	write or telephone in advance, not allowed Sat.
Green Fees	IEP36 per round (IEP46 Sat).
Cards	💳 💳 💳 💳 💳
Prof	Liam McCool
Designer	Paddy Merrigan
Facilities	⊗ ⋙ ☕ ♨ ♀ ⚲ ☕ ↟ ♨ ⚘ ♨ ⚲ ⚘ ⌇
& Leisure	hard tennis courts, heated indoor swimming pool, squash, sauna, solarium, gymnasium.
Location	1.5m E of Ballyconnell

▶

Hotel	★★★★ 67% Slieve Russell Hotel Golf and Country Club, BALLYCONNELL ☎ 049 9526 444 159 ⇋ ↟

BELTURBET   Map 01 C4

Belturbet Erne Hill ☎ 049 9522287 & 9524044
Beautifully maintained parkland course with predominantly family membership and popular with summer visitors.
9 holes, 5480yds, Par 68, SSS 65, Course record 64.
Club membership 200.
Visitors   must contact in advance.
Societies   must contact secretary in advance.
Green Fees not confirmed.
Designer   Eddie Hackett
Facilities   ⓑ ▆ ♀ 🛆 🖅 🏌 ⚲ 𝄞

Hotel	★★★★ 67% Slieve Russell Hotel Golf and Country Club, BALLYCONNELL ☎ 049 9526 444 159 ⇋ ↟

BLACKLION   Map 01 C5

Blacklion Toam ☎ 072 53024
Parkland course established in 1962, with coppices of woodland and mature trees. The lake comes into play on two holes and there are some magnificent views of the lake, islands and surrounding hills. It has been described as one of the best maintained scenic inland courses in Ireland.
9 holes, 5614mtrs, Par 72, SSS 69.
Club membership 250.
Visitors   groups of 8 or more must contact in advance on Thu or Sat. No societies Sun.
Societies   must contact in advance.
Green Fees not confirmed.
Designer   Eddie Hackett
Facilities   ⓑ ▆ ♀ 🛆 𝄞
& Leisure   fishing, snooker.

Hotel	★★★ 71% Sligo Park Hotel, Pearse Rd, SLIGO ☎ 071 60291 110 ⇋ ↟

CAVAN   Map 01 C4

County Cavan Drumelis
☎ 049 4331541 & 049 4371313 Fax 049 31541
e-mail: info@cavangolf.ie
Parkland course.
18 holes, 5519mtrs, Par 70, SSS 69, Course record 64.
Club membership 830.
Visitors   welcome but restricted at weekends.
Societies   contact for details.
Green Fees IEP16 per 18 holes(IEP18 weekends).
Cards   ▦ ▦
Prof   Ciaran Carroll
Designer   Eddie Hackett
Facilities   ⊗ ⫞ ⓑ ▆ ♀ 🛆 ☎ 🖅 𝄞 ⚲
Location   On Killeshandra rd,out of Cavan town

Hotel	★★★ 65% Kilmore Hotel, Dublin Rd, CAVAN ☎ 049 4332288 39 ⇋ ↟

VIRGINIA   Map 01 C4

Virginia ☎ 049 47235 & 48066
9 holes, 4139mtrs, Par 64, SSS 62, Course record 57.
Club membership 500.
Visitors   may not play Thu & Sun.
Societies   must apply in writing to secretary.
Green Fees not confirmed.
Facilities   🛆 🖅 🏠
& Leisure   fishing.
Location   By Lough Ramor

Hotel	★★★ 61% Conyngham Arms Hotel, SLANE ☎ 041 24155 16rm(15 ⇋ ↟)

CO CLARE

BODYKE   Map 01 B3

East Clare ☎ 061 921322 Fax 061 921717
e-mail: eastclaregolfclub@eircon.net
Beside Lough Derg, East Clare was opened in June 1992 as a 9-hole course in 148 acre site with natural trees and water on well-drained land. An 18-hole championship course designed by Arthur Spring is in preparation.
18 holes, 5922yds, Par 70, SSS 70.
Club membership 500.
Visitors   no restrictions unless there is a club competition or a society playing.
Societies   apply in writing, deposit required.
Green Fees IEP15.
Cards   ▦ ▆ ▦ ▮
Designer   Dr Arthur Spring
Facilities   ⓑ ▆ 🛆 🖅 ⚲ 🏌 𝄞

Hotel	★★★ 67% West County Conference, Leisure Hotel, Clare Rd, ENNIS ☎ 065 6823000 152 ⇋ ↟

CLONLARA   Map 01 B3

Clonlara Golf & Leisure ☎ 061 354141 Fax 061 354143
A 12-hole parkland course, Par 47, on the banks of the River Shannon with views of Clare Hills. Set in grounds of 63 acres surrounding the 17th century Landscape House, there is also a leisure complex for self-catering holidays.
12 holes, 5187mtrs, Par 71, SSS 69.
Club membership 100.
Visitors   players only no accompanying persons.
Societies   welcome subject to availability prior notice required.
Green Fees not confirmed.
Designer   Noel Cassidy
Facilities   ⓑ ▆ ♀ 🛆 🖅 🏠 𝄞
& Leisure   hard tennis courts, fishing, sauna, games room, childrens play area.
Location   7m NE of Limerick

Hotel	★★★★ 71% Castletroy Park Hotel, Dublin Rd, LIMERICK ☎ 061 335566 107 ⇋ ↟

ENNIS   Map 01 B3

Ennis Drumbiggle ☎ 065 6824074 Fax 065 6841848
e-mail: egc@eircom.net
On rolling hills, this immaculately manicured course presents
an excellent challenge to both casual visitors and aspiring
scratch golfers, with tree-lined fairways and well protected
greens.
18 holes, 5338mtrs, Par 70, SSS 69, Course record 65.
Club membership 1000.
Visitors   advisable to contact in advance, course available
              Mon-Sat at most times.
Societies   apply in writing/telephone
Green Fees   not confirmed.
Prof   Martin Ward
Facilities   ⊗ 〗⫙ �🄫 ♥ ⚑ ☖ ⚐ ⚒ ⚸
Location   Close to town, well signposted

Hotel   ★★★ 68% Temple Gate Hotel, The Square,
              ENNIS ☎ 065 6823300 73 ⇆ 🄫

Woodstock Golf and Country Club Shanaway Rd
☎ 065 6829463 & 6842406 Fax 065 6820304
This parkland course stands on 155 acres of land and
includes 4 hole where water is a major hazard. The course ia
playable all year and the sand based greens offer a consistent
surface for putting
*Woodstock Golf & Country Club: 18 holes, 5864mtrs, Par
71, SSS 71.*
Club membership 250.
Visitors   booking advisable at weekends.
Societies   advisable to telephone in advance.
Green Fees   not confirmed.
Cards   ▱▱ ▰
Designer   Arthur Spring
Facilities   ⊗ 〗⫙ 🄫 ♥ ⚑ ☖ ⚐ ⚒ ⚸
& Leisure   heated indoor swimming pool, sauna,
              gymnasium.
Location   Off N85

Hotel   ★★★ 67% West County Conference,
              Leisure Hotel, Clare Rd, ENNIS
              ☎ 065 6823000 152 ⇆ 🄫

KILKEE   Map 01 B3

Kilkee East End
☎ 065 9056048 & 9056977 Fax 065 9656977
e-mail: kilkeegolfclub@eircom.net
Well established course on the cliffs of Kilkee Bay, with
beautiful views. Spectacular cliff-top holes.
18 holes, 6500yds, Par 72, SSS 71, Course record 68.
Club membership 390.
Visitors   must book in advance.
Societies   apply in writing/telephone/fax/e-mail
Green Fees   IEP20 per round.
Cards   ▱▱ ▰ ▱ ▱
Designer   Eddie Hackett
Facilities   ⊗ 〗⫙ 🄫 ♥ ⚑ ☖ ⚐ ⚒ ⚸
& Leisure   squash, sauna.
Location   On Cilff-Edge,East End,Kilkee

Hotel   ★★ 64% Halpin's Hotel, Erin St, KILKEE
              ☎ 065 56032 12 ⇆ 🄫

Ocean Cove Golf & Leisure Hotel Kilkee Bay
☎ 065 9083111 Fax 065 9083123
A typical coastal course surrounded on two sides by the
Atlantic Ocean and the sea can be seen from nearly every
hole. A number of greens are situated in a spectacular
position along the edge of the Clare Cliffs.
18 holes, 5265metres, Par 69, SSS 69.
Club membership 500.
Visitors   must contact in advance, may not play
              competition days,
Societies   apply in writing
Green Fees   not confirmed.
Facilities   ⚑ ☖ ⚐ ⚸
& Leisure   squash, gymnasium.

Hotel   ★★★ 61% Ocean Cove Golf &
              Leisure Hotel, KILKEE
              ☎ 065 6823000 50 ⇆ 🄫

KILRUSH   Map 01 B3

Kilrush Parknamoney ☎ 065 51138 Fax 065 52633
e-mail: kelgolf@iol.ie
Parkland course that was extended to 18 holes in the summer
of 1994.
18 holes, 5986yds, Par 70, SSS 70, Course record 68.
Club membership 425.
Visitors   welcome, contact in advance.
Societies   by prior arrangement.
Green Fees   not confirmed.
Designer   Arthur Spring
Facilities   ⊗ 〗⫙ 🄫 ♥ ⚑ ☖ ⚐ ⚒ ⚸

Hotel   ★★ 64% Halpin's Hotel, Erin St, KILKEE
              ☎ 065 56032 12 ⇆ 🄫

LAHINCH   Map 01 B3

Lahinch ☎ 065 81003 Fax 065 81592
e-mail: lgc@iol.ie
Originally designed by Tom Morris and later modified
by Dr Alister MacKenzie, Lahinch has hosted every
important Irish amateur fixture and the Home
Internationals. The par five 5th - The Klondike - is
played along a deep valley and over a huge dune; the par
three 6th may be short, but calls for a blind shot over the
ridge of a hill to a green hemmed in by hills on three
sides.
Old Course: 18 holes, 6696yds, Par 72, SSS 73.
Castle Course: 18 holes, 5594yds, Par 70, SSS 70.
Club membership 1840.
Visitors   must contact in advance.
Societies   apply in writing
Green Fees   not confirmed.
Cards   ▱▱ ▰ ▱▰
Prof   R McCavery
Designer   Alister MacKenzie
Facilities   ⊗ 〗⫙ 🄫 ♥ ⚑ ☖ ⚐ ⚸
Location   2m W of Ennisstymon on N67

Hotel   ★★ 70% Sheedy's Restaurant & Hotel,
              LISDOONVARNA
              ☎ 065 7074026 11 ⇆ 🄫

MILLTOWN MALBAY   Map 01 B3

Spanish Point ☎ 065 7084198 & 7084219 e-mail: dkfitzgerald@tinet.ie
A 9-hole links course with 3 elevated greens and 4 elevated tees. Overlooking Spanish Point beach.
9 holes, 4600mtrs, Par 64, SSS 63, Course record 59.
Club membership 410.
Visitors   contact in advance. Not before 1pm Sun.
Societies   apply in writing to the secretary.
Green Fees   IEP15 per day (IEP17 weekends & bank holidays).
Facilities   ⬛🍴♀⚲🏌♂
Location   2m SW of Miltown Malbay, on N67

Hotel   ★★★ 67% West County Conference, Leisure Hotel, Clare Rd, ENNIS
             ☎ 065 6823000 152 ⇌ ☏

NEWMARKET-ON-FERGUS   Map 01 B3

Dromoland Castle Golf & Country Club
☎ 061 368444 & 368144 Fax 061 363355/368498
e-mail: dromolandgc@tinet.ie
Set in 200 acres of parkland, the course is enhanced by numerous trees and a lake. Three holes are played around the lake which is in front of the castle.
18 holes, 6098yds, Par 71, SSS 72, Course record 67.
Club membership 500.
Visitors   must contact in advance.
Societies   contact in writing.
Green Fees   not confirmed.
Cards   ▦ ▦ ▦ 🔳
Prof   Philip Murphy
Designer   Wigginton
Facilities   ⊗ �🍴 ⬛ 🍴♀⚲🏌♂🏠🏌↗ 🚣🚣♂
& Leisure   hard tennis courts, fishing, sauna, solarium, gymnasium.
Location   2m N, on main Limerick/Galway rd

Hotel   ★★★ 63% Clare Inn Golf and Leisure Hotel, NEWMARKET-ON-FERGUS
             ☎ 065 6823000 182 ⇌ ☏

SHANNON AIRPORT   Map 01 B3

Shannon ☎ 061 471849 Fax 061 471507
e-mail: shannongolfclub@eircom.net
Superb parkland course with tree-lined fairways, strategically placed bunkers, water hazards and excellent greens, offering a challenge to all levels of players - including the many famous golfers who have played here.
18 holes, 6874yds, Par 72, SSS 74, Course record 65.
Club membership 1000.
Visitors   must contact in advance & have handicap certificate. Restricted play at certain times.
Societies   must contact in writing.
Green Fees   not confirmed.
Cards   ▦ ▦
Prof   Artie Pyke
Designer   John Harris
Facilities   ⊗ �🍴 ⬛ 🍴♀⚲🏠🏌↗ 🚣🚣♂
Location   2m from Shannon Airport

Hotel   ★★★ 69% Fitzpatrick Bunratty Hotel, BUNRATTY ☎ 061 361177 115 ⇌ ☏

CO CORK

BANDON   Map 01 B2

Bandon Castlebernard ☎ 023 41111 Fax 023 44690
e-mail: bandongolfclub@eircom.net
Lovely parkland course in pleasant rural surroundings.
18 holes, 5663mtrs, Par 70, SSS 69, Course record 66.
Club membership 900.
Visitors   welcome but may not play during club competitions. Must contact in advance.
Societies   must apply in writing or telephone well in advance.
Green Fees   IEP20 per day (IEP25 weekends & bank holidays).
Prof   Paddy O'Boyle
Facilities   ⊗ �🍴 ⬛ 🍴♀⚲🏠🏌♂
& Leisure   hard tennis courts.
Location   2.5km W

Hotel   ★★★ 65% Inishannon House Hotel, INISHANNON ☎ 021 775121
             12 ⇌ ☏ Annexe1 ⇌ ☏

BANTRY   Map 01 B2

Bantry Bay Bantry Bay
☎ 027 50579 & 50583 Fax 027 50579
e-mail: secretary@bantrygolf.com
Designed by Christy O'Connor Jnr and extended in 1997 to 18 holes, this challenging and rewarding course is idyllically set at the head of Bantry Bay. Testing holes include the par 5 of 487mtrs and the little par 3 of 127mtrs where accuracy is all-important.
18 holes, 5910mtrs, Par 71, SSS 72, Course record 71.
Club membership 600.
Visitors   advance booking recommended. At weekends and bank holidays visitors between 11.30-1.30pm and 3-4.30pm. Catering Mar-Oct only.
Societies   must apply in writing.
Green Fees   not confirmed.
Designer   Christy O'Connor/Eddie Hackett
Facilities   ⊗ �🍴 ⬛ 🍴♀⚲🏌↗🚣🚣♂
Location   3km N of Bantry town on the N71 Glengarrif road

Hotel   ★★★ 61% Westlodge Hotel, BANTRY
             ☎ 027 50360 90 ⇌ ☏

BLARNEY   Map 01 B2

Muskerry Carrigrohane
☎ 021 4385297 Fax 021 4385297
An adventurous game is guaranteed at this course, with its wooded hillsides and the meandering Shournagh River coming into play at a number of holes. The 15th is a notable hole - not long, but very deep - and after that all you need to do to get back to the clubhouse is stay out of the water.
18 holes, 6327yds, Par 71, SSS 71.
Club membership 763.
                                                    ▶

Visitors	may not play Wed afternoon & Thu morning. Some limited opportunities at weekends after 3.30pm & members hour 12.30-1.30pm daily. Must contact in advance.
Societies	must telephone in advance and then confirm in writing.
Green Fees	IEP25 per round(IEP28 weekends & bank holidays).
Prof	W M Lehane
Designer	Dr A McKenzie
Facilities	⊗ ∭ ⓑ ♥ ♀ ⚐ ⚑ ⚑ ⚐ ♂
Location	2.5m W of Blarney

| Hotel | ★★★ 68% Christy's Hotel, BLARNEY ☎ 021 385011 49 ⇌ ⚑ |

CARRIGALINE   Map 01 B2

Fernhill Hotel & Golf Club
☎ 021 4372226 Fax 021 4371011 e-mail: fernhill@iol.ie
Parkland course.
18 holes, 5000mtrs, Par 69, SSS 68.
Club membership 150.

Visitors	available any time.
Societies	telephone in advance.
Green Fees	IEP14(IEP16 weekends).
Cards	⊟ ▆ ▦ ⒫
Prof	Wayne O'Callaghan
Designer	M L Bowes
Facilities	⊗ ∭ ⓑ ♥ ♀ ⚐ ⚑ ⚐ ♂
& Leisure	hard tennis courts, heated indoor swimming pool, fishing, sauna, 3 hole academy.
Location	2m from Ringaskiddy

CASTLETOWNBERE   Map 01 A2

Berehaven Millcove ☎ 027 70700 Fax 027 70700
Seaside links founded in 1902. Moderately difficult with four
holes over water.
9 holes, 2398mtrs, Par 68, SSS 66, Course record 63.
Club membership 150.

Visitors	welcome. Please check for major events.
Societies	telephone in advance.
Green Fees	IEP15 per day.
Cards	▦
Facilities	⊗ ∭ ⓑ ♥ ♀ ⚐ ⚑ ⚐ ♂
& Leisure	hard tennis courts, sauna.
Location	2m E on Glen Garriff Rd

| Hotel | ★★★▲▲ 75% Sea View Hotel, BALLYLICKEY ☎ 027 50073 & 50462 Fax 027 51555 17 ⇌ ⚑ |

CHARLEVILLE   Map 01 B2

Charleville ☎ 063 81257 & 81515 Fax 063 81274
e-mail: charlevillegolf@eircom.net
Wooded parkland course offering not too strenuous walking.
*West Course: 18 holes, 6212yds, Par 71, SSS 69, Course
record 65.*
East Course: 9 holes, 6702yds, Par 72, SSS 72.
Club membership 1000.

| Visitors | only prebooked at weekends. |
| Societies | contact in advance. |

Charleville Golf Club

Green Fees	not confirmed.
Cards	⊟ ▆ ▦
Prof	David Keating
Designer	Eddie Connaughton
Facilities	⊗ ∭ ⓑ ♥ ♀ ⚐ ⚑ ⚐ ♂ ⚑ ⚐ ♂ ⚑
Location	2m W from town centre

| Hotel | ★★★▲▲ Longueville House Hotel, MALLOW ☎ 022 47156 & 47306 Fax 022 47459 22 ⇌ ⚑ |

CLONAKILTY   Map 01 B2

Dunmore Dunmore, Muckross ☎ 023 33352
9 holes, 4464yds, Par 64, SSS 61, Course record 57.

| Location | 3.5m S of Clonakilty |
| **Telephone for further details** | |

| Hotel | ★ 60% Courtmacsherry, COURTMACSHERRY ☎ 023 46198 12rm(9 ⇌1 ⚑) |

CORK   Map 01 B2

Cork Little Island ☎ 021 4353451 Fax 021 4353410
This championship-standard course is always kept in
superb condition and is playable all year round. It has
many memorable and distinctive features including holes
at the water's edge and holes in a disused quarry.
18 holes, 5910mtrs, Par 72, SSS 72, Course record 67.
Club membership 750.

Visitors	may not play 12.30-2pm or on Thu (Ladies Day), and only after 2pm Sat & Sun.
Societies	must contact in advance.
Green Fees	IEP50 per day(IEP55 per round weekends).
Cards	⊟ ▆ ▦ ⒫
Prof	Peter Hickey
Designer	Alister Mackenzie
Facilities	⊗ ∭ ⓑ ♥ ♀ ⚐ ⚑ ⚐ ♂
Location	5m E, on N25 of Cork City

| Hotel | ★★★★ 69% Jurys Hotel, Western Rd, CORK ☎ 021 276622 185 ⇌ ⚑ |

Fitzpatrick Silver Springs Tivoli ☎ 021 507533 & 505128
Five Par 4s and 4 Par 3s make up this short 9-hole course.
The 4th has a 189 metre drive with out of bounds on the
righthand side. The 8th is the longest holes, with a 301 metre
drive.
9 holes, 1786mtrs, Par 32, Course record 26.
Club membership 84.

▶

Visitors no restrictions.
Societies apply by telephone.
Green Fees not confirmed.
Cards 🖃 ▪️🖃
Prof Freddy Twomey
Designer Eddie Hackett
Facilities ⊗ 〣 🏠 ▪️ ♀ ⚒ ⛳ ⊷ ⚒
& Leisure hard tennis courts, heated indoor swimming pool, squash, sauna, solarium, gymnasium.
Location 1m E of city centre off Tivoli bypass

Hotel ★★★★ 65% Silver Springs Moran Hotel, Tivoli, CORK ☎ 021 507533 109 ⇄ 🐾

Fota Island Carrigtwohill
☎ 021 4883700 Fax 021 4883713
e-mail: reservations@fotaisland.ie
Fota Island Golf Club is in the heart of the 780 acre island in Cork Harbour which is recognised as one of Ireland's most outstanding landscapes. The course is gently undulating parkland routed among mature woodlands with occasional views of the harbour. The overall design is very traditional, featuring pot bunkers and undulating putting surfaces. The 10th and 18th holes are narrow Par 5's that require great accuracy and shotmaking skills. Fota has hosted the Irish Club Professional Championship, the Irish PGA Championship and no fewer than three Irish Amateur Opens.
18 holes, 6500yds, Par 71, SSS 71, Course record 67.
Club membership 400.
Visitors advisable to contact in advance. Metal spikes and blue jeans not permitted.
Societies contact in advance.
Green Fees IEP45 per round(Mon), IEP55 Tues-Thur), IEP65(Fri-Sun) reductions in winter.
Cards 🖃 ▪️🖃
Prof Kevin Morris
Designer Jeff Hoves
Facilities ⊗ 〣 🏠 ▪️ ♀ ⚒ 🏠 ⛳ ➘ ⚒ ⚒ ⛏
Location Off N25 E of Cork City. Take exit for Cobh, course 500m on right

Hotel ★★★ 66% Midleton Park, MIDLETON ☎ 021 631767 40 ⇄ 🐾

The Ted McCarthy Municipal Golf Course Blackrock
☎ 021 294280
Municipal course which stretches alongside the river estuary, with some holes across water.
18 holes, 4818mtrs, Par 67, SSS 66, Course record 63.
Club membership 380.
Visitors please contact in advance, may not play mornings at weekends.
Societies please telephone in advance.
Green Fees IEP13 per day(IEP14 weekends & bank holidays).

Designer E Hackett
Facilities ⊗ 〣 🏠 ▪️ ♀ ⚒ 🏠 ⛳ ⚒
Location 2m from city centre

Hotel ★★★★ 65% Silver Springs Moran Hotel, Tivoli, CORK ☎ 021 507533 109 ⇄ 🐾

DONERAILE   Map 01 B2

Doneraile ☎ 022 24137 & 23427 (sec)
Parkland.
9 holes, 5528yds, Par 68, SSS 67.
Club membership 650.
Visitors May play weekdays only.
Societies welcome.
Green Fees IEP15 per round.
Facilities ⊗ by prior arrangement 〣 by prior arrangement 🏠 ▪️ ♀ ⚒ ⚒
Location Off T11

Hotel ★★★ 63% Springfort Hall Hotel, MALLOW ☎ 022 21278 50 ⇄ 🐾

DOUGLAS   Map 01 B2

Douglas ☎ 021 895297 Fax 895297
e-mail: admin@douglasgolfclub.ie
Level inland course overlooking the city of Cork. Suitable for golfers of all ages and abilities. The course is under re-development and the measurements/details given below may have changed.
18 holes, 5607mtrs, Par 72, SSS 69.
Club membership 850.
Visitors Contact in advance. May not play Sat or Sun am or Tues(ladies day).Reserved for members 12.30-2 pm.
Societies must contact in writing, by end of Jan.
Green Fees not confirmed.
Prof Gary Nicholson
Facilities ⊗ 〣 🏠 ▪️ ♀ ⚒ 🏠 ⛳ ⚒ ⛏
Location 6km east of Cork City.

Hotel ★★★★ 69% Jurys Hotel, Western Rd, CORK ☎ 021 276622 185 ⇄ 🐾

FERMOY   Map 01 B2

Fermoy Corrin Cross
☎ 025 32694 (office) & 31472 (shop) Fax 025 33072
Rather exposed heathland course, bisected by a road.
18 holes, 5596mtrs, Par 70, SSS 69.
Club membership 950.
Visitors contact in advance, must telephone in advance for weekends bookings ▶

Societies advisable to write or telephone in advance.
Green Fees not confirmed.
Prof Brian Moriarty
Designer John Harris
Facilities ⊗ ⅷ 🄑 ♨ ♀ 🄐 🏠 ⛳ 🚜 ⚙
Location 2m SW

Hotel ★★★🏊 Longueville House Hotel, MALLOW
☎ 022 47156 & 47306 Fax 022 47459 22 ⇄ ♖

GLENGARRIFF　　　　　　　　Map 01 B2

Glengarriff ☎ 027 63150 Fax 027 63575
Founded 1935.
9 holes, 2042mtrs, Par 66, SSS 62.
Club membership 300.
Visitors welcome, details not supplied
Societies apply to club.
Green Fees not confirmed.
Facilities 🄑 ♨ ♀ 🄐 ⛳ ⚙
Location On N71

Hotel ★★★ 61% Westlodge Hotel, BANTRY
☎ 027 50360 90 ⇄ ♖

KANTURK　　　　　　　　　　Map 01 B2

Kanturk Fairyhill ☎ 029 50534
Scenic parkland course set in the heart of the Duhallow
region with superb mountain views. It provides a good test of
skill for golfers of all standards, with tight fairways requiring
accurate driving and precise approach shots to small and
tricky greens.
18 holes, 5721mtrs, Par 72, SSS 70, Course record 73.
Club membership 550.
Visitors Ladies ring Wed. Please ring in advance.
Societies apply in writing or telephone the Secretary.
Green Fees IEP12 per day (IEP15 weekends & bank
holidays).
Designer Richard Barry
Facilities 🄐 ⚙
Location 1m from Kanturk on Fairyhill road, 2m off main
Mallow/Killarney road from Ballymacquirke
Cross

Guesthouse ♦♦♦♦♦ Assolas Country House, KANTURK
☎ 029 50015 6 ⇄ ♖ Annexe3 ⇄ ♖

KINSALE　　　　　　　　　　Map 01 B2

Kinsale Farrangalway ☎ 021 774722 Fax 021 773114
e-mail: kinsaleg@indigo.ie
In addition to the existing 9-hole (Ringenane) course, a new
18-hole (Farrangalway) course was opened in 1994. Set in
unspoilt farmland and surrounded by peaceful rolling
countryside, it offers a stiff yet fair challenge to be enjoyed
by all standards of golfers. New putting green.
Farrangalway: 18 holes, 6609yds, Par 71, SSS 71, Course
record 70.
Ringenane: 9 holes, 5332yds, Par 70, SSS 68.
Club membership 780.
Visitors welcome but may not be able to play at
weekends. Contact in advance.
Societies apply in writing.
Green Fees not confirmed.
Cards 🌐🌐
Prof Ger Broderick

Designer Jack Kenneally
Facilities ⊗ ⅷ 🄑 ♨ ♀ 🄐 🏠 ⛳ 🚜 ⚙
Location On main Cork/Kinsale rd

Hotel ★★★ 68% Trident Hotel, Worlds End,
KINSALE ☎ 021 4772301 58 ⇄ ♖

Old Head ☎ 021 4778444 Fax 021 4778022 e-
mail: info@oldheadgolf.ie
Opened for play in 1997 and designed by Ron Kirby and Joe
Carr, the Old Head course is spectacularly situated on a
promontory jutting out into the Atlantic. As well as bringing
the sea and cliffs into play, you have to contend with strong
prevailing winds - a fine test for all serious golfers.
18 holes, 7200yds, Par 72, SSS 73.
Club membership 250.

Visitors tee time must be booked in advance.
Societies pre booking necessary, rates for groups over 24.
Green Fees not confirmed.
Cards 🌐 🌐 🌐 🌐
Prof David Murray
Designer R Kirby/J Carr/P Merrigan/E Hackett
Facilities ⊗ ⅷ 🄑 ♨ ♀ 🄐 🏠 ⛳ 🚜 ⚙ ♟
Location From Cork city/airport, follow R600 to Kinsale,
then signed to golf course

Hotel ★★★ 73% Actons Hotel, Pier Rd, KINSALE
☎ 021 4772135 76 ⇄ ♖

LITTLE ISLAND　　　　　　　Map 01 B2

Harbour Point Clash Rd
☎ 021 4353094 Fax 021 4354408 e-mail: hpoint@iol.ie
A new championship-standard course in rolling countryside
on the banks of the River Lee at Cork's scenic harbour. A
distinctive and testing course for every standard of golfer.
18 holes, 5883metres, Par 72, SSS 71, Course record 71.
Visitors must contact in advance.
Societies telephone for bookings.
Green Fees IEP24 per 18 holes(IEP27 weekends).
Cards 🌐🌐
Prof Morgan O'Donovan
Designer Patrick Merrigan
Facilities ⊗ ⅷ 🄑 ♨ ♀ 🄐 🏠 ⛳ ⚓ 🚜 ⚙ ♟
Location 5m E of Cork, take Rosslare road E from Cork
city & exit at Little Island

Hotel ★★★★ 65% Silver Springs Moran Hotel,
Tivoli, CORK ☎ 021 507533 109 ⇄ ♖

MACROOM
Map 01 B2

Macroom Lackaduve ☎ 026 41072 Fax 026 41391
e-mail: mcroomgc@iol.ie
A particularly scenic parkland course located on undulating ground along the banks of the River Sullane. Bunkers and mature trees make a variable and testing course and the 12th has a 50 yards carry over the river to the green.
18 holes, 5574mtrs, Par 72, SSS 70, Course record 68.
Club membership 650.
Visitors   Booking essential for weekends.
Societies   Telephone in advance.
Green Fees IEP20 per round(IEP25 weekends).
Cards   💳 💳
Designer   Jack Kenneally
Facilities   ⊗ ⊪ ⓑ ♥ ♀ 占 ⚑ ♨ ⚐
Location   Through castle entrance in town square

Hotel   ★★ 72% Castle Hotel, Main St, MACROOM
☎ 026 41074 42 ⇄ ⋔

MALLOW
Map 01 B2

Mallow Ballyellis ☎ 022 21145 Fax 022 42501
e-mail: golfmall@gofree.indigo.ie
Mallow Golf Club was first established in the late 1800's. A well wooded parkland course overlooking the Blackwater Valley, Mallow is straightforward, but no less of a challenge for it. The front nine is by far the longer, but the back nine is demanding in its call for accuracy and the par 3 18th provides a tough finish.
18 holes, 5769metres, Par 72, SSS 71, Course record 67.
Club membership 1400.

Visitors   must contact in advance.
Societies   apply in advance.
Green Fees IEP20 per round (IEP25 weekends & bank holidays).
Cards   💳 💳
Prof   Sean Conway
Designer   D W Wishart
Facilities   ⊗ ⊪ ⓑ ♥ ♀ 占 ⚑ ♨ ⚐
& Leisure   hard tennis courts, squash, sauna.
Location   1m E of Mallow town

Hotel   ★★★⚜ Longueville House Hotel,
MALLOW ☎ 022 47156 & 47306
Fax 022 47459 22 ⇄ ⋔

MIDLETON
Map 01 C2

East Cork Gortacrue
☎ 021 4631687 & 4631273 Fax 021 4613695
A well wooded course calling for accuracy of shots.
18 holes, 5491yds, Par 69, SSS 67, Course record 64.
Club membership 640.
Visitors   may not play Sun mornings.
Societies   must telephone.
Green Fees IEP15.
Prof   Don MacFarlane
Designer   E Hackett
Facilities   ⊗ ⊪ ⓑ ♥ ♀ 占 ⚑ ♨ ⚐ ⚐
Location   On the A626

Hotel   ★★★ 66% Midleton Park, MIDLETON
☎ 021 631767 40 ⇄ ⋔

MITCHELSTOWN
Map 01 B2

Mitchelstown Limerick Rd ☎ 025 24072 & 087 2650110
Attractive, gently undulating parkland course set in the Golden Vale, noted for the quality of the greens, the magnificent views of the Galtee Mountains and its friendly atmosphere. Ideal for golfers seeking tranquility and a golfing challenge.
18 holes, 5160mtrs, Par 67, SSS 68, Course record 65.
Club membership 400.
Visitors   advisable to check in advance (information line 025 24231)
Societies   apply in writing or telephone.
Green Fees IEP15(IEP20 weekends).
Designer   David Jones
Facilities   ⊗ ⓑ ♥ ♀ 占 ⚐
Location   0.75m on Limerick rd from Mitchelstown

Hotel   ★★★⚜ Longueville House Hotel, MALLOW
☎ 022 47156 & 47306 Fax 022 47459 22 ⇄ ⋔

MONKSTOWN
Map 01 B2

Monkstown Parkgariffe, Monkstown
☎ 021 4841376 Fax 021 4841376
Undulating parkland course with five tough finishing holes.
18 holes, 5441mtrs, Par 70, SSS 68, Course record 66.
Club membership 960.
Visitors   restricted weekends, must contact in advance.
Societies   apply in writing or telephone. Large groups (24+) should book before Xmas.
Green Fees IEP30 per day.
Prof   Batt Murphy
Facilities   ⊗ ⊪ ⓑ ♥ ♀ 占 ⚑ ♨ ⚐ ⚐
Location   0.5m SE of Monkstown village

Hotel   ★★★★ 69% Jurys Hotel, Western Rd,
CORK ☎ 021 276622 185 ⇄ ⋔

Looking for a driving range?
See the index at the back of the guide

Entries with a green background
identify courses considered to be
particularly interesting

OVENS   Map 01 B2

Lee Valley Golf & Country Club Clashanure
☎ 021 7331721 Fax 021 7331695
e-mail: leevalleygolfclub@eircom.net
An undulating test of all golfing abilities designed by Ryder Cup star Christy O'Connor Junior. Seven of the 18 holes have water and the unusual feature of two fairy forts which are over 300 years old - can they be blamed for errors on the testing Par 5 8th and 12th holes?! The 508yard, Par 5 8th is already regarded as one of the best holes in Ireland with its spectacular lake a feature from tee to green.
18 holes, 6434yds, Par 72, SSS 70, Course record 62.
Club membership 400.

Visitors	telephone in advance. Avoid Sat/Sun before 11.15am.
Societies	telephone in advance.
Green Fees	not confirmed.
Prof	John Savage
Designer	Christy O'Connor
Facilities	⊗ Ⅲ ⅃ ❤ ⅄ ⚲ 🏠 ⚑ ⚐ 🏌 ⚘ ⚷
Location	8m from Cork on Cork/Killarney road N22

Hotel	★★ 72% Castle Hotel, Main St, MACROOM ☎ 026 41074 42 ⇄ 🅡

SKIBBEREEN   Map 01 B2

Skibbereen & West Carbery Licknavar
☎ 028 21227 Fax 028 22994
Slightly hilly course in scenic location.
18 holes, 6004yds, Par 71, SSS 69, Course record 66.
Club membership 700.

Visitors	advisable to contact club secretary for dates in writing.
Societies	apply in writing or telephone.
Green Fees	IEP18(IEP20weekends).
Cards	🌐 ⬛ 🔳 🔲 🌐 🌐 🔳 🌀
Designer	Jack Kenneally
Facilities	⊗ Ⅲ ⅃ ❤ ⅄ ⚲ 🏠 ⚑ 🏌 ⚘ ⚷
Location	1m W on Baltimore road

Hotel	★★★ 64% Baltimore Harbour Hotel & Leisure Cntr, BALTIMORE ☎ 028 20361 64 ⇄ 🅡

YOUGHAL   Map 01 C2

Youghal Knockaverry
☎ 024 92787 & 92861 Fax 024 92641
e-mail: youghalgolfclub@tinet.ie
For many years the host of various Golfing Union championships, Youghal offers a good test of golf and is well maintained for year-round play. There are panoramic views of Youghal Bay and the Blackwater estuary.
18 holes, 5646mtrs, Par 70, SSS 69, Course record 67.
Club membership 827.

Visitors	may not play Wed (Ladies Day) and should contact in advance for weekends.
Societies	must apply in writing a few months in advance.
Green Fees	not confirmed.
Cards	🌐 🔳
Prof	Liam Burns
Designer	Cd. Harris
Facilities	⊗ Ⅲ ⅃ ❤ ⅄ ⚲ 🏠 ⚑ 🏌 ⚘ ⚷

Location	Located on the N25 main road from Rosslare, between Waterford and Cork City
Hotel	★★ 66% Devonshire Arms Hotel and Restaurant, Pearse Square, YOUGHAL ☎ 024 92827 & 92018 Fax 024 92900 10 ⇄ 🅡

CO DONEGAL

BALLINTRA   Map 01 B5

Donegal Murvagh, Laghy
☎ 073 34054 Fax 073 34377
e-mail: info@donegalgolfclub.ie
This massive links course was opened in 1973 and provides a world-class facility in peaceful surroundings. It is a very long course with some memorable holes, including five par 5s, calling for some big hitting. Donegal is the home club of former Curtis Cup captain, Maire O'Donnell.
18 holes, 6243mtrs, Par 73, SSS 73, Course record 68.
Club membership 750.

Visitors	must contact in advance, limited availability at weekends.
Societies	must contact in advance.
Green Fees	IEP30 per day(IEP40 Fri-Sun & bank holidays).
Cards	🌐 🔳
Prof	Leslie Robinson
Designer	Eddie Hackett
Facilities	⊗ Ⅲ ⅃ ❤ ⅄ ⚲ 🏠 ⚑ ⚘ ⚷
Location	6m S of Donegal on Ballyshannon road

Hotel	★★★ 77% Sand House Hotel, ROSSNOWLAGH ☎ 072 51777 46 ⇄ 🅡

BALLYBOFEY   Map 01 C5

Ballybofey & Stranorlar Stranorlar ☎ 074 31093
A most scenic course incorporating pleasant valleys backed by mountains with three of its holes bordered by a lake. There are three Par 3s on the first nine and two on the second. The most difficult hole is the long uphill Par 4 16th. The only Par 5 is the 7th.
18 holes, 5366mtrs, Par 68, SSS 68, Course record 64.
Club membership 450.

Visitors	may play on weekdays. Advisable to book in advance
Green Fees	not confirmed.
Facilities	⅄ ⚲
& Leisure	squash.
Location	0.25m from Stranorlar

Hotel	★★★ 70% Kee's Hotel, Stranorlar, BALLYBOFEY ☎ 074 31018 53 ⇄ 🅡

> AA Hotels that have special arrangements with golf courses are listed at the back of the guide

BALLYLIFFEN   Map 01 C6

Ballyliffin Clonmany ☎ 077 76119 Fax 077 76672
e-mail: ballyliffingolfclub@eircom.net
The Old course is a links course with rolling fairways, surrounded by rolling hills and bounded on one side by the ocean. Nick Faldo said 'This is the most natural golf links I have ever played.' It has an old-fashioned charm with its uniquely contoured fairways. The new 18-hole course, the Glashedy (opened summer 1995), offers a modern (and arguably 'fairer') championship test.
Old Links: 18 holes, 6604yds, Par 72, SSS 72, Course record 66.
Glashedy Links: 18 holes, 7135yds, Par 72, SSS 74, Course record 68.
Club membership 1200.

Visitors	telephone in advance.
Societies	telephone in advance.
Green Fees	Old Links: IEP24 (IEP27 weekends); Glashedy: IEP35 (IEP40 weekends).
Cards	💳 💳
Designer	Tom Craddock/Pat Ruddy
Facilities	⊗ 🍴 🛏 🕭 ♀ 🎣 🏠 ⛳ 🏌 🛺 ∅
Location	30mins from Derry city

Guesthouse ◆◆◆◆ Mount Royd Country Home, CARRIGANS ☎ 074 40163 4 ↟

BUNCRANA   Map 01 C6

Buncrana Municipal Railway Rd, Ballmacarry
☎ 077 62279
A 9-hole course with a very challenging Par-3 3rd with all carry out of bounds on either side.
9 holes, 2125yds, Par 62, SSS 60, Course record 59.
Club membership 100.

Visitors	during open competitions only visitors with club handicaps.Telephone in advance to make arrangements for weekends.
Societies	write in advance/telephone.
Green Fees	IEP6-IEP10 per 18 holes..
Facilities	🛏 🕭

Guesthouse ◆◆◆◆ Mount Royd Country Home, CARRIGANS ☎ 074 40163 4 ↟

North West Lisfannon, Fahan
☎ 077 61027 & 61715 Fax 077 63284
e-mail: nwgc13@hotmail.com
A traditional-style links course on gently rolling sandy terrain with some long par 4s. Good judgement is required on the approaches and the course offers a satisfying test coupled with undemanding walking.
18 holes, 5968yds, Par 70, SSS 70, Course record 64.
Club membership 580.

Visitors	contact in advance for weekends. Wed - Ladies Day
Societies	telephone in advance.
Green Fees	IEP15 (IEP20 weekends).
Prof	Seamus McBriarty
Designer	Thompson Dudley
Facilities	⊗ 🍴 🛏 🕭 ♀ 🎣 🏠 🏌 ∅
Location	1m S of Buncanna

Guesthouse ◆◆◆◆ Mount Royd Country Home, CARRIGANS ☎ 074 40163 4 ↟

BUNDORAN   Map 01 B5

Bundoran ☎ 072 41302 Fax 072 42014
This popular course, acknowledged as one of the best in the country, runs along the high cliffs above Bundoran beach and has a difficult par of 70. Designed by Harry Vardon, it offers a challenging game of golf in beautiful surroundings and has been the venue for a number of Irish golf championships.
18 holes, 5688mtrs, Par 70, SSS 70, Course record 66.
Club membership 700.

Visitors	must contact in advance for prior booking.
Societies	must contact in advance.
Green Fees	IEP20 per round (IEP25 weekends & bank holidays).
Prof	David T Robinson
Designer	Harry Vardon
Facilities	🛏 🕭 ♀ 🎣 🏠 🏌 🛺 ∅
Location	Just off Main St, Bundoran on the Sligo/Derry road, 22m N of Sligo
Hotel	★★★ 77% Sand House Hotel, ROSSNOWLAGH ☎ 072 51777 46 ⇄ ↟

CRUIT ISLAND   Map 01 B5

Cruit Island Kincasslagh ☎ 075 43296 Fax 075 48028
A links course on a small island. It is perched along the cliffs overlooking the Atlantic. The course is short but always challenging as the wind blows 90% of the time. It is crowned by a magnificent 6th hole which is played across a cove to an island green. With the prevailing wind in your face and the Atlantic waves crashing in front, it is not for the fainthearted.
9 holes, 4833mtrs, Par 68, SSS 66, Course record 62.
Club membership 350.

Visitors	restricted Sun & Thu mornings for Club competitions.
Societies	apply in writing to secretary.
Green Fees	IEP15.
Cards	💳 💳
Designer	Michael Doherty
Facilities	🛏 🕭 ♀ 🎣 ∅
Location	8km N of Dungloe
Hotel	★★★ 65% Arnold's Hotel, DUNFANAGHY ☎ 074 36208 30 ⇄ ↟

DUNFANAGHY   Map 01 C6

Dunfanaghy Kill ☎ 074 36335 Гɑʌ 074 36335
e-mail: dough@rircom.net
Overlooking Sheephaven Bay, the course has a flat central area with three difficult streams to negotiate. At the Port-na-Blagh end there are five marvellous holes, including one across the beach, while at the Horn Head end, the last five holes are a test for any golfer.
18 holes, 5066mtrs, Par 68, SSS 66, Course record 63.
Club membership 335.

Visitors	must book in advance, time sheet in operation all year.
Societies	must telephone in advance.
Green Fees	not confirmed.
Designer	Harry Vardon
Facilities	🛏 🕭 ♀ 🎣 🏠 🏌 🛺 ∅
Location	On N56

▶

Hotel ★★★ 65% Arnold's Hotel, DUNFANAGHY
☎ 074 36208 30 ⇆ ♜

GREENCASTLE
Map 01 C6

Greencastle Moville ☎ 077 81013
18 holes, 5118mtrs, Par 69, SSS 67.
Telephone for further details

Hotel ★★★ 68% Trinity Hotel, 22-24 Strand Rd,
DERRY CITY ☎ 028 7127 1271 40 ⇆ ♜

GWEEDORE
Map 01 B6

Gweedore Derrybeg ☎ 075 31140
This 9-hole links course provides plenty of challenge with
two subtle Par 3s and the Par 5 5th/14th at 556yards into the
prevailing west wind is a monster.
9 holes, 6201yds, Par 71, SSS 69.
Club membership 175.
Visitors golf club must be notified if large numbers wish
to play.Telephone club for tee off weekend
times.
Societies apply in writing.
Green Fees £10 per round(IEP12 weekends).
Facilities ㊐ ♥ ♀ ♨ ♂

LETTERKENNY
Map 01 C5

Letterkenny Barnhill ☎ 074 21150 Fax 074 21175
The fairways are wide and generous, but the rough, when
you find it, is short, tough and mean. The flat and untiring
terrain on the shores of Lough Swilly provides good holiday
golf. Many interesting holes include the intimidating 1st with
its high tee through trees and the tricky dog-leg of the 2nd
hole. The last 7 holes are on undulating ground, steep climb
from 11th green to 12th tee.
18 holes, 6239yds, Par 70, SSS 71, Course record 65.
Club membership 700.
Visitors preferred Mon-Fri, except Wed evenings after
5pm. Advisable to contact in advance for
weekends and bank holidays.
Societies apply by writing or telephone.
Green Fees IEP£20 per day(IEP£25 weekends & bank
holidays).
Designer Eddie Hacket
Facilities ㊐ ⅏ ㏒ ♥ ♀ ♨ 🏠 ⛳ ♂
Location 2m from town on Rathmelton road

Hotel ★★★ 70% Kee's Hotel, Stranorlar,
BALLYBOFEY ☎ 074 31018 53 ⇆ ♜

MOVILLE
Map 01 C6

Redcastle Redcastle ☎ 077 82073 Fax 077 82214
e-mail: redcastle.hotel@oceanfree.net
A testing course enjoying a picturesque setting on the shores
of Loch Foyle. The two challenging Par 3 holes should be
approached with the necessary respect.
9 holes, 3076yds, Par 36.
Club membership 200.
Visitors welcome except club times advisable to
telephone.
Societies enquiries welcome by telephone or in writing.
Green Fees IEP£11(IEP£15 weekends & bank holidays).

Cards 🃏 ▬ ▬ 🃏
Facilities ㊐ ⅏ ㏒ ♥ ♀ 🏠 ⛳ 🦅 ♂
& Leisure hard tennis courts, heated indoor swimming
pool, fishing, sauna, gymnasium.
Location Main Londonderry/Moville road

NARIN
Map 01 B5

Narin & Portnoo ☎ 075 45107 Fax 075 45107
Seaside links with every hole presenting its own special
feature. The Par 4 5th, for instance, demands a perfectly
placed drive to get a narrow sight of the narrow entrance to
the elevated green. Cross winds from the sea can make some
of the Par 4s difficult to reach with two woods.
18 holes, 5322mtrs, Par 69, SSS 68, Course record 63.
Club membership 600.
Visitors contact in advance for weekend tee times.
Societies telephone in advance.
Green Fees IEP£20(IEP£25 weekends & bank holidays).
Facilities ㏒ ♥ ♀ ♨ 🏠 🦅 ♂
Location 6m from Ardara

Hotel ★★★ 63% Abbey Hotel, The Diamond,
DONEGAL ☎ 073 21014 49 ⇆ ♜

PORTSALON
Map 01 C6

Portsalon ☎ 074 59459 Fax 074 59459
Another course blessed by nature. The golden beaches of
Ballymastocker Bay lie at one end, while the beauty of
Lough Swilly and the Inishowen Peninsula beyond is a
distracting but pleasant feature to the west. Situated on the
Fanad Peninsula, this lovely links course provides untiring
holiday golf at its best.
18 holes, 5880yds, Par 69, SSS 68.
Club membership 400.
Visitors telephone in advance.
Societies telephone in advance.
Green Fees IEP£20(IEP£25 weekends & bank holidays).
Designer Pat Ruddy
Facilities ㊐ ⅏ ㏒ ♥ ♀ ♨ 🦅 ♂
Location 20m N of Letterkenny

Hotel ★★★≜≜ 73% Fort Royal Hotel, Fort Royal,
RATHMULLAN ☎ 074 58100
11 ⇆ ♜ Annexe4 ⇆

RATHMULLAN
Map 01 C6

Otway Saltpans ☎ 074 58319
9 holes, 4234yds, Par 64, SSS 60, Course record 60.
Location W shore of Loch Swilly
Telephone for further details

Hotel ★ 59% Pier Hotel, RATHMULLAN
☎ 074 58178 & 58115 Fax 074 58115 10 ⇆ ♜

ROSAPENNA
Map 01 C6

Rosapenna Downings ☎ 074 55301 Fax 074 55128
e-mail: rosapenna@tinet.ie
Dramatic links course offering a challenging round.
Originally designed by Tom Morris and later modified by
James Braid and Harry Vardon, it includes such features as
bunkers in mid fairway. The best part of the links runs in the
▶

low valley along the ocean.
18 holes, 6271yds, Par 70, SSS 71.
Club membership 200.
Visitors   no restrictions.
Societies   must contact in advance.
Green Fees IEP25 per round(IEP30 weekends).
Cards   🖃 📰 📟 🔲
Designer   Old Tom Morris
Facilities   ⅶ 🖤 ♀ ♨ 📆 ⌇ ⇌ ♣ ⚐
& Leisure   hard tennis courts, heated indoor swimming pool.

Hotel   ★★★ 65% Arnold's Hotel, DUNFANAGHY
      ☎ 074 36208 30 ⇌ 🐾

CO DUBLIN

BALBRIGGAN   Map 01 D4

Balbriggan Blackhall ☎ 01 8412229 Fax 01 8413927
A parkland course with great variations and good views of the Mourne and Cooley mountains.
18 holes, 5922mtrs, Par 71, SSS 71.
Club membership 650.
Visitors   must contact in advance. With member only at weekends.
Societies   must apply in writing.
Green Fees IEP23 per round.
Designer   Paramoir
Facilities   ⊗ ⅶ 🖿 🖤 ♀ ♨ 🐾 ⇌ ⚐
Location   1km S off Balbriggan on N1

Hotel   ★★★ 61% Boyne Valley Hotel & Country Club, Stameen, Dublin Rd, DROGHEDA
      ☎ 041 9837737   35 ⇌ 🐾

BALLYBOUGHAL   Map 01 D4

Hollywood Lakes
☎ 01 8433406 & 8433407 Fax 01 8433002
e-mail: austinbrogan@hotmail
A parkland course opened in 1992 with large USGA-type, sand-based greens and tees. There are water features on seven holes. The front nine requires accuracy while the second nine includes a 636yard Par 5.
18 holes, 6246mtrs, Par 72, SSS 72, Course record 67.
Club membership 630.
Visitors   welcome Mon-Fri but may only play weekends from 1pm.
Societies   telephone then write in advance.
Green Fees IEP20 (IEP25 weekends).
Cards   📟
Designer   Mel Flanagan
Facilities   ⊗ ⅶ 🖿 🖤 ♀ ♨ 📆 ⌇ 🐾 ⇌ ⚐ ♣
Location   3m off main Dublin/Belfast road

Hotel   ★★★ 70% Marine Hotel, Sutton Cross, DUBLIN 13 ☎ 01 8390000   51 ⇌ 🐾

Entries with a green background
identify courses considered to be
particularly interesting

BRITTAS   Map 01 D4

Slade Valley Lynch Park
☎ 01 4582183 & 4582739 Fax 01 4582784
This is a course for a relaxing game, being fairly easy and in pleasant surroundings.
18 holes, 5388mtrs, Par 69, SSS 68, Course record 65.
Club membership 800.
Visitors   must contact in advance.
Societies   telephone in advance.
Green Fees IEP17 per round.
Cards   🖃 📟
Prof   John Dignam
Designer   W Sullivan & D O Brien
Facilities   ⊗ ⅶ 🖿 🖤 ♀ ♨ 📆 ⌇ ⚐
Location   9m SW of Dublin on N81

Hotel   ★★★ 66% Downshire House Hotel, BLESSINGTON ☎ 045 865199
      14 ⇌ 🐾 Annexe11 ⇌ 🐾

CASTLEKNOCK   Map 01 D4

Elm Green ☎ 01 8200797 Fax 01 8226662
Located a short distance from Dublin, beside Phoenix Park, with a fine layout, tricky greens and year round playability.
18 holes, 5796yds, Par 71, SSS 66, Course record 65.
Club membership 400.
Visitors   must book in advance.
Societies   telephone in advance.
Green Fees not confirmed.
Cards   🖃 📰 📟
Prof   Arnold O'Connor/Paul McGavan
Designer   Eddie Hackett
Facilities   ⊗ 🖿 🖤 ♨ 📆 ⌇ ⇌ ⚐ ♣
& Leisure   pitch and putt course..
Location   Off Navan Rd, 15 mins from city centre

Hotel   ★★★ 70% Finnstown Country House Hotel, Newcastle Rd, LUCAN
      ☎ 01 6280644   25 ⇌ 🐾 Annexe26 ⇌ 🐾

Luttrellstown Castle Dublin15
☎ 01 8089988 Fax 01 8089989
e-mail: golf@luttrellstown.ie
Set in the grounds of the magnificent 560-acre Luttrellstown Castle estate, this championship course has retained the integrity of a mature and ancient parkland. It is renowned for the quality of its greens and the log-built Clubhouse which provides excellent facilities.
18 holes, 6032mtrs, Par 72, SSS 73, Course record 66.
Club membership 400.
Visitors   bookings made in advance only, no denims.
Societies   must phone in advance.
Green Fees IEP60 per round (IEP65 weekends).
Cards   🖃 📰 📟
Prof   Edward Doyle
Designer   N Bielenberg
Facilities   ⊗ ⅶ 🖿 🖤 ♀ ♨ 📆 ⌇ ⇌ 🐾 ⇌ ⚐ ♣
& Leisure   hard tennis courts, heated outdoor swimming pool, fishing, clay shooting.
Location   Porterstown rd   ▶

Hotel   ★★★ 70% Finnstown Country House Hotel, Newcastle Rd, LUCAN
☎ 01 6280644   25 ⇄ ♠ Annexe26 ⇄ ♠

CLOGHRAN   Map 01 D4

Forrest Little ☎ 01 8401183
Testing parkland course.
18 holes, 5865mtrs, Par 70, SSS 70.
Visitors   preferred weekday mornings.
Green Fees not confirmed.
Prof   Tony Judd
Facilities   ♀ 🖥 ⚐
Location   6m N of Dublin on N1

Hotel   ★★★ 70% Marine Hotel, Sutton Cross,
DUBLIN 13 ☎ 01 8390000 51 ⇄ ♠

DONABATE   Map 01 D4

Balcarrick Corballis
☎ 01 8436228 & 8436957 Fax 01 8436957
Splendid 18-hole parkland course located close to the sea. A strong prevailing wind often plays a big part on every hole. Many challenging holes, notably the 7th - nicknamed 'Amen Corner'.
18 holes, 6273mtrs, Par 73, SSS 71.
Club membership 750.
Visitors   must contact in advance.
Societies   telephone in advance.
Green Fees not confirmed.
Prof   Stephen Rayfus
Designer   Barry Langan
Facilities   ⊗ �)Ⅲ ⛳ ⚑ ♀ 🏖 🖥

Hotel   ★★★ 69% Posthouse Dublin Airport, Dublin Airport, DUBLIN ☎ 01 8080500 249 ⇄ ♠

Corballis Public Corballis ☎ 01 8436583
Well maintained coastal course with excellent greens.
18 holes, 4971yds, Par 65, SSS 64.
Visitors   no restrictions.
Societies   apply in writing or telephone.
Green Fees not confirmed.
Facilities   ⛳ 🏖 🖥 ⚐ 🏌 ℒ

Hotel   ★★★ 69% Posthouse Dublin Airport, Dublin Airport, DUBLIN ☎ 01 8080500 249 ⇄ ♠

Donabate Balcarrick ☎ 01 8436346 & 8436001
18 holes, 5704yds, Par 70, SSS 69, Course record 67.
Telephone for further details

Hotel   ★★★ 69% Posthouse Dublin Airport, Dublin Airport, DUBLIN ☎ 01 8080500 249 ⇄ ♠

The Island Corballis
☎ 01 8436104 & 8436205 Fax 01 8436860 e-mail: islandgc@iol.ie
Links course on a promontory, with sea inlets separating some of the fairways. Accuracy as well as length of shots are required on some holes and sand hills provide an additional challenge.
18 holes, 6078mtrs, Par 71, SSS 72, Course record 67.
Club membership 800.

The Island Golf Club

Visitors   must contact in advance. Preferred on Mon, Tue & Fri limited availability on all other days. Telephone for appointment.
Societies   must apply in advance.
Green Fees May-Oct: IEP60 per round (IEP70 weekends) Nov-Apr: IEP50 per round (IEP60 weekends).
Cards   🔲 🔲
Prof   Kevin Kelliher
Designer   Hackett/Hawtree
Facilities   ⊗)Ⅲ ⛳ ⚑ ♀ 🏖 🖥 ⚐ 🏌 🏖 ℒ
Location   Take main Dublin/Belfast road N1, pass airport, take turn for Donabate/Portrane, follow signs

Hotel   ★★★ 69% Posthouse Dublin Airport, Dublin Airport, DUBLIN
☎ 01 8080500 249 ⇄ ♠

DUBLIN   Map 01 D4

Carrickmines Carrickmines ☎ 01 2955972
Meadowland course.
9 holes, 6100yds, Par 71, SSS 69.
Club membership 500.
Visitors   may not play Wed or Sat.
Societies   contact for details.
Green Fees IEP23 per 18 holes;IEP13 per 9 holes(IEP26/IEP15 Sunday).
Facilities   ⛳ ⚑ ♀ 🏖 ℒ
Location   7m S of Dublin

Hotel   ★★★ 68% Royal Marine Hotel, Marine Rd, DUN LAOGHAIRE ☎ 01 2801911 103 ⇄ ♠

Castle Woodside Dr, Rathfarnham
☎ 01 4904207 Fax 01 4920264
A tight, tree-lined parkland course which is very highly regarded by all who play there.
18 holes, 5732mtrs, Par 70, SSS 70, Course record 63.
Club membership 1200.
Visitors   welcome but may not play at weekends & bank holidays.
Societies   must apply in writing 6 months in advance.
Green Fees not confirmed.
Prof   David Kinsella
Designer   Barcroft-Pickman & Hood
Facilities   ⊗)Ⅲ ⛳ ⚑ ♀ 🏖 🖥 ℒ
Location   Off Dodder Park Road

▶

Hotel ★★★★ 72% Jurys Hotel Dublin, Pembroke Rd, Ballsbridge, DUBLIN 4 ☎ 01 6605000 294 ➪ 🐾

Clontarf Donnycarney House, Malahide Rd
☎ 01 8331892 Fax 01 8331933
The nearest golf course to Dublin city, with a historic building as a clubhouse, Clontarf is a parkland type course bordered on one side by a railway line. There are several testing and challenging holes including the 12th, which involves playing over a pond and a quarry.
18 holes, 5317mtrs, Par 69, SSS 68, Course record 64.
Club membership 1100.
Visitors welcome daily but must contact in advance.
Societies Tue & Fri. Must contact in advance.
Green Fees IEP26(IEP35 weekends).
Prof Mark Callan
Designer Harry Colt
Facilities ⊗ �𝕄 🏌 ♨ ♀ 🛆 🏠 ⊶ ✓
Location 2.5m N via Fairview

Hotel ★★★ 67% Jurys Skylon Hotel, Drumcondra Rd, DUBLIN 9 ☎ 01 8379121 92 ➪ 🐾

Corrstown Corrstown, Kilsallaghan
☎ 01 8640533 & 8640534 Fax 01 8640537
e-mail: corrstowngolfclub@eircom.net
The 18 hole course has a small river meandering through, coming into play at several holes culminating in a challenging Island green finish. Orchard course has mature trees and rolling pastureland offering golfers a relaxing enjoyable game.
River Course: 18 holes, 6077mtrs, Par 72, SSS 71, Course record 69.
Orchard Course: 9 holes, 5584mtre, Par 70, SSS 69.
Club membership 1050.
Visitors advisable to contact in advance. May play weekends after 1pm on River Course. Visitors welcome anytime on Orchard Course.
Societies telephone or write in advance.
Green Fees not confirmed.
Prof Pat Gittens
Designer Eddie Connaughton
Facilities ⊗ �𝕄 🏌 ♨ ♀ 🛆 🏠 ⊶ ✓
Location 10 minutes W of Dublin Airport via St Margarets

Hotel ★★★ 67% Jurys Skylon Hotel, Drumcondra Rd, DUBLIN 9 ☎ 01 8379121 92 ➪ 🐾

Deer Park Hotel & Golf Course Howth D13
☎ 01 8322624 Fax 01 8392405
e-mail: sales@deerpark.iol.ie
Claiming to be Ireland's largest golf/hotel complex, be warned that its popularity makes it quite busy at times and only hotel residents can book tee-off times.
St Fintans: 9 holes, 3373yds, Par 37.
Deer Park: 18 holes, 6830yds, Par 72.
Grace O'Malley: 9 holes, 3130yds, Par 35.
Short Course: 12 holes, 1810yds, Par 36.
Club membership 350.
Visitors no restrictions. There may be delays especially Sun mornings.
Societies must contact by telephone.
Green Fees not confirmed.
Cards 💳 ▬ ▭ 📄
Designer Fred Hawtree

Facilities & Leisure ⊗ ⟫ 🏌 ♨ ♀ 🛆 ⊶ 🏠 ✓ hard tennis courts, heated indoor swimming pool, sauna.
Location On right 0.5m before Howth Harbour

Hotel ★★★ 70% Marine Hotel, Sutton Cross, DUBLIN 13 ☎ 01 8390000 51 ➪ 🐾

Edmonstown Edmondstown Rd, Edmondstown
☎ 01 4931082 Fax 01 4933152 e-mail: edmondgc@iol.ie
A popular and testing parkland course situated at the foot of the Dublin Mountains in the suburbs of the city. An attractive stream flows in front of the 4th and 6th greens calling for an accurate approach shot.
18 holes, 5393mtrs, Par 70, SSS 70.
Club membership 750.

Visitors must contact in advance as there are daily times reserved for members. Limited times after 3.30pm weekends.
Societies must contact in advance.
Green Fees IEP30 weekdays(IEP35 weekends & bank holidays).
Cards 💳 ▬
Prof Andrew Crofton
Designer McEvoy/Cooke
Facilities ⊗ ⟫ 🏌 ♨ ♀ 🛆 🏠 ⊶ 🐾 ⚓ ✓

Hotel ★★★ 68% Jurys Montrose Hotel, Stillorgan Rd, DUBLIN ☎ 01 2693311 179 ➪ 🐾

Elm Park Golf & Sports Club Nutley House, Nutley Ln, Dennybrook ☎ 01 2693438 Fax 01 2694505
Interesting parkland course requiring a degree of accuracy, particularly as half of the holes involve crossing the stream.
18 holes, 5355mtrs, Par 69, SSS 68, Course record 64.
Club membership 1750.
Visitors must contact in advance.
Societies apply in advance.
Green Fees not confirmed.
Prof Seamus Green
Facilities ⊗ ⟫ 🏌 ♨ ♀ 🛆 🏠 ⊶ ✓
& Leisure hard and grass tennis courts.
Location 3m from city centre

Hotel ★★★★ 72% Jurys Hotel Dublin, Pembroke Rd, Ballsbridge, DUBLIN 4 ☎ 01 6605000 294 ➪ 🐾

Foxrock Torquay Rd, Foxrock ☎ 01 2895668 & 2893992
A well-treed parkland course.
9 holes, 5667mtrs, Par 70, SSS 69.
Club membership 650.
Visitors welcome but contact in advance, no green fees Tue & weekends. ▶

Societies apply in writing to William Daly.
Green Fees not confirmed.
Prof David Walker
Facilities ♀⬥🏠🚩

Hotel ★★★ 68% Royal Marine Hotel, Marine Rd,
DUN LAOGHAIRE ☎ 01 2801911 103 ⇌ 🏴

Grange Rathfarnham ☎ 01 4932889
Wooded parkland course which provides both interest
and challenge.
18 holes, 5517mtrs, Par 68, SSS 69.
Visitors preferred on weekdays.
Green Fees not confirmed.
Prof W Sullivan
Facilities ♀🏠
Location 6m from city centre

Hotel ★★★ 68% Jurys Montrose Hotel,
Stillorgan Rd, DUBLIN
☎ 01 2693311 179 ⇌ 🏴

Howth St Fintan's, Carrickbrack Rd, Sutton
☎ 01 8323055 Fax 01 8321793
A heathland course with scenic views of Dublin Bay. It is
very hilly and presents a good challenge to the novice or
expert golfer.
18 holes, 5618mtrs, Par 72, SSS 69.
Club membership 1200.
Visitors contact in advance. May not play Wed and
weekends.
Societies must contact in advance.
Green Fees IEP35 per round.
Prof John McGuirk
Designer James Braid
Facilities ⬥🏠✓
Location 9m NE of City Centre, 2m from Sutton Cross,
on Sutton side of Hill of Howth

Hotel ★★★ 70% Marine Hotel, Sutton Cross,
DUBLIN 13 ☎ 01 8390000 51 ⇌ 🏴

Milltown Lower Churchtown Rd
☎ 01 4976090 Fax 01 4976008 e-mail: millgolf@iol.ie
Level parkland course on the outskirts of the city.
18 holes, 5638mtrs, Par 71, SSS 69, Course record 64.
Club membership 1400.
Visitors must contact in advance but may not play
weekends.
Societies apply in writing.
Green Fees not confirmed.
Cards 💳 💳 💳
Prof John Harnett
Designer Freddie Davis
Facilities ⊗ �🍴 ⬥ 💷 ♀⬥🏠🚩✓
Location Lower Churchtown Road, Dublin 14

Hotel ★★★★ 72% Jurys Hotel Dublin,
Pembroke Rd, Ballsbridge, DUBLIN 4
☎ 01 6605000 294 ⇌ 🏴

Newlands Clondalkin 22
☎ 01 4593157 & 4593498 Fax 01 4593498
Mature parkland course offering a testing game.
18 holes, 5714mtrs, Par 71, SSS 70.
Club membership 1000.

Visitors must contact in advance and may play Mon,
Thu, Fri and Wed mornings only.
Societies must contact in writing.
Green Fees IEP40 per round.
Prof Karl O'Donnell
Designer James Braid
Facilities ⊗ ⍟ ⬥ 💷 ♀⬥🏠🚩✓

Hotel ★★★ 68% Jurys Green Isle Hotel, Naas Rd,
DUBLIN 22 ☎ 01 4593406 90 ⇌ 🏴

The Open Golf Centre Newton House, St Margaret's
☎ 01 8640324 Fax 01 8341400 e-mail: rwwright@iol.ie
A 27-hole Pay and Play parkland course that is testing for the
low handicap golfer but not too intimidating for high
handicapper.
*Yellow & Red Course: 18 holes, 5973yds, Par 71, SSS 69,
Course record 66.*
Blue Course: 9 holes, 2479yds, Par 31.
Visitors no restrictions. Booking essential.
Societies telephone for booking form.
Green Fees not confirmed.
Cards 💳 💳 💳
Prof Roger Yates
Designer M Hawtree
Facilities ⬥🏠🚩🏋✓🍴
Location Adjacent to Dublin airport

Hotel ★★★ 70% Marine Hotel, Sutton Cross,
DUBLIN 13 ☎ 01 8390000 51 ⇌ 🏴

Rathfarnham Newtown ☎ 01 4931201 & 4931561
Fax 01 4931561 e-mail: rgc@oceanfree.net
Parkland course designed by John Jacobs in 1962.
9 holes, 5815mtrs, Par 71, SSS 70, Course record 69.
Club membership 685.
Visitors must contact in advance, by arrangement only.
Societies restricted to Mon, Wed & Fri.
Green Fees IEP22.50 per round (IEP28 Sun).
Prof Brian O'Hara
Designer John Jacobs
Facilities ⬥ 💷 ♀⬥🏠✓

Hotel ★★★★ 72% Jurys Hotel Dublin,
Pembroke Rd, Ballsbridge, DUBLIN 4
☎ 01 6605000 294 ⇌ 🏴

Royal Dublin North Bull Island, Dollymount
☎ 01 8336346 Fax 01 8336504
e-mail: jlambe@theroyaldublingolfclub.com

A popular course with visitors, for its design subtleties,
for the condition of the links and the friendly
atmosphere. Founded in 1885, the club moved to its ▶

present site in 1889 and received its Royal designation in 1891. A notable former club professional was Christie O'Connor, who was appointed in 1959 and immediately made his name. Along with its many notable holes, Royal Dublin has a fine and testing finish. The 18th is a sharply dog-legged par 4, with out of bounds along the right-hand side. The decision to try the long carry over the 'garden' is one many visitors have regretted.
18 holes, 6002mtrs, Par 72, SSS 71, Course record 63. Club membership 800.

Visitors	must contact in advance & have handicap certificate. May not play Wed, Sat until 3.30 summer.
Societies	must book one year in advance.
Green Fees	IEP75 per round Mon-Thu (IEP85 Fri-Sun).
Cards	〰 ▆ ▆▆
Prof	Leonard Owens
Designer	H S Colt
Facilities	⊗ ⑭ 🐴 ▆ ♀ ♨ 🏠 ⛳ ↘ ♂
Location	3.5m NE of city centre

Hotel	★★★ 69% Longfield's Hotel, Fitzwilliam St, DUBLIN 2 ☎ 01 6761367 24 ⇄ ♗

St Anne's North Bull Island, Dollymount ☎ 01 8336471
Links course, recently extended from 9 holes to 18.
18 holes, 5652mtrs, Par 70, SSS 69. Club membership 500.

Visitors	telephone for restrictions.
Societies	must apply in writing.
Green Fees	not confirmed.
Facilities	♀ ♨ ♂

Hotel	★★★ 69% Longfield's Hotel, Fitzwilliam St, DUBLIN 2 ☎ 01 6761367 24 ⇄ ♗

St Margaret's Golf & Country Club St Margaret's
☎ 01 8640400 Fax 01 8640289 e-mail: sales@stmargarets.net

A championship standard course which measures nearly 7,000 yards off the back tees, but flexible teeing offers a fairer challenge to the middle and high handicap golfer. The modern design makes wide use of water hazards and mounding. The Par 5 8th hole is set to become notorious - featuring lakes to the left and right of the tee and a third lake in front of the green. Ryder Cup player, Sam Torrance, has described the 18th as 'possibly the strongest and most exciting in the world'.
18 holes, 6917yds, Par 73, SSS 73, Course record 69. Club membership 200.

Visitors	telephone in advance.
Societies	apply in writing or telephone
Green Fees	not confirmed.
Cards	〰 ▆ ▆▆ ▆
Designer	Craddock/Ruddy
Facilities	⊗ ⑭ 🐴 ▆ ♀ ♨ 🏠 ⛳ ↘ ♂ ♗
Location	9m NW of city centre

Hotel	★★★ 70% Marine Hotel, Sutton Cross, DUBLIN 13 ☎ 01 8390000 51 ⇄ ♗

Stackstown Kellystown Rd, Rathfarnham
☎ 01 4942338 & 4941993 Fax 01 4933934
Pleasant course in scenic surroundings.
18 holes, 5925mtrs, Par 72, SSS 72, Course record 68. Club membership 1042.

Visitors	preferred Mon-Fri.
Societies	telephone in advance and confirm in writing.
Green Fees	not confirmed.
Prof	Michael Kavanach
Facilities	⊗ 🐴 ▆ ♀ ♨ 🏠 ↘ ♂ ♗
& Leisure	sauna, snooker.
Location	9m S of city centre

Hotel	★★★ 68% Jurys Montrose Hotel, Stillorgan Rd, DUBLIN ☎ 01 2693311 179 ⇄ ♗

DUN LAOGHAIRE   Map 01 D4

Dun Laoghaire Eglinton Park, Tivoli Rd
☎ 01 2803916 Fax 01 2804868 e-mail: dlgc@iol.ie
This is a well wooded parkland course, not long, but requiring accurate club selection and placing of shots. The course was designed by Harry Colt in 1918.
18 holes, 5298mtrs, Par 69, SSS 68, Course record 63. Club membership 1118.

Visitors	may play Mon,Tue & Fri.Restricted on all other days.
Societies	must apply in writing.
Green Fees	IEP35 per round;IEP50 per 36 holes..
Cards	〰 ▆ ▆▆ ▆ ▆▆ ▆ ♫
Prof	TBC
Designer	Harry Colt
Facilities	⊗ ⑭ 🐴 ▆ ♀ ♨ 🏠 ⛳ ♂
Location	0.75m from town centre and ferry port

Hotel	★★★ 68% Royal Marine Hotel, Marine Rd, DUN LAOGHAIRE ☎ 01 2801911 103 ⇄ ♗

KILLINEY   Map 01 D4

Killiney Ballinclea Rd ☎ 01 2852823 Fax 01 2852823
The course is on the side of Killiney Hill with picturesque
views over south Dublin and the Wicklow Mountains.
9 holes, 5655mtrs, Par 70, SSS 70.
Club membership 450.
Visitors welcome Mon, Wed, Fri & Sun afternoons.
Societies Apply in writing.
Green Fees IEP30.
Prof P O'Boyle
Facilities ⓑ ⓦ 🍴 ⚲ 🏠 🍴 ⚓ 🏌

Hotel ★★★★ 65% Fitzpatrick Castle Hotel,
KILLINEY ☎ 01 2840700 113 ⇄ ⓡ

KILTERNAN   Map 01 D4

Kilternan Golf & Country Club Hotel
☎ 01 2955559 Fax 01 2955670
e-mail: kgc@kilternan-hotel.ie
Interesting and testing course overlooking Dublin Bay.
18 holes, 5223yds, Par 68, SSS 66, Course record 66.
Club membership 940.

Visitors may not play before 1.30pm at weekends.
Contact in advance.
Societies apply in writing/telephone in advance.
Green Fees not confirmed.
Cards 🔲 🔲 🔲 🔲
Designer Eddie Hackett
Facilities ⓧ 🏸 ⓑ ⓦ 🍴 ⚲ 🏠 🍴 ⚓ 🏌
& Leisure hard tennis courts, heated indoor swimming
pool, sauna, gymnasium.

Hotel ★★★★ 65% Fitzpatrick Castle Hotel,
KILLINEY ☎ 01 2840700 113 ⇄ ⓡ

LUCAN   Map 01 D4

Hermitage Ballydowd
☎ 01 6265049 & 6268491 Fax 01 6268491
Part level, part undulating course bordered by the River
Liffey and offering some surprises.
18 holes, 6034mtrs, Par 71, SSS 70.
Club membership 1100.
Visitors Must contact in advance.
Societies must telephone well in advance.
Green Fees IEP35 per round(IEP45 weekends).
Cards 🔲
Prof Simon Byrne
Designer J McKenna
Facilities ⓧ 🏸 ⓑ ⓦ 🍴 ⚲ 🏠 🍴 🏌

Hotel ★★★ 70% Finnstown Country House Hotel,
Newcastle Rd, LUCAN
☎ 01 6280644 25 ⇄ ⓡ Annexe26 ⇄ ⓡ

Lucan Celbridge Rd ☎ 01 6282106 Fax 01 6282929
Founded in 1897 as a nine hole course and extended to 18
holes in 1988, Lucan involves playing over a lane which
bisects the 1st and 7th holes. The first nine is undulating
while the back nine is flatter and features water hazards and a
538mtr 5 par 18th hole.
18 holes, 5958mtrs, Par 71, SSS 71, Course record 67.
Club membership 780.
Visitors may play Mon, Tue & Fri.
Societies must apply in writing.
Green Fees IEP30 per 18 holes(Mon,Tues,Fri).
Designer Eddie Hackett
Facilities ⓧ 🏸 ⓑ ⓦ 🍴 ⚲ 🏌
Location N4 W to Celbridge

Hotel ★★★ 64% Lucan Spa Hotel, LUCAN
☎ 01 6280495 & 6280497
Fax 01 6280841 71rm(61 ⇄ ⓡ)

MALAHIDE   Map 01 D4

Malahide Beechwood, The Grange ☎ 01 8461611
Fax 01 8461270 e-mail: malgc@clubi.ie
Splendid parkland course with raised greens and water
hazards affecting many of the holes, demanding
accuracy from tee to green.
Main Course: 18 holes, 6066mtrs, Par 71.
Club membership 1100.

Visitors must contact in advance.
Societies must contact in advance.
Green Fees IEP35 per round(IEP50 weekends).
Cards 🔲 🔲 🔲
Prof John Murray
Designer E Hackett
Facilities ⓧ 🏸 ⓑ ⓦ 🍴 ⚲ 🏠 🍴 ⚓ 🏌
Location 1m from coast road at Portmarnock

Hotel ★★★★ 77% Portmarnock Hotel & Golf
Links, Strand Rd, PORTMARNOCK
☎ 01 8460611 103 ⇄ ⓡ

PORTMARNOCK   Map 01 D4

PORTMARNOCK See page 463

Portmarnock

Portmarnock, *Co Dublin*   ☎ 01 8462968   Fax 01 8462601   Map 01 D4

(bookings) e-mail: liz@portmarnockgolfclub.ie

Universally acknowledged as one of the truly great links courses, Portmarnock has hosted many great events from the British Amateur Championship of 1949 and the Canada Cup in 1960, to 12 stagings of the revived Irish Open. Founded in 1894, the championship course offers a classic challenge. Surrounded by water on three sides and laid out in a serpentine fashion, no two successive holes play in the same direction. Unlike many courses which play nine out and nine home, Portmarnock demands a continual discernment of wind direction.

The course has some extraordinary holes including the 14th, which Henry Cotton regarded as the best hole in golf; the 15th which Arnold Palmer regards as the best par-3 in the world, and the 5th regarded as the best on the course by the late Harry Bradshaw, 40 years Portmarnock's golf professional and runner-up to AD Locke in the 1949 British Open after playing his ball from an empty bottle of stout.

Visitors must contact in advance and confirm in writing. Restricted Saturday, Sunday and public holiday. Handicap certificate required

Societies must contact in advance in writing.

Green Fees IEP100 per round Mon-Fri. IEP120 weekends & public holidays.

Facilities
Professional (Joey Purcell)

Location 12m from Dublin, 1m from village down Golf Rd.

Holes/Par/Course record 27 holes Old Course: 18 holes, 7182yds, Par 72, SSS73
New Course: 9 holes , 3370yds, Par 37

WHERE TO STAY AND EAT NEARBY

Hotels
PORTMARNOCK
★★★★ ⊛⊛ 77% Portmarnock Hotel & Golf Links.
☎ 01 8460611   103 ⇔ 🏌

Championship Course

RATHCOOLE   Map 01 D4

Beech Park Johnstown ☎ 01 4580522 Fax 01 4588365
e-mail: info@beechpark.ie
Relatively flat parkland with heavily wooded fairways.
Famous for its 'Amen Corner' (holes 10-13).
18 holes, 5730mtrs, Par 72, SSS 70, Course record 67.
Club membership 955.

Visitors   may not play weekends, telephone in advance.
Societies   apply in writing.
Green Fees   IEP30 per round(Mon,Thur,Fri).
Cards   ⬚⬚ ⬚⬚
Designer   Eddie Hackett
Facilities   ⅏ 🏋 💺 💺 👤 🏌 𝆹

Hotel   ★★★ 70% Finnstown Country House Hotel,
                 Newcastle Rd, LUCAN
                 ☎ 01 6280644 25 ➡ 🏌 Annexe26 ➡ 🏌

RUSH   Map 01 D4

Rush ☎ 01 8438177 (Office) 8437548 (Clubhouse)
Fax 01 8438177
Seaside borders three fairways on this links course. There are
28 bunkers and undulating fairways to add to the challenge
of the variable and strong winds that blow at all times and
change with the tides. There are no easy holes!
9 holes, 5598mtrs, Par 70, SSS 69.
Club membership 350.

Visitors   restricted Wed, Thu, weekends & bank holidays.
Societies   apply in writing.
Green Fees   not confirmed.
Facilities   ⊗ ⅏ 🏋 💺 💺 👤 𝆹

Hotel   ★★★ 69% Posthouse Dublin Airport, Dublin
                 Airport, DUBLIN ☎ 01 8080500 249 ➡ 🏌

SAGGART   Map 01 D4

City West Hotel & Golf Resort
☎ 01 4010500 & 4010900 (shop) Fax 01 4588565
e-mail: info@citywest-hotel.iol.ie
18 holes, 6314yds, Par 70, SSS 70, Course record 65.

Visitors   time sheet in operation, telephone in advance.
Societies   apply in writing/telephone in advance.
Green Fees   not confirmed.
Cards   ⬚⬚ ⬚⬚ ⬚⬚ ⬚⬚
Prof   Mac Gregor
Designer   Christy O'Connor Jnr
Facilities   ⊗ ⅏ 🏋 💺 💺 👤 🏌 🗑 ⚑ ⬚ 🏌 𝆹 ⚐
& Leisure   heated indoor swimming pool, fishing, sauna,
                 solarium, gymnasium.
Location   Naas road, southbound N7

Hotel   ★★★ 65% Bewley's Hotel Newlands Cross,
                 Newlands Cross, Naas Rd, DUBLIN 22
                 ☎ 01 464 0140 260 ➡ 🏌

SKERRIES   Map 01 D4

Skerries Hacketstown ☎ 01 8491567 Fax 01 8491591
e-mail: skerriesgolfclub@eircom.net
Tree-lined parkland course on gently rolling countryside,
with sea views from some holes. The 1st and 18th are
particularly challenging. The club can be busy on some days,
but is always friendly.
18 holes, 6081mtrs, Par 73, SSS 72.
Club membership 800.

Visitors   must contact in advance but may not play at
                 weekends.
Societies   must contact well in advance in writing.
Green Fees   IEP30 per round.
Cards   ⬚⬚ ⬚⬚
Prof   Jimmy Kinsella
Facilities   ⊗ ⅏ 🏋 💺 💺 👤 🏌 🗑 🏌 𝆹
Location   E of Dublin-Belfast road

Hotel   ★★★ 61% Boyne Valley Hotel & Country
                 Club, Stameen, Dublin Rd, DROGHEDA
                 ☎ 041 9837737 35 ➡ 🏌

SWORDS   Map 01 D4

Swords Open Golf Course Balheary Av, Swords
☎ 01 8409819 & 8901030 Fax 01 8409819
Parkland course situated beside the River Broadmeadow in
unspoilt countryside, 10 miles from Dublin.
18 holes, 5677mtrs, Par 71, SSS 70, Course record 67.
Club membership 425.

Visitors   timesheet bookings available all year, telephone
                 to book, may play at any time
Societies   telephone well in advance.
Green Fees   IEP10 per round (IEP15 weekends).
Designer   T Halpin
Facilities   🏋 💺 👤 🏌 𝆹
Location   5 mins from Swords

Hotel   ★★★ 67% Jurys Skylon Hotel, Drumcondra
                 Rd, DUBLIN 9 ☎ 01 8379121 92 ➡ 🏌

TALLAGHT   Map 01 D4

Ballinascorney Ballinascorney
☎ 01 4516430 Fax 01 4598445
Set in the valley of Glenasmole, this very scenic course
offers a variety of terrain, where every hole is different,
many would be considered feature holes.
18 holes, 5535yds, Par 69, SSS 67, Course record 63.

Visitors   please contact in advance, welcome weekdays
                 and weekends after 4pm.
Societies   contact for details.
Green Fees   IEP20 (IEP30 weekends & bank holidays).
Cards   ⬚⬚
Designer   Eddie Hackett
Facilities   💺 👤 🏌 ⚐ 🏌 𝆹
Location   8m SW of Dublin city centre

Hotel   ★★★ 68% Jurys Green Isle Hotel, Naas Rd,
                 DUBLIN 22 ☎ 01 4593406 90 ➡ 🏌

CO GALWAY

BALLINASLOE   Map 01 B4

Ballinasloe Rosglos ☎ 0905 42126 Fax 0905 42538
Well maintained parkland course, recently extended from a
par 68 to a par 72.
18 holes, 5865mtrs, Par 72, SSS 70, Course record 69.
Club membership 884.
Visitors   preferably Mon-Sat, contact in advance.
Societies   contact in advance.
Green Fees not confirmed.
Prof   Barry Flangan
Designer   E Hackett/E Connaughton
Facilities   ⌘ 🏠 🏌 🍴

Hotel   ★★★ 64% Haydens Gateway Business,
              Leisure Hotel, BALLINASLOE
              ☎ 065 68 23000 47 ⇥ 🐾

BALLYCONNEELY   Map 01 A4

Connemara ☎ 095 23502 & 23602 Fax 095 23662
e-mail: links@iol.ie
This championship links course is situated on the verge
of the Atlantic Ocean in a most spectacular setting, with
the Twelve Bens Mountains in the background.
Established as recently as 1973, it is a tough challenge,
due in no small part to its exposed location, with the
back 9 the equal of any in the world. The last six holes
are exceptionally long and offer a great challenge to
golfers of all abilities. Also 27 hole championship links.
18 holes, 6611mtrs, Par 72, SSS 75, Course record 67.
Club membership 970.
Visitors   advisable to book in advance.
Societies   telephone in advance.
Green Fees not confirmed.
Cards   💳 💳
Prof   Hugh O'Neill
Designer   Eddie Hackett
Facilities   ⊗ 🍽 ⌘ 🏌 🍴 ⌛ 🏠 🍴 🚩 ⚲ 🏌 ⚘ 🍴
Location   9m SW of Clifden

Hotel   ★★★ 76% Abbeyglen Castle Hotel, Sky
              Rd, CLIFDEN ☎ 095 21201 36 ⇥ 🐾

BEARNA   Map 01 B3

Bearna Golf and Country Club Corboley
☎ 091 592677 Fax 091 592674 e-
mail: bearnagc@eircom.net
Set amid the beautiful landscape of the west of Ireland
and enjoying commanding views of Galway Bay, the
golf course covers more than 100 hectares of unique
countryside. This has resulted in generously proportioned
fairways, many elevated tees and some splendid carries.
Water comes into play at thirteen holes and the final four
holes provide a memorable finish.
18 holes, 5746mtrs, Par 72, SSS 72, Course record 68.
Club membership 500.
Visitors   must telephone in advance.
Societies   contact in advance.
Green Fees IEP25 per round Mon-Thu (IEP30 Fri-Sun).
Cards   💳 💳 💳

Designer   Robert J Brown
Facilities   ⊗ ⌘ 🍴 🏌 ⌛ 🏠 🚩 ⚲ 🏌 ⚘
Location   5miles W Galway City on Spiddal Rd.

Hotel   ★★★ 65% Galway Ryan Hotel, Dublin
              Rd, GALWAY ☎ 091 753181 96 ⇥ 🐾

GALWAY   Map 01 B4

Galway Blackrock, Salthill
☎ 091 522033 Fax 091 529783
Designed by Dr Alister MacKenzie, this course is inland
by nature, although some of the fairways run close to the
ocean. The terrain is of gently sloping hillocks with
plenty of trees and furze bushes to catch out the unwary.
Although not a long course, it provided a worthy
challenge as the venue of the Celtic International
Tournament in 1984 and continues to delight the visiting
golfer.
18 holes, 6376yds, Par 70, SSS 71, Course record 67.
Club membership 1050.
Visitors   preferred on weekdays, except Tue.
Societies   must apply in writing.
Green Fees not confirmed.
Prof   Don Wallace
Designer   McKenzie
Facilities   ⊗ 🍽 ⌘ 🍴 🏌 ⌛ 🏠 🚩 ⚲ ⚘
Location   2m W in Salthill

Hotel   ★★★ 60% Lochlurgain Hotel, 22
              Monksfield, Upper Salthill, GALWAY
              ☎ 091 529595 13 ⇥ 🐾

Glenlo Abbey Bushypark
☎ 091 526666 Fax 091 527800 e-mail: glenlo@iol.ie
A parkland course overlooking the magnificent Lough Corrib
but only 10 minutes from the centre of Galway city. Nine
fairways but large double green with two flags and four tee
postions allows 18 diffent holes. The Par 3, 4th hole is on an
island-like green extending into the lough.
9 holes, 6009mtrs, Par 71, SSS 71.
Club membership 100.
Societies   telephone in advance.
Green Fees not confirmed.
Cards   💳 💳 💳 💳
Prof   Philip Murray & Bill Daly
Designer   Jeff Howes
Facilities   ⊗ 🍽 ⌘ 🍴 🏌 ⌛ 🏠 🚩 🍴 🏌 ⚘ 🍴
& Leisure fishing, clay pigeon shooting..
Location   On N59 Galway/Clifden road 4km from Galway
              City Centre

Hotel   ★★★★🏌 Glenlo Abbey Hotel, Bushypark,
              GALWAY ☎ 091 526666 45 ⇥ 🐾

GORT   Map 01 B3

Gort Kilmacduagh Rd, Castlequarter
☎ 091 632244 Fax 091 632387 e-mail: gortgolf@tinet.ie
Replacing the original 9-hole course, this new 18-hole
course, opened in June 1996, offers golfers a real challenge.
The 564yd 9th and the 516yd 17th are played into a
prevailing wind and the par 4 dog-leg 7th will test the best.
18 holes, 5705mtrs, Par 71, SSS 69.
Club membership 1060.

▶

Visitors	advisable to telephone in advance. Sun am reserved for members.
Societies	apply in writing or telephone.
Green Fees	contact secretary.
Cards	💳 💳
Designer	Christy O'Connor Jnr
Facilities	⊗ by prior arrangement 🎯 by prior arrangement 🏌 💪 ♀ 🏌 🏠 🍴 🏌 🚗 ♿

| Hotel | ★★★ 65% Galway Ryan Hotel, Dublin Rd, GALWAY ☎ 091 753181 96 ➡ 📻 |

LOUGHREA   Map 01 B3

Loughrea Bullaun Rd, Graigue
☎ 091 841049 Fax 091 847472
An excellent parkland course with good greens and extended in 1992 to 18-holes. The course has an unusual feature in that it incorporates a historic souterrain (underground shelter/food store).
18 holes, 5261metres, Par 69, SSS 67, Course record 68.
Club membership 615.

Visitors	contact in advance, may not generally play Sun.
Societies	written application required. Anytime weekdays, 9-11.30 Sat, no play Sun.
Green Fees	not confirmed.
Designer	Eddie Hackett
Facilities	⊗ 🎯 🏌 💪 ♀ 🏠 ♿

| Hotel | ★★★ 64% Haydens Gateway Business, Leisure Hotel, BALLINASLOE ☎ 065 68 23000 47 ➡ 📻 |

MOUNTBELLEW   Map 01 B4

Mountbellew Ballinasloe ☎ 0905 79259
A 9-hole wooded parkland course with 2 quarries and penalty drains to provide hazards.
9 holes, 5143mtrs, Par 69, SSS 66.
Club membership 400.

Visitors	welcome. Contact club if you wish to play at weekends.
Societies	by prior arrangement.
Green Fees	IEP10 per 18 holes.
Facilities	🏌 💪 ♀ 🏠 ♿
Location	Of N63 midway between Roscommon/Galway

| Hotel | ★★★ 64% Haydens Gateway Business, Leisure Hotel, BALLINASLOE ☎ 065 68 23000 47 ➡ 📻 |

ORANMORE   Map 01 B3

Athenry Palmerstown ☎ 091 794466 Fax 091 794971
e-mail: athenrygc@eircom.net
Wooded parkland course.
18 holes, 5687metres, Par 70, SSS 70, Course record 67.
Club membership 1000.

Visitors	advisable to telephone in advance, may not play Sun or Sat am.
Societies	must apply in writing,telephone,e-mail.
Green Fees	IEP20 per day(IEP25 weekends).reductions in winter.
Cards	💳 💳
Prof	Raymond Ryan
Designer	Eddie Hackett

Facilities	⊗ 🎯 🏌 💪 ♀ 🏠 🍴 🏌 🚗 ♿ 🏌
Location	On R348 to Athenry 10km E of Galway City

| Hotel | ★★★ 65% Galway Ryan Hotel, Dublin Rd, GALWAY ☎ 091 753181 96 ➡ 📻 |

Galway Bay Golf & Country Club Renville
☎ 091 790500 Fax 091 792510 e-mail: gbaygolf@iol.ie
A championship golf course surrounded on three sides by the Atlantic Ocean and featuring water hazards on a number of holes. Each hole has its own characteristics made more obvious by the everchanging seaside winds. The design of the course highlights and preserves the ancient historic features of the Renville Peninsula. A spectacular setting distractingly beautiful and cleverly designed mix of holes presents a real golfing challenge, demanding total concentration.
18 holes, 6091mtrs, Par 72, SSS 73, Course record 68.
Club membership 440.

Visitors	Contact in advance.
Societies	Telephone in advance.
Green Fees	not confirmed.
Cards	💳 💳 💳 💳
Prof	Eugene O'Connor
Designer	Christy O'Connor Jnr
Facilities & Leisure	⊗ 🎯 🏌 💪 ♀ 🏠 🍴 🏌 🚗 ♿ 🏌 sauna.
Location	N18 S towards Limerick/Shannon, turn right for Oranmore at rdbt, through village, follow signs

| Hotel | ★★★ 65% Galway Bay Golf & Country Club Hotel, ORANMORE ☎ 091 790500 90 ➡ 📻 |

OUGHTERARD   Map 01 B4

Oughterard ☎ 091 552131 Fax 091 552377 e-mail: golfough@iol.ie
Redesigned in 1998 to USPGA standard, incorporating natural woodland and water features.
18 holes, 6660yds, Par 70, SSS 69, Course record 67.
Club membership 1000.

Visitors	contact secretary or professional in advance.
Societies	must apply in writing.
Green Fees	not confirmed.
Cards	💳 💳 💳
Prof	Michael Ryan
Designer	P Merrigan
Facilities	⊗ 🎯 🏌 💪 ♀ 🏠 🍴 🏌 🚗 ♿ 🏌
Location	1m from Oughterard on N59 from Galway

| Hotel | ★★★ 67% Ross Lake House Hotel, Rosscahill, OUGHTERARD ☎ 091 550109 & 550154 Fax 091 550184 13 ➡ 📻 |

PORTUMNA   Map 01 B3

Portumna ☎ 0509 41059 Fax 0509 41798
Parkland course with mature trees.
18 holes, 6172mtrs, Par 71, SSS 71.
Club membership 650.

Visitors	restricted Sun & public holidays.
Societies	must contact in writing.
Green Fees	IEP15(IEP18 weekends & bank holidays).

▶

Prof Richard Clarke
Designer E Connaughton
Facilities ⊗ ⍫ ⅃ ☏ ♟ ⚐ ⌂ ⚲ ⛳ ⚑ ⚒ ⚓
Location 2.5m from town on Woodford/Ennis road

Hotel ★★★ 60% County Arms Hotel, BIRR
☎ 0509 20791 24 ⇄ ♞

RENVYLE   Map 01 A4

Renvyle House Hotel ☎ 095 43511 Fax 43515
e-mail: renvyle@iol.ie
Pebble Beach course at Renvyle House is an exceptionally
demanding 9 hole course. Exposed to Atlantic winds,
crosswinds are a regular feature. A lake comes into play on 3
holes on one of which is a drive over water. On 4 holes
pebble beach and the sea demand precision.
Pebble Beach: 9 holes, 3500yds, Par 36, Course record 34.
Club membership 250.
Visitors Must contact in advance.
Societies Telephone in advance.
Green Fees IEP10 per round:IEP15 per day.
Cards ▭▭ ▬▬ ▭▭ ▭▭
Facilities ⊗ ⍫ ⅃ ☏ ♟ ⚐ ⚲ ⚓ ⛳
& Leisure hard tennis courts, heated outdoor swimming
pool, fishing.
Location From N59 West, right into Recess, left at
Kylemore, right at Letterfrack, proceed for 5m

Hotel ★★★ 66% Renvyle House Hotel, RENVYLE
☎ 095 43511 65 ⇄ ♞

TUAM   Map 01 B4

Tuam Barnacurragh ☎ 093 28993 Fax 093 26003
Parkland course with plenty of trees and bunkers.
18 holes, 5513mtrs, Par 72, SSS 69.
Club membership 800.
Visitors preferred Mon-Fri, must contact in advance. No
visitors weekends.
Societies telephone/write in advance.
Green Fees IEP18 per round.
Prof Larry Smyth
Designer Eddie Hackett
Facilities ⊗ ⍫ ⅃ ☏ ♟ ⚐ ⌂ ⚲ ⛳ ⚑ ⚒ ⚓
Location 0.5m from town on Athenry road

Hotel ★★★ 65% Galway Ryan Hotel, Dublin Rd,
GALWAY ☎ 091 753181 96 ⇄ ♞

CO KERRY

BALLYBUNION   Map 01 A3

BALLYBUNION See page 469

Looking for a driving range?
See the index at the back of the guide

BALLYFERRITER   Map 01 A2

Ceann Sibeal ☎ 066 9156255 Fax 066 9156409
e-mail: dinglegc@iol.ie
This most westerly golf course in Europe has a magnificent
scenic location. It is a traditional links course with beautiful
turf, many bunkers, a stream that comes into play on 14 holes
and, usually, a prevailing wind.
18 holes, 6700yds, Par 72, SSS 71, Course record 72.
Club membership 432.
Visitors telephone in advance.
Societies must contact in advance.
Green Fees IEP35 per day(IEP40 weekends).
Cards ▭▭ ▬▬
Prof Dermot O'Connor
Designer Hackett/O'Connor Jnr
Facilities ⊗ ⍫ ⅃ ☏ ♟ ⚐ ⌂ ⚲ ⛳
Location 1.5m from Ballyferriter

Hotel ★★★ 72% Dingle Skellig Hotel, DINGLE
☎ 066 9150200 116 ⇄ ♞

CASTLEGREGORY   Map 01 A2

Castlegregory Stradbally ☎ 066 7139444
A links course sandwiched between the sea and a freshwater
lake and mountains on two sides. The 3rd hole is visually
superb with a 365yard drive into the wind.
9 holes, 2569mtrs, Par 68, SSS 68, Course record 67.
Club membership 341.
Visitors advisable to contact in advance.
Societies apply in advance.
Green Fees IEP18 per 18 holes.
Designer Dr Arthur Spring
Facilities ⅃ ☏ ⚲ ⛳ ⚓
& Leisure fishing.
Location On Main Tralee/Castlegregory/Conor-pass road

Hotel ★★★ 64% Abbey Gate Hotel, Maine St,
TRALEE ☎ 066 7129888 100 ⇄ ♞

GLENBEIGH   Map 01 A2

Dooks ☎ 066 9768205 Fax 066 9768476
e-mail: office@dooks.com
Old-established course on the sea shore between the
Kerry mountains and Dingle Bay. Sand dunes are a
feature (the name Dooks is a derivation of the Gaelic
word for sand bank) and the course offers a fine
challenge in a superb Ring of Kerry location.
18 holes, 6010yds, Par 70, SSS 68.
Club membership 800.
Visitors must contact in advance. Members time
reserved.
Societies contact in advance.
Green Fees IEP25 per round; IEP35 per 36 holes.
Cards ▭▭ ▬▬ ▭▭ ▭▭
Facilities ⊗ ⍫ ⅃ ☏ ♟ ⚐ ⌂ ⚲ ⛳
Location On N70, between Killorglin and Glenbeigh

Hotel ★★★ 68% Gleneagle Hotel,
KILLARNEY ☎ 064 31870 213 ⇄ ♞

KENMARE   Map 01 B2

Kenmare Kilgarvan Rd ☎ 064 41291 Fax 064 42061
Extended to a championship 18-hole course in 1993 this
challenging parkland course enjoys a magnificent setting
where the cascading waters of the Sheen and Roughty rivers
join the Atlantic. Although it can be exacting on a good
golfer, it is never unfair to the weak or the novice golfer.
18 holes, 5615yds, Par 71.
Club membership 400.
Visitors   enquire for weekends.
Societies   contact in advance.
Green Fees   not confirmed.
Designer   Eddie Hackett
Facilities   ⓑ ▬ ♀ ♁ 🏠 ☂ ♂

Hotel   ★★★★♨ Park Hotel Kenmare, KENMARE
                   ☎ 064 41200 49 ⇄ ⋒

KILLARNEY   Map 01 B2

Beaufort Churchtown, Beaufort
☎ 064 44440 Fax 064 44752 e-mail: beaufortgc@tinet.ie
A championship standard Par 71 parkland course designed
by Dr Arthur Spring. This relatively new course is in the
centre of south-west Ireland's golfing mecca. Old ruins of an
11th century castle dominate the back nine and the whole
course is overlooked by the MacGillycuddy Reeks. The Par 3
8th and Par 4 11th are two of the most memorable holes.
18 holes, 6587yds, Par 71, SSS 72, Course record 70.
Club membership 300.

Visitors   booking advisable for weekends.
Societies   advance booking essential.
Green Fees   IEP30 per round(IEP38 weekends & bank
                   holidays).
Cards   ▭ ▬ ▭
Prof   Hugh Duggan
Designer   Arthur Spring
Facilities   ⓧ ⫟ ⓑ ▬ ♀ ♁ 🏠 ☂ ⚒ ♂
Location   7m W of Killarney, off N72 w

Hotel   ★★★ 67% Castlerosse Hotel, KILLARNEY
                   ☎ 064 31144 110 ⇄ ⋒

Killarney Golf & Fishing Club Mahony's Point
☎ 064 31034 Fax 064 33065
e-mail: kgc@iol.ie or raservations@killarney-golf.com
The three courses are parkland with tree-lined fairways,
many bunkers and small lakes which provide no mean
challenge. Mahoney's Point Course has a particularly
testing par 5, 4, 3 finish and the courses call for great
skill from the tee. Killarney has been the venue for many

important events, including the 1996 Curtis Cup, and is a
favourite of many famous golfers.
*Mahony's Point: 18 holes, 5826mtrs, Par 72, SSS 72,
Course record 64.*
*Killeen: 18 holes, 6001mtrs, Par 72, SSS 72,
Course record 68.*
Lackabane: 18 holes, 6011mtrs, Par 72, SSS 72.
Club membership 1300.
Visitors   must contact in advance & have a handicap
                   certificate.
Societies   must telephone in advance/apply in writing.
Green Fees   IEP50 per round.
Cards   ▭ ▬ ▭ ▭
Prof   Tony Coveney
Designer   H Longhurst/Sir Guy Campbell
Facilities   ⓧ ⫟ ⓑ ▬ ♀ ♁ 🏠 ☂ ♂ ⚓
& Leisure   sauna, gymnasium.
Location   On N 72, Ring of Kerry road

Hotel   ★★★★ 79% Aghadoe Heights Hotel,
                   KILLARNEY ☎ 064 31766 75 ⇄ ⋒

KILLORGLIN   Map 01 A2

Killorglin Stealroe
☎ 066 9761979 Fax 066 9761437 e-mail: kilgolf@iol.ie
A parkland course designed by Eddie Hackett as a challeng-
ing but fair test of golf, surrounded by magnificent views.
18 holes, 6497yds, Par 72, SSS 71, Course record 68.
Club membership 280.
Visitors   pre booking of tee time advisable, must be
                   confirmed in writing. Deposit required.
Societies   book by telephone, confirm in writing.
Green Fees   IEP18 per round (IEP20 weekends).
Cards   ▭ ▬ ▭
Designer   Eddie Hackett
Facilities   ⓧ ⫟ ⓑ ▬ ♀ ♁ 🏠 ☂ ⚒ ♂
& Leisure   fishing.
Location   3km from Killorglin, on N70 to Tralee

Guesthouse   ◆◆◆◆ The Grove Lodge, Killarney Rd,
                   KILLORGLIN ☎ 066 9761157 10 ⇄ ⋒

PARKNASILLA   Map 01 A2

Parknasilla ☎ 064 45122 Fax 064 45323
9 holes, 5400mtrs, Par 70, SSS 69.
Location   2m E of Sneem village on Ring of Kerry road
Telephone for further details

Hotel   ★★★★ 79% Great Southern Hotel,
                   PARKNASILLA ☎ 064 45122
                   26 ⇄ ⋒ Annexe59 ⇄ ⋒

Ballybunion

Ballybunion, *Co Kerry*   ☎ 068 27146   Fax 068 27387   Map 01 A3

e-mail: bbgolfc@ioe.ie

Hailed for its excellent links courses, Ballybunion is recognised for its fine development of the natural terrain. Mr Murphy built the Old Course in 1906. With large sand dunes and an Atlantic backdrop, Ballybunion offers the golfer an exciting round of golf in a scenic location but be warned, the Old Course is difficult to play in the wind. President Clinton played Ballybunion on his historic visit to Ireland in 1998.

Although overshadowed by the Old Course, the Cashen Course designed by Robert Trent Jones is also world class. Narrow fairways, small greens and large dunes characterise the course.

Visitors must contact in advance for reservations and details, subject to availability.
Societies apply in advance
Green Fees Old Course IEP75 per round, Cashen Course IEP40 per round ⊟ ▆ ▆
Facilities ⊗ ⅏ ▙ 🍷 ♀ 🍴 🏠 ⚐ ♂
Professional (Brian O'Callaghan)
Location Sandhill Rd, Ballybunion.
Holes/Par/Course record 36 holes.
Old Course: 18 holes, 6603 yds, Par 71, SSS 72, Course record 67
Cashen Course: 18 holes, 6216 yds, Par 72, SSS 72

Championship Course

WHERE TO STAY NEARBY

Hotels
BALLYHEIGE
★★★◉ 64% The White Sands
☎ 066 7133102. 81 ⇆ ♟

TRALEE
★★★ 69% Meadowlands, Oakpark
☎ 066 718044. 27 ⇆ ♟
★★★ 64% Abbey Gate, Maine St.
☎ 066 7129888. 100 (95 ⇆ 5 ♟)

TRALEE   Map 01 A2

Tralee West Barrow ☎ 066 7136379
Fax 066 7136008 e-mail: info@traleegolfclub.com
The first Arnold Palmer designed course in Europe, the
magnificent 18-hole links are set in spectacular scenery
on the Barrow peninsula surrounded on three sides by
the sea. Perhaps the most memorable hole is the par 4
17th which plays from a high tee, across a deep gorge to
a green perched high against a backdrop of mountains.
The first 9 holes are relatively easy, but the back 9 are
very difficult and not suitable for beginners.
18 holes, 5939mtrs, Par 71, SSS 71, Course record 66.
Club membership 1190.

Visitors	may play before 4.20pm on weekdays but only between 7.30-10.30am on Wed & 11am-1.30pm on Sat & 11.30-1pm bank holidays. Must have a handicap certificate and contact in advance. May not play Sun.
Societies	weekdays only; must contact in writing.
Green Fees	IEP75 per round.
Cards	💳 ▬ 💳
Prof	David Power
Designer	Arnold Palmer
Facilities	⊗ ⫙ ⓑ � ♀ ⌕ ⌂ ⚐ ⚵
Location	8m NW of Tralee off Spa-Fenit Road
Hotel	★★★ 69% Meadowlands Hotel, Oakpark, TRALEE ☎ 066 7180444 27 ⇔ ➤

WATERVILLE   Map 01 A2

Waterville House & Golf Links
☎ 066 9474102 Fax 066 9474482
e-mail: wvgolf@iol.ie
On the western tip of the Ring of Kerry, this course is
highly regarded by many top golfers. The feature holes
are the par five 11th, which runs along a rugged valley
between towering dunes, and the par three 17th, which
features an exceptionally elevated tee. Needless to say,
the surroundings are beautiful.
18 holes, 6549yds, Par 72, SSS 72, Course record 65.

Visitors	must contact in advance.
Societies	must contact secretary/manager in advance.
Green Fees	IEP100 per round(IEP50 before 8am & after 4pm Mon-Thur).
Cards	💳 ▬ 💳
Prof	Liam Higgins
Designer	Eddie Hackett
Facilities	⊗ ⫙ ⓑ ♀ ⌂ ⚐ ⌕ ➤ ⚵ ⚐
& Leisure	heated outdoor swimming pool, fishing, sauna.
Hotel	★★★ 72% Butler Arms Hotel, WATERVILLE ☎ 066 9474144 30 ⇔ ➤

AA Hotels that have special
arrangements with golf courses are listed at
the back of the guide

ATHY   Map 01 C3

Athy Geraldine ☎ 0507 31729
A meadowland course approaching its centenary year having
been founded in 1906.
18 holes, 6159yds, Par 71, SSS 69, Course record 69.
Club membership 475.

Visitors	time sheet in operation on Sundays
Societies	contact for infromation.
Green Fees	not confirmed.
Facilities	⫙ by prior arrangement ⓑ ♀ ♀ ⌂ ⚵
Location	2m N of Athy
Guesthouse	◆◆◆◆◆ Coursetown Country House, Stradbally Rd, ATHY ☎ 0507 31101 5 ➤

CARBURY   Map 01 C4

Highfield Highfield House
☎ 0405 31021 Fax 0405 31021 e-mail: hgc@indigo.ie
A relatively flat parkland course but with interesting
undulations, especially by the fast flowing stream which runs
through many holes. The 7th doglegs over the lake, the 10th
is a great Par 5 with a challenging green, the 14th Par 3 is
over rushes onto a plateau green (out of bounds on left) and
the 18th Par 3 green is tucked between bunkers and a huge
chestnut tree.
18 holes, 5707mtrs, Par 72, SSS 69.
Club membership 500.

Visitors	welcome, must contact in advance for weekend play.
Societies	telephone or apply in writing.
Green Fees	not confirmed.
Cards	💳 ▬ 💳
Prof	Peter O'Hagan
Designer	Alan Duggan
Facilities	ⓑ ♀ ♀ ⌂ ⚐ ➤ ⚵ ♀ ⚐
Location	9m from Enfield
Hotel	★★★ 73% Keadeen Hotel, NEWBRIDGE ☎ 045 431666 55 ⇔ ➤

CASTLEDERMOT   Map 01 C3

Kilkea Castle ☎ 0503 45555 Fax 0503 45505
e-mail: kilkeagolfclub@eircom.net

A beautiful course in the grounds of a 12th-century castle -
visible from all over the course. The River Griese and ▶

two lakes create numerous water hazards. The 16th and 17th are considered to be two of the best parkland holes in the country.
18 holes, 6200mtrs, Par 71, SSS 71.
Club membership 230.
Visitors   must contact in advance for details.
Societies   welcome, contact for details.
Green Fees IEP30 per round Mon-Thur(IEP35 Fri-sun).
Cards   🖅 💳 💳 🏧
Facilities   ⌂ 🏪 🍽 ♂
& Leisure   hard tennis courts, heated indoor swimming pool, fishing, sauna, solarium, gymnasium.

DONADEA   Map 01 C4

Knockanally Golf & Country Club
☎ 045 869322 Fax 045 869322 e-mail: golf@knockanally.com
Home of the Irish International Professional Matchplay championship, this parkland course is set in a former estate, with a Palladian-style clubhouse.
18 holes, 6485yds, Par 72, SSS 72, Course record 66.
Club membership 500.
Visitors   may not play on Sun 8.30am-noon.
Societies   must contact in writing or telephone.
Green Fees IEP20 per round (IEP30 weekends & Bank holidays).
Prof   Martin Darcy
Designer   Noel Lyons
Facilities   ⊗ 🏛 🏪 💪 ♀ ⌂ 🏪 🍽 ❦ ♂
& Leisure   fishing.
Location   3m off main Dublin-Galway road between Kilcock & Enfield

Hotel   ★★★ 64% Lucan Spa Hotel, LUCAN
☎ 01 6280495 & 6280497
Fax 01 6280841 71rm(61 ⇆ 🐾)

KILDARE   Map 01 C3

Cill Dara Cill Dara, Little Curragh
☎ 045 521295 & 521433
Only 1 mile from the famous Curragh racecourse, this 9-hole parkland course is unusual in having links type soil as well as plenty of trees.
9 holes, 5738mtrs, Par 71, SSS 70, Course record 64.
Club membership 500.
Visitors   welcome, Wed is Ladies Day and may only play after 1.30pm Sun (winter) and 4pm Sun (Summer).
Societies   apply in writing to Mr M O'Boyle, Professional.
Green Fees not confirmed.
Prof   Mark O'Boyle
Facilities   ⊗ 🏛 🏪 💪 ♀ ⌂ 🏪
Location   1m E of Kildare

Hotel   ★★★ 73% Keadeen Hotel, NEWBRIDGE
☎ 045 431666   55 ⇆ 🐾

The Curragh Curragh
☎ 045 441238 & 441714 Fax 045 441714
A particularly challenging course, well wooded and with lovely scenery all around.
18 holes, 6035mtrs, Par 72, SSS 71, Course record 63.
Club membership 1040.
Visitors   must contact in advance, preferred on Mon, Wed, Thu & Fri.

Societies   apply in writing.
Green Fees not confirmed.
Prof   Gerry Burke
Facilities   ⊗ 🏛 🏪 💪 ♀ ⌂ 🏪 🍽 ♂
Location   Off N7 between Newbridge & Kildare

Hotel   ★★★ 73% Keadeen Hotel, NEWBRIDGE
☎ 045 431666   55 ⇆ 🐾

KILL   Map 01 D4

Killeen ☎ 045 866003 Fax 045 875881
e-mail: admin@killeengc.ie
Set in pleasant countryside, the attractive course is characterised by its many lakes. It provides a challenge to test the skills of the moderate enthusiast and the more experienced golfer.
18 holes, 5561mtrs, Par 71, SSS 71, Course record 70.
Club membership 170.
Visitors   please ring for tee-times
Societies   must contact in advance.
Green Fees not confirmed.
Cards   💳 🏧
Designer   Pat Ruddy/M Kelly
Facilities   ⊗ 🏛 🏪 💪 ♀ ⌂ 🏪 🍽 ♂
Location   Off N7 at Kill signposted

Hotel   ★★★ 76% Barberstown Castle, STRAFFAN
☎ 01 6288157   22 ⇆ 🐾

NAAS   Map 01 D4

Bodenstown Sallins ☎ 045 897096
Bodenstown: 18 holes, 6132mtrs, Par 71, SSS 71.
Ladyhill: 18 holes, 5428mtrs, Par 71, SSS 68.
Location   4m from town near Bodenstown graveyard
Telephone for further details

Hotel   ★★★ 66% Downshire House Hotel, BLESSINGTON ☎ 045 865199
14 ⇆ 🐾 Annexe11 ⇆ 🐾

Craddockstown Blessington Rd
☎ 045 897610 Fax 045 896968
A gradually maturing parkland course featuring four testing par 3 holes, all over 140 metres in length, sand-based greens, and many trees. Easy walking.
18 holes, 5726mtrs, Par 71, SSS 69, Course record 66.
Club membership 800.
Visitors   should ring in advance to verify tee times available, limited at weekends.
Societies   apply in writing.
Green Fees IEP18(IEP20 Fri-Sun & bank holidays).
Cards   🖅
Designer   A Spring
Facilities   ⊗ 🏛 🏪 💪 ♀ ⌂ ♂
Location   Off the main dual carriageway (N7/N97), head towards Naas, turn left on to Blessington Road

Hotel   ★★★ 63% Ambassador Hotel, KILL
☎ 045 886700   36 ⇆ 🐾

Naas Kerdiffstown
☎ 045 897509 & 874644 Fax 045 896109
Scenic parkland course well bunkered, with a substantial number of trees, greens are both sand based and natural.
18 holes, 5663mtrs, Par 71, SSS 69, Course record 65.
Club membership 1000.

Visitors may not play on Sun, Tue or Thu.
Societies must contact in advance.
Green Fees not confirmed.
Cards 💳 🪧
Designer E Hackett/A Spring
Facilities ⊗ 🅱 💺 ♀ 🏌 𝄇
Location 1m from town on Sallins-Johnstown road

Hotel ★★★ 66% Downshire House Hotel,
BLESSINGTON ☎ 045 865199
14 ⇄ ♠ Annexe11 ⇄ ♠

Woodlands Cooleragh, Coill Dubh
☎ 045 860777 Fax 045 860988
Reconstructed 9-hole course opened in 1997 offering an
interesting challenge with completely new greens, tees and
an extra 1000 yards coming into play. Extended to 18 hole
course which opened in 1999.
9 holes, 6408yds, Par 72, SSS 71.
Club membership 454.
Visitors must contact in advance, unable to play most
weekends (member competitions).
Societies telephone in advance for details.
Green Fees not confirmed.
Designer Tommy Halpin
Facilities ⊗ 🎏 🅱 💺 ♀ 🏌 🏠 𝄇
Location Off the Clane/Edenderry road

Hotel ★★★ 73% Keadeen Hotel, NEWBRIDGE
☎ 045 431666 55 ⇄ ♠

STRAFFAN   Map 01 D4

Castlewarden ☎ 01 4589254 & 4589838 Fax 01 458897
e-mail: castlewarden@clubi.ie
Founded in 1990, Castlewarden is maturing into a delightful
parkland course with water features and excellent greens.
18 holes, 6496yds, Par 72, SSS 70.
Club membership 765.
Visitors welcome contact for details. Tues Ladies Day.
Societies by prior application.
Green Fees IEP17-IEP23 per round.
Cards 🪧
Prof Gerry Egan
Designer Tommy Halpin
Facilities 🏌 🏠 🍴 𝄇
Location Between Naas/Rathcoole

Hotel ★★★ 63% Ambassador Hotel, KILL
☎ 045 886700 36 ⇄ ♠

The K Club ☎ 01 6017300 Fax 01 6017399
e-mail: golf@kclub.ie
Designed by Arnold Palmer, its 6,456 metre length is a
challenge to even the best golfers. Covering 177 acres of
prime Kildare woodland there are 14 man-made lakes as
well as the River Liffey to create water hazards. There is
the promise of a watery grave at the monster 7th (Par 5,
520 metres) and at the 17th the tee shot is to the green on
the water's edge. There is also a practise area and driving
range.
18 holes, 6163mtrs, Par 72, SSS 72, Course record 60.
Club membership 520.
Visitors contact in advance to book prefered tee
times, restricted at members times.

The K Club

Societies telephone & write in advance, societies not
allowed on weekends & Wed afternoon.
Green Fees Summer: IEP175 per round; Winter: IEP85
per round.
Cards 💳 🪧 🪧 💷
Prof Ernie Jones
Designer Arnold Palmer
Facilities ⊗ 🎏 🅱 💺 ♀ 🏌 🏠 🍴 🐾 🛶 𝄇 ⓣ
& Leisure hard tennis courts, heated indoor swimming
pool, squash, fishing, sauna, solarium,
gymnasium.
Location From Dublin take N4 and axit R406,
entrance to hotel on right in Straffan

Hotel ★★★★★⚌ The Kildare Hotel & Country
Club, STRAFFAN ☎ 01 6017200
36 ⇄ ♠ Annexe9 ⇄ ♠

CO KILKENNY

CALLAN   Map 01 C3

Callan Geraldine ☎ 056 25136 & 25949 Fax 056 55155
Meadowland course with well positioned spinneys and water
hazards. Not difficult walking and a good test for golfers of
all standards.
18 holes, 6422yds, Par 72, SSS 70, Course record 66.
Club membership 700.
Visitors welcome. Advised to contact in advance.
Societies must apply in writing.
Green Fees IEP20 per round.
Cards 💳 🪧 🪧
Prof John O'Dwyer
Designer B Moore/J Power
Facilities ⊗ 🎏 🅱 💺 ♀ 🏠 🍴 🐾 🛶 𝄇
& Leisure fishing.
Location 1m from Callan on the Knocktopher Road

Hotel ★★★ 71% Newpark Hotel, KILKENNY
☎ 056 22122 111 ⇄ ♠

> Where to stay, where to eat?
> Visit the AA internet site
> www.theAA.com

Mount Juliet

| Mount Juliet, *Co Kilkenny* | ☎ 056 73000 | Fax 056 73019 | Map 01 C3 |

e-mail: info@mountjuliet.ie

Venue for the American Express World Golf Championships in September 2002, Mount Juliet's superb 18-hole golf course was designed by Jack Nicklaus, and has also been the chosen venue for many prestigious golfing events including the Irish Open on three occasions. The course boasts a cleverly concealed drainage and irrigation system, perfect even when inclement weather would otherwise preclude play, and takes advantage of the estate's mature landscape to provide a world-class 72-par challenge for professionals and high-handicap golfers alike.

A unique three-hole golfing academy has been added to offer both novice and experienced players ample opportunity to improve their games, while a new 18-hole putting course provides an extra dimension of golfing pleasure.

Visitors welcome, no restrictions but preferable to contact in advance

Societies book in advance by telephone or in writing

Green Fees IEP50-IEP100 depending on season. Discounts for groups and hotel residents. ⊞ ▥ ▭ ▣

Facilities ⊗ ⊪ ▙ ▄ ♀♨ 🛏 ⚐ 🏌 ⛳ 🏌 ♀ ⚲
3 hole Academy Course. Professional (Ted Higgins)

Leisure tennis, indoor swimming pool, private fishing, sauna, solarium, gym, horse riding, clay target shooting

Location N9, Dublin/Waterford Rd.

Holes/Par/Course record
18 holes, 6641 yds, Par 72, SSS 72, Course record 65

Championship Course

WHERE TO STAY NEARBY

Hotels
THOMASTOWN

★★★★ ⊛⊚ ♨♨ Mount Juliet Hotel
☎ 056 73000. 32 ⇄ 🐾 Annexe 27 ⇄ 🐾

KILKENNY

★★★ 65% Kilkenny, Ormonde, Ormonde Street. ☎ 056 62000. 103 ⇄ 🐾

★★★ 71% Newpark Hotel
☎ 056 23900. 118 (86 ⇄ 🐾)

KILKENNY   Map 01 C3

Kilkenny Glendine ☎ 056 65400 Fax 056 23593
One of Ireland's most pleasant inland courses, noted for
its tricky finishing holes and its par threes. Features of
the course are its long 11th and 13th holes and the
challenge increases year by year as thousands of trees
planted over the last 30 years or so are maturing. As host
of the Kilkenny Scratch Cup annually, the course is
permanently maintained in championship condition. The
Irish Dunlop Tournament and the Irish Professional
Matchplay Championship have also been held here.
18 holes, 5857mtrs, Par 71, SSS 70, Course record 64.
Club membership 1000.
Visitors   must contact in advance.
Societies   must contact in advance.
Green Fees IEP25(IEP30 weekends & bank holidays).
Cards   💳 💳
Prof   Noel Leahy
Facilities   ⊗ ⅷ ⅃ ♥ ♀ ⅍ 🏠 ⚐ ❦ ⚒ ⚔ ⌀ ʆ
Location   1m from centre on Castlecomer road

THOMASTOWN   Map 01 C3

THOMASTOWN See page 473

![CO LAOIS banner]

ABBEYLEIX   Map 01 C3

Abbeyleix Rathmoyle ☎ 0502 31450 Fax 0502 30108
A pleasant, parkland 9 hole course.
9 holes, 5626mtrs, Par 70, SSS 69.
Club membership 300.
Visitors   welcome weekdays.
Societies apply in writing.
Green Fees not confirmed.
Facilities ♀ ⅍ ⌀

Hotel   ★★★ 71% Newpark Hotel, KILKENNY
               ☎ 056 22122 111 ⇄ 🐾

MOUNTRATH   Map 01 C3

Mountrath Knockanina
☎ 0502 32558 & 32643 (office) Fax 0502 32643
A picturesque course at the foot of the Slieve Bloom
Mountains in central Ireland. The 18 hole course has fine
fairways and well bunkered greens, the river Nore flows
through the course.
18 holes, 5493mtrs, Par 71, SSS 69, Course record 68.
Club membership 650.
Visitors   check for availability at weekends, other days no
               problem but safer to check.
Societies must contact in advance.
Green Fees IEP12.
Facilities ⊗ by prior arrangement ⅃ ♥ ♀ ⅍ ❦ ⌀
Location   1.5m from town on Dublin-Limerick road

Hotel   ★★★ 73% Keadeen Hotel, NEWBRIDGE
               ☎ 045 431666 55 ⇄ 🐾

PORTARLINGTON   Map 01 C3

Portarlington Garryhinch ☎ 0502 23115 Fax 0502 23044
Lovely parkland course designed around a pine forest. It is
bounded on the 16th and 17th by the River Barrow which
makes the back 9 very challenging.
18 holes, 5723mtrs, Par 71, SSS 70, Course record 66.
Club membership 562.
Visitors   welcome but restricted Tue-Ladies Day, Sat &
               Sun societies and club competitions. Must
               contact in advance
Societies must apply in writing.
Green Fees IEP14 per round(IEP17 weekends & bank
               holidays).
Designer   Eddie Hackett
Facilities ⊗ ⅷ ⅃ ♥ ♀ ⅍ ⌀
Location   4m from town on Mountmellick road

Hotel   ★★★ 73% Keadeen Hotel, NEWBRIDGE
               ☎ 045 431666 55 ⇄ 🐾

PORTLAOISE   Map 01 C3

The Heath
☎ 0502 46533 & 46622 (Pro shop) Fax 0502 46866
One of the oldest clubs in Ireland. The course is set in pretty
countryside and offers a good challenge.
18 holes, 5736mtrs, Par 71, SSS 69, Course record 69.
Club membership 800.
Visitors   contact in advance, preferred on weekdays.
Societies apply in writing to Tom Hannon
Green Fees IEP10 per 18 holes(IEP20 weekends).
Prof   Eddie Doyle
Facilities ⅃ ♥ ♀ ⅍ 🏠 ❦ ⌀ ʆ
Location   3m N on N7

Hotel   ★★★ 73% Keadeen Hotel, NEWBRIDGE
               ☎ 045 431666 55 ⇄ 🐾

RATHDOWNEY   Map 01 C3

Rathdowney ☎ 0505 46170 Fax 0505 46065
A 18 hole course recently opened. Undulating terrain, 12th &
15th are particularly tough par 4 holes, 6th is a challenging
par 5 (550yds) into the prevaling wind. A good test for
golfers of all abilities.
18 holes, 5894mtrs, Par 71, SSS 70, Course record 67.
Club membership 400.
Visitors   welcome. Ladies have priority on Wed, Sat &
               Sun mornings are reserved for member &
               societies.
Societies must apply in writing and pay deposit to confirm
               booking.
Green Fees IEP12 per day(IEP15 weekends).
Designer   Eddie Hackett
Facilities ⊗ by prior arrangement ⅃ ♥ ♀ ⅍ ⌀
Location   0.5m SE. Follow signs from town square

Hotel   ★★★ 71% Newpark Hotel, KILKENNY
               ☎ 056 22122 111 ⇄ 🐾

CO LEITRIM

BALLINAMORE   Map 01 C4

Ballinamore ☎ 078 44346
A very dry and very testing 9-hole parkland course along the Ballinamore/Ballyconnell Canal.
9 holes, 5680yds, Par 68, SSS 66, Course record 66.
Club membership 300.
Visitors   wellcome 6 days per week,competition on most sundays.Visitors wellcome to play in open competitions.
Societies   must contact in writing.
Green Fees IEP10 per day.
Designer   A Spring
Facilities ♥♀⚐
& Leisure fishing.

Hotel   ★★★★ 67% Slieve Russell Hotel Golf and Country Club, BALLYCONNELL
☎ 049 9526 444 159 ⇆ ⋔

CARRICK-ON-SHANNON   Map 01 C4

Carrick-on-Shannon Woodbrook ☎ 079 67015
A pleasant 9-hole course overlooking the River Shannon. A fine test of golf for both those with low and high handicaps.
9 holes, 5545mtrs, Par 70, SSS 68.
Club membership 400.
Visitors   welcome, contact in advance to avoid competitions.
Societies   must contact in advance.
Green Fees not confirmed.
Designer   Eddie Hackett
Facilities ⊗ ⑂ ⮞ ♥ ♀ ⚐ ⛳ ⚑
Location   4m W beside N4

Hotel   ★★★★ 67% Slieve Russell Hotel Golf and Country Club, BALLYCONNELL
☎ 049 9526 444 159 ⇆ ⋔

CO LIMERICK

ADARE   Map 01 B3

Adare Manor ☎ 061 396204 Fax 061 396800
e-mail: brayfab@hotmail.com
An 18-hole parkland course, Par 69, in an unusual setting. The course surrounds the ruins of a castle, a friary and an abbey.
18 holes, 5800yds, Par 69, SSS 69.
Club membership 600.
Visitors   welcome weekdays, weekends only by arrangement and subject to availability.
Societies   by prior arrangement, preferably in writing.
Green Fees not confirmed.
Designer   Ben Sayers/Eddie Hacket
Facilities ⊗ ⑂ ⮞ ♥ ♀ ⚐ ⛳ ⚑
Location   10m from Limerick City

LIMERICK   Map 01 B3

Castletroy Castletroy
☎ 061 335753 & 335261 Fax 061 335373
e-mail: cgc@iol.ie
Parkland course with out of bounds on the left of the first two holes. The long par five 10th features a narrow entrance to a green guarded by a stream. The par three 13th has a panoramic view of the course and surrounding countryside from the tee and the 18th is a daunting finish, with the drive played towards a valley with the ground rising towards the green which is protected on both sides by bunkers. In recent years the club has hosted the finals of the Irish Mixed Foursomes and the Senior Championships.
18 holes, 5802mtrs, Par 71, SSS 71.
Club membership 1062.
Visitors   must contact in advance & have handicap certificate but may not play Sun or 1-2.30pm weekdays.
Societies   apply in writing.
Green Fees not confirmed.
Cards ▨
Facilities ⊗ ⑂ ⮞ ♥ ♀ ⚐ ⛳ ⚑ ⤳ ⚒ ⚓
Location   3m from city on Dublin road

Hotel   ★★★★ 71% Castletroy Park Hotel, Dublin Rd, LIMERICK ☎ 061 335566 107 ⇆ ⋔

Limerick Ballyclough ☎ 061 415146 Fax 061 319219
e-mail: lgc@eircom.net
Tree-lined parkland course which hosted the 1991 Ladies Senior Interprovincial matches. The club are the only Irish winners of the European Cup Winners Team Championship.
18 holes, 5938mtrs, Par 72, SSS 71, Course record 63.
Club membership 1300.
Visitors   may not play after 4pm or on Tue & weekends.
Societies   must contact in writing.
Green Fees IEP35 per day.
Cards ▦ ▨
Prof   Lee Harrington
Designer   A McKenzie
Facilities ⊗ ⑂ ⮞ ♥ ♀ ⚐ ⛳ ⚑
Location   3m S on Fedamore Road

Hotel   ★★★ 73% Jurys Hotel, Ennis Rd, LIMERICK
☎ 061 327777 95 ⇆ ⋔

Limerick County Golf & Country Club Ballyneety
☎ 61 351881 Fax 61 351384 e-mail: lcgolf@iol.ie
Limerick County was designed by Des Smyth and presents beautifully because of the strategic location of the main features. It stretches over undulating terrain with one elevated section providing views of the surrounding countryside. It features over 70 bunkers with six lakes and several unique design features.
18 holes, 6712yds, Par 72, SSS 74, Course record 70.
Club membership 400.
Visitors   welcome but prebooking essential.
Societies   book by telephone or in writing.
Green Fees IEP25(IEP30 weekends).
Cards ▦ ▦ ▨ ▨
Prof   Donal McSweeney
Designer   Des Smyth
Facilities ⊗ ⑂ ⮞ ♥ ♀ ⚐ ⛳ ⚑ ⚬ ⤳ ⚒ ⚓ ⚑
Location   5m SE of Limerick on R512

▶

Hotel   ★★★ 62% Greenhills Hotel, Caherdavin,
LIMERICK ☎ 061 453033 58 ⇆ ♠

NEWCASTLE WEST   Map 01 B3

Killeline Cork Rd ☎ 069 61600 Fax 069 77428
e-mail: killeline@eircom.net
Set in 160 acres of gently contoured parkland in the heart of
the Golden Vale with views to the Galtee Mountains.
Because of its design and many mature trees, accuracy in
playing is the key to good scoring.
18 holes, 6671yds, Par 72, SSS 68.
Club membership 200.
Visitors   welcome weekdays, by arrangement weekends,
                must contact in advance
Societies   telephone in advance.
Green Fees IEP15 per round.
Cards   ▦ ▦ ▦ ▦
Prof   Kevin Dorrian
Facilities ⊗ ⅏ ⅃ ▆ ♀ ⅄ ☆ ⅋ ⅌ ⌀
& Leisure   heated indoor swimming pool, sauna, solarium,
                gymnasium.
Location   0.25m off main Limerick/Killarney route

Hotel   ★★★ 77% Dunraven Arms Hotel, ADARE
☎ 061 396633 75 ⇆ ♠

Newcastle West Ardagh ☎ 069 76500 Fax 069 76511
A new course set in 150 acres of unspoilt countryside, built
to the highest standards on sandy free draining soil. A
practice ground and driving range are included. Hazards on
the course include lakes, bunkers, streams and trees. A
signature hole is likely to be the Par 3 6th playing 185 yards
over a lake.
18 holes, 6317yds, Par 71, SSS 72, Course record 67.
Club membership 730.

Visitors   advisable to contact in advance, but available
                most days.
Societies   contact in advance.
Green Fees not confirmed.
Cards   ▦ ▦
Prof   Ger Jones
Designer   Dr Arthur Spring
Facilities ⊗ ⅏ ⅃ ▆ ♀ ⅄ ☆ ⅋ ⌀ ⌁
Location   2m off N21 between Limerick & Killarney

Hotel   ★★★ 77% Dunraven Arms Hotel, ADARE
☎ 061 396633 75 ⇆ ♠

.

LONGFORD   Map 01 C4

County Longford Glack, Dublin Rd ☎ 043 46310
Fax 043 47082 e-mail: colonggolf@eircom.net
A lovely 18-hole parkland course with lots of trees.
18 holes, 6044yds, Par 70, SSS 69, Course record 69.
Club membership 819.
Visitors   very welcome, but advisable to telephone in
                advance for Tue and Sun play.
Societies   by prior arrangement.
Green Fees not confirmed.
Facilities ⅃ ▆ ♀ ⅄ ☆ ⅋ ⅌ ⌀
Location   E of town

Hotel   ★★★ 65% Abbey Hotel, Galway Rd,
ROSCOMMON ☎ 0903 26240 & 26505
Fax 0903 26021 25 ⇆ ♠

ARDEE   Map 01 D4

Ardee Townparks ☎ 041 6853227 Fax 041 6856137
Pleasant parkland course with mature trees and a stream.
18 holes, 6100yds, Par 70, SSS 71.
Club membership 680.
Visitors   may normally play on weekdays (except Wed).
Societies   apply in writing to Secretary/Manager
Green Fees IEP20(IEP30 weekends).
Cards   ▦
Prof   Joe Frowlev
Designer   Eddie Hackett
Facilities ⊗ ⅃ ▆ ♀ ⅄ ☆ ⅋ ⅌ ⌀ ⌁
Location   400 yards from Northern end of Ardee Main
                Street

Hotel   ★★★ 71% Ballymascanlon House Hotel,
DUNDALK ☎ 042 9371124 43 ⇆

BALTRAY   Map 01 D4

County Louth ☎ 041 9822329 Fax 041 9822969
e-mail: baltray@indego.ie
Generally held to have the best greens in Ireland, this
links course was designed by Tom Simpson to have well
guarded and attractive greens without being overly
dependant on bunkers. It provides a good test for the
modern champion, notably as the annual venue for the
East of Ireland Amateur Open.
18 holes, 6613yds, Par 73, SSS 71.
Club membership 1100.
Visitors   must contact in advance.
Societies   by prior arrangement.
Green Fees not confirmed.
Cards   ▦ ▦ ▦
Prof   Paddy McGuirk
Designer   Tom Simpson   ▶

Facilities	⊗ 〗⮾ ⅃ 🛌 ♀ ⚄ 🏠 ⛳ 🏴 ⬗ 🚜 ♂
& Leisure	hard tennis courts.
Location	5m NE of Drogheda

| Hotel | ★★★ 61% Conyngham Arms Hotel, SLANE ☎ 041 24155 16rm(15 ⇄ ☏) |

DUNDALK   Map 01 D4

Ballymascanlon House Hotel
☎ 042 9371124 Fax 042 9371598
e-mail: info@ballymascanlon.com
Now a testing 18-hole parkland course with numerous water hazards and two difficult holes through woodland, this very scenic course is set at the edge of the Cooley Mountains.
18 holes, 5548yds, Par 68, SSS 66.

Visitors	must telephone in advance to check availability.
Societies	booking by telephone or letter.
Green Fees	IEP16(IEP18 Fri-Sun).
Cards	🖃 ▦ ⬛ 🖃
Designer	Craddock/Ruddy
Facilities	⊗ 〗⮾ ⅃ 🛌 ♀ ⚄ 🏠 ⛳ 🏴 ♂
& Leisure	grass tennis courts, heated indoor swimming pool, sauna, gymnasium.
Location	3m N of Dundalk on the Carlingford road

| Hotel | ★★★ 71% Ballymascanlon House Hotel, DUNDALK ☎ 042 9371124 43 ⇄ |

Dundalk Blackrock ☎ 042 9321731 Fax 042 22022
A tricky course with extensive views.
18 holes, 6115mtrs, Par 72, SSS 72.
Club membership 1300.

Visitors	must contact in advance and may not play Tue or Sun.
Societies	must apply in writing in advance.
Green Fees	IEP35 per 18 holes.
Cards	🖃 ▦
Prof	Leslie Walker
Facilities	⊗ 〗⮾ ⅃ 🛌 ♀ ⚄ 🏠 ⛳ 🏴 ♂
& Leisure	sauna.
Location	2.5m S on coast road

| Hotel | ★★★ 71% Ballymascanlon House Hotel, DUNDALK ☎ 042 9371124 43 ⇄ |

Killinbeg Killin Park ☎ 042 39303
Opened in 1991 and designed by Eddie Hackett, this undulating 18-hole parkland course has mature woodland and river features.
18 holes, 5293yds, Par 69, SSS 65, Course record 67.
Club membershtp 100.

Visitors	no restrictions.
Societies	apply by telephone or in writing in advance.
Green Fees	not confirmed.
Designer	Eddie Hackett
Facilities	⮾ ⅃ 🛌 ♀ ⚄ 🏴 ♂
Location	Bridge-a-Crinn

| Hotel | ★★★ 71% Ballymascanlon House Hotel, DUNDALK ☎ 042 9371124 43 ⇄ |

GREENORE   Map 01 D4

Greenore ☎ 042 9373212 & 9373678 Fax 042 9373678
Situated amidst beautiful scenery on the shores of Carlingford Lough, with views of the Mourne Mountains. The pine trees here are an unusual feature on a semi-links course. There are quite a number of water facilities, tight fairways and very good greens.
18 holes, 6514yds, Par 71, SSS 71.
Club membership 500.

Visitors	must contact in advance at weekends.
Societies	must contact in advance.
Green Fees	not confirmed.
Designer	Eddie Hackett
Facilities	⊗ 〗⮾ ⅃ 🛌 ⅃ ♀ ⚄ 🚜 ♂

| Hotel | ★★★ 71% Ballymascanlon House Hotel, DUNDALK ☎ 042 9371124 43 ⇄ |

TERMONFECKIN   Map 01 D4

Seapoint ☎ 041 9822333 Fax 041 9822331
e-mail: golflinks@seepoint.ie
A very long championship links course of 7,000 yards with a particularly interesting 17th hole.
18 holes, 6420mtrs, Par 72, SSS 74.
Club membership 470.

Visitors	phone in advance for restrictions.
Societies	telephone in advance.
Green Fees	IEP25(IEP35 weekends & bank holidays).
Cards	🖃 ▦
Prof	David Carroll
Designer	Des Smyth
Facilities	⊗ 〗⮾ ⅃ 🛌 ⅃ ♀ ⚄ 🏠 ⛳ 🏴 ⬗ 🚜 ♂ ⫟
Location	4m NE of Drogheda

| Hotel | ★★★ 61% Conyngham Arms Hotel, SLANE ☎ 041 24155 16rm(15 ⇄ ☏) |

CO MAYO

BALLINA   Map 01 B4

Ballina Mossgrove, Shanaghy
☎ 096 21050 Fax 096 21050
Undulating but mostly flat inland course.
18 holes, 6103yds, Par 71, SSS 69, Course record 69.
Club membership 478.

▶

Visitors welcome but may not play Sun before 3.30pm. Restrictions apply depending on competitions/society visits.
Societies apply in writing or telephone in advance.
Green Fees not confirmed.
Cards 🔲 🔲 🔲
Designer E Hackett
Facilities 🏌 ⛳ ♀ ♨ 🏌 🛒 ♂
Location 1m outside town on Bonnocolon Rd

BALLINROBE Map 01 B4

Ballinrobe Cloonagashel ☎ 092 41118 Fax 092 41889
e-mail: bgcgolf@ioi.ie
A championship parkland 18 hole course, set in the mature woodlands of a historic estate at Cloonacastle. The layout of the course incorporates seven man made lakes with the River Robe flowing at the back of the 3rd and 5th greens. Ballinrobe is full of charm and character typified by the 19th century period residence now used as the clubhouse.
18 holes, 6043mtrs, Par 73, SSS 72, Course record 69.
Club membership 570.
Visitors welcome daily, telephone to reserve Tee-time.
Societies must telephone or write to Secretary in advance.
Green Fees not confirmed.
Cards 🔲 🔲
Prof David Kearney
Designer Eddie Hackett
Facilities ⊗ 🏌 ⛳ ♀ ♨ 🍴 🏌 ⚐ 🛒 ♂ ⛏
Location Off N84 onto R331 to Claremorris

Hotel ★★★ 67% Breaffy House Hotel, CASTLEBAR ☎ 094 22033 59 ⇄ ⁅

BALLYHAUNIS Map 01 B4

Ballyhaunis Coolnaha ☎ 0907 30014 Fax 094 81829
e-mail: tmack@tinet.ie
Undulating parkland course with 9 holes, 10 greens and 18 tees.
9 holes, 5413mtrs, Par 70, SSS 68, Course record 68.
Club membership 340.
Visitors welcome all times but must avoid members competitions on Sun & Thu.
Societies must apply in writing or telephone.
Green Fees IEP10 per day.
Facilities 🏌 ⛳ ♀ ♨ ♂ ⛏
Location 3m N on N83

Hotel ★★★ 67% Breaffy House Hotel, CASTLEBAR ☎ 094 22033 59 ⇄ ⁅

BELMULLET Map 01 A5

Carne Carne ☎ 097 82292 Fax 097 81477
e-mail: carngolf@iol.ic
18 holes, 6119mtrs, Par 72, SSS 72, Course record 72.
Club membership 460.
Visitors welcome, booking essential to guarantee tee-time.
Societies booking advisable.
Green Fees not confirmed.
Designer Eddie Hackett
Facilities ⊗ 🌃 🏌 ⛳ ♀ ♨ ⚐ 🛒 ♂
Location 2m from Belmullet

CASTLEBAR Map 01 B4

Castlebar Hawthorn Av, Rocklands
☎ 094 21649 Fax 094 26088
e-mail: castlebargolf@eircom.ie
Mature testing treelined parkland course, where an accurate tee shot is essential. A steady putting stroke is needed if par is to be achieved on the course's sloping grounds.
18 holes, 5698mtrs, Par 71, SSS 70.
Club membership 950.
Visitors very welcome weekdays, must contact in advance for weekend play. No vistors on Sun.
Societies must contact in advance.
Green Fees IEP20 per day (IEP25 Fri,Sat & Sun).
Designer Peter Mcevoy
Facilities 🏌 ⛳ ♀ ♨ ♫ 🛒 ♂
Location 1m from town on Belcarra road

Hotel ★★★ 67% Breaffy House Hotel, CASTLEBAR ☎ 094 22033 59 ⇄ ⁅

CLAREMORRIS Map 01 B4

Claremorris Castlemagarrett ☎ 094 71527
e-mail: claremorris@ebookireland.com
A 9-hole parkland course on hilly terrain. A new 18-hole course is due to open in 1998 and will feature plenty of mature trees and numerous water hazards.
18 holes, 6600mtrs, Par 73, SSS 70, Course record 68.
Club membership 550.
Visitors contact club for availability.
Societies contact 094 71527 for details.
Green Fees IEP18 per round (IEP20 weekends).
Designer Tom Craddock
Facilities ⊗ by prior arrangement ⫼ by prior arrangement 🏌 ⛳ ♀ ♨ 🏌 🛒 ♂
Location 1.5m from town, on N17 S of Claremorris

Hotel ★★★ 59% Belmont Hotel, KNOCK ☎ 094 88122 64 ⇄ ⁅

KEEL Map 01 A4

Achill Achill Island, Westport ☎ 098 43456
Seaside links in a scenic location on the edge of the Atlantic Ocean.
9 holes, 2723yds, Par 70, SSS 66, Course record 69.
Club membership 200.
Visitors welcome but cannot play on some Sundays
Societies must write or telephone in advance.
Green Fees not confirmed.
Facilities ⛳ ♨ ♫ ♂
Location 15 Km towards Keel Village

Hotel ★★★ 70% Hotel Westport, The Demesne, Newport Rd, WESTPORT ☎ 098 25122 129 ⇄ ⁅

SWINFORD Map 01 B4

Swinford Brabazon Park ☎ 094 51378 Fax 094 51378
A pleasant parkland course with good views of the beautiful surrounding countryside.
9 holes, 5542mtrs, Par 70, SSS 68.
Club membership 420.

▶

Visitors must contact in advance in peak season.
Societies must apply in writing or telephone in advance.
Green Fees IEP10 per day.
Facilities ⚐ ✿

Hotel ★★★ 67% Breaffy House Hotel,
CASTLEBAR ☎ 094 22033 59 ⇄ ☏

WESTPORT Map 01 B4

Westport Carrowholly ☎ 098 28262 & 27070
Fax 098 27217 e-mail: wpgolf@iol.ie
This is a beautiful course with wonderful views of Clew
Bay, with its 365 islands, and the holy mountain called
Croagh Patrick, famous for the annual pilgrimage to its
summit. Golfers indulge in a different kind of penance
on this challenging course with many memorable holes.
Perhaps the most exciting is the par five 15th, 580 yards
long and featuring a long carry from the tee over an inlet
of Clew Bay.
18 holes, 6667yds, Par 73, SSS 71, Course record 65.
Club membership 750.
Visitors must contact in advance. No visitors during
members times.
Societies apply in writing or telephone well in
advance.
Green Fees IEP25-IEP30 per 18 holes.
Cards ▥
Prof Alex Mealia
Designer Fred Hawtree
Facilities ⊗ 〗 ▙ ▆ ♀ ⚐ 🖼 ☏ ➤ ⚒ ✿
Location 2.5m from town

Hotel ★★★ 70% Hotel Westport, The Demesne,
Newport Rd, WESTPORT
☎ 098 25122 129 ⇄ ☏

CO MEATH

BETTYSTOWN Map 01 D4

Laytown & Bettystown ☎ 041 27170 Fax 041 28506
A very competitive and trying links course, home of famous
golfer, Des Smyth.
18 holes, 5652mtrs, Par 71, SSS 70.
Club membership 950.
Visitors may not play 1-2pm. Advisable to contact in
advance.
Societies must contact in writing.
Green Fees not confirmed.
Cards ▥ ▥
Prof Robert J Browne
Facilities ⊗ 〗 ▙ ▆ ♀ ⚐ 🖼 ☏ ✿
& Leisure hard tennis courts.

Hotel ★★★ 61% Conyngham Arms Hotel, SLANE
☎ 041 24155 16rm(15 ⇄ ☏)

Entries with a green background
identify courses considered to be
particularly interesting

DUNSHAUGHLIN Map 01 D4

Black Bush Thomastown ☎ 01 8250021 Fax 01 8250400
e-mail: golf@blackbush.iol.ie
Three 9-hole courses, giving three possible 18-hole
combinations, set in lovely parkland, with a lake providing a
hazard at the 1st. Recently added creeks, trees and bunkers
make for challenging and accurate shot-making.
Black Bush: 18 holes, 6930yds, Par 73, SSS 72.
Agore: 18 holes, 6598yds, Par 71, SSS 69.
Thomastown: 18 holes, 6433yds, Par 70, SSS 68.
Club membership 950.

Visitors must contact in advance but cannot play 1-2pm
weekdays.
Societies advance booking required.
Green Fees not confirmed.
Cards ▥ ▥
Prof Shane O'Grady
Designer Bobby Browne
Facilities ⊗ 〗 ▙ ▆ ♀ ⚐ 🖼 ☏ ➤ ⚒ ✿ ☍
Location 1.5m from village on Dunshaughlin-Ratoath
raod

Hotel ★★★ 70% Finnstown Country House Hotel,
Newcastle Rd, LUCAN
☎ 01 6280644 25 ⇄ ☏ Annexe26 ⇄ ☏

KELLS Map 01 C4

Headfort ☎ 046 40857 40146 Fax 046 49282
A delightful parkland course which is regarded as one of
the best of its kind in Ireland. There are ample
opportunities for birdies, but even if these are not
achieved, Headfort provides for a most pleasant game. A
further 18 hole course has recently opened and promises
to be equally challenging.
36 holes, 6007mtrs, Par 72, SSS 71, Course record 67.
Club membership 1162.
Visitors restricted Tues Ladies Day. Must contact in
advance.
Societies must apply in writing.
Green Fees Old Course:IEP25(IEP30 weekends).New
Course:IEP35.
Cards ▥ ▥ ▥
Prof Brendan McGovern
Facilities ⊗ 〗 ▙ ▆ ♀ ⚐ 🖼 ☏ ✿

Hotel ★★★ 62% Ardboyne Hotel, Dublin Rd,
NAVAN ☎ 046 23119 29 ⇄ ☏

KILCOCK
Map 01 C4

Kilcock Gallow ☎ 01 6287592 Fax 01 6287283
A parkland course with wide, gently undulating fairways, flat greens and light rough only.
18 holes, 5775mtrs, Par 72, SSS 70, Course record 69.
Club membership 450.
Visitors   must contact in advance for weekends, no problem weekdays.
Societies   telephone for dates available.
Green Fees   IEP14 per 18 holes(IEP16 weekends & bank holidays).
Designer   Eddie Hackett
Facilities   ⊗ �𝄞 🏌 ♥ ♀ ♨ 🏌 ✓
Location   2m from end of M4

Hotel   ★★★ 64% Lucan Spa Hotel, LUCAN
☎ 01 6280495 & 6280497
Fax 01 6280841 71rm(61 ⇌ ↑)

NAVAN
Map 01 C4

Royal Tara Bellinter
☎ 046 25508 & 25244 Fax 046 25508
e-mail: info@royaltaragolfclub.com
Pleasant parkland course offering plenty of variety. Situated close to the Hill of Tara, the ancient seat of the Kings of Ireland.
New Course: 18 holes, 5757mtrs, Par 71, SSS 70.
Bellinter Nine: 9 holes, 3184yds, Par 35, SSS 35.
Club membership 1000.
Visitors   prior arrangement is advisable. Tue is ladies day.
Societies   apply in writing or telephone.
Green Fees   IEP25 per 18 holes(IEP30 weekends).
Prof   Adam Whiston
Designer   Des Smyth
Facilities   ⊗ �𝄞 🏌 ♥ ♀ ♨ 🏠 ⛳ ⚐ 🏌 ✓
Location   6m from town on N3

Hotel   ★★★ 62% Ardboyne Hotel, Dublin Rd,
NAVAN ☎ 046 23119 29 ⇌ ↑

TRIM
Map 01 C4

County Meath Newtownmoynagh
☎ 046 31463 Fax 046 37554
Originally a 9-hole course opened in 1971, it was extended to 18-holes in 1990. It is maturing into a very challenging and formidable course with four testing Par 5's. Luxurious clubhouse with panoramic views across the course.
18 holes, 6720mtrs, Par 73, SSS 72, Course record 68.
Club membership 900.
Visitors   welcome; some restrictions telephone for details.
Societies   not Sun, enquiries welcome.
Green Fees   IEP20(IEP25 Fri-Sun & bank holidays).
Cards   💳 💳 💳 💳
Prof   Robin Machin
Designer   Eddie Hackett/Tom Craddock
Facilities   ⊗ ⟨⟨ 🏌 ♥ ♀ ♨ 🏠 ✓
& Leisure   snooker.
Location   3m outside Trim on Trim/Longwood rd

Hotel   ★★★ 61% Conyngham Arms Hotel, SLANE
☎ 041 24155 16rm(15 ⇌ ↑)

CARRICKMACROSS
Map 01 C4

Mannan Castle Donaghmoyne
☎ 042 9663308 Fax 042 9663195
Parkland and picturesque, the course features the Par 3 2nd to an island green. The short Par 4 12th through the woods and the 14th to 18th, all crossing water at least once. A test of golf for both amateur and professional.
18 holes, 6500yds, Par 70, SSS 69.
Club membership 700.
Visitors   may play anytime except competition times Sat, Sun & Wed from 2-2.30pm.
Societies   apply in writing to the secretary.
Green Fees   not confirmed.
Designer   F Ainsworth
Facilities   🏌 ♥ ♀ ♨
Location   4m N

Hotel   ★★★ 71% Ballymascanlon House Hotel,
DUNDALK ☎ 042 9371124 43 ⇌

Nuremore
☎ 042 9661438 & 9664016 Fax 042 9661853 e-mail: nuremore@eircom.net
Picturesque parkland course of championship length incorporating the drumlins and lakes which are a natural feature of the Monaghan countryside. Precision is required on the 10th to drive over a large lake and between a narrow avenue of trees. Signature hole 18th.
18 holes, 6400yds, Par 71, SSS 69, Course record 67.
Club membership 200.

Visitors   welcome all times but must contact Maurice Cassidy in advance.
Societies   must contact in advance.
Green Fees   not confirmed..
Cards   💳 💳 💳 💳
Prof   Maurice Cassidy
Designer   Eddie Hackett
Facilities   ⊗ ⟨⟨ 🏌 ♥ ♀ ♨ 🏠 ⛳ ⚐ 🏌 ✓
& Leisure   hard tennis courts, heated outdoor swimming pool, squash, fishing, sauna, gymnasium.
Location   1m S of Carrickmacross, on main N2

Hotel   ★★★★ 75% Nuremore Hotel,
CARRICKMACROSS
☎ 042 9661438 72 ⇌ ↑

CASTLEBLAYNEY   Map 01 C4

Castleblayney Onomy ☎ 042 40451 Fax 042 40451
e-mail: rayben@eircom.com
Scenic course on Muckno Park estate, adjacent to Muckno
Lake and Hope Castle.
9 holes, 5378yds, Par 68, SSS 66, Course record 68.
Club membership 275.
Visitors   no visitors allowed during major weekend
         competitions.
Societies   must contact in advance.
Green Fees not confirmed.
Designer   Bobby Browne
Facilities   ฿ 🍴 ♀ ⚒
& Leisure   fishing.
Location   Situated on the Hope Castle Estate, in the town
         of Castleblayney

Hotel   ★★★ 71% Ballymascanlon House Hotel,
         DUNDALK ☎ 042 9371124   43 ⇆

CLONES   Map 01 C5

Clones Hilton Park ☎ 047 56017
Parkland course set in Drumlin country. Due to limestone
belt, the course is very dry and playable all year round. There
is a timesheet in operation on Saturday and Sunday.
9 holes, 5206mtrs, Par 68, SSS 67, Course record 62.
Club membership 330.
Visitors   must contact in advance.Timesheets i operation
         at weekends.
Societies   apply in writing.
Green Fees IEP10 per day (IEP12 weekends).
Cards   ▨ ▨
Designer   Cromwell
Facilities   ⊗ 〗 ฿ 🍴 ♀ ⚒ ✎
Location   3m from Clones on Scotshouse rd

Hotel   ★★★★ 60% Hillgrove Hotel, Old Armagh Rd,
         MONAGHAN ☎ 047 81288   44 ⇆ ⌐

MONAGHAN   Map 01 C5

Rossmore Rossmore Park, Cootehill Rd ☎ 047 71222
An undulating 18-hole parkland course amidst beautiful
countryside.
18 holes, 5590mtrs, Par 70, SSS 69, Course record 62.
Club membership 800.
Visitors   must contact in advance, telephone Pro Shop on
         047 71222.
Societies   must apply in writing.
Green Fees IEP20 per day.
Prof   Mark Nicholson
Designer   Des Smyth
Facilities   ฿ 🍴 ♀ ⚒ 🏠 ⛳ ✎ 𝆑
& Leisure   snooker & pool.
Location   2m S on Cootehill Road

Hotel   ★★★★ 60% Hillgrove Hotel, Old Armagh Rd,
         MONAGHAN ☎ 047 81288   44 ⇆ ⌐

Looking for a driving range?
See the index at the back of the guide

CO OFFALY

BIRR   Map 01 C3

Birr The Glenns ☎ 0509 20082 Fax 0509 22155
The course has been laid out over undulating parkland
utilising the natural contours of the land, which were created
during the ice age. The sandy subsoil means that the course is
playable all year round.
18 holes, 5700mtrs, Par 70, SSS 70, Course record 62.
Club membership 750.
Visitors   contact in advance.
Societies   advance contact to secretary.
Green Fees IEP15 (IEP20 weekends).
Designer   Eddie Connaughton
Facilities   ⊗ 〗 ฿ 🍴 ♀ ⚒ 🏠 ⛳ ➤ ⚒ ✎ 𝆑
Location   2 miles W of Birr town en route to Banagher)

Hotel   ★★★ 60% County Arms Hotel, BIRR
         ☎ 0509 20791 24 ⇆ ⌐

EDENDERRY   Map 01 C4

Edenderry ☎ 0405 31072
A most friendly club which offers a relaxing game in
pleasant surroundings. In 1992 the course was extended to 18
holes.
18 holes, 6029mtrs, Par 72, SSS 72, Course record 66.
Club membership 700.
Visitors   restricted Thu & weekends, ring for times.
Societies   may not play on Thu & Sun; must contact the
         secretary in writing.
Green Fees not confirmed.
Designer   Havers/Hackett
Facilities   ⚒ ✎

TULLAMORE   Map 01 C4

Tullamore Brookfield ☎ 0506 21439 Fax 0506 41806
Well wooded parkland course.
18 holes, 6500yds, Par 70, SSS 71, Course record 68.
Club membership 975.
Visitors   must contact in advance, restricted on Tue & at
         weekends.
Societies   must contact in writing.
Green Fees IEP25 per 18 holes(IEP30 Sat & bank holidays).
Cards   ▨
Prof   Donagh McArdle
Designer   James Braid/Paddy Merrigam
Facilities   ⊗ 〗 ฿ 🍴 ♀ ⚒ 🏠 ⛳ ✎
Location   2.5m SW on Kinnity road

Hotel   ★★★ 59% Prince Of Wales Hotel,
         ATHLONE ☎ 0902 72626 73 ⇆ ⌐

AA Hotels that have special
arrangements with golf courses are listed at
the back of the guide

ATHLONE
Map 01 C4

Athlone Hodson Bay ☎ 0902 92073
A picturesque course with a panoramic view of Lough Ree.
Overall, it is a tight, difficult course with some outstanding
holes and is noted for its magnificent greens. Many
championships have taken place here including the 1998 All
Ireland Cups and Shields finals.
18 holes, 5854mtrs, Par 71, SSS 71.
Club membership 1250.
Visitors must contact in advance.
Societies apply in writing.
Green Fees IEP20 per round (IEP22 weekends).
Cards
Prof Martin Quinn
Designer J McAllister
Facilities ⊗ ⅢⅢ ⒧ ■ ♀ ♨ 🕋 ☂ ♋ ♨ ♂
Location 4m from town beside Lough Ree

Hotel ★★★ 70% Hodson Bay Hotel, Hodson Bay,
ATHLONE ☎ 0902 92444 133 ⊆ 📞

BALLAGHADERREEN
Map 01 B4

Ballaghaderreen ☎ 0907 60295
Mature 9-hole course with an abundance of trees. Accuracy
off the tee is vital for a good score. Small protected greens
require a good short-iron plan. The Par 3, 5th hole at 178
yards has ruined many a good score.
9 holes, 5727yds, Par 70, SSS 67, Course record 68.
Club membership 250.
Visitors no restrictions.
Societies apply in writing or telephone during office
hours.
Green Fees IEP10 per day.
Designer Paddy Skerritt
Facilities ⒧ ■ ♨ ♂
Location 2m S of town

Hotel ★★★ 62% Markree Castle, COLLOONEY
☎ 071 67800 30 ⊆ 📞

BOYLE
Map 01 B4

Boyle Roscommon Rd ☎ 079 62594
Situated on a low hill and surrounded by beautiful scenery,
this is an undemanding course where, due to the generous
fairways and semi-rough, the leisure golfer is likely to finish
the round with the same golf ball.
9 holes, 5324yds, Par 67, SSS 66, Course record 65.
Club membership 288.
Visitors no restrictions.
Societies must contact in writing.
Green Fees IEP10 per day.
Designer E Hackett
Facilities ⊗ by prior arrangement ⅢⅢ by prior arrangement
⒧ ■ ♀ ☂
Location 2m from Boyle on the Roscommon road

Hotel ★★★ 62% Markree Castle, COLLOONEY
☎ 071 67800 30 ⊆ 📞

CASTLEREA
Map 01 B4

Castlerea Clonalis ☎ 0907 20068 & 20705
9 holes, 4974mtrs, Par 68, SSS 66, Course record 62.
Location On Dublin/Castlebar road
Telephone for further details

Hotel ★★★ 65% Abbey Hotel, Galway Rd,
ROSCOMMON ☎ 0903 26240 & 26505
Fax 0903 26021 25 ⊆ 📞

ROSCOMMON
Map 01 B4

Roscommon Mote Park
☎ 0903 26382, 26931 Fax 0903 26043
Located on the rolling pastures of the old Mote Park estate,
this recently extended 18-hole course successfully blends the
old established nine holes with an exciting and equally
demanding new 9-hole lay-out. Numerous water hazards,
notably on the tricky 13th, multi-tiered greens and an
excellent irrigation to give an all-weather surface.
18 holes, 6290mtrs, Par 72, SSS 70.
Club membership 650.
Visitors contact in advance,especially Sundays.
Societies apply in writing.
Green Fees IEP15 per day; Nov-Mar IEP10.
Designer E Connaughton
Facilities ⊗ ⅢⅢ ⒧ ■ ♀ ♨ ☂ ♋ ♂
Location 0.5m S of Roscommon town

Hotel ★★★ 65% Abbey Hotel, Galway Rd,
ROSCOMMON ☎ 0903 26240 & 26505
Fax 0903 26021 25 ⊆ 📞

STROKESTOWN
Map 01 C4

Strokestown Bumlin ☎ 078 33528
Picturesque 9-hole course set in parkland with fine views of
Cloonfinlough Lake. The three Par 3's are long and quite
testing.
9 holes, 2615mtrs, Par 68.
Club membership 250.
Visitors may play any times except during competitions.
Societies apply in writing or telephone at least 2 weeks in
advance.
Green Fees IEP10 per day.
Facilities ♨
Location 1.5m from Strokestown

Hotel ★★★ 65% Abbey Hotel, Galway Rd,
ROSCOMMON ☎ 0903 26240 & 26505
Fax 0903 26021 25 ⊆ 📞

Where to stay, where to eat?
Visit the AA internet site
www.theAA.com

CO SLIGO

BALLYMOTE   Map 01 B4

Ballymote Ballinascarrow ☎ 071 83158 & 83089
e-mail: jocon@iol.ie
Although Ballymote was founded in 1940, the course dates from 1993 and has matured well into a parkland course with ample fairways and large greens. Wonderful views of Ballinascarow Lake. Ideal for family groups.
9 holes, 5302mtrs, Par 68, SSS 67.
Club membership 250.
Visitors   must contact in advance.
Societies   telephone in advance.
Green Fees IEP10 per day.
Prof   Leslie Robinson
Designer   Eddie Hacket
Facilities   🍺🏌⚑♂
& Leisure   fishing.
Location   1m N

Hotel   ★★★ 62% Markree Castle, COLLOONEY
           ☎ 071 67800 30 ⇄ ☏

ENNISCRONE   Map 01 B5

Enniscrone ☎ 096 36297 Fax 096 36657
e-mail: enniscronegolf@eircom.ie
In a magnificent situation with breathtaking views of mountain, sea and rolling countryside, this course offers some unforgettable golf. It was host to the West of Ireland championship and the Ladies Irish Close in 1997. It offers an exciting challenge among its splendid sandhills and a particularly favourite hole is the tenth, with a marvellous view from the elevated tee and the chance of a birdie with an accurate drive.
18 holes, 6620yds, Par 72, SSS 72, Course record 66.
Club membership 750.
Visitors   must contact in advance, may not play before 11am or between 1.00 & 4pm on Sun.
Societies   must telephone in advance.
Green Fees not confirmed.
Cards   🗖🗖🗖
Prof   Charlie McGoldrick
Designer   E Hackett
Facilities   ⊗🍖🏌🍺♀♂🏠⚑🛒🍴
Location   0.5m S on Ballina road

SLIGO   Map 01 B5

County Sligo Rosses Point ☎ 071 77134 or 77186
Fax 071 77460 e-mail: cosligo@iol.ie
Now considered to be one of the top links courses in Ireland, County Sligo is host to a number of competitions, including the West of Ireland Championships and Internationals. Set in an elevated position on cliffs above three large beaches, the prevailing winds provide an additional challenge. Tom Watson described it as "a magnificent links, particularly the stretch of holes from the 14th to the 17th."
18 holes, 6043mtrs, Par 71, SSS 72, Course record 67.
Bowmore: 9 holes, 2785mtrs, Par 35, SSS 35.
Club membership 1069.

Visitors   advisable to contact in advance, available most days except Captains or Presidents days. Deposit required to secure.
Societies   must contact in writing & pay a deposit.
Green Fees IEP40 per 18 holes(IEP50 Fri-Sun).Bomore Course IEP15 per 9 holes.
Cards   🗖🗖🗖
Prof   Jim Robinson
Designer   Harry Colt
Facilities   ⊗🍖🏌🍺♀♂🏠⚑🛒🍴
Location   Off N15 to Donegal

Hotel   ★★★ 65% Tower Hotel, Quay St, SLIGO
           ☎ 071 44000 58 ⇄ ☏

Strandhill Strandhill ☎ 071 68188 Fax 071 68811
This scenic course is situated between Knocknarea Mountain and the Atlantic, offering golf in its most natural form amid the sand dunes of the West of Ireland. The 1st, 16th and 18th are Par 4 holes over 364 metres in length; the 2nd and 17th are testing Par 3s which vary according to the prevailing wind; the Par 4 13th is a testing dogleg right. This is a course where accuracy will be rewarded.
18 holes, 5516mtrs, Par 69, SSS 68.
Club membership 450.
Visitors   must contact in advance.
Societies   apply in advance.
Green Fees IEP25 per round(IEP30 weekends).
Facilities   ⊗🍖🏌🍺♀♂🏠⚑🛒🍴
Location   5m from town

Hotel   ★★★ 71% Sligo Park Hotel, Pearse Rd, SLIGO ☎ 071 60291 110 ⇄ ☏

TOBERCURRY   Map 01 B4

Tobercurry ☎ 071 85849
A 9-hole parkland course designed by Edward Hackett. The 8th hole, a Par 3, is regarded as being one of the most testing in the west of Ireland.
9 holes, 5490mtrs, Par 70, SSS 69.
Club membership 300.
Visitors   may not play on Sundays.
Societies   telephone in advance on 071 85770.
Green Fees IEP10.
Designer   Eddie Hackett
Facilities   ⊗🍖🏌🍺♀♂
Location   0.25m from Tobercurry

CO TIPPERARY

CAHIR   Map 01 C3

Cahir Park Kilcommon ☎ 052 41474 Fax 052 42717
Parkland course dissected by the River Suir which adds a challenge to the par 4 8th and par 3 16th.
18 holes, 6350yds, Par 71, SSS 71, Course record 67.
Club membership 600.
Visitors   may play any time except during competitions.
Societies   by prior arrangement, apply in writing.
Green Fees IEP18 per day(IEP20 weekends).   ▶

Prof Markus Joseph
Designer Eddie Hackett
Facilities 🍴🍺♀⚲🏠🛒✐
Location 1m from Cahir on the Clogheen road

Hotel ★★★ 67% Cahir House Hotel, The Square, CAHIR ☎ 52 42727 31 ⇔ 🏠

CARRICK-ON-SUIR   Map 01 C2

Carrick-on-Suir Garvonne
☎ 051 640047 Fax 051 640558 e-mail: cosgc@eircom.net
18 hole parkland course with the backdrop of the Comeragh Mountains on one side and views of the Suir valley on the other.
18 holes, 6061mtrs, Par 72, SSS 71, Course record 69.
Club membership 600.
Visitors may not play on Sun morning.contact in advance.
Societies contact for details.
Green Fees IEP17 per round(IEP20 weekends).
Cards 💳🟥
Designer Eddie Hackett
Facilities ⊗〗🏠🍺♀⚲🛒✐
Location 2m SW

Hotel ★★★ 74% Minella Hotel, CLONMEL ☎ 052 22388 70 ⇔ 🏠

CLONMEL   Map 01 C2

Clonmel Lyreanearla, Mountain Rd
☎ 052 24050 & 21138 Fax 052 24050
e-mail: cgc@indigo.ie
Set in the scenic, wooded slopes of the Comeragh Mountains, this is a testing course with lots of open space and plenty of interesting features. It provides an enjoyable round in exceptionally tranquil surroundings.
18 holes, 6347yards, Par 72, SSS 71.
Club membership 950.
Visitors must contact in advance.
Societies apply in advance by writing or phone.
Green Fees IEP20 per round (IEP22 weekends).
Cards 🟥
Prof Robert Hayes
Designer Eddie Hackett
Facilities ⊗〗 by prior arrangement 🏠🍺♀⚲🏠
🛒✐
Location 3m from Clonmel off N24

Hotel ★★★ 74% Minella Hotel, CLONMEL ☎ 052 22388 70 ⇔ 🏠

MONARD   Map 01 B3

Ballykisteen Ballykisteen, Limerick Junction
☎ 062 33333 Fax 062 52457
Ballykisteen is set in emerald green countryside just two miles from Tipperary. The course, with landscaped surroundings against a backdrop of mountains, lakes and streams, offers an excellent challenge for the champion golfer. The use of forward tees provide a course that is playable and enjoyable for the average golfer.
18 holes, 6765yds, Par 72, SSS 72.
Club membership 220.

Visitors no restrictions.
Societies must contact in advance.
Green Fees not confirmed.
Cards 💳
Prof David Reddan
Designer Des Smith
Facilities ⊗〗🏠🍺♀⚲🏠⛳🛒✐✐
Location On N24 2m from Tipperary towards Limerick

NENAGH   Map 01 B3

Nenagh Beechwood ☎ 067 31476 Fax 067 34808
Interesting gradients call for some careful approach shots. Some magnificent views.
18 holes, 5491mtrs, Par 69, SSS 68, Course record 64.
Club membership 600.
Visitors must contact in advance.May not play Sundays.
Societies must apply in writing.
Green Fees IEP25 per 18 holes.
Cards 🟥
Prof Gordon Morrison
Designer Eddie Hackett
Facilities ⊗〗🏠🍺♀⚲🏠⛳🛒✐
Location 3m from town on old Birr rd

Hotel ★★★ 68% Abbey Court Hotel, Dublin Rd, NENAGH ☎ 067 41111 46 ⇔ 🏠

ROSCREA   Map 01 C3

Roscrea Golf Club Derryvale
☎ 0505 21130 Fax 0505 23410
An 18-hole parkland course.
18 holes, 5750mtrs, Par 71, SSS 70, Course record 66.
Club membership 600.
Visitors telephone in advance, on Sun by arrangement.
Societies apply in writing to Hon Secretary.
Green Fees IEP14(IEP17 weekends).
Designer A Spring
Facilities ⊗〗🏠🍺♀⚲⛳✐
Location N7, Dublin side of Roscrea

Hotel ★★★ 60% County Arms Hotel, BIRR ☎ 0509 20791 24 ⇔ 🏠

TEMPLEMORE   Map 01 C3

Templemore Manna South
☎ 0504 31400 & 32923 Fax 0504 35450
e-mail: johnkm@tinet.ie
Parkland course with many mature and some newly planted trees which offers a pleasant test to visitors without being too difficult. Ideal for holidaymakers.
9 holes, 5443mtrs, Par 70, SSS 69, Course record 68.
Club membership 220.
Visitors may not play during Special Events.
Societies must contact in advance.
Green Fees IEP10 per round (IEP15 weekends & bank holidays).
Cards 🟥
Facilities ⊗〗🏠🍺♀⚲✐
& Leisure hard tennis courts.
Location 0.5m S, beside N62

Hotel ★★★ 60% County Arms Hotel, BIRR ☎ 0509 20791 24 ⇔ 🏠

THURLES   Map 01 C3

Thurles Turtulla ☎ 0504 21983 & 22466 Fax 0504 24647
18 holes, 5904mtrs, Par 72, SSS 71, Course record 65.
Location   1m from town on Cork road
Telephone for further details

Guesthouse ♦♦♦ Ach-na-Sheen Guesthouse, Clonmel Rd,
TIPPERARY ☎ 062 51298 10rm(5 ⇄ ℞)

TIPPERARY   Map 01 C3

County Tipperary Dundrum House Hotel, Dundrum
☎ 062 71116
18 holes, 6709yds, Par 72, SSS 72, Course record 70.
Location   7m W of Cashel off N8
Telephone for further details

Guesthouse ♦♦♦ Ach-na-Sheen Guesthouse, Clonmel Rd,
TIPPERARY ☎ 062 51298 10rm(5 ⇄ ℞)

Tipperary Rathanny ☎ 062 51119
Recently extended to 18-holes, this parkland course has
plenty of trees and bunkers and water at three holes to
provide additional hazards.
18 holes, 5761mtrs, Par 71, SSS 71, Course record 66.
Club membership 700.
Visitors   advisable to contact by phone, weekend play
available but limited on Sun.
Societies   apply in writing.
Green Fees not confirmed.
Facilities   ⊗ ⅷ by prior arrangement �❧ ♨ ♀ ⚴ 🏠 ⛳
🛒 ✐
Location   1m S

Guesthouse ♦♦♦ Ach-na-Sheen Guesthouse, Clonmel Rd,
TIPPERARY ☎ 062 51298 10rm(5 ⇄ ℞)

CO WATERFORD

DUNGARVAN   Map 01 C2

Dungarvan Knocknagranagh
☎ 058 41605 & 43310 Fax 058 44113
e-mail: dungarvangolf@cablesurf.com
A championship-standard course beside Dungarvan Bay,
with seven lakes and hazards placed to challenge all levels of
golfer. The greens are considered to be among the best in
Ireland.
18 holes, 6560yds, Par 72, SSS 71, Course record 66.
Club membership 900.
Visitors   welcome weekdays, booking advisable
weekends.
Societies   telephone then write to confim booking.
Green Fees not confirmed.
Prof   David Hayes
Designer   Moss Fives
Facilities   ⊗ ⅷ � ♨ ♀ ⚴ 🏠 ⛳ 🛒 ✐
& Leisure   snooker.
Location   Off N25 between Waterford & Youghal

Hotel   ★★★ 58% Lawlors Hotel, DUNGARVAN
☎ 058 41122 & 41056 Fax 058 41000 89 ⇄ ℞

Gold Coast Golf & Leisure Ballinacourty
☎ 058 42249 & 44055 Fax 058 43378
e-mail: info@cionea.com
A parkland course bordered by the Atlantic Ocean with
unrivalled panoramic views of Dungarvan Bay. The mature
tree-lined fairways of the old course are tastefully integrated
with the long and challenging newer holes to create a superb
course.
18 holes, 6171mtrs, Par 72, SSS 72, Course record 72.
Club membership 450.
Visitors   book in advance, times available throughout the
week.
Societies   apply by telephone in advance.
Green Fees IEP22 per round (IEP27 weekends).
Cards   ⬜ ⬛ ⬛ ⬜
Designer   Maurice Fives
Facilities   ⊗ ⅷ �❧ ♨ ♀ ⚴ 🏠 ⛳ 🐕 🛒 ✐ ♙
& Leisure   hard tennis courts, heated indoor swimming
pool, sauna, gymnasium.
Location   Left of N25, 2m bfore Dungarvan

Hotel   ★★★ 58% Lawlors Hotel, DUNGARVAN
☎ 058 41122 & 41056 Fax 058 41000 89 ⇄ ℞

West Waterford ☎ 058 43216 & 41475 Fax 058 44343
e-mail: info@westwaterfordgolf.com
Designed by Eddie Hackett, the course is on 150 acres of
rolling parkland by the Brickey River with a backdrop of the
Comeragh Mountains, Knockmealdowns and Drum Hills.
The first nine holes are laid out on a large plateau featuring a
stream which comes into play at the 3rd and 4th holes. The
river at the southern boundary affects several later holes.
18 holes, 6557yds, Par 72, SSS 74, Course record 70.
Club membership 300.
Visitors   pre book for tee times.
Societies   telephone or write in advance.
Green Fees IEP18 per round(IEP23 weekends & bank
holidays).
Cards   ⬜ ⬛
Designer   Eddie Hackett
Facilities   ⊗ ⅷ �❧ ♨ ♀ ⚴ 🏠 ⛳ 🐕 🛒 ✐
& Leisure   hard tennis courts.
Location   Approx 3m W of Dungarvan, off N25

Hotel   ★★★ 58% Lawlors Hotel, DUNGARVAN
☎ 058 41122 & 41056 Fax 058 41000 89 ⇄ ℞

DUNMORE EAST   Map 01 C2

Dunmore East ☎ 051 383151 Fax 051 383151
Overlooking the village of Dunmore East, with panoramic
views of the village, bay and Hook peninsula. This course
promises to offer idyllic surroundings and challenging golf
for the high or low handicap golfer.
18 holes, 6655yds, Par 72, SSS 70, Course record 69.
Club membership 300.
Visitors   welcome, no restrictions.
Societies   telephone in advance.
Green Fees not confirmed.
Prof   Derry Kiely
Designer   W H Jones
Facilities   ⊗ ⅷ �❧ ♨ ♀ ⚴ 🏠 ⛳ 🐕 🛒 ✐
Location   Follow signs to Dunmore East. After Petrol Stn
take left fork. Left at The Strand Inn & 1st right
▶

485

Hotel   ★★★ 63% Majestic Hotel, TRAMORE
             ☎ 051 381761 57 ⇄ ♠

LISMORE   Map 01 C2

Lismore Ballyin ☎ 058 54026 Fax 058 53338
e-mail: dooleybernard@eircom.net
Picturesque tree-dotted sloping course on the banks of the
Blackwater River. Rothwell's is a difficult hole with a
sloping green and trees to either side.
9 holes, 2748mtrs, Par 69, SSS 68.
Club membership 350.
Visitors   telephone in advance,especially weekends.
Societies   must apply in writing or phone.
Green Fees IEP15 per day.
Facilities ⬞ ⬞ ♀ ⬞ ♂ ⬞
Location   1 mile from Lismore on Ballyduff Road

Hotel   ★★★ 58% Lawlors Hotel, DUNGARVAN
             ☎ 058 41122 & 41056 Fax 058 41000 89 ⇄ ♠

TRAMORE   Map 01 C2

Tramore Newtown Hill ☎ 051 386170 Fax 051 390961
e-mail: tragolf@iol.ie
This course has matured nicely over the years to become a
true championship test and has been chosen as the venue for
the Irish Professional Matchplay Championship and the Irish
Amateur Championship. Most of the fairways are lined by
evergreen trees, calling for accurate placing of shots, and the
course is continuing to develop.
18 holes, 5918mtrs, Par 72, SSS 72, Course record 65.
Club membership 1200.
Visitors   pre-booking required.
Societies   contact in advance.
Green Fees IEP30 per round (IEP35 weekends & bank
                holidays).
Cards   ⬞ ⬞
Prof   Derry Kiely
Designer   Capt H C Tippet
Facilities ⊗ ⫼ ⬞ ⬞ ♀ ⬞ ⬞ ♂ ⬞ ⬞ ⬞
& Leisure   squash.
Location   0.5m from Tramore on Dungaruan coast road

Hotel   ★★★ 63% Majestic Hotel, TRAMORE
             ☎ 051 381761 57 ⇄ ♠

WATERFORD   Map 01 C2

Faithlegg House Dunmore East ☎ 051 382241
Some wicked slopes and borrows on the immaculate greens,
a huge 432yard 17th what has a host of problems and a
doglegged approach to the two-tier 18th green are just some
of the novel features on this course. Set on the banks of the
River Suir, the course has been integrated into a landscape
textured with mature trees, flowing parkland and five lakes.
18 holes, 6057mtrs, Par 72, SSS 72, Course record 69.
Club membership 65.
Visitors   no restrictions.
Societies   apply in writing or telephone at least a month in
                advance.
Green Fees not confirmed.
Prof   Ted Higgins
Facilities ♀ ⬞ ⬞ ♂

Hotel   ★★★ 62% Jurys Hotel, Ferrybank,
             WATERFORD ☎ 051 832111 98 ⇄ ♠

Waterford Newrath ☎ 051 876748 Fax 051 853405
Undulating parkland course in pleasant surroundings.
18 holes, 5722mtrs, Par 71, SSS 70, Course record 64.
Club membership 931.
Visitors   must contact in advance.
Societies   must apply in writing.
Green Fees not confirmed.
Prof   Joseph Condon
Designer   W Park/J Braid
Facilities ⊗ ⫼ ⬞ ⬞ ♀ ⬞ ⬞ ♂ ⬞ ⬞
Location   1m N

Hotel   ★★★ 62% Jurys Hotel, Ferrybank,
             WATERFORD ☎ 051 832111 98 ⇄ ♠

Waterford Castle The Island, Ballinakill
☎ 051 871633 Fax 051 871634
e-mail: golf@waterfordcastle.com
Parkland course with mature trees, 4 lakes, sandbased
tees and greens and good bunkering.
18 holes, 5827mtrs, Par 72, SSS 71, Course record 70.
Club membership 500.
Visitors   must contact in advance, pre booking required.
Societies   apply in advance.
Green Fees IEP30 per 18 holes;IEP45 per 36 holes
                (IEP35 per 18 holesweekends& bank
                holidays).
Cards   ⬞ ⬞
Designer   Den Smyth
Facilities ⬞ ⬞ ♀ ⬞ ♂ ⬞ ⬞ ⬞ ⬞
& Leisure   hard tennis courts.
Location   2m E of Waterford City, on Island
                approached by private ferry

Hotel   ★★★ 62% Jurys Hotel, Ferrybank,
             WATERFORD ☎ 051 832111 98 ⇄ ♠

CO WESTMEATH

ATHLONE   Map 01 C4

Glasson Golf & Country Club Glasson
☎ 0902 85120 Fax 0902 85444 e-mail: info@glassongolf.ie
Opened for play in 1993 the course has earned a reputation
for being one of the most challenging and scenic courses in
Ireland. Designed by Christy O'Connor Jnr it is reputedly his
best yet! Surrounded on three sides by Lough Ree the views
from everywhere on the course are breathtaking.
*Glasson Golf & Country Club: 18 holes, 6664yds, Par 72,
SSS 72, Course record 65.*
Club membership 220.
Visitors   must book in advance.
Societies   book in advance.
Green Fees IEP32 (Mon-Thur);IEP35 (Fri-Sun);IEP40(Sat).
Cards   ⬞ ⬞ ⬞ ⬞
Designer   Christy O'Connor Jnr
Facilities ⊗ ⫼ ⬞ ⬞ ♀ ⬞ ⬞ ♂ ⬞ ⬞ ⬞
Location   6m N of Athlone on N55

▶

Hotel ★★★ 59% Prince Of Wales Hotel, ATHLONE ☎ 0902 72626 73 ⇆ 📷

DELVIN   Map 01 C4

Delvin Castle Clonyn
☎ 044 64315 & 64671 Fax 044 64315
Situated in the mature parkland of Clonyn Castle, the course is well known for its unique historic setting with a 16th century ruin in the back nine holes and an imposing Victorian castle in the front nine.
18 holes, 5800mtrs, Par 70, SSS 68.
Club membership 400.
Visitors no restrictions. Advance booking recommemded.
Societies apply in writing in advance.
Green Fees IEP16 per 18 holes; IEP10 per 9 holes (IEP18 weekends & bank holidays).
Prof David Keenaghan
Designer John Day
Facilities ⊗ ⊪ ᴸ ☕ ♀ ⅄ ☎ ☂ ↺
Location On N52, Dundalk to Mullingar road

Hotel ★★★ 62% Ardboyne Hotel, Dublin Rd, NAVAN ☎ 046 23119 29 ⇆ 📷

MOATE   Map 01 C4

Moate ☎ 0902 81271 Fax 0902 81267
Extended in 1994 to 18 holes, the course is parkland with trees. Although the original 9-holes did not have water hazards the new section has lakes and many bunkers.
18 holes, 5742mtrs, Par 72, SSS 70, Course record 67.
Club membership 650.

Visitors welcome, advisable to telephone in advance.
Societies must contact in advance.
Green Fees IEP12 per round (IEP15 weekends & bank holidays).
Prof Paul Power
Designer B Browne
Facilities ⊗ ⊪ ᴸ ☕ ♀ ⅄ ☎ ☂ ↺
Location 1m N

Hotel ★★★ 59% Prince Of Wales Hotel, ATHLONE ☎ 0902 72626 73 ⇆ 📷

Mount Temple Mount Temple Village
☎ 0902 81841 & 81545 Fax 0902 81957
e-mail: mttemple@iol.ie
A traditionally built, highly-rated, all year round course with parkland and unique links-type greens and natural undulating fairways. A challenge for all levels of golfers as the wind plays a major part in the scoring on this course.
18 holes, 5950mtrs, Par 72, SSS 72, Course record 65.
Club membership 200.
Visitors welcome but must book for weekends.
Societies telephone in advance.
Green Fees IEP18 per 18 holes(IEP24 weekends & bank holidays).
Cards 💳 💳
Prof David Keenan
Designer Michael Dolan
Facilities ⊗ ⊪ ᴸ ☕ ♀ ⅄ ☎ ☂ ↺
Location 4m off N6 to Mount Temple village, 5m from Athlone

Hotel ★★★ 59% Prince Of Wales Hotel, ATHLONE ☎ 0902 72626 73 ⇆ 📷

MULLINGAR   Map 01 C4

Mullingar ☎ 044 48366 Fax 044 41499
18 holes, 6406yds, Par 72, SSS 71, Course record 63.
Location 3m S
Telephone for further details

Hotel ★★★ 59% Prince Of Wales Hotel, ATHLONE ☎ 0902 72626 73 ⇆ 📷

CO WEXFORD

ENNISCORTHY   Map 01 D3

Enniscorthy Knockmarshall ☎ 054 33191 Fax 054 37367
A pleasant course suitable for all levels of ability.
18 holes, 6115mtrs, Par 72, SSS 72.
Club membership 900.
Visitors must telephone for booking.
Societies must book in advance.
Green Fees not confirmed.
Prof Martin Sludos
Designer Eddie Hackett
Facilities ⊗ ⊪ ᴸ ☕ ♀ ⅄ ☎ ☂ ↺ ₹
Location 1m from town on New Ross road

Hotel ★ 60% Murphy-Flood's Hotel, Market Square, ENNISCORTHY ☎ 054 33413 21rm(5 ⇆13 📷)

GOREY   Map 01 D3

Courtown Kiltennel ☎ 055 25166 Fax 055 25553 e-mail: courtown@iol.ie
A pleasant parkland course which is well wooded and enjoys views across the Irish Sea near Courtown Harbour.
18 holes, 5898mtrs, Par 71, SSS 71, Course record 65.
Club membership 1200. ▶

Courtown Golf Club

Green Fees IEP25 (IEP35 weekends & bank holidays).
Cards ▨▨ ▧
Prof Johnny Young
Designer Hawtree/Taylor
Facilities 🏌🏌♀⛳🏠🍴🛒🛍🚃♂
& Leisure sauna.
Location 6m N of Rosslare Ferry Terminal

Hotel ★★★★ 78% Kelly's Resort Hotel, ROSSLARE
☎ 053 32114 Annexe99 ⇄ 🐾

St Helen's Bay Golf & Country Club St Helens, Kilrane
☎ 053 33234 & 33669 Fax 053 33803
e-mail: sthelens@iol.ie
A championship-standard golf course designed by Philip Walton. Link and parkland with water hazards, bunkers and trees incorporated generously. Overlooking the beach with accommodation on site.
18 holes, 5813mtrs, Par 72, SSS 72, Course record 69.
Club membership 450.
Visitors contact in advance.
Societies telephone in advance.
Green Fees from IEP20-IEP28.
Cards ▨▨ ▧
Designer Philip Walton
Facilities ⊗⧂🏌♀⛳🏠🍴🎾🛒🚃♂
& Leisure hard tennis courts, sauna.
Location 5 minutes from the ferryport of Rosslare

Hotel ★★★★ 67% Ferrycarrig Hotel, Ferrycarrig, WEXFORD ☎ 053 20999 103 ⇄ 🐾

Courtown Golf Club
Visitors must contact in advance.
Societies advisable to contact in advance.
Green Fees IEP25(IEP30 weekends). Reductions in winter.
Cards ▨▨ ▧
Prof John Coone
Designer Harris & Associates
Facilities ⊗⧂🏌🏌♀⛳🏠🍴🛒🚃♂
Location 3m from town, off Courtown Road

Hotel ★★★♨ Marlfield House Hotel, GOREY
☎ 055 21124 19 ⇄ 🐾

NEW ROSS　　　　　　　　　　Map 01 C3

New Ross Tinneranny ☎ 051 421433 Fax 051 420098
Recently extended to 18-holes, this well kept parkland course has an attractive backdrop of hills and mountains. Straight hitting and careful placing of shots is very important, especially on the 2nd, 6th, 10th and 15th, all of which are challenging holes.
18 holes, 5751yds, Par 71, SSS 70.
Club membership 700.
Visitors welcome, booking required for weekend play.
Societies apply to secretary/manager.
Green Fees not confirmed.
Designer Des Smith
Facilities ⊗🏌♀⛳🏠♂
Location 3m from town centre

Hotel ★★ 59% The Old Rectory Hotel, Rosbercon, NEW ROSS ☎ 051 421719 12 ⇄ 🐾

ROSSLARE　　　　　　　　　　Map 01 D2

Rosslare Rosslare Strand ☎ 053 32203 Fax 053 32263
e-mail: rgolfclb@iol.ie
This traditional links course is within minutes of the ferry terminal at Rosslare, but its popularity is not confined to visitors from Fishguard or Le Havre. It is a great favourite with the Irish too. Many of the greens are sunken and are always in beautiful condition, but the semi-blind approaches are among features of this course which provide a healthy challenge.
Old Course: 18 holes, 6601yds, Par 72, SSS 72, Course record 66.
New Course: 9 holes, 3153yds, Par 35, SSS 70.
Club membership 1000.
Visitors telephone 053 32203 ext3 in advance.
Societies apply in writing/telephone.

WEXFORD　　　　　　　　　　Map 01 D3

Wexford Mulgannon ☎ 053 42238 Fax 053 42243
Parkland course with panoramic view of the Wexford coastline and mountains.
18 holes, 6100yds, Par 72, SSS 70.
Club membership 800.
Visitors must contact in advance but may not play Thu & Sundays.
Societies must contact in writing.
Green Fees IEP22 per 18 holes,summer;IEP18 winter (IEP25 weekends & bank holidays).
Prof Damien McGrane
Facilities ⊗⧂🏌♀⛳🏠🍴🛒🚃♂

Hotel ★★★ 72% Talbot Hotel Conference & Leisure Centre, Trinity St, WEXFORD
☎ 053 22566 100 ⇄ 🐾

CO WICKLOW

ARKLOW　　　　　　　　　　Map 01 D3

Arklow Abbeylands ☎ 0402 32492 Fax 0402 32492
Scenic links course.
18 holes, 5404mtrs, Par 68, SSS 67, Course record 66.
Club membership 450.
Visitors may play Mon-Fri and 3hrs Sat 9am-12 noon, must book in advance. ▶

Societies must apply in writing or telephone in advance.
Green Fees not confirmed.
Designer Hawtree & Taylor
Facilities ⊗ ⫪ ⓛ ♥ ♀ ♨ 🏠 ⛳ ✂ ⟊
Location 0.5m from town centre

Hotel ★★★♨ Marlfield House Hotel, GOREY
☎ 055 21124 19 ⇆ 🐾

BALTINGLASS   Map 01 D3

Baltinglass Dublin Rd ☎ 0508 81350 Fax 0508 81350
On the banks of the River Slaney, the 9-hole course has 4
Par-4s over 400 yards which have to be played twice.
Reputed to be one of the hardest 9-hole courses in the
Republic.
9 holes, 5554mtrs, Par 68, SSS 69, Course record 68.
Club membership 400.
Visitors advisable to check availability for weekends.
Societies apply in writing.
Green Fees not confirmed.
Designer Lionel Hewston
Facilities ⊗ ⓛ ♥ ♀ ♨ ✂
Location 500 metres N of Baltinglass

Rathsallagh ☎ 045 403316 Fax 045 403295
e-mail: info@rathsallagh.com
Designed by Peter McEvoy and Christy O'Connor Jnr, this is
a spectacular course which will test the pro's without
intimidating the club golfer. Set in 252 acres of lush parkland
with thousands of mature trees, natural water hazards and
gently rolling landscape. The greens are of high quality, in
design, construction and condition.
18 holes, 6916yds, Par 72, SSS 74.
Club membership 270.
Visitors prior booking and neat dress is essential.Metal
spikes are prohibited.
Societies telephone in advance.
Green Fees Mon-Thu: IEP45 per round;IEP25 per 9
holes(IEP55/IEP30 fri-sun & bank holidays).
Cards 🟦 🟥 🟦
Prof Brendan McDaid
Designer McEvoy/O'Connor
Facilities ⊗ ⫪ ⓛ ♥ ♀ ♨ 🏠 ⛳ 🏇 ✂ ⟊
& Leisure hard tennis courts, heated indoor swimming
pool, sauna.
Location 15m SE of Naas off main Dublin/Carlow road

Hotel ★★★ 66% Downshire House Hotel,
BLESSINGTON ☎ 045 865199
14 ⇆ 🐾 Annexe11 ⇆ 🐾

BLAINROE   Map 01 D3

Blainroe ☎ 0404 68168 Fax 0404 69369
Parkland course overlooking the sea on the east coast,
offering a challenging round to golfers of all abilities.
18 holes, 6070mtrs, Par 72, SSS 72, Course record 71.
Club membership 868.
Visitors must contact in advance.
Societies must telephone in advance.
Green Fees IEP30 per round;IEP40 per 36
holes(IEP40/IEP50 weekends).
Cards 🟦 🟥
Prof John McDonald
Designer C Hawtree

Facilities ⊗ ⫪ ⓛ ♥ ♀ ♨ 🏠 ⛳ 🏇 ✂
Location S of Wicklow, on coast road

Hotel ★★★♨ Tinakilly Country House &
Restaurant, RATHNEW
☎ 0404 69274 52 ⇆ 🐾

BLESSINGTON   Map 01 D3

Tulfarris House Hotel & Country Club
☎ 045 867555 Fax 045 867561
Designed by Paddy Merrigan, this course is on the
Blessington lakeshore with the Wicklow Mountains as a
backdrop.
18 holes, 7116yds, Par 72, SSS 74.
Club membership 150.
Visitors tee booking advisable; may not play Sun 8-
11.30pm.
Societies must contact in writing or telephone in advance.
Green Fees IEP50 per round (IEP60 weekends & bank
holidays).
Cards 🟦 🟥 🟦 🟦
Prof A Williams
Designer Patrick Merrigan
Facilities ⊗ ⫪ ⓛ ♨ 🏠 ⛳ 🏇 🏊 ✂ ⟊
& Leisure hard tennis courts, heated indoor swimming
pool, fishing, sauna, solarium, gymnasium.
Location Via N81, 2m from Blessington village

Hotel ★★★ 66% Downshire House Hotel,
BLESSINGTON ☎ 045 865199
14 ⇆ 🐾 Annexe11 ⇆ 🐾

BRAY   Map 01 D4

Bray Ravenswell Rd ☎ 01 2862484 Fax 01 2862484
A 9-hole parkland course with plenty of trees and bunkers.
9 holes, 5761mtrs, Par 70, SSS 70, Course record 65.
Club membership 500.
Visitors restricted Mon, Sat & Sun.
Societies contact in advance.
Green Fees not confirmed.
Prof Michael Walby
Facilities ⓛ ♥ ♀ ♨ 🏠 ⛳ ✂

Hotel ★★★★ 65% Fitzpatrick Castle Hotel,
KILLINEY ☎ 01 2840700 113 ⇆ 🐾

Old Conna Ferndale Rd ☎ 01 2826055 & 2826766
Fax 01 2825611
Parkland course set in wooded terrain with panoramic views
of Irish Sea and Wicklow mountains.
18 holes, 6550yds, Par 72, SSS 72, Course record 70.
Club membership 900.
Visitors advisable to contact in advance but may not play
weekends. Smart dress essential on course & in
clubhouse.
Societies must telephone well in advance.
Green Fees IEP35 per round (IEP45 weekends).
Cards 🟦 🟥 🟦 🟦
Prof Paul McDaid
Designer Eddie Hackett
Facilities ⊗ ⫪ ⓛ ♥ ♀ ♨ 🏠 ⛳ 🏇 ✂
Location 2m from Bray

Hotel ★★★ 59% Royal Hotel & Leisure Centre,
Main St, BRAY ☎ 01 2862935 91 ⇆ 🐾

Woodbrook Dublin Rd ☎ 01 2824799 Fax 01 2821950
e-mail: woodbrook@internet-ireland.ie
Pleasant parkland with magnificent views and bracing sea
breezes which has hosted a number of events, including the
Irish Close and the Irish Open Championships. A testing
finish is provided by an 18th hole with out of bounds on both
sides.
18 holes, 6017mtrs, Par 72, SSS 71, Course record 65.
Club membership 1100.
Visitors   must contact in advance and have a handicap
               certificate.
Societies   must contact in advance.
Green Fees IEP55 (IEP65 weekends).
Cards   🔲 💳
Prof   Billy Kinsella
Designer   Peter McEvoy
Facilities   ⊗ ⫼ ┗ 🍺 ♀ ⚐ 🏠 ⛳ 🐎 ✈ ♟
Location   11m S of Dublin on N11

Hotel   ★★★ 59% Royal Hotel & Leisure Centre,
           Main St, BRAY ☎ 01 2862935 91 ⇄ �my

BRITTAS BAY   Map 01 D3

The European Club   ☎ 0404 47415 Fax 0404 47449
e-mail: info@europeanclub.com
A links course that runs through a large dunes system.
Since it was opened in 1992 it is rapidly gaining
recognition as one of Ireland's Best Courses.
18 holes, 7105yds, Par 71, SSS 73, Course record 69.
Club membership 100.
Visitors   pre-booking advised especially for
               weekends, no denim.
Societies   must book in advance.
Green Fees IEP80 per round;IEP120 per day.reductions
                 in winter..
Cards   🔲 💳
Designer   Pat Ruddy
Facilities   ⊗ ⫼ ┗ 🍺 △ ⛳ 🐎 ✈ ♟
Location   1.5m from Brittas Bay Beach

Hotel   ★★★♨ Tinakilly Country House &
           Restaurant, RATHNEW
           ☎ 0404 69274 52 ⇄ 🌚

DELGANY   Map 01 D3

Delgany ☎ 01 2874536 Fax 01 2873977
e-mail: delganygolf@eircom.net
An undulating parkland course amidst beautiful scenery.
18 holes, 5474mtrs, Par 69, SSS 68, Course record 61.
Club membership 967.
Visitors   may play Mon, Wed (until 10am), Thu & Fri.
               Contact in advance.
Societies   contact in advance.
Green Fees IEP30 per round.
Cards   🔲 💳
Prof   Gavin Kavanagh
Designer   H Vardon
Facilities   △ ⚐ ⛳ ✈ 🐎 ♟
Location   0.75m from village

Hotel   ★★★ 59% Royal Hotel & Leisure Centre,
           Main St, BRAY ☎ 01 2862935 91 ⇄ 🌚

GREYSTONES   Map 01 D3

Charlesland Golf & Country Club Hotel
☎ 01 2874350 Fax 01 2874360 e-mail: charlesland@tinet.ie
Championship length, Par 72 course with a double dog-leg at
the 9th and 18th. Water hazards at the 3rd and 11th.
18 holes, 5963mtrs, Par 72, SSS 72.
Club membership 744.
Visitors   must contact in advance.
Societies   must apply in advance.
Green Fees not confirmed.
Cards   🔲 💳
Prof   Paul Heeney
Designer   Eddie Hackett
Facilities   ⊗ ⫼ ┗ 🍺 ♀ △ ⚐ 🏠 ⛳ 🐎 ✈ ♟
& Leisure   sauna.
Location   1m S of Greystones on the road to Delgany
              village

Hotel   ★★★♨ Tinakilly Country House &
           Restaurant, RATHNEW
           ☎ 0404 69274 52 ⇄ 🌚

Greystones ☎ 01 2874136 Fax 01 2873749
A part level and part hilly parkland course.
18 holes, 5322mtrs, Par 69, SSS 68.
Club membership 995.
Visitors   may only play Mon, Tue & Fri morning. Must
               contact in advance.
Societies   must contact in writing.
Green Fees IEP25 per round (IEP30 Friday).
Cards   🔲 💳
Designer   P Merrigan
Facilities   ⊗ ⫼ ┗ 🍺 ♀ △ ⚐ 🏠 ⛳ 🐎 ✈ ♟

Hotel   ★★★♨ Tinakilly Country House &
           Restaurant, RATHNEW
           ☎ 0404 69274 52 ⇄ 🌚

KILCOOLE   Map 01 D3

KILCOOLE See page 491

Kilcoole ☎ 01 2872066 2872070 Fax 01 2871803
9 holes, 5506mtrs, Par 70, SSS 69.
Club membership 250.
Visitors   restricted Sat & Sun 8-10am.
Societies   apply in writing or telephone.
Green Fees not confirmed.
Facilities   🍺 △ ♟
Location   N11 Kilcoole/Newcastle

▶

AA Hotels that have special
arrangements with golf courses are listed at
the back of the guide

Druid's Glen

Kilcoole, *Co Wicklow* ☎ 01 2873600 Fax 01 2873699 Map 01 D3

e-mail: info@druidsglen.ie

D ruids Glen from the first tee to the eighteenth green (7000 yards in all) creates an exceptional golfing experience that is totally unique with its distinguished surroundings and spectacular views. A masterpiece of inspired planning and golfing architecture, designed by Tom Craddock and Pat Ruddy, it is the culmination of years of preparation, creating a unique inland golf course that challenges and satisfies in equal parts.

Druids Glen hosted the Murphy's Irish Open in 1996, 1997, 1998 and an unprecedented fourth time in 1999. In 2000 Druid's Glen won the title of European Golf Course of the Year. The world's top professionals and club golfers alike continue to enjoy the challenge offered here. A variety of teeing positions are available and there is a practice area, including three full-length 'academy holes'. Individual and corporate members enjoy generous reserved tee times, visitors are very welcome but it is recommended that you book well in advance.

Visitors advance booking essential
Societies advance booking essential
Green Fees IEP90 per round
Facilities ⊗ 〉〔 ⌷ ☕ ♀ ⚲ 🏠
〒 ❧ 🎣 ♂ ♞ Professional (Eamon Darcy/Ciaran Monaghan)
Location 20m S of Dublin, 3m off N11 motorway, immediately S of Glen of the Downs
Holes/Par/Course record 18 holes, 6547 yds, Par 71, SSS 73, Course record 62

Championship Course

Hotel ★★★🏊 Tinakilly Country House &
Restaurant, RATHNEW
☎ 0404 69274 52 ⇄ 🐾

RATHDRUM   Map 01 D3

Glenmalure Greenane ☎ 0404 46679 Fax 0404 46783
e-mail: golf@glenmalure-golf.ie
A moorland course with elevated tees and greens where
accuracy is required. The 3rd, known as the Helicopter Pad,
is difficult. GUI affiliated.
18 holes, 5300yds, Par 71, SSS 67, Course record 71.
Club membership 250.
Visitors unable to play Sunday 8-11am
Societies telephone at least 3 days in advance.
Green Fees not confirmed.
Designer P Suttle
Facilities ⊗ ⽊ ⅃ 🎽 ♀ ⚲ ⚑ 🏌 🛒 ⚸
Location 2m W

Hotel ★★★ 64% Woodenbridge Hotel, WOODEN
BRIDGE ☎ 0402 35146 23 ⇄ 🐾

ROUNDWOOD   Map 01 D3

Roundwood Newtown, Mountkennedy
☎ 01 2818488 & 2802555 Fax 01 2843642
e-mail: rwood@indigo.ie
Heathland and parkland course with forest and lakes set in
beautiful countryside with views of the coast and the
Wicklow Mountains.
18 holes, 6685yds, Par 72, SSS 72.
Club membership 120.
Visitors no restrictions
Societies pre booking necessary.
Green Fees IEP25 (IEP32 weekends).
Facilities 🎽 ⚲ ⚑ 🏌 🛒 ⚸
Location 2.5m off N11 at Newtown Mountkennedy on
N765

Hotel ★★★ 64% The Glendalough Hotel,
GLENDALOUGH ☎ 0404 45135 44 ⇄ 🐾

Looking for a driving range?
See the index at the back of the guide

SHILLELAGH   Map 01 D3

Coollattin Coollattin ☎ 055 29125 Fax 055 29125
Plenty of trees provide features on this 18-hole parkland
course.
18 holes, 6148yds, Par 70, SSS 68.
Club membership 840.
Visitors Must contact in advance.
Societies contact for details.
Green Fees IEP20 per round (IEP25 weekends & bank
holidays).
Prof Peter Jones
Designer Peter McEvoy
Facilities ⊗ ⽊ ⅃ 🎽 ♀ ⚲ 🏠 🛒 ⚸

Hotel ★★★🏊 Marlfield House Hotel, GOREY
☎ 055 21124 19 ⇄ 🐾

WICKLOW   Map 01 D3

Wicklow Dunbur Rd ☎ 0404 67379
Situated on the cliffs overlooking Wicklow Bay this parkland
course does not have many trees. It was extended to 18 holes
in 1994, it provides a challenging test of golf with each hole
having its own individual features.
18 holes, 5126mtrs, Par 71, SSS 70.
Club membership 500.
Visitors welcome, restrictions on Wed/Thu evening and
Sun. Recommended to call in advance for times
Societies contact for details.
Green Fees IEP25 per round.
Cards 💳
Prof Darren McLoughlin
Designer Craddock & Ruddy
Facilities ⊗ ⽊ ⅃ 🎽 ♀ ⚲ 🏠 ⚸

Hotel ★★★🏊 Tinakilly Country House &
Restaurant, RATHNEW
☎ 0404 69274 52 ⇄ 🐾

WOODENBRIDGE   Map 01 D3

Woodenbridge Woodenbridge, Arklow
☎ 0402 35202 Fax 0402 35202 e-mail: wgc@eircom.net
A level parkland course with undulating fairways and greens,
traversed by two lovely meandering rivers.
18 holes, 6400yds, Par 71, SSS 70, Course record 71.
Club membership 550.
Visitors may not play Thu and Sat, prior booking
strongly recommended.
Societies Mon, Tue & Fri only, book well in advance.
Green Fees IEP40 per round(IEP50 weekends & bank
holidays).
Cards 💳
Designer Patrick Merrigan
Facilities ⊗ ⽊ ⅃ 🎽 ♀ ⚲ 🏌 ⚸
Location 4m NW of Arklow

Hotel ★★★ 64% Woodenbridge Hotel, WOODEN
BRIDGE ☎ 0402 35146 23 ⇄ 🐾

KEY TO ATLAS

Shetland Islands

16

Orkney Islands

○	Town Names
●	Golf Course
⑩	Motorway junction
⑳	Restricted motorway junction

13   **14**   **15**
●Inverness

Aberdeen●

●Fort William

Perth●

Glasgow●   ●Edinburgh

10   **11**   **12**

Londonderry●   Larne●   ●Stranraer   Newcastle●
●Belfast   ●Carlisle

●Middlesbrough

●Kendal

●York

Leeds●   Hull●

1   Liverpool●   Manchester●   **8**   **9**

Galway●   Dublin●   **6**   **7**   ●Sheffield

Holyhead●   ●Lincoln

Limerick●   Nottingham●   Norwich●

Rosslare●

Aberystwyth●

Cork●   Birmingham●

●Cambridge

Carmarthen●   Gloucester●   Colchester●
Oxford●

Cardiff●   **4**   LONDON●   **5**
2   **3**   ●Bristol   Guildford●

Barnstaple●   Taunton●   Maidstone●   Dover●
Southampton●   Brighton●

Exeter●   Dorchester●

●Plymouth

Penzance●

Isles of Scilly   See page 16 for Channel Islands

© Automobile Association Developments Limited 2001

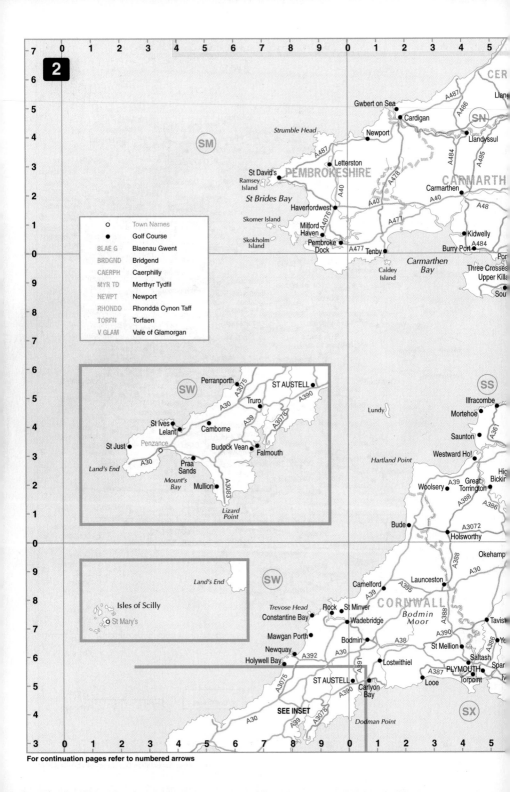

2

CER

Llan

Gwbert on Sea
Cardigan

SN

Strumble Head
Newport
Llandyssul

SM

A487

A484

A485

Letterston

St David's
PEMBROKESHIRE

CARMARTH

Ramsey
Island

A478

Carmarthen

A40

St Brides Bay

Haverfordwest

A40

A40

A48

Skomer Island
Milford
Haven

Kidwelly

A477

	Town Names
●	Golf Course
BLAE G	Blaenau Gwent
BRDGND	Bridgend
CAERPH	Caerphilly
MYR TD	Merthyr Tydfil
NEWPT	Newport
RHONDD	Rhondda Cynon Taff
TORFN	Torfaen
V GLAM	Vale of Glamorgan

Skokholm
Island
Pembroke
Dock
A477
Tenby

Burry Port
A484

Por

Caldey
Island

Carmarthen
Bay

Three Crosses
Upper Killa

Sou

Perranporth
ST AUSTELL

SW

A3075

A390

Truro

SS

Ilfracombe

A30

Mortehoe

A39

Lundy

Saunton

A361

St Ives
Lelant
Camborne

A3078

Budock Vean
Falmouth

St Just
Penzance

Westward Ho!

Land's End
A30
Praa
Sands

Hartland Point

Hig
Bickir

Mount's
Bay
Mullion

A3083

Woolsery

A39
A388

Great
Torrington

A386

Lizard
Point

Bude

A3072

Holsworthy

Okeham p

A388

A30

Land's End
SW

Camelford
A395

Launceston

A30

Isles of Scilly
St Mary's

Trevose Head
Constantine Bay
Rock
St Minver

CORNWALL

Bodmin
Moor

A388

Tavist

Mawgan Porth
Wadebridge
A390

Newquay
A392
Bodmin
A38
St Mellion

A389
Ye

A30

A391

Holywell Bay
Lostwithiel
Saltash
PLYMOUTH
Spar

A3075

A387
Torpoint
Iv

ST AUSTELL
Looe

A390
Carlyon
Bay

SX

SEE INSET
A30
A391
A3078

Dodman Point

For continuation pages refer to numbered arrows

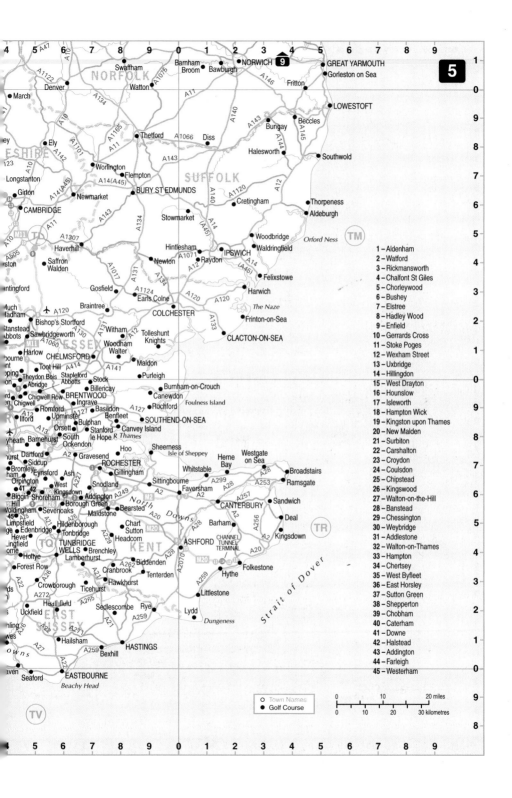

5

NORFOLK
SUFFOLK
ESSEX
KENT
EAST SUSSEX

Swaffham
Barnham Broom
Bawburgh
NORWICH
GREAT YARMOUTH
Gorleston on Sea
Denver
Watton
Fritton
March
LOWESTOFT
Ely
Thetford
Diss
Bungay
Beccles
Halesworth
Southwold
Worlington
Flempton
Longstanton
Newmarket
BURY ST EDMUNDS
Girton
Cretingham
Thorpeness
CAMBRIDGE
Stowmarket
Aldeburgh
Haverhill
Woodbridge
Orford Ness
Saffron Walden
Hintlesham
Waldringfield
Newton
IPSWICH
Raydon
Gosfield
Felixstowe
Earls Colne
Harwich
Braintree
The Naze
Bishop's Stortford
COLCHESTER
Frinton-on-Sea
Sawbridgeworth
Witham
Tolleshunt Knights
Harlow
Woodham Walter
CLACTON-ON-SEA
CHELMSFORD
Maldon
Toot Hill
Theydon Bois
Stapleford Abbotts
Stock
Purleigh
Abridge
Billericay
Burnham-on-Crouch
Chigwell Row
BRENTWOOD
Canewdon
Chigwell
Ingrave
Rochford
Foulness Island
Romford
Basildon
Ilford
Upminster
Benfleet
SOUTHEND-ON-SEA
Orsett
Bulphan
Stanford
Canvey Island
South
le Hope
R. Thames
Barnehurst
Ockendon
Sheerness
Hoo
Isle of Sheppey
Westgate on Sea
Sidcup
Gravesend
Herne Bay
Bromley
ROCHESTER
Whitstable
Broadstairs
Eynsford
Ash
Gillingham
Sittingbourne
Ramsgate
Orpington
West
Snodland
Faversham
Shoreham
Kingsdown
Addington
Sandwich
Borough Green
Bearsted
CANTERBURY
Sevenoaks
Maidstone
Deal
Hildenborough
Chart Sutton
Barham
Hever
Tonbridge
Headcorn
Kingsdown
Edenbridge
ASHFORD
CHANNEL TUNNEL TERMINAL
Holtye
TUNBRIDGE WELLS
Brenchley
Forest Row
Lamberhurst
Biddenden
Folkestone
Crowborough
Cranbrook
Tenterden
Hythe
Heathfield
Ticehurst
Hawkhurst
Littlestone
Uckfield
Sedlescombe
Rye
Lydd
Dungeness
Hailsham
HASTINGS
Seaford
Bexhill
EASTBOURNE
Beachy Head

North Downs

Strait of Dover

1 – Aldenham
2 – Watford
3 – Rickmansworth
4 – Chalfont St Giles
5 – Chorleywood
6 – Bushey
7 – Elstree
8 – Hadley Wood
9 – Enfield
10 – Gerrards Cross
11 – Stoke Poges
12 – Wexham Street
13 – Uxbridge
14 – Hillingdon
15 – West Drayton
16 – Hounslow
17 – Isleworth
18 – Hampton Wick
19 – Kingston upon Thames
20 – New Malden
21 – Surbiton
22 – Carshalton
23 – Croydon
24 – Coulsdon
25 – Chipstead
26 – Kingswood
27 – Walton-on-the-Hill
28 – Banstead
29 – Chessington
30 – Weybridge
31 – Addlestone
32 – Walton-on-Thames
33 – Hampton
34 – Chertsey
35 – West Byfleet
36 – East Horsley
37 – Sutton Green
38 – Shepperton
39 – Chobham
40 – Caterham
41 – Downe
42 – Halstead
43 – Addington
44 – Farleigh
45 – Westerham

○ Town Names
● Golf Course

0   10   20 miles
0   10   20   30 kilometres

6

Point of Ayre
Seascale

A17

Isle of Man   Ramsey
A3   Maughold Head

ISLE
OF
MAN

Peel A4
A2
Sile
Onchan
A1   DOUGLAS
A3
A5
Port St Mary
Port Erin   Castletown
Dreswick Point

SC

I r i s h
S e a

Carmel Head
Amlwch   Great
Ormes
Head
Holyhead   Llandudno   Prestaty
COLWYN   Rhyl
Anglesey   BAY
Holy Island   Llangefni   Conwy   Abergele   Rhu
Beaumaris   St A
Rhosneigr   Penmaenmawr   Bodelwyddan   C
Llanfairfechan
A55   Bangor
ISLE OF   Denbigh
ANGLESEY   Caernarfon
CONWY   A543
Caernarfon   A4086
Bay   Betws-y-coed   DENBI
SH   A470   R
A498
Morfa   A499   A5
Nefyn   A487
Lleyn Peninsula   A497   Porthmadog
Criccieth   A4212
Pwllheli   Bala
A494
Harlech   A470
Abersoch   GWYNEDD
Bardsey   A496
Island

Dolgellau   A470
A458

○ Town Names   A487   POWY
● Golf Course

Machynlleth   A470
Aberdyfi   A493   Caersw
Cardigan Bay   Ne
0   10   20 miles   Borth   A487   A44   Llanidloes   A470
0   10   20   30 kilometres   SN Aberystwyth   A470
CEREDIGION   A470

Llanrhystud
2

Llandulas

For continuation pages refer to numbered arrows

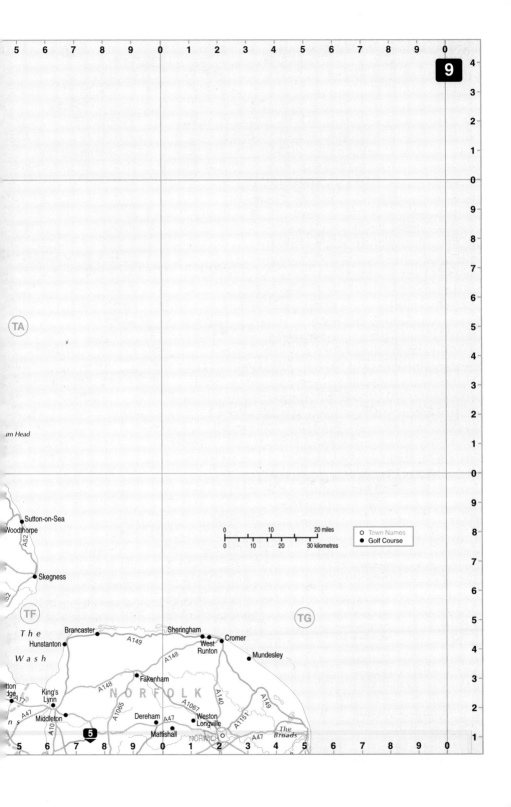

5　6　7　8　9　0　1　2　3　4　5　6　7　8　9　0

9

4
3
2
1
0
9
8
7
6

TA

5
4
3
2

ırn Head

1
0
9

Sutton-on-Sea
Woodthorpe
A52

| 0 | | 10 | | 20 miles |
| 0 | 10 | 20 | | 30 kilometres |

○ Town Names
● Golf Course

8
7

Skegness

6

TF

TG

5
4

The
Wash

Brancaster
Hunstanton
A149

Sheringham
West
Runton
Cromer

Mundesley

3

tton
dge
A17

King's
Lynn

A148

Fakenham

N O R F O L K

A140

A149

2

A47
n s
Middleton
A10

A1065

A148

Dereham
A47

Weston
Longville

A1151

1

5

Mattishall

NORWICH ○

A47

*The
Broads*

5　6　7　8　9　0　1　2　3　4　5　6　7　8　9　0

8 9 0 1 2 13 3 4 5 6 7 8 9 0 1 14 2 3

-4
-3
-2
-1
0
9
8
7
6
5
4
3
2
1
0
9
8
7
6
5
4
3
2
1

Tiree
Ulva
Iona
Isle of Mull
Craignure
Oban
Dalmally
A849
NM
A85
A816
Firth of Lorne
Lismore
Eriska
A828
ARGYLL
AND BUTE
A819
Luing
Inveraray
A83
Scarba
Colonsay
Scalasaig
Oronsay
Lochgilphead
A886
A815
A814
Luss
A82
Helensburgh
Cardross
Gourock
Dunoon
DUMB
Jura
Sound of Jura
A846
Tighnabruaich
Innellan
Port
Bannatyne
Greenock
Port Glasgow
Kilmacolm
Bis
Bridge of Wei
Johns
Lochwinno
Uplaw
Skelmorlie
Tarbert
Coul Point
A847
Islay
Rothesay
Kingarth
Largs
Millport
Kilbirnie
West
Kilbride
Sound
of Bute
A844
A78
A760
B
A737
Gigha
Gigha
Island
NR
A83
Kintyre
Kilbrannan Sound
Lochranza
Sannox
A841
NORTH
AYRSHIRE
Stevenston
Irvine
Port Ellen
Carradale
Arran
Brodick
Machrie
Lamlash
Holy I
Whiting
Bay
KILMARN
Firth of
Clyde
Ba
Troon
Prestwick
Ayr
Blackwaterfoot
Machrihanish
Patna
Southend
Mull of
Kintyre
Maybo
Turnberry
Ailsa Craig
Girvan
SOUTH
AYRSHIR

North Channel
NW

Newton Stew
Loch Ryan
A71
A714
Stranraer
A77
A75
Glenluce
Wig
Portpatrick
A176
A747
Luce Bay
M
Mull of
Galloway

○ Town Names
● Golf Course
C EDIN   City of Edinburgh
C GLAS   City of Glasgow
CLACKS   Clackmannanshire
W DUNS   West Dunbartonshire
E DUNS   East Dunbartonshire
E RENS   East Renfrewshire
INVER   Inverclyde
N LANS   North Lanarkshire
RENS   Renfrewshire

0   10   20 miles
0   10   20   30 kilometres

8 9 0 1 2 3 4 5 6 7 8 9 0 1 6 2 3

For continuation pages refer to numbered arrows

15

2 3 4 5 6 7 8 9 0 1 2 3 4 5 6 7

Island of Stroma
Duncansby Head
A836

Noss Head
Wick

ND

Lybster

Lossiemouth
Spey Cullen
Garmouth Bay Buckie Banff Macduff Fraserburgh
Elgin A98 Inverallochy
(A92) A90
A941 A96
Keith NJ A97 Turriff A950
Rothes A952 (A92)
Dufftown A95 (A90) Peterhead
MORAY A920 Huntly A947 (A952)
A95 A96 Cruden Bay
A941 A97 A920 Ellon
Insch Oldmeldrum
ABERDEENSHIRE A90 Newburgh on Ythan
A939 Inverurie (A92)
Alford Newmachar
A944 Kemnay Kintore
A939 A97 A944 ABERDEEN CITY
Tarland Torphins A980 Peterculter A93 ABERDEEN
A93 Aboyne
Ballater Banchory Portlethen
A957 A90
Stonehaven

Auchenblae A92

NO
shee
(al of) Edzell A90
ANGUS Brechin
Kirriemuir Montrose
A935
A932
Alyth Forfar A933 Lunan Bay

○ Town Names
● Golf Course

0   10   20 miles
0   10   20   30 kilometres

2 3 4 5 12 6 7 8 9 0 1 2 3 4 5 6 7 8

16

0   10   20 miles
0   10   20   30 kilometres

HY

HP

Westray

Yell

Mainland

Island of
Whalsay

Mainland

KIRKWALL

LERWICK

Stromness

HU

Hoy

ND

Orkney
Islands

Shetland
Islands

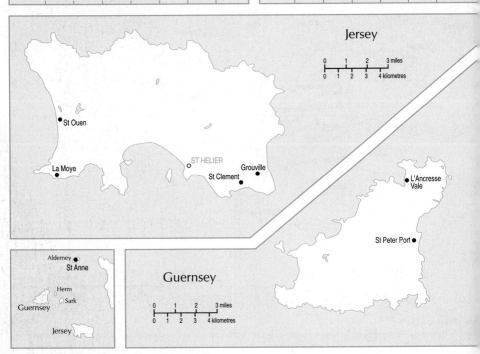

Jersey

0   1   2   3 miles
0   1   2   3   4 kilometres

St Ouen

ST HELIER

Grouville

La Moye

St Clement

L'Ancresse
Vale

St Peter Port

Alderney
St Anne

Herm

Guernsey

Guernsey

Sark

0   1   2   3 miles
0   1   2   3   4 kilometres

Jersey

AA Hotels

with special arrangements for golf

The following index lists hotels, inspected and rated by the AA, that have a special arrangement with a golf course or courses. These hotels may have their own golf course attached to the hotel or nearby, or they may offer discounted green fees, reserved tee times or other golfing packages to residents. This list was believed correct at our press date, please contact the hotels directly for information on golfing packages or arrangements. Further details of these and other hotels can be found in the AA Hotel Guide, published annually. For the most up-to-date information visit the AA web site: www.theAA.com

ENGLAND

ABBOT'S SALFORD
Salford Hall Hotel 01386 871300

ALBRIGHTON
Lea Manor Hotel 1902 373266

ALDEBURGH
The Brudenell 01728 452071

ALDEBURGH
Wentworth Hotel 01728 452312

ALDEBURGH
White Lion Hotel 01728 452720

ALDERMINSTER
Ettington Park Hotel 01789 450123

ALFRISTON
Deans Place 01323 870248

ALNWICK
White Swan Hotel 01665 602109

ALTARNUN
Penhallow Manor Hotel
01566 86206

ALTRINCHAM
Cresta Court Hotel 0161 927 7272

ALTRINCHAM
Quality Hotel 0161 928 7121

AMBLESIDE
Nanny Brow Country House
015394 32036

AMBLESIDE
Regent Hotel 015394 32254

AMESBURY
Antrobus Arms Hotel 01980 623163

ANDOVER
Esseborne Manor 01264 736444

ANDOVER
Quality Hotel Andover 01264 369111

ASCOT
The Berystede 0870 400 8111

ASCOT
The Royal Berkshire Hotel
01344 623322

ASHBURTON
Holne Chase Hotel 01364 631471

ASHBURTON
The Lavender House Hotel
01364 652697

ASHFORD
Eastwell Manor 01233 213000

AXMINSTER
Fairwater Head Hotel 01297 678349

AXMINSTER
Lea Hill Hotel 01404 881881

AYLESBURY
Hartwell House 01296 747444

BALSALL COMMON
Nailcote Hall 024 7646 6174

BAMBURGH
The Mizen Head Hotel
01668 214254

BAMBURGH
Victoria Hotel 01668 214431

BAMBURGH
Waren House Hotel 01668 214581

BANBURY
Banbury House 01295 259361

BANBURY
Wroxton House Hotel 01295 730777

BARLBOROUGH
Hotel Ibis 01246 813222

BARNSTAPLE
Barnstaple Hotel 01271 376221

BARNSTAPLE
Park Hotel 01271 372166

BARNSTAPLE
Royal & Fortescue Hotel
01271 324446

BARNSTAPLE
The Imperial 01271 345861

BARTON
Barton Grange Hotel
01772 862551

BASINGSTOKE
Hanover International Hotel & Club
01256 764161

BASINGSTOKE
Ringway Hotel 01256 796700

BASSENTHWAITE
Castle Inn Hotel 017687 76401

BATH
Lansdown Grove Hotel
01225 483888

BATH
The Bath Spa Hotel 0870 400 822

BATH
The Francis 0870 400 822

BATH
Wentworth House Hotel
01225 33919

BEACONSFIELD
The Bellhouse 01753 88721

BEAMINSTER
Bridge House Hotel 01308 86220

BELFORD
Blue Bell Hotel 01668 21354

BERWICK-UPON-TWEED
Marshall Meadows Country House
Hotel 01289 33113

BIDEFORD
Royal Hotel 01237 47200

BIDEFORD
Yeoldon Country House Hotel
01237 47440

BIGBURY-ON-SEA
Henley Hotel 01548 81024

BIRKENHEAD
Bowler Hat Hotel 0151 652 493

BIRMINGHAM
Express by Holiday Inn Castle
Bromwich 0121 747 663

BIRMINGHAM
Oxford Hotel 0121 449 329

BIRMINGHAM
Posthouse Birmingham Great Barr
0870 400 900

BIRMINGHAM AIRPORT
Novotel Birmingham Airport
0121 782 700

BISHOP'S STORTFORD
Down Hall Country House Hotel
01279 73144

BOLTON ABBEY
The Devonshire Arms Country House
Hotel 01756 71044

BORROWDALE
Borrowdale Hotel 017687 7722

BOSCASTLE
The Wellington Hotel 01840 250202

BOUGHTON STREET
The Garden Hotel & Restaurant
01227 751411

BOURNEMOUTH
Belvedere Hotel 01202 297556

BOURNEMOUTH
Burley Court Hotel 01202 552824

BOURNEMOUTH
Cumberland Hotel 01202 290722

BOURNEMOUTH
Queens Hotel 01202 554415

BOURNEMOUTH
The Connaught Hotel 01202 298020

BOURTON-ON-THE-WATER
Chester House Hotel & Motel
01451 820286

BOURTON-ON-THE-WATER
Dial House Hotel 01451 822244

BOVEY TRACEY
Coombe Cross Hotel 01626 832476

BOVEY TRACEY
Edgemoor Hotel 01626 832466

BRACKNELL
Coppid Beech 01344 303333

BRADFORD
Apperley Manor 0113 250 5626

BRADFORD
Cedar Court Hotel Bradford
01274 406606

BRADFORD
Courtyard by Marriott
Leeds/Bradford 0113 285 4646

BRADFORD
Midland Hotel 01274 735735

BRADFORD-ON-AVON
Leigh Park Hotel 01225 864885

BRADFORD-ON-AVON
Woolley Grange 01225 864705

BRAMHALL
County Hotel Bramhall
0161 455 9988

BRAMPTON
Farlam Hall Hotel 016977 46234

BRAMPTON
The Tarn End House Hotel
01697 72340

BRANDESBURTON
Burton Lodge Hotel 01964 542847

BRANSTON
Branston Hall Hotel 01522 793305

BRAY
Chauntry House Hotel & Restaurant
01628 673991

BRIDGNORTH
Falcon Hotel 01746 763134

BRIDGWATER
Walnut Tree Hotel 01278 662255

BRIDLINGTON
Expanse Hotel 01262 675347

BRIDPORT
Haddon House Hotel 01308 423626

BRIDPORT
Roundham House Hotel
01308 422753

BRIGHTON
Brighton Hotel 01273 820555

BRIGHTON
Old Ship Hotel 01273 329001

BRISTOL
Aztec Hotel 01454 201090

BRISTOL
Bristol Marriott City Centre
0117 929 4281

BRISTOL
Bristol Marriott Royal Hotel
0117 925 5100

BRISTOL
Henbury Lodge Hotel
0117 950 2615

BRISTOL
Redwood Lodge Hotel
01275 393901

BRIXHAM
Berryhead Hotel 01803 853225

BRIXHAM
Maypool Park 01803 842442

BRIXHAM
Quayside Hotel 01803 855751

BROCKENHURST
Rhinefield House 01590 622922

BROME
The Cornwallis Country Hotel &
Restaurant 01379 870326

BROMLEY
Bromley Court Hotel 020 8461 8600

BROMSGROVE
Hanover International Hotel & Club
01527 576600

BROXTON
Broxton Hall Country House Hotel
01829 782321

BROXTON
De Vere Carden Park Hotel
01829 731000

BUCKINGHAM
Villiers Hotel 01280 822444

BUDE
Atlantic House Hotel 01288 352451

BUDE
Camelot Hotel 01288 352361

BUDE
Falcon Hotel 01288 352005

BUDE
Hotel Penarvor 01288 352036

BUDE
Maer Lodge Hotel 01288 353306

BUDE
Stamford Hill Hotel 01288 352709

BURFORD
The Inn For All Seasons
01451 844324

BURNHAM
Burnham Beeches 01628 429955

BURNHAM
Grovefield Hotel 01628 603131

BURNLEY
Oaks Hotel 01282 414141

BURRINGTON
Northcote Manor 01769 560501

BUXTON
Buckingham Hotel 01298 70481

BUXTON
Palace Hotel 01298 22001

BUXTON
Portland Hotel & Park Restaurant
01298 71493

CADNAM
Bartley Lodge 023 8081 2248

CAMBRIDGE
Royal Cambridge Hotel
01223 351631

CANTERBURY
County Hotel 01227 766266

CANTERBURY
The Chaucer 0870 400 8106

CARLISLE
County Hotel 01228 531316

CARLISLE
Crown Hotel 01228 561888

CARLISLE
The Crown & Mitre 01228 525491

CASTLE DONINGTON
The Priest House on the River
01332 810649

CHALE
Clarendon Hotel & Wight Mouse Inn
01983 730431

CHARD
Lordleaze Hotel 01460 61066

CHELTENHAM
Cheltenham Park Hotel
01242 222021

CHELTENHAM
The Greenway 01242 862352

CHELTENHAM
The Prestbury House Hotel &
Restaurant 01242 529533

CHENIES
The Bedford Arms Chenies
01923 283301

CHESHUNT
Cheshunt Marriott Hotel
01992 451245

CHESTER
Grosvenor Pulford Hotel
01244 570560

CHESTER
The Chester Crabwell Manor Hotel
01244 851666

CHICHESTER
The Ship Hotel 01243 778000

CHIDEOCK
Chideock House Hotel
01297 489242

CHIPPING
The Gibbon Bridge Hotel
01995 61456

CHIPPING CAMPDEN
Cotswold House 01386 840330

CHOLLERFORD
Swallow George Hotel
01434 681611

CHORLEY
Park Hall Hotel 01257 452090

CHURT
Frensham Pond Hotel 01252 795161

CHURT
Pride of the Valley Hotel
01428 605799

CLACTON-ON-SEA
Esplanade Hotel 01255 220450

CLEATOR
Ennerdale Country House Hotel
01946 813907

CLEOBURY MORTIMER
The Redfern Hotel 01299 270395

CLEVEDON
Walton Park Hotel 01275 874253

CLIMPING
Bailiffscourt Hotel 01903 723511

CLITHEROE
Shireburn Arms Hotel 01254 826518

COLCHESTER
Posthouse Colchester 0870 400 9020

COLERNE
Lucknam Park 01225 742777

CONSTANTINE BAY
Treglos Hotel 01841 520727

COPTHORNE
Copthorne Hotel London Gatwick
01342 348800

CORNHILL-ON-TWEED
Tillmouth Park Country House Hotel
01890 882255

CRATHORNE
Crathorne Hall Hotel 01642 700398

CROYDE
Kittiwell House Hotel & Restaurant
01271 890247

DARLINGTON
Blackwell Grange 01325 509955

DARLINGTON
Croft Spa Hotel 01325 720319

DARLINGTON
Devonport Hotel 01325 332255

DARTFORD
Rowhill Grange Hotel & Spa
01322 615136

DARTMOUTH
Royal Castle Hotel 01803 833033

DARTMOUTH
Stoke Lodge Hotel 01803 770523

DARTMOUTH
The Dart Marina Hotel
0870 400 8134

DAVENTRY
Hanover International Hotel & Club
01327 307000

DAWLISH
Langstone Cliff Hotel
01626 868000

DERBY
Hotel Ristorante La Gondola
01332 332895

DERBY
Menzies Mickleover Court
0870 6003013

DOVER
The Churchill 01304 203633

DROITWICH
The Hadley Bowling Green Inn
01905 620294

DURHAM
Bowburn Hall Hotel 0191 377 0311

DURHAM
Durham Marriott Hotel, Royal
County 0191 386 6821

EAST GRINSTEAD
Woodbury House Hotel
01342 313657

EASTBOURNE
Chatsworth Hotel 01323 411016

EASTBOURNE
Grand Hotel 01323 412345

EASTBOURNE
Hydro Hotel 01323 720643

EASTBOURNE
Langham Hotel 01323 731451

EASTBOURNE
Lansdowne Hotel 01323 725174

EASTBOURNE
New Wilmington Hotel
01323 721219

EGHAM
Runnymede Hotel & Spa
01784 436171

ELSTREE
Edgwarebury Hotel 020 8953 8227

ELY
The Nyton Hotel 01353 662459

EMBLETON
Dunstanburgh Castle Hotel
01665 576111

EMPINGHAM
The White Horse Inn 01780 460221

EPWORTH
Red Lion Hotel 01427 872208

EVESHAM
Northwick Hotel 01386 40322

EVESHAM
The Mill At Harvington
01386 870688

EVESHAM
Wood Norton Hall 01386 420007

EWEN
Wild Duck Inn 01285 770310

EXETER
Gipsy Hill Hotel 01392 465252

EXETER
Lord Haldon Hotel 01392 832483

EXETER
Royal Clarence 01392 319955

EXETER
The Southgate 0870 400 8333

EXMOUTH
Royal Beacon Hotel 01395 264886

FAIRFORD
Bull Hotel 01285 712535

FALMOUTH
Falmouth Beach Resort Hotel
01326 312999

FALMOUTH
Falmouth Hotel 01326 312671

FALMOUTH
Green Lawns Hotel 01326 312734

FALMOUTH
Gyllyngdune Manor Hotel
01326 312978

FALMOUTH
Park Grove Hotel 01326 313276

FALMOUTH
Penmere Manor 01326 211411

FALMOUTH
Penmorvah Manor 01326 250277

FALMOUTH
Royal Duchy Hotel 01326 313042

FAREHAM
Lysses House Hotel 01329 822622

FAREHAM
Posthouse Fareham 0870 400 9028

FAREHAM
Solent Hotel 01489 880000

FARINGDON
Sudbury House Hotel & Conference
Centre 01367 241272

FARNHAM
Bishop's Table Hotel 01252 710222

FELIXSTOWE
Orwell Hotel 01394 285511

FERNDOWN
The Dormy 01202 872121

FOREST ROW
Ashdown Park Hotel 01342 824988

FOWNHOPE
Green Man Inn 01432 860243

FRINTON-ON-SEA
Maplin Hotel 01255 673832

GILLAN
Tregildry Hotel 01326 231378

GISBURN
Stirk House Hotel 01200 445581

GLOSSOP
Wind in the Willows Hotel
01457 868001

GLOUCESTER
Hatton Court 01452 617412

GOODRICH
Ye Hostelrie Hotel 01600 890241

GRANTHAM
Kings Hotel 01476 590800

GRANTHAM
Swallow Hotel 01476 593000

GRASMERE
Michael's Nook Country House Hotel
& Rest. 015394 35496

GRASMERE
Rothay Garden Hotel 015394 35334

GRASMERE
The Swan 0870 400 8132

GRASMERE
Wordsworth Hotel 015394 35592

GREAT YARMOUTH
Imperial Hotel 01493 842000

GRIMSBY
Humber Royal 01472 240024

GUILDFORD
The Manor 01483 222624

HADLEY WOOD
West Lodge Park Hotel
020 8216 3900

HALIFAX
The Rock Inn Hotel 01422 379721

HARROGATE
The White House 01423 501388

HARROW WEALD
Grim's Dyke Hotel 020 8385 3100

HASTINGS & ST LEONARDS
Royal Victoria Hotel 01424 445544

HEBDEN BRIDGE
Carlton Hotel 01422 844400

HELMSLEY
Feversham Arms Hotel
01439 770766

HELMSLEY
Pheasant Hotel 01439 771241

HELMSLEY
The Carlton Lodge Hotel
01439 770557

HELMSLEY
The Crown Hotel 01439 770297

HEREFORD
Ancient Camp Inn 01981 250449

HEREFORD
Graftonbury Garden Hotel
01432 268826

HETHERSETT
Park Farm Hotel 01603 810264

HEXHAM
Beaumont Hotel 01434 602331

HINCKLEY
Hanover International Hotel & Club
01455 631122

HINCKLEY
Sketchley Grange Hotel
01455 251133

HINTON CHARTERHOUSE
Homewood Park Hotel
01225 723731

HOLMFIRTH
Old Bridge Hotel 01484 681212

HONITON
Combe House Hotel at Gittisham
01404 540400

HOPE COVE
Cottage Hotel 01548 561555

HORLEY
Stanhill Court Hotel 01293 862166

HORNCASTLE
Admiral Rodney Hotel 01507 523131

HOUNSLOW
The Renaissance London Heathrow
Hotel 020 8897 6363

HUDDERSFIELD
Old Golf House Hotel 01422 379311

HUDDERSFIELD
The Lodge Hotel 01484 431001

HUNMANBY
Wrangham House Hotel
01723 891333

HUNSTRETE
Hunstrete House Hotel
01761 490490

HYTHE
Stade Court 01303 268263

HYTHE
The Hythe Imperial Hotel
01303 267441

ILKLEY
The Craiglands Hotel 01943 430001

IPSWICH
County Hotel Ipswich 01473 209988

IPSWICH
Novotel Ipswich 01473 232400

IVYBRIDGE
Glazebrook House Hotel &
Restaurant 01364 73322

KENILWORTH
Chesford Grange Hotel
01926 859331

KESWICK
Keswick Country House Hotel
017687 72020

KESWICK
Skiddaw Hotel 017687 72071

KETTERING
Kettering Park Hotel 01536 416666

KING'S LYNN
Stuart House Hotel 01553 772169

KINGSBRIDGE
Buckland-Tout-Saints 01548 853055

KINGTON
Burton Hotel 01544 230323

KIRKBURTON
Hanover International Hotel
01484 607788

KIRKBY LONSDALE
Hipping Hall 015242 71187

KIRKBY LONSDALE
Plough Hotel 015395 67227

KIRKBYMOORSIDE
George & Dragon Hotel
01751 433334

KNUTSFORD
Cottons Hotel 01565 650333

KNUTSFORD
Mere Court Hotel & Conference
Centre 01565 831000

LANGHO
Northcote Manor 01254 240555

LAVENHAM
The Swan 0870 400 8116

LEA MARSTON
Lea Marston Hotel & Leisure
Complex 01675 470468

LEATHERHEAD
Bookham Grange Hotel
01372 452742

LEEDS
Crowne Plaza Leeds 0113 244 2200

LEEDS
Haley's Hotel & Restaurant
0113 278 4446

LEICESTER
Hermitage Hotel 0116 256 9955

LEICESTER
Leicester Stage Hotel 0116 288 6161

LENHAM
Chilston Park Hotel 01622 859803

LEOMINSTER
Royal Oak Hotel 01568 612610

LEOMINSTER
Talbot Hotel 01568 616347

LEWES
White Hart Hotel 01273 476694

LICHFIELD
Little Barrow Hotel 01543 414500

LIFTON
Arundell Arms 01566 784666

LONDON SW1
The Millennium Knightsbridge
020 7235 4377

LONDON W1
Claridge's 020 7629 8860

LONDON W1
The Westbury Hotel 020 7629 7755

LONG MELFORD	**MARCH**	**NANTWICH**
The Bull 01787 378494	Olde Griffin Hotel 01354 652517	Rookery Hall 01270 610016
LOOE	**MARKET HARBOROUGH**	**NEWBURY**
Fieldhead Hotel 01503 262689	Three Swans Hotel 01858 466644	The Vineyard at Stockcross
LOOE	**MAWGAN PORTH**	01635 528770
Hannafore Point Hotel	Tredragon Hotel 01637 860213	**NEWCASTLE UPON TYNE**
01503 263273	**MAWNAN SMITH**	"Newcastle Marriott Hotel, Gosforth
LOOE	Budock Vean-The Hotel on the River	Park " 0191 236 4111
Rivercroft Hotel & Apartments	01326 252100 & Freephone	**NEWCASTLE UPON TYNE**
01503 262251	**MAWNAN SMITH**	Whites Hotel 0191 281 5126
LOSTWITHIEL	Meudon Hotel 01326 250541	**NEWICK**
Lostwithiel Hotel Golf & Country	**MAWNAN SMITH**	Newick Park Country Estate
Club 01208 873550	Trelawne Hotel 01326 250226	01825 723633
LOSTWITHIEL	**MERIDEN**	**NEWQUAY**
Restormel Lodge Hotel	Manor Hotel 01676 522735	Barrowfield Hotel 01637 878878
01208 872223	**MIDHURST**	**NEWQUAY**
LOUGHBOROUGH	Spread Eagle Hotel and Health Spa	Cedars Hotel 01637 874225
Quality Hotel 01509 211800	01730 816911	**NEWQUAY**
LOWER BEEDING	**MIDSOMER NORTON**	Esplanade Hotel 01637 873333
South Lodge Hotel 01403 891711	Centurion Hotel 01761 417711	**NEWQUAY**
LOWER SLAUGHTER	**MILFORD ON SEA**	Glendorgal Hotel 01637 874937
Lower Slaughter Manor	South Lawn Hotel 01590 643911	**NEWQUAY**
01451 820456	**MILFORD ON SEA**	Headland Hotel 01637 872211
LOWER SLAUGHTER	Westover Hall Hotel 01590 643044	**NEWQUAY**
Washbourne Court Hotel	**MILTON COMMON**	Hotel Bristol 01637 875181
01451 822143	The Oxford Belfry 01844 279381	**NEWQUAY**
LOWESTOFT	**MILTON KEYNES**	Hotel Riviera 01637 874251
Hotel Hatfield 01502 565337	Posthouse Milton Keynes	**NEWQUAY**
LOWESTOFT	0870 400 9057	Philema Hotel 01637 872571
Ivy House Farm 01502 501353	**MILTON KEYNES**	**NEWQUAY**
LUDLOW	Quality Hotel & Suites Milton Keynes	Porth Veor Manor Hotel
Dinham Hall Hotel 01584 876464	01908 561666	01637 873274
LYDFORD	**MINEHEAD**	**NEWQUAY**
Lydford House 01822 820347	Channel House Hotel 01643 703229	Trebarwith Hotel 01637 872288
LYME REGIS	**MINEHEAD**	**NORTH WALTHAM**
Bay Hotel 01297 442059	Periton Park Hotel 01643 706885	Premier Lodge (Basingstoke)
LYMPSHAM	**MINEHEAD**	0870 700 1312
Batch Country Hotel 01934 750371	Wyndcott Hotel 01643 704522	**NORTHAMPTON**
LYNDHURST	**MORECAMBE**	Courtyard by Marriott Northampton
Crown Hotel 023 8028 2922	Strathmore Hotel 01524 421234	01604 622777
LYNDHURST	**MORETON**	**NORTHAMPTON**
Forest Lodge Hotel 023 8028 3677	Leasowe Castle Hotel 0151 606 9191	Lime Trees Hotel 01604 632188
LYTHAM ST ANNES	**MORETON-IN-MARSH**	**NORTHAMPTON**
Clifton Arms 01253 739898	Manor House Hotel 01608 650501	Northampton Marriott Hotel
LYTHAM ST ANNES	**MORTEHOE**	01604 768700
Glendower Hotel 01253 723241	Lundy House Hotel 01271 870372	**NORTHWICH**
MAIDENHEAD	**MOUSEHOLE**	Quality Hotel Northwich
Elva Lodge Hotel 01628 622948	Old Coastguard Hotel 01736 731222	01606 44443
MAIDENHEAD	**MULLION**	**NORTON**
Ye Olde Bell Hotel 01628 825881	Mullion Cove Hotel 01326 240328	The Hundred House Hotel
MALVERN	**MULLION**	01952 730353
Foley Arms Hotel 01684 573397	Polurrian Hotel 01326 240421	**NOTTINGHAM**
MALVERN	**MUNDFORD**	Bestwood Lodge 0115 920 3011
The Cottage in the Wood Hotel	Lynford Hall Hotel 01842 878351	**NOTTINGHAM**
01684 575859	**NAILSWORTH**	Nottingham Gateway 0115 979 4949
MANCHESTER	Egypt Mill Hotel 01453 833449	**NUNNEY**
Le Meridien Victoria & Albert	**NANTWICH**	The George at Nunney
0870 400 8505	Crown Hotel & Restaurant	01373 836458
MANCHESTER	01270 625283	**OAKHAM**
The Waterside Hotel 0161 445 0225		Hambleton Hall 01572 756991

OAKHAM
Whipper-in Hotel   01572 756971

OKEHAMPTON
Ashbury Hotel   01837 55453

OKEHAMPTON
Manor House Hotel   01837 53053

OKEHAMPTON
White Hart Hotel   01837 52730

ONNELEY
Wheatsheaf Inn at Onneley
01782 751581

ORMSKIRK
Beaufort Hotel   01704 892655

OSWESTRY
Pen-y-Dyffryn Country Hotel
01691 653700

OTTERBURN
The Otterburn Tower Hotel
01830 520620

OXFORD
Hawkwell House   01865 749988

PAIGNTON
Torbay Holiday Motel 01803 558226

PAINSWICK
Painswick Hotel   01452 812160

PENKRIDGE
Quality Hotel Stafford 01785 712459

PENRITH
North Lakes Hotel   01768 868111

PENRITH
The George Hotel   01768 862696

PERRANPORTH
Beach Dunes Hotel   01872 572263

PETTY FRANCE
Petty France Hotel   01454 238361

PICKERING
White Swan   01751 472288

PICKHILL
Nags Head Country Inn
01845 567391

PLYMOUTH
Grand Hotel   01752 661195

PLYMOUTH
Grosvenor Park Hotel 01752 229312

PLYMOUTH
Kitley House Hotel   01752 881555

PLYMOUTH
New Continental Hotel
01752 220782

POCKLINGTON
Yorkway Motel Ltd   01759 303071

POOLE
Haven Hotel   01202 707333

POOLE
Mansion House Hotel 01202 685666

POOLE
Salterns Hotel   01202 707321

POOLE
Sandbanks Hotel   01202 707377

PORLOCK
Anchor Hotel & Ship Inn
01643 862753

PORTSMOUTH
Portsmouth Marriott Hotel
023 9238 3151

PORTSMOUTH
Westfield Hall Hotel 023 9282 6971

PRESTON
Preston Marriott Hotel
01772 864087

PULBOROUGH
Chequers Hotel   01798 872486

READING
Holiday Inn   0118 925 9988

READING
Millennium Madejski Hotel Reading
0118 925 3500

READING
Royal County Hotel   0118 958 3455

REDDITCH
Montville Hotel and Restaurant
01527 544411

REDHILL
Nutfield Priory   01737 824400

REDWORTH
Redworth Hall Hotel   01388 770600

RENISHAW
Sitwell Arms Hotel   01246 435226

RICHMOND
King's Head Hotel   01748 850220

RINGWOOD
Tyrrells Ford Country House Hotel
01425 672646

RIPON
Ripon Spa Hotel   01765 602172

ROMSEY
Potters Heron Hotel   023 8026 6611

ROSS-ON-WYE
Chase Hotel   01989 763161

ROSS-ON-WYE
Chasedale Hotel   01989 562423

ROSS-ON-WYE
King's Head Hotel   01989 763174

ROSS-ON-WYE
Orles Barn Hotel and Restaurant
01989 562155

ROSS-ON-WYE
Pencraig Court Hotel 01989 770306

ROSS-ON-WYE
Pengethley Manor   01989 730211

ROYAL TUNBRIDGE WELLS
The Spa Hotel   01892 520331

SALCOMBE
Bolt Head Hotel   01548 843751

SALCOMBE
Soar Mill Cove Hotel 01548 561566

SALCOMBE
South Sands Hotel   01548 843741

SALCOMBE
Sunny Cliff Hotel   01548 842207

SALCOMBE
Tides Reach Hotel   01548 843466

SALISBURY
Milford Hall Hotel   01722 417411

SALISBURY
Rose & Crown Hotel   01722 399955

SANDIWAY
Nunsmere Hall Country House Hotel
01606 889100

SANDWICH
The Blazing Donkey Country Hotel
& Inn   01304 617362

SAUNTON
Preston House Hotel 01271 890472

SAUNTON
Saunton Sands Hotel 01271 890212

SCARBOROUGH
Crown Hotel   01723 373491

SCOTCH CORNER
Quality Hotel Scotch Corner
01748 850900

SEAHOUSES
Bamburgh Castle Hotel
01665 720283

SEATON
Seaton Heights Hotel   01297 20932

SEAVIEW
Springvale Hotel & Restaurant
01983 612533

SEDGEFIELD
Hardwick Hall Hotel   01740 620253

SEDLESCOMBE
Brickwall Hotel   01424 870253

SEVENOAKS
Royal Oak Hotel   01732 451109

SHANKLIN
Luccombe Hall Hotel 01983 862719

SHEFFIELD
Beauchief Hotel   0114 262 0500

SHIPDHAM
Pound Green Hotel   01362 820940

SHIPLEY
Marriott Hollins Hall Hotel &
Country Club   01274 530053

SHREWSBURY
Albrighton Hall Hotel 01939 291000

SIDMOUTH
Belmont Hotel   01395 512555

SIDMOUTH
Devoran Hotel   01395 513151

SIDMOUTH
Fortfield Hotel   01395 512403

SIDMOUTH
Hunters Moon Hotel 01395 513380

SIDMOUTH
Kingswood Hotel   01395 516367

SIDMOUTH
Mount Pleasant Hotel 01395 514694

SIDMOUTH
Riviera Hotel 01395 515201

SIDMOUTH
Royal Glen Hotel 01395 513221

SIDMOUTH
Salcombe Hill House Hotel
01395 514697

SIDMOUTH
Sidmount Hotel 01395 513432

SIDMOUTH
The Royal York & Faulkner Hotel
01395 513043 & 0800 220714

SIDMOUTH
Victoria Hotel 01395 512651

SIDMOUTH
Westbourne Hotel 01395 513774

SIDMOUTH
Westcliff Hotel 01395 513252

SKIPTON
Coniston Hall Lodge 01756 748080

SKIPTON
Hanover International Hotel & Club
01756 700100

SOUTH BRENT
Brookdale House Restaurant & Hotel
01548 821661

SOUTH NORMANTON
Swallow Hotel 01773 812000

SOUTHAMPTON
De Vere Grand Harbour
023 8063 3033

SOUTHPORT
Balmoral Lodge Hotel 01704 544298

SPENNYMOOR
Whitworth Hall 01388 811772

ST AGNES
Rose in Vale Country House Hotel
01872 552202

ST ALBANS
Sopwell House Hotel & Country Club
01727 864477

ST ALBANS
St Michael's Manor 01727 864444

ST AUSTELL
Boscundle Manor Hotel
01726 813557

ST AUSTELL Cliff
Head Hotel 01726 812345

ST IVES
Carbis Bay Hotel 01736 795311

ST IVES
Garrack Hotel & Restaurant
01736 796199

ST IVES
Olivers Lodge Hotel 01480 463252

ST IVES
Pedn-Olva Hotel 01736 796222

ST IVES
Porthminster Hotel 01736 795221

ST KEYNE
The Old Rectory 01579 342617

ST MARY'S
Star Castle Hotel 01720 422317

ST NEOTS
Abbotsley Golf Hotel & Country Club
01480 474000

STAFFORD
The Moat House 01785 712217

STAFFORD
Tillington Hall Hotel 01785 253531

STEEPLE ASTON
The Holt Hotel 01869 340259

STEVENAGE
Novotel Stevenage 01438 346100

STEYNING
The Old Tollgate Restaurant & Hotel
01903 879494

STOCKPORT
Bredbury Hall Hotel & Country Club
0161 430 7421

STOKE D'ABERNON
Woodlands Park Hotel
01372 843933

STOKE GABRIEL
Gabriel Court Hotel 01803 782206

STOKENCHURCH
The Kings Arms 01494 609090

STON EASTON
Ston Easton Park 01761 241631

STONE
Stone House Hotel 01785 815531

STONEHOUSE
Stonehouse Court 01453 825155

STOW-ON-THE-WOLD
Fosse Manor 01451 830354

STOW-ON-THE-WOLD
Grapevine Hotel 01451 830344

STOW-ON-THE-WOLD
Old Stocks Hotel 01451 830666

STOW-ON-THE-WOLD
The Royalist at Stow-on-the-Wold
01451 830670

STOW-ON-THE-WOLD
The Unicorn 01451 830257

STOW-ON-THE-WOLD
Wyck Hill House Hotel
01451 831936

STRATFORD-UPON-AVON
Billesley Manor Hotel 01789 279955

STRATFORD-UPON-AVON
Charlecote Pheasant 01789 279954

STRATFORD-UPON-AVON
Stratford Manor 01789 731173

STRATFORD-UPON-AVON
The Alveston Manor 0870 400 8181

STRATFORD-UPON-AVON
The Falcon Hotel 01789 279953

STROUD
Burleigh Court 01453 883804

STROUD
The Bell Hotel & Restaurant
01453 763556

SUNDERLAND
Quality Hotel 0191 519 1999

SUNDERLAND
Swallow Hotel 0191 529 2041

SUTTON COLDFIELD
Quality Hotel Sutton Court
0121 354 4991

SWINDON
Posthouse Swindon 0870 400 9079

SWINDON
Stanton House Hotel 01793 861777

SWINDON
Villiers Inn 01793 814744

SYMONDS YAT [EAST]
Forest View Hotel 01600 890210

TALLAND BAY
Talland Bay Hotel 01503 272667

TAPLOW
Cliveden 01628 668561

TARPORLEY
The Wild Boar 01829 260309

TAUNTON
Farthings Hotel and Restaurant
01823 480664

TAUNTON
The Mount Somerset Hotel
01823 442500

TELFORD
Buckatree Hall Hotel 01952 641821

TELFORD
Clarion Hotel Madeley Court
01952 680068

TELFORD
Valley Hotel 01952 432247

TELFORD
White House Hotel 01952 604276

TETBURY
Calcot Manor 01666 890391

TETBURY
Hare & Hounds Hotel 01666 880233

THORNE
Belmont Hotel 01405 812320

THORNTON WATLASS
Buck Inn 01677 422461

THORPE
The Peveril of the Peak
0870 400 8109

THORPE MARKET
Elderton Lodge Hotel & Langtry
Restaurant 01263 833547

THURLESTONE
Thurlestone Hotel 01548 560382

TIVERTON
The Tiverton Hotel 01884 256120

TORPOINT
Whitsand Bay Hotel, Golf & Country
Club 01503 230276

TORQUAY
Corbyn Head Hotel & Orchid
Restaurant   01803 213611

TORQUAY
Grand Hotel   01803 296677

TORQUAY
Kistor Hotel   01803 212632

TORQUAY
Livermead Cliff Hotel 01803 299666

TORQUAY
Norcliffe Hotel   01803 328456

TORQUAY
The Imperial   01803 294301

TORQUAY
The Osborne Hotel   01803 213311

TORQUAY
Torcroft Hotel   01803 298292

TOTLAND BAY
Sentry Mead Hotel   01983 753212

TRING
Pendley Manor   01442 891891

TROUTBECK [NEAR WINDERMERE]
Mortal Man Hotel   015394 33193

TRURO
Alverton Manor   01872 276633

TUTBURY
Ye Olde Dog & Partridge Hotel
                        01283 813030

TWO BRIDGES
Prince Hall Hotel   01822 890403

UCKFIELD
Buxted Park Country House Hotel
                        01825 732711

UMBERLEIGH
Rising Sun Inn   01769 560447

UPHOLLAND
Quality Hotel Skelmersdale
                        01695 720401

VENTNOR
Eversley Hotel   01983 852244

VENTNOR
Hillside Hotel   01983 852271

VENTNOR
The Royal Hotel   01983 852186

VENTNOR
Ventnor Towers Hotel 01983 852277

VERYAN
The Nare Hotel   01872 501111

WADEBRIDGE
The Molesworth Arms Hotel
                        01208 812055

WALSALL
Beverley Hotel   01922 614967

WALSALL
The Fairlawns at Aldridge
                        01922 455122

WALTERSTONE
Allt-yr-Ynys Country House Hotel
                        01873 890307

WALTHAM ABBEY
Swallow Hotel   01992 717170

WAREHAM
Kemps Country House Hotel
                        01929 462563

WAREHAM
Worgret Manor Hotel 01929 552957

WARMINSTER
Bishopstrow House   01985 212312

WARRINGTON
Daresbury Park Hotel 01925 267331

WARWICK
Ardencote Manor Hotel & Country
Club   01926 843111

WATERGATE BAY
Tregurrian Hotel   01637 860540

WATTON
Broom Hall Country Hotel
                        01953 882125

WELLS
Swan Hotel   01749 836300

WELLS
The Market Place Hotel
                        01749 836300

WELWYN
Quality Hotel Welwyn 01438 716911

WENTBRIDGE
Wentbridge House Hotel
                        01977 620444

WEST BEXINGTON
Manor Hotel   01308 897616

WESTON-SUPER-MARE
Beachlands Hotel   01934 621401

WEYMOUTH
Hotel Prince Regent 01305 771313

WEYMOUTH
Moonfleet Manor   01305 786948

WHICKHAM
Gibside Arms Hotel 0191 488 9292

WHITBY
Dunsley Hall   01947 893437

WHITBY
Saxonville Hotel   01947 602631

WILLITON
Curdon Mill   01984 656522

WILLITON
The Masons Arms Hotel
                        01984 639200

WILMSLOW
Stanneylands Hotel 01625 525225

WIMBORNE MINSTER
Beechleas Hotel & Restaurant
                        01202 841684

WINCHESTER
Lainston House Hotel 01962 863588

WINCHESTER
Marwell Hotel & Conference Centre
                        01962 777681

WINCHESTER
The Winchester Royal 01962 840840

WINDERMERE
Beech Hill Hotel   015394 42137

WINDERMERE
Cedar Manor Hotel & Restaurant
                        015394 43192

WINDERMERE
Gilpin Lodge Country House Hotel &
Restaurant   015394 88818

WINDERMERE
Langdale Chase Hotel 015394 32201

WINDERMERE
Lindeth Fell Country House Hotel
                        015394 43286

WINDERMERE
Lindeth Howe Country House Hotel
& Restaurant   015394 45759

WINDERMERE
Wild Boar Hotel   015394 45225

WINDSOR
Christopher Hotel   01753 852359

WINDSOR
The Castle Hotel   0870 400 8300

WOLVERHAMPTON
Quality Hotel Wolverhampton
                        01902 429216

WOOLACOMBE
Little Beach Hotel   01271 870398

WOOLACOMBE
Woolacombe Bay Hotel
                        01271 870388

WOOTTON BASSETT
Marsh Farm Hotel   01793 848044

WORKSOP
Clumber Park Hotel   01623 835333

YARMOUTH
George Hotel   01983 760331

YORK
Dean Court Hotel   01904 625082

YORK
Heworth Court Hotel 01904 425156

YORK
Jacobean Lodge Hotel
                        01904 762749

YORK
Swallow Hotel   01904 701000

CHANNEL ISLANDS
PERELLE
L'Atlantique Hotel   01481 264056

ST BRELADE
Hotel La Place   01534 744261

ST HELIER
Pomme D'Or Hotel   01534 880110

ST LAWRENCE
Hotel Cristina   01534 758024

ST MARTIN
Green Acres Hotel   01481 235711

ST PETER
Mermaid Hotel   01534 741255

ST PETER PORT
Old Government House Hotel
01481 724921

ISLE OF MAN
DOUGLAS
The Empress Hotel   01624 661155
PORT ERIN
Cherry Orchard Hotel
01624833811

SCOTLAND
ABERDEEN
Aberdeen Marriott Hotel
01224 770011

ABERDEEN
Copthorne Hotel Aberdeen
01224 630404

ABERDEEN
Mariner Hotel   01224 588901

ABERDEEN
Maryculter House Hotel
01224 732124

ABERDEEN
The Marcliffe at Pitfodels
01224 861000

ABERDEEN
Westhill Hotel   01224 740388

AUCHENCAIRN
Balcary Bay Hotel   01556 640217

AUCHTERARDER
Cairn Lodge   01764 662634

AVIEMORE
Aviemore Highlands Hotel
01479 810771

AVIEMORE
Freedom Inn   01479 810781

AYR
Grange Hotel   01292 265679

AYR
Quality Hotel Ayr   01292 263268

BALLOCH
Cameron House Hotel 01389 755565

BANCHORY
Burnett Arms Hotel   01330 824944

BANFF
Banff Springs Hotel   01261 812881

BEAULY
Priory Hotel   01463 782309

BLAIRGOWRIE
Angus Hotel   01250 872455

BLAIRGOWRIE
Kinloch House Hotel   01250 884237

BRIDGE OF ALLAN
Royal Hotel   01786 832284

BRORA
Royal Marine Hotel   01408 621252

BRORA
The Links Hotel   01408 621225

BUCKIE
Mill House Hotel   01542 850233

CAIRNDOW
Cairndow Stagecoach Inn
01499 600286

CALLANDER
Dalgair House Hotel   01877 330283

CALLANDER
Roman Camp Country House Hotel
01877 330003

CARNOUSTIE
Carnoustie Golf Resort & Spa Hotel
01241 411999

CARRUTHERSTOWN
Hetland Hall Hotel   01387 840201

CASTLE DOUGLAS
Douglas Arms   01556 502231

CASTLE DOUGLAS
Imperial Hotel   01556 502086

CASTLE DOUGLAS
King's Arms Hotel   01556 502626

CASTLE DOUGLAS
Urr Valley Hotel   01556 502188

CLACHAN-SEIL
Willowburn Hotel   01852 300276

COMRIE
Royal Hotel   01764 679200

CONTIN
Coul House Hotel   01997 421487

CRAIGELLACHIE
Craigellachie Hotel   01340 881204

CRIEFF
Crieff Hydro   01764 655555

CRUDEN BAY
Red House Hotel   01779 812215

CUPAR
Eden House Hotel   01334 652510

DORNOCH
Burghfield House Hotel
01862 810212

DRYMEN
Buchanan Arms Hotel and Leisure
Club   01360 660588

DRYMEN
Winnock Hotel   01360 660245

DUMFRIES
Station Hotel   01387 254316

DUNDEE
Sandford Country House Hotel
01382 541802

DUNFERMLINE
King Malcolm   01383 722611

DUNFERMLINE
Pitbauchlie House Hotel
01383 722282

DUNFERMLINE
The Hideaway Lodge & Restaurant
01383 725474

DUNOON
Enmore Hotel   01369 702230

DUNOON
Esplanade Hotel   01369 704070

DUNOON
Lyall Cliff Hotel   01369 702041

DUNOON
Royal Marine Hotel   01369 705810

EAST KILBRIDE
Crutherland Country House Hotel
01355 577000

EDINBURGH
Braid Hills Hotel   0131 447 8888

EDINBURGH
Carlton Hotel   0131 472 3000

EDINBURGH
Dalhousie Castle And Spa
01875 820153

EDINBURGH
Orwell Lodge Hotel   0131 229 1044

EDINBURGH
Salisbury View Hotel 0131 667 1133

EDINBURGH
Swallow Royal Scot Hotel
0131 334 9191

EDZELL
Glenesk Hotel   01356 648319

ELGIN
Mansion House Hotel 01343 548811

ERISKA
Isle of Eriska   01631 720371

ERSKINE
The Erskine Bridge Hotel
0141 812 0123

FENWICK
Fenwick Hotel   01560 600478

FORFAR
Idvies House Hotel   01307 818787

FORRES
Ramnee Hotel   01309 672410

FREUCHIE
Lomond Hills Hotel   01337 857329

GALASHIELS
Abbotsford Arms Hotel
01896 752517

GALASHIELS
Kingsknowes Hotel   01896 758375

GALASHIELS
Woodlands House Hotel &
Restaurants   01896 754722

GATEHOUSE OF FLEET
Murray Arms Hotel   01557 814207

GLASGOW
Sherbrooke Castle Hotel
0141 427 4227

GLASGOW
The Ewington   0141 423 1152

GLENFARG
The Glenfarg Hotel & Restaurant
01577 830241

GLENLUCE
Kelvin House Hotel   01581 300303

GLENROTHES
Balgeddie House Hotel
01592 742511

GLENROTHES
Rescobie House Hotel & Restaurant
01592 749555

HALKIRK
Ulbster Arms Hotel   01847 831206

HOWWOOD
Bowfield Hotel & Country Club
01505 705225

INVERNESS
Smithton Hotel   01463 791999

JOHNSTONE
Lynnhurst Hotel   01505 324331

KELSO
The Roxburghe Hotel & Golf Course
01573 450331

KILLIN
Dall Lodge Country House Hotel
01567 820217

KINROSS
Green Hotel   01577 863467

KIRKCUDBRIGHT
Royal Hotel   01557 331213

KIRKCUDBRIGHT
Selkirk Arms Hotel   01557 330402

LADYBANK
Fernie Castle   01337 810381

LARGS
Willowbank Hotel   01475 672311

LOCHCARRON
Lochcarron Hotel   01520 722226

LOCHEARNHEAD
Lochearnhead Hotel   01567 830229

LOCHINVER
Inver Lodge Hotel   01571 844496

LOCKERBIE
Kings Arms Hotel   01576 202410

LOCKERBIE
The Dryfesdale Country House Hotel
01576 202427

LUNDIN LINKS
Old Manor Hotel   01333 320368

MELROSE
George & Abbotsford Hotel
01896 822308

MOFFAT
Beechwood Country House Hotel
01683 220210

MONTROSE
Links Hotel   01674 671000

MONTROSE
Montrose Park Hotel   01674 663400

MUIR OF ORD
Ord House Hotel   01463 870492

MUIR OF ORD
The Dower House   01463 870090

NAIRN
Boath House   01667 454896

NAIRN
Claymore House Hotel
01667 453731

NEWTON STEWART
Bruce Hotel   01671 402294

NEWTON STEWART
Creebridge House Hotel
01671 402121

NEWTON STEWART
Kirroughtree House   01671 402141

NORTH BERWICK
Nether Abbey Hotel   01620 892802

NORTH BERWICK
The Marine   0870 400 8129

PEEBLES
Castle Venlaw Hotel   01721 720384

PEEBLES
Kingsmuir Hotel   01721 720151

PEEBLES
Park Hotel   01721 720451

PEEBLES
Peebles Hydro Hotel   01721 720602

PERTH
Kinfauns Castle   01738 620777

PERTH
Murrayshall Country House Hotel
01738 551171

PERTH
Quality Hotel Perth   01738 624141

PETERHEAD
Palace Hotel   01779 474821

PITLOCHRY
Dundarach Hotel   01796 472862

PORT ASKAIG
Port Askaig Hotel   01496 840245

PORT WILLIAM
Corsemalzie House Hotel
01988 860254

PORTMAHOMACK
Caledonian Hotel   01862 871345

PORTPATRICK
Fernhill Hotel   01776 810220

PORTREE
Cuillin Hills Hotel   01478 612003

PORTREE
Royal Hotel   01478 612525

POWFOOT
Powfoot Golf Hotel   01461 700254

PRESTWICK
Parkstone Hotel   01292 477286

RENFREW
Glynhill Hotel & Leisure Club
0141 886 5555

ROSEBANK
Popinjay Hotel   01555 860441

ST BOSWELLS
Dryburgh Abbey Hotel
01835 822261

ST FILLANS
Achray House Hotel   01764 685231

STRACHUR
Creggans Inn   01369 860279

STRANRAER
Corsewall Lighthouse Hotel
01776 853220

STRANRAER
North West Castle Hotel
01776 704413

STRONTIAN
Kilcamb Lodge Hotel   01967 402257

TAIN
Mansfield House Hotel
01862 892052

TAIN
Morangie House Hotel
01862 892281

TANGASDALE
Isle of Barra Hotel   01871 810383

THORNHILL
Trigony House Hotel
01848 331211

TOBERMORY
Highland Cottage   01688 302030

TOMINTOUL
The Gordon Hotel   01807 580206

TONGUE
Ben Loyal Hotel   01847 611216

TROON
Marine Hotel   01292 314444

TURNBERRY
Malin Court   01655 331457

UPHALL
Houstoun House Hotel and Country
Club   01506 853831

UPLAWMOOR
Uplawmoor Hotel   01505 850565

WICK
Mackay's Hotel   01955 602323

WALES
ABERDYFI
Harbour Hotel   01654 767250

ABERDYFI
Penhelig Arms Hotel Restaurant
01654 767215

ABERDYFI
Trefeddian Hotel   01654 767213

ABERGAVENNY
Llansantffraed Court Hotel
01873 840678

ABERGELE
Kinmel Manor Hotel   01745 832014

ABERPORTH
Hotel Penrallt   01239 810227

ABERSOCH
Deucoch Hotel   01758 712680

ABERSOCH
Neigwl Hotel   01758 712363

ABERSOCH
The White House Hotel
01758 713427

ABERYSTWYTH	**DOLGELLAU**	**LLANGOLLEN**
Belle Vue Royal Hotel 01970 617558	Penmaenuchaf Hall Hotel	The Wild Pheasant Hotel &
ABERYSTWYTH	01341 422129	Restaurant 01978 860629
Four Seasons Hotel 01970 612120	**DOLGELLAU**	**LLANGYBI**
ABERYSTWYTH	Plas Dolmelynllyn 01341 440273	Cwrt Bleddyn Hotel & Country Club
Groves Hotel 01970 617623	**EGLWYSFACH**	01633 450521
ABERYSTWYTH	Ynyshir Hall 01654 781209	**LLYSWEN**
Marine Hotel 01970 612444	**EWLOE**	Griffin Inn 01874 754241
ABERYSTWYTH	De Vere St Davids Park	**LLYSWEN**
Richmond Hotel 01970 612201	01244 520800	Llangoed Hall 01874 754525
AMLWCH	**GWBERT-ON-SEA**	**MACHYNLLETH**
Lastra Farm Hotel 01407 830906	Cliff Hotel 01239 613241	Wynnstay Hotel 01654 702941
AMLWCH	**HAVERFORDWEST**	**MERTHYR TYDFIL**
Trecastell Hotel 01407 830651	Hotel Mariners 01437 763353	Tregenna Hotel 01685 723627
AMMANFORD	**HAVERFORDWEST**	**MISKIN**
Mill at Glynhir 01269 850672	Wolfscastle Country Hotel	Miskin Manor Hotel 01443 224204
BALA	01437 741688	**MOLD**
Plas Coch Hotel 01678 520309	**HAY-ON-WYE**	Beaufort Park Hotel 01352 758646
BETWS-Y-COED	The Swan-at-Hay Hotel	**MONMOUTH**
The Royal Oak Hotel 01690 710219	01497 821188	Riverside Hotel 01600 715577
BRIDGEND	**KNIGHTON**	**NEWPORT**
Coed-Y-Mwstwr Hotel 01656 860621	The Knighton Hotel 01547 520530	Newport Lodge Hotel 01633 821818
BRIDGEND	**LANGLAND BAY**	**PEMBROKE**
Heronston Hotel 01656 668811	Wittemberg Hotel 01792 369696	Lamphey Court Hotel 01646 672273
BUILTH WELLS	**LLANARMON DYFFRYN CEIRIOG**	**PEMBROKE**
Pencerrig Gardens Hotel	West Arms Hotel 01691 600665	Lamphey Hall Hotel 01646 672394
01982 553226	**LLANBEDR**	**PONTERWYD**
CAERNARFON	Ty Mawr Hotel 01341 241440	The George Borrow Hotel
Seiont Manor Hotel 01286 673366	**LLANBERIS**	01970 890230
CAERNARFON	Royal Victoria Hotel 01286 870253	**PONTYPRIDD**
Stables Hotel 01286 830711	**LLANDEILO**	Llechwen Hall Hotel 01443 742050
CARDIFF	White Hart Inn 01558 823419	**PORTHCAWL**
Cardiff Marriott Hotel	**LLANDRILLO**	Glenaub Hotel 01656 788242
029 2039 9944	Tyddyn Llan Country Hotel &	**RHOSSILI**
CARDIFF	Restaurant 01490 440264	Worms Head Hotel 01792 390512
New House Country Hotel	**LLANDRINDOD WELLS**	**RHYL**
029 2052 0280	Hotel Metropole 01597 823700	Hotel Marina 01745 342371
CARDIFF	**LLANDUDNO**	**SAUNDERSFOOT**
St Mellons Hotel & Country Club	Bodysgallen Hall Hotel	Jalna Hotel 01834 812282
01633 680355	01492 584466	**SAUNDERSFOOT**
CARMARTHEN	**LLANDUDNO**	Rhodewood House Hotel
Falcon Hotel 01267 234959	Epperstone Hotel 01492 878746	01834 812200
CHEPSTOW	**LLANDUDNO**	**SAUNDERSFOOT**
Beaufort Hotel 01291 622497	Esplanade Hotel 0800 318688	St Brides Hotel 01834 812304
CHEPSTOW	(freephone)	**ST DAVID'S**
The Old Course Hotel 01291 626261	**LLANDUDNO**	Grove Hotel 01437 720341
CHIRK	Risboro Hotel 01492 876343	**ST DAVID'S**
Moreton Park Lodge 01691 776666	**LLANDUDNO**	St Non's Hotel 01437 720239
CONWY	St George's Hotel 01492 877544	**ST DAVID'S**
The Castle Hotel 01492 592324	**LLANDUDNO**	Warpool Court Hotel 01437 720300
CRICCIETH	St Tudno Hotel and Restaurant	**TALSARNAU**
Caerwylan Hotel 01766 522547	01492 874411	Estuary Motel 01766 771155
CRICCIETH	**LLANDUDNO**	**TALSARNAU**
Lion Hotel 01766 522460	Tan-Lan Hotel 01492 860221	Tregwylan Hotel 01766 770424
CRICKHOWELL	**LLANGAMMARCH WELLS**	**TAL-Y-BONT**
Bear Hotel 01873 810408	Lake Country House Hotel	Lodge Hotel 01492 660766
CRICKHOWELL	01591 620202	**TENBY**
Gliffaes Country House Hotel	**LLANGOLLEN**	Atlantic Hotel 01834 842881
01874 730371 & 0800	Bryn Howel Hotel & Restaurant	**TENBY**
	01978 860331	Fourcroft Hotel 01834 842886

TENBY
Heywood Mount Hotel
01834 842087

TENBY
Panorama Hotel & Restaurant
01834 844976

TENBY
Penally Abbey Country House
01834 843033

TENBY
Tenby House Hotel   01834 842000

TINTERN
Parva Farmhouse Hotel & Restaurant
01291 689411

TREARDDUR BAY
Trearddur Bay Hotel   01407 860301

TREFRIW
Hafod Country Hotel   01492 640029

TREFRIW
Princes Arms Hotel   01492 640592

WELSHPOOL
Golfa Hall Hotel   01938 553399

WHITEBROOK
The Crown at Whitebrook
01600 860254

NORTHERN IRELAND
AGHADOWEY
Brown Trout Golf & Country Inn
028 7086 8209

BALLYMENA
Adair Arms Hotel   028 2565 3674

BALLYMENA
Galgorm Manor   028 2588 1001

BANGOR
Clandeboye Lodge Hotel
028 9185 2500

BANGOR
Marine Court Hotel   028 9145 1100

BANGOR
Royal Hotel   028 9127 1866

CARNLOUGH
Londonderry Arms Hotel
028 2888 5255

CRAWFORDSBURN
Old Inn   028 9185 3255

DUNGANNON
The Cohannon Inn   028 8772 4488

ENNISKILLEN
Killyhevlin Hotel   028 6632 3481

IRVINESTOWN
Mahons Hotel   028 6862 1656

LONDONDERRY
Trinity Hotel   028 7127 1271

PORTAFERRY
Portaferry Hotel   028 4272 8231

REPUBLIC OF IRELAND
ABBEYLEIX
Abbeyleix Manor Hotel 0502 30111

ADARE
Dunraven Arms Hotel   061 396633

ADARE
Fitzgeralds Woodlands House Hotel
061 605100

AHERLOW
Aherlow House   062 56153

ARDARA
Nesbitt Arms   075 41103

ARDMORE
Round Tower Hotel   024 94494

ARTHURSTOWN
Dunbrody Country House &
Restaurant   051 389600

ASHFORD
Cullenmore Hotel   0404 40187

ATHLONE
Hodson Bay Hotel   0902 92444

ATHLONE
Prince Of Wales Hotel 0902 72626

ATHLONE
Royal Hoey Hotel   0902 72924

BALLINASLOE
Haydens Gateway Business, Leisure
Hotel   065 68 23000

BALLINLOUGH
Whitehouse Hotel   0907 40112

BALLYBOFEY
Kee's Hotel   074 31018

BALLYCOTTON
Bay View Hotel   021 646746

BALLYHEIGE
The White Sands Hotel
066 7133 102

BALLYLICKEY
Sea View Hotel   027 50073

BALTIMORE
Baltimore Harbour Hotel & Leisure
Cntr   028 20361

BALTIMORE
Casey's of Baltimore Hotel
028 20197

BARNA
The Twelve Pins Hotel   091 592368

BETTYSTOWN
Neptune Beach Hotel & Leisure Club
041 9827107

BIRR
County Arms Hotel   0509 20791

BLARNEY
Christy's Hotel   021 385011

BRAY
Royal Hotel & Leisure Centre
01 2862935

BUNBEG
Ostan Gweedore   075 31177

BUNRATTY
Fitzpatrick Bunratty Hotel
061 361177

CAHERCIVEEN
Caherciveen Park Hotel 066 9472543

CAHIR
Cahir House Hotel   052 42727

CARLOW
Dolmen Hotel   0503 42002

CARLOW
Seven Oaks Hotel   0503 31308

CASTLEBAR
Breaffy House Hotel   094 22033

CASTLEBAR
Welcome Inn Hotel   094 22288

CASTLECONNELL
Castle Oaks House Hotel 061 377666

CAVAN
Kilmore Hotel   049 4332288

CLONAKILTY
The Lodge & Spa at Inchydoney
Island   023 33143

CLONMEL
Minella Hotel   052 22388

CORK
Arbutus Lodge Hotel   021 501237

CORK
Hayfield Manor   021 315600

CORK
Imperial Hotel   021 274040

CORK
Jurys Hotel   021 276622

CORK
Metropole Hotel & Leisure Centre
021 508122

CORK
The Kingsley Hotel   021 4800500

COURTMACSHERRY
Courtmacsherry   023 46198

COURTOWN HARBOUR
Courtown Hotel   055 25210

DONEGAL
Abbey Hotel   073 21014

DUBLIN
Abberley Court Hotel   01 4596000

DUBLIN
Herbert Park Hotel   01 6672200

DUBLIN
Radisson SAS St Helen's Hotel
01 2186000

DUBLIN
Red Cow Moran Hotel   01 4593650

DUBLIN
Stillorgan Park Hotel 01 2881621

DUBLIN
The Clarence   01 4070800

DUBLIN
The Fitzwilliam Hotel 01 4787000

DUNDALK
Fairways Hotel & Leisure Centre
042 9321500

DUNFANAGHY
Arnold's Hotel   074 36208

DUNGARVAN	**KINSALE**	**RENVYLE**
Lawlors Hotel 058 41122	Actons Hotel 021 4772135	Renvyle House Hotel 095 43511
ENNIS	**KINSALE**	**ROSCOMMON**
Magowna House Hotel	Trident Hotel 021 4772301	Abbey Hotel 0903 26240
065 6839009	**KNOCK**	**ROSSCARBERY**
ENNIS	Belmont Hotel 094 88122	Celtic Ross Hotel 023 48722
West County Conference, Leisure	**LAHINCH**	**ROSSLARE**
Hotel 065 6823000	Aberdeen Arms Hotel 065 81100	Kelly's Resort Hotel 053 32114
ENNISCORTHY	**LEIXLIP**	**ROSSNOWLAGH**
Murphy-Flood's Hotel 054 33413	Leixlip House Hotel 01 6242268	Sand House Hotel 072 51777
ENNISCORTHY	**LIMERICK**	**SHANNON**
Riverside Park Hotel 054 37800	Castletroy Park Hotel 061 335566	Quality Shannon Hotel 061 364588
FERMOY	**LIMERICK**	**SLIGO**
Castlehyde Hotel 025 31865	Limerick Ryan Hotel 061 453922	Sligo Park Hotel 071 60291
GALWAY	**LIMERICK**	**SLIGO**
Ardilaun House Hotel Conference	South Court Business & Leisure	Tower Hotel 071 44000
centre and LC 091 521433	Hotel 065 6823000	**STRAFFAN**
GALWAY	**LISMORE**	Barberstown Castle 01 6288157
Galway Bay Hotel Conference &	Ballyrafter House Hotel 058 54002	**TEMPLEGLANTINE**
Leisure Centre 091 520520	**LUCAN**	The Devon Inn Hotel 069 84122
GALWAY	Finnstown Country House Hotel	**TRALEE**
Menlo Park Hotel 091 761122	01 6280644	Meadowlands Hotel 066 7180444
GOREY	**LUCAN**	**TRAMORE**
Marlfield House Hotel 055 21124	Lucan Spa Hotel 01 6280495	Majestic Hotel 051 381761
KENMARE	**MACROOM**	**WATERFORD**
Riversdale House Hotel 064 41299	Castle Hotel 026 41074	Bridge Hotel 051 877222
KENMARE	**MALLOW**	**WATERFORD**
Sheen Falls Lodge 064 41600	Longueville House Hotel 022 47156	Dooley's Hotel 051 873531
KILKEE	**MALLOW**	**WATERFORD**
Ocean Cove Golf & Leisure Hotel	Springfort Hall Hotel 022 21278	Granville Hotel 051 305555
065 6823000	**MAYNOOTH**	**WATERFORD**
KILL	Moyglare Manor 01 6286351	Ivory's Hotel 051 358888
Ambassador Hotel 045 886700	**MIDLETON**	**WATERFORD**
KILLARNEY	Midleton Park 021 631767	Jurys Hotel 051 832111
Aghadoe Heights Hotel 064 31766	**NEW ROSS**	**WATERFORD**
KILLARNEY	Clarion Brandon House Hotel and	Tower Hotel 051 875801
Cahernane Hotel 064 31895	LeisureCentre 051 421703	**WATERVILLE**
KILLARNEY	**NEWBRIDGE**	Butler Arms Hotel 066 9474144
Castlerosse Hotel 064 31144	Keadeen Hotel 045 431666	**WESTPORT**
KILLARNEY	**NEWMARKET-ON-FERGUS**	Clew Bay Hotel 098 28088
Gleneagle Hotel 064 31870	Clare Inn Golf and Leisure Hotel	**WESTPORT**
KILLARNEY	065 6823000	Hotel Westport 098 25122
International Hotel 064 31816	**PORTMARNOCK**	**WESTPORT**
KILLARNEY	Portmarnock Hotel & Golf Links	The Olde Railway Hotel 098 25166
Killarney Court Hotel 064 37070	01 8460611	**WEXFORD**
KILLARNEY	**PORTUMNA**	Ferrycarriq Hotel 053 20999
Lake Hotel 064 31035	Shannon Oaks Hotel & Country Club	**WEXFORD**
KILLINEY	0509 41777	Talbot Hotel Conference & Leisure
Court Hotel 01 2851622	**RATHMULLAN**	Centre 053 22566
KILTIMAGH	Fort Royal Hotel 074 58100	**WEXFORD**
Cill Aodain Hotel 094 81761	**RATHNEW**	Whitford House Hotel 053 43444
KINGSCOURT	Tinakilly Country House &	**WOODENBRIDGE**
Cabra Castle 042 9667030	Restaurant 0404 69274	Woodenbridge Hotel 0402 35146

Golf
driving ranges

ABINGDON Drayton Park Golf Course 231
ABRIDGE Abridge Golf and Country Club 82
ADDINGTON Addington Court 98
ADDINGTON West Malling Golf Club 98
ALNMOUTH Alnmouth Golf Club 202
ALTON Worldham Park Golf Course 122
ALTRINCHAM Altrincham Golf Club 110
ANDOVER Hampshire Golf Club 122
ASCOT Lavender Park Golf Centre 18
ASCOT Mill Ride Golf Club 18
ASCOT The Berkshire Golf Club 17
ASH The London Golf Club 144
ASHFORD Homelands Bettergolf Centre 145
AUGHTON The Oaks Golf Club 292
AYLESBURY Aylesbury Golf Centre 25
BAGSHOT Windlesham Golf Course 238
BARHAM Broome Park Golf Club 145
BARNHAM BROOM Barnham Broom Hotel,
  Golf, Conference, Leisure 192
BARNSLEY Sandhill Golf Club 302
BASINGSTOKE Dummer Golf Club 123
BATH Lansdown Golf Club 221
BAWBURGH Bawburgh Golf Club 192
BAWTRY Austerfield Park Golf Club 303
BEACONSFIELD Beaconsfield Golf Club 25
BEDFORD Mowsbury Golf Club 14
BEDFORD The Bedford Golf Club 14
BELCHALWELL Dorset Heights Golf Club 72
BELFORD Belford Golf Club 203
BELLINGHAM Bellingham Golf Club 203
BELTON Belton Woods Hotel 172
BERE REGIS East Dorset Golf Club 72
BERWICK-UPON-TWEED Berwick-upon-
  Tweed (Goswick) Golf Club 203
BEWDLEY Wharton Park Golf Club 287
BIDDENDEN Chart Hills Golf Club 145
BIDFORD-ON-AVON
  Bidford Grange Golf Club 268
BILLERICAY Stock Brook Golf &
  Country Club 83
BINFIELD Blue Mountain Golf Centre 18
BISHAMPTON Vale Golf Club 287
BISHOP'S STORTFORD Great Hadham Golf &
  Country Club 136
BLACKAWTON Dartmouth Golf &
  Country Club 64
BLACKPOOL De Vere Blackpool
  (Herons Reach Golf Course) 158
BLETCHLEY Windmill Hill Golf Course 26
BODMIN Lanhydrock Golf Club 44
BOLDON Boldon Golf Club 264
BOTCHESTON Forest Hill Golf Club 167
BOTLEY Botley Park Hotel, Golf &
  Country Club 123
BOURNE Toft Hotel Golf Club 173
BOW BRICKHILL Woburn Golf & Country
  Club 27

BRAINTREE Towerlands Golf Club 84
BRAMLEY Bramley Golf Club 238
BRANDON City of Coventry-Brandon Wood
  Golf Club 268
BREADSALL Marriott Breadsall Priory Hotel &
  Country Club 59
BRENCHLEY Moatlands Golf Club 146
BRENTWOOD Warley Park Golf Club 84
BRIDGWATER Cannington Golf Course 221
BRIDLINGTON Bridlington Links 293
BRIGHOUSE Willow Valley Golf & Country
  Club 309
BRISTOL Bristol and Clifton Golf Club 24
BROMSGROVE Bromsgrove Golf Centre 288
BROXBOURNE Hertfordshire Golf & Country
  Club 136
BULPHAN Langdon Hills Golf Centre 84
BURGESS HILL Burgess Hill Golf Centre 259
BURNHAM The Lambourne Club 26
BURTON UPON TRENT Branston Golf &
  Country Club 227
BURTON UPON TRENT The Craythorne 227
BUSHEY Bushey Golf & Country Club 137
BUSHEY Hartsbourne Golf & Country Club 137
BUXTON Cavendish Golf Club 60
CALNE Bowood Golf & Country Club 282
CALVERTON Ramsdale Park Golf Centre 207
CALVERTON Springwater Golf Club 208
CAMBERLEY Camberley Heath Golf Club 238
CAMBERLEY Pine Ridge Golf Club 239
CAMBRIDGE The Gog Magog Golf Club 32
CAMELFORD Bowood Park Golf Course 282
CANNOCK Beau Desert Golf Club 227
CANVEY ISLAND Castle Point Golf Club 85
CARSHALTON Oaks Sports Centre 100
CASTLE COMBE The Manor House Golf Club at
  Castle Combe 283
CATERHAM Happy Valley Golf Club 239
CHACOMBE Cherwell Edge Golf Club 198
CHADDLEWORTH West Berkshire Golf Course 19
CHALFONT ST GILES Oakland Park Golf Club 28
CHAPMANSLADE Thoulstone Park Golf
  Course 283
CHARD Windwhistle Golf, Squash & Country
  Club 222
CHART SUTTON The Ridge Golf Club 147
CHELMSFORD Channels Golf Club 85
CHESSINGTON Chessington Golf Club 100
CHESTER Carden Park Hotel Golf Resort & Spa 36
CHESTER Vicars Cross Golf Club 37
CHESTERFIELD Grassmoor Golf Centre 60
CHESTER-LE-STREET Roseberry Grange
  Golf Course 79
CHICHESTER Chichester Golf Club 259
CHIDDINGFOLD Chiddingfold Golf Course 239
CHIPPING NORTON Lyneham Golf Course 213
CHIPSTEAD Chipstead Golf Club 239
CHRISTCHURCH Iford Bridge Golf Course 74
CIRENCESTER Cirencester Golf Club 93

CLEETHORPES Tetney Golf Club 173
CLEOBURY MORTIMER Cleobury Mortimer
  Golf Club 218
CLITHEROE Clitheroe Golf Club 160
COBHAM Silvermere Golf Club 240
COLCHESTER Colchester & Lexden Golf
  Centre 86
COLCHESTER Colchester Golf Club 86
COLCHESTER Stoke by Nayland Golf Club 86
COLEFORD Forest Hills Golf Club 94
COLLINGTREE Collingtree Park Golf Course 199
COLMWORTH Colmworth & North Bedfordshire
  Golf Course 15
CONGRESBURY Mendip Spring Golf Club 222
COOKHAM Winter Hill Golf Club 19
COTTINGHAM Cottingham Golf Club 293
COVENTRY Ansty Golf Centre 275
CRANLEIGH Fernfell Golf & Country Club 240
CRANLEIGH Wildwood Country Club 240
CRAWLEY Tilgate Forest Golf Centre 260
CRETINGHAM Cretingham Golf Club 233
CRONDALL Oak Park Golf Club 124
CROSBY-ON-EDEN Eden Golf Course 55
CROYDON Selsdon Park Hotel Golf Course 101
DARLINGTON Stressholme Golf Club 80
DARTFORD Birchwood Park Golf Centre Ltd 147
DEAL Royal Cinque Ports Golf Club 147
DENHAM Buckinghamshire Golf Club 28
DEREHAM The Norfolk Golf & Country Club 193
DIBDEN Dibden Golf Centre 125
DIDCOT Hadden Hill Golf Club 214
DITCHLING Mid Sussex Golf Club 254
DROITWICH Ombersley Golf Club 289
DUDLEY Swindon Golf Club 276
DURHAM Ramside Hall Golf Club 80
EARLS COLNE The Essex Golf & Country Club 87
EASINGWOLD Easingwold Golf Club 295
EAST GOSCOTE Beedles Lake Golf Centre 167
EAST HORSLEY Drift Golf Club 241
EDENBRIDGE Edenbridge Golf & Tennis
  Centre 148
EDENBRIDGE Sweetwoods Park 148
EFFINGHAM Effingham Golf Club 241
ELSTREE Elstree Golf Club 137
ENTON GREEN West Surrey Golf Club 241
EPPING Nazeing Golf Club 87
EPPING The Epping Golf Course 87
EPSOM Horton Park Golf & Country Club 241
ERLESTOKE Erlestoke Sands Golf Course 284
EXETER Woodbury Park Golf Club 66
EYNSFORD Austin Lodge Golf Club 148
FALMOUTH Falmouth Golf Club 45
FARINGDON Carswell Golf & Country Club 214
FARLEIGH Farleigh Court Golf Club 242
FARNHAM Blacknest Golf Club 242
FARRINGTON GURNEY Farrington Golf Club 223
FAVERSHAM Boughton Golf 148
FERNDOWN Dudsbury Golf Club 74
FERNDOWN Ferndown Forest Golf Club 74

FOLKESTONE Etchinghill Golf Course 148
FRITTON Caldecott Hall Golf & Leisure 194
FROME Frome Golf Club 223
FROME Orchardleigh Golf Club 223
GAINSBOROUGH Gainsborough Golf Club 174
GARFORTH Garforth Golf Club 310
GARSTANG Garstang Country Hotel & Golf Club 161
GEDNEY HILL Gedney Hill Golf Course 174
GILLINGHAM Gillingham Golf Club 149
GLOUCESTER Brickhampton Court Golf Club 94
GLOUCESTER Jarvis Gloucester Hotel & Country Club 95
GODALMING Broadwater Park Golf Club 243
GOODWOOD Marriott Goodwood Park Hotel & Country Club 260
GOSFORTH Parklands 265
GRAVELEY Chesfield Downs Golf Club 138
GREAT CASTERTON Rutland County Golf Club 217
GREAT DURNFORD High Post Golf Club 284
GREENFORD Lime Trees Park Golf Club 103
GREETHAM Greetham Valley Golf Club 217
GUILDFORD Merrist Wood Golf Club 243
GUILDFORD Roker Park Golf Course 244
HADLEY WOOD Hadley Wood Golf Club 104
HAILSHAM Wellshurst Golf & Country Club 255
HALESWORTH Halesworth Golf Club 233
HALSTOCK Halstock Golf Enterprises 75
HARLOW North Weald Golf Club 88
HARPENDEN Harpenden Golf Club 138
HARROGATE Rudding Park Hotel and Golf 296
HASTINGS & ST LEONARDS Hastings Golf Course 255
HAYWARDS HEATH Haywards Heath Golf Club 261
HAYWARDS HEATH Paxhill Park Golf Club 261
HEATHFIELD Horam Park Golf Course 256
HEMEL HEMPSTEAD Little Hay Golf Complex 139
HEMINGFORD ABBOTS Hemingford Abbots Golf Course 33
HENLEY-IN-ARDEN Henley Golf & Country Club 268
HENLEY-ON-THAMES Aspect Park Golf Centre 214
HEVER Hever Golf Club 150
HEXHAM De Vere Slaley Hall Hotel, Golf Resort & Spa 205
HIGH BICKINGTON Libbaton Golf Club 66
HIGHWORTH Wrag Barn Golf & Country Club 284
HINDHEAD Hindhead Golf Club 244
HOO Deangate Ridge Golf Club 150
HORNCASTLE Horncastle Golf Club 175
HORSHAM Horsham Golf & Fitness 261
HORSLEY Horsley Lodge Golf Club 62
HORTON-CUM-STUDLEY Studley Wood Golf Club 215
HOUNSLOW Airlinks Golf Club 104
HOVE West Hove Golf Club Ltd 253
HOWDEN Boothferry Park Golf Club 297
HOYLAKE Royal Liverpool Golf Club 107
HUDDERSFIELD Bradley Park Golf Course 311
HUDDERSFIELD Huddersfield Golf Club Ltd 311
HURN Parley Golf Course 75

HURSTPIERPOINT Singing Hills Golf Course 261
HYTHE Sene Valley Golf Club 151
IPSWICH Fynn Valley Golf Club 234
IVER Iver Golf Club 29
IVER Richings Park Golf & Country Club 29
IVYBRIDGE Dinnaton Sporting & Country Club 68
KENILWORTH Kenilworth Golf Club 268
KEYNSHAM Stockwood Vale Golf Club 224
KIBWORTH Kibworth Golf Club 168
KIDDERMINSTER Wyre Forest Golf Club 289
KING'S LYNN Eagles Golf Centre 195
KINGSWOOD Kingswood Golf Club 244
KINGTON Kington Golf Club 133
KIRBY MUXLOE Kirby Muxloe Golf Club 168
KIRKBY IN ASHFIELD Notts Golf Club 208
KIRTLINGTON Kirtlington Golf Club 215
KNOWLE Copt Heath Golf Club 276
KNUTSFORD Mere Golf & Country Club 39
LANDFORD Hamptworth Golf & Country Club 284
LANGPORT Long Sutton Golf Course 224
LAUNCESTON Trethorne Golf Club 46
LEA MARSTON Lea Marston Hotel & Leisure Complex 269
LEATHERHEAD Pachesham Park Golf Centre 244
LEEDS Cookridge Hall Golf & Country Club 312
LEEDS Leeds Golf Centre 313
LEEDS Moor Allerton Golf Club 313
LEEDS Oulton Park Golf Course 314
LEEK WOOTTON The Warwickshire 269
LEE-ON-THE-SOLENT Lee-on-Solent Golf Club 127
LEICESTER Humberstone Heights Golf Club 169
LEICESTER Western Golf Course 169
LETCHWORTH Letchworth Golf Club 139
LEYLAND Leyland Golf Club 162
LICHFIELD Seedy Mill Golf Club 228
LINGFIELD Lingfield Park Golf Club 245
LIPHOOK Old Thorns Hotel, Golf & Country Club 127
LITTLE GADDESDEN Ashridge Golf Club 139
LIVERPOOL The Childwall Golf Club 188
LONDON E4 West Essex Golf Club 181
LONDON N14 Trent Park Golf Club 181
LONDON N9 Lee Valley Leisure Golf Course 454
LONDON NW4 The Metro Golf Centre 182
LONDON SE28 Riverside Golf Course 184
LONDON SW15 Richmond Park Golf Course 184
LONDON SW18 Central London Golf Centre 184
LONG ASHTON Woodspring Golf & Country Club 224
LONG EATON Trent Lock Golf Centre 208
LONGHORSLEY Linden Hall 205
LONGSTANTON Cambridge Golf Club 33
LOSTWITHIEL Lostwithiel Hotel, Golf & Country Club 47
LOUDWATER Wycombe Heights Golf Centre 30
LUTON Stockwood Park Golf Club 156
LUTTERWORTH Kilworth Springs Golf Course 170
LUTTERWORTH Lutterworth Golf Club 170
LYDD Lydd Golf Club 152
LYTHAM ST ANNES Royal Lytham & St Annes Golf Club 163
MAIDENHEAD Bird Hills Golf Course 19
MALDON Forrester Park Golf Club 89

MANCHESTER Blackley Golf Club 115
MANNINGS HEATH Mannings Heath Golf Club 262
MARLOW Harleyford Golf 30
MATFEN Matfen Hall Country House Hotel & Golf Club 206
MAWGAN PORTH Merlin Golf Course 47
MENTMORE Mentmore Golf & Country Club 30
MERIDEN Marriott Forest of Arden Golf & Country Club 279
MERIDEN Stonebridge Golf Centre 277
MIDDLESBROUGH Middlesbrough Municipal Golf Centre 298
MIDDLETON Manchester Golf Club 116
MIDDLETON Middleton Hall Golf Club 195
MILTON COMMON The Oxfordshire Golf Club 215
MILTON KEYNES Abbey Hill Golf Club 30
MINCHINHAMPTON Minchinhampton Golf Club 95
MORLEY Morley Hayes Golf Course 63
MORTIMER Wokefield Park Golf Club 20
MUNDESLEY Mundesley Golf Club Ltd 196
NEW MILLS New Mills Golf Club 63
NEW MILTON Chewton Glen Hotel 129
NEWCASTLE-UNDER-LYME Keele Golf Club 229
NEWDIGATE Rusper Golf Course 245
NEWTON ABBOT Dainton Park Golf Club 67
NEWTON AYCLIFFE Oakleaf Golf Club 81
NORTHALLERTON Romanby Golf & Country Club 298
NORTHAMPTON Brampton Heath Golf Centre 200
NORTHAMPTON Delapre Golf Complex 200
NORTHAMPTON Northamptonshire County Golf Club 201
NORTHWOOD Sandy Lodge Golf Club 106
NORWICH De Vere Dunston Hall Hotel 196
NORWICH Marriott Sprowston Manor Hotel & Country Club 196
NORWICH Wensum Valley Hotel, Golf & Country Club 197
NUNEATON Purley Chase Golf Club 270
OAKSEY Oaksey Park Golf & Leisure 285
OCKLEY Gatton Manor Hotel Golf & Country Club 245
OGBOURNE ST GEORGE Ogbourne Downs Golf Club 285
OKEHAMPTON Ashbury Golf Course 68
OLLERTON Rufford Park Golf Centre 210
ORMSKIRK Hurlston Hall Golf Club 164
ORPINGTON Chelsfield Lakes Golf Centre 106
ORPINGTON Cray Valley Golf Club 106
ORPINGTON Lullingstone Park Golf Course 106
ORPINGTON Ruxley Park Golf Centre 107
OSWESTRY Mile End Golf Course 218
OTTERSHAW Foxhills 246
OWER Paultons Golf Centre 129
OXTON Oakmere Park 211
PANNAL Pannal Golf Club 298
PENRITH Penrith Golf Club 57
PERTON Perton Park Golf Club 230
PETERBOROUGH Elton Furze Golf Club 34
PIDLEY Lakeside Lodge Golf Club 34
PLYMOUTH Elfordleigh Hotel Golf &

Country Club 69
PONTEFRACT Mid Yorkshire Golf Course 316
POOLE Parkstone Golf Club 75
PORTSMOUTH Great Salterns Public Course 129
PORTSMOUTH Southsea Golf Club 130
POULTON-LE-FYLDE Poulton Le Fylde Golf
Club 165
PRESTBURY Prestbury Golf Club 41
PRESTON Preston Golf Club 166
PRESTWICH Heaton Park Golf Centre 117
PULBOROUGH West Sussex Golf Club 262
RADCLIFFE ON TRENT Cotgrave Place Golf &
Country Club 211
RADLETT Porters Park Golf Club 140
RAINHILL Blundells Hill Golf Club 189
RAMSEY Old Nene Golf & Country Club 34
RAYDON Brett Vale Golf Club 235
READING Hennerton Golf Course 21
REDBOURN Redbourn Golf Club 140
REDDITCH Abbey Hotel Golf & Country Club 290
REIGATE Reigate Hill Golf Club 248
RICHMOND UPON THAMES The Richmond
Golf Club 107
RICKMANSWORTH Moor Park Golf Club 140
ROCHDALE Castle Hawk Golf Club 117
ROCHESTER Rochester & Cobham Park
Golf Club 153
ROCK St Enodoc Golf Club 49
ROMFORD Risebridge Golf Centre 108
ROSS-ON-WYE South Herefordshire
Golf Club 134
ROSS-ON-WYE The Ross-on-Wye Golf Club 134
ROTHERHAM Grange Park Golf Club 304
ROTHERHAM Phoenix Golf Club 304
ROYSTON Heydon Grange Golf &
Country Club 140
ROYSTON Kingsway Golf Centre 177
RUGBY Whitefields Hotel Golf &
Country Club 270
RUISLIP Ruislip Golf Club 108
SAFFRON WALDEN Saffron Walden
Golf Club 90
SALTASH China Fleet Country Club 52
SALTBURN-BY-THE-SEA Hunley Hall Golf
Club & Hotel 299
SANDWICH Prince's Golf Club 153
SANDWICH Royal St George's Golf Club 155
SAUNTON Saunton Golf Club 69
SCUNTHORPE Forest Pines Golf Club 176
SEAFORD Seaford Golf Club 256
SEAGRAVE Park Hill Golf Club 171
SEASCALE Seascale Golf Club 57
SEDGEFIELD Knotty Hill Golf Centre 82
SEDGLEY Sedgley Golf Centre 277
SEDLESCOMBE Sedlescombe Golf Course 258
SHEDFIELD Marriott Meon Valley Hotel &
Country Club 130
SHEFFIELD Concord Park Golf Club 305
SHEFFIELD Hillsborough Golf Club 306
SHEFFIELD Rother Valley Golf Centre 306
SHEFFORD Beadlow Manor Hotel & Golf &
Country Club 17
SHEPPERTON American Golf at Sunbury 248
SHIPLEY Marriott Hollins Hall Hotel &
Country Club 317

SHREWSBURY Shrewsbury Golf Club 219
SINDLESHAM Bearwood Golf Club 21
SITTINGBOURNE The Oast Golf Centre 154
SITTINGBOURNE Upchurch River Valley
Golf Centre 154
SLINFOLD Slinfold Park Golf & Country Club 263
SNODLAND Oastpark Golf Course 154
SOLIHULL Robin Hood Golf Club 277
SOUTH OCKENDON Belhus Park Golf Course 90
SOUTH OCKENDON Top Meadow
Golf Course 90
SOUTHAMPTON Chilworth Golf Club 131
SOUTHPORT Hillside Golf Club 190
ST AUSTELL Porthpean Golf Club 49
ST AUSTELL St Austell Golf Club 49
ST MELLION St Mellion Hotel, Golf &
Country Club 51
ST MINVER Roserrow Golf & Country Club 52
ST NEOTS Abbotsley Golf Hotel &
Country Club 35
STANDISH Standish Court Golf Club 119
STANFORD-LE-HOPE St Clere's Hall Golf Club 91
STANTON BY DALE Erewash Valley 63
STAVERTON Staverton Park Golf Club 201
STEVENAGE Stevenage Golf Centre 142
STOCK Crondon Park Golf Club 91
STOKE POGES Stoke Poges Golf Club 31
STOKE-ON-TRENT Trentham Golf Club 230
STONE Izaak Walton Golf Club 231
STOWMARKET Stowmarket Golf Club 236
STRATFORD-UPON-AVON Stratford Oaks 272
STRATFORD-UPON-AVON Welcombe Hotel and
Golf Course 272
SUTTON ON SEA Sandilands Golf Club 180
SWINDON Broome Manor Golf Complex 285
TADLEY Bishopswood Golf Course 131
TADMARTON Tadmarton Heath Golf Club 216
TAMWORTH Tamworth Municipal Golf Club 231
TARPORLEY Portal Golf & Country Club 41-2
TAUNTON Oake Manor Golf Club 225
TAUNTON Taunton Vale Golf Club 225
TEDBURN ST MARY Fingle Glen Golf Centre 70
TELFORD Telford Golf & Country Club 220
TELFORD The Shropshire 219-20
TEWKESBURY Tewkesbury Park Hotel Golf &
Country Club 96
THORNBURY Thornbury Golf Centre 96
THORNEY Thorney Golf Centre 29
TICEHURST Dale Hill Hotel & Golf Club 258
TILSWORTH Tilsworth Golf Centre 17
TOLLARD ROYAL Rushmore Park Golf Club 286
TOLLESHUNT KNIGHTS Five Lakes Hotel Golf &
Country Club 91
TOOT HILL Toot Hill Golf Club 92
TORKSEY Millfield Golf Course 180
TRURO Killiow Golf Club 52
TWICKENHAM Twickenham Golf Centre 109
UCKFIELD East Sussex National Golf Club 257
UCKFIELD Piltdown Golf Club 258
UPHOLLAND Beacon Park Public
Golf Centre 166
UTTOXETER Manor Golf Club 231
VERWOOD Crane Valley Golf Club 77
VIRGINIA WATER Wentworth Club 247
WADEBRIDGE St Kew Golf Course 53

WALLSEND Wallsend Golf Club 267
WALSALL Calderfields Golf Academy 280
WALTON-ON-THAMES Burhill Golf Club 248
WARE Whitehill Golf Course 142
WARWICK Warwick Golf Club 273
WASHINGTON George Washington Hotel Golf &
Country Club 267
WATERSTOCK Waterstock Golf Course 216
WATTON Richmond Park Golf Club 198
WAVENDON Wavendon Golf Centre 31
WELLS Wells (Somerset) Golf Club 226
WELWYN GARDEN CITY Mill Green
Golf Club 144
WEST BYFLEET West Byfleet Golf Club 250
WEST CHILTINGTON West Chiltington
Golf Club 263
WEST CLANDON Clandon Regis Golf Club 250
WEST END Windlemere Golf Club 250
WEST KINGSDOWN Woodlands Manor
Golf Club 157
WESTERHAM Westerham Golf Club 156
WESTON-UNDER-REDCASTLE Hawkstone Park
Hotel & Golf Centre 220
WETHERBY Wetherby Golf Club 318
WEXHAM STREET Wexham Park Golf Club 32
WHETSTONE Whetstone Golf Club 171
WHITCHURCH Hill Valley Golf &
Country Club 220
WHITTLEBURY Whittlebury Park Golf &
Country Club 202
WICK Tracy Park Golf & Country Club 97
WILMSLOW Mottram Hall 43
WILMSLOW Styal Golf Club 43
WILSON Breedon Priory Golf Centre 172
WIMBORNE Canford Magna Golf Club 77
WINCHESTER South Winchester Golf Club 132
WING Aylesbury Vale Golf Club 32
WISHAW The De Vere Belfry 271
WITHAM Benton Hall Golf Course 92
WITNEY Witney Lakes Golf Course 216
WOKING Hoebridge Golf Centre 250
WOKING Pyrford Golf Club 251
WOKINGHAM Downshire Golf Course 22
WOKINGHAM Sand Martins Golf Club 22
WOLVERHAMPTON Three Hammers
Short Course 281
WOODBRIDGE Seckford Golf Course 236
WOODBRIDGE Ufford Park Hotel
Golf & Leisure 236
WOODHALL SPA Woodhall Spa Golf Club 179
WOODHAM WALTER Warren Golf Club 92
WOOTTON BASSETT The Wiltshire Golf Club 286
WORCESTER Bank House Hotel Golf &
Country Club 291
WORKSOP Bondhay Golf & Country Club 212
WORTHING Worthing Golf Club 264
WYBOSTON Wyboston Lakes 17
YEOVIL Yeovil Golf Club 226
YORK Forest of Galtres Golf Club 301
YORK Forest Park Golf Club 301
YORK Swallow Hall Golf Course 302

CHANNEL ISLANDS

LA MOYE La Moye Golf Club 319

L'ANCRESSE VALE Royal Guernsey Golf Club 319
ST OUEN Les Mielles Golf & Country Club 320
ST PETER PORT St Pierre Park Golf Club 319

ISLE OF MAN

DOUGLAS Mount Murray Hotel &
  Country Club 320

NORTHERN IRELAND

ARMAGH County Armagh Golf Club 434
BALLYCLARE Greenacres Golf Course 432
BALLYGALLY Cairndhu Golf Club 432
BALLYMENA Galgorm Castle Golf &
  Country Club 432
BANBRIDGE Banbridge Golf Club 438
BANGOR Blackwood Golf Centre 405
BELFAST Mount Ober Golf & Country Club 437
ENNISKILLEN Ashwoods Golf Centre 443
ENNISKILLEN Castle Hume Golf Course 443
HOLYWOOD Holywood Golf Club 440
KILKEEL Kilkeel Golf Club 442
KILLYLEAGH Ringdufferin Golf Course 442
LIMAVADY Benone Tourist Complex 444
LIMAVADY Radisson Roe Park Hotel &
  Golf Resort 444
LONDONDERRY Foyle International
  Golf Centre 445
LURGAN Craigavon Golf & Ski Centre 436
MAZE Down Royal Park Golf Course 434
NEWTOWNABBEY Ballyearl Golf &
  Leisure Centre 434
WHITEHEAD Bentra Municipal Golf Course 434

REPUBLIC OF IRELAND

ARDEE Ardee Golf Club 476
ARKLOW Arklow Golf Club 488
BALLINASLOE Ballinasloe Golf Club 465
BALLINROBE Ballinrobe Golf Club 478
BALLYBOUGHAL Hollywood Lakes Golf Club 457
BALLYCONNEELY Connemara Golf Club 465
BALLYCONNELL Slieve Russell Hotel Golf and
  Country Club 446
BALLYHAUNIS Ballyhaunis Golf Club 478
BALTINGLASS Rathsallagh Golf &
  Country Club 489
BIRR Birr Golf Club 481
BLESSINGTON Tulfarris House Hotel &
  Country Club 489
CARBURY Highfield Golf Course 470
CASTLEKNOCK Elm Green Golf Course 457
CASTLEKNOCK Luttrellstown Castle Golf &
  Country Club 457
CASTLETOWNBERE Berehaven Golf Club 450
CAVAN County Cavan Golf Course 447
CHARLEVILLE Charleville Golf Club 450
CORK Fota Island Golf Course 451
DOUGLAS Douglas Golf Club 451
DUBLIN St Margaret's Golf & Country Club 461
DUBLIN The Open Golf Centre 460
DUNGARVAN Gold Coast Golf Club 485
DUNSHAUGHLIN Black Bush Golf Club 479
ENNISCORTHY Enniscorthy Golf Club 487

ENNISCRONE Enniscrone Golf Club 483
GALWAY Glenlo Abbey Golf Course 465
GREYSTONES Charlesland Golf & Country
  Club Hotel 490
KILCOOLE Druids Glen Golf Club 490
KILKENNY Kilkenny Golf Club 474
KILLARNEY Killarney Golf & Fishing Club 468
KINSALE Old Head Golf Links 452
LIMERICK Limerick County Golf &
  Country Club 475
LISMORE Lismore Golf Club 486
LITTLE ISLAND Harbour Point Golf Club 452
MIDLETON East Cork Golf Club 453
MONAGHAN Rossmore Golf Club 481
MONARD Ballykisteen Golf & Country Club 484
MONKSTOWN Monkstown Golf Club 453
MULLINGAR Mullingar Golf Club 487
NEWCASTLE WEST Newcastle West Golf Club 476
ORANMORE Athenry Golf Club 466
ORANMORE Galway Bay Golf & Country Club 466
OUGHTERARD Oughterard Golf Club 466
OVENS Lee Valley Golf & Country Club 454
PORTLAOISE The Heath Golf Club 474
ROSAPENNA Rosapenna Golf Club 456
SAGGART City West Hotel & Golf Resort 464
STRAFFAN The K Club 472
TERMONFECKIN Seapoint Golf Club 477
THOMASTOWN Mount Juliet Hotel &
  Golf Club 473
THURLES Thurles Golf Club 485
TIPPERARY County Tipperary Golf Course 485
WATERFORD Waterford Castle Golf Club 486
WATERVILLE Waterville House & Golf Links 470

SCOTLAND

ALYTH Strathmore Golf Centre 376
ALYTH The Alyth Golf Club 1894 376
AUCHTERARDER The Gleneagles Hotel 379
BANNOCKBURN Brucefields Family
  Golfing Centre 393
BARRY Panmure Golf Club 330
BURNTISLAND Burntisland Golf House Club 356
CRIEFF Crieff Golf Club 378
CRUDEN BAY Cruden Bay Golf Club 326
CUMBERNAULD Westerwood Hotel Golf &
  Country Club 375
DORNOCH The Carnegie Club 364
EDINBURGH Bruntsfield Links Golfing Society 336
EDINBURGH Marriott Dalmahoy Hotel Golf &
  Country Club 337
EDZELL Edzell Golf Club 332
ELGIN Elgin Golf Club 371
ELIE Golf House Club 358
ERISKA Isle of Eriska 334
GIRVAN Brunston Castle Golf Course 388
GLASGOW Cowglen Golf Club 340
GRETNA Gretna Golf Club 344
GULLANE Gullane Golf Club 351
HAMILTON Strathclyde Park Golf Club 392
HUNTLY Huntly Golf Club 327
INVERNESS Loch Ness Golf Course 366
KELSO The Roxburghe Golf Course 385
KIRKCUDBRIGHT Brighouse Bay Golf Course &
  Driving Range 344

LEUCHARS Drumoig Hotel & Golf Course 359
LUSS Loch Lomond Golf Club 335
NAIRN The Nairn Golf Club 367
NEWMACHAR Newmachar Golf Club 328
NORTH BERWICK Whitekirk Golf Course 352
PENICUIK Glencorse Golf Club 370
PERTH Murrayshall Country House Hotel &
  Golf Course 381
PORT ELLEN Machrie Hotel & Golf Links 398
SALINE Saline Golf Club 363
SPEY BAY Spey Bay Golf Course 372
ST ANDREWS Dukes Course 362
ST ANDREWS St Andrews Links Trust 361
STIRLING Stirling Golf Club 394
TROON Royal Troon Golf Club 387
TURNBERRY Turnberry Hotel, Golf Courses
  and Spa 389
WHITBURN Polkemmet Country Park 396

WALES

ABERGAVENNY Wernddu Golf Centre 418
ABERSOCH Abersoch Golf Club 414
BETTWS NEWYDD Alice Springs Golf Club 418
BODELWYDDAN Kimnel Park Golf Course 411
BRECON Cradoc Golf Club 424
BRIDGEND Southerndown Golf Club 403
CAERLEON Caerleon Golf Course 421
CAERPHILLY Mountain Lakes & Castell Heights 405
CAERPHILLY Virginia Park Golf Club 405
CAERSWS Mid-Wales Golf Centre 424
CAERWENT Dewstow Golf Club 418
CARDIFF Cottrell Park Golf CLub 406
CHEPSTOW Marriott St Pierre Hotel and
  Country Club 419
CHIRK Chirk Golf Club 429
CWMBRAN Green Meadow Golf &
  Country Club 428
HOLYHEAD Holyhead Golf Club 402
KIDWELLY Glyn Abbey Golf Club 408
LLANRHYSTUD Penrhos Golf &
  Country Club 409
MAESYCWMMER Bryn Meadows Golf &
  Country Hotel 405
MARGAM Lakeside Golf Course 420
MOLD Padeswood & Buckley Golf Club 413
NEWPORT Parc Golf Course 422
NEWPORT The Celtic Manor Resort 421
NORTHOP Northop Country Park Golf Club 413
OAKDALE Oakdale Golf Course 406
PENARTH Glamorganshire Golf Club 429
PENCOED St Mary's Hotel Golf &
  Country Club 403
PENRHYS Rhondda Golf Club 425
PONTYCLUN Vale of Glamorgan Hotel Golf &
  Country Club 426
PORTHCAWL Royal Porthcawl Golf Club 404
PYLE Pyle & Kenfig Golf Club 404
ST ASAPH Llannerch Park Golf Course 412
SWANSEA Clyne Golf Club 427
WREXHAM Clays Farm Golf Centre 430

Index *of Golf Courses*

A

Abbeydale, Sheffield 296
Abbeydale, Sheffield 305
Abbey Hill, Milton Keynes 30
Abbey Hotel Golf & Country Club,
    Redditch 290
Abbeyleix, Abbeyleix 474
Abbey View, St Albans 141
Abbotsley Golf & Squash Club,
    St Neots 35
Aberdare, Aberdare 425
Aberdelghy, Lisburn 433
Aberdour, Aberdour 356
Aberdovey, Aberdyfi 415
Aberfeldy, Aberfeldy 376
Aberfoyle, Aberfoyle 393
Abergele, Abergele 409
Abernethy, Nethy Bridge 368
Abersoch, Abersoch 414
Aberystwyth, Aberystwyth 408
Aboyne, Aboyne 325
Abridge Golf and Country Club,
    Abridge 82-3
Accrington & District, Accrington 157
Achill, Keel 478
Adare Manor, Adare 475
The Addington, Addington 98
Addington Court, Addington 98
Addington Palace, Addington 98
Airdrie, Airdrie 374
Airlinks, Hounslow 104
Aldeburgh, Aldeburgh 232
Aldenham Golf and Country Club,
    Aldenham 135
Alderley Edge, Alderley Edge 36
Alderney, Alderney 319
Alder Root, Winwick 44
Aldwark Manor, Aldwark 295
Aldwickbury Park, Harpenden 138
Alexandra, Glasgow 340
Alford, Alford 325
Alfreton, Alfreton 59
Alice Springs, Bettws Newydd 418
Allendale, Allendale 202
Allerton Park, Liverpool 188
Allestree Park, Derby 61
Alloa, Alloa 341-2
Allt-y-Graban, Pontlliw 426
Alnesbourne Priory, Ipswich 234
Alness, Alness 363
Alnmouth, Alnmouth 202
Alnmouth Village, Alnmouth 202
Alnwick, Alnwick 202-3
Alresford, Alresford 121
Alsager Golf & Country Club,
    Alsager 36
Alston Moor, Alston 53
Alton, Alton 121-2
Altrincham, Altrincham 110-11
Alva, Alva 342
Alwoodley, Alwoodley 307
Alyth, Alyth 376
American Golf at Sunbury,
    Shepperton 248
Ampfield Par Three, Ampfield 122
Andover, Andover 122

Anglesey, Rhosneigr 402
Annanhill, Kilmarnock 347
Anstruther, Anstruther 356
Ansty Golf Centre, Coventry 275
Appleby, Appleby-in-Westmorland 53
Aquarius, SE22 East Dulwich 184
Arbroath, Arbroath 329-30
Arcot Hall, Cramlington 204
Ardee, Ardee 476
Ardeer, Stevenston 374
Ardglass, Ardglass 438
Arkley, Barnet 99
Arklow, Arklow 488-9
Army, Aldershot 121
Arrowe Park, Birkenhead 185
Arscott, Shrewsbury 219
Ashbourne, Ashbourne 59
Ashburnham, Burry Port 407
Ashbury, Okehampton 68
Ashby Decoy, Scunthorpe 176
Ashdown Forest Golf Hotel,
    Forest Row 255
Ashford, Ashford 145
Ashford Manor, Ashford 237
Ashley Wood, Blandford Forum 73
Ashridge, Little Gaddesden 139
Ashton & Lea, Preston 165
Ashton-in-Makerfield,
    Ashton-in-Makerfield 111
Ashton on Mersey, Sale 118
Ashton-under-Lyne,
    Ashton-under-Lyne 111
Ashwoods Golf Centre, Enniskillen 443
Askernish, Askernish 400
Aspect Park, Henley-on-Thames 214
Aspley Guise & Woburn Sands,
    Aspley Guise 14
Astbury, Congleton 37
Athenry, Oranmore 466
Atherstone, Atherstone 268
Athlone, Athlone 482
Athy, Athy 470
Auchenblae, Auchenblae 325
Auchmill, Aberdeen 324
Auchterarder, Auchterarder 377
Auchterderran, Cardenden 356
Austerfield Park, Bawtry 303
Austin Lodge, Eynsford 148
Avisford Park, Arundel 258-9
Avro, Woodford 121
Axe Cliff, Axmouth 64
Aylesbury Golf Centre, Aylesbury 25
Aylesbury Park, Aylesbury 25
Aylesbury Vale, Wing 32

B

Baberton, Edinburgh 336
Backworth, Backworth 264
Bacup, Bacup 158
Badgemore Park,
    Henley-on-Thames 214-15
Bagden Hall Hotel & Golf Course,
    Huddersfield 311
Baildon, Baildon 307
Bakewell, Bakewell 59
Bala, Bala 416

Balbirnie Park, Markinch 362
Balbriggan, Balbriggan 457
Balcarrick, Donabate 458
Ballaghaderreen, Ballaghaderreen 482
Ballards Gore, Canewdon 85
Ballater, Ballater 325
Ballina, Ballina 477-8
Ballinamore, Ballinamore 475
Ballinascorney, Tallaght 464
Ballinasloe, Ballinasloe 465
Ballinrobe, Ballinrobe 478
Ballochmyle, Mauchline 347-8
Ballybofey & Stranorlar, Ballybofey 454
Ballybunion, Ballybunion 469
Ballycastle, Ballycastle 432
Ballyclare, Ballyclare 432
Ballyearl Golf & Leisure Centre,
    Newtownabbey 434
Ballyhaunis, Ballyhaunis 478
Ballykisteen, Monard 484
Ballyliffin, Ballyliffen 455
Ballymascanlon House Hotel,
    Dundalk 477
Ballymena, Ballymena 432
Ballymote, Ballymote 483
Balmoral, Belfast 436
Balnagask, Aberdeen 324
Baltinglass, Baltinglass 489
Bamburgh Castle, Bamburgh 203
Banbridge, Banbridge 438-9
Banchory, Banchory 326
Bandon, Bandon 449
Bangor, Bangor 439
Bank House Hotel Golf & Country
    Club, Worcester 291
Banstead Downs, Banstead 238
Bantry Bay, Bantry 449
Bargoed, Bargoed 405
Barkway Park, Royston 140
Barlaston, Stone 231
Barnard Castle, Barnard Castle 78
Barnehurst, Barnehurst 99
Barnham Broom Hotel, Golf,
    Conference, Leisure, Barnham
    Broom 192
Barnsley, Barnsley 302
Baron Hill, Beaumaris 402
Barrow, Barrow-in-Furness 54
Barshaw, Paisley 383
Barton-on-Sea, Barton-on-Sea 122-3
Basildon, Basildon 83
Basingstoke, Basingstoke 123
Batchwood Hall, St Albans 141
Bath, Bath 221
Bathgate, Bathgate 395
Bawburgh, Bawburgh 192
Baxenden & District, Accrington 157
Beacon Park, Upholland 166
Beaconsfield, Beaconsfield 25-6
Beadlow Manor Hotel & Golf &
    Country Club, Shefford 17
Beamish Park, Beamish 78
Bearna Golf and Country Club,
    Bearna 465
Bearsden, Bearsden 348
Bearsted, Bearsted 145
Bearwood, Sindlesham 21-2

Index *of Golf Courses*

Beauchief Public, Sheffield 305
Beau Desert, Cannock 227
Beaufort, Killarney 468
Beccles, Beccles 232
Beckenham Place Park,
    Beckenham 99
Bedale, Bedale 295
Bedford & County, Bedford 14
Bedford, Bedford 14
Bedfordshire, Bedford 14
Bedlingtonshire, Bedlington 203
Beech Park, Rathcoole 464
Beedles Lake, East Goscote 167-8
Beeston Fields, Nottingham 209
Beith, Beith 372
Belfairs, Southend-on-Sea 90
Belford, Belford 203
The Belfry, Wishaw 271
Belleisle, Ayr 388
Bellingham, Bellingham 203
Bellshill, Bellshill 374
Belmont Lodge, Hereford 133
Belton Park, Grantham 174
Belton Woods Hotel, Belton 172
Belturbet, Belturbet 447
The Belvoir Park, Newtownbreda 438
Benone, Limavady 444
Ben Rhydding, Ilkley 311
Bentham, Bentham 295
Bentley, Brentwood 84
Benton Hall, Witham 92
Bentra Municipal, Whitehead 434
Berehaven, Castletownbere 450
Berkhamsted, Berkhamsted 135
Berkshire, Ascot 17-18
Berwick-upon-Tweed (Goswick),
    Berwick-upon-Tweed 203-4
Betchworth Park, Dorking 240
Betws-y-Coed, Betws-y-Coed 410
Beverley & East Riding, Beverley 292
Bexleyheath, Bexleyheath 100
Bicester Golf & Country Club,
    Chesterton 213
Bidford Grange, Bidford-on-Avon 268
Bidston, Wallasey 190
Bigbury, Bigbury-on-Sea 64
Biggar, Biggar 391
Billingham, Billingham 78
Bingley St Ives, Bingley 307
Birch Grove, Colchester 86
Birch Hall, Unstone 63
Birchwood, Warrington 42
Birchwood Park, Dartford 147
Bird Hills, Maidenhead 19-20
Birley Wood, Sheffield 305
Birr, Birr 481
Birstall, Birstall 167
Birtley, Birtley 264
Bishop Auckland, Bishop Auckland 78
Bishopbriggs, Bishopbriggs 348-9
Bishop's Stortford, Bishop's
    Stortford 135-6
Bishopswood, Tadley 131-2
Blackburn, Blackburn 158
Black Bush, Dunshaughlin 479
Blackley, Manchester 115

Blacklion, Blacklion 447
Blackmoor, Bordon 123
Blacknest, Farnham 242
Blackpool North Shore, Blackpool 158
Blackwell, Bromsgrove 288
Blackwell Grange, Darlington 79
Blackwood, Blackwood 405
Blackwood Golf Centre, Bangor 439
Blainroe, Blainroe 489
Blair Atholl, Blair Atholl 377
Blairbeth, Burnside 391
Blairgowrie, Blairgowrie 377
Blankney, Blankney 172
Bloxwich, Walsall 280
Blue Mountain Golf Centre,
    Binfield 18-19
Blundells Hill, Rainhill 189
Blyth, Blyth 204
Boat of Garten, Boat of Garten 363-4
Bodenstown, Naas 471
Bognor Regis, Bognor Regis 259
Boldmere, Sutton Coldfield 278
Boldon, Boldon 264
Bolton, Bolton 111
Bonar Bridge-Ardgay, Bonar
    Bridge 364
Bondhay Golf & Country Club,
    Worksop 212
Bonnyton, Eaglesham 354
Boothferry Park, Howden 297
Bootle, Bootle 186
Borris, Borris 446
Borth & Ynyslas, Borth 408
Boston, Boston 173
Bothwell Castle, Bothwell 391
Botley Park Hotel, Golf & Country
    Club, Botley 123-4
Boughton, Faversham 148
Bow Brickhill, Woburn 27
Bowood Golf & Country Club,
    Calne 282-3
Bowood Park, Camelford 45
Bowring, Huyton 187
Boxmoor, Hemel Hempstead 138-9
Boyce Hill, Benfleet 83
Boyle, Boyle 482
Brackenwood, Bebington 185
Brackley Municipal, Walkden 120
Bradford (Hawksworth), Guiseley 310
Bradford Moor, Bradford 308
Bradley Park, Huddersfield 311
Braehead, Alloa 342
Braemar, Braemar 326
Braid Hills, Edinburgh 336
Brailes, Upper Brailes 273
Braintree, Braintree 83-4
Bramall Park, Bramhall 112-13
Bramcote Hills, Nottingham 209
Bramhall, Bramhall 113
Bramley, Bramley 238
Brampton, Brampton 54
Brampton Heath, Northampton 200
Brampton Park, Brampton 32
Bramshaw, Lyndhurst 128
Brancepeth Castle, Durham 80
Brandhall, Birmingham 273
Brandon, Leeds 312

Branshaw, Keighley 312
Branston, Burton-upon-Trent 227
Braxted Park, Witham 92
Bray, Bray 489
Brean, Burnham-on-Sea 222
Brechin, Brechin 330, 332
Brecon, Brecon 423-4
Breedon Priory, Wilson 172
Breightmet, Bolton 112
Brent Valley, W7 Hanwell 185
Brett Vale, Raydon 235
Brickendon Grange, Brickendon 136
Brickhampton Court, Gloucester 94-5
Bridge of Allan, Bridge of Allan 393
Bridgnorth, Bridgnorth 217
Bridlington, Bridlington 292
Bridlington Links, Bridlington 293
Bridport & West Dorset, Bridport 73
Briggens House Hotel, Stanstead
    Abbots 142
Brighouse Bay, Kirkcudbright 344
Bright Castle, Downpatrick 440
Brighton & Hove, Brighton & Hove 252
Brinkworth, Wootton Bassett 286
Bristol, Almondsbury 93
Bristol and Clifton, Bristol 24
British Golf Museum, St Andrews 362
British Steel Port Talbot, Port
    Talbot 421
Broadstone (Dorset), Broadstone 73-4
Broadwater Park, Godalming 243
Broadway, Broadway 288
Brocton Hall, Brocton 227
Brodick, Brodick 397
Broke Hill, Halstead 149
Brokenhurst Manor, Brockenhurst 124
Bromborough, Bromborough 186
Bromley, Bromley 100
Bromsgrove Golf Centre,
    Bromsgrove 288
Brookdale, Failsworth 114
Brookmans Park, Brookmans
    Park 136
Broome Manor Golf Complex,
    Swindon 285
Broome Park, Barham 145
Broomieknowe, Bonnyrigg 369
Brora, Brora 364
Brough, Brough 293
Brown Trout Golf & Country Inn,
    Aghadowey 443
Brucefields Family Golfing Centre,
    Bannockburn 393
Brunston Castle, Girvan 388, 390
Bruntsfield Links Golfing Society,
    Edinburgh 336
Brynhill, Barry 428
Bryn Meadows Golf & Country Hotel,
    Maesycwmmer 405-6
Bryn Morfydd Hotel, Denbigh 411
Buchanan Castle, Drymen 394
Buckingham, Buckingham 26
Buckinghamshire, Denham 28
Buckpool, Buckie 370
Bude & North Cornwall, Bude 44
Budock Vean Golf & Country House
    Hotel, Budock Vean 44

Builth Wells, Builth Wells 424
Bulbury Woods, Slepe 76
Bull Bay, Amlwch 402
Bulwell Forest, Nottingham 209
Buncrana Municipal, Buncrana 455
Bundoran, Bundoran 455
Bungay & Waveney Valley, Bungay 233
Bunsay Downs, Woodham Walter 92
Burford, Burford 213
Burgess Hill, Burgess Hill 259
Burghill Valley, Hereford 133
Burghley Park, Stamford 178
Burhill, Walton-on-Thames 248, 250
Burley, Burley 124
Burnham & Berrow, Burnham-
on-Sea 222
Burnham Beeches, Burnham 26
Burnham-on-Crouch, Burnham-
on-Crouch 85
Burnley, Burnley 159
Burntisland Golf House Club,
Burntisland 356
Burslem, Stoke-on-Trent 230
The Burstead, Billericay 83
Burton-upon-Trent, Burton-upon-
Trent 227
Bury, Bury 113
Bury St Edmunds, Bury St
Edmunds 233
Bushey Golf & Country Club,
Bushey 137
Bushey Hall, Bushey 137
Bushfoot, Portballintrae 434
Bush Hill Park, N21 Winchmore
Hill 182
Bute, Kingarth 398
Buxton & High Peak, Buxton 60

C

C & L Golf & Country Club,
Greenford 103
Cadmore Lodge Hotel & Country Club,
Tenbury Wells 291
Caerleon, Caerleon 421
Caernarfon, Caernarfon 416
Caerphilly, Caerphilly 405
Caerwys Nine of Clubs, Caerwys 413
Cahir Park, Cahir 483-4
Caird Park, Dundee 347
Cairndhu, Ballygally 432
Calcot Park, Reading 21
Caldecott Hall Golf & Leisure,
Fritton 194
Calderbraes, Uddingston 393
Calderfields, Walsall 280
Caldwell, Uplawmoor 355
Caldy, Caldy 186
Callan, Callan 472
Callander, Callander 394
Calverley, Pudsey 316
Camberley Heath, Camberley 238-9
Cambridge, Longstanton 33
Cambridge Meridian, Toft 36
Cambridgeshire Moat House,
Bar Hill 32
Came Down, Dorchester 74

Camperdown, Dundee 347
Campsie, Lennoxtown 349
Cams Hall, Fareham 125-6
Canford Magna, Wimborne 77-8
Canmore, Dunfermline 357
Cannington, Bridgwater 221-2
Cannock Park, Cannock 228
Canons Brook, Harlow 88
Canterbury, Canterbury 146-7
Canwick Park, Lincoln 175
Cape Cornwall Golf & Country Club,
St Just (near Land's End) 49
Caprington, Kilmarnock 347
Carden Park Hotel, Chester 36
Cardiff, Cardiff 406
Cardigan, Cardigan 408-9
Cardross, Cardross 333
Carholme, Lincoln 175
Carlisle, Carlisle 54-5
Carlow, Carlow 446
Carluke, Carluke 391
Carlyon Bay Hotel, Carlyon Bay 45
Carmarthen, Carmarthen 408
Carnalea, Bangor 439
Carne, Belmullet 478
The Carnegie Club, Dornoch 364
Carnoustie Golf Links, Carnoustie 331
Carnwath, Carnwath 391
Carradale, Carradale 333
Carrbridge, Carrbridge 364
Carrickfergus, Carrickfergus 433
Carrick Knowe, Edinburgh 336
Carrickmines, Dublin 458
Carrick-on-Shannon, Carrick-on-
Shannon 475
Carrick-on-Suir, Carrick-on-Suir 484
Carswell, Faringdon 214
Carus Green, Kendal 56
Castle, Dublin 458-9
Castlebar, Castlebar 478
Castleblayney, Castleblayney 481
Castle Douglas, Castle Douglas 342
Castle Eden & Peterlee, Hartlepool 81
Castlegregory, Castlegregory 467
Castle Hawk, Rochdale 117-18
Castle Hume, Enniskillen 443
Castle Point, Canvey Island 85
Castlerea, Castlerea 482
Castlerock, Castlerock 444
Castletown Golf Links, Castletown 320
Castletroy, Limerick 475
Castlewarden, Straffan 472
Cathcart Castle, Clarkston 354
Cathkin Braes, Burnside 391
Catterick, Catterick Garrison 295
Cave Castle Golf Hotel, South
Cave 294
Cavendish, Buxton 60
Cawder, Bishopbriggs 349
Ceann Sibeal, Ballyferriter 467
Celtic Manor Resort, Newport 421-2
Central London Golf Centre, SW18
Wandsworth 184
Chadwell Springs, Ware 142
Chalgrave Manor, Chalgrave 14-15
Channels, Chelmsford 85
Chapel-en-le-Frith, Chapel-en-

le-Frith 60
Charlesland Golf & Country Club Hotel,
Greystones 490
Charleville, Charleville 450
Charnock Richard, Chorley 159
Charnwood Forest, Woodhouse
Eaves 172
Chart Hills, Diddenden 145-6
Chartridge Park, Chartridge 28
Cheadle, Cheadle 113
Chedington Court, Beaminster 72
Chelmsford, Chelmsford 85
Chelsfield Lakes Golf Centre,
Orpington 106
Cherry Lodge, Biggin Hill 100
Cherwell Edge, Chacombe 198
Chesfield Downs, Graveley 138
Chesham & Ley Hill, Chesham 28
Cheshunt, Cheshunt 137
Chessington, Chessington 100-1
Chester, Chester 36-7
Chesterfield, Chesterfield 60
Chester-le-Street, Chester-le-
Street 78-9
Chestfield (Whitstable), Whitstable 157
Chevin, Duffield 62
Chewton Glen Hotel, New Milton 129
Chichester, Chichester 259
Chiddingfold, Chiddingfold 239
Chigwell, Chigwell 85-6
The Childwall, Liverpool 188
Chiltern Forest, Aylesbury 25
Chilwell Manor, Nottingham 210
Chilworth, Southampton 131
China Fleet Country Club, Saltash 52
Chippenham, Chippenham 283
Chipping Norton, Chipping Norton 213
Chipping Sodbury, Chipping
Sodbury 93
Chipstead, Chipstead 239-40
Chirk Golf Club, Chirk 429
Chislehurst, Chislehurst 101
Chobham, Chobham 240
Chorley, Chorley 159
Chorleywood, Chorleywood 137
Chorlton-cum-Hardy, Manchester 115
Chulmleigh, Chulmleigh 65
Churchill and Blakedown,
Blakedown 287
Church Stretton, Church Stretton 217
Churston, Churston Ferrers 65
Cilgwyn, Llangybi 409
Cill Dara, Kildare 471
Cirencester, Cirencester 93-4
City of Coventry-Brandon Wood,
Brandon 268
City of Derry, Londonderry 444
City of Newcastle, Newcastle upon
Tyne 265
City of Wakefield, Wakefield 318
City West Hotel & Golf Resort,
Saggart 464
Clacton, Clacton-on-Sea 86
Clandeboye, Bangor 439
Clandon Regis, West Clandon 250
Claremorris, Claremorris 478
Clays Farm Golf Centre, Wrexham 430

Index *of Golf Courses*

Clayton, Bradford 308
Cleckheaton & District, Cleckheaton 309
Cleethorpes, Cleethorpes 173
Cleeve Hill, Cleeve Hill 94
Cleobury Mortimer, Cleobury Mortimer 218
Clevedon, Clevedon 222
Cleveland, Redcar 299
Cliff Hotel, Gwbert-on-Sea 409
Cliftonville, Belfast 436
Clitheroe, Clitheroe 160
Clober, Milngavie 349
Clones, Clones 481
Clonlara Golf & Leisure, Clonlara 447
Clonmel, Clonmel 484
Clontarf, Dublin 459
The Club at Meyrick Park, Bournemouth 73
Clydebank & District, Clydebank 395
Clyne, Swansea 427
Cobtree Manor Park, Maidstone 152
Cochrane Castle, Johnstone 382-3
Cockermouth, Cockermouth 55
Cocksford, Tadcaster 300-1
Cocks Moors Woods, Birmingham 274
Coed-Y-Mwstwr, Bridgend 403
Colchester & Lexden Golf Centre, Colchester 86
Colchester, Colchester 86
Cold Ashby, Cold Ashby 199
Collingtree Park, Collingtree 199
Colmworth & North Bedfordshire, Colmworth 15
Colne, Colne 160
Colne Valley, Earls Colne 87
Colonsay, Scalasaig 398
Colvend, Colvend 343
Colville Park, Motherwell 375-6
Comrie, Comrie 378
Concord Park, Sheffield 305
Congleton, Congleton 37
Connemara, Ballyconneely 465
Consett & District, Consett 79
Conwy (Caernarvonshire), Conwy 410
Cooden Beach, Bexhill 252
Cookridge Hall Golf & Country Club, Leeds 312
Coollattin, Shillelagh 492
Coombe Hill, Kingston upon Thames 105
Coombe Wood, Kingston upon Thames 105
Copt Heath, Knowle 276-7
Copthorne, Copthorne 259
Corballis Public, Donabate 458
Corby Public, Corby 199
Corhampton, Corhampton 124
Cork, Cork 450
Corrie, Sannox 397
Corrstown, Dublin 459
Cosby, Cosby 167
Costessy Park, Norwich 196
Cotgrave Place Golf & Country Club, Radcliffe-on-Trent 211
Cotswold Edge, Wotton-under-Edge 98

Cotswold Hills, Cheltenham 93
Cottesmore, Crawley 260
Cottingham, Cottingham 293
Cottrell Park, Cardiff 406
Coulsdon Manor Hotel, Coulsdon 101
County Armagh, Armagh 434
County Cavan, Cavan 447
County Longford, Longford 476
County Louth, Baltray 476-7
County Meath, Trim 480
County Sligo, Sligo 483
County Tipperary, Tipperary 485
Courtown, Gorey 487-8
Coventry, Coventry 275-6
Coventry Hearsall, Coventry 276
Cowal, Dunoon 334
Cowdenbeath, Cowdenbeath 356
Cowdray Park, Midhurst 262
Cowes, Cowes 281
Cowglen, Glasgow 340
Coxmoor, Sutton in Ashfield 212
Craddockstown, Naas 471
Cradoc, Brecon 424
Craigavon Golf & Ski Centre, Lurgan 436
Craigentinny, Edinburgh 336
Craigie Hill, Perth 381
Craigmillar Park, Edinburgh 336
Craignure, Craignure 399
Crail Golfing Society, Crail 357
Crane Valley, Verwood 77
Craythorne, Burton-upon-Trent 227
Cray Valley, Orpington 106
Creigiau, Creigiau (Creiyiau) 407
Cretingham, Cretingham 233
Crewe, Crewe 37
Crews Hill, Enfield 102-3
Criccieth, Criccieth 416
Cricklade Hotel & Country Club, Cricklade 283
Crieff, Crieff 378
Croham Hurst, Croydon 101
Crompton & Royton, Oldham 117
Crondon Park, Stock 91
Crook, Crook 79
Crookhill Park Municipal, Conisbrough 303
Crosland Heath, Huddersfield 311
Crowborough Beacon, Crowborough 253
Crow Wood, Muirhead 376
Cruden Bay, Cruden Bay 326
Cruit Island, Cruit Island 455
Cuddington, Banstead 238
Cullen, Cullen 370
Cupar, Cupar 357
The Curragh, Kildare 471
Cushendall, Cushendall 433

D

Dainton Park, Ipplepen 67-8
Dalbeattie, Dalbeattie 343
Dale Hill Hotel & Golf Club, Ticehurst 258
Dalmally, Dalmally 333-4
Dalmilling, Ayr 388

Dalmuir Municipal, Clydebank 395
Dalmunzie, Spittal of Glenshee 380
Darenth Valley, Shoreham 154
Darlington, Darlington 79
Dartford, Dartford 147
Dartmouth, West Bromwich 280
Dartmouth Golf & Country Club, Blackawton 64
Darwen, Darwen 160
Datchet, Datchet 19
Davenport, Poynton 40-1
Daventry & District, Daventry 199
Davyhulme Park, Manchester 115
Deane, Bolton 112
Dean Farm, Kingsley 127
Deangate Ridge, Hoo 150
Dean Wood, Upholland 166
Deer Park Golf & Country Club, Livingston 396
Deer Park Hotel & Golf Course, Dublin 459
Deeside, Aberdeen 324
Delamere Forest, Delamere 38
Delapre Golf Complex, Northampton 200
Delgany, Delgany 490
Delvin Castle, Delvin 487
Denbigh, Denbigh 411
Denham, Denham 28
Denton, Denton 113-14
Dereham, Dereham 193
Derllys Court, Carmarthen 408
De Vere Belfry, Wishaw 271
De Vere Blackpool (Herons Reach), Blackpool 158-9
De Vere Dunston Hall Hotel, Norwich 196
De Vere Slaley Hall, Golf Resort & Spa, Hexham 205
Dewlands Manor, Crowborough 253-4
Dewsbury District, Mirfield 315
Dewstow, Caerwent 418
Dibden, Dibden 125
Didsbury, Manchester 115
Dinas Powis, Dinas Powis 429
Dinnaton Sporting & Country Club, Ivybridge 68
Dinsdale Spa, Middleton St George 81
Disley, Disley 38
Diss, Diss 194
Dolgellau, Dolgellau 416
Dollar, Dollar 342
Donabate, Donabate 458
Donaghadee, Donaghadee 440
Doncaster, Doncaster 303
Doncaster Town Moor, Doncaster 303
Donegal, Ballintra 454
Doneraile, Doneraile 451
Donnington Valley, Newbury 20
Dooks, Glenbeigh 467
Doon Valley, Patna 348
Dore & Totley, Sheffield 305
Dorking, Dorking 240-1
Dorset Heights, Belchalwell 72
Douglas, Douglas (Co Cork) 451
Douglas, Douglas (Isle of Man) 320
Douglas Park, Bearsden 348

Index of Golf Courses

Douglas Water, Rigside 393
Downes Crediton, Crediton 65
Downfield, Dundee 347
Downpatrick, Downpatrick 440
Down Royal Park, Maze 434
Downshire, Wokingham 22
Drayton Park, Abingdon 213
Drayton Park, Tamworth 231
Driffield, Great Driffield 293
Drift, East Horsley 241
Droitwich, Droitwich 288
Dromoland Castle Golf & Country
    Club, Newmarket-on-Fergus 449
Druids Glen, Kilcoole, 491
Druids Heath, Aldridge 273
Drumoig Hotel & Golf Course,
    Leuchars 359
Drumpellier, Coatbridge 374
Duddingston, Edinburgh 336, 338
Dudley, Dudley 276
Dudmoor Farm, Christchurch 74
Dudsbury, Ferndown 74
Duff House Royal, Banff 326
Dufftown, Dufftown 370-1
Dukes Course, St Andrews 362
Duke's Dene, Woldingham 251
Dukinfield, Ashton-under-Lyne 111
Dullatur, Cumbernauld 375
Dulwich & Sydenham Hill, SE21
Dulwich 184
Dumbarton, Dumbarton 395
Dumfries & County, Dumfries 343
Dumfries & Galloway, Dumfries 343
Dummer, Basingstoke 123
Dunaverty, Southend 335
Dunbar, Dunbar 351
Dunblane New Golf Club,
    Dunblane 394
Dundalk, Dundalk 477
Dundas Parks, South Queensferry 340
Dunfanaghy, Dunfanaghy 455-6
Dunfermline, Dunfermline 357
Dungannon, Dungannon 445
Dungarvan, Dungarvan 485
Dunham Forest, Altrincham 111
Dunkeld & Birnam, Dunkeld 378
Dun Laoghaire, Dun Laoghaire 461
Dunmore, Clonakilty 450
Dunmore East, Dunmore East 485-6
Dunmurry, Belfast 436-7
Dunnerholme, Askam-in-Furness 54
Dunnikier Park, Kirkcaldy 359
Dunning, Dunning 378
Duns, Duns 384
Dunscar, Bolton 112
Dunstable Downs, Dunstable 15
Dunstanburgh Castle, Embleton 204
Dunwood Manor, Romsey 130
Durham City, Durham 80
Durness, Durness 365
Duxbury Jubilee Park, Chorley 159-60
Dyke, Brighton & Hove 252
Dyrham Park Country Club, Barnet 99

E

Eagles, King's Lynn 195

Eaglescliffe and District, Eaglescliffe 80
Ealing, Greenford 103
Earlswood, Neath 420
Easingwold, Easingwold 295-6
East Berkshire, Crowthorne 19
East Bierley, Bradford 308
Eastbourne Downs, Eastbourne 254
East Brighton, Brighton & Hove 252-3
East Clare, Bodyke 447
East Cork, Midleton 453
East Devon, Budleigh Salterton 64
East Dorset, Bere Regis 72-3
Easter Moffat, Airdrie 374
Eastham Lodge, Eastham 186
East Herts, Buntingford 136-7
East Kilbride, East Kilbride 391
East Renfrewshire, Newton
    Mearns 354
East Sussex National, Uckfield 257
Eastwood, Newton Mearns 354-5
Eaton, Chester 37
Eaton, Norwich 196
Eccleston Park, Rainhill 189
Eden, Crosby-on-Eden 55-6
Edenbridge Golf & Country Club,
    Edenbridge 148
Edenderry, Edenderry 481
Edenmore, Magheralin 442
Edgbaston, Birmingham 274
Edmonstown, Dublin 459
Edwalton Municipal, Nottingham 210
Edzell, Edzell 332
Effingham, Effingham 241
Effingham Park, Copthorne 259-60
Elderslie, Johnstone 383
Elemore, Houghton-le-Spring 265
Elfordleigh, Plymouth 69
Elgin, Elgin 371
Elland, Elland 309
Ellesborough, Aylesbury 25
Ellesmere, Worsley 121
Ellesmere Port, Ellesmere Port 38
Elm Green, Castleknock 457
Elm Park Golf & Sports Club,
    Dublin 459
Elsham, Elsham 174
Elstree, Elstree 137-8
Eltham Warren, SE9 Eltham 183
Elton Furze, Peterborough 34
Ely City, Ely 33
Enderby, Enderby 168
Enfield, Enfield 103
Enmore Park, Enmore 223
Ennis, Ennis 448
Enniscorthy, Enniscorthy 487
Enniscrone, Enniscrone 483
Enniskillen, Enniskillen 443
Entry Hill, Bath 221
Enville, Enville 228
Epping, Epping 87
Epsom, Epsom 241
Erewash Valley, Stanton-by-Dale 63
Erlestoke Sands, Erlestoke 284
Erskine, Bishopton 382
Esporta, Dougalston, Milngavie 350
Essex Golf & Country Club, Earls
    Colne 87

Etchinghill, Folkestone 148-9
The European Club, Brittas Bay 490
Evesham, Fladbury 289
Executive Golf Club at Cranbrook,
    Cranbrook 147
Exeter Golf & Country Club, Exeter 66
Eyemouth, Eyemouth 384

F

Fairfield, Manchester 115
Fairhaven, Lytham St Annes 162
Fairwood Park, Upper Killay 427
Faithlegg House, Waterford 486
Fakenham, Fakenham 194
Falkirk, Falkirk 355
Falkirk Tryst, Larbert 355
Falkland, Falkland 358
Falmouth, Falmouth 45
Farleigh Court, Farleigh 242
Farnham, Farnham 242-3
Farnham Park, Farnham 243
Farnham Park, Stoke Poges 31
Farrington, Farrington Gurney 223
Farthingstone Hotel & Golf Course,
    Farthingstone 199
Faversham, Faversham 148
Felixstowe Ferry, Felixstowe 233
Feltwell, Thetford 197
Fereneze, Barrhead 354
Fermoy, Fermoy 451-2
Ferndown, Ferndown 74
Ferndown Forest, Ferndown 75
Fernfell Golf & Country Club,
    Cranleigh 240
Fernhill Hotel & Golf Club,
    Carrigaline 450
Filey, Filey 296
Filton, Bristol 24
Finchley, NW7 Mill Hill 182-3
Fingle Glen, Tedburn St Mary 70
Fintona, Fintona 445
Fishwick Hall, Preston 165
Fitzpatrick Silver Springs, Cork 450-1
Five Lakes Hotel Golf & Country Club,
    Tolleshunt Knights 91
Flackwell Heath, Flackwell Heath 28-9
Flamborough Head, Flamborough 293
Fleetwood, Fleetwood 160
Fleming Park, Eastleigh 125
Flempton, Flempton 233
Flint, Flint 413
Flixton, Urmston 120
Forest of Dean Golf Club and Bells
    Hotel, Coleford 94
Forest of Galtres, York 301
Forest Hill, Botcheston 167
Forest Hills, Coleford 94
Forest Park, York 301
Forest Pines - Briggate Lodge Inn
    Hotel, Scunthorpe 176-7
Forfar, Forfar 332
Formby, Formby 187
Formby Ladies, Formby 187
Forres, Forres 371
Forrester Park, Maldon 89
Forrest Little, Cloghran 458

Fort Augustus, Fort Augustus 365
Fortrose & Rosemarkie, Fortrose 365
Fortwilliam, Belfast 437
Fort William, Fort William 365
Fosseway Country Club, Midsomer Norton 224
Fota Island, Cork 451
Foxhills, Ottershaw 246
Foxrock, Dublin 459-60
Foyle International Golf Centre, Londonderry 445
Fraserburgh, Fraserburgh 327
Freshwater Bay, Freshwater 281-2
Frilford Heath, Frilford 214
Frinton, Frinton-on-Sea 87-8
Frodsham, Frodsham 38
Frome Golf Centre, Frome 223
Fulford, York 301
Fulford Heath, Wythall 292
Fulneck, Pudsey 316
Fulwell, Hampton 104
Furness, Barrow-in-Furness 54
Furzeley, Denmead 125
Fynn Valley, Ipswich 234

G

Gainsborough, Gainsborough 174
Gairloch, Gairloch 365
Galashiels, Galashiels 384
Galgorm Castle Golf & Country Club, Ballymena 432-3
Galway, Galway 465
Galway Bay Golf & Country Club, Oranmore 466
Ganstead Park, Hull 294
Ganton, Ganton 296
Garesfield, Chopwell 264
Garforth, Garforth 310
Garmouth & Kingston, Garmouth 371
Garstang Country Hotel & Golf Club, Garstang 161
Gatehouse, Gatehouse-of-Fleet 343-4
Gathurst, Shevington 118
Gatley, Gatley 114
Gatton Manor Hotel Golf & Country Club, Ockley 245-6
Gaudet Luce, Droitwich 288-9
Gay Hill, Hollywood 289
Gedney Hill, Gedney Hill 174
George Washington Hotel Golf & Country Club, Washington 267
Gerrards Cross, Gerrards Cross 29
Ghyll, Barnoldswick 158
Gifford, Gifford 351
Gigha, Gigha Island 334
Gillingham, Gillingham 149
Girton, Girton 33
Girvan, Girvan 390
Glamorganshire, Penarth 429
Glasgow, Irvine 372-3
Glasson Golf & Country Club, Athlone 486-7
Gleddoch Golf and Country Club, Langbank 383
Glen, North Berwick 352
Glenbervie Clubhouse, Larbert 355

Glencorse, Penicuik 370
Glencruitten, Oban 335
Gleneagles, Auchterarder 379
Glengarriff, Glengarriff 452
Glen Gorse, Oadby 170
Glenlo Abbey, Galway 465
Glenmalure, Rathdrum 492
Glenrothes, Glenrothes 358
Glossop and District, Glossop 62
Glyn Abbey, Kidwelly 408
Glynhir, Ammanford 407
Glynneath, Glynneath 420
Goal Farm, Pirbright 246
Gog Magog, Cambridge 32-3
Gold Coast Golf & Leisure, Dungarvan 485
Goldenhill, Goldenhill 228
Golf House Club, Elie 358
Golspie, Golspie 366
Goodwood, Goodwood 260
Goring & Streatley, Streatley 22
Gorleston, Gorleston-on-Sea 194
Gort, Gort 465-6
Gosfield Lake, Gosfield 88
Gosforth, Gosforth 265
Gosport & Stokes Bay, Gosport 126
Gotts Park, Leeds 312
Gourock, Gourock 369
Gower, Three Crosses 427
Grange, Dublin 460
Grange Fell, Grange-over-Sands 56
Grangemouth, Polmont 355
Grange-over-Sands, Grange-over-Sands 56
Grange Park, Rotherham 304
Grange Park, St Helens 189
Grantown-on-Spey, Grantown-on-Spey 366
Grassmoor Golf Centre, Chesterfield 60
Great Barr, Birmingham 274
Great Hadham Golf & Country Club, Bishop's Stortford 136
Great Harwood, Great Harwood 161
Great Lever & Farnworth, Bolton 112
Great Salterns Public Course, Portsmouth & Southsea 129-30
Great Yarmouth & Caister, Great Yarmouth 194-5
Greenacres, Ballyclare 432
Greenburn, Fauldhouse 395
Greencastle, Greencastle 456
Green Haworth, Accrington 158
Green Hotel, Kinross 380
Greenisland, Carrickfergus 433
Green Meadow Golf & Country Club, Cwmbran 428
Greenock, Greenock 369
Greenock Whinhill, Greenock 369
Greenore, Greenore 477
Greenway Hall, Stoke-on-Trent 230
Greetham Valley, Greetham 217
Gretna, Gretna 344
Greystones, Greystones 490
Griffin, Dunstable 15
Grimsby, Grimsby 174
Grims Dyke, Pinner 107

Guildford, Guildford 243
Gullane, Gullane 351, 353
Gweedore, Gweedore 456

H

Habberley, Kidderminster 289
Hadden Hill, Didcot 214
Haddington, Haddington 351-2
Hadley Wood, Hadley Wood 104
Haggs Castle, Glasgow 341
Hagley Golf & Country Club, Stourbridge 277-8
Haigh Hall, Wigan 121
Hainault Forest, Chigwell Row 86
Hainsworth Park, Brandesburton 292
Hale, Hale 114
Halesowen, Halesowen 276
Halesworth, Halesworth 233-4
Halifax, Halifax 310
Halifax Bradley Hall, Holywell Green 310-11
Hallamshire Golf Club Ltd, Sheffield 305-6
Hall Garth Golf & Country Club Hotel, Darlington 79-80
Hallowes, Dronfield 61
Halstock, Halstock 75
Haltwhistle, Greenhead 204-5
Hamilton, Hamilton 392
Ham Manor, Angmering 258
Hampshire, Andover 122
Hampstead, N2 East Finchley 181
Hamptworth Golf & Country Club, Landford 284-5
Handsworth, Birmingham 274
Hanging Heaton, Dewsbury 309
Hankley Common, Tilford 248
Happy Valley, Caterham 239
Harborne, Birmingham 274
Harborne Church Farm, Birmingham 274
Harbour Point, Little Island 452
Harburn, West Calder 396
Harewood Downs, Chalfont St Giles 26, 28
Harleyford, Marlow 30
Harpenden, Harpenden 138
Harpenden Common, Harpenden 138
Harrogate, Harrogate 296
Hartland Forest, Woolsery 72
Hartlepool, Hartlepool 81
Hartley Wintney, Hartley Wintney 126
Hartsbourne Golf & Country Club, Bushey 137
Hartswood, Brentwood 84
Harwich & Dovercourt, Harwich 88
Harwood, Bolton 112
Hassocks, Hassocks 261
Haste Hill, Northwood 106
Hastings, Hastings & St Leonards 255
Hatchford Brook, Birmingham 274-5
Hatfield London Country Club, Essendon 138
Haverfordwest, Haverfordwest 422
Haverhill, Haverhill 234
Hawarden, Hawarden 413

Index of Golf Courses

Hawick, Hawick 384-5
Hawkhurst, Hawkhurst 149
Hawkstone Park Hotel, Weston-under Redcastle 220
Haydock Park, Newton-le-Willows 189
Hayling, Hayling Island 120 7
Hayston, Kirkintilloch 349
Haywards Heath, Haywards Heath 261
Hazel Grove, Hazel Grove 114
Hazelhead Public, Aberdeen 324
Hazlemere, High Wycombe 29
Headfort, Kells 479
Headingley, Leeds 312-13
Headley, Bradford 308
The Heath, Portlaoise 474
Heathpark, West Drayton 110
Heaton Moor, Stockport 118
Heaton Park Municipal, Prestwich 117
Hebden Bridge, Hebden Bridge 310
Helen's Bay, Bangor 439-40
Helensburgh, Helensburgh 334
Hellidon Lakes Hotel & Country Club, Hellidon 200
Helmsdale, Helmsdale 366
Helsby, Helsby 38-9
Hemingford Abbots, Hemingford Abbots 33
Henbury, Bristol 24
Hendon, NW7 Mill Hill 183
Henley, Henley-on-Thames 215
Henley Golf & Country Club, Henley-in Arden 268
Hennerton, Reading 21
Hereford Municipal, Hereford 133
Herefordshire, Wormsley 135
Hermitage, Lucan 462
Herne Bay, Herne Bay 150
Hertfordshire, Broxbourne 136
The Hesketh, Southport 190
Hessle, Hessle 293
Heswall, Heswall 187
Hever, Hever 150
Heworth, Felling 264
Heworth, York 302
Hexham, Hexham 205
Heydon Grange Golf & Country Club, Royston 140-1
Heyrose, Knutsford 39
Heysham, Heysham 161
Hickleton, Hickleton 304
High Beech, Loughton 89
Highbullen Hotel, Chittlehamholt 64
Highcliffe Castle, Highcliffe 75
High Elms, Downe 102
Highfield, Carbury 470
Highgate, N6 Highgate 181
High Post, Great Durnford 284
Highwoods, Bexhill 252
Highworth Community Golf Centre, Highworth 284
Hill Barn Municipal, Worthing 263
Hillingdon, Hillingdon 104
Hillsborough, Sheffield 306
Hillside, Southport 190
Hilltop, Birmingham 275
Hill Valley, Whitchurch 220-1
Hilton Park, Milngavie 350

Hilton Puckrup Hall, Tewkesbury 96
Himley Hall Golf Centre, Himley 228
Hinckley, Hinckley 168
Hindhead, Hindhead 244
Hindley Hall, Hindley 114
Hintlesham Hall, Hintlesham 234
Hirsel, Coldstream 384
Hirst Priory, Crowle 173
Hoar Cross Hall Health Spa Golf Academy, Burton-upon-Trent 227
Hobson Municipal, Burnopfield 78
Hockley, Winchester 132
Hoebridge Golf Centre, Woking 250-1
Holland Bush, Lesmahagow 392
Hollingbury Park, Brighton & Hove 253
Hollywood Lakes, Ballyboughal 457
Holme Hall, Scunthorpe 177
Holsworthy, Holsworthy 66-7
Holtye, Holtye 256
Holyhead, Holyhead 402
Holywell, Brynford 412
Holywell Bay, Holywell Bay 46
Holywood, Holywood 440
Homelands Bettergolf Centre, Ashford 145
Home Park, Hampton Wick 104
Honiton, Honiton 67
Hopeman, Hopeman 371
Horam Park, Heathfield 256
Horncastle, Horncastle 175
Hornsea, Hornsea 294
Horsenden Hill, Greenford 103
Horsforth, Leeds 313
Horsham, Horsham 261
Horsley Lodge, Horsley 62
Horton Park Country Club, Epsom 241-2
Houghton-le-Spring, Houghton-le-Spring 265
Houghwood Golf, St Helens 189
Houldsworth, Stockport 119
Hounslow Heath Municipal, Hounslow 105
Howley Hall, Morley 315
Howth, Dublin 460
Hoylake, Hoylake 187
Huddersfield, Huddersfield 311
Hull, Hull 294
Humberstone Heights, Leicester 169
Hunley Hall Golf Club & Hotel, Saltburn-by-the-Sea 299
Hunstanton, Hunstanton 195
Huntercombe, Nuffield 215
Huntly, Huntly 327
Hurdwick, Tavistock 70
Hurlston Hall, Ormskirk 164
Hurtmore, Godalming 243
Huyton & Prescot, Huyton 188
Hythe Imperial, Hythe 150-1

I

Ifield Golf & Country Club, Crawley 260
Iford Bridge, Christchurch 74
Ilford, Ilford 105
Ilfracombe, Ilfracombe 67
Ilkley, Ilkley 312

Immingham, Immingham 175
Inco, Clydach 426
Ingestre Park, Weston 232
Ingol, Preston 165
Innellan, Innellan 334
Innerleithen, Innerleithen 385
Inmsh, Insch 327
Inverallochy, Inverallochy 327
Inveraray, Inveraray 334
Invergordon, Invergordon 366
Inverness, Inverness 366
Inverurie, Inverurie 327
Ipswich, Ipswich 234-5
Irvine, Irvine 373
Irvine Ravenspark, Irvine 373
The Island, Donabate 458
Isle of Eriska, Eriska 334
Isle of Purbeck, Swanage 76-7
Isle of Skye, Sconser 400
Isle of Wedmore, Wedmore 226
Iver, Iver 29
Izaak Walton, Stone 231

J

Jarvis Gloucester Hotel & Country Club, Gloucester 95
Jedburgh, Jedburgh 385
John O'Gaunt, Sandy 16

K

Kanturk, Kanturk 452
The K Club, Straffan 472
Kedleston Park, Kedleston 62
Keele Golf Club, Newcastle-under-Lyme 229
Keighley, Keighley 312
Keith, Keith 371
Kelso, Kelso 385
Kemnay, Kemnay 327
Kendal, Kendal 56
Kenilworth, Kenilworth 268-9
Kenmare, Kenmare 468
Kenmore, Kenmore 380
Keswick, Keswick 56
Kettering, Kettering 200
Kibworth, Kibworth 168-9
Kidderminster, Kidderminster 289
Kilbirnie Place, Kilbirnie 373
Kilcock, Kilcock 480
Kilcoole, Kilcoole 490, 492
Kilkea Castle, Castledermot 470-1
Kilkee, Kilkee 448
Kilkeel, Kilkeel 442
Kilkenny, Kilkenny 474
Killarney Golf & Fishing Club, Killarney 468
Killeen, Kill 471
Killeline, Newcastle West 476
Killin, Killin 394
Killinbeg, Dundalk 477
Killiney, Killiney 462
Killiow Park, Truro 52
Killorglin, Killorglin 468
Killymoon, Cookstown 445
Kilmacolm, Kilmacolm 369
Kilmarnock (Barassie), Barassie 388

Index *of Golf Courses*

Kilrea, Kilrea 444
Kilrush, Kilrush 448
Kilspindie, Aberlady 350
Kilsyth Lennox, Kilsyth 375
Kilternan Golf & Country Club Hotel,
    Kilternan 462
Kilton Forest, Worksop 212
Kilworth Springs, Lutterworth 169
Kimnel Park, Bodelwyddan 411
King Edward Bay Golf & Country Club,
    Onchan 321
Kinghorn, Kinghorn 358
King James VI, Perth 381
Kingsdown, Kingsdown 284
Kingsknowe, Edinburgh 338
Kings Links, Aberdeen 324
King's Lynn, King's Lynn 195
Kings Norton, Alvechurch 287
Kingsthorpe, Northampton 201
Kingsway, Royston 141
Kingsway, Scunthorpe 177
Kings Wood, Hatfield 304
Kingswood, Kingswood 244
Kington, Kington 133-4
Kingussie, Kingussie 367
Kinsale, Kinsale 452
Kintore, Kintore 328
Kirby Muxloe, Kirby Muxloe 168-9
Kirkby-Liverpool Municipal,
    Liverpool 188
Kirkby Lonsdale, Kirkby Lonsdale 57
Kirkbymoorside, Kirkbymoorside 297
Kirkcaldy, Kirkcaldy 359
Kirkcudbright, Kirkcudbright 344
Kirkhill, Glasgow 341
Kirkistown Castle, Cloughey 440
Kirriemuir, Kirriemuir 332
Kirtlington, Kirtlington 215
Kirton Holme, Boston 173
Knaresborough, Knaresborough 297
Knebworth, Knebworth 139
Knighton, Knighton 424
Knighton Heath, Bournemouth 73
Knights Grange, Winsford 43-4
Knightswood, Glasgow 341
Knock, Dundonald 437
Knockanally Golf & Country Club,
    Donadea 471
Knole Park, Sevenoaks 153
Knott End, Knott End-on-Sea 161
Knotty Hill Golf Centre, Sedgefield 82
Knowle, Bristol 24
Knutsford, Knutsford 39
Kyles of Bute, Tighnabruaich 335

L

Ladbrook Park, Tanworth-in-Arden 273
Ladybank, Ladybank 359
Lahinch, Lahinch 448
Lakeside, Margam 420
Lakeside Lodge, Pidley 34
Laleham, Chertsey 239
Lamberhurst, Lamberhurst 151
Lambourne, Burnham 26
Lamlash, Lamlash 397
La Moye, La Moye 319-20

Lanark, Lanark 392
Lancaster Golf Club, Lancaster 161
Langdon Hills Golf Centre,
    Bulphan 84-5
Langholm, Langholm 345
Langland Bay, Swansea 427
Langley Park, Beckenham 99
Lanhydrock, Bodmin 44
Lansdown, Bath 221
Lansil, Lancaster 162
Largs, Largs 373
Larkhall, Larkhall 392
Larne, Larne 433
Lauder, Lauder 385-6
Launceston, Launceston 46
Lavender Park, Ascot 18
Laytown & Bettystown,
    Bettystown 479
Leadhills, Leadhills 392
Lea Marston Hotel & Leisure Complex,
    Lea Marston 269
Leamington & County, Leamington
    Spa 269
Leasowe, Wallasey 192
Leatherhead, Leatherhead 244
Leckford, Leckford 127
Leeds, Leeds 313
Leeds Castle, Maidstone 152
Leeds Golf Centre, Leeds 313
Leek, Leek 228
Leen Valley Golf Centre, Hucknall 208
Lee-on-Solent, Lee-on-the-Solent 127
Lee Park, Liverpool 188
Lees Hall, Sheffield 306
Lee Valley Golf & Country Club,
    Ovens 454
Lee Valley Leisure, N9 Lower
    Edmonton 181
Leicestershire, Leicester 169
Leigh, Warrington 42
Leighton Buzzard, Leighton
    Buzzard 15
Lenzie, Lenzie 349
Leominster, Leominster 134
Leslie, Leslie 359
Les Mielles Golf & Country Club,
    St Ouen 320
Letchworth, Letchworth 139
Letham Grange, Arbroath 330
Lethamhill, Glasgow 341
Letterkenny, Letterkenny 456
Leven Links, Leven 360
Lewes, Lewes 256
Leyland, Leyland 162
Libbaton, High Bickington 66
Liberton, Edinburgh 338
Lickey Hills, Birmingham 275
Lightcliffe, Halifax 310
Lilleshall Hall, Lilleshall 218
Lilley Brook, Cheltenham 93
Limerick, Limerick 475
Limerick County Golf & Country Club,
    Limerick 475-6
Lime Trees Park, Greenford 103
Limpsfield Chart, Limpsfield 245
Lincoln, Torksey 180
Linden Hall, Longhorsley 205

Lindrick, Worksop 212
Lingdale, Woodhouse Eaves 172
Lingfield Park, Lingfield 245
Links, Newmarket 235
Links Country Park Hotel & Golf Club,
    West Runton 198
Linlithgow, Linlithgow 395-6
Linn Park, Glasgow 341
Liphook, Liphook 127
Lisburn, Lisburn 433
Lismore, Lismore 486
Little Aston, Sutton Coldfield 278
Little Chalfont, Little Chalfont 30
Littlehampton, Littlehampton 261-2
Little Hay, Hemel Hempstead 139
Littlehill, Bishopbriggs 349
Little Lakes Golf and Country Club,
    Bewdley 287
Littlestone, Littlestone 151
Llandrindod Wells, Llandrindod
    Wells 424
Llandudno (Maesdu), Llandudno 410
Llanfairfechan, Llanfairfechan 411
Llangefni (Public), Llangefni 402
Llanishen, Cardiff 406
Llannerch Park, St Asaph 412
Llantrisant & Pontyclun, Talbot
    Green 426
Llanwern, Llanwern 421
Llanymynech, Pant 219
Lobden, Whitworth 167
Lochcarron, Lochcarron 367
Lochgelly, Lochgelly 360
Lochgilphead, Lochgilphead 334-5
Loch Lomond, Luss 335
Lochmaben, Lochmaben 345
Loch Ness, Inverness 366
Lochore Meadows, Lochgelly 360
Lochranza, Lochranza 397
Lochwinnoch, Lochwinnoch 383
Lockerbie, Lockerbie 345
The London, Ash 144-5
Long Ashton, Long Ashton 224
Longcliffe, Loughborough 169
Longley Park, Huddersfield 311
Longniddry, Longniddry 352
Longridge, Longridge 162
Long Sutton, Langport 224
Looe, Looe 46-7
Lostwithiel Hotel, Golf & Country Club,
    Lostwithiel 47
Lothianburn, Edinburgh 338
Loudoun, Galston 347
Loughrea, Loughrea 466
Loughton, Loughton 89
Louth, Louth 176
Lowes Park, Bury 113
Low Laithes, Ossett 315
Lucan, Lucan 462
Ludlow, Ludlow 218
Luffenham Heath, Ketton 168
Luffness New, Aberlady 350
Lullingstone Park, Orpington 106-7
Lundin, Lundin Links 360
Lundin Ladies, Lundin Links 360, 362
Lurgan, Lurgan 436
Lutterworth, Lutterworth 170

Index *of Golf Courses*

Luttrellstown Castle, Castleknock 457-8
Lybster, Lybster 367
Lydd, Lydd 152
Lydney, Lydney 95
Lyme Regis, Lyme Regis 75
Lymm, Lymm 39
Lyneham, Chipping Norton 213-14
Lyshott Heath, Millbrook 16
Lytham Green Drive, Lytham St Annes 162

M

Macclesfield, Macclesfield 40
McDonald, Ellon 327
Machrie Bay, Machrie 397
Machrie Hotel, Port Ellen 398-9
Machrihanish, Machrihanish 335
Machynlleth, Machynlleth 425
Macroom, Macroom 453
Maesteg, Maesteg 403
Magdalene Fields, Berwick-upon-Tweed 204
Mahee Island, Ardmillan 438
Maidenhead, Maidenhead 20
Malahide, Malahide 462
Malden, New Malden 106
Maldon, Maldon 89
Malkins Bank, Sandbach 41
Malone, Belfast 437
Mallow, Mallow 453
Mallusk, Newtownabbey 434
Malone, Belfast 437
Malton & Norton, Malton 297
Manchester, Middleton 116
Mangotsfield, Bristol 24
Mannan Castle, Carrickmacross 480
Mannings Heath, Mannings Heath 262
Mannings Heath Hotel, Lower Beeding 262
Manor, Uttoxeter 231
Manor, Kearsley 115
Manor, Laceby 175
Manor of Groves Golf & Country Club, Sawbridgeworth 141-2
Manor House, Castle Combe 283
Manor House Hotel, Moretonhampstead 68
Mansfield Woodhouse, Mansfield Woodhouse 209
Mapledurham, Reading 21
Mapperley, Nottingham 210
March, March 33
Market Drayton, Market Drayton 218
Market Harborough, Market Harborough 170
Market Rasen & District, Market Rasen 176
Market Rasen Race Course (Golf Course), Market Rasen 176
Marlborough, Marlborough 285
Marple, Stockport 119
Marriott Breadsall Priory Hotel & Country Club, Breadsall 59
Marriott Dalmahoy Hotel & Country Club, Edinburgh 337
Marriott Forest of Arden Hotel Golf and

Country Club, Meriden 279
Marriott Goodwood Park Hotel & Country Club, Goodwood 260
Marriott Hanbury Manor Golf & Country Club, Ware 143
Marriott Hollins Hall Hotel & Country Club, Shipley 317
Marriott Meon Valley Hotel & Country Club, Shedfield 130-1
Marriott St Pierre Hotel & Country Club, Chepstow 419
Marriott Sprowston Manor Hotel & Country Club, Norwich 196
Marriott Tudor Park Hotel & Country Club, Maidstone 152
Marriott Worsley Park Hotel & Country Club, Manchester 115-16
Marsden, Marsden 314-15
Marsden Park, Nelson 164
Maryport, Maryport 57
Masham, Masham 297-8
Massereene, Antrim 432
Matfen Hall, Matfen 206
Matlock, Matlock 62
Mattishall, Mattishall 195
Maxstoke Park, Coleshill 268
Maybole Municipal, Maybole 390
Maylands Golf Club & Country Park, Romford 108
Maywood, Risley 63
Mellor & Townscliffe, Mellor 116
Melrose, Melrose 386
Meltham, Meltham 315
Melton Mowbray, Melton Mowbray 170
Mendip, Gurney Slade 223-4
Mendip Spring, Congresbury 222-3
Mentmore Golf & Country Club, Mentmore 30
Meole Brace, Meole Brace 218
Merchants of Edinburgh, Edinburgh 338
Mere Golf & Country Club, Knutsford 39
Merlin, Mawgan Porth 47-8
Merrist Wood, Guildford 243-4
Merthyr Tydfil, Merthyr Tydfil 417
The Metro Golf Centre, NW4 Hendon 182
Mickleover, Derby 61
Middlesborough, Middlesborough 298
Middlesborough Municipal, Middlesborough 298
Middleton Hall, Middleton 195
Middleton Park Municipal, Leeds 313
Mid Herts, Wheathampstead 144
Mid Kent, Gravesend 149
Mid Sussex, Ditchling 254
Mid-Wales Golf Centre, Caersws 424
Mid Yorkshire, Pontefract 316
Mile End, Oswestry 218-19
Milford, Guildford 244
Milford Haven, Milford Haven 422-3
Millfield, Torksey 180
Mill Green, Welwyn Garden City 144
Mill Hill, NW7 Mill Hill 183
Millport, Great Cumbrae Island 372
Mill Ride, Ascot 18

Milltown, Dublin 460
Milnathort, Milnathort 380-1
Milngavie, Milngavie 350
Minchinhampton (New Course), Minchinhampton 95
Minchinhampton (Old Course), Minchinhampton 95
Minehead & West Somerset, Minehead 225
Minto, Minto 386
Mitcham, Mitcham 105-6
Mitchelstown, Mitchelstown 453
Moate, Moate 487
Moatlands, Brenchley 146
Moffat, Moffat 345
Mold, Pantymwyn 414
Monifieth, Monifieth 332
Monkstown, Monkstown 453
Monmouth, Monmouth 418
Monmouthshire, Abergavenny 417-18
Montrose Links Trust, Montrose 333
Moor Allerton, Leeds 313
Moore Place, Esher 242
Moor Hall, Sutton Coldfield 278
Moor Park, Rickmansworth 140
Moors Valley, Ashley Heath 122
Moortown, Leeds 313-14
Moray, Lossiemouth 372
Morecambe, Morecambe 164
Morlais Castle, Merthyr Tydfil 417
Morley Hayes, Morley 63
Morpeth, Morpeth 206
Morriston, Swansea 427
Mortehoe & Woolacombe, Mortehoe 68
Mortonhall, Edinburgh 338
Moseley, Birmingham 275
Mottram Hall, Wilmslow 43
Mountain Ash, Mountain Ash 425
Mountain Lakes & Castell Heights, Caerphilly 405
Mountbellew, Mountbellew 466
Mount Ellen, Gartcosh 375
Mount Juliet Golf Course, Thomastown 473
Mount Murray Hotel & Country Club, Douglas 320-1
Mount Ober Golf & Country Club, Belfast 437
Mount Oswald, Durham 80
Mount Pleasant, Lower Stondon 15-16
Mountrath, Mountrath 474
Mount Temple, Moate 487
Mount Wolseley Hotel, Golf & Country Club, Tullow 446
Mowsbury, Bedford 14
Moyola Park, Castledawson 443-4
Much Hadham, Much Hadham 139
Muckhart, Muckhart 342
Muir of Ord, Muir of Ord 367
Mullingar, Mullingar 487
Mullion, Mullion 48
Mundesley, Mundesley 196
Murcar, Aberdeen 324
Murrayfield, Edinburgh 338
Murrayshall Country House Hotel, Perth 381

Index *of Golf Courses*

Muskerry, Blarney 449-50
Musselburgh, Musselburgh 352
Musselburgh Links, The Old Course, Musselburgh 352
Muswell Hill, N22 Wood Green 182
Muthill, Muthill 381
Mytton Fold Hotel & Golf Complex, Langho 162

N

Naas, Naas 471-2
Nairn, Nairn 367
Nairn Dunbar, Nairn 367-8
Narin & Portnoo, Narin 456
Naunton Downs, Naunton 96
Nazeing, Epping 87
Neath, Neath 420-1
Nefyn & District, Morfa Nefyn 416-17
Nelson, Nelson 164
Nenagh, Nenagh 484
Nevill, Royal Tunbridge Wells 156
Newark, Newark-on-Trent 209
Newbattle, Dalkeith 369-70
Newbiggin-by-the-Sea, Newbiggin-by-the-Sea 206
Newbold Comyn, Leamington Spa 269
Newburgh on Ythan, Newburgh on Ythan 328
Newbury & Crookham, Newbury 21
Newcastleton, Newcastleton 386
Newcastle-under-Lyme, Newcastle under-Lyme 229
Newcastle United, Newcastle upon Tyne 265
Newcastle West, Newcastle West 476
New Cumnock, New Cumnock 348
New Forest, Lyndhurst 128-9
New Galloway, New Galloway 345
Newlands, Dublin 460
Newmachar, Newmachar 328
New Mills, New Mills 63
New North Manchester, Middleton 117
Newport, Newport (Gwent) 422
Newport, Newport (Isle of Wight) 282
Newport (Pemb), Newport (Pembrokeshire) 423
Newquay, Newquay 48
New Ross, New Ross 488
Newry, Newry 442
Newton Abbot (Stover), Newton Abbot 68
Newton Green, Newton 236
Newtonmore, Newtonmore 368
Newton Stewart, Newton Stewart 345-6
Newtownstewart, Newtownstewart 445
New Zealand, Addlestone 237
Niddry Castle, Broxburn 350
Nizels, Hildenborough 150
The Norfolk Golf & Country Club, Dereham 193-4
Normanby Hall, Normanby 176
Normanton, Normanton 315
Northampton, Northampton 201
Northamptonshire County,

Northampton 201
North Berwick, North Berwick 352
Northcliffe, Shipley 317
North Downs, Woldingham 252
Northenden, Manchester 116
North Foreland, Broadstairs 146
North Hants, Fleet 126
North Inch, Perth 381-2
North Middlesex, N20 Whetstone 182
Northop Country Park, Northop 413
North Oxford, Oxford 215
North Shore Hotel & Golf Club, Skegness 177
Northumberland, Newcastle upon Tyne 265-6
North Wales, Llandudno 410
North Warwickshire, Meriden 277
North Weald, Harlow 88
North West, Buncrana 455
North Wilts, Bishops Cannings 282
Northwood, Northwood 106
North Worcestershire, Birmingham 275
Norton, Stockton-on-Tees 82
Nottingham City, Nottingham 210
Notts, Kirkby in Ashfield 208
Nuneaton, Nuneaton 270
Nuremore, Carrickmacross 480

O

Oadby, Oadby 170
Oakdale, Harrogate 296
Oakdale, Oakdale 406
Oake Manor, Taunton 225
Oakland Park, Chalfont St Giles 28
Oakleaf, Newton Aycliffe 81
Oakmere Park, Oxton 211
Oak Park, Crondall 124-5
Oakridge, Nuneaton 270
Oaks, Aughton 292
Oaksey Park Golf & Leisure, Oaksey 285
Oaks Sports Centre, Carshalton 100
The Oast Golf Centre, Sittingbourne 154
Oastpark, Snodland 154
Ocean Cove Golf & Leisure Hotel, Kilkee 448
Ogbourne Downs, Ogbourne St George 285
Okehampton, Okehampton 69
Old Colwyn, Colwyn Bay 410
Old Conna, Bray 489
Old Fold Manor, Barnet 99
Oldham, Oldham 117
Old Head, Kinsale 452
Old Links, Bolton 112
Old Meldrum, Oldmeldrum 328
Old Nene Golf & Country Club, Ramsey 34-5
Old Padeswood, Mold 413
Old Rectory, Llangattock 424-5
Old Thorns Hotel, Golf & Country Club, Liphook 127-8
Olton, Solihull 277
Omagh, Omagh 445-6
Ombersley, Droitwich 289

Onneley, Onneley 229
The Open Golf Centre, Dublin 460
Orchardleigh, Frome 223
Orkney, Kirkwall 399
Ormeau, Belfast 437
Ormonde Fields Golf and Country Club, Codnor 61
Ormskirk, Ormskirk 164
Orsett, Orsett 89
Orton Meadows, Peterborough 34
Osborne, East Cowes 281
Oswestry, Oswestry 219
Otley, Otley 315
Otter Valley Golf Centre, Upottery 71
Otway, Rathmullan 456
Oughterard, Oughterard 466
Oulton Park, Leeds 314
Oundle, Oundle 201
Outlane, Outlane 316
Overstone Park, Northampton 201
Owston Park, Doncaster 303
The Oxfordshire, Milton Common 215
Oxley Park, Wolverhampton 280-1

P

Pachesham Park Golf Complex, Leatherhead 244-5
Padbrook Park, Cullompton 65
Padeswood & Buckley, Mold 413
Painswick, Painswick 96
Painthorpe House, Wakefield 318
Paisley, Paisley 383
Palacerigg, Cumbernauld 375
Panmure, Barry 330
Pannal, Pannal 298
Panshanger Golf & Squash Complex, Welwyn Garden City 144
Parc, Newport 422
Park Hill, Seagrave 171
Parklands, Gosforth 265
Parknasilla, Parknasilla 468
Parkstone, Poole 75-6
Parkwood, Westerham 156
Parley, Hurn 75
Pastures, Mickleover 62-3
Patshull Park Hotel Golf & Country Club, Pattingham 229-30
Paultons Golf Centre, Ower 129
Pavenham Park, Pavenham 16
Paxhill Park, Haywards Heath 261
Peacehaven, Newhaven 256
Peebles, Peebles 386
Peel, Peel 321
Penmaenmawr, Penmaenmawr 411
Penn, Wolverhampton 281
Pennard, Southgate 426-7
Pennyhill Park Hotel & Country Club, Bagshot 237
Penrhos Golf & Country Club, Llanrhystud 409
Penrith, Penrith 57
Penwortham, Preston 165-6
Penycae, Ruabon 429-30
Peover, Knutsford 39
Perivale Park, Greenford 103
Perranporth, Perranporth 48

Index *of Golf Courses*

Perton Park, Perton 230
Peterborough Milton, Peterborough 34
Peterculter, Peterculter 325
Peterhead, Peterhead 328-9
Petersfield (New Course),
  Petersfield 129
Petersfield (Old Course),
  Petersfield 129
Peterstone, Cardiff 406
Phoenix, Rotherham 304
Pike Hills, Copmanthorpe 295
Piltdown, Uckfield 258
Pine Ridge, Camberley 239
Pinner Hill, Pinner 107
Pitcheroak, Redditch 290
Pitlochry, Pitlochry 382
Pitreavie, Dunfermline 358
Plassey, Eyton 429
Pleasington, Pleasington 165
Polkemmet Country Park,
  Whitburn 396
Pollok, Glasgow 341
Polmont, Polmont 356
Pontardawe, Pontardawe 421
Pontefract & District, Pontefract 316
Ponteland, Ponteland 206
Pontnewydd, Cwmbran 428
Pontypool, Pontypool 428
Pontypridd, Pontypridd 426
Portadown, Portadown 436
Portal Golf & Country Club,
  Tarporley 41-2
Portarlington, Portarlington 474
Port Bannatyne, Port Bannatyne 398
Porters Park, Radlett 140
Port Glasgow, Port Glasgow 369
Porthmadog, Porthmadog 417
Porthpean, St Austell 49
Portlethen, Portlethen 329
Portmarnock, Portmarnock 463
Portobello, Edinburgh 338-9
Portpatrick, Portpatrick 346
Port St Mary, Port St Mary 321
Portsalon, Portsalon 456
Portsmouth, Waterlooville 132
Portstewart, Portstewart 445
Portumna, Portumna 466-7
Potters Bar, Potters Bar 139
Poulton-le-Fylde, Poulton-le-Fylde 165
Poulton Park, Warrington 42
Poultwood, Tonbridge 156
Powfoot, Cummertrees 343
Praa Sands, Praa Sands 48-9
Prenton, Birkenhead 185
Prestatyn, Prestatyn 411-12
Prestbury, Prestbury 41
Preston, Preston 166
Prestonfield, Edinburgh 339
Prestwich, Prestwich 117
Prestwick, Prestwick 390
Prestwick St Cuthbert, Prestwick 390
Prestwick St Nicholas, Prestwick 390
Prince's, Sandwich 153
Priskilly Forest, Letterston 422

Prudhoe, Prudhoe 206
Pryors Hayes, Oscroft 40
Pumpherston, Livingston 396
Purley Chase, Nuneaton 270
Purley Downs, Purley 107
Puttenham, Puttenham 246
Pwllheli, Pwllheli 417
Pyecombe, Pyecombe 263
Pyle & Kenfig, Pyle 404
Pype Hayes, Sutton Coldfield 278
Pyrford, Woking 251

Q

Queensbury, Bradford 308
Queen's Park, Bournemouth 73
Queen's Park, Crewe

R

Radcliffe-on-Trent, Radcliffe-on-
  Trent 211
Radisson Roe Park Hotel & Golf
  Resort, Limavady 444
Radyr, Cardiff 407
RAF St Athan, Barry 428
Raglan Parc, Raglan 420
Ralston, Paisley 383
Ramsdale Park Golf Centre,
  Calverton 207-8
Ramsey, Ramsey (Cambs) 35
Ramsey, Ramsey (Isle of Man) 321
Ramside Hall, Durham 80
Ranfurly Castle, Bridge of Weir 382
Rathdowney, Rathdowney 474
Rathfarnham, Dublin 460
Ratho Park, Ratho 340
Rathsallagh, Baltinglass 489
Ravelston, Edinburgh 339
Raven Hall Hotel Golf Course,
  Ravenscar 298
Ravensworth, Gateshead 265
Rawdon Golf & Lawn Tennis Club,
  Rawdon 316-17
Reading, Reading 21
Reaseheath, Nantwich 40
Reay, Reay 368
Redbourn, Redbourn 140
Redcastle, Moville 456
Reddish Vale, Stockport 119
Redditch, Redditch 290-1
Redhill & Reigate, Redhill 246
Regent Park, Bolton 112
Reigate Heath, Reigate 246
Reigate Hill, Reigate 248
Renfrew, Renfrew 383-4
Renishaw Park, Renishaw 63
Renvyle House Hotel, Renvyle 467
Retford, Retford 211
Rhondda, Penrhys 425-6
Rhos-on-Sea, Llandudno 410
Rhuddlan, Rhuddlan 412
Rhyl, Rhyl 412
Richings Park Golf & Country Club,
  Iver 29

Richmond, Richmond 299
Richmond, Richmond upon
  Thames 107
Richmond Park, SW15 Putney 184
Richmond Park, Watton 198
Rickmansworth Public Course,
  Rickmansworth 140
Riddlesden, Riddlesden 317
The Ridge, Chart Sutton 147
Ringdufferin Golf Course,
  Killyleagh 442
Ringway, Altrincham 111
Ripon City, Ripon 299
Risebridge Golf Centre, Romford 108
Rishton, Rishton 166
Riverside, SE28 Woolwich 184
Robin Hood, Solihull 277
Rochdale, Rochdale 118
Rochester & Cobham Park,
  Rochester 153
Rochford Hundred, Rochford 90
Rockmount, Carryduff 440
Rodway Hill, Gloucester 95
Roker Park, Guildford 244
Rolls of Monmouth, Monmouth 420
Romanby, Northallerton 298
Romford, Romford 108
Romiley, Romiley 118
Romney Warren, Littlestone 151
Romsey, Romsey 130
Rookery Park, Lowestoft 235
Rosapenna, Rosapenna 456-7
Roscommon, Roscommon 482
Roscrea Golf Club, Roscrea 484
Roseberry Grange, Chester-le-
  Street 79
Roserrow Golf & Country Club,
  St Minver 52
Rossendale, Haslingden 161
Rosslare, Rosslare 488
Rossmore, Monaghan 481
Ross-on-Wye, Ross-on-Wye 134
Rothbury, Rothbury 206
Rotherham Golf Club Ltd,
  Rotherham 304-5
Rother Valley Golf Centre,
  Sheffield 306
Rothes, Rothes 372
Rothesay, Rothesay 398
Rothley Park, Rothley 170
Roundhay, Leeds 314
Roundwood, Roundwood 492
Routenburn, Largs 373
Rowany, Port Erin 321
Rowlands Castle, Rowlands
  Castle 130
Roxburghe, Kelso 385
Royal Aberdeen, Aberdeen 324
Royal Ascot, Ascot 18
Royal Ashdown Forest, Forest
  Row 255
The Royal Belfast, Holywood 442
Royal Birkdale, Southport 191
Royal Blackheath, SE9 Eltham 183

Royal Burgess, Edinburgh 339
Royal Cinque Ports, Deal 147-8
Royal County Down, Newcastle 441
Royal Cromer, Cromer 193
Royal Dornoch, Dornoch 364-5
Royal Dublin, Dublin 460-1
Royal Eastbourne, Eastbourne 254
Royal Epping Forest, E4
  Chingford 180-1
Royal Guernsey, L'Ancresse Vale 319
Royal Jersey, Grouville 319
Royal Liverpool, Hoylake 187
Royal Lytham and St Annes, Lytham
  St Annes 163
Royal Mid-Surrey, Richmond upon
  Thames 107-8
Royal Musselburgh, Prestonpans 354
Royal North Devon, Westward
  Ho! 71-2
Royal Norwich, Norwich 196
Royal Porthcawl, Porthcawl 404
Royal Portrush, Portrush 435
Royal St Davids, Harlech 416
Royal St George's, Sandwich 155
Royal Tara, Navan 480
Royal Tarlair, Macduff 328
Royal Troon, Troon 387
Royal West Norfolk, Brancaster 193
Royal Wimbledon, SW19
  Wimbledon 184-5
Royal Winchester, Winchester 132
Royal Worlington & Newmarket,
  Worlington 237
Royston, Royston 141
Rudding Park Hotel & Golf,
  Harrogate 296-7
Ruddington Grange, Ruddington 211
Rufford Park Golf Centre,
  Ollerton 210-11
Rugby, Rugby 270
Ruislip, Ruislip 108
Runcorn, Runcorn 41
Rush, Rush 464
Rushcliffe, East Leake 208
Rushden, Wellingborough 201-2
Rushmere, Ipswich 235
Rushmore Park Golf Club, Tollard
  Royal 286
Rusper, Newdigate 245
Rutherford Castle Golf Club, West
  Linton 388
Ruthin-Pwllglas, Ruthin 412
Rutland County, Great Casterton 217
Ruxley Park Golf Centre,
  Orpington 107
Ryburn, Sowerby 318
Ryde, Ryde 282
Rye, Rye 256
Rye Hill, Banbury 213
Ryhope, Sunderland 266
Ryston Park, Denver 193
Ryton, Ryton 266

S

Saddleworth, Uppermill 120
Saffron Walden, Saffron Walden 90
St Andrews Links, St Andrews 361
St Andrews Major, Barry 428-9
St Anne's, Dublin 461
St Annes Old Links, Lytham
  St Annes 162, 164
St Augustine's, Ramsgate 153
St Austell, St Austell 49
St Bees, St Bees 57
St Boswells, St Boswells 386
St Clement, St Clement 320
St Clere's Hall, Stanford-le-Hope 91
St David's City, St David's 423
St Deiniol, Bangor 416
St Enodoc, Rock 49
St Fillans, St Fillans 382
St George's Hill, Weybridge 250
St Giles, Newtown 425
St Helen's Bay Golf & Country Club,
  Rosslare 488
St Idloes, Llanidloes 425
St Ives (Cambs), St Ives 35
St Kew, Wadebridge 53
St Margaret's Golf & Country Club,
  Dublin 461
St Mary's Hotel Golf & Country Club,
  Pencoed 403-4
St Medan, Monreith 345
St Mellion, St Mellion 51
St Mellons, Cardiff 407
St Melyd, Prestatyn 412
St Michael Jubilee, Widnes 43
St Michael's, Leuchars 359
St Neots, St Neots 35
St Pierre Park Golf Club, St Peter
  Port 319
Sale, Sale 118
Saline, Saline 363
Salisbury & South Wilts, Salisbury 285
Saltburn by the Sea, Saltburn-by-the-
  Sea 300
Saltford, Saltford 225
Sandford Springs, Kingsclere 127
Sandhill, Barnsley 302-3
Sandilands, Sutton on Sea 180
Sandiway, Sandiway 41
Sand Martins, Wokingham 22
Sand Moor, Leeds 314
Sandwell Park, West Bromwich 280
Sandy Lodge, Northwood 106
Sanquhar, Sanquhar 346
Sapey, Upper Sapey 134-5
Saron, Llandyssul 409
Saunton, Saunton 69
Scarborough North Cliff,
  Scarborough 300
Scarborough South Cliff,
  Scarborough 300
Scarcroft, Scarcroft 317
Scathingwell, Tadcaster 301
Scoonie, Leven 360

Scotscraig, Tayport 363
Scrabo, Newtownards 442
Scraptoft, Scraptoft 171
Seacroft, Skegness 177
Seaford, Seaford 256, 258
Seaford Head, Seaford 258
Seaham, Seaham 81
Seahouses, Seahouses 207
Seapoint, Termonfeckin 477
Seascale, Seascale 57
Seaton Carew, Seaton Carew 81-2
Seckford, Woodbridge 236
Sedbergh, Sedbergh 57
Sedgley Golf Centre, Sedgley 277
Sedlescombe, Sedlescombe 258
Seedy Mill, Lichfield 228-9
Selby, Selby 300
Selkirk, Selkirk 386
Selsdon Park, Croydon 101-2
Selsey, Selsey 263
Sene Valley, Hythe 151
Serlby Park, Serlby 212
Settle, Settle 300
Severn Meadows, Highley 218
Shandon Park, Belfast 437
Shanklin & Sandown, Sandown 282
Shannon, Shannon Airport 449
Shaw Hill Hotel Golf & Country Club,
  Chorley 160
Sheerness, Sheerness 153-4
Shendish Manor, Hemel
  Hempstead 139
Sherborne, Sherborne 76
Sherdley Park, St Helens 189-90
Sheringham, Sheringham 197
Sherwood Forest, Mansfield 209
Shetland, Lerwick 400
Shifnal, Shifnal 219
Shillinglee Park, Godalming 243
Shipley, Bingley 308
Shipton, Cheltenham 93
Shirehampton Park, Bristol 25
Shirenewton, Chepstow 418
Shirland, Shirland 63
Shirley, Solihull 277
Shirley Park, Croydon 102
Shiskine, Blackwaterfoot 397
Shooters Hill, SE18 Woolwich 184
Shortlands, Bromley 100
Shotts, Shotts 376
Shrewsbury, Shrewsbury 219
Chrigley Hall Hotel, Macclesfield 40
Shrivenham Park, Shrivenham 216
The Shropshire, Telford 219-20
Sickleholme, Bamford 59
Sidcup, Sidcup 108
Sidmouth, Sidmouth 69
Silecroft, Silecroft 58
Silkstone, Silkstone 306
Silloth on Solway, Silloth 58
Silsden, Silsden 317
Silverdale, Silverdale 166
Silverknowes, Edinburgh 339
Silvermere, Cobham 240

Index of Golf Courses

Sinfin, Derby 61
Singing Hills, Hurstpierpoint 261
Sittingbourne & Milton Regis, Sittingbourne 154
Sitwell Park, Rotherham 305
Skeabost, Skeabost Bridge 400
Skelmorlie, Skelmorlie 373-4
Skerries, Skerries 464
Skibbereen & West Carbery, Skibbereen 454
Skipton, Skipton 300
Slade Valley, Brittas 457
Sleaford, Sleaford 178
Slieve Russell Hotel Golf & Country Club, Ballyconnell 446-7
Slinfold Park Golf & Country Club, Slinfold 263
Sonning, Sonning 22
Southampton, Southampton 131
South Beds, Luton 16
South Bradford, Bradford 308
Southerndown, Bridgend 403
Southerness, Southerness 346
Southern Valley, Gravesend 149
Southfield, Oxford 216
South Herefordshire, Ross-on-Wye 134
South Herts, N20 Whetstone 182
South Kyme, South Kyme 178
South Leeds, Leeds 314
South Moor, Stanley 82
South Pembrokeshire, Pembroke Dock 423
Southport & Ainsdale, Southport 190
Southport Municipal, Southport 190
Southport Old Links, Southport 190
Southsea, Portsmouth & Southsea 130
South Shields, South Shields 266
South Staffordshire, Wolverhampton 281
Southwick Park Naval Recreation Centre, Southwick 131
South Winchester, Winchester 132
Southwold, Southwold 235-6
Southwood, Farnborough 126
Spa, Ballynahinch 438
Spalding, Spalding 178
Spanish Point, Milltown Malbay 449
Spey Bay, Spey Bay 372
Springfield Park, Rochdale 118
Springhead Park, Hull 294
Springs Hotel, Wallingford 216
Springwater, Calverton 208
Stackstown, Dublin 461
Staddon Heights, Plymouth 69
Stafford Castle, Stafford 230
Stamford, Stalybridge 118-19
Stand, Whitefield 120
Standish Court, Standish 119
Stanedge, Chesterfield 60
Stanley Park Municipal, Blackpool 159
Stanmore, Stanmore 109
Stanton on the Wolds, Keyworth 208

Stapleford Abbotts, Stapleford Abbotts 91
Staverton Park, Staverton 201
Stevenage Golf Centre, Stevenage 142
Stinchcombe Hill, Dursley 94
Stirling, Stirling 394
Stock Brook Golf & Country Club, Billericay 83
Stockley Park, Uxbridge 110
Stockport, Stockport 119
Stocksbridge & District, Stocksbridge 306
Stocksfield, Stocksfield 207
Stocks Hotel Golf & Country Club, Aldbury 135
Stockwood Park, Luton 156
Stockwood Vale, Keynsham 224
Stoke Albany, Market Harborough 170
Stoke-by-Nayland, Colchester 86-7
Stoke Poges, Stoke Poges 31
Stoke Rochford, Stoke Rochford 178
Stone, Stone 231
Stonebridge Golf Centre, Meriden 277
Stoneham, Southampton 131
Stonehaven, Stonehaven 329
Stoneleigh Deer Park, Stoneleigh 272
Stony Holme Municipal, Carlisle 55
Stornoway, Stornoway 399
Stourbridge, Stourbridge 278
Stowmarket, Stowmarket 236
Strabane, Strabane 446
Strandhill, Sligo 483
Stranraer, Stranraer 346
Stratford Oaks, Stratford-upon-Avon 272
Stratford-upon-Avon, Stratford-upon-Avon 272
Strathaven, Strathaven 393
Strathclyde Park, Hamilton 392
Strathlene, Buckie 370
Strathmore Golf Centre, Alyth 376-7
Strathpeffer Spa, Strathpeffer 368
Strathtay, Strathtay 382
Strawberry Hill, Twickenham 109
Stressholme, Darlington 80
Strokestown, Strokestown 482
Stromness, Stromness 399
Studley Wood, Horton-cum-Studley 215
Sturminster Marshall, Sturminster Marshall 76
Styal, Wilmslow 43
Sudbrook Moor, Grantham 174
Sudbury, Wembley 110
The Suffolk Golf & Country Club, Bury St Edmunds 233
Summerhill, Hay-on-Wye 424
Sundridge Park, Bromley 100
Sunningdale, Sunningdale 23
Sunningdale Ladies, Sunningdale 22
Surbiton, Surbiton 109
Sutton Bridge, Sutton Bridge 178
Sutton Coldfield, Sutton Coldfield 278
Sutton Green, Sutton Green 248

Sutton Park, Hull 294
Swaffham, Swaffham 197
Swallow Hall, York 302
Swansea Bay, Neath 421
Swanston, Edinburgh 339
Swarland Hall, Swarland 207
Sweetwoods Park, Edenbridge 148
Swindon, Dudley 276
Swinford, Swinford 478-9
Swinley Forest, Ascot 18
Swinton Park, Swinton 120
Swords Open Golf Course, Dublin 464

T

Tadmarton Heath, Tadmarton 216
Tain, Tain 368
Tall Pines, Backwell 221
Tamworth Municipal, Tamworth 231
Tandragee, Tandragee 436
Tandridge, Tandridge 248
Tankersley Park, High Green 304
Tapton Park Municipal, Chesterfield 61
Tarbert, Tarbert 335
Tarland, Tarland 329
Taunton & Pickeridge, Taunton 225
Taunton Vale, Taunton 225-6
Tavistock, Tavistock 70
Taymouth Castle, Kenmore 380
The Ted McCarthy Municipal Golf Course, Cork 451
Teeside, Stockton-on-Tees 82
Tehidy Park, Camborne 44-5
Teignmouth, Teignmouth 70-1
Teign Valley, Christow 65
Telford Golf & Country Club, Telford 220
Temple, Maidenhead 20
Templemore, Templemore 484
Temple Newsam, Leeds 314
Tenby, Tenby 423
Tenterden, Tenterden 154
Test Valley, Overton 129
Tetney, Cleethorpes 173
Tewkesbury Park Hotel Golf & Country Club, Tewkesbury 96
Thames Ditton & Esher, Esher 242
Thetford, Thetford 197
Theydon Bois, Theydon Bois 91
Thirsk & Northallerton, Thirsk 301
Thornbury Golf Centre, Thornbury 96-7
Thorndon Park, Ingrave 88
Thorne, Thorne 307
Thorney, Thorney 35-6
Thorney Park, Iver 29
Thornhill, Thornhill 346
Thornhurst Park, Doncaster 303
Thornton, Thornton 363
Thorpe Hall, Southend-on-Sea 90
Thorpeness Golf Club & Hotel, Thorpeness 236
Thorpe Wood, Peterborough 34
Thoulstone Park, Chapmanslade 283

Three Hammers Short Course, Wolverhampton 281
Three Locks, Milton Keynes 30-1
Three Rivers, Purleigh 89
Thurles, Thurles 485
Thurlestone, Thurlestone 71
Thurso, Thurso 368
Tidworth Garrison, Tidworth 285-6
Tilgate Forest Golf Centre, Crawley 260
Tillicoultry, Tillicoultry 342
Tilsworth, Tilsworth 17
Tinsley Park Municipal Golf, Sheffield 306
Tipperary, Tipperary 485
Tiverton, Tiverton 71
Tobercurry, Tobercurry 483
Tobermory, Tobermory 399
Todmorden, Todmorden 318
Toft Hotel, Bourne 173
Toot Hill, Toot Hill 92
Top Meadow, South Ockendon 90
Torphin Hill, Edinburgh 339
Torphins, Torphins 329
Torquay, Torquay 71
Torrance House, East Kilbride 392
Torrington, Great Torrington 71
Torvean, Inverness 367
Torwoodlee, Galashiels 384
Towerlands, Braintree 84
Towneley, Burnley 159
Tracy Park, Wick 97-8
Traditions, Woking 251
Traigh, Arisaig 363
Tralee, Tralee 470
Tramore, Tramore 486
Tredegar Park, Newport 422
Tredegar and Rhymney, Tredegar 403
Trefloyne, Tenby 423
Tregenna Castle Hotel, Golf & Country Club, St Ives 49
Treloy, Newquay 48
Trentham, Stoke-on-Trent 230
Trentham Park, Stoke-on-Trent 230-1
Trent Lock Golf Centre, Long Eaton 208
Trent Park, N14 Southgate 181-2
Trethorne, Launceston 46
Trevose, Constantine Bay 45
Troon Municipal, Troon 390
Truro, Truro 52-3
Tuam, Tuam 467
Tulfarris House Hotel & Country Club, Blessington 489
Tullamore, Tullamore 481
Tulliallan, Kincardine 358
Tunbridge Wells, Royal Tunbridge Wells 156
Tunshill, Milnrow 117
Turnberry Hotel Golf Courses, Turnberry 389
Turnhouse, Edinburgh 339-40
Turriff, Turriff 329
Turton, Bromley Cross 113

Twickenham, Twickenham 109
Tylney Park, Rotherwick 130
Tynemouth, Tynemouth 267
Tyneside, Ryton 266
Tyrrells Wood, Leatherhead 245
Tytherington, Macclesfield 40

U

Ufford Park Hotel Golf & Leisure, Woodbridge 236
Ullesthorpe, Ullesthorpe 171
Ulverston, Ulverston 58
Upavon, Upavon 286
Upchurch River Valley Golf Centre, Sittingbourne 154
Uphall, Uphall 396
Upminster, Upminster 109
Upton-by-Chester, Chester 37
Uttoxeter, Uttoxeter 231
Uxbridge, Uxbridge 110

V

Vale of Glamorgan Golf & Country Club, Pontyclun 426
Vale Golf Club, Bishampton 287
Vale of Leven, Bonhill 395
Vale of Llangollen, Llangollen 411
Ventnor, Ventnor 282
Verulam, St Albans 141
Vicars Cross, Chester 37
The Village Golf Course, Wike 318
Virginia, Virginia 447
Virginia Park Golf Club, Caerphilly 405
Vivary Park Municipal, Taunton 226
Vogrie, Gorebridge 370

W

Wakefield, Wakefield 318
Waldringfield Heath, Waldringfield 236
Wallasey, Wallasey 192
Wallsend, Wallsend 267
Walmer & Kingsdown, Kingsdown 151
Walmersley, Bury 113
Walmley, Sutton Coldfield 278, 280
Walsall, Walsall 280
Walton Hall, Warrington 42
Walton Heath, Walton-on-the-Hill 249
Wanstead, E11 Leytonstone & Wanstead 181
Wareham, Wareham 77
Warkworth, Warkworth 207
Warley Park, Brentwood 84
Warley Woods, Birmingham 275
Warren, Wallasey 192
Warren, Woodham Walter 92-3
Warren, Dawlish Warren 66
Warrenpoint, Warrenpoint 443
Warrington, Warrington 42-3
Warwick, Warwick 273
The Warwickshire, Leek Wootton 269-70
Waterbridge, Down St Mary 66

Waterford, Waterford 486
Waterford Castle, Waterford 486
Waterhall, Brighton & Hove 253
Waterlooville, Waterlooville 132
Waterstock, Waterstock 216
Waterville House & Golf Links, Waterville 470
Wath, Rawmarsh 304
Wavendon Golf Centre, Wavendon 31
Weald of Kent, Headcorn 150
Weald Park, Brentwood 84
Wearside, Sunderland 267
Welbeck Manor & Sparkwell Golf Course, Sparkwell 70
Welcombe Hotel, Stratford-upon-Avon 272-3
Wellingborough, Wellingborough 202
Wellow, East Wellow 125
Wellshurst Golf & Country Club, Hailsham 255
Wells (Somerset), Wells 226
Welshpool, Welshpool 425
Welwyn Garden City, Welwyn Garden City 144
Wensum Valley Hotel, Golf & Country Club, Norwich 197
Wentworth, Virginia Water 247
Wenvoe Castle, Wenvoe 429
Wergs, Wolverhampton 281
Wernddu Golf Centre, Abergavenny 418
Werneth, Oldham 117
Werneth Low, Hyde 114
West Berkshire, Chaddleworth 19
West Bowling, Bradford 308-9
West Bradford, Bradford 309
West Byfleet, West Byfleet 250
West Chiltington, West Chiltington 263
West Cornwall, Lelant 46
West Derby, Liverpool 188
West End, Halifax 310
Westerham, Westerham 156
Westerhope, Newcastle upon Tyne 266
Western, Leicester 169
Western Gailes, Irvine 373
Westerwood Hotel Golf & Country Club, Cumbernauld 375
West Essex, E4 Chingford 181
Westgate and Birchington, Westgate on Sea 157
West Herts, Watford 142
Westhill, Aberdeen 325
West Hill, Brookwood 238
Westhoughton, Westhoughton 120
West Hove, Brighton & Hove 253
West Kent, Downe 102
West Kilbride, West Kilbride 374
West Lancashire, Blundellsands 186
West Linton, West Linton 388
West Lothian, Linlithgow 396
West Malling, Addington 144
West Middlesex, Southall 109
West Monmouthshire, Nantyglo 403

Index *of Golf Courses*

Westonbirt, Westonbirt 97
Weston Park, Weston Longville 198
Weston-super-Mare, Weston-super-Mare 226
Weston Turville Golf & Squash Club, Weston Turville 31
Westport, Westport 479
Westray, Westray 399
West Surrey, Enton Green 241
West Sussex, Pulborough 262-3
West Waterford, Dungarvan 485
West Wilts, Warminster 286
Westwood (Leek), Leek 228
Wetherby, Wetherby 318
Wexford, Wexford 488
Wexham Park, Wexham Street 32
Weybrook Park, Basingstoke 123
Weymouth, Weymouth 77
Whalley, Whalley 166
Whalsay, Island of Whalsay 400
Wharton Park, Bewdley 287
Wheathill, Somerton 225
Wheatley, Doncaster 303
Whetstone, Whetstone 171-2
Whickham, Whickham 267
Whipsnade Park, Whipsnade 17
Whiston Hall, Whiston 232
Whitburn, South Shields 266
Whitby, Whitby 301
Whitchurch, Cardiff 407
Whitecraigs, Newton Mearns 355
Whitefield, Whitefield 120-1
Whitefields Hotel Golf & Country Club, Rugby 270, 272
Whitehall, Nelson 406
Whitehead, Whitehead 434
Whitehill, Ware 142
Whitekirk, North Berwick 352, 354
Whiteleaf, Princes Risborough 31
Whitemoss, Dunning 378
Whitewebbs Park, Enfield 103
Whiting Bay, Whiting Bay 398
Whitley Bay, Whitley Bay 267
Whitsand Bay Hotel Golf & Country Club, Torpoint 52
Whitstable & Seasalter, Whitstable 157
Whittaker, Littleborough 115
Whittington Heath, Lichfield 229
Whittlebury Park Golf & Country Club,

Whittlebury 202
Wick, Wick 368-9
Wicklow, Wicklow 492
Widnes, Widnes 43
Wigan, Wigan 121
Wigtown & Bladnoch, Wigtown 346
Wigtownshire County, Glenluce 344
Wildwood Country Club, Cranleigh 240
Willesley Park, Ashby-de-la-Zouch 167
Williamwood, Glasgow 341
William Wroe Municipal, Flixton 114
Willingdon, Eastbourne 254-5
Willow Valley Golf & Country Club, Brighouse 309
Wilmslow, Wilmslow 43
Wilpshire, Wilpshire 167
Wilton, Redcar 299
Wiltshire, Wootton Bassett 286
Wimbledon Common, SW19
Wimbledon 185
Wimbledon Park, SW19
Wimbledon 185
Windermere, Bowness-on-Windermere 54
Windlemere, West End 250
Windlesham, Bagshot 238
Windmill Hill, Bletchley 26
Windmill Village Hotel Golf & Leisure Club, Coventry 276
Windwhistle Golf, Squash & Country Club, Chard 222
Windyhill, Bearsden 348
Winterfield, Dunbar 351
Winter Hill, Cookham 19
Wirral Ladies, Birkenhead 185-6
Wishaw, Wishaw 376
Withernsea, Withernsea 294
Withington, Manchester 116
Witney Lakes, Witney 216-17
Wokefield Park, Mortimer 20
Woking, Woking 251
Wollaton Park, Nottingham 210
Wolstanton, Newcastle-under-Lyme 229
Woodbridge, Woodbridge 237
Woodbrook, Bray 490
Woodbury Park, Exeter 66
Woodcote Park, Coulsdon 101
Woodenbridge, Woodenbridge 492

Woodford, Woodford Green 110
Woodhall Hills, Pudsey 316
Woodhall Spa, Woodhall Spa 179
Woodham Golf & Country Club, Newton Aycliffe 81
Woodlake Park Golf & Country Club, Pontypool 428
Woodlands, Naas 472
Woodlands, Bristol 25
Woodlands Manor, West Kingsdown 157
Woodsome Hall, Fenay Bridge 309-10
Woodspring Golf & Country Club, Long Ashton 224
Woodstock Golf and Country Club, Ennis 448
Woodthorpe Hall, Woodthorpe 180
Wooler, Wooler 207
Woolton, Liverpool 188
Worcester Golf & Country Club, Worcester 291
Worcestershire, Malvern Wells 290
Worfield, Worfield 221
Workington, Workington 58
Worksop, Worksop 212
Worldham Park, Alton 122
Worlebury, Weston-super-Mare 226
Worplesdon, Woking 251
Worsley, Manchester 116
Worthing, Worthing 264
Wortley, Wortley 307
Wrag Barn Golf & Country Club, Highworth 284
Wrangaton (S Devon), South Brent 70
Wrekin, Wellington 220
Wrexham, Wrexham 430
Wrotham Heath, Borough Green 146
Wyboston Lakes, Wyboston 17
Wycombe Heights Golf Centre, Loudwater 30
Wyke Green, Isleworth 105
Wyre Forest, Kidderminster 289

Y

Yelverton, Yelverton 72
Yeovil, Yeovil 226-7
York, York 302
Youghal, Youghal 454